IF FOUND, please notify and arrange return to owner. This text is an important study guide for the owner's career and/or exam preparation.

Name: ______________________

Address: ______________________

City, State, ZIP: ______________________

Telephone: (____) ______________ E-mail: ______________

Gleim Publications, Inc., offers five university-level study systems:

Auditing & Systems Exam Questions and Explanations with Exam Prep Software
Business Law/Legal Studies Exam Questions and Explanations with Exam Prep Software
Federal Tax Exam Questions and Explanations with Exam Prep Software
Financial Accounting Exam Questions and Explanations with Exam Prep Software
Cost/Managerial Accounting Exam Questions and Explanations with Exam Prep Software

The following is a list of Gleim examination review systems:

CIA Review: Part I, Internal Audit Role in Governance, Risk, and Control
CIA Review: Part II, Conducting the Internal Audit Engagement
CIA Review: Part III, Business Analysis and Information Technology
CIA Review: Part IV, Business Management Skills

CFM Review: Corporate Financial Management
CMA Review: Part 1, Business Analysis
CMA Review: Part 2, Management Accounting and Reporting
CMA Review: Part 3, Strategic Management
CMA Review: Part 4, Business Applications

CPA Review: Financial
CPA Review: Auditing
CPA Review: Business
CPA Review: Regulation

EA Review: Part 1, Individuals
EA Review: Part 2, Sole Proprietorships and Partnerships
EA Review: Part 3, Corporations, Fiduciaries, Estate and Gift Tax, and Trusts
EA Review: Part 4, IRS Administration and Other Topics

Order forms are provided at the back of this book or contact us at www.gleim.com or (800) 87-GLEIM.

All orders must be prepaid. Shipping and handling charges will be added to all orders. Library and company orders may be purchased on account. Add applicable sales tax to shipments within Florida. All payments must be in U.S. funds and payable on a U.S. bank. Please write or call for prices and availability of all foreign country shipments. Orders will usually be shipped the day your request is received. Allow 10 days for delivery in the United States. Please contact us if you do not receive your shipment within 2 weeks.

Gleim Publications, Inc. guarantees the immediate refund of all resalable texts and unopened software and audios purchased directly from Gleim Publications, Inc. if they are returned within 30 days. Shipping and handling charges are nonrefundable. Returns of books purchased from bookstores and other resellers should be made to the respective bookstore or reseller.

Groundwood Paper and Highlighters — All Gleim books are printed on high quality groundwood paper. We recommend you use a non-bleed-through (dry) highlighter (e.g., the Avery *Glidestick*™ -- ask for it at your local office supply store) when highlighting page items within these books.

REVIEWERS AND CONTRIBUTORS

Garrett Gleim, B.S., University of Pennsylvania, is one of our vice presidents. Mr. Gleim coordinated the production staff, reviewed the manuscript, and provided production assistance throughout the project.

John F. Rebstock, CIA, B.S., Fisher School of Accounting, University of Florida, specializes in ensuring that our answer explanations and Knowledge Transfer Outlines are user-friendly. Mr. Rebstock reviewed portions of the manuscript.

A PERSONAL THANKS

This manual would not have been possible without the extraordinary effort and dedication of Julie Cutlip, Teresa Soard, Polly Werner, and Heather Williams, who typed the entire manuscript and all revisions; and drafted, scanned, and laid out the diagrams and illustrations in this book.

The authors appreciate the proofreading and production assistance of Justin Ash, Clint Berg, Katharine Cicatelli, Richard Dellifraine, Emily Gorovsky, Seth Kaye, Jean Marzullo, Shane Rapp, Cara Richardson, and Sonia Santana.

The authors also appreciate the critical reading assistance of Scott Grubbs, Thomas McDuffie, Erica Malinowski, and April Woodbury.

Finally, we appreciate the encouragement, support, and tolerance of our families throughout this project.

Twelfth Edition

FINANCIAL ACCOUNTING

Exam Questions and Explanations

by

Irvin N. Gleim, Ph.D., CPA, CIA, CMA, CFM

and

William A. Collins, Ph.D., CPA

with the assistance of
Grady M. Irwin, J.D.

ABOUT THE AUTHORS

Irvin N. Gleim is Professor Emeritus in the Fisher School of Accounting at the University of Florida and is a member of the American Accounting Association, Academy of Legal Studies in Business, American Institute of Certified Public Accountants, Association of Government Accountants, Florida Institute of Certified Public Accountants, the Institute of Internal Auditors, and the Institute of Management Accountants. He has had articles published in the *Journal of Accountancy, The Accounting Review,* and *The American Business Law Journal* and is author/coauthor of numerous accounting and aviation books and CPE courses.

William A. Collins is Professor at the Joseph M. Bryan School of Business and Economics, University of North Carolina at Greensboro. He is a member of the American Accounting Association, the American Institute of Certified Public Accountants, and the Florida Institute of Certified Public Accountants. He has authored and coauthored articles that have been published in the *Journal of Accountancy*, *The Accounting Review*, *Journal of Accounting Research*, and *Internal Auditor*. Monographs coauthored by him have been published by the Financial Accounting Standards Board and the Institute of Internal Auditors. Professor Collins also annually authors and presents continuing education seminars dealing with the authoritative accounting and reporting standards.

Gleim Publications, Inc.
P.O. Box 12848
University Station
Gainesville, Florida 32604
(800) 87-GLEIM or (800) 874-5346
(352) 375-0772
FAX: (352) 375-6940
Internet: www.gleim.com
E-mail: admin@gleim.com

ISSN: 1091-451X
ISBN: 1-58194-425-X

This is the first printing of the twelfth edition of ***Financial Accounting Exam Questions and Explanations***. Please e-mail update@gleim.com with FIN EQE 12-1 as the subject or text. You will receive our current update as a reply. Updates are available until the next edition is published.

EXAMPLE:

To:	update@gleim.com
From:	your e-mail address
Subject:	FIN EQE 12-1

First Printing: July 2005

ACKNOWLEDGMENTS

Material from Uniform Certified Public Accountant Examination questions and unofficial answers, copyright © 1972 - 2002 by the American Institute of Certified Public Accountants, Inc. is reprinted and/or adapted with permission.

The authors also appreciate and thank The Institute of Internal Auditors, Inc. for permission to use The Institute's Certified Internal Auditor Examination questions, copyright © 1978 - 1996 by The Institute of Internal Auditors, Inc.

The authors also appreciate and thank the Institute of Certified Management Accountants for permission to use questions from past CMA examinations, copyright © 1979 - 1996 by the Institute of Management Accountants.

The authors also acknowledge the Florida State Board of Accountancy and its written professional examination as a source of questions.

Visit our website (www.gleim.com) for the latest updates and information on all of our products.

PREFACE FOR ACCOUNTING STUDENTS

The purpose of this study manual is to help you understand financial accounting principles and procedures, and their applications. In turn, these skills will enable you to perform better on your undergraduate examinations, as well as look ahead to (and prepare for) professional examinations.

One of the major benefits of this study manual is comprehensive coverage of financial accounting topics. Accordingly, when you use this study manual to help prepare for financial accounting courses and examinations, you are assured of covering virtually all topics that could reasonably be expected to be studied in typical college or university intermediate and advanced financial accounting courses.

The question-and-answer format is designed and presented to facilitate effective study. Students should be careful not to misuse this text by referring to the answers before independently answering each question. Use the bookmark provided at the back of this book to cover the answers.

The majority of the questions are from past CIA, CMA, and CPA examinations. Although a citation for the source of each question is provided, a substantial number have been modified to accommodate changes in professional pronouncements, to clarify questions, and/or to emphasize a financial accounting concept or its application. In addition, hundreds of publisher-written questions test areas covered in current textbooks but not directly tested on accounting certification examinations. Finally, we are pleased to use questions submitted by accounting professors.

Note that this study manual should not be relied upon to prepare for the professional examinations. You should use review manuals specifically developed for each examination. Gleim's *CIA Review*, *CMA/CFM Review*, *CPA Review*, and *EA Review* are up-to-date and comprehensively cover all material necessary for successful completion of these examinations. An order form for these and other Gleim books is provided at the back of this book.

Thank you for your interest in this study manual. We deeply appreciate the many letters and suggestions received from accounting students and educators during the past years, as well as from CFM, CIA, CMA, and CPA candidates. Please send us your suggestions, comments, and corrections concerning this edition. The last page of this book has been designed to help you note corrections and suggestions throughout your study process. Please photocopy it or tear it out and mail it to us with your suggestions.

Please read the Introduction carefully. It is very short but nonetheless very important.

Good Luck on Your Exams,

Irvin N. Gleim
William A. Collins

July 2005

Gleim Publications' Customer Service Procedures

To continue providing our customers with first-rate service, we request that questions about our books and software be sent to us via mail, e-mail, or fax. The appropriate staff member will give each question thorough consideration and a prompt response. Questions concerning orders, prices, shipments, or payments will be handled via telephone by our competent and courteous customer service staff.

Thank you.

PREFACE FOR ACCOUNTING PRACTITIONERS

The first purpose of this study manual is to permit you to assess your technical proficiency concerning financial accounting standards and special skills. The second purpose is to facilitate your review and update of financial accounting standards and techniques with our compendium of objective questions. The third purpose is to provide CPE credit for your self-assessment and review/update study effort in conjunction with the Gleim CPE program.

This approach to CPE is both motivating and intense. You should be continually challenged to answer each question correctly. When you answer a question incorrectly or have difficulty, you should pursue a complete understanding by reading the answer explanation and consulting reference sources as necessary.

Most of the questions in *Financial Accounting Exam Questions and Explanations* were taken from various professional examinations, but many have been revised, adapted, etc., to provide broader, up-to-date coverage of the financial accounting body of technical knowledge. While many are from the CPA exam, others are from the CIA and CMA exams. Thus, you have an opportunity to consider the appropriateness of pursuing these other accounting certifications. In addition, hundreds of publisher questions cover material not directly tested on the accounting certification examinations.

Practitioners interested in multiple certification will find the discussion of the CIA and CMA/CFM certification programs in the Introduction to be useful. If, as you work through this study book and take the open-book CPE final exams, you find you need to refer to a current textbook, Appendix A contains a list of current titles. Also, be sure to read carefully the introductory pages of your Financial Accounting CPE final exam booklet.

Finally, we ask for any supplemental comments, reactions, suggestions, etc., that you may have as you complete our CPE program. The last page of this study book has been designed to help you note corrections and suggestions throughout your study process. Please attach it to the Course Evaluation form included with your CPE program.

Thank you for your interest, and we look forward to hearing from you. If you would like information on other CPE programs available from Gleim, please call us for a free brochure or visit our website at www.gleim.com/CPE.

Best Wishes in Your CPE Endeavors,

Irvin N. Gleim
William A. Collins

July 2005

P.S. Please check out our new Online CPE, which offers the following advantages:

- You will know your results INSTANTLY.
- Print out your certificate from the Internet IMMEDIATELY.
- Corporate packages also available.

Visit www.gleim.com/CPE

TABLE OF CONTENTS

CONTRIBUTING PROFESSORS

We are especially grateful to the following professors who submitted questions for this and previous editions. Their participation has made *Financial Accounting Exam Questions and Explanations* truly a community project. We welcome further submissions of questions either for the Thirteenth Edition of *Financial Accounting Exam Questions and Explanations* or for future editions of our other exam questions and explanations books.

Barnhart, James R. .... Ball State University
Bayes, Paul E. .... East Tennessee State University
Boze, Ken M. .... University of Alaska, Anchorage
Broome, O. Whitfield, Jr. .... University of Virginia - Clear Lake
Bruno, Joan D. .... University of Houston
Bush, H. Francis .... Virginia Military Institute
Cerepak, John .... Fairleigh Dickinson University
Derstine, Robert P. .... Villanova University
Emig, James M. .... Villanova University
Flesher, D.L. .... University of Mississippi
Hall, J.O. .... Western Kentucky University
Helling, Alene G. .... Stark Technical College
Higley, Wayne M. .... Siebens Forum
Hora, Judith A. .... University of San Diego
Kame, Donald G. .... Stark Technical College
Krueger, LaVern E. .... University of Missouri - Kansas City
Lockett, Pete .... Cal State LA
Mantooth, J.W. .... University of Science and Arts of Oklahoma
McBrayer, Phil .... High Point College
Miller, Tim .... Murray State University
Oddo, Alfonso R. .... Niagara University
O'Keefe, Ruth R. .... Jacksonville University
Phillips, T.J., Jr. .... Louisiana Tech University
Posey, Roderick B. .... University of Southern Mississippi
Schultz, Sally .... SUNY College at New Paltz
Spede, Edward C. .... Virginia Commonwealth University
Sperry, John B. .... Virginia Commonwealth University
Trebby, James P. .... Marquette University
Venkateswar, Sankaran .... Trinity University

INTRODUCTION

The format and content of this study manual are innovative in the accounting text market. The first purpose is to provide accounting students with a well-organized, comprehensive compendium of objective questions covering the topics taught in typical financial accounting undergraduate courses. The second purpose is to provide accounting professionals with a comprehensive presentation of objective questions for self-diagnostic use and/or review of financial accounting pronouncements and procedures.

The Gleim exam question and explanation books really work! You can pretest yourself before class to see if you are strong or weak in the assigned area. You can retest after class to see if you really understand the material. The questions in these books cover **all** topics in your related courses, so you will encounter few questions on your exams for which you will not be well prepared.

The titles and organization of Study Units 1 through 30 are based on the current financial accounting textbooks listed in Appendix A. Appendix A contains the table of contents of each of the listed books with cross-references to study units and subunits in this book. Some textbooks may have been inadvertently omitted. If you are using a textbook that is not included in our list, please fax, mail, or e-mail us the table of contents so that we may provide you with a cross-reference. In your correspondence to us, please include your name, address, school, professor, and course name.

OUR USE OF SUBUNITS

Each study unit of this book is divided into subtopics to assist your study program. We call these subtopics "subunits." Subunits permit broad and perhaps overwhelming topics to be divided into more manageable components.

Choosing subunits and arranging questions within them was difficult. Thus, topics and questions may overlap somewhat. The number of questions offers comprehensive coverage but does not present an insurmountable task. We define each subunit narrowly enough to cover a single topic but broadly enough to prevent questions from being repetitious.

Within each subunit, the multiple-choice questions are presented in a sequence moving from the general to the specific, elementary to advanced, etc., to provide an effective learning sequence. Duplicate questions and redundant explanations have been kept to a minimum.

SOURCES OF OBJECTIVE QUESTIONS

Past CIA, CMA, and CPA examinations and sample questions are the primary sources of questions included in this study manual.

Gleim Publications will continue to prepare questions (coded in this text as *Publisher*) based upon the content of financial accounting textbooks, ARBs, APBs, SFASs, SOPs, etc. These *Publisher* questions were developed to review topics not adequately covered by questions from the other sources. We will continue to develop challenging, current questions to provide you with complete review materials. Also, professionals and professors from schools around the country have contributed questions. See page viii for a list of their names. We invite professors and students to submit questions for future editions.

IDENTIFICATION OF THE SOURCE OF EACH QUESTION

The source of each question appears in the first line of its answer explanation, in the column to the right of the question. Summary of source codes:

CIA	Certified Internal Auditor Examination
CMA	Certified Management Accountant Examination
CPA	Uniform Certified Public Accountant Examination
Publisher	Your authors
Individual name	Name of professional or professor who contributed the question

If you, your professor, or your classmates wish to submit questions, we will consider using them in future editions. Please send questions you develop, complete with answers and explanations, to the following e-mail address: accounting@gleim.com. Alternatively, you can mail questions to the following address:

Gleim Publications, Inc.
EQE Question Bank
P.O. Box 12848, University Station
Gainesville, FL 32604

Writing and analyzing multiple-choice questions is an excellent way to prepare yourself for your exams. We will make every effort to consider, edit, and use questions you submit. However, we ask that you send us only serious, complete, carefully considered efforts.

UNIQUENESS OF OBJECTIVE QUESTIONS

The major advantage of objective questions is their ability to cover a large number of topics with little time and effort when compared to essay questions and/or computational problems.

A multiple-choice question is actually a series of statements of which all but one are incorrect given the facts of the question. The advantage of multiple-choice questions over true-false questions is that they require more analysis and result in a lower score for those with little or no knowledge. Random guessing on questions with four answer choices results in an expected grade of 25%, whereas random guessing on a true-false test results in an expected grade of 50%.

Students and practitioners both like multiple-choice questions. Because they present alternative answers from which only one needs to be selected, students find them relatively easy to answer. Professors also like objective questions because they are easy to grade and because much more material can be tested in the same period of time. Most professors will also ask students to complete essay or computational questions.

ANSWER EXPLANATIONS ALONGSIDE THE QUESTIONS

Our format presents objective questions and their answer explanations side by side. The answer explanations are to the right of each question. The example below is from the CPA exam.

8. At December 31, 2004 and 2005, Apex Co. had 3,000 shares of $100 par, 5% cumulative preferred stock outstanding. No dividends were in arrears as of December 31, 2003. Apex did not declare a dividend during 2004. During 2005, Apex paid a cash dividend of $10,000 on its preferred stock. Apex should report dividends in arrears in its 2005 financial statements as a(n)

A. Accrued liability of $15,000.

B. Disclosure of $15,000.

C. Accrued liability of $20,000.

D. Disclosure of $20,000.

Answer (D) is correct. (*CPA, adapted*)

REQUIRED: The amount and means of reporting preferred dividends in arrears.

DISCUSSION: Dividends in arrears on preferred stock are not an obligation of the company and are not recognized in the financial statements. However, the aggregate and per share amounts of arrearages in cumulative preferred dividends should be disclosed on the face of the balance sheet or in the notes (APB 10). The aggregate amount in arrears is $20,000 [(2 years × 5% × $100 par × 3,000 shares) – $10,000 paid in 2005].

Answers (A) and (C) are incorrect because dividends in arrears do not meet recognition criteria. Answers (B) is incorrect because $15,000 is the arrearage for 1 year.

The format in this study manual is designed to facilitate your study of objective questions, their answers, and the answer explanations. The intent is to save you time and effort by eliminating the need to turn pages back and forth from questions to answers.

Be careful, however. Do not misuse this format by consulting the answers before you have answered the questions. Misuse of the readily available answers will give you a false sense of security and result in poor performance on examinations and decreased benefit from your studies. The best way to use this study manual is to cover the answer explanations with the bookmark provided for this purpose in the back of the book (or a sheet of paper) as you read and answer each question. As a crucial part of the learning process, you must honestly commit yourself to an answer before looking at the answer explanation. Whether you are right or wrong, your memory of the correct answer will be reinforced by this process.

OVERVIEW OF ACCOUNTING CERTIFICATION PROGRAMS

The CPA (Certified Public Accountant) exam is the grandparent of all the professional accounting examinations. Its origin was in the 1896 public accounting legislation of New York. In 1917, the American Institute of CPAs (AICPA) began to prepare and grade a uniform CPA exam. It is currently used to measure the technical competence of those applying to be licensed as CPAs in all 50 states, Guam, Puerto Rico, the Virgin Islands, and the District of Columbia. More than 100,000 candidates sit for the CPA exam each year. In April 2004, the CPA exam switched to a computerized format. It is available as often as six days per week for two of every three months. This new exam places greater emphasis on auditing and other attestation services, the assessment of such skills as research and communications, general business knowledge, and information technology.

The CIA (Certified Internal Auditor), CMA (Certified Management Accountant), and CFM (Certified Financial Manager) examinations are relatively new certification programs compared with the CPA exam. The CMA exam was first administered in 1972, and the first CIA exam was in 1974. The CFM exam was first administered in December 1996. Why were these certification programs begun? Generally, the requirements of the CPA designation instituted by the boards of accountancy, especially the necessity for public accounting experience, led to the development of the CIA, CMA, and CFM programs. The IRS Enrolled Agent (EA) certification is available for tax specialists.

Certification is important to professional accountants because it provides

1. Participation in a recognized professional group
2. An improved professional training program arising out of the certification program
3. Recognition among peers for attaining the professional designation
4. An extra credential for the employment market/career ladder
5. The personal satisfaction of attaining a recognized degree of competency

These reasons hold particularly true in the accounting field due to wide recognition of the CPA designation. Accountants and accounting students are often asked whether they are CPAs. Thus, there is considerable pressure for accountants to become *certified.*

A new development is multiple certifications, which is important for the same reasons as initial certification. Accounting students and recent graduates should plan for career progression and expanded opportunities by obtaining multiple certifications. The table of selected CIA, CMA, CFM, and CPA examination data on the following page provides an overview of these accounting examinations. Additional information about the IRS enrolled agent (EA) exam is available at www.gleim.com.

RATIONALE FOR ACCOUNTING CERTIFICATION PROGRAMS

The primary purpose of professional exams is to measure the technical competence of candidates. Competence includes technical knowledge, ability to apply such knowledge with good judgment, and comprehension of professional responsibility. Additionally, the nature of these exams (low pass rate, broad and rigorous coverage, etc.) has several very important effects.

1. Candidates are forced to learn all of the material that should have been presented and learned in a good accounting educational program.

2. Candidates must integrate the topics and concepts that are presented in individual courses in accounting education programs.

3. The content of each exam provides direction to accounting education programs; i.e., what is tested will be taught to accounting students.

EXAMINATION CONTENT

The content of these examinations is specified by their governing boards with lists of topics to be tested. In the Gleim review manuals – *CIA Review, CMA/CFM Review, CPA Review, and EA Review* – the material tested is divided into subtopics called study units. A study unit is a more manageable undertaking than an overall part of each exam. The listings of topics on pages 6 through 8 provide an overview of the content of these exams.

CIA, CMA/CFM, CPA EXAMINATION SUMMARY

	CIA	CMA/CFM	CPA
Sponsoring Organization	Institute of Internal Auditors 247 Maitland Avenue Altamonte Springs, FL 32701 (407) 937-1100 www.theiia.org	Institute of Management Accountants 10 Paragon Drive Montvale, NJ 07645-1718 (201) 573-9000 (800) 638-4427 www.imanet.org	American Institute of Certified Public Accountants Harborside Financial Center 201 Plaza Three Jersey City, NJ 07311-3881 (201) 938-3750 www.aicpa.org
Passing Score	75%	70%	75%
Average Pass Rate by Exam Part	35%-40%	55%	40%-45%
Cost	$380 (50% student discount)	$460 (50% student discount; requires IMA membership)	$500-$800 (varies by state)
Year Examination Was First Administered	1974	1972	1917
Major Exam Sections and Length	I. Internal Audit Role in Governance, Risk, and Control (3-1/2 hours) II. Conducting the Internal Audit Engagement (3-1/2 hours) III. Business Analysis and Information Technology (3-1/2 hours) IV. Business Management Skills (3-1/2 hours)	1. Business Analysis (3 hours) 2. Management Accounting and Reporting (4 hours) 2. CFM. Corporate Financial Management (3 hours) 3. Strategic Management (3 hours) 4. Business Applications (3 hours)	1. Business Environment & Concepts (2-1/2 hours) 2. Auditing & Attestation (4-1/2 hours) 3. Regulation (3 hours) 4. Financial Accounting & Reporting (4 hours)
Length of Exam	14 hours	13 hours CMA and 12 hours CFM	14 hours
When Administered	Mid-May and Mid-Nov	On Demand	Jan-Feb Apr-May July-Aug Oct-Nov
Candidates Sitting for Exam:	Total number of candidates sitting for two examinations; many are repeaters.		
1990	4,363	4,839	143,572
1991	4,547	6,404	140,042
1992	4,961	7,464	136,541
1993	5,103	7,879	140,100
1994	4,557	8,259	131,000
1995	4,649	8,675	126,000
1996	4,646	8,679	122,232
1997	5,169	*5,456	121,437
1998	7,972	*5,276	116,906
1999	11,724	*4,950	126,770
2000	15,912	*4,823	115,423
2001	19,451	*5,791	106,079
2002	26,147	*5,100	108,900
2003	31,539	*5,200	108,700
2004	30,634	*6,644	**100,000

*Does not include double-counting which occurred in previous years.
**Exam parts, not candidates for three calendar quarters, which is about a 50% drop from 2000 and 2003 levels.

Other professional accounting-related designations include CBA (Certified Bank Auditor), CDP (Certificate in Data Processing), CFA (Chartered Financial Analyst), CFE (Certified Fraud Examiner), CISA (Certified Information Systems Auditor), Enrolled Agent (one enrolled to practice before the IRS).

LISTING OF *CIA REVIEW* STUDY UNITS

Part I: Internal Audit's Role in Governance, Risk, and Control

1. Introduction to Internal Auditing
2. Charter, Independence, and Objectivity
3. Standards and Proficiency
4. Internal Audit Roles and Responsibilities
5. Control I
6. Control II
7. Planning and Supervising the Engagement
8. Managing the Internal Audit Activity I
9. Managing the Internal Audit Activity II
10. Engagement Procedures

Part II: Conducting the Internal Audit Engagement

1. Engagement Information
2. Working Papers
3. Communicating Results and Monitoring Progress
4. Specific Engagements
5. Information Technology I
6. Information Technology II
7. Statistics and Sampling
8. Other Engagement Tools
9. Ethics
10. Fraud

Part III: Business Analysis and Information Technology

1. Business Performance
2. Managing Resources and Pricing
3. Financial Accounting -- Basic Concepts
4. Financial Accounting -- Assets, Liabilities, and Equity
5. Financial Accounting -- Special Topics
6. Finance
7. Managerial Accounting
8. Regulatory, Legal, and Economic Issues
9. Information Technology I
10. Information Technology II

Part IV: Business Management Skills*

1. Structural Analysis and Strategies
2. Industry and Market Analysis
3. Environments and Strategic Decisions
4. Global Business Issues
5. Motivation and Communications
6. Organizational Structure and Effectiveness
7. Managing Groups
8. Influence and Leadership
9. Time Management
10. Conflict and Negotiation

*Persons who have passed the CPA or CMA exams (and many other professional exams) are not required to take Part IV of the CIA exam.

The explosive growth in the number of candidates sitting for the CIA exam (see previous page) is certainly the result of a combination of factors including the Sarbanes-Oxley legislation and the Enron/WorldCom scandals.

Each of the four parts consists of 80 multiple-choice questions and is 3 1/2 hours in length (8:30 - 12:00 and 1:30 - 5:00).

The first two parts of the CIA exam focus on the theory and practice of internal auditing. The body of knowledge of internal auditing and the auditing skills to be tested consist of

1. The typical undergraduate auditing class (as represented by auditing texts, e.g., Arens and Loebbecke, Taylor and Glezen, etc.)
2. Internal auditing textbooks (e.g., Sawyer and Dittenhofer, *Sawyer's Internal Auditing*, and Ratliff, Wallace, Sumners, McFarland, and Loebbecke, *Internal Auditing: Principles and Techniques*)
3. Various IIA (Institute of Internal Auditors) pronouncements (e.g., The IIA *Code of Ethics*, Standards for the International Professional Practice of Internal Auditing, and Practice Advisories)
4. Reasoning ability, communications, problem-solving, and relations with auditees in an audit context (i.e., the questions may cover audit topics, but test audit skills)

The remaining 50% of the exam, parts III and IV, assures that internal auditors are conversant with topics, methods, and techniques ranging from individual and organizational behavior to economics.

Management cannot personally observe the functioning of all officers, employees, and specialized functions (finance, marketing, operations, etc.). Each has a unique perspective. Only internal auditing is in a position to take a total organizational perspective.

Listing of *CMA/CFM REVIEW* Study Units

Part 1: Business Analysis*

1. Microeconomics
2. Macroeconomics
3. International Business Environment
4. Risk Assessment and Internal Control
5. Internal Auditing
6. Decision Making Under Uncertainty
7. Linear Programming
8. Other Quantitative Methods
9. The Accounting Standard-Setting Environment
10. Financial Statement Analysis

Part 2CMA: Management Accounting and Reporting

1. Cost and Managerial Accounting Terminology
2. Process Costing and Overhead
3. Other Product Costing Topics
4. Cost Behavior
5. Budgeting
6. Quality, the Balanced Scorecard, and Control
7. Standard Costs and Variance Analysis
8. Responsibility Accounting
9. Information Systems I
10. Information Systems II
11. Conceptual Framework
12. Financial Statements
13. Current Assets and Investments
14. Long-Lived Assets
15. Liabilities
16. Liabilities -- Special Issues
17. Equity
18. Other Income Items
19. Other Reporting Issues
20. SEC Requirements and Audit Committees

*Persons who have passed the CPA exam are not required to take Part 1 of the CMA exam.

**CMAs in good standing need only pass this part to earn the CFM designation.

Part 2CFM: Corporate Financial Management**

1. The Accounting Standard-Setting Environment
2. Working Capital Policy and Management
3. Long-Term Capital Financing
4. Financial Markets and Interest Rates
5. Investment Banking and Commercial Banking
6. Financial Statement Analysis
7. Business Combinations and Restructurings
8. Risk Management
9. External Financial Environment
10. Employee Benefit Plans and Deferred Taxes

Part 3: Strategic Management

1. Strategic Planning
2. Manufacturing Paradigms and Process Performance
3. Working Capital Finance
4. Capital Structure Finance
5. Risk and Return
6. Decision Analysis
7. Cost-Volume-Profit Analysis
8. Capital Budgeting
9. The Strategic Role of Marketing
10. Marketing Basics

Part 4: Business Applications

1. Organizational Theory
2. Organizational Theory and Decentralization
3. Motivation and the Directing Process
4. Motivation and Managing
5. Communication
6. Behavioral Issues
7. Ethics as Tested on the CMA Exam
8. CMA Part 1 Review
9. CMA Part 2 Review
10. CMA Part 3 Review

The CMA and CFM exams have broader coverage than the CPA exam in several areas. For example:

1. CMA topics like risk management, finance, management, and marketing are covered lightly, if at all, on the CPA exam.
2. The CMA exam tests internal auditing to a greater degree than does the CPA exam.
3. The CMA exam tests business ethics, but not business law.

CMA questions are generally more analysis-oriented than CPA questions. On the CPA exam, the typical requirement is the solution of an accounting problem, e.g., consolidated worksheet, funds statement, etc.

The CMA exam is given in a computer-based format. Parts 1, 2, and 3 consist of multiple-choice questions that test all levels of cognitive skills. Part 4 consists of approximately 6 essay questions that test knowledge and skills with respect to all material covered in Parts 1, 2, and 3, plus organization management and communication, behavioral issues, and ethical considerations.

LISTING OF *CPA REVIEW* STUDY UNITS

Business Environment and Concepts

1. Proprietorships and General Partnerships
2. Noncorporate Limited Liability Entities
3. Corporations: Formation, Powers, and Financing
4. Corporations: Governance and Fundamental Changes
5. Economic Concepts I
6. Economic Concepts II
7. Working Capital Policy and Management
8. Long-Term Capital Financing
9. Financial Statement Analysis
10. Risk Management
11. IT and Business Information Systems
12. IT Controls
13. Hardware, Software, and Data
14. Processing Modes, Databases, and Networks
15. E-Commerce
16. Planning and Budgeting
17. Business Performance
18. Cost Behavior and Definitions
19. Product Costing and Related Topics
20. Standard Costs and Variance Analysis

Regulation

1. AICPA Ethics
2. CPAs and the Law
3. Agency
4. Contracts
5. Debtor-Creditor Relationships
6. Government Regulation of Business
7. Negotiable Instruments, Bank Transactions, and Related Topics
8. Sales
9. Secured Transactions
10. Real Property and Insurance
11. Gross Income
12. Deductions
13. Tax Computations and Tax Procedures
14. Property Transactions
15. Corporate Taxable Income
16. Corporate Tax Computations
17. Corporate Tax Special Topics
18. S Corporations
19. Partnerships
20. Estates and Trusts

Financial Accounting and Reporting

1. Concepts and Standards
2. Financial Statements
3. Income Statement Items
4. Financial Statement Disclosure
5. Cash and Investments
6. Receivables
7. Inventories
8. Property, Plant, and Equipment
9. Intangibles and Other Assets
10. Payables and Taxes
11. Employee Benefits
12. Long-Term Liabilities
13. Leases and Contingencies
14. Equity
15. Business Combinations
16. Foreign Currency Issues and Other Topics
17. Governmental Concepts
18. Fund Accounting and Reporting
19. Not-for-Profit Concepts
20. Not-for-Profit Accounting and Reporting

Auditing and Attestation

1. Engagement Responsibilities
2. Risk Assessment
3. Strategic Planning Issues
4. Internal Control Concepts and Information Technology
5. Internal Control -- Sales-Receivables-Cash Receipts Cycle
6. Internal Control -- Purchases-Payables-Cash Disbursements Cycle
7. Internal Control -- Payroll and Other Cycles
8. Tests of Controls
9. Internal Control Communications
10. Evidence -- Objectives and Nature
11. Evidence -- The Sales-Receivables-Cash Cycle
12. Evidence -- The Purchases-Payables-Inventory Cycle
13. Evidence -- Other Assets, Liabilities, and Equities
14. Evidence -- Key Considerations
15. Evidence -- Sampling
16. Reports -- Standard, Qualified, Adverse, and Disclaimer
17. Reports -- Other Modifications
18. Review, Compilation, and Special Reports
19. Related Reporting Topics
20. Governmental Audits

Computer Administered CPA Exam (effective April 2004)

The CPA exam is now an on-demand test administered at hundreds of Prometric testing centers throughout the United States. The quality, integrity, and prestige of the CPA exam increased and the exam became easier for candidates to prepare for and pass. Computerization of the CPA exam is a win-win development. Every aspect of the exam is explained and analyzed in *CPA Review: A System for Success.* Faculty and student organizations should order this book in bulk for distribution.

WHEN TO SIT FOR THE EXAMS

Sit for all examinations as soon as you can. The CIA, CMA, and CFM exams can be taken in your last undergraduate quarter or semester, and all are offered with a 50% reduction in fees to full-time students. In many states, you may also take the CPA exam in your last quarter or semester. The EA exam does not have an educational requirement. If you are graduating in May, consider taking the CIA exam in May and the CPA, CMA, CFM, and EA exams by the end of the year. Your preparation program for all of these exams is very synergistic and not appreciably more work than preparing for just the CPA exam.

EXAMINATION PASS RATES

The pass rates on the CIA and CMA exams are about the same and are somewhat higher than the pass rate on the CPA exam. Nationally, the pass rate on the CPA exam averages about 40%-45% on each of the four parts. The pass rates on the CIA and CMA exams range from 35%-65% per part (see the tables below).

Many schools and CPA review courses advertise the quality of their programs by reporting pass rates. Obviously, the best rates are emphasized. Thus, the reported percentage may be that for first-time candidates, all candidates, candidates passing a specific section of the examination, candidates completing the examination, or even candidates successfully completing the exam after a specified number of sittings.

CIA Exam Pass Rates						
	5/02	11/02	5/03	11/03	5/04	11/04
Part I	38.1	33.2	41.3	33.1	39.8	34.3
Part II	41.0	34.2	45.0	33.9	42.2	34.6
Part III	39.0	45.4	42.7	33.6	42.7	32.8
Part IV	32.6	27.6	37.4	29.9	45.6	39.9

CMA Exam Pass Rates (revised exam, small numbers)	
Part 1	68%
Part 2	48%
Part 3	50%
Part 4	64%

IRS Special Enrollment Examination Pass Statistics

For those who sit for all four parts of the EA exam in recent years, about 20% pass all four parts; 15%-20% pass one, two, or three parts; and about 50% fail all four parts. The vast majority of candidates attempting to pass remaining parts are successful.

Remember, if you do not pass all four parts on your first sitting, you must pass the remaining parts within the following 3-year period or you will lose credit for the parts previously passed.

Reasons for the Low Pass Rates

Although a very high percentage of serious candidates successfully complete each of the examinations, the 35%-55% CPA, CIA, and CMA pass rates warrant an explanation. First, the pass rates are low (relative to bar and medical exams) because these examinations reflect the high standards of the accounting profession, which contribute greatly to the profession's reputation and also attract persons with both competence and aspiration.

Second, the pass rates are low because most accounting educational programs are at the undergraduate rather than graduate level. Undergraduate students are generally less career-oriented than graduate students. Undergraduates may look on their program as a number of individual courses required for graduation rather than as an integrated program to prepare them for professional practice.

Third, the pass rates are low because accounting programs and curricula at most colleges and universities are not given the budgetary priority they deserve. Accounting faculties are often understaffed for the number of accounting majors, the number and nature of accounting courses (problem-oriented vs. descriptive), etc., relative to other faculties. However, you cannot use this as an excuse or reason for not achieving your personal goals. You must do your best to improve your control systems and study resources.

COST TO OBTAIN AND MAINTAIN PROFESSIONAL CERTIFICATION

The cost to take the CIA exam for members of The Institute of Internal Auditors (The IIA) is a $60 registration fee plus a $70-per-part examination fee, which totals $340 (assuming you pass all parts the first time you take them). Full-time students save 50%. Nonmembers pay a $75 registration fee plus a $95-per-part examination fee. Nonmembers must also include a $50 processing fee when they submit their CPE report every 2 years. Membership in The IIA is not required. Membership dues vary from $30 to $115. See The IIA website at www.theiia.org for more information.

The cost to take the CMA/CFM exam is $115 for each of the parts and a $75 credentialing fee plus Institute of Management Accountants (IMA) membership dues, which vary from $35 for students to $175 for regular members. Membership in the IMA is required. Students may take each part of the examination once at a reduced fee of $57.50 per part and do NOT pay a credentialing fee. See the IMA website at www.imanet.org for more information.

The cost of the CPA exam varies by state. The table on page 12 lists the URL for each state board. Most states require an annual fee to maintain the CPA certificate and/or license. See www.cpa-exam.org for more information.

For the IRS EA exam, the fee for applicants taking all four parts of the 2004 examination was $55. For applicants taking fewer than four parts, the examination fee was $45. These fees are nonrefundable, but a credit may be granted toward the next year's examination fee under some circumstances, e.g., illness or death in the family, as explained in the instructions for Form 2587, the application form to be filed with the IRS. See the IRS website at www.irs.gov/taxpros/agents/ for more information.

WHERE TO TAKE THE CPA EXAM

If you are not going to practice public accounting, you may wish to become certified in a state that

1. Issues a CPA certificate separate from a license to practice
2. Does **not** require experience to receive a CPA certificate
3. Does **not** require continuing professional education of CPA certificate holders
4. Does **not** require residency to sit for the CPA exam

You may also be concerned with the 150-hour requirement to sit for the CPA exam. Consult your state board contact information on page 12.

STEPS TO BECOME A CPA

1. Decide when you are going to take the CPA exam (the sooner, the better!).
2. Determine the state board to which you will apply to sit for the CPA exam. Read "Where to Take the CPA Exam" above.
3. Obtain, complete, and submit your application form, including transcripts, etc.
4. Commit to thorough, systematic preparation for the exam as described in *CPA Review: A System for Success*, also available on our website at **www.gleim.com/accounting/cpa/systemforsuccess.php**
5. Work systematically through each study unit in the four Gleim *CPA Review* books (*Business*, *Auditing*, *Regulation*, and *Financial*).
6. Use Gleim's ***CPA Test Prep*** software: over 6,000 CPA questions, all updated to current tax law, FASB Statements, etc.
7. Sit for and PASS the CPA exam while you are in control, as described in Study Units 6 and 7 of *CPA Review: A System for Success.* Gleim will make it easy. Call (800) 87-GLEIM for more information.

STATE BOARDS OF ACCOUNTANCY

All 50 states (and the District of Columbia, Guam, Puerto Rico, and the Virgin Islands) have an administrative agency that administers the laws and rules which regulate the practice of public accounting in each state. Each of these 54 jurisdictions contracts with the AICPA to use the AICPA's Uniform CPA Examination.

While the 54 jurisdictions agree on using the same examination, the rules and procedures for applying to take the exam and becoming licensed to practice public accounting vary considerably. Accordingly, you should call or write to your state board for a CPA exam application form. With the form, you will receive that board's rules, regulations, and directions to you as a CPA candidate.

The following page contains a list of the state boards, their addresses, phone numbers, and websites. Please visit our website at www.gleim.com for the most current information regarding CPA requirements by state. If you have any questions, please check with your state board for final verification.

STATE BOARDS OF ACCOUNTANCY CONTACT INFORMATION

NOTE: Contact your State Board for complete up-to-date information.

STATE BOARD • ADDRESS		Telephone #	Website
AK	P.O. Box 110806 • Juneau, AK 99811-0806	(907) 465-3811	www.dced.state.ak.us/occ/pcpa.htm
AL	P.O. Box 300375 • Montgomery, AL 36130-0375	(334) 242-5700	www.asbpa.state.al.us
AR	101 East Capitol, Suite 430 • Little Rock, AR 72201	(501) 682-1520	www.state.ar.us/asbpa
AZ	100 N. 15th Avenue, Room 165 • Phoenix, AZ 85007	(602) 364-0900	www.accountancy.state.az.us/
CA	2000 Evergreen St., Suite 250 • Sacramento, CA 95815-3832	(916) 263-3680	www.dca.ca.gov/cba
CO	1560 Broadway, Suite 1340 • Denver, CO 80202	(303) 894-7800	www.dora.state.co.us/accountants
CT	30 Trinity Street • Hartford, CT 06115	(860) 509-6179	www.sots.state.ct.us/SBOA/SBOAindex.html
DC	941 N. Capital St., NE Rm 7200 • Washington, DC 20002	(202) 442-4461	www.dcra.dc.gov/information/build_pla/occupational/accountancy/index.shtm
DE	Cannon Building, Suite 203, 861 Silver Lake Blvd. • Dover, DE 19904	(302) 744-4500	www.professionallicensing.state.de.us
FL	240 NW 76th Drive, Suite A • Gainesville, FL 32607	(352) 333-2500	www.state.fl.us/dbpr/cpa/index.shtml
GA	237 Coliseum Drive • Macon, GA 31217-3858	(478) 207-1400	www.sos.state.ga.us/plb/accountancy/
GU	Suite 508, GCIC Building 414 W. Soledad Ave. • Hagatna, GU 96910-5014	(671) 477-1050	www.guam.net/gov/gba/
HI	P.O. Box 3469 • Honolulu, HI 96801-3469	(808) 586-2696	www.state.hi.us/dcca/pvl/areas_accountancy.html
IA	1920 SE Hulsizer Avenue • Ankeny, IA 50021-3961	(515) 281-4126	www.state.ia.us/iacc
ID	P.O. Box 83720 • Boise, ID 83720-0002	(208) 334-2490	www.state.id.us/boa
IL	505 E. Green, Room 216 Champaign, IL 61820-5723	(217) 333-1565	www.illinois-cpa-exam.com
IN	302 West Washington St., E034 • Indianapolis, IN 46204-2246	(317) 232-5987	www.state.in.us/pla/bandc/accountancy/
KS	900 SW Jackson St., Suite 556 • Topeka, KS 66612-1239	(785) 296-2162	www.ksboa.org
KY	332 W. Broadway, Suite 310 • Louisville, KY 40202-2115	(502) 595-3037	cpa.state.ky.us
LA	601 Poydras St., Suite 1770 • New Orleans, LA 70139	(504) 566-1244	www.cpaboard.state.la.us
MA	239 Causeway St., Suite 450 • Boston, MA 02114	(617) 727-1806	www.state.ma.us/reg/boards/pa
MD	500 N. Calvert Street, 3rd Floor • Baltimore, MD 21202-3651	(410) 230-6322	www.dllr.state.md.us/license/occprof/account.html
ME	35 State House Station • Augusta, ME 04333	(207) 624-8603	www.state.me.us/pfr/olr/categories/cat01.htm
MI	P.O. Box 30018 • Lansing, MI 48909-7518	(517) 241-9249	www.michigan.gov/cis/0,1607,7-154-10557_12992_13878-40080--,00.html
MN	85 East 7th Place, Suite 125 • St. Paul, MN 55101	(612) 296-7938	www.boa.state.mn.us
MO	P.O. Box 613 • Jefferson City, MO 65102	(573) 751-0012	www.ded.mo.gov/regulatorylicensing/professionalregistration/account/
MS	5 Old River Place, Suite 104 • Jackson, MS 39202-3449	(601) 354-7320	www.msbpa.state.ms.us
MT	P.O. Box 200513 • Helena, MT 59620-0513	(406) 841-2389	www.discoveringmontana.com/dli/pac
NC	P.O. Box 12827 • Raleigh, NC 27605-2827	(919) 733-4222	www.cpaboard.state.nc.us/
ND	2701 S. Columbia Rd. • Grand Forks, ND 58201-6029	(800) 532-5904	www.state.nd.us/ndsba
NE	P.O. Box 94725 • Lincoln, NE 68509-4725	(402) 471-3595	www.nol.org/home/BPA
NH	6 Chenell Drive, Suite 220 • Concord, NH 03301	(603) 271-3286	www.nh.gov/accountancy/
NJ	P.O. Box 45000 • Newark, NJ 07101	(973) 504-6380	www.state.nj.us/lps/ca/nonmed.htm
NM	1650 University NE, Suite 400-A • Albuquerque, NM 87102	(505) 841-9108	www.rld.state.nm.us/b&c/accountancy/index.htm
NV	200 South Virginia St., Suite 670 • Reno, NV 89501-2408	(775) 786-0231	www.nvaccountancy.com
NY	89 Washington Avenue, 2nd Floor East Mezzanine • Albany, NY 12234-1000	(518) 474-3817 ext. 160	www.op.nysed.gov/cpa.htm
OH	77 South High St., 18th Floor • Columbus, OH 43215-6128	(614) 466-4135	www.acc.ohio.gov
OK	4545 Lincoln Blvd., Suite 165 • Oklahoma City, OK 73105-3413	(405) 521-2397	www.youroklahoma.com/oab
OR	3218 Pringle Road SE, Suite 110 • Salem, OR 97302-6307	(503) 378-4181	www.boahost.com/index.lasso
PA	124 Pine Street, 1st Floor • Harrisburg, PA 17101-2649	(717) 783-1404	www.dos.state.pa.us/bpoa/accbd/mainpage.htm
PR	Box 9023271, Old San Juan Station • San Juan, PR 00902-3271	(787) 722-4816	www.estado.gobierno.pr/contador.htm
RI	233 Richmond St., Suite 236 • Providence, RI 02903-4236	(401) 222-3185	www.dbr.state.ri.us/account.html
SC	P.O. Box 11329 • Columbia, SC 29211-1329	(803) 896-4770	www.llr.state.sc.us/POL/accountancy/INDEX.ASP
SD	301 E. 14th St., Suite 200 • Sioux Falls, SD 57104	(605) 367-5770	www.state.sd.us/dcr/accountancy
TN	500 James Robertson Pkwy., 2nd Floor • Nashville, TN 37243-1141	(615) 741-2550	www.state.tn.us/commerce/boards/tnsba/index.html
TX	333 Guadalupe Tower III, Suite 900 • Austin, TX 78701-3900	(512) 305-7800	www.tsbpa.state.tx.us
UT	P.O. Box 146741 • Salt Lake City, UT 84114-6741	(801) 530-6396	www.dopl.utah.gov
VA	3600 West Broad Street, Suite 696 • Richmond, VA 23230-4916	(804) 367-8505	www.boa.state.va.us
VI	Office of Boards and Commissions Golden Rock Shopping Center • Christiansted, St. Croix, VI 00820	(340) 773-4305	www.dlca.gov.vi
VT	26 Terrace St, Drawer 09 • Montpelier, VT 05609-1106	(802) 828-2191	www.vtprofessionals.org/opr1/accountants
WA	P.O. Box 9131 • Olympia, WA 98507-9131	(360) 753-2585	www.cpaboard.wa.gov
WI	P.O. Box 8935 • Madison, WI 53708-8935	(608) 266-5511	www.drl.state.wi.us
WV	122 Capitol Street, Suite 100 • Charleston, WV 25301	(304) 558-3557	www.state.wv.us/wvboa/
WY	2020 Carey Avenue • Cheyenne, WY 82002-0610	(307) 777-7551	cpaboard.state.wy.us

CPA Examination Services, a division of the National Association of State Boards of Accountancy, processes the CPA exam applications in many states, and issues Notices To Schedule (NTS) to all CPA candidates. Call (800) 877-EXAM

USING EXAM QUESTION AND EXPLANATION BOOKS TO IMPROVE GRADES

Use the other Gleim exam question books to ensure your understanding of each topic you study in your accounting and business law courses. Access the largest bank of exam questions (including thousands from past certification exams) that is widely used by professors. Get immediate feedback on your study effort while you take your "practice" tests.

AUDITING & SYSTEMS EXAM QUESTIONS AND EXPLANATIONS (Twelfth Edition)

FINANCIAL ACCOUNTING EXAM QUESTIONS AND EXPLANATIONS (Twelfth Edition)

COST/MANAGERIAL ACCOUNTING EXAM QUESTIONS AND EXPLANATIONS (Seventh Edition)

FEDERAL TAX EXAM QUESTIONS AND EXPLANATIONS (Fifteenth Edition)

Individual
1. Gross Income
2. Exclusions from Gross Income
3. Business Expenses and Losses
4. Limitations on Losses
5. Other Deductions for AGI
6. Deductions from AGI
7. Individual Tax Computations
8. Credits

Property
9. Basis
10. Depreciation, Amortization, and Depletion
11. Capital Gains and Losses
12. Sale of Business Property
13. Nontaxable Property Transactions

Other Entities
14. Partnerships: Formation and Operation
15. Partnerships: Distributions, Sales, and Exchanges
16. Corporate Formations and Operations
17. Advanced Corporate Topics
18. Income Taxation of Estates, Trusts, and Tax-Exempt Organizations

Other Topics
19. Accounting Methods
20. Employment Taxes and Withholding
21. Wealth Transfer Taxes
22. Preparer Rules
23. Federal Tax Process and Procedure

BUSINESS LAW/LEGAL STUDIES EXAM QUESTIONS AND EXPLANATIONS (Sixth Edition)

Introduction
1. The American Legal System
2. The American Court System
3. Civil Litigation and Procedure
4. Constitutional Law
5. Administrative Law
6. Criminal Law and Procedure
7. Tort Law
8. Contracts: The Agreement
9. Contracts: Consideration
10. Contracts: Capacity, Legality, Mutuality, and Statute of Frauds
11. Contracts: Interpretation, Conditions, Discharge, and Remedies
12. Contracts: Third-Party Rights and Duties
13. Sale of Goods: The Sales Contract, Interpretation, and Risk of Loss
14. Sale of Goods: Performance, Remedies, and Warranties
15. Negotiable Instruments: Types, Negotiation, and Holder in Due Course
16. Negotiable Instruments: Liability, Bank Transactions, and EFTs
17. Negotiable Instruments: Documents of Title and Letters of Credit
18. Secured Transactions
19. Suretyship
20. Bankruptcy
21. Personal Property and Bailments
22. Computers and the Law
23. Real Property: Interests and Rights
24. Real Property: Transactions
25. Mortgages
26. Creditor Law and Liens
27. Landlord and Tenant
28. Wills, Estate Administration, and Trusts
29. Agency
30. Partnerships and Other Entities
31. Corporations: Nature, Formation, and Financing
32. Corporations: Operations and Management
33. Federal Securities Regulation
34. Insurance
35. Environmental Law
36. Antitrust
37. Consumer Protection
38. Employment Regulation
39. International Business Law
40. Accountants' Legal Responsibilities

INCREASE YOUR COMPETITIVENESS!

After graduation, you will be competing with graduates from schools across the country in the job market. Make sure you measure up to the standards your counterparts at other schools measure up to (which will be tested on the CPA and other certification exams).

Gleim's ***Exam Questions and Explanations Test Prep*** software is a powerful knowledge transfer tool for students and professors. The software allows students to test themselves interactively with all of the multiple-choice questions from the corresponding *Exam Questions and Explanations* book. Professors use the same software to generate quizzes and exams.

CITATIONS TO AUTHORITATIVE PRONOUNCEMENTS

Throughout the book, we refer to authoritative accounting pronouncements by the following abbreviations:

ARB - Fifty-one Accounting Research Bulletins were issued by the AICPA's Committee on Accounting Procedure from 1939 to 1959. ARB 43 is a codification of the first 42 ARBs and consists of numerous chapters. References to ARB 43 indicate the pertinent chapter number.

APB - Thirty-one APB Opinions were published by the AICPA's Accounting Principles Board from 1959 to 1973.

SFAS - Statements of Financial Accounting Standards are pronouncements of the Financial Accounting Standards Board (FASB), established in 1973. Many SFASs supersede prior SFASs, APB Opinions, and Accounting Research Bulletins.

SGAS - Forty-six Statements of Governmental Accounting Standards have been issued by the Governmental Accounting Standards Board (GASB), established in 1984.

FASB Interpretations - Financial Accounting Standards Board Interpretations interpret existing pronouncements rather than establish new, superseding, or amending positions.

SFAC - FASB Statements of Financial Accounting Concepts establish financial accounting and reporting objectives and concepts. SFACs are included in the other accounting literature section of the GAAP hierarchy for nongovernmental entities, which is subordinate to the categories of established accounting principles. Relevant other accounting literature is considered only in the absence of established principles. They were designed for use by the FASB in developing their other authoritative pronouncements.

SOP - Statements of Position are pronouncements of the Accounting Standards Executive Committee of the AICPA. SOPs were originally intended to provide accounting practitioners with guidance on unusual and specialized topics. SOPs cleared by the FASB are included in category (b) of the GAAP hierarchy for financial statements of nongovernmental entities. In the future, the content of AICPA SOPs will be limited to matters not appropriate for FASB pronouncements, e.g., personal financial statements.

The number following each acronym is the number of the pronouncement. The first time an authoritative pronouncement is cited, its complete title is given in italics. When the pronouncement is referred to again in the related series of questions, the title is usually omitted.

COVERAGE OF AUTHORITATIVE PRONOUNCEMENTS

Most of the authoritative pronouncements from the AICPA and the FASB currently in effect are covered in this book. The following listing of Study Units 1 through 30 indicates where coverage of each pronouncement can be found:

Study Unit 1 - Conceptual Framework
ARB 43-3A
SFAC 1, 2, 5, 6

Study Unit 2 - The Accounting Process

Study Unit 3 - Comprehensive Income and the Statement of Income
ARB 43-2A
APB 9, 13, 30
SFAS 16, 130, 144, 145, 154

Study Unit 4 - Present Value and Future Value
APB 21
SFAC 7

Study Unit 5 - Current Assets, Cash, Accounts Receivable, and Short-Term Notes Receivable
ARB 43-1A, 3A
APB 6, 12
SFAS 5, 140

Study Unit 6 - Inventory
ARB 43-4
SFAS 48, 49, 151

Study Unit 7 - Property, Plant, and Equipment
APB 6, 29
SFAS 34, 42, 58, 62, 144, 153
FASB Interpretation No. 30

Study Unit 8 - Depreciation and Depletion
ARB 43-9

Study Unit 9 - Intangible Assets and Research and Development Costs
SFAS 2, 45, 68, 86, 142, 144
FASB Interpretation No. 6
AICPA SOP 93-7, 97-2, 98-1, 98-5

Study Unit 10 - Investments in Debt Securities, Equity Securities, and Derivatives
APB 18
SFAS 91, 107, 114, 115, 133, 138, 149
FASB Interpretation No. 35

Study Unit 11 - Current Liabilities, Compensated Absences, and Contingencies
ARB 43-3A
SFAS 5, 6, 43, 49, 78
FASB Interpretation No. 14, 45
AICPA SOP 96-1

Study Unit 12 - Long-Term Liabilities
APB 14, 21, 26
SFAS 15, 47, 84, 140, 143, 145, 146, 150
FASB Interpretation No. 47

Study Unit 13 - Pensions, Other Postretirement Benefits, and Postemployment Benefits
SFAS 35, 87, 88, 106, 112, 132(R)

Study Unit 14 - Leases
SFAS 13, 22, 23, 27, 28, 29, 91, 98, 145
FASB Interpretation No. 19, 23, 24, 26, 27

Study Unit 15 - Corporate Equity
ARB 43-7A, 7B
APB 6, 9, 10, 12, 29
AICPA SOP 76-3
SFAS 15, 116, 150

Study Unit 16 - EPS and Share-Based Payment
SFAS 123(R), 128, 129

Study Unit 17 - Accounting for Income Taxes
SFAS 37, 109
APB 2, 4, 23

Study Unit 18 - Accounting Changes and Error Corrections
APB 9
SFAS 16, 154
FASB Interpretation No. 1

Study Unit 19 - Statement of Cash Flows
SFAS 95, 102, 104, 115
ARB 43-3A

Study Unit 20 - Accounting for Changing Prices
SFAS 89

Study Unit 21 - Financial Statement Disclosures
APB 22
AICPA SOP 94-6
SFAS 7, 57, 95, 131

Study Unit 22 - Long-Term Construction-Type Contracts, Installment Sales, and Consignments
ARB 45
APB 10
AICPA SOP 81-1
SFAC 5

Study Unit 23 - Financial Statement Analysis Based on Percentage Relationships

Study Unit 24 - GAAP Accounting for Partnerships

Study Unit 25 - Business Combinations, Consolidations, and Branch Accounting
ARB 51
APB 6
SFAS 72, 94, 141, 142, 147
FASB Interpretation No. 4, 21, 46

Study Unit 26 - Interim Financial Reporting
APB 28
SFAS 16, 154
FASB Interpretation No. 18

Study Unit 27 - Foreign Currency Translation and Transactions
SFAS 52, 133, 137, 138
FASB Interpretation No. 37

Study Unit 28 - Accounting for State and Local Government Entities
[Statements and Interpretations of the Governmental Accounting Standards Board (GASB) and AICPA and FASB pronouncements specifically made applicable to state and local governments by the GASB constitute officially established accounting principles for state and local governmental accounting.]

Study Unit 29 - Not-for-Profit Organizations
SFAS 93, 116, 117, 124, 136
SFAC 4
AICPA SOP 98-2
Audit and Accounting Guides for Not-for-Profit Organizations and Health Care Organizations

Study Unit 30 - Specialized Accounting Issues
AICPA SOP 75-2, 78-9, 82-1
SFAS 19, 25, 50, 51, 60, 61, 63, 65, 66, 67, 69, 71, 90, 91, 92, 97, 101, 145, 152
FASB Interpretation No. 36
AICPA Statements on Standards for Attestation Engagements

ARB, APB, AND FASB PRONOUNCEMENT CROSS-REFERENCE

The following listing of pronouncements directs you to the study unit in this study manual related to the coverage of each pronouncement listed. The study unit number follows the pronouncement title. Most pronouncements are covered by at least two multiple-choice questions. The index can also be helpful in locating questions on specific topics.

Pronouncement	Gleim Study Unit(s)	Accounting Research Bulletins
ARB 43		
1A	5	Rules Adopted by Membership
1B	15	Profits or Losses on Treasury Stock
2A	3	Comparative Financial Statements
3A	1, 5, 11	Current Assets and Current Liabilities
4	6	Inventory Pricing
7A	15	Quasi-Reorganization
7B	15	Stock Dividends and Stock Splits
9	8	Depreciation
10A	3	Real and Personal Property Taxes
11	3	Government Contracts
ARB 45	22	Long-Term Construction Contracts
ARB 46	15	Discontinuance of Dating Retained Earnings
ARB 51	25	Consolidated Financial Statements
		Accounting Principles Board Opinions
APB 2 and 4	17	Accounting for the "Investment Credit"
APB 6	5, 7, 15, 25	Status of Accounting Research Bulletins
APB 9	3, 15, 18	Reporting the Results of Operations
APB 10	15, 22	Omnibus Opinion-1966
APB 12	5, 13, 15	Omnibus Opinion-1967
APB 13	3	Amending Paragraph 6 of APB Opinion No. 9, Application to Commercial Banks
APB 14	12	Convertible Debt and Debt Issued with Stock Purchase Warrants
APB 18	10	Equity Method for Investments in Common Stock
APB 21	4, 12	Interest on Receivables and Payables
APB 22	21	Disclosure of Accounting Policies
APB 23	17	Accounting for Income Taxes-Special Areas
APB 26	12	Early Extinguishment of Debt
APB 28	26	Interim Financial Reporting
APB 29	7, 15	Accounting for Nonmonetary Transactions
APB 30	3	Reporting the Results of Operations

Pronouncement	Gleim Study Unit(s)	Statements of Financial Accounting Standards
SFAS 2	9	Accounting for Research and Development Costs
SFAS 5	5, 11	Accounting for Contingencies
SFAS 6	11	Classification of Short-Term Obligations Expected to be Refinanced
SFAS 7	21	Accounting and Reporting by Development Stage Enterprises
SFAS 13	14	Accounting for Leases
SFAS 15	12, 15	Accounting by Debtors and Creditors for Troubled Debt Restructurings
SFAS 16	3, 18, 26	Prior Period Adjustments
SFAS 19	30	Financial Accounting and Reporting by Oil and Gas Producing Companies
SFAS 22	14	Changes in the Provisions of Lease Agreements Resulting from Refundings of Tax-Exempt Debt
SFAS 23	14	Inception of the Lease
SFAS 25	30	Suspension of Certain Accounting Requirements for Oil and Gas Producing Companies
SFAS 27	14	Classification of Renewals or Extensions of Existing Sales-Type or Direct Financing Leases
SFAS 28	14	Accounting for Sales with Leasebacks
SFAS 29	14	Determining Contingent Rentals
SFAS 34	7	Capitalization of Interest Cost
SFAS 35	13	Accounting and Reporting by Defined Benefit Pension Plans
SFAS 37	17	Balance Sheet Classification of Deferred Income Taxes
SFAS 42	7	Determining Materiality for Capitalization of Interest Cost
SFAS 43	11	Accounting for Compensated Absences
SFAS 45	9	Accounting for Franchise Fee Revenue
SFAS 47	12	Disclosure of Long-Term Obligations
SFAS 48	6	Revenue Recognition When Right of Return Exists
SFAS 49	6, 11	Accounting for Product Financing Arrangements
SFAS 50	30	Financial Reporting in the Record and Music Industry
SFAS 51	30	Financial Reporting by Cable Television Companies
SFAS 52	27	Foreign Currency Translation
SFAS 57	21	Related Party Disclosures
SFAS 58	7	Capitalization of Interest Cost in Financial Statements that Include Investments Accounted for by the Equity Method
SFAS 60	30	Accounting and Reporting by Insurance Enterprises
SFAS 61	30	Accounting for Title Plant
SFAS 62	7	Capitalization of Interest Cost in Situations Involving Certain Tax-Exempt Borrowings and Certain Gifts and Grants
SFAS 63	30	Financial Reporting by Broadcasters
SFAS 65	30	Accounting for Certain Mortgage Banking Activities
SFAS 66	30	Accounting for Sales of Real Estate
SFAS 67	30	Accounting for Costs and Initial Rental Operations of Real Estate Projects
SFAS 68	9	Research and Development Arrangements
SFAS 69	30	Disclosures about Oil and Gas Producing Activities
SFAS 71	30	Accounting for the Effects of Certain Types of Regulation
SFAS 72	25	Accounting for Certain Acquisitions of Banking or Thrift Institutions (Applies only if the institutions are mutual enterprises)
SFAS 78	11	Classification of Obligations that Are Callable by the Creditor
SFAS 84	12	Induced Conversions of Convertible Debt
SFAS 86	9	Accounting for the Costs of Computer Software to Be Sold, Leased, or Otherwise Marketed
SFAS 87	13	Employers' Accounting for Pensions
SFAS 88	13	Employers' Accounting for Settlements and Curtailments of Defined Benefit Pension Plans and for Termination Benefits
SFAS 89	20	Financial Reporting and Changing Prices
SFAS 90	30	Regulated Enterprises - Accounting for Phase-in Plans, Abandonments, and Disallowances of Plant Costs
SFAS 91	10, 14, 30	Accounting for Nonrefundable Fees and Costs Associated with Originating and Acquiring Loans
SFAS 92	30	Regulated Enterprises - Accounting for Phase-in Plans
SFAS 93	29	Recognition of Depreciation by Not-for-Profit Organizations
SFAS 94	25	Consolidation of All Majority-Owned Subsidiaries
SFAS 95	19, 21	Statement of Cash Flows
SFAS 97	30	Accounting and Reporting by Insurance Enterprises for Certain Long-Duration Contracts and for Realized Gains and Losses from the Sale of Investments

Pronounce-ment	Gleim Study Unit(s)	Statements of Financial Accounting Standards
SFAS 98	14	Accounting for Leases - Sale-Leaseback Transactions Involving Real Estate; Sales-Type Leases of Real Estate; Definition of the Lease Term; Initial Direct Costs of Direct Financing Leases
SFAS 101	30	Regulated Enterprises - Accounting for the Discontinuation of Application of FASB Statement No. 71
SFAS 102	19	Statement of Cash Flows - Exemption of Certain Enterprises and Classification of Cash Flows from Certain Securities Acquired for Resale
SFAS 104	19	Statement of Cash Flows - Net Reporting of Certain Cash Receipts and Cash Payments and Classification of Cash Flows from Hedging Transactions
SFAS 106	13	Employers' Accounting for Postretirement Benefits Other than Pensions
SFAS 107	10, 21	Disclosures about Fair Value of Financial Statements
SFAS 109	17	Accounting for Income Taxes
SFAS 110	13	Reporting by Defined Benefit Pension Plans of Investment Contracts
SFAS 111	18	Revision of FASB Statement No. 32 and Technical Corrections
SFAS 112	13	Employers' Accounting for Postemployment Benefits
SFAS 113	30	Accounting and Reporting for Reissuance of Short-Duration and Long-Duration Contracts
SFAS 114	10	Accounting by Creditors for Impairment of a Loan
SFAS 115	10, 19	Accounting for Certain Investments in Debt and Equity Securities
SFAS 116	15, 29	Accounting for Contributions Received and Contributions Made
SFAS 117	29	Financial Statements of Not-for-Profit Organizations
SFAS 118	12	Accounting by Creditors for Impairment of a Loan-Income Recognition and Disclosures
SFAS 120	30	Accounting and Reporting by Mutual Life Insurance Enterprises and by Insurance Enterprises for Certain Long-Duration Participating Contracts
SFAS 123(R)	15	Accounting for Share-Based Payment
SFAS 124	29	Accounting for Certain Investments Held by Not-for-Profit Organizations
SFAS 126	10	Exemption from Certain Required Disclosures about Financial Instruments
SFAS 128	16	Earnings Per Share
SFAS 129	16	Disclosure of Information about Capital Structure
SFAS 130	3	Reporting Comprehensive Income
SFAS 131	21	Disclosures about Segments of an Enterprise and Related Information
SFAS 132(R)	13	Employers' Disclosure about Pensions and Other Postretirement Benefits
SFAS 133	10, 27	Accounting for Derivative Instruments and Hedging Activities
SFAS 134	30	Accounting for Mortgage-Backed Securities Retained after the Securitization of Mortgage Loans Held for Sale by a Mortgage Banking Enterprise
SFAS 135	13	Rescission of FASB Statement No. 75 and Technical Corrections
SFAS 136	29	Transfer of Assets to a Not-for-Profit Organization or Charitable Trust that Raises Contributions for Others
SFAS 137	10, 27	Accounting for Derivative Instruments and Hedging Activities - Deferral of the Effective Date of FASB Statement No. 133
SFAS 138	10, 27	Accounting for Certain Derivative Instruments and Certain Hedging Activities
SFAS 139	30	Rescission of FASB Statement No. 53 and Amendments to FASB Statements No. 63, 89, and 121
SFAS 140	5, 12	Accounting for Transfers and Servicing of Financial Assets and Extinguishments of Liabilities (a replacement of SFAS 125)
SFAS 141	25	Business Combinations
SFAS 142	9, 25	Goodwill and Other Intangible Assets
SFAS 143	12	Accounting for Asset Retirement Obligations
SFAS 144	3, 7, 9	Accounting for Impairment or Disposal of Long-Lived Assets
SFAS 145	3, 12, 14, 30	Rescission of FASB Statements 4, 44, and 64; Amendment of FASB Statement No. 13; and Technical Corrections
SFAS 146	12	Accounting for Costs Associated with Exit or Disposal Activities
SFAS 147	25	Acquisitions of Certain Financial Institutions
SFAS 148	15	Accounting for Stock-Based Compensation-Transition and Disclosure
SFAS 149	10	Amendment of Statement 133 on Derivative Instruments and Hedging Activities
SFAS 150	12	Accounting for Certain Financial Instruments with Characteristics of Liabilities and Equity
SFAS 151	6	Inventory Costs
SFAS 152	30	Accounting for Real Estate Time-Sharing Transactions
SFAS 153	7	Exchanges of Nonmonetary Assets
SFAS 154	18, 26	Accounting Changes and Error Corrections

Pronouncement	Gleim Study Unit(s)	FASB Interpretations
No. 1	18	Accounting Changes Related to the Cost of Inventory
No. 4	25	Applicability of SFAS 2 to Business Combinations Accounted for by the Purchase Method
No. 6	9	Applicability of SFAS 2 to Computer Software
No. 7	21	Applying SFAS 7 in Financial Statements of Established Operating Enterprise
No. 8	11	Classification of a Short-Term Obligation Repaid Prior to Being Replaced by a Long-Term Security
No. 9	25	Applying APB 16 and 17 When a Savings and Loan Association or Similar Institution is Acquired in a Business Combination Accounted for by the Purchase Method (Applies only if the institutions are mutual enterprises)
No. 14	11	Reasonable Estimation of the Amount of Loss
No. 18	26	Accounting for Income Taxes in Interim Periods
No. 19	14	Lessee Guarantee of the Residual Value of Leased Property
No. 21	25	Accounting for Leases in a Business Combination
No. 23	14	Leases of Certain Property Owned by a Governmental Unit or Authority
No. 24	14	Leases Involving only Part of a Building
No. 26	14	Accounting for Purchase of a Leased Asset by the Lessee during the Term of the Lease
No. 27	14	Accounting for a Loss on a Sublease
No. 30	7	Accounting for Involuntary Conversions of Nonmonetary Assets to Monetary Assets
No. 33	30	Applying SFAS 34 to Oil and Gas Producing Operations Accounted for by the Full Cost Method
No. 35	10	Criteria for Applying the Equity Method of Accounting for Investments in Common Stock
No. 36	30	Accounting for Exploratory Wells in Progress at the End of a Period
No. 37	27	Accounting for Translation Adjustments upon Sale of Part of an Investment in a Foreign Entity
No. 39	21	Offsetting of Amounts Related to Certain Contracts
No. 40	30	Applicability of GAAP to Mutual Life Insurance and Other Enterprises
No. 41	21	Offsetting of Amounts Related to Certain Repurchase and Reverse Repurchase Agreements
No. 43	30	Real Estate Sales
No. 45	11	Guarantor's Accounting and Disclosure Requirements for Guarantees, Including Indirect Guarantees of Indebtedness to Others
No. 46	25	Consolidation of Variable Interest Entities (Revised December 2003)
		Statements of Financial Accounting Concepts
SFAC 1	1	Objectives of Financial Reporting by Business Enterprises
SFAC 2	1	Qualitative Characteristics: Criteria for Selecting and Evaluating Financial Accounting and Reporting Policies
SFAC 4	29	Objectives of Financial Reporting by Nonbusiness Organizations
SFAC 5	1	Recognition and Measurement in Financial Statements of Business Enterprises
SFAC 6	1	Elements of Financial Statements
SFAC 7	1	Using Cash Flow Information and Present Value in Accounting Measurements
		Selected Statements of Position
81-1	22	Accounting for Performance of Construction-Type and Certain Production-Type Contracts
82-1	30	Accounting and Financial Reporting for Personal Financial Statements
93-7	9	Advertising Costs
94-6	21	Disclosure of Certain Significant Risks and Uncertainties
96-1	11	Environmental Remediation Liabilities
97-2	9	Software Revenue Recognition
98-1	9	Accounting for the Costs of Computer Software Developed or Obtained for Internal Use
98-2	28, 29	Accounting for the Costs of Activities of Not-for-Profit Organizations and State and Local Governmental Entities That Include Fund Raising
98-5	9	Reporting on the Costs of Start-Up Activities

STUDY UNIT ONE
CONCEPTUAL FRAMEWORK

The conceptual framework is a coherent set of interrelated objectives and fundamental concepts. This framework is contained in the **Statements of Financial Accounting Concepts (SFACs)**. These Statements do not themselves establish the accounting and reporting standards for particular items and events. Instead, their purpose is to describe concepts and relationships as a basis for developing a consistent set of standards defining accounting and reporting requirements.

The **primary objective of financial reporting** by business enterprises is to provide **useful information** to investors and creditors in making rational economic decisions. The usefulness of the information is based on the assumptions that investors and creditors have a reasonable understanding of business and economic activities, and they are willing to study the information presented with reasonable diligence. Information should be useful to investors and creditors in estimating the total future cash flows that they will receive from their investment and credit decisions. Because investors' and creditors' cash flows are related to those of the enterprise, financial accounting should provide information that helps to estimate future net cash inflows to the enterprise.

The primary focus of financial accounting by business enterprises is information about **earnings**. These earnings are based on the **accrual basis** rather than the cash basis of accounting because it usually provides a better indication of an enterprise's present and continuing ability to generate cash flows. Financial accounting should also provide information about an enterprise's financial position (its assets, liabilities, and equity) and the effects of transactions, events, and circumstances that change the enterprise's financial position.

The primary purpose of **accrual accounting** is to describe an enterprise's earning process during an accounting period. It is considered to be a better description of this process than the cash basis. Under accrual accounting, the financial effects of transactions and other events and circumstances that have cash consequences for an entity are recorded in the accounting periods in which those transactions, events, and circumstances occur, not just in the periods when cash is received or paid.

Financial reporting by business enterprises is not an end in itself; it is intended to provide information that is useful in making reasoned choices among alternative uses of scarce resources in the conduct of business and economic activities. The underlying **objectives of financial reporting** should be responsive to the economic, legal, political, and social environment in which reporting takes place. These objectives also are affected by the characteristics and limitations of the kinds of information that financial reporting can provide. Financial information (1) pertains to business enterprises rather than to industries or the economy as a whole; (2) often results from estimated, rather than exact, measures; (3) largely reflects the financial effects of transactions and events that have already occurred; (4) is usually only one part of the information needed by investors and creditors in formulating their decisions; and (5) is provided and used at a cost.

The most important characteristic of financial information is its **usefulness** for decision making. The two most important qualities that make accounting information useful are relevance and reliability (the primary decision-specific qualities). Accounting information is **relevant** if it is capable of making a difference in a decision. To be relevant, information must be timely as well as possess predictive value or feedback value. Accounting information is **reliable** if it is reasonably free of error and bias and represents what it purports to represent. The user also should have assurance that the information possesses that representational quality. Moreover, reliable information is verifiable and neutral. **Comparability** (including consistency) is a secondary quality that interacts with relevance and reliability to contribute to usefulness. Accounting information also is subject to two pervasive constraints. The first constraint is that the **benefits** of the information should exceed the **costs** of providing the information. The second is that the qualities of information are subject to a **materiality** threshold.

Financial statements are the principal means of communicating financial information to investors and creditors. A full set reports financial position, earnings (net income), comprehensive income, cash flows, and investments by and distributions to owners. **Elements** of financial statements are broad classes of items. For business enterprises, they include assets, liabilities, equity, revenues, expenses, gains, losses, investments by owners, distributions to owners, and comprehensive income. The traditional financial statements use a financial (not physical) **capital maintenance concept** to distinguish a return **on** capital from a return **of** capital.

The **statement of financial position** (balance sheet) presents information about an entity's resources (assets), its obligations to creditors (liabilities), and its residual ownership interests (equity) at a moment in time. **Assets** are probable future economic benefits obtained or controlled by a particular entity as a result of past transactions or events. **Liabilities** represent probable future sacrifices of economic benefits arising from present obligations of an entity to transfer assets or provide services to another entity in the future as a result of past transactions or events. **Equity** of a business enterprise (**net assets** of a nonprofit entity) is the residual interest in assets that remains after deducting liabilities.

Recognition is the formal recording of an item in the financial statements. The item is recorded as a numerical effect on a particular account when the fundamental recognition criteria are met. These criteria require that the item meet the definition of an element and have a relevant attribute that can be quantified in monetary units with sufficient reliability.

An **attribute** is a trait or an aspect of what is to be measured. Assets and liabilities are measured by different attributes, depending on the nature of the item and the relevance and reliability of the attribute measured. The attributes currently used include the following:

1. Historical cost -- the amount of cash, or its equivalent, paid to acquire an asset. It is commonly adjusted after acquisition for amortization or other allocations.
2. Historical proceeds -- the amount of cash, or its equivalent, received when the obligation was incurred. It may be adjusted for amortization or other allocations.
3. Current (replacement) cost -- the amount of cash, or its equivalent, that would have to be paid if the same or an equivalent asset were acquired currently.
4. Current market value (exit value) -- the amount of cash, or its equivalent, that could be obtained by selling an asset in an orderly liquidation.
5. Net realizable value -- the nondiscounted amount of cash, or its equivalent, into which an asset is expected to be converted in the due course of business, minus direct costs, if any, necessary to make that conversion.

6. Settlement value -- the nondiscounted amount of cash, or its equivalent, expected to be paid to liquidate an obligation in the due course of business, plus any necessary direct costs.
7. Present (or discounted) value of future cash flows --the net present value of future cash inflows into which an asset is expected to be converted in the due course of business, or the net present value of future cash outflows expected to be required to satisfy a liability in the due course of business.

The **statement of earnings** contemplated by the conceptual framework is similar to the statement of income used in current practice except that it excludes the cumulative effects of changes in accounting principles. The statement of earnings measures the extent to which asset inflows (revenues and gains) associated with cash-to-cash cycles substantially completed during the period are equal to or less than asset outflows (expenses and losses) associated, directly or indirectly, with the same cycles. **Revenues** are increases in an entity's assets or decreases in its liabilities, or a combination of both, during an accounting period that directly result from the entity's ongoing principal operations. **Gains** are similar to revenues except that they result from peripheral or incidental transactions of an entity. Gains do not include revenues or investments by owners. **Expenses** are decreases in an entity's assets or increases in its liabilities, or a combination of both, during an accounting period that directly result from the entity's ongoing principal operations. **Losses** are similar to expenses except that they result from peripheral or incidental transactions of an entity. Losses do not include expenses or distributions to owners.

Revenues and gains ordinarily are measured by the exchange value of the assets or liabilities involved. Recognition of revenues depends on whether they are realized or realizable and whether an earning process is substantially complete. **Realized** means that products (goods or services) or other assets are exchanged for cash or claims to cash (receivables). **Realizable** means that the related assets held are readily convertible to known amounts of cash or claims to cash. **Readily convertible** means that the assets held are interchangeable units for which quoted prices are available in an active market. **Earned** means that the entity has substantially accomplished the activities that constitute its ongoing major or central operations. However, gains ordinarily do not flow from an earning process. Thus, for gain recognition, being realized or realizable is more important than being earned.

Depending on the primary operations of an entity, revenues and gains may be recognized at different times in the operating cycle:

1. Revenues from manufacturing and selling activities and gains and losses from sales of other assets are most commonly recognized at the **time of delivery**.
2. When services are rendered or rights to use assets extend continuously over time and reliable contractual prices exist, revenues are commonly recognized based on the **passage of time**.
3. If a product is contracted for before production and reasonable estimates of total profit and percentage of completion exist, revenues may be recognized as production takes place on a **percentage-of-completion basis.**
4. If products are readily realizable because they are salable at reliably determinable prices without significant effort, revenues and some gains or losses may be recognized at **completion of production**.
5. If collectibility of receivables is doubtful, revenues and gains may be recognized on the basis of **cash received**.
6. Exchanges in which nonmonetary assets are received that are not readily convertible to cash may result in revenues or gains or losses because they have been **earned** and the transactions are **complete**.
7. Gains and losses may result when nonmonetary assets are received or distributed in **nonreciprocal exchanges**.

Expenses and losses are generally recognized when assets are used up in delivering or producing goods, rendering services, or other activities that constitute ongoing major operations (consumption of benefit), or when previously recognized assets are expected to provide little further benefit (loss of future benefit). A **consumption of benefit** is recognized (1) upon recognition of revenues that result directly and jointly from the same transaction or other event as the expense; (2) based on a systematic and rational allocation to the periods in which the related assets are expected to provide benefits; or (3) during the period in which cash is spent or liabilities are incurred for goods and services that are used up simultaneously with acquisition or soon thereafter. A **loss of future benefit** is recognized when (1) a recognized asset's future economic benefits have been reduced or eliminated, or (2) a liability has been incurred or increased without a corresponding increase in related economic benefits.

The **statement of cash flows** provides information about the cash receipts and cash payments of an entity during an accounting period. These cash receipts and cash payments are associated with operating activities, investing activities, and financing activities. In addition, significant financing and investing activities that do not directly affect cash flows must be disclosed.

The **statement of investments by and distributions to owners** includes an entity's capital rather than income transactions with owners during an accounting period. **Investments by owners** are increases in the equity of a business enterprise that result from transfers to it from other entities of something valuable to obtain or increase their ownership interests (or equity). **Distributions to owners** are decreases in the equity of a business enterprise that result from transferring assets, rendering services, or incurring liabilities by the enterprise to its owners.

Comprehensive income is the change in equity of a business enterprise during the period from nonowner sources. It differs from earnings because it encompasses both cumulative accounting adjustments recognized during the period and certain nonowner changes in equity (e.g., the changes in fair value of available-for-sale securities).

Absent market-based measurements, estimated cash flows often measure an asset or a liability. Thus, the FASB has established a framework that uses **cash flows** and **present value** for measurements at initial recognition, for fresh-start purposes, and for applications of the interest method.

Generally accepted accounting principles (GAAP) are the "conventions, rules, and procedures necessary to define accepted accounting practice at a particular time." They include both the broad guidelines and the detailed practices and procedures promulgated by the profession that provide uniform standards to measure financial presentations (**SAS 69**, *The Meaning of "Present Fairly in Conformity with Generally Accepted Accounting Principles" in the Independent Auditor's Report)*. NOTE: The FASB is expected to move the hierarchy to a FASB standard. GAAP hierarchies have been established for nongovernmental entities, state and local governments, and federal governmental entities. In the **GAAP hierarchy for nongovernmental entities**, the highest category (officially established accounting principles) includes FASB Statements and Interpretations, APB Opinions, and AICPA Accounting Research Bulletins. The next category includes FASB Technical Bulletins, and, if cleared by the FASB, AICPA Audit and Accounting Guides and AICPA Statements of Position. The third category includes consensus positions of the FASB Emerging Issues Task Force and, if cleared by the FASB, AICPA Accounting Standards Executive Committee (AcSEC) Practice Bulletins. The fourth category includes AICPA Accounting Interpretations, questions and answers published by the FASB staff, and industry practices widely recognized and prevalent. The fifth category includes other accounting literature, such as the SFACs.

NOTE: Pursuant to the evaluation required by the Sarbanes-Oxley Act of 2002, the SEC has reaffirmed the FASB as the standard-setting body for nongovernmental entities.

QUESTIONS

1.1 Objectives of Financial Reporting

1. What are the Statements of Financial Accounting Concepts (SFAC) intended to establish?

A. Generally accepted accounting principles in financial reporting by business enterprises.

B. The meaning of "present fairly in accordance with generally accepted accounting principles."

C. The objectives and concepts for use in developing standards of financial accounting and reporting.

D. The hierarchy of sources of generally accepted accounting principles.

Answer (C) is correct. *(CPA, adapted)*

REQUIRED: The purpose of the SFACs.

DISCUSSION: SFACs define the objectives, qualitative characteristics, and other concepts that guide the Financial Accounting Standards Board (FASB) in developing sound accounting principles. They do not establish accounting and reporting requirements. Thus, in the GAAP hierarchy for nongovernmental entities promulgated by Statement of Auditing Standards (SAS) 69, *The Meaning of "Present Fairly in Conformity with Generally Accepted Accounting Principles" in the Independent Auditor's Report* (codified as AU 411 in AICPA Professional Standards, Volume 1), the SFACs are classified as other accounting literature (the lowest category), not as established accounting principles (the four highest categories). Hence, they are not covered by the AICPA's Conduct Rule 203, *Accounting Principles*, which applies only to officially established accounting principles [category (a)]. NOTE: The FASB is expected to move the hierarchy to a FASB standard.

Answer (A) is incorrect because SFACs are intended to guide the development of promulgated GAAP. Answer (B) is incorrect because AU 411 (SAS 69) clarifies the meaning of "present fairly in accordance with generally accepted accounting principles." Answer (D) is incorrect because AU 411 establishes the hierarchy of sources of GAAP.

2. According to the FASB conceptual framework, the objectives of financial reporting for business enterprises are based on

A. The need for conservatism.

B. Reporting on management's stewardship.

C. Generally accepted accounting principles.

D. The needs of the users of the information.

Answer (D) is correct. *(CPA, adapted)*

REQUIRED: The objectives of financial reporting for business enterprises.

DISCUSSION: SFAC 1, *Objectives of Financial Reporting by Business Enterprises*, states that an objective of financial reporting is to provide information that is useful to present and potential investors, creditors, and other users in making rational investment, credit, and similar decisions.

Answer (A) is incorrect because conservatism is a qualitative characteristic. Answer (B) is incorrect because financial reporting provides information that is helpful in evaluating management's stewardship but does not directly provide information about that performance. Answer (C) is incorrect because GAAP governs how to account for items in the financial statements.

3. Which of the following statements reflects the basic purposes of financial reporting?

A. The primary focus of financial reporting is information about an enterprise's resources.

B. The best indication of an enterprise's ability to generate favorable cash flows is information based on previous cash receipts and payments.

C. Financial accounting is expressly designed to measure directly the value of a business enterprise.

D. Investment and credit decisions often are based, at least in part, on evaluations of the past performance of an enterprise.

Answer (D) is correct. *(Publisher)*

REQUIRED: The true statement about the basic purposes of financial reporting.

DISCUSSION: SFAC 1 states that, although investment and credit decisions reflect investors' and creditors' expectations about future enterprise performance, those expectations are commonly based, at least in part, on evaluations of past enterprise performance.

Answer (A) is incorrect because the primary focus of financial reporting is information about earnings and its components (not resources). Answer (B) is incorrect because the best indication of an enterprise's present and continuing ability to generate favorable cash flows is information about enterprise earnings based on accrual (not cash basis) accounting. Answer (C) is incorrect because financial accounting is not designed to measure the value of a business enterprise directly, but the information provided may be helpful to those who wish to estimate its value.

4. The information provided by financial reporting pertains to

A. Individual business enterprises, rather than to industries or an economy as a whole or to members of society as consumers.

B. Individual business enterprises and industries, rather than to an economy as a whole or to members of society as consumers.

C. Individual business enterprises and an economy as a whole, rather than to industries or to members of society as consumers.

D. Individual business enterprises, industries, and an economy as a whole, rather than to members of society as consumers.

Answer (A) is correct. *(CPA, adapted)*

REQUIRED: The economic level(s) to which the information provided by financial reporting pertains.

DISCUSSION: According to SFAC 1, financial reporting pertains essentially to individual business enterprises. Information about industries and economies in which an industry operates is usually provided only to the extent necessary for understanding the individual business enterprise.

5. During a period when an enterprise is under the direction of a particular management, its financial statements will directly provide information about

A. Both enterprise performance and management performance.

B. Management performance but not directly provide information about enterprise performance.

C. Enterprise performance but not directly provide information about management performance.

D. Neither enterprise performance nor management performance.

Answer (C) is correct. *(CPA, adapted)*

REQUIRED: The information directly provided by financial statements.

DISCUSSION: Financial reporting provides information about an enterprise's performance during a period when it was under the direction of a particular management but does not directly provide information about that management's performance. Financial reporting does not try to separate the impact of a particular management's performance from the effects of prior management actions, general economic conditions, the supply and demand for an enterprise's inputs and outputs, price changes, and other events.

6. The best indication of an enterprise's present and continuing ability to generate favorable cash flows is information about enterprise earnings based on which of the following?

A. Cash accounting basis.

B. Modified cash accounting basis.

C. Accrual accounting basis.

D. Tax accounting basis.

Answer (C) is correct. *(Publisher)*

REQUIRED: The basis that best indicates an enterprise's ability to generate favorable cash flows.

DISCUSSION: SFAC 1 states that information about enterprise earnings based on accrual accounting generally provides a better indication of the enterprise's present and continuing ability to generate favorable cash flows than would information limited to the financial effects of cash receipts and payments. Accrual accounting attempts to record the financial effects on an enterprise of transactions and other events and circumstances that have cash consequences in the periods in which those transactions, events, and circumstances occur, rather than only in the periods in which cash is received or paid by the enterprise.

7. The primary current source of generally accepted accounting principles for nongovernmental U.S. entities is the

A. Securities and Exchange Commission.

B. Financial Accounting Foundation.

C. Financial Accounting Standards Board.

D. American Institute of Certified Public Accountants.

Answer (C) is correct. *(Publisher)*

REQUIRED: The institution primarily responsible for the establishment of generally accepted accounting principles.

DISCUSSION: The FASB was created as a seven-member, full-time autonomous board with the responsibility of establishing financial accounting standards. It is charged to be responsive to the needs and viewpoints of the entire economic community, not just the public accounting profession, and it operates in full view of the public through a due process system. Pursuant to the evaluation required by the Sarbanes-Oxley Act of 2002, the SEC has reaffirmed the FASB as the standard-setting body for nongovernmental entities.

Answer (A) is incorrect because, although the SEC is influential in the establishment of GAAP, it is not the primary source. Answer (B) is incorrect because, although the FAF is influential in the establishment of GAAP, it is not the primary source. Answer (D) is incorrect because, although the AICPA is influential in the establishment of GAAP, it is not the primary source.

8. Which of the following statements about accrual accounting is false?

A. Accrual accounting is concerned with the process by which cash expended on resources and activities is returned as more (or perhaps less) cash to the enterprise, not just with the beginning and end of that process.

B. Accrual accounting recognizes that buying, producing, selling, and other operations of an enterprise during a period often do not coincide with the cash receipts and payments of the period.

C. Accrual accounting attempts to record the financial effects on an enterprise of transactions and other events and circumstances that have cash consequences for an enterprise.

D. Accrual accounting is primarily concerned with the cash receipts and cash payments of an enterprise.

Answer (D) is correct. *(Publisher)*

REQUIRED: The false statement about accrual accounting.

DISCUSSION: Accrual accounting attempts to record the financial effects on an enterprise of transactions and other events and circumstances that have cash consequences in the periods in which those transactions, events, and circumstances occur, rather than only in the periods in which cash is received or paid by the enterprise. Thus, the focus of accrual accounting is not primarily on the actual cash receipts and cash payments. It is concerned with the process by which cash expended on resources is returned as more (or perhaps less) cash to the enterprise, not just with the beginning and end of the process.

9. The FASB's conceptual framework explains both financial and physical capital maintenance concepts. Which capital maintenance concept is applied to currently reported net income, and which is applied to comprehensive income?

	Currently Reported Net Income	Comprehensive Income
A.	Financial capital	Physical capital
B.	Physical capital	Physical capital
C.	Financial capital	Financial capital
D.	Physical capital	Financial capital

Answer (C) is correct. *(CPA, adapted)*

REQUIRED: The capital maintenance concept(s) applicable to currently reported net income and comprehensive income.

DISCUSSION: The financial capital maintenance concept is the traditional basis of financial statements, including comprehensive income (a return on financial capital). Under this concept, a return on investment (defined in terms of money) results only if the financial amount of net assets at the end of the period exceeds the amount at the beginning after excluding transactions with owners. Under a physical capital concept, a return on investment (in terms of physical capital) results only if the physical productive capacity (or the resources to achieve that capacity) at the end of the period exceeds the capacity at the beginning after excluding transactions with owners. The latter concept requires many assets to be measured at current (replacement) cost. Under the financial capital concept, price changes, if recognized, are holding gains and losses included in return on capital. Under the physical capital concept, those changes are recognized directly in equity.

10. In the hierarchy of generally accepted accounting principles for nongovernmental entities, APB Opinions have the same authority as AICPA

A. Statements of Position (SOP).

B. Audit and Accounting Guides.

C. Issues Papers.

D. Accounting Research Bulletins (ARBs).

Answer (D) is correct. *(CPA, adapted)*

REQUIRED: The AICPA pronouncement with the same authority as APB Opinions.

DISCUSSION: In the GAAP hierarchy for nongovernmental entities, the first four categories consist of established accounting principles. The highest category (officially established accounting principles) contains pronouncements by bodies designated by the AICPA to establish such principles pursuant to the AICPA's *Code of Professional Conduct.* This category includes FASB Statements (SFASs) and Interpretations, APB Opinions, and ARBs.

Answer (A) is incorrect because SOPs are in a lower category of established accounting principles. Answer (B) is incorrect because Audit and Accounting Guides are in a lower category of established accounting principles. Answer (C) is incorrect because Issues Papers are considered other accounting literature (the lowest category).

11. FASB Interpretations of Statements of Financial Accounting Standards have the same authority as

A. Statements of Financial Accounting Concepts.

B. Consensus positions of the Emerging Issues Task Force.

C. Technical Bulletins.

D. Statements of Financial Accounting Standards (SFASs).

Answer (D) is correct. *(CPA, adapted)*

REQUIRED: The pronouncements having the same authority as FASB Interpretations.

DISCUSSION: In the GAAP hierarchy for nongovernmental entities, the highest category (officially established accounting principles) includes SFASs and Interpretations, APB Opinions, and AICPA Accounting Research Bulletins. Mandatory SEC pronouncements applying only to SEC registrants also have the highest authority.

Answer (A) is incorrect because SFACs are included in the lowest category. Answer (B) is incorrect because EITF positions are included in the third highest category. Answer (C) is incorrect because FASB Technical Bulletins are included in the second highest category.

12. The operating cycle of a business is the span of time that

A. Coincides with the economy's business cycle, which runs from one trough of the economy's business activity to the next.

B. Corresponds with its natural business year, which runs from one trough of the particular firm's business activity to the next.

C. Is set by the industry's trade association, usually on an average length of time for all firms that are members of the association.

D. Runs from cash disbursement for items of inventory through their sale to the realization of cash from sale.

Answer (D) is correct. *(CPA, adapted)*

REQUIRED: The operating cycle of a business.

DISCUSSION: As stated in ARB 43, Chapter 3A, *Current Assets and Current Liabilities*, the average amount of time from cash disbursement to the realization of cash from sale is the operating cycle of the business.

Answer (A) is incorrect because financial reporting is geared toward a business enterprise's business cycle, not the economy's. Answer (B) is incorrect because it defines the firm's fiscal year rather than its operating cycle. One operating cycle may last 12 months or more, although usually the fiscal year of the business includes a number of operating cycles. Answer (C) is incorrect because the operating cycle of a business is determined by the firm's transactions, not by reference to an industry trade association estimate.

13. The business reason usually given for a business to select a fiscal year different from the calendar year is

A. The firm's owners may have a personal preference.

B. Tax laws favor firms that employ a fiscal year other than the calendar year.

C. The fiscal year-end is selected to coincide with the low points in sales, production, and inventories, which may occur at some period other than the calendar year-end.

D. Public accounting firms might not be able to handle the workload if all their clients were to report on a calendar-year basis.

Answer (C) is correct. *(CMA, adapted)*

REQUIRED: The most common reason for selecting a fiscal year different from the calendar year.

DISCUSSION: A fiscal year is a 12-month period that ends at a date other than December 31. The business's natural business year is normally chosen. A natural year runs from one low point in a firm's business activity to the same low point 12 months later.

Answer (A) is incorrect because personal preference is a less compelling reason than matching the period chosen with the entity's normal business cycle. Answer (B) is incorrect because, in the long-term, choice of a fiscal year provides no tax advantage. Answer (D) is incorrect because an entity should choose a reporting period based on its normal business cycle, not the convenience of accounting firms.

14. The primary purpose of the statement of financial position of a business enterprise is to reflect

A. The fair value of the firm's assets at some moment in time.

B. The status of the firm's assets in case of forced liquidation of the firm.

C. The firm's potential for growth in stock values in the stock market.

D. Items of value, debts, and net worth.

Answer (D) is correct. *(CMA, adapted)*

REQUIRED: The primary purpose of the statement of financial position (balance sheet).

DISCUSSION: In conformity with GAAP, the statement of financial position or balance sheet of a business enterprise presents three major financial accounting elements: assets (items of value), liabilities (debts), and equity (net worth). According to SFAC 6, *Elements of Financial Statements*, assets are probable future economic benefits resulting from past transactions or events. Liabilities are probable future sacrifices of economic benefits arising from present obligations as a result of past transactions or events. Equity of a business enterprise is the residual interest in the assets after deduction of liabilities.

Answer (A) is incorrect because assets are reported in the balance sheet using various measurement attributes, including but not limited to fair values. Answer (B) is incorrect because the balance sheet usually does not report forced liquidation values. Answer (C) is incorrect because the future value of a company's stock is more dependent upon future operations and investors' expectations than on the data found in the balance sheet.

15. What is the purpose of information presented in notes to the financial statements?

A. To provide disclosures required by generally accepted accounting principles.

B. To correct improper presentation in the financial statements.

C. To provide recognition of amounts not included in the totals of the financial statements.

D. To present management's response to auditor comments.

Answer (A) is correct. *(CPA, adapted)*

REQUIRED: The purpose of information presented in notes to the financial statements.

DISCUSSION: Notes are an integral part of the basic financial statements. Notes provide information essential to understanding the financial statements, including disclosures required by GAAP (SFAC 5, *Recognition and Measurement in Financial Statements of Business Enterprises*).

Answer (B) is incorrect because notes may not be used to rectify an improper presentation. Answer (C) is incorrect because disclosure in notes is not a substitute for recognition in financial statements for items that meet recognition criteria. Answer (D) is incorrect because management's response to auditor comments is not an appropriate subject of financial reporting.

1.2 Qualitative Characteristics

16. SFAC 2, *Qualitative Characteristics of Accounting Information*, identifies the two primary qualities that make accounting information useful for decision making as

A. Neutral and verifiable.

B. Fair and precise.

C. Relevant and reliable.

D. Consistent and comparable.

Answer (C) is correct. *(J. Cerepak)*

REQUIRED: The two primary qualities that make accounting information useful.

DISCUSSION: SFAC 2 identifies relevance and reliability as the two primary qualities that make accounting information useful for decision making. Relevance is the capacity of information to make a difference in the user's decision. Reliability provides assurance that the information is reasonably free from error and bias and that it represents what it purports to represent.

Answer (A) is incorrect because neutrality and verifiability are ingredients of reliability. Answer (B) is incorrect because, while accounting information should be fairly presented, precision is not always possible when estimates are necessary. Answer (D) is incorrect because consistency and comparability are secondary qualities that interact with the two primary qualities to contribute to usefulness.

17. According to Statements of Financial Accounting Concepts, neutrality is an ingredient of

	Reliability	Relevance
A.	Yes	Yes
B.	Yes	No
C.	No	Yes
D.	No	No

Answer (B) is correct. *(CPA, adapted)*

REQUIRED: The quality of which neutrality is an ingredient.

DISCUSSION: The primary quality of reliability assures that information is reasonably free from error and bias and faithfully represents what it purports to represent. Its ingredients are representational faithfulness, verifiability, and neutrality. Neutrality is the absence of bias intended to reach a predetermined result or induce a certain behavior.

18. According to SFAC 2, materiality is a pervasive concept that relates to

	Relevance	Reliability
A.	No	No
B.	Yes	No
C.	No	Yes
D.	Yes	Yes

Answer (D) is correct. *(Publisher)*

REQUIRED: The relationship of materiality to relevance and reliability.

DISCUSSION: In accordance with SFAC 2, materiality is a pervasive concept that relates to both of the primary decision-specific qualities: relevance and reliability.

19. Which of the following is considered a pervasive constraint by SFAC 2?

A. Benefits > costs.

B. Conservatism.

C. Timeliness.

D. Verifiability.

Answer (A) is correct. *(CPA, adapted)*

REQUIRED: The accounting quality that is a pervasive constraint.

DISCUSSION: All accounting information is subject to two quantitative constraints: materiality and benefits > costs. If a reasonable person relying on the information would not have changed his/her judgment as a result of an omission or misstatement, it is not considered material. The constraint of benefits > costs states that the benefits of information must exceed the cost of obtaining it.

Answer (B) is incorrect because conservatism is defined as a prudent reaction to uncertainty. Answer (C) is incorrect because timeliness is an ingredient of relevance. Answer (D) is incorrect because verifiability is an ingredient of reliability.

20. Materiality is one of the pervasive concepts discussed in SFAC 2. Which of the following statements is true with regard to materiality?

A. Materiality judgments generally may be based solely on the magnitude of the item.

B. The nature and magnitude of an item as well as the circumstances in which the judgment has to be made are integral aspects of a materiality judgment.

C. Relevant items are always material.

D. Materiality judgments generally may be made without consideration of the magnitude of the item involved.

Answer (B) is correct. *(Publisher)*

REQUIRED: The true statement with regard to materiality.

DISCUSSION: In accordance with SFAC 2, the basis for a materiality judgment is generally not sufficient unless the nature of the item, the circumstances in which the judgment has to be made, and the magnitude of the item are all considered.

Answer (A) is incorrect because the magnitude of the item is only one aspect of a materiality judgment. Answer (C) is incorrect because materiality is a pervasive concept that relates to the qualitative characteristic of relevance. Information may be relevant because it can make a difference in a single investment decision, but it may be too small (immaterial) to make that difference matter over an accounting period. Answer (D) is incorrect because the magnitude of the item is only one aspect of a materiality judgment.

21. Under SFAC 2, the ability, through consensus among measurers, to ensure that information represents what it purports to represent is the definition of the concept of

A. Relevance.

B. Verifiability.

C. Comparability.

D. Feedback value.

Answer (B) is correct. *(CPA, adapted)*

REQUIRED: The term that describes the ability to ensure that information represents what it purports to represent.

DISCUSSION: Verifiability is defined as the ability, through consensus among measurers, to ensure that information represents what it purports to represent. It is easily confused with representational faithfulness, which is the agreement between a description and what it purports to measure. However, representational faithfulness concerns the validity of the measurement, whereas verifiability relates to the application of the measurement rule.

Answer (A) is incorrect because relevance (a primary decision-specific quality) is the capacity of the information to make a difference in a decision. Answer (C) is incorrect because comparability (a secondary interactive quality) is the quality of information that enables users to identify similarities in and differences between two sets of data. Answer (D) is incorrect because feedback value (an ingredient of relevance) is the quality of information that enables users to confirm or correct prior expectations.

22. According to the FASB conceptual framework, which of the following situations violates the concept of reliability?

A. Financial statements were issued 9 months late.

B. Data on segments having the same expected risks and growth rates are reported to analysts estimating future profits.

C. Financial statements included property with a carrying amount increased to management's estimate of market value.

D. Management reports to shareholders regularly refer to new projects undertaken, but the financial statements never report project results.

Answer (C) is correct. *(CPA, adapted)*

REQUIRED: The situation violating the concept of reliability.

DISCUSSION: Reliability is defined as the quality of information that provides assurance that the information is reasonably free from error and bias and faithfully represents what it purports to represent. In accordance with GAAP, the carrying amount of property should not be increased to market value. If it is reported at markup value, it is misrepresented, which violates the concept of reliability.

Answer (A) is incorrect because the situation relates to relevance, which is the capacity of information to make a difference in a decision. Answer (B) is incorrect because the situation relates to relevance, which is the capacity of information to make a difference in a decision. Answer (D) is incorrect because the situation relates to relevance, which is the capacity of information to make a difference in a decision.

23. Factors that might influence a decision maker's judgment as to what accounting information is useful include

A. The decision to be made.

B. The information already possessed.

C. The decision maker's capacity to process the information.

D. All of the answers are correct.

Answer (D) is correct. *(Publisher)*

REQUIRED: The factors that influence a decision maker's judgment as to the usefulness of accounting information.

DISCUSSION: The judgment by a decision maker as to what accounting information can be useful includes

1. The type of decision to be made;
2. The methods by which the decision would be made;
3. The information already possessed or attainable from other sources; and
4. The decision maker's capacity, either alone or with professional help, to process the information. See SFAC 2.

24. Accounting information that enables decision makers to confirm or correct prior expectations is said to have

A. Predictive value.

B. Representational faithfulness.

C. Feedback value.

D. Comparability.

Answer (C) is correct. *(CMA, adapted)*

REQUIRED: The characteristic of accounting information enabling confirmation or correction of prior expectations.

DISCUSSION: The primary quality of relevance is the capacity of information to make a difference in a decision. It is composed of (1) predictive value, (2) feedback value, and (3) timeliness. Feedback value is the quality of information that permits users to confirm or correct prior expectations.

Answer (A) is incorrect because predictive value enables users to predict the outcome of future events. Answer (B) is incorrect because representational faithfulness is the agreement between a measure or description and the phenomenon that it purports to represent. Answer (D) is incorrect because comparability enables users to identify similarities in and differences between two sets of economic phenomena.

25. According to the FASB conceptual framework, which of the following relates to both relevance and reliability?

A. Comparability.

B. Feedback value.

C. Verifiability.

D. Timeliness.

Answer (A) is correct. *(CPA, adapted)*

REQUIRED: The item that relates to both relevance and reliability.

DISCUSSION: Comparability (a secondary interactive quality) is the quality of information that enables users to identify similarities in and differences between two sets of data. Comparability interacts with relevance and reliability to contribute to the usefulness of information (SFAC 2).

Answer (B) is incorrect because feedback value is an ingredient of the primary quality of relevance but not of reliability. Answer (C) is incorrect because verifiability is an ingredient of the primary quality of reliability but not of relevance. Answer (D) is incorrect because timeliness is an ingredient of the primary quality of relevance but not of reliability.

26. According to SFAC 2, an interim earnings report is expected to have which of the following?

	Predictive Value	Feedback Value
A.	No	No
B.	Yes	Yes
C.	Yes	No
D.	No	Yes

Answer (B) is correct. *(CPA, adapted)*

REQUIRED: The qualitative value(s) expected in an interim earnings report.

DISCUSSION: According to SFAC 2, an interim earnings report gives feedback on past performance and provides a basis for predicting annual earnings before the year-end. Feedback value is the quality of information that permits users to confirm or correct prior expectations. An interim earnings report enables a user to match its information with the prior predictions of the firm's earnings capacity. Predictive value is the quality of information that permits users to increase the probability of making correct forecasts. An interim earnings report has predictive value as well as feedback value because it serves to enhance a forecast of annual earnings.

27. Consolidated financial statements are prepared when a parent-subsidiary relationship exists in recognition of the accounting concept of

A. Materiality.

B. Entity.

C. Verifiability.

D. Going concern.

Answer (B) is correct. *(CPA, adapted)*

REQUIRED: The accounting concept recognized in consolidated financial statements.

DISCUSSION: Consolidated financial statements should reflect the economic activities of a business enterprise measured without regard to the boundaries of the legal entity. Accounting information pertains to a business enterprise, the boundaries of which are not necessarily those of the legal entity. For instance, a parent and subsidiary are legally separate but are treated as a single business enterprise in consolidated statements. A business enterprise also may be required to consolidate an entity that is not a subsidiary, according to FASB Interpretation No. 46 (revised December 2003), *Consolidation of Variable Interest Entities*.

Answer (A) is incorrect because materiality requires reporting of information that has a value significant enough to affect decisions of those using the financial statements. Answer (C) is incorrect because verifiability means having an existence independent of the observer. Answer (D) is incorrect because the going concern concept assumes that the business entity will continue to operate in the absence of evidence to the contrary, but it is not a reason for preparing consolidated statements.

28. During the lifetime of a business enterprise, accountants produce financial statements at arbitrary moments in time in accordance with which basic accounting concept?

A. Verifiability.

B. Periodicity.

C. Conservatism.

D. Matching.

Answer (B) is correct. *(CPA, adapted)*

REQUIRED: The basic accounting concept requiring financial statements to be issued at arbitrary moments in time.

DISCUSSION: A basic feature of the financial accounting process is that information about the economic activities of the business enterprise should be issued at regular intervals. These time periods should be of equal length to facilitate comparability. They should also be of relatively short duration, e.g., 1 year, to provide business information useful for decision making.

Answer (A) is incorrect because verifiability is a qualitative characteristic, not a concept of the timing of financial statements. Answer (C) is incorrect because conservatism is a qualitative characteristic. It is "a prudent reaction to uncertainty to try to ensure that uncertainties and risks inherent in business situations are adequately considered" (SFAC 2). Answer (D) is incorrect because matching (another term for associating cause and effect) requires costs to be recognized as expenses on the basis of their direct association with specific revenues to the extent possible.

29. When a company makes a change in accounting principle, prior-year financial statements are not generally restated to reflect the change. The Accounting Principles Board decided that this procedure would prevent a dilution of public confidence in financial statements but recognized that this procedure conflicts with the accounting concept of

A. Materiality.

B. Conservatism.

C. Verifiability.

D. Comparability.

Answer (D) is correct. *(CPA, adapted)*

REQUIRED: The accounting concept conflicting with the procedure for changes in accounting principle.

DISCUSSION: APB 20, *Accounting Changes*, requires that most changes in accounting principle be recognized by including the cumulative effect of the change in net income of the period of the change, i.e., no restatement of prior-period financial statements. This procedure conflicts with the concept of consistency or comparability, which requires that similar events be accounted for similarly in successive periods, i.e., requiring restatement of prior-year statements for accounting changes.

Answer (A) is incorrect because the materiality concept states that accounting information may be ignored if it is not significant enough to affect users' decisions. Answer (B) is incorrect because conservatism is a qualitative characteristic. It is "a prudent reaction to uncertainty to try to ensure that uncertainties and risks inherent in business situations are adequately considered" (SFAC 2). Answer (C) is incorrect because verifiability is a qualitative ingredient of reliability not related to consistency of financial statements.

30. Continuation of an accounting entity in the absence of evidence to the contrary is an example of the basic concept of

A. Accounting entity.

B. Consistency.

C. Going concern.

D. Substance over form.

Answer (C) is correct. *(CPA, adapted)*

REQUIRED: The concept regarding the continuation of a business entity.

DISCUSSION: A basic feature of financial accounting is that the business entity is assumed to be a going concern in the absence of evidence to the contrary. The going concern concept is based on the empirical observation that many enterprises have an indefinite life.

Answer (A) is incorrect because the accounting entity concept refers to the business enterprise, which may or may not be synonymous with the legal entity. The emphasis is also on the separation of the entity from its ownership. Answer (B) is incorrect because the consistency principle requires that similar events be accounted for similarly in succeeding accounting periods to facilitate comparability between periods. Answer (D) is incorrect because the concept of substance over form requires accounting treatment to be based upon the economic substance of events rather than upon the legal form.

31. The concept of consistency is sacrificed in the accounting for which of the following income statement items?

A. Discontinued operations.

B. Loss on disposal of a component of an entity.

C. Extraordinary items.

D. Cumulative effect of changes in accounting principle.

Answer (D) is correct. *(CPA, adapted)*

REQUIRED: The income statement item that sacrifices consistency.

DISCUSSION: Changes in accounting principles ordinarily are accounted for by means of a cumulative effect adjustment in the year of change with no restatement of prior-year statements. Thus, similar events are not accounted for in the same way in succeeding accounting periods.

Answer (A) is incorrect because principles may be consistently observed in the current period in relation to the preceding period even though operations have been discontinued. Unusual transactions or events do not result in lack of consistency. Answer (B) is incorrect because principles may be consistently observed in the current period in relation to the preceding period even though a component of an entity has been disposed of. Unusual transactions or events do not result in lack of consistency. Answer (C) is incorrect because principles may be consistently observed in the current period in relation to the preceding period even though an extraordinary item has been recognized. Unusual transactions or events do not result in lack of consistency.

32. Which of the following accounting concepts states that an accounting transaction should be supported by sufficient evidence to allow two or more qualified individuals to arrive at essentially similar measures and conclusions?

A. Matching.

B. Verifiability.

C. Periodicity.

D. Stable monetary unit.

Answer (B) is correct. *(CPA, adapted)*

REQUIRED: The accounting concept described.

DISCUSSION: The essence of reliability is that accounting measures represent what they purport to represent. The measurements of financial accounting transactions must be able to be corroborated by outside or independent persons; i.e., accounting information is verifiable if it is capable of independent replication.

Answer (A) is incorrect because matching involves recognizing costs as expenses on the basis of direct association with revenues, e.g., cost of goods sold. Answer (C) is incorrect because periodicity requires accounting information to be reported at regular intervals to foster comparability and at relatively short intervals to provide useful information. Answer (D) is incorrect because the stable monetary unit concept assumes that the unit of measure (e.g., the U.S. dollar) does not fluctuate.

33. Uncertainty and risks inherent in business situations should be adequately considered in financial reporting. This statement is an example of the concept of

A. Conservatism.

B. Completeness.

C. Neutrality.

D. Representational faithfulness.

Answer (A) is correct. *(CPA, adapted)*

REQUIRED: The accounting concept promoted by adequately considering uncertainty and risks.

DISCUSSION: SFAC 2 defines conservatism as "a prudent reaction to uncertainty to try to ensure that uncertainty and risks inherent in business situations are adequately considered." However, it does not connote a consistent and deliberate understatement of net assets and profits. Thus, conservatism is not meant to introduce a bias into financial reporting. For example, if two estimates are equally likely, conservatism requires use of the less optimistic. But if these estimates are not equally likely, use of the more pessimistic is not required by the concept of conservatism.

Answer (B) is incorrect because completeness (an ingredient of reliability) requires the inclusion in reported accounting information of everything material that is needed for adequate representation. Answer (C) is incorrect because neutrality is that ingredient of reliability which implies an absence of bias. Answer (D) is incorrect because representational faithfulness means that the accounting information represents what it purports to represent.

34. The concept of verifiability is complied with when an accounting transaction occurs that

A. Involves an arm's-length transaction between two independent interests.

B. Furthers the objectives of the company.

C. Is promptly recorded in a fixed amount of dollars.

D. Allocates revenues or expense items in a rational and systematic manner.

Answer (A) is correct. *(CPA, adapted)*

REQUIRED: The accounting transaction that complies with the concept of verifiability.

DISCUSSION: Verifiability is an ingredient of reliability of accounting information (SFAC 2). The essence of verifiability is that a measurement of accounting information should be capable of independent replication. The existence of an arm's-length transaction between independent interests suggests that the requisite reliability is present in the transaction.

Answer (B) is incorrect because verifiability relates to the reliability of accounting measurement, not to the particular objectives of any company. Answer (C) is incorrect because recording at a fixed dollar amount does not guarantee the reliability of the measurement. Answer (D) is incorrect because rational and systematic allocation is a specific means of expense recognition. Systematic and rational allocation of expenses is undertaken when a direct means of associating cause and effect (expense and revenue) is lacking.

1.3 Elements of Financial Statements

35. Under SFAC 6, *Elements of Financial Statements*, interrelated elements of financial statements that are directly related to measuring the performance and status of an enterprise include

	Distribution to Owners	Notes to Financial Statements
A.	Yes	Yes
B.	Yes	No
C.	No	Yes
D.	No	No

Answer (B) is correct. *(CPA, adapted)*

REQUIRED: The financial statement element(s) directly related to measuring status and performance of an entity.

DISCUSSION: The elements of financial statements directly related to measuring the performance and status of both business enterprises and not-for-profit organizations are assets, liabilities, equity of a business or net assets of a not-for-profit organization, revenues, expenses, gains, and losses. The elements of investments by owners, distributions to owners, and comprehensive income relate only to business enterprises. Information disclosed in notes or parenthetically on the face of financial statements amplifies or explains information recognized in the financial statements.

36. According to the FASB conceptual framework, which of the following is an essential characteristic of an asset?

A. The claims to an asset's benefits are legally enforceable.

B. An asset is tangible.

C. An asset is obtained at a cost.

D. An asset provides future benefits.

Answer (D) is correct. *(CPA, adapted)*

REQUIRED: The essential characteristic of an asset.

DISCUSSION: One of the three essential characteristics of an asset is that the transaction or event giving rise to the enterprise's right to or control of its assets has already occurred; it is not expected to occur in the future. A second essential characteristic of an asset is that an enterprise can obtain the benefits of, and control others' access to, the asset. The third essential characteristic is that an asset must embody a probable future benefit that involves a capacity to contribute to future net cash inflows (SFAC 6).

Answer (A) is incorrect because claims to an asset's benefits may not be legally enforceable, for example, in the case of goodwill. Answer (B) is incorrect because some assets are intangible. Answer (C) is incorrect because assets may be obtained through donations or investments by owners.

37. An essential characteristic of a liability is that

A. The obligated enterprise must pay cash to a recipient entity.

B. It must be legally enforceable.

C. The identity of the recipient entity must be known to the obligated entity before the time of settlement.

D. The obligation must have arisen as the result of a previous transaction.

Answer (D) is correct. *(Publisher)*

REQUIRED: The characteristic that is essential to the existence of a liability.

DISCUSSION: SFAC 6 defines three essential characteristics of a liability: (1) It represents an obligation that requires settlement by probable future transfer or use of assets; (2) the enterprise has little or no discretion to avoid the obligation; and (3) the transaction or other event giving rise to the obligation has already occurred.

Answer (A) is incorrect because liabilities often require the payment of cash, but they could also be satisfied through the use of other assets or the provision of services. Answer (B) is incorrect because liabilities are usually but not always legally enforceable. Answer (C) is incorrect because the identity of the recipient must be known only by the time of settlement, not before.

38. According to the FASB's conceptual framework, asset valuation accounts are

A. Assets.

B. Neither assets nor liabilities.

C. Part of equity.

D. Liabilities.

Answer (B) is correct. *(CPA, adapted)*

REQUIRED: The conceptual framework's definition of asset valuation accounts.

DISCUSSION: Asset valuation accounts are separate items sometimes found in financial statements that reduce or increase the carrying amount of an asset. The conceptual framework considers asset valuation accounts (e.g., an allowance for bad debts) to be part of the related asset account. They are not considered to be assets or liabilities in their own right (SFAC 6).

Answer (A) is incorrect because asset valuation accounts are part of the related asset accounts but are not assets. Answer (C) is incorrect because asset valuation accounts are part of the related asset accounts but are not part of equity. Answer (D) is incorrect because asset valuation accounts are part of the related asset accounts but are not liabilities.

39. A stated purpose of SFAC 6, *Elements of Financial Statements*, is to

A. Define three classes of net assets for businesses.

B. Define the elements necessary for presentation of financial statements of both business and not-for-profit organizations.

C. Apply the comprehensive income concept to not-for-profit organizations.

D. Apply its principles to reporting by state and local governmental units.

Answer (B) is correct. *(Publisher)*

REQUIRED: The stated purpose of SFAC 6.

DISCUSSION: SFAC 6 defines 10 interrelated elements of financial statements that are directly related to measuring the performance and status of an entity. Of these, seven are found in statements of both business and not-for-profit entities: assets, liabilities, equity or net assets, revenues, expenses, gains, and losses. Investments by owners, distributions to owners, and comprehensive income are elements of financial statements of business enterprises only.

Answer (A) is incorrect because SFAC 6 defines three classes of net assets of not-for-profit entities and the changes therein during the period. Answer (C) is incorrect because the comprehensive income concept is not applicable to not-for-profit organizations. Answer (D) is incorrect because SFAC 6 does not apply its principles to reporting by state and local governmental units. GASB Concepts Statements apply to such entities.

40. According to the FASB conceptual framework, an entity's revenue may result from

A. A decrease in an asset from primary operations.

B. An increase in an asset from incidental transactions.

C. An increase in a liability from incidental transactions.

D. A decrease in a liability from primary operations.

Answer (D) is correct. *(CPA, adapted)*

REQUIRED: The possible source of revenue.

DISCUSSION: According to SFAC 6, revenues are inflows or other enhancements of assets or settlements of liabilities from activities that constitute the entity's ongoing major or central operations. Thus, a revenue may result from a decrease in a liability from primary operations, for example, by delivering goods that were paid for in advance.

Answer (A) is incorrect because a decrease in an asset from primary operations results in an expense. Answer (B) is incorrect because an increase in an asset from incidental transactions results in a gain. Answer (C) is incorrect because an increase in a liability from incidental transactions results in a loss.

41. Which of the following best describes the distinction between expenses and losses?

A. Losses are reported net of related tax effect, whereas expenses are not reported net of tax.

B. Losses are extraordinary charges, whereas expenses are ordinary charges.

C. Losses are material items, whereas expenses are immaterial items.

D. Losses result from peripheral or incidental transactions, whereas expenses result from ongoing major or central operations of the entity.

Answer (D) is correct. *(CIA, adapted)*

REQUIRED: The distinction between expenses and losses.

DISCUSSION: SFAC 6 defines expenses as "outflows or other using up of assets or incurrences of liabilities (or a combination of both) from delivering or producing goods, rendering services, or carrying out other activities that constitute the entity's ongoing major or central operations." Losses are defined as "decreases in equity (net assets) from peripheral or incidental transactions of an entity and from all other transactions and other events and circumstances affecting the entity except those that result from expenses or distributions to owners."

1.4 Recognition and Measurement

42. Recognition is the process of formally incorporating an item into the financial statements of an entity as an asset, liability, revenue, or expense. Recognition criteria include all of the following except

A. Measurability with sufficient reliability.

B. Definitions of elements of financial statements.

C. Decision usefulness.

D. Relevance.

Answer (C) is correct. *(CMA, adapted)*

REQUIRED: The item not included in the recognition criteria.

DISCUSSION: SFAC 5, *Recognition and Measurement in Financial Statements of Business Enterprises*, states that an item and information about the item should be recognized when the following four fundamental recognition criteria are met: (1) The item meets the definition of an element of financial statements; (2) it has a relevant attribute measurable with sufficient reliability (measurability); (3) the information about the item is capable of making a difference in user decisions (relevance); and (4) the information is representationally faithful, verifiable, and neutral (reliability). Decision usefulness is the most important quality in the hierarchy of accounting qualities given in SFAC 2, not a specific recognition criterion.

43. According to the FASB conceptual framework, which of the following statements conforms to the realization concept?

A. Equipment depreciation was assigned to a production department and then to product unit costs.

B. Depreciated equipment was sold in exchange for a note receivable.

C. Cash was collected on accounts receivable.

D. Product unit costs were assigned to cost of goods sold when the units were sold.

Answer (B) is correct. *(CPA, adapted)*

REQUIRED: The statement that conforms to the realization concept.

DISCUSSION: The term "realization" is used most precisely in accounting and financial reporting with regard to sales of assets for cash or claims to cash. According to SFACs 5 and 6, the terms "realized" and "unrealized" identify revenues or gains and losses on assets sold and unsold, respectively. Thus, the sale of depreciated equipment for a claim to cash meets the definition of realization.

Answer (A) is incorrect because assigning costs to products is allocation, not realization. Answer (C) is incorrect because realization occurred when the accounts receivable (claims to cash) were recognized. Answer (D) is incorrect because assigning costs to products is allocation, not realization.

44. Revenues of an entity are usually measured by the exchange values of the assets or liabilities involved. Recognition of revenue does not occur until

A. The revenue is realizable.

B. The revenue is realized and earned.

C. Products or services are exchanged for cash or claims to cash.

D. The entity has substantially accomplished what it agreed to do.

Answer (B) is correct. *(CMA, adapted)*

REQUIRED: The appropriate timing of the recognition of revenue.

DISCUSSION: In accordance with SFAC 5, revenues should be recognized when they are realized or realizable and earned. Revenues are realized when products, merchandise, or other assets are exchanged for cash or claims to cash. Revenues are realizable when related assets received or held are readily convertible to known amounts of cash or claims to cash. Revenues are earned when the entity has substantially accomplished what it must do to be entitled to the benefits represented by the revenues.

45. The Star Company is a service enterprise that requires customers to place their orders 2 weeks in advance. Star bills its customers on the fifteenth day of the month following the date of service and requires that payment be made within 30 days of the billing date. Conceptually, Star should recognize revenue from its services at the date when

A. A customer places an order.

B. The service is provided.

C. A billing is mailed.

D. A customer's payment is received.

Answer (B) is correct. *(CIA, adapted)*

REQUIRED: The date at which a catering service should recognize revenue.

DISCUSSION: Revenues should be recognized when they are realized or realizable and earned. The most common time at which these two conditions are met is when the product or merchandise is delivered or services are rendered to customers.

46. For a monthly fee, Roach Co. visits its customers' premises and performs pest control services. If customers experience problems between regularly scheduled visits, Roach makes service calls at no additional charge. Instead of paying monthly, customers may pay an annual fee in advance. For a customer who pays the annual fee in advance, Roach should recognize the related revenue

A. When the cash is collected.

B. At the end of the fiscal year.

C. At the end of the contract year after all of the services have been performed.

D. Evenly over the contract year as the services are performed.

Answer (D) is correct. *(CPA, adapted)*

REQUIRED: The timing of recognition of revenue.

DISCUSSION: Accrual-based revenue should be recognized when realized or realizable and earned. When the earning process involves service, these conditions are usually met when the services are rendered. Because these services entail monthly visits, the annual payment should be recognized evenly over the period in which the services are performed.

Answer (A) is incorrect because recognition when cash is collected is appropriate when the cash basis is used. Answer (B) is incorrect because the revenue should be recognized evenly over the contract year. Answer (C) is incorrect because the revenue should be recognized evenly over the contract year.

47. The selling price for a product is reasonably assured, the units are interchangeable, and the costs of selling and distributing the product are insignificant. To recognize revenue from the product as early in the revenue cycle as is permitted by GAAP, the revenue recognition method that should be used is the

A. Cash method.

B. Completion-of-production method.

C. Percentage-of-completion method.

D. Cost recovery method.

Answer (B) is correct. *(CMA, adapted)*

REQUIRED: The revenue recognition method allowing proper recognition of revenue prior to the sale of the merchandise.

DISCUSSION: Revenue is to be recognized when the conditions of "realized or realizable" and "earned" are met. If products or other assets, such as precious metals or certain agricultural products, are readily realizable because they are salable at reliably determinable prices without significant effort, revenues may be recognized when production is completed or when prices of the asset change.

48. An acceptable method for recognizing profit when the collection of cash is in doubt is the

A. Percentage-of-completion method.

B. Installment method.

C. Completed-contract method.

D. Consignment method.

Answer (B) is correct. *(CMA, adapted)*

REQUIRED: The method of recognizing profit.

DISCUSSION: Revenue is to be recognized when it is realized or realizable and earned. If no reasonable basis exists for estimating the degree of collectibility of assets to be received for products, services, or other assets, revenues and gains may be recognized on the basis of cash received. Thus, the installment method or the cost recovery method may be used (APB 10).

Answer (A) is incorrect because the percentage-of-completion method is not an acceptable method for recognizing profit when the collection of cash is in doubt. Answer (C) is incorrect because the completed-contract method is not an acceptable method for recognizing profit when the collection of cash is in doubt. Answer (D) is incorrect because the consignment method is not an acceptable method for recognizing profit when the collection of cash is in doubt.

49. Under a royalty agreement with another enterprise, a company will receive royalties from the assignment of a patent for 2 years. The royalties received should be reported as revenue

A. At the date of the royalty agreement.

B. In the period earned.

C. In the period received.

D. Evenly over the life of the royalty agreement.

Answer (B) is correct. *(CPA, adapted)*

REQUIRED: The timing of recognition of royalty revenue.

DISCUSSION: In accordance with SFAC 5, revenues should be recognized when they are realized or realizable and earned. Revenues are realized when products, merchandise, or other assets are exchanged for cash or claims to cash. Revenues are realizable when related assets received or held are readily convertible to known amounts of cash or claims to cash. Revenues are earned when the entity has substantially accomplished what it must do to be entitled to the benefits represented by the revenues. Earning embraces the activities that give rise to revenue, for example, allowing other entities to use enterprise assets (such as patents) or the occurrence of an event specified in a contract (such as production using the patented technology).

50. Determining periodic earnings and financial position depends on measuring economic resources and obligations and changes in them as these changes occur. This explanation pertains to

A. Disclosure.

B. Accrual accounting.

C. Materiality.

D. The matching concept.

Answer (B) is correct. *(CPA, adapted)*

REQUIRED: The accounting concept described.

DISCUSSION: A basic feature of financial accounting is that it is an accrual system under which the determination of periodic earnings and financial position is dependent upon the measurement of all economic resources and obligations (e.g., receivables and payables) and changes in them as the changes occur.

Answer (A) is incorrect because disclosure pertains to the requirement that the user of financial statements be provided with sufficient information to avoid being misled. Answer (C) is incorrect because accounting data are material if they are sufficiently significant to be included in the accounting system. Answer (D) is incorrect because the matching concept concerns the association of cause and effect, that is, of costs with revenues.

51. Which of the following is not a theoretical basis for the allocation of expenses?

A. Systematic allocation.

B. Cause and effect.

C. Profit maximization.

D. Immediate recognition.

Answer (C) is correct. *(CPA, adapted)*

REQUIRED: The accounting concept that is not a theoretical basis for allocation of expenses.

DISCUSSION: Profit maximization is not a theoretical basis for the allocation of expense. The allocation of expenses on such a basis would subvert the purpose of GAAP to present fairly the results of operations and financial position because expenses would not be reported.

Answer (A) is incorrect because expenses are to be recognized by a systematic and rational allocation if causal relations are generally identifiable but particular amounts cannot be related directly to specific revenues or periods. Answer (B) is incorrect because expenses should be recognized in a particular period if they have a direct association with that period or with specific revenues recognized in that period. Answer (D) is incorrect because immediate recognition is appropriate when costs have no discernible future benefits or there is no other theoretically sound basis for allocation of the expenses.

52. Costs that can be reasonably associated with specific revenues but not with specific products should be

A. Charged to expense in the period incurred.

B. Allocated to specific products based on the best estimate of the production processing time.

C. Expensed in the period in which the related revenue is recognized.

D. Capitalized and then amortized over a period not to exceed 60 months.

Answer (C) is correct. *(CPA, adapted)*

REQUIRED: The time to recognize costs that can be reasonably associated with specific revenues but not with specific products.

DISCUSSION: The expense recognition principle of "associating cause and effect" or "matching" applies when a direct cause-and-effect relationship can be demonstrated between costs and particular revenues. A typical example of expenses recognized by the association of cause and effect is cost of goods sold. Association of costs with revenues can also be applied to services. Association of costs with specific products is not necessary.

Answer (A) is incorrect because immediate recognition is permitted only if no cause-and-effect relationship can be demonstrated and there is no other basis on which to expense the costs. Answer (B) is incorrect because a systematic and rational allocation of costs (based on processing time or length of asset service) is made if only a general (not direct) cause-and-effect relationship exists between costs and revenues. Answer (D) is incorrect because a systematic and rational allocation of costs (based on processing time or length of asset service) is made if only a general (not direct) cause-and-effect relationship exists between costs and revenues.

53. Some costs cannot be directly related to particular revenues but are incurred to obtain benefits that are exhausted in the period in which the costs are incurred. An example of such a cost is

A. Salespersons' monthly salaries.

B. Salespersons' commissions.

C. Transportation to customers.

D. Prepaid insurance.

Answer (A) is correct. *(CPA, adapted)*

REQUIRED: The costs not directly related to particular revenues but incurred to obtain benefits exhausted in the same period in which they are incurred.

DISCUSSION: Expenses should be recognized when there is a consumption of benefit. The consumption of benefit may occur when the expenses are matched with the revenues, when they are allocated on a systematic and rational basis to the periods in which the related assets are expected to provide benefits, or when the cash is spent or liabilities are incurred for goods and services that are used up either simultaneously with the acquisition or soon after. Salespersons' monthly salaries is an example of a cost that cannot be directly related to particular revenues but is incurred to obtain benefits that are exhausted in the period in which the cost is incurred.

Answer (B) is incorrect because these costs are recognized upon recognition of revenues that result directly and jointly from the same transaction or other events as the cost. Answer (C) is incorrect because these costs are recognized upon recognition of revenues that result directly and jointly from the same transaction or other events as the cost. Answer (D) is incorrect because prepaid insurance benefits a number of accounting periods. Its cost should thus be allocated on a systematic and rational basis to the accounting periods benefitted.

54. When bad debt expense is estimated on the basis of the percentage of past actual losses from bad debts to past net credit sales, and this percentage is adjusted for anticipated conditions, the accounting concept of

A. Matching is being followed.

B. Matching is not being followed.

C. Substance over form is being followed.

D. Going concern is not being followed.

Answer (A) is correct. *(CPA, adapted)*

REQUIRED: The item describing bad debt expense estimated based on past and expected future experience.

DISCUSSION: When bad debt expense is estimated on the basis of net credit sales, a cost (bad debt expense) is being directly associated with a revenue of the period (net credit sales). This practice applies the expense recognition principle of "associating cause and effect," also known as matching.

Answer (B) is incorrect because matching is being followed. Answer (C) is incorrect because substance over form refers to that feature of financial accounting that emphasizes the economic substance of a transaction rather than its legal form; e.g., a lease may actually be a purchase. Answer (D) is incorrect because the going concern concept refers to the assumption that the enterprise is going to continue in operation and liquidation values do not have to be used.

55. Why are certain costs of doing business capitalized when incurred and then depreciated or amortized over subsequent accounting cycles?

A. To reduce the federal income tax liability.

B. To aid management in the decision-making process.

C. To match the costs of production with revenues as earned.

D. To adhere to the accounting concept of conservatism.

Answer (C) is correct. *(CPA, adapted)*

REQUIRED: The reason certain costs are capitalized and then depreciated or amortized.

DISCUSSION: If costs benefit more than one accounting period, they should be systematically and rationally allocated to all periods benefitted. This is done by capitalizing the costs and depreciating or amortizing them over the periods in which the asset helps generate revenue. The term "matching" is most narrowly defined as the expense recognition principle of associating cause and effect, but it is sometimes used more broadly (as here) to apply to the entire process of expense recognition or even of income determination.

Answer (A) is incorrect because capitalization and depreciation of costs on the financial statements have no effect on federal income tax liability. Answer (B) is incorrect because expense recognition principles are applied to benefit all users of financial statements, not merely management. Answer (D) is incorrect because the accounting concept of conservatism requires a prudent approach to uncertainty but without the introduction of bias into financial reporting. Thus, the more conservative approach might be to recognize all costs immediately.

56. Which of the following is an example of the expense recognition principle of associating cause and effect?

A. Allocation of insurance cost.

B. Sales commissions.

C. Depreciation of fixed assets.

D. Officers' salaries.

Answer (B) is correct. *(CPA, adapted)*

REQUIRED: The example of associating cause and effect for expense recognition.

DISCUSSION: If a direct cause-and-effect relationship can be established between costs and revenues, the costs should be recognized as expenses when the related revenue is recognized. Costs of products sold or services provided and sales commissions are examples of costs that can be associated with specific revenues.

Answer (A) is incorrect because allocation of insurance cost is an example of allocating costs among several periods on a systematic and rational basis. Answer (C) is incorrect because depreciation is an example of allocating costs among several periods on a systematic and rational basis. Answer (D) is incorrect because officers' salaries are expenses that are recognized immediately. They provide no discernible future benefits, and there is no other more useful basis of allocation.

57. Which of the following is an application of the principle of systematic and rational allocation?

A. Amortization of intangible assets.

B. Sales commissions.

C. Research and development costs.

D. Officers' salaries.

Answer (A) is correct. *(CPA, adapted)*

REQUIRED: The application of the concept of systematic and rational allocation.

DISCUSSION: The expense recognition principle of systematic and rational allocation is applied to the amortization of intangible assets because of the absence of a direct means of associating cause and effect. The costs benefit a number of periods (they generate revenue in those periods) and should be systematically and rationally allocated.

Answer (B) is incorrect because sales commissions directly relate to particular revenues and should be recognized as an expense when the related revenues are recognized. Answer (C) is incorrect because research and development costs are expensed in the period incurred. Answer (D) is incorrect because officers' salaries are expensed in the period incurred.

58. A patent, purchased in year 1 and amortized over a 15-year life, was determined to be worthless in year 6. The write-off of the asset in year 6 is an application of which of the following principles?

A. Associating cause and effect.

B. Immediate recognition.

C. Systematic and rational allocation.

D. Objectivity.

Answer (B) is correct. *(CPA, adapted)*

REQUIRED: The accounting principle of which the write-off of a patent is an example.

DISCUSSION: The patent was being amortized in a systematic and rational manner. When it was determined that the costs associated with the patent (recorded as an asset) no longer provided discernible benefits, the remaining unamortized costs were written off; that is, the loss was recognized immediately.

Answer (A) is incorrect because it is a method of deferring costs to future periods that is not appropriate when a cost has no discernible future benefit. Answer (C) is incorrect because it is a method of amortizing the patent. Answer (D) is incorrect because objectivity is a quality of accounting information, not an accounting principle. Moreover, it was rejected in favor of verifiability for inclusion in the hierarchy of qualitative characteristics in SFAC 2.

59. Which of the following is not a basis for the immediate recognition of a cost during a period?

A. The cost provides no discernible future benefit.

B. The cost recorded in a prior period no longer produces discernible benefits.

C. The federal income tax savings using the immediate write-off method exceed the savings obtained by allocating the cost to several periods.

D. Allocation of the cost on the basis of association with revenue or among several accounting periods is considered to serve no useful purpose.

Answer (C) is correct. *(CPA, adapted)*

REQUIRED: The item that should not be immediately recognized as an expense.

DISCUSSION: In applying the principles of expense recognition, costs are analyzed to determine whether they can be associated with revenue on a cause-and-effect basis, e.g., cost of goods sold. If not, a systematic and rational allocation should be attempted, e.g., depreciation. If neither principle is applicable, only then are costs recognized as expenses in the period incurred or in which a loss is discerned. Accordingly, even though federal income tax savings could be obtained by the immediate write-off method, GAAP might require another treatment of the expense.

60. Items reported in financial statements are measured by different attributes. The unit of measurement is money unadjusted for changes in purchasing power over time. According to SFAC 5,

A. Units of constant general purchasing power should replace nominal units of money.

B. A single attribute should be selected for measuring all assets and liabilities.

C. The use of different measurement attributes should continue.

D. Current practice is based on a single attribute with several major exceptions.

Answer (C) is correct. *(Publisher)*

REQUIRED: The approach of SFAC 5 to measurement attributes and the unit of measurement.

DISCUSSION: SFAC 5 characterizes current practice as based on different attributes: historical cost (historical proceeds), current cost, current market value, net realizable (settlement) value, and present (or discounted) value of future cash flows. SFAC 5 suggests that use of different attributes will continue.

Answer (A) is incorrect because, unless inflation increases to an intolerable level, nominal units of money will continue to be used. Answer (B) is incorrect because use of different attributes will continue. Answer (D) is incorrect because use of different attributes will continue.

61. SFAC 5 states that items currently reported in financial statements are measured by different attributes. The amount of cash or its equivalent that would have to be paid if the same or an equivalent asset were acquired currently defines the attribute of

A. Historical cost.

B. Current cost.

C. Current market value.

D. Net realizable value.

Answer (B) is correct. *(Publisher)*

REQUIRED: The measurement attribute defined by SFAC 5.

DISCUSSION: The amount of cash or its equivalent that would have to be paid if the same or an equivalent asset were acquired currently is the definition of the measurement attribute of current (replacement) cost. Some inventories are reported in accordance with this attribute.

Answer (A) is incorrect because historical cost is the amount of cash or its equivalent paid to acquire an asset. Answer (C) is incorrect because current market value is the amount of cash or its equivalent that could be obtained by selling an asset in orderly liquidation. Answer (D) is incorrect because net realizable value is the nondiscounted amount of cash or its equivalent into which an asset is expected to be converted in due course of business minus any direct cost necessary to make that conversion.

62. According to SFAC 5, *Recognition and Measurement in Financial Statements of Business Enterprises*, the appropriate attribute for measuring long-term payables is

A. Historical cost.

B. Current cost.

C. Net realizable value.

D. Present value of future cash flows.

Answer (D) is correct. *(CMA, adapted)*

REQUIRED: The appropriate attribute to use when measuring long-term payables.

DISCUSSION: According to SFAC 5, the appropriate measurement attribute for long-term liabilities is "the present or discounted value of future cash outflows expected to be required to satisfy the liability in due course of business."

Answer (A) is incorrect because historical cost is an attribute of assets, not liabilities. Answer (B) is incorrect because current cost is an attribute of assets, not liabilities. Answer (C) is incorrect because net realizable value is an attribute of assets, not liabilities.

63. According to SFAC 5, *Recognition and Measurement in Financial Statements of Business Enterprises*, the appropriate attribute for measuring land currently used in a business is

A. Historical cost.

B. Current cost.

C. Net realizable value.

D. Present value of future cash flows.

Answer (A) is correct. *(CMA, adapted)*

REQUIRED: The attribute to use when measuring land currently used in a business.

DISCUSSION: According to SFAC 5, land used in a business should be valued at its historical cost. "Property, plant, and equipment and most inventories are reported at their historical cost, which is the amount of cash, or its equivalent, paid to acquire an asset, commonly adjusted after acquisition for amortization or other allocations."

64. Reporting inventory at the lower of cost or market is a departure from the accounting principle of

A. Historical cost.

B. Consistency.

C. Conservatism.

D. Full disclosure.

Answer (A) is correct. *(CPA, adapted)*

REQUIRED: The principle from which reporting inventory at the lower of cost or market is a departure.

DISCUSSION: Historical cost is the amount of cash, or its equivalent, paid to acquire an asset. Thus, the LCM rule departs from the historical cost principle when the utility of the inventory is judged no longer to be as great as its cost.

Answer (B) is incorrect because LCM does not violate the consistency principle as long as it is consistently applied. Answer (C) is incorrect because LCM yields a conservative inventory valuation. Answer (D) is incorrect because, as long as the basis of stating inventories is disclosed, LCM does not violate the full disclosure principle.

STUDY UNIT TWO
THE ACCOUNTING PROCESS

The accounting system is an information system that uses accounts to record and classify the financial effects of an entity's transactions and events, summarize these effects, and report the results in financial statements.

Accounts ordinarily are classified in accordance with the following equations:

Assets = *Liabilities + Equity*

Equity = *Contributed capital + Accumulated other comprehensive income + Retained earnings*

Retained earnings = *Retained earnings at the beginning of the period + Net income – Dividends ± Certain adjustments*

Net income = *Revenues – Expenses + Gains – Losses*

An entity's chart of accounts specifies the particular asset, liability, and equity accounts used by that entity.

The principal means of applying the balance sheet equation are (1) the debit-credit convention and (2) the double-entry convention. In accordance with the **debit-credit convention**, increases in asset accounts are debits, and decreases are credits. In contrast, increases in liabilities and equity accounts are credits, and decreases are debits. For each account, the balance equals the sum of the amounts debited and credited. In accordance with the **double-entry convention**, the dollar amount of the total debits arising from a transaction or an event must be equal to the total credits. The result of applying these conventions is that the effects both of individual transactions and events and of total transactions and events are recorded in accordance with the balance sheet equation.

Accounts are classified as either permanent (real) or temporary (nominal). Assets, liabilities, and equity are recorded in **permanent accounts** because their balances at the end of one accounting period (the balance sheet date) are carried forward as the beginning balances of the next accounting period. **Temporary accounts**, however, record the transactions and events during the accounting period that ultimately affect retained earnings (revenues, expenses, gains, losses, and dividends). Their balances are not carried forward.

Journal entries record the financial effects of transactions and events in the accounting system. For every journal entry, the total debited must equal the total credited. Every journal entry must affect at least two accounts, and the effect (debit or credit) must be posted to the particular accounts. Journal entries are recorded in books of original entry (journals). Account balances are maintained in the general ledger. Every entity will maintain a general journal and a general ledger. Many entities also will maintain special journals and subsidiary ledgers.

During an accounting period, a series of journal entries and postings will be made to record and classify the financial effects of transactions and events in accordance with generally accepted accounting principles (GAAP). These journal entries and postings are part of the **accounting cycle**. At the end of the period, the following steps are taken: (1) preparing an unadjusted trial balance; (2) preparing, recording, and posting adjusting entries; (3) preparing financial statements; and (4) preparing, recording, and posting closing entries. In addition, some entities also (1) prepare adjusted and post-closing trial balances at the end of the accounting period and (2) prepare, record, and post reversing entries at the beginning of the next accounting period.

Adjusting entries are made as of the balance sheet date to record the effects on periodic revenue and expense of prepayments (prepaid expenses and unearned revenues) and accruals (revenues earned but not yet received in cash and expenses incurred but not yet paid in cash). **Closing entries** transfer (close) temporary account balances to retained earnings. **Reversing entries** reverse the effects of adjusting entries to simplify the future recording of revenue and expense transactions related to the adjusting entries. Adjusting, closing, and reversing entries must affect at least one temporary account and at least one real account.

QUESTIONS

2.1 The Accounting System

1. The correct order of the following steps of the accounting cycle is

A. Posting, closing, adjusting, reversing.

B. Posting, adjusting, closing, reversing.

C. Posting, reversing, adjusting, closing.

D. Adjusting, posting, closing, reversing.

Answer (B) is correct. *(CIA, adapted)*

REQUIRED: The proper sequence of steps in the accounting cycle.

DISCUSSION: The order of the steps in the accounting cycle is identification and measurement of transactions and other events required to be recognized, journalization, posting from the journals to the ledgers, the development of a trial balance, adjustments to produce an adjusted trial balance, statement presentation, closing, taking a postclosing trial balance (optional), and making reversing entries (optional).

Answer (A) is incorrect because adjusting entries are made prior to closing. Answer (C) is incorrect because reversing entries are made after adjustments and closing entries. Answer (D) is incorrect because posting is done prior to adjusting.

2. A chart of accounts is

A. A flowchart of all transactions.

B. An accounting procedures manual.

C. A journal.

D. A list of names of all account titles.

Answer (D) is correct. *(Publisher)*

REQUIRED: The definition of a chart of accounts.

DISCUSSION: A chart of accounts is a listing of all account titles used within an accounting system. Business transactions affecting these accounts are initially recorded by journal entries and then posted to the individual accounts maintained in the ledger.

Answer (A) is incorrect because actual transactions are not flowcharted. Flowcharts of accounting procedures are developed by auditors and systems analysts (but are not called charts of accounts). Answer (B) is incorrect because an accounting procedures manual explains how to use the chart of accounts, e.g., whether to make adjusting entries, reversing entries, etc. Answer (C) is incorrect because a journal contains the initial recording of the transactions that affect the accounts contained in the chart of accounts.

3. As commonly used, the term "net assets" represents

A. Retained earnings of a corporation.

B. Current assets minus current liabilities.

C. Total paid-in (contributed) capital of a corporation.

D. Total assets minus total liabilities.

Answer (D) is correct. *(CPA, adapted)*

REQUIRED: The definition of net assets.

DISCUSSION: Net assets is equal to total assets minus total liabilities. It is synonymous with the net worth of an entity as expressed in the balance sheet equation: assets – liabilities = equity.

Answer (A) is incorrect because retained earnings is the cumulative income earned by a corporation minus amounts declared as dividends. Answer (B) is incorrect because current assets minus current liabilities is working capital. Answer (C) is incorrect because total paid-in (contributed) capital of a corporation is the sum of all money and property received from investors. In addition to total paid-in (contributed) capital, net assets includes retained earnings and accumulated other comprehensive income.

4. What is the purpose of nominal accounts?

A. To provide temporary accumulations of certain account balances for a meaningful period of time.

B. To facilitate accounting for small amounts.

C. To correct errors as they are detected.

D. To record all transactions initially.

Answer (A) is correct. *(Publisher)*

REQUIRED: The purpose of nominal accounts.

DISCUSSION: The primary focus of financial reporting is to account for earnings. To facilitate the calculation of earnings, nominal revenue and expense accounts are created to accumulate temporarily the components of earnings during an accounting period. At the end of the period, they are usually aggregated to determine net income. Each nominal account is reduced to a zero balance by closing it to retained earnings, a balance sheet account.

Answer (B) is incorrect because small amounts are recorded in real as well as nominal accounts. Answer (C) is incorrect because errors are corrected wherever they are found, e.g., in real accounts, nominal accounts, ledgers, or journals. Answer (D) is incorrect because all transactions are initially recorded in the books of original entry called journals.

5. What function do general ledgers serve in the accounting process?

A. Reporting.

B. Summarizing.

C. Classifying.

D. Recording.

Answer (C) is correct. *(Publisher)*

REQUIRED: The function of general ledgers in the accounting process.

DISCUSSION: General ledgers serve to classify accounting data. Transactions that have been recorded in the journals are posted to the general ledger accounts where they are classified as to the accounts that have been affected.

Answer (A) is incorrect because accounting data are reported in the financial statements. Answer (B) is incorrect because data are summarized during the adjusting and closing process. Answer (D) is incorrect because transactions are recorded in the journals.

6. A subsidiary ledger is

A. A listing of the components of account balances.

B. A backup system to protect against record destruction.

C. A listing of account balances just before closing entries are prepared.

D. All accounts of a subsidiary.

Answer (A) is correct. *(Publisher)*

REQUIRED: The definition of a subsidiary ledger.

DISCUSSION: A general or controlling ledger contains the balance for each asset, liability, and equity account. A subsidiary ledger consists of the detail of a general ledger account, e.g., the individual receivables making up accounts receivable in the aggregate.

Answer (B) is incorrect because a subsidiary ledger is not a supplementary accounting system. Answer (C) is incorrect because a listing of account balances just before closing entries are prepared is a trial balance. Answer (D) is incorrect because the term "subsidiary ledger" relates to a specific general ledger account, not the accounting systems of a subsidiary company.

7. An example of a nominal account is

A. Customer deposits.

B. Capital stock.

C. Petty cash.

D. Sales returns.

Answer (D) is correct. *(Publisher)*

REQUIRED: The item that is an example of a nominal account.

DISCUSSION: Sales returns is a nominal account because it is used to accumulate the amount of sales returns for a given period. At the end of the period, the balance of sales returns is brought to zero; i.e., the account is closed at the end of the year. Nominal accounts usually are closed to retained earnings. They exist for an accounting period for the purpose of determining the effect on equity of net income. (An exception is cash dividends payable, a nominal account sometimes debited when cash dividends are declared. It does not affect net income.)

Answer (A) is incorrect because customer deposits are a real account (balance sheet account) and is not closed at the end of an accounting period. The nonzero balances in real accounts at the end of one accounting period become the beginning balances of the next period. Answer (B) is incorrect because capital stock is a real account (balance sheet account) and is not closed at the end of an accounting period. The nonzero balances in real accounts at the end of one accounting period become the beginning balances of the next period. Answer (C) is incorrect because petty cash is a real account (balance sheet account) and is not closed at the end of an accounting period. The nonzero balances in real accounts at the end of one accounting period become the beginning balances of the next period.

8. The term "double-entry system" refers to

A. The use of real and nominal accounts.

B. The recording of each transaction in two parts.

C. The use of two journals.

D. The use of a journal and a ledger.

Answer (B) is correct. *(Publisher)*

REQUIRED: The nature of a double-entry system.

DISCUSSION: In the double-entry system, each transaction is composed of two parts, debits and credits. The debits must equal the credits, and the sum of all debits for all transactions in a double entry system must equal the sum of all credits.

Answer (A) is incorrect because the distinction between real and nominal accounts is based on the relative permanence of accounts rather than the double entry, self-balancing attribute of accounting systems. Answer (C) is incorrect because many journals may be used, e.g., general journal, sales journal, cash receipts journal, and cash payments journal. Answer (D) is incorrect because, even though journals and ledgers are parts of all double entry systems, they have nothing to do with the term "double entry."

9. In the equation, assets + expenses + losses = liabilities + revenues + gains + capital, the expenses and revenues are

A. Contra asset and contra liability accounts, respectively, that assist analysis of the financial progress of the firm.

B. Incorrectly stated because their signs are reversed; i.e., both are contra items that should have negative signs in the formula.

C. Adjustments to capital that are postponed until the end of a specific accounting period to determine their net effect on capital for that period.

D. Incorrectly included in the formula because assets = liabilities + capital.

Answer (C) is correct. *(Publisher)*

REQUIRED: The status of expenses and revenues in the basic accounting equation.

DISCUSSION: Expenses and revenues are adjustments to retained earnings (an equity or capital account) that are not made immediately upon their occurrence but, instead, are postponed until the end of a specific accounting period to determine their net effect on capital for that period, i.e., at the time of computation of net income. They are initially recorded in nominal accounts.

Answer (A) is incorrect because contra asset and contra liability accounts reduce the related accounts; e.g., accumulated depreciation offsets the related asset account. Answer (B) is incorrect because expenses are debits and thus positive on the left-hand side of the equation; revenues are credits and thus positive on the right-hand side of the equation. Answer (D) is incorrect because the debits to assets equal the sum of the credits to liabilities and capital accounts, but the given equation is also correct.

10. What are real accounts?

A. Nonfictitious accounts.

B. Accounts in existence.

C. Balance sheet accounts.

D. Income statement accounts.

Answer (C) is correct. *(Publisher)*

REQUIRED: The definition of real accounts.

DISCUSSION: Real accounts are not closed at the end of the year and can carry forward nonzero balances from one accounting period to the next. Real accounts are typically balance sheet accounts and are also called permanent accounts.

Answer (A) is incorrect because "nonfictitious accounts" has no accounting meaning. Answer (B) is incorrect because nominal accounts can also exist. Answer (D) is incorrect because income statement accounts are nominal accounts.

11. Why are adjusting entries necessary?

A. To record revenues and expenses.

B. To make debits equal credits.

C. To close nominal accounts at year-end.

D. To correct erroneous balances in accounts.

Answer (A) is correct. *(Publisher)*

REQUIRED: The rationale for adjusting entries.

DISCUSSION: Adjusting entries are used to adjust expenses (and the related asset or liability accounts) or revenues (and the related asset or liability accounts) to year-end amounts. Adjusting entries are needed to properly reflect revenues recognized when they are realized or realizable and earned and expenses recognized in accordance with the expense recognition principles. Accrual adjusting entries are made when the expense or revenue is recognized prior to the payment or receipt of cash. Deferral adjusting entries are necessary when the expense or revenue is recognized after the payment or receipt of cash.

Answer (B) is incorrect because all transactions result in equal debits and credits, and the cumulative balances of debits and credits are always equal. Answer (C) is incorrect because it relates to closing entries. Answer (D) is incorrect because it relates to correcting entries.

12. Closing entries

A. Transfer the balances in all of the nominal accounts to equity.

B. Must be made after the reversing entries but before the adjusting entries.

C. Close out all of the accounts in the general ledger.

D. Must be followed by reversing entries.

Answer (A) is correct. *(Publisher)*

REQUIRED: The true statement about closing entries.

DISCUSSION: Closing entries transfer the balances in all the nominal accounts to the retained earnings account. This process usually involves closing amounts to the income summary account and then to retained earnings.

Answer (B) is incorrect because closing entries are made after adjusting entries and before reversing entries. Answer (C) is incorrect because closing entries close only nominal accounts. Answer (D) is incorrect because reversing entries are not required. They merely facilitate accounting for certain transactions in the next accounting period.

13. Which of the following statements is a true description of reversing entries?

A. The recording of reversing entries is a mandatory step in the accounting cycle.

B. Reversing entries are made at the end of the next accounting period, after recording regular transactions of the period.

C. Reversing entries are identical to the adjusting entries made in the previous period.

D. Reversing entries are the exact opposite of the adjustments made in the previous period.

Answer (D) is correct. *(CIA, adapted)*

REQUIRED: The best description of reversing entries.

DISCUSSION: Reversing entries are made at the beginning of a period to reverse the effects of adjusting entries made at the end of the preceding period. They are optional entries made for the sake of convenience in recording the transactions of the period. In order for reversing entries to reverse the prior adjustments, they must be the exact opposite of the adjustments made in the previous period.

Answer (A) is incorrect because reversing entries are optional. Answer (B) is incorrect because reversing entries are made at the beginning of the next accounting period. Answer (C) is incorrect because reversing entries are the exact opposite of the adjustments made in the previous period.

14. Compared with the accrual basis of accounting, the cash basis of accounting understates income by the net decrease during the accounting period of

	Accounts Receivable	Accrued Expenses
A.	Yes	Yes
B.	Yes	No
C.	No	No
D.	No	Yes

Answer (D) is correct. *(CPA, adapted)*

REQUIRED: The cash-basis item(s), if any, the net decrease of which understates income compared with accrual-basis accounting.

DISCUSSION: A net decrease in accounts receivable indicates that cash collected exceeded accrual-basis revenue from receivables in the current period. A net decrease in accrued expenses indicates that cash paid for expenses exceeded the current period's accrual-basis expenses. Thus, a net decrease in receivables results in an overstatement of cash-basis income compared with accrual-basis income, and a net decrease in accrued expenses results in an understatement.

15. To calculate net sales, <List A> must be <List B> cash receipts from customers.

	List A	List B
A.	An increase in net accounts receivable	Added to
B.	An increase in net accounts receivable	Subtracted from
C.	An increase in net accounts payable	Added to
D.	An increase in net accounts payable	Subtracted from

Answer (A) is correct. *(CIA, adapted)*

REQUIRED: The calculation of net sales.

DISCUSSION: To convert from the cash basis (cash receipts) to the accrual basis (net sales), the increase in net accounts receivable must be added to cash receipts from customers.

Answer (B) is incorrect because a decrease in receivables would be subtracted from cash receipts. Answer (C) is incorrect because changes in accounts payable are not included in the calculation of net sales. Answer (D) is incorrect because changes in accounts payable are not included in the calculation of net sales.

16. On April 1, Julie began operating a service proprietorship with an initial cash investment of $1,000. The proprietorship provided $3,200 of services in April and received a payment of $2,500 in May. The proprietorship incurred expenses of $1,500 in April that were paid in June. During May, Julie drew $500 from her capital account. What was the proprietorship's income for the 2 months ended May 31 under the following methods of accounting?

	Cash-Basis	Accrual-Basis
A.	$500	$1,200
B.	$1,000	$1,700
C.	$2,000	$1,200
D.	$2,500	$1,700

Answer (D) is correct. *(CPA, adapted)*

REQUIRED: The income for a proprietorship under the cash basis and accrual basis.

DISCUSSION: Under the cash basis, $2,500 of income is recognized for the payments received in May for the services rendered in April. The $1,500 of expenses is not recognized until June. Under the accrual basis, the $3,200 of income and the $1,500 of expenses incurred in April but not paid until June are recognized. The net income is $1,700 under the accrual basis. The cash investment and capital withdrawal are ignored because they do not affect net income.

Answer (A) is incorrect because the $500 withdrawal should not be recognized in the computation of net income under either method, and the $1,500 of expenses should not be recognized under the cash basis. Answer (B) is incorrect because the cash basis does not recognize the $1,500 in expenses until June. Answer (C) is incorrect because the $500 withdrawal should not be recognized in the computation of net income under either method.

17. Hahn Co. prepared financial statements on the cash basis of accounting. The cash basis was modified so that an accrual of income taxes was reported. Are these financial statements in accordance with the modified cash basis of accounting?

A. Yes.

B. No, because the modifications are illogical.

C. No, because there is no substantial support for recording income taxes.

D. No, because the modifications result in financial statements equivalent to those prepared under the accrual basis of accounting.

Answer (A) is correct. *(CPA, adapted)*

REQUIRED: The true statement about whether cash-basis statements may be modified for accrual of income taxes.

DISCUSSION: A comprehensive basis of accounting other than GAAP includes the cash basis. Modifications of the cash basis having substantial support, such as accruing income taxes or recording depreciation on fixed assets, may be made when preparing financial statements on the cash basis (AU 623).

Answer (B) is incorrect because accrual of quarterly income taxes is a logical modification of the cash basis of accounting. Answer (C) is incorrect because substantial support exists for accrual of a reasonably estimable expense such as income taxes. Answer (D) is incorrect because a modification of the cash basis that accrues income taxes, but incorporates no other accruals or deferrals, will not result in financial statements equivalent to those prepared under the accrual basis.

18. Income tax-basis financial statements differ from those prepared under GAAP in that income tax-basis financial statements

A. Do not include nontaxable revenues and nondeductible expenses in determining income.

B. Include detailed information about current and deferred income tax liabilities.

C. Contain no disclosures about capital and operating lease transactions.

D. Recognize certain revenues and expenses in different reporting periods.

Answer (D) is correct. *(CPA, adapted)*

REQUIRED: The difference between income tax-basis financial statements and those prepared under GAAP.

DISCUSSION: Income tax-basis financial statements and those prepared under GAAP differ when the tax basis of an asset or a liability and its reported amount in the GAAP-based financial statements are not the same. The result will be taxable or deductible amounts in future years when the reported amount of the asset is recovered or the liability is settled. Thus, certain revenues and expenses are recognized in different periods. An example is subscriptions revenue received in advance, which is recognized in taxable income when received and in financial income when earned in a later period. Another example is a warranty liability, which is recognized as an expense in financial income when a product is sold and in taxable income when the expenditures are made in a later period.

Answer (A) is incorrect because, even if financial statements are prepared on the income tax basis, permanent difference items, e.g., nondeductible expenses, are included as revenues or expenses in the income statement. They do not have to be presented in a special category of the income statement. Answer (B) is incorrect because detailed information about current and deferred income tax liabilities is necessary whether financial statements are prepared on the income-tax basis or in conformity with GAAP. Temporary differences, which result in deferred tax amounts, arise under either basis of accounting. Answer (C) is incorrect because lease disclosures are the same under either basis of accounting.

2.2 Deferrals and Accruals

19. How would the proceeds received from the advance sale of nonrefundable tickets for a theatrical performance be reported in the seller's financial statements before the performance?

A. Revenue for the entire proceeds.

B. Revenue to the extent of related costs expended.

C. Unearned revenue to the extent of related costs expended.

D. Unearned revenue for the entire proceeds.

Answer (D) is correct. *(CPA, adapted)*

REQUIRED: The reporting of the proceeds received from the advance sale of nonrefundable tickets.

DISCUSSION: Revenue is recognized when it is realized or realizable and earned. The entire proceeds should be reported as unearned revenue because the earning process will not be complete until the performance has been given even though the tickets are not refundable. "Revenues are considered to have been earned when the entity has substantially accomplished what it must do to be entitled to the benefits represented by the revenues" (SFAC 5).

Answer (A) is incorrect because revenue is recognized when it is realized or realizable and earned. Answer (B) is incorrect because revenue is recognized when it is realized or realizable and earned. Answer (C) is incorrect because the entire proceeds should be credited to unearned revenue.

20. An adjusting entry that records the earned portion of unearned revenue previously recorded always includes a

A. Debit to an account in the asset category.

B. Credit to an account in the asset category.

C. Credit to an account in the equity category.

D. Credit to an account in the liability category.

Answer (C) is correct. *(CMA, adapted)*

REQUIRED: The effect of an adjusting entry that records the earned portion of unearned revenue previously recorded.

DISCUSSION: When cash from customers is collected in advance, a credit is made to the unearned revenue account. When the revenue is earned, usually on the basis of production and delivery, the unearned revenue account must then be debited, with a corresponding credit to a revenue account (an equity account).

21. A company that sprays chemicals in residences to eliminate or prevent infestation of insects requires that customers prepay for 3 months' service at the beginning of each new quarter. Which term appropriately describes the prepayment from the perspective of the service provider?

A. Unearned revenue.

B. Earned revenue.

C. Accrued revenue.

D. Prepaid expense.

Answer (A) is correct. *(CIA, adapted)*

REQUIRED: The classification of collected fees that pertain to a future period.

DISCUSSION: Under the revenue recognition principle, revenue is recognized (reported as revenue) in the period in which it is earned; therefore, when it is received in advance of its being earned, the amount applicable to future periods is deferred. The amount unearned (received in advance) is considered a liability because it represents an obligation to perform a service in the future arising from a past transaction. Unearned revenue is revenue that has been received but not earned.

Answer (B) is incorrect because the revenue is not earned. The company has not performed the related services for the customer. Answer (C) is incorrect because accrued revenue is revenue that has been earned but not received. The company reports revenue that has been received but not earned. Answer (D) is incorrect because the customer reports a prepaid expense (expense paid but not incurred); the company reports unearned revenue (revenue received but not earned).

22. An accrued expense can best be described as an amount

A. Paid and currently matched with earnings.

B. Paid and not currently matched with earnings.

C. Not paid and not currently matched with earnings.

D. Not paid and currently matched with earnings.

Answer (D) is correct. *(CPA, adapted)*

REQUIRED: The best description of an accrued expense.

DISCUSSION: An accrued expense is one that has been incurred but not paid. Thus, it should be charged (matched) against revenue in the current period and recorded as a liability.

Answer (A) is incorrect because an expense paid in the same period in which it is incurred is not accrued and does not require an adjusting entry. Answer (B) is incorrect because it describes a deferral of expense. Answer (C) is incorrect because an amount neither paid nor incurred requires no original entry and no adjusting entry.

23. On November 1, year 1, Fitz Co. paid $3,600 to renew its insurance policy for 3 years. On December 31, year 1, Fitz's unadjusted trial balance showed a balance of $90 for prepaid insurance and $4,410 for insurance expense. What amounts should be reported for prepaid insurance and insurance expense in Fitz's December 31, year 1 financial statements?

	Prepaid Expense	Insurance Expense
A.	$3,300	$1,200
B.	$3,400	$1,200
C.	$3,400	$1,100
D.	$3,490	$1,010

Answer (C) is correct. *(CPA, adapted)*

REQUIRED: The amounts reported for prepaid insurance and insurance expense.

DISCUSSION: At year-end, the expense and prepaid insurance accounts should be adjusted to reflect the expired amounts. The entry to record the insurance renewal included a debit to insurance expense for $3,600. The balance in prepaid insurance has expired. The 3-year prepayment is amortized at $100 per month ($3,600 ÷ 36 months), or $200 for year 1. Consequently, insurance expense for the year should be $1,100 [$90 prepaid insurance balance + ($4,410 – $3,400 unexpired amount of the November 1 prepayment)]. The $3,400 unexpired amount should be reported as prepaid insurance.

Answer (A) is incorrect because an asset balance of $3,300 and an expense of $1,200 assume the renewed policy has been in effect for 3 months. Answer (B) is incorrect because an expense of $1,200 assumes the renewed policy has been in effect for 3 months. Answer (D) is incorrect because the unadjusted prepaid insurance balance ($90) represents an expired amount.

24. An analysis of Patrick Corp.'s unadjusted prepaid expense account at December 31, year 2 revealed the following:

- An opening balance at $1,500 for Patrick's comprehensive insurance policy. Patrick had paid an annual premium of $3,000 on July 1, year 1.
- A $3,200 annual insurance premium payment made July 1, year 2.
- A $2,000 advance rental payment for a warehouse Thrift leased for 1 year beginning January 1, year 3.

In its December 31, year 2 balance sheet, what amount should Patrick report as prepaid expenses?

A. $5,200

B. $3,600

C. $2,000

D. $1,600

Answer (B) is correct. *(CPA, adapted)*

REQUIRED: The amount reported for prepaid expenses.

DISCUSSION: The $1,500 beginning balance of prepaid insurance expired on June 30, year 2, leaving a $0 balance. The $3,200 annual insurance premium paid on July 1, year 2 should be allocated equally to year 2 and year 3, leaving a $1,600 prepaid insurance balance. The $2,000 advance rental payment is an expense that is wholly deferred until year 3. Consequently, the total of prepaid expenses at year-end is $3,600 ($1,600 + $2,000).

Answer (A) is incorrect because half of the $3,200 of prepaid insurance should be expensed in year 2. Answer (C) is incorrect because half of the $3,200 of prepaid insurance should not be expensed in year 2. Answer (D) is incorrect because the prepaid rent is deferred until year 3.

25. On February 12, year 1, Gleem Publishing, Inc. purchased the copyright to a book for $15,000 and agreed to pay royalties equal to 10% of book sales, with a guaranteed minimum royalty of $60,000. Gleem had book sales of $750,000 in year 1. In its year 1 income statement, what amount should Gleem report as royalty expense?

A. $60,000

B. $75,000

C. $76,500

D. $90,000

Answer (B) is correct. *(CPA, adapted)*

REQUIRED: The royalty expense for the year.

DISCUSSION: The year 1 royalty expense is equal to 10% of book sales, with a guaranteed minimum royalty of $60,000. Thus, year 1 royalty expense is $75,000 (10% × $750,000 book sales).

Answer (A) is incorrect because $60,000 is the guaranteed minimum royalty, which is less than 10% of book sales. Answer (C) is incorrect because $76,500 includes 10% of the purchase price of the copyright. Answer (D) is incorrect because the copyright purchase price is not included in royalty expense.

26. Cathay Co. owns a royalty interest in an oil well. The contract stipulates that Cathay will receive royalty payments semiannually on January 31 and July 31. The January 31 payment will be for 20% of the oil sold to jobbers between the previous June 1 and November 30, and the July 31 payment will be for oil sold between the previous December 1 and May 31. Royalty receipts for year 2 amounted to $80,000 and $100,000 on January 31 and July 31, respectively. On December 31, year 1, accrued royalty revenue receivable amounted to $15,000. Production reports show the following oil sales:

June 1, year 1 - November 30, year 1	$400,000
December 1, year 1 - May 31, year 2	500,000
June 1, year 2 - November 30, year 2	425,000
December 1, year 2 - December 31, year 2	70,000

What amount should Cathay report as royalty revenue for year 2?

A. $179,000

B. $180,000

C. $184,000

D. $194,000

Answer (C) is correct. *(CPA, adapted)*

REQUIRED: The royalty revenue for year 2.

DISCUSSION: The royalty revenue for year 2 is 20% of year 2 oil sales. Given that 12/1/year 1 - 5/31/year 2 oil sales equaled $500,000 and that the accrued royalty for December year 1 was $15,000, oil sales for that month must have been $75,000 ($15,000 accrued ÷ 20%). Hence, oil sales for year 2 are $920,000 [($500,000 – $75,000) + $425,000 + $70,000]. Thus, royalty revenue for year 2 is $184,000 (20% × $920,000).

Answer (A) is incorrect because $179,000 incorrectly computes part of the revenue with the sales from 6/1/year 1 - 11/30/year 1 instead of 1/1/year 1 - 5/31/year 2. Answer (B) is incorrect because $180,000 is the royalty payments received in year 2. Answer (D) is incorrect because $194,000 is the royalty payments received in year 2, plus 20% of December year 2's sales.

27. The following information pertains to Falcon Co.'s current year sales:

Cash sales	
Gross	$160,000
Returns and allowances	7,000
Credit sales	
Gross	$240,000
Discounts	11,000

On January 1, customers owed Falcon $70,000. On December 31, customers owed Falcon $60,000. Falcon uses the direct write-off method for bad debts. No bad debts were recorded in the current year. Under the cash basis of accounting, what amount of net revenue should Falcon report for the current year?

A. $153,000

B. $340,000

C. $382,000

D. $392,000

Answer (D) is correct. *(CPA, adapted)*

REQUIRED: The revenue under the cash basis of accounting.

DISCUSSION: Under the cash basis of accounting, revenue is recognized when cash is received. Falcon had $153,000 ($160,000 – $7,000) in net cash sales and $229,000 ($240,000 – $11,000) in net credit sales. Given that accounts receivable decreased, cash collections thereon must have exceeded net credit sales by $10,000 ($70,000 – $60,000). No adjustment for bad debts is needed because no bad debts were recorded. Accordingly, net revenue is $392,000 ($153,000 + $229,000 + $10,000).

Answer (A) is incorrect because $153,000 equals net cash sales. Answer (B) is incorrect because $340,000 equals total gross sales minus ending accounts receivable. Answer (C) is incorrect because $382,000 does not reflect an adjustment for the change in receivables.

28. Windy Co. must determine the December 31, year 2 year-end accruals for advertising and rent expenses. A $500 advertising bill was received January 7, year 3. It related to costs of $375 for advertisements in December year 2 issues and $125 for advertisements in January year 3 issues of the newspaper. A store lease, effective December 16, year 1, calls for fixed rent of $1,200 per month, payable 1 month from the effective date and monthly thereafter. In addition, rent equal to 5% of net sales over $300,000 per calendar year is payable on January 31 of the following year. Net sales for year 2 were $550,000. In its December 31, year 2 balance sheet, Windy should report accrued liabilities of

A. $12,500

B. $12,875

C. $13,100

D. $13,475

Answer (D) is correct. *(CPA, adapted)*

REQUIRED: The accrued liabilities reported at year-end.

DISCUSSION: The $375 of advertising expense should be accrued in year 2 because this amount can be directly related to events in that period. The $125 amount is related to events in year 3 and should not be accrued in year 2. The fixed rental is due at mid-month. Thus, the fixed rental for the last half month of year 2 ($1,200 ÷ 2 = $600) and the rental based on annual sales [5% × ($550,000 – $300,000) = $12,500] should also be accrued, for a total of $13,475 ($375 + $600 + $12,500).

Answer (A) is incorrect because $12,500 omits the half-month of the fixed rental and the advertising bill for December. Answer (B) is incorrect because $12,875 omits the half-month of the fixed rental. Answer (C) is incorrect because $13,100 excludes the advertising bill for December.

29. Larsen Corp. pays commissions to its sales staff at the rate of 3% of net sales. Sales staff are not paid salaries but are given monthly advances of $15,000. Advances are charged to commission expense, and reconciliations against commissions are prepared quarterly. Net sales for the year ended March 31 were $15 million. The unadjusted balance in the commissions expense account on March 31 was $400,000. March advances were paid on April 3. In its income statement for the year ended March 31, what amount should Larsen report as commission expense?

A. $465,000

B. $450,000

C. $415,000

D. $400,000

Answer (B) is correct. *(CPA, adapted)*

REQUIRED: The commission expense for the year.

DISCUSSION: Sales commissions should be recognized as an expense when the related revenues are earned. Given that the enterprise pays commissions at a rate of 3% of net sales, commission expense is $450,000 (3% × $15,000,000 net sales).

Answer (A) is incorrect because $465,000 is the sum of commission expense and one monthly advance. Answer (C) is incorrect because $415,000 equals the unadjusted balance in commissions expense plus one monthly advance. Answer (D) is incorrect because $400,000 is the unadjusted balance in commissions expense.

30. Jay Corp.'s trademark was licensed to John Co. for royalties of 15% of sales of the trademarked items. Royalties are payable semiannually on March 15 for sales in July through December of the prior year, and on September 15 for sales in January through June of the same year. Jay received the following royalties from John:

	March 15	September 15
Year 1	$10,000	$15,000
Year 2	12,000	18,000

John estimated that sales of the trademarked items would total $90,000 for July through December year 2. In Jay's year 2 income statement, the royalty revenue should be

A. $31,500

B. $30,000

C. $43,500

D. $46,500

Answer (A) is correct. *(CPA, adapted)*

REQUIRED: The amount of royalty revenue to be reported.

DISCUSSION: The royalty revenue for year 2 is $31,500 [$18,000 received in September year 2 + ($90,000 × 15%) to be received in March year 3 for sales in year 2].

Answer (B) is incorrect because $30,000 includes $12,000 that was received in March year 2 but was applicable to year 1 sales and omits the $13,500 ($90,000 × 15%) attributable to sales for July through December year 2. Answer (C) is incorrect because $43,500 includes $12,000 that was received in March year 2 but was applicable to year 1 sales. Answer (D) is incorrect because $46,500 includes $15,000 that was received in September year 1 and was applicable to year 1 sales.

31. Seri Co.'s professional fees expense account had a balance of $92,000 at December 31, year 1, before considering year-end adjustments relating to the following:

- Consultants were hired for a special project at a total fee not to exceed $65,000. Seri has recorded $55,000 of this fee based on billings for work performed in year 1.
- The attorney's letter requested by the auditors, dated January 28, year 2, indicated that legal fees of $6,000 were billed on January 15, year 2 for work performed in November year 1 and that unbilled fees for December year 1 were $9,000.

What amount should Seri report for professional fees expense for the year ended December 31, year 1?

A. $117,000

B. $107,000

C. $98,000

D. $92,000

Answer (B) is correct. *(CPA, adapted)*

REQUIRED: The professional fees expense for the year.

DISCUSSION: The enterprise should recognize an expense only for the work done by the consultants and attorneys in year 1. Thus, no adjustment is necessary for the consulting fees, but the legal fees, billed and unbilled, for November and December year 1 should be debited to the account. The professional fees expense for the year is therefore $107,000 ($92,000 + $6,000 + $9,000).

Answer (A) is incorrect because $117,000 includes the maximum fee that may be payable to the consultants. Answer (C) is incorrect because $98,000 excludes the attorneys' fees for December. Answer (D) is incorrect because $92,000 excludes the attorneys' fees for November and December.

32. Dix Company sells subscriptions to a specialized directory that is published semiannually and shipped to subscribers on April 15 and October 15. Subscriptions received after the March 31 and September 30 cutoff dates are held for the next publication. Cash from subscribers is received evenly during the year and is credited to deferred revenues from subscriptions. Data relating to year 2 are as follows:

Deferred revenues from subscriptions, balance 12/31/year 1	$1,500,000
Cash receipts from subscribers	7,200,000

In its December 31, year 2 balance sheet, Dix should report deferred revenues from subscriptions of

A. $1,800,000

B. $3,300,000

C. $3,600,000

D. $5,400,000

Answer (A) is correct. *(CPA, adapted)*

REQUIRED: The balance to be reported as deferred revenues from subscriptions at year-end.

DISCUSSION: The deferred revenues from subscriptions account records subscription fees received that have not been earned. The balance in this account in the December 31, year 2 balance sheet should reflect the subscription fees received after the September 30 cutoff date. Because cash from subscribers is received evenly during the year, $1,800,000 [$7,200,000 × (3 months ÷ 12 months)] should be reported as deferred revenues from subscriptions.

Answer (B) is incorrect because $3,300,000 is the sum of the existing deferred revenues balance and the fees received after the September 30 cutoff. Answer (C) is incorrect because $3,600,000 equals 6 months of fees. Answer (D) is incorrect because $5,400,000 equals 9 months of fees.

33. Based on current year sales of music recorded by an artist under a contract with Cyber Music, the artist earned $200,000 after an adjustment of $16,000 for anticipated returns. In addition, Cyber paid the artist $150,000 in the current year as a reasonable estimate of the amount recoverable from future royalties to be earned by the artist. What amount should Cyber report in its current year income statement for royalty expense?

A. $200,000

B. $216,000

C. $350,000

D. $366,000

Answer (A) is correct. *(CPA, adapted)*

REQUIRED: The royalty expense.

DISCUSSION: Income is earned by the artist and an expense is incurred by Cyber based on net sales (sales – returns). Amounts paid in advance and recoverable from future royalties are classified as prepaid expenses. Thus, Cyber should report royalty expense of $200,000.

Answer (B) is incorrect because $216,000 includes the adjustment of $16,000 for anticipated returns. Answer (C) is incorrect because $350,000 includes the prepayment. Answer (D) is incorrect because $366,000 includes the prepayment and the adjustment of $16,000 for anticipated returns.

34. Boland Co.'s advertising expense account had a balance of $160,000 at December 31, year 1, before any necessary year-end adjustment relating to the following:

- Included in the $160,000 is the $15,000 cost of printing catalogs for a sales promotional campaign in January year 2.
- Radio advertisements broadcast during December year 1 were billed to Boland on January 2, year 2. Boland paid the $12,000 invoice on January 11, year 2.

What amount should Boland report as advertising expense in its income statement for the year ended December 31, year 1?

A. $133,000

B. $145,000

C. $157,000

D. $172,000

Answer (C) is correct. *(CPA, adapted)*

REQUIRED: The amount to be reported as advertising expense.

DISCUSSION: Advertising expense should be recognized when the promotions occur. It should include the $12,000 for radio advertisements broadcast in December. The $15,000 cost of printing catalogs should not be included because the expense relates to year 2 income. Hence, year 1 advertising expense is $157,000 ($160,000 – $15,000 + $12,000).

Answer (A) is incorrect because $133,000 results from subtracting the radio expenses. Answer (B) is incorrect because $145,000 does not include the radio expenses. Answer (D) is incorrect because $172,000 includes the catalog expenses that relate to year 2 income.

35. Amy.com sells 1- and 2-year subscriptions for its electronic book-of-the-month download business. Subscriptions are collected in advance and credited to sales. An analysis of the recorded sales activity revealed the following:

	Year 1	Year 2
Sales	$420,000	$500,000
Minus cancelations	20,000	30,000
Net sales	$400,000	$470,000
Subscriptions expirations:		
Year 1	$120,000	
Year 2	155,000	$130,000
Year 3	125,000	200,000
Year 4		140,000
	$400,000	$470,000

In Amy.com's December 31, year 2 balance sheet, the balance for unearned subscription revenue should be

A. $470,000

B. $465,000

C. $400,000

D. $340,000

Answer (B) is correct. *(CPA, adapted)*

REQUIRED: The balance for unearned subscription revenue.

DISCUSSION: The earning process for subscription revenue is complete upon production and delivery. The balance for unearned subscription revenue should reflect the advance collections for which production and delivery have not yet occurred. Thus, the unexpired subscriptions as of December 31, year 2 total $465,000 ($125,000 + $200,000 + $140,000), which is the balance for unearned subscription revenue.

Answer (A) is incorrect because $470,000 equals net sales for year 2. Answer (C) is incorrect because $400,000 equals net sales for year 1. Answer (D) is incorrect because $340,000 omits the year 1 sales of subscriptions that will expire in year 3.

36. In its year 2 financial statements, Cris Co. reported interest expense of $85,000 in its income statement and cash paid for interest of $70,000 in its cash flow statement. There was no prepaid interest or interest capitalization at either the beginning or the end of year 2. Accrued interest at December 31, year 1 was $20,000. What amount should Cris report as accrued interest payable in its December 31, year 2 balance sheet?

A. $5,000

B. $20,000

C. $15,000

D. $35,000

Answer (D) is correct. *(CPA, adapted)*

REQUIRED: The accrued interest payable at year-end.

DISCUSSION: The cash paid for interest was $70,000, including $20,000 of interest paid for year 1. Consequently, $50,000 ($70,000 – $20,000) of the cash paid for interest related to year 2. Interest payable is therefore $35,000 ($85,000 – $50,000).

Answer (A) is incorrect because $5,000 results from adding the $20,000 to $70,000 and subtracting the $85,000 interest expense. Answer (B) is incorrect because $20,000 is the interest paid in year 2 that related to year 1. Answer (C) is incorrect because $15,000 is the difference between the interest expense and cash paid.

37. Qwik Co.'s officers' compensation expense account had a balance of $490,000 at December 31, year 1 before any appropriate year-end adjustment relating to the following:

- No salary accrual was made for the week of December 25-31, year 1. Officers' salaries for this period totaled $18,000 and were paid on January 5, year 2.
- Bonuses to officers for year 1 were paid on January 31, year 2 in the total amount of $175,000.

The adjusted balance for officers' compensation expense for the year ended December 31, year 1 should be

A. $683,000

B. $665,000

C. $508,000

D. $490,000

Answer (A) is correct. *(CPA, adapted)*

REQUIRED: The adjusted balance in the officers' compensation expense account.

DISCUSSION: The officers' compensation expense account should include the entire compensation expense incurred in year 1. Accordingly, it should include the $490,000 previously recorded in the account, the $18,000 of accrued salaries, and the $175,000 of accrued bonuses. The adjusted balance should therefore be $683,000 ($490,000 + $18,000 + $175,000).

Answer (B) is incorrect because $665,000 does not include salaries accrued at year-end. Answer (C) is incorrect because $508,000 does not include the bonuses. Answer (D) is incorrect because $490,000 does not include the bonuses and the accrued salaries.

38. Kiddie Kare Co. offers three payment plans on its 12-month contracts. Information on the three plans and the number of children enrolled in each plan for the June 1, year 1 through May 31, year 2 contract year follows:

Plan	Initial Payment per Child	Monthly Fees per Child	Number of Children
#1	$500	$ --	15
#2	200	30	12
#3	--	50	9
			36

Kiddie received $9,900 of initial payments on June 1, year 1 and $5,670 of monthly fees during the period June 1 through December 31, year 1. In its December 31, year 1 balance sheet, what amount should Kiddie report as deferred revenues?

A. $5,670

B. $5,775

C. $4,125

D. $9,900

Answer (C) is correct. *(CPA, adapted)*

REQUIRED: The amount reported as deferred revenues.

DISCUSSION: Unearned (deferred) revenues relate to the portion of the contracts for which services have not been performed (the earning process has not been completed). At December 31, year 1, deferred revenues should equal $4,125 [9,900 prepayments received × (5 months ÷ 12 months)].

Answer (A) is incorrect because $5,670 is the total of monthly fees collected in year 1. Answer (B) is incorrect because $5,775 is the portion of prepayments earned in year 1. Answer (D) is incorrect because $9,900 equals the total prepayments.

39. Under Best Co.'s accounting system, all insurance premiums paid are debited to prepaid insurance. For interim financial reports, Best makes monthly estimated charges to insurance expense with credits to prepaid insurance. Additional information for the year ended December 31, year 2 is as follows:

Prepaid insurance at December 31, year 1	$110,000
Charges to insurance expense during year 2 (including a year-end adjustment of $10,500)	437,500
Prepaid insurance at December 31, year 2	120,500

What was the total amount of insurance premiums paid by Best during year 2?

A. $327,500

B. $427,000

C. $437,500

D. $448,000

Answer (D) is correct. *(CPA, adapted)*

REQUIRED: The total amount of insurance premiums paid.

DISCUSSION: The company debits prepaid insurance for all insurance premiums paid and credits the account when it charges insurance expense. Thus, total debits equal insurance premiums paid. The asset account had total credits (charges to expense) of $437,500 and increased by $10,500 ($120,500 ending balance – $110,000 beginning balance). Consequently, total debits (premiums paid) must have been $448,000 ($437,500 total charges to insurance expense + $10,500 increase in the asset account).

Answer (A) is incorrect because $327,500 equals total credits minus the beginning balance. Answer (B) is incorrect because $427,000 results from subtracting, not adding, the difference between the beginning and ending balances. Answer (C) is incorrect because $437,500 equals total credits to the account.

40. O'Hara Co. owns an office building and leases the offices under a variety of rental agreements involving rent paid in advance monthly or annually. Not all tenants make timely payments of their rent. O'Hara's balance sheets contained the following data:

	Year 1	Year 2
Rentals receivable	$19,200	$24,800
Unearned rentals	64,000	48,000

During year 2, O'Hara received $160,000 cash from tenants. What amount of rental revenue should O'Hara record for year 2?

A. $181,600

B. $170,800

C. $144,000

D. $133,200

Answer (A) is correct. *(CPA, adapted)*

REQUIRED: The rental revenue for the current year.

DISCUSSION: The ending balance in the rental receivable was $5,600 higher than the beginning balance ($24,800 – $19,200). Thus, revenues exceeded cash receipts. The ending balance in unearned rent was $16,000 less than the beginning balance ($64,000 – $48,000), again indicating that revenues exceeded cash receipts. Rental revenue is $181,600 ($160,000 + $5,600 + $16,000).

Answer (B) is incorrect because $170,800 equals the cash received plus 50% of the sum of the increase in rentals receivable and the decrease in unearned rentals. Answer (C) is incorrect because $144,000 equals the cash received minus the decrease in unearned rentals. Answer (D) is incorrect because $133,200 equals the cash received, minus the decrease in unearned rentals, minus 50% of the sum of the increase in rentals receivable and the decrease in unearned rentals.

41. Vanel Co. sells equipment service contracts that cover a 2-year period. The sales price of each contract is $600. Vanel's past experience is that, of the total dollars spent for repairs on service contracts, 40% is incurred evenly during the first contract year and 60% evenly during the second contract year. Vanel sold 1,000 contracts evenly throughout year 1. In its December 31, year 1 balance sheet, what amount should Vanel report as deferred service contract revenue?

A. $540,000

B. $480,000

C. $360,000

D. $300,000

Answer (B) is correct. *(CPA, adapted)*

REQUIRED: The amount of deferred service contract revenue reported on the balance sheet.

DISCUSSION: Revenue should be recognized when it is realized or realizable and earned. Service contract revenue should be recognized as the services are provided. Assuming that services are provided in proportion to the incurrence of expenses, 40% of revenue should be recognized in the first year of a service contract. Given that expenses are incurred evenly throughout the year, revenue will also be recognized evenly. Moreover, given that Dunne sold 1,000 contracts evenly throughout year 1, total revenue will be $600,000 (1,000 × $600), and the average contract must have been sold at mid-year. Thus, the elapsed time of the average contract must be half a year, and revenue earned in year 1 must equal $120,000 (40% × $600,000 total revenue × .5 year). Deferred revenue at year-end will equal $480,000 ($600,000 – $120,000).

Answer (A) is incorrect because $540,000 assumes the average contract has been outstanding for 3 months. Answer (C) is incorrect because $360,000 equals the second year's revenue for all contracts. Answer (D) is incorrect because $300,000 is the amount deferred if 50% of expenses are expected to be incurred each year and the average contract has been outstanding for 1 year.

42. Delect Co. provides repair services for the AZ195 TV set. Customers prepay the fee on the standard 1-year service contract. The year 1 and year 2 contracts were identical, and the number of contracts outstanding was substantially the same at the end of each year. However, Delect's December 31, year 2 deferred revenue balance on unperformed service contracts was significantly less than the balance at December 31, year 1. Which of the following situations might account for this reduction in the deferred revenue balance?

A. Most year 2 contracts were signed later in the calendar year than were the year 1 contracts.

B. Most year 2 contracts were signed earlier in the calendar year than were the year 1 contracts.

C. The year 2 contract contribution margin was greater than the year 1 contract contribution margin.

D. The year 2 contribution margin was less than the year 1 contract contribution margin.

Answer (B) is correct. *(CPA, adapted)*

REQUIRED: The situation that might explain the reduction in the deferred revenue balance.

DISCUSSION: Revenue should be recognized when it is realized or realizable and earned. Service contract fees are not earned until the services are provided. Thus, the fees collected in advance should be reported as unearned (deferred) revenue in the liability section of the balance sheet until the services are provided. The earlier a service contract is signed, the longer the time to provide the service and earn the revenue. Completion of the earning process reduces the deferred revenue balance. Thus, if most contracts outstanding on December 31, year 2 were signed earlier in the period than those outstanding a year earlier, the deferred revenue balance should have decreased.

Answer (A) is incorrect because, if most year 2 contracts were signed later in the calendar year than were the year 1 contracts, the deferred revenue balance would have increased. Answer (C) is incorrect because the contribution margin relates to profit, not revenue. Answer (D) is incorrect because the contribution margin relates to profit, not revenue.

2.3 Journal Entries

43. In reviewing a set of journal entries, an auditor encounters an entry composed of a debit to interest expense and a credit to interest payable. The purpose of this journal entry is to record

A. An accrued expense.

B. A deferred expense.

C. A contingent liability.

D. An unexpired cost.

Answer (A) is correct. *(CIA, adapted)*

REQUIRED: The purpose of a journal entry that debits an expense and credits a payable.

DISCUSSION: An accrued expense is one that has been incurred in the current period but has not yet been paid. The journal entry to record an accrued expense requires a debit to an expense account and a credit to a payable account.

Answer (B) is incorrect because a deferred expense is a prepayment and is recorded as an asset. Answer (C) is incorrect because interest expense is not a contingent liability. Answer (D) is incorrect because an unexpired cost is an asset.

44. In performing an audit, an auditor encounters an adjusting journal entry recorded at year-end that contains a debit to rental revenue and a credit to unearned rental revenue. The purpose of this journal entry is to record

A. An accrued revenue.

B. An unexpired cost.

C. An expired cost.

D. A deferred revenue.

Answer (D) is correct. *(CIA, adapted)*

REQUIRED: The purpose of a journal entry that debits rental revenue and credits unearned rental revenue.

DISCUSSION: Revenues should be recognized when realized or realizable and earned. If rental fees are collected before the revenue is earned and a credit is made to rental revenue, an adjusting entry may be necessary at year-end. The purpose of the journal entry is to adjust both rental revenue and unearned rental revenue to reflect the rental fees collected that had not been earned during this accounting period.

Answer (A) is incorrect because an accrued revenue is reflected as a receivable. Answer (B) is incorrect because an unexpired cost is recorded as an asset. Answer (C) is incorrect because an expired cost is charged to expense.

45. On October 1, year 1, a company sold services to a customer and accepted a note in exchange with a $120,000 face amount and an interest rate of 10%. The note requires that both the principal and interest be paid at the maturity date, December 1, year 2. The company's accounting period is the calendar year. What adjusting entry (related to this note) will be required at December 31, year 1 on the company's books?

A. Deferred interest income $3,000
   Interest receivable $3,000

B. Interest income $3,000
   Interest receivable $3,000

C. Interest receivable $3,000
   Deferred interest income $3,000

D. Interest receivable $3,000
   Interest income $3,000

Answer (D) is correct. *(CIA, adapted)*

REQUIRED: The adjusting entry related to a note receivable.

DISCUSSION: Interest receivable should be debited and interest income credited for the interest on the note accrued (earned but not paid) at year-end [(10% × $120,000) × (3 months ÷ 12 months) = $3,000].

46. What is the purpose of the following entry?

Supplies $XXX
   Supplies expense $XXX

A. To recognize supplies used, if purchases of supplies are recorded in supplies.

B. To recognize supplies on hand, if purchases of supplies are recorded in supplies expense.

C. To record the purchase of supplies during or at the end of the period.

D. To close the expense account for supplies at the end of the period.

Answer (B) is correct. *(CIA, adapted)*

REQUIRED: The purpose of the given entry.

DISCUSSION: The debit to supplies and credit to supplies expense is an end-of-period adjusting entry. Assuming the acquisition of supplies was debited to expense, an adjusting entry is needed to record the supplies on hand and to recognize the correct amount of expense.

Answer (A) is incorrect because, if purchases are initially recorded in a real account, the entry to record use of supplies is

Supplies expense
   Supplies

Answer (C) is incorrect because the correct entry to record the purchase of supplies is

Supplies or Supplies expense
   Cash or Accounts payable

Answer (D) is incorrect because the entry to close supplies expense is

Income summary
   Supplies expense

47. On December 31, earned but unpaid wages amounted to $15,000. What reversing entry could be made on January 1?

A. Wages expense $15,000
   Wages payable $15,000

B. Prepaid wages $15,000
   Wages expense $15,000

C. Wages expense $15,000
   Prepaid wages $15,000

D. Wages payable $15,000
   Wages expense $15,000

Answer (D) is correct. *(Publisher)*

REQUIRED: The reversing entry for an accrual of wages expense.

DISCUSSION: The accrual of an expense requires a debit to expense and a credit to a liability. Accordingly, the reversing entry is to debit the liability and credit expense. The purpose of reversing this accrual of expense is to avoid having to apportion the first cash disbursement in the next period between the liability and expense accounts.

Answer (A) is incorrect because it is the adjusting rather than the reversing entry. Answer (B) is incorrect because it reflects an adjusting entry when wages have been prepaid and the original debit was to an expense account (which is not frequently found in practice). Answer (C) is incorrect because it is the reversing entry for an adjusting entry that occurs when wages have been prepaid and the original debit was to an expense account.

48. A 3-year insurance policy was purchased on October 1 for $6,000, and prepaid insurance was debited. Assuming a December 31 year-end, what is the reversing entry at the beginning of the next period?

A. None is required.

B. Cash $6,000
   Prepaid insurance $6,000

C. Prepaid insurance $5,500
   Insurance expense $5,500

D. Insurance expense $500
   Prepaid insurance $500

Answer (A) is correct. *(Publisher)*

REQUIRED: The reversing entry when a prepaid expense was debited to an asset account.

DISCUSSION: Given that the original entry recorded the prepaid insurance as an asset, the adjusting entry will debit expense and credit the asset for the amount of insurance that has expired. Accordingly, at the beginning of the year, the unexpired insurance will be in an asset account. Thus, no reversing entry is required.

Answer (B) is incorrect because it is the opposite (not a reversing entry) of the entry made to record the purchase of the 3-year insurance policy. Answer (C) is incorrect because it is the correct adjusting entry if the original entry had debited insurance expense rather than prepaid insurance. Answer (D) is incorrect because it is the correct adjusting entry (which requires no reversing entry).

49. A consulting firm started and completed a project for a client in December of year 1. The project has not been recorded on the consulting firm's books, and the firm will not receive payment from the client until February year 2. The adjusting entry that should be made on the books of the consulting firm on December 31, year 1, the last day of the firm's fiscal year, is

A. Cash in transit $XXX
   Consulting revenue $XXX

B. Consulting revenue receivable $XXX
   Consulting revenue $XXX

C. Unearned consulting revenue $XXX
   Consulting revenue $XXX

D. Consulting revenue receivable $XXX
   Unearned consulting revenue $XXX

Answer (B) is correct. *(CMA, adapted)*

REQUIRED: The adjusting entry necessary to record consulting revenue.

DISCUSSION: Revenues should be recognized when they are realized or realizable and earned. Consulting revenue is realized and earned when the consulting service has been performed. Thus, for a consulting project that was started and completed during year 1, an adjusting entry should be made at year-end to record both a receivable and the revenue. The journal entry is a debit to consulting revenue receivable and a credit to consulting revenue.

Answer (A) is incorrect because cash in transit is not an account. Answer (C) is incorrect because the unearned revenue account is used only if the client prepays. Answer (D) is incorrect because the revenue was earned during the period.

Questions 50 and 51 are based on the following information. Louviere Co. prepares monthly financial statements. The clerical staff is paid every 2 weeks on the Monday following the end of the 2-week (10 working days) pay period ending on the prior Friday. The last pay period ended on Friday, November 19. The next payday is Monday, December 6 for the pay period ending December 3. The total clerical payroll for a 2-week period is $30,000, income tax withholding averages 15%, and Social Security taxes amount to 7.65%. None of the clerical staff's earnings will exceed the maximum limit for Social Security taxes.

50. The adjusting entry required to accrue Louviere's payroll as of November 30 is to

A. Debit wage expense for $21,000 and credit wages payable for $21,000.

B. Debit wage expense for $30,000, credit payroll tax expense for $1,950, and credit wages payable for $28,050.

C. Debit wage expense for $21,000, credit income tax withholding payable for $3,150, credit payroll taxes payable for $1,606.50, and credit wages payable for $16,243.50.

D. Debit wage expense for $30,000, credit income tax withholding payable for $4,500, credit payroll taxes payable for $1,950, and credit wages payable for $23,550.

Answer (C) is correct. *(CMA, adapted)*

REQUIRED: The adjusting entry necessary to accrue the payroll.

DISCUSSION: The 7 days included in the period from November 20 through November 30 represents 70% of the 10 working days in a 2-week pay period. Thus, $21,000 in wages expense should be accrued ($30,000 × 70%). Of this amount, $3,150 ($21,000 × 15%) must be credited to income tax withholding payable, $1,606.50 ($21,000 × 7.65%) to payroll tax payable, and the remainder, $16,243.50, to wages payable.

Answer (A) is incorrect because wages payable must be reduced by income tax withholding and Social Security. Answer (B) is incorrect because the period from November 20 through November 30 includes only 7 working days, not the full 2-week period. Answer (D) is incorrect because the period from November 20 through November 30 includes only 7 working days, not the full 2-week period.

51. Louviere is also required to record an accrual for its obligation for payroll tax expenses. This adjusting entry should be to

A. Debit payroll tax expense for $1,955 and credit payroll taxes payable for $1,955.

B. Debit payroll tax expense for $1,606.50 and credit payroll taxes payable for $1,606.50.

C. Debit payroll tax expense for $6,450 and credit payroll taxes payable for $6,450.

D. Debit payroll tax expense for $4,515 and credit payroll taxes payable for $4,515.

Answer (B) is correct. *(CMA, adapted)*

REQUIRED: The adjusting entry necessary to accrue the company's obligation for Social Security taxes.

DISCUSSION: In addition to the Social Security taxes that must be withheld from employees' wages and remitted to the tax collection agency, the employer must also accrue and remit an equivalent amount as the employer's share. Thus, an additional expense of $1,606.50 ($21,000 × 7.65%) must be accrued.

52. Dunlap Company sublet a portion of its warehouse for 5 years at an annual rental of $15,000, beginning on March 1. The tenant paid 1 year's rent in advance, which Dunlap recorded as a credit to unearned rental income. Dunlap reports on a calendar-year basis. The adjustment on December 31 of the first year should be

A. No entry.

B.

Unearned rental income	$2,500	
Rental income		$2,500

C.

Rental income	$2,500	
Unearned rental income		$2,500

D.

Unearned rental income	$12,500	
Rental income		$12,500

Answer (D) is correct. *(CPA, adapted)*

REQUIRED: The adjusting entry at year-end for unearned rental income.

DISCUSSION: Given that the sublessor originally recorded the $15,000 received as a credit to a liability account, the adjusting entry is to debit the liability account and credit revenue for the revenue earned, which equals $1,250 a month ($12,500) for 10 months.

Answer (A) is incorrect because an adjusting entry is needed for all deferrals and accruals. Answer (B) is incorrect because the rental income to be recognized is for 10 months at $1,250 a month, not for 2 months. Answer (C) is incorrect because the debit and credit entries are switched, and the rental income to be recognized should be for 10 months, not 2 months.

53. Hurlburt Corporation renewed an insurance policy for 3 years beginning July 1, year 1 and recorded the $81,000 premium in the prepaid insurance account. The $81,000 premium represents an increase of $23,400 from the $57,600 premium charged 3 years ago. Assuming Hurlburt's records its insurance adjustments only at the end of the calendar year, the adjusting entry required to reflect the proper balances in the insurance accounts at December 31, year 1, Hurlburt's year-end is to

A. Debit insurance expense for $13,500 and credit prepaid insurance for $13,500.

B. Debit prepaid insurance for $13,500 and credit insurance expense for $13,500.

C. Debit insurance expense for $67,500 and credit prepaid insurance for $67,500.

D. Debit insurance expense for $23,100 and credit prepaid insurance for $23,100.

Answer (D) is correct. *(CMA, adapted)*

REQUIRED: The entry to adjust the prepaid insurance account assuming annual adjustments.

DISCUSSION: The $57,600 premium paid 3 years ago was equivalent to a rate of $1,600 per month ($57,600 ÷ 36 months). On January 1, year 1, the prepaid insurance account would have had a balance of $9,600 ($1,600 × 6 months). On July 1, the prepaid insurance account would have been debited for an additional $81,000 covering the next 36 months at a monthly rate of $2,250 ($81,000 ÷ 36 months). The expense for year 1 is therefore $23,100 [$9,600 + (6 months × $2,250)]. The adjusting entry is to debit insurance expense and credit prepaid insurance for $23,100.

Answer (A) is incorrect because $13,500 is the expense for the last 6 months of the year. Answer (B) is incorrect because, if the initial payment is debited to a real account, the adjustment requires a debit to a nominal account and a credit to the real account. Answer (C) is incorrect because $67,500 is the ending balance in prepaid insurance.

54. After a successful drive aimed at members of a specific national association, Online Publishing Company received a total of $180,000 for 3-year subscriptions beginning April 1, year 1, and recorded this amount in the unearned revenue account. Assuming Online records adjustments only at the end of the calendar year, the adjusting entry required to reflect the proper balances in the accounts at December 31, year 1 is to

A. Debit subscription revenue for $135,000 and credit unearned revenue for $135,000.

B. Debit unearned revenue for $135,000 and credit subscription revenue for $135,000.

C. Debit subscription revenue for $45,000 and credit unearned revenue for $45,000.

D. Debit unearned revenue for $45,000 and credit subscription revenue for $45,000.

Answer (D) is correct. *(CMA, adapted)*

REQUIRED: The year-end adjusting entry.

DISCUSSION: The company initially debited cash and credited unearned revenue, a liability account, for $180,000. Subscriptions revenue should be recognized when it is realized or realizable and the earning process is substantially complete. Because 25% (9 months ÷ 36 months) of the subscription period has expired, 25% of the realized but unearned revenue should be recognized. Thus, the adjusting entry is to debit unearned revenue and credit subscription revenue for $45,000.

Answer (A) is incorrect because $135,000 would be the debit to the revenue account if it had been credited initially. Answer (B) is incorrect because a $135,000 debit to the unearned revenue account would be appropriate if 75% of the subscription period had elapsed. Answer (C) is incorrect because $45,000 would be the debit to the revenue account if it had been credited initially and if 75% of the subscription period had elapsed.

55. A machine costing $27,000 with a residual value of $2,000 is to be depreciated on a straight-line basis over 5 years. What is the year-end adjusting entry?

A. Depreciation expense	$5,000	
Machine		$5,000
B. Depreciation expense	$5,000	
Cash		$5,000
C. Machine	$27,000	
Cash		$20,000
Depreciation expense		5,000
Residual value		2,000
D. Depreciation expense	$5,000	
Accumulated depreciation		$5,000

Answer (D) is correct. *(Publisher)*

REQUIRED: The year-end adjusting entry to depreciate a machine.

DISCUSSION: At year-end, depreciation expense is debited, and accumulated depreciation (a contra asset account) is credited. The amount of depreciation is 20% (1 year ÷ 5 years) of the depreciation base of $25,000 ($27,000 machine cost – $2,000 residual value).

Answer (A) is incorrect because the credit is not made directly to the asset but to the contra account, accumulated depreciation. Answer (B) is incorrect because cash is expended when the machine is purchased, not each year when depreciation is recorded. Answer (C) is incorrect because $27,000 was the machine's cost, depreciation expense is a debit rather than a credit, and residual value is not separately recorded.

STUDY UNIT THREE
COMPREHENSIVE INCOME AND THE STATEMENT OF INCOME

Comprehensive income includes all changes in equity of a business enterprise except those changes resulting from investments by owners and distributions to owners. Comprehensive income includes two major categories, net income and other comprehensive income.

Net income encompasses the results of operations classified as income from continuing operations (including operating and nonoperating items), discontinued operations, and extraordinary items. Components of comprehensive income not included in the determination of net income are included in **other comprehensive income (OCI)**. Each component of other comprehensive income is displayed net of tax, or one amount is shown for the aggregate tax effect on other comprehensive income, but the tax effect on each component must be disclosed.

SFAS 130, *Reporting Comprehensive Income*, requires that an enterprise report comprehensive income when it has items of OCI (but the terms "comprehensive income" and "other comprehensive income" are not required to be used). The components of comprehensive income should be reported in a financial statement that is displayed with the same prominence as other financial statements that constitute a full set of financial statements. However, SFAS 130 does not prescribe a specific format. Moreover, an entity is not required to report comprehensive income if it has no items of OCI in any period for which financial statements are presented.

When an enterprise has items of OCI, SFAS 130 requires that a **total amount for comprehensive income** for the period be displayed in the financial statement in which the components of OCI are reported. A combined statement of income and comprehensive income may be used to meet this requirement. An alternative is to present separate statements for net income and comprehensive income. The items included in net income are displayed in the customary manner, and net income is reported as a classification within comprehensive income. A third possibility is to report comprehensive income in a **statement of changes in equity**. This option is the most popular because many entities already present a statement of changes in equity to meet the requirement to disclose changes in (1) the separate amounts in equity and (2) the number of equity securities. These disclosures must be made when financial position and results of operations are reported. They may be made in the basic statements, in the notes, or in separate statements (**APB 12**, *Omnibus Opinion - 1967*).

SFAS 130 further requires the display of the total of **accumulated other comprehensive income** as a component of equity separate from additional paid-in capital and retained earnings. The accumulated balances of each component are disclosed on the face of the balance sheet, in a statement of changes in equity, or in notes to the financial statements. Under existing accounting standards, OCI is classified separately into (1) foreign currency items (translation adjustments; hedging gains and losses on a net investment in a foreign operation, accounted for as translation adjustments; and gains and losses on derivatives designated, qualifying, and effective as foreign-currency cash flow hedging instruments), (2) minimum pension liability adjustments, (3) unrealized gains and losses on available-for-sale securities (except those that are hedged items in a fair value hedge), and (4) the effective portions (minus amounts reclassified into earnings) of gains or losses on derivatives designated and qualifying as cash flow hedges of a recognized asset or liability or of a forecasted transaction. In addition, to avoid double counting, **reclassification adjustments** (except for minimum pension liability adjustments) are necessary when an item included in net income was included in OCI for the same or a prior period. SFAS 130 also requires that a total for comprehensive income be reported in condensed financial statements of interim periods.

The **capital maintenance approach** requires that income be determined by finding the change in equity after adjusting for investments by, and distributions to, owners. However, this approach does not provide the detail of the **transaction approach** to income determination, under which each component of income is measured and reported. Accordingly, revenue, expense, gain, and loss transactions are recognized. Furthermore, the presentation must contain additional classifications. Thus, to increase the usefulness of the information contained in the **statement of income**, different classifications of income are prescribed under GAAP. The major classifications are (1) income from continuing operations (SFAS 144), (2) discontinued operations (SFAS 144), and (3) extraordinary items (APB 30). Although GAAP do not require entities to report categories of income from continuing operations, the conceptual framework and actual reporting practices suggest that the categories exist. The two categories of income from continuing operations frequently reported are operating income and other revenues and expenses. In effect, operating and nonoperating sections may be presented.

Income (loss) from continuing operations includes the income effects (revenues, expenses, gains, and losses) of all transactions and events not classified as discontinued operations or extraordinary items. The primary focus of income from continuing operations is on the income effects directly related to the principal business activities of the enterprise.

Income (loss) from continuing operations may be presented in a single-step or a multiple-step format (or some mixture). In the **single-step format**, revenues and gains are grouped separately from expenses and losses. Income from continuing operations is then calculated in a single step as the difference between the subtotals of the two groups. In the **multiple-step format**, certain revenues and expenses are assigned to an operating section. The most common subtotals in this section are gross profit (margin) or loss (net sales revenue – cost of sales) and operating income or loss (gross profit or loss – operating expenses). In the **nonoperating section**, the income effects of significant recurring transactions not directly related to primary operations and gains and losses that do not meet the criteria of discontinued operations or extraordinary items are commonly grouped as other revenues and gains and other expenses and losses. The net total of these other items is added to, or subtracted from, operating income (loss) to determine the subtotal, **pretax income (loss) from continuing operations**. Income (loss) from continuing operations is then determined by subtracting (adding) the **aggregate tax effect** applicable to pretax income (loss) from continuing operations. [The caption title may vary depending on whether the entity has a discontinued operation or extraordinary item. For example, if an extraordinary item but not a discontinued operation is to be reported, the foregoing caption would be income (loss) before extraordinary item.]

The **discontinued operations** caption reports operating results for current and prior periods in the income statements (statements of activities) of a business enterprise (not-for-profit organization) if a component of the entity has been disposed of, or is **classified as held for sale** based on the criteria described in Study Unit 7. A **component of an entity** encompasses operations and cash flows that are clearly distinguishable for operating and financial reporting purposes from the rest of the entity. A component may be a reportable segment or an operating segment, a reporting unit, a subsidiary, or an asset group. This presentation is allowed if the component's operations and cash flows have been or will be eliminated from the entity's ongoing operations as a result of the disposal, and the entity will have no significant continuing involvement after the disposal. **Operating results** (including the gain or loss on disposal) are reported in discontinued operations in the period(s) when they occur. Operating results include any loss for a writedown to **fair value minus cost to sell** of a long-lived asset held for sale or a gain arising from an increase in fair value minus cost to sell (but limited to the losses previously recognized). The results of discontinued operations, minus (plus) income tax (benefit), are reported separately in a caption before extraordinary items (if any). The **gain or loss on disposal** must be disclosed on the face of the financial statements or in the notes. **Amounts previously reported in discontinued operations** in a prior period may require adjustment in the current period. If such an adjustment is **directly related** to a prior-period disposal of a component, it is reported currently in discontinued operations as a separate item, and its nature and amount are disclosed. If a long-lived asset or disposal group is not a component, a gain or loss on its sale is included in **income from continuing operations**.

Extraordinary items are material gains or losses reported net of taxes after income from continuing operations and discontinued operations. The criteria for classifying a gain or loss as extraordinary are that the event or transaction giving rise to the gain or loss must be both unusual in nature and infrequent in occurrence in the environment in which the enterprise operates.

The **statement of retained earnings** is a basic financial statement. Most entities report the changes in retained earnings in a separate statement or in a statement of equity. According to APB 9, the income statement and the statement of retained earnings (presented separately or combined) are designed to broadly reflect the results of operations. The statement of retained earnings consists of beginning retained earnings, with any prior-period adjustments (net of tax); net income (loss); dividends paid or declared; and certain other rare items, e.g., quasi-reorganizations. The final figure is ending retained earnings. Furthermore, the retained earnings balance is sometimes divided into **appropriated and unappropriated** amounts. However, APB 9 states that "transfers to and from accounts properly designated as appropriated retained earnings (such as general purpose contingency reserves or provisions for replacement costs of fixed assets)" are always excluded from the determination of net income.

QUESTIONS

3.1 Comprehensive Income

1. When a business enterprise provides a full set of general-purpose financial statements reporting financial position, results of operations, and cash flows, comprehensive income and its components should

A. Appear as a part of discontinued operations and extraordinary items.

B. Be reported net of related income tax effects, in total and individually.

C. Appear in a supplemental schedule in the notes to the financial statements.

D. Be displayed in a financial statement that has the same prominence as other financial statements.

Answer (D) is correct. *(CPA, adapted)*

REQUIRED: The presentation of comprehensive income and its components.

DISCUSSION: If an enterprise that reports a full set of financial statements has items of other comprehensive income (OCI), it must display comprehensive income and its components in a financial statement having the same prominence as the other statements included in the full set. No particular format is required, but net income must be displayed as a component of comprehensive income in that statement.

Answer (A) is incorrect because discontinued operations and extraordinary items are components of net income, which is itself a component of comprehensive income. Answer (B) is incorrect because the components of OCI are displayed either (1) net of related tax effects or (2) before the related tax effects with one amount shown for the aggregate tax effect related to the total of OCI. No amount is displayed for the tax effect related to total comprehensive income. Answer (C) is incorrect because comprehensive income and its components must be displayed in a financial statement given the same prominence as other financial statements included in the full set of financial statements.

2. Which of the following items should be reported as a component of other comprehensive income (OCI)?

A. Unrealized loss on an investment classified as a trading security.

B. Unrealized loss on an investment classified as an available-for-sale security.

C. Realized loss on an investment classified as an available-for-sale security.

D. Cumulative effect of a change in accounting principle.

Answer (B) is correct. *(Publisher)*

REQUIRED: The item properly classified as a component of OCI.

DISCUSSION: Comprehensive income includes all changes in equity of a business entity except those changes resulting from investments by owners and distributions to owners. Comprehensive income includes two major categories: net income and OCI. Net income includes the results of operations classified as income from continuing operations, discontinued operations and extraordinary items. Components of comprehensive income not included in the determination of net income are included in OCI, for example, unrealized gains and losses on available-for-sale securities (except those that are hedged items in a fair value hedge).

Answer (A) is incorrect because unrealized gains and losses on trading securities is a component of net income. Answer (C) is incorrect because realized gains and losses on available-for-sale securities is a component of net income. Answer (D) is incorrect because the cumulative effect of a change in accounting principle is a component of net income.

3. On December 31, year 1, the last day of its fiscal year, Smart Company purchased 2,000 shares of available-for-sale securities at a price of $10 per share. These securities had a fair value of $24,000 and $30,000 on December 31, year 2 and December 31, year 3, respectively. No dividends were paid, and all of the securities were sold on December 31, year 3. Smart recognizes all holding gains and losses on available-for-sale securities before recognizing realized gain. If Smart's tax rate is 25%, the total after-tax effect on comprehensive income in year 3 of the foregoing transactions was

A. $10,000

B. $7,500

C. $4,500

D. $3,000

Answer (C) is correct. *(Publisher)*

REQUIRED: The total after-tax effect on comprehensive income of a sale of available-for-sale securities in year 3.

DISCUSSION: Smart paid $20,000 for the shares. Thus, its after-tax holding gain in year 2 was $3,000 [($24,000 fair value – $20,000) × (1.0 – .25 tax rate)]. Because the shares were classified as available-for-sale, the $3,000 holding gain was included in OCI, not net income. Smart's after-tax holding gain in year 3 was $4,500 [($30,000 – $24,000) × (1.0 – .25)]. Moreover, its realized after-tax gain in year 3 included in net income was $7,500 [($30,000 – $20,000) × (1.0 .25)]. The recognition of these amounts in year 2 and year 3 necessitates a reclassification adjustment to prevent double counting. This adjustment to OCI is equal to, but opposite in sign from, the realized gain recognized in net income. Accordingly, the after-tax effect on comprehensive income in year 3 of the sale of the available-for-sale securities is $4,500 ($7,500 realized gain + $4,500 holding gain – $7,500 reclassification adjustment).

Answer (A) is incorrect because $10,000 is the pre-tax realized gain recognized in net income in year 3. Answer (B) is incorrect because $7,500 is the amount of the reclassification adjustment and the realized after-tax gain. Answer (D) is incorrect because $3,000 is the after-tax holding gain in year 2.

4. Rock Co.'s financial statements had the following balances at December 31:

Extraordinary gain	$ 50,000
Foreign currency translation gain	100,000
Net income	400,000
Unrealized gain on available-for-sale equity securities	20,000

What amount should Rock report as comprehensive income for the year ended December 31?

A. $400,000

B. $420,000

C. $520,000

D. $570,000

Answer (C) is correct. *(Publisher)*

REQUIRED: The comprehensive income to be reported on December 31.

DISCUSSION: Comprehensive income includes all changes in equity of a business enterprise except those changes resulting from investments by owners and distributions to owners. Comprehensive income includes two major categories: net income and other comprehensive income (OCI). Net income includes the results of continuing and discontinued operations and extraordinary items. Components of comprehensive income not included in the determination of net income are included in OCI, for example, unrealized gains and losses on available-for-sale securities (except those that are hedged items in a fair value hedge) and foreign currency items. Thus, Rock's comprehensive income equals $520,000 ($400,000 net income + $100,000 translation gain + $20,000 unrealized gain on available-for-sale securities).

Answer (A) is incorrect because foreign currency items and unrealized gains on available-for-sale equity securities are components of OCI. Answer (B) is incorrect because foreign currency items are a component of OCI. Answer (D) is incorrect because the extraordinary gain is already included in the net income amount of $400,000.

3.2 Income from Continuing Operations

5. APB 9, *Reporting the Results of Operations,* concludes that the all-inclusive income statement concept

A. Is synonymous with the current operating concept, and both are acceptable under GAAP.

B. Is generally more appropriate than the current operating concept.

C. Is not appropriate. The current operating concept is a generally accepted accounting principle.

D. Produces an interactive income statement that avoids the problems associated with the changing value of currencies.

Answer (B) is correct. *(Publisher)*

REQUIRED: The true statement about the all-inclusive income statement concept.

DISCUSSION: In the calculation of net income, the all-inclusive approach includes all transactions that affect equity during the current period except (1) transactions with owners, (2) prior-period adjustments, and (3) certain items that are reported initially in other comprehensive income. The current operating concept includes only the ordinary, normal, recurring operations in the net income of the current period. Other items are direct adjustments to retained earnings. APB 9 adopts the all-inclusive approach. The all-inclusive concept was strengthened by SFAS 16, which limits prior-period adjustments in most instances to corrections of errors. As a result, most revenue, expense, gain, and loss items are included in continuing operations in the income statement.

Answer (A) is incorrect because APB 9 rejected the current operating concept. Answer (C) is incorrect because APB 9 rejected the current operating concept. Answer (D) is incorrect because an "interactive income statement" does not exist in financial accounting.

6. Under GAAP, comparative financial statements are

A. Required for at least the current and the prior year.

B. Required for at least the current and the prior 2 years.

C. Recommended for at least the current and the prior year.

D. Neither required nor recommended.

Answer (C) is correct. *(S. Rubin)*

REQUIRED: The position of GAAP concerning comparative financial statements.

DISCUSSION: ARB 43, Ch. 2A, states that presenting financial statements of two or more periods is ordinarily desirable. This position is commonly understood to be a recommendation rather than a requirement.

Answer (A) is incorrect because comparative financial statements are not required. Answer (B) is incorrect because comparative financial statements are not required. Answer (D) is incorrect because comparative financial statements are recommended.

7. Select the best order for the following items appearing in income statements:

1. Extraordinary items
2. Income from continuing operations
3. Discontinued operations
4. Prior-period adjustments
5. Taxes on income from continuing operations
6. Dividends
7. Net income
8. Revenues
9. Expenses
10. Income from continuing operations before income tax

A. 9 - 10 - 8 - 7 - 6 - 2 - 4

B. 8 - 6 - 7 - 1 - 2 - 5

C. 9 - 10 - 8 - 6 - 3 - 2 - 1 - 4

D. 8 - 9 - 10 - 5 - 2 - 3 - 1 - 7

Answer (D) is correct. *(Publisher)*

REQUIRED: The order of items appearing in income statements.

DISCUSSION: The order of appearance in income statements of the items is

8. Revenues
9. Expenses
10. Income from continuing operations before income tax
5. Taxes on income from continuing operations
2. Income from continuing operations
3. Discontinued operations
1. Extraordinary items
7. Net income

Prior-period adjustments (4) and dividends (6) appear only in retained earnings statements.

8. On December 31, year 1, Salo Corp.'s balance sheet accounts increased by the following amounts compared with those at the end of the prior year:

Assets	$178,000
Liabilities	62,000
Capital stock	125,000
Additional paid-in capital	17,000

Salo had no accumulated other comprehensive income (OCI), and the only charge to retained earnings during year 1 was for a dividend payment of $34,000. Net income for year 1 was

A. $60,000

B. $34,000

C. $8,000

D. $26,000

Answer (C) is correct. *(CPA, adapted)*

REQUIRED: The net income for the year given the increases in assets, liabilities, and paid-in capital.

DISCUSSION: Assets equal the sum of liabilities and equity (contributed capital, retained earnings, and accumulated other comprehensive income). To calculate net income, the first step is to add the dividend payment ($34,000) to the increase in assets ($178,000). The excess of this sum ($212,000) over the increase in liabilities ($62,000) gives the total increase in equity ($150,000). Given no accumulated OCI, the excess of this amount over the combined increases in the capital accounts ($142,000) equals the increase in retained earnings ($8,000) arising from net income.

Answer (A) is incorrect because $60,000 equals the dividend payment plus the excess of the sum of the increases in liabilities, capital stock, and additional paid-in capital over the increase in assets. Answer (B) is incorrect because $34,000 is the dividend payment. Answer (D) is incorrect because $26,000 is the excess of the sum of the increases in liabilities, capital stock, and additional paid-in capital over the increase in assets.

9. The major distinction made between the multiple-step and single-step income statement formats is the separation of

A. Operating and nonoperating data.

B. Income tax expense and administrative expenses.

C. Cost of goods sold expense and administrative expenses.

D. The effect on income taxes due to extraordinary items and the effect on income taxes due to income before extraordinary items.

Answer (A) is correct. *(CIA, adapted)*

REQUIRED: The major distinction between the multiple-step and single-step income statement formats.

DISCUSSION: Within the income from continuing operations classification, the single-step income statement provides one grouping for revenue items and one for expense items. The single-step is the one subtraction necessary to arrive at income from continuing operations prior to the effect of income taxes. In contrast, the multiple-step income statement matches operating revenues and expenses separately from nonoperating items. This format emphasizes subtotals such as gross profit, gross margin (or loss), and operating income or operating profit (or loss) within the presentation of income from continuing operations.

Answer (B) is incorrect because both formats separate these items. Answer (C) is incorrect because both formats separate these items. Answer (D) is incorrect because both formats separate these items.

10. On January 1 of the current year, Bricks and Mortar Co. (B&M) installed cabinets to display its merchandise in customers' stores. B&M expects to use these cabinets for 5 years. Its current-year multi-step income statement should include

A. One-fifth of the cabinet costs in cost of goods sold.

B. One-fifth of the cabinet costs in selling expenses.

C. All of the cabinet costs in cost of goods sold.

D. All of the cabinet costs in selling expenses.

Answer (B) is correct. *(CPA, adapted)*

REQUIRED: The costs included in the determination of current net income.

DISCUSSION: The cost of the cabinets is a selling expense. However, because the cabinets will provide benefits over a 5-year period, their cost should be allocated systematically and rationally over that period, for example, by the straight-line method. In effect, periodic depreciation of the cabinets should be recognized as a selling expense.

Answer (A) is incorrect because selling costs are not inventoried. Answer (C) is incorrect because selling costs are not inventoried. Answer (D) is incorrect because the cost should be allocated to the periods benefited.

11. In Baer Food Co.'s year 3 single-step income statement, the section titled *Revenues* consisted of the following:

Net sales revenue	$187,000
Discontinued operations:	
Income from operations of component unit (including gain on disposal of $21,600)	18,000
Income tax	(6,000)
Interest revenue	10,200
Gain on sale of equipment	4,700
Total revenues	$213,900

In the revenues section of the year 3 income statement, Baer Food should have reported total revenues of

A. $213,900

B. $209,200

C. $203,700

D. $201,900

Answer (D) is correct. *(CPA, adapted)*

REQUIRED: The total revenues.

DISCUSSION: This single-step income statement classifies the items included in income from continuing operations as either revenues or expenses. Discontinued operations is a classification in the income statement separate from continuing operations. Hence, total revenues (including interest and the gain) were $201,900 ($213,900 – $12,000 results from discontinued operations).

Answer (A) is incorrect because $213,900 equals reported total revenues. Answer (B) is incorrect because $209,200 excludes the gain. Answer (C) is incorrect because $203,700 excludes the interest.

12. Henderson Corp. reports operating expenses in two categories: (1) selling and (2) general and administrative. The adjusted trial balance on December 31 included the following expense and loss accounts:

Accounting and legal fees	$120,000
Advertising	150,000
Freight out	80,000
Interest	70,000
Loss on sale of long-term investment	30,000
Officers' salaries	225,000
Rent for office space	220,000
Sales salaries and commissions	140,000

One-half of the rented premises is occupied by the sales department. Henderson's total selling expenses for the year are

A. $480,000

B. $400,000

C. $370,000

D. $360,000

Answer (A) is correct. *(CPA, adapted)*

REQUIRED: The total selling expenses.

DISCUSSION: Within the categories of expenses presented, the $150,000 of advertising, the $80,000 of freight out, 50% of the $220,000 rent for office space, and the $140,000 of sales salaries and commissions should be classified as selling expenses. Total selling expenses are therefore $480,000. The costs of accounting and legal fees, officers' salaries, and 50% of rent for office space are general and administrative expenses. Interest and the loss on sale of the long-term investment are nonoperating items.

Answer (B) is incorrect because $400,000 excludes the freight-out expense. Answer (C) is incorrect because $370,000 excludes 50% of the rent for office space. Answer (D) is incorrect because $360,000 excludes the advertising and freight-out expenses and includes the entire rent for the office.

13. A company has a 40% gross margin, general and administrative expenses of $50, interest expense of $20, and net income of $70 for the year just ended. If the corporate tax rate is 30%, the level of sales revenue for the year just ended was

A. $170

B. $255

C. $350

D. $425

Answer (D) is correct. *(CIA, adapted)*

REQUIRED: The sales revenue for the year.

DISCUSSION: Net income before taxes is $100 [$70 NI ÷ (1.0 – .3 tax rate)]. Hence, the gross margin (sales – cost of sales) is $170 ($100 NI before taxes + $20 interest + $50 G&A expenses). Sales must then be $425 ($170 gross margin ÷ 40% gross margin ratio).

Answer (A) is incorrect because $170 is the gross margin. Answer (B) is incorrect because $255 is the cost of goods sold. Answer (C) is incorrect because $350 assumes pre-tax net income was $70.

14. The effect of a material transaction that is infrequent in occurrence but not unusual in nature should be presented separately as a component of income from continuing operations when the transaction results in a

	Gain	Loss
A.	Yes	Yes
B.	Yes	No
C.	No	No
D.	No	Yes

Answer (A) is correct. *(CPA, adapted)*

REQUIRED: The circumstances in which an infrequent but not unusual transaction is shown as a separate component of income from continuing operations.

DISCUSSION: To be classified as an extraordinary item, a transaction must be both unusual in nature and infrequent in occurrence within the environment in which the business operates. If an item meets one but not both of these criteria, it should be presented separately as a component of income from continuing operations. Whether the transaction results in a gain or a loss does not affect this presentation.

15. Carlisle Co.'s income statement for the year ended December 31, year 1 reported net income of $148,200. The auditor raised questions about the following amounts that had been included in net income:

Unrealized holding loss on available-for-sale securities	$(10,800)
Gain on early retirement of bonds payable (net of $22,000 tax effect)	44,000
Adjustment to profits of prior years for errors in depreciation (net of $7,500 tax effect)	(15,000)
Loss from fire (net of $14,000 tax effect)	(28,000)

The loss from the fire was an infrequent but not unusual occurrence in Carlisle's line of business. Carlisle's December 31, year 1 income statement should report net income of

A. $130,000

B. $132,200

C. $163,200

D. $174,000

Answer (D) is correct. *(CPA, adapted)*

REQUIRED: The net income.

DISCUSSION: The unrealized holding loss on available-for-sale securities should have been debited to other comprehensive income (an equity account), not included in the determination of net income (SFAS 115, *Accounting for Certain Investments in Debt and Equity Securities*). The gain on early retirement of bonds payable was properly included as an ordinary gain absent evidence clearly supporting classification of the gain as extraordinary. The fire loss was also properly included as an ordinary loss, but the adjustment for depreciation errors should have been charged directly to retained earnings as a prior-period adjustment (SFAS 16, *Prior-Period Adjustments*). Thus, reported net income should have been $174,000 ($148,200 + $10,800 + $15,000).

Answer (A) is incorrect because $130,000 improperly excludes the gain on early retirement of bonds. Answer (B) is incorrect because $132,200 results from subtracting the gain on early retirement of bonds and adding back the fire loss. Answer (C) is incorrect because $163,200 fails to adjust for improper recognition of the unrealized holding loss on the available-for-sale securities.

16. Which of the following statements about APB 9, *Reporting the Results of Operations*, is true?

A. APB 9 is applicable to banks.

B. Commercial banks are exempt from APB 9.

C. Banks issue a statement of condition rather than an income statement.

D. The controller of the currency specifies the detailed format of commercial bank income statements.

Answer (A) is correct. *(Publisher)*

REQUIRED: The true statement about APB 9 with regard to commercial banks.

DISCUSSION: APB 9 applies to income statements of all profit-oriented entities. An amendment by APB 13 made APB 9 applicable to financial statements issued by commercial banks. The deferral of APB 9's applicability was simply a courtesy extended by the APB to an AICPA committee that was studying financial reporting by banks.

Answer (B) is incorrect because APB 9 governs income statements of commercial banks issued for public reporting purposes. Answer (C) is incorrect because a statement of condition is a bank's balance sheet. Answer (D) is incorrect because APB 9 governs income statements of commercial banks issued for public reporting purposes.

3.3 Discontinued Operations

17. For the purpose of reporting discontinued operations, a component of an entity is

A. An operating segment or one level below an operating segment.

B. A set of operations and cash flows clearly distinguishable from the rest of the entity for operational and financial reporting purposes.

C. A separate major line of business or class of customer.

D. A significant disposal group.

Answer (B) is correct. *(Publisher)*

REQUIRED: The nature of a component of an entity.

DISCUSSION: According to SFAS 144, a component of an entity is a set of operations and cash flows clearly distinguishable from the rest of the entity for operational and financial reporting purposes. It may be, but is not limited to, a reportable segment or an operating segment, a reporting unit, a subsidiary, or an asset group. The results of operations of a component that has been disposed of or is classified as held for sale are reported in discontinued operations if (1) its operations and cash flows have been or will be eliminated from the ongoing operations of the entity as a result of the disposal and (2) the entity will have no significant continuing post-disposal involvement in the component's operations.

Answer (A) is incorrect because a component of an entity is not restricted to a reporting unit, that is, an operating segment as defined in SFAS 131 or one level below an operating segment as defined in SFAS 142. Answer (C) is incorrect because, under the pronouncement superseded by SFAS 144, reporting of a discontinued operation was limited to a separate major line of business or class of customer. Answer (D) is incorrect because the criteria for the reporting of discontinued operations does not emphasize either the significance of a component or any quantitative threshold.

18. Good Fast Foods (GFF) operates entity-owned stores and has franchise agreements with entrepreneurs in the East, South, and West Regions. During the current year, GFF committed to a plan to sell the entity-owned stores in the East and South Regions to its franchisees. These stores are classified as held for sale. In the East Region, GFF will receive future fees based on revenues from the stores and will continue to be significantly involved in post-sale operations. In the South Region, GFF will have no post-sale involvement in the operations of the stores, and their operations and cash flows will be eliminated from GFF's ongoing operations. Assuming that each store to be sold is a component of the entity, GFF is required to report the results of operations of which stores classified as held for sale in discontinued operations?

	East Region	South Region
A.	Yes	Yes
B.	Yes	No
C.	No	Yes
D.	No	No

Answer (C) is correct. *(Publisher)*

REQUIRED: The components of the entity, if any, the operating results of which must be reported in discontinued operations.

DISCUSSION: The results of operations of a component that has been disposed of or is classified as held for sale are reported in discontinued operations if (1) its operations and cash flows have been or will be eliminated from the ongoing operations of the entity as a result of the disposal and (2) the entity will have no significant continuing post-disposal involvement in the component's operations (SFAS 144). These criteria are met for the stores classified as held for sale in the South Region but not the East Region.

19. On April 30, year 1, Deer Corp. committed to a plan to sell a component of the entity. As a result, the component's operations and cash flows will be eliminated from the entity's operations, and the entity will have no significant continuing post-disposal involvement in the component's operations. For the period January 1 through April 30, year 1, the component had revenues of $500,000 and expenses of $800,000. The assets of the component were sold on October 15, year 1, at a loss for which no tax benefit is available. In its income statement for the year ended December 31, year 1, how should Deer report the component's operations from January 1 to April 30, year 1?

A. $500,000 and $800,000 should be included with revenues and expenses, respectively, as part of continuing operations.

B. $300,000 should be reported as part of the loss on disposal of a component.

C. $300,000 should be reported as an extraordinary loss.

D. $300,000 should be included in the determination of income or loss from operations of a discontinued component.

Answer (D) is correct. *(CPA, adapted)*

REQUIRED: The proper reporting of a loss related to operations of a discontinued component.

DISCUSSION: The results of operations of a component that has been disposed of or is classified as held for sale, together with any loss on a writedown to fair value minus cost to sell (or a gain from recoupment thereof), minus applicable income taxes (benefit), should be reported separately as a component of income (discontinued operations) before extraordinary items. These results should be reported in the period(s) when they occur (SFAS 144). Thus, the operating results of the component from January 1, year 1 through October 15, year 1 and the loss on disposal are included in the determination of income or loss from operations of the discontinued component.

Answer (A) is incorrect because discontinued operations should not be reported as part of continuing operations. Answer (B) is incorrect because discontinued operations should be presented in two categories: income or loss from operations of the discontinued component and the applicable income taxes (benefit). The loss on disposal is included in the determination of income or loss from the discontinued component. Answer (C) is incorrect because income or loss from discontinued operations should be reported separately as a component of income before extraordinary items.

20. On January 1, year 2, Dart, Inc. entered into an agreement to sell the assets and product line of its Jay Division, which met the criteria for classification as an operating segment. The sale was consummated on December 31, year 2 and resulted in a gain on disposal of $400,000. The division's operations resulted in losses before income tax of $225,000 in year 2 and $125,000 in year 1. Dart's income tax rate is 30% for both years, and the criteria for reporting a discontinued operation have been met. In a comparative statement of income for year 2 and year 1, under the caption discontinued operations, Dart should report a gain (loss) of

	Year 2	Year 1
A.	$122,500	$(87,500)
B.	$122,500	$0
C.	$(157,500)	$(87,500)
D.	$(157,500)	$0

Answer (A) is correct. *(CPA, adapted)*

REQUIRED: The amounts reported for discontinued operations in comparative statements.

DISCUSSION: When a component (e.g., an operating segment) has been disposed of or is classified as held for sale, and the criteria for reporting a discontinued operation have been met, the income statement of a business enterprise for current and prior periods must report its operating results in discontinued operations. The gain from operations of the component for year 2 equals the $225,000 operating loss for year 2, plus the $400,000 gain on disposal. The pretax gain is therefore $175,000 ($400,000 – $225,000). The after-tax amount is $122,500 [$175,000 × (1 – 30%)]. Because year 1 was prior to the time that the component was classified as held for sale, the $125,000 of operating losses would have been reported under income from continuing operations in the year 1 income statement as originally issued. This loss is now attributable to discontinued operations, and the year 1 financial statements presented for comparative purposes must be reclassified. In the reclassified 2001 income statement, the $125,000 pretax loss should be shown as an $87,500 [$125,000 × (1 – 30%)] loss from discontinued operations.

Answer (B) is incorrect because the comparative statement of income for year 2 and year 1 should report a loss on discontinued operations for year 1. Answer (C) is incorrect because an after-tax loss of $157,500 for year 2 does not consider the gain on disposal. Answer (D) is incorrect because the comparative statement of income for year 2 and year 1 should report a loss on discontinued operations for year 1, and an after-tax loss of $157,500 for year 2 does not consider the gain on disposal.

21. A business enterprise disposed of a component of the entity during its fiscal year that ended on December 31, year 1. The results of operations of this component were properly reported in discontinued operations. Which of the following adjustments recognized in year 2 to amounts previously reported in discontinued operations in year 1 most likely should be reported in continuing operations?

A. The resolution of a contingency involving adjustment of the purchase price as provided for in the terms of the disposal.

B. The resolution of a contingency involving an environmental liability directly related to the predisposal operations of the component.

C. The settlement of a pension benefit obligation to employees affected by the sale of the component at the time of the sale and at the discretion of the employer.

D. The settlement of a pension benefit obligation to employees affected by the sale of the component as a condition of the sale but more than 1 year after the disposal because of the occurrence of unexpected events.

Answer (C) is correct. *(Publisher)*

REQUIRED: The adjustment to amounts previously recognized in discontinued operations that most likely should be reported in discontinued operations.

DISCUSSION: According to SFAS 144, amounts previously reported in discontinued operations in a prior period may require adjustment in the current period. If such an adjustment is directly related to a prior-period disposal of a component, it is reported currently in discontinued operations as a separate item, and its nature and amount are disclosed. A settlement of an employee benefit plan obligation is directly related to the disposal given a demonstrated direct cause-and-effect relationship. Moreover, the settlement should occur no later than 1 year after the disposal unless delayed by events or circumstances not within the entity's control. However, if the timing of a settlement is at the discretion of the employer, the mere coincidence that settlement occurred at the time of sale does not, by itself, establish a cause-and-effect relationship. Thus, a discretionary settlement of a pension benefit obligation at the time of sale is the least likely to qualify for reporting in discontinued operations and the most likely to be reported in continuing operations.

Answer (A) is incorrect because the direct-relationship criterion for current reporting is met. Answer (B) is incorrect because the direct-relationship criterion for current reporting is met. Answer (D) is incorrect because settlement of a pension benefit obligation as a condition of the disposal meets the direct-relationship criterion for current reporting. The criterion is met even if the settlement occurred more than 1 year after the sale, provided that the delay was the result of events or circumstances beyond the entity's control.

22. During January year 1, Doe Corp. agreed to sell the assets and product line of its Hart division. The sale was completed on January 15, year 2 and resulted in a gain on disposal of $900,000. Hart's operating losses were $600,000 for year 1 and $50,000 for the period January 1 through January 15, year 2. Disregarding income taxes, and assuming that the criteria for reporting a discontinued operation are met, what amount of net gain (loss) should be reported in Doe's comparative year 2 and year 1 income statements?

	Year 2	Year 1
A.	$0	$250,000
B.	$250,000	$0
C.	$850,000	$(600,000)
D.	$900,000	$(650,000)

Answer (C) is correct. *(CPA, adapted)*

REQUIRED: The amounts reported in comparative statements for discontinued operations.

DISCUSSION: The results of operations of a component classified as held for sale are reported separately in the income statement under discontinued operations in the periods when they occur. Thus, in its year 1 income statement, Doe should recognize a $600,000 loss. For year 2, a gain of $850,000 should be recognized ($900,000 – $50,000).

Answer (A) is incorrect because $250,000 is the net gain for year 1 and year 2. However, the results for year 2 may not be anticipated, and the results for year 1 should not be deferred. Answer (B) is incorrect because $250,000 is the net gain for year 1 and year 2. However, the results for year 2 may not be anticipated, and the results for year 1 should not be deferred. Answer (D) is incorrect because the operating loss for January year 2 should be recognized in year 2.

3.4 Extraordinary Items

23. A transaction that is unusual in nature and infrequent in occurrence should be reported separately

A. After income from continuing operations and before discontinued operations.

B. As part of income from continuing operations.

C. In the notes but not in the income statement.

D. After discontinued operations and before net income.

Answer (D) is correct. *(CPA, adapted)*
REQUIRED: The reporting of a transaction that is unusual in nature and infrequent in occurrence.
DISCUSSION: A transaction that is unusual in nature and infrequent in occurrence in the environment in which the entity operates is classified as an extraordinary item. The following is the order of items to be reported separately in the income statement: income from continuing operations, discontinued operations, extraordinary items, and net income.

24. An extraordinary item should be reported separately on the income statement as a component of income

	Net of Income Taxes	Before Discontinued Operations
A.	Yes	Yes
B.	Yes	No
C.	No	No
D.	No	Yes

Answer (B) is correct. *(CPA, adapted)*
REQUIRED: The presentation of an extraordinary item.
DISCUSSION: Extraordinary items should be reported separately in the income statement, net of tax, after discontinued operations but before net income.

25. During the current year, both Raim Co. and Cane Co. suffered losses due to the flooding of the Mississippi River. Raim is located 2 miles from the river and sustains flood losses every 2 to 3 years. Cane, which has been located 50 miles from the river for the past 20 years, has never before had flood losses. How should the flood losses be reported in each company's current-year income statement?

	Raim	Cane
A.	As a component of income from continuing operations	As an extraordinary item
B.	As a component of income from continuing operations	As a component of income from continuing operations
C.	As an extraordinary item	As a component of income from continuing operations
D.	As an extraordinary item	As an extraordinary item

Answer (A) is correct. *(CPA, adapted)*
REQUIRED: The reporting of flood losses in the income statement.
DISCUSSION: For Raim, flood losses are neither unusual nor infrequent in the environment in which it operates. Thus, these losses should be classified as a separate component of income from continuing operations, not net of tax as an extraordinary item. For Cane, the flood losses meet the criteria of an extraordinary item because they are unusual and infrequent: Cane had never before suffered flood losses.

26. In year 1, hail damaged several of Toncan Co.'s vans. Hailstorms had frequently inflicted similar damage to Toncan's vans. Over the years, Toncan had saved money by not buying hail insurance and either paying for repairs, or selling damaged vans and then replacing them. In year 1, the damaged vans were sold for less than their carrying amount. How should the hail damage cost be reported in Toncan's year 1 financial statements?

A. The actual year 1 hail damage loss as an extraordinary loss, net of income taxes.

B. The actual year 1 hail damage loss in continuing operations, with no separate disclosure.

C. The expected average hail damage loss in continuing operations, with no separate disclosure.

D. The expected average hail damage loss in continuing operations, with separate disclosure.

Answer (B) is correct. *(CPA, adapted)*

REQUIRED: The reporting of hail damage costs when a company is uninsured and sells the damaged item for a loss.

DISCUSSION: Because Toncan sold its damaged vans for less than their carrying amount, the company suffered a loss. Because this occurrence is not unusual or infrequent, the actual loss should be included in continuing operations with no separate disclosure.

Answer (A) is incorrect because a frequent occurrence does not meet the definition of an extraordinary item. Answer (C) is incorrect because Toncan should report the actual loss incurred in year 1. Answer (D) is incorrect because Toncan should report the actual loss, and a separate disclosure is not needed.

27. In the current year, Teller Co. incurred losses arising from its guilty plea in its first antitrust action and from a substantial increase in production costs caused when a major supplier's workers went on strike. Which of these losses should be reported as an extraordinary item?

	Antitrust Action	Production Costs
A.	No	No
B.	No	Yes
C.	Yes	No
D.	Yes	Yes

Answer (C) is correct. *(CPA, adapted)*

REQUIRED: The loss(es), if any, reported as an extraordinary item.

DISCUSSION: APB 30 specifically states that the effects of a strike are not extraordinary. However, a loss from the company's first antitrust action is clearly infrequent and most likely unusual, that is, abnormal and of a type unrelated to the typical activities of the entity in the environment in which it operates.

28. Which one of the following material events is most likely to be classified as an extraordinary item on an income statement?

A. A write-down of obsolete inventories.

B. A loss from disposal of a component of an entity as a result of a newly enacted law.

C. A loss from sale of property, plant, or equipment used in a business that results from an expropriation.

D. A gain or loss from the exchange of foreign currency due to a major devaluation.

Answer (C) is correct. *(CMA, adapted)*

REQUIRED: The item that is classified as extraordinary.

DISCUSSION: Examples of transactions that are not extraordinary items include (1) write-down of receivables, inventories, equipment leased to others, deferred R&D costs, or other intangible assets; (2) gains or losses from exchange or translation of foreign currencies; (3) gains or losses on disposal of a component of an entity; (4) other gains or losses on sale or abandonment of property, plant, or equipment used in the business; (5) effects of strikes, including those against competitors and suppliers; and (6) adjustment of accruals on long-term contracts. However, gains and losses, such as those in (1) and (4) that (a) result from a major casualty, an expropriation, or a prohibition under a newly enacted law or regulation and (b) clearly meet the criteria for extraordinary treatment, are classified as extraordinary items.

Answer (A) is incorrect because a write-down of inventories as a result of obsolescence is unlikely to meet the criteria for extraordinary treatment. Answer (B) is incorrect because disposal of a component of an entity is accounted for and presented in the income statement under SFAS 144. SFAS 144 applies even if the gain or loss (1) results from a major casualty, an expropriation, or a prohibition under a newly enacted law or regulation and (2) clearly meets the criteria for extraordinary treatment. Answer (D) is incorrect because foreign currency transaction gains and losses are unlikely to meet the criteria for extraordinary treatment.

29. In open market transactions, Gold Corp. simultaneously sold its long-term investment in Iron Corp. bonds and purchased its own outstanding bonds. The broker remitted the net cash from the two transactions. Gold's gain on the purchase of its own bonds exceeded its loss on the sale of the Iron bonds. Gold should report the

A. Two transactions as extraordinary gains.

B. Two transactions in income before extraordinary items.

C. Effect of its own bond transaction gain in income before extraordinary items and report the Iron bond transaction as an extraordinary loss.

D. Effect of its own bond transaction as an extraordinary gain and report the Iron bond transaction loss in income before extraordinary items.

Answer (B) is correct. *(CPA, adapted)*

REQUIRED: The reporting of the sale of a long-term investment in bonds and an extinguishment of debt.

DISCUSSION: APB 26 requires that differences between the reacquisition prices and the net carrying amounts of extinguished debt be recognized currently as gains or losses in income of the period of extinguishment. Transactions are presumed to be ordinary and usual unless a pronouncement specifically states otherwise or the evidence clearly supports classification as extraordinary. No currently effective pronouncement classifies these transactions as extraordinary. No evidence indicates that the sale of securities and the extinguishment of debt are clearly infrequent and unusual in the environment in which the entity operates. Thus, the gain on the bond purchase and the loss on the sale of bonds should be reported in income before extraordinary items.

Answer (A) is incorrect because the extinguishment resulted in an ordinary gain, and the sale of securities in an ordinary loss. Answer (C) is incorrect because the extinguishment resulted in an ordinary gain, and the sale of securities in an ordinary loss. Answer (D) is incorrect because the extinguishment resulted in an ordinary gain, and the sale of securities in an ordinary loss.

30. Kent Co. incurred the following infrequent losses during the current year:

- A $300,000 loss was incurred on disposal of one of four dissimilar factories.
- A major currency devaluation caused a $120,000 foreign currency transaction loss on an amount remitted by a customer.
- Inventory valued at $190,000 was made worthless by a competitor's unexpected product innovation.

In its current-year income statement, what amount should Kent report as losses that are not considered extraordinary?

A. $610,000

B. $490,000

C. $420,000

D. $310,000

Answer (A) is correct. *(CPA, adapted)*

REQUIRED: The amount of losses not considered extraordinary.

DISCUSSION: To be classified as an extraordinary item, a transaction must be both unusual in nature and infrequent in occurrence in the environment in which the business operates. APB 30 specifies six items that are not usually considered extraordinary. These items include gains and losses on disposal of a component of an entity; gains and losses from exchange or translation of foreign currencies, including those resulting from major devaluations and revaluations; and write-downs of receivables and inventories. Hence, the amount of ordinary losses is $610,000 ($300,000 + $120,000 + $190,000).

Answer (B) is incorrect because $490,000 omits the foreign currency transaction loss. Answer (C) is incorrect because $420,000 omits the inventory write-off. Answer (D) is incorrect because $310,000 omits the loss on disposal of the factory. A gain or loss on disposal of a component of an entity is reported in discontinued operations.

31. Nikoto Steel Co. had the following unusual financial events occur during the current year:

- Bonds payable were retired 5 years before their scheduled maturity, resulting in a $260,000 gain. Nikoto has frequently retired bonds early when interest rates declined significantly.
- A steel forming plant suffered $255,000 in losses from hurricane damage. This was the fourth similar loss sustained in a 5-year period at that location.
- Nikoto's steel transportation operating segment was sold at a net loss of $350,000. This transaction was Nikoto's first divestiture of one of its component units.

Before income taxes, what amount should be reported as the gain (loss) from extraordinary items in the current year?

A. $0

B. $5,000

C. $(90,000)

D. $(350,000)

Answer (A) is correct. *(CPA, adapted)*

REQUIRED: The amount disclosed as the gain (loss) from extraordinary items.

DISCUSSION: APB 26 requires that differences between the reacquisition prices and the net carrying amounts of extinguished debt be recognized currently as gains or losses in income of the period of extinguishment. Transactions are presumed to be ordinary and usual unless a pronouncement specifically states otherwise or the evidence clearly supports classification as extraordinary. No currently effective pronouncement classifies this transaction as extraordinary, and no evidence clearly supports that classification. The extinguishment of debt is not clearly infrequent and unusual in the environment in which the entity operates. Thus, the gain on the bond purchase should be reported in income before extraordinary items. The divestiture of a component unit is reported as a discontinued operation. The hurricane damage, which is unusual but not infrequent, is reported separately as a component of income from continuing operations. Hence, no extraordinary item is reported.

Answer (B) is incorrect because $5,000 is the net of the extinguishment gain and the $255,000 hurricane loss reported in continuing operations. Answer (C) is incorrect because $(90,000) is the net of the loss from discontinued operations and the extinguishment gain. Answer (D) is incorrect because $(350,000) is the loss from discontinued operations.

3.5 Statement of Retained Earnings

32. The major segments of the statement of retained earnings for a period are

A. Dividends declared, prior-period adjustments, and changes due to treasury stock transactions.

B. Prior-period adjustments, before tax income or loss, income tax, and dividends paid.

C. Net income or loss from operations, dividends paid, and extraordinary gains and losses.

D. Net income or loss, prior-period adjustments, and dividends paid or declared.

Answer (D) is correct. *(CMA, adapted)*

REQUIRED: The major segments of the statement of retained earnings.

DISCUSSION: The statement of retained earnings is a basic financial statement. APB 9, *Reporting the Results of Operations*, states that the income statement and the statement of retained earnings (presented separately or combined) are designed to broadly reflect the "results of operations." The statement of retained earnings consists of beginning retained earnings adjusted for any prior-period adjustments (net of tax), with further adjustments for net income (loss), dividends paid or declared, and certain other rare adjustments, e.g., quasi-reorganizations and certain treasury stock transactions. The final figure is ending retained earnings.

Answer (A) is incorrect because net income (loss) is a major segment of the retained earnings statement. Treasury stock transactions result in changes in retained earnings only in limited circumstances. Answer (B) is incorrect because after-tax net income is reflected in the statement of retained earnings. Answer (C) is incorrect because operating income and extraordinary gains and losses should be included in the determination of after-tax net income.

33. Which of the following should be reflected, net of applicable income taxes, in the statement of equity as an adjustment of the opening balance in retained earnings?

A. Correction of an error in previously issued financial statements.

B. Cumulative effect of a change in depreciation method.

C. Loss on disposal of a component of an entity.

D. Extraordinary item.

Answer (A) is correct. *(CPA, adapted)*

REQUIRED: The item treated as an adjustment to beginning retained earnings.

DISCUSSION: According to SFAS 16, *Prior Period Adjustments*, the correction of an error occurring in a prior period should be accounted for as a prior-period adjustment. It should be charged or credited net of tax to retained earnings and reported as an adjustment in the statement of equity. It is not included in net income for the current period.

Answer (B) is incorrect because a change in depreciation method is a change in estimate that is accounted for prospectively. Answer (C) is incorrect because a discontinued operation is reported under a separate caption in the income statement. Answer (D) is incorrect because an extraordinary item is reported under a separate caption in the income statement.

34. Omicron Co. made a justifiable change in its method of accounting for long-term contracts. The cumulative effect of this change in accounting principle should be reported in comparative financial statements

A. In the income statement between discontinued operations and extraordinary items, net of tax.

B. As a component of income from continuing operations.

C. As an adjustment of the beginning balance of retained earnings for the current period.

D. By retrospective application if practicable.

Answer (D) is correct. *(Publisher)*

REQUIRED: The proper reporting of a change in accounting principle.

DISCUSSION: Retrospective application is required for a change in accounting principle unless it is impracticable to determine either the cumulative effect or the period-specific effects of the change. Accordingly, the beginning balances of assets, liabilities, and retained earnings for the first period presented are adjusted to reflect the cumulative effect of applying the new principle on all prior periods. Each prior period presented is then adjusted to reflect the period-specific effects.

Answer (A) is incorrect because retrospective application is required for a change in accounting principle unless it is impracticable to determine either the cumulative effect or the period-specific effects of the change. Answer (B) is incorrect because retrospective application is required for a change in accounting principle unless it is impracticable to determine either the cumulative effect or the period-specific effects of the change. Answer (C) is incorrect because retrospective application is required for a change in accounting principle unless it is impracticable to determine either the cumulative effect or the period-specific effects of the change.

STUDY UNIT FOUR
PRESENT VALUE AND FUTURE VALUE

This chapter covers basic concepts related to the time value of money, that is, present values (PV) and future values (FV). Present value and future value are used in accounting for investments, long-term liabilities, pensions and other employment benefits, and leases.

Money has a **time value**. Thus, the value (worth) of an amount of money is greater the earlier it is received. For example, $500 to be received immediately is worth more than $500 to be received 2 years from now. Furthermore, if amounts of money are to be received at different times, the amount to be received later must be greater than the amount to be received earlier if they are to have the same value (worth). The difference is interest. Interest may be classified as simple and compound. Simple interest includes only interest earned on a principal amount of money. Compound interest includes both interest on a principal amount and interest earned during previous interest periods. Both present value and future value are based on compound interest.

Present value is the present equivalent (value) of a future amount(s) of money. Present value is calculated by discounting the future amount(s) to determine the present equivalent. This calculation removes the total compound interest included in the future amount(s). The formula for determining the present value (PV) of a future amount of money (FV) to be received at time, *t*, at an applicable interest (discount) rate, *i*, is $PV_{t=0} = FV_{t=n} \times [1 \div (1 + i)^n]$. For example, the present value of \$121 to be received in 2 years discounted at an annual interest rate of 10% is \$100 $\{PV_{t=0} = \$121_{t=2} \times [1 \div (1 + .1)^2]\}$.

Future value is the future equivalent (value) of a present sum of money. Future value is calculated by multiplying the present value by the applicable interest rate for the appropriate number of interest periods. The formula for determining the future value (FV) at time, *t*, of a present sum (PV) at an applicable interest rate, *i*, is $FV_{t=n} = PV_{t=0} \times (1 + i)^n$. For example, the future value of \$100 to be invested for 2 years at 10% compounded annually is \$121 $[FV_{t=2} = \$100 \times (1 + .1)^2]$.

SFAC 7, *Using Cash Flow Information and Present Value in Accounting Measurements*, provides a conceptual framework for the use of present value. With regard to accounting measurements for initial-recognition or fresh-start purposes, this framework states that present value should attempt to reflect fair value. The framework also describes the conditions under which an interest method of amortization should be considered.

SFAC 7 introduced the **expected cash flow approach** to measuring present value. This approach focuses on explicit assumptions about the range of expected cash flows and their respective probabilities. In contrast with the traditional approach, the expected cash flow method permits the use of present value when the timing of cash flows is uncertain.

QUESTIONS

4.1 Conceptual Framework

1. According to SFAC 7, *Using Cash Flow Information and Present Value in Accounting Measurements*, the objective of present value is to estimate fair value when used to determine accounting measurements for

	Initial-Recognition Purposes	Fresh-Start Purposes
A.	No	No
B.	Yes	Yes
C.	Yes	No
D.	No	Yes

Answer (B) is correct. *(Publisher)*

REQUIRED: The objective of present value in initial-recognition and fresh-start measurements.

DISCUSSION: SFAC 7 states that the objective of present value in initial-recognition or fresh-start measurements is to estimate fair value. "Present value should attempt to capture the elements that, taken together, would comprise a market price if one existed, that is, fair value." A present value measurement includes five elements: estimates of cash flows, expectations about their variability, the time value of money (the risk-free interest rate), the price of uncertainty inherent in an asset or liability, and other factors (e.g., illiquidity or market imperfections). Fair value encompasses all these elements using the estimates and expectations of participants in the market.

2. The expected cash flow approach to measuring present value promulgated by SFAC 7

A. Uses a single set of estimated cash flows.

B. Is limited to assets and liabilities with contractual cash flows.

C. Focuses on explicit assumptions about the range of expected cash flows and their respective probabilities.

D. Focuses on the single most likely amount or best estimate.

Answer (C) is correct. *(Publisher)*

REQUIRED: The nature of the expected cash flow approach.

DISCUSSION: The traditional approach to calculating present value employs one set of estimated cash flows and one interest rate. This approach is expected to continue to be used in many cases, for example, when contractual cash flows are involved. However, SFAC 7 describes the expected cash flow approach, which is applicable in more complex circumstances, such as when no market or no comparable item exists for an asset or liability. The expected cash flow results from multiplying each possible estimated amount by its probability and adding the products. The expected cash flow approach emphasizes explicit assumptions about the possible estimated cash flows and their probabilities. The traditional method merely includes those uncertainties in the choice of interest rate. Moreover, by allowing for a range of possibilities, the expected cash flow method permits the use of present value when the timing of cash flows is uncertain.

Answer (A) is incorrect because the traditional present value measurement approach uses a single set of estimated cash flows and a single interest rate. Answer (B) is incorrect because the expected cash flow approach may also apply when the timing of cash flows is uncertain or when nonfinancial assets and liabilities are to be measured and no market or comparable item exists for them. Answer (D) is incorrect because some current accounting applications use the estimated mode (single most likely amount or best estimate), but the expected cash flow approach arrives at an estimated mean by probabilistically weighting a range of possible estimated amounts.

4.2 Present Value

3. On July 1, Dichter Company obtained a $2,000,000, 180-day bank loan at an annual rate of 12%. The loan agreement requires Dichter to maintain a $400,000 compensating balance in its checking account at the lending bank. Dichter would otherwise maintain a balance of only $200,000 in this account. The checking account earns interest at an annual rate of 6%. Based on a 360-day year, the effective interest rate on the borrowing is

A. 12%

B. 12.67%

C. 13.33%

D. 13.5%

Answer (B) is correct. *(CPA, adapted)*

REQUIRED: The annual effective interest rate on a loan requiring a compensating balance.

DISCUSSION: The effective interest rate on the 180-day borrowing is equal to the net interest cost divided by the net available proceeds of $1,800,000 ($2,000,000 loan – $200,000 increase in the compensating balance). The net interest cost is equal to the gross interest cost minus the incremental interest revenue. The gross interest cost is $120,000 [$2,000,000 × 12% × (6 ÷ 12)]. Because the incremental interest revenue is $6,000 [$200,000 × 6% × (6 ÷ 12)], the net interest cost is $114,000 ($120,000 – $6,000). The 6-month effective interest rate is therefore 6.33% ($114,000 ÷ $1,800,000). The annual effective interest rate is 12.67% (6.33% × 2).

Answer (A) is incorrect because 12% is the annual rate. Answer (C) is incorrect because the interest revenue from the checking account must be included in the calculations. Answer (D) is incorrect because the interest revenue from the checking account must be included in the calculations.

4. The relationship between the present value of a future sum and the future value of a present sum can be expressed in terms of their respective interest factors. If the present value of $200,000 due at the end of 8 years, at 10%, is $93,300, what is the approximate future value of $200,000 invested for the same length of time and at the same rate?

A. $93,300

B. $200,000

C. $293,300

D. $428,724

Answer (D) is correct. *(CIA, adapted)*

REQUIRED: The approximate future value of an amount.

DISCUSSION: The interest factor for the future value of a present sum is equal to the reciprocal of the interest factor for the present value of a future sum. Thus, the future value is $428,724 [($200,000 ÷ $93,300) × $200,000].

Answer (A) is incorrect because $93,300 is the present value of $200,000 to be received in 8 years. Answer (B) is incorrect because $200,000 is the present value, not the future value, of $200,000 invested today. Answer (C) is incorrect because the addition of the present and future values has no accounting meaning.

5. A company purchased some large machinery on a deferred payment plan. The contract calls for $40,000 down on January 1 and $40,000 at the beginning of each of the next 4 years. There is no stated interest rate in the contract, and there is no established exchange price for the machinery. What should be recorded as the cost of the machinery?

A. $200,000.

B. $200,000 plus the added implicit interest.

C. Future value of an annuity due for 5 years at an imputed interest rate.

D. Present value of an annuity due for 5 years at an imputed interest rate.

Answer (D) is correct. *(CIA, adapted)*

REQUIRED: The cost of machinery acquired under a deferred payment plan.

DISCUSSION: The contract calls for an annuity due because the first annuity payment is due immediately. In an ordinary annuity (annuity in arrears), each payment is due at the end of the period. According to APB 21, *Interest on Receivables and Payables*, an interest rate must be imputed in the given circumstances to arrive at the present value of the machinery.

Answer (A) is incorrect because the implicit interest should be subtracted from the $200,000 in total payments. Answer (B) is incorrect because the implicit interest should be subtracted from the $200,000 in total payments. Answer (C) is incorrect because the present value, not the future value, is the appropriate concept.

6. On September 1, year 1, a company purchased a new machine that it does not have to pay for until September 1, year 3. The total payment on September 1, year 3 will include both principal and interest. Assuming interest at a 10% rate, the cost of the machine will be the total payment multiplied by what time value of money factor?

A. Present value of annuity of $1.

B. Present value of $1.

C. Future amount of annuity of $1.

D. Future amount of $1.

Answer (B) is correct. *(CPA, adapted)*

REQUIRED: The time value of money factor to compute current cost when payment is to be made in a lump sum at a future date.

DISCUSSION: The cost of the machine to the company on 9/1/year 1 is the present value of the payment to be made on 9/1/year 3. To obtain the present value, i.e., today's price, the future payment is multiplied by the present value of $1 for two periods at 10%.

Answer (A) is incorrect because the present value of an annuity determines the value today of a series of future payments (not merely one payment). Answer (C) is incorrect because the future value of an annuity determines the amount available at a specified time in the future after a series of deposits (investments). Answer (D) is incorrect because the future value of a dollar determines how much will be available at a specified time in the future based on the single investment (deposit) today.

7. The computation of the current value of an asset using the present value of future cash flows method does not include the

A. Cost of alternate uses of funds given up.

B. Productive life of the asset.

C. Applicable interest rate.

D. Future amounts of cash receipts or cash savings.

Answer (A) is correct. *(CPA, adapted)*

REQUIRED: The information not used in computing current value by the present value of future cash flows method.

DISCUSSION: The present value of future cash flows is one technique for computing current value of an asset. To calculate the current value of an asset (using the "present value" method) requires (1) the discount period (the productive life of the asset), (2) the discount rate (the applicable interest rate), and (3) the future values (the future amounts of cash receipts or cash savings). This method does not take into account opportunity costs (costs of giving up alternate uses of funds).

8. On July 1, Goblette Company sold some machinery to another company. The two companies entered into an installment sales contract at a predetermined interest rate. The contract required five equal annual payments with the first payment due on July 1, the date of sale. What present value concept is appropriate for this situation?

A. Present value of an annuity due of $1 for five periods.

B. Present value of an ordinary annuity of $1 for five periods.

C. Future amount of an annuity due of $1 for five periods.

D. Future amount of $1 for five periods.

Answer (A) is correct. *(CPA, adapted)*

REQUIRED: The present value concept appropriate for an installment sale with the first payment due immediately.

DISCUSSION: The contract calls for five equal annual payments with the first due immediately. Ordinary annuity tables assume the first payment occurs at the end of the first time period. An annuity in which the first payment occurs at the beginning of the first period is called an "annuity due" or an "annuity in advance."

The number of payments earning interest in an annuity due is one less than the number earning interest in an ordinary annuity because there is no interest on the first payment. Accordingly, the present value of an annuity due of $1 for five periods can be calculated by taking the present value of an ordinary annuity of $1 for four periods and adding $1. Hence, a special table for an annuity due or the method described above can be used in this situation.

Answer (B) is incorrect because the question describes an annuity due (not an ordinary annuity) for five periods. Answer (C) is incorrect because a present value computation is required. Answer (D) is incorrect because a present value computation is required.

9. In the determination of a present value, which of the following relationships is true?

A. The lower the discount rate and the shorter the discount period, the lower the present value.

B. The lower the future cash flow and the shorter the discount period, the lower the present value.

C. The higher the discount rate and the longer the discount period, the lower the present value.

D. The higher the future cash flow and the longer the discount period, the lower the present value.

Answer (C) is correct. *(Publisher)*

REQUIRED: The true relationship between the discount period, discount rate, and present value.

DISCUSSION: As the discount rate increases, the present value decreases. Also, as the discount period increases, the present value decreases.

Answer (A) is incorrect because, as the discount period decreases, the present value increases. Answer (B) is incorrect because, as the discount period decreases, the present value increases. Answer (D) is incorrect because increased future cash flows increase the present value.

10. For which of the following transactions would the use of the present value of an annuity due concept be appropriate in calculating the present value of the asset obtained or liability owed at the date of incurrence?

A. A capital lease is entered into with the initial lease payment due 1 month subsequent to the signing of the lease agreement.

B. A capital lease is entered into with the initial lease payment due upon the signing of the lease agreement.

C. A 10-year 8% bond is issued on January 2 with interest payable semiannually on July 1 and January 1 yielding 7%.

D. A 10-year 8% bond is issued on January 2 with interest payable semiannually on July 1 and January 1 yielding 9%.

Answer (B) is correct. *(CPA, adapted)*

REQUIRED: The transaction for which the present value of an annuity due concept would be appropriate.

DISCUSSION: In an annuity due, the first payment is made at the beginning of the first period and is therefore not discounted. In an ordinary annuity, the first payment is made at the end of the first period and therefore is discounted. For annuities due, the first payment is included in the computation at its face value.

Answer (A) is incorrect because, in this case, the initial payment is not due immediately. Answer (C) is incorrect because, in this case, the initial payment is not due immediately. Answer (D) is incorrect because, in this case, the initial payment is not due immediately.

11. Stone Co. is considering the acquisition of equipment. To buy the equipment, the cost is $15,192. To lease the equipment, Stone must sign a noncancelable lease and make five payments of $4,000 each. The first payment will be paid on the first day of the lease. At the time of the last payment, Stone will receive title to the equipment. The present value of an ordinary annuity of $1 is as follows:

	Present Value		
No. of Periods	10%	12%	16%
1	0.909	0.893	0.862
2	1.736	1.690	1.605
3	2.487	2.402	2.246
4	3.170	3.037	2.798
5	3.791	3.605	3.274

The interest rate implicit in this lease is approximately

A. 10%

B. 12%

C. Between 10% and 12%.

D. 16%

Answer (D) is correct. *(CPA, adapted)*

REQUIRED: The interest rate implicit in a lease.

DISCUSSION: Present value tables may be used to determine the interest rate if the present value is already known. The present value is divided by the periodic amount to find the interest factor. The interest factor may then be found in the present-value-of-an-ordinary-annuity table in the row corresponding to the number of periods over which the annuity is payable.

In this question, the series of payments is an annuity due, and an adjustment must be made before using the ordinary annuity table. The first payment is due immediately, so its present value (face amount) of $4,000 is deducted from the given present value of the annuity. The row for n – 1 periods (4) should then be used.

Present value	$15,192
Minus first payment	(4,000)
	$11,192
Divided by annuity amount	÷ 4,000
Present value factor	2.798

The present value factor of 2.798 is found under 16% in the row for four periods.

12. Harry Rawlings wants to withdraw $10,000 (including principal) from an investment fund at the end of each year for 5 years. How should he compute his required initial investment at the beginning of the first year if the fund earns 6% compounded annually?

A. $10,000 times the amount of an annuity of $1 at 6% at the end of each year for 5 years.

B. $10,000 divided by the amount of an annuity of $1 at 6% at the end of each year for 5 years.

C. $10,000 times the present value of an annuity of $1 at 6% at the end of each year for 5 years.

D. $10,000 divided by the present value of an annuity of $1 at 6% at the end of each year for 5 years.

Answer (C) is correct. *(CPA, adapted)*

REQUIRED: The computation for the initial investment required at a given rate to permit withdrawal of a fixed amount at the end of each of a series of years.

DISCUSSION: The question requires a present value rather than a future value, i.e., today's equivalent of $10,000 at the end of each of the next 5 years. The table used is for the present value of an ordinary annuity. The interest factor corresponding to 6% for five periods is multiplied by $10,000 to provide the answer.

Answer (A) is incorrect because the question requires a present value rather than a future value calculation. "Amount of an annuity" is synonymous with future value of an annuity. Answer (B) is incorrect because the question requires a present value rather than a future value calculation. "Amount of an annuity" is synonymous with future value of an annuity. Answer (D) is incorrect because $10,000 must be multiplied (rather than divided) by the present value of an ordinary annuity of $1 for 6% and five periods.

13. Chambers Company bought Machine 1 on March 5, year 1 for $5,000 cash. The estimated salvage was $200 and the estimated life was 11 years. On March 5, year 2, the company learned that it could purchase a different machine for $8,000 cash. It would save the company an estimated $250 per year. The new machine would have no estimated salvage and an estimated life of 10 years. The company could sell Machine 1 for $3,000 on March 5, year 2. Ignoring income taxes, which of the following calculations would best assist the company in deciding whether to purchase the new machine?

A. (Present value of an annuity of $250) + $3,000 – $8,000

B. (Present value of an annuity of $250) – $8,000

C. (Present value of an annuity of $250) + $3,000 – $8,000 – $5,000

D. (Present value of an annuity of $250) + $3,000 – $8,000 – $4,800

Answer (A) is correct. *(CPA, adapted)*

REQUIRED: The calculation that would best assist the company in deciding whether to purchase the new machine.

DISCUSSION: The sale of the first machine for $3,000 and the purchase of the new machine for $8,000 on 3/5/year 2 results in an incremental cost to the company of $5,000. If the present value of the future savings from the second machine exceeds $5,000 [the formula presented in answer (A)], the company should purchase the new machine. Note that the remaining estimated useful life of the first machine is the same as that of the second. Note also that the cost of Machine 1 should be ignored because it is a sunk cost.

Answer (B) is incorrect because it fails to consider the resale value of Machine 1 on 3/5/year 2. Answer (C) is incorrect because it improperly considers the sunk cost of Machine 1. Answer (D) is incorrect because it improperly considers the sunk cost of Machine 1.

14. On July 1, year 1, Ahmed signed an agreement to operate as a franchisee of Teacake Pastries, Inc. for an initial franchise fee of $240,000. On the same date, Ahmed paid $80,000 and agreed to pay the balance in four equal annual payments of $40,000 beginning July 1, year 2. The down payment is not refundable and no future services are required of the franchisor. Ahmed can borrow at 14% for a loan of this type.

Present value of $1 at 14% for 4 periods	0.59
Future amount of $1 at 14% for 4 periods	1.69
Present value of an ordinary annuity of $1 at 14% for 4 periods	2.91

Ahmed should record the acquisition cost of the franchise on July 1, year 1 at

A. $270,400

B. $240,000

C. $196,400

D. $174,400

Answer (C) is correct. *(CPA, adapted)*

REQUIRED: The acquisition cost of a franchise to be paid for in installments.

DISCUSSION: The acquisition cost would have been recorded at $240,000 if this amount of cash had been paid immediately. Given that the $240,000 is to be paid in installments, the acquisition cost is equal to the down payment of $80,000 plus the present value of the series of four annuity payments beginning 1 year after the date of purchase. The proper interest factor to be employed is the present value of an ordinary annuity of $1 at 14% for four periods, or 2.91.

$ 40,000
× 2.91
$116,400
+ 80,000
$196,400

15. On January 1, year 1, Saucerer Company bought a building with an assessed value of $220,000 on the date of purchase. Saucerer gave as consideration a $400,000 noninterest-bearing note due on January 1, year 4. There was no established exchange price for the building, and the note had no ready market. The prevailing rate of interest for a note of this type at January 1, year 1 was 10%. The present value of $1 at 10% for three periods is 0.75. What amount of interest expense should be included in Saucerer's year 1 income statement?

A. $22,000

B. $30,000

C. $33,333

D. $40,000

Answer (C) is correct. *(CPA, adapted)*

REQUIRED: The interest expense on a noninterest-bearing note.

DISCUSSION: The purchase of a building without an established exchange price should be recorded at the fair market value of the consideration given. A noninterest-bearing note should be recorded at its fair market value or present value of the future cash flows discounted at the prevailing rate of interest. The note and building should therefore be recorded at $300,000 ($400,000 × 0.75). The difference between the face amount and the present value is recorded as a discount and amortized to interest expense over the life of the note. The amount of interest expense for the first year is $33,333 [$100,000 discount ÷ 3 years].

Answer (A) is incorrect because $22,000 results from applying the interest rate to the assessment value of the building. Answer (B) is incorrect because $30,000 is the carrying amount of the note times the 10% interest rate. Answer (D) is incorrect because $40,000 fails to consider the present value of the note.

16. On January 1, year 1, Kaban Company exchanged equipment for a $200,000 noninterest-bearing note due on January 1, year 4. The prevailing rate of interest for a note of this type at January 1, year 1 was 10%. The present value of $1 at 10% for three periods is 0.75. What amount of interest revenue should be included in Kaban's year 2 income statement?

A. $7,500

B. $15,000

C. $16,667

D. $20,000

Answer (C) is correct. *(CPA, adapted)*

REQUIRED: The interest revenue for a noninterest-bearing note in the second year.

DISCUSSION: A noninterest-bearing note should be recorded at its fair value, which is the present value of the future cash flows discounted at the prevailing rate of interest. Kaban Company's note should therefore be recorded at $150,000 ($200,000 × 0.75) on 1/1/year 1. The difference between the future (face) amount and the present value is recorded as a discount and amortized to interest revenue over the life of the note. The amount of interest revenue for year 2 is $16,667 [$50,000 discount ÷ 3 years].

Answer (A) is incorrect because $7,500 is one-half of the carrying amount of the note during year 1 times the 10% interest rate. Answer (B) is incorrect because $15,000 is the carrying amount of the note during year 1 times the 10% interest rate. Answer (D) is incorrect because $20,000 fails to consider the present value of the note.

17. Risoner Company plans to purchase a machine with the following conditions:

- Purchase price = $300,000.
- The down payment = 10% of purchase price with remainder financed at an annual interest rate of 16%.
- The financing period is 8 years with equal annual payments made every year.
- The present value of an annuity of $1 per year for 8 years at 16% is 4.3436.
- The present value of $1 due at the end of 8 years at 16% is .3050.

The annual payment (rounded to the nearest dollar) is

A. $39,150

B. $43,200

C. $62,160

D. $82,350

Answer (C) is correct. *(CIA, adapted)*

REQUIRED: The annual payment (rounded to the nearest dollar).

DISCUSSION: The periodic payment is found by dividing the amount to be accumulated ($300,000 price – $30,000 down payment = $270,000) by the interest factor for the present value of an ordinary annuity for 8 years at 16%. Consequently, the payment is $62,160 ($270,000 ÷ 4.3436).

Answer (A) is incorrect because $39,150 is based on dividing ($270,000 × 1.16) by 8 (years). Answer (B) is incorrect because $43,200 is 16% of $270,000. Answer (D) is incorrect because $82,350 reflects multiplication by the present value of a sum due (.305) instead of dividing by the present value of an annuity (4.3436).

18. On December 30 of the current year, Azrael, Inc. purchased a machine from Abiss Corp. in exchange for a noninterest-bearing note requiring eight payments of $20,000. The first payment was made on December 30, and the others are due annually on December 30. At date of issuance, the prevailing rate of interest for this type of note was 11%. Present value factors are as follows:

Period	Present Value of Ordinary Annuity of $1 at 11%	Present Value of Annuity in Advance of $1 at 11%
7	4.712	5.231
8	5.146	5.712

On Azrael's current year December 31 balance sheet, the note payable to Abiss was

A. $94,240

B. $102,920

C. $104,620

D. $114,240

Answer (A) is correct. *(CPA, adapted)*

REQUIRED: The carrying amount of a noninterest-bearing note payable at the date of issuance.

DISCUSSION: The payment terms of this purchase agreement provide for a $20,000 initial payment and seven equal payments of $20,000 to be received at the end of each of the next 7 years. The note payable, however, should reflect only the present value of the seven future payments. The present value factor to be used is the present value of an ordinary annuity for seven periods at 11%, or 4.712. The note payable should be recorded at $94,240 ($20,000 × 4.712).

Answer (B) is incorrect because $102,920 uses the factor for eight periods rather than seven. Answer (C) is incorrect because the factor for an ordinary annuity should be used. Answer (D) is incorrect because the factor used should be for an ordinary annuity of seven periods, not an annuity in advance for eight periods.

19. Potter Corporation is contemplating the purchase of a new piece of equipment with a purchase price of $500,000. It plans to make a 10% down payment and will receive a loan for 25 years at 10% interest. The present value interest factor for an annuity of $1 per year for 25 years at 10% is 9.0770. The annual payment required on the loan will be

A. $18,000

B. $49,576

C. $45,000

D. $55,084

Answer (B) is correct. *(CIA, adapted)*

REQUIRED: The annual payment required on the loan.

DISCUSSION: The corporation plans a 10% down payment on equipment with a purchase price of $500,000. The amount of the loan will therefore equal $450,000. Because the loan will be financed at 10% for 25 years, the annual payments can be calculated by dividing the amount of the initial loan by the present value interest factor for an annuity of $1 per year for 25 years at 10%. The annual payment required is equal to $49,576 ($450,000 ÷ 9.0770).

Answer (A) is incorrect because $18,000 results from allocating the $450,000 equally over 25 years. Answer (C) is incorrect because $45,000 results from multiplying $450,000 by the 10% interest. Answer (D) is incorrect because $55,084 results if the $50,000 down payment is not removed before the annual payment is calculated.

20. Based on 8% interest compounded annually from day of deposit to day of withdrawal, what is the present value today of $4,000 to be received 6 years from today?

Periods	Present Value of $1 Discounted at 8% per Period
1	.926
2	.857
3	.794
4	.735
5	.681

A. $4,000 × 0.926 × 6.

B. $4,000 × 0.794 × 2.

C. $4,000 × 0.681 × 0.926.

D. Cannot be determined from the information given.

Answer (C) is correct. *(CPA, adapted)*

REQUIRED: The present value today of an amount to be received at a given future date.

DISCUSSION: To calculate the present value of an amount to be received 6 years from today when present value factors for only five periods are available, multiply $4,000 by the present value of $1 factor for five periods. This discounts the $4,000 back 5 years. This new product should then be discounted back one additional year, i.e., multiplied by the present value factor for one period.

Answer (A) is incorrect because the $4,000 should first be discounted for 5 years; then that amount should be discounted for 1 additional year. Answer (B) is incorrect because the $4,000 should first be discounted for 5 years; then that amount should be discounted for 1 additional year. Answer (D) is incorrect because the present value can be determined from the information given.

21. Murray is planning a project that will cost $22,000. The annual cash inflow, net of income taxes, will be $5,000 a year for 7 years. The present value of $1 at 12% is as follows:

Period	Present Value of $1 at 12%
1	.893
2	.797
3	.712
4	.636
5	.567
6	.507
7	.452

Using a rate of return of 12%, what is the present value of the cash flow generated by this project?

A. $22,600

B. $22,820

C. $34,180

D. $35,000

Answer (B) is correct. *(CPA, adapted)*

REQUIRED: The present value of the cash flow generated by the project.

DISCUSSION: If the cash inflow, net of taxes, at the end of each of 7 years is $5,000, and if the discount rate is 12%, the present value of this series of cash flows will be equal to the present value of an ordinary annuity of $5,000 for 7 years at 12%. The interest factor for the present value of an ordinary annuity is equal to the sum of the interest factors for the present value of $1 for the same period. The interest factor for an ordinary annuity of $5,000 for seven periods is 4.564. The present value is $22,820 ($5,000 × 4.564).

The alternative is to calculate the present value of each $5,000 cash flow using the interest factor for the present value of $1 at 12% for each of the periods one through seven. The sum of these products is equal to the present value of an ordinary annuity of $5,000 for seven periods at 12%.

$5,000	×	.893	=	$ 4,465
5,000	×	.797	=	3,985
5,000	×	.712	=	3,560
5,000	×	.636	=	3,180
5,000	×	.567	=	2,835
5,000	×	.507	=	2,535
5,000	×	.452	=	2,260
5,000	×	4.564	=	$22,820

Answer (A) is incorrect because the present value of the cash flow is equal to the annual inflow times the sum of the present value factors. Answer (C) is incorrect because the present value of the cash flow is equal to the annual inflow times the sum of the present value factors. Answer (D) is incorrect because the present value of the cash flow is equal to the annual inflow times the sum of the present value factors.

4.3 Future Value

22. Jarvis wants to invest equal semiannual payments in order to have $10,000 at the end of 20 years. Assuming that Jarvis will earn interest at an annual rate of 6% compounded semiannually, how would the periodic payment be calculated?

A. $10,000 divided by the future amount of an ordinary annuity of 40 payments of $1 each at an interest rate of 3% per period.

B. $10,000 divided by the present value of an ordinary annuity of 40 payments of $1 each at an interest rate of 3% per period.

C. The future amount of an ordinary annuity of 20 payments of $1 each at an interest rate of 6% per period divided into $10,000.

D. The present value of an ordinary annuity of 40 payments of $1 each at an interest rate of 3% per period divided by $10,000.

Answer (A) is correct. *(CPA, adapted)*

REQUIRED: The method of calculating the periodic payment to accumulate a known future amount.

DISCUSSION: The question involves future value because it requires computation of the periodic amount of an annuity that must be invested to produce a given future amount. Accordingly, the appropriate factor reflecting the compound interest effect will be derived from the formula for the future value of an ordinary annuity of $1. This factor multiplied by the periodic payment is equal to the desired future value. If the payment is unknown, it may be calculated by dividing the known future amount ($10,000) by the appropriate factor derived from the future amount of an ordinary annuity formula. If the payments are to be made semiannually for 20 years, 40 compounding periods are involved. If the interest rate is 6% per annum, the semiannual interest rate is 3%.

Answer (B) is incorrect because the question calls for a future value computation. Answer (C) is incorrect because 40 semiannual payments are to be made at an interest rate of 3% per period (not 20 payments at 6%). Answer (D) is incorrect because the question calls for a future value computation.

23. On March 15, year 1, Kathleen Corp. adopted a plan to accumulate $1,000,000 by September 1, year 5. Kathleen plans to make four equal annual deposits to a fund that will earn interest at 10% compounded annually. Kathleen made the first deposit on September 1, year 1. Future value and future amount factors are as follows:

Future value of $1 at 10% for four periods	1.46
Future amount of ordinary annuity of $1 at 10% for four periods	4.64
Future amount of annuity in advance of $1 at 10% for four periods	5.11

Kathleen should make four annual deposits (rounded) of

A. $250,000

B. $215,500

C. $195,700

D. $684,930

Answer (C) is correct. *(CPA, adapted)*

REQUIRED: The amount of an annuity in advance that would generate a future sum.

DISCUSSION: The depositor wishes to have $1,000,000 at the end of a 4-year period (from 9/1/year 1 to 9/1/year 5). The amount will be generated from four equal annual payments (an annuity) to be made starting at the beginning of the 4-year period. The annual payment for this annuity can be calculated in advance by dividing the desired future amount of $1,000,000 by the factor for the future amount of an annuity in advance of $1 at 10% for four periods. Each annual deposit should therefore equal $195,700 ($1,000,000 ÷ 5.11).

Answer (A) is incorrect because $250,000 does not take into account the interest. Answer (B) is incorrect because $215,500 is computed using the future value factor of an ordinary annuity instead of an annuity in advance (annuity due). Answer (D) is incorrect because $684,930 is computed using the future value factor of $1 instead of the future value factor of an annuity in advance.

24. If the amount to be received in 4 years is $137,350, and given the correct factor from the 10% time-value-of-money table below, what is the current investment?

Periods	FVIF	PVIF	FVIF of Ordinary Annuity	PVIF of Ordinary Annuity
1	1.1000	.9091	1.0000	.9091
2	1.2100	.8264	2.1000	1.7355
3	1.3310	.7513	3.3100	2.4869
4	1.4641	.6830	4.6410	3.1699
5	1.6105	.6029	6.1051	3.7908

A. $30,034.33

B. $43,329.44

C. $93,810.05

D. $201,094.14

Answer (C) is correct. *(CIA, adapted)*

REQUIRED: The current investment required to receive a future amount of money at a given interest rate.

DISCUSSION: The current investment is the present value of the given future amount. It equals the future amount multiplied by the factor for the present value of $1 for four periods at 10%. Accordingly, the current investment is $93,810.05 ($137,350 × .6830).

25. A pension fund is projecting the amount necessary today to fund a retiree's pension benefits. The retiree's first annual pension check will be in 10 years. Payments are expected to last for a total of 20 annual payments. Which of the following best describes the computation of the amount needed today to fund the retiree's annuity?

A. Present value of $1 for 10 periods, times the present value of an ordinary annuity of 20 payments, times the annual annuity payment.

B. Present value of $1 for nine periods, times the present value of an ordinary annuity of 20 payments, times the annual annuity payment.

C. Future value of $1 for 10 periods, times the present value of an ordinary annuity of 20 payments, times the annual annuity payment.

D. Future value of $1 for nine periods, times the present value of an ordinary annuity of 20 payments, times the annual annuity payment.

Answer (B) is correct. *(CIA, adapted)*

REQUIRED: The formula to compute the amount needed today to fund a pension that will begin in the future.

DISCUSSION: Multiplying the annual annuity pension payment times the present value of an ordinary annuity of 20 payments factor results in a present value determination 1 year prior to the start of the payments, or 9 years hence. Multiplying the present value of ordinary annuity pension payments by a present value of $1 factor for 9 years results in the amount needed today to fund the retiree's annuity.

26. An actuary has determined that Jaykay Company should have $90,000,000 accumulated in a fund 20 years from now to be able to meet its pension obligations. An interest rate of 8% is considered appropriate for all pension fund calculations involving an interest component. Jaykay wishes to calculate how much it should contribute at the end of each of the next 20 years for the pension fund to have its required balance in 20 years. Which set of instructions correctly describes the procedures necessary to compute the annual amount the company should contribute to the fund?

A. Divide $90,000,000 by the interest factor for the present value of an ordinary annuity for n=20, i=8%.

B. Multiply $90,000,000 by the interest factor for the present value of an ordinary annuity for n=20, i=8%.

C. Divide $90,000,000 by the interest factor for the future value of an ordinary annuity for n=20, i=8%.

D. Multiply $90,000,000 by the interest factor for the future value of an ordinary annuity for n=20, i=8%.

Answer (C) is correct. *(CIA, adapted)*

REQUIRED: The set of instructions that correctly describes the procedures necessary to compute the annual amount the company should contribute to the fund.

DISCUSSION: The future value of an annuity equals the appropriate interest factor (for n periods at an interest rate of i), which is derived from standard tables, times the periodic payment. The $90,000,000 amount is the future value of the funding payments. The amount of each funding payment can be calculated by dividing the future value of the funding payments by the interest factor for future value of an ordinary annuity for n equals 20 and i equals 8%.

Answer (A) is incorrect because the $90,000,000 is a future value figure. The interest factor to be used for the division process should be a future value factor, not a present value factor. Answer (B) is incorrect because the $90,000,000 is a future value figure. The factor to be used should be a future value factor. That factor should be used in a division, rather than a multiplication, process. Answer (D) is incorrect because the $90,000,000 should be divided by the appropriate interest factor.

27. A loan is to be repaid in eight annual installments of $1,875. The interest rate is 10%. The present value of an ordinary annuity for eight periods at 10% is 5.33. Identify the computation that approximates the outstanding loan balance at the end of the first year.

A. $1,875 × 5.33 = $9,994

B. $1,875 × 5.33 = $9,994; $9,994 – $1,875 = $8,119

C. $1,875 × 5.33 = $9,994; $1,875 – $999 = $876; $9,994 – $876 = $9,118

D. $1,875 × 8 = $15,000; $15,000 – ($1,875 – $1,500) = $14,625

Answer (C) is correct. *(CIA, adapted)*

REQUIRED: The computation approximating the outstanding loan balance at the end of year one.

DISCUSSION: If the present value of an ordinary annuity of $1 for eight periods at 10% is 5.33, then the present value for $1,875 is $9,994 (5.33 × $1,875). This figure is the original amount of the loan. If the interest rate is 10%, the interest on the principal for year one will be approximately $999. Accordingly, the first installment will have an interest component of $999 and a principal component of $876 ($1,875 – $999 interest). The first payment will therefore reduce the principal balance of $9,994 by $876 to $9,118.

Answer (A) is incorrect because it gives the present value of the annuity, not the loan balance at the end of year one. Answer (B) is incorrect because it improperly deducts both principal and interest for year one in arriving at the principal balance. Answer (D) is incorrect because it does not take into account the time value of money.

Questions 28 and 29 are based on the following information. Present value, amount of $1, and ordinary annuity information are presented below. All values are for four periods with an interest rate of 8%.

Amount of $1	1.36
Present value of $1	0.74
Amount of an ordinary annuity of $1	4.51
Present value of an ordinary annuity of $1	3.31

28. Cara Galadon decides to create a fund to earn 8% compounded annually that will enable her to withdraw $5,000 per year each June 30, beginning in 2004 and continuing through 2007. Cara wishes to make equal contributions on June 30 of each of the years 2000 through 2003. Which equation would be used to compute the balance that must be in the fund on June 30, 2003 for Cara to meet her objective?

A. $X = $5,000 × 3.31

B. $X = $5,000 × (3.31 + 1.00)

C. $X = $5,000 × 1.36

D. $X = $5,000 × 4.51

Answer (A) is correct. *(CIA, adapted)*

REQUIRED: The equation to compute the balance in the fund on a given date to permit withdrawals at equal intervals over a stated period.

DISCUSSION: The fund balance on 6/30/03 should be equal to the present value of four equal annual payments of $5,000 each discounted at a rate of 8%. If the factor for the present value of an ordinary annuity of $1 for four periods at 8% is 3.31, the present value of an ordinary annuity of $5,000 for four periods discounted at 8% is $5,000 × 3.31.

Answer (B) is incorrect because it gives the present value of an annuity due for five periods. Answer (C) is incorrect because it gives the future value in four periods of $5,000 invested today. Answer (D) is incorrect because it is the future value of an annuity of four annual deposits of $5,000.

29. Pippen wants to accumulate $50,000 by making equal contributions at the end of each of 4 succeeding years. Which equation would be used to compute Pippen's annual contribution to achieve the $50,000 goal at the end of the fourth year?

A. $X = $50,000 ÷ 4.51

B. $X = $50,000 ÷ 4.00

C. $X = $12,500 ÷ 1.36

D. $X = $50,000 ÷ 3.31

Answer (A) is correct. *(CIA, adapted)*

REQUIRED: The equation to compute the annual year-end payment necessary to accumulate a stated amount at the end of a stated period.

DISCUSSION: Use the factor for the amount of an ordinary annuity of $1 for four periods at 8% (4.51). If an investment of $1 at 8% at the end of each of four periods would generate a future amount of 4.51, an investment of $X per period for four periods at 8% would generate the necessary $50,000. The required annual payment is equal to $50,000 ÷ 4.51.

Answer (B) is incorrect because it does not take into account interest to be earned. Answer (C) is incorrect because it gives the present value of $12,500 to be received four periods hence. Answer (D) is incorrect because it gives the amount of the periodic payment needed to produce an ordinary annuity with a present value of $50,000.

STUDY UNIT FIVE
CURRENT ASSETS, CASH, ACCOUNTS RECEIVABLE, AND SHORT-TERM NOTES RECEIVABLE

In its statement of financial position (balance sheet), an enterprise displays its assets, liabilities, and equity at a moment in time. If the balance sheet is classified, assets and liabilities are differentiated as current and noncurrent. **Current assets** include cash and other assets that are reasonably expected to be realized in cash or sold or consumed within 1 year from the balance sheet date or the normal operating cycle, whichever is longer. Current assets commonly include cash; cash equivalents; short-term receivables; prepaid expenses; and certain individual trading, available-for-sale, and held-to-maturity securities. **Current liabilities** include those obligations that are expected to be satisfied by the payment of cash, the use of current assets other than cash, or the creation of new current liabilities within 1 year from the balance sheet date or the normal operating cycle, whichever is longer. **Working capital** is equal to the difference between current assets and current liabilities.

All **cash** balances on hand and on deposit that are readily available for current operating purposes are reported as cash. Restricted cash is reported under a separate caption. Because it is the most liquid, cash usually is the first asset listed on the balance sheet. However, cash and cash equivalents may be reported as a combined amount. **Cash equivalents** are short-term, highly liquid investments that are bought and sold for cash management purposes.

Short-term receivables represent amounts owed to an enterprise that are expected to be collected within 1 year or the operating cycle, whichever is longer. Receivables may be classified as (1) trade receivables, which arise when an enterprise sells goods or services on credit, or (2) nontrade receivables, which primarily arise when an enterprise lends money on a short-term basis. Receivables also may be classified as accounts receivable or notes receivable. **Accounts receivable** ordinarily consist of unwritten promises by credit customers. They normally do not include an interest component unless they become overdue. In contrast, **notes receivable** customarily are formal written agreements that include an interest component.

SFAS 140, *Accounting for Transfers and Servicing of Financial Assets and Extinguishments of Liabilities*, adopts a **financial-components approach** based on control. After a transfer, an entity recognizes the assets it controls and the liabilities it has incurred, derecognizes the assets it no longer controls, and derecognizes extinguished liabilities. For example, a **servicing asset or liability** is normally recognized pursuant to an undertaking to service financial assets. A transfer of financial assets (or a portion of an asset) over which the transferor surrenders control is a **sale** to the extent that the consideration does not consist of a beneficial interest in the transferred assets. The transferor surrenders **control** when (1) the transferred assets are isolated from the transferor and are therefore presumed to be beyond the reach of the transferor and its creditors, even in bankruptcy; (2) neither a regular transferee nor a holder of a beneficial interest in a qualifying special-purpose entity (e.g., certain trusts) is subject to a condition that both constrains its right to pledge or exchange the transferred interests, and provides more than a trivial benefit to the transferor; and (3) the transferor does not maintain effective control over the transferred assets through (a) an agreement entered into concurrently with the transfer that both entitles and obligates the transferor to repurchase or redeem substantially the same assets on substantially the agreed terms before their maturity and at a fixed or determinable price, or (b) the ability to unilaterally cause the holder to return specific assets, except through a cleanup call (e.g., an option held by a servicer to repurchase the transferred assets if they fall to a level at which servicing costs are burdensome relative to benefits). After completing a transfer of financial assets, the transferor allocates the previous carrying amount between the assets sold and the retained interests based on their **fair values** at the transfer date. If a transfer of financial assets qualifies as a sale, the transferor (seller) must (1) derecognize all assets sold; (2) recognize all assets obtained and liabilities incurred in consideration as proceeds; (3) initially measure the assets obtained and liabilities incurred at fair value, if practicable; and (4) recognize any gain or loss in earnings. The transferee initially recognizes assets obtained and liabilities incurred at fair value. When the conditions for surrender of control are met, a **transfer of receivables with recourse** is accounted for as a sale, with the proceeds reduced by the fair value of the recourse obligation. If the transfer does not meet the criteria for a sale, the parties account for the transfer as a **secured borrowing with a pledge** of noncash collateral.

Most short-term receivables are trade accounts receivable, and GAAP require that they be reported at their **net realizable value**, which is most often recorded as the gross accounts receivable offset by an allowance for uncollectible accounts. The allowance account is credited (increased) when bad debt expense is recognized. The allowance is debited (decreased) when a specific account is recognized as being uncollectible. **SFAS 5**, *Accounting for Contingencies*, requires that **bad debt expense** be recognized. For most credit-granting enterprises, it is probable that gross accounts receivable are overstated, and the amounts can be reasonably estimated. GAAP allow two methods for estimating bad debt expense. The income statement approach calculates bad debt expense as a percentage of sales reported on the income statement. An equal amount is credited to the allowance account. The balance sheet approach estimates the balance that should be recorded in the allowance account relative to the gross accounts receivable balance. Bad debt expense is the amount necessary to adjust the allowance.

QUESTIONS

5.1 Current Assets

1. On Geo's April 30, 2003 balance sheet, a note receivable was reported as a noncurrent asset, and its accrued interest for 10 months was reported as a current asset. Which of the following terms would fit Geo's note receivable?

A. Both principal and interest amounts are payable on June 30, 2003 and 2004.

B. Principal and interest are due December 31, 2003.

C. Both principal and interest amounts are payable on December 31, 2003 and 2004.

D. Principal is due June 30, 2004, and interest is due June 30, 2003 and 2004.

Answer (D) is correct. *(CPA, adapted)*

REQUIRED: The terms explaining classification of a note receivable as a noncurrent asset and its accrued interest as a current asset.

DISCUSSION: A noncurrent note receivable is not expected to be converted into cash within 1 year or one operating cycle, whichever is longer. Because the principal is due more than 1 year from the balance sheet date, it must be regarded as noncurrent. However, the accrued interest is a current asset because it is due in 2 months.

2. Grown Company is a leading producer of medicinal herbs. From the time the herbs are planted until the crop is cured and sold, a period of 4 years will have passed. The basis for the segregation of current assets will be

A. Assets that may be immediately realized.

B. Assets that may be realized in cash within 1 year.

C. Assets that are directly used in the production of herbs.

D. Assets that are realized in cash, sold, or consumed during the 4-year period from seeding to sale of the crop.

Answer (D) is correct. *(Publisher)*

REQUIRED: The proper basis for classifying assets as current.

DISCUSSION: ARB 43, Chapter 3A, *Current Assets and Current Liabilities*, defines current assets as those reasonably expected to be realized in cash, sold, or consumed during the operating cycle of the business or within 1 year, whichever is longer. The operating cycle is the time between the acquisition of materials or services and the final cash realization from the earning process. Grown's operating cycle is 4 years, and the assets realized in cash, sold, or consumed during the 4-year period should be categorized as current.

Answer (A) is incorrect because it is not based on the appropriate time period: the longer of 1 year or the operating cycle. Answer (B) is incorrect because it is not based on the appropriate time period: the longer of 1 year or the operating cycle. Answer (C) is incorrect because the 1-year or operating-cycle rule applies to all assets of the enterprise.

3. At October 31, year 1, Dingo, Inc. had cash accounts at three different banks. One account balance is segregated solely for a November 15, year 1 payment into a bond sinking fund. A second account, used for branch operations, is overdrawn. The third account, used for regular corporate operations, has a positive balance. How should these accounts be reported in Dingo's October 31, year 1 classified balance sheet?

A. The segregated account should be reported as a noncurrent asset, the regular account should be reported as a current asset, and the overdraft should be reported as a current liability.

B. The segregated and regular accounts should be reported as current assets, and the overdraft should be reported as a current liability.

C. The segregated account should be reported as a noncurrent asset, and the regular account should be reported as a current asset net of the overdraft.

D. The segregated and regular accounts should be reported as current assets net of the overdraft.

Answer (A) is correct. *(CPA, adapted)*

REQUIRED: The proper reporting of three cash accounts.

DISCUSSION: Current assets include cash available for current operations and items that are the equivalent of cash. Hence, the account used for regular operations is current. Cash that is restricted to use for other than current operations, designated for the acquisition or construction of noncurrent assets, or segregated for the liquidation of long-term debts is noncurrent. "Even though not actually set aside in special accounts, funds that are clearly to be used in the near future for the liquidation of long-term debts, payments to sinking funds, or for other similar purposes should also, under this concept, be excluded from current assets" (ARB 43, Chapter 3A). The overdraft should be treated as a current liability and not netted against the other cash balances. If the company had another account in the same bank with a positive balance, netting would be appropriate because the bank would have a right of offset.

Answer (B) is incorrect because the segregated account is noncurrent. Answer (C) is incorrect because the overdraft should not be netted. Answer (D) is incorrect because the segregated account is noncurrent and the overdraft should not be netted.

4. The following is Azzura Corp.'s June 30, year 1 trial balance:

Cash overdraft		$ 10,000
Accounts receivable, net	$ 35,000	
Inventory	58,000	
Prepaid expenses	12,000	
Land held for resale	100,000	
Property, plant, and equipment, net	95,000	
Accounts payable and accrued expenses		32,000
Common stock		25,000
Additional paid-in capital		150,000
Retained earnings		83,000
	$300,000	$300,000

Additional information:

- Checks amounting to $30,000 were written to vendors and recorded on June 29, year 1, resulting in a cash overdraft of $10,000. The checks were mailed on July 9, year 1.
- Land held for resale was sold for cash on July 15, year 1.
- Gold issued its financial statements on July 31, year 1.

In its June 30, year 1 balance sheet, what amount should Azzura report as current assets?

A. $225,000
B. $205,000
C. $195,000
D. $125,000

Answer (A) is correct. *(CPA, adapted)*
REQUIRED: The amount reported for current assets on the balance sheet.
DISCUSSION: Current assets include cash; inventory; receivables; certain individual trading, held-to-maturity, and available-for-sale securities; and prepaid expenses. Examples of prepaid expenses are insurance, interest, rent, and taxes that are reasonably expected to be realized in cash, sold, or consumed within 1 year, or the normal operating cycle of the business, whichever is longer. Thus, Azzura's current assets include $20,000 of cash ($30,000 of checks mailed in the next period but prematurely recorded – $10,000 overdraft), net accounts receivable ($35,000), inventory ($58,000), prepaid expenses ($12,000), and the land held for resale (treated as a current asset because it was held for immediate sale). The total is $225,000.
Answer (B) is incorrect because $205,000 does not include the $20,000 in cash. Answer (C) is incorrect because $195,000 reflects the $30,000 of checks not mailed at 6/30/year 1. Answer (D) is incorrect because $125,000 does not include the land held for resale, which was realized in cash after the balance sheet date.

5.2 Working Capital

5. A characteristic of all assets and liabilities included in working capital is that they are

A. Cash equivalents.
B. Current.
C. Monetary.
D. Marketable.

Answer (B) is correct. *(CPA, adapted)*
REQUIRED: The characteristic of all assets and liabilities included in working capital.
DISCUSSION: Working capital is defined by ARB 43, Chapter 3A, as the excess of current assets over current liabilities. Working capital identifies the relatively liquid portion of the capital of the enterprise available for meeting obligations within the operating cycle of the firm.
Answer (A) is incorrect because, although assets and liabilities may be any combination of monetary, marketable, or cash equivalents in addition to cash, they must be current to be part of working capital. Answer (C) is incorrect because, although assets and liabilities may be any combination of monetary, marketable, or cash equivalents in addition to cash, they must be current to be part of working capital. Answer (D) is incorrect because, although assets and liabilities may be any combination of monetary, marketable, or cash equivalents in addition to cash, they must be current to be part of working capital.

6. The following transactions occurred during a company's first year of operations:

I. Purchased a delivery van for cash
II. Borrowed money by issuance of short-term debt
III. Purchased treasury stock

Which of the items above caused a change in the amount of working capital?

A. I only.
B. II and III only.
C. I and III only.
D. I, II, and III.

Answer (C) is correct. *(CIA, adapted)*

REQUIRED: The items that caused a change in the amount of working capital.

DISCUSSION: Working capital is computed by deducting total current liabilities from total current assets. The purchase of a delivery van for cash reduces current assets and has no effect on current liabilities. The borrowing of cash by incurring short-term debt increases current assets by the same amount as it increases current liabilities; hence, it will have no effect on working capital. The purchase of treasury stock decreases current assets but has no effect on current liabilities. Thus, the purchases of the van and treasury stock affect working capital.

7. Current liabilities are best defined as those obligations

A. The liquidation of which will require the use of resources properly classifiable as current assets within the next operating cycle or 1 year, whichever is longer.
B. The liquidation of which will require the use of cash or increase current liabilities within the next operating cycle or 1 year, whichever is longer.
C. The liquidation of which is reasonably expected to require the use of current assets or the creation of other current liabilities within the next operating cycle or 1 year, whichever is longer.
D. Involving commitments made within the next operating cycle or 1 year, whichever is longer.

Answer (C) is correct. *(Publisher)*

REQUIRED: The correct description of current liabilities.

DISCUSSION: ARB 43, Chapter 3A, defines current liabilities as obligations the liquidation of which is reasonably expected to require the use of existing resources properly classifiable as current assets or the creation of other current liabilities during the next operating cycle or year, whichever is longer. SFAS 78, *Classification of Obligations That Are Callable by the Creditor*, amends ARB 43 to include as current liabilities (1) obligations that by their terms are or will be due on demand within 1 year (or the operating cycle, if longer) and (2) obligations that are or will be callable by the creditor because of a violation of a debt covenant at the balance sheet date.

Answer (A) is incorrect because liabilities are also current if their liquidation requires creation of other current liabilities. Answer (B) is incorrect because liabilities are current if they are settled with any current assets, not just cash. Answer (D) is incorrect because commitments made during the longer of the next year or the operating cycle may not even be liabilities at the balance sheet date.

8. Which of the following items enter into the determination of working capital?

A. Inventory of finished products that as of the balance sheet date has been held by a manufacturer for 1 year of a 3-year aging cycle.
B. Cash value of life insurance policies pledged as collateral against 90-day bank notes.
C. Cash held by an investment banker to be used to acquire in the open market an additional 25% of a 55%-owned subsidiary.
D. U.S. Treasury bills maturing 60 days after the balance sheet date, the proceeds of which, by direction of the board of directors, will be used to retire long-term debts.

Answer (A) is correct. *(Publisher)*

REQUIRED: The item that is considered part of working capital.

DISCUSSION: Working capital is the excess of current assets over current liabilities. An asset is current if it is reasonably expected to be realized in cash, sold, or consumed during the longer of 1 year or the normal operating cycle of the business. The operating cycle is the average time elapsing between the acquisition of materials or services entering into the earning process and the final cash realization. If a manufacturer's inventory must undergo a 3-year aging process before it can be sold, the inventory should be classified as a current asset because it will be sold during the current operating cycle.

Answer (B) is incorrect because the cash surrender value of life insurance policies is a long-term investment. Answer (C) is incorrect because cash is not a current asset if it is restricted to purchase noncurrent assets. Answer (D) is incorrect because Treasury bills are not current assets if they are restricted to pay long-term debts.

9. A service company's working capital at the beginning of May of the current year was $70,000. The following transactions occurred during May:

Performed services on account	$30,000
Purchased supplies on account	5,000
Consumed supplies	4,000
Purchased office equipment for cash	2,000
Paid short-term bank loan	6,500
Paid salaries	10,000
Accrued salaries	3,500

What is the amount of working capital at the end of May?

A. $80,500

B. $78,500

C. $50,500

D. $47,500

Answer (A) is correct. *(CIA, adapted)*

REQUIRED: The amount of working capital.

DISCUSSION: Working capital is the excess of total current assets (CA) over total current liabilities (CL). Thus, working capital at the end of May equals $80,500 computed as follows:

		CA*	CL*
Beginning working capital	$70,000		
Performed services on account	30,000	I	N
Purchased supplies on account	-0-	I	I
Consumed supplies	(4,000)	D	N
Purchased office equipment	(2,000)	D	N
Paid short-term bank loan	-0-	D	D
Paid salaries	(10,000)	D	N
Accrued salaries	(3,500)	N	I
Working capital, end of January	$80,500		

* N = no effect; I = increase; D = decrease

Answer (B) is incorrect because $78,500 does not include the consumed supplies, the cash purchase of office equipment, and the accrued salaries, and includes the supplies purchased on account and the repayment of the short-term bank loan. Answer (C) is incorrect because $50,500 does not include the services performed on account. Answer (D) is incorrect because $47,500 does not include the services performed on account and accrued salaries and includes the repayment of short-term loan.

10. Griffin Corp. declared a $50,000 cash dividend on May 19, year 1 to shareholders of record on May 30, year 1, payable on June 9, year 1. As a result of this cash dividend, working capital

A. Was not affected.

B. Decreased on June 9.

C. Decreased on May 30.

D. Decreased on May 19.

Answer (D) is correct. *(CPA, adapted)*

REQUIRED: The effect of a cash dividend on working capital.

DISCUSSION: On May 19, the date of declaration, retained earnings is debited and dividends payable credited. The declaration decreases working capital because a current liability is increased.

Answer (A) is incorrect because working capital was decreased on May 19. Answer (B) is incorrect because, when payment is made, both a current liability (dividends payable) and a current asset (cash) are decreased, which has no net effect on working capital. Answer (C) is incorrect because no entry is made on the record date.

11. Comparative balance sheets for a company are presented below:

Assets	12/31/yr 2	12/31/yr 1
Cash	$ 35,000	$ 30,000
Accounts receivable	80,000	75,000
Inventory	230,000	240,000
Equipment	620,000	12,000
Accumulated depreciation	(220,000)	(200,000)
Intangibles	150,000	140,000
Total assets	$895,000	$885,000
Liabilities and equity		
Accounts payable	$ 50,000	$ 60,000
Taxes payable	30,000	25,000
Salaries payable	55,000	70,000
Bonds payable (due year 5)	400,000	400,000
Discount on bonds payable	(4,000)	(5,000)
Common stock	270,000	250,000
Retained earnings	94,000	85,000
Total liabilities and equity	$895,000	$885,000

What is the increase in working capital for the year ended December 31, year 2?

A. $5,000

B. $10,000

C. $20,000

D. $29,000

Answer (C) is correct. *(CIA, adapted)*

REQUIRED: The increase in working capital for the current year.

DISCUSSION: Working capital is the excess of current assets over current liabilities. The change in working capital is equal to the aggregate change in those accounts classified as current assets and current liabilities. Increases in current assets and decreases in current liabilities increase (are sources of) working capital. Decreases in current assets and increases in current liabilities decrease (are uses of) working capital. The change in working capital for the year is presented below:

Working Capital Accounts	Increase (Decrease)
Cash	$ 5,000
Accounts receivable	5,000
Inventory	(10,000)
Accounts payable	10,000
Taxes payable	(5,000)
Salaries payable	15,000
Increase in working capital	$20,000

Answer (A) is incorrect because $5,000 does not include the change in salaries payable. Answer (B) is incorrect because $10,000 is the increase in total assets. Answer (D) is incorrect because $29,000 is the increase in working capital plus the increase in retained earnings.

5.3 Cash

12. Smartchip Corp. has supplied the following list of its bank accounts and cash as of its fiscal year-end of June 30:

Checking account (compensating balance of $12,000 with no restriction)	$ 32,000
Savings account	20,000
Certificate of deposit, 6 months	50,000
Money market (30-day certificate)	25,000
Payroll checking account	2,000
Certificate of deposit, 2 years	50,000
Petty cash	1,000
	$180,000

The amount reported as "cash on hand" as of June 30 should be

A. $55,000

B. $180,000

C. $105,000

D. $75,000

Answer (A) is correct. *(C. Garfinkle)*

REQUIRED: The amount of cash on hand at year-end.

DISCUSSION: The cash account on the balance sheet should include coin and currency on hand, deposits in checking and savings accounts, and near-cash assets such as undeposited checks. To be classified as cash, an asset must be readily available for use by the business; i.e., its use should not be restricted. The money market account and the certificates of deposit are not considered readily available and should be classified as investments. The cash on hand thus equals $55,000 ($32,000 checking + $20,000 savings + $2,000 payroll + $1,000 petty cash). The $12,000 compensating balance is unrestricted and available.

Answer (B) is incorrect because $180,000 includes the money market account and certificates of deposit. Answer (C) is incorrect because $105,000 includes the 6-month certificate of deposit. Answer (D) is incorrect because $75,000 is the sum of the money market account and the 2-year certificate of deposit.

13. The objective of a petty cash system is to

A. Facilitate office payment of small, miscellaneous items.

B. Cash checks for employees.

C. Account for cash sales.

D. Account for all cash receipts and disbursements.

Answer (A) is correct. *(Publisher)*

REQUIRED: The objective of a petty cash system.

DISCUSSION: In an imprest petty cash system, a specific amount of money, e.g., $1,000, is set aside in the care of a petty cash custodian to pay office expenses that are too small to pay by check or to record in the accounting system as they occur. The entry is to debit petty cash and to credit cash. Periodically, the fund is reimbursed for all expenditures based on expense receipts, and journal entries are made to reflect the transactions. However, entries are made to the petty cash account only to establish the fund, to change its amount, or to adjust the balance if it has not been reimbursed at year-end.

Answer (B) is incorrect because, if necessary, a separate check cashing fund should be established with daily bank deposits of checks cashed. Answer (C) is incorrect because petty cash systems are for cash disbursements, not cash sales. Answer (D) is incorrect because petty cash systems are for cash disbursements, not cash receipts.

14. On January 1, a company establishes a petty cash account and designates one employee as petty cash custodian. The original amount included in the petty cash fund is $500, and it will be used to make small cash disbursements. The fund will be replenished on the first of each month, after the petty cash custodian presents receipts for disbursements to the general cashier. The following disbursements are made in January:

Office supplies	$127
Postage	83
Entertainment	84

The balance in the petty cash box at the end of January is $196.

The entry required at the end of January is

A.

Office supplies expense	$127	
Postage expense	83	
Entertainment expense	84	
Cash		$294

B.

Office supplies expense	$127	
Postage expense	83	
Entertainment expense	84	
Petty cash		$294

C.

Office supplies expense	$127	
Postage expense	83	
Entertainment expense	84	
Cash over and short	10	
Cash		$304

D.

Office supplies expense	$127	
Postage expense	83	
Entertainment expense	84	
Cash		$284
Cash over and short		10

Answer (C) is correct. *(CIA, adapted)*

REQUIRED: The entry for petty cash fund disbursements.

DISCUSSION: Each expense item is recognized, cash is credited for the total expenditures plus the cash shortage ($127 + $83 + $84 + $10 = $304), and the discrepancy is debited to the cash over and short account. The discrepancy is the original balance of the fund, minus total documented expenditures, minus the ending balance of the fund ($500 – $294 – $196 = $10).

Answer (A) is incorrect because this entry does not recognize that $10 is missing from the petty cash fund. Answer (B) is incorrect because this entry credits petty cash rather than cash and does not recognize that $10 is missing from the petty cash fund. Answer (D) is incorrect because this entry credits the cash account for the wrong amount ($284 rather than $304) and credits the cash over and short account rather than debiting it.

15. Usually, if the petty cash fund is not reimbursed just prior to year-end and an appropriate adjusting entry is not made,

A. A complete audit is necessary.

B. The petty cash account should be returned to the company cashier.

C. Expenses will be overstated and cash will be understated.

D. Cash will be overstated and expenses understated.

Answer (D) is correct. *(Publisher)*

REQUIRED: The effect of not reimbursing the petty cash fund prior to year-end and not making the appropriate adjusting entry.

DISCUSSION: When the petty cash fund is established, petty cash is debited and cash credited. As monies are expended, expense receipts are obtained. The petty cash fund consists of the cash and expense receipts. Upon reimbursement of the petty cash fund, the various expenses are debited and cash is credited. If the petty cash fund is not reimbursed at year-end and an adjusting entry debiting expenses and crediting cash is not made, the cash account will be overstated and expenses understated because petty cash is a component of the cash account.

Answer (A) is incorrect because complete audits are usually undertaken only if fraud is suspected. Petty cash is ordinarily not material. Answer (B) is incorrect because the petty cash cannot be returned to the cashier. At least some of the cash will usually have been expended. Answer (C) is incorrect because expenses will be understated and cash overstated.

16. Nefertiti Corporation had the following transactions in its first year of operations:

Sales (90% collected in first year)	$1,500,000
Bad debt write-offs	60,000
Disbursements for costs and expenses	1,200,000
Disbursements for income taxes	90,000
Purchases of fixed assets	400,000
Depreciation on fixed assets	80,000
Proceeds from issuance of common stock	500,000
Proceeds from short-term borrowings	100,000
Payments on short-term borrowings	50,000

What is the cash balance at the end of the first year?

A. $150,000

B. $170,000

C. $210,000

D. $280,000

Answer (C) is correct. *(CPA, adapted)*

REQUIRED: The cash balance at year-end.

DISCUSSION: The cash balance may be determined by setting up a T account and appropriately debiting or crediting the account for each of the transactions listed. The beginning balance is $0 for the first year of operations. The sales collections give rise to a debit of $1,350,000 (.9 × $1,500,000). The bad debt write-offs and depreciation on fixed assets are not cash transactions. The disbursements for costs and expenses, taxes, fixed assets, and debt service are all credits. The proceeds from stock and short-term borrowings are debits. At the end of the year, therefore, the account has a debit balance of $210,000.

Cash (in 000s)

Sales	$1,350	Disbursements	$1,200
Stock	500	Taxes	90
Loan	100	FA	400
		Loan	50
	$ 210		

Answer (A) is incorrect because $150,000 results from a credit to the cash account for the bad debt write-offs. Answer (B) is incorrect because $170,000 results from a debit to cash for 100% (instead of 90%) of sales and credits bad debt and depreciation but not the loan payment. Answer (D) is incorrect because $280,000 incorrectly debits cash for 100% of sales for the year and credits cash for depreciation on fixed assets.

17. Bank reconciliations are usually prepared on a monthly basis upon receipt of the bank statement to identify either bank errors or items that need to be adjusted on the depositor's books. The adjustments should be made for

A. Deposits in transit and outstanding checks.

B. All items except deposits in transit, outstanding checks, and bank errors.

C. Deposits in transit, outstanding checks, and bank errors.

D. All items except bank errors, NSF checks, outstanding checks, and deposits in transit.

Answer (B) is correct. *(Publisher)*

REQUIRED: The adjustments made as a result of a bank reconciliation.

DISCUSSION: Deposits in transit and outstanding checks are reconciling items that have no effect on the correctness of either the depositor's or the bank's accounting records. They reflect a timing difference between the two sets of books as to when cash receipts and disbursements are recognized. Thus, they require no adjustment by the bank or the depositor. Bank errors must be corrected by the bank, not the depositor. All other items must be adjusted on the depositor's books.

Answer (A) is incorrect because deposits in transit and outstanding checks do not require adjustment on either the bank's or depositor's books. Answer (C) is incorrect because deposits in transit, outstanding checks, and bank errors do not require adjustment on either the bank's or depositor's books. Answer (D) is incorrect because NSF checks require a debit to a receivable and a credit to cash on the depositor's books.

18. A proof of cash, also known as a four-column bank reconciliation, is

A. A reconciliation of beginning balances, deposits-receipts, checks-disbursements, and ending balances.

B. Bank reconciliations for four selected periods.

C. Reconciliation of beginning balances, receipts, and disbursements, usually for 1 month.

D. Reconciliation of the beginning account balance and the ending account balance, taking into account deposits in transit, outstanding checks, and other reconciling items.

Answer (A) is correct. *(Publisher)*

REQUIRED: The description of a proof of cash.

DISCUSSION: The proof of cash adds a time dimension to a bank reconciliation. Instead of reconciling a balance per bank and a balance per depositor at a given date, the proof of cash reconciles the beginning balance, receipts, disbursements, and the ending balance for a period according to the bank statement with the respective amounts according to the books. The proof of cash actually includes four reconciliations.

Answer (B) is incorrect because a proof of cash contains only two bank reconciliations (for the beginning and ending balances). Answer (C) is incorrect because the ending balance is also reconciled. Answer (D) is incorrect because it describes a bank reconciliation.

19. Puddie Company maintains two checking accounts. A special account is used for the weekly payroll only, and the general account is used for all other disbursements. Every week, a check in the amount of the net payroll is drawn on the general account and deposited in the payroll account. The company maintains a $10,000 minimum balance in the payroll account. On a monthly bank reconciliation, the payroll account should

A. Show a zero balance per the bank statement.

B. Show a $10,000 balance per the bank statement.

C. Reconcile to $10,000.

D. Be reconciled jointly with the general account in a single reconciliation.

Answer (C) is correct. *(CPA, adapted)*

REQUIRED: The true statement concerning the monthly bank reconciliation of the payroll account.

DISCUSSION: Because a minimum balance of $10,000 is maintained, the check drawn on the general account is deposited to the special account before any payroll checks are written. The balance in the special account recorded by the bank, minus any outstanding checks, plus any bank charges not yet recorded on the company's books should equal $10,000.

Answer (A) is incorrect because the balance per bank statement should be equal to $10,000, plus the amount of any outstanding checks, minus any bank charges not recorded in the company's books. Answer (B) is incorrect because the balance per bank statement should be equal to $10,000, plus the amount of any outstanding checks, minus any bank charges not recorded in the company's books. Answer (D) is incorrect because each checking account reflected in the formal accounting system should be separately reconciled with the related bank statement.

20. Piquet Corp.'s checkbook balance on December 31, year 1 was $5,000. In addition, Piquet held the following items in its safe on that date:

Check payable to Piquet Corp., dated January 2, year 2, in payment of a sale made in December year 1, not included in December 31 checkbook balance.	$1,000
Check payable to Piquet Corp., deposited December 15 and included in December 31 checkbook balance, but returned by Bank on December 30 stamped "NSF." The check was redeposited on January 2, year 2 and cleared on January 9.	600
Check drawn on Piquet Corp.'s account, payable to a vendor, dated and recorded in Piquet's books on December 31 but not mailed until January 10, year 2.	700

The proper amount to be shown as cash on Piquet's balance sheet at December 31, year 1 is

A. $5,100

B. $5,700

C. $5,400

D. $6,100

Answer (A) is correct. *(CPA, adapted)*

REQUIRED: The amount to be recorded as cash on the year-end balance sheet.

DISCUSSION: The December 31 checkbook balance is $5,000. The $1,000 check dated 1/2/year 2 is properly not included in this balance because it is not negotiable at year-end. The $600 NSF check should not be included in cash because it is a receivable. The $700 check that was not mailed until January 10 should be added to the balance. This predated check is still within the control of the company and should not decrease the cash account. Consequently, the cash balance to be reported on the 12/31/year 1 balance sheet is $5,100.

Balance per checkbook	$5,000
Add: Predated check	700
Deduct: NSF check	(600)
Cash balance 12/31/year 1	$5,100

Answer (B) is incorrect because $5,700 does not include the deduction for the NSF check. Answer (C) is incorrect because $5,400 includes the postdated check but not the predated check. Answer (D) is incorrect because $6,100 includes the postdated check.

21. The following information is shown in the accounting records of a company:

Balances as of January 1, year 1

Cash	$62,000
Merchandise inventory	86,000
Accounts receivable	67,000
Accounts payable	53,000

Balances as of December 31, year 1

Merchandise inventory	$78,000
Accounts receivable	91,000
Accounts payable	48,000

Total sales and cost of goods sold for year 1 were $798,000 and $583,000, respectively. All sales and all merchandise purchases were made on credit. Various operating expenses of $107,000 were paid in cash. Assume that there were no other pertinent transactions. The cash balance on December 31, year 1 is

A. $108,000

B. $149,000

C. $256,000

D. $305,000

Answer (B) is correct. *(CIA, adapted)*

REQUIRED: The cash balance at year-end.

DISCUSSION: Cash collected from customers equals $774,000 ($798,000 credit sales – $24,000 increase in A/R). The amount of purchases is $575,000 ($583,000 CGS – $8,000 decrease in inventory). Disbursements to suppliers totaled $580,000 ($575,000 Pur. + $5,000 decrease in A/P). The cash collected is added to the beginning balance in the cash account. The disbursements to suppliers and for operating expenses are subtracted to arrive at an ending cash balance of $149,000.

Accounts Receivable

	$ 67,000		
Sales	798,000	Collections	$774,000
	$ 91,000		

Merchandise Inventory

	$ 86,000		
Purchases	575,000	CGS	$583,000
	$ 78,000		

Accounts Payable

			$ 53,000
Disburse.	$580,000	Purchases	575,000
			$ 48,000

Cash

	$ 62,000		
Collections	774,000	Disburse.	$580,000
		Disburse.	107,000
	$149,000		

Answer (A) is incorrect because $108,000 is the excess of total sales over cost of goods sold and operating expenses. Answer (C) is incorrect because $256,000 does not include a credit to cash for the operating expenses. Answer (D) is incorrect because $305,000 appears to be a random number.

22. An organization is reconciling its bank statement with internal records. The cash balance per the bank statement is $20,000, while the cash balance per the organization's books is $18,000. There are $2,000 of bank charges not yet recorded, $3,000 of outstanding checks, $5,000 of deposits in transit, and $6,000 of bank credits and collections not yet recorded in the organization's books. If there are no bank or book errors, what is the organization's actual cash balance?

A. $20,000

B. $22,000

C. $24,000

D. $29,000

Answer (B) is correct. *(CIA, adapted)*

REQUIRED: The cash balance given no bank or book errors.

DISCUSSION: The balance per bank is $20,000, which includes the bank charges, credits, and collections not recorded on the books. Adding deposits in transit and subtracting outstanding checks results in an actual cash balance of $22,000 ($20,000 + $5,000 – $3,000).

Answer (A) is incorrect because $20,000 is the balance per bank. Answer (C) is incorrect because $24,000 equals the balance per bank, plus bank credits and collections, minus bank charges. Answer (D) is incorrect because $29,000 results from adding the deposits in transit to the balance per bank.

23. A company shows a cash balance of $35,000 on its bank statement dated November 1. As of November 1, there are $11,000 of outstanding checks and $7,500 of deposits in transit. The cash balance on the company books as of November 1 is

A. $24,000

B. $31,500

C. $42,500

D. $53,500

Answer (B) is correct. *(CIA, adapted)*

REQUIRED: The cash balance on the company books.

DISCUSSION: The $35,000 cash balance on the November 1 bank statement does not reflect either the $11,000 of outstanding checks or the $7,500 of deposits in transit. Adding the deposits in transit and subtracting the outstanding checks result in a cash balance per books of $31,500 ($35,000 + $7,500 – $11,000).

Answer (A) is incorrect because $24,000 does not include the $7,500 of deposits in transit. Answer (C) is incorrect because $42,500 does not include the $11,000 of outstanding checks. Answer (D) is incorrect because $53,500 results from adding the $11,000 of outstanding checks and the $7,500 of deposits in transit.

24. In preparing its bank reconciliation at December 31, year 1, Rhein Company has available the following data:

Balance per bank statement, 12/31/year 1	$38,075
Deposit in transit, 12/31/year 1	5,200
Outstanding checks, 12/31/year 1	6,750
Amount erroneously credited by bank to Rhein's account, 12/28/year 1	400
Bank service charges for December	75

Rhein's adjusted cash in bank balance at December 31, year 1 is

A. $36,525

B. $36,450

C. $36,125

D. $36,050

Answer (C) is correct. *(CPA, adapted)*

REQUIRED: The adjusted cash in bank balance.

DISCUSSION: The balance per bank statement at December 31 is $38,075. As indicated below, the $5,200 deposit in transit should be added to this amount. The $6,750 in outstanding checks and the $400 that was erroneously credited by the bank to Rhein's account should be deducted. The $75 bank service charges are already included in the December 31 bank statement balance. The adjusted cash in bank balance at December 31 is $36,125.

Balance per statement	$38,075
Add: Deposit in transit	5,200
Deduct: Outstanding checks	(6,750)
Bank error	(400)
Adjusted cash in bank	$36,125

Answer (A) is incorrect because $36,525 does not include the deduction for the bank error. Answer (B) is incorrect because $36,450 does not include the deduction for the bank error and incorrectly includes the bank service charges. Answer (D) is incorrect because $36,050 incorrectly includes the deduction for bank service charges.

5.4 Accounts Receivable

25. Which of the following statements is not valid in determining balance sheet disclosure of accounts receivable?

A. Accounts receivable should be identified on the balance sheet as pledged if they are used as security for a loan even though the loan is shown on the same balance sheet as a liability.

B. That portion of installment accounts receivable from customers coming due more than 12 months from the balance sheet date usually would be excluded from current assets.

C. Allowances may be deducted from the accounts receivable for discounts, returns, and adjustments to be made in the future on accounts shown in the current balance sheet.

D. Trade receivables are best shown separately from nontrade receivables when amounts of each are material.

Answer (B) is correct. *(CPA, adapted)*

REQUIRED: The invalid statement concerning balance sheet disclosure of accounts receivable.

DISCUSSION: Current assets are reasonably expected to be realized in cash or to be sold or consumed within 12 months or the operating cycle of the business, whichever is longer. If the ordinary trade receivables of the business fall due more than 12 months from the balance sheet date, the operating cycle is clearly longer than 12 months, and the trade receivables should be included in current assets.

Answer (A) is incorrect because accounts receivable pledged or used as security for a loan should be presented with relevant information disclosed in a note or in a parenthetical explanation. Answer (C) is incorrect because various allowance or valuation accounts may be set up as contra accounts to receivables to arrive at the net realizable value of receivables in the balance sheet. Allowances may be made for discounts granted to customers, returned merchandise, collection expenses, and uncollectible accounts. Answer (D) is incorrect because, if the different categories of receivables are material in amount, they should be segregated in the balance sheet.

26. On a balance sheet, what is the preferable presentation of notes receivable or accounts receivable from officers, employees, or affiliated companies?

A. As trade notes and accounts receivable if they otherwise qualify as current assets.

B. As assets but separately from other receivables.

C. As offsets to capital.

D. By means of disclosure in the notes.

Answer (B) is correct. *(CPA, adapted)*

REQUIRED: The preferable balance sheet presentation of receivables from officers, employees, or affiliated companies.

DISCUSSION: The basic principle is that, if the different categories of receivables are material in amount, they should be presented separately in the balance sheet. Receivables from officers, employees, or affiliated companies are assets and should be presented in the balance sheet as such. If these receivables are material, they should be segregated from other classifications of receivables. See ARB 43, Chapter 1A, *Rules Adopted by Membership.*

Answer (A) is incorrect because such receivables, if material, should be separately classified even though they qualify as current assets. Answer (C) is incorrect because such receivables are assets and should not be presented in the equity section. Answer (D) is incorrect because such receivables are assets that should be included in the body of the balance sheet. Presentation by note disclosure would understate financial position.

Questions 27 and 28 are based on the following information. A company recorded two sales on March 1 of $20,000 and $30,000 under credit terms of 3/10, n/30. Payment for the $20,000 sale was received March 10. Payment for the $30,000 sale was received on March 25.

---

27. Under the gross method and the net method, net sales in the March income statement should appear as which of the following amounts?

	Gross Method	Net Method
A.	$48,500	$48,500
B.	$48,500	$49,400
C.	$49,400	$48,500
D.	$49,400	$49,400

Answer (C) is correct. *(Publisher)*

REQUIRED: The net sales under the gross and the net methods.

DISCUSSION: The gross method accounts for receivables at their face amount. If a discount is taken, a sales discount is recorded and classified as an offset to sales in the income statement to yield net sales. The expression "3/10, n/30" means that a 3% discount may be taken if payment is made within 10 days of the invoice. The $20,000 payment was received during this period. The $30,000 payment was not. Under the gross method, a $600 sales discount offsets the $50,000 of gross sales to give net sales of $49,400. The net method records receivables net of the applicable discount. If the payment is not received during the discount period, an interest revenue account such as sales discounts forfeited is credited at the end of the discount period or when the payment is received. Consequently, both sales would be recorded net of discount ($48,500), and $900 (3% of $30,000) would be recorded as an interest income item. The gross and net methods have the same income effect. The difference is in how they present items in the income statement.

Answer (A) is incorrect because the gross method net sales of $48,500 includes the $900 discount lost. Answer (B) is incorrect because the net sales amounts should be reversed. Answer (D) is incorrect because the net method records receivables net of all applicable discounts.

28. What are gross sales for the month of March?

	Gross Method	Net Method
A.	$50,000	$50,000
B.	$50,000	$48,500
C.	$49,400	$48,500
D.	$48,500	$50,000

Answer (B) is correct. *(Publisher)*

REQUIRED: The gross sales under the gross and the net methods.

DISCUSSION: The gross method records March sales at the gross amount ($50,000). Because the $20,000 receivable was paid within the discount period, sales discount is debited for $600 at the payment date. The net method records March sales at the net amount ($48,500, or $50,000 minus 3% of $50,000). The $30,000 receivable was not paid within the discount period, and the following entry must also be made:

Accounts receivable	$900	
Sales discounts forfeited		$900

Answer (A) is incorrect because the net method records sales at the net amount. Answer (C) is incorrect because the gross method records sales at the gross amount. Answer (D) is incorrect because the gross sales amounts should be reversed.

29. Lin Co., a distributor of machinery, bought a machine from the manufacturer in November for $10,000. On December 30, Lin sold this machine to Zee Hardware for $15,000 under the following terms: 2% discount if paid within 30 days, 1% discount if paid after 30 days but within 60 days, or payable in full within 90 days if not paid within the discount periods. However, Zee has the right to return this machine to Lin if Zee is unable to resell the machine before expiration of the 90-day payment period, in which case Zee's obligation to Lin is canceled. In Lin's net sales for the year ended December 31, how much should be included for the sale of this machine to Zee?

A. $0

B. $14,700

C. $14,850

D. $15,000

Answer (A) is correct. *(CPA, adapted)*

REQUIRED: The sales revenue to be recognized when a right of return exists.

DISCUSSION: SFAS 48, *Revenue Recognition When Right of Return Exists*, states that the sale may be recognized at the time of sale if all of the following conditions are met:

1. The seller's price is substantially fixed or determinable.
2. The buyer has paid the seller, or the buyer is obligated to pay, and the obligation is not contingent on resale.
3. The buyer's obligation to the seller is unchanged by damage to or theft of or destruction of the product.
4. The buyer has economic substance apart from the seller.
5. The seller does not have any significant obligations regarding resale of the product by the buyer.
6. The amount of future returns can be reasonably estimated.

The buyer has the right to return the machine to the seller, and the obligation to pay is contingent on resale. Thus, the second condition is not met, and no recognition of sales revenue and cost of sales is allowable.

30. Henry Stores, Inc. had sales of $2,000,000 during December. Experience has shown that merchandise equaling 7% of sales will be returned within 30 days and an additional 3% will be returned within 90 days. Returned merchandise is readily resalable. In addition, merchandise equaling 15% of sales will be exchanged for merchandise of equal or greater value. What amount should Henry report for net sales in its income statement for the month of December?

A. $1,800,000

B. $1,700,000

C. $1,560,000

D. $1,500,000

Answer (A) is correct. *(CPA, adapted)*

REQUIRED: The amount of net sales.

DISCUSSION: Net sales equal gross sales minus net returns and allowances. No adjustments are made for anticipated exchanges for merchandise of equal or greater value. Hence, net sales equal $1,800,000 [$2,000,000 – (10% x $2,000,000)].

Answer (B) is incorrect because $1,700,000 equals sales minus 15% of sales. Answer (C) is incorrect because $1,560,000 equals sales, minus 15% of sales, minus 7% of sales. Answer (D) is incorrect because $1,500,000 equals net sales minus 15% of sales.

31. Clarion, Inc. sells to wholesalers on terms of 2/15, net 30. Clarion has no cash sales but 50% of Clarion's customers take advantage of the discount. Clarion uses the gross method of recording sales and trade receivables. An analysis of Clarion's trade receivables balances at December 31, year 1 revealed the following:

Age	Amount	Collectible
0-15 days	$200,000	100%
16-30 days	120,000	95%
31-60 days	10,000	90%
Over 60 days	5,000	$500
	$335,000	

In its December 31, year 1, balance sheet, what amount should Clarion report for allowance for discounts?

A. $2,000

B. $3,240

C. $3,350

D. $4,000

Answer (A) is correct. *(CPA, adapted)*

REQUIRED: The amount to be reported as an allowance for discounts.

DISCUSSION: The allowance for discounts should include an estimate of the expected discount based on the eligible receivables. According to the analysis, receivables equal to $200,000 are still eligible. Based on past experience, 50% of the customers take advantage of the discount. Thus, the allowance should be $2,000 [$200,000 x 50% x 2% (the discount percentage)].

Answer (B) is incorrect because $3,240 assumes that 50% of all collectible amounts are eligible for the discount. Answer (C) is incorrect because $3,350 assumes that 50% of the total gross receivables are eligible for the discount. Answer (D) is incorrect because $4,000 assumes 100% of eligible customers will take the discount.

32. Which of the following is a method to generate cash from accounts receivable?

	Assignment	Factoring
A.	Yes	No
B.	Yes	Yes
C.	No	Yes
D.	No	No

Answer (B) is correct. *(CPA, adapted)*

REQUIRED: The method(s) of generating cash from accounts receivable.

DISCUSSION: Methods of generating cash from accounts receivable include both assignment and factoring. Assignment occurs when specifically named accounts receivable are pledged as collateral for a loan. The accounts receivable remain those of the assignor. However, when cash is collected from these accounts receivable, the cash must be remitted to the assignee. Accounts receivable are factored when they are sold outright to a third party. This sale may be with or without recourse.

Answer (A) is incorrect because factoring is a way to generate cash from accounts receivable. Answer (C) is incorrect because assignment is a way to generate cash from accounts receivable. Answer (D) is incorrect because both assignment and factoring are ways to generate cash from accounts receivable.

33. Monte Company's usual sales terms are net 60 days, FOB shipping point. Sales, net of returns and allowances, totaled $2,300,000 for the year ended December 31, year 1, before year-end adjustment. Additional data are as follows:

- On December 27, year 1, Monte authorized a customer to return, for full credit, goods shipped and billed at $50,000 on December 15, year 1. The returned goods were received by Monte on January 4, year 2, and a $50,000 credit memo was issued on the same date.
- Goods with an invoice amount of $80,000 were billed to a customer on January 3, year 2. The goods were shipped on December 31, year 1.
- On January 5, year 2, a customer notified Monte that goods billed and shipped on December 23, year 1 were lost in transit. The invoice amount was $100,000.

Monte's adjusted net sales for year 1 should be

A. $2,330,000
B. $2,280,000
C. $2,250,000
D. $2,230,000

Answer (A) is correct. *(CPA, adapted)*

REQUIRED: The adjusted net sales for the year.

DISCUSSION: Prior to adjustment, sales net of returns and allowances were $2,300,000. The goods returned ($50,000) should be recorded in the year in which the return was authorized (year 1) rather than the year in which the credit memo was issued (year 2). The $80,000 item billed in January should be added to the December sales because the shipment occurred in December. The company's terms are FOB shipping point, which means title and risk of loss normally pass to the buyer at the time and place of shipment. For this reason, the goods lost in transit are not an adjustment to sales because the buyer held title and bore the risk of loss at the point of shipment. Thus, Monte's adjusted net sales for year 1 should be $2,330,000 ($2,300,000 – $50,000 + $80,000).

Answer (B) is incorrect because $2,280,000 incorrectly deducts the $100,000 of goods lost in transit and does not include the deduction for the returned goods. Answer (C) is incorrect because $2,250,000 does not include the $80,000 item shipped in December. Answer (D) is incorrect because $2,230,000 incorrectly deducts the $100,000 of goods lost in transit and does not deduct the $50,000 of goods returned.

34. On January 1, Davis College assigned $500,000 of accounts receivable to the Scholastic Finance Company. Davis gave a 14% note for $450,000 representing 90% of the assigned accounts and received proceeds of $432,000 after deduction of a 4% fee. On February 1, Davis remitted $80,000 to Scholastic, including interest for 1 month on the unpaid balance. As a result of this $80,000 remittance, accounts receivable assigned and notes payable will be decreased by what amounts?

	A/R Assigned	Notes Payable
A.	$80,000	$74,750
B.	$80,000	$80,000
C.	$72,000	$74,750
D.	$74,750	$80,000

Answer (A) is correct. *(A.G. Helling)*

REQUIRED: The decrease in assigned accounts receivable and notes payable when cash is collected and remitted to the assignor.

DISCUSSION: When assigned accounts receivable are collected, the cash should be remitted to the assignee. The accounts receivable assigned account should be decreased for the amount collected ($80,000), and the note should be decreased by the amount remitted ($80,000) minus interest [$450,000 × 14% × (1 ÷ 12) = $5,250].

Answer (B) is incorrect because notes payable should be decreased by the amount remitted. Answer (C) is incorrect because accounts receivable should be decreased by the amount collected. Answer (D) is incorrect because notes payable should be decreased by the amount remitted, and the accounts receivable should be decreased by the amount collected.

35. In accounting for the transfer of financial assets, which of the following is the approach underlying the accounting prescribed by SFAS 140, *Accounting for Transfers and Servicing of Financial Assets and Extinguishments of Liabilities*?

A. Financial-components approach.

B. The risks-and-rewards approach.

C. Inseparable-unit approach.

D. Linked-presentation approach.

Answer (A) is correct. *(Publisher)*
REQUIRED: The conceptual approach underlying the accounting for transfers of financial assets.
DISCUSSION: SFAS 140, *Accounting for Transfers and Servicing of Financial Assets and Extinguishments of Liabilities*, adopts a financial-components approach based on control. After a transfer, an entity recognizes the financial and servicing assets it controls and the liabilities it has incurred; derecognizes financial assets it no longer controls; derecognizes extinguished liabilities; and, if the transfer qualifies as a sale, recognizes any gain or loss in earnings.
Answer (B) is incorrect because the risks-and-rewards approach was rejected by the FASB. It is consistent with viewing each financial asset as an indivisible unit. Answer (C) is incorrect because the inseparable-unit approach was rejected by the FASB. It is consistent with viewing each financial asset as an indivisible unit. Answer (D) is incorrect because the linked-presentation approach was rejected by the FASB. It is consistent with viewing each financial asset as an indivisible unit.

36. A transfer of financial assets in accordance with SFAS 140, *Accounting for Transfers and Servicing of Financial Assets and Extinguishments of Liabilities*, may be treated as a sale if the transferor surrenders control of the assets. Which of the following is one of the criteria that must be met before control is deemed to be surrendered?

A. The transferred assets are isolated from the transferor and its creditors except in bankruptcy.

B. The transferee cannot pledge or exchange the transferred assets.

C. The transferor is not a party to an agreement that both entitles and obligates it to repurchase or redeem the securities prior to maturity.

D. The consideration received by the transferor consists solely of beneficial interests in the transferred assets.

Answer (C) is correct. *(Publisher)*
REQUIRED: The criterion that must be met before control over transferred financial assets is deemed to be surrendered.
DISCUSSION: A transfer of financial assets (or a portion) over which the transferor relinquishes control is a sale to the extent it receives consideration other than beneficial interests in the assets. The transferor relinquishes control only if (1) the transferred assets are isolated from the transferor and are therefore presumed to be beyond the reach of the transferor and its creditors, even in bankruptcy; (2) neither a regular transferee nor a holder of a beneficial interest in a qualifying SPE (e.g., certain trusts) is subject to a condition that both constrains its right to pledge or exchange the transferred interests and provides more than a trivial benefit to the transferor; and (3) the transferor does not maintain effective control over the transferred assets through (a) an agreement entered into concurrently with the transfer that both entitles and obligates the transferor to repurchase or redeem substantially the same assets on substantially the agreed terms before their maturity and at a fixed or determinable price, or (b) the ability unilaterally to cause the holder to return specific assets, except through a cleanup call.
Answer (A) is incorrect because control is not surrendered if the transferor's creditors can reach the assets in bankruptcy. Answer (B) is incorrect because the transferee is able to pledge or exchange the assets if control is surrendered. Answer (D) is incorrect because the transfer is accounted for as a sale only to the extent consideration other than beneficial interests in the assets is received by the transferor.

37. If a transfer of financial assets meets the criteria for recognition as a sale, the transferor should

A. Account for any gain or loss in other comprehensive income.

B. Initially measure at fair value any assets obtained and liabilities incurred, if practicable.

C. Allocate the previous carrying amount to the assets obtained and liabilities incurred.

D. Recognize liabilities in accordance with SFAS 5, *Accounting for Contingencies*.

Answer (B) is correct. *(Publisher)*
REQUIRED: The accounting for a transfer of financial assets that meets the criteria for recognition as a sale.
DISCUSSION: The transferor should derecognize all assets sold; recognize all assets obtained and liabilities incurred in consideration as proceeds; initially measure at fair value any assets obtained and liabilities incurred, if practicable; and recognize any gain or loss in earnings (SFAS 140).
Answer (A) is incorrect because the transferor should recognize any gain or loss in earnings. Answer (C) is incorrect because fair value accounting should be used, if practicable. Answer (D) is incorrect because, if fair value measurement of assets is not practicable, they are recorded at zero. If fair value measurement of liabilities is not practicable, no gain is recognized, and the liabilities are recorded at the greater of (1) the excess, if any, of (a) the fair value of assets obtained minus the fair value of other liabilities incurred, over (b) the sum of the carrying amounts of the assets transferred, or (2) the amount determined under SFAS 5.

38. Seller Co. transferred loans to Buyer Co. in a transaction appropriately accounted for as a sale and did not retain a servicing interest. The loans had a fair value of $1,650 and a carrying amount of $1,500. Seller also received an option to call (purchase) the same or similar loans from Buyer and undertook to repurchase delinquent loans. Furthermore, the loans had a fixed rate, but Seller agreed to provide Buyer a return at a variable rate. Thus, the transaction effectively included an interest rate swap. The following are the relevant fair values:

Cash received	$1,575
Interest rate swap	60
Recourse obligation	90
Call option	105

Seller should recognize a gain of

A. $45

B. $90

C. $150

D. $240

Answer (C) is correct. *(Publisher)*

REQUIRED: The gain on a sale of financial assets.

DISCUSSION: The gain equals the net proceeds (cash, derivatives, or other assets obtained in a transfer of financial assets, minus liabilities incurred) minus the carrying amount of the assets derecognized. Any asset obtained that is not an interest in the transferred assets is included in the proceeds. Moreover, any derivative obtained concurrently with the transfer of financial assets is an asset obtained (or liability incurred) and is part of the proceeds. Thus, the cash received and the fair values of the interest rate swap and the call option are debited as part of the proceeds. Any liability incurred, even if related to the assets transferred, reduces the proceeds, so the recourse obligation should be credited. After crediting the carrying amount of the loans sold and measuring assets and liabilities at fair value, Seller should recognize a gain on sale (a credit) of $150 ($1,575 cash + $60 interest rate swap + $105 call option – $90 recourse obligation – $1,500 carrying amount).

Answer (A) is incorrect because $45 omits the call option. Answer (B) is incorrect because $90 omits the interest rate swap. Answer (D) is incorrect because $240 omits the recourse obligation.

39. Lender Bank made a large loan to a major borrower and then transferred an undivided interest in this loan to Student Union Bank. The transfer was on a nonrecourse basis, and Lender continued to service the loan. Student Union is not a major competitor of Lender. Lender should account for this transfer as a secured borrowing if the participation agreement

A. Allows Student Union Bank to pledge its participation interest.

B. Does not grant Lender the right of first refusal on the sale of Student Union's participation interest.

C. Does not allow Student Union to sell its participation interest.

D. Prohibits Student Union from selling its participation interest to banks that are direct, major competitors of Lender.

Answer (C) is correct. *(Publisher)*

REQUIRED: The condition under which a loan participation should be accounted for as a secured borrowing.

DISCUSSION: A transfer of financial assets, such as a loan participation agreement, should be accounted for as a sale if the transferor (originating lender) surrenders control over the participation interest transferred to the transferee (participating bank). If control is not surrendered, the transfer should be accounted for as a secured borrowing. Control is not surrendered if the participation agreement constrains the participating bank from pledging or exchanging its participation interest.

Answer (A) is incorrect because the right to exchange or pledge participation interests is consistent with the relinquishment of control. Answer (B) is incorrect because failing to grant Lender the right of first refusal on the sale of Student Union's participation interest is not a constraint on the transferee that permits the transferor to retain control. Indeed, a right of first refusal is not such a constraint. Answer (D) is incorrect because a prohibition on sale to the transferor's competitors is not a constraint on the transferee if other willing buyers exist.

40. Athens Corporation sold an 80% pro rata interest in a $2,000,000 note receivable to Sparta Company for $1,920,000. The note was originally issued at its face amount. Future benefits and costs of servicing the note are immaterial. If the provisions of SFAS 140 are followed, the amount of gain or loss Athens should recognize on this transfer of a partial interest is

A. ($80,000)

B. $0

C. $320,000

D. $400,000

Answer (C) is correct. *(Publisher)*

REQUIRED: The amount of gain or loss to be recognized on a transfer of a partial interest in a loan.

DISCUSSION: The fair value of the note is $2,400,000 ($1,920,000 ÷ 80%). The carrying amount is $2,000,000. Given no servicing asset or liability, Athens should debit cash for $1,920,000, reduce the carrying amount of the note receivable by $1,600,000 ($2,000,000 × 80%), and recognize a gain of $320,000 ($1,920,000 – $1,600,000).

Answer (A) is incorrect because a loss of $80,000 is equal to the $1,920,000 cash received minus the $2,000,000 carrying amount of the note. Answer (B) is incorrect because a gain should be recognized equal to the pro rata (80%) difference between the fair value and the carrying amount of the note. Answer (D) is incorrect because $400,000 is equal to 100% of the difference between the fair value and the carrying amount of the note.

41. On the last day of its fiscal year, Originator Co. transferred long-term loans to Transferee Co. in a transaction appropriately accounted for as a sale and retained a servicing asset. These loans have a 10% yield, a fair value of $220,000 (including servicing), and a carrying amount of $200,000. Originator sold the entire principal and the right to receive interest income at 8% for $198,000. The fee for continuing to service the loans is a portion of the interest income not transferred. The remainder of the interest income not transferred is an interest-only strip receivable. The latter has substantial prepayment risk and is not subject to SFAS 133, *Accounting for Derivative Instruments*. The following are the relevant fair values:

Cash	$198,000
Interest-only strip receivable	13,200
Servicing asset	8,800
	$220,000

Which of the following is an appropriate entry to reflect an aspect of this sale of loan receivables?

A. Interest-only strip $1,200
Other comprehensive income $1,200

B. Cash $198,000
Loss 2,000
Loan receivables $200,000

C. Interest-only strip $13,200
Servicing asset 8,800
Loan receivables $22,000

D. Servicing asset $800
Other comprehensive income $800

Answer (A) is correct. *(Publisher)*

REQUIRED: The proper entry to record an aspect of a sale of receivables given retention of an interest-only strip and a servicing asset.

DISCUSSION: The previous carrying amount should be allocated among the loan receivables sold and the retained interests (the servicing asset and the interest-only strip). The amounts allocated include $180,000 to the loan receivables sold [($198,000 ÷ $220,000) × $200,000], $12,000 to the interest-only strip [($13,200 ÷ $220,000) × $200,000], and $8,000 to the servicing asset [($8,800 ÷ $220,000) × $200,000]. The gain on the sale of the loans is therefore $18,000 ($198,000 cash – $180,000 allocated carrying amount). The interest-only strip and the servicing asset are initially debited as assets for their allocated amounts, with an offsetting credit to loan receivables. Furthermore, the interest-only strip should be adjusted at the balance sheet date (in this case, also the date of the sale) to reflect its fair value. A financial asset subject to a substantial prepayment risk should be measured subsequent to initial recognition in the same way as investments in trading or available-for-sale securities. Given that the interest-only strip is a long-term asset, it should be treated in the same way as an available-for-sale security, that is, by a debit to the asset (or an allowance account) and a credit to other comprehensive income for the amount necessary to reflect the fair value at the balance sheet date ($13,200 – $12,000 = $1,200).

Answer (B) is incorrect because a gain should be recognized. Answer (C) is incorrect because the servicing asset is a retained interest and initially should be recorded at its allocated portion of the carrying amount. It is subsequently measured by amortizing that portion in proportion to, and over the period of, estimated net servicing income. Answer (D) is incorrect because the servicing asset is a retained interest and initially should be recorded at its allocated portion of the carrying amount. It is subsequently measured by amortizing that portion in proportion to, and over the period of, estimated net servicing income.

5.5 Allowance for Uncollectible Accounts and Bad Debt Expense

42. When may an asset valuation allowance, such as the allowance for uncollectible accounts, be shown on the credit side of the balance sheet?

A. Never.

B. When they have to be repaid.

C. In the airline industry.

D. When it exceeds 10% of the accounts receivable balance.

Answer (A) is correct. *(Publisher)*

REQUIRED: The circumstances in which an asset valuation allowance may be shown on the credit side of the balance sheet.

DISCUSSION: APB 12, *Omnibus Opinion - 1967*, states that all allowance accounts must be shown contra to the related asset accounts. Thus, they are never reported as liabilities or elsewhere on the credit side of the balance sheet. They are subtracted from the related assets (or asset groups), with proper disclosure.

Answer (B) is incorrect because valuation accounts are not repaid. Answer (C) is incorrect because there are no industry exceptions for presentation of asset valuation accounts. Answer (D) is incorrect because the materiality of the account does not affect its classification as a contra asset.

43. When the allowance method of recognizing uncollectible accounts is used, the entries at the time of collection of a small account previously written off

A. Increase the allowance for uncollectible accounts.

B. Increase net income.

C. Decrease the allowance for uncollectible accounts.

D. Have no effect on the allowance for uncollectible accounts.

Answer (A) is correct. *(CPA, adapted)*

REQUIRED: The effect of the collection of an account previously written off.

DISCUSSION: When an account receivable is written off, both accounts receivable and the allowance for uncollectible accounts are decreased. When an account previously written off is collected, the account must be reinstated by increasing both accounts receivable and the allowance. Accounts receivable is then decreased by the amount of cash collected.

Answer (B) is incorrect because neither write-off nor reinstatement and collection affects bad debt expense or net income. Answer (C) is incorrect because the allowance is increased. Answer (D) is incorrect because the allowance is increased.

44. A method of estimating uncollectible accounts that emphasizes asset valuation rather than income measurement is the allowance method based on

A. Aging the receivables.

B. Direct write-offs.

C. Gross sales.

D. Credit sales minus returns and allowances.

Answer (A) is correct. *(CPA, adapted)*

REQUIRED: The method of estimating uncollectible accounts that emphasizes asset valuation.

DISCUSSION: Under the allowance method, accounts are estimated in two ways. One method emphasizes asset valuation. The other emphasizes income measurement. The method that emphasizes asset valuation is based on an aging of the receivables to determine the balance in the allowance for uncollectible accounts. Bad debt expense is the amount necessary to adjust the allowance account to this estimated balance. The method emphasizing the income statement recognizes bad debt expense as a percentage of sales. The corresponding credit is to the allowance for uncollectible accounts. Both methods are acceptable under GAAP.

Answer (B) is incorrect because the direct write-off method is not a means of estimation. Answer (C) is incorrect because an estimate based on these figures focuses on the income measurement. Answer (D) is incorrect because an estimate based on these figures focuses on the income measurement.

45. When the allowance method of recognizing uncollectible accounts is used, the entry to record the write-off of a specific account

A. Decreases both accounts receivable and the allowance for uncollectible accounts.

B. Decreases accounts receivable and increases the allowance for uncollectible accounts.

C. Increases the allowance for uncollectible accounts and decreases net income.

D. Decreases both accounts receivable and net income.

Answer (A) is correct. *(CPA, adapted)*

REQUIRED: The effect of the write-off of a specific uncollectible account.

DISCUSSION: The entry to record bad debt expense under the allowance method is to debit bad debt expense and credit the allowance account. When a specific account is then written off, the allowance is debited and accounts receivable credited. Net income is affected when bad debt expense is recognized, not at the time of the write-off. Because accounts receivable and the allowance account are decreased by the same amount, a write-off of an account also has no effect on the net amount of accounts receivable.

Answer (B) is incorrect because the allowance for uncollectible accounts decreases. Answer (C) is incorrect because the allowance for uncollectible accounts decreases, and net income is not affected. Answer (D) is incorrect because net income is not affected.

46. Which method of recording uncollectible accounts expense is consistent with accrual accounting?

	Allowance	Direct Write-Off
A.	Yes	Yes
B.	Yes	No
C.	No	Yes
D.	No	No

Answer (B) is correct. *(CPA, adapted)*

REQUIRED: The method(s) of recording uncollectible accounts expense consistent with accrual accounting.

DISCUSSION: Accrual accounting records the financial effects of transactions and other events and circumstances when they occur, not when their cash effects occur. Thus, the allowance method is consistent with accrual accounting because it recognizes bad debt expense when sales transactions occur, not when a final determination about their cash effects (the extent of uncollectibility) is made. The direct write-off method is not consistent with accrual accounting because recognition of bad debt expense is deferred until a final determination is made about the cash collectible from a particular receivable.

47. Turner Co. estimates its uncollectible accounts expense to be 2% of credit sales. Turner's credit sales for year 1 were $1,000,000. During year 1, Turner wrote off $18,000 of uncollectible accounts. Turner's allowance for uncollectible accounts had a $15,000 balance on January 1, year 1. In its December 31, year 1 income statement, what amount should Turner report as bad debt expense?

A. $23,000

B. $20,000

C. $18,000

D. $17,000

Answer (B) is correct. *(CPA, adapted)*

REQUIRED: The uncollectible accounts expense as a percentage of sales.

DISCUSSION: When bad debt expense is estimated on the basis of net credit sales, a cost (bad debt expense) is being directly associated with a revenue of the period (net credit sales). Thus, uncollectible accounts expense is $20,000 (2% × $1,000,000 credit sales).

Answer (A) is incorrect because $23,000 assumes that $20,000 is the required ending balance in the allowance account (expense = write-offs + the change in the allowance). Answer (C) is incorrect because $18,000 equals the write-offs for year 1. Answer (D) is incorrect because $17,000 is the ending balance in the allowance account.

48. William Co. determined that the net realizable value (NRV) of its accounts receivable at December 31, year 1, based on an aging of the receivables, was $650,000. Additional information is as follows:

Allowance for uncollectible accounts -- 1/1/year 1	$ 60,000
Uncollectible accounts written off during year 1	36,000
Uncollectible accounts recovered during year 1	4,000
Accounts receivable at 12/31/year 1	700,000

What is William's bad debt expense for year 1?

A. $10,000

B. $22,000

C. $30,000

D. $42,000

Answer (B) is correct. *(CPA, adapted)*

REQUIRED: The uncollectible accounts expense.

DISCUSSION: The allowance for uncollectible accounts before year-end adjustment is $28,000 ($60,000 beginning balance – $36,000 write-offs + $4,000 recovered). The balance should be $50,000 ($700,000 year-end A/R – $650,000 NRV based on aging). Thus, the allowance account should be credited and bad debt expense debited for $22,000 ($50,000 desired balance – $28,000).

Answer (A) is incorrect because $10,000 is the difference between gross and net accounts receivable ($50,000) and the balance in the allowance account at the beginning of the year ($60,000). Answer (C) is incorrect because $30,000 equals $50,000 minus the difference between the $60,000 allowance and the $36,000 written off, reduced by the $4,000 recovered. Answer (D) is incorrect because $42,000 equals the $60,000 allowance, plus $36,000 written off, reduced by $4,000 recovered, minus $50,000.

49. The following information relates to Soward Co.'s accounts receivable for year 1:

Accounts receivable, 1/1/year 1	$1,300,000
Credit sales for year 1	2,700,000
Sales returns for year 1	75,000
Accounts written off during year 1	40,000
Collections from customers during year 1	2,150,000
Estimated future sales returns at 12/31/year 1	50,000
Estimated uncollectible accounts at 12/31/year 1	220,000

What amount should Soward report for accounts receivable, before allowances for sales returns and uncollectible accounts, at December 31, year 1?

A. $1,850,000

B. $1,775,000

C. $1,735,000

D. $815,000

Answer (C) is correct. *(CPA, adapted)*

REQUIRED: The year-end balance in accounts receivable.

DISCUSSION: The $1,735,000 ending balance in accounts receivable is equal to the $1,300,000 beginning debit balance, plus debits for $2,700,000 of credit sales, minus credits for $2,150,000 of collections, $40,000 of accounts written off, and $75,000 of sales returns. The $220,000 of estimated uncollectible receivables and the $50,000 of estimated sales returns are not relevant because they affect the allowance accounts but not gross accounts receivable.

Accounts Receivable (in 000s)

1/1/year 1	$1,300	Sales returns	75
Credit sales	2,700	Collections	$2,150
		Write-off	40
	$1,735		

Answer (A) is incorrect because $1,850,000 does not subtract write-offs and sales returns from accounts receivable. Answer (B) is incorrect because $1,775,000 does not subtract write-offs from accounts receivable. Answer (D) is incorrect because estimated future sales returns and uncollectible accounts affect their respective allowance accounts, not gross accounts receivable.

50. The following information pertains to Eire Co.'s accounts receivable at December 31, year 2:

Days Outstanding	Amount	Estimated % Uncollectible
0 - 60	$240,000	1%
61 - 20	180,000	2%
Over 120	200,000	6%
	$620,000	

During year 2, Eire wrote off $14,000 in receivables and recovered $8,000 that was written off in prior years. Its December 31, year 1 allowance for uncollectible accounts was $44,000. Under the aging method, what amount of allowance for uncollectible accounts should Eire report at December 31, year 2?

A. $18,000

B. $20,000

C. $26,000

D. $38,000

Answer (A) is correct. *(CPA, adapted)*

REQUIRED: The allowance for uncollectible accounts under the aging method.

DISCUSSION: The aging schedule determines the allowance for uncollectible accounts based on year-end accounts receivable, their age, and their estimated collectibility. This year-end amount is $18,000 [(1% × $240,000) + (2% × $180,000) + (6% × $200,000)].

Answer (B) is incorrect because $20,000 equals the beginning balance, plus the recovery, minus write-offs, minus the amount determined by the aging schedule ($44,000 + $8,000 – $14,000 – $18,000). Answer (C) is incorrect because $26,000 equals the beginning balance minus the amount determined by the aging schedule ($44,000 – $18,000). Answer (D) is incorrect because $38,000 equals the beginning balance, plus the recovery, minus write-offs ($44,000 + $8,000 – $14,000).

51. An analysis and aging of Hom Company's accounts receivable at December 31, disclosed the following:

Accounts receivable	$850,000
Allowance for uncollectible accounts per books	50,000
Amounts deemed uncollectible	64,000

The net realizable value (NRV) of the accounts receivable at December 31 should be

A. $836,000

B. $800,000

C. $786,000

D. $736,000

Answer (C) is correct. *(CPA, adapted)*

REQUIRED: The NRV of accounts receivable.

DISCUSSION: The NRV of accounts receivable is equal to the $850,000 gross accounts receivable minus the $64,000 estimate of the accounts estimated to be uncollectible. The $50,000 balance in the allowance account is not used because it is an unadjusted balance.

Answer (A) is incorrect because $836,000 is the gross accounts receivable account, minus the amount deemed uncollectible, plus the allowance for uncollectible accounts. Answer (B) is incorrect because $800,000 is the gross accounts receivable account minus the allowance for uncollectible accounts. Answer (D) is incorrect because $736,000 is the gross accounts receivable account minus the allowance for uncollectible accounts and the amount deemed uncollectible.

52. The following accounts were abstracted from Pika Co.'s unadjusted trial balance at December 31:

	Debit	Credit
Accounts receivable	$2,000,000	
Allowance for uncollectible accounts	16,000	
Net credit sales		$6,000,000

Pika estimates that 3% of the gross accounts receivable will become uncollectible. After adjustment at December 31, the allowance for uncollectible accounts should have a credit balance of

A. $180,000

B. $164,000

C. $44,000

D. $60,000

Answer (D) is correct. *(CPA, adapted)*

REQUIRED: The ending balance in the allowance for uncollectible accounts.

DISCUSSION: The allowance for uncollectible accounts at year-end should have a credit balance of $60,000. This amount is equal to the $2,000,000 of accounts receivable multiplied by the 3% that is estimated to become uncollectible.

Answer (A) is incorrect because $180,000 is equal to 3% of net credit sales. Answer (B) is incorrect because $164,000 equals 3% of net credit sales minus the unadjusted balance in the allowance account. Answer (C) is incorrect because $44,000 equals 3% of accounts receivable minus the unadjusted balance in the allowance account.

5.6 Notes Receivable

53. How should unearned discounts, finance charges, and unearned interest included in the face amount of notes receivable be presented in the balance sheet?

A. As a deferred credit.

B. As deductions from the related receivables.

C. In the notes to the financial statements.

D. As a current liability.

Answer (B) is correct. *(Publisher)*

REQUIRED: The proper presentation of unearned discounts, finance charges, and unearned interest.

DISCUSSION: APB 6, *Status of Accounting Research Bulletins,* states that unearned discounts (except for cash discounts, quantity discounts, etc.), finance charges, and unearned interest included in the face amount of notes receivable should be shown as contra items to the face amounts of the related receivables in the balance sheet. Thus, a note receivable should be recorded at its net amount, that is, as a debit for the face amount and a credit for the unearned discount, finance charge, or unearned interest.

Answer (A) is incorrect because APB 6 requires presentation as deductions from the related receivables, not as a deferred credit. Answer (C) is incorrect because APB 6 requires presentation as deductions from the related receivables, not in the notes. Answer (D) is incorrect because APB 6 requires presentation as deductions from the related receivables, not as a current liability.

54. Holder Co. has an 8% note receivable dated June 30, year 1 in the original amount of $300,000. Payments of $100,000 in principal plus accrued interest are due annually on July 1; year 2, year 3, and year 4. In its June 30, year 3 balance sheet, what amount should Holder report as a current asset for interest on the note receivable?

A. $0

B. $8,000

C. $16,000

D. $24,000

Answer (C) is correct. *(CPA, adapted)*

REQUIRED: The amount reported as a current asset for interest on a note receivable.

DISCUSSION: Current assets are those reasonably expected to be realized in cash, sold, or consumed during the longer of the operating cycle of a business or 1 year. Given that the date of the balance sheet is 6/30/year 3, the interest to be paid on the next day, 7/1/year 3, should be classified as a current asset.

Answer (A) is incorrect because $16,000 of interest is reported as a current asset. Answer (B) is incorrect because $8,000 is the interest to be earned in year 4. Answer (D) is incorrect because $24,000 is the interest earned in year 2.

55. On August 15, Benet Co. sold goods for which it received a note bearing the market rate of interest on that date. The 4-month note was dated July 15. Note principal, together with all interest, is due November 15. When the note was recorded on August 15, which of the following accounts increased?

A. Unearned discount.

B. Interest receivable.

C. Prepaid interest.

D. Interest revenue.

Answer (B) is correct. *(CPA, adapted)*

REQUIRED: The account that increased when the note was recorded.

DISCUSSION: Because the note bears interest at a reasonable rate, its present value at the date of issuance is the face amount. Hence, the note should be recorded at this amount. Interest receivable may also be debited and unearned interest revenue credited, although the simple alternative is to debit cash and credit interest revenue when payment is received.

Answer (A) is incorrect because the note bears interest at the market rate. Thus, no discount from its face value is recorded. Answer (C) is incorrect because no prepayment of interest has been made. Answer (D) is incorrect because interest revenue has not yet been earned.

56. A 90-day, 15% interest-bearing note receivable is sold to a bank after being held for 30 days. The proceeds are calculated using an 18% interest rate. The note receivable has been

	Discounted	Pledged
A.	No	Yes
B.	No	No
C.	Yes	No
D.	Yes	Yes

Answer (C) is correct. *(CPA, adapted)*

REQUIRED: The proper description of the sale of a note receivable.

DISCUSSION: A note receivable sold before maturity has been discounted. A pledge is a security transaction in which the collateral to secure a debt is held by the secured party. No security has been given in this case.

Answer (A) is incorrect because the note has been discounted but not pledged. Answer (B) is incorrect because the note has been discounted. Answer (D) is incorrect because the note has not been pledged.

57. On November 1, year 1, Love Co. discounted with recourse at 10% a 1-year, noninterest-bearing, $20,500 note receivable maturing on January 31, year 2. What amount of contingent liability for this note must Love disclose in its financial statements for the year ended December 31, year 1?

A. $0

B. $20,000

C. $20,333

D. $20,500

Answer (D) is correct. *(CPA, adapted)*

REQUIRED: The amount to be disclosed in the financial statements for a contingent liability.

DISCUSSION: When a note receivable is discounted with recourse, the discounting firm is responsible for its full amount ($20,500) if it is not paid. Consequently, this amount should be disclosed in the notes to the financial statements.

Answer (A) is incorrect because a note receivable should disclose the full potential liability. Answer (B) is incorrect because Love may be responsible for the full amount of the note receivable ($20,500). Answer (C) is incorrect because Love may be responsible for the full amount of the note receivable ($20,500).

58. Ayn, Inc. accepted from a customer an $80,000, 90-day, 12% interest-bearing note dated August 31. On September 30, Ayn discounted the note at the Nadir State Bank at 15%. However, the proceeds were not received until October 1. In Ayn's September 30 balance sheet, the amount receivable from the bank, based on a 360-day year, includes accrued interest revenue of

A. $340

B. $400

C. $600

D. $800

Answer (A) is correct. *(CPA, adapted)*

REQUIRED: The accrued interest revenue recognized when a note is discounted.

DISCUSSION: As determined below, the interest received by Ayn if it had held the 90-day note to maturity would have been $2,400. The discount fee charged on a note with a maturity amount of $82,400 ($80,000 face amount + $2,400 interest) discounted at 15% for 60 days is $2,060. The difference of $340 ($2,400 interest – $2,060 discount fee) should be reflected as accrued interest revenue at the balance sheet date because the cash proceeds were not received until the next period.

$80,000 × 12% × 90 ÷ 360 =	$2,400	interest
$82,400 × 15% × 60 ÷ 360 =	(2,060)	discount fee
Accrued interest revenue	$ 340	

Answer (B) is incorrect because the accrued interest revenue is the difference between the interest on the note if held to maturity minus the discounted amount of the note. Answer (C) is incorrect because the accrued interest revenue is the difference between the interest on the note if held to maturity minus the discounted amount of the note. Answer (D) is incorrect because the accrued interest revenue is the difference between the interest on the note if held to maturity minus the discounted amount of the note.

59. Jayne Corp. discounted its own $50,000, 1-year note at a bank, at a discount rate of 12%, when the prime rate was 10%. In reporting the note on Jayne's balance sheet prior to the note's maturity, what rate should Jayne use for the accrual of interest?

A. 10.0%

B. 10.7%

C. 12.0%

D. 13.6%

Answer (D) is correct. *(CPA, adapted)*

REQUIRED: The effective rate of interest on a discounted note.

DISCUSSION: The note had a face amount of $50,000. The proceeds from discounting the note were $44,000 [$50,000 – ($50,000 × .12 × 1 year)]. Thus, Jayne paid $6,000 interest ($50,000 – $44,000) on $44,000 for 1 year. The effective interest rate was thus 13.6% ($6,000 ÷ $44,000).

Answer (A) is incorrect because the rate used for the accrual of interest is the effective interest rate. Answer (B) is incorrect because the rate used for the accrual of interest is the effective interest rate. Answer (C) is incorrect because the rate used for the accrual of interest is the effective interest rate.

60. Halen, Inc. received from a customer a 1-year, $500,000 note bearing annual interest of 8%. After holding the note for 4 months, Halen discounted the note at Regional Bank at an effective interest rate of 10%. What amount of cash did Halen receive from the bank?

A. $540,000

B. $520,667

C. $504,000

D. $486,000

Answer (C) is correct. *(CPA, adapted)*

REQUIRED: The amount of cash received when a note is discounted.

DISCUSSION: The maturity amount of the note is $540,000 [$500,000 face amount + (8% × $500,000)]. The discount fee is $36,000 [10% × $540,000 × (8 ÷12)]. Consequently, the proceeds equal $504,000 ($540,000 – $36,000).

Answer (A) is incorrect because $540,000 is the maturity value. Answer (B) is incorrect because $520,667 assumes a nominal rate of 10% and a discount rate of 8%. Answer (D) is incorrect because $486,000 results from discounting the note for 1 year.

61. On August 1, year 1, Beethoven Corp.'s $500,000 1-year, noninterest-bearing note due July 31, year 2, was discounted at Gray Bank at 10.8%. Beethoven uses the straight-line method of amortizing bond discount. What carrying amount should Beethoven report for notes payable in its December 31, year 1 balance sheet?

A. $500,000

B. $477,500

C. $468,500

D. $446,000

Answer (C) is correct. *(CPA, adapted)*

REQUIRED: The carrying amount reported for notes payable.

DISCUSSION: The discount is $54,000 (10.8% × $500,000). Hence, the carrying amount on August 1 was $446,000. Given straight-line amortization of the discount, the carrying amount at year-end is $468,500 {$500,000 – [$54,000 – ($54,000 × 5/12)]}.

Answer (A) is incorrect because $500,000 is the face amount of the note payable. Answer (B) is incorrect because $477,500 will be the carrying amount after 7 months. Answer (D) is incorrect because $446,000 was the carrying amount on August 1.

62. Sap Co. purchased from Azalea Co. a $20,000, 8%, 5-year note that required five equal annual year-end payments of $5,009. The note was discounted to yield a 9% rate to Sap. At the date of purchase, Sap recorded the note at its present value of $19,485. What should be the total interest revenue earned by Sap over the life of this note?

A. $5,045

B. $5,560

C. $8,000

D. $9,000

Answer (B) is correct. *(CPA, adapted)*

REQUIRED: The total interest revenue earned on a discounted note receivable.

DISCUSSION: Sap Co. will receive cash of $25,045 (5 × $5,009). Hence, interest revenue is $5,560 ($25,045 – $19,485 present value).

Answer (A) is incorrect because $5,045 does not include the discount amortization. Answer (C) is incorrect because $8,000 equals $20,000 times 8% nominal interest for 5 years. Answer (D) is incorrect because $9,000 equals $20,000 times the 9% yield rate for 5 years.

63. Punn Co. has been forced into bankruptcy and liquidated. Unsecured claims will be paid at the rate of $.30 on the dollar. Mega Co. holds a noninterest-bearing note receivable from Punn in the amount of $50,000, collateralized by machinery with a liquidation value of $10,000. The total amount to be realized by Mega on this note receivable is

A. $25,000

B. $22,000

C. $15,000

D. $10,000

Answer (B) is correct. *(CPA, adapted)*

REQUIRED: The amount to be realized from a liquidation claim.

DISCUSSION: The $50,000 note receivable is secured to the extent of $10,000. The remaining $40,000 is unsecured, and Mega will be paid on this claim at the rate of $.30 on the dollar.

Secured claim	$10,000
Unsecured ($40,000 × .3)	12,000
	$22,000

Answer (A) is incorrect because $25,000 equals 30% of the note receivable plus the liquidation value of the collateral [($50,000 × .3) + $10,000]. Answer (C) is incorrect because $15,000 is the amount that would be realized if no collateral had been pledged (.3 × $50,000). Answer (D) is incorrect because $10,000 is the liquidation value of the collateral.

STUDY UNIT SIX
INVENTORY

Inventory is defined as tangible personal property that is held for sale in the ordinary course of business (finished goods), that is in the process of production for such sale (work-in-process), or that is to be consumed in the production of goods or services available for sale (raw materials and supplies). The basic rule is that inventory includes goods to which the enterprise has legal title. The focus of this study unit is on goods held by a merchandising company for sale in the ordinary course of business.

GAAP require that inventory be stated at the **lower of cost or market (LCM)** with certain exceptions that allow inventory to be stated above cost. However, accounting for inventories is primarily based on **cost**, that is, the expenditures and charges necessary to make the inventory salable. Many considerations are involved in determining this acquisition and production cost. Thus, **variable overheads** are allocated based on actual usage of facilities, and **fixed overheads** are allocated based on **normal capacity** (production expected over multiple periods under normal circumstances). When production is **abnormally high**, the per-unit allocation of fixed overhead must be reduced to avoid overstating inventory cost. But if production is **abnormally low**, the allocation to inventoriable cost is not increased. **Unallocated overheads** and abnormal freight, handling costs, spoilage, and similar items are expensed as incurred. **General and administrative expenses** are usually expensed as incurred, and **selling costs** are never inventoried (**SFAS 151**, *Inventory Costs*). The cost of inventory subject to **purchase discounts** may be recorded at either the gross amount or net of the purchase discount.

Inventory costing ordinarily is determined in accordance with certain **cost flow assumptions**. The purpose is not to measure the actual costs of the specific goods that are sold. Instead, the primary purpose of cost flow assumptions is to provide information about the relationship of the cost of goods sold to the sales revenue generated by their sale. The most common cost flow assumptions are that (1) the oldest goods are sold first (first-in, first-out or **FIFO**); (2) the newest goods acquired are sold first (last-in, first-out or **LIFO**); and (3) a mixture of goods are sold (**weighted average** or moving weighted average). The cost flow assumptions may be applied in either a perpetual or a periodic inventory accounting system.

Reporting LCM inventory at market indicates that the utility of the goods has decreased. **Market** is defined as replacement cost subject to a maximum (ceiling) and a minimum (floor). The maximum is net realizable value; the minimum is net realizable value minus normal profit.

Any cost flow method permitted for annual financial statements is permitted for interim financial statements. In addition, GAAP permit use of the **gross profit method** to determine inventory for interim financial statements. The gross profit method also may be appropriate in other accounting applications.

A form of LIFO, **dollar-value LIFO**, often is used to cost inventories consisting of similar (but not identical) items. A primary advantage of this form is that LIFO liquidations are minimized. Dollar-value LIFO costs inventory items in terms of dollars of constant purchasing power rather than in terms of physical units. Two variations of dollar-value LIFO are the double-extension method and the link-chain method.

Retail stores are permitted to use a **retail method** to cost inventories. The most common retail methods are the lower-of-average-cost-or-market method (the conventional retail method) and the dollar-value LIFO retail method.

For certain transactions, a sale of inventory may not be recognized at the time the transaction occurs. According to **SFAS 48**, *Revenue Recognition When a Right to Return Exists*, when a selling company gives the buyer a right of return, a sale of inventory is recognized at the time of sale only if (1) the seller's price is substantially fixed or determinable; (2) the buyer has paid, or is obligated to pay, the seller and the obligation is not contingent on resale by the buyer; (3) the buyer's obligation to the seller is unchanged by damage to, theft of, or destruction of the product; (4) the buyer has economic substance apart from the seller; (5) the seller does not have any significant obligations regarding resale of the product by the buyer; and (6) the amount of future returns can be reasonably estimated. According to **SFAS 49**, *Accounting for Product Financing Arrangements*, when a sponsoring enterprise undertakes to sell a product to another enterprise and to repurchase the product at a price equal to the original price plus holding and financing costs, the transaction is treated as a product financing arrangement (borrowing), not as a sale of inventory.

Under **ARB 43, Chap. 4**, *Inventory Pricing*, a firm commitment to purchase inventory in the future is not recorded at the time of the agreement. However, a loss is accrued when the market price of inventory subject to a firm commitment drops below the commitment price. Losses on firm commitments are measured in the same manner as inventory losses. A **firm commitment** is "an agreement with an unrelated party, binding on both parties and usually legally enforceable." It has certain characteristics. Thus, "The agreement specifies all significant terms, including the quantity to be exchanged, the fixed price, and the timing of the transaction. The fixed price may be expressed as a specified amount of an entity's functional currency or of a foreign currency. It also may be expressed as a specified interest rate or specified effective yield." Furthermore, "the agreement includes a disincentive for nonperformance that is sufficiently large to make performance probable" (SFAS 133).

QUESTIONS

6.1 General Concepts

1. Inventory is defined as those goods held for sale in the ordinary course of business, in the process of production for such sale, and to be consumed in the production of goods or services available for sale. Which item would not be properly classified as inventory?

A. Manufacturing supplies.

B. Raw materials.

C. Office supplies.

D. Work-in-process.

Answer (C) is correct. *(Publisher)*

REQUIRED: The item that is not properly classified as inventory.

DISCUSSION: Office supplies are neither held for sale nor consumed in the production of goods or services available for sale.

Answer (A) is incorrect because manufacturing supplies are consumed in the production of goods and may be classified as inventory. Answer (B) is incorrect because finished goods, raw materials, and work-in-process are the traditional components of inventory of a manufacturing entity. Answer (D) is incorrect because finished goods, raw materials, and work-in-process are the traditional components of inventory of a manufacturing entity.

2. Inventories can be valued using different costing methods. All of the following methods of inventory valuation are acceptable for financial reporting purposes except

A. Dollar-value LIFO method.

B. Full absorption cost method.

C. Weighted-average cost method.

D. Base-stock method.

Answer (D) is correct. *(CMA, adapted)*

REQUIRED: The unacceptable inventory valuation method.

DISCUSSION: The acceptable methods of inventory valuation specified in ARB 43 include FIFO, LIFO, weighted average, retail inventory, and weighted moving average. ARB 43 also requires the use of the absorption method of inventory valuation. The base-stock method is not acceptable under GAAP or for tax purposes. The base-stock method assumes that a minimum amount of inventory is always required. Accordingly, the inventory base or minimum amount is considered a long-term investment to be recorded at its original cost. Last-in, first-out (LIFO) has the same effect if base levels of inventory are not sold.

Answer (A) is incorrect because dollar-value LIFO is an inventory valuation method acceptable for financial reporting purposes under GAAP. Answer (B) is incorrect because full absorption cost is an inventory valuation method acceptable for financial reporting purposes under GAAP. Answer (C) is incorrect because weighted-average cost is an inventory valuation method acceptable for financial reporting purposes under GAAP.

3. According to the net method, which of the following items should be included in the cost of inventory?

	Freight Costs	Purchase Discounts Not Taken
A.	Yes	No
B.	Yes	Yes
C.	No	Yes
D.	No	No

Answer (A) is correct. *(CPA, adapted)*

REQUIRED: The items that should be included as inventoriable cost.

DISCUSSION: ARB 43, Chap. 4, *Inventory Pricing*, states that cost is "the sum of the applicable expenditures and charges directly or indirectly incurred in bringing an article to its existing condition and location." Freight costs (but not abnormal amounts) are therefore an inventoriable cost. Under the net method, purchase discounts are treated as reductions in the invoice prices of specific purchases. Accordingly, goods available for sale reflect the purchase price net of the discount, and a purchase discount not taken is recognized as an item of interest expense.

Answer (B) is incorrect because, under the net method, purchase discounts not taken are an interest expense. Answer (C) is incorrect because freight costs are part of inventory costs, but purchase discounts not taken under the net method are not inventory costs. Answer (D) is incorrect because freight costs are included in the cost of inventory.

4. In pricing inventory, cost may be determined under any one of several assumptions as to the flow of cost factors. The major objective in selecting a method should be to choose the one that, under the circumstances, most clearly reflects the

A. Current value of the inventory.

B. Periodic income.

C. Future utility of the inventory.

D. Conservative accounting assumption.

Answer (B) is correct. *(Publisher)*

REQUIRED: The principal reason for choosing from among the various inventory cost flow assumptions.

DISCUSSION: ARB 43, Chap. 4, *Inventory Pricing*, states that the inventory cost flow method used by a firm should be the one that most clearly reflects periodic income. Periodic income is best reflected when costs are recognized in the same period as the related revenues.

Answer (A) is incorrect because, although it is an objective of inventory pricing, the major objective is to reflect income clearly. Answer (C) is incorrect because, although it is an objective of inventory pricing, the major objective is to reflect income clearly. Answer (D) is incorrect because, although it is an objective of inventory pricing, the major objective is to reflect income clearly.

5. All of the following should be disclosed when reporting inventories except

A. The use of the lower of cost or market method, if applicable.

B. Classifications of inventory items.

C. The method(s) used for determining the cost.

D. An estimated amount of obsolete inventory included in the total inventory valuation.

Answer (D) is correct. *(CMA, adapted)*

REQUIRED: The item not a required disclosure.

DISCUSSION: ARB 43 states that the basis of stating inventories (e.g., lower of cost or market) must be disclosed. If a significant change is made in that basis, required disclosures are the nature of the change and any material effect on income. ARB 43 also requires disclosure of inventories stated above cost and accrued net losses on firm purchase commitments. Moreover, APB 22 states that disclosures required regarding accounting policies include those relating to inventory pricing and composition (classification) of inventories.

Answer (A) is incorrect because disclosures should include the use of the LCM method. Answer (B) is incorrect because disclosures should include the use of classifications based on the types of inventory items. Answer (C) is incorrect because disclosures should include the methods used for determining inventory cost.

6. The following information applied to Atlas Co. for the current year:

Merchandise purchased for resale	$800,000
Freight-in	20,000
Freight-out	10,000
Purchase returns	4,000

The company's current-year inventoriable cost was

A. $800,000

B. $806,000

C. $816,000

D. $826,000

Answer (C) is correct. *(CPA, adapted)*

REQUIRED: The amount of inventoriable cost.

DISCUSSION: Inventoriable cost is the sum of the applicable expenditures and charges directly or indirectly incurred in bringing all items of inventory to their existing condition and location. Thus, inventoriable cost includes the $800,000 cost of the merchandise purchased, plus the $20,000 of freight-in, minus the $4,000 of purchase returns. Freight-out is not a cost incurred in bringing the inventory to a salable condition. The inventoriable cost for Atlas during the current year is $816,000 ($800,000 + $20,000 – $4,000).

Answer (A) is incorrect because $800,000 is the amount of gross purchases. Answer (B) is incorrect because $806,000 incorrectly includes freight-out as a cost instead of freight-in. Answer (D) is incorrect because $826,000 incorrectly includes freight-out.

7. The following costs were incurred by Parthos Co., a manufacturer, during the current year:

Accounting and legal fees	$ 50,000
Freight-in	350,000
Freight-out	320,000
Officers' salaries	300,000
Insurance	170,000
Sales representatives' salaries	430,000

What amount of these costs should be reported as general and administrative expenses for the current year?

A. $520,000

B. $1,100,000

C. $1,270,000

D. $1,620,000

Answer (A) is correct. *(CPA, adapted)*

REQUIRED: The amount to be reported as general and administrative expenses for the year.

DISCUSSION: General and administrative expenses are incurred for the direction of the enterprise as a whole and are not related wholly to a specific function, e.g., selling or manufacturing. They include accounting, legal, and other fees for professional services; officers' salaries; insurance; wages of office staff; miscellaneous supplies; utilities' costs; and office occupancy costs. Thus, the general and administrative expenses for Parthos equaled $520,000 ($50,000 + $300,000 + $170,000).

Answer (B) is incorrect because $1,100,000 does not include insurance and incorrectly includes the sales representatives' salaries and freight-out (selling costs). Answer (C) is incorrect because freight-out costs and sales representatives' salaries are included. Answer (D) is incorrect because freight costs and sales representatives' salaries are not considered general and administrative costs.

8. Aramis Co.'s inventory at December 31, year 1 was $1,500,000 based on a physical count priced at cost and before any necessary adjustment for the following:

- Merchandise costing $90,000, shipped FOB shipping point from a vendor on December 30, year 1, was received and recorded on January 5, year 2.
- Goods in the shipping area were excluded from inventory although shipment was not made until January 4, year 2. The goods, billed to the customer FOB shipping point on December 30, year 1, had a cost of $120,000.

What amount should Aramis report as inventory in its December 31, year 1 balance sheet?

A. $1,500,000

B. $1,590,000

C. $1,620,000

D. $1,710,000

Answer (D) is correct. *(CPA, adapted)*

REQUIRED: The year-end inventory.

DISCUSSION: The inventory balance prior to adjustments was $1,500,000. The merchandise shipped FOB shipping point to Aramis should be included because title passed when the goods were shipped. The goods in the shipping area should be included because title did not pass until the goods were shipped on January 4, year 2, even though the customer was billed in year 1. Thus, the inventory should be $1,710,000 ($1,500,000 + $90,000 + $120,000).

Answer (A) is incorrect because $1,500,000 excludes the $90,000 of goods shipped by a vendor and the $120,000 of goods not shipped until January 4. Answer (B) is incorrect because $1,590,000 results from failing to include the $120,000 of goods not shipped until January 4. Answer (C) is incorrect because $1,620,000 does not include the $90,000 of goods shipped by a vendor FOB shipping point.

9. On July 1, Clio Company recorded purchases of inventory of $40,000 and $50,000 under credit terms of 2/15, net 30. The payment due on the $40,000 purchase was remitted on July 14. The payment due on the $50,000 purchase was remitted on July 25. Under the net method and the gross method, these purchases should be included at what respective net amounts in the determination of cost of goods available for sale?

	Net Method	Gross Method
A.	$90,000	$90,000
B.	$89,200	$88,200
C.	$88,200	$89,200
D.	$88,200	$88,200

Answer (C) is correct. *(Publisher)*

REQUIRED: The amounts at which net purchases should be valued under the net and gross methods.

DISCUSSION: The 2/15, net 30 credit phrase indicates that a 2% discount may be taken if payment is made within 15 days of the invoice date and that payment is overdue if not made within 30 days.

Under the net method, purchases are recorded net of any discount. Purchase discounts not taken are reflected as an expense in purchase discounts lost. The $90,000 in purchases should be recorded net of the 2% discount at $88,200 ($39,200 + $49,000) to determine cost of goods available for sale.

Under the gross method, purchases are recorded at their gross amount and offset by a purchase discounts account for discounts taken. Net purchases included in the determination of cost of goods available for sale are equal to the gross purchase amount of $90,000 less the $800 ($40,000 × 2%) discount taken. Net purchases equal $89,200 under the gross method.

10. In theory, the cash discounts allowed on purchased merchandise (purchase discounts) in a periodic inventory system should be

A. Deducted from purchases in determination of goods available for sale.

B. Deducted from cost of goods sold in the income statement.

C. Shown as other income in an income statement.

D. Deducted from inventory on the balance sheet at year-end.

Answer (A) is correct. *(D.G. Kame)*

REQUIRED: The theoretically correct treatment of cash discounts earned on the purchase of merchandise.

DISCUSSION: In theory, cash discounts on purchases should be treated as reductions in the invoiced prices of specific purchases so that goods available for sale reflects the purchase price net of the discounts. It is consistent with this approach to record any purchase discounts not taken as a financial expense in the income statement.

Answer (B) is incorrect because the purchase discounts should be reflected in goods available for sale, which is allocated to either cost of goods sold or ending inventory. Answer (C) is incorrect because the purchase discounts should be reflected in goods available for sale, which is allocated to either cost of goods sold or ending inventory. Answer (D) is incorrect because the purchase discounts should be reflected in goods available for sale, which is allocated to either cost of goods sold or ending inventory.

11. Le Sud Retailers purchased merchandise with a list price of $20,000, subject to trade discounts of 20% and 10%, with no cash discounts allowable. Le Sud should record the cost of this merchandise as

A. $14,000

B. $14,400

C. $15,600

D. $20,000

Answer (B) is correct. *(CPA, adapted)*

REQUIRED: The amount to be recorded as cost of inventory subject to trade discounts.

DISCUSSION: When inventory is subject to cash discounts, the purchases may be reflected either net of these discounts or at the gross prices. However, purchases should always be recorded net of trade discounts. A chain discount is the application of more than one trade discount to a list price. Chain discounts should be applied in steps as indicated below.

List price	$20,000
20% discount	(4,000)
	$16,000
10% discount	(1,600)
Cost of merchandise	$14,400

Answer (A) is incorrect because $14,000 applies both discounts to the retail price. Answer (C) is incorrect because $15,600 assumes the 10% discount is applied to the 20% discount. Answer (D) is incorrect because $20,000 is the list price, and it fails to reflect the discounts.

12. On June 1, Halle Corp. sold merchandise with a list price of $5,000 to Bonn on account. Halle allowed trade discounts of 30% and 20%. Credit terms were 2/15, n/40, and the sale was made FOB shipping point. Halle prepaid $200 of delivery costs for Bonn as an accommodation. On June 12, Halle received from Bonn a remittance in full payment amounting to

A. $2,744

B. $2,940

C. $2,944

D. $3,140

Answer (C) is correct. *(CPA, adapted)*

REQUIRED: The amount received as a remittance in full payment.

DISCUSSION: Inventory sold should always be invoiced net of trade discounts. Remittances paid during the cash or purchase discount period should be net of these discounts. When goods are shipped FOB shipping point, they become the purchaser's inventory at the time of shipment. Thus, the purchaser is responsible for the payment of delivery costs. As indicated below, the remittance received by Halle should amount to $2,944.

List price	$5,000
30% trade discount	(1,500)
	$3,500
20% trade discount	(700)
	$2,800
2% cash discount	(56)
	$2,744
Delivery costs	200
	$2,944

Answer (A) is incorrect because $2,744 excludes the delivery costs. Answer (B) is incorrect because $2,940 includes a 2% cash discount on the delivery costs. Answer (D) is incorrect because $3,140 includes a 2% discount on the delivery costs and double counts the delivery costs.

13. On December 28, Nord Manufacturing Co. purchased goods costing $50,000. The terms were FOB destination. Some costs incurred in connection with the sale and delivery of the goods were

Packaging for shipment	$1,000
Shipping	1,500
Special handling charges	2,000

These goods were received on December 31. In Nord's December 31 balance sheet, what amount of cost should be included in inventory?

A. $54,500

B. $53,500

C. $52,000

D. $50,000

Answer (D) is correct. *(CPA, adapted)*

REQUIRED: The amount of cost for goods included in inventory.

DISCUSSION: FOB destination means that title passes upon delivery at the destination, the seller bears the risk of loss, and the seller is responsible for the expense of delivering the goods to the designated point. Consequently, the costs incurred for sale and delivery (packaging, shipping, and handling costs) rather than to make the inventory salable are not included in the inventory. The amount that should be included is therefore the purchase price of $50,000.

Answer (A) is incorrect because the packaging, shipping, and handling costs should not be included. Answer (B) is incorrect because the shipping and handling costs should not be included. Answer (C) is incorrect because the handling costs should not be included.

14. Inventory may properly be stated above cost

A. When its market value or its net realizable value exceeds its cost.

B. When cost is determined under the first-in, first-out method.

C. When cost is determined under the last-in, first-out method.

D. Only in exceptional cases.

Answer (D) is correct. *(CMA, adapted)*

REQUIRED: The justification for stating inventory above cost.

DISCUSSION: ARB 43, Chap. 4, *Inventory Pricing,* states that only in exceptional cases may inventories be stated above cost. Examples are precious metals that have a fixed monetary value with no additional cost of marketing, and fungible (interchangeable) agricultural, mineral, and other products that have an immediate marketability at quoted prices and for which it may be difficult to obtain appropriate costs.

Answer (A) is incorrect because inventory may be stated at market value or net realizable value (sales price – costs of completion and disposal) when these amounts are less (not more) than cost in accordance with the lower of cost or market rule. Answer (B) is incorrect because FIFO is based on cost flow assumptions. It reflects cost, not amounts above cost. Answer (C) is incorrect because LIFO is based on cost flow assumptions. It reflects cost, not amounts above cost.

15. The following information pertains to Hague Corp.'s year 2 cost of goods sold:

Inventory, 12/31/year 1	$180,000
Year 2 purchases	248,000
Year 2 write-off of obsolete inventory	68,000
Inventory, 12/31/year 2	60,000

The inventory written off became obsolete because of an unexpected and unusual technological advance by a competitor. In its year 2 income statement, what amount should Hague report as cost of goods sold?

A. $436,000

B. $368,000

C. $300,000

D. $248,000

Answer (C) is correct. *(CPA, adapted)*

REQUIRED: The cost of goods sold for the year.

DISCUSSION: As indicated in the T-account analysis below, cost of goods sold equals purchases plus any decrease in inventory or minus any increase in inventory (purchases minus the change in inventory). The write-off of obsolete inventory is a loss, not a component of CGS. Thus, cost of goods sold is $300,000.

Inventory			
12/31/01	$180,000	Obsolescence	$68,000
Purchases	248,000	CGS	300,000
	$ 60,000		

Answer (A) is incorrect because $436,000 results from adding obsolete inventory to, not subtracting it from, beginning inventory. Answer (B) is incorrect because $368,000 includes the obsolete inventory in CGS. Answer (D) is incorrect because $248,000 equals purchases.

16. Madrid Corp.'s trial balance for the year ended December 31, year 1 included the following:

	Debit	Credit
Sales		$600,000
Cost of sales	$240,000	
Administrative expenses	60,000	
Loss on sale of equipment	36,000	
Sales commissions	40,000	
Interest revenue		20,000
Freight-out	12,000	
Loss on early retirement of long-term debt	40,000	
Bad debt expense	12,000	
Totals	$440,000	$620,000

Other information:

Finished goods inventory:	
January 1, year 1	$400,000
December 31, year 1	360,000

In Madrid's year 1 multiple-step income statement, the cost of goods manufactured was

A. $200,000

B. $212,000

C. $280,000

D. $292,000

Answer (A) is correct. *(CPA, adapted)*

REQUIRED: The cost of goods manufactured.

DISCUSSION: Cost of goods sold equals beginning finished goods inventory, plus cost of goods manufactured, minus ending finished goods inventory. Rearranging this equation, we get cost of goods manufactured equals cost of goods sold, plus ending finished goods inventory, minus beginning finished goods inventory, or $200,000 ($240,000 cost of goods sold + $360,000 ending finished goods inventory – $400,000 beginning finished goods inventory).

Answer (B) is incorrect because $212,000 includes the freight-out. Answer (C) is incorrect because $280,000 subtracts ending finished goods and adds beginning finished goods. Answer (D) is incorrect because $292,000 subtracts ending finished goods inventory and adds beginning finished goods. It also includes the freight-out.

17. When a company sells its products and gives the buyer the right to return the product, revenue from the sale should be recognized at the time of sale only if certain criteria are met. According to SFAS 48, *Revenue Recognition When Right of Return Exists*, which one of the following is not a criterion?

A. The seller does not have significant obligations for future performance to directly bring about the resale of the product by the buyer.

B. The buyer acquiring the product for resale has economic substance apart from that provided by the seller.

C. The buyer's obligation to the seller would not be changed in the event of physical destruction of the product.

D. The seller's price to the buyer is contingent upon the ultimate selling price received when the product is resold.

Answer (D) is correct. *(CMA, adapted)*

REQUIRED: The item not a criterion for the recognition of a sale when the right of return exists.

DISCUSSION: SFAS 48 states that revenue may be recognized at the time of sale if all of the following conditions are met:

1. The seller's price is substantially fixed or determinable.
2. The buyer has paid the seller, or the buyer is obligated to pay, and the obligation is not contingent on resale.
3. The buyer's obligation to the seller is unchanged by damage to or theft of or destruction of the product.
4. The buyer has economic substance apart from the seller.
5. The seller does not have any significant obligations regarding resale of the product by the buyer.
6. The amount of future returns can be reasonably estimated.

Thus, the seller's price must not be contingent on the resale price; the seller's price must be substantially fixed or determinable.

Answer (A) is incorrect because the seller may not have significant future obligations. Answer (B) is incorrect because the buyer must have economic substance apart from the seller. Answer (C) is incorrect because risk of loss must reside with the buyer.

18. Lew Co. sold 200,000 corrugated boxes for $2 each. Lew's cost was $1 per unit. The sales agreement gave the customer the right to return up to 60% of the boxes within the first six months, provided an appropriate reason was given. It was reasonably estimated that 5% of the boxes would be returned. Lew absorbed an additional $10,000 to process the returns and expects to resell the boxes. What amount should Lew report as operating profit from this transaction?

A. $170,000

B. $179,500

C. $180,000

D. $200,000

Answer (C) is correct. *(CPA, adapted)*

REQUIRED: The amount reported as operating profit.

DISCUSSION: SFAS 48, *Revenue Recognition When Right of Return Exists*, states that the sale may be recognized at the time of sale if all of the following conditions are met:

1. The seller's price is substantially fixed or determinable.
2. The buyer has paid the seller, or the buyer is obligated to pay, and the obligation is not contingent on resale.
3. The buyer's obligation to the seller is unchanged by damage to, or theft or destruction of, the product.
4. The buyer has economic substance apart from the seller.
5. The seller does not have any significant obligations regarding resale of the product by the buyer.
6. The amount of future returns can be reasonably estimated.

Assuming that these six conditions are met, Lew Co.'s revenues were $400,000 (200,000 boxes × $2), cost of goods sold was $200,000 (200,000 boxes × $1), and gross profit was $200,000 ($400,000 – $200,000). Cost of goods sold equals cost of goods manufactured (or purchases for a retailer) adjusted for the change in finished goods inventory. Because a reasonable estimate of returns could be made, Lew subtracts a 5% allowance (5% × $200,000) to arrive at operating profit. Lew will also incur an additional $10,000 to process the returns. Thus, operating profit is $180,000 ($200,000 gross profit – $10,000 additional processing cost – $10,000 allowance for returns).

Answer (A) is incorrect because $170,000 results from subtracting the cost of the returned boxes twice. Answer (B) is incorrect because $179,500 results from an additional subtraction for 5% of the $10,000 processing cost. Answer (D) is incorrect because $200,000 is the gross profit.

19. Application rates for fixed production overheads best reflect anticipated fluctuations in production over a cycle of years when they are computed under the concept of

A. Maximum capacity.

B. Normal capacity.

C. Practical capacity.

D. Expected actual capacity.

Answer (B) is correct. *(CPA, adapted)*

REQUIRED: The concept of capacity for best applying overheads over a cycle of years.

DISCUSSION: Normal capacity is the production level that will approximate demand over a period of years that includes seasonal, cyclical, and trend variations. Deviations in one year will be offset in other years. Moreover, normal capacity is expected to be achieved under normal circumstances, including loss of capacity because of planned maintenance. Consequently, GAAP require allocation of fixed production overheads to conversion cost based on normal capacity (SFAS 151, *Inventory Costs*).

Answer (A) is incorrect because maximum (theoretical or ideal) capacity is the level at which output is maximized assuming perfectly efficient operations at all times. This level is impossible to maintain and results in underapplied overheads. Answer (C) is incorrect because practical capacity is the maximum level at which output is produced efficiently. It usually also results in underapplied overheads. Answer (D) is incorrect because expected actual capacity is a short-run output level. It minimizes under- or overapplied overheads but does not provide a consistent basis for assigning overhead cost. Per-unit overheads will fluctuate because of short-term changes in the expected production level.

6.2 Cost Flow Assumptions: FIFO, LIFO, Weighted Average

20. The weighted average for the year inventory cost flow method is applicable to which of the following inventory systems?

	Periodic	Perpetual
A.	Yes	Yes
B.	Yes	No
C.	No	Yes
D.	No	No

Answer (B) is correct. *(CPA, adapted)*

REQUIRED: The applicability of the weighted-average cost flow method to periodic and perpetual inventory systems.

DISCUSSION: The weighted-average method determines an average cost only once (at the end of the period) and is therefore applicable only to a periodic system. In contrast, the weighted moving average method requires determination of a new weighted-average cost after each purchase and thus applies only to a perpetual system.

21. The LIFO inventory cost flow method may be applied to which of the following inventory systems?

	Periodic	Perpetual
A.	No	No
B.	No	Yes
C.	Yes	Yes
D.	Yes	No

Answer (C) is correct. *(CPA, adapted)*

REQUIRED: The applicability of LIFO to periodic and perpetual inventory systems.

DISCUSSION: In a periodic system, a purchases account is used, and the beginning inventory remains unchanged during the accounting period. Cost of goods sold is determined at year-end. It is the difference between the goods available for sale (beginning inventory + purchases) and ending inventory.

In a perpetual system, purchases are directly recorded in the inventory account. Cost of goods sold is determined as the goods are sold. LIFO may be applied to both a periodic and a perpetual system, but the amount of cost of goods sold may vary with the system chosen.

22. The cost of materials has risen steadily over the year. Which of the following methods of estimating the ending balance of the materials inventory account will result in the highest net income, assuming all other variables remain constant?

A. Last-in, first-out (LIFO).

B. First-in, first-out (FIFO).

C. Weighted average.

D. Specific identification.

Answer (B) is correct. *(CIA, adapted)*

REQUIRED: The inventory flow assumption yielding the highest net income given rising prices.

DISCUSSION: Net income will be higher when cost of goods sold is lower, other factors held constant. Cost of goods sold equals beginning inventory, plus purchases, minus ending inventory. Accordingly, cost of goods sold will be lowest when the ending inventory is highest. Ending inventory is highest under FIFO because the older, less expensive items are deemed to have been sold, leaving the more expensive items in the ending inventory.

Answer (A) is incorrect because LIFO yields the lowest net income. Answer (C) is incorrect because weighted average averages inventory, so it results in a lower net income than FIFO. Answer (D) is incorrect because, under specific identification, the newest (most expensive) items are sold first, resulting in a higher cost of goods sold and lower income.

23. The operations of a firm may be viewed as a continual series of transactions or as a series of separate ventures. The inventory valuation method that views a firm as a series of separate ventures is

A. First-in, first-out.

B. Last-in, first-out.

C. Weighted average.

D. Specific identification.

Answer (D) is correct. *(CMA, adapted)*

REQUIRED: The inventory valuation method that views a firm as a series of separate ventures.

DISCUSSION: When specific inventory is clearly identified from the time of purchase through the time of sale and is costed on that basis, the firm's operations may be viewed as a series of separate ventures or transactions. Much business activity, however, involves goods whose identity is lost between the time of acquisition and the time of sale. Moreover, if items of inventory are interchangeable, the use of specific identification may not result in the most useful financial information. For these reasons, other inventory cost flow assumptions essentially view the firm as a continual series of transactions.

Answer (A) is incorrect because FIFO views the firm's activities as a continual series of transactions. Answer (B) is incorrect because LIFO views the firm's activities as a continual series of transactions. Answer (C) is incorrect because weighted average views the firm's activities as a continual series of transactions.

Questions 24 through 28 are based on the following information. Toulouse Co. began the month of November with 150 baubles on hand at a cost of $4.00 each. These baubles sell for $7.00 each. The following schedule presents the sales and purchases of this item during the month of November.

	Purchases		
Date of Transaction	Quantity Received	Unit Cost	Units Sold
November 5			100
November 7	200	$4.20	
November 9			150
November 11	200	4.40	
November 17			220
November 22	250	4.80	
November 29			100

24. If Toulouse uses FIFO inventory pricing, the value of the inventory on November 30 would be

A. $936

B. $1,012

C. $1,046

D. $1,104

Answer (D) is correct. *(CMA, adapted)*

REQUIRED: The value of the ending inventory using the FIFO method of inventory costing.

DISCUSSION: Under FIFO, the ending inventory consists of the most recent inventory purchased. The beginning inventory included 150 units and purchases totaled 650 units, a total of 800 units. Sales equaled 570 units (100 + 150 + 220 + 100). Thus, ending inventory was 230 units (800 – 570). Under FIFO, these units are valued at the cost of the most recent 230 units purchased, or $4.80. Ending inventory is therefore $1,104 (230 × $4.80).

Answer (A) is incorrect because $936 is based on periodic LIFO. Answer (B) is incorrect because $1,012 is based on the weighted-average unit cost of $4.40, not $4.80. Answer (C) is incorrect because $1,046 is the ending inventory under perpetual LIFO.

25. If Toulouse uses perpetual moving-average inventory pricing, the sale of 220 items on November 17 will be recorded at a unit cost of

A. $4.00

B. $4.16

C. $4.20

D. $4.32

Answer (D) is correct. *(CMA, adapted)*

REQUIRED: The unit cost of the items sold on November 17 under the perpetual moving-average method.

DISCUSSION: The beginning inventory consisted of 150 units at $4.00 each. Following the November 5 sale, the inventory valuation was $200 (50 units × $4). The November 7 purchase added 200 units at $4.20, after which the moving average unit cost was $4.16 {[$200 + (200 units × $4.20)] ÷ (50 units + 200 units)}. The November 9 sale of 150 units left 100 units at $4.16. Adding $416 (100 units × $4.16) to the $880 purchase on November 11 brought the total inventory to 300 units with a total cost of $1,296, or $4.32 each. Thus, $4.32 was the unit cost of items sold on November 17.

Answer (A) is incorrect because $4.00 was the cost of the beginning inventory. Answer (B) is incorrect because $4.16 was the unit cost of the items sold on November 9. Answer (C) is incorrect because $4.20 would have been the cost if the perpetual LIFO method had been used for the November 9 sale.

26. If Toulouse uses weighted-average inventory pricing, the gross profit for November will be

A. $1,046

B. $1,482

C. $1,516

D. $1,528

Answer (B) is correct. *(CMA, adapted)*

REQUIRED: The gross profit if the weighted-average method is used.

DISCUSSION: The value of the total goods available for sale is determined as follows:

Beginning inventory	150	×	$4.00	=	$ 600.00
Nov. 7 purchase	200	×	$4.20	=	840.00
Nov. 11 purchase	200	×	$4.40	=	880.00
Nov. 22 purchase	250	×	$4.80	=	1,200.00
Total available	800				$3,520.00

The weighted-average unit cost is $4.40 ($3,520 ÷ 800 units available). The cost of goods sold and total sales are therefore $2,508 ($4.40 × 570 units sold) and $3,990 ($7 × 570 units), respectively. Consequently, gross profit is $1,482 ($3,990 – $2,508).

Answer (A) is incorrect because $1,046 is the ending inventory under perpetual LIFO. Answer (C) is incorrect because $1,516 is based on perpetual LIFO. Answer (D) is incorrect because $1,528 is based on the moving-average method.

27. Refer to the information on page 128. If Toulouse uses periodic LIFO inventory pricing, the cost of goods sold for November will be

A. $2,416

B. $2,444

C. $2,474

D. $2,584

Answer (D) is correct. *(CMA, adapted)*

REQUIRED: The cost of goods sold using periodic LIFO.

DISCUSSION: The value of the goods available for sale is as follows:

Beginning inventory	150 × $4.00 =	$ 600.00
Nov. 7 purchase	200 × $4.20 =	840.00
Nov. 11 purchase	200 × $4.40 =	880.00
Nov. 22 purchase	250 × $4.80 =	1,200.00
Total available	800	$3,520.00

The ending inventory consists of 230 units. Under periodic LIFO, these are costed at the prices paid for the earliest 230 units purchased, or 150 units at $4.00 and 80 units at $4.20, a total of $936. Hence, cost of goods sold is $2,584 ($3,520 goods available – $936 EI).

Answer (A) is incorrect because $2,416 is based on the FIFO method. Answer (B) is incorrect because $2,444 is based on the moving-average method. Answer (C) is incorrect because $2,474 is based on perpetual LIFO.

28. Refer to the information on page 128. If Toulouse uses perpetual LIFO inventory pricing, the value of the inventory at November 30 will be

A. $936

B. $1,012

C. $1,046

D. $1,076

Answer (C) is correct. *(CMA, adapted)*

REQUIRED: The value of the inventory.

DISCUSSION: Under perpetual LIFO, the inventory valuation is recalculated as follows after every purchase and sale. The 230 units in ending inventory consist of 150 units at $4.80 each, 30 units at $4.20 each, and 50 units from the beginning inventory at $4.00 each.

Date	Receipts	Sales	Ending Inventory
11-1	150 @ $4.00 = $600		$ 600.00
11-5		100 @ $4.00 = $400	200.00
11-7	200 @ $4.20 = $840		1,040.00
11-9		150 @ $4.20 = $630	410.00
11-11	200 @ $4.40 = $880		1,290.00
11-17		200 @ $4.40 = $880 20 @ $4.20 = $84	326.00
11-22	250 @ $4.80 = $1,200		1,526.00
11-29		100 @ $4.80 = $480	1,046.00

Answer (A) is incorrect because $936 is based on periodic LIFO. Answer (B) is incorrect because $1,012 is based on the weighted-average method. Answer (D) is incorrect because $1,076 is based on the moving-average method.

29. During periods of inflation, a perpetual inventory system will result in the same dollar amount of ending inventory as a periodic inventory system under which of the following inventory valuation methods?

	FIFO	LIFO
A.	Yes	No
B.	Yes	Yes
C.	No	Yes
D.	No	No

Answer (A) is correct. *(CPA, adapted)*

REQUIRED: The effect of perpetual and periodic inventory systems on the dollar amount of ending inventory.

DISCUSSION: In periods of inflation, a perpetual inventory system will result in the same dollar amount of ending inventory as a periodic inventory system assuming a FIFO cost flow. Under both perpetual and periodic systems, the same units are deemed to be in ending inventory. During periods of inflation, a perpetual inventory system will generate a dollar amount different from that of a periodic inventory system assuming a LIFO inventory cost flow. These two methods assume that different units are in the LIFO ending inventory. The periodic system determines the cost of sales only at year-end, but the perpetual system determines cost of sales as the sales take place. Thus, the perpetual system assumes that layers of inventory may be liquidated during a year even though inventory quantities are restored by later purchases. The periodic system does not make this assumption.

Answer (B) is incorrect because LIFO periodic and LIFO perpetual inventory valuation methods result in different ending inventory amounts. They assume that different units are in ending inventory. Answer (C) is incorrect because LIFO periodic and LIFO perpetual inventory valuation methods result in different ending inventory amounts. They assume that different units are in ending inventory. FIFO perpetual and FIFO periodic methods assume that the same units are in ending inventory. Answer (D) is incorrect because FIFO periodic and FIFO perpetual inventory valuation methods assume that the same units are in ending inventory, resulting in the same ending inventory amount.

30. A company had 2,000 units of opening inventory that cost $20 per unit. On May 1, 2,000 units were purchased at a cost of $22 each, and on September 1, another 2,000 units were purchased at a cost of $24 each. If 4,000 units were sold during the year, the company will report cost of goods sold of <List A> if the <List B> method of inventory valuation is used.

	List A	List B
A.	$88,000	LIFO
B.	$92,000	Weighted average
C.	$84,000	FIFO
D.	$88,000	FIFO

Answer (C) is correct. *(CIA, adapted)*

REQUIRED: The proper match of cost of goods sold and inventory valuation method.

DISCUSSION: Under FIFO, the first items purchased are presumed to be the first sold. If 6,000 units were available and 4,000 units were sold, FIFO cost of goods sold equals $84,000 [(2,000 × $20) BI + (2,000 × $22) May 1 purchase].

Answer (A) is incorrect because cost of goods sold is $88,000 under the weighted-average method. Under LIFO, cost of goods sold is $92,000 ($48,000 + $44,000). The 2,000 most recently purchased units are presumed to have been sold. Answer (B) is incorrect because the weighted-average unit cost of all items available for sale is $22 [($40,000 + $44,000 + $48,000) ÷ 6,000]. Given that 4,000 units were sold, cost of goods sold is $88,000 (4,000 × $22) under this method. Answer (D) is incorrect because FIFO cost of goods sold is $84,000. Under the weighted-average method, cost of goods sold is $88,000.

31. Ordinarily, which inventory costing method approximates most closely the current cost for each of the following?

	Cost of Goods Sold	Ending Inventory
A.	LIFO	FIFO
B.	LIFO	LIFO
C.	FIFO	FIFO
D.	FIFO	LIFO

Answer (A) is correct. *(CPA, adapted)*

REQUIRED: The appropriate inventory costing method.

DISCUSSION: The LIFO basis assumes that the most recently purchased items are the first to be sold. Thus, LIFO is a better approximation of current cost of goods sold than FIFO. According to SFAS 89, if "turnover is rapid and material amounts of depreciation are not allocated to inventory, cost of goods sold measured on a LIFO basis may provide an acceptable approximation of cost of goods sold, measured at current cost, provided that the effect of any LIFO inventory liquidations (that is, decreases in earlier years' LIFO layers) is excluded." However, the FIFO basis more closely approximates the current cost of ending inventory because it assumes the most recent purchases are the last to be sold.

32. In a periodic inventory system that uses the weighted-average cost flow method, the beginning inventory is the

A. Net purchases minus the ending inventory.

B. Net purchases minus the cost of goods sold.

C. Total goods available for sale minus the net purchases.

D. Total goods available for sale minus the cost of goods sold.

Answer (C) is correct. *(CPA, adapted)*

REQUIRED: The beginning inventory in a periodic system using weighted-average cost.

DISCUSSION: In a periodic system, beginning inventory is equal to the total goods available for sale minus net purchases, regardless of the cost flow method used.

Answer (A) is incorrect because it states the difference between the beginning inventory and the cost of goods sold. Answer (B) is incorrect because this difference is the change in inventory valuation during the period. Answer (D) is incorrect because goods available minus cost of sales equals ending inventory.

33. The acquisition cost of a heavily used raw material changes frequently. The carrying amount of the inventory of this material at year-end will be the same if perpetual records are kept as it would be under a periodic inventory method only if the carrying amount is computed under the

A. Weighted-average method.

B. First-in, first-out method.

C. Last-in, first-out method.

D. Base-stock method.

Answer (B) is correct. *(CPA, adapted)*

REQUIRED: The cost flow assumption giving the same year-end carrying amount under both perpetual and periodic inventory systems.

DISCUSSION: Under FIFO, the oldest goods are assumed to have been sold first, and it would not matter whether the cost of goods sold was determined at the point of sale (perpetual) or at year-end (periodic).

Answer (A) is incorrect because, under this method, different goods are assumed to be sold if the determination is made at the time of sale (perpetual) rather than at year-end (periodic). Answer (C) is incorrect because, under this method, different goods are assumed to be sold if the determination is made at the time of sale (perpetual) rather than at year-end (periodic). Answer (D) is incorrect because, under this method, different goods are assumed to be sold if the determination is made at the time of sale (perpetual) rather than at year-end (periodic).

34. Which of the following factors would not be considered in the selection of LIFO as an inventory costing method?

A. Tax benefits.

B. Matching.

C. Physical flow.

D. Improved cash flow.

Answer (C) is correct. *(Publisher)*

REQUIRED: The factor that would not be considered.

DISCUSSION: Inventory costing methods are based on cost flow assumptions, not physical flow assumptions. If a LIFO physical flow were actually followed, the first goods purchased might never be sold. In most cases, they would deteriorate from damage, obsolescence, etc.

Answer (A) is incorrect because tax benefits do arise from LIFO. Less taxable income is reported in periods of rising prices. Answer (B) is incorrect because LIFO permits the matching of current costs (the most recent inventory purchases) with current revenues. Answer (D) is incorrect because the tax benefits arising from LIFO in periods of rising prices improve cash flow relative to FIFO.

35. Munich Co. uses the average-cost inventory method for internal reporting purposes and LIFO for financial statement and income tax reporting. At December 31, the inventory was $750,000 using average cost and $640,000 using LIFO. The unadjusted credit balance in the LIFO reserve account on the same date was $70,000. What adjusting entry should Munich record to adjust from average cost to LIFO at December 31?

	Cost of Goods Sold	Debit	Credit
A.	Cost of goods sold	$110,000	
	Inventory		$110,000
B.	Cost of goods sold	$110,000	
	LIFO reserve		$110,000
C.	Cost of goods sold	$40,000	
	Inventory		$40,000
D.	Cost of goods sold	$40,000	
	LIFO reserve		$40,000

Answer (D) is correct. *(CPA, adapted)*

REQUIRED: The journal entry to adjust from average cost to LIFO.

DISCUSSION: The LIFO reserve account is an allowance that adjusts the inventory balance stated according to the method used for internal reporting purposes to the LIFO amount appropriate for external reporting. If the LIFO effect is $110,000 ($750,000 average cost – $640,000 LIFO cost) and the account has a $70,000 credit balance, it must be credited for $40,000, with a corresponding debit to cost of goods sold.

Answer (A) is incorrect because the balance in the reserve account should equal $110,000, and inventory should not be adjusted. Answer (B) is incorrect because the balance in the reserve account should be $110,000. Answer (C) is incorrect because inventory should not be adjusted.

36. Which of the following is not valid as it applies to inventory costing methods?

A. If inventory quantities are to be maintained, part of the earnings must be invested (plowed back) in inventories when FIFO is used during a period of rising prices.

B. LIFO tends to smooth out the net income pattern because it matches current cost of goods sold with current revenue, if inventories remain at constant quantities.

C. When a firm using the LIFO method fails to maintain its usual inventory position (reduces stock on hand below customary levels), there may be a matching of old costs with current revenue.

D. FIFO, but not LIFO, permits some control by management over the amount of net income for a period through controlled purchases.

Answer (D) is correct. *(CPA, adapted)*

REQUIRED: The invalid statement concerning inventory valuation.

DISCUSSION: Under LIFO, the most recent purchases are included in cost of goods sold. Management could affect net income with an end-of-period purchase that would immediately alter cost of goods sold. A last-minute FIFO purchase included in the ending inventory would have no such effect.

Answer (A) is incorrect because maintenance of inventory quantities results in an increased dollar investment in inventory when FIFO is used during inflationary times. Answer (B) is incorrect because LIFO smooths income in a period of rising prices. The inflated current costs are matched with current sales prices. Answer (C) is incorrect because LIFO results in matching old, lower costs with current revenues when inventory is liquidated. If sales exceed purchases, a firm liquidates earlier, lower-priced LIFO layers.

37. The Poirot Company began operations on January 1 of the year before last and uses the FIFO method in costing its raw material inventory. Management is contemplating a change to the LIFO method and is interested in determining what effect such a change will have on net income. Accordingly, the following information has been developed:

Final Inventory	Year 1	Year 2
FIFO	$240,000	$270,000
LIFO	200,000	210,000
Net Income (per FIFO)	$120,000	$170,000

Based upon the above information, a change to the LIFO method in Year 2 would result in net income for Year 2 of

A. $110,000

B. $150,000

C. $170,000

D. $230,000

Answer (A) is correct. *(CPA, adapted)*

REQUIRED: The second-year net income after a change from FIFO to LIFO in the second year of operations.

DISCUSSION: In the first year of operations, beginning inventory is the same under FIFO and LIFO. The amount of purchases in any year is also the same. The difference in the first year was that FIFO ending inventory was $40,000 greater ($240,000 FIFO – $200,000 LIFO). Thus, FIFO net income was also $40,000 greater. The difference in income in the second year is equal to the $20,000 difference between the FIFO inventory change and the LIFO inventory change (FIFO: $270,000 – $240,000 = $30,000 change; LIFO: $210,000 – $200,000 = $10,000 change; $30,000 – $10,000 = $20,000 difference). Because a change from FIFO to LIFO will be treated as a cumulative effect-type accounting change, the $170,000 FIFO net income will decrease by $60,000 ($40,000 cumulative effect on beginning retained earnings + $20,000). Net LIFO income will therefore be $110,000 ($170,000 – $60,000). In some cases, the cumulative effect on beginning retained earnings of a change from FIFO to LIFO may not be included in the calculation of net income. The reason is that the cumulative effect may not be determinable (APB 20, *Accounting Changes*). For Poirot, however, this concern does not arise.

Answer (B) is incorrect because $150,000 incorrectly adds the difference from Year 1 to the net income under LIFO for Year 2. Answer (C) is incorrect because $170,000 is the income for Year 2 under FIFO. Answer (D) is incorrect because $230,000 incorrectly adds the difference between LIFO and FIFO to FIFO net income, instead of subtracting the difference from FIFO net income.

6.3 Lower of Cost or Market

38. Which of the following statement(s) is(are) true when a company applying the lower-of-cost-or-market method reports its inventory at replacement cost?

I. The original cost is less than replacement cost.

II. The net realizable value is equal to or greater than replacement cost.

A. I only.

B. II only.

C. Both I and II.

D. Neither I nor II.

Answer (B) is correct. *(CPA, adapted)*

REQUIRED: The value of inventory under the lower-of-cost-or-market rule.

DISCUSSION: ARB 43, Chap. 4, *Inventory Pricing*, defines market as current replacement cost subject to maximum and minimum values. The maximum is net realizable value; the minimum is net realizable value minus normal profit. When replacement cost is within this range, it is used as the market value. Consequently, only statement II is correct.

Answer (A) is incorrect because replacement cost must be lower than original cost. Answer (C) is incorrect because replacement cost must be lower than original cost. Answer (D) is incorrect because replacement cost must not exceed net realizable value.

39. The lower-of-cost-or-market (LCM) rule for inventories may be applied to total inventory, to major categories of inventory, or to each item. Which application usually results in the lowest inventory amount?

A. All applications result in the same amount.

B. Total inventory.

C. Groups of similar items.

D. Separately to each item.

Answer (D) is correct. *(CPA, adapted)*

REQUIRED: The application of the LCM rule that usually results in the lowest amount.

DISCUSSION: Applying the LCM rule to each item of inventory produces the lowest valuation for each item and therefore the lowest and most conservative valuation for the total inventory. The reason is that aggregating items results in the inclusion of some items at amounts greater than LCM. For example, if item A (cost $2, market $1) and item B (cost $3, market $4) are aggregated for LCM purposes, the inventory valuation is $5. If the rule is applied separately to A and B, the LCM valuation is $4.

Answer (A) is incorrect because each application results in a different amount. Answer (B) is incorrect because grouping all items results in a higher valuation than applying the LCM rule to individual items. Answer (C) is incorrect because grouping some items results in a higher valuation than applying the LCM rule to individual items.

40. Metz Co. is selecting its inventory system in preparation for its first year of operations. Thread intends to use either the periodic weighted-average method or the perpetual moving-average method, and to apply the lower-of-cost-or-market (LCM) rule either to individual items or to the total inventory. Inventory prices are expected to increase throughout the year, although a few individual prices will decrease. What inventory system should Metz select if it wants to maximize the inventory carrying amount at the balance sheet date?

	Inventory Method	Cost or Market Application
A.	Perpetual	Total inventory
B.	Perpetual	Individual item
C.	Periodic	Total inventory
D.	Periodic	Individual item

Answer (A) is correct. *(CPA, adapted)*

REQUIRED: The inventory system that maximizes the inventory carrying amount at year-end.

DISCUSSION: The weighted-average inventory pricing system is applicable to a periodic inventory system. The weighted-average unit cost is equal to the total cost of goods available for sale divided by the number of units available for sale. The moving-average system is applicable only to perpetual inventories. It requires that a new weighted average be computed after every purchase. This moving average is based on remaining inventory held and the new inventory purchased. In a period of rising prices, the moving-average method results in a higher unit and total ending inventory because the most recent purchases are given greater weight in the calculation. ARB 43, Chap. 4, *Inventory Pricing*, permits application of the LCM rule to each item in the inventory, to the inventory as a whole, or to the total of the component of each major category. Applying the LCM rule to the total inventory will maximize the carrying amount because the reduction in the inventory will equal only the excess of aggregate cost over aggregate market. LCM applied on an individual item basis recognizes all of the inventory declines but none of the gains.

Answer (B) is incorrect because the moving-average method and applying the LCM rule to the total inventory result in a higher ending inventory. Answer (C) is incorrect because the moving-average method and applying the LCM rule to the total inventory result in a higher ending inventory. Answer (D) is incorrect because the moving-average method and applying the LCM rule to the total inventory result in a higher ending inventory.

41. The replacement cost of an inventory item is below the net realizable value and above the net realizable value minus the normal profit margin. The original cost of the inventory item is below the net realizable value minus the normal profit margin. Under the lower-of-cost-or-market (LCM) method, the inventory item should be measured at

A. Net realizable value.

B. Net realizable value minus the normal profit margin.

C. Original cost.

D. Replacement cost.

Answer (C) is correct. *(CPA, adapted)*

REQUIRED: The measurement of an inventory item under the lower-of-cost-or-market method.

DISCUSSION: When replacement cost is below the NRV and above the NRV minus the normal profit margin, market equals replacement cost. Given that the original cost of the inventory item is below market, the original cost should be used to measure the inventory item under the LCM method.

Answer (A) is incorrect because the replacement cost, given the circumstances, is designated as market. Answer (B) is incorrect because the replacement cost, given the circumstances, is designated as market. Answer (D) is incorrect because cost is below market.

42. The original cost of an inventory item is below both replacement cost and net realizable value. The net realizable value minus normal profit margin is below the original cost. Under the lower-of-cost-or-market (LCM) method, the inventory item should be measured at

A. Replacement cost.

B. Net realizable value.

C. Net realizable value minus normal profit margin.

D. Original cost.

Answer (D) is correct. *(CPA, adapted)*

REQUIRED: The measured of inventory under the LCM method.

DISCUSSION: ARB 43, Chap. 4, *Inventory Pricing*, defines market as current replacement cost subject to a ceiling and a floor. The maximum is net realizable value, and the minimum is net realizable value minus normal profit. When replacement cost is within this range, it is used as market. The original cost is above the NRV minus normal profit margin but below the NRV and the replacement cost. Thus, market must be the NRV (if it is less than replacement cost) or the replacement cost (which is greater than NRV minus normal profit), and LCM is equal to original cost.

Answer (A) is incorrect because replacement cost is greater than original cost. Answer (B) is incorrect because the NRV is greater than original cost. Answer (C) is incorrect because net realizable value minus normal profit margin is less than original cost.

43. Lorraine Co. has determined its fiscal year-end inventory on a FIFO basis to be $400,000. Information pertaining to that inventory follows:

Estimated selling price	$408,000
Estimated cost of disposal	20,000
Normal profit margin	60,000
Current replacement cost	360,000

Lorraine records losses that result from applying the lower-of-cost-or-market (LCM) rule. At its year-end, what should be the net carrying amount of Lorraine's inventory?

A. $400,000

B. $388,000

C. $360,000

D. $328,000

Answer (C) is correct. *(CPA, adapted)*

REQUIRED: The net carrying amount of the ending inventory.

DISCUSSION: Under the LCM method, market is current replacement cost subject to a maximum (ceiling) equal to net realizable value and a minimum (floor) equal to net realizable value minus a normal profit. NRV equals selling price minus costs of completion and disposal. Here, original cost is $400,000 and replacement cost is $360,000. The LCM method uses the lower of the two, $360,000, to measure inventory. However, the inventory measure cannot exceed the NRV of $388,000 ($408,000 selling price – $20,000 cost of disposal). Furthermore, the inventory carrying amount cannot be lower than NRV minus normal profit or $328,000 ($388,000 NRV – $60,000 normal profit). Because the lower of cost or market ($360,000) is between $388,000 (ceiling) and $328,000 (floor), the net carrying amount is $360,000.

Answer (A) is incorrect because $400,000 is the original cost. Answer (B) is incorrect because $388,000 is the NRV (ceiling). Answer (D) is incorrect because $328,000 is the NRV minus normal profit (floor).

44. Based on a physical inventory taken at year-end, Brussels Co. determined its raw materials inventory on a FIFO basis at $26,000 with a replacement cost of $20,000. Brussels estimated that, after further processing costs of $12,000, the raw materials could be sold as finished goods for $40,000. The company's normal profit margin is 10% of sales. Under the lower-of-cost-or-market (LCM) rule, what amount should Brussels report as raw materials inventory at the balance sheet date?

A. $28,000

B. $26,000

C. $24,000

D. $20,000

Answer (C) is correct. *(CPA, adapted)*

REQUIRED: The amount reported for inventory under the LCM rule.

DISCUSSION: ARB 43, Chap. 4, *Inventory Pricing*, defines market as current replacement cost subject to a ceiling and a floor. The maximum is net realizable value, and the minimum is net realizable value minus normal profit. When replacement cost is within this range, it is used as market. Cost is given as $26,000. Net realizable value is $28,000 ($40,000 selling price – $12,000 additional processing costs), and net realizable amount minus a normal profit equals $24,000 [$28,000 – (10% × $40,000)]. Because the lowest amount in the range ($24,000) exceeds replacement cost ($20,000), it is used as market. Because market ($24,000) is less than cost ($26,000), it is also the inventory measurement.

Answer (A) is incorrect because $28,000 is the NRV. Answer (B) is incorrect because $26,000 is the cost. Answer (D) is incorrect because $20,000 is the replacement cost.

Questions 45 through 47 are based on the following information. The data below concerns items in Stockholm Co.'s inventory.

Per Unit	Gear	Stuff	Wickets
Historical cost	$190.00	$106.00	$53.00
Selling price	217.00	145.00	73.75
Cost to distribute	19.00	8.00	2.50
Current replacement cost	203.00	105.00	51.00
Normal profit margin	32.00	29.00	21.25

45. The limits to the market measurement (i.e., the ceiling and the floor) that should be used in the lower-of-cost-or-market (LCM) comparison of gear are

A. $217 and $198.

B. $217 and $185.

C. $198 and $166.

D. $185 and $166.

Answer (C) is correct. *(CMA, adapted)*

REQUIRED: The limits of the market measurement for gear.

DISCUSSION: ARB 43, Chap. 4, *Inventory Pricing*, defines market as current replacement cost subject to a maximum equal to net realizable value and a minimum equal to net realizable value minus a normal profit. Net realizable value is equal to selling price minus costs of completion and disposal. For gear, the net realizable value is $198 ($217 selling price – $19 distribution cost). Net realizable value minus normal profit is $166 ($198 net realizable value – $32 normal profit).

Answer (A) is incorrect because $217 is the selling price, and $198 is the NRV. Answer (B) is incorrect because $217 is the selling price, and $185 is the selling price minus normal profit. Answer (D) is incorrect because the ceiling equals the net realizable value, not selling price minus normal profit.

46. The cost amount that should be used in the lower-of-cost-or-market (LCM) comparison of stuff is

A. $105

B. $106

C. $108

D. $137

Answer (B) is correct. *(CMA, adapted)*

REQUIRED: The cost amount for stuff.

DISCUSSION: The cost amount used in the LCM comparison is the historical cost of an item. Thus, for stuff, the historical cost of $106 is compared with market.

Answer (A) is incorrect because $105 is the current replacement cost, not the historical cost. Answer (C) is incorrect because $108 is the net realizable value minus the normal profit margin, not the historical cost. Answer (D) is incorrect because net realizable value ($137) is not used in the calculation of historical cost.

47. The market amount that should be used to measure the wickets on the basis of the lower-of-cost-or-market (LCM) rule is

A. $51.00

B. $53.00

C. $50.00

D. $71.25

Answer (A) is correct. *(CMA, adapted)*

REQUIRED: The market amount for wickets.

DISCUSSION: Net realizable value for wickets is $71.25 ($73.75 selling price – $2.50 distribution cost). The net realizable value minus normal profit is $50 ($71.25 net realizable value – $21.25 normal profit margin). The $51 replacement cost falls between the $71.25 ceiling and the $50 floor and is the appropriate market value. Because the $51 market value is lower than the $53 historical cost, it should be the basis of valuation for the wickets.

Answer (B) is incorrect because $53 is the historical cost. Answer (C) is incorrect because $50 is the floor. It is used only if replacement cost is lower. Answer (D) is incorrect because $71.25 is the net realizable value. It is used as the market amount only if replacement cost is greater.

6.4 Gross Margin Method

48. Which of the following methods of inventory valuation is allowable at interim dates but not at year-end?

A. Weighted average.

B. Estimated gross profit rates.

C. Retail method.

D. Specific identification.

Answer (B) is correct. *(CPA, adapted)*

REQUIRED: The inventory valuation method permitted at interim dates but not at year-end.

DISCUSSION: APB 28, *Interim Financial Reporting,* permits using the estimated gross profit method to determine inventory for interim statements provided that adequate disclosure is made of reconciliations with the annual physical inventory at year-end. Any method allowable at year-end is also allowable at an interim date.

Answer (A) is incorrect because the weighted average method is allowable at year-end. Answer (C) is incorrect because the retail method is allowable at year-end. Answer (D) is incorrect because the specific identification method is allowable at year-end.

49. Norway Co. maintains a markup of 60% based on cost. The company's selling and administrative expenses average 30% of sales. Annual sales amounted to $960,000. Norway's cost of goods sold and operating profit for the year are

	Cost of Goods Sold	Operating Profit
A.	$576,000	$96,000
B.	$576,000	$288,000
C.	$600,000	$72,000
D.	$600,000	$288,000

Answer (C) is correct. *(CPA, adapted)*

REQUIRED: The estimated cost of goods sold and operating profit.

DISCUSSION: A markup of 60% based on cost is equal to the fraction 60% markup ÷ 100% cost. Because retail is equal to markup plus cost, a markup on retail is equal to the 60% markup divided by the total of the 100% cost plus the 60% markup. Norway's markup on retail is therefore 37.5% [60% ÷ (100% + 60%)]. If the markup on retail is 37.5%, cost of goods sold must be 62.5% (1 – .375) of sales. Thus, cost of goods sold must be $600,000 ($960,000 sales × 62.5%). Selling and administrative expenses average 30% of sales and are estimated to be $288,000 ($960,000 sales × 30%). Accordingly, operating profit is $72,000 ($960,000 sales – $600,000 CGS – $288,000 S&A expenses).

Answer (A) is incorrect because cost of goods sold is based on a 60% markup from cost, not sales, and the $96,000 operating profit is based on the incorrect cost of goods sold. Answer (B) is incorrect because cost of goods sold is based on a 60% markup from cost, not sales, and the $288,000 is the selling and administrative expenses. Answer (D) is incorrect because $288,000 is the selling and administrative expenses.

50. The following information is available for Sweden Company for its most recent year:

Net sales	$3,600,000
Freight-in	90,000
Purchase discounts	50,000
Ending inventory	240,000

The gross margin is 40% of net sales. What is the cost of goods available for sale?

A. $1,680,000

B. $1,920,000

C. $2,400,000

D. $2,440,000

Answer (C) is correct. *(CPA, adapted)*

REQUIRED: The cost of goods available for sale.

DISCUSSION: Because the gross margin equals 40% of net sales, cost of goods sold equals 60% of net sales, or $2,160,000. Cost of goods available for sale equals the cost of goods sold plus the cost of the goods in ending inventory. Hence, cost of goods available for sale equals $2,160,000 plus $240,000, or $2,400,000 (BI + PUR = GAFS* = CGS + EI). Freight-in and purchase discounts are not used to estimate CGS or GAFS in the gross margin approach.

Ending inventory	$ 240,000
Cost of goods sold	2,160,000
Goods available for sale*	$2,400,000

Answer (A) is incorrect because $1,680,000 is gross margin plus ending inventory. Answer (B) is incorrect because $1,920,000 is cost of goods sold minus ending inventory. Answer (D) is incorrect because $2,440,000 is cost of goods available for sale plus freight-in and minus purchase discounts.

51. The following information is available for the Sibelius Company for the 3 months ended March 31 of this year:

Merchandise inventory, January 1 of this year	$ 900,000
Purchases	3,400,000
Freight-in	200,000
Sales	4,800,000

The gross margin recorded was 25% of sales. What should be the merchandise inventory at March 31?

A. $700,000

B. $900,000

C. $1,125,000

D. $1,200,000

Answer (B) is correct. *(CPA, adapted)*

REQUIRED: The estimated ending inventory using the gross profit method.

DISCUSSION: If the gross profit margin is 25% of sales, cost of goods sold equals 75% of sales. Ending inventory is equal to goods available for sale minus cost of goods sold.

Beginning inventory	$ 900,000
Purchases	3,400,000
Freight-in	200,000
Goods available for sale	$4,500,000
CGS (1 – .25) × ($4,800,000)	(3,600,000)
Ending inventory	$ 900,000

Answer (A) is incorrect because $700,000 excludes freight-in. Answer (C) is incorrect because ending inventory is goods available for sale minus cost of goods sold. Answer (D) is incorrect because $1,200,000 is the gross margin.

52. A store uses the gross profit method to estimate inventory and cost of goods sold for interim reporting purposes. Past experience indicates that the average gross profit rate is 25% of sales. The following data relate to the month of March:

Inventory cost, March 1	$25,000
Purchases during the month at cost	67,000
Sales	84,000
Sales returns	3,000

Using the data above, what is the estimated ending inventory at March 31?

A. $20,250

B. $21,000

C. $29,000

D. $31,250

Answer (D) is correct. *(CIA, adapted)*

REQUIRED: The estimated ending inventory value based on a 25% gross margin ratio.

DISCUSSION: The gross profit rate is 25% of sales. Thus, estimated cost of goods sold is 75% (1 – .25) of sales. Subtracting estimated cost of goods sold from total goods available for sale leaves an estimated ending inventory figure of $31,250.

Beginning inventory	$25,000
Purchases	67,000
Goods available for sale	$92,000
Estimated CGS (1 – .25) × ($84,000 – $3,000)	(60,750)
Estimated ending inventory	$31,250

Answer (A) is incorrect because $20,250 is the gross margin. Answer (B) is incorrect because $21,000 is the gross margin without considering sales returns. Answer (C) is incorrect because $29,000 fails to consider sales returns.

53. Finland Co. prepares monthly income statements. A physical inventory is taken only at year-end; hence, month-end inventories must be estimated. All sales are made on account. The rate of markup on cost is 50%. The following information relates to the month of June:

Accounts receivable, June 1	$20,000
Accounts receivable, June 30	30,000
Collection of accounts receivable during June	50,000
Inventory, June 1	36,000
Purchases of inventory during June	32,000

The estimated cost of the June 30 inventory is

A. $24,000

B. $28,000

C. $38,000

D. $44,000

Answer (B) is correct. *(CPA, adapted)*

REQUIRED: The estimated cost of ending inventory assuming a 50% markup on cost.

DISCUSSION: To determine inventory cost, cost of sales must be determined. Sales can be derived from a T-account analysis of accounts receivable; that is, the beginning balance ($20,000) plus credit sales equals the collections ($50,000) plus the ending balance ($30,000). Thus, sales equal $60,000 ($50,000 + $30,000 – $20,000). Because sales equal cost of sales plus the 50% markup on cost, sales equal 150% of cost. Cost of sales therefore equals $40,000 ($60,000 sales ÷ 1.5). Cost of sales deducted from the cost of goods available for sale equals the ending inventory.

Beginning inventory	$36,000
Purchases	32,000
Goods available for sale	$68,000
Cost of goods sold	(40,000)
Ending inventory	$28,000

Answer (A) is incorrect because sales are incorrectly computed. Answer (C) is incorrect because $38,000 results from a markup based on sales instead of cost. Answer (D) is incorrect because sales are incorrectly computed.

54. Dart Company's accounting records indicated the following information:

Beginning inventory	$ 500,000
Purchases during the year	2,500,000
Sales during the year	3,200,000

A physical inventory taken on at year-end, resulted in an ending inventory of $575,000. Dart's gross profit on sales has remained constant at 25% in recent years. Dart suspects some inventory may have been taken by a new employee. At the balance sheet date, what is the estimated cost of missing inventory?

A. $25,000

B. $100,000

C. $175,000

D. $225,000

Answer (A) is correct. *(CPA, adapted)*
REQUIRED: The missing inventory estimated based on a gross margin ratio.
DISCUSSION: To estimate the missing inventory, the estimated cost of goods sold is subtracted from the cost of goods available for sale to estimate the amount of inventory that should be on hand. Given that the gross margin is 25% of sales, 75% of sales, or $2,400,000, is the estimated cost of goods sold.

Beginning balance	$ 500,000
Purchases	2,500,000
Cost of goods available	$3,000,000
Estimated cost of goods sold [$3,200,000 sales × (1 – .25)]	(2,400,000)
Estimated year-end balance	$ 600,000
Physical inventory year-end	(575,000)
Estimated theft loss	$ 25,000

Answer (B) is incorrect because $100,000 is the difference between estimated ending inventory and actual beginning inventory. Answer (C) is incorrect because $175,000 is the ending physical inventory minus beginning inventory, plus purchases, minus cost of goods sold. Answer (D) is incorrect because $225,000 is the gross margin minus actual ending inventory.

55. A firm experienced a flood loss in the current year that destroyed all but $6,000 of inventory (at cost). Data available are below:

	Prior Year	Current (to Date of Flood)
Sales	$100,000	$40,000
Purchases	70,000	35,000
Cost of goods sold	60,000	
Ending inventory	10,000	

What is the approximate inventory lost?

A. $10,000

B. $15,000

C. $16,000

D. $21,000

Answer (B) is correct. *(CIA, adapted)*
REQUIRED: The approximate inventory lost to fire.
DISCUSSION: Based on the prior-year figures, the ratio of cost of goods sold to sales is 60% ($60,000 ÷ $100,000). This ratio can be used to approximate current-year cost of goods sold (60% × $40,000 current-year sales = $24,000). As indicated below, this estimate is deducted from goods available to determine estimated inventory at the time of the fire ($21,000). Given actual remaining inventory of $6,000, the inventory lost to fire is $15,000.

Beginning inventory	$10,000
Purchases	35,000
Cost of goods available	$45,000
Estimated cost of goods sold	(24,000)
Estimated inventory	$21,000
Actual inventory	(6,000)
Approximate inventory destroyed	$15,000

Answer (A) is incorrect because $10,000 is the ending inventory for the prior year and the beginning inventory in the current year. Answer (C) is incorrect because $16,000 is the current year beginning inventory plus the actual ending inventory of $6,000. Answer (D) is incorrect because $21,000 is the estimated ending inventory.

6.5 Retail Inventory Methods

56. The retail inventory method is characterized by

A. The recording of sales at cost.

B. The recording of purchases at selling price.

C. The reporting of year-end inventory at retail in the financial statements.

D. The recording of markups at retail and markdowns at cost.

Answer (B) is correct. *(CIA, adapted)*
REQUIRED: The characteristic of the retail inventory method.
DISCUSSION: In the retail inventory method, records of the beginning inventory and net purchases are maintained at both cost and retail. Sales at retail are deducted from the sum of beginning inventory and purchases at retail to provide ending inventory at retail. This figure is adjusted to cost using a cost-to-price (retail) ratio.

Answer (A) is incorrect because sales are not recorded at cost. Answer (C) is incorrect because inventory must be reported at cost per GAAP. Answer (D) is incorrect because both markups and markdowns should be recorded at retail.

57. With regard to the retail inventory method, which of the following is the most accurate statement?

A. Accountants usually ignore net markups and net markdowns in computing the cost-price percentage.

B. Accountants usually include both net markups and net markdowns in computing the cost-price percentage.

C. This method results in a lower ending inventory cost if net markups are included but net markdowns are excluded in computing the cost-price percentage.

D. It is not adaptable to LIFO costing.

Answer (C) is correct. *(CPA, adapted)*

REQUIRED: The most accurate statement concerning the retail inventory method.

DISCUSSION: The cost-retail ratio is lower if retail (the denominator) is increased. Excluding markdowns increases the denominator, thus decreasing the ratio applied to ending inventory stated at retail, and also decreasing ending inventory stated at cost. Excluding markdowns approximates lower of cost or market and is characteristic of the conventional retail method.

Answer (A) is incorrect because accountants usually include net markups but not net markdowns in computing the denominator of the cost-retail ratio. Answer (B) is incorrect because accountants usually include net markups but not net markdowns in computing the denominator of the cost-retail ratio. Answer (D) is incorrect because the retail method is adaptable to FIFO, LIFO, average cost, or lower of cost or market.

58. Under the retail inventory method, freight-in would be included in the calculation of the goods available for sale for which of the following?

	Cost	Retail
A.	No	No
B.	No	Yes
C.	Yes	No
D.	Yes	Yes

Answer (C) is correct. *(CPA, adapted)*

REQUIRED: The calculation that includes freight-in when determining goods available for sale.

DISCUSSION: In the retail inventory method, records of the components of net purchases (purchases, freight-in, and purchase returns and allowances) are kept at cost and are included with beginning inventory in the calculation of the goods available for sale at cost. Records are kept at retail only for net purchases, not its components, because retail prices are usually set to cover a variety of costs, such as freight-in. Consequently, freight-in, a component of net purchases, is explicitly and directly included only in the calculation of goods available for sale at cost.

59. The retail inventory method includes which of the following in the calculation of both cost and retail amounts of goods available for sale?

A. Purchase returns.

B. Sales returns.

C. Net markups.

D. Freight-in.

Answer (A) is correct. *(CPA, adapted)*

REQUIRED: The element common to calculation of goods available for sale at cost and at retail.

DISCUSSION: In the retail inventory method, records are kept of beginning inventory and net purchases at both cost and retail. Purchase returns are deducted in the calculation of net purchases at both cost and retail because the return of goods reduces both total cost and the total sales price of the purchased goods.

Answer (B) is incorrect because sales returns is an element of retail only. Answer (C) is incorrect because markups and markdowns affect only retail. Answer (D) is incorrect because freight-in is an element of cost; there is no retail counterpart.

60. If the retail method is used to approximate a lower-of-average-cost-or-market valuation, which of the following describes the proper treatment of net additional markups and markdowns in the cost-retail ratio calculation?

A. Net additional markups should be included in the ratio; net markdowns should be excluded.

B. Net additional markups should be excluded from the ratio; net markdowns should be included.

C. Both net additional markups and markdowns should be included in the ratio calculation.

D. Both net additional markups and markdowns should be excluded from the ratio calculation.

Answer (A) is correct. *(S. Venkateswar)*

REQUIRED: The treatment of markups and markdowns in computing the cost-retail ratio under a lower-of-average-cost-or-market approach.

DISCUSSION: The cost-retail ratio based on a lower of average cost or market valuation approach should include net additional markups but not net markdowns. Including net additional markups and excluding net markdowns approximates lower of cost or market. The reason is that increasing the denominator of the ratio (BI at retail + Pur at retail + Markups) while holding the numerator (BI at cost + Pur at cost) constant gives a more conservative (a lower) valuation.

61. In the retail inventory method, when computing the cost-retail ratio, under what flow assumption(s) is beginning inventory excluded from both cost and retail?

A. FIFO only.

B. LIFO only.

C. Weighted-average cost or weighted-average lower of cost or market.

D. Both FIFO and LIFO.

Answer (D) is correct. *(Publisher)*

REQUIRED: The flow assumption(s) requiring that beginning inventory be excluded in determining the cost-retail ratio.

DISCUSSION: Under both FIFO and LIFO, the cost-retail ratio must be computed for purchases, not goods available for sale. For FIFO, beginning inventory is excluded because ending inventory includes only goods from current purchases. For LIFO, the layers of goods from the purchases of separate accounting periods must be considered separately.

Answer (A) is incorrect because FIFO excludes beginning inventory in determining the cost-retail ratio. Answer (B) is incorrect because LIFO excludes beginning inventory in determining the cost-retail ratio. Answer (C) is incorrect because weighted average includes beginning inventory as well as purchases.

62. Using the retail inventory method, when is the cost-retail ratio based only on the cost and retail values of beginning inventory?

A. When FIFO is used and sales exceed purchases at retail.

B. When FIFO is used and sales are less than purchases at retail.

C. When LIFO is used and sales exceed purchases at retail.

D. When LIFO is used and sales are less than purchases at retail.

Answer (C) is correct. *(Publisher)*

REQUIRED: The circumstances in which the cost-retail ratio is based only upon beginning inventory cost and retail values.

DISCUSSION: If LIFO is used and sales exceed purchases at retail, the ending inventory will be less than beginning inventory. Ending inventory will consist entirely of values from beginning inventory and should be converted from retail to cost using the cost-retail ratio that existed in the beginning inventory.

Answer (A) is incorrect because, under FIFO, ending inventory includes goods purchased during the period. Answer (B) is incorrect because, under FIFO, ending inventory includes goods purchased during the period. Answer (D) is incorrect because, under LIFO, when sales are less than purchases at retail, the ending inventory will include beginning inventory plus a layer of goods purchased during the period.

63. The accounting records of Saraphina Co. contain the following amounts on November 30, the end of its fiscal year:

	Cost	Retail
Beginning inventory	$ 68,000	$100,000
Purchases	262,000	400,000
Net markups		50,000
Net markdowns		110,000
Sales		360,000

Saraphina's ending inventory as of November 30, computed by the conventional retail method, is:

A. $80,000

B. $60,000

C. $54,400

D. $48,000

Answer (D) is correct. *(CMA, adapted)*

REQUIRED: The ending inventory under the conventional retail method.

DISCUSSION: The lower-of-cost-or-market retail method includes net markups but not net markdowns in the determination of goods available for sale. The approximate LCM (conventional) retail method is a weighted-average method. Accordingly, the numerator of the cost-retail ratio is the sum of the beginning inventory at cost plus purchases at cost, and the denominator is the sum of beginning inventory at retail, purchases at retail, and net markups.

	Cost	Retail
Beginning inventory	$ 68,000	$100,000
Purchases	262,000	400,000
Markups, net		50,000
Goods available	$330,000	$550,000
Sales		(360,000)
Markdowns, net		(110,000)
Ending inventory -- retail		$ 80,000
Cost-retail ratio ($330 ÷ $550 = 60%)		× .6
Ending inventory at cost		$ 48,000

Answer (A) is incorrect because $80,000 is ending inventory at retail. Answer (B) is incorrect because $60,000 incorrectly uses a 75% cost-retail ratio. Answer (C) is incorrect because $54,400 incorrectly uses a 68% cost-retail ratio.

64. Dublin Co. uses the conventional retail inventory method to account for inventory. The following information relates to current-year operations:

	Average Cost	Retail
Beginning inventory and purchases	$600,000	$920,000
Net markups		40,000
Net markdowns		60,000
Sales		780,000

What amount should be reported as cost of sales for the year?

A. $480,000

B. $487,500

C. $520,000

D. $525,000

Answer (D) is correct. *(CPA, adapted)*

REQUIRED: The cost of sales based on the conventional retail inventory method.

DISCUSSION: The lower-of-cost-or-market retail method includes net markups but not net markdowns in the determination of goods available for sale. The approximate LCM (conventional) retail method is a weighted-average method. Accordingly, the numerator of the cost-retail ratio is the sum of the beginning inventory at cost plus purchases at cost, and the denominator is the sum of beginning inventory at retail, purchases at retail, and net markups. The numerator of the ratio (goods available at cost) is given as $600,000, and the denominator (goods available at retail) is $960,000 ($920,000 BI and purchases + $40,000 net markups). Ending inventory at retail is $120,000 ($960,000 goods available at retail – $60,000 net markdowns – $780,000 sales). Hence, ending inventory at cost is $75,000 [$120,000 EI at retail × ($600,000 ÷ $960,000) cost-retail ratio], and cost of sales must be $525,000 ($600,000 BI and purchases at cost – $75,000 EI at cost).

Answer (A) is incorrect because $480,000 results from subtracting ending inventory at retail from the sum of beginning inventory and purchases at cost. Answer (B) is incorrect because $487,500 omits net markdowns from the computation. Answer (C) is incorrect because $520,000 assumes net markdowns are deducted in determining the cost-retail ratio.

65. Londinium Ltd. values its inventory by using the retail method (FIFO basis, lower of cost or market). The following information is available for the year just ended:

	Cost	Retail
Beginning inventory	$ 80,000	$140,000
Purchases	297,000	420,000
Freight-in	4,000	
Shortages		8,000
Markups (net)		10,000
Markdowns (net)		2,000
Sales		400,000

At what amount would Londinium report its ending inventory?

A. $112,000

B. $113,400

C. $117,600

D. $119,000

Answer (A) is correct. *(CPA, adapted)*

REQUIRED: The ending inventory at cost using the retail method (FIFO basis, LCM).

DISCUSSION: Under FIFO, ending inventory is composed of the latest purchases. Thus, in calculating the cost-retail ratio, only current purchases are included. To approximate the lower of cost or market, the denominator of the ratio includes net markups but not net markdowns.

	Cost	Retail
Purchases	$297,000	$420,000
Freight-in	4,000	
Markups, net		10,000
Adjusted purchases	$301,000	$430,000
Beginning inventory	80,000	140,000
Goods available	$381,000	$570,000
Net markdowns		(2,000)
Shortages		(8,000)
Sales		(400,000)
Ending inventory -- retail		$160,000
Cost-retail ratio ($301,000 ÷ $430,000 = 70%)		× .7
Ending inventory		$112,000

Answer (B) is incorrect because $113,400 fails to consider net markdowns in retail ending inventory. Answer (C) is incorrect because $117,600 ignores the effects of shortages in retail ending inventory. Answer (D) is incorrect because $119,000 incorrectly includes net markups in retail ending inventory.

66. Riga PLC uses a calendar year and the LIFO retail inventory method (assuming stable prices). Information relating to the computation of the inventory at December 31 is as follows:

	Cost	Retail
Beginning inventory	$ 150	$ 300
Purchases (net)	1,650	4,860
Net markups		830
Net markdowns		970
Sales		4,180

What should be the ending inventory at cost at December 31 using the LIFO retail inventory method?

A. $252

B. $333

C. $339

D. $840

Answer (C) is correct. *(K. Boze)*

REQUIRED: The ending inventory at cost using the LIFO retail inventory method.

DISCUSSION: Under the LIFO retail method (assuming stable prices), markups and markdowns are included in the calculation of the cost-retail ratio because the lower of cost or market is not being approximated. The markups and markdowns are usually assumed to apply only to purchases, and the ratio applies only to the LIFO layer added from the current purchases. Hence, the cost-retail ratio excludes beginning inventory and includes only purchases, markups, and markdowns. As indicated below, this ratio is 35%. The ending inventory will consist of a layer at 35% and a layer at the previous year's ratio.

	Cost	Retail
Purchases	$1,650	$4,860
Markups		830
Markdowns		(970)
Adjusted purchases	$1,650	$4,720
Beginning inventory	150	300
Goods available	$1,800	$5,020
Sales		(4,180)
Ending inventory -- retail		$ 840

Current cost-retail ratio ($1,650 ÷ $4,720 = 35%)

BI layer at cost	$ 150
Current layer at cost = ($840 – $300) × .35	189
Ending inventory at cost	$ 339

Answer (A) is incorrect because $252 is the ending inventory based on the conventional retail method. Answer (B) is incorrect because $333 results from using a cost-retail ratio equal to purchases at cost divided by purchases at retail. Answer (D) is incorrect because $840 is the retail ending inventory.

67. Tirana Co. uses the first-in, first-out retail method of inventory valuation. The following information is available:

	Cost	Retail
Beginning inventory	$12,000	$ 30,000
Purchases	60,000	110,000
Net additional markups		10,000
Net markdowns		20,000
Sales revenue		90,000

If the lower-of-cost-or-market (LCM) rule is disregarded, what would be the estimated cost of the ending inventory?

A. $24,000

B. $20,800

C. $20,000

D. $19,200

Answer (A) is correct. *(CPA, adapted)*

REQUIRED: The ending inventory using the FIFO version of the retail inventory method.

DISCUSSION: Under FIFO, ending inventory consists of purchases because beginning inventory is assumed to be sold first. Both markdowns and markups are used to calculate the cost-retail ratio because LCM is not being approximated.

	Cost	Retail
Purchases	$60,000	$110,000
Markups		10,000
Markdowns		(20,000)
Adjusted purchases	$60,000	$100,000
Beg. inv. 1/1	12,000	30,000
Goods available	$72,000	$130,000
Sales		(90,000)
Ending inventory -- retail		$ 40,000
Cost-retail ratio ($60,000 ÷ $100,000)		× .6
Ending inventory -- FIFO		$ 24,000

Answer (B) is incorrect because $20,800 incorrectly uses a 52% cost-retail ratio. Answer (C) is incorrect because $20,000 incorrectly uses a 50% cost-retail ratio. Answer (D) is incorrect because $19,200 incorrectly uses a 48% cost-retail ratio.

6.6 Dollar-Value LIFO

68. Estimates of price-level changes for specific inventories are required for which of the following inventory methods?

A. Conventional retail.

B. Dollar-value LIFO.

C. Weighted-average cost.

D. Average cost retail.

Answer (B) is correct. *(CPA, adapted)*

REQUIRED: The inventory method for which estimates of price-level changes for specific inventories are required.

DISCUSSION: Dollar-value LIFO accumulates inventoriable costs of similar (not identical) items. These items should be similar in the sense of being interchangeable, having similar uses, belonging to the same product line, or constituting the raw materials for a given product. Dollar-value LIFO determines changes in ending inventory in terms of dollars of constant purchasing power rather than units of physical inventory. This calculation uses a specific price index for each year. The ending inventory is deflated by the current-year index to arrive at base-year cost. This amount is then compared to the beginning inventory stated at base-year cost to determine what layers are to be in the ending inventory. Each layer is then inflated by the relevant price index for the year it was created to determine the aggregate ending inventory valuation.

Answer (A) is incorrect because retail inventory methods calculate ending inventory at retail and then adjust it to cost by applying a cost-retail ratio. Answer (C) is incorrect because weighted-average cost method computes ending inventory based on an average cost determined at year-end. Answer (D) is incorrect because retail inventory methods calculate ending inventory at retail and then adjust it to cost by applying a cost-retail ratio.

69. The double-extension method and the link-chain method are two variations of which of the following inventory cost flow methods?

A. Moving average.

B. FIFO.

C. Dollar-value LIFO.

D. Conventional (lower-of-cost-or-market) retail.

Answer (C) is correct. *(CPA, adapted)*

REQUIRED: The inventory cost flow method of which the double-extension method and the link-chain method are variations.

DISCUSSION: The double-extension method and the link-chain method are variations of dollar-value LIFO. In dollar-value LIFO, similar (rather than identical) dollar-value pools of inventory are accumulated. Each layer of inventory is stated in dollar-value terms based on the price index for the relevant year. The link-chain version uses beginning-of-the-year costs as the denominator of the index for each year after the base year. Each successive year's index is multiplied by the cumulative index. The double-extension version uses the base-year prices in the annual index. The two methods are mutually exclusive.

70. Which of the following inventory cost flow methods could use dollar-value pools?

A. Conventional (lower-of-cost-or-market) retail.

B. Weighted average.

C. FIFO.

D. LIFO.

Answer (D) is correct. *(CPA, adapted)*

REQUIRED: The cost flow assumption using dollar-value pools.

DISCUSSION: A modification of LIFO may be employed to account for dollar-value pools of similar items rather than identical items. This method overcomes a difficulty with traditional LIFO: Some items may be liquidated below the LIFO base while the value of similar items may increase. Dollar-value LIFO prevents the loss of the advantages of LIFO when the mixture of similar items changes.

71. When the double-extension approach to the dollar-value LIFO inventory method is used, the inventory layer added in the current year is multiplied by an index number. Which of the following correctly states how components are used in the calculation of this index number?

A. In the numerator, the average of the ending inventory at base-year cost and at current-year cost.

B. In the numerator, the ending inventory at current-year cost, and, in the denominator, the ending inventory at base-year cost.

C. In the numerator, the ending inventory at base-year cost, and, in the denominator, the ending inventory at current-year cost.

D. In the denominator, the average of the ending inventory at base-year cost and at current-year cost.

Answer (B) is correct. *(CPA, adapted)*

REQUIRED: The true statement of how components are used in the calculation of an index number under the double-extension method.

DISCUSSION: An enterprise applying dollar-value LIFO may calculate price indexes rather than use externally determined numbers. The double-extension approach states ending inventory at current-year cost and then divides that amount by the base-year cost to determine the index for the current year. Hence, this method extends the quantity of the inventory at both current-year and base-year unit cost. The indexes determined in this way are then multiplied by the appropriate inventory layers stated at base-year cost.

Answer (A) is incorrect because the numerator is the current-year cost. Answer (C) is incorrect because the numerator is the current-year cost and the denominator is the base-year cost. Answer (D) is incorrect because the denominator is the base-year cost.

72. The dollar-value LIFO inventory cost flow method involves computations based on

	Inventory Pools of Similar Items	A Specific Price Index for Each Year
A.	No	Yes
B.	No	No
C.	Yes	No
D.	Yes	Yes

Answer (D) is correct. *(CPA, adapted)*

REQUIRED: The computations required for dollar-value LIFO inventory.

DISCUSSION: Dollar-value LIFO accumulates inventoriable costs of similar (not identical) items. These items should be similar in the sense of being interchangeable, having similar uses, belonging to the same product line, or constituting the raw materials for a given product. Dollar-value LIFO determines changes in ending inventory in terms of dollars of constant purchasing power rather than units of physical inventory. This calculation uses a specific price index for each year. The ending inventory is deflated by the current-year index to arrive at base-year cost. This amount is then compared to the beginning inventory stated at base-year cost to determine what layers are to be in the ending inventory. Each layer is then inflated by the relevant price index for the year it was created to determine the aggregate ending inventory valuation.

Answer (A) is incorrect because dollar-value LIFO uses inventory pools of similar items. Answer (B) is incorrect because dollar-value LIFO uses inventory pools and a price index. Answer (C) is incorrect because this method uses a price index.

73. Dollar-value LIFO is used to minimize the problem of LIFO liquidation caused by technological change. When technological change occurs and a new or improved product is added, a reconstructed cost must be established. Which price would not be used as a reconstructed cost?

A. The price of the product at the base date of the inventory.

B. The price to the firm if no prior costs can be determined.

C. The price at the item's first availability if it did not exist at the inventory base date.

D. The price of the item at the end of the year in which it is added to the company inventory.

Answer (D) is correct. *(Publisher)*

REQUIRED: The price that would not be used as a reconstructed cost for dollar-value LIFO.

DISCUSSION: Reconstructed cost problems arise when technological change alters the nature of inventory accounted for under dollar-value LIFO. Under dollar-value LIFO, the price used for the new product is either the price in effect when LIFO was adopted by the company, the price at the product's first availability, or, if those prices are not available, the price that the company first paid for the goods. Use of the year-end price would be consistent with the FIFO rather than the LIFO flow assumption.

Answer (A) is incorrect because the price of the product at the base date of the inventory may be used as a reconstructed cost. Answer (B) is incorrect because the price to the firm if no prior costs can be determined may be used as a reconstructed cost. Answer (C) is incorrect because the price at the item's first availability if it did not exist at the inventory base date may be used as a reconstructed cost.

Questions 74 and 75 are based on the following information. Minsk Company adopted the dollar-value last-in, first-out (LIFO) method of inventory valuation at December 31, year 1. Inventory balances and price indices are shown below.

December 31	Ending Inventory at End-of-Year Prices	Price Index at December 31
Year 1	$240,000	100
Year 2	275,000	110
Year 3	300,000	120

74. Minsk Company's ending inventory as of December 31, year 2 computed by the dollar-value LIFO method was

A. $240,000

B. $250,000

C. $251,000

D. $275,000

Answer (C) is correct. *(CMA, adapted)*

REQUIRED: The dollar-value LIFO inventory for year 2.

DISCUSSION: The first step is to convert the year 2 ending inventory into base-year prices. Dividing by the price index for year 2 results in an inventory value of $250,000 ($275,000 ÷ 1.1). This amount consists of two layers: $240,000 purchased during the base year (year 1) and $10,000 acquired in the current year (year 2). The latter amount must be converted back into year-end prices because this merchandise was not purchased during the base year. The year 2 increment therefore has a dollar-value LIFO valuation of $11,000 ($10,000 × 1.1). Total inventory is $251,000 ($240,000 + $11,000).

Answer (A) is incorrect because $240,000 does not include the year 2 layer. Answer (B) is incorrect because $250,000 includes the year 2 layer at base-year prices. Answer (D) is incorrect because $275,000 is the ending inventory at end-of-year prices.

75. Minsk Company ending inventory as of December 31, year 3 computed by the dollar-value LIFO method would be

A. $240,000

B. $250,000

C. $251,000

D. $300,000

Answer (C) is correct. *(CMA, adapted)*

REQUIRED: The dollar-value LIFO inventory for year 3.

DISCUSSION: The first step is to convert the year 3 ending inventory at year-end prices into base-year prices. Dividing by the price index for year 3 results in an inventory value at base-year prices of $250,000 ($300,000 ÷ 1.2). This figure is exactly the same as that for year 2. Thus, no increment was added during year 3, and the dollar-value LIFO ending inventory for year 3 is the same as at the end of year 2 ($251,000). This amount consists of a $240,000 layer purchased in year 1 and an $11,000 layer purchased in year 2. Under LIFO, the assumption is that nothing is still on hand from year 3 purchases because the inventory stated in base-year prices is the same as at the end of the preceding year.

Answer (A) is incorrect because $240,000 does not include the year 2 layer. Answer (B) is incorrect because $250,000 includes the year 2 layer at base-year prices. Answer (D) is incorrect because $300,000 is the ending inventory at end-of-year prices.

76. Which of the following is an advantage of the dollar-value LIFO method over the specific-goods LIFO method?

A. The dollar-value LIFO method may be used only for identical inventory items.

B. Under dollar-value LIFO, new inventory items are entered into the inventory pool at their entry year cost.

C. Under dollar-value LIFO, a given inventory item may experience a unit count decrease, but no liquidation need be recorded.

D. Under dollar-value LIFO, updating of the cost basis of old inventory items is facilitated.

Answer (C) is correct. *(D.L. Flesher)*

REQUIRED: The advantage of the dollar-value LIFO method.

DISCUSSION: The dollar-value LIFO method is applicable to pools of similar but not identical inventory items. The method deals with layers of inventory, not with individual inventory items. Thus, when a given inventory item experiences a unit count decrease, but the overall pool of inventory does not decrease, no liquidation is recorded.

Answer (A) is incorrect because dollar-value LIFO is used for inventory pools composed of similar but not identical items. Answer (B) is incorrect because new inventory items are placed in the pool at the substituted item's base-year price. Answer (D) is incorrect because no LIFO method permits an updating of old inventory items.

6.7 Purchase Commitments

77. Net losses on firm purchase commitments for goods for inventory result from a contract price that exceeds the current market price. If a firm expects that losses will occur when the purchase is effected, expected losses, if material,

A. Should be recognized in the accounts and separately disclosed as losses on the income statement of the period during which the decline in price takes place.

B. Should be recognized in the accounts and separately disclosed as net unrealized losses on the balance sheet at the end of the period during which the decline in price takes place.

C. Should be recognized in the accounts and separately disclosed as net unrealized losses on the balance sheet at the end of the period during which the contract is executed.

D. Should not be recognized in the accounts until the contract is executed and need not be separately disclosed in the financial statements.

Answer (A) is correct. *(CMA, adapted)*

REQUIRED: The accounting treatment of losses arising from a firm (noncancelable) purchase commitment not yet exercised.

DISCUSSION: ARB 43, Chap. 4, *Inventory Pricing*, requires the accrual of a loss in the current year's income statement on goods subject to a firm purchase commitment if the market price of these goods declines below the commitment price. This loss should be measured in the same manner as inventory losses. Disclosure of the loss is also required. The entry is to debit an estimated loss and to credit an estimated liability. However, a gain on a noncancelable, unhedged firm commitment is not recognized. Furthermore, GAAP do not currently require recognition of an asset and liability when the firm commitment is entered into.

When a previously unrecognized firm commitment is designated as a hedged item in accordance with SFAS 133, *Accounting for Derivative Instruments and Hedging Activities*, an asset or liability is recognized related to a gain or loss, respectively, recognized on the firm commitment.

Answer (B) is incorrect because the losses should be recognized in the determination of net income. Answer (C) is incorrect because the losses should be recognized in the determination of net income. Answer (D) is incorrect because, if a loss arises out of a firm, noncancelable, and unhedged commitment, it should be recognized in the current year.

78. At the beginning of its fiscal year, Ankara Corp. signed a 3-year, noncancelable purchase contract, which allows it to purchase up to 500,000 units of a component annually from Cairo Company at $.10 per unit and guarantees a minimum annual purchase of 100,000 units. During the year, the component unexpectedly became obsolete. Ankara had 250,000 units of this inventory at year-end and believes they can be sold as scrap for $.02 per unit. What amount of probable loss from the purchase commitment should Ankara report in its income statement?

A. $24,000

B. $20,000

C. $16,000

D. $8,000

Answer (C) is correct. *(CPA, adapted)*

REQUIRED: The amount of probable loss from the purchase commitment.

DISCUSSION: ARB 43, Chap. 4, *Inventory Pricing*, requires the accrual of a loss in the current year's income statement on goods subject to a firm purchase commitment if the market price of these goods declines below the commitment price. This loss should be measured in the same manner as inventory losses. Disclosure of the loss is also required. Consequently, given that 200,000 units must be purchased over the next 2 years for $20,000 (200,000 × $.10) and the parts can be sold as scrap for $4,000 (200,000 × $.02), the amount of probable loss from the purchase commitment is $16,000 ($20,000 – $4,000).

Answer (A) is incorrect because $24,000 includes the purchase commitment for the current year. Answer (B) is incorrect because $20,000 excludes the net realizable value of the parts from the calculation. Answer (D) is incorrect because $8,000 excludes the probable loss expected in the last year of the purchase commitment.

79. During the year, the Lisbon Company signed a noncancelable contract to purchase 2,000 pounds of a raw material at $64 per pound during the forthcoming year. On December 31, the market price of the raw material is $52 per pound, and the selling price of the finished product is expected to decline accordingly. The financial statements prepared for the year should report

A. An appropriation of retained earnings for $24,000.

B. Nothing regarding this matter.

C. A footnote describing the expected loss on the purchase commitment.

D. A loss of $24,000 in the income statement.

Answer (D) is correct. *(Publisher)*

REQUIRED: The proper financial statement treatment of a loss on inventory that the firm is committed to purchase.

DISCUSSION: ARB 43, Chap. 4, requires recognition in the income statement of a material loss on a purchase commitment as if the inventory were already owned. Losses on firm purchase commitments are measured in the same way as inventory losses. If the cost is $128,000 and the market price is $104,000, a $24,000 loss should be disclosed.

Answer (A) is incorrect because net income is to be charged for purchase commitment losses in the year market prices decline below commitment prices. Appropriating retained earnings does not affect net income. Answer (B) is incorrect because net income is to be charged for purchase commitment losses in the year market prices decline below commitment prices. Answer (C) is incorrect because net income is to be charged for purchase commitment losses in the year market prices decline below commitment prices.

6.8 Product Financing Arrangements

80. Guinea Corp. produced 1,000 units of its product that it sold for cash to Moresby Corp. In a related transaction, Guinea agreed to repurchase the 1,000 units at a specified price at a future date. The price specified in the agreement is not subject to change based on future market fluctuations except for fluctuations resulting from finance and holding costs incurred by Moresby. In accounting for these transactions, Guinea should

A. Record the sale in an ordinary manner and remove the inventory from the balance sheet.

B. Record the sale, remove the inventory from the balance sheet, and disclose the purchase commitment in the notes to the financial statements.

C. Continue to carry the inventory on the books and record a valuation account to be reported as a reduction to the inventory account on the balance sheet, rather than record a sale.

D. Record a liability and continue to carry the inventory on the books rather than record a sale.

Answer (D) is correct. *(Publisher)*

REQUIRED: The proper accounting treatment of a sale of inventory coupled with a repurchase agreement.

DISCUSSION: The transaction is, in substance, a financing arrangement. In essence, the future reacquisition of the inventory is a return of collateral upon payment of a debt. Guinea should account for the transaction as if it were a financing arrangement, not record a sale (SFAS 49, *Accounting for Product Financing Arrangements*).

Answer (A) is incorrect because it is appropriate for a sale. The Guinea-Moresby transactions are, in substance, a financing arrangement. Answer (B) is incorrect because it is appropriate for a sale. The Guinea-Moresby transactions are, in substance, a financing arrangement. Answer (C) is incorrect because the transaction must be accounted for by recording a liability and finance charges rather than by reducing inventory.

81. Naples Company bought a product on behalf of Rome Corporation, and, in a related transaction, Rome agreed to buy the product from Naples at a specified price at a specified date in the future. Rome should record an asset and a related obligation at the date that

A. The agreement is signed.

B. Naples acquires the product.

C. Naples ships the product to Rome.

D. Rome receives the product.

Answer (B) is correct. *(Publisher)*

REQUIRED: The date on which a product financing arrangement should be recorded.

DISCUSSION: The transaction is essentially a financing arrangement because Rome has acquired rights in the product without an immediate expenditure. Rome should record the asset and the related liability when Naples acquires the product. Naples is acting for Rome, and Rome should treat the goods received by Naples as if Rome itself had received them.

Answer (A) is incorrect because purchases are not ordinarily recorded until title to the goods passes. Answer (C) is incorrect because Rome should record the inventory and liability when Naples acquires the product, not later. Answer (D) is incorrect because Rome should record the inventory and liability when Naples acquires the product, not later.

82. A sponsoring enterprise enters into an agreement whereby it sells a product to another enterprise and agrees to repurchase that product at specified prices at later dates. If the specified prices fluctuate solely because of changes in purchasing, financing, and holding costs, the transaction should be treated as which of the following?

A. A borrowing.

B. A consignment.

C. A sale and repurchase.

D. Not recorded.

Answer (A) is correct. *(Publisher)*

REQUIRED: The correct accounting treatment of a product financing arrangement.

DISCUSSION: According to SFAS 49, *Accounting for Product Financing Arrangements*, such an arrangement "is a transaction in which an enterprise sells and agrees to repurchase inventory with the repurchase price equal to the original price plus carrying and financing costs, or other similar transactions." It should be treated as a borrowing if the specified prices do not fluctuate except to cover changes in purchasing, financing, and holding costs.

Answer (B) is incorrect because a consignment is the consigner's inventory physically located at the consignee's place of operations. Answer (C) is incorrect because a sale and repurchase describes the form of the transaction, not the substance. Answer (D) is incorrect because liabilities must be recorded.

6.9 Inventory Errors

83. On December 31, the last day of its current fiscal year, Latvia Co. shipped merchandise with a list price of $90,000 to Prague Company. The goods were sold on account with terms of net 30 days, F.O.B. shipping point. Due to an oversight, the sale was not recorded until January, and the merchandise, which was sold at a 25% markup, was included in Latvia's perpetual inventory on December 31. As a result, Latvia's income before taxes for the year ended December 31 was understated by

A. $90,000

B. $72,000

C. $67,500

D. $18,000

Answer (D) is correct. *(CMA, adapted)*

REQUIRED: The amount by which pretax income was understated because of failure to record a sale.

DISCUSSION: Given that terms were FOB shipping point, the title and risk of loss passed to the buyer at the time and place of shipment, i.e., on December 31. Thus, the sale should have been recorded and the inventory should not have been shown on Latvia's financial statements. The failure to record the sale understated revenues by $90,000. Cost of goods sold would also have been understated by the cost of the inventory. Because the goods were sold at a 25% markup (125% of cost), cost must have been $72,000 ($90,000 ÷ 125%). The net effect on income is $18,000 ($90,000 – $72,000 CGS).

Answer (A) is incorrect because $90,000 is the effect on sales. Answer (B) is incorrect because $72,000 is the effect on cost of goods sold. Answer (C) is incorrect because $67,500 is the cost based on a 25% markup on sales.

84. Heidelberg Co.'s beginning inventory at January 1 was understated by $52,000, and its ending inventory was overstated by $104,000. As a result, Heidelberg's cost of goods sold for the year was

A. Understated by $52,000.

B. Overstated by $52,000.

C. Understated by $156,000.

D. Overstated by $156,000.

Answer (C) is correct. *(CPA, adapted)*

REQUIRED: The misstatement of cost of goods sold.

DISCUSSION: When beginning inventory is understated, cost of goods sold will be understated. When ending inventory is overstated, cost of goods sold will be understated. Thus, Heidelberg Co.'s inventory is understated by $156,000 ($52,000 + $104,000).

Answer (A) is incorrect because the overstatement of ending inventory also understates cost of goods sold. Answer (B) is incorrect because the error understates cost of goods sold. Answer (D) is incorrect because the error understates cost of goods sold.

85. If ending inventory is underestimated due to an error in the physical count of items on hand, then cost of goods sold for the period will be <List A> and net earnings will be <List B>.

	List A	List B
A.	Underestimated	Underestimated
B.	Underestimated	Overestimated
C.	Overestimated	Underestimated
D.	Overestimated	Overestimated

Answer (C) is correct. *(CIA, adapted)*

REQUIRED: The effect on cost of goods sold and net earnings of an error in counting inventory.

DISCUSSION: Cost of goods sold equals beginning inventory, plus purchases, minus ending inventory. If the ending inventory is underestimated, the cost of goods sold will be overestimated. If cost of goods sold is overestimated, net earnings will be underestimated.

86. The following inventory valuation errors have been discovered for Lithuania Corporation:

- The year 1 year-end inventory was overstated by $23,000.
- The year 2 year-end inventory was understated by $61,000.
- The year 3 year-end inventory was understated by $17,000.

The reported income before taxes for Knox was

Year	Income before Taxes
Year 1	$138,000
Year 2	254,000
Year 3	168,000

Reported income before taxes for year 1, year 2, and year 3, respectively, should have been

A. $161,000, $170,000, and $212,000.

B. $115,000, $338,000, and $124,000.

C. $161,000, $338,000, and $90,000.

D. $115,000, $338,000, and $212,000.

Answer (B) is correct. *(CMA, adapted)*

REQUIRED: The reported income after correction of inventory errors.

DISCUSSION: Cost of sales equals beginning inventory, plus purchases or cost of goods manufactured, minus ending inventory. Hence, over (under) statement of inventory affects cost of sales and income. The year 1 pretax income was affected by the $23,000 year 1 overstatement of year-end inventory. This error understated year 1 cost of sales and overstated pretax income. The corrected income is $115,000 ($138,000 – $23,000). The same $23,000 error caused year 2 income to be understated by overstating beginning inventory. In addition, the $61,000 understatement of year 2 year-end inventory also caused year 2 income to be understated. Thus, the corrected year 2 pretax income is $338,000 ($254,000 + $23,000 + $61,000). The $61,000 understatement at the end of year 2 caused year 3 income to be overstated by understating beginning inventory. Income for year 3 is understated by the $17,000 of year-end inventory understatement. Accordingly, the corrected income is $124,000 ($168,000 – $61,000 + $17,000).

Answer (A) is incorrect because year 1 income of $161,000 results from adding, not subtracting, the $23,000 overstatement of ending inventory. Similarly, year 2 income of $170,000 results from subtracting, not adding, the $23,000 overstatement of beginning inventory and the $61,000 understatement of ending inventory. Finally, year 3 income of $212,000 results from adding, not subtracting, the $61,000 understatement of beginning inventory and subtracting, not adding, the understatement of ending inventory. Answer (C) is incorrect because year 3 income of $90,000 results from subtracting, not adding, the $17,000 understatement of ending inventory. Answer (D) is incorrect because year 3 pre-tax income should be $124,000.

STUDY UNIT SEVEN
PROPERTY, PLANT, AND EQUIPMENT

Property, plant, and equipment (PP&E) are tangible assets held for use in long-term operations. PP&E include land, land improvements, buildings, machinery, equipment, furniture, fixtures, natural resources subject to depletion, leasehold improvements, leased assets held under capital leases, non-current assets under construction, and other depreciable assets. PP&E normally are recorded at **historical cost minus a provision for depreciation or depletion** (amortized cost). Historical cost includes the purchase price plus other costs necessary to make the asset ready for its intended use. Costs incurred subsequent to acquisition that significantly improve the future service potential of an asset by increasing the quality or quantity of its output or its estimated useful life are capitalized when incurred. Conversely, costs incurred to maintain an asset's operating condition are expensed when incurred.

SFAS 34, *Capitalization of Interest Cost*, requires capitalization of material interest costs for assets constructed for internal use, assets constructed for sale or lease as discrete products, and investments accounted for on the equity basis while the investee has activities in progress necessary to begin its planned principal operations. Capitalization of interest for a qualifying asset is required when (1) expenditures have been made, (2) activities are underway to prepare the asset for its intended use, and (3) interest cost is being incurred. The amount of interest cost to be capitalized is intended to be the portion of interest costs incurred during a qualifying asset's acquisition period that theoretically could have been avoided if expenditures for the asset had not been made. The amount of interest capitalized in an accounting period is determined by applying the capitalization rate to the **average amount of accumulated expenditures** for the asset during the period. The **capitalization** rate is based on rates applicable to borrowings outstanding during the period. The interest rate on construction loans specific to the qualifying asset is ordinarily used as the capitalization rate to the extent average accumulated expenditures for the period do not exceed the amount of the construction loan. A weighted-average rate on other borrowings outstanding during the period is used to the extent average accumulated expenditures for the period exceed the amount of the construction loan.

SFAS 144, *Accounting for the Impairment or Disposal of Long-Lived Assets*, applies to the long-lived assets of an entity that are to be held and used or disposed of. These assets may be included in a group with other assets and liabilities. The unit of accounting is the group. If a long-lived asset(s) is to be held and used, the **asset group** is the lowest level at which identifiable cash flows are largely independent of those of other groups. If a long-lived asset(s) is to be disposed of by sale or otherwise, the **disposal group** constitutes assets to be disposed of together in one transaction and directly associated liabilities to be transferred in the same transaction. A **long-lived asset (asset group) to be held and used** is impaired when its carrying amount is greater than its **fair value**. However, a loss equal to this excess is recognized only when the carrying amount is not **recoverable**, that is, when the carrying amount exceeds the sum of the undiscounted cash flows expected to arise from the use and disposition of the asset (asset group). Recoverability is tested when events or changes in circumstances provide indicators that the carrying amount of the asset (asset group) may not be recoverable. An impairment loss decreases only the carrying amounts of the long-lived assets in the group on a pro rata basis according to their relative carrying amounts. However, the carrying amount of a given long-lived asset is not reduced below its fair value (if determinable without undue cost and effort). The carrying amount of a long-lived asset adjusted for an impairment loss is its **new cost basis**. A previously recognized impairment loss may not be reversed. **Estimates of future cash flows employed in the recoverability test** are based on existing service potential and include only those directly associated with and expected to arise as a direct result of the use and disposition of the asset (asset group). The estimates must be based on the entity's own reasonable **assumptions** about its use of the asset (asset group) and all available evidence. The estimates are made for the **remaining useful life** as determined from the perspective of the entity. The remaining useful life is that of the **primary asset** of the group. An entity **reports** an impairment loss in income from continuing operations before income taxes. **Long-lived assets to be disposed of other than by sale**, for example, by abandonment, exchange, or a distribution to owners in a spinoff, are classified as held and used until disposal.

An asset (disposal group) is classified as **held for sale** when (1) a level of management with authority to approve the action has committed to a plan to sell, (2) the asset is available for immediate sale in its current condition on usual and customary terms, (3) actions (such as actively seeking a buyer) have begun to complete the plan, (4) completion of sale within 1 year is probable (but this condition need not be met if certain events or circumstances occur that the entity cannot control), (5) the asset is actively marketed at a price reasonably related to current fair value, and (6) there is little likelihood of significant change in or withdrawal of the plan. Whenever the foregoing conditions are not met, the asset or disposal group must be **reclassified** as held and used. **Measurement** is at the **lower of carrying amount or fair value minus cost to sell**. An asset classified as held for sale is not depreciated, but expenses related to the liabilities of a disposal group are accrued. **Costs to sell** are the incremental direct costs. A loss is recognized for a write-down to fair value minus cost to sell. A gain is recognized for any subsequent increase, but only to the extent of previously recognized losses for write-downs. The loss or gain adjusts only the carrying amount of a long-lived asset even if it is included in a disposal group. **Changes to a plan of sale** may occur because of circumstances previously regarded as unlikely that result in a decision not to sell. In these circumstances, the asset (disposal group) is **reclassified as held and used**. A **reclassification adjustment** to the carrying amount is included in income from continuing operations in the period of the decision not to sell. If a **long-lived asset** is held for sale, it is **reported** separately in the balance sheet. If a **disposal group** is held for sale, its assets and liabilities are reported separately in the balance sheet and are not offset and presented as a single amount.

Monetary assets include cash and such assets as short- or long-term receivables whose amounts are fixed in terms of cash. **Nonmonetary assets** are such assets as inventory; investments in stock; and property, plant, and equipment. The value of these assets in terms of cash may change over time (APB 29). **Nonmonetary transactions** generally involve only nonmonetary assets. However, a transaction that includes cash (termed **boot**) should still be classified as nonmonetary, provided that the boot is less than 25% of the fair value of the exchange (EITF 86-29). Accounting for **monetary transactions** should be based on the **fair value** of the assets involved, with gain or loss recognized immediately. Fair value of the asset relinquished generally is used unless the fair value of the asset received is more evident. Accounting for nonmonetary transactions also should be based on fair value. However, accounting for nonmonetary transactions should be based on the **carrying amount** of the asset relinquished when the transaction is (1) an exchange in which neither the fair value of the asset relinquished nor the fair value of the asset received is determinable within reasonable limits, (2) an exchange of **inventory** sold in the same line of business that is undertaken to facilitate sales to customers other than the parties to the exchange, or (3) an exchange that lacks commercial substance. An exchange **lacks commercial substance** when an entity's cash flows are not expected to change significantly. Cash flows do not change significantly when (1) the configuration (risk, timing, and amount) of the entity's future cash flows is not expected to change significantly as a result of the exchange, or (2) the **entity-specific values** of the assets involved do not differ significantly (**SFAS 153**, *Exchanges of Nonmonetary Assets*). In addition, when boot is received equal to less than 25% of the fair value of the exchange, the recipient should adjust the carryover basis for the portion of the gain equal to the total gain times the ratio of the boot to the sum of the boot plus the fair value of the asset received. However, the full amount of any loss is recognized as an adjustment of the carryover basis.

QUESTIONS

7.1 Acquisition Cost

1. Property, plant, and equipment are conventionally presented in the balance sheet at

A. Replacement cost minus accumulated depreciation.

B. Historical cost minus salvage value.

C. Original cost adjusted for general price-level changes.

D. Historical cost minus depreciated portion thereof.

Answer (D) is correct. *(CPA, adapted)*

REQUIRED: The conventional balance sheet presentation of property, plant, and equipment.

DISCUSSION: Property, plant, and equipment are recorded at their acquisition cost. They are then measured in accordance with SFAC 5 at their historical cost attribute. When property, plant, and equipment are used in normal operations, this historical cost must be allocated (depreciated) on a systematic and rational basis to the accounting periods in which they are used. Land is an exception because it is not depreciated.

Answer (A) is incorrect because historical cost rather than replacement cost is the attribute at which property, plant, and equipment are measured. Answer (B) is incorrect because assets appear in the balance sheet at historical cost with an offset for accumulated depreciation (not salvage value). Answer (C) is incorrect because the basic financial statements are not adjusted for price-level changes.

2. A contributed plant asset for which the fair value has been determined, and for which incidental costs were incurred in acceptance of the asset, should be recorded at an amount equal to its

A. Incidental costs incurred.

B. Fair value and incidental costs incurred.

C. Carrying amount on books of donor and incidental costs incurred.

D. Carrying amount on books of donor.

Answer (B) is correct. *(CPA, adapted)*

REQUIRED: The amount at which a contributed plant asset should be recorded.

DISCUSSION: A contributed plant asset should be debited at its fair value plus any incidental costs necessary to make the asset ready for its intended use. Contributions received ordinarily should be credited as revenues or gains in the periods they are received. However, a credit to a revenue or gain is not required for contributions by governments to business enterprises (SFAS 116, *Accounting for Contributions Received and Contributions Made*).

3. Charging the cost of ordinary repairs to the machinery and equipment asset account during the current year

A. Understates net income for the current year.

B. Understates equity at the end of the current year.

C. Does not affect the total assets at the end of the current year.

D. Does not affect the total liabilities at the end of the current year.

Answer (D) is correct. *(CMA, adapted)*

REQUIRED: The effect of charging the cost of ordinary repairs to the machinery and equipment asset account.

DISCUSSION: When an asset is acquired, the expenses of maintaining the asset are expenses of the period in which the ordinary repairs are rendered. Charging such ordinary repairs to the machinery and equipment asset account overstates total assets, the current year's net income, and equity. Liabilities are not affected.

Answer (A) is incorrect because net income is overstated (not understated). Answer (B) is incorrect because equity is overstated (not understated). Answer (C) is incorrect because assets are overstated.

4. When fixed assets are self-constructed, which costs should be expensed in the period of construction?

A. Excess of construction costs over third-party selling price.

B. Fixed and variable overhead costs.

C. Fees paid to outside consultants.

D. Cost of safety devices required by government agencies.

Answer (A) is correct. *(Publisher)*

REQUIRED: The costs of self-constructed fixed assets that should be expensed in the period of construction.

DISCUSSION: An asset should not be recorded in excess of its fair value. Thus, a self-constructed fixed asset should not be capitalized at an amount greater than that at which the asset could be purchased from a third party. Any excess cost is a loss that should not be deferred to future periods and should be expensed.

Answer (B) is incorrect because some fixed costs may be expensed rather than capitalized when the construction reduces normal production. Answer (C) is incorrect because expenditures directly related to the construction of fixed assets should be capitalized. Answer (D) is incorrect because expenditures directly related to the construction of fixed assets should be capitalized.

5. According to current authoritative literature, write-ups of property, plant, and equipment to reflect current appraisals are

A. Permissible only during times of rapidly increasing prices.

B. Permissible provided current value evidence is sufficiently objective.

C. Usually not acceptable in financial statements.

D. Permitted in statements of unconsolidated United States domestic subsidiaries.

Answer (C) is correct. *(Publisher)*

REQUIRED: The permissibility of write-ups of property, plant, and equipment to reflect current appraisals.

DISCUSSION: APB 6, *Status of Accounting Research Bulletins*, states that property, plant, and equipment should not be written up by an entity to reflect appraisal, market, or current values that are above cost to the business. The exceptions to this rule are minor.

Answer (A) is incorrect because write-ups to reflect current appraisals are usually not permissible. Answer (B) is incorrect because APB 6 makes no exception for circumstances in which evidence of current value is sufficiently objective. Answer (D) is incorrect because write-ups to reflect current appraisals are usually not permissible.

6. On January 2, Novation Corp. replaced its boiler with a more efficient one. The following information was available on that date:

Purchase price of new boiler	$120,000
Carrying amount of old boiler	10,000
Fair value of old boiler	4,000
Installation cost of new boiler	16,000

The old boiler was sold for $4,000. What amount should Novation capitalize as the cost of the new boiler?

A. $136,000

B. $132,000

C. $126,000

D. $120,000

Answer (A) is correct. *(CPA, adapted)*

REQUIRED: The amount to be capitalized as the cost of the replacement asset.

DISCUSSION: When a fixed asset is replaced, the new asset should be recorded at its purchase price plus any incidental costs necessary to make the asset ready for its intended use. Consequently, the replacement boiler should be recorded at $136,000 ($120,000 purchase price + $16,000 installation cost). In addition, the $10,000 carrying amount of the old boiler should be removed from the accounts, and a loss of $6,000 ($4,000 proceeds – $10,000 carrying amount) should be recognized.

Answer (B) is incorrect because $132,000 improperly deducts the fair value of the old boiler. Answer (C) is incorrect because $126,000 results from deducting the carrying amount of the old boiler. Answer (D) is incorrect because $120,000 does not consider the installation costs.

7. A machine with an original estimated useful life of 10 years is moved to another location in the factory after it has been in service for 3 years. The efficiency of the machine is increased for its remaining useful life. The reinstallation costs should be capitalized if the remaining useful life of the machine is

	5 Years	10 Years
A.	No	No
B.	No	Yes
C.	Yes	No
D.	Yes	Yes

Answer (D) is correct. *(CPA, adapted)*

REQUIRED: The proper treatment of reinstallation costs that increase a machine's efficiency.

DISCUSSION: Costs that significantly improve the future service potential of an asset by increasing the quality or quantity of its output should be capitalized even though the machine's useful life is not extended. The reinstallation cost should be capitalized whether the remaining useful life is 5 or 10 years.

8. Chapeau Co. incurred costs to modify its building and to rearrange its production line. As a result, an overall reduction in production costs is expected. However, the modifications did not increase the building's market value, and the rearrangement did not extend the production line's life. Should the building modification costs and the production line rearrangement costs be capitalized?

	Building Modification Costs	Production Line Rearrangement Costs
A.	Yes	No
B.	Yes	Yes
C.	No	No
D.	No	Yes

Answer (B) is correct. *(CPA, adapted)*

REQUIRED: The accounting for building modification costs and production line rearrangement costs.

DISCUSSION: A rearrangement is the movement of existing assets to provide greater efficiency or to reduce production costs. If the rearrangement expenditure benefits future periods, it should be capitalized. If the building modification costs likewise improve future service potential, they too should be capitalized.

Answer (A) is incorrect because the production line rearrangement costs should be capitalized. Answer (C) is incorrect because the building modification costs and production line rearrangement costs should be capitalized. Answer (D) is incorrect because the building modification costs should be capitalized.

9. A building suffered uninsured fire damage. The damaged portion of the building was refurbished with higher quality materials. The cost and related accumulated depreciation of the damaged portion are identifiable. To account for these events, the owner should

A. Reduce accumulated depreciation equal to the cost of refurbishing.

B. Record a loss in the current period equal to the sum of the cost of refurbishing and the carrying amount of the damaged portion of the building.

C. Capitalize the cost of refurbishing and record a loss in the current period equal to the carrying amount of the damaged portion of the building.

D. Capitalize the cost of refurbishing by adding the cost to the carrying amount of the building.

Answer (C) is correct. *(CPA, adapted)*

REQUIRED: The proper accounting for a substitution.

DISCUSSION: When a substantial portion of a productive asset is replaced and the cost and related accumulated depreciation associated with the old component are identifiable, the substitution method of accounting is used. Under this approach, the asset account and accumulated depreciation should be reduced by the appropriate amounts and a gain or loss recognized. In this instance, the damages were uninsured, and a loss equal to the carrying amount of the damaged portion of the building should be recognized. In addition, the cost of refurbishing should be capitalized in the asset account.

10. During year 1, Kapital Company spent $2,700,000 to rearrange and $1,200,000 to reinstall the assembly line at one of its plants in order to convert the plant over to the manufacture of a new company product beginning in year 2. The $1,200,000 in reinstallation costs were charged to the related machinery and equipment, which has an average remaining useful life of 15 years. The new product has an expected life of 9 years. The $2,700,000 in rearrangement costs should be charged in year 1 to

A. A deferred expense account and expensed at a rate of $300,000 per year beginning in year 2.

B. A deferred expense account that is never amortized.

C. An expense account.

D. Factory machinery and equipment and depreciated over 15 years.

Answer (A) is correct. *(CIA, adapted)*

REQUIRED: The proper accounting for rearrangement costs.

DISCUSSION: Costs that significantly improve the future service potential of an asset by increasing the quality or quantity of its output should be capitalized. Because the rearrangement and reinstallation costs were incurred to increase the productivity of the assembly line, both costs should be capitalized as part of the related machinery and equipment. These capitalized costs should then be amortized over the expected 9-year life of the new product. Thus, the $2,700,000 in rearrangement costs should be debited to either the asset account or a deferred expense account and then expensed over the 9 years at a rate of $300,000 per year.

Answer (B) is incorrect because the rearrangement costs should be capitalized and amortized over 9 years. Answer (C) is incorrect because the rearrangement costs increase the quality or quantity of output so the costs should not be treated as an expense. Answer (D) is incorrect because the rearrangement costs benefit the new product which has an expected life of 9 years; therefore, the cost should not be amortized over 15 years (the life of the old equipment).

11. An expenditure subsequent to acquisition of assembly-line manufacturing equipment benefits future periods. The expenditure should be capitalized if it is a

	Betterment	Rearrangement
A.	No	No
B.	No	Yes
C.	Yes	No
D.	Yes	Yes

Answer (D) is correct. *(CPA, adapted)*

REQUIRED: The type(s) of expenditure that should be capitalized.

DISCUSSION: A betterment occurs when a replacement asset is substituted for an existing asset, and the result is increased productivity, capacity, or expected useful life. A rearrangement is the movement of existing assets to provide greater efficiency or to reduce production costs. If the betterment or rearrangement expenditure benefits future periods, it should be capitalized.

12. During the current year, Murdock Company made the following expenditures relating to plant machinery and equipment:

- Renovation of a group of machines at a cost of $100,000 to secure greater efficiency in production over their remaining 5-year useful lives. The project was completed on December 31.
- Continuing, frequent, and low-cost repairs at a cost of $70,000.
- Replacement of a broken gear on a machine at a cost of $10,000.

What total amount should be charged to repairs and maintenance for the current year?

A. $70,000

B. $80,000

C. $170,000

D. $180,000

Answer (B) is correct. *(CPA, adapted)*

REQUIRED: The amount to be charged to repair and maintenance expense.

DISCUSSION: Repair and maintenance costs are incurred to maintain plant assets in operating condition. The continuing, frequent, and low-cost repairs and the replacement of a broken gear meet the definition of repairs and maintenance expense. Accordingly, the amount that should be charged to repairs and maintenance is $80,000 ($70,000 + $10,000). The renovation cost increased the quality of production during the expected useful life of the group of machines. Hence, this $100,000 cost should be capitalized.

Answer (A) is incorrect because the cost of a broken gear should also be charged to repairs and maintenance. Answer (C) is incorrect because the renovation of machines should not be charged to repairs and maintenance; it should be capitalized. The broken gear should be included in repairs and maintenance. Answer (D) is incorrect because the renovation of machines should be capitalized, not charged to repairs and maintenance.

13. On November 2, Corley Co. incurred the following costs for one of its printing presses:

Purchase of collating and stapling attachment	$168,000
Installation of attachment	72,000
Replacement parts for overhaul of press	52,000
Labor and overhead in connection with overhaul	28,000

The overhaul resulted in a significant increase in production. Neither the attachment nor the overhaul increased the estimated useful life of the press. What amount of the above costs should be capitalized?

A. $0

B. $168,000

C. $240,000

D. $320,000

Answer (D) is correct. *(CPA, adapted)*

REQUIRED: The amount of costs to be capitalized.

DISCUSSION: Expenditures that increase the quality or quantity of a machine's output should be capitalized whether or not its useful life is extended. Thus, the amount of the cost to be capitalized equals $320,000 ($168,000 + $72,000 + $52,000 + $28,000).

Answer (A) is incorrect because $320,000 of costs should be capitalized. Answer (B) is incorrect because all of the costs associated with the purchase of the parts and the overhaul should be capitalized. Answer (C) is incorrect because the cost of replacement parts and labor and overhead should also be capitalized.

14. Meriadoc Co. purchased a machine costing $125,000 for its manufacturing operations and paid shipping costs of $20,000. It spent an additional $10,000 testing and preparing the machine for use. What amount should Meriadoc record as the cost of the machine?

A. $155,000

B. $145,000

C. $135,000

D. $125,000

Answer (A) is correct. *(CPA, adapted)*

REQUIRED: The amount to be recorded as the acquisition cost of the machine.

DISCUSSION: The amount to be recorded as the acquisition cost of a machine includes all costs necessary to prepare it for its intended use. Thus, the cost of a machine used in the manufacturing operations of a company includes the cost of testing and preparing the machine for use and the shipping costs. The acquisition cost is $155,000 ($125,000 + $20,000 + $10,000).

Answer (B) is incorrect because $145,000 does not include the $10,000 cost of testing and preparation. Answer (C) is incorrect because $135,000 does not include the shipping costs. Answer (D) is incorrect because $125,000 does not include the shipping, testing, and preparation costs.

15. On July 1, year 1, Colman Company sold land with a carrying amount of $75,000 to Monte Company in exchange for $50,000 in cash and a note calling for five annual $10,000 payments beginning on June 30, year 2, and ending on June 30, year 6. The fair value of the land is uncertain, and Monte can borrow long-term funds at 11%. What should be the amount capitalized as acquisition cost of the land by Monte Company? (The present value of $1 for five periods at 11% is 0.59345, and the present value of an ordinary annuity of $1 for five periods at 11% is 3.6959.)

A. $55,935

B. $75,000

C. $86,959

D. $100,000

Answer (C) is correct. *(S. Schultz)*

REQUIRED: The cost at which an asset should be capitalized when acquired under a financing agreement.

DISCUSSION: The acquisition of land should be recorded at fair value. When the fair value of the asset received is uncertain, the fair value of the assets transferred is used. The assets transferred included $50,000 in cash and a note. Given that Monte can borrow long-term funds at 11%, the market value of the note can be approximated by imputing an 11% rate and using it to calculate the present value of the five equal annual payments. The present value of this ordinary annuity is $36,959 ($10,000 payment × 3.6959), and the land should be recorded at $86,959 ($50,000 + $36,959).

Answer (A) is incorrect because $55,935 is the $50,000 in cash plus the present value of $10,000 to be received in 5 years. Answer (B) is incorrect because $75,000 is Colman Company's carrying amount of the land. Answer (D) is incorrect because $100,000 is the $50,000 in cash plus $50,000 of payments which should have been calculated at present value.

16. On December 1 of the current year, Horton Co. purchased a tract of land as a factory site for $300,000. The old building on the property was razed, and salvaged materials resulting from demolition were sold. Additional costs incurred and salvage proceeds realized during December were as follows:

Cost to raze old building	$25,000
Legal fees for purchase contract and to record ownership	5,000
Title guarantee insurance	6,000
Proceeds from sale of salvaged materials	4,000

In Horton's current year balance sheet dated December 31, what amount should be reported as land?

A. $311,000

B. $321,000

C. $332,000

D. $336,000

Answer (C) is correct. *(CPA, adapted)*

REQUIRED: The amount to be reported as the cost of land.

DISCUSSION: When land is acquired as a factory site, the cost of the land should include the purchase price of the land and such additional expenses as legal fees, title insurance, recording fees, subsequent assumption of encumbrances on the property, and the costs incurred in preparing the property for its intended use. Because the land was purchased as a factory site, the cost of razing the old building, minus any proceeds received from the sale of salvaged materials, should be capitalized as part of the land account. Thus, the amount to be reported as land is $332,000 ($300,000 + $5,000 + $6,000 + $25,000 – $4,000).

Answer (A) is incorrect because $311,000 excludes the net cost of razing the old building. Answer (B) is incorrect because $321,000 excludes the legal fees and title insurance. Answer (D) is incorrect because $336,000 excludes the proceeds of razing the old building.

17. Land was purchased to be used as the site for the construction of a plant. A building on the property was sold and removed by the buyer so that construction on the plant could begin. The proceeds from the sale of the building should be

A. Classified as other income.

B. Deducted from the cost of the land.

C. Netted against the costs to clear the land and expensed as incurred.

D. Netted against the costs to clear the land and amortized over the life of the plant.

Answer (B) is correct. *(CPA, adapted)*

REQUIRED: The treatment of proceeds from the sale of a building removed to prepare for construction.

DISCUSSION: Land obtained as a plant site should be recorded at its acquisition cost. This cost includes the purchase price of the land and any additional expenses such as legal fees, title insurance, recording fees, assumption of encumbrances on the property, and any other costs incurred in preparing the property for its intended use. Because the intended use of the land was as a site for the construction of a plant, the proceeds from the sale of the building removed to prepare the land for construction should be deducted from the cost of the land.

18. During the current year, Hamilton Co. had the following transactions pertaining to its new office building:

Purchase price of land	$120,000
Legal fees for contracts to purchase land	4,000
Architects' fees	16,000
Demolition of the old building on site	10,000
Sale of scrap from old building	6,000
Construction cost of new building (fully completed)	700,000

In Hamilton's current year balance sheet dated December 31, what amounts should be reported as the cost of land and cost of building?

	Land	Building
A.	$120,000	$720,000
B.	$124,000	$720,000
C.	$128,000	$716,000
D.	$130,000	$724,000

Answer (C) is correct. *(CPA, adapted)*

REQUIRED: The amounts reported as the cost of land and cost of building.

DISCUSSION: The cost of the land should include the purchase price of the land and additional expenses such as legal fees, title insurance, recording fees, subsequent assumption of encumbrances on the property, and the costs incurred in preparing the property for its intended use. Because the land was purchased as the site of an office building, the cost of razing the old building, minus any proceeds received from the sale of salvaged materials, should be capitalized as part of the land account. Thus, land should be reported as $128,000 ($120,000 + $4,000 + $10,000 – $6,000). The architects' fees are included in the cost of the building, which should be reported as $716,000 ($700,000 + $16,000).

Answer (A) is incorrect because a $120,000 land cost omits the legal fees and the net demolition cost, and a $720,000 building cost improperly includes the legal fees. Answer (B) is incorrect because a $124,000 land cost omits the legal fees or the net demolition cost, and a $720,000 building cost improperly includes the legal fees. Answer (D) is incorrect because a $130,000 land cost includes the gross demolition cost but not the legal fees. A $724,000 building cost includes the legal fees and the net demolition cost.

19. On July 1 of the current year, Degas Co. purchased a tract of land for $1,200,000. Degas incurred additional costs of $300,000 during the remainder of the year in preparing the land for sale. The tract was subdivided into residential lots as follows:

Lot Class	Number of Lots	Sales Price per Lot
A	100	$24,000
B	100	16,000
C	200	10,000

Using the relative sales value method, what amount of costs should be allocated to the Class A lots?

A. $300,000

B. $375,000

C. $600,000

D. $720,000

Answer (C) is correct. *(CPA, adapted)*

REQUIRED: The amount of costs allocated using the relative sales value method.

DISCUSSION: The relative sales value method allocates cost based on the relative value of assets in a group. The total sales value of the lots is $6,000,000 [($24,000 × 100) + ($16,000 × 100) + ($10,000 × 200)]. Class A represents 40% of the total value ($2,400,000 ÷ $6,000,000). Total costs equal $1,500,000 ($1,200,000 + $300,000). Thus, the amount of costs allocated to Class A is $600,000 ($1,500,000 × .40).

Answer (A) is incorrect because $300,000 equals the additional costs incurred. Answer (B) is incorrect because $375,000 equals 25% of the total cost. Class A represents 25% of the lots but 40% of the total value. Answer (D) is incorrect because $720,000 equals 48% of the total cost. Class A's sales price per lot is 48% of the sum of the unit sales prices of Classes A, B, and C.

7.2 Capitalization of Interest

20. According to SFAS 34, *Capitalization of Interest Costs*, interest should be capitalized for assets that are

A. In use or ready for their intended use in the earning activities of the enterprise.

B. Being constructed or otherwise being produced as discrete projects for an enterprise's own use.

C. Not being used in the earning activities of the enterprise and not undergoing the activities necessary to get them ready for use.

D. Routinely produced.

Answer (B) is correct. *(CMA, adapted)*

REQUIRED: The types of assets for which interest should be capitalized.

DISCUSSION: SFAS 34 requires capitalization of material interest costs for assets constructed for internal use and those constructed for sale or lease as discrete projects. It does not apply to products routinely produced for inventory, assets in use or ready for use, assets not being used or being prepared for use, and idle land.

Answer (A) is incorrect because interest is not capitalized for assets in use or ready for use. Answer (C) is incorrect because assets not being used and being prepared for use are not subject to interest capitalization rules. Answer (D) is incorrect because capitalized interest should not be added to routinely produced inventory.

21. During the current year, Elbridge Co. constructed machinery for its own use and for sale to customers. Bank loans financed these assets both during construction and after construction was complete. How much of the interest incurred should be reported as interest expense in the current year income statement?

	Interest Incurred for Machinery for Elbridge's Own Use	Interest Incurred for Machinery Held for Sale
A.	All interest incurred	All interest incurred
B.	All interest incurred	Interest incurred after completion
C.	Interest incurred after completion	Interest incurred after completion
D.	Interest incurred after completion	All interest incurred

Answer (D) is correct. *(CPA, adapted)*

REQUIRED: The interest incurred reported as interest expense.

DISCUSSION: In accordance with SFAS 34, interest should be capitalized for two types of assets: those constructed or otherwise produced for an enterprise's own use, including those constructed or produced by others; and those intended for sale or lease that are constructed or produced as discrete products (e.g., ships). SFAS 58, *Capitalization of Interest Cost in Financial Statements That Include Investments Accounted for by the Equity Method*, adds equity-based investments to the list of qualifying assets. Machinery constructed for a company's own use qualifies for capitalization of interest if relevant expenditures have been made, activities necessary to prepare the asset for its intended use are in progress, and interest is being incurred. Machinery routinely constructed for sale to others does not qualify. Thus, interest incurred for machinery held for sale and interest incurred after an asset has been completed should be expensed.

22. During a calendar-year company's second quarter, the following expenditures were made relative to a qualifying asset on which interest is to be capitalized: $80,000 on April 1, $90,000 on May 1, and $100,000 incurred uniformly during the period. What was the average amount of accumulated expenditures for this quarterly accounting period?

A. $180,000

B. $190,000

C. $240,000

D. $270,000

Answer (B) is correct. *(Publisher)*

REQUIRED: The average accumulated expenditures.

DISCUSSION: To determine the average accumulated expenditures on which interest is to be capitalized, the expenditures must be weighted by the portion of the accounting period for which they were incurred. The $80,000 expended on April 1 was incurred during the entire period. The $90,000 expended on May 1 was incurred for two-thirds of the period. The $100,000 incurred uniformly throughout is equivalent to an expenditure of $50,000 for the whole period. The average amount of accumulated expenditures is equal to $190,000 [($80,000 × 1) + ($90,000 × 2/3) + ($100,000 × 1/2)].

Answer (A) is incorrect because $180,000 assumes the whole $100,000 is included and none of the $90,000. Answer (C) is incorrect because $240,000 assumes that the whole $100,000 is included. Answer (D) is incorrect because $270,000 is not the average amount of accumulated expenditures; it is the sum of the three interest expenditures.

23. Which one of the following ways of determining an interest rate should be used when the average accumulated expenditures for the constructed asset exceed the amounts of specific new borrowings associated with the asset?

A. Average rate of return on equity for the last 5 years.

B. Cost of capital rate for the company.

C. Prime interest rate.

D. Weighted average of the interest rates applicable to the other borrowings of the company.

Answer (D) is correct. *(CMA, adapted)*

REQUIRED: The method of determining the interest rate.

DISCUSSION: The actual interest rate on specific new borrowings is used to capitalize construction expenditures to the extent of the new borrowings. If average accumulated construction expenditures for the period exceed the specific new borrowings related to the construction, interest on other borrowings must be capitalized. SFAS 34 requires a weighted-average interest rate to be used to capitalize interest costs on accumulated construction expenditures in excess of the specific new borrowings associated with the asset.

Answer (A) is incorrect because average rate of return on equity for the last 5 years is not specified by SFAS 34. Answer (B) is incorrect because cost of capital rate for the company is not specified by SFAS 34. Answer (C) is incorrect because prime interest rate is not specified by SFAS 34.

24. Harbor Co. began constructing a building for its own use in January of the current year. During the current year, Harbor incurred interest of $100,000 on specific construction debt, and $40,000 on other borrowings. Interest computed on the weighted-average amount of accumulated expenditures for the building during the current year was $80,000. What amount of interest cost should Harbor capitalize?

A. $40,000

B. $80,000

C. $100,000

D. $140,000

Answer (B) is correct. *(CPA, adapted)*

REQUIRED: The amount of interest capitalized.

DISCUSSION: Material interest costs incurred for the construction of certain assets for internal use are capitalized. The interest to be capitalized is determined by applying an appropriate rate to the average qualifying expenditures accumulated during a given period. Thus, $80,000 of the interest incurred on the construction is capitalized.

Answer (A) is incorrect because $40,000 equals interest on other borrowings. Answer (C) is incorrect because $100,000 equals the total interest on specific construction debt. Answer (D) is incorrect because $140,000 equals the sum of interest on other borrowings and the total interest on specific construction debt.

25. Which of the following is not an accurate statement of a criterion that must be met before interest is required to be capitalized in accordance with the provisions of SFAS 34?

A. Expenditures relative to a qualifying asset have been made.

B. Activities necessary to prepare the asset for its intended use are in progress.

C. Interest cost is incurred on borrowings.

D. Debt is incurred for the project.

Answer (D) is correct. *(Publisher)*

REQUIRED: The criterion not required by SFAS 34.

DISCUSSION: Capitalization of interest for a qualifying asset is required when expenditures have been made, activities are in progress to ready the asset for its intended use, and interest cost is being incurred. The mere incurrence of debt is not sufficient. Capitalized interest is limited to interest on borrowings. Accordingly, the incurrence of debt, such as trade payables, upon which no interest cost is being incurred, is not sufficient to meet the required criteria, even if qualifying expenditures have been made and the appropriate activities are in progress.

26. Which of the following items should not have been capitalized?

A. The cost of reinstalling or rearranging equipment to facilitate more efficient future production.

B. The cost of removing an old building from land that was purchased with the intent of constructing a new office building on the site.

C. The estimated cost of equity capital during the construction period of a new office building.

D. The cost of a new hospital wing.

Answer (C) is correct. *(CIA, adapted)*

REQUIRED: The item that should not have been capitalized.

DISCUSSION: SFAS 34 requires the capitalization of interest on debt incurred as a cost of acquiring an asset during the period in which an asset is being constructed for the company's own use. Imputed interest on equity capital is not capitalized. The view of the FASB is that recognizing the cost of equity capital would not conform to the current accounting framework.

Answer (A) is incorrect because such a cost will benefit future periods and thus should be capitalized. Answer (B) is incorrect because the removal cost is associated with preparing land for its intended use and therefore should be capitalized. Answer (D) is incorrect because a new hospital wing is an addition and should be capitalized.

27. SFAS 62, *Capitalization of Interest Cost in Situations Involving Certain Tax-Exempt Borrowings and Certain Gifts and Grants*, amends SFAS 34 to require the offsetting of related interest income and interest expense in situations involving acquisition of qualifying assets financed with the proceeds of tax-exempt borrowings. SFAS 62 applies

A. To assets acquired with gifts and grants that are restricted by the donor or grantor to the acquisition of particular assets to the extent funds are available.

B. When those funds are externally restricted to the financing of specific qualifying assets.

C. Only if the funds are used for nonqualifying assets.

D. If the interest earned is less than 50% of the related interest expense.

Answer (B) is correct. *(Publisher)*

REQUIRED: The condition under which interest income from funds raised by tax-exempt borrowings and not yet expended for qualifying assets may offset capitalizable interest expense.

DISCUSSION: Ordinarily, interest income earned should not be offset against interest costs in determining the amount of interest to be capitalized. An exception is provided by SFAS 62 when qualifying assets are financed with the proceeds of tax-exempt borrowings, and the funds are externally restricted to the acquisition of specified qualifying assets or to the servicing of the debt related to those assets.

Answer (A) is incorrect because the interest earned from investments of gifts and grants is considered an addition to the gift or grant by SFAS 62. Answer (C) is incorrect because the funds must be used for qualifying assets (as specified in SFAS 62). Answer (D) is incorrect because no limits exist on the amount of interest income that can offset interest expense.

28. SFAS 42, *Determining Materiality for Capitalization of Interest Cost*, amended SFAS 34 in which of the following ways?

A. It set new materiality standards based on the remote, reasonably possible, and probable standards.

B. It constituted a minor wording change to avoid new tests of materiality for interest capitalization.

C. It provided a detailed cost benefit formula to determine if interest cost needs to be capitalized.

D. It concluded that interest cost does not need to be capitalized if the rollover effect occurring from amortizing previously capitalized interest approximates interest costs planned in the future.

Answer (B) is correct. *(Publisher)*

REQUIRED: The true statement regarding the effect of SFAS 42 on capitalization of interest costs.

DISCUSSION: SFAS 34 implies that interest may not have to be capitalized when the net income over a series of years is approximately the same whether interest is capitalized or expensed. This situation could occur when amortization equals the annual interest expense. SFAS 42 corrects this implication by requiring interest to be capitalized on qualifying assets when the usual materiality requirements are met.

Answer (A) is incorrect because SFAS 42 reaffirms that SFAS 34 does not establish new tests of materiality. Answer (C) is incorrect because SFAS 34 requires interest cost on certain qualifying assets to be capitalized regardless of cost-benefit analysis. Answer (D) is incorrect because SFAS 34 requires interest cost on certain qualifying assets to be capitalized regardless of the effect on net income.

29. SFAS 58, *Capitalization of Interest Cost in Financial Statements That Include Investments Accounted for by the Equity Method*, clarifies when interest may be capitalized on equity method investments and other assets. SFAS 58 concludes that interest may be capitalized on

A. Equity method investments in activities in progress necessary to the commencement of the planned principal operations when the activities include the use of funds to acquire qualifying assets.

B. Assets that are not included in the consolidated balance sheet of a parent company with consolidated subsidiaries.

C. Investments accounted for by the equity method after the planned principal operations of the investee begin.

D. Investments in regulated investees that are capitalizing the cost of both debt and equity capital.

Answer (A) is correct. *(Publisher)*

REQUIRED: The qualifying assets on which interest may be capitalized under SFAS 58.

DISCUSSION: SFAS 58 applies to investments in joint ventures, unconsolidated subsidiaries, and investees accounted for under the equity method. If these investees are in the process of commencing planned principal operations and they are using funds to acquire qualifying assets for their operations, interest may be capitalized as part of the investment.

Answer (B) is incorrect because SFAS 58 specifically prohibits capitalizing interest on assets that are not included in the consolidated balance sheet of a parent company with consolidated subsidiaries. Answer (C) is incorrect because SFAS 58 specifically prohibits capitalizing interest on investments accounted for by the equity method after the planned principal operations of the investee begin. Answer (D) is incorrect because SFAS 58 specifically prohibits capitalizing interest on investments in regulated investees that are capitalizing the cost of both debt and equity capital.

7.3 Impairment and Disposal

30. SFAS 144, *Accounting for the Impairment or Disposal of Long-Lived Assets*, requires testing for possible impairment of a long-lived asset (asset group) that an entity expects to hold and use

A. At each interim and annual balance sheet date.

B. At annual balance sheet dates only.

C. Periodically.

D. Whenever events or changes in circumstances indicate that its carrying amount may not be recoverable.

Answer (D) is correct. *(Publisher)*

REQUIRED: The appropriate time for testing impairment of a long-lived asset (asset group) to be held and used.

DISCUSSION: A long-lived asset (asset group) to which SFAS 144 applies is tested for recoverability whenever events or changes in circumstances indicate that its carrying amount may not be recoverable. The carrying amount is not recoverable when it exceeds the sum of the undiscounted cash flows expected to result from the use and disposition of the asset (asset group). If the carrying amount is not recoverable, an impairment loss is recognized equal to the excess of the carrying amount over the fair value.

31. On January 2, year 1, Clarinette Co. purchased assets for $400,000 that were to be depreciated over 5 years using the straight-line method with no salvage value. Taken together, these assets have identifiable cash flows that are largely independent of the cash flows of other asset groups. At the end of year 2, Clarinette, as the result of certain changes in circumstances indicating that the carrying amount of these assets may not be recoverable, tested them for impairment. It estimated that it will receive net future cash inflows (undiscounted) of $100,000 as a result of continuing to hold and use these assets, which had a fair value of $80,000 at the end of year 2. Thus, the impairment loss to be reported at December 31, year 2, is

A. $0

B. $140,000

C. $160,000

D. $400,000

Answer (C) is correct. *(Publisher)*

REQUIRED: The carrying amount given estimated future net cash inflows and the fair value.

DISCUSSION: The carrying amount at December 31, year 2 is $240,000 {$400,000 cost – [2 years × ($400,000 ÷ 5 years)]}, but the recoverable amount is only $100,000. Hence, the SFAS 144 test for recognition of an impairment loss has been met. This loss is measured by the excess of the carrying amount over the fair value. Clarinette should therefore recognize a loss of $160,000 ($240,000 – $80,000 fair value).

Answer (A) is incorrect because the test for recognition of impairment has been met. Answer (B) is incorrect because $140,000 is the excess of the carrying amount over the undiscounted future net cash inflows. Answer (D) is incorrect because $400,000 is the purchase price of the assets.

32. Tera Corporation owns a plant that produces baubles for a specialized market niche. This plant is part of a an asset group that is the lowest level at which identifiable cash flows are largely independent of those of Tera's other holdings. The asset group includes long-lived assets X, Y, and Z, which are to be held and used. It also includes current assets and liabilities that are not subject to SFAS 144, *Accounting for the Impairment or Disposal of Long-Lived Assets*. The sum of the undiscounted cash flows expected to result from the use and eventual disposition of the asset group is $3,200,000, and its fair value is $2,900,000. The following are the carrying amounts ($000 omitted) of the assets and liabilities included in the asset group:

Current assets	$ 600
Liabilities	(200)
Long-lived asset X	1,500
Y	900
Z	600

If the fair value of X is determinable as $1,400,000 without undue cost and effort, what should be the carrying amount of Z?

A. $440,000

B. $500,000

C. $600,000

D. $660,000

Answer (A) is correct. *(Publisher)*

REQUIRED: The carrying amount of Z.

DISCUSSION: An impairment loss decreases only the carrying amounts of the long-lived assets in the group on a pro rata basis according to their relative carrying amounts. However, the carrying amount of a given long-lived asset is not reduced below its fair value if that fair value is determinable without undue cost and effort. Because the total carrying amount of the asset group of $3.4 million ($600 – $200 + $1,500 + $900 + $600) exceeds the $3.2 million sum of the undiscounted cash flows expected to result from the use and eventual disposition of the asset group, the carrying amount is not recoverable. Hence, an impairment loss equal to the excess of the total carrying amount of the group over its fair value ($3.4 million – $2.9 million = $500,000) must be recognized and allocated pro rata to the long- lived assets. The amounts allocated to X, Y, and Z are $250,000 [($1,500 ÷ $3,000) × $500], $150,000 [($900 ÷ $3,000) × $500], and $100,000 [($600 ÷ $3,000) × $500], respectively. The preliminary adjusted carrying amounts of X, Y, and Z are therefore $1,250,000 ($1,500 – $250), $750,000 ($900 – $150), and $500,000 ($600 – $100), respectively. However, the fair value of X determined without undue cost and effort is $1,400,000. Accordingly, $150,000 ($1,400 fair value of X – $1,250 preliminary adjusted carrying amount of X) must be reallocated to Y and Z. The amounts reallocated to Y and Z are $90,000 [($750 ÷ $1,250) × $150] and $60,000 [($500 ÷ $1,250) × $150], respectively. Thus, the carrying amount of Z should be $440,000 ($600 – $100 – $60).

Answer (B) is incorrect because $500,000 is the preliminary adjusted carrying amount of Z. Answer (C) is incorrect because $600,000 is the carrying amount of Z before reduction for a proportionate share of the impairment loss. Answer (D) is incorrect because $660,000 is the carrying amount of Z before reduction for a proportionate share of the impairment loss plus (rather than minus) Z's share of the reallocated amount.

33. SFAS 144, *Accounting for the Impairment or Disposal of Long-Lived Assets*, provides guidance for the recognition and measurement of impairment losses on long-lived assets to be held and used. It applies to

A. Goodwill.

B. An asset group.

C. A financial instrument.

D. Any intangible asset not being amortized.

Answer (B) is correct. *(Publisher)*
REQUIRED: The item to which SFAS 144 applies.
DISCUSSION: SFAS 144 applies to the long-lived assets of an entity that are to be held and used or disposed of, including those that are part of a group with other assets and liabilities not subject to SFAS 144. The unit of accounting for such a long-lived asset is the asset group. If a long-lived asset(s) is to be held and used, the asset group is the lowest level at which identifiable cash flows are largely independent of those of other groups. Under SFAS 144, if the carrying amount of a long-lived asset (asset group) is not recoverable, a loss equal to the excess of that carrying amount over the fair value is recognized.
Answer (A) is incorrect because SFAS 144 does not apply to goodwill, which is tested for impairment at the reporting unit level (SFAS 142). Answer (C) is incorrect because SFAS 144 does not apply to financial instruments, servicing assets, deferred tax assets, and certain long-lived assets subject to pronouncements applicable to specialized industries (such as marketed software or oil and gas). Answer (D) is incorrect because SFAS 144 does not apply to an intangible asset not being amortized that is to be held and used (SFAS 142).

34. To determine whether an impairment loss must be recognized, estimates of future cash flows are used to test the recoverability of the carrying amount of a long-lived asset (asset group) to be held and used. The estimates of future cash flows for an asset group should be based on

A. The service potential expected to exist at relevant times in the future.

B. Assumptions developed by disinterested third parties.

C. The remaining useful life of the primary asset of the group.

D. All future expenditures exclusive of interest needed to produce the expected service potential if the asset group is under development.

Answer (C) is correct. *(Publisher)*
REQUIRED: The basis of cash flow estimates used in the recoverability test.
DISCUSSION: The estimates are made for the remaining useful life as determined from the perspective of the entity. The remaining useful life is that of the primary asset of the group, that is, the principal depreciable tangible asset or amortizable intangible asset that is the most significant component of the asset group for generating cash flows. Whether a given asset is primary is determined by such considerations as whether the other group assets would have been acquired without it, the cost of replacing it, and its useful life in relation to the other group assets. If the primary asset does not have the longest remaining useful life, estimates should assume the sale of the group at the end of the primary asset's remaining useful life.
Answer (A) is incorrect because the estimates of future cash flows are based on the existing service potential at the time of the test for recoverability, which is a function of the remaining useful life of the asset (asset group), ability to produce cash flows, and (for tangible assets) physical output. Answer (B) is incorrect because the estimates of future cash flows must be based on the entity's own assumptions about its use of the asset (asset group) and all available evidence. Answer (D) is incorrect because, if the asset (asset group) is under development, the cash flow estimates reflect all future expenditures necessary to produce the expected service potential. These expenditures include capitalizable interest.

35. Measuring the impairment loss on a long-lived asset (asset group) to be held and used requires a determination of its fair value. In appropriate circumstances, this fair value may be based on

I. The sum of the individual fair values of the assets and liabilities of the asset group
II. The prices of similar assets or groups
III. Present value estimates

A. I and III only.

B. I and II only.

C. II and III only.

D. I, II, and III.

Answer (C) is correct. *(Publisher)*
REQUIRED: The possible bases for a fair value estimate.
DISCUSSION: Quoted market prices in active markets are the best evidence of fair value but may not be available for a long-lived asset (asset group). Thus, fair value may need to be estimated. Such estimates should be based on the best information available, such as prices for similar assets (groups) and the results of other valuation methods. The present value methods described in SFAC 7 are often the best available means of estimating fair value. In particular, the expected present value method may be the most appropriate when the cash flows of a long-lived asset (asset group) are uncertain as to timing and amount. The fair value of an asset group or a disposal group is the amount at which the whole group could be transferred in one current transaction. This fair value is therefore not the sum of the fair values of the individual assets and liabilities.

36. An impairment loss on a long-lived asset (asset group) to be held and used is reported by a business enterprise in

A. Discontinued operations.

B. Extraordinary items.

C. Other comprehensive income.

D. Income from continuing operations.

Answer (D) is correct. *(Publisher)*

REQUIRED: The reporting of an impairment loss on a long-lived asset (asset group) to be held and used.

DISCUSSION: An impairment loss is included in income from continuing operations before income taxes by a business enterprise (income from continuing operations in the statement of activities by a not-for-profit organization). When a subtotal for "income from operation" is reported, the impairment loss is included.

Answer (A) is incorrect because a long-lived asset (asset group) to be held and used is not a discontinued operation. Answer (B) is incorrect because an impairment loss does not meet the criteria for an extraordinary item (unusual in nature and infrequent in the environment in which the entity operates). Answer (C) is incorrect because an impairment loss is reported in the income statement. Items reported in OCI have bypassed the income statement.

37. If a long-lived asset satisfies the criteria for classification as held for sale,

A. Its carrying amount is the cost at the acquisition date if the asset is newly acquired.

B. It is not depreciated.

C. Interest attributable to liabilities of a disposal group to which the asset belongs is not accrued.

D. It is classified as held for sale even if the criteria are not met until after the balance sheet date but before issuance of the financial statements.

Answer (B) is correct. *(Publisher)*

REQUIRED: The treatment of a long-lived asset that meets the criteria for classification as held for sale.

DISCUSSION: A long-lived asset is not depreciated (amortized) while it is classified as held for sale and measured at the lower of carrying amount or fair value minus cost to sell. The reason is that depreciation (amortization) would reduce the carrying amount below fair value minus cost to sell. Furthermore, fair value minus cost to sell must be evaluated each period, so any future decline will be recognized in the period of decline.

Answer (A) is incorrect because the carrying amount of a newly acquired long-lived asset classified as held for sale is its fair value minus cost to sell at the acquisition date. Answer (C) is incorrect because interest and other expenses attributable to liabilities of a disposal group to which the asset belongs are accrued. Answer (D) is incorrect because, if the criteria are not met until after the balance sheet date but before issuance of the financial statements, the long-lived asset continues to be classified as held and used in those statements.

38. A long-lived asset is measured at the lower of carrying amount or fair value minus cost to sell if it is to be

I. Held for sale
II. Abandoned
III. Exchanged for a similar productive asset
IV. Distributed to owners in a spinoff

A. I only.

B. I and III only.

C. II, III, and IV only.

D. I, II, III, and IV.

Answer (A) is correct. *(Publisher)*

REQUIRED: The circumstances in which a long-lived asset is measured at the lower of carrying amount or fair value minus cost to sell.

DISCUSSION: Disposal of a long-lived asset may be other than by sale, e.g., by abandonment, exchange, or distribution to owners in a spinoff. When disposal is to be other than by sale, the asset continues to be classified as held and used until disposal. A long-lived asset to be held and used is measured at the lower of its carrying amount or fair value if the carrying amount is not recoverable. An asset that meets the criteria for classification as held for sale is measured at the lower of its carrying amount or fair value minus cost to sell.

39. A long-lived asset (disposal group) classified as held for sale should be accounted for by

A. Subtracting expected future operating losses from its fair value.

B. Recognizing a write-down to fair value minus cost to sell as a credit to other comprehensive income.

C. Recognizing a gain for any increase in fair value minus cost to sale.

D. Adjusting only a long-lived asset for write-downs to, or increases in, fair value minus cost to sell.

Answer (D) is correct. *(Publisher)*

REQUIRED: The accounting for a long-lived asset classified as held for sale.

DISCUSSION: A loss is recognized for a write-down to fair value minus cost to sell. A gain is recognized for any subsequent increase but only to the extent of previously recognized losses for write-downs. The loss or gain adjusts only the carrying amount of a long-lived asset even if it is included in a disposal group.

Answer (A) is incorrect because a long-lived asset (disposal group) is measured at fair value minus cost to sell. Answer (B) is incorrect because a write-down to fair value minus cost to sell is recognized as a loss (a debit) in the income statement. Answer (C) is incorrect because the gain is limited to the cumulative loss previously recognized for write-downs.

40. An entity may decide not to sell a long-lived asset (disposal group) classified as held for sale. It should therefore reclassify the long-lived asset (disposal group) as held and used. As a result of reclassification,

A. The disposal group will be measured at the lower of carrying amount or fair value at the date of the decision not to sell.

B. The results of operations of a reclassified component of an entity will be reported prospectively in continuing operations.

C. Depreciation on individual reclassified long-lived assets is reflected in their measurement.

D. Any assets removed from a disposal group that are to be sold must continue to be measured as a group.

Answer (C) is correct. *(Publisher)*

REQUIRED: The result of reclassifying a long-lived asset (disposal group) after a decision not to sell.

DISCUSSION: Changes to a plan of sale may occur because of circumstances previously regarded as unlikely that result in a decision not to sell. In these circumstances, the asset (disposal group) is reclassified as held and used. A reclassified long-lived asset is measured individually at the lower of (1) carrying amount before the asset (disposal group) was classified as held for sale, minus any depreciation (amortization) that would have been recognized if it had always been classified as held and used or (2) fair value at the date of the decision not to sell.

Answer (A) is incorrect because individual long-lived assets are measured at the lower of carrying amount before classification as held for sale, adjusted for depreciation (amortization) that would otherwise have been recognized, or fair value at the date of the decision not to sell. Answer (B) is incorrect because, when a component of an entity is reclassified as held and used, its results of operations previously reported in discontinued operations are reclassified and included in income from continuing operations for all periods presented. Answer (D) is incorrect because, if the assets removed from a disposal group that are to be sold do not meet the criteria for classification as held for sale as a group, they are measured individually at the lower of their carrying amounts or fair values minus cost to sell at the date of removal.

41. How should a long-lived asset or disposal group classified as held for sale be reported?

A. The major classes of assets and liabilities must be separately disclosed on the face of the balance sheet.

B. Assets and liabilities of a disposal group may not be presented as one amount.

C. A long-lived asset may be aggregated with similar items on the balance sheet if separate disclosure is made in the notes.

D. The income statement must separately present a loss for a write-down to fair value minus cost to sell.

Answer (B) is correct. *(Publisher)*

REQUIRED: The reporting of a long-lived asset or disposal group classified as held for sale.

DISCUSSION: If a disposal group is held for sale, its assets and liabilities are reported separately in the balance sheet and are not offset and presented as a single amount.

Answer (A) is incorrect because the major classes of assets and liabilities held for sale are separately disclosed on the face of the balance sheet or in the notes. Answer (C) is incorrect because, if a long-lived asset is held for sale, it is reported separately in the balance sheet. Answer (D) is incorrect because the entity must disclose in the notes a loss recognized for a write-down to fair value minus cost to sell, and, if not separately presented on the income statement, the caption that includes the loss.

42. A state government condemned Epirus Co.'s parcel of real estate. Epirus will receive $1,500,000 for this property, which has a carrying amount of $1,150,000. Epirus incurred the following costs as a result of the condemnation:

Appraisal fees to support a $1,500,000 value	$5,000
Attorney fees for the closing with the state	7,000
Attorney fees to review contract to acquire replacement property	6,000
Title insurance on replacement property	8,000

What amount of cost should Epirus use to determine the gain on the condemnation?

A. $1,162,000

B. $1,164,000

C. $1,168,000

D. $1,176,000

Answer (A) is correct. *(CPA, adapted)*

REQUIRED: The amount of cost used to determine the gain on the condemnation.

DISCUSSION: FASB Interpretation No. 30, *Accounting for Involuntary Conversions of Nonmonetary Assets to Monetary Assets*, requires that gain or loss be recognized even though an enterprise reinvests or is obligated to reinvest the monetary assets in replacement nonmonetary assets. The determination of the gain is based on the carrying amount ($1,150,000) and the costs incurred as a direct result of the condemnation ($5,000 appraisal fees and $7,000 attorney fees), a total of $1,162,000. Because the recipient is not obligated to reinvest the condemnation proceeds in other nonmonetary assets, the costs associated with the acquisition of the replacement property (attorney fees and title insurance) should be treated as part of the consideration paid for that property.

Answer (B) is incorrect because $1,164,000 includes the costs associated with the replacement property but not the costs incurred as a direct result of the condemnation. Answer (C) is incorrect because $1,168,000 includes the attorney fees associated with the replacement property. Answer (D) is incorrect because $1,176,000 includes the costs associated with the replacement property.

43. On July 1 of the current year, one of Damon Co.'s delivery vans was destroyed in an accident. On that date, the van's carrying amount was $2,500. On July 15 of the current year, Damon received and recorded a $700 invoice for a new engine installed in the van in May, and another $500 invoice for various repairs. In August, Damon received $3,500 under its insurance policy on the van, which it plans to use to replace the van. What amount should Damon report as gain (loss) on disposal of the van in its current-year income statement?

A. $1,000

B. $300

C. $0

D. $(200)

Answer (B) is correct. *(CPA, adapted)*

REQUIRED: The gain (loss) on disposal of the van.

DISCUSSION: Gain (loss) is recognized on an involuntary conversion equal to the difference between the proceeds and the carrying amount. The carrying amount includes the carrying amount at July 1 ($2,500) plus the capitalizable cost ($700) of the engine installed in May. This cost increased the carrying amount because it improved the future service potential of the asset. Ordinary repairs, however, are expensed. Consequently, the gain is $300 [$3,500 – ($2,500 + $700)].

Answer (A) is incorrect because $1,000 results from expensing the cost of the engine. Answer (C) is incorrect because gain (loss) is recognized on an involuntary conversion. Answer (D) is incorrect because $(200) assumes the cost of repairs increased the carrying amount.

7.4 Coinsurance

44. When an insurance policy has a coinsurance clause, the minimum amount recoverable by the insured is never limited by the

A. Insured's loss.

B. Coinsurance requirement.

C. Face amount of the policy.

D. Carrying amount of the asset.

Answer (D) is correct. *(Publisher)*

REQUIRED: The response not a limitation on amounts recoverable under a coinsurance clause.

DISCUSSION: A coinsurance clause requires the insured to have at least a specified percentage of the value of the property insured or the insurance company will pay only a proportionate part of a partial loss. The amount that can be recovered on a partial loss when an insurance policy has a coinsurance clause is the lowest of three amounts: the insured's loss, the calculated amount based on the coinsurance requirement, or the face amount of the policy. The carrying amount of the asset determines only the accounting gain or loss on the insurance settlement.

Answer (A) is incorrect because the insured's loss is a limitation on recovery under a policy with a coinsurance clause. Answer (B) is incorrect because the coinsurance requirement is a limitation on recovery under a policy with a coinsurance clause. Answer (C) is incorrect because the face amount of the policy is a limitation on recovery under a policy with a coinsurance clause.

45. Caldera Corporation carries a $50,000 fire insurance policy on its office building in downtown Magma. The policy has an 80% coinsurance clause. The building, having a carrying amount of $50,000 and a fair value of $75,000, sustained $30,000 of fire damage last year. How much can Caldera collect on the insurance policy?

A. $20,000

B. $36,000

C. $30,000

D. $25,000

Answer (D) is correct. *(C. Dugopolski)*

REQUIRED: The amount collectible under a fire insurance policy with a coinsurance clause.

DISCUSSION: Under an 80% coinsurance clause, the property must be insured for at least 80% of its fair value (insurable value). If a lesser amount is carried, the insured becomes a coinsurer. The insurance company is thus liable for only a proportionate amount of any partial loss. Thus, Caldera can collect $25,000 from its insurance company.

$$\frac{\$50{,}000 \textit{ face amount}}{80\% \times \$75{,}000 \textit{ FMV}} \times \$30{,}000 \textit{ loss} = \$25{,}000$$

Answer (A) is incorrect because $20,000 is the difference between the amount of insurance carried and the cost of the damage. Answer (B) is incorrect because $36,000 is more than the cost of the damage. Answer (C) is incorrect because $30,000 is the full amount of the damages. It should be prorated because Caldera has not met the coinsurance requirement.

46. On July 1, a fire destroyed $200,000 of Gabon Company's $600,000 inventory (fair values). Gabon carried a $240,000 fire insurance policy with an 80% coinsurance clause. What is the maximum amount of insurance that Gabon can collect as a result of this loss?

A. $200,000

B. $192,000

C. $160,000

D. $100,000

Answer (D) is correct. *(CPA, adapted)*

REQUIRED: The amount recoverable when the insurance carried does not meet the coinsurance requirement.

DISCUSSION: Under a coinsurance agreement, the amount recoverable equals the amount of the loss times the ratio of the face amount of the insurance policy to the coinsurance requirement (i.e., to the percentage of insurance required times the fair value of the insured assets). Gabon Company can collect a maximum of $100,000.

$$\frac{\$240{,}000 \textit{ face amount}}{80\% \times \$600{,}000 \textit{ FMV}} \times \$200{,}000 \textit{ loss} = \$100{,}000$$

The amount recoverable is limited to the lowest of (1) the coinsurance amount calculated above, (2) the face amount of the policy, or (3) the amount of the casualty loss.

Answer (A) is incorrect because $200,000 is the total damages subject to the coinsurance clause. Answer (B) is incorrect because $192,000 is 80% of the $240,000 face amount of the policy. Answer (C) is incorrect because $160,000 is 80% of the $200,000 in damage.

47. If four separate carriers have written fire insurance policies totaling $60,000 on a single property with a cash value of $100,000, what fraction of a loss of $20,000 would be collectible from a carrier whose $30,000 policy contains a 90% coinsurance clause?

A. 60/90

B. 30/90

C. 30/60

D. 20/100

Answer (B) is correct. *(CPA, adapted)*

REQUIRED: The fraction of a loss collectible from a carrier whose policy contains a 90% coinsurance clause.

DISCUSSION: If two or more insurers have insured the same asset, and the various policies have different coinsurance percentages, the amount recoverable from each policy is determined by multiplying the loss by a percentage equal to the face amount of the policy divided by the greater of the coinsurance amount or the aggregate face amount of all the policies.

The property had an insurable value of $100,000, but the fire insurance policies totaled only $60,000. Given that the policy in question had a 90% coinsurance clause, the percentage collectible from that carrier is $30,000 (the face amount of the policy) divided by $90,000 (the greater of the coinsurance requirement or the total value of all the policies).

Answer (A) is incorrect because 60/90 is the total amount of coverage over the coinsurance requirement. Answer (C) is incorrect because 30/60 is the face amount of one of the policies over the total amount of coverage from all of the carriers. Answer (D) is incorrect because 20/100 is the amount of loss over the fair value of the insured property.

7.5 Exchange of Nonmonetary Assets

48. Departure from the use of fair values in accounting for a nonmonetary exchange transaction is acceptable when there is an insignificant difference between the

I. Risk, timing, and amount of the future cash flows of the asset(s) received and the risk, timing, and amount of the future cash flows of the asset(s) transferred.

II. Entity-specific value of the asset(s) received and the entity-specific value of the asset(s) transferred.

A. Both I and II.

B. I only.

C. II only.

D. Neither I nor II.

Answer (A) is correct. *(Publisher)*

REQUIRED: The appropriate departures, if any, from fair value in accounting for a nonmonetary exchange.

DISCUSSION: Accounting for both monetary and nonmonetary transactions generally should be based on fair value of the assets involved, with gain or loss recognized immediately. However, accounting for nonmonetary transactions should be based on the carrying amount of the asset relinquished when the transaction is (1) an exchange in which neither the fair value of the asset relinquished nor the fair value of the asset received is determinable within reasonable limits; (2) an exchange of inventory to be sold in the same line of business that is undertaken to facilitate sales to customers; or (3) an exchange that lacks commercial substance. An exchange lacks commercial substance when an entity's cash flows are not expected to change significantly. Cash flows do not change significantly when (1) the configuration (risk, timing, and amount) of the future cash flows of the asset(s) received does not significantly differ from the future cash flows of the asset(s) transferred, or (2) the entity-specific value of the asset(s) received does not significantly differ from the entity-specific value of the asset(s) transferred. Entity-specific value is determined in the context of the entity's use of the assets.

49. When an exchange of inventory items between an enterprise and another entity is undertaken to serve the needs of the enterprise's customers, the enterprise should record the inventory items received based on the

A. Carrying amount of the inventory items relinquished.

B. Fair value of the inventory items relinquished.

C. Carrying amount of the inventory items received.

D. Fair value of the inventory items received.

Answer (A) is correct. *(Publisher)*

REQUIRED: The proper accounting for an exchange of inventory items undertaken to serve customer needs.

DISCUSSION: According to APB 29, *Accounting for Nonmonetary Transactions*, as amended by SFAS 153, *Exchanges of Nonmonetary Assets*, accounting for both monetary and nonmonetary transactions generally should be based on the fair value of the assets involved, with gain or loss recognized immediately. The fair value of the asset relinquished should be used unless the fair value of the asset received is more evident. However, accounting for nonmonetary transactions should be based on the carrying amount of the asset relinquished when the transaction is (1) an exchange in which neither the fair value of the asset relinquished nor the fair value of the asset received is determinable within reasonable limits; (2) an exchange of inventory undertaken to facilitate sales to customers; or (3) an exchange that lacks commercial substance.

50. Iona Co. and Siena Co. exchanged goods, held for resale, with equal fair values. Each will use the other's goods to promote its own products. The retail price of the wicket that Iona gave up is less than the retail price of the womble received. What gain should Iona recognize on the nonmonetary exchange?

A. A gain is not recognized.

B. A gain equal to the difference between the retail prices of the womble received and the wicket.

C. A gain equal to the difference between the retail price and the cost of the wicket.

D. A gain equal to the difference between the fair value and the cost of the wicket.

Answer (D) is correct. *(CPA, adapted)*

REQUIRED: The gain to be recognized on a nonmonetary exchange of inventory.

DISCUSSION: Accounting for both monetary and nonmonetary transactions generally should be based on fair value of the assets involved, with gain or loss recognized immediately. In certain circumstances, however, the accounting for a nonmonetary transaction should be based on the carrying amount of the asset relinquished. These circumstances include an exchange of a product or property held for sale in the ordinary course of business for a product to be sold in the same line of business. The exchange also must be designed to facilitate sales to customers other than the parties to the exchange. Because Iona will use the womble received to promote its own product, the requirement that the product be used to facilitate sales to customers other than Iona or Siena is not met. Facilitation entails, for example, meeting immediate inventory needs or reducing transportation costs (APB 29). Hence, Iona should record a gain equal to the difference between the fair value (the same for both assets) and the cost (carrying amount) of the asset surrendered.

Answer (A) is incorrect because a gain should be recognized. Answer (B) is incorrect because fair value, not retail prices, is the appropriate basis at which the asset received should be recognized. Answer (C) is incorrect because fair value, not retail prices, is the appropriate basis at which the asset received should be recognized.

51. Jaffa Co. and Istria Co. exchanged similar trucks with fair values in excess of carrying amounts. In addition, Jaffa paid Istria to compensate for the difference in truck values. The amount paid was 20% of the fair value of the exchange. The exchange did not have commercial substance. As a consequence, Istria recognized

A. A gain equal to the difference between the fair value and carrying amount of the truck given up.

B. A gain determined by the proportion of the cash received to the total consideration.

C. A loss determined by the proportion of cash received to the total consideration.

D. Neither a gain nor a loss.

Answer (B) is correct. *(CPA, adapted)*

REQUIRED: The gain or loss, if any, to be recognized on a nonmonetary exchange of similar trucks involving boot if the transaction lacked commercial substance.

DISCUSSION: Accounting for both monetary and nonmonetary transactions generally should be based on fair value of the assets involved, with gain or loss recognized immediately. In certain circumstances, however, the accounting for a nonmonetary transaction should be based on the carrying amount of the asset relinquished. These circumstances include an exchange that lacks commercial substance. In addition, when the transaction includes a cash component (termed boot), if the boot is less than 25% of the fair value of the exchange, the recipient of the boot should adjust the carryover basis for the portion of the gain equal to the total gain times the ratio of the boot to the sum of the boot and the fair value of the asset received. However, the full amount of a loss is recognized as an adjustment of the carryover basis.

Answer (A) is incorrect because the proportion of the gain recognized is equal to the ratio of the boot to the sum of the boot and the fair value of the asset received. Answer (C) is incorrect because a gain should be recognized. Answer (D) is incorrect because a gain should be recognized.

52. Horn Co. and Book Co. exchanged nonmonetary assets in a transaction that did not have commercial substance for either party. Horn paid cash to Book that was equal to 15% of the fair value of the exchange. To the extent that the amount of cash exceeds a proportionate share of the carrying amount of the asset surrendered, a realized gain on the exchange should be recognized by

	Horn	Book
A.	Yes	Yes
B.	Yes	No
C.	No	Yes
D.	No	No

Answer (C) is correct. *(CPA, adapted)*

REQUIRED: The party(ies), if any, that should recognize a realized gain on a nonmonetary transaction involving boot that lacked commercial substance.

DISCUSSION: The accounting for a nonmonetary transaction should be based on the carrying amount of the asset(s) relinquished when the exchange lacks commercial substance. In addition, when the transaction includes a cash component (termed boot), if the boot is less than 25% of the fair value of the exchange, the recipient of the boot should adjust the carryover basis for the portion of the gain equal to the total gain times the ratio of the boot to the sum of the boot and the fair value of the asset received. However, the full amount of a loss is recognized as an adjustment of the carryover basis. In contrast, the payer of boot should measure the asset received at an amount equal to the carrying amount of the asset relinquished plus the amount of boot.

Answer (A) is incorrect because the payer of boot measures the asset received at an amount equal to the carrying amount of the asset relinquished plus the amount of boot. Only the recipient recognizes a proportionate gain. Answer (B) is incorrect because the payer of boot measures the asset received at an amount equal to the carrying amount of the asset relinquished plus the amount of boot. Only the recipient recognizes a proportionate gain. Answer (D) is incorrect because the recipient of boot should recognize a gain.

53. Hagen Co. exchanged a truck with a carrying amount of $12,000 and a fair value of $20,000 for a truck and $5,000 cash. The fair value of the truck received was $15,000. The exchange was not considered to have commercial substance. At what amount should Hagen record the truck received in the exchange?

A. $7,000

B. $9,000

C. $12,000

D. $15,000

Answer (D) is correct. *(CPA, adapted)*

REQUIRED: The amount at which a nonmonetary asset should be recorded in a transaction involving boot that lacked commercial substance.

DISCUSSION: A transaction involving nonmonetary assets and boot is classified as monetary if the boot equals or exceeds 25% of the fair value of the exchange. In this exchange, the $5,000 of boot equals 25% of the $20,000 ($5,000 + $15,000) fair value of the exchange. Thus, the exchange is classified as monetary. Accounting for monetary transactions should be based on the fair value of the assets involved, with gain or loss recognized immediately. Hagen should record the truck received at its $15,000 fair value. Hagen also should record an $8,000 gain equal to the difference between the $20,000 fair value received and the $12,000 carrying amount of the truck relinquished.

Answer (A) is incorrect because $7,000 is equal to the $12,000 carrying amount of the asset relinquished minus the $5,000 boot received. Answer (B) is incorrect because $9,000 is equal to the $12,000 carrying amount of the truck relinquished, minus the $5,000 boot received, plus the $2,000 (25% × $8,000) proportionate gain that would have been recognized had the transaction been classified as nonmonetary. Answer (C) is incorrect because $12,000 is equal to the carrying amount of the truck relinquished.

54. In an exchange of assets, Junger Co. received equipment with a fair value equal to the carrying amount of the equipment given up. Junger also contributed cash equal to 10% of the fair value of the exchange. If the exchange is not considered to have commercial substance, Junger should recognize

A. A loss equal to the cash (boot) given up.

B. A loss determined by the proportion of cash paid to the total transaction value.

C. A gain determined by the proportion of cash paid to the total transaction value.

D. Neither gain nor loss.

Answer (A) is correct. *(CPA, adapted)*

REQUIRED: The gain or loss to be recognized in a nonmonetary transaction involving boot that lacked commercial substance.

DISCUSSION: The accounting for a nonmonetary transaction should be based on the carrying amount of the asset(s) relinquished when the exchange lacks commercial substance. In addition, when the transaction includes a cash component (termed boot), if the boot is less than 25% of the fair value of the exchange, the recipient of the boot should adjust the carryover basis for the portion of the gain equal to the total gain times the ratio of the boot to the sum of the boot and the fair value of the asset received. However, the full amount of any loss is recognized as an adjustment of the carryover basis. In this situation, a loss should be recognized because the carrying amount of the asset relinquished plus the boot paid is greater than the fair value of the asset received. An asset should not be recognized at an amount higher than its fair value.

Answer (B) is incorrect because, when a loss is indicated, the entire loss should be recognized. Answer (C) is incorrect because a loss equal to the amount of cash given up should be recognized. Answer (D) is incorrect because a loss equal to the amount of cash given up should be recognized.

55. Bell and Mayo are independent companies. Each owns a tract of land being held for development. However, each would prefer to build on the other's land. Accordingly, the companies agreed to exchange their land. From an independent appraisal report and the companies' records, the following information was obtained:

	Bell's Land	Mayo's Land
Cost and carrying amount	$ 80,000	$50,000
Fair value based on appraisal	100,000	85,000

Based on the difference in appraisal values, Mayo paid $15,000 to Bell. If Mayo did not consider the exchange to have commercial substance, at what amount should Mayo record the receipt of the land from Bell?

A. $100,000

B. $85,000

C. $65,000

D. $50,000

Answer (C) is correct. *(W. Higley)*

REQUIRED: The amount at which the asset received should be recorded by the payer of boot in a nonmonetary exchange lacking commercial substance.

DISCUSSION: Accounting for a nonmonetary transaction should be based on the carrying amount of the asset(s) relinquished when the exchange lacks commercial substance. In addition, when the transaction includes a cash component (termed boot), if the boot is less than 25% of the fair value of the exchange, the recipient of the boot should adjust the carryover basis for the portion of the gain equal to the total gain times the ratio of the boot to the sum of the boot plus the fair value of the asset received. In contrast, the payer of boot should record the asset received at an amount equal to the carryover basis of the nonmonetary asset relinquished plus the boot paid. In this situation, because the boot equals 15% ($15,000 ÷ $100,000) of the fair value of the exchange, Mayo should record the land received from Bell at $65,000 ($50,000 carrying amount + $15,000 boot).

Answer (A) is incorrect because $100,000 is the fair value of the land received, the amount at which the land would be recorded if the exchange had commercial substance. Answer (B) is incorrect because $85,000 is the fair value of the land Mayo exchanged. Answer (D) is incorrect because $50,000 is the carrying amount of the land Mayo exchanged.

56. Minor Baseball Company had a player contract with Doe that was recorded in its accounting records at $145,000. Better Baseball Company had a player contract with Smith that was recorded in its accounting records at $140,000. Minor traded Doe to Better for Smith by exchanging player contracts. The fair value of each contract was $150,000. Evidence suggested that the contract exchange lacked commercial substance. At what amount should the contracts be valued in accordance with generally accepted accounting principles at the time of the exchange of the player contracts?

	Minor	Better
A.	$140,000	$140,000
B.	$140,000	$145,000
C.	$145,000	$140,000
D.	$150,000	$150,000

Answer (C) is correct. *(CPA, adapted)*

REQUIRED: The amount at which to record an asset received in a nonmonetary exchange transaction that lacked commercial substance.

DISCUSSION: The accounting for a nonmonetary transaction should be based on the carrying amount of the asset(s) relinquished when the exchange lacks commercial substance. An exchange lacks commercial substance when an entity's cash flows are not expected to change significantly. Cash flows do not change significantly when (1) the configuration (risk, timing, and amount) of the entity's future cash flows is not expected to change significantly as a result of the exchange, or (2) the entity-specific values of the assets involved do not differ significantly. Thus, Minor should record its contract with Smith at $145,000, and Better should record its contract with Doe at $140,000.

Answer (A) is incorrect because Minor should record its contract with Smith at $145,000, its previously recorded (carryover) amount for its contract with Doe. Answer (B) is incorrect because Minor should record its contract with Smith at $145,000, and Better should record its contract with Doe at $140,000. Answer (D) is incorrect because $150,000, the fair value of each contract, should be recorded if the exchange has commercial substance.

57. Essen Co. and Potsdam Co. are fuel oil distributors. To facilitate delivery of oil to their customers, Essen and Potsdam exchanged ownership of 1,200 barrels of oil without physically moving the oil. Essen paid Potsdam $30,000 to compensate for a difference in the grade of oil. On the date of the exchange, costs and fair values of the oil were as follows:

	Essen Co.	Potsdam Co.
Cost	$100,000	$126,000
Fair values	120,000	150,000

What amount of gain from the transaction should Potsdam report in its income statement?

A. $0

B. $4,800

C. $24,000

D. $30,000

Answer (B) is correct. *(CPA, adapted)*

REQUIRED: The gain to be recognized in a nonmonetary exchange involving boot that facilitated sales to customers.

DISCUSSION: Accounting for an exchange of nonmonetary assets should be based on the carrying amount of the asset relinquished when the exchange involves inventory exchanged to facilitate sales to customers other than the parties to the exchange. In addition, when the transaction includes a cash component (termed boot), if the boot is less than 25% of the fair value of the exchange, the recipient of the boot should adjust its carryover basis for the portion of the gain equal to the total gain times the ratio of the boot to the sum of the boot and the fair value of the asset received. The boot in this exchange is equal to 20% [$30,000 ÷ ($30,000 + $120,000)]. Thus, Potsdam should record a $4,800 proportionate gain equal to 20% of the $24,000 ($150,000 – $126,000) difference between the fair value of the exchange and the cost of the inventory relinquished. Moreover, it should debit inventory for $100,800 ($126,000 carrying amount – $30,000 cash received + $4,800 gain recognized). The following is the journal entry to record the transaction:

	Debit	Credit
Cash	$ 30,000	
Inventory received	100,800	
Inventory relinquished		$126,000
Gain		4,800

Answer (A) is incorrect because a proportionate gain should be recognized. Answer (C) is incorrect because $24,000 is the total potential gain. Answer (D) is incorrect because $30,000 is the amount of boot.

58. On July 1 of the current year, Trey Co. exchanged a truck for 25 shares of Deuce Corp.'s common stock. The fair value of this stock is not readily determinable. On that date, the truck's carrying amount was $2,500, and its fair value was $3,000. Also, the carrying amount of Deuce's stock was $60 per share. On December 31 of the current year, Deuce had 250 shares of common stock outstanding and its carrying amount per share was $50. Trey cannot exercise significant influence over Deuce. What amount should Trey report in its December 31 current-year balance sheet as investment in Deuce?

A. $3,000

B. $2,500

C. $1,500

D. $1,250

Answer (A) is correct. *(CPA, adapted)*

REQUIRED: The amount reported for stock received in exchange for a nonmonetary asset.

DISCUSSION: Accounting for nonmonetary transactions usually should be based on the fair values of the assets or services involved (APB 29). The exceptions arise when (1) the fair value of neither the asset(s) received nor the asset(s) relinquished is determinable within reasonable limits, (2) the exchange facilitates sales of inventory to customers, or (3) the exchange lacks commercial substance. No exception applies because the fair value of the asset relinquished is known, inventory is not involved, and no facts indicate that the exchange lacks commercial substance. Accordingly, the exchange is measured on July 1 at the $3,000 fair value of the asset relinquished. Moreover, this investment in equity securities is subsequently reported at cost (the fair value of the truck on July 1) because (1) their fair value is not readily determinable (SFAS 115, *Accounting for Certain Investments in Debt and Equity Securities*), and (2) the equity method does not apply because Trey cannot exercise significant influence over Deuce (APB 18).

Answer (B) is incorrect because $2,500 is the truck's carrying amount, not its fair value. Answer (C) is incorrect because $1,500 was the carrying amount of 25 shares of Deuce's stock on July 1 on Deuce's books. Answer (D) is incorrect because $1,250 is the carrying amount of 25 shares of Deuce's stock on December 31 on Deuce's books.

59. An entity disposes of a nonmonetary asset in a nonreciprocal transfer. A gain or loss should be recognized on the disposition of the asset when the fair value of the asset transferred is determinable and the nonreciprocal transfer is to

	Another Entity	A Shareholder of the Entity
A.	No	Yes
B.	No	No
C.	Yes	No
D.	Yes	Yes

Answer (D) is correct. *(CPA, adapted)*

REQUIRED: The circumstances under which gain or loss should be recorded in a nonreciprocal transfer.

DISCUSSION: A nonreciprocal transfer is a transfer of assets or services in one direction. APB 29 states that a nonreciprocal transfer of a nonmonetary asset to a shareholder or to another entity should be recorded at the fair value of the asset transferred, and a gain or loss should be recognized on the transfer. However, an exception to this general rule is provided for distributions of nonmonetary assets to owners in a spin-off or other form of reorganization or liquidation or in a plan that is in substance the rescission of a prior business combination. In such cases, the transaction should be measured at the recorded amount (after any reduction for an impairment of value determined in accordance with SFAS 144) of the nonmonetary assets distributed.

60. Orr Corporation owned 1,000 shares of Vee Corporation. These shares were purchased for $9,000. On September 15, Orr declared a property dividend of one share of Vee for every ten shares of Orr held by a shareholder. On that date, when the market price of Vee was $14 per share, 9,000 shares of Orr were outstanding. This transaction did not constitute a spin-off or other form of reorganization or liquidation and was not part of a plan that was in substance a rescission of a prior business combination. What gain and net reduction in retained earnings would result from this property dividend?

	Gain	Net Reduction in Retained Earnings
A.	$0	$8,100
B.	$0	$12,600
C.	$4,500	$3,600
D.	$4,500	$8,100

Answer (D) is correct. *(CPA, adapted)*

REQUIRED: The gain and net reduction in retained earnings from a property dividend.

DISCUSSION: The Vee shares had a carrying amount of $9 per share ($9,000 ÷ 1,000 shares). Because 900 shares were distributed by Orr as a property dividend (9,000 shares ÷ 10), the shares used as a property dividend had an aggregate carrying amount of $8,100. The fair value of the 900 shares on the date of declaration was $12,600 (900 shares × $14 per share).

Given that the transaction is not effectively a reorganization, liquidation, or rescission of a business combination, a nonreciprocal transfer of a nonmonetary asset to a shareholder should be recorded at the fair value of the asset transferred, and a gain or loss should be recognized on the disposition (APB 29). The gain is $4,500 ($12,600 fair value – $8,100 carrying amount). The net reduction in retained earnings is $8,100 ($12,600 dividend – $4,500 gain). The journal entries are

Retained earnings	$12,600	
Property dividend payable		$12,600
Property dividend payable	$12,600	
Investment in Vee		$ 8,100
Gain on Vee disposition		4,500

Answer (A) is incorrect because a gain must be recognized when a shareholder receives a nonreciprocal transfer of a nonmonetary asset, and retained earnings should be reduced. Answer (B) is incorrect because a gain must be recognized when a shareholder receives a nonreciprocal transfer of a nonmonetary asset, and retained earnings should be reduced. Answer (C) is incorrect because $3,600 is the gain if the full amount of the $9,000 of Vee Corporation stock is subtracted from the $12,600 dividend.

61. Tioga City owned a vacant plot of land zoned for industrial use. Tioga gave this land to Haile Corp. solely as an incentive for Haile to build a factory on the site. The land had a fair value of $300,000 at the date of the gift. This nonmonetary transaction is most likely to be reported by Haile as

A. An extraordinary gain.
B. Donated capital.
C. A credit to retained earnings.
D. A memorandum entry.

Answer (B) is correct. *(CPA, adapted)*

REQUIRED: The accounting for a contributed asset.

DISCUSSION: Under SFAS 116, *Accounting for Contributions Received and Contributions Made*, contributions received ordinarily should be accounted for as revenues and gains at fair value, but SFAS 116 does not apply to tax exemptions, abatements, or incentives, or to transfers of assets from a government to a business enterprise. Nevertheless, SFAS 116 does not preclude accounting for this contribution as a revenue or gain. Indeed, such treatment would have the virtue of being consistent with the accounting for most contributions. However, contributions have often been accounted for by crediting donated capital, an additional paid-in capital account. This approach is not currently prohibited by GAAP.

Answer (A) is incorrect because a contribution most likely does not meet the criteria of an extraordinary item. It is not unusual. Answer (C) is incorrect because a contribution from a government is not recorded directly in retained earnings. It should be reported in the income statement or as contributed capital. Answer (D) is incorrect because a contribution should be recognized in the accounts.

STUDY UNIT EIGHT
DEPRECIATION AND DEPLETION

Depreciation is the systematic allocation of the productive capacity (depreciable base) of a long-lived, tangible, productive asset to the service (useful) life of the asset. The **depreciable base** of a long-lived tangible asset normally equals its original (historical) cost minus any estimated salvage value. The **service life** of an asset may be time-based or activity-based. The service life is time-based when the depreciation method allocates the depreciable base to the accounting periods that define the expected useful life of the asset. It is activity-based when the depreciation method allocates the depreciable base to the units of product or the output of service units (machine hours, miles driven, etc.) that define the expected useful life of the asset.

Allocation methods permissible under GAAP include the straight-line, double-declining-balance (DDB), sum-of-the-years'-digits (SYD), and units-of-output methods. Annuity methods are not permissible. The straight-line, DDB, and SYD methods allocate the depreciable base to accounting periods. The units-of-product and units-of-service methods allocate the depreciable base to activity-based service lives.

The straight-line, units-of-product, and units-of-service methods allocate a **constant amount** of the depreciable base to each accounting period, unit of product, or unit of service, respectively. In contrast, DDB and SYD are **accelerated methods**; they allocate a greater amount of the depreciable base to earlier accounting periods. These methods may be more appropriate when the expected productivity or revenue-earning capabilities of the asset are greater in the earlier years or when maintenance charges tend to increase over time.

Depreciation may be accounted for as a **periodic expense** (depreciation expense) or **capitalized** as an asset (e.g., work-in-progress or construction-in-progress). The credit ordinarily is to accumulated depreciation, a contra asset. Net carrying amount of the asset equals the original cost of the asset minus accumulated depreciation.

An entity must **disclose** depreciation expense for the period and balances of major classes of depreciable assets (by nature or function) and accumulated depreciation (either by major classes of depreciable assets or in total) in the financial statements or notes. Depreciation expense and accumulated depreciation should be the amounts at the balance sheet date.

Group depreciation and composite depreciation are **aggregate depreciation methods**. They are applied to an aggregation of long-lived, tangible, productive assets that are depreciated as if they were a single asset. The group method applies to an aggregation of similar assets; the composite method applies to an aggregation of dissimilar assets.

Depletion is the systematic allocation of the depletable base of a natural resource (a wasting asset) to the estimated units of the resource expected to be produced. The depletable base of a natural resource equals its original cost, plus any estimated reclamation costs, minus any estimated salvage value.

QUESTIONS

8.1 Depreciation Concepts

1. Depreciation of a plant asset is the process of

A. Asset valuation for statement of financial position purposes.

B. Allocation of the asset's cost to the periods of use.

C. Fund accumulation for the replacement of the asset.

D. Asset valuation based on current replacement cost data.

Answer (B) is correct. *(CMA, adapted)*

REQUIRED: The purpose of depreciation of fixed assets.

DISCUSSION: In accounting, depreciation is the systematic and rational allocation of the cost of the productive capacity of a fixed asset to the accounting periods the asset benefits. The asset's historical cost minus expected salvage value is the basis for the allocation.

Answer (A) is incorrect because depreciation is a process of cost allocation, not valuation. Answer (C) is incorrect because depreciation allocates cost; it does not provide for replacement. Answer (D) is incorrect because depreciation is a process of cost allocation, not valuation.

2. On January 2, Rio Corp. bought machinery under a contract that required a down payment of $10,000, plus 24 monthly payments of $5,000 each, for total cash payments of $130,000. The cash equivalent price of the machinery was $110,000. The machinery has an estimated useful life of 10 years and estimated salvage value of $5,000. Rio uses straight-line depreciation. In its income statement for the year ended December 31, what amount should Rio report as depreciation for this machinery?

A. $10,500

B. $11,000

C. $12,500

D. $13,000

Answer (A) is correct. *(CPA, adapted)*

REQUIRED: The depreciation on the machinery.

DISCUSSION: The cash equivalent price of the machinery (present value), reduced by the salvage value, equals the depreciable base. The excess of the total cash to be paid over the cash equivalent price of the machinery will be recognized as interest expense, not depreciation. Accordingly, straight-line depreciation is $10,500 [($110,000 cash equivalent price – $5,000 salvage value) ÷ 10 years].

Answer (B) is incorrect because $11,000 does not allow for the salvage value. Answer (C) is incorrect because $12,500 is based on the total cash payments minus salvage value. Answer (D) is incorrect because $13,000 is based on the total cash payments with no allowance for salvage value.

3. A depreciable asset has an estimated 15% salvage value. At the end of its estimated useful life, the accumulated depreciation will equal the original cost of the asset under which of the following depreciation methods?

	Straight-Line	Productive-Output
A.	Yes	No
B.	Yes	Yes
C.	No	Yes
D.	No	No

Answer (D) is correct. *(CPA, adapted)*

REQUIRED: The method(s) under which accumulated depreciation will equal cost at the end of a salvageable asset's useful life.

DISCUSSION: The straight-line and productive-output depreciation methods both deduct estimated salvage value from the original cost to determine the depreciable base. At the end of the asset's estimated useful life, the accumulated depreciation will equal the cost minus the salvage value under each of these methods. The net carrying amount (cost – accumulated depreciation) will equal the salvage value.

4. Net income is understated if, in the first year, estimated salvage value is excluded from the depreciation computation when using the

	Straight-Line Method	Production or Use Method
A.	Yes	No
B.	Yes	Yes
C.	No	No
D.	No	Yes

Answer (B) is correct. *(CPA, adapted)*

REQUIRED: The depreciation method(s) that understate(s) net income if estimated salvage value is excluded from the computation.

DISCUSSION: Under the straight-line method, the depreciable base of an asset is allocated uniformly over the time periods of the estimated use of the asset. Under the production or use method, the depreciable base is allocated as a constant per-unit amount as goods are produced. For both methods, the depreciable base is equal to the original cost minus the salvage value. Thus, if the estimated salvage value is excluded from the depreciable base calculated using either method, the amount of depreciation will be overstated. The result will be an understatement of net income.

5. Depreciation is computed on the original cost minus estimated salvage value under which of the following depreciation methods?

	Double-Declining Balance	Productive-Output
A.	No	No
B.	No	Yes
C.	Yes	Yes
D.	Yes	No

Answer (B) is correct. *(CPA, adapted)*

REQUIRED: The method(s) under which depreciation is computed on original cost minus estimated salvage value.

DISCUSSION: Under the productive-output method, depreciation is determined by allocating the original cost minus the estimated salvage value to the projected units of output during the expected life of the asset. Under the double-declining-balance method, depreciation is determined by multiplying the carrying amount at the beginning of each period by a constant rate that is equal to twice the straight-line rate of depreciation. Each year, the carrying amount of the asset decreases by the depreciation expense recognized. The double-declining-balance calculation does not include salvage value in calculating depreciation. However, the asset may not be depreciated below the amount of the estimated salvage value.

6. When appreciation has been recorded on property, plant, and equipment, APB 6, *Status of Accounting Research Bulletins*, states that depreciation

A. Should be based on the appreciated amounts.

B. Should be based on the historical cost.

C. If taken on written-up assets, should be charged directly to the appraisal capital account and not flow through the income account.

D. Cannot be charged on write-ups without verifiable objective evidence (e.g., a formal property appraisal report) that the asset's value has changed significantly from its historical cost.

Answer (A) is correct. *(Publisher)*

REQUIRED: The true statement about depreciation on recorded appreciation of property, plant, and equipment.

DISCUSSION: According to APB 6, when appreciation on an asset has been recorded, depreciation should be based on the appreciated amount rather than on the historical cost. However, "property, plant, and equipment should not be written up by an entity to reflect appraisal, market, or current values that are above cost to the entity."

Answer (B) is incorrect because the depreciation should be based on the appreciated amount. Answer (C) is incorrect because the depreciation expense should flow through the income statement and not be charged directly to equity. Answer (D) is incorrect because the depreciation on the recorded appreciation should be recorded regardless of any formal property appraisal reports.

7. Which of the following statements is the assumption on which straight-line depreciation is based?

A. The operating efficiency of the asset decreases in later years.

B. Service value declines as a function of time rather than use.

C. Service value declines as a function of obsolescence rather than time.

D. Physical wear and tear are more important than economic obsolescence.

Answer (B) is correct. *(CPA, adapted)*

REQUIRED: The assumption on which straight-line depreciation is based.

DISCUSSION: Under the straight-line method, depreciation expense is a constant amount for each period of the estimated useful life of the asset. The straight-line method ignores fluctuations in the use of an asset and in maintenance and service charges. The carrying amount is dependent upon the length of time the asset has been held rather than the amount of use.

Answer (A) is incorrect because, if operating efficiency declines over time, an accelerated depreciation method may be appropriate. Answer (C) is incorrect because, if obsolescence determines service value, a write-down method based on market values may be appropriate. Answer (D) is incorrect because physical wear and tear is a justification for an activity method of depreciation, e.g., depreciation based on hours of machine use.

8. In which of the following situations is the units-of-production method of depreciation most appropriate?

A. An asset's service potential declines with use.

B. An asset's service potential declines with the passage of time.

C. An asset is subject to rapid obsolescence.

D. An asset incurs increasing repairs and maintenance with use.

Answer (A) is correct. *(CPA, adapted)*

REQUIRED: The situation in which the units-of-production method of depreciation is most appropriate.

DISCUSSION: The units-of-production depreciation method allocates asset cost based on the level of production. As production varies, so will the credit to accumulated depreciation. Consequently, when an asset's service potential declines with use, the units-of-production method is the most appropriate method.

Answer (B) is incorrect because the straight-line method is appropriate when an asset's service potential declines with the passage of time. Answer (C) is incorrect because an accelerated method is best when an asset is subject to rapid obsolescence. Answer (D) is incorrect because the units-of-production method does not allow for increasing repairs and maintenance.

9. Which of the following reasons provides the best theoretical support for accelerated depreciation?

A. Assets are more efficient in early years and initially generate more revenue.

B. Expenses should be allocated in a manner that "smooths" earnings.

C. Repairs and maintenance costs will probably increase in later periods, so depreciation should decline.

D. Accelerated depreciation provides easier replacement because of the time value of money.

Answer (A) is correct. *(CPA, adapted)*

REQUIRED: The best theoretical basis for accelerated depreciation.

DISCUSSION: Accelerated depreciation methods result in decreasing depreciation charges over the life of the asset. Depreciation charges are greatest in the early years when the asset is presumably more efficient and generates more revenue. The effect of accelerated depreciation under this assumption is to match expenses and revenues more realistically.

Answer (B) is incorrect because the smoothing of earnings is not a proper justification for making a choice among generally accepted accounting principles. Accounting theory requires that the results of operations be presented fairly, even though such presentation might produce considerable fluctuations in earnings. Answer (C) is incorrect because, although an anticipated increase in maintenance costs is a practical justification for accelerated depreciation, it is not the best theoretical support. Answer (D) is incorrect because depreciation for financial reporting purposes has no effect on cash flow.

10. Under which of the following depreciation methods is it possible for depreciation expense to be higher in the later years of an asset's useful life?

A. Straight-line.

B. Activity method based on units of production.

C. Sum-of-the-years'-digits.

D. Declining-balance.

Answer (B) is correct. *(CIA, adapted)*

REQUIRED: The depreciation method under which higher depreciation is possible later in an asset's useful life.

DISCUSSION: Under the activity method, depreciation is a function of use, not the passage of time. If the estimated activity level (stated, for example, in units of production) is higher in the later years of the asset's useful life, depreciation expense will be higher.

Answer (A) is incorrect because the straight-line method results in a constant depreciation expense. Answer (C) is incorrect because depreciation expense diminishes over time when an accelerated method, e.g., SYD or declining-balance method, is used. Answer (D) is incorrect because depreciation expense diminishes over time when an accelerated method, e.g., SYD or declining-balance method, is used.

11. Caracas Corp. purchased a computer on January 1 for $108,000. It was estimated to have a 4-year useful life and a salvage value of $18,000. The double-declining-balance (DDB) method is to be used. The amount of depreciation to be reported at the end of the first year is

A. ($108,000 – $18,000)(25% × 2)

B. ($108,000 – $18,000)(25% × 1/2)

C. ($108,000)(25% × 2)

D. ($108,000)(25% × 1/2)

Answer (C) is correct. *(CIA, adapted)*

REQUIRED: The computation to calculate the amount of depreciation under the double-declining-balance method.

DISCUSSION: When using a declining-balance method, a constant rate is applied to the changing carrying amount of the asset. The carrying amount for the first period's calculation is the acquisition cost ($108,000). The constant rate for the DDB method is twice the straight-line rate [(100% ÷ 4 years) × 2].

Answer (A) is incorrect because the salvage value is ignored in computing depreciation by use of a declining-balance method until the later years of the life. The asset should not be depreciated below its salvage value. Answer (B) is incorrect because the salvage value is ignored. Furthermore, the rate used should be twice the straight-line rate. Answer (D) is incorrect because the rate used should be twice the straight-line rate.

12. On the first day of its current fiscal year, Santiago Corporation purchased equipment costing $400,000 with a salvage value of $80,000. Depreciation expense for the year was $160,000. If Santiago uses the double-declining-balance (DDB) method of depreciation, what is the estimated useful life of the asset?

A. 5

B. 4

C. 2.5

D. 2

Answer (A) is correct. *(J. Hora)*

REQUIRED: The estimated useful life of an asset being depreciated using the DDB method.

DISCUSSION: DDB uses a depreciation rate that is twice the straight-line rate. In the first year of this equipment's life, the DDB depreciation rate is 40% ($160,000 ÷ $400,000). The straight-line rate is therefore 20% (40% ÷ 2). Accordingly, the expected useful life of the asset is 5 years.

Answer (B) is incorrect because 4 years assumes salvage value is subtracted from the cost to determine the depreciable base used to calculate DDB depreciation. Answer (C) is incorrect because 2.5 years is equivalent to a straight-line rate of 40% and a DDB rate of 80%. Hence, DDB depreciation would be $320,000 (80% × $400,000). Answer (D) is incorrect because, if the useful life were 2 years, the depreciation expense would be $320,000 [(100% × $400,000 cost) – $80,000 salvage].

13. Quito Co. acquired a fixed asset with an estimated useful life of 5 years and no salvage value for $15,000 at the beginning of year 1. For financial statement purposes, how would the depreciation expense calculated using the double-declining-balance (DDB) method compare with that calculated using the sum-of-the-years'-digits (SYD) method in year 1 and year 2, respectively?

	Year 1	Year 2
A.	Lower	Lower
B.	Lower	Higher
C.	Higher	Lower
D.	Higher	Higher

Answer (C) is correct. *(CIA, adapted)*

REQUIRED: The comparison for 2 years of DDB and SYD depreciation expense.

DISCUSSION: DDB is an accelerated depreciation method that determines periodic depreciation expense by multiplying the carrying amount at the beginning of each period by a constant rate that is equal to twice the straight-line rate of depreciation. Each year the carrying amount of the asset decreases by the depreciation expense recognized. Salvage value is ignored in determining the carrying amount except as a floor beneath which the asset may not be depreciated. SYD depreciation multiplies a constant depreciable base (cost – salvage value) by the SYD fraction. The SYD fraction's numerator is the number of years of the useful life (n) minus the prior years elapsed. The formula to compute the denominator in the SYD method is

$$n\left[\frac{(n+1)}{2}\right]$$

For a 5-year estimated useful life, the denominator of the fraction is 15 [5(5 + 1) ÷ 2].

DDB: Year 1 = $15,000(.4) = $6,000
Year 2 = $9,000(.4) = $3,600

SYD: Year 1 = $15,000(5 ÷ 15) = $5,000
Year 2 = $15,000(4 ÷ 15) = $4,000

Answer (A) is incorrect because DDB depreciation is higher in year 1. Answer (B) is incorrect because DDB depreciation is higher in year 1 and lower in year 2. Answer (D) is incorrect because DDB depreciation is lower in year 2.

14. Lima Company is depreciating an asset with a 5-year useful life. It cost $100,000 and has no salvage value. If the <List A> method is used, depreciation expense in the second year will be <List B>.

	List A	List B
A.	Sum-of-years'-digits	$20,000
B.	Sum-of-years'-digits	$40,000
C.	Double-declining balance	$16,000
D.	Double-declining-balance	$24,000

Answer (D) is correct. *(CIA, adapted)*

REQUIRED: The proper match of depreciation method and expense amount.

DISCUSSION: The DDB method uses twice the straight-line rate. In the first year of the asset's life, depreciation expense was $40,000 ($100,000 × 20% × 2). In the second year, the depreciation base is reduced by the amount of depreciation expense already taken in the first year, so depreciation expense in the second year is $24,000 [2 × 20% × ($100,000 – $40,000)].

Answer (A) is incorrect because depreciation in the second year will be $20,000 under the straight-line method of depreciation. Under the SYD method, it is $26,667 [(4 ÷ 15) × $100,000]. Answer (B) is incorrect because SYD depreciation in the second year is $26,667. Answer (C) is incorrect because $16,000 assumes the declining-balance method is used with the straight-line rate.

15. Ottawa Corp. uses the sum-of-the-year's-digits method of depreciation. In the third year of use of an asset with a 4-year estimated useful life, the portion of the depreciation cost for the asset that the organization will expense is

A. 10%

B. 20%

C. 30%

D. 33.33%

Answer (B) is correct. *(CIA, adapted)*

REQUIRED: The SYD depreciation in the third year.

DISCUSSION: The SYD fraction (remaining years of the useful life at the beginning of the year ÷ the sum of the years of the useful life) is applied to the constant depreciable base (cost – salvage). For the third year of use of an asset with a 4-year life, the percentage of the depreciable base to be recognized is 20% [2 years ÷ (1 + 2 + 3 + 4)].

Answer (A) is incorrect because 10% results from calculating the portion of depreciable cost to expense in any given year using the end of the current year in the numerator. Answer (C) is incorrect because 30% uses the digit of the current year in the numerator. Answer (D) is incorrect because 33.33% calculates the denominator as the sum of the years up to the end of the current year.

16. A machine with a 5-year estimated useful life and an estimated 10% salvage value was acquired on January 1, year 1. On December 31, year 4, accumulated depreciation using the sum-of-the-years'-digits method is

A. (Original cost – salvage value) × (1 ÷ 15).

B. (Original cost – salvage value) × (14 ÷ 15).

C. Original cost × (14 ÷ 15).

D. Original cost × (1 ÷ 15).

Answer (B) is correct. *(CPA, adapted)*

REQUIRED: The accumulated depreciation at the end of 4 years under the SYD method.

DISCUSSION: SYD depreciation is calculated on a constant depreciable base equal to the original cost minus the salvage value, multiplied by the SYD fraction. The SYD fraction's numerator is the number of years of the useful life of the asset minus the prior years elapsed. The denominator is the sum of the digits of the total years of the expected useful life. In this case, the denominator is 15 (1 + 2 + 3 + 4 + 5). Thus, the accumulated depreciation at the end of the fourth year is (14 ÷ 15) of the depreciable base (original cost – salvage value), that is, the sum of the depreciation amounts calculated for each of the 4 years, or [(5 ÷ 15) + (4 ÷ 15) + (3 ÷ 15) + (2 ÷ 15)] times the depreciable base.

Answer (A) is incorrect because (original cost – salvage value) × (1 ÷ 15) is the depreciation for year 5. Answer (C) is incorrect because original cost × (14 ÷ 15) is the accumulated depreciation on December 31, year 4, assuming no salvage value. Answer (D) is incorrect because original cost × (1 ÷ 15) is the depreciation for year 5 assuming no salvage value.

17. Tunis Company purchased a van for $45,000. The estimated useful life of the van is 5 years or 80,000 miles, and the salvage value is $5,000. Actual mileage driven in the first year was 20,000 miles. Which of the following methods will result in the highest depreciation for the first year?

A. Straight-line.

B. Productive-output.

C. Sum-of-the-years'-digits.

D. Double-declining-balance.

Answer (D) is correct. *(J. Emig)*

REQUIRED: The method that will result in the highest depreciation for the first year.

DISCUSSION: Under the straight-line, productive-output, and SYD methods, the depreciable base is $40,000 ($45,000 original cost – $5,000 estimated salvage value). Under the straight-line method, this base is allocated equally to the 5 years, resulting in a depreciation expense of $8,000. Under the units-of-output method, the $40,000 is allocated evenly across the estimated mileage to produce a depreciation charge of $.50 per mile. Thus, first-year depreciation expense is $10,000 ($.50 × 20,000 miles). Under SYD, the depreciable base is multiplied by the SYD factor (years remaining at the beginning of the year ÷ the sum of the digits). SYD depreciation expense in the first year is therefore $13,333 [$40,000 × (5 ÷ 15)]. Under the DDB method, the $45,000 original cost is multiplied by a rate that is equal to twice the straight-line rate (2 × 20% = 40%). The result is a depreciation expense of $18,000 (40% × $45,000) in the first year.

Answer (A) is incorrect because straight-line depreciation is $8,000. Answer (B) is incorrect because productive-output depreciation is $10,000. Answer (C) is incorrect because SYD depreciation is $13,333.

18. On January 1, year 1, Nairobi, Inc. purchased equipment having an estimated salvage value equal to 20% of its original cost at the end of a 10-year life. The equipment was sold December 31, year 5 for 50% of its original cost. If the equipment's disposition resulted in a reported loss, which of the following depreciation methods did Nairobi use?

A. Double-declining-balance.

B. Sum-of-the-years'-digits.

C. Straight-line.

D. Composite.

Answer (C) is correct. *(CPA, adapted)*

REQUIRED: The method that would result in a reported loss upon disposition.

DISCUSSION: The straight-line method of depreciation yields the lowest amount of depreciation for the early part of the depreciable life of the asset. Because only 50% of the original cost was received and straight-line accumulated depreciation equaled 40% of cost {[(100% – 20%) ÷ 10 years] × 5 years} at the time of sale, a 10% loss [50% – (100% – 40%)] results.

Answer (A) is incorrect because the DDB method results in 5-year accumulated depreciation that is greater than 50% of cost. Answer (B) is incorrect because the SYD method results in 5-year accumulated depreciation that is greater than 50% of cost. Answer (D) is incorrect because the composite method of depreciation applies to the weighted average of multiple useful lives of assets, whereas only one asset is mentioned in this question. Moreover, it recognizes no gain or loss on disposition.

19. According to current authoritative literature, all of the following disclosures should be made in the financial statements or notes regarding depreciable assets and their corresponding methods of depreciation except

A. Balances of major classes of depreciable assets, by nature or function at the balance sheet date.

B. Accumulated depreciation, either by major classes of depreciable assets or in total, at the balance sheet date.

C. A general description of the method(s) used in computing depreciation for major classes of depreciable assets.

D. The depreciation lives by major class of assets used in computing depreciation.

Answer (D) is correct. *(Publisher)*

REQUIRED: The disclosure not required in the financial statements or notes regarding depreciable assets and their corresponding depreciation methods.

DISCUSSION: APB 12 requires disclosure of

1) Depreciation expense for the period
2) Balances of major classes of depreciable assets at the financial statement date
3) Amount of accumulated depreciation as of the financial statement date
4) General description of methods used in computing depreciation

APB 12 does not require disclosure of the estimated useful lives employed in depreciation calculations.

8.2 Depreciation Calculations

20. Pretoria Company acquired a new machine at a cost of $400,000 and incurred costs of $4,000 to have the machine shipped to its factory. Pretoria also paid $9,000 to construct and prepare a site for the new machine and $7,000 to install the necessary electrical connections. Pretoria estimates that the useful life of this new machine will be 5 years and that it will have a salvage value of $30,000 at the end of that period. Assuming that Pretoria acquired the machine on January 1 and will take a full year's depreciation, the proper amount of depreciation expense to be recorded by Pretoria if it uses the double-declining-balance method is

A. $148,000

B. $168,000

C. $160,000

D. $161,600

Answer (B) is correct. *(CMA, adapted)*

REQUIRED: The proper amount of depreciation under the double-declining-balance (DDB) method.

DISCUSSION: The acquisition cost of the machine includes all costs necessary to prepare it for its intended use. Hence, the depreciable cost is $420,000 ($400,000 invoice price + $4,000 delivery expense + $9,000 site preparation + $7,000 electrical work). Under the DDB method, salvage value is ignored at the beginning. Thus, the full $420,000 will be subject to depreciation. Given a 5-year life, the annual straight-line rate is 20%, and the DDB rate is 40%. Depreciation for the first year is therefore $168,000 (40% × $420,000).

Answer (A) is incorrect because $148,000 assumes that the depreciable cost is the invoice price minus salvage value. Answer (C) is incorrect because the depreciable cost of the machine was $420,000, not the $400,000 invoice price. Answer (D) is incorrect because $161,600 assumes a depreciable cost of $404,000, which does not include the site preparation and electrical costs.

21. Sydney Co. purchased a machine that was installed and placed in service on January 1, year 1 at a cost of $480,000. Salvage value was estimated at $80,000. The machine is being depreciated over 10 years by the double-declining-balance method. For the year ended December 31, year 2, what amount should Sydney report as depreciation expense?

A. $96,000

B. $76,800

C. $64,000

D. $61,440

Answer (B) is correct. *(CPA, adapted)*

REQUIRED: The DDB depreciation expense reported in the second year.

DISCUSSION: DDB is an accelerated depreciation method that determines periodic depreciation expense by multiplying the carrying amount at the beginning of each period by a constant rate that is equal to twice the straight-line rate of depreciation. Given that this machine has a 10-year useful life, the DDB rate is 20%. Each year the carrying amount of the asset decreases by the depreciation expense recognized. Salvage value is ignored in determining the carrying amount except as a floor beneath which the asset may not be depreciated. The carrying amount at the end of the first year was $384,000 [(100% – 20%) × $480,000 cost]. Thus, second-year depreciation is $76,800 (20% × $384,000).

Answer (A) is incorrect because $96,000 was the first-year depreciation. Answer (C) is incorrect because $64,000 assumes that salvage value is included in the calculation. Answer (D) is incorrect because $61,440 will be the third-year depreciation.

22. Khartoum Co. purchased equipment on January 2, year 1 for $50,000. The equipment had an estimated 5-year service life. Khartoum's policy for 5-year assets is to use the 200%-double-declining-balance depreciation method for the first 2 years of the asset's life and then switch to the straight-line depreciation method. In its December 31, year 3 balance sheet, what amount should Khartoum report as accumulated depreciation for equipment?

A. $30,000

B. $38,000

C. $39,200

D. $42,000

Answer (B) is correct. *(CPA, adapted)*

REQUIRED: The amount of accumulated depreciation to be reported in the balance sheet.

DISCUSSION: Under the DDB method, the assets are depreciated at a constant rate of 40% (200% × 20% straight-line rate). This rate is applied in each of the first 2 years. For year 3, straight-line is used based on the remaining carrying amount. The calculation is as follows:

Year 1:	$50,000 × 40%	$20,000
Year 2:	($50,000 – $20,000) × 40%	12,000
Year 3:	($50,000 – $20,000 – $12,000) ÷ 3	6,000
		$38,000

Answer (A) is incorrect because $30,000 equals the accumulated straight-line depreciation for 3 years. Answer (C) is incorrect because $39,200 equals DDB depreciation for 3 years. Answer (D) is incorrect because $42,000 includes third-year straight-line depreciation calculated without regard to DDB depreciation previously taken.

23. Spiro Corp. uses the sum-of-the-years'-digits method to depreciate equipment purchased in January year 1 for $20,000. The estimated salvage value of the equipment is $2,000 and the estimated useful life is four years. What should Spiro report as the asset's carrying amount as of December 31, year 3?

A. $1,800

B. $2,000

C. $3,800

D. $4,500

Answer (C) is correct. *(CPA, adapted)*

REQUIRED: The asset's carrying amount as of December 31, year 3.

DISCUSSION: The sum-of-the-year's digits (SYD) method multiplies a constant depreciable base (cost – salvage) by a declining fraction. It is a declining-rate, declining-charge method. The SYD fraction's numerator is the number of years of the useful life (n) minus the prior years elapsed. The formula to compute the (sum of the years' digits) denominator is

$$n\left[\frac{(n+1)}{2}\right]$$

Consequently, the depreciable base is $18,000 ($20,000 – $2,000), the numerator is 1 year (4 – 3), and the denominator is 10 {[4 × (4 + 1)] ÷ 2}. The depreciation for the last year is $1,800 [$18,000 × (1 ÷ 10)], so the declining balance after 3 years of the 4-year period (year 1-year 3) is $3,800 ($1,800 remaining depreciable base + $2,000 salvage value).

Answer (A) is incorrect because $1,800 is the final-year SYD depreciation. Answer (B) is incorrect because $2,000 is the salvage value. Answer (D) is incorrect because $4,500 is the annual straight-line depreciation.

Questions 24 and 25 are based on the following information.

Since year 1, Canberra Company has replaced all of its major manufacturing equipment and now has the following equipment recorded in the appropriate accounts. Canberra uses a calendar year as its fiscal year.

- A forge purchased January 1, year 1 for $100,000. Installation costs were $20,000, and the forge has an estimated 5-year life with a salvage value of $10,000.
- A grinding machine costing $45,000 purchased January 1, year 2. The machine has an estimated 5-year life with a salvage value of $5,000.
- A lathe purchased January 1, year 4 for $60,000. The lathe has an estimated 5-year life with a salvage value of $7,000.

24. Using the straight-line depreciation method, Canberra's year 4 depreciation expense is

A. $45,000

B. $40,334

C. $40,600

D. $40,848

Answer (C) is correct. *(CMA, adapted)*

REQUIRED: The year 4 depreciation expense using the straight-line method.

DISCUSSION: The straight-line method allocates the depreciation evenly over the estimated useful life of an asset. The depreciable cost equals cost minus salvage value for each asset, and dividing that amount by the life of the asset gives the periodic depreciation as follows:

Asset	Cost	Salvage	C – S	Life	Expense
Forge	$120,000	$10,000	$110,000	5	$22,000
Grind	45,000	5,000	40,000	5	8,000
Lathe	60,000	7,000	53,000	5	10,600
Total					$40,600

Answer (A) is incorrect because $45,000 does not take into account the deduction for salvage value. Answer (B) is incorrect because $40,334 is based on the sum-of-the-years'-digits method. Answer (D) is incorrect because $40,848 is based on the double-declining-balance method.

25. Using the double-declining-balance method, Canberra's year 4 depreciation expense is

A. $36,464

B. $40,334

C. $40,600

D. $40,848

Answer (D) is correct. *(CMA, adapted)*

REQUIRED: The year 4 depreciation expense using the double-declining-balance method.

DISCUSSION: The DDB method allocates a series of decreasing depreciation charges over an asset's life. A percentage that is double the straight-line rate is multiplied each year times an asset's remaining carrying amount at the beginning of the year. Given that each asset has a 5-year life, the straight-line rate is 20%. The DDB rate is therefore 40%. The forge was purchased in year 1 at a total cost of $120,000. The depreciation for each year is calculated as follows:

Year	Carrying Amount	%	Expense
Year 1	$120,000	40%	$48,000
Year 2	72,000	40%	28,800
Year 3	43,200	40%	17,280
Year 4	25,920	40%	10,368

For the grinding machine, the calculations are

Year	Carrying Amount	%	Expense
Year 2	$45,000	40%	$18,000
Year 3	27,000	40%	10,800
Year 4	16,200	40%	6,480

The year 4 calculation for the new lathe requires multiplying the $60,000 cost times 40% to yield a $24,000 expense. Adding the year 4 expense for each of the three machines ($10,368 + $6,480 + $24,000) produces total depreciation of $40,848.

Answer (A) is incorrect because $36,464 is based on the double-declining-balance method but with salvage value deducted from the initial depreciable base. Answer (B) is incorrect because $40,334 is based on the sum-of-the-years'-digits method. Answer (C) is incorrect because $40,600 is based on the straight-line method.

Questions 26 through 28 are based on the following information.

Samoa Corporation's schedule of depreciable assets at December 31, year 3 is shown in the next column. Samoa takes a full year's depreciation expense in the year of an asset's acquisition and no depreciation expense in the year of an asset's disposition. The estimated useful life of each depreciable asset is 5 years.

Asset	Cost	Accumulated Depreciation	Acquisition Date	Salvage Value
A	$100,000	$ 64,000	Year 2	$20,000
B	55,000	36,000	Year 1	10,000
C	70,000	33,600	Year 1	14,000
	$225,000	$133,600		$44,000

26. Samoa depreciates asset A on the double-declining-balance method. How much depreciation expense should Samoa record in year 4 for asset A?

A. $32,000

B. $24,000

C. $14,400

D. $1,600

Answer (C) is correct. *(CPA, adapted)*

REQUIRED: The current depreciation expense.

DISCUSSION: DDB depreciation equals carrying amount at the beginning of the year times twice the straight-line rate. Salvage value is considered only as the floor beneath which the carrying amount may not be reduced. Asset A has a useful life of 5 years, so the straight-line rate is 20%. The DDB rate is 40% (2 × 20%). The carrying amount is $36,000 ($100,000 cost – $64,000 accumulated depreciation). Annual depreciation expense for its third year is thus $14,400 (.4 × $36,000).

Answer (A) is incorrect because $32,000 is first-year depreciation after subtracting salvage value from the depreciable base. Answer (B) is incorrect because $24,000 was the year 2 depreciation. Answer (D) is incorrect because $1,600 will be the difference between 12/31/year 4 carrying amount and the salvage value that will be the year 5 depreciation.

27. Using the same depreciation method as used in year 1, year 2, and year 3, how much depreciation expense should Samoa record in year 4 for asset B?

A. $6,000

B. $9,000

C. $12,000

D. $15,000

Answer (A) is correct. *(CPA, adapted)*

REQUIRED: The current depreciation expense.

DISCUSSION: The cost of asset B was $55,000, and the depreciation accumulated after 3 years of its 5-year life is $36,000. Under the straight-line method, depreciation would have totaled $27,000 [3 × .2 × ($55,000 – $10,000 salvage value)]. DDB depreciation would have been $43,120 (40% of a declining carrying amount each year). The SYD method multiplies a fraction (the years remaining ÷ the SYD) times a constant depreciable base (cost – salvage). The SYD is 15 [n(n + 1) ÷ 2 = 5(5 + 1) ÷ 2]. Total SYD depreciation after 3 years is $36,000. Thus, SYD should be used and year 4 depreciation is $6,000 [(2 ÷ 15) × $45,000].

Year 1:	[(5 ÷ 15) × ($55,000 – $10,000)]	=	$15,000
Year 2:	[(4 ÷ 15) × ($55,000 – $10,000)]	=	12,000
Year 3:	[(3 ÷ 15) × ($55,000 – $10,000)]	=	9,000
			$36,000

Answer (B) is incorrect because $9,000 was the third-year SYD depreciation. Answer (C) is incorrect because $12,000 was the second-year depreciation. Answer (D) is incorrect because $15,000 was the first-year depreciation.

28. Samoa depreciates asset C by the straight-line method. On June 30, year 4, Samoa sold asset C for $28,000 cash. How much gain or (loss) should Samoa record in year 4 on the disposal of asset C?

A. $2,800

B. $(2,800)

C. $(5,600)

D. $(8,400)

Answer (D) is correct. *(CPA, adapted)*

REQUIRED: The gain (loss) on disposal of asset C.

DISCUSSION: Asset C had a carrying amount at the time of its disposition of $36,400 ($70,000 cost – $33,600 accumulated depreciation), given that no depreciation was recognized in the year of sale. The loss on the transaction was $8,400 ($36,400 carrying amount – $28,000 cash received).

Answer (A) is incorrect because $2,800 assumes that a year's depreciation was taken in year 4. Answer (B) is incorrect because $(2,800) assumes depreciation was taken for the first half of the year. Answer (C) is incorrect because $(5,600) equals the accumulated depreciation balance minus the cash received.

Questions 29 and 30 are based on the following information. Roswell Company has the following information on one of its vehicles purchased on January 1, year 1:

Vehicle cost	$ 50,000
Useful life, years, estimated	5
Useful life, miles, estimated	100,000
Salvage value, estimated	$ 10,000
Actual miles driven, year 1	30,000
year 2	20,000
year 3	15,000
year 4	25,000
year 5	12,000

No estimates were changed during the life of the asset.

29. The year 3 depreciation expense for the vehicle using the sum-of-the-years'-digits (SYD) method was

A. $6,000

B. $8,000

C. $10,000

D. $16,000

Answer (B) is correct. *(CMA, adapted)*

REQUIRED: The year 3 depreciation expense under the SYD method.

DISCUSSION: Under the SYD method, the amount to be depreciated is $40,000 ($50,000 original cost – $10,000 salvage). The portion expensed each year is based on a fraction, the denominator of which is the summation of the years of life of the asset being depreciated. For an asset with a 5-year life, the denominator is 15 (5 + 4 + 3 + 2 + 1). The numerator equals the years remaining at the beginning of the year. For year 3, the fraction is 3 ÷ 15, and depreciation expense is $8,000 [$40,000 × (3 ÷ 15)].

Answer (A) is incorrect because $6,000 is based on the units-of-production method. Answer (C) is incorrect because $10,000 omits the vehicle's salvage value from the calculation. Answer (D) is incorrect because $16,000 is the double-declining-balance method depreciation for year 3 if the salvage value is subtracted from the cost.

30. Using the units-of-production method, what was the year 5 depreciation expense?

A. $4,000

B. $4,800

C. $5,000

D. $6,000

Answer (A) is correct. *(CMA, adapted)*

REQUIRED: The depreciation expense for year 5 under the units-of-production method.

DISCUSSION: Under the units-of-production method, periodic depreciation is based on the proportion of expected total production that occurred. For the years 1 through 4, the total depreciation was $36,000 {($50,000 – $10,000) × [(30,000 + 20,000 + 15,000 + 25,000) ÷ 100,000]}. Hence, the remaining depreciable base was $4,000 ($50,000 cost – $10,000 salvage – $36,000). Given that the 12,000 miles driven in year 5 exceeded the remaining estimated production of 10,000 miles (100,000 – 30,000 – 20,000 – 15,000 – 25,000), only the $4,000 of the remaining depreciable base should be recognized in year 5.

Answer (B) is incorrect because $4,800 is based on a year 5 rate of 12% (12,000 miles ÷ 100,000 miles of estimated usage). It ignores the effects of depreciation expense deducted in prior years. Answer (C) is incorrect because $5,000 assumes that depreciation is based on original cost without regard to salvage value. Answer (D) is incorrect because $6,000 is based on a 12% rate and ignores salvage value.

31. On July 1, year 1, Tungushka Corporation purchased factory equipment for $100,000. Salvage value was estimated at $4,000. The equipment will be depreciated over 10 years using the double-declining-balance method. Counting the year of acquisition as one-half year, Tungushka should record year 2 depreciation expense of

A. $17,280

B. $18,000

C. $16,000

D. $20,000

Answer (B) is correct. *(CPA, adapted)*

REQUIRED: The DDB depreciation expense for an asset acquired in mid-year.

DISCUSSION: Using DDB when an asset is acquired in mid-year requires that each year's DDB depreciation be allocated to the accounting period in which it falls. Accordingly, the first year's depreciation must be prorated between the last half of year 1 and the first half of year 2. The second year's must be prorated between the second half of year 2 and the first half of year 3, etc. The year 2 depreciation expense is the sum of half of the first and half of the second year's depreciation. The DDB depreciation for years one and two computed below is based on the asset cost of $100,000 and a 10-year life (resulting in a DDB rate of 20%).

Year 1: $100,000 × 20% = $20,000
Year 2: ($100,000 – $20,000) × 20% = $16,000

50% × $20,000	=	$10,000
50% × $16,000	=	8,000
		$18,000

Answer (A) is incorrect because $17,280 is calculated by using a depreciable base of $100,000 reduced by the salvage value of $4,000. Answer (C) is incorrect because $16,000 is the total depreciation for the second year of the asset's life without proration. Answer (D) is incorrect because $20,000 is the total depreciation for the first year of the asset's life without proration.

32. Melbourne Co. uses straight-line depreciation for its property, plant, and equipment, which, stated at cost, consisted of the following:

	12/31/year 2	12/31/year 1
Land	$ 25,000	$ 25,000
Buildings	195,000	195,000
Machinery and equipment	695,000	650,000
	$915,000	$870,000
Minus accumulated depreciation	400,000	370,000
	$515,000	$500,000

Melbourne's depreciation expense for year 2 and year 1 was $55,000 and $50,000, respectively. What amount was debited to accumulated depreciation during year 2 because of property, plant, and equipment retirements?

A. $40,000

B. $25,000

C. $20,000

D. $10,000

Answer (B) is correct. *(CPA, adapted)*

REQUIRED: The amount that was debited to accumulated depreciation because of retirements.

DISCUSSION: When an asset is depreciated, a debit is made to depreciation expense and a credit to accumulated depreciation. An equipment retirement results in a debit to accumulated depreciation. During year 2, accumulated depreciation increased by $30,000 despite recognition of a $55,000 expense (a credit). Consequently, a $25,000 ($55,000 – $30,000) debit must have been made to the accumulated depreciation account.

Answer (A) is incorrect because $40,000 is equal to $55,000 minus the $15,000 increase in net property, plant, and equipment. Answer (C) is incorrect because $20,000 is the difference between year 1 depreciation ($50,000) and the $30,000 increase in accumulated depreciation. Answer (D) is incorrect because $10,000 is equal to $55,000 minus the $45,000 increase in the gross property, plant, and equipment.

33. On January 2, year 1, Osaka Co. purchased a machine for $800,000 and established an annual depreciation charge of $100,000 over an 8-year life. At the beginning of year 4, after issuing its year 3 financial statements, Osaka concluded that $250,000 was a reasonable estimate of the sum of the undiscounted net cash inflows expected to be recovered through use of the machine for the period January 1, year 4 through December 31, year 8. The machine's fair value was $200,000 at the beginning of year 4. In Osaka's December 31, year 4 balance sheet, the machine should be reported at a carrying amount of

A. $0

B. $100,000

C. $160,000

D. $400,000

Answer (C) is correct. *(CPA, adapted)*

REQUIRED: The carrying amount of an asset.

DISCUSSION: The asset should be written down to fair value if the carrying amount is not recoverable (SFAS 144). Because the carrying amount ($800,000 cost – $300,000 accumulated depreciation = $500,000) exceeded the recoverable amount ($250,000) at the beginning of year 4, Osaka should have recognized an impairment loss of $300,000 ($500,000 carrying amount – $200,000 fair value at the beginning of year 4). Accordingly, the new carrying amount was $200,000, and the new annual depreciation expense for the remaining 5-year useful life (year 4 – year 8) was $40,000 ($200,000 ÷ 5 years). The machine should be reported at a carrying amount of $160,000 ($200,000 – $40,000 depreciation) on December 31, year 4.

Answer (A) is incorrect because the machine still has a carrying amount. Answer (B) is incorrect because $100,000 results from subtracting the originally computed annual depreciation from the new carrying amount. Answer (D) is incorrect because $400,000 assumes no impairment.

34. Auckland Co. determined that, because of obsolescence, equipment with an original cost of $1,800,000 and accumulated depreciation on the first day of the current fiscal year of $840,000 had suffered impairment and, as a result, should have a carrying amount of only $600,000 (the fair value) as of the beginning of the year. In addition, the remaining useful life of the equipment was reduced from 8 years to 3. In its year-end balance sheet, what amount should Auckland report as accumulated depreciation?

A. $200,000

B. $1,040,000

C. $1,200,000

D. $1,400,000

Answer (D) is correct. *(CPA, adapted)*

REQUIRED: The accumulated depreciation given on impairment loss and a change in estimate.

DISCUSSION: The carrying amount of the equipment before the impairment was $960,000 ($1,800,000 – $840,000). After the impairment, the carrying amount should be $600,000; therefore, $360,000 ($960,000 – $600,000) of additional accumulated depreciation should be recorded to reflect the impairment loss (assuming the entry is to debit the loss and credit accumulated depreciation). In addition, the depreciation for the year should be $200,000 ($600,000 ÷ 3). Hence, the accumulated depreciation in the year-end balance sheet is $1,400,000 ($840,000 + $360,000 impairment loss + $200,000 depreciation for the year).

Answer (A) is incorrect because $200,000 is the depreciation for the year. Answer (B) is incorrect because $1,040,000 is the sum of the accumulated depreciation at the beginning of the year and the revised annual depreciation. Answer (C) is incorrect because $1,200,000 is the accumulated depreciation before adjusting the useful life and claiming current-year depreciation.

8.3 Aggregate Depreciation Methods

35. Asuncion Company, which uses the composite depreciation method for its fleet of trucks, cars, and campers, retired one of its trucks and received cash from a salvage company. The net carrying amount of these composite asset accounts was decreased by the

A. Cash proceeds received and original cost of the truck.

B. Cash proceeds received.

C. Original cost of the truck minus the cash proceeds.

D. Original cost of the truck.

Answer (B) is correct. *(CPA, adapted)*

REQUIRED: The effect of a retirement on the net carrying amount of a composite asset account.

DISCUSSION: Because both composite and group methods use weighted averages of useful lives and depreciation rates, early and late retirements are expected to offset each other. Consequently, gains and losses on retirements of single assets are treated as adjustments of accumulated depreciation. The entry is to credit the asset at cost, debit cash for any proceeds received, and debit accumulated depreciation for the difference. (A credit is unlikely. Proceeds of a retirement rarely exceed original cost.) Thus, the net carrying amount of the composite asset accounts is decreased by the amount of cash received. The net carrying amount of total assets is unchanged.

36. Which of the following uses the straight-line depreciation method?

	Group Depreciation	Composite Depreciation
A.	No	No
B.	Yes	No
C.	Yes	Yes
D.	No	Yes

Answer (C) is correct. *(CPA, adapted)*

REQUIRED: The method(s) using straight-line depreciation.

DISCUSSION: Both composite and group depreciation use the straight-line method. Both methods aggregate groups of assets. The composite method is used for a collection of dissimilar assets with varying useful lives, whereas the group method deals with similar assets. Each method involves the calculation of a total depreciable cost for all the assets included in one account and of a weighted-average estimated useful life.

37. When depreciation is calculated for similar articles of small value, either the retirement or the replacement system may be used. Under which of these two systems would the cost of the replacement assets purchased be capitalized?

	Retirement	Replacement
A.	Yes	Yes
B.	Yes	No
C.	No	Yes
D.	No	No

Answer (B) is correct. *(Publisher)*

REQUIRED: The system(s) under which the cost of replacement assets is capitalized.

DISCUSSION: Both retirement and replacement systems are used when depreciation must be calculated for similar articles of small value. These systems are principally used by public utilities for assets such as poles and telephones.

Under the retirement system, the cost of the replacement assets is capitalized in the asset account. The cost of the assets retired minus their salvage value is charged to depreciation expense as they are retired.

Under the replacement system, the cost of the old assets is maintained in the asset account. The cost of the newly acquired assets minus the salvage value of the replaced assets is charged to depreciation expense.

38. The inventory (appraisal) method of depreciation computes depreciation as

A. A means of valuing fixed assets at current replacement cost.

B. Systematic and rational.

C. The difference between the value at the beginning of the year, plus additions, and the inventory at the end of the year.

D. Usually requiring the use of an accumulated depreciation account.

Answer (C) is correct. *(Publisher)*

REQUIRED: The true statement about the inventory (appraisal) method of depreciation.

DISCUSSION: The inventory depreciation method is a means of accounting for numerous small items such as hand tools. Depreciation in any one year is the carrying amount at the beginning of the year, plus acquisitions, minus the amount on hand at the end of the year. This method is similar to the periodic system of accounting for merchandise inventory.

Answer (A) is incorrect because depreciation methods are used to allocate cost, not to value assets. Answer (B) is incorrect because the inventory method is not a systematic and rational amortization of cost over several periods. Answer (D) is incorrect because an accumulated depreciation account is ordinarily not used.

Questions 39 through 41 are based on the following information.

For its first year of operations, Falkland Co. decided to use the composite method of depreciation and prepared the schedule of machinery owned presented in the opposite column.

	Total Cost	Estimated Salvage Value	Estimated Life in Years
Machine X	$550,000	$50,000	20
Machine Y	200,000	20,000	15
Machine Z	40,000	--	5

39. Falkland computes depreciation on the straight-line method. Based upon the information presented, the composite life of these assets (in years) should be

A. 13.3

B. 16.0

C. 17.6

D. 20.0

Answer (B) is correct. *(CPA, adapted)*

REQUIRED: The composite life of the assets in years.

DISCUSSION: The composite or average useful life of the assets is essentially a weighted average. As illustrated below, the annual straight-line depreciation for each asset should be calculated. The total cost, estimated salvage value, and depreciable base of the assets should then be computed. Dividing the composite depreciable base ($720) by the total annual straight-line depreciation ($45) gives the composite life (16 years) of these assets.

	Total Cost	Salvage Value	Dep. Base	Est. Life	Annual S-L Dep.
X	$550	$50	$500	20	$25
Y	200	20	180	15	12
Z	40	0	40	5	8
	$790	$70	$720		$45

Answer (A) is incorrect because 13.3 is the average useful life of the three assets. Answer (C) is incorrect because 17.6 ignores salvage value. Answer (D) is incorrect because 20 is the estimated life of asset X.

40. At the start of the fifth year of operations, Falkland sold machine Z for $10,000. Determine the depreciation expense and the ending balance in the accumulated depreciation account that should be recorded for year five.

A. $45,000 and $225,000.

B. $45,000 and $195,000.

C. $42,500 and $222,500.

D. $42,500 and $192,500.

Answer (D) is correct. *(Publisher)*

REQUIRED: The calculation of depreciation expense and accumulated depreciation under the composite method when an asset is sold.

DISCUSSION: The straight-line depreciation rate is 6.25% ($45,000 ÷ $720,000). When an asset included in a composite group is sold, the original cost of that asset minus the amount received for it is debited to the accumulated depreciation account. No gain or loss is recorded. The depreciation rate is multiplied by the depreciable base of the remaining assets to determine the depreciation expense.

The depreciation expense for the fifth year is equal to $42,500 [($720,000 – $40,000) × 6.25%]. The accumulated depreciation at the start of year five ($180,000) is increased by the $42,500 depreciation expense and decreased by $30,000 ($40,000 original cost – $10,000 cash received), leaving a year-end balance of $192,500.

Answer (A) is incorrect because $45,000 is the annual straight-line depreciation, and $225,000 is the accumulated depreciation if the machine is not sold. Answer (B) is incorrect because $45,000 is the original annual depreciation, and $195,000 equals the accumulated depreciation after 4 years, plus the original annual depreciation, minus $30,000 ($40,000 cost of Z – $10,000 sale price). Answer (C) is incorrect because $222,500 reflects a failure to deduct the accumulated depreciation associated with machine Z.

41. Assume that, in addition to the sale of machine Z for $10,000 at the start of year 5, Falkland purchased machine W for $60,000 to replace the machine that was sold. Machine W is expected to last 5 years with an expected salvage value of $10,000. If machine W is included in the composite asset group, the depreciation expense for the fifth year should be equal to which of the following amounts?

A. $42,500

B. $45,000

C. $45,625

D. $46,250

Answer (C) is correct. *(Publisher)*

REQUIRED: The depreciation expense under the composite method when a new asset is added.

DISCUSSION: When machine Z was sold, the depreciable base of the composite group was decreased from $720,000 to $680,000. The purchase of machine W adds $50,000 to the depreciable base. This increase is the original cost ($60,000) minus the salvage value ($10,000). The new depreciable base ($730,000) is multiplied by the straight-line depreciation rate (6.25%), resulting in year 5 depreciation of $45,625. Once a composite rate has been set, it continues to be used unless significant changes occur in the estimated lives or the composition of the assets through additions and retirements.

Answer (A) is incorrect because $42,500 is the depreciation expense excluding the new asset. Answer (B) is incorrect because $45,000 fails to consider the effects of both the sale of Z and the purchase of W. Answer (D) is incorrect because $46,250 fails to exclude the salvage value from the new asset's depreciable base.

8.4 Depletion

42. Budapest Co., a calendar-year entity, purchased the rights to a copper mine on July 1. Of the total purchase price, $2.8 million was appropriately allocable to the copper. Estimated reserves were 800,000 tons of copper. Budapest expects to extract and sell 10,000 tons of copper per month. Production began immediately. The selling price is $25 per ton. Budapest uses percentage depletion (15%) for tax purposes. To aid production, Budapest also purchased some new equipment on July 1. The equipment cost $76,000 and had an estimated useful life of 8 years. After all the copper is removed from this mine, however, the equipment will be of no use to Budapest and will be sold for an estimated $4,000. If sales and production conform to expectations, what is Budapest's depletion expense on this mine for financial accounting purposes for the calendar year?

A. $105,000
B. $210,000
C. $215,400
D. $420,000

Answer (B) is correct. *(CPA, adapted)*
REQUIRED: The annual depletion expense for financial accounting purposes assuming accurate estimates of sales and production.
DISCUSSION: Depletion expense is based on the units-of-production method. Assuming total reserves of 800,000 tons at a price of $2.8 million, the depletion charge per ton is $3.50. If 10,000 tons are extracted in each of the last 6 months of the year (60,000 tons), the depletion charge should be $210,000. The equipment cost is not included in the depletion base and is depreciated separately.
Answer (A) is incorrect because $105,000 is the depletion expense for 3 months. Answer (C) is incorrect because $215,400 includes depreciation of the equipment based on the units-of-production method. Answer (D) is incorrect because $420,000 is the 15% tax depletion.

43. In January, Manila Co., a calendar-year enterprise, purchased a mineral mine for $2,640,000 with removable ore estimated at 1.2 million tons. After it has extracted all the ore, Manila will be required by law to restore the land to its original condition at an estimated cost of $180,000. Manila believes it will be able to sell the property afterwards for $300,000. During the year, Manila incurred $360,000 of development costs preparing the mine for production and removed and sold 60,000 tons of ore. In its annual income statement, what amount should Manila report as depletion?

A. $135,000
B. $144,000
C. $150,000
D. $159,000

Answer (B) is correct. *(CPA, adapted)*
REQUIRED: The amount of depletion to be reported.
DISCUSSION: The depletion base is the purchase price of the land ($2,640,000), minus the value of the land after restoration ($300,000 – $180,000 = $120,000), plus any costs necessary to prepare the property for the extraction of ore ($360,000). This depletion base must be allocated over the 1.2 million tons of ore that the land is estimated to yield. Accordingly, Manila's depletion charge per ton is $2.40 [($2,640,000 – $120,000 + $360,000) ÷ 1,200,000]. Manila should report $144,000 ($2.40 × 60,000 tons removed) as depletion in its annual income statement.
Answer (A) is incorrect because $135,000 does not include the $180,000 restoration costs. Answer (C) is incorrect because $150,000 does not consider the restoration costs and the residual value of the land. Answer (D) is incorrect because $159,000 adds the $180,000 restoration cost instead of deducting the $120,000 net residual value of the land.

STUDY UNIT NINE
INTANGIBLE ASSETS AND RESEARCH AND DEVELOPMENT COSTS

SFAS 142, *Goodwill and Other Intangible Assets*, defines an **intangible asset** as a nonfinancial asset without physical substance. If an intangible asset is acquired individually or with other assets but not in a business combination, it is initially recognized and measured at fair value. The costs of **internally developed intangible assets** and goodwill are expensed when incurred if they are not specifically identifiable, have indeterminate lives, or are inherent in a continuing business and related to the entity as a whole. The **useful life** of an asset is the period during which it is expected to contribute either directly or indirectly to the future cash flows of the reporting entity. An intangible asset with a **finite useful life** to the reporting entity is amortized over that useful life. If the useful life is finite but not precisely known, the best estimate is the amortization period. The **pattern of consumption of economic benefits**, if it can be reliably ascertained, is reflected in the method of amortization. Otherwise, the **straight-line method** is required. The **amortizable amount** equals the amount initially assigned minus the residual value, which is the estimated fair value to the entity at the end of the asset's useful life, minus disposal costs. The **residual value** is zero unless a third party has committed to purchase the asset or it can be ascertained from an exchange transaction in an existing market for the asset that is expected to exist at the end of the useful life. The useful life should be reevaluated each reporting period. An amortized intangible asset is reviewed for **impairment** when events or changes in circumstances indicate that its carrying amount may not be recoverable. An impairment loss is recognized only if the carrying amount is **not recoverable** and is greater than the asset's fair value. Thus, the test for recognition is met if the sum of the undiscounted expected future cash flows from the asset is less than the carrying amount. The measure of any loss recognized is the excess of that carrying amount over the fair value. This loss is irreversible. An intangible asset with an **indefinite useful life** is not amortized. A nonamortized intangible asset is tested for impairment at least annually. It is tested more often if events or changes in circumstances suggest that the asset may be impaired. However, the impairment test differs from that for amortized intangible assets. If the carrying amount exceeds the fair value of the asset, that excess is the recognized loss. This loss is irreversible. **Goodwill** is not amortized. However, all goodwill acquired in a business combination is assigned to a reporting unit(s) and tested for impairment at least annually. **Potential impairment** of goodwill is deemed to exist only if the carrying amount (including goodwill) of a reporting unit is greater than its fair value. Thus, accounting for goodwill is based on the units of the combined entity into which the acquired entity was absorbed. A **reporting unit** is an operating segment or a component, which is one level below an operating segment. If a potential impairment is found, the carrying amount of reporting-unit goodwill is compared with its implied fair value. An impairment loss not exceeding the carrying amount of goodwill is then recognized equal to any excess of that carrying amount over the implied fair value. This loss is irreversible. The **implied fair value** of reporting-unit goodwill is estimated by allocating the fair value of the reporting unit to its assets and liabilities (including unrecognized intangible assets). The excess of that fair value over the amounts assigned equals the implied fair value. As part of testing goodwill for impairment, acquired assets, assumed liabilities, and assets and liabilities considered by the reporting entity to be part of its corporate assets and liabilities are **assigned at the acquisition date** to the reporting unit if (1) the assets are used in, or the liabilities are related to, the reporting unit's operations, and (2) the assets and liabilities are included in determining the reporting unit's fair value. The amounts of assets used in, or relating to, multiple reporting units should be divided among them based on a method that is reasonable, supportable, and consistently applied. As part of testing goodwill for impairment, all **goodwill is assigned at the acquisition date** to the reporting units that will benefit from the business combination. The method used for this assignment should be reasonable, supportable, consistently applied, and consistent with the objectives of the assignment. The assignment, in principle, should be done in the same manner as the determination of goodwill in a business combination. In accordance with this concept, the fair value of the acquired business (or a part) included in the reporting unit would be the "**purchase price**." This amount would be allocated to the assets acquired and liabilities assumed related to that business (or a part). The excess "price" is the goodwill assigned. If no assets acquired or liabilities assumed are assigned to a reporting unit, the goodwill to be assigned might equal the change in the fair value of the reporting unit as a result of the combination.

Franchise fees may be capitalized or expensed, depending upon the nature of the fees. The initial franchise fee includes the cost of establishing the franchise relationship and providing some initial services. The franchisee capitalizes this fee and amortizes the cost over the estimated useful life if it is finite. The continuing franchise fee includes the consideration paid for the continuing rights granted by the franchise arrangement and for general or specific services during its life. The franchisee expenses this fee as incurred. The franchisor recognizes franchise fee revenue at the earliest time that the franchisor has substantially performed or satisfied all material services or conditions relating to the franchise arrangement. The earliest time ordinarily is the commencement of operations by the franchisee, unless the franchisor can demonstrate that substantial performance of all obligations occurred previously.

Organization costs are those incurred in the formation of a business entity. For federal income tax purposes, the minimum amortization period is 5 years. However, for financial accounting purposes, **SOP 98-5**, *Reporting on the Costs of Start-Up Activities*, requires nongovernmental entities to expense start-up costs and organization costs as incurred.

SOP 93-7, *Reporting on Advertising Costs*, states that advertising costs should be expensed, either as incurred or when advertising first occurs. The primary costs are production and communication. However, **direct response advertising** costs should be capitalized (deferred) if the primary purpose is to elicit sales from customers who respond specifically to the advertising, and probable future economic benefits result. A second exception is for expenditures **subsequent to recognition** of related revenue. An example is a manufacturer's obligation to repay retailers for costs of advertising that involve the manufacturer's products. This type of cost should be accrued and expensed when related revenues are recognized.

Research is planned search or critical investigation aimed at discovery of new knowledge with the hope that such knowledge will aid in the development of a new product or service ("product"), or a new process or technique ("process"), or in the significant improvement of an existing product or process. **Development** is the translation of research findings or other knowledge into a plan or design for a new product or process or for the significant improvement of an existing product or process, whether for sale or use.

R&D costs are charged to expense when incurred. Disclosure of total R&D costs charged to expense is required for each period for which an income statement is presented. R&D costs include materials, equipment, and facilities; salaries, wages, and other related personnel costs; costs of externally acquired intangible assets; contract services; and a reasonable allocation of indirect costs. The costs of materials, equipment, facilities, and intangible assets purchased from others that have alternative future uses (including other R&D projects) are capitalized when acquired or produced. These costs are expensed as R&D when consumed or depreciated as part of R&D activities. The costs of assets that are acquired or produced for a specific R&D project and that have no alternative future uses are expensed.

Activities typically classified as R&D (unless conducted for others under a contractual arrangement) include (1) laboratory research aimed at discovery of new knowledge; (2) searching for applications of new research findings or other knowledge; (3) conceptual formulation and design of possible product or process alternatives; (4) testing in search for or evaluation of product or process alternatives; (5) modification of the formulation or design of a product or process; (6) design, construction, and testing of preproduction prototypes and models; (7) design of tools, jigs, molds, and dies involving new technology; (8) design, construction, and operation of a pilot plant that is not of a scale economically feasible to the enterprise for commercial production; and (9) engineering activity required to advance the design of a product until it meets specific functional and economic requirements and is ready for manufacture.

Activities typically not classified as R&D include (1) engineering follow-through in an early phase of commercial production; (2) quality control during commercial production, including routine testing of products; (3) troubleshooting in connection with breakdowns during commercial production; (4) routine, ongoing efforts to refine, enrich, or otherwise improve upon the qualities of an existing product; (5) adaptation of an existing capability to a particular requirement or customer's need as part of a continuing commercial activity; (6) seasonal or other periodic design changes to existing products; (7) routine design of tools, jigs, molds and dies; (8) activity, including design and construction engineering, related to the construction, relocation, rearrangement, or start-up of facilities or equipment other than pilot plants and facilities or equipment whose sole use is for a particular R&D project; and (9) legal work in connection with patent applications or litigation, and the sale or licensing of patents.

SFAS 86, *Accounting for the Costs of Computer Software to Be Sold, Leased, or Otherwise Marketed*, applies to software developed internally or purchased. All costs are expensed as R&D until technological feasibility has been established for the product. Thereafter, all costs are capitalized and amortized using the straight-line method over the estimated remaining life of the product. They are subsequently reported at the lower of unamortized cost or net realizable value. Capitalization ends when the product is available for general release. **SOP 98-1**, *Accounting for the Costs of Computer Software Developed or Obtained for Internal Use*, requires that software costs be expensed as incurred during the preliminary project stage. During the application development stage, internal and external costs are capitalized. During the post-implementation/operation stage, internal and external training and maintenance costs are expensed as incurred. Under **SOP 97-2**, *Software Revenue Recognition*, if a software arrangement does **not require significant production, modification, or customization**, revenue is recognized when persuasive evidence of an arrangement exists, delivery has occurred, the vendor's fee is fixed or determinable, and collectibility is probable. If a software arrangement **requires significant production, modification, or customization**, the accounting for **long-term construction contracts** ordinarily should be used. Thus, separate accounting for different elements is not permitted unless an exception applies. Software arrangements may have **multiple elements**, for example, other software, upgrades or enhancements, postcontract customer support (PCS), or services. If long-term construction contract accounting is not used, the vendor's fee is allocated to the elements based on **vendor-specific objective evidence of fair values**. If sufficient evidence of this kind does not exist, all revenue is deferred until sufficient evidence exists or all elements have been delivered. Certain exceptions apply. For example, if the only undelivered element is PCS or services not requiring significant production, the entire fee is recognized ratably over the contract period or over the period the services are to be performed, respectively. If a delivered element is sold only with another element(s) qualifying for separate accounting and vendor-specific objective evidence of fair value exists for each undelivered element but not for a delivered element(s), **residual accounting** is used. It defers the total fair value of the undelivered elements and recognizes the difference between the fee and the deferred amount as revenue from the delivered elements. Regardless of whether contract accounting is used, a **service element** must be separately accounted for when the services are not essential to the functionality of another element and are described in the contract so that the total price is expected to vary with the inclusion or exclusion of the services.

QUESTIONS

9.1 Intangible Assets

1. A recognized intangible asset is amortized over its useful life

A. Unless the pattern of consumption of the economic benefits of the asset is not reliably determinable.

B. If that life is determined to be finite.

C. Unless the precise length of that life is not known.

D. If that life is indefinite but not infinite.

Answer (B) is correct. *(Publisher)*

REQUIRED: The circumstances in which a recognized intangible asset is amortized.

DISCUSSION: A recognized intangible asset is amortized over its useful life if that useful life is finite, that is, unless the useful life is determined to be indefinite. The useful life of an intangible asset is indefinite if no foreseeable limit exists on the period over which it will contribute, directly or indirectly, to the reporting entity's cash flows (SFAS 142).

Answer (A) is incorrect because an intangible asset is amortizable if its useful life is finite. If the pattern of consumption of the economic benefits of such an intangible asset is not reliably determinable, the straight-line amortization method is applied. Answer (C) is incorrect because, if the precise length of the useful life is not known, an intangible asset with a finite useful life is amortized over the best estimate of its useful life. Answer (D) is incorrect because a recognized intangible asset is not amortized if its useful life is indefinite.

2. Amortization of intangible assets, such as copyrights or patents, is the accounting process of

A. Determining the cash flow from operations for the current period.

B. Systematically allocating the cost of the intangible asset to the periods of use.

C. Accumulating a fund for the replacement of the asset at the end of its useful life.

D. Systematically reflecting the change in general price levels over the current period.

Answer (B) is correct. *(CMA, adapted)*

REQUIRED: The meaning of amortization.

DISCUSSION: Amortization is a means of allocating an initial cost to the periods that benefit from that cost. It is similar to depreciation, a term associated with long-lived tangible assets, and depletion, which is associated with natural resources.

Answer (A) is incorrect because amortization is an allocation process that is not cash-based. Answer (C) is incorrect because no funding is associated with amortization. Answer (D) is incorrect because amortization has nothing to do with changes in price levels.

3. How are intangible assets different from deferred charges?

A. They are noncurrent assets.

B. They represent costs deferred to future periods.

C. They are disclosed in the notes rather than presented in the balance sheet.

D. They represent a well-defined group of items with specific financial reporting guidelines.

Answer (D) is correct. *(Publisher)*

REQUIRED: The difference between intangible assets and deferred charges.

DISCUSSION: Intangible assets are assets other than financial assets, for example, patents, copyrights, acquired customer lists, or broadcast licenses, that lack physical substance. SFAS 142, *Goodwill and Other Intangible Assets,* prescribes the proper accounting treatment for them. By contrast, deferred charges are a collection of noncurrent assets that are not property, plant, and equipment; investments; or intangible assets. Deferred charges are usually not classifiable elsewhere, and no authoritative pronouncements deal with the general topic of deferred charges.

Answer (A) is incorrect because both intangible assets and deferred charges are noncurrent assets. Answer (B) is incorrect because both intangible assets and deferred charges represent costs deferred to future periods. Answer (C) is incorrect because both intangible assets and deferred charges are presented in the balance sheet.

4. Which of the following assets, if any, acquired this year in an exchange transaction is (are) potentially amortizable?

	Goodwill	Trademarks
A.	No	No
B.	No	Yes
C.	Yes	Yes
D.	Yes	No

Answer (B) is correct. *(CPA, adapted)*

REQUIRED: The currently acquired assets that are potentially amortizable.

DISCUSSION: Under SFAS 142, goodwill is tested for impairment at least annually but is never amortized. Trademarks, however, may be amortized, but only if they have finite useful lives.

5. Vair Publishing Company owns a copyright. A material amount of legal fees and other costs it incurred in successfully defending a copyright suit should be

A. Capitalized as part of the cost of the copyright and amortized over the remaining useful life of the copyright.

B. Charged to an expense account in the period incurred.

C. Charged to a loss account in the period incurred.

D. Capitalized in a separate asset account and amortized over 40 years.

Answer (A) is correct. *(CIA, adapted)*

REQUIRED: The accounting for material legal fees and other costs incurred in defending a copyright suit.

DISCUSSION: Legal fees and other costs incurred in successfully defending a suit are to be charged to the copyright account because the suit preserves the legal rights of the holder. Accordingly, these expenditures meet the definition of an asset in SFAC 6 because they provide "probable future economic benefits obtained or controlled by a particular entity as a result of past transactions or events." Because the useful life of a copyright is legally limited, that life is finite, and the copyright is amortizable. Thus, the balance in the copyright account is amortized over the remaining useful life of the copyright. The legal duration of a publisher's copyright is 95 years from publication or 120 years from creation, but that period may greatly exceed the copyright's useful life.

Answer (B) is incorrect because the costs should be capitalized and amortized over the remaining useful life of the copyright. Answer (C) is incorrect because the costs should be capitalized and amortized over the remaining useful life of the copyright. Answer (D) is incorrect because the costs should be charged to the copyright account and amortized over the remaining useful life of the copyright. The facts given do not indicate that the useful life is 40 years.

6. Intangible assets acquired singly from other enterprises or individuals should be recorded at their cost at the date of acquisition. Cost may not be measured by which of the following?

A. Net carrying amount of the previous owner.

B. Amount of cash disbursed.

C. Present value of amounts to be paid for liabilities incurred.

D. Fair value of other assets distributed.

Answer (A) is correct. *(Publisher)*

REQUIRED: The method not allowed to measure the cost of intangible assets.

DISCUSSION: If cash is the consideration given in an exchange transaction, the cash paid is the measure of the transaction. If noncash consideration (noncash assets, liabilities incurred, or equity interests issued) is given, the measurement is based on the more reliably measurable of the fair value of the consideration given or the fair value of the asset or net assets acquired (SFAS 142). Furthermore, the only objective of present value used in initial recognition and fresh-start measurements is to estimate fair value in the absence of a market price (SFAC 7). Consequently, only the carrying amount of the previous owner is not a proper measurement of cost.

7. In accordance with generally accepted accounting principles, which of the following methods of amortization is required for amortizable intangible assets if the pattern of consumption of economic benefits is not reliably determinable?

A. Sum-of-the-years'-digits.

B. Straight-line.

C. Units-of-production.

D. Double-declining-balance.

Answer (B) is correct. *(CPA, adapted)*

REQUIRED: The method of amortization of intangible assets if the pattern of consumption of economic benefits is not reliably determinable.

DISCUSSION: The default method of amortization of intangible assets is the straight-line method (SFAS 142).

Answer (A) is incorrect because sum-of-the-years'-digits may be used only if it is reliably determined to reflect the pattern of consumption of the economic benefits of the intangible asset. Answer (C) is incorrect because units-of-production may be used only if it is reliably determined to reflect the pattern of consumption of the economic benefits of the intangible asset. Answer (D) is incorrect because double-declining-balance may be used only if it is reliably determined to reflect the pattern of consumption of the economic benefits of the intangible asset.

8. Which of the following is not a consideration in determining the useful life of an intangible asset?

A. Legal, regulatory, or contractual provisions.

B. Provisions for renewal or extension.

C. Expected actions of competitors.

D. Initial cost.

Answer (D) is correct. *(CPA, adapted)*

REQUIRED: The consideration not used in determining the useful life of an intangible asset.

DISCUSSION: Initial cost is not a factor relevant to estimating the useful life of an intangible asset because it has no causal connection with the asset's contribution to the future cash flows of the reporting entity. The relevant factors for determining the useful life of an intangible asset include the expected use of the asset; the useful life of a related asset or assets; legal, regulatory, or contractual provisions that may limit the useful life or that may permit renewal or extension without substantial cost; economic factors (e.g., obsolescence, competition, or demand); and expenditures for maintenance (SFAS 142).

9. When should leaseholds and leasehold improvements be amortized over different periods?

A. When the useful life of the leasehold improvement is less than the term of the leasehold.

B. When the term of the leasehold exceeds 40 years.

C. When the term of the leasehold is less than the useful life of the leasehold improvement.

D. If the company is in the development stage.

Answer (A) is correct. *(Publisher)*

REQUIRED: The appropriate time for amortization periods of leaseholds and leasehold improvements to differ.

DISCUSSION: A leasehold refers to the property under lease. Leasehold improvements should be amortized over their useful life if it is less than the term of the lease. But if the useful life is greater than the term of the lease, the improvement should be amortized over the life of the lease because the property will revert to the lessor at the end of the lease. If an option exists for renewal of the lease and the lessee intends to renew, the leasehold improvements should be amortized over the option period as well, but not to exceed their useful life.

Answer (B) is incorrect because a leasehold should be amortized in the same way as other similar property. There is no minimum or maximum period. Answer (C) is incorrect because, when the term of the lease is less than the improvement's useful life, amortization should occur over the shorter period. Answer (D) is incorrect because SFAS 7, *Accounting and Reporting by Development Stage Enterprises*, requires the same amortization by development stage companies as by established operating companies.

10. On January 1, year 1, Chertco acquired an intangible asset for $500,000 and properly began amortizing it using the straight-line method over its estimated useful life of 10 years. The asset has no residual value. At December 31, year 4, a significant change in the business climate caused Chertco to assess the recoverability of the carrying amount of the intangible asset. Chertco estimated that the undiscounted future net cash inflows from the intangible asset would be $325,000 and that its fair value was $275,000. SFAS 144, *Accounting for the Impairment or Disposal of Long-Lived Assets*, applies. Accordingly, for the year ended December 31, year 4, Chertco should recognize an impairment loss of

A. $175,000

B. $50,000

C. $25,000

D. $0

Answer (D) is correct. *(Publisher)*

REQUIRED: The impairment loss.

DISCUSSION: Events or changes in circumstances may indicate that the entity should assess the recoverability of the carrying amount of a recognized intangible asset subject to SFAS 144. In that case, the entity should estimate the undiscounted future net cash inflows to be generated by the asset. If these cash flows are less than the carrying amount, an impairment loss, measured by the excess of the carrying amount over the fair value, is recognized. However, Chertco should recognize no impairment loss because the estimated undiscounted future net cash inflows ($325,000) exceed the carrying amount {$500,000 – [4 years × ($500,000 ÷ 10 years)] = $300,000}.

Answer (A) is incorrect because $175,000 assumes no amortization. Answer (B) is incorrect because $50,000 is the excess of the estimated undiscounted future net cash inflows over the fair value. Answer (C) is incorrect because $25,000 (carrying amount – fair value) would be the impairment loss if the carrying amount were not fully recoverable.

9.2 Goodwill

11. Which of the following costs of goodwill should be capitalized and amortized?

	Maintaining Goodwill	Developing Goodwill
A.	Yes	No
B.	No	No
C.	Yes	Yes
D.	No	Yes

Answer (B) is correct. *(CPA, adapted)*

REQUIRED: The costs of goodwill that should be capitalized and amortized.

DISCUSSION: SFAS 141, *Business Combinations*, requires that the cost of goodwill arising from a business combination be capitalized. SFAS 142 prohibits amortization of goodwill. Moreover, the cost of internally developing, maintaining, or restoring intangible assets (including goodwill) that are not specifically identifiable, have indeterminate useful lives, or are inherent in a continuing business and related to an enterprise as a whole should be expensed as incurred.

12. Vanadium Co. is considering the sale of its business. Its cumulative earnings for the past 5 years were $900,000, including extraordinary gains of $20,000. The annual earnings based on an average rate of return on investment for this industry would have been $152,000. If excess earnings are to be capitalized at 10%, implied goodwill should be

A. $240,000

B. $280,000

C. $880,000

D. $900,000

Answer (A) is correct. *(CPA, adapted)*

REQUIRED: The amount of implied goodwill based on capitalization of excess earnings.

DISCUSSION: One method of computing goodwill is to assign the cost of the acquired entity to the assets acquired and liabilities assumed based on their estimated fair values. Goodwill is the excess of the cost of the acquired entity over the net amount assigned. This method is applied for accounting purposes. A second method is to compute goodwill by capitalizing excess earnings. The latter method is used to value a business rather than to account for it. Past earnings provide estimates of future earnings; thus, the extraordinary gains of $20,000 should be excluded. Given ordinary earnings of $880,000 over the past 5 years, the average annual earnings were $176,000. Given also that annual earnings based on an average industry rate of return were $152,000, the excess earnings were $24,000. Implied goodwill capitalized at 10% is $240,000 ($24,000 ÷ 10%).

Answer (B) is incorrect because $280,000 results from including the $10,000 extraordinary gain in earnings for the past 5 years. Answer (C) is incorrect because $880,000 equals the past 5 years' earnings minus extraordinary gains. Answer (D) is incorrect because $900,000 equals the cumulative earnings for the past 5 years.

13. A business broker is attempting to value Chadco, a software company. Average earnings over the last 6 years have been $132,000 and are relatively stable. The original investment was $480,000, and the current fair value of the net assets is $820,000. What is the amount of implied goodwill if the average earnings rate in this industry is 10% of investment?

A. $132,000

B. $480,000

C. $500,000

D. $1,320,000

Answer (C) is correct. *(Publisher)*

REQUIRED: The implied goodwill given average annual earnings and the average rate of return.

DISCUSSION: Given that the industry average earnings rate is 10% and average earnings are $132,000, the overall value of the company is $1,320,000 ($132,000 ÷ 10%). Because the fair value of the net assets is $820,000, the value of the company includes $500,000 of implied goodwill ($1,320,000 – $820,000).

Answer (A) is incorrect because $132,000 equals the average earnings. Answer (B) is incorrect because $480,000 equals the original investment. Answer (D) is incorrect because $1,320,000 is the overall value of the company.

14. When a business is acquired, the purchaser calculates goodwill associated with the acquisition as the difference between the purchase price and the

A. Carrying amount of the net assets acquired.

B. Fair value of the net assets acquired.

C. Carrying amount of the net tangible assets acquired.

D. Fair value of the net tangible assets acquired.

Answer (B) is correct. *(CIA, adapted)*

REQUIRED: The calculation of goodwill.

DISCUSSION: A business combination is accounted for as a purchase, and goodwill may be recorded. Goodwill is defined as the "excess of the cost of an acquired entity over the net of the amounts assigned to assets acquired and liabilities assumed." That excess includes acquired intangible assets that do not meet SFAS 141's criteria for separate recognition. According to SFAS 141, the cost of the acquired entity is allocated to the assets acquired and liabilities assumed based on their estimated fair values at the acquisition date.

Answer (A) is incorrect because goodwill is the difference between the purchase price and the fair value of the net assets acquired. The calculation of the latter amount includes (1) tangible assets, and (2) intangible assets that meet the SFAS 141 criteria for separate recognition. Answer (C) is incorrect because goodwill is the difference between the purchase price and the fair value of the net assets acquired. The calculation of the latter amount includes (1) tangible assets, and (2) intangible assets that meet the SFAS 141 criteria for separate recognition. Answer (D) is incorrect because goodwill is the difference between the purchase price and the fair value of the net assets acquired. The calculation of the latter amount includes (1) tangible assets, and (2) intangible assets that meet the SFAS 141 criteria for separate recognition.

15. On January 2, year 1, Paye Co. purchased Shef Co. at a cost that resulted in recognition of goodwill of $200,000 having an expected benefit period of 10 years. Shef is treated as a reporting unit, and the entire amount of the recognized goodwill is assigned to it. During the first quarter of year 1, Shef spent an additional $80,000 on expenditures designed to maintain goodwill. Due to these expenditures, at December 31, year 1, Shef estimated that the benefit period of goodwill was 40 years. In its consolidated December 31, year 1 balance sheet, what amount should Paye report as goodwill?

A. $180,000

B. $200,000

C. $252,000

D. $280,000

Answer (B) is correct. *(CPA, adapted)*

REQUIRED: The amount of goodwill in the balance sheet.

DISCUSSION: Goodwill is not recorded except when a business is purchased. Thus, only the $200,000 recognized at the purchase date should be recorded as goodwill. It should not be amortized but should be tested for impairment at the reporting-unit level. The facts given suggest that the fair value of the reporting unit (Shef) is not less than its carrying amount. Hence, no impairment of goodwill has occurred, and goodwill is unchanged at $200,000. Moreover, the cost of internally developing, maintaining, or restoring intangible assets (including goodwill) that are not specifically identifiable, have indeterminate useful lives, or are inherent in a continuing business and related to an enterprise as a whole should be expensed as incurred.

Answer (A) is incorrect because $180,000 results when goodwill is amortized on the straight-line basis over 10 years. Answer (C) is incorrect because $252,000 results from amortizing an additional $80,000 of expenditures to maintain goodwill over 10 years. Answer (D) is incorrect because $280,000 results from adding $80,000 of expenditures for the maintenance of goodwill.

16. What is the proper treatment of the recorded goodwill when an entity disposes of a portion of a reporting unit that constitutes a stand-alone acquired business?

A. All of the carrying amount of the goodwill of the reporting unit should be considered part of the cost of the assets sold.

B. The total carrying amount of the goodwill acquired with the business should be considered part of the cost of the assets sold.

C. Goodwill cannot be considered sold; it should be written off as a loss.

D. Goodwill cannot be sold; it should be amortized over its original useful life.

Answer (B) is correct. *(Publisher)*

REQUIRED: The true statement about goodwill when a portion of a reporting unit is sold.

DISCUSSION: If part of a reporting unit is to be disposed of and that part constitutes a business, goodwill related to the business is included in the carrying amount to be disposed of. The goodwill of the business and the goodwill retained by the reporting unit are determined based on relative fair values. However, when the business was not integrated with the other activities of the reporting unit, for example, because it is operated as a stand-alone entity, no allocation of the goodwill acquired with the business is made, and its carrying amount should be included in the carrying amount of the business to be disposed of (SFAS 142).

9.3 Patents

17. A purchased utility patent has a remaining legal life of 15 years. It should be

A. Expensed in the year of acquisition.

B. Amortized over 15 years regardless of its useful life.

C. Amortized over its useful life if less than 15 years.

D. Amortized over 40 years.

Answer (C) is correct. *(CPA, adapted)*

REQUIRED: The period over which a patent should be amortized.

DISCUSSION: An intangible asset should be amortized over its useful life if that life is finite. A utility patent (the most common category) issued by the federal government after June 1995 is valid and legally enforceable for 20 years from the date of application. Thus, the useful life is limited by legal provisions, and the patent (an intangible asset) is therefore amortizable because its useful life is finite.

Answer (A) is incorrect because an intangible asset acquired from another should be recorded as an asset. Answer (B) is incorrect because the amortization period is not to exceed the useful life. Answer (D) is incorrect because the remaining legal life of the patent is only 15 years.

18. Legal fees incurred by a company in defending its patent rights should be capitalized when the outcome of litigation is

	Successful	Unsuccessful
A.	Yes	Yes
B.	Yes	No
C.	No	No
D.	No	Yes

Answer (B) is correct. *(CPA, adapted)*

REQUIRED: The condition for capitalizing legal fees incurred in defending a patent.

DISCUSSION: Legal fees incurred in the successful defense of a patent should be capitalized as part of the cost of the patent and then amortized over its remaining useful life because a patent's life is finite. Legal fees incurred in an unsuccessful defense should be expensed as incurred.

19. Espion Corp. bought Patent X for $80,000 and Patent Z for $120,000. Espion also paid acquisition costs of $10,000 for Patent X and $14,000 for Patent Z. Both patents were challenged in legal actions. Espion paid $40,000 in legal fees for a successful defense of Patent X and $60,000 in legal fees for an unsuccessful defense of Patent Z. What amounts should Espion capitalize for patents?

A. $324,000

B. $224,000

C. $130,000

D. $90,000

Answer (C) is correct. *(CPA, adapted)*

REQUIRED: The amount capitalized for patents.

DISCUSSION: When an intangible asset is acquired externally, it should be recorded at its cost at the date of acquisition. Cost is measured by the more reliably determinable of the fair value of the consideration given or the fair value of the net assets acquired. Moreover, an exchange transaction for which the consideration is cash is measured by the amount paid. Legal fees incurred in the successful defense of a patent should be capitalized as part of the cost of the patent and then amortized over its remaining useful life. Amortization is appropriate for a patent because its useful life is finite. Legal fees incurred in an unsuccessful defense should be expensed as the costs are incurred. Hence, the cost of Patent X ($80,000 + $10,000) and the legal fees for its successful defense ($40,000) should be capitalized in the amount of $130,000. The costs associated with Patent Z should be written off immediately. The unsuccessful defense suggests that no asset exists.

Answer (A) is incorrect because $324,000 includes all costs associated with Patent Z. Answer (B) is incorrect because $224,000 equals the total acquisition costs for Patents X and Z but excludes legal fees. Answer (D) is incorrect because $90,000 excludes the legal fees for a successful defense of Patent X.

20. On January 2, year 1, Valhalla Corp. purchased a utility patent for a new consumer product for $180,000. At the time of purchase, the patent was valid for 15 years; however, the patent's useful life was estimated to be only 10 years due to the competitive nature of the product, with no residual value. On December 31, year 4, the product was permanently withdrawn from sale under governmental order because of a potential health hazard in the product. Thus, no future positive cash flows will result from use of the patent, and its fair value is zero. What amount should Valhalla charge against income during year 4, assuming straight-line amortization is appropriately recorded at the end of each year?

A. $18,000

B. $108,000

C. $126,000

D. $144,000

Answer (C) is correct. *(CPA, adapted)*

REQUIRED: The amount charged against income when a product is permanently withdrawn from sale.

DISCUSSION: A patent is an amortizable intangible asset because its useful life is finite. The straight-line method of amortization is used if the pattern of consumption of the economic benefits cannot be reliably determined. Because the patent was written off at the end of year 4, the amount charged against income is equal to amortization expense plus the carrying amount of the asset at the time of the write-off. Amortization expense is $18,000 ($180,000 cost ÷ 10 years useful life). The remaining carrying amount of the asset is $108,000 ($180,000 cost – 4 years of amortization expense). This amount reflects an impairment loss ($108,000 carrying amount – $0 fair value) calculated in accordance with SFAS 144 on an amortizable intangible asset when (1) the carrying amount is not recoverable and (2) the fair value of the asset is zero. Thus, the amount charged against income is $126,000 ($18,000 + $108,000).

Answer (A) is incorrect because $18,000 includes only amortization expense. Answer (B) is incorrect because $108,000 includes only the carrying amount of the asset before recognition of the impairment loss. Answer (D) is incorrect because $144,000 bases amortization on a 15-year useful life.

21. Freya Co. has two patents that have allegedly been infringed by competitors. After investigation, legal counsel informed Freya that it had a weak case for Patent P and a strong case for Patent Q. Freya incurred additional legal fees to stop infringement on Patent Q. Both patents have a remaining legal life of 8 years. How should Freya account for these legal costs incurred relating to the two patents?

A. Expense costs for Patent P and capitalize costs for Patent Q.

B. Expense costs for both Patent P and Patent Q.

C. Capitalize costs for both Patent P and Patent Q.

D. Capitalize costs for Patent P and expense costs for Patent Q.

Answer (A) is correct. *(CPA, adapted)*

REQUIRED: The accounting for legal costs incurred.

DISCUSSION: Legal fees incurred in a successful defense of a patent should be capitalized and amortized. Legal fees incurred in an unsuccessful defense should be expensed as incurred. Hence, Freya should expense costs for Patent P and capitalize costs for Patent Q.

Answer (B) is incorrect because Freya should capitalize costs for Patent Q. Answer (C) is incorrect because Freya should expense costs for Patent P. Answer (D) is incorrect because Freya should expense costs for Patent P and capitalize costs for Patent Q.

9.4 Franchises

22. On January 2, year 1, Fafnir Co. purchased a franchise with a finite useful life of 10 years for $50,000. An additional franchise fee of 3% of franchise operation revenues must be paid each year to the franchisor. Revenues from franchise operations amounted to $400,000 during year 1. The pattern of consumption of benefits of the franchise is not reliably determinable, and the residual value is zero. In its December 31, year 1 balance sheet, what amount should Fafnir report as an intangible asset-franchise?

A. $33,000

B. $43,800

C. $45,000

D. $50,000

Answer (C) is correct. *(CPA, adapted)*

REQUIRED: The amount of the intangible asset that is recorded for a franchise.

DISCUSSION: Intangible assets acquired other than in a business combination are initially recognized and measured based on their fair value. This "cost" should be based on the more reliably measurable of the fair value of the consideration given or the fair value of the assets acquired. Franchise fees are capitalized and amortized over the finite useful life. Absent information about the fair value of the assets acquired, the capitalizable amount equals the consideration given, that is, the initial fee and other expenditures necessary to acquire the franchise. Future franchise fees are expensed as incurred. Because the pattern of consumption of benefits of the franchise is not reliably determinable, the straight-line method of amortization should be used. Thus, given no residual value, the amount that should be reported as an intangible asset is $45,000 [$50,000 – ($50,000 ÷ 10)].

Answer (A) is incorrect because $33,000 results from subtracting the additional franchise fee. Answer (B) is incorrect because $43,800 includes amortization of the additional franchise fee. Answer (D) is incorrect because $50,000 is the unamortized initial fee.

23. Helsing Co. bought a franchise from Anya Co. on January 1, year 1 for $204,000. An independent consultant retained by Helsing estimated that the remaining useful life of the franchise was a finite period of 50 years and that the pattern of consumption of benefits of the franchise is not reliably determinable. Its unamortized cost on Anya's books on January 1, year 1 was $68,000. What amount should be amortized for the year ended December 31, year 1, assuming no residual value?

A. $5,100

B. $4,080

C. $3,400

D. $1,700

Answer (B) is correct. *(CPA, adapted)*

REQUIRED: The first-year amortization expense of the cost of a franchise.

DISCUSSION: A franchise is an intangible asset. The initial measurement of an intangible asset acquired other than in a business combination is at fair value. Thus, the "cost" to be amortized should be based on the more reliably measurable of the fair value of the consideration given or the fair value of the assets acquired. If the useful life is finite, the intangible asset is amortized over that period. Moreover, if the consumption pattern of benefits of the intangible asset is not reliably determinable, the straight-line method of amortization is used. Accordingly, given no residual value, the amortization expense is $4,080 ($204,000 consideration given ÷ 50-year finite useful life).

Answer (A) is incorrect because $5,100 is based on a 40-year period. Answer (C) is incorrect because $3,400 is the difference between the $204,000 franchise price and Anya's $68,000 unamortized cost, divided by 40 years. Answer (D) is incorrect because $1,700 equals the unamortized cost on Anya's books amortized over 40 years.

24. On December 31, year 1, Sigrid Corp. authorized Vortigern to operate as a franchisee for an initial franchise fee of $300,000. Of this amount, $120,000 was received upon signing the agreement, and the balance, represented by a note, is due in three annual payments of $60,000 each, beginning December 31, year 2. The present value on December 31, year 1 of the three annual payments appropriately discounted is $144,000. According to the agreement, the nonrefundable down payment represents a fair measure of the services already performed by Sigrid; however, substantial future services are required of Sigrid. Collectibility of the note is reasonably certain. In Sigrid's December 31, year 1 balance sheet, unearned franchise fees from Vortigern's franchise should be reported as

A. $300,000

B. $264,000

C. $180,000

D. $144,000

Answer (D) is correct. *(CPA, adapted)*

REQUIRED: The amount at which the franchisor should report unearned franchise fees.

DISCUSSION: SFAS 45, *Accounting for Franchise Fee Revenue*, states that franchise fee revenue should ordinarily be recognized at the earliest time when the franchisor has substantially performed or satisfied all material services or conditions relating to the franchise sale. The earliest time usually is the commencement of operations by the franchisee unless it can be demonstrated that substantial performance of all obligations occurred previously. Hence, Sigrid should recognize $120,000 of revenue. The note is a long-term receivable that should be reported at its present value. However, this amount ($144,000) should be recorded as unearned revenue because the franchisor has not substantially performed (completed the earning process).

Answer (A) is incorrect because $300,000 is the total initial fee. Answer (B) is incorrect because $264,000 includes $120,000 for services already performed. Answer (C) is incorrect because $180,000 is the undiscounted total of the annual payments.

25. Each of Thaumatic Co.'s 42 new franchisees contracted to pay an initial franchise fee of $60,000. By December 31, year 1, each franchisee had paid a nonrefundable $20,000 fee and signed a note to pay $20,000 principal plus the market rate of interest on December 31, year 2, and December 31, year 3. Experience indicates that two franchisees will default on the additional payments. Services for the initial fee will be performed in year 2. What amount of net unearned franchise fees would Thaumatic report at December 31, year 1?

A. $1,600,000

B. $2,420,000

C. $2,440,000

D. $2,520,000

Answer (C) is correct. *(CPA, adapted)*

REQUIRED: The net unearned franchise fees reported at year-end by the franchisor.

DISCUSSION: SFAS 45, *Accounting for Franchise Fee Revenue*, states that franchise fee revenue should ordinarily be recognized at the earliest time when the franchisor has substantially performed or satisfied all material services or conditions relating to the franchise sale. Thaumatic should not recognize revenue from initial franchise fees because the related services will not be performed until year 2, and the earning process is therefore not complete. The franchisor should recognize the cash received (42 × $20,000 = $840,000), a net receivable for the principal amounts estimated to be collected (40 × $40,000 = $1,600,000), and unearned franchise fees ($840,000 + $1,600,000 = $2,440,000).

Answer (A) is incorrect because $1,600,000 is the principal amount that the franchisor estimates will be collected. Answer (B) is incorrect because $2,420,000 omits the nonrefundable fee paid by one franchisee. Answer (D) is incorrect because $2,520,000 is based on the assumption that all franchisees will pay in full.

26. Which of the following should be expensed as incurred by the franchisee for a franchise with an estimated useful life of 10 years?

A. Amount paid to the franchisor for the franchise.

B. Periodic payments to a company, other than the franchisor, for that company's franchise.

C. Legal fees paid to the franchisee's lawyers to obtain the franchise.

D. Periodic payments to the franchisor based on the franchisee's revenues.

Answer (D) is correct. *(CPA, adapted)*

REQUIRED: The payment that should be expensed as incurred by the franchisee.

DISCUSSION: Payments under a franchise agreement made to a franchisor based on the franchisee's revenues do not create benefits in future periods and should not be treated as an asset. These payments should be treated as operating expenses in the period in which incurred.

Answer (A) is incorrect because it represents a cost of acquiring the franchise. This cost benefits future periods and should therefore be capitalized and amortized over the useful life of the franchise. Answer (B) is incorrect because it represents a cost of acquiring the franchise. This cost benefits future periods and should therefore be capitalized and amortized over the useful life of the franchise. Answer (C) is incorrect because it represents a cost of acquiring the franchise. This cost benefits future periods and should therefore be capitalized and amortized over the useful life of the franchise.

9.5 R&D and Similar Costs

27. On January 1, year 1, SOP Corp. incurred organization costs of $24,000. SOP is amortizing these costs so as to obtain the maximum allowable deduction for federal income tax purposes. For financial accounting purposes, what portion of the organization costs will SOP defer to years subsequent to year 1?

A. $23,400

B. $19,200

C. $4,800

D. $0

Answer (D) is correct. *(Publisher)*

REQUIRED: The deferred organization costs if amortization is the maximum allowable for tax purposes.

DISCUSSION: Organization costs are those incurred in the formation of a business entity. For federal income tax purposes, the minimum amortization period is 5 years. However, for financial accounting purposes, SOP 98-5 requires nongovernmental entities to expense all start-up costs and organization costs as incurred.

28. Which advertising costs are most likely to be capitalized?

A. Costs of production.

B. Expenditures subsequent to recognition of related revenue.

C. Expenditures for idea development.

D. Costs of communication.

Answer (B) is correct. *(Publisher)*

REQUIRED: The capitalizable advertising costs.

DISCUSSION: SOP 93-7, *Reporting on Advertising Costs*, states that advertising costs should be expensed, either as incurred or when advertising first occurs. The primary costs are production and communication. However, direct response advertising costs should be capitalized (deferred) if the primary purpose is to elicit sales from customers who respond specifically to the advertising, and probable future economic benefits result. A second exception is for expenditures subsequent to recognition of related revenue. An example is a manufacturer's obligation to repay retailers for costs of advertising that involve the manufacturer's products. This type of cost should be accrued and expensed when related revenues are recognized.

Costs of production, including idea development, art work, copywriting, printing, and hiring personnel, and costs of communication such as television, radio, and magazines are expensed unless they are direct response costs or expenditures subsequent to recognition of related revenue.

29. SFAS 2, *Accounting for Research and Development Costs*, differentiates research and development activities from activities not considered research and development. Which one of the following is not considered a research and development activity?

A. Laboratory research intended for the discovery of a new product.

B. Testing in search of product processing alternatives.

C. Modification of the design of a process.

D. Periodic design changes to existing products.

Answer (D) is correct. *(CMA, adapted)*

REQUIRED: The item not considered an R&D activity.

DISCUSSION: SFAS 2 requires that R&D costs be expensed as incurred. Research is planned search or critical investigation aimed at discovery of new knowledge with the hope that such knowledge will be useful in developing a new product or service or a new process or technique or in bringing about a significant improvement in an existing product or process. Development is the translation of research findings or other knowledge into a plan or design for a new product or process or for a significant improvement in an existing product or process whether intended for sale or use. Seasonal or other periodic design changes in existing products do not meet either of these definitions.

30. Le Sud Co. made the following expenditures relating to product THX-1138:

- Legal costs to file a patent on the product – $10,000. Production of the finished product would not have been undertaken without the patent.
- Special equipment to be used solely for development of the product – $60,000. The equipment has no other use and has an estimated useful life of 4 years.
- Labor and material costs incurred in producing a prototype model – $200,000.
- Cost of testing the prototype – $80,000.

What is the total amount of costs that will be expensed when incurred?

A. $280,000

B. $295,000

C. $340,000

D. $350,000

Answer (C) is correct. *(CPA, adapted)*

REQUIRED: The total amount of costs that will be expensed when incurred.

DISCUSSION: R&D costs are expensed as incurred. SFAS 2 specifically excludes legal work in connection with patent applications or litigation and the sale or licensing of patents from the definition of R&D. Thus, the legal costs of filing a patent should be capitalized. The company's R&D costs include the cost of equipment used solely for a specific project and those incurred for the design, construction, and testing of preproduction prototypes. Thus, the total amount of costs that will be expensed when incurred is $340,000 ($60,000 + $200,000 + $80,000).

Answer (A) is incorrect because $280,000 omits the cost of the special equipment. Answer (B) is incorrect because $295,000 includes 1 year's straight-line depreciation on the special equipment instead of the full cost. Answer (D) is incorrect because $350,000 includes the legal costs of filing a patent.

31. During the current year, Narn Co. incurred the following costs:

Research and development services performed by Molari Corp. for Narn	$150,000
Design, construction, and testing of preproduction prototypes and models	200,000
Testing in search for new products of process alternatives	175,000

In its current-year income statement, what should Narn report as research and development expense?

A. $150,000

B. $200,000

C. $350,000

D. $525,000

Answer (D) is correct. *(CPA, adapted)*

REQUIRED: The R&D expense.

DISCUSSION: Research is planned search or critical investigation aimed at discovery of new knowledge useful in developing a new product, service, process, or technique, or in bringing about a significant improvement to an existing product, etc. Development is translation of research findings or other knowledge into a plan or design for a new or improved product or process. R&D expenses include R&D performed under contract by others; design, construction, and testing of prototypes; and testing in search for new products (SFAS 2). Thus, R&D expense of $525,000 ($150,000 + $200,000 + $175,000) should be recognized.

Answer (A) is incorrect because $150,000 does not include design, construction, and testing of preproduction prototypes or testing in search of new products. Answer (B) is incorrect because $200,000 does not include R&D performed under contract by others or testing in search for new products. Answer (C) is incorrect because $350,000 does not include testing in search for new products.

32. Jakar Co. made the following expenditures during the current year:

Costs to develop computer software for internal use in Jakar's general management information system	$200,000
Costs of market research activities	150,000

What amount of these expenditures should Jakar report in its current-year income statement as research and development expenses?

A. $350,000

B. $200,000

C. $150,000

D. $0

Answer (D) is correct. *(CPA, adapted)*

REQUIRED: The amount of research and development expenses.

DISCUSSION: SFAS 2 states that costs of market research are not R&D costs. FASB Interpretation No. 6, *Applicability of FASB No. 2 to Computer Software*, states that costs to develop software for the company's own general management information system are also not R&D costs.

Answer (A) is incorrect because R&D expenses do not include costs to develop software for internal use in a general management information system or the costs of market research. Answer (B) is incorrect because R&D costs do not include costs to develop software for internal use in a general management information system. Answer (C) is incorrect because R&D costs do not include market research costs.

33. In the current year, Devlin Research Station incurred the following costs:

Direct costs of doing contract research and development work for the government to be reimbursed by governmental unit	$400,000
Research and development costs not included above were	
Depreciation	$300,000
Salaries	700,000
Indirect costs appropriately allocated	200,000
Materials	180,000

What was Devlin's total research and development expense in the current year?

A. $1,080,000

B. $1,380,000

C. $1,580,000

D. $1,780,000

Answer (B) is correct. *(CPA, adapted)*

REQUIRED: The total research and development expense.

DISCUSSION: Under SFAS 2, materials used in R&D, compensation costs of personnel, and indirect costs appropriately allocated are R&D costs that should be expensed immediately. The costs of equipment and facilities that are used for R&D activities and have alternative future uses, whether for other R&D projects or otherwise, are to be capitalized as tangible assets when acquired or constructed. Depreciation on this equipment is to be expensed as R&D expense. However, SFAS 2 does not apply to R&D activities conducted for others. Hence, the reimbursable costs are not expensed. The total R&D expense is therefore $1,380,000 ($300,000 + $700,000 + $200,000 + $180,000).

Answer (A) is incorrect because $1,080,000 omits the depreciation. Answer (C) is incorrect because $1,580,000 includes the reimbursable costs of R&D conducted for others but omits the indirect costs. Answer (D) is incorrect because $1,780,000 includes the reimbursable costs of R&D conducted for others.

34. On December 31, year 1, Byte Co. had capitalized software costs of $600,000 with an economic life of four years. Sales for year 2 were 10% of expected total sales of the software. At December 31, year 2, the software had a net realizable value of $480,000. In its December 31, year 2 balance sheet, what amount should Byte report as net capitalized cost of computer software?

A. $432,000

B. $450,000

C. $480,000

D. $540,000

Answer (B) is correct. *(CPA, adapted)*

REQUIRED: The net capitalized cost of computer software at year-end.

DISCUSSION: SFAS 86, *Accounting for the Costs of Computer Software to Be Sold, Leased, or Otherwise Marketed*, applies to software to be "sold, leased, or otherwise marketed as a separate product or as part of a product or process." After technological feasibility has been established for a software product, all software production costs incurred until the product is available for general release to customers must be capitalized and subsequently reported at the lower of unamortized cost or net realizable value. The amortization of capitalized software costs is determined separately for each product. The annual amortization is the greater of the amount determined using the ratio of current gross revenues to the sum of current gross revenues and anticipated future gross revenues, or the straight-line method over the remaining estimated economic life, including the current reporting period. At year-end, the unamortized cost of each software product must be compared with the net realizable value (NRV) of that software product. Any excess of unamortized cost over NRV must be written off. The amount of amortization under the straight-line method is used because it is greater than the amount determined using the 10% ratio of current sales to expected total sales. Thus, Byte Co. had an unamortized cost of software of $450,000 [$600,000 capitalized cost – ($600,000 ÷ 4)] at December 31, year 2. The $450,000 unamortized cost is lower than the $480,000 NRV, so $450,000 is the amount reported in the year-end balance sheet.

Answer (A) is incorrect because $432,000 equals the NRV at December 31, year 2 minus amortization calculated as 10% of NRV. Answer (C) is incorrect because $480,000 is the NRV at December 31, year 2. Answer (D) is incorrect because $540,000 assumes amortization at 10% with no adjustment for NRV.

35. Miller Co. incurred the following computer software costs for the development and sale of software programs during the current year:

Planning costs	$ 50,000
Design of the software	150,000
Substantial testing of the project's initial stages	75,000
Production and packaging costs for the first month's sales	500,000
Costs of producing product masters after technological feasibility was established	200,000

The project was not under any contractual arrangement when these expenditures were incurred. What amount should Miller report as research and development expense for the current year?

A. $200,000

B. $275,000

C. $500,000

D. $975,000

Answer (B) is correct. *(CPA, adapted)*

REQUIRED: The R&D expense.

DISCUSSION: According to SFAS 86, R&D costs of software are all costs incurred to establish technological feasibility. Technological feasibility is established when the enterprise has completed all planning, designing, coding, and testing necessary to establish that the product can be produced to meet its design specifications, including functions, features, and technical performance requirements. Consequently, Miller's R&D cost is $275,000 ($50,000 planning + $150,000 design + $75,000 initial testing).

Answer (A) is incorrect because $200,000 does not include the cost for substantial testing of the project's initial stages. Answer (C) is incorrect because production and packaging costs for the first month's sales are capitalized as inventory. Answer (D) is incorrect because $975,000 includes production and packaging costs for the first month's sales and costs of producing product masters after technological feasibility was established. These amounts are capitalized as inventory.

36. According to SOP 98-1, *Accounting for the Costs of Computer Software Developed or Obtained for Internal Use*, certain costs of internal-use software not qualifying as R&D costs should be capitalized in which stage(s), if any, of software development?

	Preliminary Project Stage	Application Development Stage	Post-Implementation Operation Stage
A.	Yes	Yes	Yes
B.	Yes	Yes	No
C.	No	Yes	No
D.	No	No	No

Answer (C) is correct. *(Publisher)*

REQUIRED: The stage(s), if any, of development of internal-use software in which costs are capitalized.

DISCUSSION: SOP 98-1 states that certain internal and external development costs of internal-use software not qualifying as R&D costs should be expensed during the preliminary project and post-implementation/operation stages. However, they should be capitalized during the application development stage. Costs capitalizable include external direct costs of materials and services consumed, payroll and payroll-related costs for employees to the extent they spend time directly on the project, and interest costs. Furthermore, costs to develop or obtain software allowing for access or conversion of old data by a new system are also capitalized.

37. During year 1, Scios Co. incurred $204,000 of research and development costs in its laboratory to develop a patent that was granted on July 1, year 1. Legal fees and other costs associated with registration of the patent totaled $41,000. The estimated economic life of the patent is 10 years. What amount should Scios capitalize for the patent on July 1, year 1?

A. $0

B. $41,000

C. $204,000

D. $245,000

Answer (B) is correct. *(CPA, adapted)*

REQUIRED: The amount to be capitalized for an internally developed patent.

DISCUSSION: SFAS 2 requires that R&D costs be expensed as they are incurred. Legal fees and registration fees are excluded from the definition of R&D by SFAS 2. Thus, the $41,000 in legal fees and other costs associated with the registration of the patent should be capitalized. The $204,000 in R&D costs should be expensed.

Answer (A) is incorrect because legal fees and other costs associated with the registration of the patent should be capitalized. Answer (C) is incorrect because legal fees and other costs associated with the registration of the patent should be capitalized, whereas R&D costs must be expensed as incurred. Answer (D) is incorrect because R&D costs must be expensed as incurred.

Questions 38 and 39 are based on the following information. During year 1, Microcomp Corp. incurred costs to develop and produce a routine, low-risk computer software product, as described below.

Completion of detail program design	$13,000
Costs incurred for coding and testing to establish technological feasibility	10,000
Other coding costs after establishment of technological feasibility	24,000
Other testing costs after establishment of technological feasibility	20,000
Costs of producing product masters for training materials	15,000
Duplication of computer software and training materials from product masters (1,000 units)	25,000
Packaging product (500 units)	9,000

38. In Microcomp's December 31, year 1 balance sheet, what amount should be reported in inventory?

A. $25,000

B. $34,000

C. $40,000

D. $49,000

Answer (B) is correct. *(CPA, adapted)*

REQUIRED: The amount reported in inventory.

DISCUSSION: SFAS 86 states that costs incurred internally in creating a computer software product must be charged to expense when incurred as R&D until technological feasibility has been established. Thereafter, all software production costs incurred until the product is available for general release to customers must be capitalized and amortized. The costs of duplicating the software, documentation, and training materials from the product masters and of physically packaging the product for distribution are capitalized as inventory. Hence, inventory should be reported at $34,000 ($25,000 duplication costs + $9,000 packaging costs).

Answer (A) is incorrect because $25,000 excludes packaging costs. Answer (C) is incorrect because $40,000 excludes packaging costs but includes costs of producing product masters. Answer (D) is incorrect because $49,000 includes costs of producing product masters.

39. In Microcomp's December 31, year 1 balance sheet, what amount should be capitalized as software cost subject to amortization?

A. $54,000

B. $57,000

C. $59,000

D. $69,000

Answer (C) is correct. *(CPA, adapted)*

REQUIRED: The amount capitalized as software cost subject to amortization.

DISCUSSION: SFAS 86 specifies that costs incurred internally in creating a computer software product shall be charged to expense when incurred as research and development until technological feasibility has been established for the product. Thereafter, all software production costs incurred until the product is available for general release to customers shall be capitalized and subsequently reported at the lower of unamortized cost or net realizable value. Hence, the costs of completing the detail program design and establishing technological feasibility are expensed, the costs of duplicating software and training materials and packaging the product are inventoried, and the costs of coding and other testing after establishing technological feasibility and the costs of producing product masters are capitalized and amortized. The amount capitalized as software cost subject to amortization is therefore $59,000 ($24,000 + $20,000 + $15,000).

Answer (A) is incorrect because $54,000 equals inventoriable costs plus the other testing costs. Answer (B) is incorrect because $57,000 is the sum of the costs expensed and the costs inventoried. Answer (D) is incorrect because $69,000 assumes the costs of coding and testing to establish feasibility are capitalized and amortized.

40. If a company constructs a laboratory building to be used as a research and development facility, the cost of the laboratory building is matched against earnings as

A. Research and development expense in the period(s) of construction.

B. Depreciation deducted as part of research and development costs.

C. Depreciation or immediate write-off depending on company policy.

D. An expense at such time as productive research and development has been obtained from the facility.

Answer (B) is correct. *(CPA, adapted)*

REQUIRED: The proper treatment of the cost of a laboratory building used as an R&D facility.

DISCUSSION: The costs of equipment and facilities that are used for R&D activities and have alternative future uses, whether for other R&D projects or otherwise, are to be capitalized as tangible assets when acquired or constructed. The depreciation of a facility such as a laboratory building used for R&D is an R&D expense.

Answer (A) is incorrect because the cost should be matched against earnings in the period of construction only if the building is usable for a particular research project and has no alternative use. Answer (C) is incorrect because a company has no discretion regarding R&D costs. Answer (D) is incorrect because a company has no discretion regarding R&D costs.

41. On January 1, year 1, Cybience purchased equipment for use in developing a new product. Cybience uses the straight-line depreciation method. The equipment could provide benefits over a 10-year period. However, the new product development is expected to take 5 years, and the equipment can be used only for this project. Cybience's year 1 expense equals

A. The total cost of the equipment.

B. One-fifth of the cost of the equipment.

C. One-tenth of the cost of the equipment.

D. Zero.

Answer (A) is correct. *(CPA, adapted)*

REQUIRED: The expense for equipment usable only for developing a new product.

DISCUSSION: The costs of materials, equipment, or facilities that are acquired or constructed for a particular R&D project and that have no alternative future uses and therefore no separate economic values are R&D costs when incurred. R&D costs are expensed in full when incurred.

42. SOP 97-2, *Software Revenue Recognition*, applies to determination of the amounts and timing of revenue recognition that is not incidental to another product or service as a whole. Under SOP 97-2, if a software arrangement requires significant production, modification, or customization, what is the usual method of accounting?

A. Separate accounting for the elements of the arrangement.

B. Long-term construction contract accounting.

C. Residual accounting.

D. Separate accounting only for the service element.

Answer (B) is correct. *(Publisher)*

REQUIRED: The usual method of accounting for a software arrangement that requires significant production, modification, or customization.

DISCUSSION: If a software arrangement requires significant production, modification, or customization, the accounting for long-term construction contracts (percentage-of-completion method or completed-contract method, as appropriate) ordinarily should be used. Thus, separate accounting for different elements is not permitted unless an exception applies.

Answer (A) is incorrect because, with certain exceptions, if long-term construction contract accounting is not used, the vendor's fee is allocated to the elements based on vendor-specific objective evidence of fair values. If sufficient evidence of this kind does not exist, all revenue is deferred until sufficient evidence exists or all elements have been delivered. Answer (C) is incorrect because residual accounting is used if a delivered element is sold only with another element(s) qualifying for separate accounting and vendor-specific objective evidence of fair value exists for each undelivered element but not for a delivered element(s). This method is appropriate if all other recognition criteria are met and the fair value of all undelivered elements is less than the arrangement fee. Residual accounting defers the total fair value of the undelivered elements and recognizes the difference between the fee and the deferred amount as revenue from the delivered elements. Answer (D) is incorrect because, regardless of whether long-term construction contract accounting is used, a service element must be separately accounted for when the services are not essential to the functionality of another element and are described in the contract such that the total price is expected to vary with the inclusion or exclusion of the services.

Questions 43 and 44 are based on the following information. Partnership A advances $1 million to Corporation B to perform research and development. The terms of the agreement specify that B must repay the funds upon successful completion of the project.

43. Corporation B accounts for the $1 million as

A. A liability.

B. Income from operations.

C. Deferred contract revenue.

D. Shareholders' equity.

Answer (C) is correct. *(E. Spede/J. Sperry)*

REQUIRED: The classification of an R&D advance in the accounts of the recipient.

DISCUSSION: SFAS 68, *Research and Development Arrangements*, indicates how a company is to treat R&D advances. If the enterprise is obligated to repay any of the funds provided by the other party regardless of the outcome of the project, the enterprise recognizes a liability. If repayment depends solely on the results of the R&D having future economic benefit, the enterprise accounts for its obligation as a contract to perform R&D for others. Given that B must repay only on successful completion of the project, the advance should be recorded as deferred contract revenue.

Answer (A) is incorrect because the enterprise is not obligated to repay if the R&D has no future economic benefit. Answer (B) is incorrect because no services have yet been performed. Answer (D) is incorrect because the transaction is a contract to perform services, not an investment by Partnership A.

44. Partnership A accounts for the $1 million as

A. Accounts receivable.

B. Research and development expense.

C. Deferred research and development costs.

D. Advances on contract.

Answer (B) is correct. *(E. Spede/J. Sperry)*

REQUIRED: The classification of the advance in the accounts of the lender.

DISCUSSION: If repayment to the enterprise of any advance to other parties depends solely on the results of the R&D having future economic benefits, the advance is accounted for as a cost incurred by the enterprise. Furthermore, the costs are charged to R&D expense. B's repayment depends solely on the successful completion of the R&D, and Partnership A should treat the advance as R&D expense.

Answer (A) is incorrect because Corporation B does not have an unconditional obligation to repay the advance. Answer (C) is incorrect because, when repayment depends solely on the results of the R&D having future economic benefits, the advance must be expensed. Answer (D) is incorrect because, when repayment depends solely on the results of the R&D having future economic benefits, the advance must be expensed.

STUDY UNIT TEN
INVESTMENTS IN DEBT SECURITIES, EQUITY SECURITIES, AND DERIVATIVES

In financial statements presented in accordance with GAAP, business enterprises (investors) account for investments in **debt securities** in accordance with **SFAS 115**, *Accounting for Certain Investments in Debt and Equity Securities*. They account for investments in equity securities of other business enterprises (investees) depending on their ability to exert significant influence or control over operating and financial policies of the investees. Investments in investees over which the investor cannot exert significant influence or control are accounted for (1) as either trading or available-for-sale securities in accordance with SFAS 115, or (2) under the **cost method** described in **APB 18**, *Equity Method for Investments in Common Stock*, if fair values are not readily determinable. Investors that hold (directly or indirectly) less than 20% of an investee's outstanding voting interests at a balance sheet date are presumed not to be able to exert significant influence. An investor holding (directly or indirectly) at least 20% but not more than 50% of an investee's outstanding voting interests at a balance sheet date is presumed to be able to exert **significant influence**. In the latter case, the investor applies the equity method. If the investor (parent company) has control over the investee (subsidiary), the investment is presented on a consolidated basis in accordance with **SFAS 94**, *Consolidation of All Majority-Owned Subsidiaries*, unless control does not rest with the majority owner. Greater-than-50% ownership of the investee's outstanding voting interests provides control. Consolidated financial statements are covered in Study Unit 25. Entities account for derivative instruments in accordance with **SFAS 133**, *Accounting for Derivative Instruments and Hedging Activities*, as amended.

SFAS 115 addresses the accounting and reporting for (1) investments in equity securities accounted for on a nonequity basis that have readily determinable fair values and (2) all investments in debt securities. SFAS 115 requires business entities to classify these investments at acquisition as securities held to maturity, trading securities, or securities available for sale. **Securities held to maturity** are debt securities that the reporting entity has the positive intent and ability to hold to maturity. A debt security is not classified as held to maturity if the enterprise has the intent to hold the security for an indefinite period. Securities held to maturity are measured at amortized cost and classified as either current or noncurrent. Unrealized (holding) gains and losses are not recognized. Cash flows from purchases, sales, and maturities are reported gross as cash flows from investing activities. **Trading securities** are equity securities with readily determinable fair values and debt securities not classified as held to maturity that are bought and held principally to sell in the near term. These securities usually are actively and frequently traded to generate profit on short-term differences in price. Trading securities are measured at fair value and classified as current or noncurrent (SFAS 135). Unrealized holding gains and losses are included in the determination of income. Cash flows from purchases, sales, and maturities are reported gross as cash flows from operating activities. **Available-for-sale securities** are debt securities and equity securities with readily determinable fair values that are not classified as either held to maturity or trading securities, respectively. They are measured at fair value and classified as either current or noncurrent. Unrealized gains and losses are excluded from the determination of net income, except for all or part of the unrealized holding gains or losses on an available-for-sale security designated as being hedged in a **fair value hedge**. The latter are included in the determination of net income during the period of the hedge in accordance with SFAS 133. Accordingly, most unrealized holding gains and losses are reported net of tax in **other comprehensive income**, a separate component of equity. Cash flows from purchases, sales, and maturities are reported gross as cash flows from investing activities.

Reclassifications of securities are accounted for at fair value. At the time of transfer from the trading category, the unrealized holding gain or loss will have already been included in the determination of net income and is not reversed. At the time of transfer into the trading category, the unrealized holding gain or loss is immediately included in the determination of income. At the time of transfer into the available-for-sale category from the held-to-maturity category, the unrealized holding gain or loss is recognized as other comprehensive income. At the time of transfer into the held-to-maturity category from the available-for-sale category, the unrealized holding gain or loss continues to be recognized as other comprehensive income but is amortized over the remaining life of the security as an adjustment of yield.

SFAS 115 does not affect the methods used for reporting and measuring dividend and interest income, including amortization of discount and premium, and realized gains and losses. Investments ordinarily are recorded at **fair value at acquisition**. The fair value of an equity instrument at acquisition usually equals its cost. Income on equity instruments equals the investor's proportionate interest in dividends declared by the investee. The fair value of a long-term **bond** at acquisition equals the total associated cash flows discounted at the yield rate in effect at acquisition. The total associated cash flows are the maturity (face) amount payable at the end of the bond's term and the periodic interest payments. Interest payments equal the maturity amount times the coupon (face) rate. The difference between total cash flows and their present value equals total interest revenue. Under the **interest method**, total interest revenue is allocated to each interest period to reflect a constant interest rate equal to the yield rate at issuance. Under the straight-line method, a constant amount of interest revenue is allocated to each interest period. GAAP require the interest method unless straight-line results do not differ materially from the interest method. Bonds with a yield rate equal to the coupon rate are issued at par value. Interest revenue on bonds issued at par equals the periodic interest payment. Bonds with a yield rate greater than the coupon rate are issued at a discount. Interest revenue on bonds issued at a discount is greater than the periodic interest payment and increases over time. Bonds with a yield rate less than the coupon rate are issued at a premium. Interest revenue on bonds issued at a premium is less than the periodic interest payment and decreases over time.

APB 18 requires the use of the **equity method** when an investor exerts **significant influence** over the investee. An equity-based investment in equity securities is initially recorded at cost. The investment account subsequently is adjusted for investment income or loss equal to the investor's proportionate share of the declared income or loss of the investee, adjusted for amortization of certain acquisition differentials and intercompany gains and losses. Acquisition differentials are (1) differences between fair values and carrying amounts of tangible and intangible assets acquired and liabilities assumed (amortizable) and (2) goodwill recognized. However, equity method goodwill is **not amortized**. Moreover, it is not separately reviewed for impairment. It is not separable from the investment. These adjustments are similar to those made in preparing consolidated financial statements. The investment account also is reduced by the investor's proportionate share of dividends declared by the investee.

SFAS 133, as amended, requires that entities recognize all derivatives as either **assets or liabilities** and measure them at fair value. A **derivative** is a financial instrument or other contract that (1) has (a) one or more underlyings and (b) one or more notional amounts or payment provisions, or both; (2) requires either no initial net investment or an immaterial net investment; and (3) requires or permits net settlement. An **underlying** may be a specified interest rate, security price, commodity price, foreign exchange rate, index of prices or rates, or other variable. A **notional amount** is a number of currency units, shares, bushels, pounds, or other units specified. **Settlement** of a derivative is based on the interaction of the notional amount and the underlying.

SFAS 133 permits the designation of certain derivatives as **hedges** of (1) the exposure to changes in the fair value of a recognized asset or liability or an unrecognized firm commitment; (2) the exposure to the variability of the cash flows of a recognized asset or liability or a forecasted transaction; or (3) the foreign currency exposure of (a) a net investment in a foreign operation, (b) an unrecognized firm commitment, (c) a recognized asset or liability, or (d) a forecasted transaction. An entity electing to designate a derivative as a hedge must establish at its inception the method for assessing the effectiveness of the hedge and the measurement approach for determining any ineffective aspect of the hedge. Gains and losses from changes in fair value of a derivative not designated as a hedge are included in earnings in the period of change.

A **fair value hedge** includes a hedge of an exposure to changes in the fair value of a **recognized asset or liability** or an **unrecognized firm commitment**. A **foreign currency fair value hedge** includes a hedge of a foreign currency exposure of either an unrecognized firm commitment or a recognized asset or liability (including an available-for-sale security). Gains and losses arising from changes in fair value of a derivative classified as either a fair value or a foreign currency fair value hedge are included in the determination of **earnings** in the period of change. They are offset by losses or gains on the hedged item attributable to the risk being hedged. Thus, earnings of the period of change are affected only by the net gain or loss attributable to the ineffective aspect of the hedge.

A **cash flow hedge** is a hedge of an exposure to variability in the cash flows of a **recognized asset or liability** or a **forecasted transaction**. A **foreign currency cash flow hedge** is a hedge of the foreign currency exposure to variability in the functional-currency equivalent cash flows associated with a forecasted transaction, a recognized asset or liability, an unrecognized firm commitment, or a forecasted interentity transaction (e.g., a forecasted sale to a foreign subsidiary). The accounting treatment of gains and losses arising from changes in fair value of a derivative designated as either a cash flow or a foreign currency cash flow hedge varies for the effective and ineffective portions. The effective portion initially is reported in **other comprehensive income**. It is reclassified into earnings when the forecasted transaction affects earnings. The ineffective portion is immediately included in earnings.

Ordinarily, **nonderivatives** may not be designated as hedging instruments. The two exceptions are for nonderivative financial instruments that hedge the foreign currency exposure of an unrecognized firm commitment (a fair value hedge) or a **net investment in a foreign operation**. In the latter case, the gain or loss on a hedging derivative (or the foreign currency transaction gain or loss on a nonderivative hedging instrument) is reported as a component of the cumulative translation adjustment in other comprehensive income.

Embedded derivatives must be accounted for separately from the related host contract if the following three conditions are met: (1) The economic characteristics and risks of the embedded derivative instrument are **not clearly and closely related** to the economic characteristics of the host; (2) the hybrid instrument is **not remeasured at fair value** under otherwise applicable GAAP, with changes in fair value reported in earnings as they occur; and (3) a freestanding instrument with the same terms as the embedded derivative would be subject to the requirements of SFAS 133. If an embedded derivative is accounted for separately, the host contract is accounted for based on the accounting standards that are applicable to instruments of its type. The **separated derivative** should be accounted for under SFAS 133. If separating the two instruments is impossible, the entire contract must be measured at fair value, with gains and losses recognized in earnings. It may not be designated as a hedging instrument because nonderivatives usually do not qualify as hedging instruments.

QUESTIONS

10.1 Available-for-Sale, Held-to-Maturity, and Trading Securities

1. Investments in equity securities that have readily determinable fair values may be classified as

I. Available-for-sale securities
II. Held-to-maturity securities
III. Trading securities

A. I only.

B. I and II only.

C. I and III only.

D. I, II, and III.

Answer (C) is correct. *(Publisher)*
REQUIRED: The possible classification(s) of equity securities.
DISCUSSION: SFAS 115, *Certain Investments in Debt and Equity Securities*, applies to equity securities with readily determinable fair values. Equity securities held principally for sale in the near term are classified as trading securities. Equity securities not classified as trading securities are classified as available-for-sale securities. Held-to-maturity securities are debt securities only.

2. Investments in debt securities should be classified as held-to-maturity securities if the reporting entity has the

	Ability to Hold to Maturity	Intent to Hold to Maturity
A.	Yes	Yes
B.	Yes	No
C.	No	Yes
D.	No	No

Answer (A) is correct. *(Publisher)*
REQUIRED: The condition(s) necessary for classifying debt securities as held-to-maturity.
DISCUSSION: Under SFAS 115, a reporting enterprise must have both the positive intent and the ability to hold debt securities until maturity to classify them as held-to-maturity.

3. Investments in trading securities should be valued on the statement of financial position at

A. Acquisition cost.

B. Lower of cost or market for the portfolio.

C. Lower of cost or market for individual securities.

D. Fair value.

Answer (D) is correct. *(CMA, adapted)*
REQUIRED: The valuation of trading securities on the balance sheet.
DISCUSSION: Trading securities are those held principally for sale in the near term. They may be classified as current or noncurrent and consist of debt securities and equity securities with readily determinable fair values. Unrealized holding gains and losses on trading securities are reported in earnings. On a statement of financial position, these securities are reported at fair value, which is "the amount at which a financial instrument could be exchanged in a current transaction between willing parties, other than in a forced or liquidation sale."

4. Investments in available-for-sale securities should be valued on the statement of financial position at

A. Acquisition cost.

B. Lower of cost or market for the portfolio.

C. Lower of cost or market for individual securities.

D. Fair value.

Answer (D) is correct. *(CMA, adapted)*
REQUIRED: The valuation of available-for-sale securities on the balance sheet.
DISCUSSION: Available-for-sale securities are investments in debt securities that are not classified as held-to-maturity or trading securities and in equity securities with readily determinable fair values that are not classified as trading securities. They are measured at fair value in the balance sheet.

5. Investments in debt securities classified as held-to-maturity securities should be valued at

A. Acquisition cost.

B. Amortized cost.

C. Lower of cost or market.

D. Fair value.

Answer (B) is correct. *(Publisher)*

REQUIRED: The attribute for measuring held-to-maturity securities.

DISCUSSION: SFAS 115 requires that debt securities classified as held-to-maturity be valued at amortized cost. In this respect, SFAS 115 does not depart from prior practice.

Answer (A) is incorrect because the acquisition cost of held-to-maturity securities is adjusted for amortization. Answer (C) is incorrect because held-to-maturity securities are written down below amortized cost only when a decline in fair value below amortized cost is other than temporary. Answer (D) is incorrect because debt securities classified as held-to-maturity are reported at amortized cost.

6. A decline in the value of an available-for-sale security below its amortized cost basis that is deemed to be other than temporary should

A. Be accumulated in a valuation allowance.

B. Be treated as a realized loss and included in the determination of net income for the period.

C. Not be realized until the security is sold.

D. Be treated as an unrealized loss and included in the equity section of the balance sheet as a separate item.

Answer (B) is correct. *(CMA, adapted)*

REQUIRED: The accounting for a nontemporary impairment of an available-for-sale security.

DISCUSSION: Any other-than-temporary decline in the value of an available-for-sale security below its amortized cost basis should be considered a realized loss. The amortized cost basis should be written down to fair value and is not adjusted for subsequent recoveries in fair value. Realized gains and losses should be included in income in the period in which they occur. However, if a security has been the hedged item in a fair value hedge, its amortized cost basis will reflect adjustments in its carrying amount for changes in fair value attributable to the hedged risk. The amortized cost basis should be distinguished from the fair value, which equals the cost basis plus or minus the net unrealized holding gain or loss. The cost basis, not the fair value, is used to determine the amount of any other-than-temporary decline in fair value that will be treated as a realized loss.

Answer (A) is incorrect because a valuation allowance is used to record changes in fair value regarded as temporary. Answer (C) is incorrect because a permanent decline in fair value is treated as a realized loss. Answer (D) is incorrect because a permanent decline in fair value is treated as a realized loss.

7. When the fair value of investments in debt securities exceeds their carrying amounts, held-to-maturity securities and available-for-sale securities should be reported at the end of the year at

	Held-to-Maturity Securities	Available-for-Sale Securities
A.	Fair value	Amortized cost
B.	Amortized cost	Fair value
C.	Amortized cost	Amortized cost
D.	Fair value	Fair value

Answer (B) is correct. *(CPA, adapted)*

REQUIRED: The proper reporting of held-to-maturity and available-for-sale debt securities.

DISCUSSION: Held-to-maturity securities should be reported at their amortized cost, and available-for-sale and trading securities should be reported at fair value.

8. The amount by which the fair value of an equity security exceeds its cost should be accounted for in other comprehensive income when the security is classified as

	Trading	Available-for-Sale
A.	No	No
B.	No	Yes
C.	Yes	Yes
D.	Yes	No

Answer (B) is correct. *(CPA, adapted)*

REQUIRED: The accounting for the excess of fair value over cost.

DISCUSSION: SFAS 115 requires recognition in earnings of unrealized holding gains and losses on trading securities. Unrealized holding gains and losses on available-for-sale securities are recognized in other comprehensive income, assuming these securities are not being hedged in a fair value hedge.

9. Nola Co. has a portfolio of marketable equity securities that it does not intend to sell in the near term. How should Nola classify these securities, and how should it report unrealized gains and losses from these securities?

	Classify as	Report as a
A.	Trading securities	Component of income from continuing operations
B.	Available-for-sale securities	Other comprehensive income
C.	Trading securities	Other comprehensive income
D.	Available-for-sale securities	Component of income from continuing operations

Answer (B) is correct. *(CPA, adapted)*

REQUIRED: The proper classification of certain marketable equity securities and the reporting of unrealized gains and losses.

DISCUSSION: Marketable equity securities may be classified as either trading or available-for-sale. Equity securities that are not expected to be sold in the near term should be classified as available-for-sale. These securities should be reported at fair value, with unrealized holding gains and losses excluded from earnings and reported in other comprehensive income, assuming these securities are not being hedged in a fair value hedge.

10. On December 31, year 1, Ott Co. had investments in trading securities as follows:

	Cost	Fair Value
Man Co.	$10,000	$ 8,000
Kemo, Inc.	9,000	11,000
Fenn Corp.	11,000	9,000
	$30,000	$28,000

Ott's December 31, year 1 balance sheet should report the trading securities as

A. $26,000

B. $28,000

C. $29,000

D. $30,000

Answer (B) is correct. *(CPA, adapted)*

REQUIRED: The amount at which the trading securities should be reported.

DISCUSSION: Trading securities are reported at fair value, and unrealized holding gains and losses are included in earnings. Consequently, the securities should be reported as $28,000.

Answer (A) is incorrect because $26,000 is the lower of cost or fair value determined on an individual security basis. Answer (C) is incorrect because $29,000 is the average of the aggregate cost and aggregate fair value. Answer (D) is incorrect because $30,000 is the aggregate cost.

11. Zinc Co.'s adjusted trial balance at December 31, year 1 includes the following account balances:

Common stock, $3 par	$600,000
Additional paid-in capital	800,000
Treasury stock, at cost	50,000
Accumulated other comprehensive income: net unrealized loss on available-for-sale equity securities	20,000
Retained earnings: appropriated for uninsured earthquake losses	150,000
Retained earnings: unappropriated	200,000

What amount should Zinc report as total equity in its December 31, year 1 balance sheet?

A. $1,680,000

B. $1,720,000

C. $1,780,000

D. $1,820,000

Answer (A) is correct. *(CPA, adapted)*

REQUIRED: The total equity.

DISCUSSION: Total credits to equity equal $1,750,000 ($600,000 common stock at par + $800,000 additional paid-in capital + $350,000 retained earnings). Total debits equal $70,000 ($50,000 cost of treasury stock + $20,000 unrealized loss on available-for-sale securities). Thus, total equity equals $1,680,000.

Answer (B) is incorrect because $1,720,000 treats the unrealized loss as a credit. Answer (C) is incorrect because $1,780,000 treats the treasury stock as a credit. Answer (D) is incorrect because $1,820,000 treats the treasury stock and the unrealized loss as credits.

12. On January 2, year 1, Adam Co. purchased as a long-term investment 10,000 shares of Mill Corp.'s common stock for $40 a share. These securities were properly classified as available for sale. On December 31, year 1, the market price of Mill's stock was $35 a share, reflecting a temporary decline in market price. On January 28, year 2, Adam sold 8,000 shares of Mill stock for $30 a share. For the year ended December 31, year 2, Adam should report a realized loss on disposal of a long-term investment of

A. $100,000

B. $80,000

C. $60,000

D. $40,000

Answer (B) is correct. *(CPA, adapted)*

REQUIRED: The loss on disposal of a long-term investment.

DISCUSSION: A realized loss or gain is recognized when an individual security is sold or otherwise disposed of. The investment was acquired for $40 per share. Because the shares were purchased as a long-term investment, they should be classified as available-for-sale securities. Thus, the temporary decline in fair value at 12/31/year 1 was debited to other comprehensive income and was not included in earnings. Accordingly, the realized loss included in earnings at 12/31/year 2 was $80,000 [8,000 shares × ($40 – $30)].

Answer (A) is incorrect because $100,000 assumes disposal of 10,000 shares. Answer (C) is incorrect because $60,000 is the fair value of the remaining shares. Answer (D) is incorrect because $40,000 was the amount of the temporary decline in value of 8,000 shares at 12/31/year 1.

13. The following information was extracted from Gil Co.'s December 31, year 1 financial statements:

Noncurrent assets:	
Long-term investments in available-for-sale equity securities (at fair value)	$96,450
Accumulated other comprehensive income:	
Net unrealized loss on long-term investments in available-for-sale equity securities	(19,800)

Historical cost of the long-term investments in available-for-sale equity securities was

A. $63,595

B. $76,650

C. $96,450

D. $116,250

Answer (D) is correct. *(CPA, adapted)*

REQUIRED: The historical cost of the available-for-sale securities.

DISCUSSION: The existence of a debit balance for a classification of a separate component of equity (accumulated other comprehensive income) signifies that the available-for-sale securities are reported at fair value that is less than historical cost. The difference is the net unrealized loss balance. Hence, historical cost must have been $116,250 ($96,450 available-for-sale securities at fair value + $19,800 net unrealized loss).

Answer (A) is incorrect because $63,595 is a nonsense figure. Answer (B) is incorrect because $76,650 results from subtracting the unrealized loss instead of adding. Answer (C) is incorrect because $96,450 ignores the unrealized loss balance.

14. On January 10, year 1, Box, Inc. purchased equity securities of Knox, Inc. and Scot, Inc. Box classified both securities as noncurrent and available-for-sale. At December 31, year 1, the cost of each investment was greater than its fair value. The loss on the Knox investment was considered permanent and that on Scot was considered temporary. How should Box report the effects of these investing activities in its year 1 income statement?

I. Excess of cost of Knox stock over its market value.

II. Excess of cost of Scot stock over its market value.

A. An unrealized loss equal to I plus II.

B. An unrealized loss equal to I only.

C. A realized loss equal to I only.

D. No income statement effect.

Answer (C) is correct. *(CPA, adapted)*

REQUIRED: The income statement effects of permanent and temporary declines in value of available-for-sale securities.

DISCUSSION: If a decline in fair value of an available-for-sale security is other than temporary, its cost basis is written down to fair value. The write-down is a realized loss and is included in the determination of earnings. A temporary decline in the fair value of available-for-sale securities is treated as an unrealized holding loss. It is excluded from the determination of earnings and recognized in other comprehensive income, given that these securities are not being hedged in a fair value hedge.

Answer (A) is incorrect because the loss on Knox securities is permanent and therefore a realized loss that is included in the determination of earnings. Answer (B) is incorrect because the loss on Knox securities is permanent and therefore a realized loss that is included in the determination of earnings. Answer (D) is incorrect because the loss on Knox securities is permanent and therefore a realized loss that is included in the determination of earnings.

15. Data regarding Ball Corp.'s available-for-sale securities follow:

	Cost	Fair Value
December 31, year 1	$150,000	$130,000
December 31, year 2	150,000	160,000

Differences between cost and fair values are considered temporary. The decline in fair value was properly accounted for at December 31, year 1. Ball's year 2 statement of changes in equity would report an increase of

A. $30,000

B. $20,000

C. $10,000

D. $0

Answer (A) is correct. *(CPA, adapted)*

REQUIRED: The increase reported in the statement of changes in equity because of a change in the fair value of available-for-sale securities.

DISCUSSION: Unrealized holding gains and losses on available-for-sale securities classified as temporary are excluded from earnings, assuming these securities are not being hedged in a fair-value hedge. They are reported in other comprehensive income. At 12/31/year 2, the fair value was greater than the cost. Consequently, the net amount reported (an unrealized net holding gain) is a credit of $10,000 ($160,000 fair value – $150,000 cost). At 12/31/year 1, the balance would have been a debit of $20,000 ($150,000 cost – $130,000 fair value). Thus, the change from a debit of $20,000 to a credit of $10,000 increases accumulated other comprehensive income and therefore total equity by $30,000.

Answer (B) is incorrect because $20,000 is the excess of cost over fair value on December 31, year 1. Answer (C) is incorrect because $10,000 is the excess of fair value over cost on 12/31/year 2. Answer (D) is incorrect because equity increases when other comprehensive income is credited.

16. On December 1, year 1, Wall Company purchased equity securities and properly classified them as trading securities. Pertinent data are as follows:

Security	Cost	Fair Value at 12/31/year 1
A	$39,000	$36,000
B	50,000	55,000
C	96,000	85,000

On December 31, year 1, Wall reclassified its investment in security C from trading to available-for-sale because Wall intends to retain security C. What net loss on its securities should be included in Wall's income statement for the year ended December 31, year 1?

A. $0

B. $9,000

C. $11,000

D. $14,000

Answer (B) is correct. *(CPA, adapted)*

REQUIRED: The net loss to be included in net income when a trading security is reclassified.

DISCUSSION: Unrealized holding gains and losses on trading securities are included in earnings, and reclassification is at fair value. Furthermore, "for a security transferred from the trading category, the unrealized holding gain or loss at the date of transfer will have already been recognized in earnings and shall not be reversed" (SFAS 115). Thus, the net unrealized holding loss at 12/31/year 2 recognized in income is $9,000 ($3,000 loss on A – $5,000 gain on B + $11,000 loss on C).

Answer (A) is incorrect because $0 ignores the unrealized losses. Answer (C) is incorrect because $11,000 ignores the loss on A and the gain on B. Answer (D) is incorrect because $14,000 ignores the gain on B.

10.2 Investments in Bonds

17. When bond interest payments are sent to the owner of the bonds by the debtor, the bonds are called

A. Participating bonds.

B. Coupon bonds.

C. Registered bonds.

D. Debenture bonds.++

Answer (C) is correct. *(Publisher)*

REQUIRED: The bonds on which interest payments are sent to the owner by the debtor.

DISCUSSION: Registered bonds are issued in the name of the owner. Thus, interest payments are sent directly to the owner. When the owner sells registered bonds, the bond certificates must be surrendered and new certificates issued. They differ from coupon (bearer) bonds, which can be freely transferred and have a detachable coupon for each interest payment.

Answer (A) is incorrect because such bonds participate in excess earnings of the debtor as defined in the contractual agreement. Answer (B) is incorrect because the debtor does not keep records of the owners of coupon (bearer) bonds. Answer (D) is incorrect because as opposed to secured bonds.

18. Bonds that investors may present for payment prior to maturity are

A. Callable bonds.

B. Redeemable bonds.

C. Convertible bonds.

D. Income bonds.

Answer (B) is correct. *(Publisher)*

REQUIRED: The type of bond that may be presented for payment prior to maturity.

DISCUSSION: Redeemable bonds may be presented for payment by the creditor prior to the maturity date. The bonds usually are redeemable only after a specified period of time.

Answer (A) is incorrect because callable bonds are the opposite; the debtor may call the bonds for redemption. Answer (C) is incorrect because convertible bonds may be exchanged, usually at the option of the creditor, for common stock or other equity securities. Answer (D) is incorrect because the distinctive feature of income bonds is that interest is paid only if income is earned by the debtor.

19. Loan origination fees are charged to the borrower in connection with originating, refinancing, or restructuring a loan (e.g., points, lending fees, etc.). Loan origination fees should be

A. Recognized in income when collected.

B. Recognized in income on a straight-line basis during the life of the loan but over no more than 5 years.

C. Deferred and recognized in income over the life of the loan using the straight-line method.

D. Deferred and recognized in income over the life of the loan by the interest method.

Answer (D) is correct. *(Publisher)*

REQUIRED: The lender accounting procedure for loan origination fees.

DISCUSSION: SFAS 91, *Accounting for Nonrefundable Fees and Costs Associated With Originating and Acquiring Loans*, requires that loan origination fees be recognized in income over the life of the loan using the interest method. The objective is to achieve a constant effective yield over the life of the loan.

Answer (A) is incorrect because the fees are deferred, not recognized immediately. Answer (B) is incorrect because the effective interest method is used, not straight-line amortization. Answer (C) is incorrect because the effective interest method is used, not straight-line amortization.

20. An investor purchased a bond classified as a long-term investment between interest dates at a discount. At the purchase date, the carrying amount of the bond is more than the

	Cash Paid to Seller	Face Amount of Bond
A.	No	Yes
B.	No	No
C.	Yes	No
D.	Yes	Yes

Answer (B) is correct. *(CPA, adapted)*

REQUIRED: The carrying amount of a bond purchased at a discount between interest dates.

DISCUSSION: At the date of purchase, the carrying amount of the bond equals its face amount minus the discount. The cash paid equals the initial carrying amount plus accrued interest. Hence, the initial carrying amount is less than the cash paid by the amount of the accrued interest and less than the face amount by the amount of the discount.

21. On January 1, Welling Company purchased 100 of the $1,000 face amount, 8%, 10-year bonds of Mann, Inc. The bonds mature on January 1 in 10 years, and pay interest annually on January 1. Welling purchased the bonds to yield 10% interest.

Present value of $1 at 8% for 10 periods	0.4632
Present value of $1 at 10% for 10 periods	0.3855
Present value of an annuity of $1 at 8% for 10 periods	6.7101
Present value of an annuity of $1 at 10% for 10 periods	6.1446

How much did Welling pay for the bonds?

A. $87,707

B. $92,230

C. $95,477

D. $100,000

Answer (A) is correct. *(CPA, adapted)*

REQUIRED: The present value to the investor (price paid) of an investment in long-term bonds.

DISCUSSION: An investment in a bond should be recorded at its fair value, i.e., the present value of its cash flows discounted at the market (yield) rate of interest. The present value of the investment has two components: the value of the periodic cash interest payments and the value of the bond proceeds at maturity. The interest payment at 8% on each bond will be $80 per year for 10 years. Applying a present value factor of 6.1446 (annuity, 10 periods, 10%) gives a present value of the periodic interest payments of $491.57. The proceeds of each bond at maturity of $1,000 are multiplied by a factor of .3855 (10%, 10 periods) for a present value of $385.50. The resulting total price per bond of $877.07 ($491.57 + $385.50) multiplied by 100 bonds gives a total payment of $87,707.

Answer (B) is incorrect because $92,230 is based on a present value of an annuity factor of 6.7101. Answer (C) is incorrect because $95,477 results from using a present value factor of .4632. Answer (D) is incorrect because $100,000 is the face amount of the bonds, which were purchased at a discount.

22. On September 1, the Consul Company acquired $10,000 face amount, 8% bonds of Envoy Corporation at 104. The bonds were dated May 1, and mature in 5 years on April 30, with interest payable each October 31 and April 30. What entry should Consul make to record the purchase of the bonds?

A. Investment in bonds $10,400
Interest receivable 266
Cash $10,666

B. Investment in bonds $10,666
Cash $10,666

C. Investment in bonds $10,666
Accrued interest receivable $ 266
Cash 10,400

D. Investment in bonds $10,000
Premium on bonds 666
Cash $10,666

Answer (A) is correct. *(CPA, adapted)*

REQUIRED: The entry to record a bond purchased at a premium with accrued interest.

DISCUSSION: At 104, the price paid for the bonds is $10,400 in the absence of any accrued interest. Because the bonds were purchased between interest dates, cash interest accrued for the 4 months from May 1 to September 1 (date of purchase) must be computed and included in the purchase price. The interest for 4 months at 8% is $266.67 [(4 ÷ 12) × 8% × $10,000], which is recorded as interest receivable and added to the $10,400 purchase price for a total amount paid of $10,666. When interest is received on October 31, the $266 in interest receivable will be credited.

Answer (B) is incorrect because interest receivable should be debited for $266. Answer (C) is incorrect because interest receivable should be debited for $266. Answer (D) is incorrect because the premium paid was $400. The interest receivable of $266 should be recorded separately from bond premium.

23. Cap Corp. reported accrued investment interest receivable of $38,000 and $46,500 at January 1 and December 31, year 1, respectively. During year 1, cash collections from the investments included the following:

Capital gains distributions	$145,000
Interest	152,000

What amount should Cap report as interest revenue from investments for year 1?

A. $160,500

B. $153,500

C. $152,000

D. $143,500

Answer (A) is correct. *(CPA, adapted)*

REQUIRED: The interest revenue from debt investments.

DISCUSSION: When a receivable increases, revenue exceeds collections. Given that the accrued interest receivable balance increased by $8,500 ($46,500 – $38,000), and interest collected equaled $152,000, interest revenue equals $160,500 ($152,000 + $8,500). Capital gains distributions do not affect interest.

Answer (B) is incorrect because $153,500 equals capital gains plus the increase in accrued interest receivable. Answer (C) is incorrect because $152,000 equals collections. Answer (D) is incorrect because $143,500 equals collections of interest minus the increase in accrued interest receivable.

24. On March 1, year 1, Clark Co. issued bonds at a discount. Clark incorrectly used the straight-line method instead of the effective interest method to amortize the discount. How were the following amounts, as of December 31, year 1, affected by the error?

	Bond Carrying Amount	Retained Earnings
A.	Overstated	Overstated
B.	Understated	Understated
C.	Overstated	Understated
D.	Understated	Overstated

Answer (C) is correct. *(CPA, adapted)*

REQUIRED: The effects of the error on the bond carrying amount and retained earnings.

DISCUSSION: The straight-line method records the same amount of expense (cash interest paid + proportionate share of discount amortization) for each period. The effective interest method applies a constant rate to an increasing bond carrying amount (face amount – discount + accumulated discount amortization), resulting in an increasing amortization of discount and increasing interest expense. Accordingly, in the first 10 months of the life of the bond, since straight-line amortization of discount is greater than under the interest method, interest expense is also greater. The effects are an understatement of unamortized discount, an overstatement of the carrying amount of the bonds, an understatement of net income, and an understatement of retained earnings.

Answer (A) is incorrect because the error understates retained earnings. Answer (B) is incorrect because the error overstates the carrying amount. Answer (D) is incorrect because the error overstates the carrying amount and understates retained earnings.

25. On July 1, year 1, York Co. purchased as a long-term investment $1 million of Park, Inc.'s 8% bonds for $946,000, including accrued interest of $40,000. The bonds were purchased to yield 10% interest and were properly classified as securities. The bonds mature on January 1, year 8 and pay interest annually on January 1. York uses the effective interest method of amortization. In its December 31, year 1 balance sheet, what amount should York report as investment in bonds?

A. $911,300

B. $916,600

C. $953,300

D. $960,600

Answer (A) is correct. *(CPA, adapted)*

REQUIRED: The amount reported as bond investment at year-end.

DISCUSSION: The bond investment's original balance was $906,000 ($946,000 price – $40,000 accrued interest) because the carrying amount does not include accrued interest. Under the effective interest method, interest income equals the yield or effective interest rate times the carrying amount of the bonds at the beginning of the interest period. The amortization of premium or discount is the difference between this interest income and the periodic cash payments. For the period 7/1 to 12/31/year 1, interest income is $45,300 [(6 ÷ 12) × 10% × $906,000], and the actual interest is $40,000 [(6 ÷ 12) × 8% × $1,000,000]. Hence, the carrying amount at year-end is $911,300 [$906,000 + ($45,300 – $40,000)].

Answer (B) is incorrect because $916,600 amortizes the discount for 12 months. Answer (C) is incorrect because $953,300 includes the accrued interest. Answer (D) is incorrect because $960,600 includes the accrued interest and amortizes the discount for 12 months.

26. On July 1, year 1, Pell Co. purchased Green Corp. 10-year, 8% bonds with a face amount of $500,000 for $420,000. The bonds mature on June 30, year 9 and pay interest semiannually on June 30 and December 31. Using the interest method, Pell recorded bond discount amortization of $1,800 for the 6 months ended December 31, year 1. From this long-term investment, Pell should report year 1 revenue of

A. $16,800

B. $18,200

C. $20,000

D. $21,800

Answer (D) is correct. *(CPA, adapted)*

REQUIRED: The interest revenue when amortization of bond discount is known.

DISCUSSION: Interest income for a bond issued at a discount is equal to the sum of the periodic cash flows and the amount of bond discount amortized during the interest period. The periodic cash flows are equal to $20,000 ($500,000 face amount × 8% coupon rate × .5 year). The discount amortization is given as $1,800. Thus, revenue for the 6-month period from 7/1 to 12/31/year 1 is $21,800 ($20,000 + $1,800).

Answer (A) is incorrect because $16,800 is 50% of 8% of $420,000. Answer (B) is incorrect because $18,200 equals the cash flow minus discount amortization. Answer (C) is incorrect because $20,000 equals the cash flow.

27. On July 1, year 1, Cody Co. paid $1,198,000 for 10%, 20-year bonds with a face amount of $1 million. Interest is paid on December 31 and June 30. The bonds were purchased to yield 8%. Cody uses the effective interest rate method to recognize interest income from this investment. The bonds are properly classified as held-to-maturity. What should be reported as the carrying amount of the bonds in Cody's December 31, year 1 balance sheet?

A. $1,207,900

B. $1,198,000

C. $1,195,920

D. $1,193,050

Answer (C) is correct. *(CPA, adapted)*

REQUIRED: The amount reported as bond investment at year-end.

DISCUSSION: Under the effective interest method, interest income equals the yield or effective interest rate times the carrying amount of the bonds at the beginning of the interest period. The amortization of premium or discount is the difference between this interest income and the periodic cash payments. For year 1, interest income is $47,920 [(6 ÷ 12) × 8% × $1,198,000], and interest received is $50,000 [(6 ÷ 12) × 10% × $1,000,000]. Hence, the carrying amount at year-end is $1,195,920 [$1,198,000 – ($50,000 – $47,920)].

Answer (A) is incorrect because $1,207,900 equals the investment if interest income is determined using a 10% rate, and the difference between actual interest and interest income is added to the carrying amount. Answer (B) is incorrect because $1,198,000 is the carrying amount before adjustment for the premium amortization. Answer (D) is incorrect because $1,193,050 assumes that interest income is based on a 10% rate and that the bonds have been outstanding for 3 months.

28. In year 1, Lee Co. acquired, at a premium, Enfield, Inc. 10-year bonds as a long-term investment. At December 31, year 1, Enfield's bonds were quoted at a small discount. Which of the following situations is the most likely cause of the decline in the bonds' fair value?

A. Enfield issued a stock dividend.

B. Enfield is expected to call the bonds at a premium, which is less than Lee's carrying amount.

C. Interest rates have declined since Lee purchased the bonds.

D. Interest rates have increased since Lee purchased the bonds.

Answer (D) is correct. *(CPA, adapted)*

REQUIRED: The most likely cause of a decline in a bond's fair value.

DISCUSSION: Bonds selling at a premium have a nominal rate in excess of the market rate. Bonds selling at a discount have a nominal rate less than the market rate. Thus, interest rates in the market must have increased in order for a bond originally acquired at a premium to be currently quoted at a discount.

Answer (A) is incorrect because a stock dividend has no effect on quoted fair values of bonds. Answer (B) is incorrect because bonds expected to be called at a premium would not be quoted at a discount. Answer (C) is incorrect because, if interest rates decline below the stated rate, the bonds will be quoted at a higher premium.

29. When bonds with detachable stock warrants are purchased, the price should be allocated between the warrants and the bonds based upon their relative market values at issuance. The amount debited to investment in stock warrants relative to the total amount paid

A. Increases the premium on the investment in bonds.

B. Increases the discount on investment in bonds.

C. Increases either any premium on the bonds or any discount on the bonds.

D. Has no effect on the investment of bond premium or discount as the warrants are purchased separately.

Answer (B) is correct. *(Publisher)*

REQUIRED: The effect on the carrying amount of bonds of debiting investment in stock warrants.

DISCUSSION: The portion of the price allocated to the detachable stock warrants decreases the allocation to investment in bonds. Thus, amounts debited to investment in stock warrants increase the discount or decrease the premium recorded for the investment in bonds.

10.3 Equity Method

30. X Company owns 15% of the voting stock of Y Co., and it owns 25% of the voting stock of Z Co. Under what circumstances should X account for each investment using the equity method?

	Investment in Y	Investment in Z
A.	In all cases	In all cases
B.	Never	In all cases
C.	Never	Only if X has the ability to exercise significant influence over Z
D.	Only if X has the ability to exercise significant influence over Y	Only if X has the ability to exercise significant influence over Z

Answer (D) is correct. *(S. Rubin)*

REQUIRED: The circumstances in which the equity method of accounting for a stock investment should be used.

DISCUSSION: APB 18, *Equity Method for Investments in Common Stock*, prescribes the equity method when an investee has the ability to exercise significant influence. An investment of 20% or more of the voting stock of an investee leads to a presumption that an investor has the ability to exercise significant influence. An investment of less than 20% leads to a presumption that an investor does not have such ability. However, those presumptions can be overcome by predominant evidence to the contrary. See FASB Interpretation No. 35, *Criteria for Applying the Equity Method of Accounting for Investments in Common Stock*.

31. Current authoritative literature states that the equity method of accounting for investments in common stock

A. Should be used in accounting for investments in common stock of corporate joint ventures.

B. Should be used only for investments in common stock of unconsolidated domestic subsidiaries reported in consolidated financial statements.

C. Is a valid substitute for consolidation.

D. May not be used when accounting for an investment of less than 25% of the voting stock of an investee.

Answer (A) is correct. *(Publisher)*

REQUIRED: The true statement about the equity method.

DISCUSSION: Investors should account for investments in common stock of corporate joint ventures by the equity method because it best enables them to reflect the underlying nature of their investments. Usually, the investors have the ability to exert significant influence on the operation of the joint venture.

Answer (B) is incorrect because investments in which the investor has significant influence must be accounted for by the equity method whether the unconsolidated subsidiaries are domestic or foreign. Answer (C) is incorrect because APB 18 states that application of the equity method is not a valid substitute for consolidation. Answer (D) is incorrect because the equity method would most likely be used if ownership were 20% or greater.

32. When an investor uses the equity method to account for investments in common stock, the investment account will be increased when the investor recognizes

A. A proportionate interest in the net income of the investee.

B. A cash dividend received from the investee.

C. Periodic amortization of the goodwill related to the purchase.

D. Depreciation related to the excess of fair value over the carrying amount of the investee's depreciable assets at the date of purchase by the investor.

Answer (A) is correct. *(CPA, adapted)*

REQUIRED: The basis for increasing the investment account when the investor uses the equity method.

DISCUSSION: Under the equity method, the investor's share of the investee's net income is accounted for as an addition to the carrying amount of the investment on the investor's books. Losses and dividends are reflected as reductions of the carrying amount.

Answer (B) is incorrect because recognition of a cash dividend received from the investee reduces the carrying amount. Answer (C) is incorrect because goodwill is not amortized (SFAS 142). Moreover, equity method goodwill is not separately reviewed for impairment because it is not separate from the investment. Answer (D) is incorrect because recognition of depreciation related to the excess of fair value over the carrying amount of the investee's depreciable assets at the date of purchase by the investor reduces the carrying amount.

33. When the equity method is used to account for investments in common stock, which of the following affects the investor's reported investment income?

	Goodwill Amortization Related to the Purchase	Cash Dividends from Investee
A.	Yes	Yes
B.	No	Yes
C.	No	No
D.	Yes	No

Answer (C) is correct. *(CPA, adapted)*

REQUIRED: The transaction(s) affecting the investor's reported investment income when the equity method is used.

DISCUSSION: The difference between the cost of an investment and the investee's underlying equity should be accounted for as if the investee were a consolidated subsidiary (APB 18). Thus, the difference is assigned first to any undervalued or overvalued assets, with the remainder allocated to goodwill. Amortization of goodwill is prohibited by SFAS 142 and therefore does not reduce investment income. Moreover, equity method goodwill is not separately reviewed for impairment because it is not separate from the investment. The receipt of a cash dividend from the investee also does not affect equity-based earnings.

34. In its financial statements, Pulham Corp. uses the equity method of accounting for its 30% ownership of Angles Corp. At December 31, year 1, Pulham has a receivable from Angles. How should the receivable be reported in Pulham's year 1 financial statements?

A. None of the receivable should be reported, but the entire receivable should be offset against Angles' payment to Pulham.

B. 70% of the receivable should be separately reported, with the balance offset against 30% of Angles' payment to Pulham.

C. The total receivable should be disclosed separately.

D. The total receivable should be included as part of the investment in Angles, without separate disclosure.

Answer (C) is correct. *(CPA, adapted)*

REQUIRED: The method of reporting a receivable from a 30%-owned company.

DISCUSSION: According to SFAS 57, *Related Party Disclosures*, related parties include an enterprise and its equity-based investees. A receivable from a related party should be separately disclosed in full.

Answer (A) is incorrect because elimination of intercompany transactions is inappropriate except in the case of combined or consolidated statements. Moreover, a general principle of accounting is that assets and liabilities should not be offset in the balance sheet unless a right of offset exists (APB 10, *Omnibus Opinion -- 1966*). Answer (B) is incorrect because elimination of intercompany transactions is inappropriate except in the case of combined or consolidated statements. Moreover, a general principle of accounting is that assets and liabilities should not be offset in the balance sheet unless a right of offset exists (APB 10, *Omnibus Opinion -- 1966*). Answer (D) is incorrect because the investment balance equals cost plus the investor's share of earnings and losses, minus any return of the investment. Also, separate disclosure is required.

35. FASB Interpretation No. 35 applies to the criterion stated in APB 18 for applying the equity method of accounting to investments of 50% or less. That criterion is the ability to exercise significant influence over the investee. A 20% or greater ownership is a presumptive indication of that ability. An investor who owns 30% of the voting common stock of the investee is most likely to exercise significant influence when

A. The investor and investee sign an agreement under which the investor surrenders significant rights.

B. The investor tries and fails to obtain representation on the investee's board of directors.

C. Opposition by the investee, such as litigation or complaints to governmental regulatory authorities, challenges the investor's exercise of significant influence.

D. The majority ownership of the investee is spread among a large group of shareholders who have objectives with respect to the investee that differ from those of the investor.

Answer (D) is correct. *(Publisher)*

REQUIRED: The situation that indicates ability to exercise significant influence.

DISCUSSION: If the investor owns 20% to 50% of an investee and the remainder of the ownership is spread among a large group of shareholders, the investee will be able to exert significant influence even though most of the other owners have objectives contrary to those of the investor. The presumption of significant influence could be overcome by evidence that majority ownership is held by a small number of shareholders who operate the investee without regard to the investor's views.

Answer (A) is incorrect because this is a specific example given in FASB Interpretation No. 35 of an inability to exercise significant influence over an investee. Answer (B) is incorrect because this is a specific example given in FASB Interpretation No. 35 of an inability to exercise significant influence over an investee. Answer (C) is incorrect because this is a specific example given in FASB Interpretation No. 35 of an inability to exercise significant influence over an investee.

36. On January 2, year 1, Well Co. purchased 10% of Rea, Inc.'s outstanding common shares for $400,000. Well is the largest single shareholder in Rea, and Well's officers are a majority on Rea's board of directors. Rea reported net income of $500,000 for year 1, and paid dividends of $150,000. In its December 31, year 1 balance sheet, what amount should Well report as investment in Rea?

A. $450,000

B. $435,000

C. $400,000

D. $385,000

Answer (B) is correct. *(CPA, adapted)*

REQUIRED: The amount reported in the investment account.

DISCUSSION: The equity method should be used because Well Co. exercises significant influence over Rea. The investment in Rea equals $435,000 [$400,000 investment + (10% × $500,000 net income) – (10% × $150,000 of dividends)].

Answer (A) is incorrect because $450,000 does not deduct Well's dividends. Answer (C) is incorrect because $400,000 does not include Well's share of net income or deduct Well's dividends. Answer (D) is incorrect because $385,000 does not include Well's share of net income.

37. An investor uses the equity method to account for an investment in common stock. After the date of acquisition, the investment account of the investor is

A. Not affected by its share of the earnings or losses of the investee.

B. Not affected by its share of the earnings of the investee but is decreased by its share of the losses of the investee.

C. Increased by its share of the earnings of the investee but is not affected by its share of the losses of the investee.

D. Increased by its share of the earnings of the investee and is decreased by its share of the losses of the investee.

Answer (D) is correct. *(CPA, adapted)*

REQUIRED: The effect(s) on an equity-based investment in common stock of investee earnings and losses.

DISCUSSION: After the date of acquisition, an equity-based investment-in-common-stock account of an investor is increased by its share of the earnings of the investee, decreased by its share of the losses of the investee, and decreased by its share of cash dividends received from the investee.

38. Which procedure mentioned below is a requirement in the application of the equity method of accounting for investments?

A. The investor's share of extraordinary items should be classified in a similar manner, if material, in the income statement of the investor.

B. The difference between the cost of an investment and the amount of the underlying equity in net assets of the investee should be permanently capitalized in the balance sheet of the investor.

C. Even if the percentage ownership of the investee's common stock held by the investor falls below the level needed to exercise significant influence, the equity method should still be employed.

D. The investor should continue using the equity method even when the investee's losses are large enough to cause the investment account to be reduced below a zero balance.

Answer (A) is correct. *(Publisher)*

REQUIRED: The proper procedure in applying the equity method.

DISCUSSION: The income statement of an investor reflects investment income resulting from the investor's share of the earnings of the investee company. APB 18 specifies that the investor's share of the investee's extraordinary items should be reported as extraordinary items in the investor's income statement.

Answer (B) is incorrect because the difference between the cost of an investment and the investee's underlying equity should be assigned first to any undervalued or overvalued assets, with the remainder allocated to goodwill, which is nonamortizable. Moreover, equity method goodwill is not separately reviewed for impairment. Answer (C) is incorrect because, if an investment falls below the level needed to exert significant influence, the investor should discontinue use of the equity method and change to the fair-value method (assuming the stock has a readily determinable fair value). Answer (D) is incorrect because, when the investment account is reduced to zero by the losses of the investee, the investor should discontinue using the equity method.

39. The investor's accounting procedure under the equity method is to debit the investment account to record investee income and credit the investment account to record investee dividends. In substance, the net effect is to

A. Recognize only distributed income of the investee.

B. Not consider distributed income of the investee as income.

C. Increase the investment account for investee distributed income.

D. Recognize both distributed and undistributed income of the investee.

Answer (D) is correct. *(Publisher)*

REQUIRED: The substance of the entries to record investee income and dividends under the equity method.

DISCUSSION: The traditional journal entries for the equity method are

Investment in investee	$XXX	
Investment income		$XXX
Cash	$XXX	
Investment in investee		$XXX

If they are compounded into a single entry, the net effect is to debit the investment account for undistributed income, to debit cash for distributed income, and to credit investment income for total income.

Answer (A) is incorrect because it describes the cost method. Answer (B) is incorrect because both distributed and undistributed income are recognized by the investor. Answer (C) is incorrect because the investment account is increased for all investee income, not just distributed income.

40. In accordance with APB 18, *Equity Method for Investments in Common Stock*, which of the following is false?

A. Company A owns 19% of Company B's voting common stock and acquires 1% more. Company A's investment, results of operations (current and prior periods presented), and retained earnings should be adjusted retroactively.

B. Depending on the circumstances, an investor may be required to account for an investment in voting common stock under the fair-value method even though the investor owns more than 20% of the voting common stock.

C. Company A owns 20% of Company B's voting common stock and sells 1%. Company A's investment, results of operations (current and prior periods presented), and retained earnings should be adjusted retroactively.

D. One of the disclosures necessary under the equity method of accounting for investments is the difference, if any, between the amount at which an investment is carried and the amount of underlying equity in net assets and the accounting treatment of the difference.

Answer (C) is correct. *(Publisher)*

REQUIRED: The false statement regarding the equity method of investment accounting.

DISCUSSION: When an investor accounts for an investment by the equity method (at a level of 20% ownership or greater) and subsequently sells shares such that significant influence is no longer presumed to be exerted over the investee, the investor should account for the stock using the fair-value method described in SFAS 115, assuming the stock has a readily determinable fair value. The change is accounted for on a prospective basis; no retroactive adjustment is made. The carrying amount of the investment subsequently will be changed by transactions in the stock and by changes in its fair value. Moreover, the carrying amount will be reduced by dividends in future periods to the extent they exceed the investor's share of investee earnings. Subsequent dividends not exceeding the investor's share of investee earnings are accounted for as income.

Answer (A) is incorrect because achieving a level of significant influence subsequent to the initial purchase of an investment requires retroactive application of the equity method. Answer (B) is incorrect because, when significant influence cannot be exerted over the investee despite 20% or greater ownership, the fair-value method should be used if the stock has a readily determinable fair value. Answer (D) is incorrect because APB 18 specifically requires disclosure of the difference, if any, between the amount in the investment account and the underlying equity in the net assets of the investee and the method by which the difference is being amortized.

41. Peel Co. received a cash dividend from a common stock investment with a readily determinable fair value. Should Peel report an increase in the investment account if it accounts for the security as available-for-sale or uses the equity method of accounting?

	Available-for-Sale	Equity
A.	No	No
B.	Yes	Yes
C.	Yes	No
D.	No	Yes

Answer (A) is correct. *(CPA, adapted)*

REQUIRED: The effect of a cash dividend on the investment account.

DISCUSSION: If a stock investment is classified as available-for-sale, it is accounted for using the fair-value method described in SFAS 115. Hence, dividends from an investee should be accounted for by the investor as dividend income unless a liquidating dividend is received. Thus, assuming that the dividend is not liquidating, it has no effect on the investment account. Under the equity method, cash dividends decrease the investment account because the dividend is considered to be a return of investment.

42. On January 1, year 1, Point, Inc. purchased 10% of Iona Co.'s common stock. Point purchased additional shares, bringing its ownership up to 40% of Iona's common stock outstanding on August 1, year 1. During October year 1, Iona declared and paid a cash dividend on all of its outstanding common stock. How much income from the Iona investment should Point's year 1 income statement report?

A. 10% of Iona's income for January 1 to July 31, year 1, plus 40% of Iona's income for August 1 to December 31, year 1.

B. 40% of Iona's income for August 1 to December 31, year 1 only.

C. 40% of Iona's year 1 income.

D. Amount equal to dividends received from Iona.

Answer (A) is correct. *(CPA, adapted)*

REQUIRED: The income from an investment that has increased from less than 20% to more than 20% during the period.

DISCUSSION: Once the ownership percentage increased from 10% to 40%, Point was presumed to exercise significant influence over Iona; therefore, the investment should be accounted for retroactively under the equity method. Given that Point held 10% of Iona's common stock for the first 7 months of the year, it should recognize in earnings 10% of Iona's income for that period. It should recognize 40% of Iona's income for the balance of the year. Point's share of the dividend is credited to the investment account and is not included in earnings.

Answer (B) is incorrect because adoption of the equity method is retroactive to the acquisition of the first shares of stock of the investee. Answer (C) is incorrect because Point held only 10% of Iona's stock for the January-July period. Answer (D) is incorrect because Iona's dividends do not affect Point's net income.

43. A corporation that uses the equity method of accounting for its investment in a 40%-owned investee that earned $20,000 and paid $5,000 in dividends made the following entries:

Investment in subsidiary	$8,000	
Equity in earnings of subsidiary		$8,000
Cash	$2,000	
Dividend revenue		$2,000

What effect will these entries have on the parent's statement of financial position?

A. Investment understated, retained earnings understated.

B. Investment overstated, retained earnings overstated.

C. Investment overstated, retained earnings understated.

D. Financial position will be fairly stated.

Answer (B) is correct. *(CPA, adapted)*

REQUIRED: The effect of an error in recording investment income or dividends received.

DISCUSSION: In the case of 40% ownership, the equity method of accounting for the investment in the investor's books should be applied. The 40% share of the investee's $20,000 net income ($8,000) is correctly recorded.

Dividends received from an investee must be recorded in the books of the investor as a decrease in the carrying amount of the investment and an increase in assets (cash). Hence, dividend revenue was incorrectly credited with the $2,000 dividend resulting in an overstatement of retained earnings. The investment account should have been credited for $2,000. Thus, the effect on the investment account is also an overstatement.

44. Moss Corp. owns 20% of Dobro Corp.'s preferred stock and 80% of its common stock. Dobro's stock outstanding at December 31, year 1 is as follows:

10% cumulative preferred stock	$100,000
Common stock	700,000

Dobro reported net income of $60,000 for the year ended December 31, year 1. What amount should Moss record as equity in earnings of Dobro for the year ended December 31, year 1?

A. $40,000

B. $48,000

C. $48,400

D. $50,000

Answer (A) is correct. *(CPA, adapted)*

REQUIRED: The equity of a parent in the earnings of a subsidiary.

DISCUSSION: The equity method generally applies when the investor holds at least 20% of the investee's voting interests. Hence, it requires Moss to record its share of Dobro's earnings available to common shareholders. When an investee has outstanding cumulative preferred stock, the investor should calculate its share of the investee's net income after deducting the preferred dividends, whether or not declared (APB 18). Thus, the equity of Moss in Dobro's earnings available to common shareholders is $40,000 {80% × [$60,000 – (10% × $100,000)]}. Moss is also entitled to preferred dividends of $2,000 (20% × 10% × $100,000). However, the equity method is not applicable to nonvoting interests. Because preferred stock is normally nonvoting, the equity method does not apply to it, and Moss should not record its equity in cumulative dividends. The total equity in the earnings of Dobro is therefore $40,000.

Answer (B) is incorrect because $48,000 equals 80% of Dobro's net income. Answer (C) is incorrect because $48,400 equals 80% of Dobro's net income plus 20% of a 20% share of the preferred dividends. Answer (D) is incorrect because $50,000 equals Dobro's net income minus the preferred dividends.

45. Park Co. uses the equity method to account for its January 1, year 1 purchase of Tun, Inc.'s common stock. On January 1, year 1, the fair values of Tun's FIFO inventory and land exceeded their carrying amounts. How do these excesses of fair values over carrying amounts affect Park's reported equity in Tun's year 1 earnings?

	Inventory Excess	Land Excess
A.	Decrease	Decrease
B.	Decrease	No effect
C.	Increase	Increase
D.	Increase	No effect

Answer (B) is correct. *(CPA, adapted)*

REQUIRED: The effect on equity in investee earnings of the excess of the fair values of the investee's FIFO inventory and land over their carrying amounts.

DISCUSSION: The equity method of accounting requires the investor's proportionate share of the investee's reported net income to be adjusted for certain acquisition differentials. Thus, the difference at the date of acquisition of the investee's stock between the fair value and carrying amount of inventory is such an adjustment when the inventory is sold. A similar adjustment for land is required when the land is sold. Assuming that the FIFO inventory was sold in year 1 and the land was not, Park's proportionate share of Tun's reported net income is decreased by the inventory differential allocated at the date of acquisition.

46. On January 2, year 1, Kean Co. purchased a 30% interest in Pod Co. for $250,000. On this date, Pod's equity was $500,000. The carrying amounts of Pod's net assets approximated their fair values except for land, for which fair value exceeded its carrying amount by $200,000. Pod reported net income of $100,000 for year 1 and paid no dividends. Kean accounts for this investment using the equity method. In its December 31, year 1 balance sheet, what amount should Kean report as investment in subsidiary?

A. $210,000

B. $220,000

C. $276,000

D. $280,000

Answer (D) is correct. *(CPA, adapted)*

REQUIRED: The amount reported as investment in subsidiary under the equity method.

DISCUSSION: The purchase price is allocated to the fair value of the net assets acquired, with the remainder allocated to goodwill. The fair value of Kean's 30% interest in Pod's net assets is $210,000 [30% × ($500,000 + $200,000)]. Goodwill is $40,000 ($250,000 – $210,000). The equity method requires the investor's share of subsequent net income reported by the investee to be adjusted for the difference at acquisition between the fair value and the carrying amount of the investee's net assets when the net assets are sold or consumed in operations. The land is assumed not to be sold, and the equity method goodwill is not amortized or separately reviewed for impairment. Thus, Kean's share of Pod's net income is $30,000 (30% × $100,000 declared income), and the investment account at year-end is $280,000 ($250,000 acquisition balance + $30,000 investment income).

Answer (A) is incorrect because $210,000 equals the fair value of the identifiable net assets acquired. Answer (B) is incorrect because $220,000 equals the price minus Kean's equity in Pod's net income. Answer (C) is incorrect because $276,000 assumes amortization of goodwill over 10 years.

47. Green Corp. owns 30% of the outstanding common stock and 100% of the outstanding noncumulative nonvoting preferred stock of Axel Corp. In year 1, Axel declared dividends of $100,000 on its common stock and $60,000 on its preferred stock. Green exercises significant influence over Axel's operations. What amount of dividend revenue should Green report in its income statement for the year ended December 31, year 1?

A. $0

B. $30,000

C. $60,000

D. $90,000

Answer (C) is correct. *(CPA, adapted)*

REQUIRED: The dividend revenue reported given declaration of common and preferred dividends by an investee.

DISCUSSION: An investment in common stock enabling the investor to exercise significant influence over the operations and management of the investee should be accounted for by the equity method. A 20% or greater ownership is presumed to permit such influence. Under the equity method, the receipt of a cash dividend from the investee should be credited to the investment account. It is a return of, not a return on, the investment. However, the equity method is not applicable to preferred stock. Thus, Green should report $60,000 of revenue when the preferred dividends are declared.

Answer (A) is incorrect because the preferred dividends should be credited to revenue. Answer (B) is incorrect because the cash dividends on common stock should be credited to the investment account. Answer (D) is incorrect because the cash dividends on common stock should be credited to the investment account.

48. Sage, Inc. bought 40% of Adams Corp.'s outstanding common stock on January 2, year 1 for $400,000. The carrying amount of the net assets at the purchase date totaled $900,000. Fair values and carrying amounts were the same for all items except for plant and inventory, for which fair values exceeded their carrying amounts by $90,000 and $10,000, respectively. The plant has an 18-year life. All inventory was sold during year 1. During year 1, Adams reported net income of $120,000 and paid a $20,000 cash dividend. What amount should Sage report in its income statement from its investment in Adams for the year ended December 31, year 1?

A. $48,000

B. $42,000

C. $36,000

D. $32,000

Answer (B) is correct. *(CPA, adapted)*

REQUIRED: The amount reported as investment income.

DISCUSSION: Sage holds 40% of the investee's stock and is assumed to exercise significant influence. It should therefore account for the investment on the equity basis by recognizing its proportionate share of the investee's net income. To determine the amount of investment income the investor should report, the investee's net income of $120,000 should be adjusted for the $10,000 excess of fair value over the carrying amount of the inventory acquired because this inventory was sold. The investee's reported net income also should be adjusted for the share of the difference between the fair value and carrying amount of the plant that has been consumed (depreciated), or $5,000 ($90,000 difference ÷ 18 years). No goodwill is recognized because the $400,000 purchase price equals a proportionate share of the fair value of the net assets {[40% × ($900,000 + $90,000 + $10,000)] = $400,000}. Thus, Sage should report investment income of $42,000 [40% × ($120,000 – $10,000 – $5,000)].

Answer (A) is incorrect because $48,000 equals the proportionate share of the investee's reported net income. Answer (C) is incorrect because $36,000 adjusts the reported net income for the dividend disclosed and does not adjust for the plant depreciation. Answer (D) is incorrect because $32,000 includes a $10,000 adjustment for goodwill amortization. Goodwill is not amortized.

49. On January 1, year 1, Mega Corp. acquired 10% of the outstanding voting stock of Penny, Inc. On January 2, year 2, Mega gained the ability to exercise significant influence over financial and operating control of Penny by acquiring an additional 20% of Penny's outstanding stock. The two purchases were made at prices proportionate to the value assigned to Penny's net assets, which equaled their carrying amounts. For the years ended December 31, year 1 and year 2, Penny reported the following:

	Year 1	Year 2
Dividends paid	$200,000	$300,000
Net income	600,000	650,000

In year 2, what amounts should Mega report as current-year investment income and as an adjustment, before income taxes, to year 1 investment income?

	Year 2 Investment Income	Adjustment to Year 1 Investment Income
A.	$195,000	$160,000
B.	$195,000	$120,000
C.	$195,000	$40,000
D.	$105,000	$40,000

Answer (C) is correct. *(CPA, adapted)*

REQUIRED: The amounts reported as current-year investment income and as an adjustment, before income taxes, to the previous year's investment income.

DISCUSSION: When ownership of an investee reaches the level of significant influence, the investor must adopt the equity method. The investor must also retroactively adjust the carrying amount of the investment, results of operations, and retained earnings as if the equity method had been in effect during all of the previous periods in which any percentage was held. Consequently, Mega should report year 2 investment income before taxes equal to $195,000 (30% × $650,000 net income reported by Penny for year 2). Ignoring taxes, it should retroactively adjust year 1 investment income by $40,000 [(10% interest held in year 1 × $600,000 investee net income in year 1) – (10% × $200,000 dividends paid by investee in year 1)].

Answer (A) is incorrect because $160,000 equals 30% of Penny's year 1 net income minus 10% of Penny's year 1 dividends. Answer (B) is incorrect because $120,000 equals 30% of Penny's year 1 net income minus 30% of Penny's year 1 dividends. Answer (D) is incorrect because $105,000 equals Mega's share of year 2 net income minus its share of dividends.

50. Pare, Inc. purchased 10% of Tot Co.'s 100,000 outstanding shares of common stock on January 2, year 1 for $50,000. On December 31, year 1, Pare purchased an additional 20,000 shares of Tot for $150,000. There was no goodwill as a result of either acquisition, and Tot had not issued any additional stock during year 1. Tot reported earnings of $300,000 for year 1. What amount should Pare report in its December 31, year 1 balance sheet as investment in Tot?

A. $170,000

B. $200,000

C. $230,000

D. $290,000

Answer (C) is correct. *(CPA, adapted)*

REQUIRED: The amount reported in the investment account.

DISCUSSION: Given that Pare owned 30% of Tot at year-end, Pare can presumably exercise significant influence. Thus, the equity method should be used. Although Pare held 20% or greater ownership only on the last day of year 1, the adoption of the equity method must be retroactive. However, the retroactive effect is based on the percentage of ownership held prior to the adoption of the equity method. Consequently, Pare should recognize its equity in the earnings of Tot as if the equity method had been in effect since 1/2/year 1. Accordingly, its share of Tot's year 1 earnings will be $30,000 (10% × $300,000), and the investment account balance at year-end will be $230,000 ($150,000 + $50,000 + $30,000).

Answer (A) is incorrect because $170,000 results from subtracting the equity in Tot's earnings. Answer (B) is incorrect because $200,000 ignores the equity in Tot's earnings. Answer (D) is incorrect because $290,000 assumes Pare held a 30% interest throughout the year.

51. On July 1, year 1, Denver Corp. purchased 3,000 shares of Eagle Co.'s 10,000 outstanding shares of common stock for $20 per share. On December 15, year 1, Eagle paid $40,000 in dividends to its common shareholders. Eagle's net income for the year ended December 31, year 1 was $120,000, earned evenly throughout the year. In its year 1 income statement, what amount of income from this investment should Denver report?

A. $36,000

B. $18,000

C. $12,000

D. $6,000

Answer (B) is correct. *(CPA, adapted)*

REQUIRED: The income reported from an investment in common stock.

DISCUSSION: Denver Corp.'s purchase of 30% of Eagle presumably allows it to exercise significant influence. Hence, it should apply the equity method. The investor's share of the investee's income is a function of the percentage of ownership and the length of time the investment was held. The income from this investment was therefore $18,000 [$120,000 × .30 × (6 ÷ 12)].

Answer (A) is incorrect because $36,000 assumes Denver owned the stock for the full year. Answer (C) is incorrect because $12,000 equals 30% of the dividend. Dividends do not affect income under the equity method. Answer (D) is incorrect because $6,000 equals 50% of 30% of the dividends.

52. Pear Co.'s income statement for the year ended December 31, year 1, as prepared by Pear's controller, reported income before taxes of $125,000. The auditor questioned the following amounts that had been included in income before taxes:

Equity in earnings of Cinn Co.	$40,000
Dividends received from Cinn	8,000
Adjustments to profits of prior years for arithmetical errors in depreciation	(35,000)

Pear owns 40% of Cinn's common stock. Pear's December 31, year 1 income statement should report income before taxes of

A. $85,000

B. $117,000

C. $120,000

D. $152,000

Answer (D) is correct. *(CPA, adapted)*

REQUIRED: The amount reported as income before taxes on the income statement.

DISCUSSION: Under the equity method, the investor's share of the investee's net income is accounted for as an addition to the carrying amount of the investment, and losses and dividends are reflected as reductions. Consequently, the equity in earnings of Cinn Co. was correctly included in income, but the dividends received should have been excluded. In addition, error corrections related to earlier periods are treated as prior-period adjustments and are not included in net income. Thus, income before taxes should have been $152,000 ($125,000 – $8,000 dividends + $35,000 depreciation error).

Answer (A) is incorrect because $85,000 subtracts the equity in earnings of Cinn Co. and includes the dividends and the effects of the prior-period adjustment. Answer (B) is incorrect because $117,000 includes the prior-period adjustment. Answer (C) is incorrect because $120,000 equals the computed income, minus the equity in the earnings of Cinn, plus the depreciation error.

53. Band Co. uses the equity method to account for its investment in Guard, Inc. common stock. How should Band record a 2% stock dividend received from Guard?

A. As dividend revenue at Guard's carrying amount of the stock.

B. As dividend revenue at the market value of the stock.

C. As a reduction in the total cost of Guard stock owned.

D. As a memorandum entry reducing the unit cost of all Guard stock owned.

Answer (D) is correct. *(CPA, adapted)*

REQUIRED: The entry to record a stock dividend received from an equity investee.

DISCUSSION: No entries are made to record the receipt of stock dividends. However, a memorandum entry should be made in the investment account to record additional shares owned. This treatment applies whether the investment is accounted for by the fair-value method or the equity method.

Answer (A) is incorrect because the receipt of a stock dividend is not a revenue. The shareholder has the same proportionate interest in the investee. Answer (B) is incorrect because the receipt of a stock dividend is not a revenue. The shareholder has the same proportionate interest in the investee. Answer (C) is incorrect because the cost per share, not the total cost, is reduced.

10.4 Financial Instrument Disclosures

54. According to SFAS 107, *Disclosures about Fair Value of Financial Instruments*, which of the following is a financial instrument?

A. Merchandise inventory.

B. Deferred subscription revenue.

C. A note payable in U.S. Treasury bonds.

D. A warranty payable.

Answer (C) is correct. *(Publisher)*

REQUIRED: The item meeting the definition of a financial instrument.

DISCUSSION: SFAS 107 defines a financial instrument as cash, evidence of an ownership interest in an entity, or a contract that both (1) imposes on one entity a contractual obligation (a) to deliver cash or another financial instrument to a second entity or (b) to exchange financial instruments on potentially unfavorable terms with the second entity, and (2) conveys to that second entity a contractual right (a) to receive cash or another financial instrument from the first entity or (b) to exchange other financial instruments on potentially favorable terms with the first entity. A note payable in U.S. Treasury bonds gives the holder the contractual right to receive and imposes on the issuer the contractual obligation to deliver bonds that are themselves financial instruments. Thus, given that one entity has a contractual obligation to deliver another financial instrument and the second entity has a contractual right to receive another financial instrument, the note payable in U.S. Treasury bonds meets the definition of a financial instrument.

Answer (A) is incorrect because, although the sale of inventory could result in the receipt of cash, the holder of the inventory has no current contractual right to receive cash. Answer (B) is incorrect because this obligation will result in the delivery of goods or services. Answer (D) is incorrect because this obligation will result in the delivery of goods or services.

55. Whether recognized or unrecognized in an entity's financial statements, disclosure of the fair values of the entity's financial instruments is required when

A. It is practicable to estimate those values.

B. The entity maintains accurate cost records.

C. Aggregated fair values are material to the entity.

D. Individual fair values are material to the entity.

Answer (A) is correct. *(CPA, adapted)*

REQUIRED: The circumstances in which disclosure of the fair values of the entity's financial instruments is required.

DISCUSSION: SFAS 107, *Disclosures about Fair Value of Financial Instruments*, as amended by SFAS 133, requires certain entities to disclose the fair value of financial instruments, whether or not they are recognized in the balance sheet, if it is practicable to estimate such fair values. If estimating fair value is not practicable, disclosures include information pertinent to estimating the fair value of the financial instrument or class of financial instruments, such as the carrying amount, effective interest rate, and maturity. The reasons that estimating the fair value is not practicable should also be disclosed.

Answer (B) is incorrect because the disclosure requirement is based on a practicability standard, not record keeping. Answer (C) is incorrect because the disclosure requirement is based on a practicability standard, not materiality. Answer (D) is incorrect because the disclosure requirement is based on a practicability standard, not materiality.

56. Disclosure of information about significant concentrations of credit risk is required for

A. Most financial instruments.

B. Financial instruments with off-balance-sheet credit risk only.

C. Financial instruments with off-balance-sheet market risk only.

D. Financial instruments with off-balance-sheet risk of accounting loss only.

Answer (A) is correct. *(CPA, adapted)*

REQUIRED: The financial instruments for which disclosure of significant concentrations of credit risk is required.

DISCUSSION: SFAS 107 requires the disclosure of information about the fair value of financial instruments, whether recognized or not (certain nonpublic entities and certain instruments, such as leases and insurance contracts, are exempt from the disclosure requirements). In accordance with an amendment by SFAS 133, SFAS 107 also requires disclosure of all significant concentrations of credit risk for most financial instruments (except for obligations for deferred compensation, certain instruments of a pension plan, insurance contracts, warranty obligations and rights, and unconditional purchase obligations).

10.5 Derivatives and Hedges

57. To the extent the hedge is effective, a loss arising from the decrease in fair value of a derivative is included in current earnings if the derivative qualifies and is designated as a

	Fair-value Hedge	Cash-flow Hedge
A.	Yes	No
B.	No	Yes
C.	Yes	Yes
D.	No	No

Answer (A) is correct. *(Publisher)*

REQUIRED: The treatment of a loss arising from a decrease in fair value of a derivative qualified and designated as either a fair-value or a cash-flow hedge.

DISCUSSION: A fair-value hedge includes a hedge of an exposure to changes in the fair value of a recognized asset or liability or of an unrecognized firm commitment. Changes in both (1) the fair value of a derivative that qualifies and is designated as a fair-value hedge and (2) the fair value of the hedged item attributable to the hedged risk are included in earnings in the period of change. Thus, the net effect on earnings is limited to the ineffective portion, i.e., the difference between the changes in fair value. A cash-flow hedge includes a hedge of an exposure to variability in the cash flows of a recognized asset or liability or a forecasted transaction. Changes in the fair value of a derivative that qualifies and is designated as a cash-flow hedge are recognized as a component of other comprehensive income to the extent the hedge is effective. The ineffective portion of the hedge is recognized in current earnings. The changes accumulated in other comprehensive income are reclassified to earnings in the period(s) the hedged transaction affects earnings. For example, accumulated amounts related to a forecasted purchase of equipment are reclassified as the equipment is depreciated.

58. Garcia Corporation has entered into a binding agreement with Hernandez Company to purchase 400,000 pounds of Colombian coffee at $2.53 per pound for delivery in 90 days. This contract is accounted for as a

A. Financial instrument.

B. Firm commitment.

C. Forecasted transaction.

D. Fair value hedge

Answer (B) is correct. *(Publisher)*

REQUIRED: The type of transaction defined.

DISCUSSION: A firm commitment is an agreement with an unrelated party, binding on both parties and usually legally enforceable, that specifies all significant terms and includes a disincentive for nonperformance.

Answer (A) is incorrect because a financial instrument does not involve the delivery of a product. Answer (C) is incorrect because a forecasted transaction is a transaction that is expected to occur for which no firm commitment exists. Answer (D) is incorrect because the transaction does not hedge an exposure to risk.

59. Herbert Corporation was a party to the following transactions during November and December of the current year. Which of these transactions most likely resulted in an investment in a derivative subject to the accounting prescribed by SFAS 133, *Accounting for Derivative Instruments and Hedging Activities*?

A. Purchased 1,000 shares of common stock of a public corporation for cash based on the assumption that the stock would increase in value.

B. Purchased a term life insurance policy on the company's chief executive officer to protect the company from the effects of an untimely demise of this officer.

C. Agreed to cosign the note of its 100%-owned subsidiary to protect the lender from the possibility that the subsidiary might default on the loan.

D. Based on its forecasted need to purchase 300,000 bushels of wheat in 3 months, entered into a 3-month forward contract to purchase 300,000 bushels of wheat to protect itself from changes in wheat prices during the period.

Answer (D) is correct. *(Publisher)*

REQUIRED: The transaction resulting in an investment in a derivative instrument.

DISCUSSION: SFAS 133 defines a derivative as a financial instrument or other contract that (1) has (a) one or more underlyings and (b) one or more notional amounts or payment provisions, or both; (2) requires either no initial net investment or an immaterial net investment; and (3) requires or permits net settlement. An underlying may be a specified interest rate, security price, commodity price, foreign exchange rate, index of prices or rates, or other variable. A notional amount is a number of currency units, shares, bushels, pounds, or other units specified. Settlement of a derivative is based on the interaction of the notional amount and the underlying. The purchase of the forward contract as a hedge of a forecasted need to purchase wheat meets the criteria prescribed by SFAS 133.

Answer (A) is incorrect because this stock purchase involves an initial net investment equal to the fair value of the stock. Answer (B) is incorrect because traditional life insurance contracts are exempt from the provisions of SFAS 133. Answer (C) is incorrect because financial guarantees are exempt from the provisions of SFAS 133.

60. On October 1, year 1, Bordeaux, Inc., a calendar year-end firm, invested in a derivative designed to hedge the risk of changes in fair value of certain assets, currently valued at $1.5 million. The derivative is structured to result in an effective hedge. However, some ineffectiveness may result. On December 31, year 1, the fair value of the hedged assets has decreased by $350,000; the fair value of the derivative has increased by $325,000. Bordeaux should recognize a net effect on year 1 earnings of

A. $0

B. $25,000

C. $325,000

D. $350,000

Answer (B) is correct. *(Publisher)*

REQUIRED: The net effect on earnings of a partially effective hedge of changes in fair value of a recognized asset.

DISCUSSION: A hedge of an exposure to changes in the fair value of a recognized asset or liability is classified as a fair value hedge. Gains and losses arising from changes in fair value of a derivative classified as a fair value hedge are included in the determination of earnings in the period of change. They are offset by losses or gains on the hedged item attributable to the risk being hedged. Thus, earnings of the period of change are affected only by the net gain or loss attributable to the ineffective aspect of the hedge. The ineffective portion is equal to $25,000 ($350,000 – $325,000).

61. At the beginning of period 1, Forecast Corporation enters into a qualifying cash flow hedge of a transaction it expects to occur at the beginning of period 4. Forecast assesses hedge effectiveness by comparing the change in present value (PV) of the expected cash flows associated with the forecasted transaction with all of the hedging derivative's gain or loss (change in fair value). The change in those cash flows that occurs for any reason has been designated as the hedged risk. The following information about the periodic changes hedging relationship is available:

Period	Change in Fair Value of the Derivative	Change in PV of Expected Cash Flows from the Forecasted Transaction
1	$50,000	$(48,000)
2	47,000	(51,000)
3	(81,000)	80,000

Given that the hedge is effective to the extent it offsets the change in the present value of the expected cash flows on the forecasted transaction, Forecast should

A. Recognize a loss of $2,000 in earnings for period 1.

B. Report a balance in other comprehensive income (OCI) of $16,000 at the end of period 3.

C. Recognize a gain of $47,000 in earnings for period 2.

D. Record other comprehensive income of $97,000 for period 2.

Answer (B) is correct. *(Publisher)*

REQUIRED: The appropriate accounting for a cash flow hedge of a forecasted transaction.

DISCUSSION: The effective portion of a cash flow hedge of a forecasted transaction is included in OCI until periods in which the forecasted transaction affects earnings. At the end of period 3, the net change in the hedging derivative's fair value is $16,000 ($50,000 + $47,000 – $81,000), and the change in the PV of the expected cash flows on the forecasted transaction is $(19,000) ($80,000 – $48,000 – $51,000). Thus, the hedge is effective at the end of period 3 to the extent it offsets $16,000 of the net $19,000 decrease in the cash flows of the forecasted transaction that are expected to occur in period 4.

Answer (A) is incorrect because Forecast should recognize earnings for period 1 of $2,000. The increase in fair value of the derivative exceeds the decrease in PV of the cash flows by $2,000. The derivative is adjusted to fair value by a $50,000 debit, OCI is credited for $48,000, and earnings is credited for $2,000. Answer (C) is incorrect because the entry for period 2 is to debit the derivative for $47,000, debit earnings for $2,000, and credit OCI for $49,000 ($50,000 + $47,000 – $48,000 credit in period 1). At the end of period 2, OCI should have a credit balance of $97,000 (the extent of the hedge's effectiveness). Answer (D) is incorrect because the entry for period 2 is to debit the derivative for $47,000, debit earnings for $2,000, and credit OCI for $49,000 ($50,000 + $47,000 – $48,000 credit in period 1). At the end of period 2, OCI should have a credit balance of $97,000 (the extent of the hedge's effectiveness).

Questions 62 and 63 are based on the following information. As part of its risk management strategy, a copper mining company sells futures contracts to hedge changes in fair value of its inventory. On March 12, the commodity exchange spot price is $0.81/lb.; the futures price for mid-June is $0.83/lb. On that date, the company, a calendar year-end firm, sells 200 futures contracts on the commodity exchange at $0.83/lb. for delivery in June. Each contract is for 25,000 lbs. The company designates these contracts as a fair-value hedge of 5 million lbs. of current inventory for which a mid-June sale is expected. The average cost of this inventory is $0.58/lb. The company documents (1) the hedging relationship between the futures contracts and its inventory, (2) its objectives and strategy for undertaking the hedge, and (3) its conclusion that the hedging relationship will be highly effective. On March 31, the mid-June commodity exchange futures price is $0.85/lb.

62. In the March 31 statement of financial position, the company should record the value of the futures contracts as a(n)

A. $100,000 asset.

B. $100,000 liability.

C. $4,250,000 liability.

D. $4,250,000 asset.

Answer (B) is correct. *(Publisher)*

REQUIRED: The amount at which the futures contracts should be recorded on the March 31 statement of financial position.

DISCUSSION: SFAS 133 requires that derivative instruments be recorded as assets and liabilities and measured at fair value. At March 12, the inception of the futures contracts, the fair value of the futures contracts was $0 because the contracts were entered into at the futures price at that date. On March 31, the fair value of the futures contract is equal to the change in the futures price between the inception price and the March 31 price. Given that the futures contracts created an obligation to deliver 5 million lbs. (25,000 lbs. × 200 contracts) of copper at $0.83/lb. and that the price had risen to $0.85/lb. at the date of the financial statements, the company should record a loss and a liability of $100,000 [5 million lbs. × ($0.83 – $0.85)].

Answer (A) is incorrect because the futures contracts should be recorded as a liability. Answer (C) is incorrect because the contracts should be measured at the $100,000 change in the futures price rather than at the March 31 futures price. Answer (D) is incorrect because the futures contracts should be recorded as a liability, and the contracts should be measured at the $100,000 change in the futures price rather than at the March 31 futures price.

63. If, on March 31, the company concluded that the hedge was 100% effective, the company should record the value of the hedged copper inventory in the March 31 statement of financial position at

A. $4,350,000

B. $4,250,000

C. $3,000,000

D. $2,900,000

Answer (C) is correct. *(Publisher)*
REQUIRED: The amount at which the hedged copper inventory should be recorded on the statement of financial position.
DISCUSSION: For a fair-value hedge, changes in the fair value of the hedged item attributable to the hedged risk are reflected as adjustments to the carrying amount of the hedged recognized asset or liability or the previously unrecognized firm commitment on the statement of financial position. The adjustments to carrying amount are accounted for in the same manner as other components of the carrying amount of the asset or liability. Thus the inventory should be recorded at $3,000,000 [(5 million lbs. × $0.58) original cost + $100,000 gain in fair value].

10.6 Impairment of a Loan

64. SFAS 114, *Accounting by Creditors for Impairment of a Loan*, requires recognition of an impairment when it is probable that a creditor will be unable to collect

	Contractual Principal Payments	Contractual Interest Payments
A.	Yes	No
B.	Yes	Yes
C.	No	Yes
D.	No	No

Answer (B) is correct. *(Publisher)*
REQUIRED: The payments the noncollection of which justify recognition of impairment of a loan.
DISCUSSION: SFAS 114 requires a creditor to recognize impairment of a loan when it is probable that the creditor will not be able to collect all amounts due in accordance with the terms of the loan. All amounts include both principal and interest payments.

65. Which of the following may be used to measure impairment of a loan?

I. Observable market price
II. Present value of future cash flows discounted at the loan's effective interest rate
III. Present value of future cash flows discounted at the loan's current market interest rate

A. Both I and II.

B. Both I and III.

C. II only.

D. III only.

Answer (A) is correct. *(Publisher)*
REQUIRED: The measure(s) of the impairment of a loan.
DISCUSSION: A creditor measures impairment of a loan based on the present value of expected future cash flows discounted at the loan's effective rate. As a practical expedient, however, a creditor may use the loan's observable market price or the fair value of the collateral if the value of the loan is collateral dependent.

10.7 Cash Surrender Value

66. An increase in the cash surrender value of a life insurance policy owned by a company is recorded by

A. Decreasing annual insurance expense.

B. Increasing investment income.

C. Recording a memorandum entry only.

D. Decreasing a deferred charge.

Answer (A) is correct. *(CPA, adapted)*
REQUIRED: The proper recording of an increase.
DISCUSSION: The cash surrender value of the policy is an asset of the company. Thus, part of the premium paid is not expense. As the cash surrender value increases, the annual insurance expense decreases.
Answer (B) is incorrect because investment income is not affected by life insurance. Answer (C) is incorrect because, as the cash surrender value increases, the annual insurance expense decreases. Answer (D) is incorrect because, as the cash surrender value increases, the annual insurance expense decreases.

67. On January 2, year 1, Beal, Inc. acquired a $70,000 whole-life insurance policy on its president. The annual premium is $2,000. The company is the owner and beneficiary. Beal charged officer's life insurance expense as follows:

Year	Life Insurance Expense
1	$2,000
2	1,800
3	1,500
4	1,100
Total	$6,400

In Beal's December 31, year 4 balance sheet, the investment in cash surrender value should be

A. $0

B. $1,600

C. $6,400

D. $8,000

Answer (B) is correct. *(CPA, adapted)*

REQUIRED: The investment in cash surrender value.

DISCUSSION: Cash surrender value is the loan value or surrender value of a whole-life insurance policy. It is equal to the difference between the premiums paid and the life insurance expense recognized. Because the total of premiums paid is $8,000 (4 years × $2,000) and the total life insurance expense is $6,400, the investment in cash surrender value is $1,600. This amount is classified as a noncurrent asset on a classified balance sheet because management purchases life insurance policies for the life insurance aspect rather than as a short-term investment.

Answer (A) is incorrect because the excess of the premiums over the expenses is the cash surrender value. Answer (C) is incorrect because $6,400 is the total insurance expense for 4 years. Answer (D) is incorrect because $8,000 is the sum of the premiums for 4 years.

68. In year 1, Chain, Inc. purchased a $1 million life insurance policy on its president, of which Chain is the beneficiary. Information regarding the policy for the year ended December 31, year 6 follows:

Cash surrender value, 1/1/year 6	$ 87,000
Cash surrender value, 12/31/year 6	108,000
Annual advance premium paid 1/1/year 6	40,000

During year 6, dividends of $6,000 were applied to increase the cash surrender value of the policy. What amount should Chain report as life insurance expense for year 6?

A. $40,000

B. $21,000

C. $19,000

D. $13,000

Answer (C) is correct. *(CPA, adapted)*

REQUIRED: The life insurance expense to be reported.

DISCUSSION: Life insurance expense is equal to the excess of the premiums paid over the increase in cash surrender value and dividends received. Because the dividends were applied to increase the cash surrender value, they were therefore not received. Hence, Chain's life insurance expense is $19,000.

Premium	$40,000
Less:	
Increase in cash surrender value ($108,000 – $87,000)	(21,000)
Life insurance expense	$19,000

Answer (A) is incorrect because $40,000 is the premium paid. Answer (B) is incorrect because $21,000 is the change in the cash surrender value. Answer (D) is incorrect because $13,000 results from subtracting the dividends applied.

69. In year 1, Gar Corp. collected $300,000 as beneficiary of a key person life insurance policy carried on the life of Gar's controller, who had died in year 1. The life insurance proceeds are not subject to income tax. At the date of the controller's death, the policy's cash surrender value was $90,000. What amount should Gar report as revenue in its year 1 income statement?

A. $0

B. $90,000

C. $210,000

D. $300,000

Answer (C) is correct. *(CPA, adapted)*

REQUIRED: The revenue reported from collection of life insurance.

DISCUSSION: Upon receipt of life insurance proceeds, cash is debited for the amount received. Cash surrender value is credited for the amount of the asset on the books, and the balancing credit is to insurance income (a revenue account). Hence, revenue equals $210,000 ($300,000 cash – $90,000 cash surrender value).

Answer (A) is incorrect because cash collected exceeded the asset. Answer (B) is incorrect because $90,000 is the cash surrender value. Answer (D) is incorrect because $300,000 equals the cash collected.

STUDY UNIT ELEVEN
CURRENT LIABILITIES, COMPENSATED ABSENCES, AND CONTINGENCIES

Current liabilities, as defined under **ARB 43**, Chapter 3A, include those obligations that are expected to be satisfied by the (1) payment of cash, (2) use of current assets other than cash, or (3) creation of new current liabilities within 1 year from the balance sheet date (or operating cycle, if longer). Thus, current liabilities include obligations to pay for items to be used in producing goods or providing services (e.g., accounts payable); obligations to pay for operations directly related to the operating cycle (e.g., wages payable, taxes payable); collections in advance of delivering goods or providing services (e.g., deferred rent revenue); and other obligations, satisfaction of which is expected to occur within 1 year (or **operating cycle**, if longer) from the balance sheet date (e.g., short-term debt, current portion of long-term debt, payments required under sinking-fund requirements, and agency obligations).

Current liabilities also include (1) obligations whose terms render or will render them **due on demand** within 1 year (or the operating cycle, if longer) even though their liquidation may not be expected during that year (or operating cycle, if longer) and (2) long-term obligations that are, or will be, **callable** at the balance sheet date because the debtor has violated a provision of the debt agreement, and it is not cured within any specified grace period. However, such long-term obligations are not classified as current liabilities if either the creditor has waived or subsequently lost the right to demand repayment for more than 1 year (or operating cycle, if longer), or it is probable that the violation will be cured during a grace period. Furthermore, current liabilities do not include (1) obligations that are expected to be satisfied using **noncurrent assets** and (2) short-term obligations that an enterprise intends, and has demonstrated the ability, to **refinance on a long-term basis**.

In addition to being classified in accordance with the substance of the transactions affecting them, **current liabilities may be classified** based on whether (1) the liabilities are definite or contingent (e.g., accounts payable are definite; warranty payables are contingent); (2) the values of the liabilities are known or must be estimated (e.g., wages payable are known; warranties payable are estimated); and (3) the identities of the creditors are known or yet to be known (e.g., accounts payable creditors are known; the specific creditors who will make claims under a warranty are not known until they do so).

A **warranty** is a written guarantee of the integrity of a product or service and an undertaking by the seller to repair or replace a product, refund all or part of the price, or provide additional service. It is customarily offered for a limited time, such as 90 days. A warranty may or may not be separable from the product or service. When the **warranty is not separable**, the liability is treated as a loss contingency. Hence, the criteria for accrual of a loss contingency stated in SFAS 5 apply. If incurrence of warranty expense is probable, the amount can be reasonably estimated, and the amount is material, accrual accounting methods should be used. Otherwise, warranty expense should be recorded as incurred, that is, on the cash basis. The accounting for **separately extended warranty and product maintenance contracts** applies when the contract is separately priced. Revenue is deferred and is ordinarily recognized on the straight-line basis over the term of the contract. Costs are not deferred and amortized unless directly related. The main example is the cost of commissions. Furthermore, if service costs are not incurred on a straight-line basis, revenue recognition over the contract's term should be proportionate to the estimated service costs. Under **FASB Interpretation No. 45**, *Guarantor's Accounting and Disclosure Requirements for Guarantees, Including Indirect Guarantees of Indebtedness of Others*, a product warrantor (a guarantor) must **disclose** (1) its accounting policy, (2) its method of calculating the liability, and (3) a reconciliation of the changes in the total for the period. Also, other disclosures required by the Interpretation must be made except for the maximum potential amount of future payments.

Under **SFAS 6**, *Classification of Short-Term Obligations Expected to be Refinanced*, if an enterprise intends to refinance short-term obligations on a long-term basis and demonstrates an ability to consummate the refinancing, the obligation should be reclassified as **noncurrent**. The ability to consummate the refinancing may be demonstrated by a post-balance-sheet-date issuance of long-term obligations or equity securities. The ability to refinance may also be shown by entering into a financing agreement that meets the following criteria: (1) The agreement does not expire within the longer of 1 year or the operating cycle; (2) it is noncancelable by the lender; (3) no violation of the agreement exists at the balance sheet date; and (4) the lender is financially capable of honoring the agreement.

Compensated absences are absences from work (e.g., illness, vacations, holidays) for which employees will be paid. Under **SFAS 43**, *Accounting for Compensated Absences*, accrual of a liability for compensated absences is required when (1) the compensation relates to services already provided, (2) payment is probable, (3) the amount can be reasonably estimated, and (4) the benefits either vest or accumulate. However, accrual of compensated absences for **sick pay benefits** are required only if the benefits vest.

A **contingency** is an existing condition, situation, or set of circumstances involving uncertainty as to possible loss or gain to an enterprise that ultimately will be resolved when one or more future events occur or fail to occur. A loss (gain) contingency involves either a potentially overstated (understated) asset or a potentially understated (overstated) liability.

According to **SFAS 5**, *Accounting for Contingencies*, accrual of a contingent loss is required if information available prior to the issuance of financial statements indicates that it is **probable** that an asset is overstated or a liability is understated and the amount of the loss can be **reasonably estimated**. If the estimate of the loss is stated within a given range and an amount within that range is considered to be a better estimate than any other, that amount must be accrued. If no amount within the range is considered to be a better estimate than any other, the minimum of the range must be accrued. Disclosure of the nature of the loss also is required, and disclosure of the amount accrued is required if nondisclosure might make the financial statements misleading.

If the existence of a contingent loss is not both probable and reasonably estimable, but is at least **reasonably possible**, disclosure of the nature of the contingency and an estimate of the potential loss or range of loss, if available, are required. If an estimate cannot be made, the disclosure must include a statement to that effect.

Disclosure ordinarily is not required if the possibility of a loss is **remote**. However, disclosure of the nature and amount of remote contingencies involving **guarantees** is required, for example, (1) direct or indirect guarantees of the indebtedness of others, (2) obligations of commercial banks under standby letters of credit, and (3) guarantees to repurchase receivables that have been sold or otherwise assigned. **FASB Interpretation No. 45** states that the essence of a guarantee is a **noncontingent obligation** to be ready to perform after a triggering event or condition. It is coupled with a **contingent obligation** to make payments if such an event or condition occurs. Thus, recognition of a liability at the inception of a guarantee is required even when it is not probable that payments will be made. The **initial measurement** ordinarily is at **fair value**. If a contingent loss and liability also are required to be recognized under SFAS 5, the liability recognized by the guarantor is the greater of the fair value measurement or the contingent liability amount. However, the Interpretation does not address **subsequent measurement**. **Examples** are a stand-alone guarantee given for a premium (debit cash or a receivable), a stand-alone guarantee to an unrelated party without consideration (debit expense), or an operating (not a capital) lessee's guarantee of residual value (debit prepaid rent). However, the requirement for recognition of a noncontingent obligation does not apply to certain guarantees, e.g., product warranties, derivatives, or obligations payable in the guarantor's equity shares. The Interpretation requires many **disclosures**, such as the terms of the guarantee, how it arose, the triggering events, and maximum payments.

When a loss contingency involves an unasserted claim or assessment, neither accrual nor disclosure is required unless it is probable that a claim or assessment will be asserted. Also, **general or unspecified business risks** are not considered loss contingencies. Thus, no accrual or disclosure is required.

Contingent gains are not recognized until they are realized, but the existence of contingent gains must be disclosed. However, care should be taken to avoid misleading implications as to the likelihood of realization.

Under **SOP 96-1**, *Environmental Remediation Liabilities*, the liabilities are those measured under enacted laws and existing regulations and policies. Their measurement also depends on the technology expected to be approved to complete the remediation. This SOP applies the criteria stated in **SFAS 5**. The probability criterion is satisfied if commencement of litigation or the assertion of a claim or an assessment has occurred or, based on the available information, is probable. The available information should indicate that the litigation, claim, or assessment will probably have an unfavorable outcome. Factors considered in estimating costs are the extent and types of hazardous substances at a site, the available technologies, changes in standards of what is acceptable remediation, and the degree of responsibility and financial position of other **potentially responsible parties (PRPs)**. **Measurement** of the liability includes the entity's allocable share for a specific site plus its share of amounts that will not be paid by other PRPs or the government. The costs included are incremental direct costs and compensation and benefits of employees devoting significant time directly to remediation. The measurement is based on the entity's estimates of the costs of all elements of the remediation at the time they are expected to be performed. Discounting is permitted if the aggregate liability (or a component thereof) and the amount and timing of cash payments are reliably determinable.

QUESTIONS

11.1 Current Liabilities

1. Delhi Co. is preparing its financial statements for the year ended December 31, year 1. Accounts payable amounted to $360,000 before any necessary year-end adjustment related to the following:

- At December 31, year 1, Delhi has a $50,000 debit balance in its accounts payable to Madras, a supplier, resulting from a $50,000 advance payment for goods to be manufactured to Delhi's specifications.
- Checks in the amount of $100,000 were written to vendors and recorded on December 29, year 1. The checks were mailed on January 5, year 2.

What amount should Delhi report as accounts payable in its December 31, year 1 balance sheet?

A. $510,000

B. $410,000

C. $310,000

D. $210,000

Answer (A) is correct. *(CPA, adapted)*

REQUIRED: The amount of accounts payable reported after year-end adjustments.

DISCUSSION: The ending accounts payable balance should include amounts owed as of 12/31/year 1, on trade payables. Although Delhi wrote checks for $100,000 to various vendors, that amount should still be included in the accounts payable balance because the company had not surrendered control of the checks at year-end. The advance to the supplier was erroneously recorded as a reduction of (debit to) accounts payable. This amount should be recorded as a prepaid asset, and accounts payable should be credited (increased) by $50,000. Thus, accounts payable should be reported as $510,000 ($360,000 + $50,000 + $100,000).

Answer (B) is incorrect because $410,000 does not include the $100,000 in checks not yet mailed at year-end. Answer (C) is incorrect because $310,000 does not include the $100,000 in checks, and it reflects the subtraction, not the addition, of the $50,000 advance. Answer (D) is incorrect because $210,000 results from subtracting the advance payment and the checks.

2. Seoul Corp. had the following liabilities at December 31, year 1:

Accounts payable	$ 110,000
Unsecured notes, 8%, due 7/1/year 2	800,000
Accrued expenses	70,000
Contingent liability	900,000
Deferred income tax liability	50,000
Senior bonds, 7%, due 3/31/year 2	2,000,000

The contingent liability is an accrual for possible losses on a $2 million lawsuit filed against Seoul. Seoul's legal counsel expects the suit to be settled in year 3 and has estimated that Seoul will be liable for damages in the range of $900,000 to $1,500,000. The deferred income tax liability is not related to an asset for financial reporting and is expected to reverse in year 3. What amount should Seoul report in its December 31, year 1 balance sheet for current liabilities?

A. $1,015,000

B. $1,880,000

C. $2,980,000

D. $3,030,000

Answer (C) is correct. *(CPA, adapted)*

REQUIRED: The amount reported for current liabilities.

DISCUSSION: ARB 43, Chapter 3A, defines a current liability as an obligation that will be either liquidated using a current asset or replaced by another current liability. SFAS 78 amends ARB 43 to include the following as current liabilities: (1) obligations that, by their terms, are or will be due on demand within 1 year (or the operating cycle if longer) and (2) obligations that are or will be callable by the creditor within 1 year because of a violation of a debt covenant. Thus, the current liabilities are calculated as

Accounts payable	$ 110,000
Unsecured notes, 8%, due 7/1/year 2	800,000
Accrued expenses	70,000
Senior bonds, 7%, due 3/31/year 2	2,000,000
	$2,980,000

Answer (A) is incorrect because $1,015,000 excludes the senior bonds due within 1 year and includes the deferred income tax liability that will not reverse within 1 year. Whether a deferred tax asset or liability is current depends on the classification of the related asset or liability. If it is not related to an asset or liability, the expected reversal date of the temporary difference determines the classification. Answer (B) is incorrect because $1,880,000 includes the contingent liability not expected to be settled until year 3 and excludes the senior bonds. Answer (D) is incorrect because $3,030,000 includes the deferred income tax liability not expected to reverse until year 3.

3. Wilk Co. reported the following liabilities at December 31, year 1:

Accounts payable-trade	$ 750,000
Short-term borrowings	400,000
Bank loan, current portion $100,000	3,500,000
Other bank loan, matures June 30, year 2	1,000,000

The bank loan of $3,500,000 was in violation of the loan agreement. The creditor had not waived the rights under the loan. What amount should Wilk report as current liabilities at December 31, year 1?

A. $1,250,000

B. $2,150,000

C. $2,250,000

D. $5,650,000

Answer (D) is correct. *(CPA, adapted)*

REQUIRED: The current liabilities to be reported at year-end.

DISCUSSION: SFAS 78 classifies obligations as liabilities when they are callable by the creditor within 1 year because of a violation of a debt covenant. Long-term debt need not be classified as current if it is probable that a violation existing at the balance sheet date will be cured within a specified grace period. Absent a probable cure of Wilk's violation of the long-term loan agreement, current liabilities to be reported at year-end are $5,650,000 ($750,000 trade payables + $400,000 short-term borrowings + $3,500,000 bank loan + $1,000,000 other bank loan due within 1 year).

Answer (A) is incorrect because both the entire $3,500,000 bank loan and the other bank loan must be included as current liabilities. Answer (B) is incorrect because the $3,500,000 bank loan must be included as a current liability. Answer (C) is incorrect because the entire $3,500,000 bank loan must be recorded as a current liability.

4. On March 31, year 1, Koala Co. received an advance payment of 60% of the sales price for special order goods to be manufactured and delivered within 5 months. At the same time, Koala subcontracted for production of the special-order goods at a price equal to 40% of the main contract price. What liabilities should be reported in Koala's March 31, year 1 balance sheet?

	Deferred Revenues	Payables to Subcontractor
A.	None	None
B.	60% of main contract price	40% of main contract price
C.	60% of main contract price	None
D.	None	40% of main contract price

Answer (C) is correct. *(CPA, adapted)*

REQUIRED: The liabilities to be reported in the balance sheet.

DISCUSSION: The 60% advance payment is a deferred revenue (liability) because it has been realized but not earned. The entity has not substantially accomplished what it must do to be entitled to the benefits represented by the prepayment. The agreement with the subcontractor does not create a liability because the entity has no current obligation to transfer assets or provide services. That obligation will not arise until the subcontractor has performed.

Answer (A) is incorrect because the 60% prepayment should be credited to deferred revenue. Answer (B) is incorrect because Koala has no liability to the subcontractor. Answer (D) is incorrect because the 60% prepayment should be credited to deferred revenue, and Koala has no liability to the subcontractor.

5. Nepal Co. requires advance payments with special orders for machinery constructed to customer specifications. These advances are nonrefundable. Information for year 2 is as follows:

Customer advances--balance 12/31/year 1	$236,000
Advances received with orders in year 2	368,000
Advances applied to orders shipped in year 2	328,000
Advances applicable to orders canceled in year 2	100,000

In Nepal's December 31, year 2 balance sheet, what amount should be reported as a current liability for advances from customers?

A. $0

B. $176,000

C. $276,000

D. $296,000

Answer (B) is correct. *(CPA, adapted)*

REQUIRED: The current liability for advances.

DISCUSSION: The amount of $176,000 ($236,000 beginning balance + $368,000 advances received – $328,000 advances credited to revenue after shipment of orders – $100,000 for canceled orders) should be reported as a current liability for customer advances. Deposits or other advance payments are liabilities because they involve a probable future sacrifice of economic benefits arising from a current obligation. The advances applicable to canceled orders are not refundable. Thus, no future sacrifice of economic benefits is necessary.

Answer (A) is incorrect because deposits or other advance payments should be recognized as liabilities. Answer (C) is incorrect because $276,000 includes $100,000 applicable to orders canceled. Answer (D) is incorrect because $296,000 results from subtracting advances received and adding advances applied to shipments and advances for canceled orders.

6. Harare Company maintains escrow accounts and pays real estate taxes for its mortgage customers. Escrow funds are kept in interest-bearing accounts. Interest, minus a 10% service fee, is credited to the customer's account and used to reduce future escrow payments. Additional information follows:

Escrow accounts liability, 1/1/year 1	$ 700,000
Escrow payments received during year 1	1,580,000
Real estate taxes paid during year 1	1,720,000
Interest on escrow funds during year 1	50,000

What amount should Harare report as escrow accounts liability in its December 31, year 1 balance sheet?

A. $510,000

B. $515,000

C. $605,000

D. $610,000

Answer (C) is correct. *(CPA, adapted)*

REQUIRED: The amount of escrow accounts liability.

DISCUSSION: The liability at the beginning of the year was $700,000. Escrow payments of $1,580,000 were credited and taxes paid of $1,720,000 were debited to the account during the year. Furthermore, interest of $45,000 [$50,000 – (10% × $50,000) service fee] was credited. Thus, the year-end balance was $605,000 ($700,000 + $1,580,000 – $1,720,000 + $45,000).

Answer (A) is incorrect because $510,000 results from debiting $50,000 rather than crediting $45,000. Answer (B) is incorrect because $515,000 results from debiting $45,000 rather than crediting $45,000. Answer (D) is incorrect because $610,000 omits the adjustment for the service fee.

7. On July 1, year 1, Wessex County issued real estate tax assessments for its fiscal year ended June 30, year 2. On September 1, year 1, Milan Co. purchased a warehouse in Wessex County. The purchase price was reduced by a credit for accrued realty taxes. Milan did not record the entire year's real estate tax obligation, but instead records tax expenses at the end of each month by adjusting prepaid real estate taxes or real estate taxes payable, as appropriate. On November 1, year 1, Milan paid the first of two equal installments of $24,000 for real estate taxes. What amount of this payment should Milan record as a debit to real estate taxes payable?

A. $8,000

B. $16,000

C. $20,000

D. $24,000

Answer (B) is correct. *(CPA, adapted)*

REQUIRED: The amount to be debited to real estate taxes payable.

DISCUSSION: The credit balance in real estate taxes payable at 11/1/year 1 is $16,000. This amount reflects accrued real estate taxes of $4,000 a month [(2 × $24,000) ÷ 12 months] for 4 months (July through October). This payable should be debited for $16,000 when the real estate taxes are paid.

Answer (A) is incorrect because the $8,000 includes real estate taxes for September and October only. Answer (C) is incorrect because $20,000 includes real estate taxes for November. Answer (D) is incorrect because $24,000 equals 6 months of real estate taxes.

8. Hudson Hotel collects 15% in city sales taxes on room rentals, in addition to a $2 per room, per night, occupancy tax. Sales taxes for each month are due at the end of the following month, and occupancy taxes are due 15 days after the end of each calendar quarter. On January 3, year 2, Hudson paid its November year 1 sales taxes and its fourth quarter year 1 occupancy taxes. Additional information pertaining to Hudson's operations is

Year 1	Room Rentals	Room Nights
October	$100,000	1,100
November	110,000	1,200
December	150,000	1,800

What amounts should Hudson report as sales taxes payable and occupancy taxes payable in its December 31, year 1 balance sheet?

	Sales Taxes	Occupancy Taxes
A.	$39,000	$6,000
B.	$39,000	$8,200
C.	$54,000	$6,000
D.	$54,000	$8,200

Answer (B) is correct. *(CPA, adapted)*

REQUIRED: The sales taxes payable and occupancy taxes payable.

DISCUSSION: Hudson presumably paid its October sales taxes during year 1, but it did not pay sales taxes for November and December and occupancy taxes for October, November, and December until year 2. Consequently, it should accrue a liability for sales taxes in the amount of $39,000 [15% × ($110,000 November rentals + $150,000 December rentals)] and a liability for occupancy taxes in the amount of $8,200 [$2 × (1,100 + 1,200 + 1,800) room nights].

Answer (A) is incorrect because $6,000 excludes October room nights. Answer (C) is incorrect because $54,000 includes October room rentals, and $6,000 excludes October room nights. Answer (D) is incorrect because $54,000 includes October room rentals.

9. Florence Co.'s payroll for the month ended January 31 is summarized as follows:

Total wages	$10,000
Federal income tax withheld	1,200

All wages paid were subject to FICA taxes. Assume FICA tax rates were 7% each for employee and employer. Florence remits payroll taxes on the 15th of the following month. In its financial statements for the month ended January 31, what amounts should Florence report as total payroll tax liability and as payroll tax expense?

	Liability	Expense
A.	$1,200	$1,400
B.	$1,900	$1,400
C.	$1,900	$700
D.	$2,600	$700

Answer (D) is correct. *(CPA, adapted)*

REQUIRED: The amounts reported as total payroll tax liability and as payroll tax expense.

DISCUSSION: The payroll liability is $2,600 ($1,200 federal income tax withheld + $700 employer's FICA + $700 employees' FICA). The payroll tax expense consists of the employer's share of FICA. The employees' share is considered a withholding, not an expense.

Answer (A) is incorrect because $1,200 does not include employer and employee shares of current FICA taxes, and $1,400 includes the employees' share of FICA taxes. Answer (B) is incorrect because $1,900 does not include $700 of FICA taxes, and $1,400 includes the employees' share of FICA taxes. Answer (C) is incorrect because $1,900 does not include $700 of FICA taxes.

10. According to SFAS 78, *Classification of Obligations That Are Callable by the Creditor*, long-term obligations that are or will become callable by the creditor because of the debtor's violation of a provision of the debt agreement at the balance sheet date should be classified as

A. Long-term liabilities.

B. Current liabilities unless the creditor has waived the right to demand repayment for more than 1 year from the balance sheet date.

C. Contingent liabilities until the violation is corrected.

D. Current liabilities unless it is reasonably possible that the violation will be corrected within the grace period.

Answer (B) is correct. *(CMA, adapted)*

REQUIRED: The proper classification of long-term debt callable by the creditor because of a violation of an agreement.

DISCUSSION: ARB 43, Chapter 3A, defines a current liability as an obligation that will be either liquidated using a current asset or replaced by another current liability. SFAS 78 amends ARB 43 to include as current liabilities (1) obligations that by their terms are or will be due on demand within 1 year (or the operating cycle, if longer) and (2) obligations that are or will be callable by the creditor within 1 year because of a violation of a debt covenant. An exception exists, however, if the creditor has waived or subsequently lost the right to demand repayment for more than 1 year (or the operating cycle, if longer) from the balance sheet date.

Answer (A) is incorrect because this kind of obligation should be classified as a current liability. Answer (C) is incorrect because the liability is not contingent. Answer (D) is incorrect because the obligation may be classified as noncurrent if it is probable that the violation will be corrected within the grace period.

11. Sudan Co. sells major household appliance service contracts for cash. The service contracts are for a 1-year, 2-year, or 3-year period. Cash receipts from contracts are credited to unearned service contract revenues. This account had a balance of $1,440,000 at December 31, year 1 before year-end adjustment. Service contract costs are charged as incurred to the service contract expense account, which had a balance of $360,000 at December 31, year 1. Outstanding service contracts at December 31, year 1 expire as follows:

During year 2	$300,000
During year 3	450,000
During year 4	200,000

What amount should be reported as unearned service contract revenues in Sudan's December 31, year 1 balance sheet?

A. $1,080,000

B. $950,000

C. $590,000

D. $490,000

Answer (B) is correct. *(CPA, adapted)*

REQUIRED: The amount to be reported as unearned service contract revenues at year-end.

DISCUSSION: Unearned service contract revenues relate to outstanding contracts for which the agreed service has not yet been provided. Thus, the amount to be reported as unearned service contract revenues is the $950,000 ($300,000 + $450,000 + $200,000) of service contracts outstanding at 12/31/year 1.

Answer (A) is incorrect because $1,080,000 is the difference between the unearned service contract revenue before adjustment and the balance in the service contract expense account. Answer (C) is incorrect because $590,000 is the difference between the $360,000 balance in service contract expense and the $950,000 of unearned service contract revenue reported in the 12/31/year 1 balance sheet. Answer (D) is incorrect because $490,000 is the change in the unearned service contract revenue account ($1,440,000 – $950,000).

12. On January 3, year 1, North Company issued long-term bonds due January 3, year 6. The bond covenant includes a call provision that is effective if the firm's current ratio falls below 2:1. On June 30, year 1, the fiscal year-end for the company, its current ratio was 1.5:1. The bonds should be reported on the financial statements as a

A. Long-term debt because their maturity date is January 3, year 6.

B. Long-term debt if it is reasonably possible that North can cure the covenant violation before the end of any allowed grace period.

C. Current liability if the covenant violation is not cured.

D. Current liability, regardless of any action by the bondholder, because the company was in violation of the covenant on the balance sheet date.

Answer (C) is correct. *(R.B. Posey)*

REQUIRED: The proper classification of callable obligations.

DISCUSSION: SFAS 78, *Classification of Obligations That Are Callable by the Creditor*, states that long-term obligations that are callable by the creditor because of the debtor's violation of the debt agreement at the balance sheet date shall be classified as current liabilities.

Answer (A) is incorrect because the violation of the debt agreement would allow the creditor to accelerate the maturity date. Answer (B) is incorrect because the debt should be classified as current unless it is probable that the violation will be cured within any grace period. Answer (D) is incorrect because a creditor's waiver of the right to demand repayment of the debt would allow North to classify the bonds as long-term.

11.2 Bonus and Profit Sharing

13. Karachi Corp. has an incentive compensation plan under which a branch manager receives 10% of the branch's income after deduction of the bonus but before deduction of income tax. Branch income for the year before the bonus and income tax was $165,000. The tax rate was 30%. The annual bonus amounted to

A. $11,907

B. $15,000

C. $16,500

D. $18,000

Answer (B) is correct. *(CPA, adapted)*

REQUIRED: The bonus computed on pretax income after deduction of the bonus.

DISCUSSION: The bonus is equal to 10% of the annual pretax income of $165,000 after the bonus has been deducted. Solving the equation given below, the bonus is equal to $15,000.

$$\begin{aligned} B &= .10(\$165{,}000 - B) \\ B &= \$16{,}500 - .1B \\ 1.1B &= \$16{,}500 \\ B &= \$15{,}000 \end{aligned}$$

Answer (A) is incorrect because $11,907 is the bonus computed on after-tax income, assuming the bonus is deducted to determine taxable income. Answer (C) is incorrect because $16,500 is 10% of the branch income before deducting the bonus and income taxes. Answer (D) is incorrect because $18,000 is 10% of the sum of pretax, pre-bonus branch income plus the bonus.

14. Alpha, Inc. has a bonus plan covering all employees. The total bonus is equal to 10% of Alpha's preliminary (prebonus, pretax) income reduced by the income tax (computed on the preliminary income minus the bonus itself). Alpha's preliminary income for the year is $200,000, and the income tax rate is 40%. How much is the bonus for the year?

A. $12,000

B. $12,500

C. $18,818

D. $20,000

Answer (B) is correct. *(CPA, adapted)*

REQUIRED: The amount of a bonus computed on after-tax income before deducting the bonus.

DISCUSSION: The problem requires setting up simultaneous equations because it has two unknowns, the bonus and the tax. Set the tax (T) equal to 40% of income of $200,000 minus the bonus. Set the bonus (B) equal to 10% of the $200,000 income minus taxes. Solve for T and then substitute the resulting value for T in the bonus equation.

$$\begin{aligned} T &= .4(\$200{,}000 - B) \\ T &= \$80{,}000 - .4B \\ B &= .1(\$200{,}000 - T) \\ B &= \$20{,}000 - .1(\$80{,}000 - .4B) \\ B &= \$12{,}000 + .04B \\ .96B &= \$12{,}000 \\ B &= \$12{,}500 \end{aligned}$$

Answer (A) is incorrect because $12,000 is 10% of the difference between preliminary income and 40% of preliminary income. Answer (C) is incorrect because $18,818 equals 10% of the difference between preliminary income and the bonus. Answer (D) is incorrect because $20,000 is 10% of preliminary income.

11.3 Unredeemed Coupons/Premiums

15. A department store sells gift certificates that may be redeemed for merchandise. Each certificate expires 3 years after issuance. The revenue from the gift certificates should be recognized

A. Evenly over 3 years from the date of issuance.

B. In the period the certificates are sold.

C. In the period the certificates expire.

D. In the period the certificates are redeemed or in the period they expire if they are allowed to lapse.

Answer (D) is correct. *(CIA, adapted)*

REQUIRED: The timing of revenue recognition for gift certificates.

DISCUSSION: SFAC 5, *Recognition and Measurement in Financial Statements of Business Enterprises*, states that revenue should be recognized when realized or realizable and earned. Revenue from gift certificates is realized when the cash is received. It is earned when the certificates are redeemed or allowed to lapse. Thus, the criteria of being both realized and earned are satisfied when the certificates are redeemed or allowed to lapse.

16. Conch Shell Company sells gift certificates, redeemable for merchandise, that expire 1 year after their issuance. Conch Shell has the following information pertaining to its gift certificates sales and redemptions:

Unredeemed at 12/31/year 1	$150,000
Year 2 sales	500,000
Year 2 redemptions of prior-year sales	50,000
Year 2 redemptions of current-year sales	350,000

Conch Shell's experience indicates that 10% of gift certificates sold will not be redeemed. In its December 31, year 2 balance sheet, what amount should Conch Shell report as unearned revenue?

A. $250,000

B. $200,000

C. $150,000

D. $100,000

Answer (D) is correct. *(CPA, adapted)*

REQUIRED: The amount reported as unearned revenue at year-end.

DISCUSSION: Because the certificates expire after 1 year, all revenue from sales prior to year 2 has been earned. Hence, the unearned revenue balance for gift certificate sales at the end of year 2 relates solely to year 2 sales. Given year 2 sales of $500,000 and redemptions of $350,000, $150,000 of certificates are unredeemed at year-end. However, 10% of total certificates sold in year 2 (10% × $500,000 = $50,000) are not expected to be redeemed. Accordingly, unearned revenue is $100,000 ($150,000 – $50,000).

Answer (A) is incorrect because $250,000 is the sum of the beginning and ending balances. Answer (B) is incorrect because $200,000 assumes that none of the certificates reflected in the beginning balance have lapsed but that 10% of the certificates sold in year 2 are expected to lapse. Answer (C) is incorrect because $150,000 does not consider the 10% of certificates sold in year 2 that are estimated not to be redeemed.

17. In June year 1, Haifa Retailers sold refundable merchandise coupons. Haifa received $10 for each coupon redeemable from July 1 to December 31, year 1 for merchandise with a retail price of $11. At June 30, year 1, how should Haifa report these coupon transactions?

A. Unearned revenues at the merchandise's retail price.

B. Unearned revenues at the cash received amount.

C. Revenues at the merchandise's retail price.

D. Revenues at the cash received amount.

Answer (B) is correct. *(CPA, adapted)*

REQUIRED: The proper reporting of refundable merchandise coupons.

DISCUSSION: Revenue should not be recognized until it is realized or realizable and earned. Because the earning process is not complete until the coupons lapse or are redeemed, an unearned revenue (liability) account should be credited at the time of sale for the amount received.

Answer (A) is incorrect because the transaction is measured at the amount received, not the nominal retail price. Answer (C) is incorrect because revenue should not be recognized until it is realized or realizable and earned. Answer (D) is incorrect because revenue should not be recognized until it is realized or realizable and earned.

18. Amman Company records stamp service revenue and provides for the cost of redemptions in the year stamps are sold to licensees. Amman's past experience indicates that only 80% of the stamps sold to licensees will be redeemed. Amman's liability for stamp redemptions was $6 million at December 31, year 1. Additional information for year 2 is as follows:

Stamp service revenue from stamps sold to licensees	$4,000,000
Cost of redemptions (stamps sold prior to 1/1/year 2)	2,750,000

If all the stamps sold in year 2 were presented for redemption in year 3, the redemption cost would be $2,250,000. What amount should Amman report as a liability for stamp redemptions at December 31, year 2?

A. $7,800,000

B. $5,500,000

C. $5,050,000

D. $3,250,000

Answer (C) is correct. *(CPA, adapted)*

REQUIRED: The reported liability for stamp redemptions at year-end.

DISCUSSION: The liability for stamp redemptions at the beginning of year 2 is given as $6 million. This liability would be increased in year 2 by $2.25 million if all stamps sold in year 2 were presented for redemption. However, because only 80% are expected to be redeemed, the liability should be increased by $1,800,000 ($2,250,000 × 80%). The liability was decreased by the $2,750,000 attributable to the costs of redemptions. Thus, the liability for stamp redemptions at 12/31/year 2 is $5,050,000 ($6,000,000 + $1,800,000 – $2,750,000).

Answer (A) is incorrect because $7,800,000 omits the year 2 redemptions from the calculation. Answer (B) is incorrect because $5,500,000 assumes a 100% redemption rate. Answer (D) is incorrect because $3,250,000 omits the expected year 3 redemptions from the calculation.

19. Negev Co. frequently distributes coupons to promote a new product. On October 1, year 1, Negev mailed 1 million coupons for $.90 off each box of the product purchased. Negev expects 240,000 of these coupons to be redeemed before the December 31, year 1 expiration date. It takes 30 days from the redemption date for Negev to receive the coupons from the retailers. Negev reimburses the retailers an additional $.10 for each coupon redeemed. As of December 31, year 1, Negev had paid retailers $100,000 related to these coupons and had 100,000 coupons on hand that had not been processed for payment. What amount should Negev report as a liability for coupons in its December 31, year 1 balance sheet?

A. $140,000

B. $116,000

C. $100,000

D. $90,000

Answer (A) is correct. *(CPA, adapted)*

REQUIRED: The liability for coupons at year-end.

DISCUSSION: The company pays $1.00 ($.90 + $.10) for the redemption of a coupon, and it expects 240,000 to be redeemed at a total cost of $240,000 (240,000 × $1.00). Given that payments of $100,000 have been made, the liability at year-end must be $140,000 ($240,000 – $100,000). The cost associated with the unprocessed coupons on hand does not reduce the liability because payment for these coupons has not yet been made.

Answer (B) is incorrect because $29,000 ignores the additional $.05 per coupon paid to retailers. Answer (C) is incorrect because $100,000 is the cost of the coupons on hand that have not yet been processed for payment. Negev expects to receive additional redeemed coupons for 30 days after the balance sheet date. Answer (D) is incorrect because $90,000 equals $.90 times 100,000 coupons.

20. In packages of its products, the Kirghiz Company includes coupons that may be presented to grocers for discounts of certain products on or before a stated expiration date. The grocers are reimbursed when they send the coupons to Kirghiz. In the company's experience, 40% of such coupons are redeemed, and 1 month usually elapses between the date a grocer receives a coupon from a consumer and the date Kirghiz receives it. During year 1, Kirghiz issued two series of coupons as follows:

Issued on	Total Face Amount	Consumer Expiration Date	Amount Disbursed as of 12/31/year 1
1/1/year 1	$100,000	6/30/year 1	$34,000
7/1/year 1	120,000	12/31/year 1	40,000

The company's December 31, year 1 balance sheet should include a liability for unredeemed coupons of

A. $0

B. $8,000

C. $14,000

D. $48,000

Answer (B) is correct. *(CPA, adapted)*

REQUIRED: The year-end liability for unredeemed coupons.

DISCUSSION: No liability should be reported for unredeemed coupons at December 31 with regard to the coupons issued on 1/1/year 1 because more than 1 month has elapsed since their expiration date. The total estimated liability for the coupons issued on 7/1/year 1 is equal to $48,000 (40% × $120,000 total face amount of coupons issued) minus the $40,000 disbursed as of 12/31/year 1. Consequently, the liability is $8,000 ($48,000 – $40,000).

Answer (A) is incorrect because the amount disbursed was less than the total estimated liability. Answer (C) is incorrect because $14,000 assumes that less than 1 month has elapsed since the expiration date of the coupons issued on 1/1/year 1. Answer (D) is incorrect because $48,000 is the total estimated liability for the coupons issued on 7/1/year 1.

11.4 Warranties

21. Kamchatka sells a durable good to a customer on January 1, year 1, and the customer is automatically given a 1-year warranty. The customer also buys an extended warranty package, extending the coverage for an additional 2 years to the end of year 3. At the time of the original sale, the company expects warranty costs to be incurred evenly over the life of the warranty contracts. The customer has only one warranty claim during the 3-year period, and the claim occurs during year 2. The company will recognize revenue from the sale of the extended warranty

A. On January 1, year 1.

B. In years 2 and 3.

C. At the time of the claim in year 2.

D. December 31, year 3, when the warranty expires.

Answer (B) is correct. *(CIA, adapted)*

REQUIRED: The recognition of revenue from the sale of an extended warranty.

DISCUSSION: Because warranty costs are expected to be incurred evenly over the life of the warranty contracts, the revenue should be recognized on the straight-line basis over the life of the extended warranty contract.

Answer (A) is incorrect because the recognition of revenue from the sale of the extended warranty is deferred until the extended warranty period begins. Answer (C) is incorrect because the revenue should be recognized evenly over the life of the contract. It is not related to the timing of the claims. Answer (D) is incorrect because revenue is recognized over the life of the warranty, not at expiration.

22. San Marino Co. sells appliances that include a 3-year warranty. Service calls under the warranty are performed by an independent mechanic under a contract with San Marino. Based on experience, warranty costs are estimated at $30 for each machine sold. When should San Marino recognize these warranty costs?

A. Evenly over the life of the warranty.

B. When the service calls are performed.

C. When payments are made to the mechanic.

D. When the machines are sold.

Answer (D) is correct. *(CPA, adapted)*

REQUIRED: The proper recording of warranty costs.

DISCUSSION: Under the accrual method, a provision for warranty costs is made when the related revenue is recognized. Revenue is recognized when the machines are sold, so warranty costs also should be recognized.

Answer (A) is incorrect because the accrual method matches the costs and the related revenues. Answer (B) is incorrect because, when the warranty costs can be reasonably estimated, the accrual method should be used. Recognizing the costs when the service calls are performed is the cash basis. Answer (C) is incorrect because recognizing costs when paid is the cash basis.

23. Salvador Co. sold 800,000 electronic can openers in year 1. Based on past experience, the company estimated that 10,000 of the 800,000 would prove to be defective and that 60% of these would be returned for replacement under the company's warranty. The cost to replace an electronic can opener is $6.00.

On January 1, year 1, the balance in the company's estimated liability for warranties account was $3,000. During year 1, 5,000 electronic can openers were replaced under the warranty. The estimated liability for warranties reported on December 31, year 1 should be

A. $6,000

B. $9,000

C. $36,000

D. $39,000

Answer (B) is correct. *(O. Broome, Jr.)*

REQUIRED: The year-end estimated liability for warranties.

DISCUSSION: At the time of the sale of each electronic can opener, it is probable that a warranty liability has been incurred and its amount can be reasonably estimated. Consequently, a warranty expense should be recognized with a corresponding credit to an estimated liability for warranties account. As indicated below, the 1/1/year 1 balance in this account is $3,000. It was increased during year 1 by $36,000 (10,000 estimated defective can openers x 60% estimated replacement rate x $6 replacement fee). The account should be decreased by $30,000 (5,000 openers replaced x $6). Thus, the ending balance is $9,000.

Estimated Liability for Warranties

		$ 3,000	1/1/year 1
Replacements	$30,000	36,000	Warranty expense
		$ 9,000	12/31/year 1

Answer (A) is incorrect because $6,000 is the balance if you ignore the $3,000 balance already in the account. Answer (C) is incorrect because $36,000 is the estimated liability recorded when the can openers are sold. Answer (D) is incorrect because $39,000 is the balance in the estimated liability for warranties account before it is adjusted for the actual replacement costs incurred.

24. During year 1, Brunei Co. introduced a new product carrying a 2-year warranty against defects. The estimated warranty costs related to dollar sales are 2% within 12 months following the sale and 4% in the second 12 months following the sale. Sales and actual warranty expenditures for the years ended December 31, year 1 and year 2 are as follows:

	Sales	Actual Warranty Expenditures
Year 1	$150,000	$2,250
Year 2	250,000	7,500
	$400,000	$9,750

What amount should Brunei report as estimated warranty liability in its December 31, year 2 balance sheet?

A. $2,500

B. $3,250

C. $11,250

D. $14,250

Answer (D) is correct. *(CPA, adapted)*

REQUIRED: The estimated warranty liability at the end of the second year.

DISCUSSION: Because this product is new, the beginning balance in the estimated warranty liability account at the beginning of year 1 is $0. For year 1, the estimated warranty costs related to dollar sales are 6% (2% + 4%) of sales, or $9,000 ($150,000 x 6%). For year 2, the estimated warranty costs are $15,000 ($250,000 x 6%). These amounts are charged to warranty expense and credited to the estimated warranty liability account. This liability account is debited for expenditures of $2,250 and $7,500 in year 1 and year 2, respectively. Hence, the estimated warranty liability at 12/31/year 2 is $14,250.

Estimated Liability for Warranties

		$ 0	1/1/year 2
Year 1 expenditures	$2,250	9,000	Year 1 expense
Year 2 expenditures	$7,500	15,000	Year 2 expense
		$14,250	12/31/year 2

Answer (A) is incorrect because $2,500 is equal to 10% of year 2 sales. Answer (B) is incorrect because $3,250 is equal to 2% of year 1 sales, plus 4% of year 2 sales, minus the $9,750 in actual expenses incurred. Answer (C) is incorrect because $11,250 is the sum of year 1's actual expenditures of $2,250 and the year 1 warranty expense of $9,000.

25. The selling price of a new company's units is $20,000 each. The buyers are provided with a 2-year warranty that is expected to cost the company $500 per unit in the year of the sale and $1,500 per unit in the year following the sale. The company sold 160 units in the first year of operation and 200 units in the second year. Actual payments for warranty claims were $40,000 and $260,000 in years one and two, respectively. The amount charged to warranty expense during the second year of operation is

A. $100,000

B. $260,000

C. $340,000

D. $400,000

Answer (D) is correct. *(CIA, adapted)*

REQUIRED: The amount charged to warranty expense during the second year of operation.

DISCUSSION: Under the accrual method, the total estimated warranty costs are charged to operating expense in the year of sale. The total estimated warranty cost per unit is $2,000 ($500 + $1,500). In year two, 200 units were sold, so the warranty expense recognized is $400,000.

Answer (A) is incorrect because $100,000 is the expected amount of warranty claims for the first year of the warranty from second-year sales. Answer (B) is incorrect because $260,000 is the actual amount of claims in the second year. Answer (C) is incorrect because $340,000 is the expected amount of warranty claims in the second year.

11.5 Refinancing of Short-Term Debt

26. At December 31, year 1, Telemark Co. owed notes payable of $1,750,000, due on May 15, year 2. Telemark expects to retire this debt with proceeds from the sale of 100,000 shares of its common stock. The stock was sold for $15 per share on March 10, year 2, prior to the issuance of the year-end financial statements. In Telemark's December 31, year 1 balance sheet, what amount of the notes payable should be excluded from current liabilities?

A. $0

B. $250,000

C. $1,500,000

D. $1,750,000

Answer (C) is correct. *(CPA, adapted)*

REQUIRED: The amount of notes payable that should be excluded from current liabilities.

DISCUSSION: If an enterprise intends to refinance short-term obligations on a long-term basis and demonstrates an ability to consummate the refinancing, the obligation should be excluded from current liabilities and reclassified as noncurrent. The ability to consummate the refinancing may be demonstrated by a post-balance-sheet-date issuance of long-term obligations or equity securities. Thus, $1,500,000 (100,000 shares × $15) of the notes payable should be excluded from current liabilities and reclassified as noncurrent.

Answer (A) is incorrect because $1,500,000 should be excluded from current liabilities. Answer (B) is incorrect because $250,000 is the amount that should be classified as a current liability. Answer (D) is incorrect because $1,750,000 is the full amount of notes payable, which should be allocated between current and noncurrent liabilities.

27. Scotia, Inc. has $1 million of notes payable due June 15, year 2. At the financial statement date of December 31, year 1, Scotia signed an agreement to borrow up to $1 million to refinance the notes payable on a long-term basis. The financing agreement called for borrowings not to exceed 80% of the value of the collateral Scotia was providing. At the date of issue of the December 31, year 1 financial statements, the value of the collateral was $1.2 million, and was not expected to fall below this amount during year 2. In its December 31, year 1 balance sheet, Scotia should classify the notes payable as

	Short-term Obligations	Long-term Obligations
A.	$0	$1,000,000
B.	$40,000	$960,000
C.	$200,000	$800,000
D.	$1,000,000	$0

Answer (B) is correct. *(CPA, adapted)*

REQUIRED: The proper classification of notes payable subject to a refinancing agreement.

DISCUSSION: The portion of debt scheduled to mature in the following fiscal year ordinarily should be classified as a current liability. However, if an enterprise intends to refinance short-term obligations on a long-term basis and demonstrates an ability to consummate the refinancing, the obligation should be excluded from current liabilities and classified as noncurrent. Scotia has signed an agreement to borrow up to $1 million to refinance the notes payable on a long-term basis, but the borrowings may not exceed 80% of the value of the collateral. Consequently, Scotia has demonstrated an ability to refinance $960,000 ($1,200,000 collateral × 80% ceiling) of the notes payable. This amount should be classified as a long-term obligation. The remaining $40,000 ($1,000,000 – $960,000) should be reported as a short-term obligation.

Answer (A) is incorrect because Scotia has not demonstrated an ability to refinance $40,000 of the notes payable. Answer (C) is incorrect because Scotia has demonstrated an ability to refinance $960,000 of the notes payable. Answer (D) is incorrect because Scotia has demonstrated an ability to refinance $960,000 of the notes payable.

28. On December 31, year 1, Lapp Co. had a $750,000 note payable outstanding, due July 31, year 2. Lapp borrowed the money to finance construction of a new plant. Lapp planned to refinance the note by issuing long-term bonds. Because Lapp temporarily had excess cash, it prepaid $250,000 of the note on January 12, year 2. In February year 2, Lapp completed a $1.5 million bond offering. Lapp will use the bond offering proceeds to repay the note payable at its maturity and to pay construction costs during year 2. On March 3, year 2, Lapp issued its year 1 financial statements. What amount of the note payable should Lapp include in the current liabilities section of its December 31, year 1 balance sheet?

A. $750,000

B. $500,000

C. $250,000

D. $0

Answer (C) is correct. *(CPA, adapted)*

REQUIRED: The amount that should be classified as short-term obligations.

DISCUSSION: The portion of debt scheduled to mature in the following fiscal year ordinarily should be classified as a current liability. However, if an enterprise intends to refinance short-term obligations on a long-term basis and demonstrates an ability to consummate the refinancing, the obligation should be excluded from current liabilities and classified as noncurrent. One method of demonstrating the ability to refinance is to issue long-term obligations or equity securities after the balance sheet date but before (1) settlement of the short-term obligations and (2) issuance of the financial statements. Lapp intended, and demonstrated an ability, to refinance $500,000 of the note payable. Thus, the portion prepaid ($250,000) is a current liability because the assets used for the prepayment were current. The remaining $500,000 should be classified as noncurrent.

Answer (A) is incorrect because $750,000 includes the $500,000 that was refinanced. Answer (B) is incorrect because $500,000 is the amount that should be reclassified as noncurrent. Answer (D) is incorrect because $250,000 should be classified as a current liability.

29. Included in Sapporo Corp.'s liability account balances at December 31, year 3 were the following:

14% note payable issued October 1, year 3, maturing September 30, year 4	$125,000
16% note payable issued April 1, year 1, payable in six equal annual installments of $50,000 beginning April 1, year 2	200,000

Sapporo's December 31, year 3 financial statements were issued on March 31, year 4. On January 15, year 4, the entire $200,000 balance of the 16% note was refinanced by issuance of a long-term obligation payable in a lump sum. In addition, on March 10, year 4, Sapporo consummated a noncancelable agreement with the lender to refinance the 14%, $125,000 note on a long-term basis, on readily determinable terms that have not yet been implemented. Both parties are financially capable of honoring the agreement, and there have been no violations of the agreement's provisions. On the December 31, year 3 balance sheet, the amount of the notes payable that Sapporo should classify as short-term obligations is

A. $175,000

B. $125,000

C. $50,000

D. $0

Answer (D) is correct. *(CPA, adapted)*

REQUIRED: The amount that should be classified as short-term obligations.

DISCUSSION: If an enterprise intends to refinance short-term obligations on a long-term basis and demonstrates an ability to consummate the refinancing, the obligation should be excluded from current liabilities and reclassified as noncurrent. The ability to consummate the refinancing may be demonstrated by a post-balance-sheet-date issuance of long-term obligations or equity securities. Thus, the 16% note payable should be classified as noncurrent. The ability to refinance may also be shown by entering into a financing agreement that meets the following criteria: (1) The agreement does not expire within the longer of 1 year or the operating cycle; (2) it is noncancelable by the lender; (3) no violation of the agreement exists at the balance sheet date; and (4) the lender is financially capable of honoring the agreement (SFAS 6). For this reason, the 14% note payable is also excluded from short-term obligations. The amount of the notes payable classified as short-term is therefore $0.

Answer (A) is incorrect because $175,000 is the sum of the installment payment of $50,000 due 4/1/year 3 and the $125,000 of the 14% note. Answer (B) is incorrect because $125,000 is the amount of the 14% note. Answer (C) is incorrect because $50,000 is the installment payment on the 16% note due 4/1/year 3.

11.6 Compensated Absences

30. If the payment of employees' compensation for future absences is probable, the amount can be reasonably estimated, and the obligation relates to rights that vest, the compensation should be

A. Recognized when paid.

B. Accrued if attributable to employees' services whether or not already rendered.

C. Accrued if attributable to employees' services already rendered.

D. Accrued if attributable to employees' services not already rendered.

Answer (C) is correct. *(CPA, adapted)*

REQUIRED: The additional criterion to be met to accrue an expense for compensated absences.

DISCUSSION: SFAS 43 requires an accrual when four criteria are met: (1) The payment of compensation is probable, (2) the amount can be reasonably estimated, (3) the benefits either vest or accumulate, and (4) the compensation relates to employees' services that have already been rendered.

Answer (A) is incorrect because the cash basis is not appropriate for recognizing expenses related to compensated absences. Answer (B) is incorrect because the services must have been previously rendered. Answer (D) is incorrect because the services must have been previously rendered.

31. At December 31, year 1, Murmansk Co. estimates that its employees have earned vacation pay of $100,000. Employees will receive their vacation pay in year 2. Should Murmansk accrue a liability at December 31, year 1 if the rights to this compensation accumulated over time or if the rights are vested?

	Accumulated	Vested
A.	Yes	No
B.	No	No
C.	Yes	Yes
D.	No	Yes

Answer (C) is correct. *(CPA, adapted)*

REQUIRED: The effect of accumulation and vesting on accrual of a liability for vacation pay.

DISCUSSION: SFAS 43, *Accounting for Compensated Absences*, requires an accrual for compensated services when the compensation relates to services previously provided, the benefits either vest or accumulate, and payment is both probable and reasonably estimable. The single exception is for sick pay benefits, which must be accrued only if the rights vest.

Answer (A) is incorrect because vesting meets one of the criteria for accrual of a liability. Answer (B) is incorrect because either vesting or accumulation meets one of the criteria for accrual of a liability. Answer (D) is incorrect because accumulation meets one of the criteria for accrual of a liability.

32. SFAS 43, *Accounting for Compensated Absences*, establishes the requirements for employers to accrue a liability for employees' compensation for future absences. The item that would require accrual under the provisions of this statement is

A. Stock compensation.

B. Termination benefits.

C. Postretirement benefits.

D. Vacation pay based on past service.

Answer (D) is correct. *(CMA, adapted)*

REQUIRED: The item that requires accrual under the provisions of SFAS 43.

DISCUSSION: SFAS 43 describes the accounting for compensated absences such as sick pay benefits, holidays, and vacations. The criteria for accrual are that the obligation arose from past services, the employees' rights vest or accumulate, payment is probable, and an amount can be reasonably estimated.

Answer (A) is incorrect because SFAS 43 does not apply to stock compensation plans, which are addressed by SFAS 123 (revised 2004), *Share-Based Payment.* Answer (B) is incorrect because SFAS 43 does not apply to special or contractual termination benefits. Answer (C) is incorrect because SFAS 43 does not apply to pension and other postretirement benefits.

33. On January 1, year 1, Toledo Co. decided to grant its employees 10 vacation days and 5 sick days each year. Vacation days, but not sick days, may be carried over to the next year. However, sick pay benefits are vested. Each employee received payment for an average of 3 sick days in year 1. During year 1, each of Toledo's six employees earned $100 per day and earned 10 vacation days. These vacation days were taken during year 2. What amount should Toledo report for accrued compensated absence expense for the year ended December 31, year 1?

A. $0

B. $6,000

C. $7,200

D. $9,000

Answer (C) is correct. *(CPA, adapted)*

REQUIRED: The accrued compensated absence expense.

DISCUSSION: SFAS 43 requires an accrual for compensated services when the compensation relates to services previously provided, the benefits either vest or accumulate, and payment is both probable and reasonably estimable. The single exception is for sick pay benefits, which must be accrued only if the rights vest. Accordingly, Toledo should report accrued compensated absence expense of $7,200 [(10 days × 6 employees × $100) vacation pay + (2 days × 6 employees × $100) sick pay].

Answer (A) is incorrect because Toledo must accrue accumulated vacation pay and vested sick pay benefits. Answer (B) is incorrect because $6,000 omits sick pay. Answer (D) is incorrect because $9,000 includes 5 days of sick pay per employee.

34. Berne Co. has an employee benefit plan for compensated absences that gives employees 10 paid vacation days and 10 paid sick days. Both vacation and sick days can be carried over indefinitely. Employees can elect to receive payment in lieu of vacation days; however, no payment is given for sick days not taken. At December 31 of the current year, Berne's unadjusted balance of liability for compensated absences was $21,000. Berne estimated that there were 150 vacation days and 75 sick days available at December 31. Berne's employees earn an average of $100 per day. In its December 31, balance sheet, what amount of liability for compensated absences is Berne required to report?

A. $36,000

B. $22,500

C. $21,000

D. $15,000

Answer (D) is correct. *(CPA, adapted)*
REQUIRED: The amount of liability for compensated absences.
DISCUSSION: SFAS 43 requires accrual of vacation benefits earned but not yet taken. It does not require a liability to be accrued for future sick pay unless the rights are vested. Thus, the estimated vacation days available at December 31 require a liability of $15,000 (150 days × $100).
Answer (A) is incorrect because $36,000 is the sum of the $15,000 liability for compensated absences and the unadjusted balance of liability for compensated absences. Answer (B) is incorrect because the sick days are not required to be included in the liability for compensated absences. Answer (C) is incorrect because $21,000 is the unadjusted balance of liability for compensated absences.

11.7 Contingencies

35. According to SFAS 5, *Accounting for Contingencies*, a loss contingency should be accrued on a company's records only if it is

A. Reasonably possible that a liability has been incurred and the amount of the loss is known.

B. Probable that a liability has been incurred and the amount of the loss is unknown.

C. Probable that a liability has been incurred and the amount of the loss can be reasonably estimated.

D. Remotely probable that a liability has been incurred but the amount of the loss can be reasonably estimated.

Answer (C) is correct. *(CMA, adapted)*
REQUIRED: The circumstance under which a loss contingency should be accrued.
DISCUSSION: Loss contingencies should be accrued when information available prior to issuance of financial statements indicates that it is probable that an asset has been impaired or a liability has been incurred, and the amount of loss can be reasonably estimated. Probable is defined as a condition in which future events are likely to occur.
Answer (A) is incorrect because an event is reasonably possible if the chance of occurrence is more than remote but less than probable. Accrual requires that the event be probable. Answer (B) is incorrect because the amount of the loss must be capable of reasonable estimation. Answer (D) is incorrect because an event is remote if the chance of occurrence is slight.

36. At December 31 of the current year, Cadiz Co. awaits judgment on a lawsuit for a competitor's infringement of its patent. Legal counsel believes it is probable that Cadiz will win the suit and indicated the most likely award together with a range of possible awards. How should the lawsuit be reported in the company's current-year financial statements?

A. In note disclosure only.

B. By accrual for the most likely award.

C. By accrual for the lowest amount of the range of possible awards.

D. Neither in note disclosure nor by accrual.

Answer (A) is correct. *(CPA, adapted)*
REQUIRED: The proper treatment of a gain contingency.
DISCUSSION: SFAS 5 provides for recognition of loss but not gain contingencies if certain criteria are met. Gain contingencies are disclosed in a note but are not recognized until realized.
Answer (B) is incorrect because only losses may be accrued when the loss is probable and reasonably estimated. Answer (C) is incorrect because only losses may be accrued when the loss is probable and reasonably estimated. Answer (D) is incorrect because the gain contingency should be disclosed.

37. Management can estimate the amount of loss that will occur if a foreign government expropriates some company assets. If expropriation is reasonably possible, a loss contingency should be

A. Disclosed but not accrued as a liability.

B. Disclosed and accrued as a liability.

C. Accrued as a liability but not disclosed.

D. Neither accrued as a liability nor disclosed.

Answer (A) is correct. *(CPA, adapted)*

REQUIRED: The reporting of a loss contingency that is reasonably possible.

DISCUSSION: A contingent loss that is reasonably possible but not probable is disclosed but not accrued. The disclosure should describe the nature of the contingency and provide an estimate of the loss or range of loss or state that an estimate cannot be made (SFAS 5).

Answer (B) is incorrect because a contingent loss is accrued only if it is probable and reasonably estimable. Answer (C) is incorrect because, if a loss is reasonably possible, it is disclosed but not accrued. Answer (D) is incorrect because, if a loss is reasonably possible, it is disclosed but not accrued.

38. A manufacturer of household appliances may incur a loss due to the discovery of a defect in one of its products. The occurrence of the loss is reasonably possible, and the resulting costs can be reasonably estimated. This possible loss should be

	Accrued	Disclosed in Notes
A.	Yes	No
B.	Yes	Yes
C.	No	Yes
D.	No	No

Answer (C) is correct. *(CPA, adapted)*

REQUIRED: The proper accounting for a contingent loss that is reasonably possible and reasonably estimable.

DISCUSSION: SFAS 5 requires that a contingent loss be accrued when two conditions are met: (1) It is probable that, at a balance sheet date, an asset is overstated or a liability has been incurred, and (2) the amount of the loss can be reasonably estimated. If both conditions are not met, but the probability of the loss is at least reasonably possible, the amount of the loss must be disclosed. This loss is reasonably possible and reasonably estimable, and it therefore should be disclosed but not accrued as a liability. The financial statements should disclose the nature of the loss contingency and the amount or range of the possible loss. If an estimate cannot be made, the note should so state.

39. When reporting contingencies

A. A guarantee of another's indebtedness is accrued as a loss contingency only if the loss is considered imminent.

B. Disclosure of a loss contingency is to be made if there is a remote possibility that the loss has been incurred.

C. Disclosure of a loss contingency must include a dollar estimate of the loss.

D. A loss that is probable but not estimable must be disclosed with a notation that the amount of the loss cannot be estimated.

Answer (D) is correct. *(CMA, adapted)*

REQUIRED: The true statement about reporting contingencies.

DISCUSSION: SFAS 5 prescribes the accounting for contingencies. Contingencies are divided into three categories: probable (likely to occur), reasonably possible, and remote. When contingent losses are probable and the amount can be reasonably estimated, the amount of the loss should be charged against income. If the amount cannot be reasonably estimated but the loss is at least reasonably possible, full disclosure should be made, including a statement that an estimate cannot be made.

Answer (A) is incorrect because a loss contingency is accrued when (1) it is probable (not necessarily imminent) that an asset has been impaired or a liability incurred and (2) the loss is reasonably estimable. Moreover, SFAS 5 requires that a guarantee of another's indebtedness be disclosed even if the possibility of loss is remote. Answer (B) is incorrect because remote contingencies ordinarily need not be disclosed. Answer (C) is incorrect because disclosure need not include an amount when that amount cannot be reasonably estimated.

40. Geneva Co. is currently being sued by a customer. A reasonable estimate can be made of the costs that would result from a ruling unfavorable to the company, and the amount involved is material. The company's managers, lawyers, and auditors agree that there is only a remote likelihood of an unfavorable ruling. This contingency

A. Should be disclosed in a note.

B. Should be disclosed as a parenthetical comment in the balance sheet.

C. Need not be disclosed.

D. Should be disclosed by an appropriation of retained earnings.

Answer (C) is correct. *(Publisher)*

REQUIRED: The proper treatment of a loss contingency that is reasonably estimable but remote in probability.

DISCUSSION: Losses arising from litigation should be accrued if both probable and reasonably estimable and should be disclosed if reasonably possible. Because the likelihood of this loss from litigation is remote, the contingent loss is required to be neither accrued nor disclosed.

41. On December 20, an uninsured property damage loss was caused by a company car's being driven on company business by a company sales agent. The company did not become aware of the loss until January 25, but the amount of the loss was reasonably estimable before the financial statements were issued. The company's December 31 financial statements should report an estimated loss as

A. A disclosure but not an accrual.

B. An accrual.

C. Neither an accrual nor a disclosure.

D. An appropriation of retained earnings.

Answer (B) is correct. *(CPA, adapted)*

REQUIRED: The manner of disclosure of a loss contingency.

DISCUSSION: A loss contingency is an existing condition, situation, or set of circumstances involving uncertainty as to the impairment of an asset's value or the incurrence of a liability as of the balance sheet date. Resolution of the uncertainty depends on the occurrence or nonoccurrence of one or more future events. A loss should be debited and either an asset valuation allowance or a liability credited when the loss contingency is both probable and reasonably estimable. The loss should be accrued even though the company was not aware of the contingency at the balance sheet date.

Answer (A) is incorrect because disclosure alone would suffice only if the loss had occurred after December 31. Answer (C) is incorrect because a loss that is both probable and reasonably estimable must always be disclosed. Accrual depends on the timing of the loss. Answer (D) is incorrect because the loss must be charged to income.

42. Ace Co. settled litigation on February 1, year 2 for an event that occurred during year 1. An estimated liability was determined as of December 31, year 1. This estimate was significantly less than the final settlement. The transaction is considered to be material. The year-end financial statements for year 1 have not been issued. How should the settlement be reported in Ace's year 1 financial statements?

A. Disclosure only of the settlement.

B. Only an accrual of the settlement.

C. Neither a disclosure nor an accrual.

D. Both a disclosure and an accrual.

Answer (D) is correct. *(CPA, adapted)*

REQUIRED: The proper treatment of a loss contingency.

DISCUSSION: SFAS 5 requires that a contingent loss be accrued when, based on information available prior to the issuance of the financial statements, two conditions are met: (1) It is probable that an asset has been impaired or a liability has been incurred at a balance sheet date, and (2) the amount of the loss can be reasonably estimated. Because the liability was settled before the financial statements were issued, it was certain that a liability had been incurred, and the amount could be specifically determined. Thus, the contingent loss must be accrued. Disclosure of the amount of the accrual is necessary to keep the financial statements from being misleading, given that the settlement was significantly greater than expected.

Answer (A) is incorrect because the settlement amount must also be accrued. Answer (B) is incorrect because the settlement must also be disclosed. Answer (C) is incorrect because the settlement must be disclosed and accrued.

43. During year 1, Strasbourg Corp. guaranteed a supplier's $500,000 loan from a bank. At the time of the guarantee, the likelihood of default was not probable. On October 1, year 2, Strasbourg was notified that the supplier had defaulted on the loan and filed for bankruptcy protection. Counsel believes Strasbourg will probably have to pay between $250,000 and $450,000 under its guarantee. As a result of the supplier's bankruptcy, Strasbourg entered into a contract in December year 2 to retool its machines so that it could accept parts from other suppliers. Retooling costs are estimated to be $300,000. What amount should Strasbourg report as a contingent liability in its December 31, year 2 balance sheet?

A. $250,000

B. $450,000

C. $550,000

D. $750,000

Answer (A) is correct. *(CPA, adapted)*

REQUIRED: The amount reported as a contingent liability.

DISCUSSION: SFAS 5 requires that a contingent loss be accrued when two conditions are met: It is probable that at a balance sheet date an asset is overstated or a liability has been incurred, and the amount of the loss can be reasonably estimated. According to FASB Interpretation No. 14, *Reasonable Estimation of the Amount of a Loss*, if the estimate is stated within a given range, and no amount within that range appears to be a better estimate than any other, the minimum of the range should be accrued. Hence, the minimum amount ($250,000) of the probable payment under the guarantee should be accrued as a liability. The retooling costs will be charged to the equipment account when incurred because they significantly improve the future service of the machines.

Under FASB Interpretation No. 45, the guarantor would have recorded a noncontingent liability in year 1 for the guarantee. If a contingent liability and loss also have to be recognized, the liability is measured at the greater of the fair value or the contingent liability at the inception of the guarantee. However, the Interpretation provides no guidance about subsequent measurement.

Answer (B) is incorrect because $450,000 is the maximum amount of the estimated range of loss. Answer (C) is incorrect because $550,000 includes the retooling costs. Answer (D) is incorrect because $750,000 equals the retooling costs plus the maximum amount of the estimated range of loss.

44. In January year 2, an explosion occurred at Zurich Co.'s plant, causing damage to area properties. By March 10, year 2, no claims had yet been asserted against Zurich. However, Zurich's management and legal counsel concluded that it was reasonably possible that Zurich would be held responsible for negligence and that $3 million would be a reasonable estimate of the damages. Zurich's $5 million comprehensive public liability policy contains a $300,000 deductible clause. In Zurich's December 31, year 1 financial statements, for which the auditor's field work was completed in April year 2, how should this casualty be reported?

A. As a note disclosing a possible liability of $3 million.

B. As an accrued liability of $300,000.

C. As a note disclosing a possible liability of $300,000.

D. No note disclosure or accrual is required for year 1 because the event occurred in year 2.

Answer (C) is correct. *(CPA, adapted)*

REQUIRED: The proper accounting for a reasonably possible contingent loss covered under a liability policy.

DISCUSSION: A loss contingency involving an unasserted claim should be disclosed if it is considered probable that the claim will be asserted and at least reasonably possible that an unfavorable outcome will result. The amount of the loss to be disclosed equals the amount of the company's potential liability. The comprehensive public liability policy has a $300,000 deductible clause, and the policy is sufficient to cover the reasonable estimate of the liability. The company should therefore disclose in a note the possible loss of $300,000.

Answer (A) is incorrect because the possible loss to the company is limited to the $300,000 deductible. Answer (B) is incorrect because a reasonably possible loss should not be accrued. Answer (D) is incorrect because note disclosure is required to prevent the financial statements from being misleading even though no asset was impaired and no liability was incurred at the balance sheet date.

45. On February 5, year 2, an employee filed a $2 million lawsuit against Vienna Co. for damages suffered when one of Vienna's plants exploded on December 29, year 1. Vienna's legal counsel expects the company will lose the lawsuit and estimates the loss to be between $500,000 and $1 million. The employee has offered to settle the lawsuit out of court for $900,000, but Vienna will not agree to the settlement. In its December 31, year 1 balance sheet, what amount should Vienna report as liability from lawsuit?

A. $2,000,000

B. $1,000,000

C. $900,000

D. $500,000

Answer (D) is correct. *(CPA, adapted)*

REQUIRED: The contingent loss that should be accrued when a range of estimates is provided.

DISCUSSION: Because the loss is probable and can be reasonably estimated, it should be accrued if the amount is material. According to FASB Interpretation No. 14, *Reasonable Estimation of the Amount of a Loss*, if the estimate is stated within a given range, and no amount within that range appears to be a better estimate than any other, the minimum of the range should be accrued. Thus, Vienna should report a $500,000 contingent liability.

Answer (A) is incorrect because the minimum of the range should be accrued. Answer (B) is incorrect because the minimum of the range should be accrued. Answer (C) is incorrect because $900,000 is the proposed settlement amount.

46. On November 10, year 1, a Warsaw Corp. truck was in an accident with an auto driven by Krzyzewski. On January 10, year 2, Warsaw received notice of a lawsuit seeking $800,000 in damages for personal injuries suffered by Krzyzewski. Warsaw Corp.'s counsel believes it is reasonably possible that Krzyzewski will be awarded an estimated amount in the range between $250,000 and $500,000 and that $400,000 is a better estimate of potential liability than any other amount. Warsaw's accounting year ends on December 31, and the year 1 financial statements were issued on March 6, year 2. What amount of loss should Warsaw accrue at December 31, year 1?

A. $0

B. $250,000

C. $400,000

D. $500,000

Answer (A) is correct. *(CPA, adapted)*

REQUIRED: The proper accounting for a contingent loss that is reasonably possible and can be estimated within a range.

DISCUSSION: SFAS 5 requires that a contingent loss be accrued when it is probable that, at a balance sheet date, an asset is overstated or a liability has been incurred and the amount of the loss can be reasonably estimated. If both conditions are not met but the probability of the loss is at least reasonably possible, the amount of the loss must be disclosed. This loss is reasonably possible and reasonably estimable. Hence, it should be disclosed but not accrued.

Answer (B) is incorrect because $250,000 is the amount that would be disclosed in a note if a better estimate did not exist. Answer (C) is incorrect because $400,000 is the amount that should be disclosed. It is the best estimate. It is not accrued. Answer (D) is incorrect because $500,000 is the maximum amount of loss in the range. It is not the amount used in a note disclosure.

47. Tyrol, Inc. has a self-insurance plan. Each year, retained earnings is appropriated for contingencies in an amount equal to insurance premiums saved minus recognized losses from lawsuits and other claims. As a result of a current-year accident, Tyrol is a defendant in a lawsuit in which it will probably have to pay damages of $190,000. What are the effects of this lawsuit's probable outcome on Tyrol's current-year financial statements?

A. An increase in expenses and no effect on liabilities.

B. An increase in both expenses and liabilities.

C. No effect on expenses and an increase in liabilities.

D. No effect on either expenses or liabilities.

Answer (B) is correct. *(CPA, adapted)*

REQUIRED: The effect on the financial statements of litigation with a probable unfavorable outcome.

DISCUSSION: A loss contingency is an existing condition, situation, or set of circumstances involving uncertainty as to the impairment of an asset's value or the incurrence of a liability as of the balance sheet date. Resolution of the uncertainty depends on the occurrence or nonoccurrence of one or more future events. A loss should be debited and either an asset valuation allowance or a liability credited when the loss contingency is both probable and reasonably estimable. Thus, the company should accrue a loss and a liability. Appropriations of retained earnings have no effect on these accounting treatments.

48. Seller-Guarantor sold an asset with a carrying amount at the time of sale of $500,000 to Buyer for $650,000 in cash. Seller also provided a guarantee to Guarantee Bank of the $600,000 loan that Guarantee made to Buyer to finance the sale. The probability that Seller will become liable under the guarantee is remote. In a stand-alone arm's-length transaction with an unrelated party, the premium required by Seller to provide the same guarantee would have been $40,000. According to FASB Interpretation No. 45, *Guarantor's Accounting and Disclosure Requirements for Guarantees, Including Indirect Guarantees of the Indebtedness of Others*, the entry made by Seller at the time of the sale should include a

A. Gain of $150,000.

B. Noncontingent liability of $40,000.

C. Contingent liability of $600,000.

D. Loss of $450,000.

Answer (B) is correct. *(Publisher)*

REQUIRED: The entry made to reflect sale of an asset and the seller's guarantee of the buyer's debt.

DISCUSSION: No contingent liability results because the likelihood of payment by the guarantor is remote. However, a noncontingent liability is recognized at the inception of the seller's obligation to stand ready to perform during the term of the guarantee. This liability is initially measured at fair value. In a multiple-element transaction with an unrelated party, the fair value is estimated, for example, as the premium required by the guarantor to provide the same guarantee in a stand-alone arm's-length transaction with an unrelated party. The amount of that premium is given as $40,000. Hence, Seller debits cash for the total received ($650,000), credits the asset sold for its carrying amount ($500,000), credits the noncontingent liability for its estimated fair value ($40,000), and credits a gain for $110,000 ($650,000 – $500,000 – $40,000).

Answer (A) is incorrect because a gain of $150,000 assumes neither a noncontingent nor a contingent liability is recognized.

Answer (C) is incorrect because no contingent liability is recognized. The likelihood of payment is remote, not probable.

Answer (D) is incorrect because a loss of $450,000 assumes recognition of a contingent liability of $600,000.

49. In year 1, a contract dispute between Loch Co. and Lomond Co. was submitted to binding arbitration. In year 1, each party's attorney indicated privately that the probable award in Loch's favor could be reasonably estimated. In year 2, the arbitrator decided in favor of Loch. When should Loch and Lomond recognize their respective gain and loss?

	Loch's Gain	Lomond's Loss
A.	Year 1	Year 1
B.	Year 1	Year 2
C.	Year 2	Year 1
D.	Year 2	Year 2

Answer (C) is correct. *(CPA, adapted)*

REQUIRED: The proper accounting for a contingent gain or loss that is probable and capable of reasonable estimation.

DISCUSSION: SFAS 5 requires that a contingent loss be accrued when two conditions are met: It is probable that, at a balance sheet date, an asset is overstated or a liability has been incurred, and the amount of the loss can be reasonably estimated. In accordance with SFAS 5, gain contingencies should not be recognized until they are realized. A gain contingency should be disclosed, but care should be taken to avoid misleading implications as to the likelihood of realization. Because the award in favor of Loch is probable and can be reasonably estimated, a loss should be recognized in year 1 by Lomond. However, Loch should not recognize the gain until year 2.

50. During January of the current year, Kiev Corp. won a litigation award for $15,000 that was tripled to $45,000 to include punitive damages. The defendant, who is financially stable, has appealed only the $30,000 of punitive damages. Kiev was awarded $50,000 in an unrelated suit it filed, which is being appealed by the defendant. Counsel is unable to estimate the outcome of these appeals. In its current-year financial statements, Kiev should report what amount of pretax gain?

A. $15,000

B. $45,000

C. $50,000

D. $95,000

Answer (A) is correct. *(CPA, adapted)*

REQUIRED: The amount of pretax gain from litigation.

DISCUSSION: In accordance with SFAS 5, gain contingencies should not be recognized until they are realized. A gain contingency should be disclosed, but care should be taken to avoid misleading implications as to the likelihood of realization. Consequently, the only litigation award to be recognized in income in the current year is the $15,000 amount that has not been appealed. The other awards have not been realized because they have been appealed.

Answer (B) is incorrect because $45,000 includes the punitive damages that have been appealed. Answer (C) is incorrect because $50,000 is the amount of the award in the unrelated suit that has been appealed. Answer (D) is incorrect because $95,000 includes the punitive damages and the amount of the award in the unrelated suit. Both have been appealed.

51. In May of year 1, Caso Co. filed suit against Wayne, Inc. seeking $1.9 million damages for patent infringement. A court verdict in November year 4 awarded Caso $1.5 million in damages, but Wayne's appeal is not expected to be decided before year 6. Caso's counsel believes it is probable that Caso will be successful against Wayne for an estimated amount in the range between $800,000 and $1.1 million, with $1 million considered the most likely amount. What amount should Caso record as income from the lawsuit in the year ended December 31, year 4?

A. $0

B. $800,000

C. $1,000,000

D. $1,500,000

Answer (A) is correct. *(CPA, adapted)*

REQUIRED: The amount of income recorded from the lawsuit.

DISCUSSION: SFAS 5 requires that gain contingencies not be recognized until they are realized. Because the appeal is not expected to be decided before year 6, Caso should not record any revenue from the lawsuit in the year 4 income statement. This gain contingency should be disclosed; however, care should be taken to avoid misleading implications as to the likelihood of realization.

52. An entity may be required to recognize an environmental remediation liability. According to SOP 96-1, *Environmental Remediation Liabilities,*

A. The liability and anticipated recoveries from other potentially responsible parties (PRPs) may be offset.

B. The debit is to other comprehensive income.

C. The loss is an extraordinary item.

D. The liability may be measured by discounting certain costs.

Answer (D) is correct. *(Publisher)*

REQUIRED: The accounting for an environmental remediation liability.

DISCUSSION: The measurement of the liability is based on estimates of costs of all elements of the remediation when they are expected to be performed. Discounting is allowable if the aggregate liability (or a component) and the amounts and timing of cash payments are reliably determinable.

Answer (A) is incorrect because the balance sheet may report assets for receivables from other PRPs and for potential recoveries (at fair value) from insurers and prior owners. However, the set-off of environmental liabilities and anticipated recoveries is not usually allowed. APB 10 prohibits offsetting of assets and liabilities unless a right of offset exists. Answer (B) is incorrect because the entry to record a remediation liability ordinarily includes a debit to operating income. Answer (C) is incorrect because the criteria for treatment as an extraordinary item are not met.

STUDY UNIT TWELVE
LONG-TERM LIABILITIES

The fair (market) value of a long-term **bond** at the date of issuance equals the total cash flows associated with the bond discounted at the yield rate in effect at the date of issuance. The total cash flows associated with a bond are the maturity (face) amount payable at the end of the life of the bond and the periodic interest payments made at the end of the interest periods. The periodic interest payments equal the maturity amount multiplied by the coupon (face) rate. The difference between total cash flows and the present value of these cash flows is total interest expense. In accordance with the **interest method**, total interest expense is allocated to each interest period to reflect a constant interest rate equal to the yield rate at the time of issuance. In accordance with the straight-line method, total interest expense is allocated to each interest period to reflect a constant amount of interest expense. GAAP require the interest method unless the results of applying the straight-line method do not differ materially from those produced by the interest method.

Bonds issued at a yield rate equal to the coupon rate are issued at par (face) value. Interest expense on bonds issued at par is equal to the periodic interest payment. Bonds with a yield rate greater than the coupon rate are issued at a **discount**. Interest expense on such bonds is greater than the periodic interest payment and increases over time. Conversely, bonds with a yield rate less than the coupon rate are issued at a **premium**. Interest expense on such bonds is less than the periodic interest payment and decreases over time.

When **convertible bonds** are issued, the entire proceeds are reported as a long-term liability until the bonds are converted or redeemed. When bonds are converted under the **book value method** (the generally accepted approach), the stock issued is recorded at the carrying amount of the bonds with no recognition of gain or loss. When bonds are converted under the **market value method**, the stock issued is recorded at fair value with recognition of gain or loss equal to the difference between fair value and the carrying amount of the bonds. A debtor issuing additional securities or paying other consideration to induce conversion recognizes the fair value of the inducements (sweeteners) as an expense.

According to **APB 14**, *Convertible Debt and Debt Issued with Stock Purchase Warrants*, debt that must be surrendered to exercise attached warrants is accounted for as convertible. Thus, the entire proceeds are reported as a long-term liability until the debt is surrendered or redeemed. However, when debt is issued with detachable warrants, the proceeds are allocated between the debt and the warrants based on their relative fair values at the time of issuance. The portion allocated to the warrants is accounted for as additional paid-in-capital-warrants.

APB 26, *Early Extinguishment of Debt*, states that all debt extinguishments are fundamentally alike. The difference between the reacquisition price and the net carrying amount should be recognized in income for the period of extinguishment. **SFAS 140**, *Accounting for Transfers and Servicing of Financial Assets and Extinguishments of Liabilities*, provides for the derecognition of a liability only if it has been extinguished. Extinguishment occurs when either (1) the debtor pays the creditor and is relieved of its obligation for the liability, or (2) the debtor is legally released from being the primary obligor under the liability, either judicially or by the creditor. SFAS 140 prohibits the recognition of a gain or loss from an **in-substance defeasance**.

According to **APB 21**, *Interest on Receivables and Payables*, receivables and payables are recorded at the present value of the consideration given or received. When a **note is exchanged for property, goods, or services**, the interest rate determined by the parties in an arm's-length transaction is presumed to be fair. That presumption is overcome when no interest is stated, the stated rate is unreasonable, or the nominal amount of the note materially differs from the cash sales price of the item or the market value of the note. In these circumstances, the transaction should be recorded at the more clearly determinable of the (1) fair value of the property, goods, or services; (2) market value of the note; or (3) discounted value of future payments based on an imputed rate. If the first two values are not determinable, an interest rate is **imputed**. The prevailing rate for similar instruments of issuers with similar credit ratings normally helps determine the rate. The purpose is to estimate the rate in a similar transaction between independent parties. The stated rate may be less than the effective rate because the lender has received **other stated (or unstated) rights and privileges**. The difference between the present values of the note computed at the stated rate and the effective rate is accounted for as the cost of the rights or privileges obtained. Periodic interest is recognized at a constant rate using the **effective-interest method**.

A **troubled debt restructuring (TDR)** arises when a creditor, for economic or legal reasons related to a debtor's financial difficulties, grants a concession to the debtor that it would not otherwise consider. Troubled debt restructurings usually involve either a continuation of the debt with modified terms or an asset exchange at an amount less than the carrying amount of the debt. Under **SFAS 15**, *Accounting by Debtors and Creditors for Troubled Debt Restructurings*, when a TDR includes a **modification of terms** that results in future undiscounted cash flows less than the carrying amount of the debt, the debtor recognizes a gain equal to the difference. If the future undiscounted cash flows are greater than the carrying amount of the debt, the difference is recognized as interest using a new effective interest rate that equates the future cash payments with the carrying amount. When a TDR includes an **asset exchange**, the debtor recognizes (1) a gain or loss equal to the difference between the fair value and the carrying amount of the asset, and (2) a gain equal to the excess of the carrying amount of the debt over the fair value of the asset. **SFAS 143**, *Asset Retirement Obligations*, applies to (1) obligations associated with the retirement of tangible long-lived assets and (2) the related asset retirement cost. The fair value of a legal obligation for an ARO is recognized as a liability when incurred if fair value can be reasonably estimated. The liability is subsequently adjusted periodically for the passage of time and revisions in the original estimates of undiscounted cash flows. The related **asset retirement cost** is recorded as an increase in the carrying amount of the long-lived asset. This cost is systematically and rationally allocated over its useful life. **FASB Interpretation No. 47**, *Accounting for Conditional Asset Retirement Obligations*, clarifies that the legal obligation to be ready to perform obligation is **unconditional** even though the timing or method of settlement is conditional. Hence, a liability is recognized for a conditional ARO if its fair value can be reasonably estimated.

Under **SFAS 146**, *Accounting for Costs Associated with Exit or Disposal Activities*, **exit activities** include **restructurings**, programs planned and controlled by management that materially alter the scope of the business or how it is conducted (e.g., sale of a line of business, closure of an activity in a given location, relocation, changes in management structure, or a fundamental reorganization of operations). **Disposal activities** are those covered by SFAS 144 (Study Units 3 and 7). Among the costs subject to SFAS 146 are **one-time termination benefits** payable to involuntarily terminated current employees (but not under an ongoing benefit plan or an individual deferred compensation contract), **contract termination costs** other than those for a capital lease, and facilities consolidation and employee relocation costs. A **liability** for exit or disposal costs is ordinarily recognized and measured at **fair value** when the liability is incurred, i.e., when a **present obligation** to others exists. A present obligation exists when the entity has little discretion to avoid a future transfer of assets in settlement. **Changes in the liability** are recorded using the **credit-adjusted risk-free (CARF) rate** on which the initial measurement was based. These changes include the cumulative effect of revisions in the **timing or amount of estimated cash flows** recognized as an adjustment in the period of the change and reported in the same line item(s) as the initially recognized costs, and changes due to the **passage of time** recognized by crediting the liability and debiting an expense. **One-time termination benefits** are paid under a **plan of termination** for a specified termination event or future period. The arrangement exists when a plan has been **communicated** to employees that meets certain requirements (e.g., management's commitment to the plan and the unlikelihood of its change or withdrawal). The accounting for the liability depends on whether employees (1) must provide services until terminated and (2) will be retained beyond the **minimum retention period** (the legal notification period or a maximum of 60 days). If either criteria is **not** met, the liability is **recognized** at the **communication date** and **measured** at fair value on that date. If both criteria are met, **initial measurement** is at the communication date, the amount is the fair value on the **termination date**, and **recognition** is ratable over the service period. If a plan changes so that employees are retained beyond the minimum retention period, a liability recorded at the communication date must be adjusted by a cumulative effect accounting change. **Contract termination costs** include (1) costs to terminate prior to the completion of the contract's term or (2) continuing costs that will be incurred without economic benefit. A liability for the first type is **recognized and measured** at fair value at termination in accordance with the contract, e.g., when notice is given within a stipulated period or the entity negotiates termination. A liability for continuing costs is **recognized and measured** at fair value when the contract right is no longer used (the **cease-use date**). For an **operating lease**, the initial fair value of the liability is based on the remaining lease rentals adjusted for any recognized prepayments or deferrals and decreased by an estimate of sublease rentals reasonably obtainable, not to be reduced below zero. The liability for **other associated costs** is **recognized and measured** at fair value when the liability is incurred, ordinarily when goods or services associated with the exit or disposal activity are received. This rule applies even though the costs are in addition to other operating costs and will be incurred directly pursuant to a plan.

SFAS 150, *Accounting for Certain Financial Instruments with Characteristics of Both Liabilities and Equity*, classifies certain **freestanding financial instruments**. A freestanding instrument is separate and legally detachable from other instruments and equity transactions. However, it may consist of **more than one option or forward contract**. An example is a combination consisting solely of a written put option and a purchased call option on the issuer's equity shares. One freestanding instrument within the scope of SFAS 150 ordinarily may not be combined with another for determining whether they are liabilities.

Mandatorily redeemable financial instruments (MRFIs) are liabilities except when redemption is upon termination of the entity. They are instruments **in the form of shares** that **embody unconditional obligations** to **transfer assets** at specified or determinable times or upon an event certain to occur. An **example** of an MRFI is stock that must be redeemed upon the holder's death, a certain event. **Preferred stock** that is convertible at the holder's option for a fixed period is not an MRFI during that period.

Certain **obligations to repurchase the issuer's equity shares by transferring assets** are treated as liabilities (or, in some cases, as assets). These instruments are not in the form of outstanding shares. An instrument in this class has the following characteristics: (1) it relates to a conditional or unconditional obligation to repurchase the issuer's equity shares; (2) at inception, the instrument either **embodies that obligation** or is based on variability in the fair value of the obligation (i.e., is **indexed to the obligation**); and (3) the instrument requires or may require settlement by transferring assets. Typical **examples** are written put options and forward purchase contracts involving the issuer's equity shares that require physical settlement or net cash settlement. **Physical settlement** of an instrument occurs when each party actually delivers the full stated consideration. **Net cash settlement** means that the party with a gain on the instrument receives cash equal to the gain from the party with a loss. A **written put option** on the issuer's (writer's) equity shares is an agreement to repurchase the shares at a given price (the exercise price) within some future period. If this instrument is freestanding and requires **physical settlement**, it is accounted for as a liability. It **embodies** a conditional obligation to repurchase the issuer's equity shares that will require settlement by transferring assets if the option is "in the money." If this instrument is freestanding and requires **net cash settlement**, it is also accounted for as a liability. It is **indexed** to the conditional repurchase obligation and may require settlement by transferring assets. A freestanding **forward purchase contract** involving the issuer's equity shares that requires **physical settlement** is a liability. It **embodies an unconditional obligation** to repurchase the issuer's equity shares and requires transfer of assets. If the forward purchase contract is subject to **net cash settlement**, the obligation is conditional. Such a contract is **indexed** to the repurchase obligation and may require settlement by transferring assets. Thus, if price movements are favorable (unfavorable), the issuer of the underlying shares will receive (transfer) assets at the settlement date because the issuer will be in a gain (loss) position. During the term of the contract, the issuer will classify it as an **asset or a liability** depending on its fair value (not the fair value of the shares) at the reporting date.

Certain obligations to issue a variable number of equity shares are classified as liabilities (or, in some cases, assets). These instruments **embody conditional or unconditional obligations** that may or must be settled by issuing a variable number of equity shares, not by transferring assets. If the obligation is **conditional**, the instrument must not be an **outstanding share**. For example, preferred stock convertible to a variable number of shares of the issuer's common stock is not classified as a liability (asset) of the issuer even if it meets the other criteria. An instrument in this group is classified as a liability (an asset) when its holder is not exposed to an **owner's** risks and benefits. Furthermore, at inception, the **monetary value** of the obligation must be based **solely or predominantly** on one of the following: (1) A **known fixed monetary amount** (e.g., a payable requiring settlement with equity shares having a fair value equal to the fixed amount), (2) variations in something **not the fair value** of the issuer's equity shares (e.g., a stock index), or (3) variations with an **inverse relation** to the fair value of the issuer's equity shares (e.g., changes in the fair value of a written put option that can be net-share settled). In **net share settlement**, the loss party delivers to the gain party shares of stock with a fair value equal to the gain.

MRFIs are **initially measured** at fair value. **Subsequent measurement** given a **fixed payment amount and settlement date** is at the present value of the settlement amount. Interest cost is accrued using the rate implicit at inception. At maturity, the liability will equal the contract amount. **Subsequent measurement** given that the **payment amount or settlement date depends on specified conditions** is at the undiscounted amount of cash that would be payable under the specified conditions if settlement were at the reporting date. Interest cost is recognized for the change since the prior reporting date. **Accrued dividends** (declared or not) on the shares and any other amounts paid or payable are treated as interest cost. **Forward contracts requiring physical settlement by repurchase of a fixed number of the issuer's equity shares for cash** are a means of converting the shares into MRFIs. They are initially measured based on the fair value of the shares at inception. The measurement is adjusted for any **consideration or any unstated rights or privileges**. This amount may be determined by reference to the cash to be paid if the shares were immediately repurchased. An alternative is to discount the settlement amount at the rate implicit at inception after allowing for the consideration, etc. **Subsequent measurement** is the same as for MRFIs. An entity that has entered into this kind of forward contract or issued MRFIs must not include the affected shares of common stock in **EPS calculations**. **Other instruments** covered by SFAS 150 are measured initially at fair value. Subsequent measurement of these other instruments is also at fair value, with changes recognized in earnings, unless another pronouncement (e.g., SFAS 133) requires otherwise.

QUESTIONS

12.1 Bonds

1. Perk, Inc. issued $500,000, 10% bonds to yield 8%. Bond issuance costs were $10,000. How should Perk calculate the net proceeds to be received from the issuance?

A. Discount the bonds at the stated rate of interest.

B. Discount the bonds at the market rate of interest.

C. Discount the bonds at the stated rate of interest and deduct bond issuance costs.

D. Discount the bonds at the market rate of interest and deduct bond issuance costs.

Answer (D) is correct. *(CPA, adapted)*

REQUIRED: The net proceeds to be received from the issuance.

DISCUSSION: Bonds are sold at the sum of the present values of the maturity amount and the interest payments (if interest-bearing). The difference between the face amount and the selling price of bonds is either a discount or a premium. Bonds are sold at a discount when they sell for less than face amount, that is, when the contract (stated) interest rate is less than the market (effective) interest rate. Bonds are sold at a premium (in excess of face amount) when the stated rate exceeds the effective rate. To determine the present value of the bonds' future cash flows, the market rate of interest is used as the discount rate. The result is the market price of the bonds at the issue date. The net proceeds equal the price of the bonds minus the issue costs. Issue costs are incurred to bring a bond to market and include printing and engraving costs, legal fees, accountants' fees, underwriters' commissions, registration fees, and promotion costs.

Answer (A) is incorrect because the bonds should be discounted at the market rate, and the net proceeds equal the price (cash flows discounted at the market rate) minus the issue costs. Answer (B) is incorrect because the net proceeds equal the price (cash flows discounted at the market rate) minus the issue costs. Answer (C) is incorrect because the bonds should be discounted at the market rate.

2. York Corp.'s December 31, 2003 balance sheet contained the following items in the long-term liabilities section:

9 3/4% registered debentures, callable in 2014, due in 2019	$1,400,000
9 1/2% collateral trust bonds, convertible into common stock beginning in 2012, due in 2022	1,200,000
10% subordinated debentures ($60,000 maturing annually beginning in 2009)	600,000

What is the total amount of York's term bonds?

A. $1,200,000

B. $1,400,000

C. $2,000,000

D. $2,600,000

Answer (D) is correct. *(CPA, adapted)*

REQUIRED: The total amount of term bonds.

DISCUSSION: Term bonds mature on a single date. Hence, the registered bonds and the collateral trust bonds are term bonds, a total of $2,600,000 ($1,400,000 + $1,200,000).

Answer (A) is incorrect because the registered bonds are also term bonds. Answer (B) is incorrect because the collateral trust bonds are also term bonds. Answer (C) is incorrect because the collateral trust bonds, not the subordinated debentures, are term bonds.

3. A bond issued on June 1, year 1 has interest payment dates of April 1 and October 1. Bond interest expense for the year ended December 31, year 1 is for a period of

A. 7 months.

B. 6 months.

C. 4 months.

D. 3 months.

Answer (A) is correct. *(CPA, adapted)*

REQUIRED: The period for which interest is paid when a bond is issued between payment dates.

DISCUSSION: Interest expense should be recorded on a systematic and rational basis. The basis used is the passage of time. Because the period from June 1 to December 31 includes 7 months, 7 months of interest expense should be recorded for the year of issuance. The determination of interest expense is not dependent on the interest payment dates. The length of time outstanding determines the interest expense.

4. Cornwall Co.'s December 31, 2003 balance sheet contained the following items in the long-term liabilities section:

Unsecured	
9.375% registered bonds ($50,000 maturing annually beginning in 2007)	$550,000
11.5% convertible bonds, callable beginning in 2012, due 2023	250,000
Secured	
9.875% guaranty security bonds, due 2023	$500,000
10.0% commodity-backed bonds ($100,000 maturing annually beginning in 2008)	400,000

What are the total amounts of serial bonds and debenture bonds?

	Serial Bonds	Debenture Bonds
A.	$950,000	$800,000
B.	$950,000	$250,000
C.	$900,000	$800,000
D.	$400,000	$1,300,000

Answer (A) is correct. *(CPA, adapted)*

REQUIRED: The total amounts of serial bonds and debenture bonds.

DISCUSSION: Serial bonds mature in installments at various dates. Debentures are unsecured bonds. The commodity-backed bonds and the registered bonds are serial bonds. They total $950,000 ($550,000 + $400,000). The registered bonds and the convertible bonds are debentures. They total $800,000 ($550,000 + $250,000).

Answer (B) is incorrect because the registered bonds are also debentures. Answer (C) is incorrect because the registered bonds, not the guaranty security bonds, are serial bonds. Answer (D) is incorrect because the registered bonds are serial bonds, and the guaranty security bonds are not debentures.

5. Unamortized debt discount should be reported on the balance sheet of the issuer as a

A. Direct deduction from the face amount of the debt.

B. Direct deduction from the present value of the debt.

C. Deferred charge.

D. Part of the issue costs.

Answer (A) is correct. *(CPA, adapted)*

REQUIRED: The issuer's balance sheet presentation of unamortized discount.

DISCUSSION: APB 21, *Interest on Receivables and Payables*, requires that bond discount appear as a direct deduction from the face amount of the bond payable to report the effective liability for the bonds. Hence, the bond liability is shown net of unamortized discount.

Answer (B) is incorrect because the face amount minus the unamortized discount is equal to the present value (carrying amount) of the bond. Answer (C) is incorrect because, under APB 21, bond issue costs, not unamortized discount, appear as a deferred charge in the balance sheet. SFAC 6 suggests that issue costs be treated as an expense or in the same manner as bond discount. Answer (D) is incorrect because unamortized discount is segregated from issue costs.

6. The following information pertains to Wales Corp.'s issuance of bonds on July 1, year 1:

Face amount	$800,000
Term	10 years
Stated interest rate	6%
Interest payment dates	Annually on July 1
Yield	9%

	At 6%	At 9%
Present value of 1 for 10 periods	0.558	0.422
Future value of 1 for 10 periods	1.791	2.367
Present value of ordinary annuity of 1 for 10 periods	7.360	6.418

What should be the issue price for each $1,000 bond?

A. $1,000

B. $943

C. $864

D. $807

Answer (D) is correct. *(CPA, adapted)*

REQUIRED: The issue price for each bond.

DISCUSSION: The issue price for each bond reflects the fair value. It equals the sum of the present values of the future cash flows (principal + interest). This amount is $807 {(.422 PV of 1 for 10 periods at 9% × $1,000 face amount) + [6.418 PV of an ordinary annuity for 10 periods at 9% × (6% × $1,000) interest]}.

Answer (A) is incorrect because $1,000 is the face amount. Answer (B) is incorrect because $943 is the result of discounting the interest payments at 9% and the face amount at 6%. Answer (C) is incorrect because $864 is the result of discounting the interest payments at 6% and the face amount at 9%.

7. On January 2, year 1, Tintagel Co. issued 8% bonds with a face amount of $1 million that mature on January 2, year 6. The bonds were issued to yield 12%, resulting in a discount of $150,000. Tintagel incorrectly used the straight-line method instead of the effective-interest method to amortize the discount. How is the carrying amount of the bonds affected by the error?

	At December 31, Year 1	At January 2, Year 6
A.	Overstated	Understated
B.	Overstated	No effect
C.	Understated	Overstated
D.	Understated	No effect

Answer (B) is correct. *(CPA, adapted)*
REQUIRED: The effect of amortizing bond discount using the straight-line method.
DISCUSSION: The carrying amount of a bond issued at a discount equals its maturity amount minus the unamortized discount. Under the effective-interest method, periodic interest expense equals the carrying amount times the effective (yield) rate. Discount amortization is the excess of interest expense over actual interest paid. When bonds are issued at a discount, the carrying amount increases over time as the discount is amortized, thereby increasing interest expense and the amount of amortization. Discount amortization under the straight-line method is a constant periodic amount. Thus, in the first year, straight-line amortization of the discount exceeds the amount determined under the interest method. The effect of the error is to overstate the carrying amount by this excess. At the due date of the bonds, however, the discount is fully amortized, and the carrying amount is the same under both methods.

8. Kent Co. issued 6,000 of its 9%, $1,000 face amount bonds at 101 1/2. In connection with the sale of these bonds, Kent paid the following expenses:

Promotion costs	$ 40,000
Engraving and printing	50,000
Underwriters' commissions	400,000

What amount should Kent record as bond issue costs to be amortized over the term of the bonds?

A. $0

B. $440,000

C. $450,000

D. $490,000

Answer (D) is correct. *(CPA, adapted)*
REQUIRED: The amount to be recorded as bond issue costs.
DISCUSSION: Bond issue costs include printing costs, underwriters' commissions, attorney's fees, and promotion costs (including preparation of a prospectus). The issue costs to be amortized equal $490,000 ($40,000 promotion costs + $50,000 printing costs + $400,000 underwriters' commissions).
Answer (A) is incorrect because $490,000 of bond issue costs should be amortized. Answer (B) is incorrect because the $50,000 printing cost should be amortized. Answer (C) is incorrect because the $40,000 promotion costs should be amortized.

9. On May 1, year 1, a company issued, at 103 plus accrued interest, 500 of its 12%, $1,000 bonds. The bonds are dated January 1, year 1 and mature on January 1, year 5. Interest is payable semiannually on January 1 and July 1. The journal entry to record the issuance of the bonds and the receipt of the cash proceeds is

		Dr.	Cr.
A.	Cash	$515,000	
	Interest payable	20,000	
	Bonds payable		$500,000
	Premium on bonds payable		35,000
B.	Cash	$525,000	
	Bonds payable		$500,000
	Premium on bonds payable		15,000
	Interest payable		10,000
C.	Cash	$535,000	
	Bonds payable		$500,000
	Premium on bonds payable		15,000
	Interest payable		20,000
D.	Cash	$535,000	
	Bonds payable		$500,000
	Premium on bonds payable		35,000

Answer (C) is correct. *(CIA, adapted)*
REQUIRED: The journal entry to record the issuance of a bond at a premium plus accrued interest.
DISCUSSION: The face amount of the 500 bonds is equal to $500,000 (500 × $1,000). The cash proceeds excluding interest from the issuance of the bonds are $515,000 (103% × $500,000). The $15,000 premium is the difference between the cash issuance proceeds and the face amount of the bonds. Because the bonds were issued between interest payment dates, the issuer is also entitled to receive accrued interest for the 4 months between the prior interest date and the issuance date. The accrued interest is $20,000 [500 bonds × $1,000 face amount × 12% stated rate × (4 ÷ 12)]. The issuing company will therefore receive $535,000 in cash ($515,000 + $20,000). The resulting journal entry includes a $535,000 debit to cash, a $500,000 credit to bonds payable, a $15,000 credit to premium, and a $20,000 credit to either interest payable or interest expense.
Answer (A) is incorrect because the bond premium is $15,000 ($500,000 × .03), and interest payable should be credited. Answer (B) is incorrect because interest payable should be $20,000 [$500,000 × .12 × (4 ÷ 12)]. Answer (D) is incorrect because the premium on bonds payable should not include interest payable.

10. If the market rate of interest is <List A> the coupon rate when bonds are issued, then the bonds will sell in the market at a price <List B> the face amount, and the issuing firm will record a <List C> on bonds payable.

	List A	List B	List C
A.	Equal to	Equal to	Premium
B.	Greater than	Greater than	Premium
C.	Greater than	Less than	Discount
D.	Less than	Greater than	Discount

Answer (C) is correct. *(CIA, adapted)*

REQUIRED: The relationship of the market rate, the coupon rate, and the recording of a discount or premium.

DISCUSSION: If the market rate exceeds the coupon rate, the price of the bonds must decline to a level that equates the yield on the bonds with the market rate of interest. Accordingly, the bonds will be recorded by a debit to cash for the proceeds, a debit to discount on bonds payable, and a credit to bonds payable at face amount.

Answer (A) is incorrect because, if the market rate equals the coupon rate, the bonds will sell at a premium or discount. Answer (B) is incorrect because, if the market rate exceeds the coupon rate, the bond issue will sell at a discount. Answer (D) is incorrect because, if the market rate is less than the coupon rate, the bonds will sell at a premium.

11. How is the carrying amount of a bond payable affected by amortization of the following?

	Discount	Premium
A.	Increase	Increase
B.	Decrease	Decrease
C.	Increase	Decrease
D.	Decrease	Increase

Answer (C) is correct. *(CPA, adapted)*

REQUIRED: The effect of discount and premium amortization on the carrying amount of a bond payable.

DISCUSSION: The carrying amount of a bond payable is equal to its maturity (face) amount plus any unamortized premium or minus any unamortized discount. Amortization results in a reduction of the discount or premium. Consequently, the carrying amount of a bond is increased when discount is amortized and decreased when premium is amortized.

Answer (A) is incorrect because the carrying amount of a bond payable is increased by the amortization of a discount and decreased by the amortization of a premium. Answer (B) is incorrect because the carrying amount of a bond payable is increased by the amortization of a discount and decreased by the amortization of a premium. Answer (D) is incorrect because the carrying amount of a bond payable is increased by the amortization of a discount and decreased by the amortization of a premium.

12. Midland, Inc. had the following amounts of long-term debt outstanding at December 31, year 1:

14 1/2% term note, due year 2	$ 6,000
11 1/8% term note, due year 4	214,000
8% note, due in 11 equal annual principal payments, plus interest beginning December 31, year 2	220,000
7% guaranteed debentures, due year 5	200,000
Total	$640,000

Midland's annual sinking-fund requirement on the guaranteed debentures is $8,000 per year. What amount should Midland report as current maturities of long-term debt in its December 31, year 1 balance sheet?

A. $8,000

B. $14,000

C. $20,000

D. $26,000

Answer (D) is correct. *(CPA, adapted)*

REQUIRED: The amount to be reported as current maturities of long-term debt in the balance sheet.

DISCUSSION: A long-term liability that will become due within 1 year or the firm's operating cycle, whichever is longer, should be reclassified as a current liability, except when (1) the portion currently due will be refinanced on a long-term basis, (2) the assets that will be used to retire the currently due portion are classified as noncurrent assets, or (3) capital stock will be issued to retire the portion currently due (SFAS 6). In this case, the obligations that should be reclassified as current are the $6,000 balance of the 14 1/2% term note due in 2003 and $20,000 of the 8% note (the payment is made to reduce principal in 11 equal payments), a total of $26,000. No exception applies.

Answer (A) is incorrect because payments into a sinking fund are not considered payments made to retire debt, and $8,000 does not include the $20,000 8% and $6,000 14 1/2% notes to be reclassified as current liabilities. Answer (B) is incorrect because payments into a sinking fund are not considered payments made to retire debt, and $20,000 of the 8% note must be reclassified as current. Answer (C) is incorrect because the 14 1/2% note should be reclassified as a current liability.

13. Derry Corp.'s liability account balances at June 30, 2002 included a 10% note payable in the amount of $3.6 million. The note is dated October 1, 2001 and is payable in three equal annual payments of $1.2 million plus interest. The first interest and principal payment was made on October 1, 2002. In Derry's June 30, 2003 balance sheet, what amount should be reported as accrued interest payable for this note?

A. $270,000

B. $180,000

C. $90,000

D. $60,000

Answer (B) is correct. *(CPA, adapted)*

REQUIRED: The amount that should be reported as accrued interest payable.

DISCUSSION: Accrued interest on the note payable at the balance sheet date is the carrying amount of the note multiplied by the interest rate on the note. Because the first payment was made 10/1/02, the carrying amount of the note is $2,400,000 ($3,600,000 – $1,200,000). Also, interest has accrued for only 9 months since the first payment. As a result, accrued interest payable is $180,000 [$2,400,000 × 10% × (9 months ÷ 12 months)].

Answer (A) is incorrect because the carrying amount of the note should be reduced by the payment of $1,200,000 made on 10/1/02. Answer (C) is incorrect because the carrying amount of the note should be reduced by the first payment of $1,200,000. Also, interest should be accrued for 9 months instead of 3. Answer (D) is incorrect because interest should be accrued for 9 months instead of 3.

14. On January 2, year 1, Kerry Co. issued $4 million of 10-year, 8% bonds at par. The bonds, dated January 1, year 1, pay interest semiannually on January 1 and July 1. Bond issue costs were $500,000. In accordance with current practice, what amount of bond issue costs is unamortized at June 30, year 2?

A. $475,000

B. $450,000

C. $441,600

D. $425,000

Answer (D) is correct. *(CPA, adapted)*

REQUIRED: The amount to be recorded as unamortized bond issue costs.

DISCUSSION: Bond issue costs are customarily amortized using the straight-line method for the term of the bond, although the interest method is theoretically superior. The rationale for the current practice is that the results do not differ materially from the interest method. Thus, the amortization is $50,000 per year ($500,000 ÷ 10 years). Because the bond has been held for 18 months, $75,000 ($50,000 + $25,000) of issue costs has been amortized by 6/30/year 2. The unamortized issue costs are $425,000 ($500,000 – $75,000).

Answer (A) is incorrect because an additional full year of amortization should have been claimed. Answer (B) is incorrect because 6 more months of issue costs should have been amortized for the time between 1/1/year 2 through 6/30/year 2. Answer (C) is incorrect because $441,600 results from amortization using the interest method.

15. On January 1, 1996, Cork Corporation issued one thousand of its 9%, $1,000 callable bonds for $1,030,000. The bonds are dated January 1, 1996 and mature on December 31, 2010. Interest is payable semiannually on January 1 and July 1. The bonds can be called by the issuer at 102 on any interest payment date after December 31, 2000. The unamortized bond premium was $14,000 at December 31, 2003, and the market price of the bonds was 99 on this date. In its December 31, 2003 balance sheet, at what amounts should Cork report the carrying amount of the bonds?

A. $1,020,000

B. $1,016,000

C. $1,014,000

D. $990,000

Answer (C) is correct. *(CPA, adapted)*

REQUIRED: The carrying amount of bonds issued at a premium.

DISCUSSION: The face amount of the bonds is $1,000,000 (1,000 × $1,000), and unamortized premium is $14,000 (given). The carrying amount is thus $1,014,000. The other data are irrelevant.

Answer (A) is incorrect because $1,020,000 is the amount to be paid if the bonds are called. Answer (B) is incorrect because $1,016,000 is the issue price minus the unamortized premium ($1,030,000 – $14,000). Answer (D) is incorrect because $990,000 is the market price.

16. A company issues 10-year bonds with a face amount of $1 million, dated January 1, year 1 and bearing interest at an annual rate of 12% payable semiannually on January 1 and July 1. The full interest amount will be paid each due date. The market rate of interest on bonds of similar risk and maturity, with the same schedule of interest payments, is also 12%. If the bonds are issued on February 1, year 1, the amount the issuing company receives from the buyers of the bonds on that date is

A. $990,000

B. $1,000,000

C. $1,010,000

D. $1,020,000

Answer (C) is correct. *(CIA, adapted)*

REQUIRED: The amount received when bonds are issued subsequent to the date printed on the face of the bonds.

DISCUSSION: The amount the issuing company receives on 2/1/year 1 is the face amount of the issue plus 1 month of accrued interest, or $1,010,000 {$1,000,000 + [($1,000,000 × 12%) ÷ 12]}.

Answer (A) is incorrect because $990,000 is the result if 1 month of accrued interest is deducted from, rather than added to, the amount received. Answer (B) is incorrect because the purchasers must pay for the accrued interest from the last interest date to the issue date. They will receive 6 months' interest on July 1 despite holding the bonds for 5 months. Answer (D) is incorrect because $1,020,000 results from adding 2 months of accrued interest to the face amount.

17. On December 31, year 1, Ulster Co. issued $200,000 of 8% serial bonds, to be repaid in the amount of $40,000 each year. Interest is payable annually on December 31. The bonds were issued to yield 10% a year. The bond proceeds were $190,280 based on the present values at December 31, year 1 of the five annual payments:

Due Date	Amounts Due: Principal	Amounts Due: Interest	Present Value at 12/31/X1
12/31/X2	$40,000	$16,000	$ 50,900
12/31/X3	40,000	12,800	43,610
12/31/X4	40,000	9,600	37,250
12/31/X5	40,000	6,400	31,690
12/31/X6	40,000	3,200	26,830
			$190,280

Ulster amortizes the bond discount by the interest method. In its December 31, year 2 balance sheet, at what amount should Ulster report the carrying amount of the bonds?

A. $139,380

B. $149,100

C. $150,280

D. $153,308

Answer (D) is correct. *(CPA, adapted)*

REQUIRED: The carrying amount after year one of bonds issued at a discount.

DISCUSSION: The carrying amount of the bonds for year one equals the proceeds of $190,280. Interest expense at the 10% effective rate is $19,028. Actual interest paid is $16,000, and discount amortization is $3,028 ($19,028 – $16,000). Thus, the discount remaining at year-end is $6,692 [($200,000 face amount – $190,280 issue proceeds) – $3,028 discount amortization]. Given that $40,000 in principal is paid at year-end, the carrying amount is $153,308 ($160,000 face amount – $6,692 unamortized discount).

Answer (A) is incorrect because $139,380 is the carrying amount of the bonds at 12/31/X1 minus the present value of the bonds due 12/31/X2. Answer (B) is incorrect because $149,100 is the difference between the face amount of the bonds and the present value of the bonds due 12/31/X2. Answer (C) is incorrect because $150,280 results from reducing the carrying amount at 12/31/X1 by the payment due 12/31/X2.

18. On July 1, Dover Co. received $206,576 for $200,000 face amount, 12% bonds, a price that yields 10%. Interest expense for the 6 months ended December 31 should be

A. $12,394

B. $12,000

C. $10,328

D. $10,000

Answer (C) is correct. *(CPA, adapted)*

REQUIRED: The amount of interest expense.

DISCUSSION: Under the interest method, interest expense for the 6 months since the bond was issued is equal to the carrying amount of the bond multiplied by the effective interest rate for half a year. Thus, interest expense is $10,328 [$206,576 × 10% × (6 ÷ 12)].

Answer (A) is incorrect because $12,394 is equal to the carrying amount multiplied by the coupon rate. Answer (B) is incorrect because $12,000 is equal to the face amount multiplied by the coupon rate. Answer (D) is incorrect because $10,000 is equal to the face amount multiplied by the yield rate.

Questions 19 and 20 are based on the following information. Clare Co. issued $6 million of 12% bonds on December 1, year 1, due on December 1, year 6, with interest payable each December 1 and June 1. The bonds were sold for $5,194,770 to yield 16%.

19. If the discount were amortized by the straight-line method, Clare's interest expense for the fiscal year ended November 30, year 2 related to its $6 million bond issue would be

A. $558,954

B. $623,372

C. $720,000

D. $881,046

Answer (D) is correct. *(CMA, adapted)*

REQUIRED: The interest expense under the straight-line amortization method.

DISCUSSION: Under the straight-line method, interest expense is the sum of the periodic cash flows plus the discount amortization. The periodic cash flows are equal to $720,000 ($6,000,000 face amount × 12% coupon rate). The discount at the time of issuance was $805,230 ($6,000,000 face amount – $5,194,770 issuance price). Because the term of the bonds is 5 years, amortization by the straight-line method each year will be $161,046 ($805,230 discount ÷ 5 years). Thus, interest expense is $881,046 ($720,000 + $161,046) for the fiscal year ended 11/30/year 2. Under the straight-line method, interest expense will be the same for each year in which the bonds are outstanding. However, the straight-line method is allowable only when it does not differ materially from the interest method.

Answer (A) is incorrect because $558,954 results from subtracting the amortization of the discount. Answer (B) is incorrect because $623,372 equals the carrying amount of the bond multiplied by the coupon rate. Answer (C) is incorrect because $720,000 is interest payable.

20. If the discount were amortized by the effective-interest method, Clare's interest expense for the fiscal year ended November 30, year 2 related to its $6 million bond issue would be

A. $623,372

B. $720,000

C. $831,163

D. $835,610

Answer (D) is correct. *(CMA, adapted)*

REQUIRED: The interest expense for the first year under the effective-interest method.

DISCUSSION: Under the interest method, interest expense is equal to the carrying amount of the bonds at the beginning of the interest period times the effective interest rate. The carrying amount of the bonds at December 1, year 1 (the issuance date) was $5,194,770. The annual yield rate was 16%. Interest expense is therefore equal to $415,582 [$5,194,770 × 16% × (6 ÷ 12)] for the first 6 months of the year. For the same period, interest paid was $360,000 [$6,000,000 × 12% × (6 ÷ 12)]. Hence, the semiannual discount amortization was $55,582 ($415,582 interest expense – $360,000 interest paid), and the carrying amount of the bonds for the second 6-month period was $5,250,352 ($5,194,770 + $55,582). For this period, the semiannual interest expense was $420,028 [$5,250,352 × 16% × (6 ÷ 12)]. Total interest expense for the year is equal to $835,610 ($415,582 + $420,028).

Answer (A) is incorrect because $623,372 is equal to the carrying amount of the bond multiplied by the coupon rate. Answer (B) is incorrect because $720,000 is interest payable. Answer (C) is incorrect because $831,163 results from calculating interest expense as if interest is payable annually.

21. On July 1, 2003, Calais Company issued 500 of its 8%, $1,000 bonds for $438,000. The bonds were issued to yield 10%. The bonds are dated July 1, 2003 and mature on July 1, 2013. Interest is payable semiannually on January 1 and July 1. Using the interest method, how much of the bond discount should be amortized for the 6 months ended December 31, 2003? .

A. $3,800

B. $3,100

C. $2,480

D. $1,900

Answer (D) is correct. *(CPA, adapted)*

REQUIRED: The amount of bond discount to be amortized using the interest method.

DISCUSSION: Under the interest method, interest expense is equal to the carrying amount of the bonds at the beginning of the interest period times the yield rate. Because interest is paid semiannually, the semiannual interest rate is equal to one-half of the annual rate. Interest expense is therefore $21,900 [$438,000 × 10% × (6 ÷ 12)]. The periodic cash payment is $20,000 [$500,000 face amount × 8% stated rate × (6 ÷ 12)]. The $1,900 ($21,900 – $20,000) difference is the amount of discount to be amortized during this 6-month interest period.

Answer (A) is incorrect because $3,800 is the discount amortized for a full year. Answer (B) is incorrect because $3,100 is the difference between interest expense calculated at 10% and interest payable calculated at 10% for half a year. Answer (C) is incorrect because $2,480 is equal to the difference between interest expense calculated at 8% and interest payable calculated at 8% for half a year.

22. On January 1, 2003, Dundee Corp. issued 9% bonds in the face amount of $1 million, which mature on January 1, 2013. The bonds were issued for $939,000 to yield 10%, resulting in a bond discount of $61,000. Dundee uses the interest method of amortizing bond discount. Interest is payable annually on December 31. At December 31, 2003, Dundee's unamortized bond discount should be

A. $51,000

B. $51,610

C. $52,000

D. $57,100

Answer (D) is correct. *(CPA, adapted)*

REQUIRED: The amount of unamortized bond discount at the end of the first year.

DISCUSSION: Under the interest method, interest expense is equal to the carrying amount of the bonds at the beginning of the period times the market (yield) rate of interest. For the first year, interest expense is $93,900 ($939,000 carrying amount × 10% yield rate). The periodic interest payment is $90,000 ($1,000,000 face amount × 9% coupon rate). The $3,900 ($93,900 – $90,000) difference is the amount of bond discount to be amortized. Thus, the $61,000 unamortized bond discount at the beginning of the year should be reduced by $3,900 to a year-end balance of $57,100.

Answer (A) is incorrect because $51,000 results from reducing the discount by the face amount times the market (yield) rate less the interest payment. Answer (B) is incorrect because $51,610 results from reducing the discount by the difference between the carrying amount times the yield less the carrying amount times the coupon rate. Answer (C) is incorrect because the bond discount is reduced by the interest payment.

23. Karrie Co. has outstanding a 7%, 10-year bond with a $100,000 face amount. The bond was originally sold to yield 6% annual interest. Karrie uses the effective-interest-rate method to amortize bond premium. On June 30, year 1, the carrying amount of the outstanding bond was $105,000. What amount of unamortized premium on the bond should Karrie report in its June 30, year 2 balance sheet?

A. $1,050

B. $3,950

C. $4,300

D. $4,500

Answer (C) is correct. *(CPA, adapted)*

REQUIRED: The amount of unamortized premium.

DISCUSSION: Under the interest method, interest expense is equal to the carrying amount of the bonds at the beginning of the interest period times the market (yield) rate of interest. Interest expense for the year ended 6/30/02 is $6,300 (6% × $105,000 carrying amount), and the periodic interest payment is $7,000 (7% × $100,000). The difference ($7,000 – $6,300 = $700) is the amount of premium amortized. The unamortized premium is therefore $4,300 ($5,000 – $700).

Answer (A) is incorrect because $1,050 equals 18 months of interest payments. Answer (B) is incorrect because $3,950 equals the premium minus 18 months of interest payments. Answer (D) is incorrect because $4,500 assumes straight-line amortization and a 6/30/year 1 issue date.

24. On January 2, 2003, Ost Co. issued 9% bonds in the amount of $500,000, which mature on January 2, 2013. The bonds were issued for $469,500 to yield 10%. Interest is payable annually on December 31. Ost uses the interest method of amortizing bond discount. In its June 30, 2003 balance sheet, what amount should Ost report as bonds payable?

A. $469,500

B. $470,475

C. $471,025

D. $500,000

Answer (B) is correct. *(CPA, adapted)*

REQUIRED: The amount to be reported as bonds payable at an interim date.

DISCUSSION: Accrued interest expense is $23,475 [$469,500 × 10% × (6 ÷ 12)]. Accrued interest payable is $22,500 [$500,000 × 9% × (6 ÷ 12)]. The difference of $975 is the amount of discount amortization for the period. Bonds payable equal $470,475 ($469,500 + $975).

Answer (A) is incorrect because $469,500 is the issue price unadjusted for discount amortization. Answer (C) is incorrect because $471,025 reflects a full year's discount amortization. Answer (D) is incorrect because $500,000 is the face amount of the bonds.

12.2 Convertible Bonds

Questions 25 and 26 are based on the following information. On January 2, year 1, Kiril Co. issued 10-year convertible bonds at 105. During year 4, these bonds were converted into common stock having an aggregate par value equal to the total face amount of the bonds. At conversion, the market price of Kiril's common stock was 50% above its par value.

25. On January 2, year 1, cash proceeds from the issuance of the convertible bonds should be reported as

A. Contributed capital for the entire proceeds.

B. Contributed capital for the portion of the proceeds attributable to the conversion feature and as a liability for the balance.

C. A liability for the face amount of the bonds and contributed capital for the premium.

D. A liability for the entire proceeds.

Answer (D) is correct. *(CPA, adapted)*

REQUIRED: The proper accounting for cash proceeds received from the issuance of convertible bonds.

DISCUSSION: APB 14, *Convertible Debt and Debt Issued with Stock Purchase Warrants*, states that the entire proceeds from the issuance of convertible bonds must be reported as a liability until such time as the bonds are converted into stock.

Answer (A) is incorrect because the cash proceeds from the issuance of the convertible bonds must be treated as a liability for the entire amount. Answer (B) is incorrect because the cash proceeds from the issuance of the convertible bonds must be treated as a liability for the entire amount. Answer (C) is incorrect because the cash proceeds from the issuance of the convertible bonds must be treated as a liability for the entire amount.

26. Depending on whether the book-value method or the market-value method was used, Kiril should recognize gains or losses on conversion when using the

	Book-Value Method	Market-Value Method
A.	Either gain or loss	Gain
B.	Either gain or loss	Loss
C.	Neither gain nor loss	Loss
D.	Neither gain nor loss	Gain

Answer (C) is correct. *(CPA, adapted)*

REQUIRED: The accounting method(s) that recognizes gains or losses on the conversion of the convertible bonds.

DISCUSSION: Under the book-value method for recognizing the conversion of outstanding bonds payable to common stock, the stock issued is recorded at the carrying amount of the bonds with no recognition of gain or loss. Under the market-value method, the stock is recorded at the market value of the stock (or of the bonds). A gain or loss is recognized equal to the difference between the market value recorded and the carrying amount of the bonds payable. At the time of the conversion, Kiril's common stock had an aggregate par value equal to the total face amount of the bonds, and the market price of the stock was 50% above its par value. Thus, a loss should have been recognized upon conversion in accordance with the market-value method. The total of the credits to equity accounts exceeds the total of the debits to bonds payable and unamortized premium. The difference is the amount of the loss.

27. What is the preferred method of handling unamortized discount, unamortized issue costs, and the costs of implementing a conversion of debt into common stock?

A. Expense them in the period bonds are converted.

B. Amortize them over the remaining life of the issue retired.

C. Amortize them over a period not to exceed 40 years.

D. Charge them to paid-in capital in excess of the par value of the stock issued.

Answer (D) is correct. *(Publisher)*

REQUIRED: The preferred handling of unamortized discount, unamortized issue costs, and the costs of converting debt into common stock.

DISCUSSION: The conversion of debt into common stock is ordinarily based upon the carrying amount of the debt at the time of issuance. Because the carrying amount is based on all related accounts, the debit balances of unamortized bond discount, unamortized issue costs, and conversion costs should be considered reductions in the net carrying amount at the time of conversion. Consequently, these items should be reflected as reductions in the additional paid-in capital account.

Answer (A) is incorrect because these amounts are not expensed. In effect, each reduces the amount at which the stock is issued. Answer (B) is incorrect because these amounts are not expensed. In effect, each reduces the amount at which the stock is issued. Answer (C) is incorrect because these amounts are not expensed. In effect, each reduces the amount at which the stock is issued.

28. On July 1, after recording interest and amortization, Lancaster Co. converted $2 million of its 12% convertible bonds into 100,000 shares of $1 par value common stock. On the conversion date, the carrying amount of the bonds was $2.6 million, the market value of the bonds was $2.8 million, and Lancaster's common stock was publicly trading at $30 per share. Using the book-value method, what amount of additional paid-in capital should Lancaster record as a result of the conversion?

A. $1,900,000

B. $2,500,000

C. $2,700,000

D. $3,000,000

Answer (B) is correct. *(CPA, adapted)*

REQUIRED: The amount of additional paid-in capital reported on the conversion of bonds when the book-value method is used.

DISCUSSION: Under the book-value method for recognizing the conversion of outstanding bonds payable to common stock, the stock issued is recorded at the carrying amount of the bonds with no recognition of a gain or loss. Accordingly, the conversion should be recorded at $2.6 million. However, this amount must be allocated between common stock and additional paid-in capital. The common stock account is always valued at par value; therefore, $100,000 (100,000 shares × $1) will be credited to common stock and $2,500,000 to additional paid-in capital.

Answer (A) is incorrect because $1,900,000 equals the face amount of the bonds minus the par value of the stock. Answer (C) is incorrect because $2,700,000 is the market value of the bonds minus the par value of the stock. Answer (D) is incorrect because $3,000,000 is the market value of the stock.

29. According to SFAS 84, *Induced Conversions of Convertible Debt*, an issuer of a convertible security may attempt to induce prompt conversion of its convertible debt to equity securities by offering additional securities or other consideration as a sweetener. The additional consideration used to induce conversion should be reported as a(n)

A. Reduction of the paid-in capital recognized for the new equity securities.

B. Reduction of retained earnings.

C. Extraordinary item in the current income statement.

D. Expense of the current period, but not an extraordinary item.

Answer (D) is correct. *(CMA, adapted)*

REQUIRED: The proper treatment of a convertible debt sweetener.

DISCUSSION: A debtor may induce conversion of convertible debt by offering additional securities or other consideration to the holders of convertible debt. SFAS 84 requires that this convertible debt sweetener be recognized as an ordinary expense. It is equal to the fair value of the securities or other consideration transferred in excess of the fair value of the securities that would have been issued under the original conversion privilege.

Answer (A) is incorrect because SFAS 84 requires the sweetener to be recognized as an ordinary expense. Answer (B) is incorrect because SFAS 84 requires the sweetener to be recognized as an ordinary expense. Answer (C) is incorrect because SFAS 84 requires the sweetener to be recognized as an ordinary expense.

30. Any gains or losses from the early extinguishment of convertible debt should be

A. Recognized in current income of the period of extinguishment.

B. Treated as an increase or decrease in paid-in capital.

C. Split between a portion that is an increase (decrease) in paid-in capital and a portion recognized in current income.

D. Amortized over the remaining original life of the extinguished convertible debt.

Answer (A) is correct. *(Publisher)*

REQUIRED: The treatment of gains or losses from early extinguishment of convertible debt.

DISCUSSION: The accounting for the extinguishment of convertible debt and for ordinary debt is the same. APB 26, *Early Extinguishment of Debt*, states that a difference between the cash reacquisition price of the debt and its net carrying amount should be recognized as income in the period of extinguishment.

Answer (B) is incorrect because the debt and equity features are treated as inseparable. The convertible debt should be accounted for as if it were ordinary debt. Answer (C) is incorrect because the debt and equity features are treated as inseparable. The convertible debt should be accounted for as if it were ordinary debt. Answer (D) is incorrect because amortization was rejected by APB 26 in favor of current recognition in income of the full gain or loss.

12.3 Bonds and Warrants

31. How should the value of warrants attached to a debt security be accounted for?

A. No value assigned.

B. A separate portion of paid-in capital.

C. An appropriation of retained earnings.

D. A liability.

Answer (A) is correct. *(CPA, adapted)*

REQUIRED: The accounting for the value of warrants attached to a debt security.

DISCUSSION: Assuming the warrants are not detachable and the debt security must be surrendered to exercise the warrants, the securities are substantially equivalent to convertible debt. Under APB 14, *Convertible Debt and Debt Issued with Stock Purchase Warrants*, no portion of the proceeds from the issuance should be accounted for as attributable to the conversion feature or the warrants.

Answer (B) is incorrect because the portion of the proceeds allocable to the warrants should be accounted for as paid-in capital only if the warrants are detachable. Answer (C) is incorrect because the value of the warrants should either not be recognized or be recognized as paid-in capital. Answer (D) is incorrect because the value of the warrants should either not be recognized or be recognized as paid-in capital.

32. When bonds are issued with stock purchase warrants, a portion of the proceeds should be allocated to paid-in capital for bonds issued with

	Detachable Stock Purchase Warrants	Nondetachable Stock Purchase Warrants
A.	No	Yes
B.	No	No
C.	Yes	No
D.	Yes	Yes

Answer (C) is correct. *(CPA, adapted)*

REQUIRED: The circumstances in which proceeds from the issuance of a bond should be allocated between the bond and stock warrants.

DISCUSSION: APB 14 requires the proceeds from debt securities issued with detachable warrants to be allocated between the debt securities and the warrants based on their relative fair values at the time of issuance. The portion allocated to the warrants should be accounted for as paid-in capital. However, when debt securities are issued with nondetachable warrants, no part of the proceeds should be allocated to the warrants.

33. Bonds with detachable stock warrants were issued by Flack Co. Immediately after issue the aggregate market value of the bonds and the warrants exceeds the proceeds. Is the portion of the proceeds allocated to the warrants less than their market value, and is that amount recorded as contributed capital?

	Less than Warrants' Market Value	Contributed Capital
A.	No	Yes
B.	Yes	No
C.	Yes	Yes
D.	No	No

Answer (C) is correct. *(CPA, adapted)*
REQUIRED: The allocation of proceeds to detachable warrants and the recording of the allocation.
DISCUSSION: APB 14 requires the proceeds from debt securities issued with detachable warrants to be allocated between the debt securities and the warrants based on their relative fair values at the time of issuance. The portion allocated to the warrants should be accounted for as paid-in (contributed) capital. Assuming that the market values of both the bonds and the warrants are known and the proceeds are less than their sum, the allocation process must result in crediting paid-in (contributed) capital from stock warrants (stock warrants outstanding) for less than their market value. If the market value of the bonds is not known, the warrants will be credited at their market value.
Answer (A) is incorrect because the warrants will be credited at less than market value. Answer (B) is incorrect because the amount allocated to the warrants is credited to paid-in (contributed) capital. Answer (D) is incorrect because the warrants will be credited at less than market value, and the amount allocated to the warrants is credited to paid-in (contributed) capital.

34. On December 30, 2002, Worcester, Inc. issued 1,000 of its 8%, 10-year, $1,000 face amount bonds with detachable stock warrants at par. Each bond carried a detachable warrant for one share of Worcester's common stock at a specified option price of $25 per share. Immediately after issuance, the market value of the bonds without the warrants was $1,080,000, and the market value of the warrants was $120,000. In its December 31, 2002 balance sheet, what amount should Worcester report as bonds payable?

A. $1,000,000
B. $975,000
C. $900,000
D. $880,000

Answer (C) is correct. *(CPA, adapted)*
REQUIRED: The amount reported for bonds payable with detachable stock warrants.
DISCUSSION: The issue price of the bonds is allocated between the bonds and the detachable stock warrants based on their relative fair values. The market price of bonds without the warrants is $1,080,000, which is 90% [$1,080,000 ÷ ($1,080,000 + $120,000)] of the total fair value of the bonds without warrants plus the value of the warrants. Consequently, 90% of the issue price should be allocated to the bonds, and they should be reported at $900,000 (90% × $1,000,000) in the balance sheet.
Answer (A) is incorrect because $1,000,000 equals the total proceeds. Answer (B) is incorrect because $975,000 is the result of deducting the option price of the stock from the total proceeds. Answer (D) is incorrect because $880,000 is the result of deducting the fair value of the warrants from the total proceeds.

35. Armagh Corp. issued bonds with a face amount of $200,000. Each $1,000 bond contained detachable stock warrants for 100 shares of Armagh's common stock. Total proceeds from the issue amounted to $240,000. The market value of each warrant was $2, and the market value of the bonds without the warrants was $196,000. The bonds were issued at a discount of

A. $0
B. $678
C. $4,000
D. $40,678

Answer (B) is correct. *(CPA, adapted)*
REQUIRED: The amount of the bond discount.
DISCUSSION: The proceeds of bonds issued with detachable stock warrants must be allocated based on their relative fair values at the time of issuance. The fair values are $196,000 for the bonds and $40,000 for the warrants (200 bonds × 100 shares × 1 warrant per share × $2). Of the total proceeds of $240,000, $199,322 should be allocated to the bonds. Hence, bond discount is $678 ($200,000 face amount – $199,322 allocated proceeds).

$$\frac{\$196,000}{\$196,000 + \$40,000} \times \$240,000 = \$199,322$$

Answer (A) is incorrect because the allocation to the bonds was less than their face amount. Answer (C) is incorrect because $4,000 is the difference between the face amount and the market value of the bonds. Answer (D) is incorrect because $40,678 is the amount allocated to the warrants.

36. On March 1, 2002, Quebec Corp. issued $1 million of 10%, nonconvertible bonds at 103. They were due on February 28, 2012. Each $1,000 bond was issued with 30 detachable stock warrants, each of which entitled the holder to purchase, for $50, one share of Quebec common stock, par value $25. On March 1, 2002, the quoted market value of Quebec's common stock was $20 per share, and the market value of each warrant was $4. What amount of the bond issue proceeds should Quebec record as an increase in equity?

A. $120,000

B. $90,000

C. $30,000

D. $0

Answer (A) is correct. *(CPA, adapted)*

REQUIRED: The proceeds from bonds issued with detachable stock warrants to be recorded as equity.

DISCUSSION: When bonds are issued with detachable stock warrants, the proceeds must be allocated between the warrants and the bonds on the basis of their relative fair values. When the fair value of the warrants but not the bonds is known, paid-in capital from stock warrants should be credited (increased) for the fair value of the warrants, with the remainder credited to the bonds. Quebec issued 1,000 bonds ($1,000,000 ÷ 1,000); therefore, 30,000 warrants (1,000 bonds × 30 warrants) must also have been issued. Their fair value was $120,000 (30,000 warrants × $4), which is the amount of the credit to paid-in capital from stock warrants. The remainder of the proceeds [($1,000,000 × 103%) – $120,000 = $910,000] is allocated to bonds payable.

Answer (B) is incorrect because $90,000 equals the discount on the bonds. Answer (C) is incorrect because $30,000 is the difference between the fair value of the warrants and the discount on the bonds. Answer (D) is incorrect because stock warrants outstanding (paid-in capital from stock warrants) is an equity account.

37. Winnipeg Company issued bonds with detachable stock warrants. Each warrant granted an option to buy one share of $40 par value common stock for $75 per share. Five hundred warrants were originally issued, and $4,000 was appropriately credited to warrants. If 90% of these warrants are exercised when the market price of the common stock is $85 per share, how much should be credited to capital in excess of par on this transaction?

A. $19,350

B. $19,750

C. $23,850

D. $24,250

Answer (A) is correct. *(CPA, adapted)*

REQUIRED: The credit to capital in excess of par upon exercise of 90% of the warrants.

DISCUSSION: If 90% of the warrants are exercised, 450 shares must be issued at $75 per share. The total debit to cash is $33,750. The debit to stock warrants outstanding reflects the exercise of 90% of $4,000 of warrants, or $3,600. The par value of the common stock issued is credited for $18,000 (450 shares × $40 par). The balance of $19,350 ($33,750 + $3,600 – $18,000) is credited to capital in excess of par. The transaction is based on the exercise price, not the fair value of the stock or warrants at the time of issuance.

	Debit	Credit
Cash	$33,750	
Warrants	3,600	
Common stock at par		$18,000
Capital in excess of par		19,350

Answer (B) is incorrect because $19,750 results from assuming all of the warrants were exercised with the same amount of stock being issued. Answer (C) is incorrect because $23,850 results from issuing the stock for $85 per share instead of $75. Answer (D) is incorrect because $24,250 results from issuing the stock for $85 per share, instead of $75, and assuming all of the warrants were exercised with the same amount of stock being issued.

12.4 Extinguishment of Debt

38. An entity should not derecognize an existing liability under which of the following circumstances?

A. The entity exchanges convertible preferred stock for its outstanding debt securities. The debt securities are not canceled but are held as treasury bonds.

B. Because of financial difficulties being experienced by the entity, a creditor accepts a parcel of land as full satisfaction of an overdue loan. The value of the land is less than 50% of the loan balance.

C. The entity irrevocably places cash into a trust that will be used solely to satisfy scheduled principal and interest payments of a specific bond obligation. Because the trust investments will generate a higher return, the amount of cash is less than the carrying amount of the debt.

D. As part of the agreement to purchase a shopping center from the entity, the buyer assumes without recourse the mortgage for which the center serves as collateral.

Answer (C) is correct. *(Publisher)*

REQUIRED: The circumstances under which an existing liability should not be derecognized.

DISCUSSION: SFAS 140, *Accounting for Transfers and Servicing of Financial Assets and Extinguishments of Liabilities*, provides for the derecognition of a liability only if it has been extinguished. Extinguishment occurs when either (1) the debtor pays the creditor and is relieved of its obligation for the liability, or (2) the debtor is legally released from being the primary obligor under the liability, either judicially or by the creditor. SFAS 140 prohibits the recognition of a gain or loss from an in-substance defeasance.

Answer (A) is incorrect because the debt is extinguished when the entity exchanges convertible preferred stock for its outstanding debt securities. This exchange is at fair value (SFAS 15). Debt-equity swaps are rare because they are not tax-exempt. Answer (B) is incorrect because the debt is extinguished when a creditor accepts a parcel of land as full satisfaction of an overdue loan. Answer (D) is incorrect because the debt is extinguished when a buyer assumes without recourse the mortgage for which the property sold is collateral.

39. PPF partnership purchased land for $1,000,000 on May 1, year 1, paying $200,000 cash and giving an $800,000 note payable to Lender Bank. PPF made three annual payments on the note totaling $358,000, which included interest of $178,000. PPF then defaulted on the note. Title to the land was transferred by PPF to Lender, which canceled the note, releasing the partnership from further liability. At the time of the default, the fair value of the land approximated the note balance. In PPF's year 4 income statement, the amount of the loss should be

A. $558,000

B. $442,000

C. $380,000

D. $200,000

Answer (C) is correct. *(CPA, adapted)*

REQUIRED: The amount of the loss after default on a note and repossession of the land.

DISCUSSION: The principal of the note had been reduced to $620,000 [$800,000 – ($358,000 total payments – $178,000 interest)] at the time of default. The resultant $380,000 loss is equal to the difference between the $1,000,000 carrying amount (cost) of the land and the $620,000 carrying amount of the note.

Answer (A) is incorrect because $558,000 results from subtracting the full amount of the payments ($358,000) in determining the remaining principal. Answer (B) is incorrect because $442,000 is the note payable balance after subtracting the $178,000 of interest. Answer (D) is incorrect because $200,000 is the amount of the initial payment.

40. Paris Co. issued a 10-year, $100,000, 9% note on January 1, year 1. The note was issued to yield 10% for proceeds of $93,770. Interest is payable semiannually. The note is callable after 2 years at a price of $96,000. Due to a decline in the market rate to 8%, Paris retired the note on December 31, year 3. On that date, the carrying amount of the note was $94,582, and the discounted amount of its cash flows based on the market rate was $105,280. What amount should Paris report as gain (loss) from extinguishment of the note for the year ended December 31, year 3?

A. $9,280

B. $4,000

C. $(2,230)

D. $(1,418)

Answer (D) is correct. *(CPA, adapted)*

REQUIRED: The amount of gain (loss) from the extinguishment of a note.

DISCUSSION: The amount of gain or loss resulting from the extinguishment of debt is the difference between the amount paid and the carrying amount of the note. Thus, a loss of $1,418 ($94,582 carrying amount – $96,000 amount paid) results from the extinguishment.

Answer (A) is incorrect because $9,280 is the difference between the discounted amount based on the market rate and the call price. Answer (B) is incorrect because $4,000 is the difference between the face amount of the note and the call price. Answer (C) is incorrect because $(2,230) is the difference between the original amount received and the call price.

41. On June 2, year 1, Danube Co. issued $500,000 of 10%, 15-year bonds at par. Interest is payable semiannually on June 1 and December 1. Bond issue costs were $6,000. On June 2, year 5, Danube retired half of the bonds at 98. What is the net amount that Danube should use in computing the gain or loss on extinguishment of debt?

A. $250,000

B. $248,000

C. $247,000

D. $246,000

Answer (B) is correct. *(CPA, adapted)*

REQUIRED: The net amount used in computing the gain or loss on the extinguishment of debt.

DISCUSSION: The gain or loss on the extinguishment of debt is equal to the difference between the proceeds paid and the carrying amount of the debt. The carrying amount of the debt is equal to the face amount plus any unamortized premium or minus any unamortized discount. In addition, any unamortized issue costs are considered in effect a reduction of the carrying amount even though they are accounted for separately from the bond discount or premium. The amortization of the issue costs is $400 per year ($6,000 ÷ 15). Because accumulated amortization is $2,000 ($400 × 5), the unamortized issue costs are $4,000 ($6,000 – $2,000), of which 50% or $2,000 should be subtracted in determining the carrying amount of the bonds retired. Consequently, the net carrying amount that should be used in computing the gain or loss on this early extinguishment of debt is $248,000 ($250,000 face amount – $2,000 unamortized deferred bond issue costs).

Answer (A) is incorrect because $250,000 is half of the par value. Answer (C) is incorrect because $247,000 is half of the par value minus half of the issue costs. Answer (D) is incorrect because $246,000 results from subtracting 100% of the unamortized issue costs.

42. On July 31, 2003, Nile Co. issued $1 million of 10%, 15-year bonds at par and used a portion of the proceeds to call its 600 outstanding 11%, $1,000 face amount bonds, due on July 31, 2013, at 102. On that date, unamortized bond premium relating to the 11% bonds was $65,000. In its 2003 income statement, what amount should Nile report as gain or loss, before income taxes, from extinguishment of bonds?

A. $53,000 gain.

B. $0

C. $(65,000) loss.

D. $(77,000) loss.

Answer (A) is correct. *(CPA, adapted)*

REQUIRED: The amount to be reported for the extinguishment of bonds.

DISCUSSION: The excess of the net carrying amount of the bonds over the reacquisition price is a gain from extinguishment. The carrying amount of the bonds equals $665,000 ($600,000 face amount + $65,000 unamortized premium). The reacquisition price is $612,000 (600 × $1,000 × 1.02). Thus, the gain from extinguishment is $53,000 ($665,000 – $612,000).

Answer (B) is incorrect because the excess of the carrying amount over the reacquisition cost is a gain. Answer (C) is incorrect because $65,000 is the unamortized premium. Answer (D) is incorrect because $77,000 equals the reacquisition price of $612,000, minus the face amount of $600,000, plus $65,000 unamortized premium.

43. On June 30, 2003, Rhine Co. had outstanding 9%, $5,000,000 face amount bonds maturing on June 30, 2005. Interest was payable semiannually every June 30 and December 31. On June 30, 2003, after amortization was recorded for the period, the unamortized bond premium and bond issue costs were $30,000 and $50,000, respectively. On that date, Rhine acquired all its outstanding bonds on the open market at 98 and retired them. At June 30, 2003, what amount should Rhine recognize as gain before income taxes on redemption of bonds?

A. $20,000

B. $80,000

C. $120,000

D. $180,000

Answer (B) is correct. *(CPA, adapted)*

REQUIRED: The amount of gain from the redemption of bonds.

DISCUSSION: The amount of gain or loss on the redemption of bonds is equal to the difference between the proceeds paid and the carrying amount of the debt. The carrying amount of the bonds is equal to the face amount, plus unamortized bond premium, minus unamortized bond issue costs. Thus, the carrying amount of the bonds is $4,980,000 (5,000,000 + 30,000 – 50,000). The $80,000 gain is the difference between the carrying amount ($4,980,000) and the amount paid $4,900,000 ($5,000,000 × .98).

Answer (A) is incorrect because $20,000 results from subtracting the unamortized bond premium and bond issue costs from the face amount of the bond. Answer (C) is incorrect because the unamortized bond issue costs are added to the face amount of the bond and bond premium is subtracted to find the carrying amount. Answer (D) is incorrect because both the unamortized bond issue costs and bond premium are added to find the carrying amount of the bond.

44. On January 2, 2003, Seine Corporation entered into an in-substance debt defeasance transaction by placing cash of $875,000 into an irrevocable trust. The trust assets are to be used solely for satisfying the interest and principal payments on Seine's 6%, $1.1 million, 30-year bond payable. Seine has not been legally released under the bond agreement, but the probability is remote that Seine will be required to place additional cash in the trust. On December 31, 2002, the bond's carrying amount was $1,050,000; its fair value was $800,000. Disregarding income taxes, what amount of gain (loss) should Seine report in its 2003 income statement?

A. ($75,000)

B. $0

C. $175,000

D. $225,000

Answer (B) is correct. *(Publisher)*
REQUIRED: The amount of gain (loss) to be recognized on an in-substance defeasance.
DISCUSSION: SFAS 140 prohibits the recognition of a gain (loss) from an in-substance defeasance.
Answer (A) is incorrect because an in-substance defeasance does not result in the derecognition of a liability. Answer (C) is incorrect because an in-substance defeasance does not result in the derecognition of a liability. Answer (D) is incorrect because an in-substance defeasance does not result in the derecognition of a liability.

45. A debtor should derecognize a liability in which circumstances?

I. The debtor pays the creditor and is relieved of its obligation with respect to the liability.
II. The debtor is legally released from being the primary obligor.
III. The debtor irrevocably places cash or other assets in a trust to be used solely for satisfying scheduled payments of interest and principal of a specific obligation.

A. I only.

B. I and II only.

C. II and III only.

D. I, II, and III.

Answer (B) is correct. *(Publisher)*
REQUIRED: The circumstances in which a debtor should derecognize a liability.
DISCUSSION: Under SFAS 140, a debtor derecognizes a liability only if it has been extinguished. Extinguishment results only if the debtor pays the creditor and is relieved of its obligation with respect to the liability, or if the debtor is legally released from being the primary obligor, either judicially or by the creditor.
Answer (A) is incorrect because a legal release also permits derecognition. Answer (C) is incorrect because an in-substance defeasance (III) does not constitute an extinguishment. Answer (D) is incorrect because an in-substance defeasance (III) does not constitute an extinguishment.

46. Columbia Corporation extinguished an issue of bonds before its maturity date through a direct exchange of securities. The new issue of debt is best measured by the

A. Maturity amount of the new issue.

B. Net carrying amount of the old issue.

C. Present value of the new issue.

D. Maturity amount of the old issue.

Answer (C) is correct. *(CPA, adapted)*
REQUIRED: The best value to assign a new issue of debt used to extinguish an issue of bonds.
DISCUSSION: APB 26, *Early Extinguishment of Debt*, states that if an early extinguishment of debt is achieved by a direct exchange of new securities (a refunding), the reacquisition price is accounted for at the present value of the new securities.

47. A 15-year bond was issued in year 1 at a discount. During year 11, a 10-year bond was issued at face amount with the proceeds used to retire the 15-year bond at its face amount. The net effect of the year 11 bond transactions was to increase long-term liabilities by the excess of the 10-year bond's face amount over the 15-year bond's

A. Face amount.

B. Carrying amount.

C. Face amount minus the deferred loss on bond retirement.

D. Carrying amount minus the deferred loss on bond retirement.

Answer (B) is correct. *(CPA, adapted)*

REQUIRED: The net effect of the bond transactions.

DISCUSSION: The 10-year bond was issued at its face amount, that is, at neither a premium nor a discount. Its face amount therefore equaled its proceeds, which were used to retire the 15-year bond at its face amount. The 15-year bond was carried at a discount (face amount – unamortized discount). Consequently, net long-term liabilities must have increased by the amount of the unamortized discount on the 15-year bond, which is the excess of the 10-year bond's face amount over the carrying amount of the 15-year bond.

Answer (A) is incorrect because the face amount of the 10-year bond equaled the face amount of the 15-year bond. Answer (C) is incorrect because the loss on early extinguishment is not deferred. Answer (D) is incorrect because the loss on early extinguishment is not deferred.

12.5 Interest on Receivables and Payables

48. A company issued a noninterest-bearing note payable due in 1 year in exchange for land. Which of the following statements is true concerning the accounting for the transaction?

A. The land should be recorded at the future value of the note, and interest should be imputed at the prevailing rate on similar notes.

B. No interest should be recognized on the note, and the land should be recorded at the present value of the note.

C. Interest on the note should be imputed at the prime rate, and the land should be recorded at the discounted value of the note.

D. Interest on the note should be imputed at the prevailing rate for similar notes, and the land should be recorded at the present value of the note.

Answer (D) is correct. *(CIA, adapted)*

REQUIRED: The proper accounting for a noninterest-bearing note.

DISCUSSION: If interest on a note is not stated, it is imputed by recording the note at the fair value of the property, goods, or services exchanged, or at the fair value of the note itself. If these values are not determinable, an interest rate must be imputed. APB 21 establishes certain guidelines for imputing an interest rate. The rate should be at least equal to that at which the debtor could obtain financing of a similar nature from other sources. Other considerations are the market rate for an exchange of the note, the prime or higher rate for notes discounted with banks in light of the credit standing of the maker, and the current rates for debt instruments with substantially identical terms and risks that are traded in open markets. Accordingly, if the fair value of the note or the land is not determinable, the transaction will be recorded at the present value of the note based on an imputed rate.

Answer (A) is incorrect because the land is recorded at present value. Answer (B) is incorrect because interest should be recognized on the note. Answer (C) is incorrect because the proper discount rate is the prevailing rate for similar notes, not the prime rate.

49. When it is necessary to impute interest in connection with a note receivable, the imputed rate should be

A. Influenced by the prevailing market rate for debt instruments with substantially identical terms and risks.

B. Two-thirds of the prime rate effective at the time the note is received.

C. Equal to the rate obtainable on government securities with comparable due dates.

D. The minimum rate allowed by the Internal Revenue Code.

Answer (A) is correct. *(Publisher)*

REQUIRED: The true statement concerning imputation of an interest rate in connection with a note receivable.

DISCUSSION: APB 21 establishes certain guidelines for selecting an interest rate. The rate should be at least equal to that at which the debtor could obtain financing of a similar nature from other sources. Other considerations are the market rate for an exchange of the note, the prime or higher rate for notes discounted with banks in light of the credit standing of the maker, and the current rates for debt instruments with substantially identical terms and risks that are traded in open markets.

Answer (B) is incorrect because APB 21 does not specify any particular interest rate. Answer (C) is incorrect because APB 21 does not specify any particular interest rate. Answer (D) is incorrect because APB 21 does not specify any particular interest rate.

50. Utah Corp. lends a supplier cash that is to be repaid 5 years hence with no stated interest. At the same time, a purchase contract is entered into for the supplier's products. Utah will be required to recognize interest revenue in connection with the loan

A. Under no circumstances.

B. If the contract price is equal to the prevailing market rate.

C. If the contract price is less than the prevailing market rate.

D. If the contract price is more than the prevailing market rate.

Answer (C) is correct. *(CPA, adapted)*

REQUIRED: The circumstances in which interest revenue will be recognized.

DISCUSSION: Ordinarily, a note received solely for cash equal to its face amount is presumed to earn the stated rate of interest. However, if, in addition, some right or privilege has been exchanged, its value must be recognized in the accounts in accordance with APB 21. If the contract price is less than the market rate, Utah Corp.'s note receivable will be debited and cash credited for the amount of the loan. In addition, prepaid purchases (an asset) will be debited and discount on notes receivable will be credited for the difference between the amount lent and the present value of the note. Prepaid purchases will be treated as part of the cost of the products as they are purchased. Moreover, amortization of the discount will result in interest income under the effective-interest method over the life of the note.

Answer (A) is incorrect because Utah will recognize interest revenue if the supplier's contract price is below the market rate. Answer (B) is incorrect because, if the contract price is equal to or greater than the market rate, a loan with no stated interest would not be considered related to the purchase contract. Answer (D) is incorrect because, if the contract price is equal to or greater than the market rate, a loan with no stated interest would not be considered related to the purchase contract.

51. United Refinery Company, a refiner of peanut oil, lent $500,000 to James Barter, a peanut farmer, interest free for 5 years. The day after the loan agreement, Barter guaranteed that United Refinery could purchase up to 1 million pounds of shucked peanuts per year for the next 6 years at a price 5¢ less per pound than the prevailing market price. Barter asked for nothing in return for this price concession. United should record the loan at

A. Its face amount with no recognition of interest income over the 5-year period.

B. A discount using the average cost of capital as the rate for imputing interest.

C. Its face amount with interest income recognized each year in the amount of the price concession realized during that year.

D. A discount equal to the expected value of the price concession granted.

Answer (D) is correct. *(Publisher)*

REQUIRED: The accounting for an interest-free loan related to an unstated right or privilege.

DISCUSSION: Even though the price concession was not explicitly part of the loan agreement, the economic reality is that the noninterest-bearing loan is partial consideration for the purchase of products at less than the prevailing market price. The expected value of the price concession should be the measure of the loan discount. It is the difference between the amount of the loan and the present value of the note. The discount should be recorded as a debit to prepaid purchases and a credit to discount on notes receivable. The prepaid asset will be written off proportionally to the purchases made (debit purchases, credit prepaid purchases) during the contract term. The discount should be amortized using the interest method as interest income over the 5-year life of the loan.

Answer (A) is incorrect because APB 21 requires that the economic substance of the transaction be explicitly recognized in the accounts by recognizing the unstated right as an asset and a discount to the note receivable. Answer (B) is incorrect because the present value of the price concession should be used to discount the note. Answer (C) is incorrect because the discount on the note should be recognized as a direct deduction from the note receivable.

52. When a note receivable or a note payable has properly been recorded at its present value, any resulting discount should be disclosed in the financial statements

A. As a separate asset or liability.

B. As a deferred charge or credit.

C. In a summary caption along with any related issue costs.

D. As a direct deduction from the face amount of the note.

Answer (D) is correct. *(Publisher)*

REQUIRED: The proper financial statement disclosure of a discount related to a note receivable or payable.

DISCUSSION: APB 21 states that discount or premium is not an asset or liability separable from the related note. A discount should therefore be reported in the balance sheet as a direct deduction from the face amount of the note.

Answer (A) is incorrect because the discount is disclosed as a direct adjustment to the face amount of the note. Answer (B) is incorrect because the discount is disclosed as a direct adjustment to the face amount of the note. Answer (C) is incorrect because the discount is disclosed as a direct adjustment to the face amount of the note.

53. Which of the following is reported as interest expense?

A. Pension cost interest.

B. Postretirement healthcare benefits interest.

C. Imputed interest on a noninterest-bearing note.

D. Interest incurred to finance construction of machinery for an enterprise's own use.

Answer (C) is correct. *(CPA, adapted)*

REQUIRED: The item reported as interest expense.

DISCUSSION: When a noninterest-bearing note is exchanged for property, and neither the note nor the property has a clearly determinable exchange price, the present value of the note should be determined by discounting all future payments using an appropriately imputed interest rate. Periodic interest expense must be calculated and recognized in accordance with the effective-interest method.

Answer (A) is incorrect because interest cost for a defined benefit pension plan is reported as a component of the net periodic pension cost. Answer (B) is incorrect because interest cost for a defined benefit postretirement plan is reported as a component of the net postretirement benefit cost. Answer (D) is incorrect because interest incurred to finance construction of machinery for an enterprise's own use is capitalized.

Questions 54 and 55 are based on the following information. House Publishers offered a contest in which the winner would receive $1 million, payable over 20 years. On December 31, 2003, House announced the winner of the contest and signed a note payable to the winner for $1 million, payable in $50,000 installments every January 2. Also on December 31, 2003, House purchased an annuity for $418,250 to provide the $950,000 prize monies remaining after the first $50,000 installment, which was paid on January 2, 2004.

54. In its December 31, 2003 balance sheet, what amount should House report as note payable-contest winner, net of current portion?

A. $368,250

B. $418,250

C. $900,000

D. $950,000

Answer (B) is correct. *(CPA, adapted)*

REQUIRED: The amount of the note payable.

DISCUSSION: Noninterest-bearing notes payable should be measured at their present value rather than their face amount. Thus, House should report the note payable at $418,250 (the present value of the remaining payments).

Answer (A) is incorrect because $368,250 includes a reduction of $50,000 for the first installment. Answer (C) is incorrect because $900,000 equals the face amount of the note payable minus two installments. Answer (D) is incorrect because $950,000 equals the face amount of the note payable minus the first installment.

55. In its 2003 income statement, what should House report as contest prize expense?

A. $0

B. $418,250

C. $468,250

D. $1,000,000

Answer (C) is correct. *(CPA, adapted)*

REQUIRED: The contest prize expense.

DISCUSSION: The contest prize expense equals $468,250 ($418,250 cost of the annuity + $50,000 first installment).

Answer (A) is incorrect because $0 does not include the purchase of the annuity or the first installment as an expense in 2003. Answer (B) is incorrect because $418,250 does not include the $50,000 installment due in 2004. Answer (D) is incorrect because $1,000,000 is the face amount of the note.

56. On January 1, the Fulmar Company sold personal property to the Austin Company. The personal property had cost Fulmar $40,000. Fulmar frequently sells similar items of property for $44,000. Austin gave Fulmar a noninterest-bearing note payable in six equal annual installments of $10,000 with the first payment due beginning this December 31. Collection of the note is reasonably assured. A reasonable rate of interest for a note of this type is 10%. The present value of an annuity of $1 in arrears at 10% for six periods is 4.355. What amount of sales revenue from this transaction should be reported in Fulmar's income statement for the year of sale ended December 31?

A. $10,000

B. $40,000

C. $43,550

D. $44,000

Answer (D) is correct. *(CPA, adapted)*

REQUIRED: The amount of sales revenue to be reported in the income statement of the recipient of a noninterest-bearing note.

DISCUSSION: When a noninterest-bearing note is exchanged for property, the note, the sales price, and the cost of the property exchanged for the note should be recorded at the fair value of the property or at the market value of the note, whichever is more clearly determinable. Here, the $44,000 fair value of the property is clearly determinable because Fulmar frequently sells similar items for that amount. Consequently, $44,000 is the proper amount to be recorded as sales revenue from this transaction.

Answer (A) is incorrect because $10,000 is the amount of the annual installment. Answer (B) is incorrect because $40,000 is the original cost of the property. Answer (C) is incorrect because $43,550 is the present value of the note, but the fair value of the property is more clearly determinable.

57. The Brown Company received a 2-year, $190,000 note on January 1, year 1 in exchange for property it sold to Gray Company. According to the terms of the note, interest of 5% is payable annually on January 1, year 2 and January 1, year 3, when the face amount is also due. There was no established exchange price for the property. The prevailing rate of interest for a note of this type was 12% at the beginning of year 1 and 14% at the beginning of year 2. What interest rates should be used to calculate the amount of interest revenue from this transaction for the years ended December 31, year 1 and year 2, respectively?

A. 0% and 5%.

B. 5% and 5%.

C. 12% and 12%.

D. 12% and 14%.

Answer (C) is correct. *(CIA, adapted)*

REQUIRED: The interest rates used to calculate interest revenue for successive years if the prevailing rate changes.

DISCUSSION: When the nominal interest rate on a note is not equal to the prevailing market rate for this type of note, the face amount of the note is not equal to its fair market value or present value. In this case, the present value of the note should be determined by discounting the $190,000 maturity amount and the $9,500 annual interest payments using an appropriately imputed rate of interest. Given that 12% was the prevailing rate of interest for a note of that type at the issuance date, 12% should be used to determine both the fair market value and the interest revenue during the life of the note, regardless of fluctuations in prevailing interest rates.

Answer (A) is incorrect because the market rate of interest at the issuance date should be used to calculate the amount of interest revenue. Answer (B) is incorrect because the market rate of interest at the issuance date should be used to calculate the amount of interest revenue. Answer (D) is incorrect because the market rate of interest at the issuance date should be used to calculate the amount of interest revenue.

58. On January 1 of the current year, Parke Company borrowed $360,000 from a major customer evidenced by a noninterest-bearing note due in 3 years. Parke agreed to supply the customer's inventory needs for the loan period at less than the market price. At the 12% imputed interest rate for this type of loan, the present value of the note is $255,000 at January 1 of the current year. What amount of interest expense should be included in Parke's current-year income statement?

A. $43,200

B. $35,000

C. $30,600

D. $0

Answer (C) is correct. *(CPA, adapted)*

REQUIRED: The amount of interest expense recognized by the maker of a noninterest-bearing note.

DISCUSSION: A note issued solely for cash equal to its face amount is presumed to earn the stated rate of interest, even if that rate is zero. If, however, the parties have also exchanged stated or unstated rights or privileges, these must be recognized by determining the fair value (present value) of the note based on an appropriate interest rate. Interest income or expense should be calculated and the discount amortized using the effective interest rate. Parke agreed to supply the customer's inventory needs for the loan period at less than the market price. Hence, the initial carrying amount of the note is $255,000, with the $105,000 ($360,000 – $255,000) discount recognized as the measure of the price concession. The entry is to debit cash and credit notes payable for $360,000 and to debit discount and credit unearned revenue for $105,000. The unearned revenue is recognized as sales revenue in proportion to periodic sales to the creditor-buyer. The discount is amortized as interest expense using the effective interest method. Interest expense is equal to the carrying amount of the note at the beginning of the interest period times the 12% imputed interest rate. The interest expense for the year should therefore be $30,600 ($255,000 carrying amount × 12% imputed interest rate).

Answer (A) is incorrect because $43,200 results from applying the imputed interest rate to the face amount of the note instead of to the carrying amount. Answer (B) is incorrect because $35,000 results from recognizing interest expense using the straight-line method. Answer (D) is incorrect because interest expense must be imputed on a noninterest-bearing note.

59. On September 1, year 1, Brok Co. issued a note payable to Federal Bank in the amount of $900,000, bearing interest at 12%, and payable in three equal annual principal payments of $300,000. On this date, the bank's prime rate was 11%. The first interest and principal payment was made on September 1, year 2. At December 31, year 2, Brok should record accrued interest payable of

A. $36,000

B. $33,000

C. $24,000

D. $22,000

Answer (C) is correct. *(CPA, adapted)*

REQUIRED: The amount to be recorded as accrued interest payable.

DISCUSSION: Under the interest method, accrued interest payable is equal to the face amount of the note at the beginning of the interest period, times the stated interest rate, times the portion of the interest period that is included within the accounting period. At 9/1/year 1, the face amount of the note was $900,000. After the first $300,000 principal payment at 9/1/year 2, the face amount of the note was $600,000 ($900,000 – $300,000). Accrued interest payable for the period 9/1/year 2 to 12/31/year 2 was thus $24,000 [$600,000 face amount × 12% stated interest rate × (4 ÷ 12)]. The prime rate is irrelevant to the calculation of accrued interest payable.

Answer (A) is incorrect because $36,000 was the accrued interest payable at 12/31/year 1. Answer (B) is incorrect because $33,000 would have been the accrued interest payable at 12/31/year 1 if the interest rate had been 11%. Answer (D) is incorrect because $22,000 would have been the accrued interest payable at 12/31/year 2 if the interest rate had been 11%.

60. On January 31, 2003, Beau Corp. issued $300,000 maturity amount, 12% bonds for $300,000 cash. The bonds are dated December 31, 2002 and mature on December 31, 2012. Interest will be paid semiannually on June 30 and December 31. What amount of accrued interest payable should Beau report in its September 30, 2003 balance sheet?

A. $27,000

B. $24,000

C. $18,000

D. $9,000

Answer (D) is correct. *(CPA, adapted)*

REQUIRED: The amount of accrued interest payable that should be reported in the balance sheet.

DISCUSSION: Given that interest is paid semiannually on June 30 and December 31, the amount of each payment is $18,000 [($300,000 × 12%) ÷ 2]. On June 30, $18,000 was paid. From 7/1/03 to 9/30/03 (3 months), interest accrued. Thus, $9,000 [$18,000 × (3 ÷ 6)] of accrued interest payable should be reported.

Answer (A) is incorrect because $27,000 includes the $18,000 already paid on June 30. Answer (B) is incorrect because $24,000 includes the $18,000 already paid on June 30 and erroneously records $6,000, which is the accrued interest for 2 months. Answer (C) is incorrect because $18,000 is the amount of the semiannual interest payable.

12.6 Troubled Debt Restructurings by Debtors

61. SFAS 15, *Accounting by Debtors and Creditors for Troubled Debt Restructurings*, defined a troubled debt restructuring as one in which the

A. Fair value of cash, other assets, or an equity interest accepted by a creditor from a debtor in full satisfaction of its receivable at least equals the creditor's recorded investment in the receivable.

B. Creditor reduces the effective interest rate on the debt primarily to reflect a decrease in market interest rates in general.

C. Debtor issues, in exchange for its existing debt, new marketable debt having an effective interest rate that is at or near the current market interest rates for debt with similar maturity dates and stated interest rates issued by nontroubled debtors.

D. Creditor, for economic or legal reasons related to the debtor's financial difficulties, grants a concession to the debtor that it would not otherwise consider.

Answer (D) is correct. *(CMA, adapted)*

REQUIRED: The definition of a troubled debt restructuring under SFAS 15.

DISCUSSION: According to SFAS 15, a troubled debt restructuring occurs when the creditor, for economic or legal reasons related to the debtor's financial difficulties, grants a concession to the debtor that it would not otherwise consider. Troubled debt restructurings usually involve a continuation of debt with modified terms, a settlement at an amount less than the amount of the debt owed, or a combination. The concession involved may be imposed by law or a court, or it may arise from an agreement between the creditor and the debtor. The creditor's purpose is to reduce the loss it would otherwise incur if it did not grant the concession.

Answer (A) is incorrect because SFAS 15 lists this arrangement as an example of debt restructuring that does not qualify as troubled even if the debtor is having financial difficulties. Answer (B) is incorrect because SFAS 15 lists this arrangement as an example of debt restructuring that does not qualify as troubled even if the debtor is having financial difficulties. Answer (C) is incorrect because SFAS 15 lists this arrangement as an example of debt restructuring that does not qualify as troubled even if the debtor is having financial difficulties.

62. Which of the following situations that arise because of a debtor's financial difficulties and would not otherwise be acceptable to the creditor must be accounted for as a troubled debt restructuring?

A. Because of a court order, a creditor accepts as full satisfaction of its receivable a building the fair value of which equals the creditor's recorded investment in the receivable.

B. As part of a negotiated settlement, a creditor accepts as full satisfaction of its receivable a building the fair value of which equals the debtor's carrying amount of the payable.

C. Because of a court order, a creditor reduces the stated interest rate for the remaining original life of the debt.

D. As part of a negotiated settlement designed to maintain a relationship with a debtor, a creditor reduces the effective interest rate on debt outstanding to reflect the lower market interest rate currently applicable to debt of that risk class.

Answer (C) is correct. *(Publisher)*

REQUIRED: The situation that must be accounted for as a troubled debt restructuring.

DISCUSSION: According to SFAS 15, *Accounting by Debtors and Creditors for Troubled Debt Restructurings*, a troubled debt restructuring occurs when the creditor, for economic or legal reasons related to the debtor's financial difficulties, grants a concession to the debtor that it would not otherwise consider. Troubled debt restructurings usually involve a continuation of debt with modified terms, a settlement at an amount less than the amount of the debt owed, or a combination. A court order reducing a creditor's interest rate creates a troubled debt restructuring (assuming the reduction would not be otherwise acceptable to the creditor).

Answer (A) is incorrect because no troubled debt restructuring exists if the creditor receives full payment. Answer (B) is incorrect because no troubled debt restructuring exists if the creditor receives full payment. Answer (D) is incorrect because, if the debtor could refund the debt at the lower market rate, the creditor is not making a substantive concession.

63. According to SFAS 15, *Accounting by Debtors and Creditors for Troubled Debt Restructurings*, all of the following disclosures are required by debtors involved in a troubled debt restructuring except disclosure of

A. A description of the major changes in terms, major features of settlement, or both.

B. The aggregate gain on restructuring and the related tax effect.

C. The aggregate net gain or loss on transfer of assets.

D. The gross interest revenue that would have been recorded in the period.

Answer (D) is correct. *(CMA, adapted)*

REQUIRED: The disclosure that is not required of debtors following a troubled debt restructuring.

DISCUSSION: In addition to the items in (A) through (C), debtors must, in subsequent periods, disclose the extent to which contingent amounts are included in the carrying amount of restructured payables. The gross interest revenue that would have been recorded in the period is not a required disclosure for debtors because interest revenue is applicable to receivables, not payables.

Answer (A) is incorrect because a description of the major changes in terms or major features of settlement must be disclosed. Answer (B) is incorrect because the aggregate gain on restructuring and the related tax effect must be disclosed. Answer (C) is incorrect because the gain or loss on transfer of assets must be disclosed.

64. Casey Corp. entered into a troubled debt restructuring agreement with First State Bank. First State agreed to accept land with a carrying amount of $85,000 and a fair value of $120,000 in exchange for a note with a carrying amount of $185,000. Disregarding income taxes, what amount should Casey report as an extraordinary gain in its income statement?

A. $0

B. $35,000

C. $65,000

D. $100,000

Answer (A) is correct. *(CPA, adapted)*

REQUIRED: The extraordinary gain reported by a debtor after a troubled debt restructuring.

DISCUSSION: The debtor must recognize a gain as a result of the extinguishment of debt because the creditor settled the debt by accepting assets with a fair value less than the carrying amount of the debt. However, no extraordinary gain is recognized. An event or transaction is presumed to be ordinary and usual absent clear evidence to the contrary (APB 30). Accordingly, Casey should recognize an ordinary gain of $100,000 attributable to the $35,000 appreciation of the land ($120,000 fair value – $85,000 carrying amount) and the $65,000 excess of the carrying amount of the debt over the fair value of the land ($185,000 – $120,000).

Answer (B) is incorrect because no evidence indicates that the criteria for treatment of the gain as extraordinary have been met. Answer (C) is incorrect because no evidence indicates that the criteria for treatment of the gain as extraordinary have been met. Answer (D) is incorrect because no evidence indicates that the criteria for treatment of the gain as extraordinary have been met.

65. In 1998, May Corp. acquired land by paying $75,000 down and signing a note with a maturity amount of $1 million. On the note's due date, December 31, 2003, May owed $40,000 of accrued interest and $1 million principal on the note. May was in financial difficulty and was unable to make any payments. May and the bank agreed to amend the note as follows:

- The $40,000 of interest due on December 31, 2003 was forgiven.
- The principal of the note was reduced from $1 million to $950,000 and the maturity date extended 1 year to December 31, 2004.
- May would be required to make one interest payment totaling $30,000 on December 31, 2004.

As a result of the troubled debt restructuring, May should report a gain, before taxes, in its 2003 income statement of

A. $40,000

B. $50,000

C. $60,000

D. $90,000

Answer (C) is correct. *(CPA, adapted)*

REQUIRED: The amount of gain to be recognized from a troubled debt restructuring.

DISCUSSION: When a troubled debt restructuring is structured as a modification of terms that results in future undiscounted cash flows less than the carrying amount of the debt, a debtor should recognize a gain equal to the difference if it is material. Accordingly, May should report a gain of $60,000 ($1,000,000 principal + $40,000 accrued interest – $950,000 new principal – $30,000 interest payment). In addition, the future payments of $980,000 ($950,000 + $30,000) should be recorded as further reductions of the debt. The result is that the debt will be reduced to $0 with no interest expense recognized.

Answer (A) is incorrect because $40,000 is the amount of interest forgiven. Answer (B) is incorrect because $50,000 is the reduction of the principal forgiven. Answer (D) is incorrect because $90,000 does not include the required interest payment of $30,000 in the calculation of the gain.

66. Franco Corporation owes Chester National Bank (CNB) on a 10-year, 15% note in the amount of $100,000, plus $30,000 accrued interest. Because of financial difficulty, Franco has been unable to make annual interest payments for the past 2 years, and the note is due today. Accordingly, CNB restructured Franco Corporation's debt as follows:

- The $30,000 of accrued interest was forgiven.
- Franco was given 3 more years to pay off the debt at 8% interest. Payments are to be made annually at year-end.

Franco would properly record the restructuring and the payment for the first year as

A. An increase in interest expense of $8,000, and a gain of $2,000.

B. A decrease in accrued interest of $8,000.

C. A decrease in accrued interest of $8,000, and a gain of $2,000.

D. A decrease in accrued interest of $30,000, and a gain of $6,000.

Answer (D) is correct. *(CMA, adapted)*

REQUIRED: The entry for the restructuring of a debt if accrued interest is forgiven, the interest rate is lowered, and the payment period is extended.

DISCUSSION: According to SFAS 15, when modified terms of a restructured troubled debt provide for future undiscounted cash payments that are less than the carrying amount of the debt, the debtor should record the difference as a gain if it is material. Franco's future cash payments will total $124,000 after the restructuring ($100,000 of principal + 3 years of interest at $8,000 per year). Given a $130,000 carrying amount ($100,000 principal + $30,000 interest), the result is a gain of $6,000 ($130,000 – $124,000). Following a restructuring of this type, all future payments on the debt (principal and interest) are treated as reductions of the carrying amount. Consequently, no interest expense is recorded in the years following this restructuring. The entry to recognize the restructuring and the gain is

Note payable	$100,000	
Accrued interest	30,000	
Restructured note payable		$124,000
Gain		6,000

The entry to record the first payment is to debit restructured note payable for $8,000 and credit cash for $8,000.

Answer (A) is incorrect because no interest expense is recognized on a restructuring, and the gain is $6,000. Answer (B) is incorrect because accrued interest is reduced by $30,000 (the amount forgiven). Answer (C) is incorrect because accrued interest is reduced by $30,000, and the gain is $6,000.

67. On December 31 of the current year, X Corp. was indebted to Zyland Company on a $100,000, 10% note. Only interest had been paid to date, and the remaining life of the note was 2 years. Because X Corp. was in financial difficulties, the parties agreed that X Corp. would settle the debt on the following terms:

1. Settle one-half of the note by transferring land with a recorded amount of $40,000 and a fair value of $45,000
2. Settle one-fourth of the note by transferring 1,000 shares of $1 par common stock with a fair market value of $15 per share
3. Modify the terms of the remaining one-fourth of the note by reducing the interest rate to 5% for the remaining 2 years and reducing the principal to $15,000

What total gain should X Corp. record in the current year from this troubled debt restructuring?

A. $10,000

B. $13,500

C. $23,500

D. $28,500

Answer (D) is correct. *(T. Miller)*

REQUIRED: The total gains recorded from a troubled debt restructuring.

DISCUSSION: SFAS 15 requires that a debtor recognize a gain upon restructuring a troubled debt. X Corp. should recognize a gain of $5,000 ($45,000 fair value – $40,000 cost) when recording the land at its fair value and a gain of $5,000 when exchanging the land for a portion of the note worth $50,000 (50% x $100,000 face amount). A gain of $10,000 should be recognized on the exchange of stock with a fair market value of $15,000 (1,000 shares x $15) for the portion of the note worth $25,000 (25% x $100,000 face amount). Accordingly, the carrying amount of the balance of the note before the modification of its terms equals the remaining $25,000 principal of the original note. Because total cash payments after the restructuring will include principal of $15,000 and 2 years of interest equal to $1,500 [2 x (.05 x $15,000)], the difference between the $25,000 carrying amount and the total cash payments of $16,500 is a gain of $8,500. The total gain is therefore $28,500 ($5,000 + $5,000 + $10,000 + $8,500).

68. An enterprise incurs legal fees amounting to $2,000 in granting an equity interest to a creditor in a troubled debt restructuring. In its financial statements, the enterprise should

A. Capitalize the $2,000 and amortize it over a period not to exceed 40 years.

B. Treat the $2,000 as an expense of the period.

C. Deduct the $2,000 from the $8,000 gain resulting from the restructuring of payables.

D. Reduce by $2,000 the amount that would otherwise be recorded for the equity interest.

Answer (D) is correct. *(Publisher)*

REQUIRED: The debtor's accounting for legal fees incurred in granting an equity interest to a creditor in a troubled debt restructuring.

DISCUSSION: Under SFAS 15, legal fees and other direct costs that a debtor incurs in granting an equity interest to a creditor in a troubled debt restructuring reduce the amount otherwise recorded for the interest. Other direct costs a debtor incurs to effect a troubled debt restructuring are deducted in measuring the gain on the restructuring of the payables. If no such gain is recognized, these costs are expensed as they are incurred.

Answer (A) is incorrect because the legal fees should be applied to reduce the amount of the equity interest. Answer (B) is incorrect because it represents the proper accounting treatment of direct debt restructuring costs incurred other than in granting an equity interest. Answer (C) is incorrect because it represents the proper accounting treatment of direct debt restructuring costs incurred other than in granting an equity interest.

12.7 Asset Retirement Obligations (AROs)

69. SFAS 143, *Asset Retirement Obligations*, prescribes the accounting for obligations related to the retirement of long-lived tangible assets. A liability for an asset retirement obligation (ARO) within the scope of SFAS 143 may arise solely from

A. A plan to sell a long-lived asset.

B. The improper operation of a long-lived asset.

C. The temporary idling of a long-lived asset.

D. The acquisition, construction, development, or normal operation of a long-lived asset.

Answer (D) is correct. *(Publisher)*

REQUIRED: The source of a liability for an ARO.

DISCUSSION: An ARO is recognized for a legal obligation relating to the retirement of a tangible long-lived asset. This obligation results from the acquisition, construction, development, or normal operation of such an asset.

Answer (A) is incorrect because the scope of SFAS 143 does not extend to obligations arising (1) solely from a plan to sell or otherwise dispose of a long-lived asset covered by SFAS 144, or (2) from the improper operation of an asset. Answer (B) is incorrect because the scope of SFAS 143 does not extend to obligations arising (1) solely from a plan to sell or otherwise dispose of a long-lived asset covered by SFAS 144, or (2) from the improper operation of an asset. Answer (C) is incorrect because retirement is the nontemporary removal of the asset from service, for example, by sale, abandonment, or recycling.

70. An entity is most likely to account for an asset retirement obligation (ARO) by

A. Recognizing the fair value of the liability when it is incurred.

B. Recognizing a liability equal to the sum of the net undiscounted future cash flows associated with the ARO.

C. Decreasing the carrying amount of the related long-lived asset.

D. Decreasing the liability for the ARO to reflect the accretion expense.

Answer (A) is correct. *(Publisher)*

REQUIRED: The proper accounting for an ARO.

DISCUSSION: The fair value of the ARO liability is recognized when incurred. If a reasonable estimate of the fair value cannot be made at that time, the ARO will be recognized when such an estimate can be made. Fair value is the amount at which the ARO could be settled in a current transaction between willing parties, not in a forced or liquidation transaction. A quoted price in an active market is the best evidence of fair value. If such a price is not available, the best available information is used, such as the price of a similar liability or the result of applying present value methods.

Answer (B) is incorrect because, if a quoted market price in an active market or the price of a similar liability is not available, a present value method may be used to estimate fair value. Ordinarily, the expected cash flow method described in SFAC 7 is the only suitable present value method. Hence, probability-weighted present values, not undiscounted amounts, may be used to measure the ARO. Answer (C) is incorrect because the associated asset retirement cost (ARC) is added (debited) to the carrying amount of the tangible long-lived asset when the ARO is recognized (credited). Answer (D) is incorrect because accretion expense is debited when the ARO is credited to reflect its increase due to passage of time.

71. A business enterprise acquired a tangible long-lived asset with an asset retirement obligation (ARO) and included asset retirement cost (ARC) in the asset's carrying amount. The enterprise also recorded a liability for the ARO on the acquisition date. Subsequently, the enterprise should

A. Test the ARC for impairment but not amortize it.

B. Test the tangible long-lived asset for impairment and exclude ARC from the carrying amount for this purpose.

C. Recognize accretion expense before the periodic change in the ARO due to revised estimates of cash flows.

D. Discount upward revisions of the undiscounted estimated cash flows relating to the ARO by using the original credit-adjusted risk-free rate.

Answer (C) is correct. *(Publisher)*

REQUIRED: The subsequent accounting for a tangible long-lived asset with an ARO.

DISCUSSION: A change from one period to the next in the ARO due to passage of time is added to the liability. It is measured by applying an interest method of allocation to the ARO's beginning balance for the period. The rate is the credit-adjusted risk-free (CARF) rate used at the ARO's initial measurement. The offsetting debit is to accretion expense, which is classified as an operating item. After the periodic change resulting from the passage of time has been recognized, the periodic change in the ARO due to revised estimates of the timing or amount of the undiscounted cash flows is accounted for as an adjustment of the capitalized ARC and the carrying amount of the ARO. Increases in those estimated undiscounted cash flows are discounted using the current CARF rate, and decreases are discounted using the original CARF rate.

Answer (A) is incorrect because the ARC is expensed over its useful life using a systematic and rational method, but the entity is permitted to expense the amount that is capitalized in the same period. Answer (B) is incorrect because the carrying amount of the tangible long-lived asset includes ARC for the purpose of impairment testing. Answer (D) is incorrect because the original CARF rate is used to discount downward revisions of the undiscounted estimated cash flows relating to an ARO.

72. A business enterprise acquired a long-lived tangible asset on January 1, 2003. On that date, the enterprise recorded a liability for an asset retirement obligation (ARO) and capitalized asset retirement cost (ARC). The estimated useful life of the long-lived tangible asset is 5 years, the credit-adjusted risk-free (CARF) rate used for initial measurement of the ARO is 10%, the initial fair value of the ARO liability based on an expected present value calculation is $250,000, and no changes occur in the undiscounted estimated cash flows used to calculate that fair value. If the enterprise settles the ARO on December 31, 2007 for $420,000, what is the settlement gain or loss (rounded)?

A. $(17,372)

B. $25,000

C. $(152,628)

D. $(170,000)

Answer (A) is correct. *(Publisher)*

REQUIRED: The gain (loss) on settlement of an ARO.

DISCUSSION: Given no changes in the undiscounted estimated cash flows used to calculate the fair value of the ARO on January 1, 2003, the only adjustment to the ARO during its useful life is for the passage of time (debit accretion expense, credit ARO). This adjustment is recognized each period in an amount equal to the beginning ARO balance times the initial CARF rate. Consequently, the ARO at December 31, 2007 is

	Beginning Balance	Accretion Adjustment	Ending Balance
2003	$250,000	$25,000	$275,000
2004	275,000	27,500	302,500
2005	302,500	30,250	332,750
2006	332,750	33,275	366,025
2007	366,025	36,602.5	402,627.5

The settlement loss is $17,372 ($420,000 – $402,628 ARO balance at 12/31/07).

Answer (B) is incorrect because $25,000 is the accretion expense for 2003. Answer (C) is incorrect because $(152,628) is the difference between the ARO balance at 1/1/03 and the ARO balance at 12/31/07. Answer (D) is incorrect because $(170,000) equals the difference between the settlement amount and the initial balance.

12.8 Exit and Disposal Activities

73. Grand Corporation has decided to close its plant in Littleville. Accordingly, it will terminate the 50 employees who work at the plant. Grand gives the employees 60-days' notice on March 1 that it will close the plant on April 30. It will pay each employee $3,000 at the time that the employee stops providing services during the retention period. This one-time benefit arrangement is defined in a plan of termination that meets the criteria established by GAAP, including communication to employees. Grand should account for the one-time termination benefits by recognizing a liability

A. At the communication date at either fair value on that date or $150,000.

B. At the termination date for $150,000.

C. At the communication date at fair value on the termination date.

D. Ratably over the future service period.

Answer (A) is correct. *(Publisher)*

REQUIRED: The accounting for one-time termination benefits paid when employees stop providing services.

DISCUSSION: One-time termination benefits are paid under a one-time benefit arrangement based on a plan of termination for a specified termination event or future period. If employees need not provide services until terminated to receive the benefits, or if they will not be retained beyond the minimum retention period, the liability is recognized at the communication date. Measurement is at fair value on the communication date. However, estimates consistent with measurement at fair value are permitted. Thus, given the brevity of the discount period, the total of the undiscounted cash payments of $150,000 (50 employees × $3,000) is a reasonable estimate of the fair value.

Answer (B) is incorrect because the liability is recognized at the communication date. No exchange of benefits for future services exists. Answer (C) is incorrect because recognition and measurement are at fair value (or $150,000) on the communication date. Answer (D) is incorrect because, if employees must provide services until terminated and will be retained beyond the minimum retention period, the liability is recognized ratably over the future service period.

Questions 74 and 75 are based on the following information. Employer plans to close a plant in 18 months. All of the employees of the plant will be terminated at the time of closing. Because of its need to retain employees until closing, Employer defines a one-time benefit arrangement in a plan of termination that meets the criteria established by GAAP, including communication to employees. Under the plan, each employee who provides services for the entire 18-month period will receive a bonus of $5,000 payable 6 months after termination.

An employee who leaves voluntarily prior to closing will receive no part of the bonus. The estimated cash outflow for this one-time termination benefit is $2,000,000. Employer's credit-adjusted risk-free (CARF) rate is 3% semi-annually. Potentially relevant interest factors for the present value of $1 include the following:

3% for 1 period	.971
2 periods	.943
3 periods	.915
4 periods	.888

---

74. What is the amount of the liability recognized in the first month of the future service period?

A. $98,667

B. $107,889

C. $1,776,000

D. $1,942,000

Answer (B) is correct. *(Publisher)*

REQUIRED: The liability recognized in the first month of the future service period.

DISCUSSION: Employees may be required to provide services until terminated and be retained beyond the minimum retention period. Hence, an exchange transaction (promise of one-time benefits for rendition of services beyond a minimum period) is involved, and no present obligation exists at the communication date. In these circumstances, initial measurement of the liability is at the communication date in an amount equal to the fair value on the termination date. The liability is recognized proportionately over the future service period, that is, as employees provide services over the future service period. The termination date is 18 months after the communication date and 6 months before payment must be made. Using present value to estimate fair value, the initial measurement of the fair value at the termination date equals $2,000,000 discounted at the CARF rate of 3% for one semiannual period, or $1,942,000 ($2,000,000 × .971). Accordingly, the monthly liability recognized ratably over the future service period is $107,889 ($1,942,000 ÷ 18 months).

Answer (A) is incorrect because $98,667 results from using the present value at the communication date. Answer (C) is incorrect because $1,776,000 is the present value at the communication date. Answer (D) is incorrect because $1,942,000 is the present value at the termination date calculated at the measurement date.

75. Assume that after 6 months, Employer revises its estimate of the cash outflow for the bonus to $1,600,000 because fewer employees are likely to remain for the full service period. What is the amount of the cumulative effect change, if any, required to reflect this revised estimate?

A. $86,311

B. $129,467

C. $517,867

D. $647,334

Answer (B) is correct. *(Publisher)*

REQUIRED: The amount of the cumulative effect change.

DISCUSSION: The timing or amount of estimated cash flows may be revised. Any revisions must be measured using the CARF rate on which the initial measurement was based. The cumulative effect of this accounting change adjusts the liability in the period of change. The new present value estimate of the fair value of the one-time termination benefit at the termination date is $1,553,600 ($1,600,000 × .971 interest factor for 3% and one semiannual period). The liability that should have been recognized for the first 6 months is $517,867 [($1,553,600 ÷ 18 months) × 6 months]. The liability recognized would have been $647,334 ($107,889 recognized per month under the original estimate × 6 months). Thus, the reduction in the liability (the cumulative effect change) is $129,467 ($647,334 – $517,867).

Answer (A) is incorrect because $86,311 is the monthly amount of the liability that should be recognized given the new estimate. Answer (C) is incorrect because $517,867 is the liability that should have been recognized for the first 6 months given the new estimate. Answer (D) is incorrect because $647,334 is the liability recognized for the first 6 months under the initial estimate.

76. Employer plans to restructure operations at one of its plants and will therefore terminate 80 employees at that location. Employer communicates its plan on June 1, 2003. The plan to provide one-time termination benefits meets the criteria established by GAAP. Each employee who voluntarily leaves within 21 days will receive $8,500 in 30 days. These payments were duly made July 21, 2003. Each employee who is involuntarily terminated subsequently will receive $5,500. However, the payments for voluntary and involuntary termination benefits will not be made to more than 80 employees in total. Moreover, Employer estimates that it will reach its employee separation target within the 60-day minimum retention period. In its balance sheet dated June 30, 2003, assuming that 20 employees accept the offer for voluntary termination, Employer should report a liability for termination benefits of

A. $60,000

B. $440,000

C. $500,000

D. $680,000

Answer (C) is correct. *(Publisher)*

REQUIRED: The accounting for one-time termination benefits that include incremental voluntary benefits.

DISCUSSION: If employees need not provide services until terminated or will not be retained beyond the minimum period, the liability is recognized at the communication date at fair value on that date. Estimates consistent with fair value are permitted. Furthermore, when a plan that satisfies GAAP includes involuntary and incremental voluntary termination benefits offered for a short period, SFAS 146 applies to the former and SFAS 88 to the latter. Thus, the involuntary component (80 employees × $5,500 = $440,000) is recognized on the communication date (June 1), and measured at fair value on that date. Given the brevity of the discount period, $440,000 (undiscounted) is a reasonable estimate of fair value. The incremental voluntary component [20 employees × ($8,500 – $5,500) = $60,000] is recognized when the employees accept and the amount can be reasonably estimated (during June 2003). The amount includes lump-sum payments and the present value of future payments. Given no future payments, the $60,000 paid in July 2003 is the appropriate measure of the voluntary component (SFAS 88). The total liability is $500,000 ($440,000 + $60,000).

Answer (A) is incorrect because $60,000 is the liability for the incremental voluntary component. Answer (B) is incorrect because $440,000 is the liability for the involuntary component. Answer (D) is incorrect because $680,000 assumes no employees accepted the offer.

Questions 77 and 78 are based on the following information. Lessee Corp. enters into an operating lease of a building for 12 years at an annual rental of $150,000. The rental payment is due at the beginning of each year. After 6 years, Lessee commits to a plan to stop using the building in 1 year, but it will not terminate the lease. According to prices in an active property market, for similar properties for lessees with similar credit ratings, Lessee can reasonably expect to sublease the building for $120,000 per year. Lessee's credit-adjusted risk-free (CARF) rate is 6% annually. The following are potentially relevant present value factors for an annuity at 6%:

Annuity due (5 years)	4.465
Annuity due (6 years)	5.212
Ordinary annuity due (5 years)	4.212
Ordinary annuity due (6 years)	4.917

77. Assuming no prepayments or deferrals have been recorded, Lessee should recognize what liability for continuing costs on the cease-use date?

A. $133,950

B. $147,510

C. $631,800

D. $669,750

Answer (A) is correct. *(Publisher)*

REQUIRED: The liability on the cease-use date.

DISCUSSION: A liability for continuing costs is recognized and measured at fair value when the right under the contract is no longer used. For an operating lease, the initial fair value is based on the remaining lease rentals adjusted for any recognized prepayments or deferrals and decreased by an estimate of sublease rentals reasonably obtainable (regardless of any intent to sublease). Remaining lease rentals are not reduced below zero. Using present value to estimate the fair value of the rental payments minus the reasonably obtainable sublease payments, Lessee should recognize a liability for continuing lease costs equal to the present value of an annuity due (payments are at the beginning of each period) for 5 years [(12 – 6) – 1] discounted at 6%. Consequently, Lessee should recognize a liability of $133,950 [4.465 PV interest factor for an annuity due of 5 periods at 6% × ($150,000 annual lease rental – $120,000 annual sublease rental reasonably obtainable)].

Answer (B) is incorrect because $147,510 assumes that 6 years remain after the cease-use date and that the annuity is ordinary. Answer (C) is incorrect because $631,800 assumes that the annuity is ordinary. Also, sublease rentals are not subtracted. Answer (D) is incorrect because $669,750 does not subtract sublease rentals.

78. Assume that Lessee chose not to sublease the building for 1 year after the cease-use date but subleased the building for the subsequent term of the lease. The sublease rental per year is $135,000, with payments due at the beginning of each year. The following are potentially relevant present value factors for an annuity at 6%:

Annuity due (4 years)	3.673
Annuity due (5 years)	4.465
Ordinary annuity (4 years)	3.465
Ordinary annuity (5 years)	4.212

What is the total adjustment to the liability for continuing costs recognized at the inception of the sublease 1 year after the cease-use date?

A. $361,905 increase.

B. $78,855 decrease.

C. $66,975 decrease.

D. $55,095 decrease.

Answer (B) is correct. *(Publisher)*

REQUIRED: The total adjustment to the liability at the inception of the sublease.

DISCUSSION: The initial term of the operating lease was 12 years, Lessee used the building for 7 years, and Lessee subleased the building 1 year afterward. Hence, the term of the sublease was 4 years. The present value of an annuity due of $15,000 per year ($150,000 – $135,000) for 4 years at the 6% rate used for initial measurement of the liability is $55,095 (3.673 interest factor × $15,000). That amount is the desired balance at the inception of the sublease. Thus, the reduction in the liability is $78,855 ($133,950 balance at the cease-use date – $55,095 balance at the inception of the sublease).

Answer (A) is incorrect because a $361,905 increase equals the present value of an annuity due of $135,000 for 4 years minus the initial liability. Answer (C) is incorrect because a $66,975 decrease equals the initial liability at the inception of the sublease assuming a term of 5 years. Answer (D) is incorrect because a $55,095 decrease is the initial liability balance at the inception of the sublease.

12.9 Certain Financial Instruments

79. A freestanding combination of one written put option on the issuer's equity shares and a second option may be a liability or an asset. Assume the first option requires the entity to buy 1,000 shares of the entity's own stock at a given date for $30 per share if the market price declines below $30. The second option is a purchased call option that permits the issuer to buy 1,000 shares on the given date for $30 per share if the price rises above $31. If the fair value of the put at issuance exceeds the fair value of the call,

A. The issuer pays cash.

B. The combined instrument is classified as a liability.

C. Classification of the combined instrument depends on the settlement provision.

D. The combined instrument is a net written option classified as an asset.

Answer (B) is correct. *(Publisher)*

REQUIRED: The nature of a freestanding combination of a written put and a purchased call.

DISCUSSION: If the fair value of the put (call) at issuance exceeds the fair value of the call (put), the issuer receives (pays) cash. The combined instrument is a net written (purchased) option classified as a liability (an asset).

If the fair values are equal but opposite at issuance, the initial fair value is zero (a zero-cost collar).

Answer (A) is incorrect because the issuer receives cash. Answer (C) is incorrect because these classifications apply regardless of the settlement provision (physical, net cash, or net share). Answer (D) is incorrect because the combined instrument is classified as a liability.

80. The issuer agrees to a forward contract to repurchase 100,000 of its equity shares for $50 per share in 3 years. No other consideration is given or received, and no unstated rights or privileges are involved. The quoted market price of these shares is $42 per share at the inception of the contract, which will be physically settled in cash. How should the issuer account for this contract?

A. A memorandum entry.

B. As an asset if price movements are favorable and the contract is net-cash settled.

C. Initially debit equity and credit a liability for $5,000,000.

D. Initially debit equity and credit a liability for $4,200,000.

Answer (D) is correct. *(Publisher)*

REQUIRED: The accounting for a forward contract to repurchase equity shares for a fixed amount at a fixed settlement date with physical settlement in cash.

DISCUSSION: To recognize this unconditional obligation initially, the entity credits a liability and debits equity for $4,200,000 ($42 × 100,000 shares), the fair value of the shares at the contract's inception. Subsequently, the contract is measured at the present value of the $5,000,000 ($50 × 100,000 shares) settlement amount. The reason for subsequent measurement at present value is that the amount and settlement date are fixed. Interest cost is accrued at the 6% interest rate implicit at inception ($42 ÷ $50 = .84, the factor for the PV of $1 for 3 periods at 6%).

Answer (A) is incorrect because the issuer must recognize a liability. Answer (B) is incorrect because, if the forward purchase contract is subject to net cash settlement, the obligation is conditional. Such a contract is indexed to the repurchase obligation and may require settlement by transferring assets. Thus, if price movements are favorable (unfavorable), the issuer of the underlying shares will receive (transfer) assets at the settlement date because the issuer will be in a gain (loss) position. During the term of the contract, the issuer will classify it as an asset or a liability depending on its fair value (not the fair value of the shares) at the reporting date. For example, if the share price is $55 ($48) at the settlement date, the issuer will receive (pay) $500,000 ($200,000). Answer (C) is incorrect because the contract is accounted for at the fair value of the shares at its inception.

STUDY UNIT THIRTEEN
PENSIONS, OTHER POSTRETIREMENT BENEFITS, AND POSTEMPLOYMENT BENEFITS

Postretirement benefit plans are deferred compensation arrangements by which an employer promises to provide future benefits in exchange for current services of its employees. The primary objective of accounting for these benefits is to recognize the compensation cost over the employees' approximate service periods. Postretirement benefits include pension benefits and **other postretirement employee benefits (OPEB)**. Employer accounting for pensions is prescribed by **SFAS 87**, *Employers' Accounting for Pensions*, which primarily applies to single-employer defined benefit pension plans. Employer accounting for OPEB is prescribed by **SFAS 106**, *Employers' Accounting for Postretirement Benefits Other Than Pensions*. OPEB include health care, life insurance (other than that provided through a pension plan), tuition assistance, child care, legal services, housing subsidies, and any other benefits except pension benefits provided after retirement. "Employees" is defined as all current, retired, disabled, and former employees; their beneficiaries; and their covered dependents eligible to receive postretirement benefits. Benefits may either commence immediately upon separation or be deferred until the eligible retiree attains a certain age.

The two most common types of postretirement benefit plans are defined contribution plans and defined benefit plans. Because of the complexity of the accounting issues, the primary focus of SFASs 87 and 106 is on single-employer **defined benefit plans** that determine benefits based on a formula. Factors commonly found in a benefit formula are years of employee service rendered, employee life expectancy, level of compensation, and incidence of medical events. Total benefits are not precisely determinable, but the amount can be estimated using the formula and the anticipated effects of future events not usually controllable by the employer or the employee.

The basic elements of postretirement benefits accounting and reporting are the postretirement benefit obligation, plan assets (assets segregated and restricted to provide for postretirement benefits), and the net periodic benefit cost. For a pension plan, the principal postretirement benefit obligations are the **projected benefit obligation (PBO)** and the **accumulated benefit obligation (ABO)**. The PBO is the actuarial present value at a specific date of the benefits expected to be paid in accordance with the terms of a postretirement benefit plan. It is based on future compensation levels if they are included in the benefit formula. The ABO differs from the PBO only in that it makes no assumption about future compensation levels. For an OPEB plan, the principal postretirement benefit obligations are the **expected postretirement benefit obligation (EPBO)** and the **accumulated postretirement benefit obligation (APBO)**. The EPBO is the actuarial present value at a specific date of the benefits expected to be paid under the terms of a postretirement benefit plan. The APBO is the actuarial present value of benefits attributed to employee service provided to a specific date. After employees attain full eligibility, the EPBO and the APBO are the same.

For both pension plans and OPEB plans, net periodic benefit cost is a minimum amount required to be recognized as the cost of a benefit plan during a period. **Net periodic pension cost (NPPC)** or **net periodic postretirement benefit cost (NPPBC)** may include (1) service cost, (2) interest cost, (3) actual return on plan assets, (4) amortization of the unrecognized net gain or loss from previous periods, (5) amortization of unrecognized prior service cost, and (6) amortization of the unrecognized transition net obligation or asset. However, the determination of the actual amounts of these items differs for pension plans and OPEB plans.

Service cost is the portion of the PBO or the EPBO attributed to employee service during a period. **Interest cost** as a component of NPPC is the increase in the PBO due to the passage of time. The **actual return on plan assets** is the change in the fair value of those assets during the period adjusted for contributions, benefit payments, and expenses. However, the difference between the actual and expected returns is defined as **asset gain or loss**. Gains and losses, including asset gains and losses, are not required to be recognized in the period when they occur. Thus, the expected return is the minimum amount required to be included in the calculation of the NPPC or the NPPBC. **Prior service costs** are changes in benefits arising from a plan amendment or initiation that are attributable to employees' prior service. **Gain or loss** as a component of NPPC is essentially the net effect of the delayed recognition of the gains and losses that arise from changes in the value of the PBO or plan assets as a result of experience different from that assumed or as a result of a change in an actuarial assumption. However, the gain or loss component excludes changes in the PBO occurring during the period and deferred for later recognition. Gain or loss as a component of NPPBC is similar, except that it excludes changes in the APBO. A **transition amount** arising upon initial adoption of the plan also is amortized. For a defined benefit pension plan, the calculation is unlikely to be relevant because SFAS 87 was effective after 1986. Under SFAS 87, the likely amortization period was a maximum of 15 years. For an OPEB plan, the calculation is still relevant because SFAS 106 was effective after 1992. The transition amount is the difference between (1) the APBO and (2) the fair value of plan assets plus any recognized accrued postretirement benefit cost or minus any recognized prepaid postretirement benefit cost. Unlike the accounting prescribed by SFAS 87, SFAS 106 permits employers to elect immediate recognition in income of the transition amount as the effect of a change in accounting principle. Moreover, SFAS 106 also permits a 20-year amortization period when the average service life is less than 20 years.

Differences between amounts funded and expensed for pension obligations are recorded as prepaid pension cost (an asset) or accrued pension cost (a liability). Moreover, an employer sponsoring a defined benefit pension plan is required to recognize an **additional minimum pension liability** if either (1) a portion of the ABO is unfunded and an asset has been recognized as prepaid pension cost, or (2) the existing liability (unfunded accrued pension cost) is less than the unfunded ABO. Thus, the additional liability equals the unfunded ABO plus prepaid pension cost or minus accrued pension cost. Unlike SFAS 87, however, SFAS 106 does not require recognition of a minimum liability.

SFAS 88, *Employers' Accounting for Settlements and Curtailments of Defined Benefit Pension Plans and for Termination Benefits*, and SFAS 106 govern settlements, curtailments, and termination benefits relating to postretirement plans. A **settlement** of a postretirement plan is a transaction that is irrevocable, relieves the employer of the primary responsibility for its benefit obligation, and eliminates significant risks related to the obligation and the assets used to make the settlement. A **curtailment** is an event that significantly reduces the expected years of future service of active plan participants, or eliminates the accrual of defined benefits for some or all of the future services of a significant number of active plan participants. **Special termination benefits** are benefits offered only for a short period of time in connection with a termination of employment.

SFAS 112, *Employers' Accounting for Postemployment Benefits*, applies to all benefits provided after employment but before retirement to former or inactive employees, their beneficiaries, and their covered dependents. Postemployment benefits include salary continuation, supplemental unemployment benefits, severance benefits, disability-related benefits, job training and counseling, and the continuation of health care benefits and insurance coverage. Postemployment benefits may be paid as a result of a disability, layoff, death, or other event. Postemployment benefits are accrued if the employer's obligation is attributable to employees' services already rendered, the obligation relates to rights that vest or accumulate, payment of the compensation is probable, and the amount is reasonably estimable. If the above conditions are not met, postemployment benefits shall be accrued if it is probable that a liability has been incurred and the amount is reasonably estimable.

SFAS 35, *Accounting and Reporting by Defined Benefit Pension Plans*, applies to plans that issue financial statements except for those of state and local governments, which are covered by GASB pronouncements. The objective of these statements is to provide information useful in assessing the plan's ability to pay benefits.

SFAS 87 and SFAS 106 require many disclosures. However, these disclosure requirements have been amended. **SFAS 132 (revised 2003)**, *Employers' Disclosures about Pensions and Other Postretirement Benefits*, does not change measurement or recognition principles. It standardizes disclosures for such plans to the extent feasible. It also requires additional information on (1) changes in the benefit obligations and fair values of plan assets, (2) types of plan assets, (3) investment policies and strategies, (4) measurement dates, (5) benefits and contributions, (6) assumptions, (7) changes in obligations or assets not otherwise apparent, and (8) interim information. However, nonpublic entities may now make reduced disclosures.

QUESTIONS

13.1 Accounting and Reporting for Pensions

1. SFAS 87, *Employers' Accounting for Pensions*, establishes financial accounting and reporting standards for an employer that offers pension benefits to its employees. The provisions of SFAS 87 are applicable to

A. Any arrangement that is similar in substance to a pension plan.

B. Any written arrangement that is similar in substance to a pension plan.

C. Any arrangement that is legally defined as a pension plan.

D. Any arrangement that provides pension benefits, life insurance benefits, or health insurance benefits to retirees.

Answer (A) is correct. *(Publisher)*

REQUIRED: The arrangements to which the provisions of SFAS 87 are applicable.

DISCUSSION: The provisions of SFAS 87 are applicable to any arrangement that is similar in substance to a pension plan, regardless of form, the method of financing, or whether the plan is written or implied by the well-defined practice of paying postretirement benefits.

Answer (B) is incorrect because the arrangement may be written or implied. Answer (C) is incorrect because the provisions are applicable to any arrangement that is similar in substance to a pension plan. Answer (D) is incorrect because the provisions do not apply to life insurance benefits provided outside a pension plan or to other postretirement health and welfare benefits. SFAS 106 governs accounting for such benefits.

2. The provisions of SFAS 87 are primarily applicable to an employer's accounting for a single-employer defined benefit pension plan. SFAS 87 is based on the fundamental assumption that a defined benefit pension plan is part of an employee's compensation incurred when the

A. Defined pension benefit becomes vested.

B. Defined pension benefit is paid.

C. Defined pension benefit becomes a legal obligation.

D. Employee's services are rendered.

Answer (D) is correct. *(Publisher)*

REQUIRED: The basic assumption underlying SFAS 87.

DISCUSSION: SFAS 87 is based on the fundamental assumption that a defined benefit pension plan is part of an employee's compensation, which is incurred when the services provided to the employer by the employee are rendered. The defined pension benefit is provided in the form of a deferred payment. It is not precisely determinable. It can only be estimated based on the plan benefit formula and relevant future events such as future compensation levels, mortality rates, ages at retirement, and vesting schedules.

3. Certain accounting treatments not ordinarily allowed under GAAP are allowed in an employer's accounting for pensions. Which of the following accounting treatments is generally allowed in accounting for defined benefit pension plans?

A. The tax basis of accounting.

B. The cash or modified cash basis of accounting.

C. The offsetting of assets and liabilities.

D. The immediate recognition of all costs.

Answer (C) is correct. *(Publisher)*

REQUIRED: The accounting treatment ordinarily allowed under GAAP only for pension accounting.

DISCUSSION: SFAS 87 permits (1) the delayed recognition of certain events, (2) the reporting of a net cost, and (3) the offsetting of assets and liabilities. "Delayed recognition" means that certain changes in the pension obligation and in the value of the plan assets are not recognized as they occur. They are recognized on a systematic and gradual basis over subsequent accounting periods. "Net costs" means that various pension costs (service cost, interest, actuarial gains and losses, etc.) reflected in the income statement are reported as one expense. The "offsetting feature" means that the recognized values of the plan assets contributed to the plan are offset in the statement of financial position against the recognized liabilities.

Answer (A) is incorrect because SFAS 87 requires the accrual basis of accounting. Answer (B) is incorrect because SFAS 87 requires the accrual basis of accounting. Answer (D) is incorrect because delayed, rather than immediate, recognition is allowed for certain events.

4. SFAS 87, *Employers' Accounting for Pensions*, applies primarily to defined benefit pension plans. It defines the projected benefit obligation as the

A. Present value of benefits accrued to date based on future salary levels.

B. Present value of benefits accrued to date based on current salary levels.

C. Increase in retroactive benefits at the date of the amendment of the plan.

D. Amount of the adjustment necessary to reflect the difference between actual and estimated actuarial returns.

Answer (A) is correct. *(CMA, adapted)*

REQUIRED: The definition of the projected benefit obligation.

DISCUSSION: The projected benefit obligation (PBO) as of a date is equal to the actuarial present value of all benefits attributed by the pension benefit formula to employee service rendered prior to that date. The PBO is measured using assumptions as to future salary levels.

Answer (B) is incorrect because the accumulated benefit obligation (ABO) is the present value of benefits accrued to date based on current salary levels. Answer (C) is incorrect because prior service cost is the increase in retroactive benefits at the date of the amendment of the plan. Answer (D) is incorrect because the gain or loss component of net periodic pension cost is the amount of the adjustment necessary to reflect the difference between actual and estimated actuarial returns.

5. Timor Co. sponsors a defined benefit pension plan. The accumulated benefit obligation (ABO) arising under the plan includes benefit obligations to <List A> employees at <List B> salary levels.

	List A	List B
A.	Vested	Current
B.	Vested	Future
C.	Vested and nonvested	Current
D.	Vested and nonvested	Future

Answer (C) is correct. *(CIA, adapted)*

REQUIRED: The nature of the ABO.

DISCUSSION: The ABO is the present value of benefits accrued to date based on past and current compensation levels. Whether benefits are vested is irrelevant to the computation. Thus, the ABO includes both vested and nonvested benefits and is calculated at current, not future, salary levels.

6. An employee's right to obtain pension benefits regardless of whether (s)he remains employed is the

A. Prior service cost.

B. Defined benefit.

C. Vested interest.

D. Minimum liability.

Answer (C) is correct. *(CIA, adapted)*

REQUIRED: The term defined as the right to obtain pension benefits regardless of future employment.

DISCUSSION: Vested benefits (vested interest) are those earned pension benefits owed to an employee regardless of the employee's continued service. The employer's vested benefit obligation (VBO) is the actuarial present value of these vested benefits.

Answer (A) is incorrect because prior service cost relates to benefits for employee service provided prior to the adoption or amendment of a defined benefit pension plan. Answer (B) is incorrect because a defined benefit pension plan provides a defined pension benefit based on one or more factors, such as level of compensation, years of service, or age. Answer (D) is incorrect because a minimum liability must be recognized by an employer only if the ABO exceeds the fair value of the plan's assets.

7. Under SFAS 87, *Employers' Accounting for Pensions*, attribution of pension costs to periods of employee service for a defined benefit pension plan

A. Is based on the plan's benefit formula.

B. May be based on any acceptable actuarial cost method.

C. Is determined as a level amount or as a level percentage of compensation.

D. Should be based on a cost approach.

Answer (A) is correct. *(Publisher)*

REQUIRED: The basis for attribution of pension costs.

DISCUSSION: SFAS 87 adopted a benefits approach based on the plan's benefit formula. Thus, SFAS 87 follows the traditional accounting practice of looking to the terms of the agreement as a basis for recording an exchange. According to the FASB, the benefits approach better reflects how the costs and liabilities are incurred.

Answer (B) is incorrect because the benefit formula, not any actuarial cost method, is the basis for attribution. Answer (C) is incorrect because the approach chosen by SFAS 87 recognizes the present value of the benefits earned during the period. Because the present value of a dollar of pension benefits increases as retirement nears, the cost recognized does not remain level. Answer (D) is incorrect because the cost is based on the benefits to be paid.

8. Which of the following describes a fundamental aspect of accounting for defined benefit pension plans by employers?

A. Changes in pension assets and obligations are recognized immediately.

B. The amount of pension benefits is not precisely determinable.

C. Net periodic pension cost (NPPC) may be reported within maximum and minimum limits.

D. When underfunding occurs, immediate recognition in the balance sheet and income statement is required.

Answer (B) is correct. *(Publisher)*

REQUIRED: The statement of a fundamental aspect of pension accounting.

DISCUSSION: The total pension benefit to be provided in the form of deferred payments is not precisely determinable and can only be estimated based on the plan's benefit formula and relevant future events, many of which are not controllable by the employer. Such events include how long the employee and survivors live, years of service rendered, and levels of compensation.

Answer (A) is incorrect because certain changes in the pension obligation and in the value of the assets set aside to meet those obligations are not recognized as they occur. They are recognized on a systematic and gradual basis over subsequent accounting periods. All changes ultimately will be recognized except to the extent they may be offset by subsequent changes. Answer (C) is incorrect because SFAS 87 prescribes a standard method (not a range) for measuring NPPC. Answer (D) is incorrect because, although a liability must be recognized when the ABO exceeds plan assets, income statement recognition of the offsetting amount will be delayed.

9. In measuring pension costs and pension obligations, an employer who sponsors a defined benefit pension plan must make certain significant assumptions. Relative to these significant assumptions, the provisions of SFAS 87 require

A. The assumptions to take into consideration a right of the employer to terminate the plan.

B. The rate of return on plan assets to be based on the prime interest rate.

C. Each significant assumption to reflect the best estimate solely with respect to that individual assumption.

D. The measurements of the projected, accumulated, and vested benefit obligations to be based on the expected long-term rate of return on plan assets.

Answer (C) is correct. *(Publisher)*

REQUIRED: The true statement about the pension cost and obligation assumptions required by SFAS 87.

DISCUSSION: SFAS 87 requires that each significant assumption used reflect the best estimate of the plan's future experience solely with respect to that individual assumption. This is called an explicit approach. SFAS 87 does not allow the implicit approach, which allows the combined use of assumptions that do not individually represent the best estimates of the plan's future experience but that result in an aggregate effect presumed to approximate that obtained by the explicit approach.

Answer (A) is incorrect because the assumptions should be based on the presumption that the plan will continue in effect unless contrary evidence exists. Answer (B) is incorrect because the expected long-term rate of return should be used. Answer (D) is incorrect because the PBO, ABO, and VBO should reflect the discount rate at which these pension benefit obligations could effectively be settled.

10. Regarding the employer's reporting of the assets of a defined benefit pension plan, SFAS 87 and SFAS 132 (revised 2003), *Employers' Disclosures about Pensions and Other Postretirement Benefits*, provide that

A. Market-related value should be used for all purposes except determining asset gains and losses.

B. All assets should be measured at cost.

C. Plan assets that constitute plan investments should be measured at fair value for disclosure purposes.

D. Plan assets used in plan operations should be measured at market value.

Answer (C) is correct. *(Publisher)*

REQUIRED: The true statement about the measurement of plan assets.

DISCUSSION: For disclosure purposes under SFAS 132 (R) and for determination of the minimum liability in accordance with SFAS 87, plan investments are measured at their fair values. For calculating the expected return on plan assets and thus for determining asset gains and losses, the market-related value is used. Market-related value may be either fair value or a calculated value that recognizes changes in fair value systematically and rationally over not more than 5 years, e.g., a 5-year moving average.

Answer (A) is incorrect because market-related value is used for calculating asset gains and losses. Answer (B) is incorrect because an employer discloses plan assets at fair value and also uses fair value in calculating the minimum liability. Furthermore, the employer may use market-related value for certain purposes. Answer (D) is incorrect because plan assets used in operations, e.g., an administration building, should be reported at cost minus accumulated depreciation by the plan, not the employer-sponsor (SFAS 35).

11. SFAS 87, *Employers' Accounting for Pensions*, applies to entities that sponsor defined benefit pension plans. Under SFAS 87, they must recognize as part of net periodic pension cost the actuarial present value of the increase in pension benefits payable to employees because of their services rendered during the current period. This cost is the

A. Amortization of prior service costs.

B. Service cost.

C. Accumulated benefit obligation (ABO).

D. Projected benefit obligation (PBO).

Answer (B) is correct. *(CMA, adapted)*

REQUIRED: The term for the actuarial present value of the pension benefits attributable to employee services during the current period.

DISCUSSION: SFAS 87 defines service cost as the present value of the future benefits earned in the current period (as calculated according to the plan's benefit formula). This amount is usually calculated by the plan's actuary. Service cost is a component of net periodic pension cost. It is also a portion of the PBO.

Answer (A) is incorrect because amortization of prior service costs applies to benefits earned in earlier years that arise from amendment of a pension plan. Answer (C) is incorrect because the ABO is the same as the PBO except that it is limited to past and current compensation levels. Answer (D) is incorrect because the PBO is the actuarial present value of all future benefits attributed to past employee service at a moment in time. It is based on assumptions as to future compensation if the plan formula is based on future compensation.

12. Janney Co. sponsors a defined benefit pension plan. The discount rate used by Janney to calculate the projected benefit obligation is determined by the

	Expected Return on Plan Assets	Actual Return on Plan Assets
A.	Yes	Yes
B.	No	No
C.	Yes	No
D.	No	Yes

Answer (B) is correct. *(CPA, adapted)*

REQUIRED: The basis for determining the discount rate used to calculate the projected benefit obligation.

DISCUSSION: Assumed discount rates are used to measure the PBO. They reflect the rates at which benefits can be settled. In estimating these rates, it is appropriate to consider current prices of annuity contracts that could be used to settle pension obligations as well as the rates on high-quality fixed investments (SFAS 87). Neither the expected nor the actual return on plan assets determines the rate used to calculate the PBO.

13. Interest cost included in the net periodic pension cost recognized by an employer sponsoring a defined benefit pension plan represents the

A. Shortage between the expected and actual return on plan assets.

B. Increase in the projected benefit obligation resulting from the passage of time.

C. Increase in the fair value of plan assets resulting from the passage of time.

D. Amortization of the discount on unrecognized prior service costs.

Answer (B) is correct. *(CPA, adapted)*

REQUIRED: The definition of interest cost.

DISCUSSION: The interest cost component of net periodic pension cost is defined as the increase in the PBO resulting from the passage of time. The PBO is a discounted amount of benefits to be paid. As the time to payment is reduced, the present value increases. Interest cost is calculated by applying an appropriate discount rate to the beginning balance of the PBO for the period.

14. Net periodic pension cost recognized by an employer sponsoring a defined benefit pension plan may include a gain or loss component. Gains and losses requiring amortization

A. Result only from experience different from that assumed.

B. Result only from changes in assumptions.

C. Do not include asset gains and losses not reflected in the market-related value of plan assets.

D. Only arise from unexpected changes in the projected benefit obligation.

Answer (C) is correct. *(Publisher)*

REQUIRED: The basis for determining unrealized gains and losses.

DISCUSSION: Asset gains and losses are differences between the actual and expected return on plan assets. To the extent they are not reflected in the market-related value of plan assets (used to calculate the expected return), asset gains and losses are not subject to the required minimum amortization of gain or loss, which includes both realized and unrealized amounts.

Answer (A) is incorrect because gains and losses result from experience different from that assumed. Answer (B) is incorrect because gains and losses result from changes in assumptions. Answer (D) is incorrect because gains and losses include changes in the value of both the PBO and the plan assets.

15. Amortization of the unrecognized cumulative net gain or loss is a possible component of net periodic pension cost recognized by an employer sponsoring a defined benefit pension plan. Which of the following amortization policies is required?

A. If amortization is required, it will be over the average life expectancy of the plan's employee-participants.

B. SFAS 87 permits any systematic amortization method to be used provided the amortized amount does not exceed the prescribed minimum.

C. Amortization of a net unrecognized gain results in an increase in NPPC.

D. No amortization is required if the unrecognized net gain or loss falls within a corridor.

Answer (D) is correct. *(G. Westmoreland)*

REQUIRED: The required amortization of unrecognized net gain or loss.

DISCUSSION: SFAS 87 adopts a corridor approach to reduce the volatility of the NPPC. The cumulative unrecognized net gain or loss (excluding asset gains and losses not reflected in the market-related value of plan assets) is subject to required amortization in NPPC only to the extent it exceeds 10% of the greater of the PBO or the market-related value of plan assets.

Answer (A) is incorrect because, unless almost all participants are inactive, the amortization period is the average remaining service period of active employees expected to receive benefits under the plan. Answer (B) is incorrect because the amortized amount may be greater but not less than the minimum prescribed. Answer (C) is incorrect because gains decrease and losses increase NPPC.

16. On January 1, 2003, Whitford Co. amended its single-employer defined benefit pension plan by granting increased benefits for services provided prior to 2003. This prior service cost will be reflected in the financial statements for

A. Years before 2003 only.

B. Year 2003 only.

C. Year 2003 and years before and following 2003.

D. Year 2003 and following years only.

Answer (D) is correct. *(CPA, adapted)*

REQUIRED: The year(s) in which prior service cost will be reflected in the financial statement(s).

DISCUSSION: The amortization of prior service cost should be recognized as a component of NPPC during the future service periods of those employees active at the date of the plan amendment who are expected to receive benefits under the plan. The cost of retroactive benefits is the increase in the PBO at the date of the amendment and should be amortized by assigning an equal amount to each future period of service of each employee active at the date of the amendment who is expected to receive benefits under the plan. However, to reduce the burden of these allocation computations, any alternative amortization approach (e.g., averaging) that more rapidly reduces the unrecognized prior service cost is acceptable provided it is applied consistently.

Answer (A) is incorrect because prior service cost is not recognized as a prior-period adjustment. Answer (B) is incorrect because prior service cost is allocated to future service periods on a systematic and rational basis. Answer (C) is incorrect because prior service cost is not recognized as a prior-period adjustment.

17. Sheen Company maintains a defined benefit pension plan for its employees. For the fiscal year ended December 31 of the current year, it reported an unfunded accrued pension cost. This cost represents the amount that the

A. Cumulative net pension cost accrued exceeds contributions to the plan.

B. Cumulative net pension cost accrued exceeds the vested benefit obligation.

C. Vested benefit obligation exceeds plan assets.

D. Vested benefit obligation exceeds contributions to the plan.

Answer (A) is correct. *(CPA, adapted)*

REQUIRED: The amount that the unfunded accrued pension cost represents in a defined benefit pension plan.

DISCUSSION: The prepaid/accrued pension cost account is an asset if it has a debit balance. It is a liability if it has a credit balance. The prepaid/accrued pension cost should be recognized as a liability if the cumulative net pension cost recognized exceeds the amounts the employer has contributed to the plan.

Answer (B) is incorrect because the VBO is not used to measure the extent of funding. Answer (C) is incorrect because unfunded accrued pension cost is defined in SFAS 87 as "cumulative net pension cost accrued in excess of the employer's contributions." Answer (D) is incorrect because unfunded accrued pension cost is defined in SFAS 87 as "cumulative net pension cost accrued in excess of the employer's contributions."

18. Lowe Ltd. sponsors a defined benefit pension plan. For its fiscal year ended October 31, 2002, Lowe is subject to the minimum pension liability recognition requirement. Lowe must record an additional liability equal to the unfunded

A. Accumulated benefit obligation plus the previously recognized accrued pension cost.

B. Accumulated benefit obligation minus the previously recognized accrued pension cost.

C. Projected benefit obligation plus the previously recognized accrued pension cost.

D. Projected benefit obligation minus the previously recognized accrued pension cost.

Answer (B) is correct. *(CPA, adapted)*

REQUIRED: The amount of the additional minimum pension liability that must be recorded by an employer.

DISCUSSION: An employer sponsoring a defined benefit pension plan is required to recognize an additional minimum pension liability if either (1) a portion of the ABO is unfunded and an asset has been recognized as prepaid pension cost, or (2) the existing liability (unfunded accrued pension cost) is less than the unfunded ABO. Thus, the additional liability equals the unfunded ABO plus prepaid pension cost or minus accrued pension cost.

Answer (A) is incorrect because accrued pension cost is subtracted from, not added to, the ABO to calculate the additional minimum pension liability. Answer (C) is incorrect because the ABO, not the PBO, is used to calculate the additional minimum pension liability. Answer (D) is incorrect because the ABO, not the PBO, is used to calculate the additional minimum pension liability.

19. Which of the following defined benefit pension plan disclosures should be made in a public company's financial statements?

I. A reconciliation of the beginning and ending balances of the benefit obligation

II. A general description of the employer's funding policy

III. A reconciliation of the beginning and ending balances of the fair value of plan assets

A. I and II.

B. I and III.

C. II and III.

D. I only.

Answer (B) is correct. *(CPA, adapted)*

REQUIRED: The disclosure(s) about a defined benefit pension plan made in a public company's statements.

DISCUSSION: SFAS 132 (revised 2003), *Employers' Disclosures about Pensions and Other Postretirement Benefits*, does not change measurement or recognition principles. It standardizes disclosures for pensions and other postretirement benefits and requires additional disclosures. It also reduces required disclosures for nonpublic entities. Among other things, a public entity must disclose a reconciliation of the beginning and ending balances of the benefit obligation showing separately (1) the effects of service cost, (2) interest cost, (3) contributions by plan participants, (4) actuarial gains and losses, (5) exchange rate changes, (6) benefits paid, (7) plan amendments, (8) business combinations, (9) divestitures, (10) settlements, (11) curtailments, and (12) special termination benefits. A reconciliation of the beginning and ending balances of the fair value of plan assets is also required. It must show the effects of (1) the actual return on plan assets, (2) exchange rate changes, (3) contributions by the employer and plan participants, (4) benefits paid, (5) business combinations, (6) divestitures, and (7) settlements. However, general descriptive information about the employer's benefit plans, including employee groups covered, type of benefit formula, funding policy, type of assets held, and significant nonbenefit liabilities, is no longer required.

20. Spencer Company sponsors a defined benefit pension plan for its employees. What pension-related information should it disclose?

	Amount of Unamortized Prior Service Cost	Accumulated Other Comprehensive Income
A.	Yes	Yes
B.	Yes	No
C.	No	No
D.	No	Yes

Answer (A) is correct. *(CPA, adapted)*

REQUIRED: The disclosure(s), if any, required of an employer sponsoring a defined benefit pension plan.

DISCUSSION: Under SFAS 132 (R), a public entity must disclose the funded status of the plan, amounts not recognized in the balance sheet, and amounts recognized in the balance sheet. They include unamortized prior service cost; unrecognized net gain or loss; any unamortized, unrecognized transition amount; net prepaid assets or accrued liabilities; and any intangible asset and the accumulated OCI recognized when an additional minimum pension liability is recorded.

21. Purchase of annuity contracts is a means of transferring the risk associated with a defined benefit pension obligation from the employer to an insurer. To be treated as an annuity contract under SFAS 87, a contract must

A. Not be participating.

B. Be unconditional and irrevocable.

C. Be participating.

D. Be eligible for inclusion in plan assets.

Answer (B) is correct. *(Publisher)*

REQUIRED: The requirement for qualification as an annuity contract.

DISCUSSION: An annuity contract is a contract in which an insurance company unconditionally undertakes a legal obligation to provide specified pension benefits to specific individuals in return for a fixed consideration or premium. An annuity contract is irrevocable and involves the transfer of a significant risk from the employer to the insurance company.

Answer (A) is incorrect because, if the substance of a participating contract is that the employer remains subject to all or most of the risks and rewards associated with the obligations covered and the assets transferred to the insurer, the contract is not an annuity contract for purposes of SFAS 87. A participating annuity contract provides for the purchaser to participate in the investment performance of the insurance company. Participation is neither a requirement for treatment as an annuity contract nor a disqualification. Answer (C) is incorrect because, if the substance of a participating contract is that the employer remains subject to all or most of the risks and rewards associated with the obligations covered and the assets transferred to the insurer, the contract is not an annuity contract for purposes of SFAS 87. A participating annuity contract provides for the purchaser to participate in the investment performance of the insurance company. Participation is neither a requirement for treatment as an annuity contract nor a disqualification. Answer (D) is incorrect because nonparticipating annuity contracts are excluded from plan assets, but, in the case of a participating contract, the excess of the cost of the participating contract over an equivalent nonparticipating contract (a participation right) is recognized as an asset. Benefits covered by both nonparticipating and qualifying participating annuity contracts are also excluded from both the PBO and the ABO.

22. The employer-sponsor's measurement date for assets and obligations of a defined benefit pension plan is the

A. Beginning of the accounting period.

B. Date the actuary submits the information.

C. Date of the financial statements.

D. Date of the financial statements or a date not more than 3 months prior to that date.

Answer (D) is correct. *(Publisher)*

REQUIRED: The measurement date for pension plan assets and obligations.

DISCUSSION: The measurement of plan assets and obligations required by SFAS 87 is as of the date of the financial statements or, if used consistently from year to year, a date not more than 3 months prior to the date of the financial statements. Data for measuring plan assets and obligations may be prepared by the actuary prior to these dates and projected forward to account for subsequent events.

23. In a business combination, Ryan Co. acquired Pichardo Co., which sponsors a single-employer defined benefit pension plan. Ryan should

A. Recognize any previously existing unrecognized net gain or loss.

B. Assign part of the purchase price to the unrecognized prior service cost as an intangible asset.

C. Assign part of the purchase price to the excess of plan assets over the projected benefit obligation.

D. Recognize a previously existing unrecognized transition net asset or obligation of the plan.

Answer (C) is correct. *(Publisher)*

REQUIRED: The acquiring company's accounting when the acquired company sponsors a pension plan.

DISCUSSION: In a business combination, the acquiring entity should recognize a pension liability if the PBO of the acquired entity is in excess of its plan assets. Likewise, a pension asset should be recognized if plan assets exceed the PBO.

Answer (A) is incorrect because, in a business combination, unrecognized net gains and losses are eliminated by the assignment of part of the purchase price to a liability (excess of PBO over plan assets) or an asset (excess of plan assets over the PBO). Answer (B) is incorrect because, in a business combination, prior service costs are eliminated by the assignment of part of the purchase price to a liability (excess of PBO over plan assets) or an asset (excess of plan assets over the PBO). Answer (D) is incorrect because, in a business combination, the transition net asset or obligation of the acquired company's defined benefit plan is eliminated by the assignment of part of the purchase price to a liability (excess of PBO over plan assets) or an asset (excess of plan assets over the PBO).

24. Dawson Co. sponsors an arrangement that provides pension benefits in return for services rendered, provides an individual account for each participant, and specifies how contributions to the individual accounts are to be determined. This arrangement is a

A. Defined benefit pension plan.

B. Defined contribution plan.

C. Multiemployer plan.

D. Multiple-employer plan.

Answer (B) is correct. *(Publisher)*

REQUIRED: The type of plan defined.

DISCUSSION: A defined contribution plan specifies how contributions to an individual's account are to be determined. The benefits a participant will receive depend solely on the amount contributed, the returns earned on investments of those contributions, and forfeitures of other participants' benefits that may be allocated to his/her account. The NPPC is the contribution called for in the particular accounting period.

Answer (A) is incorrect because a defined benefit pension plan is a plan that provides a defined pension benefit based on one or more factors. Answer (C) is incorrect because a multiemployer plan is a plan to which two or more unrelated employers contribute, usually pursuant to one or more collective bargaining agreements. Assets are not segregated and may be used to provide benefits to employees of any of the participating employers. Answer (D) is incorrect because a multiple-employer plan is a pension plan to which two or more unrelated employers contribute, usually to allow pooling of assets for investment purposes and to reduce administrative costs. Assets are segregated, and contributions may be based on benefit formulas that differ.

25. The following information pertains to McNeil Co.'s defined benefit pension plan:

Actuarial estimate of projected benefit obligation at 1/1/03	$144,000
Assumed discount rate	10%
Service cost for 2003	$ 36,000
Pension benefits paid during 2003	$ 30,000

If no change in actuarial estimates occurred during 2003, McNeil's PBO at December 31, 2003 was

A. $128,400

B. $150,000

C. $158,400

D. $164,400

Answer (D) is correct. *(CPA, adapted)*

REQUIRED: The projected benefit obligation at the end of the year.

DISCUSSION: The ending balance of the PBO is the beginning balance plus the service cost and interest cost components, minus the benefits paid. The interest cost component is equal to the PBO's beginning balance times the discount rate.

Beginning PBO balance	$144,000
Service cost	36,000
Interest cost (10% × $144,000)	14,400
Benefits paid	(30,000)
Ending PBO balance	$164,400

Answer (A) is incorrect because $128,400 excludes the current year's service cost component. Answer (B) is incorrect because $150,000 excludes the interest cost component. Answer (C) is incorrect because $158,400 excludes both the service cost component and the benefits paid.

26. The following information pertains to Beltron Co.'s defined benefit pension plan for the current year:

Fair value of plan assets, beginning of year	$ 700,000
Fair value of plan assets, end of year	$1,050,000
Employer contributions	$ 220,000
Benefits paid	$ 170,000

In computing pension expense, what amount should Beltron use as actual return on plan assets?

A. $130,000

B. $300,000

C. $350,000

D. $520,000

Answer (B) is correct. *(CPA, adapted)*

REQUIRED: The actual return on plan assets.

DISCUSSION: The actual return on plan assets is based on the fair value of plan assets at the beginning and end of the accounting period adjusted for contributions and payments during the period. The actual return is $300,000 ($1,050,000 – $700,000 – $220,000 + $170,000).

Answer (A) is incorrect because $130,000 results when benefits paid to employees are not included. Answer (C) is incorrect because $350,000 is the change in the fair value of plan assets without adjustment for contributions or benefits paid. Answer (D) is incorrect because $520,000 does not deduct employer contributions.

27. At the beginning of the current year, the market-related value of the plan assets of Janeway Company's defined benefit pension plan was $1,000,000. Janeway uses a 5-year weighted-average method to determine market-related values. The company, however, had not previously experienced any asset gains and losses. The expected long-term rate of return on plan assets is 10%. The actual return during the year was $50,000. Contributions and benefits paid were $150,000 and $200,000, respectively. At year-end, the market-related value of Janeway's plan assets is

A. $1,140,000

B. $1,040,000

C. $1,000,000

D. $950,000

Answer (B) is correct. *(Publisher)*

REQUIRED: The market-related value of plan assets at year-end.

DISCUSSION: If market-related value is defined as fair value, the ending market-related value of the plan assets is the beginning value, plus the actual returns, plus the contributions, minus the benefits paid. However, in this case, the company uses an alternative method to determine market-related value. This alternative includes 20% of the sum of the differences between the actual and the expected returns (asset gains and losses) over the last 5 years. The year-end market-related value is the beginning value, plus the expected return, plus the contributions, minus the benefits paid, minus 20% of the difference between the actual return and the expected return for the current year only.

Beginning market-related value	$1,000,000
Expected return (10% × $1,000,000)	100,000
Contributions	150,000
Benefits paid	(200,000)
20% of $50,000 loss	(10,000)
Year-end market-related value	$1,040,000

Answer (A) is incorrect because $1,140,000 excludes the expected returns and benefits paid. Answer (C) is incorrect because $1,000,000 includes the entire loss. Answer (D) is incorrect because $950,000 excludes the expected return and 20% of the loss.

28. The following information relates to the current year activity of the defined benefit pension plan of Kim Company, whose stock is publicly traded:

Service cost	$240,000
Expected return on plan assets	60,000
Interest cost on pension benefit obligation	80,000
Amortization of actuarial loss	20,000
Amortization of prior service cost	10,000

Kim's pension cost for the current year is

A. $240,000

B. $260,000

C. $270,000

D. $290,000

Answer (D) is correct. *(A. Oddo)*

REQUIRED: The net periodic pension cost (NPPC) for the year.

DISCUSSION: Components of NPPC are service cost, interest cost, the expected return on plan assets, and amortization of any (1) unrecognized prior service cost, or (2) unrecognized net gain (loss). Service cost, interest cost, and the amortization of actuarial loss and prior service cost increase the net periodic pension cost. The expected return on plan assets decreases NPPC. As indicated below, NPPC is $290,000.

Service cost	$240,000
Expected return on plan assets	(60,000)
Interest cost	80,000
Amortization of actuarial loss	20,000
Amortization of prior service cost	10,000
Net periodic pension cost	$290,000

Answer (A) is incorrect because $240,000 includes only the service cost component. Answer (B) is incorrect because $260,000 excludes the amortization of prior service cost and the actual loss. Answer (C) is incorrect because $270,000 excludes the amortization of the actuarial loss.

29. Schiff Co. sponsors a defined benefit pension plan. For the current year, the expected return on plan assets was $100,000. The actual return was $150,000. The increase in the projected benefit obligation was estimated to be $600,000. The amount of the projected benefit obligation determined at year-end reflected an increase of only $400,000. If no unrecognized net gain (loss) existed at the beginning of the year, the amount of net gain (loss) subject to required amortization for the current year is

A. $0

B. $(15,000)

C. $50,000

D. $250,000

Answer (A) is correct. *(Publisher)*

REQUIRED: The amount of net gain (loss) subject to required amortization for the current year.

DISCUSSION: SFAS 87 does not require recognition of gains and losses as components of NPPC of the period in which they arise. The $50,000 asset gain ($150,000 actual return – $100,000 expected return) and the liability gain (the PBO at year-end was $200,000 less than estimated) are therefore not required to be included in NPPC of the current year. Given that no unrecognized net gain (loss) existed at the beginning of the year, the required amortization for the current year is $0.

30. The following information pertains to Hill Co.'s defined benefit pension plan:

Prepaid pension cost, January 1, 2003	$ 2,000
Service cost	19,000
Interest cost	38,000
Expected return on plan assets	22,000
Amortization of unrecognized prior service cost	52,000
Employer contributions	40,000

The fair value of plan assets exceeds the accumulated benefit obligation (ABO). In its December 31, 2003 balance sheet, what amount should Hill report as unfunded accrued pension cost?

A. $45,000

B. $49,000

C. $67,000

D. $87,000

Answer (A) is correct. *(CPA, adapted)*

REQUIRED: The unfunded accrued pension cost.

DISCUSSION: The required components of net periodic pension cost (NPPC) are (1) service cost, (2) interest cost, (3) expected return on plan assets, (4) gain or loss to the extent recognized, and (5) amortization of any unrecognized prior service cost. The NPPC is $87,000 ($19,000 service cost + $38,000 interest cost – $22,000 expected return on plan assets + $52,000 amortization of unrecognized prior service costs). The excess of the NPPC over contributions and prepaid pension cost is $45,000 ($87,000 – $40,000 – $2,000), which is the unfunded accrued pension cost. Because the fair value of plan assets exceeds the ABO, no additional liability should be recognized.

Answer (B) is incorrect because $49,000 results when prepaid pension cost is added instead of subtracted. Answer (C) is incorrect because $67,000 results when expected return on assets is not subtracted. Answer (D) is incorrect because $87,000 results when employer contributions and prepaid pension cost are not subtracted.

31. Jan Corp. amended its defined benefit pension plan, granting a total credit of $100,000 to four employees for services rendered prior to the plan's adoption. The employees, A, B, C, and D, are expected to retire from the company as follows:

"A" will retire after three years.

"B" and "C" will retire after five years.

"D" will retire after seven years.

What is the amount of prior service cost amortization in the first year?

A. $0

B. $5,000

C. $20,000

D. $25,000

Answer (C) is correct. *(CPA, adapted)*

REQUIRED: The amount of prior service cost amortization in the first year after amendment of a defined benefit pension plan.

DISCUSSION: The cost of retroactive benefits is the increase in the PBO at the date of the amendment and should be amortized by assigning an equal amount to each future period of service of each employee active at the date of the amendment who is expected to receive benefits under the plan. However, to reduce the burden of these allocation computations, any alternative amortization approach (e.g., averaging) that more rapidly reduces the unrecognized prior service cost is acceptable, provided that it is applied consistently. The total service years to be rendered by the employees equals 20 (3 + 5 + 5 + 7). Hence, the amortization percentage for the first year is 20% (4 ÷ 20), and the minimum amortization is $20,000 (20% × $100,000).

Answer (A) is incorrect because amortization of prior service cost is a component of net periodic pension cost. Answer (B) is incorrect because $5,000 is the amount assigned to each period of service by each employee. Answer (D) is incorrect because $25,000 results from assigning an equal amount to each employee.

32. At end of the year, Nickel Company's projected benefit obligation (PBO) was determined to be $1,500,000, which was $200,000 higher than had been expected. The market-related value of the defined benefit plan's assets was equal to its fair value of $1,250,000. No other gains and losses have occurred. If the average remaining service life is 20 years, the minimum required amortization of the unrecognized net gain (loss) in the next year will be

A. $20,000

B. $3,750

C. $2,500

D. $0

Answer (C) is correct. *(Publisher)*

REQUIRED: The minimum required amortization of unrecognized net gain (loss) next year.

DISCUSSION: At a minimum, amortization of the cumulative unrecognized net gain or loss (excluding asset gains and losses not yet reflected in market-related value) must be included as a component of NPPC for a year if, as of the beginning of the year, that unrecognized gain or loss exceeds 10% of the greater of the PBO or the market-related value (MRV) of plan assets. At year-end, Nickel's PBO was $200,000 greater than estimated (a $200,000 liability loss). Given that no other gain or loss has occurred, the unrecognized net loss to be amortized beginning next year is $200,000. The corridor amount is $150,000 (10% of the greater of $1,500,000 PBO or $1,250,000 MRV of plan assets). The amount outside the corridor is $50,000 ($200,000 – $150,000), and the amount to be amortized is thus $2,500 ($50,000 ÷ 20 years of average remaining service life).

Answer (A) is incorrect because $20,000 is the result of using the full $200,000 liability loss without regard to the corridor amount and assumes an amortization period of 10 years instead of 20. Answer (B) is incorrect because $3,750 is the result of using $125,000 (10% × $1,250,000 plan assets) as the corridor amount instead of $150,000. Answer (D) is incorrect because $50,000 of the liability loss must be amortized over the average remaining service life beginning the year following the loss.

33. Worldwide Co. implemented a defined benefit pension plan for its employees on January 1, 2000. During 2000 and 2001, Worldwide's contributions fully funded the plan. The following data are provided for 2003 and 2002:

	2003 Estimated	2002 Actual
Projected benefit obligation, December 31	$750,000	$700,000
Accumulated benefit obligation, December 31	520,000	500,000
Plan assets at fair value, December 31	675,000	600,000
Projected benefit obligation in excess of plan assets	75,000	100,000
Pension expense	90,000	75,000
Employer's contribution	?	50,000

What amount should Worldwide contribute to report an accrued pension liability of $15,000 in its December 31, 2003 balance sheet?

A. $50,000

B. $60,000

C. $75,000

D. $100,000

Answer (D) is correct. *(CPA, adapted)*

REQUIRED: The amount contributed to report an accrued pension liability.

DISCUSSION: The prepaid/accrued pension cost account is an asset if it has a debit balance. It is a liability if it has a credit balance. The prepaid/accrued pension cost should be recognized as a liability if the cumulative NPPC recognized exceeds the amounts the employer has contributed to the plan. No accrued/prepaid pension cost was recognized in 2000 or 2001 because the employer's contributions fully funded the plan. Accrued pension cost at the end of 2002 was $25,000 ($75,000 pension expense – $50,000 contribution). To reduce the accrued pension cost to $15,000 at the end of 2003 therefore requires overfunding of pension expense by $10,000. Hence, the contribution for 2003 should be $100,000 ($10,000 + $90,000 pension expense).

Answer (A) is incorrect because a contribution of $50,000 would result in an accrued liability of $65,000. Answer (B) is incorrect because a $60,000 contribution would result in an accrued liability of $55,000. Answer (C) is incorrect because a contribution of $75,000 would result in an accrued liability of $40,000.

34. On January 2 of the current year, Walesa Co. established a noncontributory defined benefit plan covering all employees and contributed $1,000,000 to the plan. At December 31 of the current year, Walesa determined that the current year service and interest costs for the plan were $620,000. The expected and the actual rate of return on plan assets for the current year was 10%. There are no other components of pension expense. What amount should Walesa report in its balance sheet for the current year as prepaid pension cost?

A. $280,000

B. $380,000

C. $480,000

D. $620,000

Answer (C) is correct. *(CPA, adapted)*

REQUIRED: The amount of prepaid pension cost.

DISCUSSION: Prepaid pension cost is recognized when the amount funded exceeds the amount recognized as net periodic pension cost. The net periodic pension cost is $520,000 [$620,000 service and interest costs – ($1,000,000 × 10% expected return on plan assets)]. Given that $1,000,000 was contributed, $480,000 is the prepaid pension cost ($1,000,000 – $520,000).

Answer (A) is incorrect because $280,000 is the difference between the contributed amount and the service and interest costs with 10% of $1,000,000 subtracted from the difference. Answer (B) is incorrect because $380,000 is the difference between the contributed amount and the sum of the service and interest costs. Answer (D) is incorrect because $620,000 is the sum of the service and interest costs.

35. On January 1 of the current year, Kohl Corp. adopted a defined benefit pension plan. The plan's service cost of $75,000 was fully funded at the end of the current year. Prior service cost was funded by a contribution of $30,000 in the current year. Amortization of prior service cost was $12,000 for the current year. What is the amount of Kohl's prepaid pension cost at December 31 of the current year?

A. $18,000

B. $30,000

C. $42,000

D. $45,000

Answer (A) is correct. *(CPA, adapted)*

REQUIRED: The amount of prepaid pension cost at year-end.

DISCUSSION: Prepaid pension cost is recognized when the amount funded exceeds the amount recognized as net periodic pension cost. For the initial year of the defined benefit pension plan, NPPC is equal to $87,000 ($75,000 service cost + $12,000 amortization of prior service cost). The plan's service cost was fully funded at the end of the year. The plan's prior service cost was overfunded by $18,000 ($30,000 – $12,000). Consequently, Kohl's prepaid pension cost in the year-end financial statements should be reported at $18,000.

Answer (B) is incorrect because $30,000 is the contribution for prior service cost. Answer (C) is incorrect because $42,000 is the sum of prior service cost funding and amortization. Answer (D) is incorrect because $45,000 equals service cost funding minus prior service cost funding.

36. On June 1, 2001, Cleaver Corp. established a defined benefit pension plan for its employees. The following information was available at May 31, 2003:

Projected benefit obligation	$29,000,000
Accumulated benefit obligation	24,000,000
Unfunded accrued pension cost	400,000
Plan assets at fair market value	14,000,000
Unrecognized prior service cost	3,100,000

To report the proper pension liability in Cleaver's May 31, 2003 balance sheet, what is the amount of the adjustment required?

A. $4,500,000

B. $9,500,000

C. $9,600,000

D. $1,460,000

Answer (C) is correct. *(CPA, adapted)*

REQUIRED: The amount of the adjustment required to reflect pension liability properly on the balance sheet.

DISCUSSION: The minimum liability that must be recorded on the balance sheet is equal to the amount that the ABO exceeds the fair value of the plan assets plus (minus) any unfunded prepaid (accrued) pension cost. Thus, the adjustment required is $9,600,000 ($24,000,000 ABO – $14,000,000 fair value of plan assets – $400,000 unfunded accrued pension cost).

Answer (A) is incorrect because the unfunded prior service cost is not included in the minimum liability. Answer (B) is incorrect because $9,500,000 results from calculating the additional liability based on the PBO and includes unrecognized prior service cost. Answer (D) is incorrect because $1,460,000 results from calculating the additional liability based on the PBO.

Questions 37 and 38 are based on the following information. These items pertain to Bartlett Co.'s defined benefit pension plan at December 31:

Unfunded accumulated benefit obligation (ABO)	$25,000
Unrecognized prior service cost	12,000
Net periodic pension cost	8,000

Bartlett made no contributions to the pension plan during the year.

37. At December 31, what amount should Bartlett record as additional pension liability?

A. $5,000

B. $13,000

C. $17,000

D. $25,000

Answer (C) is correct. *(CPA, adapted)*

REQUIRED: The additional pension liability.

DISCUSSION: An additional pension liability is recognized if the existing liability (unfunded accrued pension cost) is less than the unfunded ABO. No contributions were made during the year, so the entire NPPC is unfunded and should be reported as accrued pension cost. The additional pension liability is equal to the unfunded ABO minus accrued pension cost, or $17,000 ($25,000 – $8,000).

Answer (A) is incorrect because $5,000 equals the unfunded ABO minus the prior service cost and the NPPC. Answer (B) is incorrect because $13,000 equals the unfunded ABO minus the prior service cost. Answer (D) is incorrect because $25,000 is the unfunded ABO.

38. In its December 31 financial statements, what amount should Bartlett report in other comprehensive income as a result of the excess of additional pension liability over unrecognized prior service cost?

A. $5,000

B. $13,000

C. $17,000

D. $25,000

Answer (A) is correct. *(CPA, adapted)*

REQUIRED: The excess of additional pension liability over unrecognized prior service cost.

DISCUSSION: An additional pension liability is recorded by a credit to a liability and a debit to an intangible asset. However, if the amount of the additional liability exceeds the unrecognized prior service cost, the excess is debited to other comprehensive income. The excess of the additional liability over unrecognized prior service cost is $5,000 ($17,000 – $12,000).

Answer (B) is incorrect because $13,000 is the excess of the minimum liability over unrecognized prior service cost. Answer (C) is incorrect because $17,000 is the additional liability. Answer (D) is incorrect because $25,000 is the unfunded ABO.

39. Payne, Inc. implemented a defined benefit pension plan for its employees on January 2 of the current year. The following data are provided for the year, as of December 31:

Accumulated benefit obligation	$103,000
Plan assets at fair value	78,000
Net periodic pension cost	90,000
Employer's contribution	70,000

What amount should Payne record as additional minimum pension liability at December 31?

A. $0

B. $5,000

C. $20,000

D. $45,000

Answer (B) is correct. *(CPA, adapted)*

REQUIRED: The additional minimum pension liability.

DISCUSSION: SFAS 87 requires recognition of a liability that is at least equal to the unfunded ABO. For the net liability presented to equal the unfunded ABO, the company must recognize as a liability the difference between the ABO and the fair value of plan assets, plus any prepaid pension cost, or minus any accrued pension cost. Payne recognized an accrued pension cost of $20,000 ($90,000 NPPC – $70,000 contribution). Hence, the additional minimum pension liability should be $5,000 ($103,000 ABO – $78,000 fair value of plan assets – $20,000 accrued pension cost).

Answer (A) is incorrect because the full unfunded ABO has not been reflected in the accounts. Answer (C) is incorrect because $20,000 is the accrued pension cost. Answer (D) is incorrect because $45,000 equals the unfunded ABO plus the accrued pension cost.

40. On January 1 of this year, Ent Co. acquired Idiary Co. Idiary sponsors a single-employer defined benefit pension plan. At the date of the business combination, the following data were available:

Projected benefit obligation	$5,000,000
Fair value of plan assets	4,000,000
Accumulated benefit obligation	4,500,000
Unrecognized prior service cost	200,000
Prepaid pension cost	100,000

The allocation of the purchase price should be based on which of the following?

A. The only allocation related to the pension plan will be $100,000 for prepaid pension cost.

B. An allocation must be made to liabilities for the prior service cost and net loss.

C. A liability must be recognized for the excess of the projected benefit obligation over plan assets.

D. A liability must be recognized for the excess of the accumulated benefit obligation over plan assets.

Answer (C) is correct. *(Publisher)*

REQUIRED: The proper allocation of the pension-plan-related portion of the purchase price in a business combination.

DISCUSSION: In a business combination, when the acquired entity sponsors a single-employer defined benefit plan, the acquirer allocates the purchase price to the individual assets acquired and liabilities assumed. This allocation must include recognition of a liability for a PBO in excess of plan assets or an asset for plan assets in excess of the PBO. Any previously existing unrecognized net gain or loss or prior service cost is thereby eliminated. Idiary's PBO exceeded plan assets, so Ent should recognize a liability of $1,000,000 ($5,000,000 – $4,000,000).

Answer (A) is incorrect because an allocation will be made to a liability account to recognize the amount by which the PBO exceeds plan assets. Answer (B) is incorrect because unrecognized prior service cost and net gain or loss are eliminated. Answer (D) is incorrect because the difference between the PBO and plan assets is the amount of the liability that must be recorded, not the difference between the ABO and plan assets.

41. Which of the following is a provision of SFAS 35, *Accounting and Reporting by Defined Benefit Pension Plans*?

A. SFAS 35 establishes a requirement that defined benefit pension plans prepare and distribute financial statements.

B. SFAS 35 is not applicable to defined benefit pension plans that provide benefits on death, disability, or termination of employment in addition to pension benefits.

C. SFAS 35 applies only to defined benefit pension plans that are subject to the provisions of the Employee Retirement Income Security Act of 1974 (ERISA).

D. SFAS 35 applies to ongoing plans that provide pension benefits for the employees of one or more employers.

Answer (D) is correct. *(Publisher)*

REQUIRED: The item that is an SFAS 35 provision about accounting and reporting by defined benefit pension plans.

DISCUSSION: SFAS 35 establishes the accounting and reporting requirements for defined benefit pension plans themselves, as opposed to SFAS 87's requirements for reporting in the employers' financial statements. A defined benefit pension plan specifies a determinable pension benefit, usually based on such factors as age, years of service, and salary.

Answer (A) is incorrect because SFAS 35 establishes standards of accounting and reporting for those defined benefit pension plans that issue financial statements. It does not require that such statements be prepared or distributed. Answer (B) is incorrect because SFAS 35 is applicable to all defined benefit pension plans, whether or not subject to ERISA, except those of state and local governmental units, which are covered by GASB pronouncements. Answer (C) is incorrect because SFAS 35 is applicable to all defined benefit pension plans, whether or not subject to ERISA, except those of state and local governmental units, which are covered by GASB pronouncements.

42. One of the requirements of SFAS 35 is that defined benefit pension plans report the components of the change in net assets available for benefits. These components ordinarily do not include

A. Net appreciation and fair value for each significant class of investments.

B. Benefits paid to participants.

C. Contributions by the employer.

D. The change in the actuarial present value of accumulated plan benefits.

Answer (D) is correct. *(Publisher)*

REQUIRED: The item not a component of the change in net assets available for benefits of a pension plan.

DISCUSSION: The change in the present value of accumulated plan benefits is not a component of the change in net assets available for benefits. It is a change in the estimated benefits that must be satisfied by the use of the available assets.

Answer (A) is incorrect because they are components of the change in net assets available for benefits of a pension plan. Additional components are investment income (exclusive of appreciation of the fair value of investments), contributions from other sources, administrative expenses, and payments to insurance companies for beneficiaries. Answer (B) is incorrect because it is a component of the change in net assets available for benefits of a pension plan. Additional components are contributions by the employer, investment income (exclusive of appreciation of the fair value of investments), contributions from other sources, administrative expenses, and payments to insurance companies for beneficiaries. Answer (C) is incorrect because it is a component of the change in net assets available for benefits of a pension plan. Additional components are benefits paid to participants, investment income (exclusive of appreciation of the fair value of investments), contributions from other sources, administrative expenses, and payments to insurance companies for beneficiaries.

43. SFAS 35 states that the primary objective of the financial statements of a defined benefit pension plan is to provide financial information useful for assessing the plan's current and future ability to pay benefits when due. To accomplish that purpose, information about which of the following should be provided?

A. Plan resources.

B. Accumulated plan benefits of participants.

C. The results of transactions and events that affect the information regarding the plan resources and the accumulated plan benefits.

D. All of the answers are correct.

Answer (D) is correct. *(Publisher)*

REQUIRED: The information required in the financial statements of a defined benefit pension plan.

DISCUSSION: The annual financial statements of a defined benefit pension plan should include information about each of the following:

1) The net assets available for benefits as of the end of the plan year (plan assets)
2) The changes in net assets during the year
3) The actuarial present value of accumulated plan benefits as of either the beginning or end of the plan year
4) The significant factors that affect the annual change in the actuarial present value of accumulated plan benefits

The information regarding the plan resources and the accumulated plan benefits must be presented as of the same date, and the changes therein must be presented for the same period.

Answer (A) is incorrect because information about plan resources should be provided in the financial statements to be useful in assessing the plan's current and future ability to pay benefits when due. Answer (B) is incorrect because information about accumulated plan benefits of participants should be provided in the financial statements to be useful in assessing the plan's current and future ability to pay benefits when due. Answer (C) is incorrect because the results of relevant transactions and events should be provided in the financial statements to be useful in assessing the plan's current and future ability to pay benefits when due.

44. SFAS 35 requires many disclosures to be made by a defined benefit pension plan if applicable. Which of the following is usually not such a disclosure?

A. The funding policy.

B. The income tax status.

C. Identification of investments representing more than 5% of the net available assets.

D. The priority order of participants' claims.

Answer (B) is correct. *(Publisher)*

REQUIRED: The item concerning a defined benefit pension plan not required to be disclosed.

DISCUSSION: SFAS 35 requires disclosure of

1) The method of determining fair value of investments
2) The assumptions and methods underlying determination of the actuarial present value of accumulated plan benefits
3) A brief description of the plan agreement
4) Significant plan amendments during the year
5) The priority order of participants' claims to plan assets upon plan termination
6) Benefits guaranteed by the Pension Benefit Guaranty Corporation
7) The funding policy
8) The tax status of the plan if favorable status has not been obtained or maintained
9) Identification of investments representing 5% or more of net assets
10) Significant transactions with any related party

The tax status disclosure is required only if a favorable letter of determination from the IRS has not been obtained or maintained. Because almost all pension plans obtain a favorable letter of determination prior to accumulating funds, the tax status is usually not a required disclosure.

45. In accounting for a settlement, SFAS 88, *Employers' Accounting for Settlements and Curtailments of Defined Benefit Pension Plans and for Termination Benefits*, provides that

A. The settlement gain (loss) is measured by the change in the projected benefit obligation as a result of the transaction.

B. The unrecognized transition net asset or obligation is included in the calculation of the maximum settlement gain or loss.

C. A transaction must eliminate significant risks related to the obligation and the assets involved to constitute a settlement.

D. The cost of a participation right reduces the maximum gain or loss subject to recognition in a settlement.

Answer (C) is correct. *(Publisher)*

REQUIRED: The prescribed accounting for settlements.

DISCUSSION: A settlement is defined as an irrevocable action that relieves the employer (or the plan) of the primary responsibility for a PBO and eliminates significant risks related to the pension obligation and the assets used to effect the settlement.

Answer (A) is incorrect because the maximum potential settlement gain or loss is the sum of any unrecognized net gain or loss plus any remaining transition net asset. The proportion of maximum gain or loss recognized in earnings equals the percentage reduction in the PBO. Answer (B) is incorrect because the transition net obligation is regarded as prior service cost, which is unaffected by a settlement. Answer (D) is incorrect because the cost of the right to participate in the investment and other experience of an insurer from which annuities have been purchased to settle a pension obligation reduces the maximum gain (but not loss).

46. A curtailment of a defined benefit pension plan is an event that significantly reduces the expected years of future service of current employees or eliminates for a significant number of employees the accrual of defined benefits for some or all of their future service. Which statement is descriptive of a curtailment?

A. It occurs only when a plan is terminated.

B. If the amount of net curtailment loss is less than or equal to the sum of the interest cost and service cost components of net periodic pension cost, recognition is not mandatory.

C. A curtailment gain resulting from a decrease in the projected benefit obligation is offset by any unrecognized transition net obligation.

D. It involves recognition of unamortized prior service cost.

Answer (D) is correct. *(Publisher)*

REQUIRED: The statement descriptive of a curtailment.

DISCUSSION: A curtailment net gain or loss equals the combined amounts of (1) the unrecognized prior service cost associated with years of service no longer expected to be rendered and (2) the change in the PBO that does not represent a reversal of previously unrecognized net gains or losses. For this purpose, unrecognized prior service cost includes any remaining unrecognized transition net obligation (SFAS 88).

Answer (A) is incorrect because termination of a plan is not required for a curtailment. Answer (B) is incorrect because recognition is not mandatory for a settlement (not a curtailment) gain or loss. However, recognition of a settlement gain or loss is required if the cost of all settlements in a year exceeds the sum of the interest cost and the service cost components. Answer (C) is incorrect because a curtailment gain is offset only by any unrecognized net loss.

47. Pendragon Company, which sponsors a final pay, noncontributory, defined benefit pension plan, settled its vested benefit obligation of $3,000,000 by purchasing participating annuity contracts for $3,300,000. Nonparticipating annuity contracts would have cost $3,000,000. The remaining unrecognized transition net asset is $360,000, the remaining unrecognized net loss since transition is $800,000, and the projected benefit obligation is $4,000,000. Prior service cost is $600,000. The settlement gain (loss) that should be recognized is

A. $270,000

B. $(330,000)

C. $(3,550,000)

D. $(780,000)

Answer (B) is correct. *(Publisher)*

REQUIRED: The settlement gain (loss) that should be recognized.

DISCUSSION: The maximum settlement gain or loss is equal to the unrecognized net gain or loss arising subsequent to transition to SFAS 87 plus any remaining unrecognized net asset arising at transition. If the purchase of a participating annuity contract constitutes a settlement, the maximum gain is reduced by the cost of the participation rights, but the maximum loss is not adjusted. The maximum gain or loss is recognized if the entire PBO is settled. If only part is settled, a pro rata share of the maximum gain or loss is recognized equal to the percentage reduction in the PBO.

Unrecognized transition net asset	$ 360,000
Unrecognized net loss	(800,000)
Maximum loss	$(440,000)
Reduction % ($3,000,000 ÷ $4,000,000)	× .75
Settlement loss	$(330,000)

Answer (A) is incorrect because $270,000 equals the $360,000 unrecognized transition asset multiplied by the percentage reduction in the PBO. Answer (C) is incorrect because the loss should not be increased by the cost of the participation rights multiplied by the percentage reduction in the PBO. Answer (D) is incorrect because the prior service cost is not included in the calculation of settlement loss.

48. A curtailment has eliminated 50% of the estimated remaining future years of service of employees active at the date of the only amendment to Gawain Co.'s defined benefit pension plan. The unrecognized prior service cost associated with that amendment is $200,000. The curtailment eliminated 60% of the estimated remaining future years of service of employees active at the date of transition to SFAS 87. The unrecognized transition net obligation is $300,000. The curtailment reduced the projected benefit obligation by $400,000. If the unrecognized net loss subsequent to transition is $100,000, the curtailment net gain (loss) is

A. $20,000

B. $120,000

C. $(180,000)

D. $200,000

Answer (A) is correct. *(Publisher)*

REQUIRED: The curtailment net gain (loss).

DISCUSSION: The curtailment net gain or loss equals (1) the unrecognized prior service cost associated with years of service no longer expected to be rendered, plus (2) the change in the PBO that is not a reversal of previously unrecognized net gains or losses. For a curtailment, unrecognized prior service cost includes both the cost of retroactive plan amendments and any remaining unrecognized net obligation existing at the date of the initial transition to SFAS 87. The gain resulting from the decrease in the PBO is included to the extent it exceeds any remaining unrecognized net loss. Therefore, as indicated below, the curtailment net gain is $20,000.

Prior service cost (50% × $200,000)		$(100,000)
Transition net obligation (60% × $300,000)		(180,000)
PBO gain	$400,000	
Unrecognized net loss	(100,000)	
Curtailment gain		300,000
Curtailment net gain		$ 20,000

Answer (B) is incorrect because the gain must be reduced by 50% of the prior service cost. Answer (C) is incorrect because the curtailment loss must be increased by 50% of the prior service cost and reduced by the curtailment gain. Answer (D) is incorrect because the curtailment gain must also be reduced by 60% of the transition net obligation.

49. On September 1, 2003, Channing Corp. offered special termination benefits to employees who had reached the early retirement age specified in the company's pension plan. The termination benefits consisted of lump-sum and periodic future payments. Additionally, the employees accepting the company offer receive the usual early retirement pension benefits. The offer expired on November 30, 2003. Actual or reasonably estimated amounts at December 31, 2003 relating to the employees accepting the offer are as follows:

- Lump-sum payments totaling $475,000 were made on January 1, 2004.
- Periodic payments of $60,000 annually for 3 years will begin January 1, 2005. The present value at December 31, 2003 of these payments was $155,000.
- Reduction of accrued pension costs at December 31, 2003 for the terminating employees was $45,000.

In its December 31, 2003 balance sheet, Channing should report a total liability for special termination benefits of

A. $950,000

B. $1,170,000

C. $1,260,000

D. $1,310,000

Answer (C) is correct. *(CPA, adapted)*
REQUIRED: The total liability for special termination benefits.
DISCUSSION: The liability and expense arising from special termination benefits should be recognized by an employer when the employees accept the offer and the amount can be reasonably estimated. The amount should include the lump-sum payments and the present value of any future payments. Thus, Channing should report a total liability for special termination benefits of $1,260,000 ($950,000 lump-sum payments + $310,000 present value of future payments).
Answer (A) is incorrect because $950,000 excludes the present value of the annual payments. Answer (B) is incorrect because the liability should not be reduced by the reduction of accrued pension costs. Answer (D) is incorrect because the present value of the annual payments of $310,000, not the full amount of $360,000, should be included in the calculation of the liability.

50. Termination benefits are provided to employees in connection with their termination of employment. Termination benefits may be classified as either special termination benefits offered only for a short period or contractual termination benefits required by the terms of a pension plan only if a specified event occurs. The liability and loss arising from termination benefits should be recognized by an employer when the employees accept the offer and the amount can be reasonably estimated for

	Special Benefits	Contractual Benefits
A.	No	No
B.	No	Yes
C.	Yes	No
D.	Yes	Yes

Answer (C) is correct. *(Publisher)*
REQUIRED: The termination benefits that should be recognized by the employer when the employees accept the offer and the amount is reasonably estimable.
DISCUSSION: The liability and loss arising from special termination benefits should be recognized by an employer when the employees accept the offer and the amount can be reasonably estimated. The liability and loss arising from contractual termination benefits should be recognized when it is probable that employees will be entitled to benefits and the amount can be reasonably estimated (SFAS 88).

13.2 Employers' Accounting and Reporting for Postretirement Benefits Other Than Pensions

51. SFAS 106, *Employers' Accounting for Postretirement Benefits Other Than Pensions,* emphasizes an employer's accounting for a single-employer plan that defines other postretirement employee benefits (OPEB). OPEB, which are benefits other than pensions, are defined in terms of monetary amounts (e.g., a given dollar value of life insurance) or benefit coverage (e.g., amounts per day for hospitalization). The amount depends on such factors as the benefit formula, the life expectancy of the retiree and any beneficiaries and covered dependents, and the frequency and significance of events (e.g., illnesses) requiring payments. The basic elements of accounting for OPEB include

A. The expected postretirement benefit obligation (EPBO), which equals the accumulated postretirement benefit obligation (APBO) after the full eligibility date.

B. The APBO, which is the actuarial present value at a given date of the benefits projected to be earned after the full eligibility date.

C. Required recognition of a minimum liability for any excess of the EPBO over the APBO.

D. The projected benefit obligation (PBO) and the vested benefit obligation (VBO).

Answer (A) is correct. *(Publisher)*

REQUIRED: The true statement about the elements of accounting for OPEB.

DISCUSSION: The EPBO for an employee is the actuarial present value at a given date of the OPEB expected to be paid. Its measurement depends on the anticipated amounts and timing of future benefits, the costs to be incurred to provide those benefits, and the extent the costs are shared by the employee and others (such as governmental programs). The APBO for an employee is the actuarial present value at a given date of the future benefits attributable to the employee's service as of that date. Unlike the calculation of the ABO described in SFAS 87, the determination of the APBO (as well as of the EPBO and service cost) implicitly includes the consideration of future salary progression to the extent the benefit formula defines benefits as a function of future compensation levels. The full eligibility date is reached when the employee has rendered all the services necessary to earn all of the benefits expected to be received by that employee. After the full eligibility date, the EPBO and APBO are equal. Prior to that date, the EPBO exceeds the APBO.

Answer (B) is incorrect because the full eligibility date is the date when an employee has earned all the benefits expected to be received. Answer (C) is incorrect because, unlike SFAS 87, SFAS 106 does not require recognition of a minimum liability. Answer (D) is incorrect because these terms relate to pension accounting only.

52. Ethelred Co. is an employer sponsoring a defined benefit postretirement healthcare plan. Which of the following components might be included in its net periodic postretirement benefit cost (NPPBC)?

	Amortization of Unrecognized Prior Service Cost	Interest Cost
A.	No	No
B.	Yes	No
C.	No	Yes
D.	Yes	Yes

Answer (D) is correct. *(Publisher)*

REQUIRED: The true statement about the elements of NPPBC.

DISCUSSION: The six possible components of NPPBC are (1) service cost, (2) interest on the APBO, (3) expected return on plan assets, (4) amortization of unrecognized prior service cost, (5) amortization of the transition obligation or asset, and (6) the gain or loss component. The NPPBC is very similar to net periodic pension cost.

53. Li Co. is a publicly traded entity that sponsors both a pension plan and a postretirement plan providing other, nonpension benefits. The following information relates to the current year's activity of Li's defined benefit postretirement plan:

Service cost	$240,000
Return on plan assets	60,000
Interest cost on accumulated benefit obligation	80,000
Amortization of actuarial loss	20,000
Amortization of prior service cost	10,000
Amortization of transition obligation	30,000

Li's nonpension net periodic postretirement benefit cost is

A. $240,000

B. $280,000

C. $300,000

D. $320,000

Answer (D) is correct. *(A. Oddo)*

REQUIRED: The net periodic postretirement benefit cost (NPPBC) for the year.

DISCUSSION: The components of the NPPBC are service cost, interest cost, the expected return on plan assets, and amortization of (1) any unrecognized prior service cost, (2) any transition asset or obligation, and (3) any unrecognized net gain (loss). Service cost; interest cost; and the amortization of actuarial loss, prior service cost, and a transition obligation increase the NPPBC. The expected return on plan assets decreases NPPBC. As indicated below, NPPBC for the year is $320,000.

Service cost	$240,000
Return on plan assets	(60,000)
Interest cost	80,000
Amortization of actuarial loss	20,000
Amortization of prior service cost	10,000
Amortization of transition obligation	30,000
Net periodic postretirement benefit cost	$320,000

Answer (A) is incorrect because $240,000 includes only the service cost component. Answer (B) is incorrect because $280,000 excludes the amortization of the prior service cost and the amortization of the transition obligation. Answer (C) is incorrect because $300,000 excludes the amortization of the actuarial loss from the calculation of NPPBC.

54. Gallaher Co. sponsors a single-employer defined benefit postretirement plan that provides nonpension benefits. The service cost component of its net periodic postretirement benefit cost (NPPBC) is

A. Included in the APBO but not in the EPBO.

B. The portion of the EPBO attributed to employee service for a period.

C. Included in the EPBO but not the APBO.

D. Measured using implicit and explicit actuarial assumptions and present value techniques.

Answer (B) is correct. *(Publisher)*

REQUIRED: The definition of the service cost component of the NPPBC.

DISCUSSION: Service cost is the actuarial present value of benefits attributed to services rendered by employees during the period. It is the portion of the EPBO attributed to service in the period and is not affected by the level of funding.

Answer (A) is incorrect because the service cost for the most recently completed period is included in the APBO as well as the EPBO. Answer (C) is incorrect because the service cost for the most recently completed period is included in the APBO as well as the EPBO. Answer (D) is incorrect because SFAS 106 requires the use of explicit assumptions, each of which is the best estimate of a particular event.

55. Campbell Co. sponsors a single-employer defined benefit postretirement plan that provides nonpension benefits. The interest cost component of its net periodic postretirement benefit cost (NPPBC) is the

A. Increase in the EPBO because of the passage of time.

B. Increase in the APBO because of the passage of time.

C. Product of the market-related value of plan assets and the expected long-term rate of return on plan assets.

D. Change in the APBO during the period.

Answer (B) is correct. *(Publisher)*

REQUIRED: The definition of the interest cost component of the NPPBC.

DISCUSSION: Interest cost reflects the change in the APBO during the period resulting solely from the passage of time. It equals the APBO at the beginning of the period times the assumed discount rate used in determining the present value of future cash outflows currently expected to be required to satisfy the obligation.

Answer (A) is incorrect because interest cost is a function of the APBO. Answer (C) is incorrect because the expected return on plan assets is the product of the market-related value of plan assets and the expected long-term rate of return on plan assets. Answer (D) is incorrect because the change in the obligation reflects many factors, of which interest cost is one.

56. Hubbard Co. sponsors a single-employer defined benefit postretirement plan that provides nonpension benefits. Its prior service cost is the cost of benefit improvements attributable to plan participants' prior service pursuant to a plan amendment or a plan initiation that provides benefits in exchange for plan participants' prior service. Hubbard ordinarily should recognize prior service cost in net periodic postretirement benefit cost

A. By assigning an equal amount to each remaining year of service to the full eligibility date of each participant active at the amendment date who was not yet fully eligible for benefits.

B. In full in the accounting period in which the plan is amended.

C. By amortizing it over the remaining life expectancy of the participants.

D. In accordance with straight-line amortization over the average remaining years to full eligibility of the active participants.

Answer (A) is correct. *(Publisher)*

REQUIRED: The general rule for recognition of prior service cost.

DISCUSSION: The effect of a plan amendment on a participant's EPBO should be attributed to each year of service in that individual's attribution period (ordinarily from the date of hire or a later date specified by the benefit formula to the full eligibility date). This period may include years of service already rendered. The cost of benefit improvements for years of service already rendered is the increase in the APBO as a result of an amendment and measured at the date of the amendment. The general rule is that equal amounts of this cost should be assigned to each remaining year of service to the full eligibility date for each active plan participant at the date of the amendment who was not yet fully eligible.

Answer (B) is incorrect because prior service cost is deemed to provide economic benefits to the employer in future periods. Thus, recognition in full in the year of the amendment is prohibited. Answer (C) is incorrect because this treatment is appropriate only if all or almost all of the participants are fully eligible. Answer (D) is incorrect because it describes a pragmatic exception to the general rule. An alternative, consistently applied amortization method that more rapidly reduces unrecognized prior service cost is permitted to reduce complexity and detail.

57. The gain or loss components of net periodic postretirement benefit cost for single-employer defined benefit plans (SFAS 106, *Employers' Accounting for Postretirement Benefits Other Than Pensions)* and net periodic pension cost (SFAS 87, *Employers' Accounting for Pensions)* are calculated similarly. Moreover, under either pronouncement, an employer may use a systematic method of amortizing unrecognized net gain or loss other than the corridor approach described in each pronouncement. The alternative is allowable if it results in amortization at least equal to the minimum determined using that approach. Under SFAS 106, however, if an enterprise consistently recognizes gains and losses immediately,

A. Any net loss in excess of a net gain previously recognized first offsets any unrecognized prior service cost.

B. Any net gain in excess of a net loss previously recognized first offsets any unrecognized transition asset.

C. Any net loss in excess of a net gain previously recognized first offsets any unrecognized transition obligation.

D. Any net gain in excess of a net loss previously recognized first offsets any unrecognized transition obligation.

Answer (D) is correct. *(Publisher)*

REQUIRED: The proper treatment of gains or losses recognized immediately.

DISCUSSION: Under either SFAS 87 or SFAS 106, gains and losses may be recognized immediately or delayed. But SFAS 106 also provides that immediately recognized gains (losses) that do not offset previously recognized losses (gains) must first reduce any unrecognized transition obligation (asset). The transition obligation (asset) represents an underlying unfunded (overfunded) APBO. The FASB believes that gains (losses) should not be recognized until the unfunded (overfunded) APBO is recognized.

Answer (A) is incorrect because a net loss in excess of a net gain previously recognized first offsets any unrecognized transition assets. Answer (B) is incorrect because a net gain in excess of a net loss previously recognized first offsets any unrecognized transaction obligation. Answer (C) is incorrect because a net loss in excess of a net gain previously recognized first offsets any unrecognized transition assets.

58. Lee Co. maintains a single-employer defined benefit postretirement health care plan for its employees. Under the plan's terms, an excess of benefit payments over the sum of the employer's cost and the employees' contributions for a year will be recovered from increased employees' contributions in the subsequent year. However, for the current year only, Lee has decided not to adjust contributions. Lee should

A. Delay recognition of the loss by using the corridor approach.

B. Apply any systematic and rational delayed recognition approach to accounting for the loss.

C. Immediately recognize the loss in income.

D. Adjust the transition asset.

Answer (C) is correct. *(Publisher)*

REQUIRED: The treatment of a loss resulting from a temporary deviation from the plan.

DISCUSSION: A gain or loss from a temporary deviation from the substantive plan is immediately recognized in income. No delayed recognition method is appropriate because the effect of a temporary deviation (1) is not deemed to provide future economic benefits and (2) relates to benefits already paid. If the deviation is other than temporary, that is, if the employer decides to continue to bear the burden of increased costs, the implication is that the substantive plan (the plan as understood by the parties as opposed to the extant written plan) has been amended. An amendment would require accounting for prior service cost (SFAS 106).

59. Which of the following items of information should be disclosed by Purpura Company, which provides health care benefits to its retirees under a single-employer defined benefit plan?

I. The assumed health care cost trend rate used to measure the expected cost of benefits covered by the plan

II. The assumptions about the discount rate, rate of compensation increase, and expected long-term rate of return on plan assets

A. I and II.

B. I only.

C. II only.

D. Neither I nor II.

Answer (A) is correct. *(CPA, adapted)*

REQUIRED: The information that should be disclosed by an entity providing health care benefits to its retirees.

DISCUSSION: SFAS 132 (R) standardizes the disclosure requirements for pensions and other postretirement employee benefits to the extent practicable (but reduced disclosure requirements apply to nonpublic entities). These disclosures include

- "The assumed health care cost trend rate(s) for the next year used to measure the expected cost of benefits covered by the plan (gross eligible charges), and a general description of the direction and pattern of change in the assumed trend rates thereafter, together with the ultimate trend rate(s) and when that rate is expected to be achieved."
- "On a weighted-average basis, the following assumptions used in accounting for a plan: assumed discount rates, rates of compensation increase (for pay-related plans), and expected long-term rates of return on plan assets specifying, in a tabular format, the assumptions used to determine the benefit obligation and the assumptions used to determine net benefit cost."

Disclosures about assumed health care cost trend rates and certain other assumptions used in accounting for a plan must be made by public and nonpublic entities.

60. Griffin Co. provides postretirement health care benefits to employees under a single-employer defined benefit plan. To be eligible, employees must have completed at least 10 years service and be aged 55 years or older when retiring. Employees retiring from Griffin have a median age of 62, and no one has worked beyond age 65. Hurlbert is hired at 48 years old. The attribution period for accruing Griffin's expected postretirement health care benefit obligation to Hurlbert is during the period when Hurlbert is aged

A. 48 to 65.

B. 48 to 58.

C. 55 to 65.

D. 55 to 62.

Answer (B) is correct. *(CPA, adapted)*

REQUIRED: The attribution period for accruing the expected postretirement health care benefit obligation to an employee.

DISCUSSION: The attribution period begins on the date of hire unless the plan's benefit formula grants credit for service only from a later date. The end of the period is the full eligibility date. If the exception does not apply, Hurlbert's attribution is from age 48, the date of hire, to age 58, the date of full eligibility.

13.3 Postemployment Benefits

61. SFAS 112, *Employers' Accounting for Postemployment Benefits*, establishes the accounting for

A. Pension benefits provided to spouses of retired employees.

B. Salary continuation benefits provided to employees on disability leave.

C. Counseling benefits provided to employees nearing retirement age.

D. Health care benefits provided to dependents of retired employees.

Answer (B) is correct. *(Publisher)*

REQUIRED: The type of benefits accounted for under SFAS 112.

DISCUSSION: SFAS 112, *Employers' Accounting for Postemployment Benefits*, concerns accounting standards for employers who provide benefits to former or inactive employees, their beneficiaries, and their covered dependents after employment but before retirement. These benefits include, but are not limited to, salary continuation, supplemental unemployment benefits, severance benefits, disability-related benefits (including workers' compensation), job training and counseling, and continuation of benefits such as health care and life insurance coverage.

Answer (A) is incorrect because the former employees have retired and thus are not covered under SFAS 112. Answer (C) is incorrect because the employees are still employed. Answer (D) is incorrect because the former employees have retired and thus are not covered under SFAS 112.

62. Sanders Co. has determined that its payment of postemployment benefits is probable, the amount can be reasonably estimated, and the obligation relates to rights that vest or accumulate. The company's obligation for postemployment benefits should

A. Be recognized when the benefits are paid.

B. Be accrued at the date of the event giving rise to the payment of benefits.

C. Be accrued if attributable to employees' services already rendered.

D. Not be recognized.

Answer (C) is correct. *(Publisher)*

REQUIRED: The treatment of postemployment benefits by the employer.

DISCUSSION: SFAS 112 requires employers to recognize the obligation to provide postemployment benefits if the obligation is attributable to employees' services already rendered, employees' rights accumulate or vest, payment is probable, and the amount of the benefits can be reasonably estimated.

63. At December 31 of this year, Medina Corporation reasonably estimates that its obligations for postemployment benefits include

Severance pay	$120,000
Job training benefits	90,000

These benefits relate to employees' services already rendered, and payment is probable. The severance pay benefits vest; the job training benefits accumulate. In its December 31 balance sheet, Medina should report a liability for postemployment benefits of

A. $0

B. $90,000

C. $120,000

D. $210,000

Answer (D) is correct. *(Publisher)*

REQUIRED: The amount of liability that should be recorded for postemployment benefits.

DISCUSSION: According to SFAS 112, if postemployment benefits are attributable to employees' services already rendered, employees' rights accumulate or vest, payment is probable, and the amount of the benefits can be reasonably estimated, the employer should recognize a liability for the obligation. Thus, the full amount of the severance pay and job training benefits of $210,000 ($120,000 + $90,000) should be reported as a liability.

STUDY UNIT FOURTEEN
LEASES

A **lease** is an agreement between a lessor and a lessee that conveys the right to the lessee to use property, plant, or equipment for a period of time (lease term). Leases are accounted for under **SFAS 13**, *Accounting for Leases.* A **lessee** classifies a lease that transfers substantially all of the benefits and risks of ownership to the lessee as a **capital lease**. Otherwise, a lessee classifies a lease as an **operating lease**. Transfer of substantially all of the benefits and risks of ownership is indicated if at least one of the following **capitalization criteria** is met: (1) The lease transfers ownership to the lessee by the end of the lease term; (2) the lease contains a bargain purchase option; (3) the lease term is at least equal to 75% of the estimated remaining economic life of the leased property; or (4) the present value of the minimum lease payments is at least equal to 90% of the fair value of the leased property minus any investment tax credit (ITC) retained by the lessor. The latter two criteria, however, are not applicable if the lease begins within the last 25% of the total estimated useful life of the leased property.

A lessee records a **capital lease** as an asset and a liability equal to the lower of the present value of the minimum lease payments or the fair value of the leased property at the lease's inception. **Minimum lease payments** include the periodic rental payments minus any executory costs, plus either (1) the payment called for by a **bargain purchase option**, if stated in the lease, or, (2) if a bargain purchase option is not stated, any **guaranteed residual value** and any penalty imposed for not renewing the lease. However, any guarantee of residual value obtained by the lessee from an **unrelated third party** for the lessor's benefit is excluded from the lessee's minimum lease payments if the lessor specifically releases the lessee from all liability on a residual value deficiency. The **discount rate** used by the **lessor** is the rate implicit in the lease (the rate at which the sum of the present values of the minimum lease payments and the unguaranteed residual value at the beginning of the lease term equals the fair value of the leased property at the inception of the lease, minus any ITC expected to be realized by the lessor). The lessee uses **the lower** of the lessor's implicit rate (if known) or the lessee's incremental borrowing rate. The lessee amortizes the asset in accordance with its **normal depreciation policy** for owned assets. The amortization period equals the economic life of the asset given either transfer of ownership or a bargain purchase option. Otherwise, the amortization period equals the lease term. The lessee also records interest on the lease obligation in accordance with the **effective interest method** (at a constant rate).

A lessee records an **operating lease** as a property rental. Thus, only rental expense is recognized, normally in accordance with the straight-line method.

For **lessor** accounting, a lease is most commonly classified as a sales-type, direct financing, or operating lease. The lease is classified as a sales-type or a direct financing lease if (1) the lease meets at least one of the criteria indicating the transferability of the benefits and risks of ownership, (2) **collectibility** of the minimum lease payments is reasonably predictable, and (3) no material **uncertainties** exist as to unreimbursable costs yet to be incurred by the lessor. It is treated as a **direct financing** lease if the fair value of the asset is equal to its cost or carrying amount. If the fair value of the asset does not equal its cost or carrying amount, the lease is classified as a **sales-type** lease. If the lease does not meet the three conditions stated, the lessor classifies it as an operating lease. (NOTE: When the lease involves real estate, certain modifications of the rules are needed.)

In a **direct financing lease**, the lessor does not recognize a manufacturer's or dealer's profit (loss). The fair value of the leased property and its cost or carrying amount are the same at the inception of the lease. The difference between the **gross investment** (minimum lease payments + unguaranteed residual value) and the cost or carrying amount is **unearned income**. Unearned income and the **initial direct costs** are amortized to income over the lease term using the interest method so as to produce a constant rate of return on the **net investment**. It equals the gross investment, plus unamortized initial direct costs, minus unearned income.

In a **sales-type lease**, the lessor recognizes **manufacturer's or dealer's profit (loss)**. In the entry for a sales-type lease, the **asset** is credited for its cost or carrying amount. **Cost of goods sold** is debited for the cost or carrying amount, plus any initial direct costs, minus the present value of any unguaranteed residual value (a continuing investment of the lessor). **Lease payments receivable** is debited for the gross investment defined above. **Sales revenue** (price) is credited for the present value of the minimum lease payments. **Unearned income** is credited for the difference between the gross investment (lease payments receivable) and the sum of the present values of its components discounted at the rate implicit in the lease. Thus, the net investment equals gross investment minus unearned income. The unearned income is amortized to income over the lease term using the **interest method** so as to produce a constant rate of return on the net investment.

A **lessor's minimum lease payments** are the same as those for the lessee except that they include any guarantee of residual value or of rental payments beyond the lease term by a financially capable third party unrelated to the lessee or lessor.

The lessor records an **operating lease** as a rental. Income is usually recognized on the straight-line basis. **Depreciation** is based on the normal depreciation policy.

If the lease involves **real estate**, it may be classified in one of four categories: (1) land only, (2) land and building(s), (3) real estate and equipment, and (4) part of a building. SFAS 13 (as amended by SFAS 98) applies specific rules to each category.

A lessor may classify certain direct financing leases as **leveraged leases** if (1) the lease involves a long-term creditor as a third party; (2) the creditor provides substantial financing that is nonrecourse as to the general credit of the lessor; (3) the lessor's net investment first declines and then increases during the lease term; and (4) any investment tax credit retained by the lessor is accounted for as a cash flow component of the lease.

A gain on the sale in a **sale-leaseback** usually is deferred and amortized (1) in proportion to the amortization (depreciation) of the leased asset if the leaseback is classified as a capital lease or (2) in proportion to the gross rental payments expensed over the lease term if the leaseback is classified as an operating lease.

QUESTIONS

14.1 Capital Leases

1. Leases should be classified by the lessee as either operating leases or capital leases. Which of the following statements best characterizes operating leases?

A. The benefits and risks of ownership are transferred from the lessor to the lessee.

B. The lessee records an asset and a liability for the present value of the lease payments.

C. Operating leases transfer ownership to the lessee, contain a bargain purchase option, are for more than 75% of the leased property's useful life, or have lease payments with a present value in excess of 90% of the value of the leased property.

D. The lessor records lease revenue, asset depreciation, maintenance, etc., and the lessee records lease payments as rental expense.

Answer (D) is correct. *(Publisher)*

REQUIRED: The true statement about operating leases.

DISCUSSION: Operating leases are transactions in which lessees rent the right to use lessor assets without acquiring a substantial portion of the benefits and risks of ownership of those assets.

Answer (A) is incorrect because, when the benefits and risks of ownership are transferred from the lessor to the lessee, the transaction is a capital lease. Answer (B) is incorrect because the lessee records an asset and a liability for the present value of the lease payments if the transaction is accounted for as a capital lease. However, this amount may not exceed the fair value of the leased property. Answer (C) is incorrect because satisfaction of any one of these four criteria requires the lease to be treated as a capital lease.

2. The present value of minimum lease payments should be used by the lessee in determining the amount of a lease liability under a lease classified by the lessee as a(n)

	Capital Lease	Operating Lease
A.	Yes	Yes
B.	Yes	No
C.	No	No
D.	No	Yes

Answer (B) is correct. *(CPA, adapted)*

REQUIRED: The lease for which the lessee's liability is based on the present value of the minimum lease payments.

DISCUSSION: SFAS 13, *Accounting for Leases*, states that the lessee must record a capital lease as an asset and an obligation at an amount equal to the present value of the minimum lease payments. However, this amount may not exceed the fair value of the leased property. Under an operating lease, the lessee records no liability except for rental expense accrued at the end of an accounting period. Such accrual would be at settlement value rather than present value.

Answer (A) is incorrect because an operating lease does not result in a lease liability for the lessee. Answer (C) is incorrect because the lease liability under a capital lease is the present value of minimum lease payments. Answer (D) is incorrect because the lease liability under a capital lease is the present value of minimum lease payments. Also, an operating lease does not result in a lease liability.

3. GAAP require that certain lease agreements be accounted for as purchases. The theoretical basis for this treatment is that a lease of this type

A. Conveys substantially all of the benefits and risks incident to the ownership of property.

B. Is an example of form over substance.

C. Provides the use of the leased asset to the lessee for a limited period of time.

D. Must be recorded in accordance with the concept of cause and effect.

Answer (A) is correct. *(CPA, adapted)*

REQUIRED: The theoretical justification for capitalization of certain leases.

DISCUSSION: The provisions of SFAS 13 derive from the view that a lease transferring substantially all of the benefits and risks incident to the ownership of property should be accounted for as the acquisition of an asset and the incurrence of an obligation by the lessee. The lessor should account for the transaction as a sale and/or financing.

Answer (B) is incorrect because a lease is not a purchase in form, although transfer of substantially all of the benefits and risks of ownership make it similar to a purchase in substance. Answer (C) is incorrect because, although a lease is a contractual agreement covering the use of property for a specified time period, other aspects of the lease justify the capitalization treatment. Answer (D) is incorrect because the concept of cause and effect is not relevant to accounting for leases.

4. On January 1, year 1, Cutlip Co. signed a 7-year lease for equipment having a 10-year economic life. The present value of the monthly lease payments equals 80% of the equipment's fair value. The lease agreement provides for neither a transfer of title to Cutlip nor a bargain purchase option. In its year 1 income statement, Cutlip should report

A. Rent expense equal to the year 1 lease payments.

B. Rent expense equal to the year 1 lease payments minus interest.

C. Lease amortization equal to one-tenth of the equipment's fair value.

D. Lease amortization equal to one-seventh of 80% of the equipment's fair value.

Answer (A) is correct. *(CPA, adapted)*

REQUIRED: The income statement effect of the lease.

DISCUSSION: A lease is either a capital lease or an operating lease. A lease must be classified as a capital lease by a lessee if, at its inception, any one of four criteria is satisfied. Each of these criteria indicates that a substantial transfer of the benefits and risks of ownership has occurred. The following are the four criteria: (1) The lease provides for the transfer of ownership of the leased property, (2) the lease contains a bargain purchase option, (3) the lease term is 75% or more of the estimated economic life of the leased property, or (4) the present value of the minimum lease payments (excluding executory costs) is at least 90% of the fair value of the leased property to the lessor at the inception of the lease minus any related investment tax credit. (The last two criteria do not apply if the lease term begins within the last 25% of the total estimated economic life.) Because none of these criteria are satisfied, the lease must be treated as an operating lease. Under an operating lease, the lessee recognizes periodic rental expense but records neither an asset nor a liability (except for accrued rental expense at the end of a period).

Answer (B) is incorrect because Cutlip should not recognize interest on an operating lease. Answer (C) is incorrect because a capital lease requires amortization. Answer (D) is incorrect because a capital lease requires amortization.

5. Guilford Co. has leased property and accounted for the transaction as a capital lease. The amount recorded initially by Guilford as a liability should normally

A. Exceed the total of the minimum lease payments.

B. Exceed the present value of the minimum lease payments at the beginning of the lease.

C. Equal the total of the minimum lease payments.

D. Equal the present value of the minimum lease payments at the beginning of the lease.

Answer (D) is correct. *(CPA, adapted)*

REQUIRED: The amount recorded initially by the lessee as a liability.

DISCUSSION: SFAS 13 requires that the lessee record a capital lease as an asset and a liability at the present value of the minimum lease payments during the lease term. The discount rate is the lower of the lessor's implicit interest rate (if known) or the lessee's incremental borrowing rate of interest. The present value cannot exceed the fair value of the leased property at the inception of the lease.

Answer (A) is incorrect because the amount recorded initially should be a present value. Hence, it will be less than the total of the minimum lease payments. Answer (B) is incorrect because the amount recorded initially should equal the present value of the minimum lease payments. Answer (C) is incorrect because the amount recorded initially should be a present value. Hence, it will be less than the total of the minimum lease payments.

6. A 12-year capital lease expiring on December 31 specifies equal minimum annual lease payments. Part of this payment represents interest and part represents a reduction in the net lease liability. The portion of the minimum lease payment in year 10 applicable to the reduction of the net lease liability should be

A. Less than in year 8.

B. More than in year 8.

C. The same as in year 12.

D. More than in year 12.

Answer (B) is correct. *(CPA, adapted)*

REQUIRED: The trend of the change, if any, in the periodic reduction of the net lease liability.

DISCUSSION: A lease payment has two components: interest and the portion applied to the reduction of the lease obligation. The effective interest method requires that the carrying amount of the obligation at the beginning of each interest period be multiplied by the appropriate interest rate to determine the interest. The difference between the minimum lease payment and the interest is the amount of reduction in the carrying amount of the lease obligation. Because the carrying amount declines with each payment, interest in future years also declines, resulting in an increase in the amount applied to reduce the lease obligation. The year 10 minimum lease payment will therefore result in a greater reduction in the liability than the year 8 payment.

7. Quick Company's lease payments are made at the end of each period. Quick's liability for a capital lease will be reduced periodically by the

A. Minimum lease payment minus the portion of the minimum lease payment allocable to interest.

B. Minimum lease payment plus the amortization of the related asset.

C. Minimum lease payment minus the amortization of the related asset.

D. Minimum lease payment.

Answer (A) is correct. *(CPA, adapted)*

REQUIRED: The reduction of the liability for a capital lease after payments at the end of each period.

DISCUSSION: The lease liability consists of the present value of the minimum lease payments. The lease liability is reduced by the portion of the lease payment attributable to the lease liability. This amount is the lease payment minus the interest component of the payment. Thus, the liability is decreased by the minimum lease payment each period minus the portion of the payment allocable to interest.

8. Scott Co. entered into a 5-year capital lease requiring it to make equal annual payments. The reduction of the lease liability in year 2 should equal

A. The current liability shown for the lease at the end of year 1.

B. The current liability shown for the lease at the end of year 2.

C. The reduction of the lease obligation in year 1.

D. One-tenth of the original lease liability.

Answer (A) is correct. *(CPA, adapted)*

REQUIRED: The reduction of a capital lease liability in the second year.

DISCUSSION: At the inception of a capital lease, a lessee should record a fixed asset and a lease obligation equal to the present value of the minimum lease payments. However, this amount may not exceed the fair value of the leased property. In a classified balance sheet, the lease liability must be allocated between the current and noncurrent portions. The current portion at a balance sheet date is the reduction of the lease liability in the forthcoming year.

Answer (B) is incorrect because the current liability at the end of year 2 is equal to the reduction that will be recorded in year 3. Answer (C) is incorrect because the reduction of the lease liability will increase in each subsequent year. Answer (D) is incorrect because the reduction of the lease liability will increase in each subsequent year.

9. Cott, Inc. prepared an interest amortization table for a 5-year lease payable with a bargain purchase option of $2,000, exercisable at the end of the lease. At the end of the 5 years, the balance in the leases payable column of the spreadsheet was zero. Cott has asked Grant, CPA, to review the spreadsheet to determine the error. Only one error was made on the spreadsheet. Which of the following statements represents the best explanation for this error?

A. The beginning present value of the lease did not include the present value of the payment called for by the bargain purchase option.

B. Cott subtracted the annual interest amount from the lease payable balance instead of adding it.

C. The present value of the payment called for by the bargain purchase option was subtracted from the present value of the annual payments.

D. Cott discounted the annual payments as an ordinary annuity, when the payments actually occurred at the beginning of each period.

Answer (A) is correct. *(CPA, adapted)*

REQUIRED: The best explanation for an error in an interest amortization table for a lease payable with a bargain purchase option.

DISCUSSION: This lessee must record a capital lease as an asset and an obligation at an amount equal to the present value of the minimum lease payments (minimum rental payments, excluding executory costs, and the payment called for by the bargain purchase option). The effect of including the present value of the payment called for by the bargain purchase option is that, at the end of the 5-year amortization period, the lease obligation should equal that payment.

Answer (B) is incorrect because the amount of the minimum lease payment that is greater than the periodic interest is subtracted from the lease payable balance. Answer (C) is incorrect because, if the present value of the payment called for by the bargain purchase option were subtracted from the present value of the annual payments, the lease payable balance would be reduced to zero in fewer than 5 years, assuming the correct amounts were amortized each period, that is, amounts based on the correct (higher) balance of the lease obligation. At the lease's inception, the present value of the payment called for by the bargain purchase option should be added to the present value of the minimum payments. Answer (D) is incorrect because treating the lease payments as an ordinary annuity instead of an annuity due would result in higher annual payments, assuming the initial lease obligation is accurately stated. The result would be higher annual amortization that would reduce the balance below the amount of the payment called for by the bargain purchase option (but not necessarily to zero) at the end of 5 years.

10. On July 1, year 1, Maryann Company leased equipment under a 5-year, noncancelable, nonrenewable agreement. The company paid a consultant a commission of $3,000 for arranging the lease. The lessee incurred $900 in installation and $600 in pre-operational testing costs. The equipment has an expected life of 7 years and a total expected life of 10 years. The lease does not contain a bargain purchase option, and, at the expiration of the lease, the equipment reverts to the lessor. The fair value of the equipment is $300,000, and the present value of the future minimum lease payments is $280,000. At the inception of the lease, the company should classify this lease as a(n)

A. Leveraged lease.

B. Operating lease.

C. Sale and leaseback.

D. Capital lease.

Answer (D) is correct. *(P. McBrayer)*

REQUIRED: The proper classification of a lease at its inception.

DISCUSSION: A lease must be classified as a capital lease by a lessee if, at its inception, any one of four criteria is satisfied. Each of these criteria indicates that a substantial transfer of the benefits and risks of ownership has occurred. The following are the four criteria: (1) The lease provides for the transfer of ownership of the leased property, (2) the lease contains a bargain purchase option, (3) the lease term is 75% or more of the estimated economic life of the leased property, or (4) the present value of the minimum lease payments (excluding executory costs) is at least 90% of the excess of the fair value of the leased property to the lessor at the inception of the lease over any related investment tax credit. (The last two criteria do not apply if the lease term begins within the last 25% of the total estimated economic life.) None of the first three criteria are satisfied. The fourth criterion is satisfied, however, because the $280,000 present value of the future minimum lease payments is greater than 90% of the $300,000 fair value of the equipment. Hence, this lease should be classified as a capital lease.

Answer (A) is incorrect because a leveraged lease involves financing the transaction with substantial leverage (i.e., nonrecourse debt). Answer (B) is incorrect because the lease qualifies as a capital lease. Answer (C) is incorrect because no sale occurred.

11. The terms of a 6-year, noncancelable lease include a guarantee by Lessee of Lessor's 7-year bank loan obtained to finance construction of the leased equipment, a termination penalty assuring that the lease will be renewed for 3 years following the expiration of the initial lease, and an option that allows Lessor to extend the lease for 3 years following the last renewal option exercised by Lessee. The lease term as defined by current authoritative literature is

A. 6 years.

B. 7 years.

C. 9 years.

D. 12 years.

Answer (D) is correct. *(Publisher)*

REQUIRED: The number of years in the lease term.

DISCUSSION: SFAS 13, as amended by SFAS 98, states that the term of a lease includes not only the fixed noncancelable lease term but also (1) any periods covered by bargain renewal options, (2) any periods covered by ordinary renewal options preceding the date at which a bargain purchase option is exercisable, (3) any periods covered by ordinary renewal options during which a guarantee by the lessee of the lessor's debt or a loan from the lessee to the lessor related to the leased property is expected to be in effect, (4) any periods for which failure to renew the lease imposes a penalty on the lessee in an amount such that renewal appears to be reasonably assured, and (5) any periods representing renewals or extensions of the lease at the lessor's option. In no case can the lease term extend beyond the date a bargain purchase option becomes exercisable.

Here, the termination penalty covers the 3 years immediately following the initial 6-year lease term. The renewal option by Lessor at the end of the first 9 years covers an additional 3 years, resulting in a lease term of 12 years. The 7-year period of the bank loan is included in the 6-year term and the first 3-year renewal period.

Answer (A) is incorrect because 6 years includes only the fixed term. Answer (B) is incorrect because 7 years is the debt term. Answer (C) is incorrect because the lease term includes both the period that would result in a penalty to the lessee and the period that is at the option of the lessor.

12. At its inception, the lease term of Lease G is 65% of the estimated remaining economic life of the leased property. This lease contains a bargain purchase option. The lessee should record Lease G as

A. Neither an asset nor a liability.

B. An asset but not a liability.

C. An asset and a liability.

D. An expense.

Answer (C) is correct. *(CPA, adapted)*

REQUIRED: The proper accounting for a lease containing a bargain purchase option.

DISCUSSION: A lease must be classified as a capital lease by a lessee if, at its inception, any one of four criteria is satisfied. Each of these criteria indicates that a substantial transfer of the benefits and risks of ownership has occurred. One test is whether the lease contains a bargain purchase option, which is a provision that permits the lessee to purchase the leased property at a price significantly lower than the expected fair value of the property at the date the option becomes exercisable. A capital lease must be recorded by the lessee as both an asset and an obligation at an amount equal to the present value of the minimum lease payments, but this amount should not exceed the fair value at the inception of the lease.

13. On January 1, year 1, Fitzpatrick Co. signed a contract to lease equipment to Hom Co. for 8 years. The leased equipment has an estimated remaining economic life of 10 years. Collectibility of the remaining payments is reasonably predictable, and no material uncertainties exist regarding unreimbursable costs to be incurred by the lessor. The present value of the 16 equal semiannual payments in advance equaled 85% of the equipment's fair value. The contract had no provision for the lessor to transfer legal ownership of the equipment. Should Fitzpatrick recognize rent or interest revenue in year 3, and should the revenue recognized in year 3 be the same or less than the revenue recognized in year 2?

	Year 3 Revenues Recognized	Year 3 Amount Recognized Compared with Year 2
A.	Rent	The same
B.	Rent	Less
C.	Interest	The same
D.	Interest	Less

Answer (D) is correct. *(CPA, adapted)*

REQUIRED: The type of revenue recognized and the amount compared with the previous year.

DISCUSSION: A lease must be classified as a capital lease by a lessor if, at its inception, any one of the four capitalization criteria is satisfied and if, in addition, collectibility of the remaining payments is reasonably predictable, and no material uncertainties exist regarding unreimbursable costs to be incurred by the lessor. One of the capitalization criteria is that the lease term be 75% or more of the estimated economic life of the leased property, but this criterion does not apply if the lease term begins in the final 25% of the total estimated economic life. Because the lease term is 80% (8 years ÷ 10 years) of the total estimated life of the equipment, the lease is a capital lease. Whether the lessor treats the capital lease as a direct-financing or sales-type lease, it will recognize interest revenue. The amount declines over the lease term because the effective-interest method is used. As the carrying amount decreases, the interest component (applicable interest rate × carrying amount) of the periodic lease payment also decreases.

14. Zubenko Co. has leased equipment from Lessor Co. under two leases. Lease A does not contain a bargain purchase option, but the lease term is equal to 90% of the total estimated economic life of the leased property. Lease B does not transfer ownership of the property to the lessee by the end of the lease term, but the lease term is equal to 75% of the total estimated economic life of the leased property. How should Zubenko classify these leases?

	Lease A	Lease B
A.	Operating lease	Capital lease
B.	Operating lease	Operating lease
C.	Capital lease	Capital lease
D.	Capital lease	Operating lease

Answer (C) is correct. *(CPA, adapted)*

REQUIRED: The proper classification of leases.

DISCUSSION: For a lease to be classified as a capital lease by the lessee, any one of four criteria must be met. One of these criteria is that the lease term equal 75% or more of the estimated remaining economic life of the leased property, but this criterion does not apply if the lease term begins in the final 25% of the total estimated economic life. Both leases meet the 75% criterion and should be properly classified as capital leases.

15. Wilson leased a new machine having a total and remaining expected useful life of 30 years from Tehi. Terms of the noncancelable, 25-year lease were that Wilson would gain title to the property upon payment of a sum equal to the fair value of the machine at the termination of the lease. Wilson accounted for the lease as a capital lease and recorded an asset and a liability in the financial records. The asset recorded under this lease should properly be amortized over

A. 5 years (the period of actual ownership).

B. 22.5 years (75% of the 30-year asset life).

C. 25 years (the term of the lease).

D. 30 years (the total asset life).

Answer (C) is correct. *(Publisher)*

REQUIRED: The proper amortization period for a lease with a purchase option.

DISCUSSION: When a lease transfers ownership of the property to the lessee at the end of the lease or contains a bargain purchase option, the lessee will own the asset at the end of the lease. Hence, such a lease is capitalized and amortized over the expected useful life of the leased property. If, instead, the lease meets either the 75% lease term test or the 90% fair value test, it will be accounted for as a capital lease and will be amortized over the lease term, assuming the lease term does not begin in the final 25% of the total estimated economic life. Because the lease term is more than 75% of the total expected useful life of the leased property, the lease should be amortized over the lease term (25 years).

Answer (A) is incorrect because the lessee's amortization period covers the entire period of the lease. Answer (B) is incorrect because the lessee's amortization period covers the entire period of the lease. Answer (D) is incorrect because a lease is amortized over the expected useful life of the leased property only when a bargain purchase option exists or ownership is transferred at the end of the lease.

16. Douglas Co. leased machinery with an economic useful life of six years. For tax purposes, the depreciable life is seven years. The lease is for five years, and Douglas can purchase the machinery at fair market value at the end of the lease. What is the depreciable life of the leased machinery for financial reporting purposes?

A. Zero.

B. Five years.

C. Six years.

D. Seven years.

Answer (B) is correct. *(CPA, adapted)*

REQUIRED: The depreciable life of the leased machinery for financial reporting purposes.

DISCUSSION: If a lessee capitalizes a lease because the lease term is at least 75% of the expected remaining life, or the present value of the minimum lease payments is at least 90% of the fair value at the inception of the lease, the asset should be amortized over the lease term. These capitalization criteria do not apply when the beginning of the lease term is within the last 25% of the total estimated economic life. Douglas Co.'s lease is for a period that exceeds 75% of the expected remaining life (5 years ÷ 6 years = 83 1/3%). Thus, the depreciable life is the lease term of five years.

Answer (A) is incorrect because leased equipment is amortized over its depreciable life. Answer (C) is incorrect because 6 years is the economic life of the assets, not the depreciable life. Answer (D) is incorrect because 7 years is the depreciable life for tax purposes, not financial reporting purposes.

17. On January 1, year 1, Hall Co. entered into a 10-year lease for a manufacturing plant. The annual minimum lease payments are $100,000. In the notes to the December 31, year 2 financial statements, what amounts of subsequent years' lease payments should be disclosed?

	Total of Annual Disclosed Amounts for Required Period	Aggregate Amount for the Period Thereafter
A.	$100,000	$0
B.	$300,000	$500,000
C.	$500,000	$300,000
D.	$500,000	$0

Answer (C) is correct. *(CPA, adapted)*

REQUIRED: The amounts of subsequent years' lease payments to be disclosed.

DISCUSSION: SFAS 13 requires that the future minimum lease payments as of the date of the latest balance sheet presented be disclosed in the aggregate and for each of the 5 succeeding fiscal years. This disclosure is required whether the lease is classified as a capital lease or as an operating lease. Hence, the aggregate amount of the obligation is $800,000 (8 years remaining × $100,000), consisting of the future payments for the next 5 years in the amount of $500,000 (5 × $100,000), and for the period thereafter in the amount of $300,000.

18. On January 1, year 1, Rice Co. acquired a land lease for a 21-year period with no option to renew. The lease required Rice to construct a building in lieu of rent. The building, completed on January 1, year 2 at a cost of $840,000, will be depreciated using the straight-line method. At the end of the lease, the building's estimated fair value will be $420,000. What is the building's carrying amount in Rice's December 31, year 2 balance sheet?

A. $798,000

B. $800,000

C. $819,000

D. $820,000

Answer (A) is correct. *(CPA, adapted)*

REQUIRED: The building's carrying amount after 2 years.

DISCUSSION: The lease is an operating lease because it involves land only and does not transfer ownership or contain a bargain purchase option. Moreover, the general improvements to the leased property should be capitalized as leasehold improvements and amortized in accordance with the straight-line method over the shorter of their expected useful life or the lease term. Given no renewal option, the amortization period is 20 years, the shorter of the expected useful life or the remaining lease term at the date of completion. The amortizable base is $840,000 even though the building will have a fair value of $420,000 at the end of the lease. The latter amount is not a salvage value because the building will become the lessor's property when the lease expires. Consequently, year 2 straight-line amortization is $42,000 ($840,000 ÷ 20 years), and the year-end carrying amount is $798,000 ($840,000 – $42,000).

Answer (B) is incorrect because $800,000 assumes a 21-year remaining lease term at 1/1/year 2. Answer (C) is incorrect because $819,000 assumes no amortization of an amount equal to the fair value at the end of the lease term. Answer (D) is incorrect because $820,000 assumes a 21-year remaining lease term at 1/1/year 2 and no amortization of an amount equal to the fair value at the end of the lease term.

19. Terry Co. leases a building for its product showroom. The 10-year nonrenewable lease will expire on December 31, year 10. In January year 5, Terry redecorated its showroom and made leasehold improvements of $48,000. The estimated useful life of the improvements is 8 years. Terry uses the straight-line method of amortization. What amount of leasehold improvements, net of amortization, should Terry report in its June 30, year 5 balance sheet?

A. $45,600

B. $45,000

C. $44,000

D. $43,200

Answer (C) is correct. *(CPA, adapted)*

REQUIRED: The net amount of leasehold improvements reported in the balance sheet.

DISCUSSION: General improvements to leased property should be capitalized as leasehold improvements and amortized in accordance with the straight-line method over the shorter of their expected useful life or the lease term. Because the remaining lease term is less than the estimated life of the improvements, the cost should be amortized equally over 6 years. On June 30, year 5, $44,000 {$48,000 – [($48,000 ÷ 6 years) × .5 year]} should be reported for net leasehold improvements.

Answer (A) is incorrect because $45,600 assumes the amortization period is 10 years. Answer (B) is incorrect because $45,000 assumes the amortization period is 8 years. Answer (D) is incorrect because $43,200 assumes that 1 year's amortization has been recorded and that the amortization period is 10 years.

20. Schwass Corporation has leased manufacturing equipment from Riley Corporation in a transaction that is to be accounted for as a capital lease. Schwass has guaranteed Riley a residual value for the equipment. How should this guarantee be reflected in the financial statements of Schwass?

A. The full amount of the residual guarantee should be capitalized as part of the cost of the equipment.

B. The present value of the residual guarantee should be capitalized as part of the cost of the equipment.

C. The guarantee will not be reflected in the body of the financial statements but should be disclosed in the footnotes.

D. The guarantee should not be reflected in the financial statements.

Answer (B) is correct. *(CIA, adapted)*

REQUIRED: The effect of a guaranteed residual value on lessee accounting for a capital lease.

DISCUSSION: For lessee accounting, a guaranteed residual value is defined as the portion of the expected salvage value that is guaranteed by the lessee. This portion of the expected salvage value is included with the periodic rental payments in the definition of minimum lease payments. Because the lessee should record an asset and an obligation in an amount equal to the lower of the fair value of the leased property or the present value of the minimum lease payments, the guaranteed residual value is included in the capitalized cost of the equipment at an amount equal to its present value if that amount does not exceed fair value.

Answer (A) is incorrect because the present value should be capitalized as part of the cost of the equipment. Answer (C) is incorrect because the residual guarantee should be reflected in the body of the financial statements. Answer (D) is incorrect because the residual guarantee should be reflected in the body of the financial statements.

21. Jennifer Co. intends to lease a machine from Jan Corp. Jennifer's incremental borrowing rate is 14%. The prime rate of interest is 8%. Jan's implicit rate in the lease is 10%, which is known to Jennifer. Jennifer computes the present value of the minimum lease payments using which rate?

A. 8%

B. 10%

C. 12%

D. 14%

Answer (B) is correct. *(CPA, adapted)*

REQUIRED: The discount rate used by the lessee in determining the present value of minimum lease payments.

DISCUSSION: According to SFAS 13, a lessee should compute the present value of the minimum lease payments using its incremental borrowing rate unless the lessee knows the lessor's implicit rate, and the implicit rate is less than the lessee's incremental borrowing rate. Because both conditions are met, Jennifer must use the 10% implicit rate. The effect of using the lower rate is to increase the probability that the lessee will capitalize the lease.

Answer (A) is incorrect because 8% is the prime rate. Answer (C) is incorrect because 12% is the average of the implicit and incremental rates. Answer (D) is incorrect because 14% is the incremental rate, which is higher.

22. Which one of the following items is not part of the minimum lease payments recorded by the lessee?

A. The minimum rental payments called for by the lease.

B. A guarantee by the lessee of the lessor's debt.

C. The specified maximum amount of any deficiency in the lessor's realization of the residual value that the lessee is required to make up.

D. Any payment the lessee must make at the end of the lease term either to purchase the leased property or to satisfy a penalty for failure to renew the lease.

Answer (B) is correct. *(CMA, adapted)*

REQUIRED: The item that is not a component of minimum lease payments.

DISCUSSION: The lease term includes not only the fixed, noncancelable term of the lease but also those years for which there is reasonable assurance that the lease will remain in effect. A guarantee by the lessee of the lessor's debt related to the leased property provides such assurance and thus may affect the term over which the minimum lease payments are calculated. Otherwise, such a guarantee does not affect the computation of minimum lease payments.

Answer (A) is incorrect because it is an item included by the lessee in the computation of the minimum lease payments for a capital lease. Answer (C) is incorrect because it is an item included by the lessee in the computation of the minimum lease payments for a capital lease. Answer (D) is incorrect because it is an item included by the lessee in the computation of the minimum lease payments for a capital lease.

23. Equipment covered by a lease agreement is expected by the lessor to have a residual value at the end of the lease term of $20,000. As part of the lease agreement, the lessee guarantees a residual value of $12,000. In the case of excessive usage, the guaranteed residual value is $18,000. What is the amount of guaranteed residual value that should be included in the calculation of the minimum lease payments?

A. $0

B. $12,000

C. $18,000

D. $20,000

Answer (B) is correct. *(Publisher)*

REQUIRED: The amount of guaranteed residual value to be included in minimum lease payments.

DISCUSSION: FASB Interpretation No. 19, *Lessee Guarantee of the Residual Value of Leased Property*, states that the amount of guaranteed residual value to be included in the determination of minimum lease payments is the "specified maximum deficiency that the lessee is obligated to make up." In these circumstances, that amount is materially lower than the expected salvage value. Consequently, the $12,000 guarantee should be included. The additional guarantee of $6,000 ($18,000 – $12,000) in the case of excessive usage is similar to a contingent rental payment. Because it is not determinable at the lease's inception, it is not a lessee guarantee of the residual value that is includible in the minimum lease payments.

Answer (A) is incorrect because the guaranteed residual value is included in the determination of minimum lease payments. Answer (C) is incorrect because the additional guarantee of $6,000 ($18,000 – $12,000) is not included. It is contingent and thus nondeterminable. Answer (D) is incorrect because the minimum lease payments include only guaranteed residual value.

24. On October 1, the first day of its fiscal year, Heather Co., a retail outlet, entered into a lease of a building. Terms of the 5-year, noncancelable lease require monthly payments of $600 plus 1% of sales. Sales have been averaging $15,000 per month and are expected to remain constant or increase. What monthly amount(s) should be included in minimum lease payments?

A. Only the $150 payment based on expected sales.

B. Only the $600 monthly payment.

C. Both the $150 and $600 payments.

D. Neither the $150 nor $600 payments.

Answer (B) is correct. *(Publisher)*

REQUIRED: The amount(s) to be included in minimum lease payments on a lease containing a contingent payment term.

DISCUSSION: SFAS 29, *Determining Contingent Rentals*, defines contingent rentals as lease payments based on a factor that does not exist or is not measurable at the inception of the lease. Future sales do not exist at the inception of the lease and meet the definition of a contingent rental. SFAS 13 excludes contingent rentals from minimum lease payments. Because the $150 based on expected future sales is a contingent rental, only the $600 periodic payment is included in minimum lease payments.

Answer (A) is incorrect because the minimum lease payment includes only those payments that are measurable at the inception of the lease. Answer (C) is incorrect because the $150 payment is not measurable at the inception of the lease. Answer (D) is incorrect because the $600 payment is included in minimum lease payments because it is measurable.

25. Which of the following is most likely to be excluded in determining the lessee's minimum lease payments for a capital lease?

A. The guarantee of the residual value obtained by the lessee from an unrelated third party.

B. The minimum rental payments called for by the lease over the lease term.

C. The guarantee by the lessee of the residual value, excluding any residual deficiency attributable to excessive usage, of the leased property at the expiration of the lease term.

D. The payment that the lessee can be required to make upon failure to renew the lease at expiration of the lease term.

Answer (A) is correct. *(Publisher)*

REQUIRED: The item excluded by the lessee in the computation of minimum lease payments for a capital lease.

DISCUSSION: FASB Interpretation No. 19 specifically excludes any guarantee of residual value obtained by the lessee from an unrelated third party for the benefit of the lessor, provided the lessor explicitly releases the lessee from all liability for a residual value deficiency. Furthermore, amounts paid as consideration for this third-party guarantee are treated as executory costs (along with insurance, maintenance, taxes, etc.) and are also excluded.

Answer (B) is incorrect because it is an item included by the lessee in computing minimum lease payments for a capital lease. Answer (C) is incorrect because it is an item included by the lessee in computing minimum lease payments for a capital lease. Answer (D) is incorrect because it is an item included by the lessee in computing minimum lease payments for a capital lease.

26. On April 1, the first day of its fiscal year, Jaymarr Co. signed a 5-year lease for a major piece of equipment. Terms of the lease require a fixed annual payment of $12,000 plus $100 for each 1% of a specific bank's prime interest rate. If the prime interest rate is 14% on April 1, is expected to rise to 16% by July 1, and is expected to average 10% for the life of the lease, the total minimum lease payments for the life of the lease should be

A. $60,000

B. $65,000

C. $67,000

D. $68,000

Answer (C) is correct. *(Publisher)*

REQUIRED: The total minimum lease payments over the life of the lease.

DISCUSSION: SFAS 13 excludes contingent rentals from the definition of minimum lease payments. SFAS 29 defines contingent rentals as the changes in lease payments resulting from changes occurring subsequent to the inception of the lease. But lease payments that are based on a factor that exists and is measurable at the inception of the lease are not contingent rentals. Thus, total minimum lease payments for this piece of equipment should include the five annual payments of $12,000 per year ($60,000) plus $7,000, which is the sum of the five annual $1,400 payments. This amount is based on the prime interest rate (14%) existing at the inception of the lease ($100 × 14 = $1,400). As the prime rate changes during the lease term, the corresponding increase or decrease of $100 for each 1% of the prime rate should be charged or credited to income as appropriate. Minimum lease payments, however, should not be adjusted.

Answer (A) is incorrect because $60,000 excludes the $7,000 ($100 × 14 × 5) measurable at the inception of the lease. Answer (B) is incorrect because $65,000 is based on the average expected prime rate of 10%. Answer (D) is incorrect because $68,000 is based on the 16% prime rate in July.

27. On December 29, year 1, Strickland Corp. signed a 7-year capital lease for an airplane to transport its professional volleyball team around the country. The airplane's fair value was $841,500. Strickland made the first annual lease payment of $153,000 on December 31, year 1. Strickland's incremental borrowing rate was 12%, and the interest rate implicit in the lease, which was known by Strickland, was 9%. The following are the rounded present value factors for an annuity due:

9% for 7 years	5.5
12% for 7 years	5.1

What amount should Strickland report as capital lease liability in its December 31, year 1 balance sheet?

A. $841,500

B. $780,300

C. $688,500

D. $627,300

Answer (C) is correct. *(CPA, adapted)*

REQUIRED: The amount that should be reported as a capital lease liability in the balance sheet.

DISCUSSION: The capital lease liability is recorded at the present value of the minimum lease payments. The lease payments due should be discounted at the lesser of the borrower's incremental borrowing rate or the rate implicit in the lease, if known by the borrower. In this situation, the lease should be recorded at the present value of minimum lease payments discounted at the implicit rate of 9% because this rate is known by the lessee and is lower than the incremental rate. The amount is $841,500 ($153,000 × 5.5), which must then be reduced by the payment made at the inception of the lease of $153,000. The capital lease liability thus should be $688,500 ($841,500 – $153,000) in the December 31, year 1 balance sheet.

Answer (A) is incorrect because the liability must be reduced by the payment made at the inception of the lease. Answer (B) is incorrect because the present value of minimum lease payments should be discounted at 9% instead of 12%. Also, the liability should be reduced by the payment made at the inception of the lease. Answer (D) is incorrect because the lease liability should be recorded at 9% instead of 12%.

28. On January 1, year 1, Jessie Co. (lessee) entered into a 5-year lease for equipment. Jessie accounted for the acquisition as a capital lease for $120,000, which includes a $5,000 bargain purchase option. At the end of the lease, Jessie expects to exercise the bargain purchase option. Jessie estimates that the equipment's fair value will be $10,000 at the end of its 8-year life. Jessie regularly uses straight-line depreciation on similar equipment. For the year ended December 31, year 1, what amount should Jessie recognize as amortization of the asset recorded under the capital lease?

A. $13,750

B. $15,000

C. $23,000

D. $24,000

Answer (A) is correct. *(CPA, adapted)*

REQUIRED: The amortization of the asset recorded under a lease.

DISCUSSION: When a lease is capitalized because title passes to the lessee at the end of the lease term or because the lease contains a bargain purchase option, the amortization period is the estimated economic life of the underlying property. The asset recorded under the capital lease should be amortized in accordance with the lessee's normal depreciation policy for owned assets. Jessie regularly uses the straight-line method. Hence, amortization is $13,750 [($120,000 asset recorded under the lease – $10,000 salvage value) ÷ 8-year economic life].

Answer (B) is incorrect because $15,000 does not consider salvage value. Answer (C) is incorrect because $23,000 subtracts the bargain purchase option from the present value of the minimum lease payments, uses a 5-year life, and does not consider salvage value. Answer (D) is incorrect because $24,000 uses a 5-year life and does not consider salvage value.

29. Bodhran Corp. entered into a 9-year capital lease on a warehouse on December 31, year 1. The land and building are capitalized as a single unit. Lease payments of $52,000, which include real estate taxes of $2,000, are due annually, beginning on December 31, year 2, and every December 31 thereafter. Bodhran does not know the interest rate implicit in the lease; Bodhran's incremental borrowing rate is 9%. The rounded present value of an ordinary annuity for 9 years at 9% is 5.6. What amount should Bodhran report as capitalized lease liability at December 31, year 1?

A. $280,000

B. $291,200

C. $450,000

D. $468,000

Answer (A) is correct. *(CPA, adapted)*

REQUIRED: The amount reported as capitalized lease liability.

DISCUSSION: For a capital lease, the present value of the minimum lease payments should be recorded at the inception date. The minimum lease payments exclude executory costs such as insurance, maintenance, and taxes. The capitalized lease liability is therefore $280,000 [($52,000 – $2,000) × 5.6].

Answer (B) is incorrect because $291,200 is based on a $52,000 annual payment. Answer (C) is incorrect because $450,000 is the total undiscounted amount of the minimum lease payments. Answer (D) is incorrect because $468,000 is the total undiscounted amount of the minimum lease payments plus real estate taxes.

30. Law Co. leased a machine from Order Co. The lease qualifies as a capital lease and requires 10 annual payments of $10,000 beginning immediately. The lease specifies an interest rate of 12% and a purchase option of $10,000 at the end of the tenth year, even though the machine's estimated value on that date is $20,000. Law's incremental borrowing rate is 14%.

The present value of an annuity due of 1 at:
12% for 10 years is 6.328
14% for 10 years is 5.946

The present value of 1 at:
12% for 10 years is .322
14% for 10 years is .270

What amount should Law record as lease liability at the beginning of the lease term?

A. $62,160

B. $64,860

C. $66,500

D. $69,720

Answer (C) is correct. *(CPA, adapted)*

REQUIRED: The amount that should be reported as a capital lease liability.

DISCUSSION: The capital lease liability should be recorded at the present value of the minimum lease payments. The lease liability should be calculated using the lesser of the implicit interest rate, if known to the lessee, or the incremental borrowing rate of the lessee. The minimum lease payments should include the present value of the payment required by the bargain purchase option of $10,000 at 12% and the present value of an annuity due of $10,000 at 12% for 10 years. Thus, the lease liability is equal to $66,500 [($10,000 × 6.328) + ($10,000 × .322)].

Answer (A) is incorrect because the present value of the payment required by the bargain purchase option and the annual lease payments should be discounted at 12% instead of 14%. Answer (B) is incorrect because the amount of the bargain purchase option is $10,000, not the estimated value at that date. Also, the discount rate for both the option amount and the annual payments should be 12% instead of 14%. Answer (D) is incorrect because the payment required by the bargain purchase option should be included in the present value of minimum lease payments, not the estimated value of the asset at the end of the lease.

31. Collis Corporation leased equipment under a 4-year, noncancelable lease properly classified as a capital lease. The lease does not transfer ownership or contain a bargain purchase option. The equipment had an estimated economic life of 5 years and an estimated salvage value of $20,000. Terms of the lease included a guaranteed residual value of $50,000. If Collis initially recorded an asset under the lease of $240,000, the amount of amortization that should be charged each year under the lessee's usual depreciation method (straight-line) is

A. $55,000

B. $47,500

C. $44,000

D. $38,000

Answer (B) is correct. *(H.F. Bush)*

REQUIRED: The amount of amortization to be recorded on a capital lease.

DISCUSSION: The lease does not transfer ownership or contain a bargain purchase option. Accordingly, the period of amortization should be the lease term. Given that the lessee's normal depreciation policy is to apply the straight-line method, the amortization base for the asset recorded under this capital lease is equal to the $240,000 initially recorded value, minus the $50,000 guaranteed residual value, allocated equally over the 4-year lease term. Consequently, annual amortization is $47,500 [($240,000 – $50,000) ÷ 4 years].

Answer (A) is incorrect because the guaranteed residual value, not the estimated salvage value, must be subtracted from the initially recorded value. Answer (C) is incorrect because the guaranteed residual value, not the estimated salvage value, must be subtracted from the initially recorded value, and the term of the lease, not the estimated economic life, is used as the denominator in the calculation. Answer (D) is incorrect because the term of the lease, not the estimated economic life, must be used as the denominator in the calculation.

32. Allen Co. leased equipment for its entire 9-year useful life, agreeing to pay $50,000 at the start of the lease term on December 31, year 1, and $50,000 annually on each December 31 for the next 8 years. The present value on December 31, year 1 of the nine lease payments over the lease term, using the rate implicit in the lease was $316,500. Allen knows that this rate is 10%. The December 31, year 1 present value of the lease payments using Allen's incremental borrowing rate of 12% was $298,500. Allen made a timely second lease payment. What amount should Allen report as capital lease liability in its December 31, year 2 balance sheet?

A. $350,000

B. $243,150

C. $228,320

D. $0

Answer (B) is correct. *(CPA, adapted)*

REQUIRED: The amount to be reported as a capital lease liability.

DISCUSSION: The lease is a capital lease because the lease term is at least 75% of the estimated economic life of the property, and the beginning of the lease term does not fall within the last 25% of the total estimated economic life. SFAS 13 requires that the lessee use the lower of the lessor's implicit interest rate (if known) or the lessee's incremental borrowing rate of interest. Allen knows the implicit rate; therefore, the present value of the minimum lease payments of this capital lease is $316,500, the amount based on the lessor's implicit rate. After the initial payment of $50,000, which contains no interest component, is deducted, the carrying amount during year 2 is $266,500. Accordingly, the interest component of the next payment is $26,650 (10% implicit rate × $266,500), and the capital lease liability on December 31, year 2 is $243,150 [$266,500 – ($50,000 – $26,650)].

Answer (A) is incorrect because $350,000 is the sum of the nine lease payments. Answer (C) is incorrect because $228,320 is based on a 12% rate. Answer (D) is incorrect because $0 is based on the assumption that the lease is an operating lease.

33. On January 1, year 1, Hombob Co. as lessee signed a 5-year noncancelable equipment lease with annual payments of $100,000 beginning December 31, year 1. Hombob treated this transaction as a capital lease. The five lease payments have a present value of $379,000 at January 1, year 1, based on interest of 10%. What amount should Hombob report as interest for the year ended December 31, year 1?

A. $37,900

B. $27,900

C. $24,200

D. $0

Answer (A) is correct. *(CPA, adapted)*

REQUIRED: The interest to be recognized in the first year of a capital lease.

DISCUSSION: The lease liability at the inception of the lease is $379,000. Under the effective-interest method, the lease liability balance (the carrying amount) at the beginning of each year should be multiplied by the appropriate interest rate to determine the interest for that year. Accordingly, the interest for the first year is $37,900 ($10% × $379,000).

Answer (B) is incorrect because $27,900 assumes the initial payment was made immediately. Answer (C) is incorrect because $24,200 is one-fifth of the total interest ($500,000 – $379,000). Answer (D) is incorrect because interest must be accrued.

34. On December 30, year 1, Riley Corp. leased equipment under a capital lease. Annual lease payments of $20,000 are due December 31 for 10 years. The equipment's useful life is 10 years, and the interest rate implicit in the lease is 10%. The capital lease obligation was recorded on December 30, year 1 at $135,000, and the first lease payment was made on that date. What amount should Riley include in current liabilities for this capital lease in its December 31, year 1 balance sheet?

A. $6,500

B. $8,500

C. $11,500

D. $20,000

Answer (B) is correct. *(CPA, adapted)*

REQUIRED: The current liability for the capital lease.

DISCUSSION: At the inception of a capital lease, a lessee should record a fixed asset and a lease obligation equal to the present value of the minimum lease payments. In a classified balance sheet, the lease liability must be allocated between the current and noncurrent portions. The current portion at a balance sheet date is the reduction of the lease liability in the forthcoming year. A periodic lease payment has two components: interest and the reduction of the lease obligation. Under the effective interest method, the appropriate interest rate is applied to the carrying amount of the lease obligation at the beginning of the interest period to calculate interest. The portion of the minimum lease payment greater than the amount of interest is the reduction of the liability in the forthcoming year. At the beginning of year 2, the lease obligation is $115,000 ($135,000 – $20,000 initial payment). Thus, year 1 interest will be $11,500 (10% × $115,000), and the reduction of the liability when the next payment is made will be $8,500 ($20,000 – $11,500 interest).

Answer (A) is incorrect because $6,500 results from assuming that the carrying amount of the lease in year 1 will be $135,000. Answer (C) is incorrect because $11,500 is the interest. Answer (D) is incorrect because $20,000 is the full payment due.

14.2 Direct Financing and Sales-Type Leases

35. What is the difference between a direct financing lease and a sales-type lease?

A. Lessees usually amortize direct financing leases over the term of the lease and sales-type leases over the useful life of the leased asset.

B. The difference between the gross investment and the cost of the leased property to the lessor is unearned income for direct financing leases, and is part unearned income and part profit or loss for sales-type leases.

C. The lease payments receivable on the books of a lessor are recorded at their present value for sales-type leases and at their gross value for direct financing leases.

D. The lessor records the present value of the residual value of the leased property for direct financing leases, but records the undiscounted (gross) residual value for sales-type leases.

Answer (B) is correct. *(Publisher)*

REQUIRED: The difference between direct financing leases and sales-type leases.

DISCUSSION: Both direct financing and sales-type leases are accounted for by the lessee as capital leases. The difference between the two arises only for lessor accounting. In a direct financing lease, the difference between the gross investment (minimum lease payments + unguaranteed residual value) and its cost or carrying amount is recorded as unearned income. No manufacturer's or dealer's profit or loss is recognized. In a sales-type lease, the lessor records manufacturer's or dealer's profit or loss, and unearned income equals the gross investment minus the sum of the present values of its components. The cost or carrying amount, plus initial direct costs, minus the present value of the unguaranteed residual value, is debited to income when the sales price (present value of the minimum lease payments) is recognized. The difference between a direct financing and a sales-type lease is that the cost used in accounting for a direct-financing lease is ordinarily the fair value. But the cost for a sales-type lease differs from the fair value.

Answer (A) is incorrect because lessees use the same amortization methods for both kinds of leases. Answer (C) is incorrect because the receivable for the lease payments is recorded at gross on the books of the lessor for both the sales-type and direct financing leases. Answer (D) is incorrect because the undiscounted (gross) residual value is recorded by the lessor for both direct financing and sales-type leases. It is included as part of the gross investment, i.e., in lease payments receivable.

36. In a lease that is recorded as a sales-type lease by the lessor, interest income

A. Should be recognized in full as income at the lease's inception.

B. Should be recognized over the period of the lease using the straight-line method.

C. Should be recognized over the period of the lease using the effective-interest method.

D. Does not arise.

Answer (C) is correct. *(CPA, adapted)*

REQUIRED: The proper accounting for interest income in a sales-type lease.

DISCUSSION: SFAS 13 requires that the difference between the gross investment in the lease and the sum of the present values of the components of the gross investment be recorded as unearned income. This unearned income is amortized to income over the lease term using the effective-interest method, which produces a constant periodic rate of return on the net investment.

37. For a direct financing lease, the gross investment (lease payments receivable) recorded by the lessor is equal to the

A. Present value of the minimum lease payments minus the unguaranteed residual value accruing to the lessor at the end of the lease term.

B. Lower of 90% of the present value of the minimum lease payments or the fair value of the leased property.

C. Difference between the fair value of the leased property and the unearned interest income.

D. Minimum lease payments plus the unguaranteed residual value accruing to the lessor at the end of the lease term.

Answer (D) is correct. *(CMA, adapted)*

REQUIRED: The amount to be recorded as the gross investment in a direct financing lease.

DISCUSSION: The lessor should record as the gross investment in a direct financing lease the amount of the minimum lease payments plus any unguaranteed residual value. For a lessee, minimum lease payments include the minimum rental payments (excluding executory costs such as insurance, maintenance, and taxes) required during the lease term and the payment called for by a bargain purchase option. If no such option exists, the lessee's minimum lease payments equal the sum of the minimum rental payments, the amount of residual value guaranteed by the lessee, and any nonrenewal penalty imposed. The minimum lease payments calculated by the lessor are the same as those for the lessee except that they include any residual value or rental payments beyond the lease term guaranteed by a financially capable third party unrelated to the lessor or the lessee. The net investment in the lease is equal to the gross investment, plus any unamortized initial direct costs, minus the unearned income.

38. Initial direct costs incurred by the lessor under a sales-type lease should be

A. Deferred and allocated over the economic life of the leased property.

B. Expensed in the period incurred.

C. Deferred and allocated over the term of the lease in proportion to the recognition of rental income.

D. Added to the gross investment in the lease and amortized over the term of the lease as a yield adjustment.

Answer (B) is correct. *(CMA, adapted)*

REQUIRED: The accounting for initial direct costs in a sales-type lease.

DISCUSSION: SFAS 91, *Accounting for Nonrefundable Fees and Costs Associated with Originating or Acquiring Loans and Initial Direct Costs of Leases*, defines initial direct costs as having two components: (1) the lessor's external costs to originate a lease incurred in dealings with independent third parties and (2) the internal costs directly related to specified activities performed by the lessor for that lease. According to SFAS 13, in a sales-type lease, the cost, or carrying amount if different, plus any initial direct costs, minus the present value of any unguaranteed residual value, is charged against income in the same period that the sales price (present value of the minimum lease payments) is credited to income. The result is the recognition of a net profit or loss on the sales-type lease.

Answer (A) is incorrect because initial direct costs are considered an expense in the period of sale. Answer (C) is incorrect because it describes the proper treatment of initial direct costs in an operating lease. Answer (D) is incorrect because it describes the proper treatment of initial direct costs in a direct financing lease.

39. Fraser Co. has agreed to lease equipment under a direct financing lease. As lessor, Fraser has incurred a material amount of initial direct costs. What is the proper accounting for these initial direct costs by Fraser?

A. Initial direct costs must be offset against unearned income so as to produce a constant periodic rate of return on the lease.

B. Initial direct costs must be capitalized as part of the net investment in the lease.

C. Initial direct costs must be capitalized as a deferred charge and written off at the end of the lease term.

D. Initial direct costs must be written off immediately.

Answer (B) is correct. *(T.J. Phillips, Jr.)*

REQUIRED: The proper accounting for initial direct costs in a direct financing lease.

DISCUSSION: According to SFAS 98, *Accounting for Leases*, the initial direct costs of a direct financing lease "shall be amortized to income over the lease term so as to produce a constant periodic rate of return on the net investment in the lease." The net investment is the gross investment (minimum lease payments + any unguaranteed residual value), plus any unamortized initial direct costs, minus the unearned income. The unearned income equals the gross investment minus the cost or carrying amount, if different, of the leased property.

Answer (A) is incorrect because this treatment, which was prescribed by SFAS 17, *Accounting for Leases – Initial Direct Costs*, was rescinded by SFAS 91. Answer (C) is incorrect because the initial direct costs should be capitalized as part of the net investment in the lease. Answer (D) is incorrect because the initial direct costs should be capitalized as part of the net investment in the lease.

40. Mark Co. leases computer equipment to customers under direct financing leases. The equipment has no residual value at the end of the lease, and the leases do not contain bargain purchase options. Mark wishes to earn 8% interest on a five-year lease of equipment with a fair value of $323,400. The present value of an annuity due of $1 at 8% for 5 years is 4.312. What is the total amount of interest income that Mark will earn over the life of the lease?

A. $51,600

B. $75,000

C. $129,360

D. $139,450

Answer (A) is correct. *(CPA, adapted)*

REQUIRED: The interest income earned over the life of a lease.

DISCUSSION: To earn 8% interest over the lease term, the annual payment must be $75,000 ($323,400 fair value at the inception of the lease ÷ 4.312 annuity factor). Given no residual value and no bargain purchase option, total lease payments will be $375,000 ($75,000 payment × 5 years). Because no profit is recognized on a direct financing lease, the fair value is presumably the carrying amount. The difference between the gross lease payments received and their present value is the total interest of $51,600 ($375,000 – $323,400).

Answer (B) is incorrect because $75,000 is the annual lease payment. Answer (C) is incorrect because interest revenue equals the total lease payments of $375,000 minus the fair value of $323,400. Answer (D) is incorrect because interest revenue equals the total lease payments of $375,000 minus the fair value of $323,400.

41. On August 1, Mansfield Corporation leased property to Park Company for a 5-year period. The annual $20,000 lease payment is payable at the end of each year. The expected residual value at the end of the lease term is $10,000. Mansfield Company's implicit interest rate is 12%. The cost of the property to Mansfield was $50,000, which is the fair value at the lease date. The present value of an ordinary annuity of 1 for five periods is 3.605. The present value of 1 at the end of five periods is .567. At the inception of the lease, the recorded gross investment is

A. $110,000

B. $100,000

C. $72,100

D. $90,000

Answer (A) is correct. *(J.O. Hall)*

REQUIRED: The amount to be recorded as gross investment at the inception of the lease.

DISCUSSION: For a direct financing or a sales-type lease, the lessor should record the gross investment in the lease at the undiscounted sum of the minimum lease payments and any unguaranteed residual value. For a lessee, minimum lease payments include the minimum rental payments (excluding executory costs such as insurance, maintenance, and taxes) required during the lease term and the payment called for by a bargain purchase option. If no such option exists, the lessee's minimum lease payments equal the sum of the minimum rental payments, the amount of residual value guaranteed by the lessee, and any nonrenewal penalty imposed. The minimum lease payments calculated by the lessor are the same as those for the lessee except that they include any residual value or rental payments beyond the lease term guaranteed by a financially capable third party unrelated to the lessor or the lessee. Accordingly, the gross investment is the same regardless of whether any residual value is guaranteed. The five periodic payments of $20,000 equal $100,000. The expected residual value, including both guaranteed and unguaranteed portions, equals $10,000. Thus, the gross investment in this lease should be $110,000 ($100,000 + $10,000).

Answer (B) is incorrect because it fails to include the residual value in the gross investment. Answer (C) is incorrect because the annual lease payments should be recorded at their undiscounted value. Answer (D) is incorrect because the residual value is added to, not subtracted from, the undiscounted lease payments.

Questions 42 and 43 are based on the following information. Odom Company leased a machine to Rapp Company on January 1. The lease was for a 10-year period, which approximated the useful life of the machine. Odom purchased the machine for $80,000 and expects to earn a 10% return on its investment, based upon an annual rental of $11,836 payable in advance each January 1. The lease was a direct financing lease.

42. What should be the interest entry in Odom's books on December 31 of the first year of the lease?

A. Cash	$3,836	
Interest income		$3,836
B. Unearned income	$6,816	
Income		$6,816
C. Cash	$8,000	
Interest income		$8,000
D. Cash	$11,836	
Interest income		$8,000
Equipment		3,836

Answer (B) is correct. *(CPA, adapted)*

REQUIRED: The interest income from a direct financing lease during the first year of the lease.

DISCUSSION: The annual $11,836 lease payment to Odom is payable at the beginning of each period. The first payment received from Rapp reduces Odom's lease investment by the full amount of the payment, leaving a carrying amount of $68,164 ($80,000 – $11,836) at the beginning of the first year. Because the appropriate rate of return to Odom on this lease investment is 10%, interest earned in the first year is $6,816 (10% × $68,164). The difference between the gross investment and the lessor's cost or carrying amount, if different, of the leased property is reflected in the lessor's books as unearned income. Hence, the journal entry debit recognizing first-year income is to unearned income.

Answer (A) is incorrect because $3,836 is equal to the $11,836 rental payment minus $8,000 ($80,000 cost × 10%) and cash is received January 1. Answer (C) is incorrect because $8,000 is equal to the $80,000 cost unadjusted by the $11,836 initial payment × 10% and cash is received January 1. Answer (D) is incorrect because $8,000 is equal to the $80,000 cost unadjusted by the $11,836 initial payment × 10% and cash is received January 1, and equipment is not affected by the interest payment.

43. What is the initial journal entry by Odom Company to record the lease on January 1?

A. Leased property	$ 80,000	
Lease payment obligation		$68,164
Cash		11,836
B. Lease payments receivable	$ 80,000	
Leased property		$80,000
C. Lease payments receivable	$ 68,164	
Cash	11,836	
Leased property		$80,000
D. Cash	$ 11,836	
Lease payments receivable	106,524	
Leased property		$80,000
Unearned income		38,360

Answer (D) is correct. *(Publisher)*

REQUIRED: The lessor's journal entry to record a direct financing lease.

DISCUSSION: For a direct financing lease, the lessor should record the total amount of the minimum lease payments, net of executory costs (10 × $11,836 = $118,360), plus any unguaranteed residual value ($0) as the gross investment in the lease (lease payments receivable). In this case, cash must also be debited and lease payments receivable credited for the first payment ($11,836) because the payments are made at the beginning of each year. The leased property should be credited at its cost ($80,000), with the difference between the initial gross investment and cost ($118,360 – $80,000 = $38,360) recorded as unearned income.

Answer (A) is incorrect because this entry reflects the recording of the lease as a capital lease on the books of the lessee. Answer (B) is incorrect because the lease payments receivable are recorded at their gross value rather than at their present value. Answer (C) is incorrect because the lease payments receivable are recorded at their gross value rather than at their present value.

44. Which of the following disclosures is not required for lessors in direct financing and sales-type leases?

A. Future minimum lease payments for the next 5 years.

B. Initial direct costs for direct financing leases only.

C. Total contingent rentals for each period presented.

D. The gross amount of assets recorded under capital leases for each balance sheet presented.

Answer (D) is correct. *(Publisher)*

REQUIRED: The lessor disclosure not required.

DISCUSSION: Disclosure of the gross amount of assets recorded under capital leases for each balance sheet presented is required of lessees, not lessors. The required disclosures by lessors for sales-type and direct financing leases include the components of the net investment in sales-type and direct financing leases as of the date of each balance sheet presented, including the future minimum lease payments to be received; the unguaranteed residual value; the amount of unearned income; and, for direct financing leases only, initial direct costs. A lessor must also disclose future minimum lease payments to be received for each of the 5 succeeding fiscal years and total contingent rentals included in income for each period presented.

45. The excess of the fair value of leased property at the inception of the lease over its cost or carrying amount should be classified by the lessor as

A. Unearned income from a sales-type lease.

B. Unearned income from a direct financing lease.

C. Manufacturer's or dealer's profit from a sales-type lease.

D. Manufacturer's or dealer's profit from a direct financing lease.

Answer (C) is correct. *(CPA, adapted)*

REQUIRED: The classification by the lessor of the excess of the fair value of leased property over its cost or carrying amount.

DISCUSSION: According to SFAS 13, in a sales-type lease, the cost, or carrying amount if different, plus any initial direct costs, minus the present value of any unguaranteed residual value, is charged against income in the same period that the sales price (present value of the minimum lease payments) is recognized. The result is the recognition of a net profit or loss on the sales-type lease. Thus, by definition, a sales-type lease is one that gives rise to a manufacturer's or dealer's profit (or loss) because the fair value of the leased property at the inception of the lease (the present value of the minimum lease payments) differs from its cost or carrying amount.

Answer (A) is incorrect because unearned income from a sales-type lease is equal to the difference between the gross investment and the present value of its components (minimum lease payments, which include any guaranteed residual value and are netted against executory costs, and the unguaranteed residual value). The net investment for a sales-type lease equals gross investment minus unearned income. Answer (B) is incorrect because the fair value and the cost or carrying amount are the same in a direct financing lease. Answer (D) is incorrect because the fair value and the cost or carrying amount are the same in a direct financing lease.

46. Skor Co. leased equipment to Douglas Corp. on January 2, year 1 for an 8-year period expiring December 31, year 8. Equal payments under the lease are $600,000 and are due on January 2 of each year. The first payment was made on January 2, year 1. The list selling price of the equipment is $3,520,000, and its carrying cost on Skor's books is $2,800,000. The lease is appropriately accounted for as a sales-type lease. The present value of the lease payments at an imputed interest rate of 12% (Skor's incremental borrowing rate) is $3,300,000. What amount of profit on the sale should Skor report for the year ended December 31, year 1?

A. $720,000

B. $500,000

C. $90,000

D. $0

Answer (B) is correct. *(CPA, adapted)*

REQUIRED: The amount of profit on a sales-type lease.

DISCUSSION: Skor Co., the lessor, should report a profit from a sales-type lease. The gross profit equals the difference between the sales price (present value of the minimum lease payments) and the cost. Consequently, the profit on the sale equals $500,000 ($3,300,000 – $2,800,000).

Answer (A) is incorrect because $720,000 is the result of using the list selling price instead of the present value of the lease payments. Answer (C) is incorrect because $90,000 is one-eighth of the difference between the list price and the cost. Answer (D) is incorrect because a profit of $500,000 should be reported.

47. Fletcher Company leased a machine to Leavergood Company on January 1. The lease meets the criteria for a sales-type lease. Title to the asset will automatically pass to the lessee at the end of the lease term. Other details are as follows:

Lease term	10 years
Useful life of the asset	10 years
Cost of the leased property to the lessor	$55,000
Annual payment payable at the beginning of each year, beginning January 1	$10,000
Implicit interest rate	10%
Present value of an annuity due of $1 discounted for 10 years at 10%	$6.7590
Present value of $1 due in 10 years discounted at 10%	$.3855

The journal entry to record the inception of this lease on the lessor's books at January 1 is

A.

Leased machine	$67,590	
Lease obligation		$57,590
Cash		10,000

B.

Lease payments receivable	$90,000	
Cash	10,000	
Cost of sales	55,000	
Inventory		$55,000
Unearned income--leases		45,000
Sales		55,000

C.

Lease payments receivable	$90,000	
Cash	10,000	
Interest income		$32,410
Gross profit on sales-type lease		12,590
Inventory		55,000

D.

Lease payments receivable	$90,000	
Cash	10,000	
Cost of sales	55,000	
Sales		$67,590
Inventory		55,000
Unearned income--leases		32,410

Answer (D) is correct. *(CIA, adapted)*

REQUIRED: The lessor's journal entry at the inception of a sales-type lease.

DISCUSSION: For a sales-type lease, the lessor should record

1. As gross investment, the minimum lease payments plus any unguaranteed residual value (the latter element is $0 in this case)
2. As unearned income, the difference between the gross investment in the lease and the present value of its components
3. As the sales price, the present value of the minimum lease payments computed at the interest rate implicit in the lease
4. As a charge to income, the cost of the leased property, plus any initial direct costs ($0 in this case), minus the present value of the unguaranteed residual value ($0 in this case)

Because the first payment is made at the inception of the lease, the payment structure is that of an annuity due. Sales revenue is therefore equal to the $10,000 periodic payment times the present value of an annuity due of $1 discounted for 10 years at 10% ($10,000 × 6.7590 = $67,590). Given that cash is paid at the beginning of the year, the initial $10,000 cash debit immediately decreases the gross investment in the lease (lease payments receivable) from $100,000 to $90,000. The cost of the leased property ($55,000) must also be charged to cost of sales and credited to inventory. Finally, at the inception of the lease, unearned income equals the difference between the gross investment and the present value of its components ($100,000 – $67,590 = $32,410).

Answer (A) is incorrect because it is the lessee's journal entry. Answer (B) is incorrect because the sale should be recorded at the present value of the minimum lease payments, and the unearned income should be recorded as the difference between the gross lease payments receivable and the present value of this gross investment. Answer (C) is incorrect because the lease should reflect both cost of goods sold and sales, not the netted gross profit on the sales-type lease.

48. On January 1 of the current year, Clouser Co. leased a machine to Cohen Co. for 10 years, with $10,000 payments due at the beginning of each year effective at the inception of the lease. The machine cost Clouser $55,000. The lease is appropriately accounted for as a sales-type lease by Clouser. The present value of the 10 rent payments over the lease term discounted appropriately at 10% was $67,600. The estimated salvage value of the machine at the end of 10 years is equal to the disposal costs. How much interest income should Clouser record from the lease for the current year ended December 31?

A. $5,500

B. $5,760

C. $6,760

D. $7,020

Answer (B) is correct. *(CPA, adapted)*

REQUIRED: The interest income recognized by the lessor in the first year of a sales-type lease.

DISCUSSION: In accordance with the effective-interest method, the interest income is equal to the carrying amount of the net investment in the lease at the beginning of the interest period multiplied by the interest rate used to calculate the present value of the lease payments. The present value of $67,600 is reduced by the $10,000 payment made at the inception of the lease, leaving a carrying amount of $57,600. This balance multiplied by 10% yields $5,760 to be reflected as interest income for the first year of the lease.

Answer (A) is incorrect because interest income is calculated using the present value of the lease payments. The machine cost is irrelevant for this calculation. Answer (C) is incorrect because the carrying amount of the lease must first be reduced by the $10,000 payment at the inception of the lease. Answer (D) is incorrect because interest income is based on the carrying amount of the lease multiplied by the discount rate. Therefore, the amount of interest income is $5,760 [($67,600 – $10,000) × 10%].

49. Avizinis Co. manufactures equipment that is sold or leased. On December 31, year 1, Avizinis leased equipment to Anderson for a 5-year period ending December 31, year 6, at which date ownership of the leased asset will be transferred to Anderson. Equal periodic payments under the lease are $22,000 (including $2,000 of executory costs) and are due on December 31 of each year. The first payment was made on December 31, year 1. Collectibility of the remaining lease payments is reasonably assured, and Avizinis has no material cost uncertainties. The normal sales price of the equipment is $77,000, and cost is $60,000. For the year ended December 31, year 1, what amount of income should Avizinis realize from the lease transaction?

A. $17,000

B. $22,000

C. $23,000

D. $33,000

Answer (A) is correct. *(CPA, adapted)*

REQUIRED: The income to be recognized.

DISCUSSION: For a lessor to treat a lease as a capital lease, it must first meet one of four criteria. That ownership of the leased equipment transfers to the lessee at the end of the lease term is one of the four criteria. In addition, the lessor cannot treat the lease as a capital lease unless collectibility of the remaining lease payments is reasonably assured and there are no material cost uncertainties. These conditions are also met. Because the $77,000 fair value is greater than the $60,000 recorded cost of the equipment on the lessor's books, the lease should be accounted for as a sales-type lease. In a sales-type lease, two components of income may be recognized. These are the profit on the sale and interest income. The profit on the sale recorded at the inception of the lease is $17,000 ($77,000 normal sales price – $60,000 cost). At the inception of the lease, no interest income should be recorded. Thus, Avizinis should realize $17,000 of income from this lease transaction in year 1.

50. Bailey Company leased equipment to Greco, Inc. on January 1, year 2. The lease is for an 8-year period expiring December 31, year 9. The first of eight equal annual payments of $600,000 was made on January 1, year 2. Bailey had purchased the equipment on December 29, year 1 for $3,200,000. The lease is appropriately accounted for as a sales-type lease by Bailey. Assume that the present value at January 1, year 2 of all rent payments over the lease term discounted at a 10% interest rate was $3,520,000. What amount of interest income should Bailey record in year 3 (the second year of the lease period) as a result of the lease?

A. $261,200

B. $292,000

C. $320,000

D. $327,200

Answer (A) is correct. *(CPA, adapted)*

REQUIRED: The interest income during the second year of a sales-type lease.

DISCUSSION: The net investment to be recorded by the lessor at 1/1/year 2 is given as $3,520,000, the present value of the minimum lease payments discounted at 10%. The net investment is immediately reduced by the $600,000 lease payment on 1/1/year 2, resulting in a carrying amount for year 2 of $2,920,000. Interest earned for the year 2 at a rate of 10% ($2,920,000 × 10%) is $292,000. Thus, the $600,000 1/1/year 3 lease payment consists of the $292,000 interest component and a $308,000 reduction of the net investment. Because the year 3 net investment balance is $2,612,000 ($2,920,000 – $308,000), interest income for year 3 is $261,200 ($2,612,000 × 10%).

Answer (B) is incorrect because the carrying amount of the lease must be reduced by the payment on 1/1/year 3 for the amount applied to reducing the lease obligation. Answer (C) is incorrect because $320,000 is based on original cost of the leased property. Answer (D) is incorrect because interest income is calculated by the carrying amount of the lease multiplied by the discount rate. Thus, the amount of interest income is $261,200 [($2,920,000 – $308,000) × 10%].

51. On the first day of its fiscal year, Miller Co. leased certain property at an annual rental of $100,000 receivable at the beginning of each year for 10 years. The first payment was received immediately. The leased property is new, had cost $650,000, and has an estimated useful life of 13 years with no salvage value. Miller's borrowing rate is 8%. The present value of an annuity of $1 payable at the beginning of the period at 8% for 10 years is 7.247. Miller had no other costs associated with this lease. Miller should have accounted for this lease as a sale but mistakenly treated the lease as an operating lease. Thus, Miller recognized depreciation using the straight-line method, its normal policy for owned assets. What was the effect on net earnings during the first year of treating this lease as an operating lease rather than as a sale?

A. No effect.

B. Understated.

C. Overstated.

D. The effect depends on the method selected for income tax purposes.

Answer (B) is correct. *(CPA, adapted)*

REQUIRED: The effect of accounting for a lease as an operating rather than as a sales-type lease.

DISCUSSION: Accounting for the lease as an operating lease during the first year generated $50,000 of income, the $100,000 lease payment minus $50,000 of depreciation ($650,000 ÷ 13). In a sales-type lease, the lessor recognizes two income components: profit on the sale and interest income. Total income from accounting for the lease as a sale would have been $124,676 ($74,700 + $49,976). The effect of the error on net earnings was therefore an understatement.

Net investment ($100,000 × 7.247)	$724,700
Carrying amount	(650,000)
Profit on sale	$ 74,700
Net investment	$724,700
First lease payment	(100,000)
Lease balance	$624,700
Interest rate	× .08
Interest income	$ 49,976

14.3 Operating Leases

52. During January of the current year, Pauzouskie Co. made long-term improvements to a recently leased building. The lease agreement provides for neither a transfer of title to Pauzouskie nor a bargain purchase option. Moreover, the fair value of the land is less than 25% of the value of the leased property at the inception of the lease. The present value of the minimum lease payments equals 85% of the fair value of the leased property, and the lease term equals 70% of the building's economic life. Should assets be recognized for the lease and the leasehold improvements?

	Lease	Leasehold Improvements
A.	Yes	Yes
B.	No	Yes
C.	Yes	No
D.	No	No

Answer (B) is correct. *(CPA, adapted)*

REQUIRED: The item(s) for which an asset should be recognized.

DISCUSSION: A lease must be classified as a capital lease by a lessee if, at its inception, (1) the lease provides for the transfer of ownership of the leased property, (2) the lease contains a bargain purchase option, (3) the lease term is 75% or more of the estimated economic life of the leased property, or (4) the present value of the minimum lease payments (excluding executory costs) is at least 90% of the excess of the fair value of the leased property to the lessor at the inception of the lease over any related investment tax credit. (The last two criteria do not apply if the lease term begins within the last 25% of the total estimated economic life.) If a lease involves land and a building, and the fair value of the land is less than 25% of the fair value of the leased property at the inception of the lease, the land and building are deemed to be a single unit for purposes of applying criteria (3) and (4). Thus, none of the criteria are satisfied and the lessee should not recognize an asset and an obligation for the lease. However, general improvements to leased property should be capitalized as leasehold improvements and amortized in accordance with the straight-line method over the shorter of their expected useful life or the lease term.

53. On July 1, year 1, Rebstock Co. entered into a 10-year operating lease for a warehouse facility. The annual minimum lease payments are $100,000. In addition to the base rent, Rebstock pays a monthly allocation of the building's operating expenses, which amounted to $20,000 for the year ended June 30, year 2. In the notes to Rebstock's June 30, year 2 financial statements, what amounts of subsequent years' lease payments should be disclosed?

A. $100,000 per annum for each of the next 5 years and $500,000 in the aggregate.

B. $120,000 per annum for each of the next 5 years and $600,000 in the aggregate.

C. $100,000 per annum for each of the next 5 years and $900,000 in the aggregate.

D. $120,000 per annum for each of the next 5 years and $1,080,000 in the aggregate.

Answer (C) is correct. *(CPA, adapted)*

REQUIRED: The amounts of subsequent years' lease payments to be disclosed.

DISCUSSION: SFAS 13 requires that the future minimum lease payments as of the date of the latest balance sheet presented be disclosed in the aggregate and for each of the 5 succeeding fiscal years. This disclosure is required whether the lease is classified as a capital lease or as an operating lease. Thus, Rebstock should disclose that annual minimum lease payments are $100,000 for each of the next 5 years and that the aggregate is $900,000. The operating expenses are executory costs that are not included in the minimum lease payments.

Answer (A) is incorrect because the aggregate is $900,000. Answer (B) is incorrect because the operating expenses should not be included and the aggregate amount is $900,000. Answer (D) is incorrect because the operating expenses should not be included.

54. On June 1, year 1, Rogers Co. entered into a 5-year nonrenewable lease for office space, commencing on that date, and made the following payments to Rose Properties:

Bonus to obtain lease	$30,000
First month's rent	10,000
Last month's rent	10,000

In its income statement for the year ended June 30, year 1, what amount should Rogers report as rent expense?

A. $10,000

B. $10,500

C. $40,000

D. $50,000

Answer (B) is correct. *(CPA, adapted)*

REQUIRED: The amount to be reported as rent expense for an operating lease.

DISCUSSION: Rent expense is recognized as services are used. Payments that benefit the entire lease term should be amortized over the lease period. Accordingly, the rent expense will include the rent payment for June and the amount of the bonus amortized for that period. Rent expense for June year 1 thus is $10,500 {$10,000 for the month's rent + [($30,000 ÷ 5) ÷ 12 amortization of the bonus]}.

Answer (A) is incorrect because the expense should include amortization of the bonus. Answer (C) is incorrect because the bonus should be amortized over the lease term benefitted. Answer (D) is incorrect because the last month's rent payment should be deferred and expensed in the period it benefits. Also, the bonus should be amortized over the lease term.

55. On January 1 of the current year, Sharp Company leased a building to Schlachtman under an operating lease for 10 years at $50,000 per year, payable the first day of each lease year. Sharp paid $15,000 to a real estate broker as a finder's fee. The annual depreciation on the building is $12,000. Sharp incurred insurance and property tax expenses totaling $9,000 during the current year. Sharp's net rental income for the year should be

A. $27,500

B. $29,000

C. $35,000

D. $36,500

Answer (A) is correct. *(CPA, adapted)*

REQUIRED: The net rental income that should be recorded for the first year.

DISCUSSION: Net rental income is equal to the $50,000 annual payment minus any expenses incurred during the year. These expenses include $12,000 of depreciation, $9,000 for insurance and property taxes, and $1,500 ($15,000 ÷ 10 years) amortization of the finder's fee. In an operating lease, a finder's fee is an initial direct cost that should be deferred and allocated over the lease term in proportion to the recognition of rental income. Accordingly, the net rental income for the year is $27,500.

Rental income	$50,000
Depreciation	(12,000)
Insurance and property tax expenses	(9,000)
Amortization	(1,500)
Net rental income	$27,500

Answer (B) is incorrect because $29,000 excludes amortization of the finder's fee. Answer (C) is incorrect because $35,000 includes the entire finder's fee and excludes depreciation and the insurance and property tax expenses. Answer (D) is incorrect because $36,500 excludes the insurance and property tax expenses.

56. Sunhachawi Apparel, Inc. leases and operates a retail store. The following information relates to the lease for the year ended December 31, year 1:

- The store lease, an operating lease, calls for a base monthly rent of $1,500 due the first day of each month.
- Additional rent is computed at 6% of net sales over $300,000 up to $600,000 and 5% of net sales over $600,000, per calendar year.
- Net sales for year 1 were $900,000.
- Sunhachawi paid executory costs to the lessor for property taxes of $12,000 and insurance of $5,000.

For year 1, Sunhachawi's expenses relating to the store lease are

A. $71,000

B. $68,000

C. $54,000

D. $35,000

Answer (B) is correct. *(CPA, adapted)*

REQUIRED: The lessee's expenses relating to a store lease.

DISCUSSION: This lease is properly classified as an operating lease. The expenses for year 1 relating to this lease should include the fixed monthly rental payment, the contingent rental payments, and the executory costs. The year 1 expenses, as indicated below, amount to $68,000.

Monthly rent	$18,000	($1,500 × 12 months)
Additional rent	18,000	($600,000 – $300,000) × 6%
	15,000	($900,000 – $600,000) × 5%
Executory costs	12,000	(property taxes)
	5,000	(insurance)
Total expenses	$68,000	

Answer (A) is incorrect because $71,000 includes the contingent rent at 6%. Answer (C) is incorrect because $54,000 includes the contingent rent at 6% and excludes the executory costs. Answer (D) is incorrect because $35,000 excludes the contingent rent.

57. Neinus Co. leased a new electronic widget tester to Merrell for a period of 10 years. At the termination of the noncancelable lease, Merrell had the right to purchase the machine for 20% of its fair value at that time. Merrell is a financially stable company, and collectibility of the future lease payments is assured. The machine contains many technologically advanced components, and Neinus has guaranteed to repair any breakdown, no matter how minor, for the life of the lease plus an additional 10-year period. This unusual guarantee was offered by the Neinus to gain experience with the new machine in an actual use situation. The cost of meeting the terms of this guarantee cannot be reasonably estimated. According to current authoritative literature, Neinus should account for this lease as

A. A direct financing lease.

B. A leveraged lease.

C. An operating lease.

D. A sales-type lease.

Answer (C) is correct. *(Publisher)*

REQUIRED: The proper classification of the lease by the lessor.

DISCUSSION: Lessors classify leases as operating, sales-type, or direct financing. If a lease meets any one of four criteria specified in SFAS 13, collectibility of payments from the lessee is reasonably predictable, and no important uncertainties surround the amount of unreimbursable costs yet to be incurred by the lessor under the lease, the lease is classified by the lessor as either a direct financing lease or a sales-type lease. Because Merrell may purchase the machine for 20% of its fair value at the end of the lease, a bargain purchase option exists, which meets one of the four criteria specified in SFAS 13. However, the lessor has guaranteed all repairs for the next 20 years, so important uncertainties remain. The lessor must therefore classify the lease as an operating lease.

58. On January 1, year 1, Masingil Co. leased a building to Leavengood Corp. for a 10-year term at an annual rental of $50,000. At the inception of the lease, Masingil received $200,000 covering the first 2 years' rent and a security deposit of $100,000. This deposit will not be returned to Leavengood upon expiration of the lease but will be applied to payment of rent for the last 2 years of the lease. What portions of the $200,000 should be shown as a current and a long-term liability, respectively, in Masingil's December 31, year 1 balance sheet?

	Current Liability	Long-Term Liability
A.	$0	$200,000
B.	$50,000	$100,000
C.	$100,000	$100,000
D.	$100,000	$50,000

Answer (B) is correct. *(CPA, adapted)*

REQUIRED: The allocation of an advance payment between current and long-term.

DISCUSSION: Of the $200,000 received at the inception of the lease, $50,000 should be recognized as rental income for the year ended 12/31/year 1. At 12/31/year 1, the $50,000 attributable to rent for year 2 should be classified as a current liability, and the $100,000 applicable to the last 2 years of the lease should be classified as a long-term liability.

59. On December 1, year 1, King Co. leased office space for 5 years at a monthly rental of $60,000. On the same date, King paid the lessor the following amounts:

First month's rent	$ 60,000
Last month's rent	60,000
Security deposit (refundable at lease expiration)	80,000
Installation of new walls and offices	360,000

King's year 1 expense relating to use of the office space should be

A. $140,000

B. $120,000

C. $66,000

D. $60,000

Answer (C) is correct. *(CPA, adapted)*

REQUIRED: The amount to be included as rent expense in relation to the lease.

DISCUSSION: Rent expense should be recognized as the services are used. Payments that benefit future periods should be deferred and recognized when incurred. Leasehold improvements (i.e., installation of new walls and offices) should be capitalized and amortized over the term of the lease. Thus, the expense should include $60,000 rent for the first month of the lease and amortization of the leasehold improvement of $6,000 [($360,000 ÷ 5) ÷ 12]. Total expense recognized should be $66,000 ($60,000 + $6,000).

Answer (A) is incorrect because $140,000 includes the security deposit and excludes amortization of the leasehold improvements. Answer (B) is incorrect because $120,000 includes the last month's rent and excludes amortization of the leasehold improvements. Answer (D) is incorrect because $60,000 excludes amortization of the leasehold improvements.

60. Greco Co. leased office premises to Houghton, Inc. for a 5-year term beginning January 2, year 1. Under the terms of the operating lease, rent for the first year is $8,000 and rent for years 2 through 5 is $12,500 per annum. However, as an inducement to enter the lease, Greco granted Houghton the first 6 months of the lease rent-free. In its December 31, year 1 income statement, what amount should Greco report as rental income?

A. $12,000

B. $11,600

C. $10,800

D. $8,000

Answer (C) is correct. *(CPA, adapted)*

REQUIRED: The rental revenue reported for the first year of an operating lease given a varying annual rental.

DISCUSSION: For an operating lease, rent is reported as income in accordance with the lease agreement. However, if rentals vary from a straight-line basis, the straight-line basis should be used unless another systematic and rational basis is more representative of the time pattern in which the use benefit from the property is reduced. No basis other than straight-line is more representative of the reduction in the use benefit of office space. Because rent for the first year is $4,000 [$8,000 × (6 ÷ 12)], Greco should report rental revenue of $10,800 {[$4,000 + (4 × $12,500)] ÷ 5 years}.

Answer (A) is incorrect because $12,000 equals the first year's rent payment plus 6 months of free rent. Answer (B) is incorrect because $11,600 does not adjust for the 6 months of free rent. Answer (D) is incorrect because $8,000 is equal to the first year's unadjusted rental payment.

61. On July 1, year 1, Danner, Inc. leased a delivery truck from Cerrato Corp. under a 3-year operating lease. Total rent for the term of the lease will be $36,000, payable as follows:

12 months × $ 500	=	$ 6,000
12 months × $ 750	=	9,000
12 months × $1,750	=	21,000

All payments were made when due. In Cerrato's June 30, year 3 balance sheet, the accrued rent receivable should be reported as

A. $0

B. $9,000

C. $12,000

D. $21,000

Answer (B) is correct. *(CPA, adapted)*

REQUIRED: The amount to be included as rent receivable in the balance sheet.

DISCUSSION: For an operating lease, rent revenue is recognized in accordance with the straight-line method unless another systematic and rational basis is more representative of the benefits realized. Thus, monthly rent revenue of $1,000 [($6,000 + $9,000 + $21,000) ÷ 36 months] should be recognized. At 6/30/year 3 cumulative revenue recognized is $24,000 ($1,000 × 24 months). Because cumulative cash received is $15,000 ($6,000 + $9,000), an accrued receivable for the $9,000 ($24,000 – $15,000) difference should be recognized.

Answer (A) is incorrect because $9,000 is equal to rent received during the year ended 6/30/year 3. Answer (C) is incorrect because $12,000 is rent revenue recognized each year. Answer (D) is incorrect because $21,000 is equal to the rent payments to be received in the following fiscal year.

62. Clark Corp. owns an office building and normally charges tenants $30 per square foot per year for office space. Because the occupancy rate is low, Clark agreed to lease 10,000 square feet to Fletcher Co. at $12 per square foot for the first year of a 3-year operating lease. Rent for remaining years will be at the $30 rate. Fletcher moved into the building on January 1, year 1 and paid the first year's rent in advance. What amount of rental revenue should Clark report from Fletcher in its income statement for the year ended September 30, year 1?

A. $90,000

B. $120,000

C. $180,000

D. $240,000

Answer (C) is correct. *(CPA, adapted)*

REQUIRED: The amount of rent revenue to be included in the income statement.

DISCUSSION: In an operating lease, when payments differ from year to year, revenue is recognized by allocating the total amount of revenue to be received evenly over the lease term. At 9/30/year 1, the amount of revenue to be recognized is for 9 months. Thus, rent revenue is $180,000 {[$10,000 square feet × ($12 + $30 + $30)] × (9 ÷ 36)}.

Answer (A) is incorrect because $90,000 recognizes rent equal to the rental payments. Answer (B) is incorrect because $120,000 recognizes rent equal to rent payments for 12 months. Answer (D) is incorrect because $240,000 recognizes rent for 12 months.

14.4 Sale-Leaseback Transactions

63. In a sale-leaseback transaction, the seller-lessee has retained the property. The gain on the sale should be recognized at the time of the sale-leaseback when the lease is classified as a(n)

	Capital Lease	Operating Lease
A.	Yes	Yes
B.	No	No
C.	No	Yes
D.	Yes	No

Answer (B) is correct. *(CPA, adapted)*

REQUIRED: The lease for which a gain on a sale-leaseback should be recognized at the time of the transaction.

DISCUSSION: A gain on the sale in a sale-leaseback transaction normally should be deferred and amortized in proportion to the amortization of the leased asset if the leaseback is classified as a capital lease. The amortization is in proportion to the gross rental payments expensed over the lease term if the leaseback is classified as an operating lease (SFAS 28, *Accounting for Sales with Leasebacks*). The gain on the sale is normally not recognized at the time of the sale-leaseback.

64. On December 31, year 1, Svetlana Corp. sold Kenyatta Co. two airplanes and simultaneously leased them back. Additional information pertaining to the sale-leasebacks follows:

	Plane #1	Plane #2
Sales price	$600,000	$1,000,000
Carrying amount, 12/31/year 1	$100,000	$550,000
Remaining useful life, 12/31/year 1	10 years	35 years
Lease term	8 years	3 years
Annual lease payments	$100,000	$200,000

In its December 31, year 1 balance sheet, what amount should Svetlana report as deferred gain on these transactions?

A. $950,000

B. $500,000

C. $450,000

D. $0

Answer (B) is correct. *(CPA, adapted)*

REQUIRED: The amount to be recorded as deferred revenue in a sale and leaseback.

DISCUSSION: The lease of plane #1 is a capital lease because its 8-year term exceeds 75% of the 10-year estimated remaining economic life of the plane. In a sale and leaseback transaction, any profit or loss on the sale is ordinarily required to be deferred and amortized in proportion to the amortization of the leased asset if the lease is a capital lease. The amortization is in proportion to the gross rental payments expensed over the lease term if the lease is an operating lease. At the inception of this lease, the $500,000 gain ($600,000 sales price – $100,000 carrying amount) should be reported as deferred revenue. The lease of plane #2 is an operating lease that falls under an exception provided by SFAS 28. When the seller-lessee relinquishes the right to substantially all of the remaining use of the property sold and retains only a minor portion of such use (in this case, less than 10% of the remaining useful life), the seller-lessee should account for the sale and the leaseback as separate transactions based upon their respective terms. Svetlana should recognize the entire $450,000 gain ($1,000,000 sales price – $550,000 carrying amount). Thus, only the $500,000 gain from the sale of plane #1 is deferred.

Answer (A) is incorrect because $950,000 includes the gain on plane #2. Answer (C) is incorrect because $450,000 equals the gain on plane #2. Answer (D) is incorrect because the gain on plane #1 should be deferred.

65. McKenzie Co. sold its factory at a gain and simultaneously leased it back for 10 years. The factory's remaining economic life is 20 years. The lease was reported as an operating lease. At the time of sale, McKenzie should report the gain as

A. An extraordinary item, net of income tax.

B. An asset valuation allowance.

C. A separate component of shareholders' equity.

D. A deferred credit.

Answer (D) is correct. *(CPA, adapted)*

REQUIRED: The proper treatment of a gain on a sale-leaseback.

DISCUSSION: A gain on the sale in a sale-leaseback normally should be deferred and amortized. When the seller-lessee classifies the lease arising from the sale-leaseback as an operating lease, no asset is shown on the balance sheet, and the deferral cannot be presented as a contra asset. Accordingly, the usual practice is to report the gain as a deferred credit.

Answer (A) is incorrect because the gain is ordinarily deferred. Answer (B) is incorrect because an asset valuation allowance would be reported if the lease qualified as a capital lease. Answer (C) is incorrect because the gain is usually reported as a deferred credit.

66. On December 31, year 1, Joseenrique Corp. sold equipment to Dorr and simultaneously leased it back for 3 years. The following data pertain to the transaction at this date:

Sales price	$220,000
Carrying amount	150,000
Present value of lease rentals ($2,000 for 36 months at 12%)	60,800
Estimated remaining useful life	10 years

At December 31, year 1 what amount should Joseenrique report as deferred revenue from the sale of the equipment?

A. $0

B. $9,200

C. $60,800

D. $70,000

Answer (C) is correct. *(CPA, adapted)*

REQUIRED: The amount to be reported as deferred revenue in a sale-leaseback.

DISCUSSION: In an ordinary sale and leaseback, any profit or loss on the sale is amortized over the life of the lease. But SFAS 28 provides for exceptions. One exception applies when a seller-lessee retains more than a minor part but less than substantially all of the use of the property through the leaseback. If the seller-lessee in this situation realizes a profit on the sale in excess of either (1) the present value of the minimum lease payments over the lease term if the leaseback is an operating lease, or (2) the recorded amount of the leased asset if the leaseback is classified as a capital lease, the "excess" profit on the sale is recognized at the date of the sale. "Substantially all" has essentially the same meaning as the "90% test" used in determining whether a lease is a capital or operating lease (the present value of the lease payments is 90% or more of the fair value of the leased property). "Minor" refers to a transfer of 10% or less of the use of the property in the lease.

For Joseenrique Corp., the $60,800 present value of the lease rentals is greater than 10% and less than 90% of the fair value of the leased property as measured by the sales price. Thus, $9,200 in excess profit should be recognized.

Sales price	$220,000
Carrying amount	(150,000)
Profit	$ 70,000
Minus PV of lease payments	(60,800)
Profit recognized	$ 9,200

The $60,800 remaining gain on the sale-leaseback should be amortized in proportion to the gross rentals expensed over the lease term because the leaseback is classified as an operating lease (none of the criteria for a capital lease is met). At 12/31/year 1, the date of the inception of the lease, the entire $60,800 should be reported in the balance sheet as deferred revenue from the sale of the equipment.

Answer (A) is incorrect because more than a minor part but less than substantially all of the use of the property has been retained. Accordingly, only the excess profit is recognized immediately, and the remaining portion is deferred. Answer (B) is incorrect because $9,200 is the amount of profit that is recognized immediately, and $60,800 is deferred. Answer (D) is incorrect because $9,200 of the profit is recognized immediately, deferring the remaining $60,800 of revenue.

67. The following information pertains to a sale and leaseback of equipment by Joshua Co. on December 31, year 1:

Sales price	$400,000
Carrying amount	300,000
Monthly lease payment	3,250
Present value of lease payments	36,900
Estimated remaining life	25 years
Lease term	1 year
Implicit rate	12%

What amount of deferred gain on the sale should Joshua report at December 31, year 1?

A. $0

B. $36,900

C. $63,100

D. $100,000

Answer (A) is correct. *(CPA, adapted)*

REQUIRED: The amount of gain to defer resulting from a sale-leaseback transaction.

DISCUSSION: In a sale-leaseback transaction under SFAS 28, a seller will either defer all profits, recognize all profits, or recognize only excess profits. The rules for these recognition principles are based on the rights the seller retains in the property. If the seller-lessee retains substantially all rights in the property (greater than 90% of the present value of the lease payments or the useful life of the asset), all profits and losses are deferred. If minor rights are retained (less than 10% of the present value of the lease payments or the useful life of the asset), all profits and losses are recognized. If the rights retained are between these two thresholds, only excess profits are recognized. In this situation, minor rights are retained, so the entire gain of $100,000 ($400,000 sales price – $300,000 carrying amount) is recognized, and none is deferred.

Answer (B) is incorrect because $36,900 is the present value of the lease payments. Answer (C) is incorrect because $63,100 is the difference between the $100,000 gain and the present value of the minimum lease payments. Answer (D) is incorrect because $100,000 is the amount of gain recognized immediately.

68. On June 30, year 1, Travis Co. sold equipment with an estimated useful life of 11 years and immediately leased it back for 10 years. The equipment's carrying amount was $450,000; the sales price was $430,000; and the present value of the lease payments, which is equal to the fair value of the equipment, was $465,000. In its June 30, year 1 balance sheet, what amount should Travis report as deferred loss?

A. $35,000

B. $20,000

C. $15,000

D. $0

Answer (B) is correct. *(CPA, adapted)*

REQUIRED: The amount of deferred loss.

DISCUSSION: Any profit or loss on the sale in a sale-leaseback transaction is ordinarily deferred and amortized. Immediate recognition of the loss is permitted, however, when the fair value at the time of the transaction is less than the undepreciated cost (SFAS 28). Given a fair value of $465,000 and a carrying amount of $450,000, that exception does not apply. Consequently, the $20,000 ($450,000 – $430,000) excess of the carrying amount over the sales price should be deferred.

Answer (A) is incorrect because $35,000 is the excess of the fair value over the sales price. Answer (C) is incorrect because $15,000 is the excess of the fair value over the carrying amount. Answer (D) is incorrect because full recognition of the loss is not appropriate when the fair value is greater than the carrying amount.

14.5 Special Areas

69. A lease of property owned by a governmental unit or authority should be classified as an operating lease only if

A. The leased property is governmental property that can be either closed or taken possession of by a governmental agency in accordance with the lease agreement or existing statutes or regulations.

B. The leased property is nonmovable and is part of a larger facility.

C. The lease has no provision for a transfer of ownership to the lessee.

D. All of the answers are correct.

Answer (D) is correct. *(Publisher)*

REQUIRED: The condition(s) under which a lease of property from the government must be treated as an operating lease by a lessee.

DISCUSSION: FASB Interpretation No. 23, *Leases of Certain Property Owned by a Governmental Unit or Authority*, requires that a lease meeting all of the conditions specified in the other answer choices be classified as an operating lease. In addition, the leased property or equivalent property in the same service area can be neither purchased nor leased from a nongovernmental source. If all of these conditions are not met, the general criteria for classifying leases are applicable.

70. The James Company is the lessee in a lease that involves only part of a building. In the process of determining the accounting for this lease, management must determine if it has a basis for an objective determination of the fair value of the leased property. What evidence may be used to provide such a basis?

A. Only data relating to recent sales of property similar to the leased property.

B. Only data relating to recent sales of property similar to the leased property or an independent appraisal.

C. Data relating to recent sales of property similar to the leased property or an independent appraisal or estimated replacement cost data.

D. Data relating to recent sales of similar property, an independent appraisal, estimated cost information, or any valuation selected by the board of directors.

Answer (C) is correct. *(Publisher)*

REQUIRED: The evidence that may be used to provide an objective measure of the fair value of part of a building.

DISCUSSION: FASB Interpretation No. 24, *Leases Involving Only Part of a Building*, states that other evidence, such as an independent appraisal or estimated replacement cost information, may be used as a basis for an objective determination of the fair value of part of a building even if no sales of similar property have occurred.

Answer (A) is incorrect because other evidence, including both an independent appraisal and estimated replacement cost data, may be used. Answer (B) is incorrect because other evidence, including both an independent appraisal and estimated replacement cost data, may be used. Answer (D) is incorrect because any valuation selected by the board of directors would not provide an objective determination of fair value.

71. Terms of a lease involving both land and a building include retention of ownership of both elements by the lessor at the end of the lease term. The fair value of the land is $250,000, and the fair value of the building is $500,000. Current authoritative literature requires that the minimum lease payments be allocated between the two elements

A. In proportion to their fair values at the inception of the lease.

B. In proportion to their expected fair values at the end of the lease term.

C. First to the land element on the basis of its fair value at the inception of the lease with the remainder to the building element.

D. First to the building element on the basis of its fair value at the inception of the lease with the remainder to the land element.

Answer (C) is correct. *(Publisher)*

REQUIRED: The correct allocation between the land and building included in a lease.

DISCUSSION: Under SFAS 13, if a lease contains neither a bargain purchase option nor a term transferring ownership to the lessee at the termination of the lease, and if the fair value of land in the lease involving both land and a building is 25% or more of the total fair value of the leased property at the inception of the lease, the minimum lease payments should be separated by both the lessee and the lessor by determining the fair value of the land and applying the lessee's incremental borrowing rate to it to determine the annual minimum lease payments applicable to the land. The remaining minimum lease payments should be allocated to the building element.

Answer (A) is incorrect because it describes proper allocation by the lessee when either a bargain purchase option exists or ownership of the property passes to the lessee at the termination of the lease. Answer (B) is incorrect because expected fair values at the expiration of the lease term are not a relevant consideration. Answer (D) is incorrect because the building should receive the residual allocation.

72. Which of the following statements describes the proper accounting when a lease includes equipment as well as land and a building?

A. The lessor may treat the lease as a single lease if the useful life of the assets approximates the lease term.

B. The lessor must account for the equipment as a separate lease but the lessee is not required to do so.

C. The lessee must account for the equipment as a separate lease but the lessor is not required to do so.

D. Both the lessee and lessor must account for the equipment as a separate lease.

Answer (D) is correct. *(Publisher)*

REQUIRED: The accounting when a lease includes equipment, land, and a building.

DISCUSSION: If a lease involves equipment as well as land and a building (real estate), both the lessee and the lessor must first estimate the portion of the minimum lease payments that is applicable to the equipment element of the lease by whatever means are appropriate in the circumstances. The equipment portion of the lease is then classified and accounted for separately from the real estate portion.

73. Lessee has leased a new building and land from Lessor for 25 years. At the inception of the lease, the building and land have fair values of $200,000 and $25,000, respectively. The building has an expected economic life of 30 years. Which of the following statements is true regarding the Lessee's treatment of the lease?

A. Lessee should treat the lease as a capital lease even though there is no bargain purchase option and no automatic transfer of ownership at the termination of the lease.

B. Lessee should treat the lease as a capital lease only if there is either a bargain purchase option or an automatic transfer of ownership at the termination of the lease.

C. Lessee should treat the lease as a capital lease provided that the land and building are recorded in separate asset accounts and accounted for separately.

D. Lessee should treat the lease as a capital lease only if Lessor treats the transaction as a leveraged lease.

Answer (A) is correct. *(Publisher)*

REQUIRED: The true statement regarding the lessee's accounting for a lease involving land and a building.

DISCUSSION: When the lease involves both land and a building, SFAS 13 provides for a special application of the four criteria for determining whether the lessee should treat the lease as a capital or an operating lease. If the lease provides for neither a bargain purchase option nor automatic transfer of ownership at the termination of the lease, but the fair value of the land is less than 25% of the total fair value of the leased property at the inception of the lease (as in this case), the land and building should be considered a single unit for purposes of applying the 75% lease term test and the 90% fair value test. Because the lease term in this question exceeds 75% of the estimated economic life of the building, the lease should be properly classified as a capital lease by the lessee. According to SFAS 98, *Accounting for Leases – Sale-Leaseback Transactions Involving Real Estate; Sales-Type Leases of Real Estate; Definition of the Lease Term; Initial Direct Costs of Direct Financing Leases*, if the collectibility of the lease payments is reasonably predictable and no important uncertainties surround the amount of unreimbursable costs, the lessor should account for this lease as a single unit as either a direct financing lease, a leveraged lease, or an operating lease. A lease involving real estate is classified as a sales-type lease only if it results in a manufacturer's or dealer's profit (or loss) and transfers ownership.

Answer (B) is incorrect because the four tests for capital leases apply to land and building leases as well as to leases of other assets. Answer (C) is incorrect because, when the fair value of the land is less than 25% of total fair value in a capital lease, the land and building should be capitalized and amortized as a single unit. Answer (D) is incorrect because classification of a lease as a leveraged lease is possible only by a lessor and has no bearing on lessee accounting.

74. Lessor Company agreed to sell Lessee Company an asset that Lessee Company currently is accounting for as a capital lease. At the time of the purchase, the following account balances were recorded:

Leased asset, net of amortization	$31,500
Lease obligation	33,500

At what amount should Lessee record this asset, given that the price paid to Lessor was $34,000?

A. $31,500

B. $32,000

C. $33,500

D. $34,000

Answer (B) is correct. *(Publisher)*

REQUIRED: The amount at which a lessee should record the purchase of a leased asset during the lease term.

DISCUSSION: FASB Interpretation No. 26, *Accounting for Purchase of a Leased Asset by the Lessee During the Term of the Lease*, requires that the carrying amount of the leased asset be adjusted for the difference, if any, between the purchase price and the carrying amount of the lease obligation. Lessee Company should therefore record the asset at $32,000 ($31,500 + $34,000 – $33,500). If the leased asset is carried at an amount greater than the lease obligation, a loss may be recognized so that the purchased asset is not overvalued. For example, assuming the purchased asset had a fair value of $34,000, if the leased asset and obligation had been $33,500 and $31,500, respectively, a $2,000 loss would have been recognized (debit an asset for $34,000, a loss for $2,000, and the lease obligation for $31,500; credit the leased asset for $33,500 and cash for $34,000).

Answer (A) is incorrect because $31,500 is the carrying amount of the leased asset. Answer (C) is incorrect because $33,500 is the carrying amount of the lease obligation. Answer (D) is incorrect because $34,000 is the purchase price.

75. One criterion that must be met before the lease may be classified by the lessor as a sales-type lease or a direct financing lease is that "no important uncertainties surround the amount of unreimbursable costs yet to be incurred by the lessor under the lease." If the property covered by the lease is yet to be constructed by the lessor at the inception of the lease, this classification criterion should be applied at the date

A. That marks the inception of the lease.

B. That the construction of the property is completed.

C. That the lessee takes possession of the property.

D. That final payment is made to the contractor.

Answer (B) is correct. *(Publisher)*

REQUIRED: The date at which a lessor should apply the cost uncertainties criterion when the property has not yet been constructed at the inception date.

DISCUSSION: The classification of a lease is determined at the date of its inception, which is the date of the lease agreement or commitment, if earlier. However, when property covered by a lease has yet to be constructed or has not been acquired by the lessor at the date of the lease agreement or commitment (the inception of the lease), SFAS 23, *Inception of the Lease*, states that the classification criterion regarding cost uncertainties is to be applied "at the date that construction of the property is completed or the property is acquired by the lessor."

Answer (A) is incorrect because, given that the property has yet to be constructed at the inception date, the determination regarding unreimbursable costs must await completion of the project. Answer (C) is incorrect because the application of the cost uncertainties criterion by the lessor should not be later than completion of construction. Answer (D) is incorrect because the application of the cost uncertainties criterion by the lessor should not be later than completion of construction.

76. The Henson Corporation is the lessor and the Lippert Corporation is the lessee in a lease agreement. The lease is for property that has not yet been acquired by the lessor. A preliminary lease agreement has been written and approved by both parties. Only two principal provisions are yet to be negotiated. The date considered to be the inception of this lease is

A. The date of the preliminary lease agreement.

B. The date that the property is acquired by the lessor.

C. The date that the remaining two principal provisions are agreed upon in writing.

D. The date that the lessee takes possession of the property.

Answer (C) is correct. *(Publisher)*

REQUIRED: The inception date of a lease when the lease property has not yet been acquired by the lessor.

DISCUSSION: SFAS 23 defines the inception date for a lease that covers property not yet constructed or acquired by the lessor as the date of the lease agreement or any earlier commitment. The commitment must be in writing, must be signed by the interested parties, and must specifically set forth the principal lease provisions. If any of the principal provisions remains to be negotiated, the agreement does not meet the definition of a commitment.

77. When the nature of a sublease transaction is such that the original lessee is not relieved of the primary obligation under the original lease, a loss (if it occurs) should be recognized by the original lessee under which of the following conditions?

A. Never.

B. Only if the sublease was entered into as part of the disposal of a segment of a business.

C. Under all circumstances.

D. Only when the sublease is a sales-type lease.

Answer (C) is correct. *(Publisher)*

REQUIRED: The circumstances under which a loss on a sublease should be recognized.

DISCUSSION: In these circumstances, SFAS 13 "does not specifically require recognition of an indicated loss except for a sales-type loss on a sales-type sublease" (FASB Interpretation No. 27, *Accounting for a Loss on a Sublease*). However, according to this Interpretation, if the sublease is entered into as part of the disposal of a segment of a business, any gain or loss on the sublease must be recognized as part of the gain or loss on disposal. Moreover, FASB Technical Bulletin 79-15, *Accounting for Loss on a Sublease Not Involving the Disposal of a Segment*, requires recognition of a loss on operating and direct financing subleases in appropriate circumstances.

78. Under what conditions would a renewal or extension of either a sales-type or direct financing lease, that otherwise would qualify as a sales-type lease, be properly classified as a direct financing lease?

A. Under all conditions.

B. Under no conditions.

C. Under the condition that the renewal or extension occurs at or near the end of the lease term.

D. Under the condition that the renewal or extension does not occur at or near the end of the lease term.

Answer (D) is correct. *(Publisher)*

REQUIRED: The condition(s) under which a renewal or extension should be classified as a direct financing lease.

DISCUSSION: SFAS 27, *Classification of Renewals or Extensions of Existing Sales-Type or Direct Financing Leases,* states that a renewal or extension of an existing sales-type or direct financing lease, that otherwise would qualify as a sales-type lease, should be classified as a direct financing lease unless the renewal or extension occurs at or near the end of the original lease term. At or near the end of the lease term is considered to mean the last few months of the existing lease.

Answer (A) is incorrect because the sales-type classification is only appropriate under certain conditions. Answer (B) is incorrect because the sales-type classification is only appropriate under certain conditions. Answer (C) is incorrect because, under this condition, the lease should be classified as a sales-type lease.

79. The City of Medford issued tax-exempt debt to construct a building that it leased to a company. The lease was capitalized by the lessee and treated as a direct financing lease by the lessor. Terms of the lease were such that the lease obligation was essentially the same as the tax-exempt debt. If the tax-exempt debt is advance refunded and the terms of the lease are changed to pass the perceived economic advantages of the refunding through to the lessee, which of the following statements is true?

A. If the advance refunding is treated as an early extinguishment of debt, both the lessor and the lessee should recognize a gain or loss.

B. Regardless of whether the advance refunding is treated as an early extinguishment of debt, both the lessor and the lessee should recognize a gain or loss.

C. If the advance refunding is treated as an early extinguishment of debt, only the lessee should recognize a gain or loss.

D. If the advance refunding is treated as an early extinguishment of debt, only the lessor should recognize a gain or loss.

Answer (A) is correct. *(Publisher)*

REQUIRED: The true statement about the effects of advance refunding of tax-exempt debt when the provisions of a lease are changed to pass the economic advantages of the refunding through to the lessee.

DISCUSSION: SFAS 22, *Changes in the Provisions of Lease Agreements Resulting from Refundings of Tax-Exempt Debt*, applies when an advance refunding of tax-exempt debt results in a revision of lease terms of a capital lease, and the refunding is accounted for as an extinguishment of debt. In these circumstances, the lessee should adjust the lease obligation to the present value of the minimum lease payments under the revised lease using the effective interest rate applicable to the revised agreement. The lessee should also recognize any resulting gain or loss as a gain or loss on the extinguishment of debt (extraordinary).

The lessor should adjust the gross investment and the unearned interest income accounts to reflect as net investment the present value of the components of the gross investment, based on the interest rate applicable to the revised lease agreement, and should recognize the resulting adjustment as a gain or loss in the current period.

The criteria in SFAS 125, *Accounting for Transfers and Servicing of Financial Assets and Extinguishment of Liabilities,* determine whether the transaction qualifies as an extinguishment at the date of the advance refunding.

Answer (B) is incorrect because SFAS 22 states that, in these circumstances, any gain or loss should be recognized when the tax-exempt debt is considered to have been extinguished. Thus, if the advance refunding did not constitute an early extinguishment, no gain or loss should be recognized. Answer (C) is incorrect because both the lessor and the lessee should recognize a gain or loss. Answer (D) is incorrect because both the lessor and the lessee should recognize a gain or loss.

80. Which of the following statements about leveraged leases is true?

A. The lessee finances them largely by nonrecourse debt.

B. They are sales-type leases.

C. They provide depreciation expense, interest expense, and tax benefits to the lessee.

D. They provide for a creditor mortgage on the leased asset.

Answer (D) is correct. *(Publisher)*

REQUIRED: The true statement about leveraged leases.

DISCUSSION: A leveraged lease is in effect a direct financing lease in which the leased asset is financed by the lessor through a third-party long-term creditor. The third-party creditor's interest is secured either by a pledge of the lease payments or by a mortgage on the leased asset, and the debt is substantially nonrecourse as to the general credit of the lessor.

Answer (A) is incorrect because the lessor, not the lessee, finances the leased asset by nonrecourse debt. Answer (B) is incorrect because sales-type leases may not be accounted for as leveraged leases. Answer (C) is incorrect because the lessor, not the lessee, recognizes depreciation expense, interest expense, and tax benefits on a leveraged lease.

STUDY UNIT FIFTEEN
CORPORATE EQUITY

The equity accounts of a corporation include contributed capital, treasury stock, retained earnings, and items included in accumulated other comprehensive income. **Contributed capital** primarily represents the results of transactions by an enterprise in its own stock. The principal classes of stock are common and preferred. Transactions in stock may include issuances, repurchases, and retirements. GAAP do not permit the recognition of gains and losses from transactions by an enterprise in its own stock or the reporting of its holdings of its own stock (treasury stock) as an asset.

The issuance of **par-value or stated-value stock** is recorded as an increase in (credit to) capital stock equal to the number of shares issued times the par or stated value. The excess of the issuance price over the par or stated value is recorded by a credit to **additional paid-in capital**. The issuance of no-par-value stock is recorded by a credit to capital stock. The issuance price ordinarily is determined by the transaction giving rise to the issuance. For example, stock issued in exchange for cash or property is recorded at the fair value of the proceeds received, stock issued in a lump-sum transaction is recorded at the allocated amount of the lump-sum proceeds, and common stock issued upon conversion of convertible debt or preferred stock is recorded at the carrying amount or the fair value of the security converted.

Cash and property (in-kind) dividends are nonreciprocal transfers from an enterprise to its shareholders. A property dividend is recorded at the fair value of the asset transferred, with a gain or loss recognized equal to the difference between its fair value and carrying amount. Cash and property dividends are recorded as liabilities on the date of declaration by the board of directors. These liabilities are satisfied on the date of payment. Dividends on preferred stock ordinarily must be paid before dividends on common stock. In addition, dividends on preferred stock usually are cumulative. **Cumulative** unpaid dividends from previous years (dividends in arrears) are required to be paid before dividends for the current year. Moreover, dividends on preferred stock also may be, but usually are not, participating. **Participating** preferred shareholders fully or partially participate in additional dividends with common shareholders after the latter have received an initial dividend that proportionally equals the preferred shareholders' dividend for the current year.

Stock dividends and **stock splits** do not increase net assets. They also do not change the proportionate interests of shareholders. The purpose of a **stock dividend** is to provide the shareholders with additional evidence of their interests in the retained earnings of the business without distribution of cash or other assets. The purpose of a **stock split** is to materially reduce the market price per share by increasing the number of shares outstanding, thereby obtaining wider distribution and improved marketability.

According to **ARB 43**, **Chapter 7B**, a stock dividend is recognized by capitalizing retained earnings in an amount equal to the fair value of the additional shares distributed. Capitalizing retained earnings results in a debit to retained earnings and credits to common stock and additional paid-in capital. A stock split is recognized by a decrease in the par or stated value of the common stock, resulting in a proportionate increase in the number of shares of stock outstanding. In some circumstances, legal requirements of the state in which an enterprise is incorporated may require the capitalization of retained earnings when a stock split occurs. Moreover, use of the term "dividend" may be required. Under these circumstances, the stock split preferably should be described as a **split-up effected in the form of a dividend**, and retained earnings should be capitalized in an amount equal to the legal requirement, usually the par or stated value of the additional shares distributed.

The enterprise's description of the intent of the distribution normally determines whether the distribution should be accounted for as a stock dividend or a stock split. However, an issuance of shares **less than 20% or 25%** of the previously outstanding shares usually should be recognized as a stock dividend. The SEC provides that an issuance of less than 25% should be treated as a stock dividend.

When an enterprise reacquires its previously issued and outstanding shares, these shares may be retired or held as **treasury stock**. However, the stock is not an asset of the corporation, and no dividends are paid on it. To record the retirement of shares, the common stock and additional paid-in capital accounts that were credited when the stock was originally issued are debited. An excess of the amounts debited over the purchase cost is credited to additional paid-in capital arising from treasury stock transactions. An excess of the purchase cost over the amounts debited is recorded first as a debit to any additional paid-in capital arising from previous treasury stock transactions, with any remainder recorded as a debit to retained earnings.

The most common method to record shares held as treasury stock is the **cost method**. The reacquired shares are recorded at their acquisition cost as an offset to the sum of capital stock, capital surplus (additional paid-in capital), and retained earnings **(APB 6)**. When the stock is subsequently reissued for an amount greater than its acquisition cost, the excess is credited to additional paid-in capital from treasury stock transactions. If stock is subsequently reissued for an amount less than its acquisition cost, the difference is recorded first as a debit to any additional paid-in capital arising from treasury stock transactions, with any remainder debited to retained earnings.

An alternative method of accounting for shares held as treasury stock is the **par-value method.** It accounts for a treasury stock transaction as a constructive retirement. In accordance with this method, the reacquired shares first are recorded at par value as an offset to the contributed capital account representing issued stock of the same type. The additional paid-in capital and retained earnings accounts are then treated as if the reacquired shares were retired. When the treasury shares are subsequently reissued, the treasury stock account is eliminated (credited), with any excess of the reissuance price over the par value recorded as a credit to additional paid-in capital in excess of par.

In general, **SFAS 116**, *Accounting for Contributions Received and Contributions Made*, requires that contributions received be recognized as revenues or gains in the period of receipt. They should be measured at fair value. However, SFAS 116 does not apply to tax exemptions, abatements, or incentives, or to transfers of assets from a government to a business enterprise. Hence, a credit to donated capital may be allowed in these cases. **APB 9**, *Reporting the Results of Operations*, states that "adjustments or charges or credits resulting from transactions in the company's own capital stock" are excluded from the determination of net income or the results of operations. Thus, the receipt of a contribution of a company's own stock is recorded at fair value as increases in both contributed capital and treasury stock. Because these accounts offset, the transaction has no net effect on equity.

Under **ARB 43, Chapter 7A**, a **quasi-reorganization** is undertaken to reduce a deficit in retained earnings to zero. The purpose is to permit the corporation to pay dividends in the near future. This type of reorganization eliminates the accumulated deficit at a lower cost and with less difficulty than a legal reorganization.

When a corporation issues **stock rights and warrants** for no consideration, it makes a memorandum entry. When consideration is received, the issuance is credited to additional paid-in capital – rights and warrants. When securities are issued with **detachable warrants**, the proceeds are allocated between the securities and warrants based on their relative fair values at issuance. When rights and warrants are exercised and stock is issued, capital stock and additional paid-in capital are credited for the proceeds and any amount previously credited to additional paid-in capital – rights and warrants.

QUESTIONS

15.1 General

1. Which of the following is the primary element that distinguishes accounting for corporations from accounting for other legal forms of business organization (such as partnerships)?

A. The entity theory relates primarily to the other forms of business organization.

B. The corporation draws a sharper distinction in accounting for sources of capital.

C. In a corporation, retained earnings may be reduced only by the declaration of dividends.

D. Generally accepted accounting principles apply to corporations but have relatively little applicability to other forms of business organization.

Answer (B) is correct. *(CPA, adapted)*

REQUIRED: The primary distinguishing feature of accounting for corporations.

DISCUSSION: The three primary forms of business organization are the corporation, the partnership, and the proprietorship. Of the three, only the corporation sharply differentiates between contributed equity and equity earned and retained in the business. Contributed capital is reflected in the various capital stock and additional paid-in capital (additional contributed capital) accounts. Earned capital is reflected in the retained earnings accounts.

Answer (A) is incorrect because the entity theory relates primarily to the corporation. It achieves a greater degree of separation from its owners than any other form of business enterprise. Answer (C) is incorrect because retained earnings may be reduced by numerous transactions, including a net operating loss. Answer (D) is incorrect because GAAP apply to all forms of business organization.

2. The issuance of shares of preferred stock to shareholders

A. Increases preferred stock outstanding.

B. Has no effect on preferred stock outstanding.

C. Increases preferred stock authorized.

D. Decreases preferred stock authorized.

Answer (A) is correct. *(CPA, adapted)*

REQUIRED: The effect of the issuance of shares of preferred stock to shareholders.

DISCUSSION: The charter (articles of incorporation) filed with the secretary of state of the state of incorporation indicates the classes of stock that may be issued and their authorized amounts in terms of shares and/or total dollar value. When authorized shares are issued, the effect is to increase the amount of that class of stock outstanding.

Answer (B) is incorrect because the effect of the issuance of shares is to increase the stock outstanding. Answer (C) is incorrect because the issuance of shares has no effect on the preferred stock authorized. Answer (D) is incorrect because the issuance of shares has no effect on the preferred stock authorized.

3. Bier Corp. issued 400,000 shares of common stock when it began operations in year 1 and issued an additional 200,000 shares in year 2. Bier also issued preferred stock convertible to 200,000 shares of common stock. In year 3, Bier purchased 150,000 shares of its common stock and held it in treasury. At year 3, how many shares of Bier's common stock were outstanding?

A. 800,000

B. 650,000

C. 600,000

D. 450,000

Answer (D) is correct. *(CPA, adapted)*

REQUIRED: The number of shares of outstanding common stock.

DISCUSSION: Bier issued 400,000 shares of common stock in year 1 and 200,000 shares in year 2. The purchase of 150,000 shares of treasury stock decreased the number of shares of common stock outstanding in year 3 to 450,000 (400,000 + 200,000 – 150,000). The convertible preferred stock is not considered common stock.

Answer (A) is incorrect because 800,000 includes the convertible preferred stock and the treasury stock. Answer (B) is incorrect because 650,000 includes the convertible preferred stock. Answer (C) is incorrect because 600,000 includes the treasury stock.

4. The preemptive right of shareholders is the right to

A. Share equally in dividend distributions.

B. Purchase shares of stock on a pro rata basis when new issues are offered for sale.

C. Share in the distribution of assets on liquidation of the corporation.

D. Participate in the management of the corporation.

Answer (B) is correct. *(Publisher)*

REQUIRED: The definition of the preemptive right of shareholders.

DISCUSSION: The preemptive right refers to each shareholder's right to maintain proportionate ownership in the corporation if additional shares are offered for sale.

Answer (A) is incorrect because it is a shareholder right distinct from the preemptive right. Shareholders participate in management of the corporation by electing a board of directors and by voting on referendums presented by management and the directors. Answer (C) is incorrect because it is a shareholder right distinct from the preemptive right. Shareholders participate in management of the corporation by electing a board of directors and by voting on referendums presented by management and the directors. Answer (D) is incorrect because it is a shareholder right distinct from the preemptive right. Shareholders participate in management of the corporation by electing a board of directors and by voting on referendums presented by management and the directors.

5. On December 1, 2003, Circle Corp. received a contribution of 4,000 shares of its $10 par value common stock from a shareholder. On that date, the stock's market value was $70 per share. The stock was originally issued for $50 per share. By what amount does this contribution cause total equity to decrease?

A. $280,000

B. $200,000

C. $40,000

D. $0

Answer (D) is correct. *(CPA, adapted)*

REQUIRED: The decrease in equity from receipt of a contribution of the company's own stock.

DISCUSSION: Contributions received ordinarily are recorded as revenues or gains in the period received (SFAS 116). However, APB 9, *Reporting the Results of Operations*, states that "adjustments or charges or credits resulting from transactions in the company's own capital stock" are excluded from the determination of net income or the results of operations. Thus, the receipt of a contribution of a company's own stock is recorded at fair value as increases in both contributed capital and treasury stock. Because these accounts offset, the net effect on equity is $0.

Answer (A) is incorrect because $280,000 records an effect equal to the current market price. Answer (B) is incorrect because $200,000 records an effect equal to the original issuance price. Answer (C) is incorrect because $40,000 records an effect equal to the par value.

6. East Co. issued 2,000 shares of its $5 par common stock to Krannik as compensation for 1,000 hours of legal services performed. Krannik usually bills $200 per hour for legal services. On the date of issuance, the stock was trading on a public exchange at $160 per share. By what amount should the additional paid-in capital account increase?

A. $320,000

B. $310,000

C. $200,000

D. $190,000

Answer (B) is correct. *(CPA, adapted)*

REQUIRED: The increase in additional paid-in capital.

DISCUSSION: When stock is issued for property or services, the transaction is recorded at the fair value of the stock or of the property or services received. In this case, the value of the stock is used because it is more objective. The $320,000 (2,000 × $160) should be allocated as follows: $10,000 ($5 par × 2,000 shares) to common stock and $310,000 to additional paid-in capital.

Answer (A) is incorrect because $10,000 should be allocated to common stock. Answer (C) is incorrect because the value of the stock should be used to record the transaction. Answer (D) is incorrect because the value of the stock should be used to record the transaction.

Questions 7 and 8 are based on the following information. Anand Co. reported the following in its statement of equity on January 1, 2003:

Common stock, $5 par value, authorized 200,000 shares, issued 100,000 shares	$ 500,000
Additional paid-in capital	1,500,000
Retained earnings	516,000
	$2,516,000
Minus treasury stock, at cost, 5,000 shares	40,000
Total equity	$2,476,000

The following events occurred in 2003:

May 1	-- 1,000 shares of treasury stock were sold for $10,000.
July 9	-- 10,000 shares of previously unissued common stock sold for $12 per share
October 1	-- The distribution of a 2-for-1 stock split resulted in the common stock's per-share par value being halved.

Anand accounts for treasury stock under the cost method. Laws in the state of Anand's incorporation protect shares held in treasury from dilution when stock dividends or stock splits are declared.

7. In Anand's December 31, 2003 statement of equity, the par value of the issued common stock should be

A. $550,000

B. $530,000

C. $275,000

D. $265,000

Answer (A) is correct. *(CPA, adapted)*

REQUIRED: The par value of the issued common stock.

DISCUSSION: At the beginning of the year, 100,000 shares with a par value of $500,000 had been issued. These shares included the treasury stock (issued but not outstanding) accounted for at cost. Under the cost method, the par value recorded in the common stock account is unaffected by purchases and sales of treasury stock. On July 9, 10,000 shares of previously unissued common stock were sold. This transaction increased the aggregate par value to $550,000 (110,000 shares issued × $5). The 2-for-1 stock split reduced the par value per share by 50% but did not affect the aggregate par value of the issued stock. Thus, state law presumably did not require capitalization of retained earnings as a result of the stock split.

Answer (B) is incorrect because $530,000 is the par value of the issued and outstanding shares. Answer (C) is incorrect because $275,000 is half the par value of the issued stock. Answer (D) is incorrect because $265,000 is half the par value of the issued and outstanding stock.

8. The number of outstanding common shares at December 31, 2003 should be

A. 222,000

B. 220,000

C. 212,000

D. 210,000

Answer (C) is correct. *(CPA, adapted)*

REQUIRED: The number of outstanding shares.

DISCUSSION: On January 1, 2003, 95,000 shares (100,000 issued – 5,000 treasury shares) were outstanding. The treasury stock sale and the issuance of previously unissued shares increased that amount to 106,000 shares (95,000 + 1,000 + 10,000). The stock split doubled the shares outstanding to 212,000 (2 × 106,000).

Answer (A) is incorrect because 222,000 assumes 100,000 shares were outstanding on January 1. Answer (B) is incorrect because 220,000 assumes 100,000 shares were outstanding on January 1 but omits the treasury stock sale. Answer (D) is incorrect because 210,000 omits the treasury stock sale.

9. Ricky Corp. had 700,000 shares of common stock authorized and 300,000 shares outstanding at December 31, year 1. The following events occurred during year 2:

January 31	Declared 10% stock dividend
June 30	Purchased 100,000 shares
August 1	Reissued 50,000 shares
November 30	Declared 2-for-1 stock split

At December 31, year 2, how many shares of common stock did Ricky have outstanding?

A. 560,000

B. 600,000

C. 630,000

D. 660,000

Answer (A) is correct. *(CPA, adapted)*

REQUIRED: The number of outstanding shares of common stock.

DISCUSSION: Ricky had 300,000 shares outstanding at the beginning of the year. The 10% stock dividend (300,000 shares × 10% = 30,000) increased the shares outstanding to 330,000. The purchase reduced shares outstanding to 230,000. The reissuance increased these shares to 280,000. The 2-for-1 stock split increased shares outstanding to 560,000 (2 × 280,000).

Answer (B) is incorrect because 600,000 ignores all transactions except the stock split. Answer (C) is incorrect because 630,000 ignores the purchase and reissuance and assumes that the shares of the stock dividend were not split. Answer (D) is incorrect because 660,000 excludes the treasury stock purchase and the reissuance of 50,000 shares.

10. The December 31, 2002 condensed balance sheet of Moore and Daughter, a partnership, follows:

Current assets	$280,000
Equipment (net)	260,000
	$540,000
Liabilities	$140,000
Moore and Daughter, capital	400,000
	$540,000

Fair values at December 31, 2002 are as follows:

Current assets	$320,000
Equipment	420,000
Liabilities	140,000

On January 2, 2003, Moore and Daughter was incorporated, with 10,000 shares of $10 par value common stock issued. How much should be credited to additional contributed capital?

A. $640,000

B. $600,000

C. $500,000

D. $400,000

Answer (C) is correct. *(CPA, adapted)*

REQUIRED: The amount credited to additional contributed capital upon incorporation.

DISCUSSION: When assets of a partnership are contributed to a corporation in exchange for par value common stock, the contributed capital account should be credited for the fair value of the net assets. The fair value of the net assets equals $600,000 ($320,000 + $420,000 – $140,000). Of this amount, $100,000 (10,000 shares × $10 par value) should be credited to the capital stock account, with the remaining $500,000 credited to additional contributed capital.

Answer (A) is incorrect because $640,000 equals the total fair value of the assets minus the $100,000 allocated to capital stock. Answer (B) is incorrect because $600,000 is the fair value of the net assets. Answer (D) is incorrect because $400,000 is the partnership capital at its carrying amount.

11. On February 1, Lopez Corporation issued 1,000 shares of its $10 par common and 2,000 shares of its $10 par convertible preferred stock for a lump sum of $40,000. At this date, Lopez's common stock was selling for $18 per share and the convertible preferred stock for $13.50 per share. The amount of proceeds allocated to Lopez's preferred stock should be

A. $22,000

B. $24,000

C. $27,000

D. $30,000

Answer (B) is correct. *(CPA, adapted)*

REQUIRED: The proceeds to be allocated to preferred stock in a lump-sum issuance.

DISCUSSION: Given that the 1,000 shares of common stock and 2,000 shares of preferred stock were issued for a lump sum of $40,000, the proceeds should be allocated based on the relative fair values of the securities issued. The fair value of the common stock is $18,000 (1,000 shares × $18). The fair value of the preferred stock is $27,000 (2,000 shares × $13.50). Because 60% [$27,000 ÷ ($27,000 + $18,000)] of the total fair value is attributable to the preferred stock, $24,000 (60% × $40,000) of the proceeds should be allocated to this stock.

Answer (A) is incorrect because $22,000 equals the lump sum received minus the fair value of the common stock. Answer (C) is incorrect because $27,000 is the fair value of the preferred stock. Answer (D) is incorrect because $30,000 is the sum of the par values of the stock issued.

12. On September 1, Jordan Corp., a closely held corporation, issued 6% bonds with a maturity value of $120,000, together with 2,000 shares of its $5 par value common stock, for a combined cash amount of $220,000. The market value of Jordan's stock cannot be ascertained. If the bonds were issued separately, they would have sold for $80,000 on an 8% yield-to-maturity basis. What amount should Jordan record for additional paid-in capital on the issuance of the stock?

A. $150,000

B. $130,000

C. $110,000

D. $90,000

Answer (B) is correct. *(CPA, adapted)*

REQUIRED: The amount allocated to additional paid-in capital.

DISCUSSION: The proceeds of the combined issuance of different classes of securities generally should be allocated based on the relative fair values of the securities. However, if the fair value of only one class of security is known, the proceeds should be allocated first to that class of security. The remainder is allocated to the other class. The fair value of the stock is not known, so the bonds should be recorded at their fair value ($80,000), with the remainder of the proceeds ($220,000 – $80,000 = $140,000) credited to common stock at par value ($5 × 2,000 shares = $10,000) and additional paid-in capital ($140,000 – $10,000 par = $130,000).

Answer (A) is incorrect because $150,000 results from adding the par value to the total allocable to the stock. Answer (C) is incorrect because $110,000 is based on an allocation of $120,000 to the stock. Answer (D) is incorrect because $90,000 is based on an allocation of $120,000 (maturity value) to the bonds.

13. When collectibility is reasonably assured, the excess of the subscription price over the stated value of no-par common stock subscribed should be recorded as

A. No-par common stock.

B. Additional paid-in capital when the subscription is recorded.

C. Additional paid-in capital when the subscription is collected.

D. Additional paid-in capital when the common stock is issued.

Answer (B) is correct. *(CPA, adapted)*

REQUIRED: The recording of the excess of the subscription price over the stated value of no-par common stock subscribed.

DISCUSSION: The accounting for subscriptions of no-par stock with a stated value is the same as for par value stock. When stock is subscribed, the corporation recognizes an obligation to issue stock, and the subscriber undertakes the legal obligation to pay for the shares subscribed. If collectibility of the subscription price is reasonably assured on the date the subscription is received, the issuing corporation should recognize the cash collected and a subscription receivable for the remainder. In addition, the common stock subscribed account should be credited for the stated value of the shares subscribed, with the excess of the subscription price over the stated value recognized as additional paid-in capital.

Answer (A) is incorrect because the credit is to additional paid-in capital. Answer (C) is incorrect because additional paid-in capital is credited when the subscription is recorded. Answer (D) is incorrect because additional paid-in capital is credited when the subscription is recorded.

14. On December 1, 2003, shares of authorized common stock were issued on a subscription basis at a price in excess of par value. A total of 20% of the subscription price of each share was collected as a down payment on December 1, 2003, with the remaining 80% of the subscription price of each share due in 2004. Collectibility was reasonably assured. At December 31, 2003, the equity section of the balance sheet should report additional paid-in capital for the excess of the subscription price over the par value of the shares of common stock subscribed and

A. Common stock issued for 20% of the par value of the shares of common stock subscribed.

B. Common stock issued for the par value of the shares of common stock subscribed.

C. Common stock subscribed for 80% of the par value of the shares of common stock subscribed.

D. Common stock subscribed for the par value of the shares of common stock subscribed.

Answer (D) is correct. *(CPA, adapted)*

REQUIRED: The proper recording of subscribed stock in the equity section.

DISCUSSION: When stock is subscribed, the corporation recognizes an obligation to issue stock, and the subscriber undertakes the legal obligation to pay for the shares subscribed. If collectibility of the subscription price is reasonably assured on the date the subscription is received, the issuing corporation should recognize the cash collected and a subscription receivable for the remainder. In addition, the common stock subscribed account should be credited for the par value of the shares subscribed, with the excess of the subscription price over the par value recognized as additional paid-in capital.

Answer (A) is incorrect because the equity section of the balance sheet should report the common stock subscribed account for the par value of the shares subscribed and additional paid-in capital for the excess of the subscription price over the par value. Answer (B) is incorrect because the equity section of the balance sheet should report the common stock subscribed account for the par value of the shares subscribed and additional paid-in capital for the excess of the subscription price over the par value. Answer (C) is incorrect because the equity section of the balance sheet should report the common stock subscribed account for the par value of the shares subscribed and additional paid-in capital for the excess of the subscription price over the par value.

15. What is the entry to record issuance of stock after all monies have been received from a stock subscription, assuming an entry to record common stock authorized was made at the time of incorporation?

A. Common stock subscribed
    Common stock

B. Common stock subscribed
    Common stock
    Paid-in capital in excess of par

C. Common stock subscribed
    Unissued common stock

D. Stock subscriptions receivable
    Common stock subscribed
    Paid-in capital in excess of par

Answer (C) is correct. *(Publisher)*

REQUIRED: The entry to record issuance of stock after all monies have been received from a stock subscription.

DISCUSSION: If unissued stock was debited (at par value) and authorized stock was credited (also at par) at the time of incorporation, no additional entry to the latter account is needed. Accordingly, common stock subscribed should be debited and unissued common stock should be credited when full payment for the shares has been received. The difference between the authorized stock and unissued stock accounts is the amount of issued stock.

Answer (A) is incorrect because it is the entry to record the issuance of fully paid, subscribed common stock if the authorized stock and unissued stock accounts are not used. Answer (B) is incorrect because paid-in capital in excess of par value is recorded at the time of the subscription rather than the time of issuance. Answer (D) is incorrect because it is the entry to record a stock subscription when no cash is received.

16. If a subscriber to common stock defaults on the subscription and amounts already paid are forfeited, what is the journal entry in the books of the subscribed corporation?

A. Common stock subscribed
Paid-in capital in excess of par value
    Stock subscriptions receivable
    Cash

B. Common stock subscribed
Paid-in capital in excess of par value
    Stock subscriptions receivable
    Paid-in capital from stock subscription default

C. Paid-in capital in excess of par value
Common stock
    Common stock subscribed
    Cash

D. Subscriptions receivable
    Common stock subscribed
    Paid-in capital in excess of par

Answer (B) is correct. *(Publisher)*

REQUIRED: The journal entry to record a default on a common stock subscription when the payments received are forfeited.

DISCUSSION: When a subscriber defaults, the entry to record the subscription to common stock must be reversed. To the extent that payment has been received and is forfeited, paid-in capital from stock subscription default is credited for the amount forfeited.

Answer (A) is incorrect because it is the entry for a common stock subscription default when amounts previously paid in are refunded to the subscriber. Answer (C) is incorrect because common stock cannot be debited if no stock has been issued by and returned to the corporation. Answer (D) is incorrect because it is the entry to record the stock subscription when no cash is received.

17. In year 1, Veras Corp. reported $3,500,000 of appropriated retained earnings for the construction of a new office building, which was completed in year 2 at a total cost of $3,000,000. In year 2, Veras appropriated $2,400,000 of retained earnings for the construction of a new plant. Also, $4,000,000 of cash was restricted for the retirement of bonds due in year 3. In its year 2 balance sheet, Veras should report what amount of appropriated retained earnings?

A. $2,400,000

B. $2,900,000

C. $5,900,000

D. $6,400,000

Answer (A) is correct. *(CPA, adapted)*

REQUIRED: The amount of appropriated retained earnings reported.

DISCUSSION: Appropriating retained earnings is a formal way of marking a portion of retained earnings for other uses. A journal entry is used to reclassify retained earnings to appropriated retained earnings. When the appropriation is no longer necessary, the entry is reversed. The original appropriation of $3,500,000 in year 1 would have been reversed for that amount in year 2. The cash restriction is not included in appropriated retained earnings. If the amount is material, the restriction will require separate reporting of the cash item in the balance sheet, footnote disclosure, and reclassification as noncurrent. Thus, appropriated retained earnings in year 2 should be reported at $2,400,000.

Answer (B) is incorrect because $2,900,000 includes the previous year's excess of appropriated retained earnings over the actual cost. Answer (C) is incorrect because $5,900,000 includes the cash restriction and subtracts the previous year's excess of appropriated retained earnings over the actual cost. Answer (D) is incorrect because $6,400,000 includes the $4,000,000 restriction on cash for bond retirement.

18. Of the 125,000 shares of common stock issued by Maddux Corp., 25,000 shares were held as treasury stock at December 31, 2002. During 2003, transactions involving Maddux's common stock were as follows:

January 1 through October 31 -- 13,000 treasury shares were distributed to officers as part of a stock compensation plan.

November 1 -- A 3-for-1 stock split took effect.

December 1 -- Maddux purchased 5,000 of its own shares to discourage an unfriendly takeover. These shares were not retired.

At December 31, 2003, how many of Maddux's common stock were issued and outstanding?

	Shares Issued	Shares Outstanding
A.	375,000	334,000
B.	375,000	324,000
C.	334,000	334,000
D.	324,000	324,000

Answer (A) is correct. *(CPA, adapted)*

REQUIRED: The number of shares issued and outstanding.

DISCUSSION: Given that 125,000 shares have been issued and that the stock has been split 3-for-1, the shares issued at year-end equal 375,000 (3 × 125,000). At the beginning of the year, 100,000 shares were outstanding (125,000 issued – 25,000 treasury shares). After 13,000 treasury shares were distributed, 113,000 shares were outstanding, an amount that increased to 339,000 (3 × 113,000) after the stock split. The purchase on December 1 reduced the shares outstanding to 334,000 (339,000 – 5,000).

Answer (B) is incorrect because 324,000 shares would be outstanding if the 5,000-share purchase had been made before the split. Answer (C) is incorrect because shares issued exceed shares outstanding. Answer (D) is incorrect because shares issued exceed shares outstanding.

19. Galarraga Co. completed a number of capital transactions during the fiscal year ended September 30 as follows:

- An issue of 8% debentures was converted into common stock.
- An issue of $2.50 preferred stock was called and retired.
- A 10% common stock dividend was distributed on November 30.
- Warrants for 200,000 shares of common stock were exercised on September 20.

For the year-end financial statements to be sufficiently informative, Galarraga's most satisfactory method of presenting the effects of these events is

A. A formal retained earnings statement and general description in the notes to the financial statements.

B. A formal statement of changes in equity that discloses changes in the various equity accounts.

C. A detailed inclusion of each event or transaction in the statement of cash flows.

D. Comparative statements of income, financial position, and retained earnings for this year and last year.

Answer (B) is correct. *(CMA, adapted)*

REQUIRED: The most satisfactory method of presenting the effects of the listed capital transactions.

DISCUSSION: When both financial position and results of operations are presented, APB 12 requires disclosure of changes in the accounts included in equity (in addition to retained earnings). It also requires disclosure of the changes in the number of shares of equity securities during at least the most recent annual fiscal period and any subsequent interim periods presented. The required disclosure may be made in the basic financial statements, in the notes, or in a formal statement of changes in equity (which is preferable).

Answer (A) is incorrect because a general description is inadequate. Answer (C) is incorrect because events or transactions not resulting in cash flows (e.g., conversion of debt to equity or a stock dividend) are not included in the statement of cash flows. Answer (D) is incorrect because presenting disclosures about changes in equity in a separate statement gives them greater prominence than if they were contained in the basic statements.

20. At the end of year 1, Peek Corp., a newly formed company, had the following stock issued and outstanding:

- Common stock, no par, $1 stated value, 10,000 shares originally issued for $15 per share
- Preferred stock, $10 par value, 3,000 shares originally issued for $25 per share

Peek's year 1 statement of equity should report

	Common Stock	Preferred Stock	Additional Paid-In Capital
A.	$150,000	$80,000	$30,000
B.	$150,000	$75,000	$75,000
C.	$10,000	$75,000	$75,000
D.	$10,000	$30,000	$30,000

Answer (D) is correct. *(CPA, adapted)*

REQUIRED: The amounts of common stock, preferred stock, and additional paid-in capital to be reported in the statement of equity.

DISCUSSION: The common stock was issued for a total of $150,000 (10,000 shares x $15). Of this amount, $10,000 (10,000 shares x $1 stated value) should be allocated to the common stock, with the remaining $140,000 ($150,000 – $10,000) credited to additional paid-in capital. The preferred stock was issued for $75,000 (3,000 shares x $25), of which $30,000 (3,000 shares x $10 par value) should be allocated to the preferred stock and $45,000 ($75,000 – $30,000) to additional paid-in capital. In the year 1 statement of equity, Peek therefore should report $10,000 in the common stock account, $30,000 in the preferred stock account, and $185,000 ($140,000 + $45,000) as additional paid-in capital.

Answer (A) is incorrect because the excess of the issue price of the common stock over its stated value is credited to additional paid-in capital, not common stock. Answer (B) is incorrect because the excess of the issue price of the common stock over its stated value is credited to additional paid-in capital, not common stock, and the excess of the issue price of the preferred stock over its par value is credited to additional paid-in capital, not preferred stock. Answer (C) is incorrect because the excess of the issue price of the preferred stock over its par value is credited to additional paid-in capital, not preferred stock.

21. During year 1, Andrew Co. issued 5,000 shares of $100 par convertible preferred stock for $110 per share. One share of preferred stock can be converted into three shares of Andrew's $25 par common stock at the option of the preferred shareholder. On December 31, year 2, when the market value of the common stock was $40 per share, all of the preferred stock was converted. What amount should Andrew credit to common stock and to additional paid-in capital as a result of the conversion?

	Common Stock	Additional Paid-In Capital
A.	$375,000	$175,000
B.	$375,000	$225,000
C.	$500,000	$50,000
D.	$600,000	$0

Answer (A) is correct. *(CPA, adapted)*

REQUIRED: The amounts credited to common stock and additional paid-in capital.

DISCUSSION: Andrew received $550,000 (5,000 x $110) for the preferred stock converted to common stock. The par value of the 15,000 shares (5,000 x 3) of common stock is $375,000 (15,000 x $25). The remaining $175,000 ($550,000 – $375,000) is credited to additional paid-in capital.

Answer (B) is incorrect because $175,000 is credited to additional paid-in capital ($550,000 – $375,000). Answer (C) is incorrect because $500,000 is the par value of the preferred stock, not the common stock. Answer (D) is incorrect because $600,000 equals the fair value of the common stock at the date of conversion.

22. Sanders Company effects self-insurance against loss from fire by appropriating an amount of retained earnings each year equal to the amount that would otherwise be paid out as fire insurance premiums. According to current accounting literature, the procedure used by Sanders is

A. Prohibited for external reporting purposes.

B. Acceptable provided that fire losses are not charged against the appropriation.

C. Acceptable provided that fire losses are charged against the appropriation.

D. Acceptable if the amount is shown outside the equity section of the balance sheet.

Answer (B) is correct. *(Publisher)*

REQUIRED: The true statement about an appropriation of retained earnings to disclose self-insurance against fire loss.

DISCUSSION: SFAS 5, *Accounting for Contingencies*, permits no accrual of an expense prior to the occurrence of the event for which an entity self-insures because the value of the property diminishes only if the event actually occurs. But an appropriation of retained earnings is acceptable to disclose the self-insurance policy if, when a fire loss occurs, the entry appropriating retained earnings is reversed, and the loss is charged against income of the period of loss and not against retained earnings.

Answer (A) is incorrect because an appropriation of retained earnings for self-insurance is permissible. Answer (C) is incorrect because fire losses may never be charged against the appropriation of retained earnings. Answer (D) is incorrect because the procedure is acceptable only if the appropriation is shown within the equity section of the balance sheet.

23. At December 31, 2002, Chipper Corporation has the following account balances:

Common stock ($10 par, 50,000 shares issued)	$500,000
8% preferred stock ($50 par, 10,000 shares issued)	500,000
Paid-in capital in excess of par on common stock	640,000
Paid-in capital in excess of par on preferred stock	20,000
Retained earnings	600,000

The preferred stock is cumulative, nonparticipating, and has a call price of $55 per share. Chipper's journal entry to record the redemption of all preferred stock on January 2, 2003 pursuant to the call provision is

A.

Preferred stock	$500,000	
Paid-in capital in excess of par: preferred	20,000	
Discount on preferred stock	30,000	
Cash		$550,000

B.

Preferred stock	$500,000	
Paid-in capital in excess of par: preferred	20,000	
Loss on redemption of preferred stock	30,000	
Cash		$550,000

C.

Preferred stock	$500,000	
Loss on redemption of preferred stock	50,000	
Retained earnings	300,000	
Cash		$550,000
Paid-in capital in excess of par: preferred		300,000

D.

Preferred stock	$500,000	
Paid-in capital in excess of par: preferred	20,000	
Retained earnings	30,000	
Cash		$550,000

Answer (D) is correct. *(CIA, adapted)*

REQUIRED: The journal entry to record the redemption of preferred stock pursuant to the call provision.

DISCUSSION: The exercise of the call provision resulted in the redemption of the 10,000 shares of preferred stock issued and outstanding at the call price of $550,000 (10,000 shares × $55 call price per share). To eliminate the carrying amount of the preferred stock and recognize the cash paid in this transaction, the required journal entry is to debit preferred stock for $500,000, debit paid-in capital in excess of par: preferred for $20,000, and credit cash for $550,000. The difference of $30,000 ($550,000 cash – $520,000 carrying amount of the preferred stock) is charged to retained earnings. No loss is reported because GAAP do not permit the recognition of a gain or loss on transactions involving a company's own stock.

Answer (A) is incorrect because the $30,000 excess of cash paid over the carrying amount of the redeemed stock should be debited to retained earnings. Answer (B) is incorrect because the $30,000 excess of cash paid over the carrying amount of the redeemed stock should be debited to retained earnings. Answer (C) is incorrect because the $30,000 excess of cash paid over the carrying amount of the redeemed stock should be debited to retained earnings. Also, paid-in capital in excess of par: preferred should be debited for $20,000.

15.2 Cash and Property Dividends

24. On January 15, 2003, Rico Co. declared its annual cash dividend on common stock for the year ended January 31, 2003. The dividend was paid on February 9, 2003, to shareholders of record as of January 28, 2003. On what date should Rico decrease retained earnings by the amount of the dividend?

A. January 15, 2003.

B. January 31, 2003.

C. January 28, 2003.

D. February 9, 2003.

Answer (A) is correct. *(CPA, adapted)*

REQUIRED: The date to decrease retained earnings by the amount of the dividend.

DISCUSSION: Unlike stock dividends, cash dividends cannot be rescinded. A liability to the shareholders is created because the dividends must be paid once they are declared. At the declaration date, retained earnings must be debited, resulting in a decrease.

Retained earnings	$XXX	
Dividends payable		$XXX

The declaration date was January 15.

25. Glavine Corp., a company with a fiscal year-end on October 31, had sufficient retained earnings as a basis for dividends but was temporarily short of cash. Glavine declared a dividend of $100,000 on February 1, 2003 and issued promissory notes to its shareholders in lieu of cash. The notes, which were dated February 1, 2003, had a maturity date of January 31, 2004 and a 10% interest rate. How should Glavine account for the scrip dividend and related interest?

A. Debit retained earnings for $110,000 on February 1, 2003.

B. Debit retained earnings for $110,000 on January 31, 2004.

C. Debit retained earnings for $100,000 on February 1, 2003 and debit interest expense for $10,000 on January 31, 2004.

D. Debit retained earnings for $100,000 on February 1, 2003 and debit interest expense for $7,500 on October 31, 2003.

Answer (D) is correct. *(CPA, adapted)*

REQUIRED: The accounting for a scrip dividend and its related interest.

DISCUSSION: When a scrip dividend is declared, retained earnings should be debited and scrip dividends (or notes) payable should be credited for the amount of the dividend ($100,000) excluding interest. Interest accrued on the scrip dividend is recorded as a debit to interest expense up to the balance sheet date with a corresponding credit for interest payable. Thus, interest expense will be debited and interest payable credited for $7,500 [(9 ÷ 12) × $100,000 × 10%] on 10/31/03.

Answer (A) is incorrect because interest expense is recognized on the balance sheet date and on the date of payment, not on the date of declaration. Answer (B) is incorrect because $7,500 of the $10,000 interest expense should be recognized at year-end, and retained earnings should be debited on the date of declaration. Answer (C) is incorrect because $7,500 of the $10,000 interest expense should be recognized at year-end.

26. Weiss Company declared a cash dividend on its common stock on December 15, year 1, payable on January 12, year 2. How would this dividend affect equity on the following dates?

	December 15, Year 1	December 31, Year 1	January 12, Year 2
A.	Decrease	No effect	Decrease
B.	Decrease	No effect	No effect
C.	No effect	Decrease	No effect
D.	No effect	No effect	Decrease

Answer (B) is correct. *(CPA, adapted)*

REQUIRED: The effect on retained earnings of a cash dividend.

DISCUSSION: When cash dividends are declared, a liability to the shareholders is created because the dividends must be paid once they are declared. At the declaration date, retained earnings must be debited, resulting in a decrease in retained earnings. The effect is to decrease total equity (assets – liabilities) because liabilities are increased with no corresponding increase in assets. At the balance sheet date, no entry is made and there is no effect on equity. When the cash dividends are subsequently paid, the dividends payable account is debited and a cash account credited. Thus, at the payment date, equity is also not affected.

Answer (A) is incorrect because payment has no effect on equity. Answer (C) is incorrect because declaration decreases equity, but at year-end has no effect. Answer (D) is incorrect because declaration decreases equity, but payment has no effect.

27. Lunar Corp.'s outstanding capital stock at September 15 of the current year consisted of the following:

- 30,000 shares of 5% cumulative preferred stock, par value $10 per share, fully participating as to dividends. No dividends were in arrears.
- 200,000 shares of common stock, par value $1 per share.

On September 15 of the current year, Lunar declared dividends of $100,000. What was the amount of dividends payable to Lunar's common shareholders?

A. $10,000

B. $34,000

C. $40,000

D. $60,000

Answer (C) is correct. *(CPA, adapted)*

REQUIRED: The amount of dividends payable to common shareholders.

DISCUSSION: The stated rate of dividends must be paid to preferred shareholders before any amount is paid to common shareholders. Because no dividends are in arrears, this amount is $15,000 (5% × $10 par × 30,000 shares). The preferred stock is also fully participating. The preferred will participate equally in the cash dividend after a 5% return is paid on the common. The basic return to common shareholders is $10,000 (5% × 200,000 shares × $1 par). The total of the basic distributions to the shareholders is $25,000 ($15,000 + $10,000). The remaining $75,000 ($100,000 – $25,000) of the total cash dividend will be shared by all shareholders in proportion to the par values of the shares outstanding.

The aggregate par value of the preferred is $300,000 ($10 par × 30,000 shares). The aggregate par value of the common is $200,000 ($1 par × 200,000 shares). The distribution will therefore be in the ratio of 3:2, and $45,000 ($75,000 × 60%) is the participating share of the preferred shareholders. The balance of $30,000 ($75,000 – $45,000) will be paid to the common shareholders. The total amount of dividends payable on the common stock is $40,000 ($10,000 + $30,000).

Answer (A) is incorrect because $10,000 is the basic return to common shareholders. Answer (B) is incorrect because $34,000 results from assuming that no basic return is paid to the common shareholders. Answer (D) is incorrect because $60,000 is the amount paid to the preferred shareholders.

28. On June 1, Ligtenberg Company's board of directors declared a cash dividend of $1.00 per share on the 50,000 shares of common stock outstanding. The company also has 5,000 shares of treasury stock. Shareholders of record on June 15 are eligible for the dividend, which is to be paid on July 1. On June 1, the company should

A. Make no accounting entry.

B. Debit retained earnings for $50,000.

C. Debit retained earnings for $55,000.

D. Debit retained earnings for $50,000 and paid-in capital for $5,000.

Answer (B) is correct. *(CMA, adapted)*

REQUIRED: The proper journal entry on the declaration date of a dividend.

DISCUSSION: Dividends are recorded on their declaration date by a debit to retained earnings and a credit to dividends payable. The dividend is the amount payable to all shares outstanding. Treasury stock is not eligible for dividends because it is not outstanding. Thus, the June 1 entry is to debit retained earnings and credit dividends payable for $50,000 (50,000 × $1).

Answer (A) is incorrect because a liability should be recorded. Answer (C) is incorrect because the treasury stock is not eligible for a dividend. Answer (D) is incorrect because paid-in capital is not affected by the dividend declaration.

29. At December 31, 2002 and 2003, Perigel Co. had 3,000 shares of $100 par, 5% cumulative preferred stock outstanding. No dividends were in arrears as of December 31, 2001. Perigel did not declare a dividend during 2002. During 2003, Perigel paid a cash dividend of $10,000 on its preferred stock. Perigel should report dividends in arrears in its 2003 financial statements as a(n)

A. Accrued liability of $15,000.

B. Disclosure of $15,000.

C. Accrued liability of $20,000.

D. Disclosure of $20,000.

Answer (D) is correct. *(CPA, adapted)*

REQUIRED: The amount and means of reporting preferred dividends in arrears.

DISCUSSION: Dividends in arrears on preferred stock are not an obligation of the company and are not recognized in the financial statements. However, the aggregate and per-share amounts of arrearages in cumulative preferred dividends should be disclosed on the face of the balance sheet or in the notes (SFAS 129). The aggregate amount in arrears is $20,000 [(2 years × 5% × $100 par × 3,000 shares) – $10,000 paid in 2003].

Answer (A) is incorrect because dividends in arrears do not meet recognition criteria for a liability. Answer (B) is incorrect because $15,000 is the arrearage for 1 year. Answer (C) is incorrect because dividends in arrears do not meet recognition criteria for a liability.

Questions 30 and 31 are based on the following information. Millwood, Inc. was organized on September 2 with the capital structure shown. Millwood's net income for the first year ending August 31 was $450,000, but no dividends were declared.

10% cumulative preferred stock, par value $100 and liquidation value $105; authorized, issued, and outstanding 1,000 shares	$100,000
Common stock, par value $25; authorized 100,000 shares; issued and outstanding 10,000 shares	$250,000

30. How much was Millwood's carrying amount per preferred share at August 31?

A. $100

B. $105

C. $110

D. $115

Answer (D) is correct. *(CPA, adapted)*

REQUIRED: The carrying amount of a share of preferred stock when dividends are in arrears.

DISCUSSION: The carrying amount per share of cumulative preferred stock is its liquidation value plus any dividends in arrears. Thus, Millwood's carrying amount per share of preferred stock is the $105 liquidation value plus $10 ($100 × 10%) of dividends in arrears, or $115.

Answer (A) is incorrect because $100 is the par value of the preferred stock without the recognition of the liquidation value and the dividends in arrears. Answer (B) is incorrect because $105 is the liquidation value without recognition of the dividends in arrears. Answer (C) is incorrect because $110 is the par value of the stock, plus the dividends in arrears.

31. How much was Millwood's carrying amount per common share at August 31?

A. $45.00

B. $68.50

C. $69.50

D. $70.00

Answer (B) is correct. *(CPA, adapted)*

REQUIRED: The carrying amount per common share when cumulative preferred dividends are in arrears.

DISCUSSION: The preferred equity is the liquidation value of the preferred shares plus the preferred dividends in arrears. As calculated in the previous question, Millwood's carrying amount per preferred share is $115. The carrying amount of Millwood's 1,000 shares of cumulative preferred stock is therefore $115,000 ($115 × 1,000 shares). The total carrying amount of the company is $800,000 ($100,000 par value of preferred stock + $250,000 par value of common stock + retained earnings equal to $450,000 of net income). Hence, $685,000 ($800,000 – $115,000) is the carrying amount of the common stock, and carrying amount per common share is $68.50 ($685,000 ÷ 10,000 shares).

Answer (A) is incorrect because $45.00 results from net income this year. Answer (C) is incorrect because $69.50 results from reducing the value of the company by the liquidation value without the dividends in arrears. Answer (D) is incorrect because $70.00 results from reducing the value of the company by the par value of the preferred stock instead of the liquidation value plus the dividends in arrears.

32. A property dividend should be recorded in retained earnings at the property's

A. Market value at date of declaration.

B. Market value at date of issuance (payment).

C. Carrying amount at date of declaration.

D. Carrying amount at date of issuance.

Answer (A) is correct. *(CPA, adapted)*

REQUIRED: The method of accounting for the value of property dividend.

DISCUSSION: When a property dividend is declared, the property to be distributed should be restated at market value. Any gain or loss should be recognized. The declared dividend is then recorded as a debit to retained earnings and a credit to property dividends payable.

33. Instead of the usual cash dividend, Smalty Corp. declared and distributed a property dividend from its overstocked merchandise. The excess of the merchandise's carrying amount over its fair value should be

A. Ignored.

B. Reported as a separately disclosed reduction of retained earnings.

C. Reported as an extraordinary loss, net of income taxes.

D. Reported as a reduction in income before extraordinary items.

Answer (D) is correct. *(CPA, adapted)*

REQUIRED: The method of accounting for the excess of the carrying amount of a property dividend over its fair value.

DISCUSSION: APB 29, *Accounting for Nonmonetary Transactions*, requires that a nonreciprocal transfer of nonmonetary assets to owners other than one made "in a spinoff or other form of reorganization or liquidation or in a plan that is in substance the rescission of a prior business combination" be recorded at the fair value of the asset transferred on the declaration date. This property dividend qualifies as such a nonreciprocal transfer. Thus, a loss should be recognized on the disposition of the asset. This loss on merchandise is an operating item, not an extraordinary loss.

Answer (A) is incorrect because accounting for the property dividend at fair value gives rise to a loss that should be reported in the income statement. Answer (B) is incorrect because accounting for the property dividend at fair value gives rise to a loss that should be reported in the income statement. Answer (C) is incorrect because the loss does not meet the criteria of an extraordinary item.

34. On June 27, year 1, Marquis Co. distributed to its common shareholders 100,000 outstanding common shares of its investment in Chen Co., an unrelated party. The carrying amount on the books of Chen's \$1 par common stock was \$2 per share. Immediately after the distribution, the market price of Chen's stock was \$2.50 per share. In its income statement for the year ended June 30, year 1, what amount should Marquis report as gain before income taxes on disposal of the stock?

A. \$250,000

B. \$200,000

C. \$50,000

D. \$0

Answer (C) is correct. *(CPA, adapted)*

REQUIRED: The amount to be reported as gain before income taxes on disposal of stock.

DISCUSSION: When a property dividend is declared, the property to be distributed should be restated from carrying amount to fair value, with the resultant gain or loss recognized. Thus, Marquis should report a gain of \$50,000 [100,000 shares × (\$2.50 – \$2.00)].

Answer (A) is incorrect because \$250,000 is the fair value of the property dividend. Answer (B) is incorrect because \$200,000 is the book value of the property dividend. Answer (D) is incorrect because a \$50,000 gain should be recognized.

15.3 Stock Dividends and Stock Splits

35. When fractional share rights are issued as part of a stock dividend, the rights are often not exercised. The entry to record forfeiture of these rights is

A. Stock rights outstanding
    Paid-in capital from forfeiture of stock rights

B. Stock rights outstanding
    Common stock

C. Retained earnings
    Common stock

D. Stock rights outstanding
    Dividends payable

Answer (A) is correct. *(Publisher)*

REQUIRED: The journal entry to record forfeiture of stock rights.

DISCUSSION: When fractional share rights are issued as part of a stock dividend, retained earnings is debited and the stock rights outstanding account is credited. If the stock rights are forfeited, stock rights outstanding should be debited and paid-in capital from forfeiture of stock rights credited.

Answer (B) is incorrect because it is the entry to record the issuance of common stock for stock rights. Answer (C) is incorrect because it is the entry to record the issuance of common stock dividends at par. Answer (D) is incorrect because it is an entry to convert outstanding stock rights to a liability.

36. The following data are extracted from the equity section of the balance sheet of Ebbs Corporation:

	12/31/02	12/31/03
Common stock ($2 par value)	$100,000	$102,000
Paid-in capital in excess of par	50,000	58,000
Retained earnings	100,000	104,600

During 2003, the corporation declared and paid cash dividends of $15,000 and also declared and issued a stock dividend. There were no other changes in stock issued and outstanding during 2003. Net income for 2003 was

A. $4,600

B. $19,600

C. $21,600

D. $29,600

Answer (D) is correct. *(CIA, adapted)*

REQUIRED: The net income for 2003 after payment of cash and stock dividends.

DISCUSSION: The cash dividends reduced retained earnings by $15,000. The stock dividend reduced retained earnings by $10,000, as determined from the changes in the contributed capital accounts [($102,000 + $58,000) – ($100,000 – $50,000)]. Hence, as shown below, net income was $29,600.

Retained earnings

	Debit	Credit	
		$100,000	Beginning
Cash dividend	$15,000		
Stock dividend	10,000		
		29,600	Net income
		$104,600	Ending

Answer (A) is incorrect because $4,600 is the increase in retained earnings for the year. Answer (B) is incorrect because $19,600 results from not reducing retained earnings by the stock dividend. Answer (C) is incorrect because $21,600 results from reducing retained earnings for a $2,000 stock dividend.

37. The following information was abstracted from the accounts of the Moore Corp. at year-end:

Total income since incorporation	$840,000
Total cash dividends paid	260,000
Proceeds from sale of donated Travis Co. stock	90,000
Total value of stock dividends distributed	60,000
Excess of proceeds over cost of treasury stock sold	140,000

What should be the current balance of retained earnings?

A. $520,000

B. $580,000

C. $610,000

D. $670,000

Answer (A) is correct. *(CPA, adapted)*

REQUIRED: The current balance of retained earnings.

DISCUSSION: To compute the current balance, one must know which transactions affected retained earnings. Total income since incorporation ($840,000) increased retained earnings, whereas both the cash dividends and the stock dividends ($260,000 + $60,000) decreased it. Proceeds from the sale of the donated stock (given that it was not Moore Corp. stock) already would have been included in income to the extent of gain or loss. The excess of proceeds over the cost of treasury stock also does not affect retained earnings because the credit is to additional paid-in capital from treasury stock transactions. The current balance of retained earnings is therefore equal to $520,000 ($840,000 – $260,000 – $60,000).

Answer (B) is incorrect because $580,000 results from not reducing retained earnings by the value of stock dividends distributed. Answer (C) is incorrect because $610,000 results from adding the proceeds from the sale of donated stock. Answer (D) is incorrect because $670,000 results from including the proceeds from the sale of donated stock and not subtracting the total value of the stock dividends distributed.

38. Jordan Corp. declared a 5% stock dividend on its 10,000 issued and outstanding shares of $2 par value common stock, which had a fair value of $5 per share before the stock dividend was declared. This stock dividend was distributed 60 days after the declaration date. By what amount did Jordan's current liabilities increase as a result of the stock dividend declaration?

A. $0

B. $500

C. $1,000

D. $2,500

Answer (A) is correct. *(CPA, adapted)*

REQUIRED: The increase in current liabilities as a result of the stock dividend declaration.

DISCUSSION: Declaration of an issuance of fewer than 20% to 25% of the shares outstanding is a stock dividend. It is not accounted for as a liability but as a reclassification of equity. The entry is to debit retained earnings for the fair value of the stock (5% x 10,000 shares x $5 fair value = $2,500), credit stock dividend distributable at par (5% x 10,000 shares x $2 = $1,000), and credit additional paid-in capital for the excess of fair value over par value ($2,500 – $1,000 = $1,500).

39. A corporation issuing stock should charge retained earnings for the market value of the shares issued in a(n)

A. A reverse stock split.

B. 2-for-1 stock split accounted for as a stock dividend.

C. 10% stock dividend.

D. 2-for-1 stock split.

Answer (C) is correct. *(CPA, adapted)*

REQUIRED: The basis for charging retained earnings when stock is issued.

DISCUSSION: ARB 43, Chapter 7B, states that a stock dividend is a stock issuance of fewer than 20% to 25% of the shares outstanding. It generally should be accounted for by charging (debiting) retained earnings for the fair value of the stock and crediting a capital stock account for the par or stated value. A difference between the fair value and the par or stated value is credited to an additional paid-in capital account. Hence, retained earnings decreases, but total equity does not change.

Answer (A) is incorrect because a stock split or reverse stock split has no effect on the capital accounts. Answer (B) is incorrect because when an issuance exceeds 20% to 25% of the shares outstanding and capitalization of retained earnings is required by law, the transaction should be accounted for as a stock split-up effected in the form of a dividend. Retained earnings should be charged for the amount required by state law, usually the par or stated value of the shares issued. Answer (D) is incorrect because a stock split or reverse stock split has no effect on the capital accounts.

40. Unlike a stock split, a stock dividend requires a formal journal entry in the financial accounting records because stock

A. Dividends increase the relative book value of an individual's stock holding.

B. Splits increase the relative book value of an individual's stock holdings.

C. Dividends are payable on the date they are declared.

D. Dividends represent a transfer from retained earnings to capital stock.

Answer (D) is correct. *(CIA, adapted)*

REQUIRED: The reason a stock dividend requires a formal journal entry and a stock split does not.

DISCUSSION: ARB 43, Chapter 7B, states that the purpose of a stock dividend is to provide evidence to the shareholders of their interest in accumulated earnings without distribution of cash or other property.

Answer (A) is incorrect because stock dividends have no effect on total equity or on the book value of an individual shareholder's investment. Answer (B) is incorrect because stock splits have no effect on total equity or on the book value of an individual shareholder's investment. Answer (C) is incorrect because dividends, whether stock, cash, or property, are usually payable on a date different from the declaration date.

41. On December 31, 2002, the equity section of Spitz Co. was as follows:

Common stock, par value $10; authorized 30,000 shares; issued and outstanding 9,000 shares	$ 90,000
Additional paid-in capital	116,000
Retained earnings	146,000
Total equity	$352,000

On March 31, 2003, Spitz declared a 10% stock dividend. Accordingly, 900 shares were issued when the fair value was $16 per share. For the 3 months ended March 31, 2003, Spitz sustained a net loss of $32,000. The balance of Spitz's retained earnings as of March 31, 2003 should be

A. $99,600

B. $105,000

C. $108,600

D. $114,000

Answer (A) is correct. *(CPA, adapted)*

REQUIRED: The retained earnings balance after a stock dividend and incurrence of a net loss.

DISCUSSION: When the number of shares issued is fewer than 20% to 25% of the outstanding stock, the issuance generally is considered a stock dividend. Retained earnings should be debited for the fair value of the stock distributed as a stock dividend. Thus, $14,400 (900 Spitz shares × $16 fair value) should be debited to retained earnings. Retained earnings should also be decreased by the net loss of $32,000. Thus, the balance of Spitz's retained earnings as of March 31 is $99,600 ($146,000 beginning balance – $14,400 stock dividend – $32,000 net loss).

Answer (B) is incorrect because $105,000 results from reducing retained earnings by the par value of the stock dividend. Answer (C) is incorrect because $108,600 results from reducing retained earnings by the difference between the fair value and the par value. Answer (D) is incorrect because $114,000 results from not reducing retained earnings for the stock dividend.

42. Effective April 27, year 1, the shareholders of Wuerffel Corp. approved a 2-for-1 split of the company's common stock and an increase in authorized common shares from 100,000 shares (par value $20 per share) to 200,000 shares (par value $10 per share). No state legal requirements apply to this stock split. Wuerffel's equity accounts immediately before issuance of the shares were as follows:

Common stock, par value $20; 100,000 shares authorized; 50,000 shares outstanding	$1,000,000
Additional paid-in capital ($3 per share on issuance of common stock)	150,000
Retained earnings	1,350,000

The shares were issued on June 30, year 1. In Wuerffel's June 30, year 1 statement of equity, the balances of additional paid-in capital and retained earnings are

	Additional Paid-In Capital	Retained Earnings
A.	$0	$500,000
B.	$150,000	$350,000
C.	$150,000	$1,350,000
D.	$1,150,000	$350,000

Answer (C) is correct. *(CPA, adapted)*

REQUIRED: The effect of a stock split on additional paid-in capital and retained earnings.

DISCUSSION: A stock split is a nonreciprocal transfer of a company's own shares to its common shareholders in order to reduce the unit market price of the shares. The purpose is to increase the shares' marketability and broaden their distribution. Given this clear intent by Wuerffel, no transfer from retained earnings is necessary unless required by law. Hence, absent state legal requirements, the transaction described will increase the number of shares outstanding to 100,000 (50,000 shares × 2), the par value will be reduced to $10 ($20 ÷ 2), but the capital accounts will be unaffected. To effect this stock split, no formal entry is necessary because no capitalization of retained earnings occurs. Thus, additional paid-in capital ($150,000) and retained earnings ($1,350,000) will not change.

15.4 Treasury Stock Transactions

43. An amount representing the difference between the carrying amount and the proceeds from the purchase and resale of treasury stock may be reflected only in

A. Paid-in capital accounts.

B. Income, paid-in capital, and retained earnings accounts.

C. Retained earnings and paid-in capital accounts.

D. Income and retained earnings accounts.

Answer (C) is correct. *(Publisher)*

REQUIRED: The accounts affected by treasury stock transactions.

DISCUSSION: According to APB 9, *Reporting the Results of Operations*, "adjustments or charges or credits resulting from transactions in the company's own capital stock" are always excluded from the determination of net income or the results of operations. Hence, an excess of the proceeds over the carrying amount of treasury stock must be credited to additional paid-in capital. An excess of the carrying amount over the proceeds of treasury stock may be charged to either retained earnings or additional paid-in capital, depending on the circumstances (APB 6, *Status of Accounting Research Bulletins*).

Answer (A) is incorrect because retained earnings may sometimes be charged as a result of treasury stock transactions. Answer (B) is incorrect because transactions in treasury stock do not affect income. Answer (D) is incorrect because transactions in treasury stock do not affect income.

44. The acquisition of treasury stock will cause the number of shares outstanding to decrease if the treasury stock is accounted for by the

	Cost Method	Par-Value Method
A.	Yes	No
B.	No	No
C.	Yes	Yes
D.	No	Yes

Answer (C) is correct. *(CPA, adapted)*

REQUIRED: The effect of the acquisition of treasury stock on the number of shares outstanding.

DISCUSSION: When treasury stock is acquired, the effect will be to decrease the number of shares of common stock outstanding whether the treasury stock is accounted for by the cost method or the par-value method.

45. Treasury stock transactions may result in

A. Increases in the balance of retained earnings.

B. Increases or decreases in the amount of net income.

C. Decreases in the balance of retained earnings.

D. Increases or decreases in the amount of shares authorized to be issued.

Answer (C) is correct. *(J.N. McKenna)*

REQUIRED: The effect of treasury stock transactions.

DISCUSSION: Under the par-value method, when treasury shares are purchased for a price greater than the par value, retained earnings is debited for the excess of the purchase price over the par value if there is no existing paid-in capital from past treasury stock transactions or if the existing credit balance is insufficient to absorb the excess. Under the cost method, if the subsequent resale price of the treasury shares is less than the original acquisition price, it may be necessary to charge retained earnings for a portion or all of the excess of the original purchase price over the sales price.

Answer (A) is incorrect because equity credits from treasury stock transactions would affect paid-in capital accounts, not retained earnings. Answer (B) is incorrect because treasury stock transactions have no effect on net income. Answer (D) is incorrect because treasury stock transactions affect only the number of outstanding shares, not the authorized number.

46. In 2001, Phineas Co. issued $10 par value common stock for $25 per share. No other common stock transactions occurred until March 31, 2003, when Phineas acquired some of the issued shares for $20 per share and retired them. Which of the following statements correctly states an effect of this acquisition and retirement?

A. 2003 net income is decreased.

B. 2003 net income is increased.

C. Additional paid-in capital is decreased.

D. Retained earnings is increased.

Answer (C) is correct. *(CPA, adapted)*

REQUIRED: The effect of the acquisition and retirement of a company's stock for less than the issue price.

DISCUSSION: When shares of common stock are reacquired and retired, contributed capital should be debited for the amount that was credited upon the issuance of the securities. In addition, because the acquisition of a company's own shares is an equity transaction, no gain or loss should be reflected in the determination of income. The entry is to debit common stock at par ($10 × number of shares) and additional paid-in capital [($25 – $10) × number of shares], and to credit additional paid-in capital from retirement of common stock [($25 – $20) × number of shares] and cash ($20 × number of shares). The effect is to decrease additional paid-in capital.

Answer (A) is incorrect because net income is not affected. Answer (B) is incorrect because net income is not affected. Answer (D) is incorrect because retained earnings may not be increased because of treasury stock transactions.

47. Knight Corp. holds 20,000 shares of its $10 par value common stock as treasury stock reacquired in year 1 for $240,000. On December 12, year 3, Knight reissued all 20,000 shares for $380,000. Under the cost method of accounting for treasury stock, the reissuance resulted in a credit to

A. Common stock of $200,000.

B. Retained earnings of $140,000.

C. Gain on sale of investments of $140,000.

D. Additional paid-in capital of $140,000.

Answer (D) is correct. *(CPA, adapted)*

REQUIRED: The effect of the reissuance of treasury stock accounted for under the cost method.

DISCUSSION: When treasury stock accounted for under the cost method is acquired, the treasury stock account is debited for the amount of the purchase price. If it is subsequently reissued for a price greater than its carrying amount, the excess is credited to additional paid-in capital. For this transaction, the excess is $140,000 ($380,000 – $240,000).

Answer (A) is incorrect because the common stock account is unaffected by purchases and subsequent resales of treasury stock accounted for by the cost method. Answer (B) is incorrect because gains on treasury stock transactions may not be credited to retained earnings. Answer (C) is incorrect because gains on sale of investments may not be credited to income.

48. Daniel Corp. had outstanding 2,000 shares of 11% preferred stock, $50 par. On September 17 of the current year, Daniel redeemed and retired 25% of these shares for $22,500. On that date, Daniel's additional paid-in capital from preferred stock totaled $30,000. To record this transaction, Daniel should debit (credit) its capital accounts as follows:

	Preferred Stock	Additional Paid-In Capital	Retained Earnings
A.	$25,000	$ 7,500	$(10,000)
B.	$25,000	--	$ (2,500)
C.	$25,000	$(2,500)	--
D.	$22,500	--	--

Answer (C) is correct. *(CPA, adapted)*

REQUIRED: The accounting for redemption and retirement of preferred stock.

DISCUSSION: Under the cost method, the entry to record a treasury stock purchase is to debit treasury stock at cost ($22,500) and credit cash. The entry to retire this stock is to debit preferred stock at par [(25% × 2,000 shares) × $50 = $25,000], credit treasury stock at cost ($22,500), and credit additional paid-in capital from preferred stock ($2,500). No entry to retained earnings is necessary.

Answer (A) is incorrect because retained earnings is not affected. Answer (B) is incorrect because retained earnings is not affected. Answer (D) is incorrect because preferred stock is debited for the par value of the retired shares.

49. On December 31 of the current year, Remlinger Corp.'s board of directors canceled 50,000 shares of $2.50 par value common stock held in treasury at an average cost of $13 per share. Before recording the cancelation of the treasury stock, Remlinger had the following balances in its equity accounts:

Common stock	$540,000
Additional paid-in capital	750,000
Retained earnings	900,000
Treasury stock, at cost	650,000

In its balance sheet at December 31 of the current year, Remlinger should report common stock outstanding of

A. $0

B. $250,000

C. $415,000

D. $540,000

Answer (C) is correct. *(CPA, adapted)*

REQUIRED: The common stock outstanding after cancelation of the treasury stock.

DISCUSSION: The treasury shares had an aggregate par value of $125,000 (50,000 shares × $2.50). Consequently, the common stock outstanding after their retirement is $415,000 ($540,000 par value of issued common stock – $125,000).

Answer (A) is incorrect because 166,000 shares ($415,000 ÷ $2.50) of common stock remain outstanding. Answer (B) is incorrect because $250,000 is the difference between retained earnings and the cost of the treasury stock. Answer (D) is incorrect because $540,000 is the par value of the issued shares prior to cancelation of the treasury stock.

50. In year 1, Rattana Corp. acquired 6,000 shares of its own $1 par value common stock at $18 per share. In year 2, Rattana reissued 3,000 of these shares at $25 per share. Rattana uses the cost method to account for its treasury stock transactions. What accounts and amounts should Rattana credit in year 2 to record the reissuance of the 3,000 shares?

	Treasury Stock	Additional Paid-In Capital	Retained Earnings	Common Stock
A.	$54,000	--	$21,000	--
B.	$54,000	$21,000	--	--
C.	--	$72,000	--	$3,000
D.	--	$51,000	$21,000	$3,000

Answer (B) is correct. *(CPA, adapted)*

REQUIRED: The accounts and amounts to be credited when treasury stock is reissued.

DISCUSSION: Under the cost method, the treasury stock account should be debited for the purchase price. When this stock is subsequently reissued for an amount greater than its acquisition cost, the excess should be credited to additional paid-in capital. The 3,000 shares were purchased as treasury stock for $54,000 (3,000 shares × $18 per share). They were reissued for $75,000 (3,000 shares × $25 per share). Under the cost method, the carrying amount of the 3,000 shares was $54,000. When these shares are reissued, the treasury stock account should be credited for $54,000, with the remaining $21,000 ($75,000 – $54,000) credited to additional paid-in capital.

Answer (A) is incorrect because additional paid-in capital, not retained earnings, should be credited. Answer (C) is incorrect because additional paid-in capital should be credited for $21,000 and treasury stock for $54,000. Common stock is unaffected. Answer (D) is incorrect because additional paid in capital should be credited for $21,000, and retained earnings and common stock are unaffected.

51. McGlinchy Company had 100,000 shares of $4 par value common stock outstanding on June 12 of the current year. On this date, McGlinchy acquired 1,000 of its own shares as treasury stock at a cost of $12 per share. The acquisition was accounted for by the cost method. As a result of this treasury stock purchase,

A. Total assets and total equity decreased.

B. Total assets and total equity were unaffected.

C. Total assets, retained earnings, and total equity decreased.

D. Total assets were unaffected, but retained earnings decreased.

Answer (A) is correct. *(CMA, adapted)*

REQUIRED: The effect on the balance sheet of an acquisition of treasury stock accounted for by the cost method.

DISCUSSION: Under the cost method, the acquisition of treasury stock is recorded as a debit to treasury stock and a credit to cash equal to the amount of the purchase price. This transaction results in a decrease in both total assets and total equity.

Answer (B) is incorrect because both total assets and total equity decrease. Answer (C) is incorrect because retained earnings are unaffected. Answer (D) is incorrect because total assets decrease and retained earnings are unaffected.

52. Burkett, Inc. initially issued 100,000 shares of its $10 par common stock at $11 per share. During the current year, Burkett acquired 30,000 shares of its common stock at a price of $16 per share and accounted for them by the cost method. Subsequently, these shares were reissued at a price of $12 per share. Burkett had made no other issuances or acquisitions of its own common stock. What effect does the reissuance of the stock have on the following accounts?

	Additional Paid-In Capital	Retained Earnings
A.	Decrease	Decrease
B.	No effect	Decrease
C.	Decrease	No effect
D.	No effect	No effect

B

Answer (C) is correct. *(CPA, adapted)*

REQUIRED: The effect of a reissuance of treasury stock on retained earnings and additional paid-in capital.

DISCUSSION: When shares are issued for an amount greater than their par value, the difference is credited to additional paid-in capital. Under the cost method, the treasury stock account should be debited for the price of reacquired shares. If the treasury stock is subsequently reissued for an amount less than its acquisition cost but greater than its original issuance price, the difference between the acquisition cost and the reissuance price should be recorded as a decrease in additional paid-in capital from treasury stock transactions. However, if this account has a $0 balance, retained earnings is decreased. Thus, Burkett must debit cash for $360,000 ($12 reissuance price per share × 30,000 shares), debit (decrease) retained earnings for $120,000 [($16 cost per share – $12) × 30,000 shares], and credit treasury stock for $480,000 ($16 cost per share × 30,000 shares). As long as the reissuance price is greater than the original issuance price, additional paid-in capital will not be affected.

53. Mazzone Corp. acquired some of its own common shares at a price greater than both their par value and original issue price but less than their carrying amount. Mazzone uses the cost method of accounting for treasury stock. What is the impact of this acquisition on total equity and the book value per common share?

	Total Equity	Book Value per Share
A.	Increase	Increase
B.	Increase	Decrease
C.	Decrease	Increase
D.	Decrease	Decrease

Answer (C) is correct. *(CPA, adapted)*

REQUIRED: The impact of the acquisition on total equity and the book value per common share.

DISCUSSION: Under the cost method, the acquisition of treasury stock is recorded as a debit to treasury stock and a credit to cash equal to the amount of the purchase price. This transaction results in a decrease in both total assets and total equity because treasury stock is a contra equity account. Moreover, if the acquisition cost is less than the carrying amount, book value per share will increase.

54. Mulholland Corp. acquired treasury shares at an amount greater than their par value but less than their original issue price. Compared with the cost method of accounting for treasury stock, does the par value method report a greater amount for additional paid-in capital and a greater amount for retained earnings?

	Additional Paid-In Capital	Retained Earnings
A.	Yes	Yes
B.	Yes	No
C.	No	No
D.	No	Yes

Answer (C) is correct. *(CPA, adapted)*

REQUIRED: The effect of the par value method on additional paid-in capital and retained earnings compared with that of the cost method.

DISCUSSION: Under the cost method, the purchase of treasury stock has no effect on additional paid-in capital and retained earnings. Under the par value method, given that the acquisition cost is greater than par but less than the original issue price, treasury stock is debited at par and cash is credited for the purchase price. Additional paid-in capital is debited and additional paid-in capital from treasury stock transactions is credited for the difference between par value and the purchase price. Hence, additional paid-in capital and retained earnings are not affected under either method.

55. On incorporation, Genomenon, Inc. issued common stock at a price in excess of its par value. No other stock transactions occurred except that treasury stock was acquired for an amount exceeding this issue price. If Genomenon uses the par value method of accounting for treasury stock appropriate for retired stock, what is the effect of the acquisition on the following?

	Net Common Stock	Additional Paid-In Capital	Retained Earnings
A.	No effect	Decrease	No effect
B.	Decrease	Decrease	Decrease
C.	Decrease	No effect	Decrease
D.	No effect	Decrease	Decrease

Answer (B) is correct. *(CPA, adapted)*

REQUIRED: The effects of a purchase of treasury stock accounted for under the par value method.

DISCUSSION: Under the par value method, treasury stock is debited at par value, and the amount is reported as a reduction of common stock. The purchase also results in the removal of the additional paid-in capital associated with the original issue of the shares. Given that no other stock transactions occurred and that treasury stock was acquired for an amount exceeding the issue price, the balancing debit for the excess of the acquisition price over the issue price is to retained earnings. If additional paid-in capital from treasury stock transactions had been previously recorded, the balancing debit would be to that account but only to the extent of its credit balance. Thus, retained earnings is also decreased.

56. Treasury stock was acquired for cash at a price in excess of its original issue price. The treasury stock was subsequently reissued for cash at a price in excess of its acquisition price. Assuming that the par value method of accounting for treasury stock transactions is used, what is the effect on total equity of each of the following events?

	Acquisition of Treasury Stock	Reissuance of Treasury Stock
A.	Decrease	No effect
B.	Decrease	Increase
C.	Increase	Decrease
D.	No effect	No effect

Answer (B) is correct. *(CPA, adapted)*

REQUIRED: The effect on total equity of treasury stock transactions accounted for under the par value method.

DISCUSSION: The par value method treats the acquisition of treasury stock as a constructive retirement and its resale as a new issuance of stock. Thus, the acquisition of treasury stock will be reflected as a decrease in total equity. The reissuance will be accounted for as an increase in total equity.

15.5 Bankruptcies and Quasi-Reorganizations

57. Lockhart Co. filed a voluntary bankruptcy petition on August 15, year 1. The statement of affairs reflects the following amounts:

	Book Value	Estimated Current Credit
Assets:		
Assets pledged with fully secured creditors	$ 300,000	$370,000
Assets pledged with partially secured creditors	180,000	120,000
Free assets	420,000	320,000
	$ 900,000	$810,000
Liabilities:		
Liabilities with priority	$ 70,000	
Fully secured creditors	260,000	
Partially secured creditors	200,000	
Unsecured creditors	540,000	
	$1,070,000	

Assume that the assets are converted to cash at the estimated current values and the business is liquidated. What amount of cash will be available to pay unsecured nonpriority claims?

A. $240,000

B. $280,000

C. $320,000

D. $360,000

Answer (D) is correct. *(CPA, adapted)*

REQUIRED: The amount of cash available to pay unsecured nonpriority claims.

DISCUSSION: The liabilities to partially secured creditors total $200,000, and the assets pledged to secure these claims can be sold for $120,000. With respect to the $80,000 ($200,000 – $120,000) difference, these claimants have the status of general unsecured creditors. When converted to cash, the $370,000 of assets pledged with fully secured creditors and the $320,000 of free assets provide $690,000 to satisfy the $70,000 of liabilities with priority and the $260,000 of liabilities to fully secured creditors. Consequently, $360,000 ($690,000 – $70,000 – $260,000) is the amount of cash that will be available to pay unsecured nonpriority claims.

Answer (A) is incorrect because $240,000 results from reducing the remaining assets left to pay the unsecured nonpriority claims by the $120,000 that is paid to the partially secured creditors. Answer (B) is incorrect because $280,000 results from not treating the $80,000 ($200,000 – $120,000) remaining partially secured creditors claims as unsecured claims. Answer (C) is incorrect because $320,000 is the current value of the free assets.

58. Furcal Corp. was forced into bankruptcy and is in the process of liquidating assets and paying claims. Unsecured claims will be paid at the rate of $.40 on the dollar. Rocker holds a $30,000 noninterest-bearing note receivable from Furcal collateralized by an asset with a carrying amount of $35,000 and a liquidation value of $5,000. The amount to be realized by Rocker on this note is

A. $5,000

B. $12,000

C. $15,000

D. $17,000

Answer (C) is correct. *(CPA, adapted)*

REQUIRED: The total amount of cash to be realized from a partially unsecured claim.

DISCUSSION: Furcal has a secured claim for the $5,000 liquidation value of the asset. The remaining $25,000 ($30,000 note – $5,000) is an unsecured claim. Given that unsecured claims will be paid at the rate of $.40 on the dollar, Furcal will receive $10,000 ($25,000 × 40%) from its unsecured claim. The total amount to be realized is $15,000 ($5,000 + $10,000).

Answer (A) is incorrect because $5,000 is the amount of the secured claim. Answer (B) is incorrect because $12,000 results from treating the entire claim as unsecured, which would be paid $.40 on the dollar. Answer (D) is incorrect because $17,000 results from adding the $5,000 secured portion of the claim and the amount that would be paid if the entire amount were unsecured.

59. The primary purpose of a quasi-reorganization is to give a corporation the opportunity to

A. Obtain relief from its creditors.

B. Revalue understated assets to their fair values.

C. Eliminate a deficit in retained earnings.

D. Distribute the stock of a newly created subsidiary to its shareholders in exchange for part of their stock in the corporation.

Answer (C) is correct. *(CPA, adapted)*

REQUIRED: The purpose of a quasi-reorganization.

DISCUSSION: A quasi-reorganization is undertaken to reduce a deficit in retained earnings to zero. The purpose is to permit the corporation to pay dividends in the near future.

Answer (A) is incorrect because a quasi-reorganization is an accounting adjustment. It offers no relief from creditors. Answer (B) is incorrect because assets are usually written down to fair value. Answer (D) is incorrect because a quasi-reorganization does not entail an exchange of stock.

60. Perez Corp. is in liquidation under Chapter 7 of the Federal Bankruptcy Code. The bankruptcy trustee has established a new set of books for the bankruptcy estate. After assuming custody of the estate, the trustee discovered an unrecorded invoice of $2,000 for machinery repairs performed before the bankruptcy filing. In addition, a truck with a carrying amount of $40,000 was sold for $24,000 cash. This truck was bought and paid for in the year before the bankruptcy. What amount should be debited to estate equity as a result of these transactions?

A. $0

B. $2,000

C. $16,000

D. $18,000

Answer (D) is correct. *(CPA, adapted)*

REQUIRED: The amount debited to estate equity.

DISCUSSION: A trustee may continue to use the debtor's books or may open a new set. When a new set of books is opened, assets and liabilities are recorded at their carrying amounts. Any unrecorded assets or liabilities discovered by the trustee as well as the estate's gains, losses, and liquidation expenses are entered in the estate equity account. Thus, the $2,000 of repairs (a liability and an expense) and the $16,000 loss on the sale of the truck are charges to estate equity, for a total of $18,000.

Answer (A) is incorrect because $18,000 should be charged to estate equity. Answer (B) is incorrect because $2,000 does not reflect the estate's loss on the sale of the truck. Answer (C) is incorrect because $16,000 does not reflect the unrecorded liability for repairs.

61. Smokey Joe Corp., a debtor-in-possession under Chapter 11 of the Federal Bankruptcy Code, granted an equity interest to a creditor in full settlement of a $56,000 debt owed to the creditor. At the date of this transaction, the equity interest had a fair value of $50,000. What amount should Smokey Joe recognize as a gain on restructuring of debt?

A. $0

B. $6,000

C. $50,000

D. $56,000

Answer (B) is correct. *(CPA, adapted)*

REQUIRED: The amount recognized as a gain on restructuring of debt by a debtor that has granted an equity interest.

DISCUSSION: According to SFAS 15, a debtor that grants an equity interest in full settlement of a payable should account for the equity interest at fair value. The difference between the fair value of the equity interest and the carrying amount of the payable is a gain. Consequently, Smokey Joe will recognize a gain of $6,000 ($56,000 debt – $50,000 fair value of the equity interest).

Answer (A) is incorrect because a gain should be recognized. Answer (C) is incorrect because $50,000 is the fair value of the equity interest. Answer (D) is incorrect because $56,000 is the carrying amount of the debt.

62. On May 30 of the current year, Nathan Corp. paid $400,000 cash and issued 80,000 shares of its $1 par value common stock to its unsecured creditors on a pro rata basis pursuant to a reorganization plan under Chapter 11 of the bankruptcy statutes. Nathan owed these unsecured creditors a total of $1,200,000. Nathan's common stock was trading at $1.25 per share on May 30 of the current year. As a result of this transaction, Nathan's total equity had a net increase of

A. $1,200,000

B. $800,000

C. $100,000

D. $80,000

Answer (B) is correct. *(CPA, adapted)*

REQUIRED: The net increase in equity immediately after the Chapter 11 reorganization.

DISCUSSION: According to SFAS 15, a debtor that grants an equity interest in settlement of a payable should account for the equity interest at fair value. The result is an increase in equity of $100,000 (80,000 shares × $1.25). Because $400,000 in cash and a $100,000 equity interest are accepted as settlement of a $1,200,000 debt, a $700,000 ($1,200,000 – $400,000 – $100,000) gain will also be recognized and result in an increase in equity (retained earnings). Accordingly, the net increase in total equity is $800,000 ($100,000 + $700,000).

Answer (A) is incorrect because $1,200,000 is the amount of the debt. Answer (C) is incorrect because $100,000 is the increase in contributed capital. Answer (D) is incorrect because $80,000 is the increase in common stock.

63. When a company goes through a quasi-reorganization, its balance sheet carrying amounts are stated at

A. Original cost.

B. Net realizable value.

C. Replacement value.

D. Fair value.

Answer (D) is correct. *(CPA, adapted)*

REQUIRED: The amounts at which balance sheet accounts are stated after a quasi-reorganization.

DISCUSSION: ARB 43, Chapter 7A, requires that quasi-reorganization be accomplished first by revaluing assets to fair values, a process that usually increases the deficit in retained earnings. Paid-in capital or its equivalent must then be available or must be created to provide a source of capital against which the deficit may be written off.

Questions 64 and 65 are based on the following information. Alphonse Co. has sustained heavy losses over a period of time. Conditions warrant that Alphonse undergo a quasi-reorganization at July 31. Selected balance sheet items prior to the quasi-reorganization are as follows:

Inventory was recorded in the accounting records at July 31 at its market value of $6,000,000. Cost was $6,500,000.

Property, plant, and equipment was recorded in the accounting records at July 31 at $12,000,000, net of accumulated depreciation. The appraised value was $8,000,000.

Equity on July 31 was as follows:

Common stock, par value $10 per share; authorized, issued and outstanding, 700,000 shares	$7,000,000
Capital in excess of par	1,600,000
Retained earnings (deficit)	(900,000)
	$7,700,000

Under the terms of the quasi-reorganization, the par value of the common stock is to be reduced from $10 per share to $5 per share.

64. Immediately after the quasi-reorganization has been accomplished, retained earnings (deficit) should be

A. $0

B. $(200,000)

C. $(4,400,000)

D. $(4,900,000)

Answer (A) is correct. *(CPA, adapted)*

REQUIRED: The amount in retained earnings after the quasi-reorganization.

DISCUSSION: Retained earnings should have a zero balance after the quasi-reorganization, because the purpose of the procedure is to eliminate the deficit. Capital in excess of par may also have a zero balance, although that is not a requirement of the procedure.

65. Immediately after the quasi-reorganization has been accomplished, the total of equity should be

A. $3,300,000

B. $3,500,000

C. $3,700,000

D. $4,200,000

Answer (C) is correct. *(CPA, adapted)*

REQUIRED: The total equity immediately after the quasi-reorganization.

DISCUSSION: The first step in a quasi-reorganization is to revalue assets at their current fair values. The inventory is already recorded in the accounting records at its market value of $6,000,000. The property, plant, and equipment account should be reduced by $4,000,000 to reflect its appraised value. The corresponding debit will be to retained earnings, increasing the deficit to $4,900,000. To eliminate the deficit, enough capital in excess of par must be created to offset its full amount. This result is achieved by debiting the par value of the outstanding common stock and crediting capital in excess of par for $3,300,000 ($4,900,000 – $1,600,000). The final entry is a debit to capital in excess of par and a credit to retained earnings for $4,900,000.

These entries reduce total equity to $3,700,000 ($7,700,000 – $4,000,000 revaluation of assets).

Answer (A) is incorrect because $3,300,000 is the amount that is credited to capital in excess of par to reduce the deficit in retained earnings. Answer (B) is incorrect because $3,500,000 is the combined difference between cost and fair market value for the inventory and property plant and equipment. Answer (D) is incorrect because $4,200,000 results when total retained earnings is reduced by the difference between cost and fair market value for the inventory and property plant and equipment.

66. In a quasi-reorganization of a consolidated entity,

A. Only the parent company undergoes the procedure.

B. All losses should be written off against paid-in capital prior to charging retained earnings.

C. Paid-in capital cannot arise as a result of the transaction.

D. All consolidated retained earnings should be eliminated if any part of a loss is to be charged to paid-in capital.

Answer (D) is correct. *(Publisher)*

REQUIRED: The correct statement about applying a quasi-reorganization to a consolidated entity.

DISCUSSION: Consistent with the treatment of an individual enterprise, all consolidated retained earnings should be eliminated in a quasi-reorganization of a consolidated entity by a charge to paid-in capital.

Answer (A) is incorrect because the procedure may be applied to the parent or some or all subsidiaries. Answer (B) is incorrect because losses are first written off to retained earnings. The retained earnings deficit is then written off to paid-in capital. Answer (C) is incorrect because, if the legal capital is reduced by more than the deficit, paid-in capital from quasi-reorganization arises.

15.6 Rights and Warrants

67. On December 1, year 1, Lombard, Inc. issued warrants to its shareholders giving them the right to purchase additional $20 par value common shares at a price of $30. The shareholders exercised all warrants on April 1, year 2. The shares had market prices of $33, $35, and $40 on December 1, year 1; December 31, year 1; and April 1, year 2, respectively. What were the effects of the warrants on Lombard's additional paid-in capital and net income?

	Additional Paid-In Capital	Net Income
A.	Increased in year 2	No effect
B.	Increased in year 1	No effect
C.	Increased in year 2	Decreased in year 1 and year 2
D.	Increased in year 1	Decreased in year 1 and year 2

Answer (A) is correct. *(CPA, adapted)*

REQUIRED: The effects on additional paid-in capital and net income when warrants are issued and exercised.

DISCUSSION: When stock rights and warrants are issued for no consideration, only a memorandum entry is made. Consequently, common stock and additional paid-in capital are not affected. However, when warrants are exercised and stock is issued, the issuing company will reflect the proceeds as an increase in common stock and additional paid-in capital. Consequently, Lombard will increase additional paid-in capital in year 2 when stock is issued, but net income will not be affected.

Answer (B) is incorrect because only a memorandum entry is made in year 1. Answer (C) is incorrect because net income is not affected. Answer (D) is incorrect because only a memorandum entry is made in year 1, and net income is not affected.

68. Quilvio Co. issued rights to its existing shareholders without consideration. A shareholder received a right to buy one share for each 20 shares held. The exercise price was in excess of par value but less than the current market price. Retained earnings decreases when

	Rights Are Issued	Rights Are Exercised
A.	Yes	Yes
B.	Yes	No
C.	No	Yes
D.	No	No

Answer (D) is correct. *(CPA, adapted)*

REQUIRED: The effect on retained earnings when rights are issued and exercised.

DISCUSSION: When stock rights are issued for no consideration, only a memorandum entry is made. When stock rights are exercised and stock is issued, the issuing company will reflect the proceeds as an increase in common stock and additional paid-in capital. Thus, retained earnings will not be affected when rights are issued or exercised.

69. Merrilea Goings, Inc. issued preferred stock with detachable common stock warrants. The issue price exceeded the sum of the warrants' fair value and the preferred stocks' par value. The preferred stocks' fair value was not determinable. What amount should be assigned to the warrants outstanding?

A. Total proceeds.

B. Excess of proceeds over the par value of the preferred stock.

C. The proportion of the proceeds that the warrants' fair value bears to the preferred stocks' par value.

D. The fair value of the warrants.

Answer (D) is correct. *(CPA, adapted)*

REQUIRED: The amount assigned to outstanding warrants when the preferred stocks' fair value is not determinable.

DISCUSSION: When securities are issued with detachable stock warrants, the proceeds should generally be allocated between the securities and the warrants based on their relative fair values at issuance. However, if the fair value of only the warrants is known, the warrants should be recorded at fair value, with the remainder allocated to the securities.

Answer (A) is incorrect because the total proceeds need to be allocated between the warrants and the preferred stock. Answer (B) is incorrect because par value is not an appropriate basis for allocation. Answer (C) is incorrect because the fair value of the warrants is not related to the par value of the preferred stock.

70. On June 4, 2003, Bastet Co. purchased 1,000 shares of Angkor Co.'s common stock at $80 per share. On December 26, 2003, Bastet received 1,000 stock rights to purchase an additional 1,000 shares at $90 per share. The stock rights had an expiration date of May 1, 2004. On December 26, 2003, Angkor's common stock had a market value, ex-rights, of $95 per share, and the stock rights had a market value of $5 each. What amount should Bastet record on December 26, 2003 for the investment in stock rights?

A. $4,000

B. $5,000

C. $10,000

D. $15,000

Answer (A) is correct. *(CPA, adapted)*

REQUIRED: The amount to be recorded for the investment in stock rights on the balance sheet.

DISCUSSION: The $80 original cost of each share of stock should be allocated between the stock and the stock right based on their relative fair values.

Stock:	[$95 ÷ ($95 + $5)] × $80 cost =	$76
Right:	[$ 5 ÷ ($95 + $5)] × $80 cost =	4
		$80

Thus, the stock rights should be recorded at $4,000 (1,000 rights × $4) on the balance sheet.

Answer (B) is incorrect because $5,000 is the fair value of the rights. Answer (C) is incorrect because $10,000 is the difference between the cost of the 1,000 shares of stock and the exercise price for an additional 1,000 shares. Answer (D) is incorrect because $15,000 is the difference between the cost of the 1,000 shares of stock and their fair value.

71. In September 1998, Felinity Corp. made a dividend distribution of one right for each of its 240,000 shares of outstanding common stock. Each right was exercisable for the purchase of 1% of a share of Felinity's $50 variable rate preferred stock at an exercise price of $80 per share. On March 20, 2003, none of the rights had been exercised, and Felinity redeemed them by paying each shareholder $0.10 per right. As a result of this redemption, Felinity's equity was reduced by

A. $240

B. $24,000

C. $48,000

D. $72,000

Answer (B) is correct. *(CPA, adapted)*

REQUIRED: The effect on equity of the redemption of stock rights.

DISCUSSION: When rights are issued for no consideration, only a memorandum entry is made. Consequently, neither common stock nor additional paid-in capital is affected by the issuance of rights in a nonreciprocal transfer. The redemption of the rights reduces equity by the amount of their cost (240,000 × $.10 = $24,000).

Answer (A) is incorrect because $240 equals $.10 times the number of shares (2,400) that could have been purchased. Answer (C) is incorrect because, if the rights were initially credited to paid-in capital at $72,000, or $.30 each [($80 exercise price – $50 par value) ÷ 100], and paid-in capital was reduced by the redemption price of $.10 each (240,000 × $.10 = $24,000), the balance remaining would be $48,000. Answer (D) is incorrect because $72,000 assumes a price per right of $.30 [($80 exercise price – $50 par value) ÷ 100].

72. On September 1, Poilu Corp. issued rights to shareholders to subscribe to additional shares of its common stock. One right was issued for each share owned. A shareholder could purchase one additional share for 10 rights plus $15 cash. The rights expired on November 30. On September 1, the market price of a share with the right attached was $40, while the market price of one right alone was $2. Poilu's equity on August 31 included the following:

Common stock, $25 par value, 4,000 shares issued and outstanding	$100,000
Additional paid-in capital	60,000
Retained earnings	80,000

By what amount should Poilu's retained earnings decrease as a result of issuance of the stock rights on September 1?

A. $0
B. $5,000
C. $8,000
D. $10,000

Answer (A) is correct. *(CPA, adapted)*

REQUIRED: The effect on retained earnings when stock rights are issued.

DISCUSSION: When stock rights are issued for no consideration, only a memorandum entry is made. When stock rights are exercised and stock is issued, the issuing company will reflect the proceeds as an increase in common stock and additional paid-in capital. Thus, retained earnings will not be affected when rights are either issued or exercised.

Use Gleim's ***EQE Test Prep*** for interactive study and performance analysis.

STUDY UNIT SIXTEEN
EPS AND SHARE-BASED PAYMENT

SFAS 128, *Earnings per Share*, specifically applies to entities with publicly held common stock or potential common stock. Nonpublic entities that elect to present EPS information also must follow SFAS 128.

Earnings per share (EPS) is the amount of earnings attributable to a share of common stock. Investors commonly use this ratio to measure the performance of an entity over an accounting period. SFAS 128 prescribes two forms of EPS -- basic and diluted. When a loss is reported, applicable loss-per-share amounts must be presented.

Basic earnings per share (BEPS) measures earnings performance based on common stock outstanding during all or part of the reporting period. BEPS equals income available to common shareholders divided by the weighted-average number of shares of common stock outstanding.

Income available to common shareholders is determined by subtracting current dividends accumulated on cumulative preferred stock (arrearages would have been subtracted in prior periods) and current dividends declared on noncumulative preferred stock from income from continuing operations, other income components, and net income. When either a loss from continuing operations or a net loss is reported, dividends on preferred stock (if applicable) increase the amount of the loss.

The **weighted-average number of shares of common stock outstanding** is equal to the shares of common stock outstanding during the entire period, plus the shares issued or minus those reacquired during the period. The latter shares are weighted according to the portion of the period they were outstanding.

Diluted earnings per share (DEPS) measures earnings performance based on common stock and dilutive potential common stock. Potential common stock is **dilutive** if its inclusion in EPS reduces EPS or increases loss per share. DEPS is computed by (1) increasing the BEPS denominator for the weighted-average number of additional shares of common stock that would have been outstanding if the dilutive potential common stock had been issued, and (2) adding back to the BEPS numerator any dividends on convertible preferred stock and after-tax interest related to any convertible debt. The numerator also must be adjusted for other changes in income or loss, such as profit-sharing expenses, that would result from the assumed issuance of common stock. DEPS is based on the holder's most advantageous conversion rate or exercise price. Previously reported DEPS is not retroactively adjusted for subsequent conversions or changes in the market price of the common stock.

Potential common stock is a security or other contract that may entitle the holder to obtain common stock. It includes (1) convertible securities (convertible preferred stock and convertible debt), (2) stock options and warrants (and their equivalents), and (3) contingently issuable common stock. Option and warrant equivalents include nonvested stock granted to employees, stock purchase contracts, and partially paid stock subscriptions. In determining whether potential common stock is dilutive, each issue or series of issues must be considered separately and in sequence from the most dilutive to the least dilutive.

The **if-converted** method is used to determine the dilutive effect of **convertible securities.** It assumes that the convertible security was converted at the beginning of the period or time of issuance, if later. Conversion is not assumed if the effect is antidilutive. As a result, to arrive at the DEPS denominator, the BEPS denominator is increased by the weighted-average number of shares of common stock assumed to be issued. To determine the DEPS numerator, the BEPS numerator is increased by the dividends on convertible preferred stock and by the after-tax amounts of interest (after amortization of discount or premium) related to convertible debt for which the denominator was increased. The numerator is also adjusted for other changes in income or loss, such as profit-sharing expenses, that would result from the assumed issuance of common shares.

The **treasury stock method** is used to determine the dilutive effect of outstanding **call options and warrants.** Dilution occurs if the average market price for the period exceeds the exercise price. The treasury stock method assumes that (1) the options and warrants were exercised at the beginning of the period or time of issuance, if later; (2) the proceeds (price × weighted-average number of shares issuable upon exercise) were used to purchase common stock at the **average market price** during the period; and (3) to arrive at the DEPS denominator, the BEPS denominator is increased by the excess, if any, of shares issued over the shares purchased.

If a potential common stock has a dilutive effect on DEPS for **income from continuing operations,** the number of shares used to adjust the denominator for that calculation is used to adjust the denominator for the calculation of DEPS for all other reported earnings amounts. If a loss from continuing operations or a loss from continuing operations available to common shareholders is reported, potential common stock is not included in the calculation of DEPS for any reported earnings amount because the effect would be antidilutive.

If the number of common shares outstanding changes because of a **stock dividend, a stock split, or a reverse stock split**, EPS amounts for all periods presented are adjusted retroactively to reflect the change in capital structure as if it had occurred at the beginning of the first period presented. These adjustments are made even if the change occurs after the close of the current period but before the issuance of the financial statements.

All entities must present EPS amounts for both income from continuing operations and net income on the face of the income statement. An entity with a **simple capital structure** (only common stock and nondilutive potential common stock outstanding) must report BEPS amounts; an entity with a **complex capital structure** (one with some dilutive securities) must present BEPS and DEPS amounts with equal prominence. An entity that reports a **discontinued operation** or an **extraordinary item** must report the applicable EPS amount(s) on the face of the income statement or in the notes.

An entity must **disclose** (1) EPS data for all periods for which either an income statement or a summary of earnings is presented; (2) for all periods for which an income statement is presented, (a) a reconciliation by individual security of the numerators and denominators of the BEPS and DEPS computations for income from continuing operations (including income and share effects), (b) the effect of preferred dividends on the BEPS numerator, and (c) potential common shares not included in DEPS because their inclusion would have had an antidilutive effect in the periods reported; and (3) for the latest period for which an income statement is presented, any transaction occurring after the end of the most recent period but before the issuance of the financial statements that would have had a material effect on common shares or potential common shares outstanding had the transaction occurred prior to the balance sheet date. If DEPS data are reported for at least one period, they must be reported for all periods presented, even if they are equal to BEPS amounts.

SFAS 129, *Disclosure of Information about Capital Structure*, applies to both private and public entities. It continues and consolidates previously existing guidance. Thus, disclosures required include (1) rights and privileges of outstanding securities, (2) information about the number of shares issued, (3) information about liquidation preferences of preferred stock, and (4) redemption requirements for the next 5 years.

SFAS 123 (revised 2004), *Share-Based Payment*, mandates the use of a **fair-value based** method in accounting for transactions in which an entity exchanges its equity instruments for goods or services. SFAS 123R further mandates the use of a fair-value method when an entity incurs **liabilities** in exchange for goods and services, provided that the liabilities either are based on the fair value of the entity's equity instruments or may be satisfied by the issuance of equity instruments.

SFAS 123R primarily focuses on transactions in which an entity makes share-based payments, such as share options, as compensation for employee services. SFAS 123R generally requires a public entity to measure the cost of employee services received in exchange for equity instruments at the fair value of the instruments on the date of grant, estimate the number of instruments for which the requisite service is expected to be rendered, and allocate that cost to the requisite service period. The **grant date** is the date at which (1) a mutual understanding of the key terms and conditions of a share-based payment award is reached by an employer and an employee, (2) an employer becomes contingently obligated to make share-based payments to an employee who renders the requisite service, (3) any necessary approvals are obtained, and (4) subsequent changes in the market price of the underlying stock begin to either benefit or adversely affect the employee. The **requisite service period** is the period during which the employee is required to work in order to earn the compensation. It is usually the period during which the benefits vest.

If an observable market price is available for the same or similar instruments, it should be used as the grant-date fair value. More often, the grant-date fair value will be estimated using **option-pricing models** adjusted for unique characteristics of the equity instruments. If the estimate of the number of instruments for which service is expected to be rendered changes during the requisite service period, it should be accounted for as a **change in estimate**. Accordingly, the cumulative effect on the current and prior periods is recognized in compensation cost for the period of change.

Compensation cost should not be recognized for **employee share purchase plans** with certain characteristics. Moreover, if an equity award is **modified** after the grant date, the entity should recognize incremental compensation cost measured as the difference between the fair values of the modified award and the original award immediately before the modification.

SFAS 123R requires a **public entity** to recognize the compensation cost of employee services received in exchange for **liability instruments** at fair value, with adjustments at subsequent reporting dates. A **nonpublic entity** may elect to measure such liabilities at fair value or **intrinsic value** (the difference between the fair value of the underlying stock and the exercise price of an option). **Excess tax benefits**, as defined by SFAS 123R, should be recognized as additions to paid-in-capital. Cash retained as a result of these benefits should be classified as **inflows from financing activities** in a statement of cash flows.

QUESTIONS

16.1 Basic Earnings per Share

1. With respect to the computation of earnings per share, which of the following would be most indicative of a simple capital structure?

A. Common stock, preferred stock, and convertible debt outstanding.

B. Common stock, convertible preferred stock, and debt outstanding.

C. Common stock, preferred stock, and debt outstanding.

D. Common stock, preferred stock, and stock options outstanding.

Answer (C) is correct. *(CPA, adapted)*

REQUIRED: The situation most indicative of a simple capital structure.

DISCUSSION: SFAS 128, *Earnings per Share*, defines a simple capital structure as one that has only common stock outstanding. A complex capital structure is one that contains potential common stock. Potential common stock includes options, warrants, convertible securities, contingent stock requirements, and any other security or contract that may entitle the holder to obtain common stock.

Answer (A) is incorrect because a simple capital structure does not include convertible securities or stock options. Answer (B) is incorrect because a simple capital structure does not include convertible securities or stock options. Answer (D) is incorrect because a simple capital structure does not include convertible securities or stock options.

2. The disclosure requirements of SFAS 128, *Earnings per Share*, do not apply to

A. Statements presented by corporations whose capital structures contain only common stock.

B. Statements presented by wholly owned subsidiaries.

C. Statements presented by corporations whose capital structures contain both common stock and potential common stock.

D. Summaries of financial statements that purport to present the results of operations of publicly held corporations in conformity with generally accepted accounting principles.

Answer (B) is correct. *(Publisher)*

REQUIRED: The type of capital structure or financial statement presentation to which EPS disclosure requirements do not apply.

DISCUSSION: SFAS 128 applies to companies whose securities trade in a public market. SFAS 128 specifically exempts investment companies (such as mutual funds) and wholly owned subsidiaries from these disclosure requirements.

Answer (A) is incorrect because SFAS 128 applies to companies with both simple and complex capital structures. Answer (C) is incorrect because SFAS 128 applies to companies with both simple and complex capital structures. Answer (D) is incorrect because EPS data of companies subject to SFAS 128 must be presented for all periods for which an income statement or a summary of earnings is presented.

3. Earnings-per-share data must be reported on the face of the income statement for

	Income from Continuing Operations	Cumulative Effect of a Change in Accounting Principle
A.	Yes	Yes
B.	Yes	No
C.	No	No
D.	No	Yes

Answer (B) is correct. *(CPA, adapted)*

REQUIRED: The EPS data that must be reported on the face of the income statement.

DISCUSSION: SFAS 128 requires that EPS data for income from continuing operations and net income be reported on the face of the income statement. EPS data for a discontinued operation or an extraordinary item may be disclosed on the face of the income statement or in a note.

4. SFAS 128, *Earnings per Share*, requires

A. Restatement of EPS data of a prior period if the earnings of the prior period have been restated by a prior-period adjustment.

B. Dual presentation of BEPS and DEPS for the current period only.

C. The presentation of BEPS only for prior periods presented for comparative purposes.

D. Disclosure of the effect of a restatement of prior-period earnings from a prior-period adjustment in the current period, but not in EPS form.

Answer (A) is correct. *(Publisher)*

REQUIRED: The financial statement presentation of EPS required under SFAS 128.

DISCUSSION: According to SFAS 128, when the results of operations of a prior period are restated in the financial statements, the EPS data for those prior periods must also be restated.

Answer (B) is incorrect because both BEPS and DEPS must be disclosed for all periods presented if a corporation has a complex capital structure. Answer (C) is incorrect because both BEPS and DEPS must be disclosed for all periods presented if a corporation has a complex capital structure. Answer (D) is incorrect because SFAS 128 requires presentation of the effect of a prior-period adjustment on EPS for all prior periods affected by such restatement.

5. In computing the loss per share of common stock, cumulative preferred dividends not earned should be

A. Deducted from the loss for the year.

B. Added to the loss for the year.

C. Deducted from income in the year paid.

D. Added to income in the year paid.

Answer (B) is correct. *(CPA, adapted)*

REQUIRED: The effect of unearned cumulative preferred dividends on the loss-per-share calculation.

DISCUSSION: When preferred stock is cumulative, the dividend, whether earned or not, is deducted from income from continuing operations and net income, or added to any loss for the year, in computing earnings or loss, per share of common stock. When preferred stock is noncumulative, an adjustment is made for dividends declared. If the dividend is cumulative only if earned, no adjustment is necessary except to the extent of available income; that is, the preferred dividends accumulate only to the extent of net income.

Answer (A) is incorrect because it has the effect of reducing loss per share. Answer (C) is incorrect because cumulative preferred dividends are a necessary adjustment for the year in which they accumulate regardless of when they are paid. Answer (D) is incorrect because cumulative preferred dividends are a necessary adjustment for the year in which they accumulate regardless of when they are paid.

6. With regard to stock dividends and stock splits, current authoritative literature contains what general guideline for the computation of EPS?

A. If changes in common stock resulting from stock dividends, stock splits, or reverse splits have been consummated after the close of the period but before completion of the financial report, the per-share computations should be based on the new number of shares.

B. It is not necessary to give recognition to the effect on prior periods' computations of EPS for stock dividends or stock splits consummated in the current period.

C. Computations of EPS for prior periods must give recognition to changes in common shares due to stock splits, but not stock dividends, because stock dividends have an immaterial effect on EPS.

D. Footnote disclosure is necessary for anticipated stock dividends and stock splits and their effect on BEPS and DEPS.

Answer (A) is correct. *(Publisher)*

REQUIRED: The treatment of stock dividends and stock splits in the calculation of the weighted-average number of shares.

DISCUSSION: When a stock dividend, stock split, or reverse split occurs at any time before issuance of the financial statements, restatement of EPS is required for all periods presented. The purpose is to promote comparability of EPS data among reporting periods.

Answer (B) is incorrect because the effect of stock dividends and stock splits on prior-period earnings must be calculated, and EPS data should be restated for all periods presented in the financial statements. Answer (C) is incorrect because stock dividends and stock splits are treated the same for EPS purposes regardless of their amounts. Answer (D) is incorrect because a stock dividend or stock split is not accounted for or disclosed until it occurs.

7. Snell Co. had 300,000 shares of common stock issued and outstanding at December 31, 2002. No common stock was issued during 2003. On January 1, 2003, Snell issued 200,000 shares of nonconvertible preferred stock. During 2002, Snell declared and paid $75,000 of cash dividends on the common stock and $60,000 on the preferred stock. Net income for the year ended December 31, 2003 was $330,000. What is Snell's 2003 basic earnings per share?

A. $1.10

B. $0.90

C. $0.85

D. $0.65

Answer (B) is correct. *(CPA, adapted)*

REQUIRED: The amount of BEPS.

DISCUSSION: BEPS is equal to the amount of earnings available to the common shareholders divided by the weighted-average number of shares of common stock outstanding during the year. To calculate earnings available to holders of common stock, dividends on cumulative preferred stock must be subtracted from net income whether or not the dividends were declared. Earnings per common share for 2003 thus amounted to $0.90.

$$\frac{\$330{,}000 - \$60{,}000}{300{,}000} = \$0.90$$

Answer (A) is incorrect because $1.10 assumes no preferred dividends were declared. Answer (C) is incorrect because $0.85 assumes the common but not the preferred dividends were subtracted from the numerator. Answer (D) is incorrect because $0.65 assumes all dividends are subtracted from the numerator.

Questions 8 through 11 are based on the following information.

Colon Co. uses a calendar year for financial reporting. The company is authorized to issue 5 million shares of $10 par common stock. At no time has Colon issued any potentially dilutive securities. A two-for-one stock split of Colon's common stock took place on March 31, 2004. Additional information is in the next column.

Number of common shares issued and outstanding at 12/31/01	1,000,000
Shares issued as a result of a 10% stock dividend on 9/30/02	100,000
Shares issued for cash on 3/31/03	1,000,000
Number of common shares issued and outstanding at 12/31/03	2,100,000

8. The weighted-average number of common shares used in computing basic earnings per common share for 2002 on the 2003 comparative income statement was

A. 1,100,000

B. 1,050,000

C. 1,025,000

D. 1,000,000

Answer (A) is correct. *(CMA, adapted)*

REQUIRED: The weighted-average number of shares used in the BEPS computation for 2002 on the 2003 comparative income statement.

DISCUSSION: At the beginning of 2002, 1 million shares were outstanding. Another 100,000 were issued as a result of a stock dividend on September 30. The stock dividend is assumed to have occurred at the beginning of the year. Accordingly, the number of shares outstanding throughout 2002 would have been 1.1 million. No stock dividends or stock splits occurred in 2003. Thus, the same 1.1 million shares used in the BEPS calculation on the 2002 income statement would be used to determine the 2002 BEPS in the 2003 comparative statements.

Answer (B) is incorrect because 1,050,000 assumes the stock dividend affects shares outstanding for 6 months. Answer (C) is incorrect because 1,025,000 assumes the stock dividend affects shares outstanding for 3 months. Answer (D) is incorrect because 1,000,000 does not consider the stock dividend.

9. The weighted-average number of common shares used in computing BEPS for 2003 on the 2003 comparative income statement was

A. 1,600,000

B. 1,850,000

C. 2,100,000

D. 3,700,000

Answer (B) is correct. *(CMA, adapted)*

REQUIRED: The weighted-average number of shares used in computing BEPS for 2003 on the 2003 income statement.

DISCUSSION: At the beginning of 2003, 1.1 million shares were outstanding. This figure remained unchanged for 3 months until March 31 when an additional 1 million shares were issued. Hence, for the last 9 months of the year, 2.1 million shares were outstanding. Weighting the shares outstanding by the amount of time they were out standing results in a weighted average of 1,850,000 shares {[(3 ÷ 12) × 1,100,000] + [(9 ÷ 12) × 2,100,000]}.

Answer (A) is incorrect because the 1,000,000 shares issued on 3/31/03 are assumed to be outstanding for 6 months. Answer (C) is incorrect because the 1,000,000 shares issued on 3/31/03 are assumed to be outstanding for the entire year. Answer (D) is incorrect because 3,700,000 is the number of shares used in computing BEPS for 2003 on the 2004 comparative income statement.

10. The weighted-average number of common shares to be used in computing BEPS for 2004 on the 2004 comparative income statement is

A. 2,100,000

B. 3,150,000

C. 3,675,000

D. 4,200,000

Answer (D) is correct. *(CMA, adapted)*

REQUIRED: The weighted-average number of shares used in computing BEPS for 2004 on the 2004 comparative income statement.

DISCUSSION: At the beginning of 2004, 2.1 million shares were outstanding. Because of the March 31 two-for-one stock split, that number increased to 4.2 million. The stock split is assumed to have occurred on the first day of the year. Consequently, the number of shares outstanding throughout 2004 was 4.2 million.

Answer (A) is incorrect because 2,100,000 ignores the 3/31/04 stock split. Answer (B) is incorrect because 3,150,000 assumes the stock split increases shares outstanding for 6 months. Answer (C) is incorrect because 3,675,000 assumes the stock split increases shares outstanding from the date the split occurred.

11. The weighted-average number of common shares to be used on computing BEPS for 2003 on the 2004 comparative income statement is

A. 1,850,000

B. 2,100,000

C. 3,700,000

D. 4,200,000

Answer (C) is correct. *(CMA, adapted)*

REQUIRED: The weighted-average number of shares used in computing BEPS for 2003 on the 2004 comparative income statement.

DISCUSSION: A stock dividend or split occurring at any time must be treated as though it occurred at the beginning of the earliest period presented for purposes of computing the weighted-average number of shares. Thus, prior-period BEPS figures presented for comparative purposes must be retroactively restated for the effects of a stock dividend or a stock split. The number of shares used in computing the 2003 BEPS on the 2003 income statement was 1,850,000 {[(3 months ÷ 12 months) × 1,100,000 shares] + [(9 months ÷ 12 months) × 2,100,000]}. However, because of the stock split on March 31, 2004, the number of shares doubled. Thus, the BEPS calculation for 2003 on the 2004 comparative income statement should be based on 3,700,000 shares (2 × 1,850,000).

Answer (A) is incorrect because 1,850,000 is the number of shares used in computing BEPS for 2003 on the 2003 income statement. Answer (B) is incorrect because 2,100,000 ignores the 3/31/04 stock split. Answer (D) is incorrect because 4,200,000 is the number of shares used in computing BEPS for 2004 on the 2004 comparative income statement.

12. In computing earnings-per-share data, which of the following is true regarding the weighted-average computation of shares outstanding?

A. Reacquired shares should be excluded from the date of their acquisition.

B. Reacquired shares should be excluded from the beginning of the period in which they were acquired.

C. Stock dividends and stock splits consummated after the close of the period do not affect EPS computations, even though they may have been consummated before issuance of the financial statements.

D. The shares issued during the period as a result of a stock dividend are weighted according to the portion of the period for which they were actually outstanding.

Answer (A) is correct. *(Publisher)*

REQUIRED: The true statement concerning the computation of the weighted average of shares outstanding.

DISCUSSION: Reacquired shares, or treasury shares, no longer represent outstanding stock to the company as of the date of their repurchase. Thus, they should be excluded from the calculation of the weighted-average number of shares as of their reacquisition date.

Answer (B) is incorrect because, until the date of their repurchase, the shares represent outstanding ownership. Answer (C) is incorrect because stock dividends and stock splits occurring anytime before the issuance of the statements require retroactive adjustment of EPS for all periods presented. Answer (D) is incorrect because shares issued in a stock dividend are assumed to have been outstanding from the beginning of all periods presented.

13. Smith Corporation had net income for the year of $101,504 and a simple capital structure consisting of the following common shares outstanding:

Months Outstanding	Number of Shares
January - February	24,000
March - June	29,400
July - November	36,000
December	35,040
Total	124,440

Smith Corporation's basic earnings per share (rounded to the nearest cent) were

A. $2.90

B. $3.20

C. $3.26

D. $3.45

Answer (B) is correct. *(CMA, adapted)*

REQUIRED: The BEPS for a company with a simple capital structure.

DISCUSSION: BEPS equals net income divided by the weighted-average number of shares outstanding. The latter is calculated as follows:

24,000 × (2 ÷ 12)	=	4,000
29,400 × (4 ÷ 12)	=	9,800
36,000 × (5 ÷ 12)	=	15,000
35,040 × (1 ÷ 12)	=	2,920
		31,720

Accordingly, BEPS is $3.20 ($101,504 NI ÷ 31,720 shares).

Answer (A) is incorrect because $2.90 is based on the shares outstanding at year-end. Answer (C) is incorrect because $3.26 is based on an unweighted average of the four levels of shares outstanding during the year. Answer (D) is incorrect because $3.45 is based on the shares outstanding March through June.

14. The following information pertains to Tidwell Corp.'s outstanding stock for 2003:

Common stock, $5 par value	
Shares outstanding, 1/1/03	20,000
2-for-1 stock split, 4/1/03	20,000
Shares issued, 7/1/03	10,000
Preferred stock, $10 par value, 5% cumulative	
Shares outstanding, 1/1/03	4,000

How many shares should Tidwell use to calculate 2003 BEPS?

A. 40,000

B. 45,000

C. 50,000

D. 54,000

Answer (B) is correct. *(CPA, adapted)*

REQUIRED: The number of shares used to calculate BEPS.

DISCUSSION: BEPS is equal to the amount of earnings available to the common shareholders divided by the weighted-average number of shares of common stock outstanding during the year. When a stock dividend, a stock split, or a reverse split occurs other than at the beginning of a year, a retroactive adjustment for the change in capital structure should be made as of the beginning of the earliest accounting period presented. Shares outstanding during the year must then be weighted by the number of months for which they were outstanding in calculating the weighted-average number of shares to be used in determining BEPS. Hence, the new shares issued on 7/1/03 are included in year-end BEPS at their weighted average of 5,000 shares [10,000 shares × (6 months ÷ 12 months)]. Preferred stock is not included even if convertible because the BEPS calculation excludes the effects of potential common stock. Consequently, the total shares used to calculate 2003 BEPS equals 45,000 (20,000 shares outstanding at 1/1/03 + 20,000 stock-split shares + 5,000 shares issued 7/1/03).

Answer (A) is incorrect because 40,000 assumes that the stock split is not treated as though it occurred at the beginning of the period. Answer (C) is incorrect because 50,000 assumes that the shares issued on 7/1/03 were outstanding for 12 months. Answer (D) is incorrect because 54,000 includes the preferred stock and assumes that the shares issued on 7/1/03 were outstanding for 12 months.

16.2 Diluted Earnings per Share

15. In the computation of diluted earnings per share, convertible securities are

A. Ignored.

B. Recognized whether they are dilutive or antidilutive.

C. Recognized only if they are antidilutive.

D. Recognized only if they are dilutive.

Answer (D) is correct. *(CPA, adapted)*

REQUIRED: The true statement about the treatment of convertible securities in computing DEPS.

DISCUSSION: The objective of DEPS is to measure the performance of an entity during an accounting period while giving effect to all dilutive potential common shares that were outstanding during the period. Convertible securities are potential common stock.

Answer (A) is incorrect because convertible securities are not ignored. Answer (B) is incorrect because convertible securities are recognized only when they are dilutive. Answer (C) is incorrect because convertible securities are recognized only when they are dilutive.

16. In calculating annual diluted earnings per share, which of the following should not be considered?

A. The weighted-average number of common shares outstanding.

B. The amount of dividends declared on nonconvertible cumulative preferred shares.

C. The amount of cash dividends declared on common shares.

D. The number of common shares resulting from the assumed conversion of debentures outstanding.

Answer (C) is correct. *(CIA, adapted)*

REQUIRED: The information not included in the calculation of DEPS.

DISCUSSION: The numerator of the DEPS calculation represents the residual income for the period available to holders of common stock and potential common stock. A cash dividend on common stock has no effect on earnings available to common shareholders; i.e., earnings are included whether they are distributed or undistributed.

Answer (A) is incorrect because the weighted-average number of common shares outstanding is included in the denominator of DEPS. Answer (B) is incorrect because the dividend on nonconvertible cumulative preferred stock, whether declared or not, must be deducted from income from continuing operations and also from net income to arrive at earnings available to common shareholders. Answer (D) is incorrect because the assumed conversion of debentures requires adjusting both the numerator (for interest, net of tax effect) and the denominator (for the shares assumed issued) of DEPS.

17. In the computation of DEPS for a complex capital structure, which of the following is a potential common stock?

	Nonconvertible Preferred Stock	Stock Option
A.	Yes	No
B.	Yes	Yes
C.	No	Yes
D.	No	No

Answer (C) is correct. *(CPA, adapted)*

REQUIRED: The potential common stock.

DISCUSSION: SFAS 128 defines potential common stock as a security or other contract that may entitle its holder to obtain common stock during either the reporting period or some future accounting period. Potential common stocks include options, warrants, convertible preferred stock, convertible debt, and contingent stock agreements.

18. In the calculation of diluted earnings per share, a convertible bond was found to be antidilutive in 2002 and dilutive in 2003. The convertible bond is included in the computation for

	2002	2003
A.	Yes	Yes
B.	No	Yes
C.	No	No
D.	Yes	No

Answer (B) is correct. *(CPA, adapted)*

REQUIRED: The circumstances under which potential common stock is included in the determination of DEPS.

DISCUSSION: SFAS 128 states that DEPS is based on the number of common shares outstanding during the period plus the common shares that would have been outstanding if dilutive potential common shares had been issued. Thus, in a period in which the effect of potential common stock is antidilutive, it is not included in the determination of DEPS. It is included, however, in those periods in which its effect is dilutive.

19. A test to determine whether a convertible security is dilutive or antidilutive is to calculate DEPS

A. For the security alone.

B. Without inclusion of the security.

C. For the security alone and compare it with DEPS without inclusion of the security.

D. For the security alone and compare it with DEPS with inclusion of the security.

Answer (C) is correct. *(Publisher)*

REQUIRED: The method of determining whether a convertible security is dilutive or antidilutive.

DISCUSSION: To ascertain whether a convertible security's effect is dilutive or antidilutive, compute DEPS without the security and then compute the incremental effect on DEPS of the security itself. If the change in the numerator divided by the change in the denominator is less than DEPS excluding the security, the item is dilutive. For example, assuming that DEPS, without a hypothetical conversion of convertible preferred stock, is $1.00 and that the quotient of the preferred dividend added back to the numerator and the shares potentially added to the denominator is $.90, the preferred stock is dilutive. In addition, SFAS 128 requires each issue or series of issues of potential common shares be considered separately and in sequence from most to least dilutive.

Answer (A) is incorrect because both calculations are necessary to determine whether an item is dilutive. Answer (B) is incorrect because both calculations are necessary to determine whether an item is dilutive. Answer (D) is incorrect because the comparison should be made with DEPS that excludes the security.

20. When a company reports amounts for basic and diluted earnings per share,

A. They should be presented with equal prominence on the face of the income statement.

B. They need not be shown on the face of the income statement but must be disclosed in the notes to the financial statements.

C. They need to be reported for net income only.

D. BEPS should be presented on the face of the income statement. DEPS may be disclosed either on the face of the income statement or in the notes.

Answer (A) is correct. *(CMA, adapted)*

REQUIRED: The true statement about the reporting of BEPS and DEPS.

DISCUSSION: SFAS 128 requires an entity whose stock is publicly traded to report EPS information on the face of the income statement for both income from continuing operations and net income. In addition, EPS data for any discontinued operation or extraordinary item must be presented on the face of the income statement or in a note. When the entity does not have a simple capital structure, it must present BEPS and DEPS with equal prominence.

Answer (B) is incorrect because certain EPS amounts must be presented on the face of the income statement. Answer (C) is incorrect because EPS must also be presented for income from continuing operations, discontinued operations, and extraordinary items. Answer (D) is incorrect because BEPS and DEPS are to be presented on the face of the income statement with equal prominence.

21. The nature of the adjustment for stock options in the calculation of diluted earnings per share can be described as

A. Historical because earnings are historical.

B. Historical because it indicates the firm's valuation.

C. Pro forma because it indicates potential changes in the number of shares.

D. Pro forma because it indicates potential changes in earnings.

Answer (C) is correct. *(CPA, adapted)*

REQUIRED: The nature of the adjustment required for stock options in calculating DEPS.

DISCUSSION: The denominator in the DEPS calculation is adjusted for the assumed exercise of outstanding call options and warrants issued by the entity if the exercise would have a dilutive effect. The change in the number of shares has not occurred and is only assumed, so the calculation is essentially pro forma.

Answer (A) is incorrect because the conversion of stock options into common shares has not occurred, and the required adjustment is hypothetical. Answer (B) is incorrect because the conversion of stock options into common shares has not occurred, and the required adjustment is hypothetical. Answer (D) is incorrect because the assumed exercise of the options affects only the denominator of the DEPS ratio.

22. Under the treasury stock method, the DEPS calculation is based on the assumption that call options and warrants issued by the reporting entity and outstanding for the entire year were exercised at the

A. End of the period and that the funds obtained thereby were used to purchase common stock at the average market price during the period.

B. Beginning of the period and that the funds obtained thereby were used to purchase common stock at the average market price during the period.

C. End of the period and that the funds obtained thereby were used to purchase common stock at the current market price in effect at the end of the period.

D. Beginning of the period and that the funds obtained thereby were used to purchase common stock at the current market price in effect at the end of the period.

Answer (B) is correct. *(Publisher)*

REQUIRED: The proper application of the treasury stock method to the assumed exercise of options and warrants in the calculation of DEPS.

DISCUSSION: The treasury stock method of accounting for dilutive call options and warrants issued by the reporting entity assumes the exercise of outstanding options and warrants at the beginning of the period or at time of issuance, if later. The treasury stock method assumes that the proceeds from the exercise are used to purchase common stock at the average market price during the period. The incremental shares, that is, the excess of those assumed issued over those assumed purchased, are included in the DEPS denominator.

Answer (A) is incorrect because the options and warrants are assumed to have been exercised at the beginning of the period. Answer (C) is incorrect because the options and warrants are assumed to have been exercised at the beginning of the period, and the average market price during the period is used. Answer (D) is incorrect because the average market price during the period is used.

23. Deaton, Inc. had 300,000 shares of common stock issued and outstanding at December 31, 2002. On July 1, 2003, an additional 50,000 shares of common stock were issued for cash. Deaton also had issued unexercised stock options to purchase 40,000 shares of common stock at $15 per share outstanding at the beginning and end of 2003. The average market price of Deaton's common stock was $20 during 2003. What number of shares should be used in computing diluted earnings per share for the year ended December 31, 2003?

A. 325,000

B. 335,000

C. 360,000

D. 365,000

Answer (B) is correct. *(CPA, adapted)*

REQUIRED: The number of shares to be used in computing DEPS.

DISCUSSION: On July 1, 2003, 50,000 shares of common stock were issued. Hence, for the purpose of calculating Deaton's weighted-average number of shares, 300,000 shares should be considered outstanding for the first 6 months and 350,000 shares for the second 6 months, a weighted average of 325,000 shares.

Dilutive call options and warrants are included in DEPS. These options are assumed to be exercised at the beginning of the period using the treasury stock method. This method assumes the options are exercised and the $600,000 of proceeds (40,000 options × $15) is used to repurchase shares. In the DEPS computation, the assumed repurchase price is the average market price for the period ($20), so 30,000 shares are assumed to be repurchased ($600,000 ÷ $20). The difference between the shares assumed to be issued and those repurchased (40,000 – 30,000 = 10,000) is added to the weighted average of common shares outstanding to determine the DEPS denominator. Thus, 335,000 (325,000 + 10,000) shares should be used in computing DEPS for the year ending December 31, 2003.

Answer (A) is incorrect because 325,000 does not include the 10,000 shares includible due to the stock option. Answer (C) is incorrect because 360,000 includes the full 50,000 shares sold on July 1 instead of the weighted-average number of shares of 25,000. Answer (D) is incorrect because 365,000 includes the full 40,000 shares covered by the stock options instead of the amount computed under the treasury stock method.

24. In a diluted earnings-per-share computation, the effect of outstanding call options and warrants issued by the reporting entity is reflected by applying the treasury stock method. If the exercise price of these options or warrants exceeds the average market price, the computation would

A. Fairly present diluted earnings per share on a prospective basis.

B. Fairly present the maximum potential dilution of diluted earnings per share on a prospective basis.

C. Reflect the excess of the number of shares assumed issued over the number of shares assumed reacquired as the potential dilution of earnings per share.

D. Be antidilutive.

Answer (D) is correct. *(CPA, adapted)*

REQUIRED: The effect on DEPS of an exercise price above the average market price for options and warrants.

DISCUSSION: Under the treasury stock method, call options and warrants issued by the reporting entity are assumed to be exercised at the beginning of the period or at time of issuance, if later. The proceeds are then assumed to be used to reacquire common shares outstanding at the average market price for the period. The effect on the denominator in the DEPS calculation is the difference between the shares assumed to be issued and the treasury shares assumed to be acquired. If the exercise price exceeds the average market price, more shares would be purchased than issued. Because these assumed transactions would increase DEPS by decreasing the denominator, their effect would be antidilutive.

Answer (A) is incorrect because, when the exercise price exceeds the average market price, the result is antidilutive. Answer (B) is incorrect because, when the exercise price exceeds the average market price, the result is antidilutive. Answer (C) is incorrect because the number of shares reacquired would exceed the number issued.

25. How are partially paid stock subscriptions treated in the computation of EPS?

A. By use of the treasury stock method.

B. By not including them until issuance.

C. By disclosure only.

D. By use of the if-converted method.

Answer (A) is correct. *(Publisher)*

REQUIRED: The treatment of stock subscriptions in EPS computations.

DISCUSSION: SFAS 128 states that stock purchase contracts, partially paid stock subscriptions, and nonvested stock granted to employees are equivalent to stock options and warrants. Thus, the treasury stock method is used to account for partially paid stock subscriptions.

Answer (B) is incorrect because, if the stock subscriptions are dilutive, they must be included in the calculation of EPS. Answer (C) is incorrect because, if the stock subscriptions are dilutive, they must be included in the calculation of EPS. Answer (D) is incorrect because the if-converted method applies to convertible securities.

26. Troupe Company had 100,000 shares of common stock issued and outstanding at December 31, 2002. On July 1, 2003, Troupe issued a 10% stock dividend. Unexercised call options to purchase 20,000 shares of Troupe's common stock (adjusted for the 2003 stock dividend) at $20 per share were outstanding at the beginning and end of 2003. The average market price of Troupe's common stock (which was not affected by the stock dividend) was $25 per share during 2003. Net income for the year ended December 31, 2003 was $550,000. What should be Troupe's 2003 DEPS?

A. $4.82

B. $5.00

C. $5.05

D. $5.24

Answer (A) is correct. *(CPA, adapted)*

REQUIRED: The DEPS for the year given a midyear stock dividend and unexercised stock options.

DISCUSSION: A stock dividend occurring at any time before issuance of the financial statements must be reflected as a retroactive adjustment of the capital structure at the beginning of the first period presented. Hence, the 110,000 shares outstanding after the stock dividend are deemed to have been outstanding during the entire year.

The options are not antidilutive because the exercise price was less than the average market price. Accordingly, exercise of the options is assumed to have occurred at the beginning of the year at the exercise price of $20. Under the treasury stock method, the assumed proceeds of $400,000 (20,000 shares × $20) are used to repurchase 16,000 shares ($400,000 ÷ $25) at the average market price during the period. The difference between the 20,000 shares assumed to be issued and the 16,000 shares assumed to be repurchased increases the DEPS denominator from 110,000 shares to 114,000 shares. Thus, 2003 DEPS equals $4.82 ($550,000 income ÷ 114,000 shares).

Answer (B) is incorrect because $5.00 does not include the stock options in the calculation of shares outstanding for the year. Answer (C) is incorrect because $5.05 assumes the shares issued as a stock dividend were outstanding for 6 months. Answer (D) is incorrect because $5.24 assumes the shares issued as a stock dividend were outstanding for 6 months. This amount also excludes the stock options.

27. Starks Corporation has 300,000 shares of common stock outstanding. The only other securities outstanding are 10,000 shares of 9% cumulative preferred stock with detachable warrants (10 warrants per preferred share). Each warrant provides for the purchase of one share of common stock at $72. For 2003, net income was $1.6 million. During 2003, the average market price of common stock was $125. The price at December 31, 2003 was $120. What number of shares should be used to determine 2003 diluted earnings per share?

A. 340,000

B. 342,400

C. 357,600

D. 400,000

Answer (B) is correct. *(L. Krueger)*

REQUIRED: The number of shares to be used to determine DEPS.

DISCUSSION: The treasury stock method of accounting for the dilutive effect of call options and warrants issued by the reporting entity assumes they are exercised at the beginning of the period at the exercise price, with the proceeds being used to repurchase shares in the market. The assumed repurchase price is the average market price. Because the $7.2 million of hypothetical proceeds (10,000 shares of preferred × 10 warrants per share × $72 exercise price) can be used to purchase 57,600 shares ($7,200,000 ÷ 125), the DEPS denominator will be 342,400 shares (300,000 common shares outstanding + 100,000 assumed issued upon conversion – 57,600 assumed repurchased).

Answer (A) is incorrect because 340,000 is based on the 12/31/03 price of $120. Answer (C) is incorrect because 357,600 includes the 57,600 shares assumed to be repurchased. Answer (D) is incorrect because 400,000 does not adjust for treasury stock assumed to have been purchased.

28. The if-converted method of computing DEPS amounts assumes conversion of convertible securities at the

A. Beginning of the earliest period reported (or at time of issuance, if later).

B. Beginning of the earliest period reported (regardless of time of issuance).

C. Middle of the earliest period reported (regardless of time of issuance).

D. End of the earliest period reported (regardless of time of issuance).

Answer (A) is correct. *(CPA, adapted)*

REQUIRED: The conversion assumption underlying the if-converted method.

DISCUSSION: The if-converted method of computing DEPS assumes that convertible securities are included in the determination of DEPS if dilutive. Conversion is assumed to have occurred at the beginning of the earliest period reported or, if the security was issued at a later time, at the date of issuance.

29. A company's convertible debt securities are dilutive for EPS purposes. What is the effect of these securities on the calculation of BEPS and DEPS?

	BEPS	DEPS
A.	Decrease	Decrease
B.	Increase	No effect
C.	No effect	Decrease
D.	Decrease	Increase

Answer (C) is correct. *(CPA, adapted)*

REQUIRED: The effect of dilutive convertible securities on the calculation of BEPS and DEPS.

DISCUSSION: SFAS 128 requires that securities classified as potential common stock be included in the computation of the number of common shares outstanding for DEPS if the effect of the inclusion is dilutive. Dilutive potential common stock decreases DEPS. BEPS is not affected by potential common stock.

30. In the computation of DEPS, the number of common shares into which convertible preferred stock is assumed to be converted is added as an adjustment to the denominator (number of shares outstanding). If the preferred stock is preferred as to dividends, which amount should be added as an adjustment to the numerator (earnings available to common shareholders)?

A. Annual preferred dividend.

B. Annual preferred dividend times (1 – the income tax rate).

C. Annual preferred dividend times the income tax rate.

D. Annual preferred dividend divided by the income tax rate.

Answer (A) is correct. *(CPA, adapted)*

REQUIRED: The adjustment to the numerator for preferred dividends in the DEPS computation.

DISCUSSION: If a capital structure has convertible preferred stock with a dilutive effect on DEPS, the if-converted method is used. This method assumes the conversion of the preferred stock occurred at the beginning of the accounting period or at issuance, if later. The annual preferred dividend is accordingly added back to earnings available to common shareholders (the numerator of the DEPS ratio).

Answer (B) is incorrect because the tax rate is not a consideration. The preferred dividend is paid with after-tax dollars; i.e., preferred dividends are not tax-deductible. Answer (C) is incorrect because the tax rate is not a consideration. The preferred dividend is paid with after-tax dollars; i.e., preferred dividends are not tax-deductible. Answer (D) is incorrect because the tax rate is not a consideration. The preferred dividend is paid with after-tax dollars; i.e., preferred dividends are not tax-deductible.

31. In determining earnings per share, interest expense, net of applicable income taxes, on dilutive convertible debt should be

A. Added back to net income for BEPS and ignored for DEPS.

B. Added back to net income for both BEPS and DEPS.

C. Deducted from net income for DEPS.

D. Added back to net income for DEPS.

Answer (D) is correct. *(CPA, adapted)*

REQUIRED: The correct treatment of after-tax interest on dilutive convertible debt.

DISCUSSION: In accordance with the if-converted method, the DEPS calculation assumes that dilutive convertible debt is converted into common stock at the beginning of the period or at the time of issuance, if later. Given the assumed conversion, no debt would exist upon which interest could have been paid. Interest is a deduction in arriving at net income. Accordingly, that interest savings, net of tax effect, should be added back to net income in the DEPS computation.

32. During the current year, Green Corp. had the following two classes of stock issued and outstanding for the entire year:

- 100,000 shares of common stock, $1 par.
- 1,000 shares of 4% preferred stock, $100 par, convertible share for share into common stock. This stock is cumulative whether or not earned, and no preferred dividends are in arrears.

Green's current-year net income was $900,000, and its income tax rate for the year was 30%. Diluted earnings per share for the current year are

A. $9.00

B. $8.96

C. $8.91

D. $8.87

Answer (C) is correct. *(CPA, adapted)*

REQUIRED: The DEPS given convertible preferred stock.

DISCUSSION: DEPS is equal to the amount of earnings available to common shareholders and to holders of dilutive potential common stock, divided by the weighted-average number of shares of common stock and additional common shares that would have been outstanding if dilutive potential common shares had been issued. Dilution is tested by calculating EPS and the incremental effect of the potential common shares on EPS. BEPS equals income available to common shareholders (net income – cumulative preferred dividend) divided by the weighted average of common shares outstanding. Thus, BEPS is $8.96 {[$900,000 NI – (4% × 1,000 preferred shares × $100 par)] ÷ 100,000 common shares}. The incremental effect of the potential common shares equals the preferred dividends added back to the numerator if conversion is assumed divided by the potential common shares, or $4.00 ($4,000 ÷ 1,000). Because $4.00 is less than $8.96, the potential common shares are dilutive. Accordingly, the convertible preferred stock is assumed to be converted at the beginning of the year, and no dividends are deemed to have been paid. The DEPS calculation therefore adds the $4,000 preferred dividend to the BEPS numerator and the 1,000 common shares into which the preferred stock can be converted to the BEPS denominator. DEPS is $8.91 [($896,000 + $4,000) ÷ (100,000 + 1,000)].

Answer (A) is incorrect because $9.00 is equal to $900,000 net income divided by 100,000 common shares. Answer (B) is incorrect because $8.96 is equal to BEPS. Answer (D) is incorrect because $8.87 is equal to $900,000 net income minus the $4,000 preferred dividend, divided by 101,000 shares.

33. The Fleming Corporation had 200,000 shares of common stock and 10,000 shares of cumulative, 6%, $100 par preferred stock outstanding during 2003. The preferred stock is convertible at the rate of three shares of common per share of preferred. For 2003, the company had a $30,000 net loss from continuing operations. Fleming should report 2003 loss per share of

A. $(.13)

B. $(.15)

C. $(.39)

D. $(.45)

Answer (D) is correct. *(Publisher)*

REQUIRED: The loss per share given convertible preferred stock outstanding.

DISCUSSION: Potential common stock always has an antidilutive effect if an entity has a loss from continuing operations or a loss from continuing operations available to common shareholders (after an adjustment for preferred dividends). Thus, the loss per share reported should be based on common shares outstanding. When preferred stock is cumulative, the dividend, whether earned or not, is deducted from income from continuing operations and net income or added to any loss for the year in computing earnings or loss, respectively, per share of common stock. When preferred stock is noncumulative, an adjustment is made for dividends declared. If the dividend is cumulative only if earned, no adjustment is necessary except to the extent of available income; that is, the preferred dividends accumulate only to the extent of net income. Accordingly, the loss per share is $(.45) {[$30,000 + (6% × $100 × 10,000 preferred shares)] ÷ 200,000 shares of common stock}.

Answer (A) is incorrect because $(.13) includes the convertible preferred stock. Answer (B) is incorrect because $(.15) does not include the cumulative preferred dividends in the computation. Answer (C) is incorrect because $(.39) includes 200,000 shares of common stock as preferred stock convertible 3-for-1 into common stock (200,000 ÷ 3 = 66,666) and the 10,000 shares of preferred stock as common stock.

Questions 34 through 36 are based on the following information.

Collins Corp.'s capital structure was as follows:

	December 31 2002	December 31 2003
Outstanding shares of stock:		
Common	100,000	100,000
Convertible preferred	10,000	10,000
9% convertible bonds	$1,000,000	$1,000,000

During 2003, Collins paid dividends of $3.00 per share on its preferred stock. The preferred shares are convertible into 20,000 shares of common stock, and the 9% bonds are convertible into 30,000 shares of common stock. Assume that the income tax rate is 30%.

34. If net income for 2003 is $350,000, Collins should report DEPS as

A. $3.20

B. $2.95

C. $2.92

D. $2.75

Answer (D) is correct. *(CPA, adapted)*

REQUIRED: The DEPS given convertible preferred stock, convertible bonds, and net income of $350,000.

DISCUSSION: Potential common stock is included in the calculation of DEPS if it is dilutive. When two or more issues of potential common stock are outstanding, each issue is considered separately in sequence from the most to the least dilutive. This procedure is necessary because a convertible security may be dilutive on its own but antidilutive when included with other potential common shares in the calculation of DEPS. The incremental effect on EPS determines the degree of dilution. The lower the incremental effect, the more dilutive.

The incremental effect of the convertible preferred stock is $1.50 [($3 preferred dividend × 10,000) ÷ 20,000 potential common shares]. The incremental effect of the convertible debt is $2.10 {[$1,000,000 × 9% × (1.0 – 30%)] ÷ 30,000 potential common shares}. Because the $1.50 incremental effect of the convertible preferred is lower, it is the more dilutive, and its incremental effect is compared with BEPS, which equals $3.20 [($350,000 – 30,000) ÷ 100,000]. Because $1.50 is lower than $3.20, the convertible preferred is dilutive and is included in a trial calculation of DEPS. The result is $2.92 [($350,000 – $30,000 + $30,000) ÷ (100,000 + 20,000)]. However, the $2.10 incremental effect of the convertible debt is lower than the $2.92 trial calculation, so the convertible debt is also dilutive and should be included in the calculation of DEPS. Thus, DEPS is $2.75 as indicated below.

$$\frac{\$350{,}000 - \$30{,}000 + \$30{,}000 + \$63{,}000}{100{,}000 + 20{,}000 + 30{,}000} = \$2.75$$

Answer (A) is incorrect because $3.20 equals BEPS. Answer (B) is incorrect because $2.95 excludes the convertible preferred stock. Answer (C) is incorrect because $2.92 excludes the convertible debt.

35. If net income for 2003 is $245,000, Collins should report DEPS as

A. $2.15

B. $2.14

C. $2.05

D. $2.04

Answer (D) is correct. *(Publisher)*

REQUIRED: The DEPS given convertible preferred stock, convertible debt, and net income of $245,000.

DISCUSSION: The incremental effect of the convertible preferred is $1.50 and of the convertible debt is $2.10. Given net income of $245,000, BEPS equals $2.15 [($245,000 – $30,000) ÷ 100,000]. The $1.50 incremental effect of the convertible preferred stock is lower than BEPS, so it is dilutive and should be included in a trial calculation of DEPS. The result is $2.04 [($245,000 – $30,000 + $30,000) ÷ (100,000 + 20,000)]. Because the $2.10 incremental effect of the convertible debt is higher than $2.04, the convertible debt is antidilutive and should not be included in the DEPS calculation. Thus, DEPS should be reported as $2.04.

Answer (A) is incorrect because $2.15 equals BEPS. Answer (B) is incorrect because $2.14 excludes the convertible preferred stock. Answer (C) is incorrect because $2.05 includes the convertible debt.

36. If net income for 2003 is $170,000, Collins should report DEPS as

A. $1.40

B. $1.42

C. $1.56

D. $1.70

Answer (A) is correct. *(Publisher)*

REQUIRED: The DEPS given convertible preferred stock, convertible debt, and net income of $170,000.

DISCUSSION: Given net income of $170,000, BEPS equals $1.40 [($170,000 – $30,000) ÷ 100,000]. This amount is lower than both the $2.10 incremental effect of the convertible debt and the $1.50 incremental effect of the convertible preferred. Thus, both convertible securities are antidilutive, and Collins should report that DEPS is equal to BEPS. This dual presentation may be displayed on one line of the income statement.

Answer (B) is incorrect because $1.42 includes the convertible preferred stock. Answer (C) is incorrect because $1.56 includes the convertible debt. Answer (D) is incorrect because $1.70 results from not adjusting the $170,000 of net income for the $30,000 of preferred dividends in determining income available to common shareholders.

37. During all of 2003, Berlin Co. had outstanding 100,000 shares of common stock and 5,000 shares of noncumulative, $7 preferred stock. Each share of the latter is convertible into three shares of common. For 2003, Berlin had $230,000 income from continuing operations and $575,000 of extraordinary losses; no dividends were paid or declared. Berlin should report 2003 diluted earnings (loss) per share for income from continuing operations and for net income (loss), respectively, of

A. $2.30 and $(3.45).

B. $2.00 and $(3.00).

C. $2.19 and $(3.29).

D. $2.26 and $(3.39).

Answer (B) is correct. *(CPA, adapted)*

REQUIRED: The diluted earnings (loss) per share from continuing operations and net income (loss).

DISCUSSION: The noncumulative convertible preferred stock is dilutive because its assumed conversion will have no effect on the DEPS numerator and will increase the denominator by 15,000 (5,000 × 3) shares. DEPS for income from continuing operations is $2.00 ($230,000 ÷ 115,000 shares). Net loss equals the $230,000 income from continuing operations minus the $575,000 extraordinary loss, or $345,000. This amount divided by the 115,000 shares results in a diluted net loss per share of $3.00.

The effect of including the convertible preferred in the calculation of the net loss per share is antidilutive. However, SFAS 128 requires that potential common stock that is dilutive for purposes of determining DEPS from continuing operations be included in all calculations of diluted per-share amounts.

Answer (A) is incorrect because the convertible preferred stock is excluded from the calculation of shares outstanding for the year. Answer (C) is incorrect because each share of preferred stock is convertible into three shares of common stock. Answer (D) is incorrect because the number of shares outstanding is calculated as if three shares of preferred stock were convertible into one share of common stock.

38. At the beginning of the fiscal year, June 1, 2002, Piotrowski Corporation had 80,000 shares of common stock outstanding. Also outstanding was $200,000 of 8% convertible bonds that had been issued at $1,000 par. The bonds were convertible into 20,000 shares of common stock; however, no bonds were converted during the year. The company's tax rate is 34%. Piotrowski's net income for the year was $107,000. Diluted earnings per share of Piotrowski common stock for the fiscal year ended May 31, 2003 was

A. $1.07

B. $1.18

C. $1.23

D. $1.34

Answer (B) is correct. *(CMA, adapted)*

REQUIRED: The DEPS given convertible bonds outstanding.

DISCUSSION: Potential common shares that have a dilutive effect are included in the determination of DEPS. The calculation of DEPS assumes the conversion of the bonds at the beginning of the year, so the assumption is that no interest would be paid. Because bond interest was subtracted in determining net income, the DEPS numerator should be increased by the interest paid (net of tax effect). This after-tax effect was a $10,560 reduction of net income [($8% × $200,000) × (1 – 34% tax rate)]. The denominator of the DEPS calculation is 100,000 shares (80,000 common shares outstanding + 20,000 shares that would be issued if the bonds were converted as of the beginning of the year). Hence, DEPS is equal to $1.18 per share [($107,000 NI + $10,560) ÷ (80,000 + 20,000)]. The convertible bonds are dilutive because their incremental inclusion reduces the corresponding BEPS amount.

Answer (A) is incorrect because $1.07 fails to adjust the numerator for the interest savings and extra taxes. Answer (C) is incorrect because $1.23 fails to consider the additional taxes that would have to be paid on the interest savings. Answer (D) is incorrect because $1.34 equals BEPS.

39. On June 30, 2002, Kight Co. issued twenty $10,000, 7% bonds at par. Each bond was convertible into 200 shares of common stock. On January 1, 2003, 10,000 shares of common stock were outstanding. The bondholders converted all the bonds on July 1, 2003. The following amounts were reported in Kight's income statement for the year ended December 31, 2003:

Revenues	$977,000
Operating expenses	920,000
Interest on bonds	7,000
Income before income tax	50,000
Income tax at 30%	15,000
Net income	$ 35,000

What amount should Kight report as its 2003 diluted earnings per share?

A. $2.50

B. $2.85

C. $3.00

D. $3.50

Answer (B) is correct. *(CPA, adapted)*

REQUIRED: The DEPS given convertible bonds.

DISCUSSION: DEPS should be calculated even though no potential common shares were outstanding at year-end. The reason is that the purpose of DEPS is to measure the performance of the entity over the reporting period while giving effect to all potential common shares that were outstanding during the period. The bonds were converted into 4,000 (20 bonds × 200 shares) shares of common stock on July 1, 2003. Thus, the weighted-average number of shares of common stock outstanding is 12,000 shares [(10,000 × 12 ÷ 12) + (4,000 × 6 ÷ 12)]. BEPS therefore equals $2.92 ($35,000 net income ÷ 12,000). To determine if the potential common shares are dilutive, their incremental effect on EPS is calculated. This effect is equal to the after-tax interest that would be added back to net income divided by the potential common shares that would be added to the denominator. After-tax interest equals $4,900 [$7,000 × (1.0 – .30 tax rate)], and the dilutive potential common shares equal 2,000 [20 bonds × 200 shares × (6 ÷ 12 months)]. The latter computation is a weighted average because the convertible bonds were outstanding for only 6 months. The incremental effect on EPS of the assumed conversion at the beginning of the year is $2.45 ($4,900 ÷ 2,000 shares). This amount is less than BEPS, so the convertible bonds are dilutive. Thus, DEPS equals $2.85 [($35,000 + $4,900) ÷ (12,000 + 2,000)].

Answer (A) is incorrect because $2.50 is based on a numerator of $35,000. Answer (C) is incorrect because $3.00 is based on a numerator of $42,000 (not net of tax). Answer (D) is incorrect because $3.50 is based on net income of $35,000 and 10,000 shares.

40. Bilco had 10,000 shares of common stock outstanding throughout 2003. There was no potential dilution of earnings per share except that, in 2002, Bilco agreed to issue 2,000 additional shares of its stock to the former shareholders of an acquired company if the acquired company's earnings for any of the 5 years 2003 through 2008 exceed $5,000. Results of operations for 2003 were

Net income of Bilco	$10,000
Net income of acquired company	4,000
Consolidated net income	$14,000

Diluted earnings per share for 2003 on a consolidated basis is

A. $14,000 ÷ 10,000 = $1.40

B. $14,000 ÷ 12,000 = $1.17

C. $15,000 ÷ 10,000 = $1.50

D. $15,000 ÷ 12,000 = $1.25

Answer (A) is correct. *(CPA, adapted)*

REQUIRED: The consolidated DEPS when contingent shares are outstanding.

DISCUSSION: SFAS 128 provides that, if all necessary conditions have not been met at the end of the reporting period, the number of contingently issuable shares included in the DEPS denominator equals the number issuable if the end of the reporting period were the end of the contingency period. Because the acquired company earned only $4,000 for 2003, no contingent shares would be issued if the end of 2003 were the end of the contingency period. Thus, the contingent shares are disregarded. DEPS equals BEPS of $1.40 ($14,000 consolidated net income ÷ 10,000 shares issued and outstanding).

Questions 41 through 47 are based on the following information.

Carolina Company is a calendar-year entity with a complex capital structure. It calculates basic and diluted earnings per share (BEPS and DEPS, respectively) in accordance with SFAS 128, *Earnings per Share.* Carolina reported no cumulative effect of accounting changes or discontinued operations, but it had an extraordinary loss (net of tax) of $1,200,000 in the first quarter when its income before the extraordinary item was $1,000,000.

The average market price of Carolina's common stock for the first quarter was $25, the shares outstanding at the beginning of the period equaled 300,000, and 12,000 shares were issued on March 1.

At the beginning of the quarter, Carolina had outstanding $2,000,000 of 5% convertible bonds, with each $1,000 bond convertible into 10 shares of common stock. No bonds were converted.

At the beginning of the quarter, Carolina also had outstanding 120,000 shares of preferred stock paying a quarterly dividend of $.10 per share and convertible to common stock on a one-to-one basis. Holders of 60,000 shares of preferred stock exercised their conversion privilege on February 1.

Throughout the first quarter, warrants to buy 50,000 shares of Carolina's common stock for $28 per share were outstanding but unexercised. Carolina's tax rate was 30%.

41. The weighted-average number of shares used to calculate BEPS amounts for the first quarter is

A. 444,000

B. 372,000

C. 344,000

D. 300,000

Answer (C) is correct. *(Publisher)*

REQUIRED: The weighted-average number of shares used to calculate BEPS amounts for the first quarter.

DISCUSSION: The number of shares outstanding at January 1 was 300,000, 12,000 shares were issued on March 1, and 60,000 shares of preferred stock were converted to 60,000 shares of common stock on February 1. Thus, the weighted-average number of shares used to calculate BEPS amounts for the first quarter is 344,000 {300,000 + [12,000 × (1 ÷ 3)] + [60,000 × (2 ÷ 3)]}.

Answer (A) is incorrect because 444,000 is the adjusted weighted-average number of shares used in the DEPS calculation. Answer (B) is incorrect because 372,000 is the total outstanding at March 31. Answer (D) is incorrect because 300,000 equals the shares outstanding at January 1.

42. The control number for determining whether potential common shares are dilutive or antidilutive is

A. $1,000,000

B. $994,000

C. $(206,000)

D. $(1,200,000)

Answer (B) is correct. *(Publisher)*

REQUIRED: The control number for determining whether potential common shares are dilutive or antidilutive.

DISCUSSION: GAAP requires that a company use income from continuing operations (in Carolina's case, income before extraordinary item), adjusted for preferred dividends, as the control number for determining whether potential common shares are dilutive or antidilutive. Hence, the number of potential common shares used in calculating DEPS for income from continuing operations is also used in calculating the other DEPS amounts even if the effect is antidilutive with respect to the corresponding BEPS amounts. However, if the entity has a loss from continuing operations available to common shareholders, no potential common shares are included in the calculation of any DEPS amount (SFAS 128). The control number for Carolina is $994,000 {$1,000,000 income before extraordinary item – [$.10 per share dividend × (120,000 preferred shares – 60,000 preferred shares converted)]}.

Answer (A) is incorrect because $1,000,000 is unadjusted income from continuing operations. Answer (C) is incorrect because $(206,000) is the net loss available to common shareholders after subtracting the extraordinary loss. Answer (D) is incorrect because $(1,200,000) is the extraordinary loss.

43. BEPS for net income or loss is

A. $2.89

B. $(0.46)

C. $(0.60)

D. $(3.49)

Answer (C) is correct. *(Publisher)*

REQUIRED: The BEPS for net income or loss.

DISCUSSION: The weighted-average of shares used in the BEPS denominator is 344,000 {300,000 + [12,000 × (1 month ÷ 3 months)] + [60,000 × (2 months ÷ 3 months)]}. The numerator equals income before extraordinary item minus preferred dividends of $6,000 [$.10 × (120,000 preferred shares – 60,000 preferred shares converted)] minus the extraordinary loss. Thus, the numerator equals $(206,000) [$1,000,000 – $6,000 – $1,200,000]. BEPS for net loss is $(0.60) [$(206,000) ÷ 344,000 shares].

Answer (A) is incorrect because $2.89 is BEPS for income before the extraordinary item. Answer (B) is incorrect because $(0.46) uses the denominator of the DEPS calculation. Answer (D) is incorrect because $(3.49) is the BEPS amount for the extraordinary loss.

44. Refer to the information on page 396. The weighted-average number of shares used to calculate DEPS amounts for the first quarter is

A. 444,000

B. 438,000

C. 372,000

D. 344,000

Answer (A) is correct. *(Publisher)*

REQUIRED: The weighted-average number of shares used to calculate DEPS amounts for the first quarter.

DISCUSSION: The denominator of DEPS equals the weighted-average number of shares used in the BEPS calculation (344,000) plus dilutive potential common shares (assuming the control number is not a loss). The incremental shares from assumed conversion of warrants is zero because they are antidilutive. The $25 market price is less than the $28 exercise price. The assumed conversion of all the preferred shares at the beginning of the quarter results in 80,000 incremental shares {[120,000 shares × (3 ÷ 3)] – [60,000 shares × (2 ÷ 3)]}. The assumed conversion of all the bonds at the beginning of the quarter results in 20,000 incremental shares [($2,000,000 ÷ $1,000 per bond) × 10 common shares per bond]. Consequently, the weighted-average number of shares used to calculate DEPS amounts for the first quarter is 444,000 (344,000 + 0 + 80,000 + 20,000).

Answer (B) is incorrect because 438,000 assumes the hypothetical exercise of all the warrants at the beginning of the period at a price of $28 and the repurchase of shares using the proceeds at a price of $25. Answer (C) is incorrect because 372,000 is the total outstanding at March 31. Answer (D) is incorrect because 344,000 is the denominator of the BEPS fraction.

45. Refer to the information on page 396. The effect of assumed conversions on the numerator of the DEPS fraction is

A. $31,000

B. $25,000

C. $23,500

D. $17,500

Answer (C) is correct. *(Publisher)*

REQUIRED: The effect of assumed conversions on the numerator of the DEPS fraction.

DISCUSSION: If all of the convertible preferred shares are assumed to be converted on January 1, $6,000 of dividends [$.10 × (120,000 – 60,000) preferred shares] will not be paid. Furthermore, if the bonds are assumed to be converted on January 1, interest of $17,500 {[5% × $2,000,000 ÷ 4] × (1.0 – .3 tax rate)} will not be paid. Accordingly, the effect of assumed conversions on the numerator of the DEPS fraction is an addition of $23,500 ($6,000 + $17,500) to the income available to common shareholders.

Answer (A) is incorrect because $31,000 disregards the tax shield provided by bond interest. Answer (B) is incorrect because $25,000 equals one quarter's bond interest payment. Answer (D) is incorrect because $17,500 is the effect of the assumed conversion of the bonds alone.

46. Refer to the information on page 396. The difference between BEPS and DEPS for the extraordinary item is

A. $2.89

B. $2.10

C. $.79

D. $.60

Answer (C) is correct. *(Publisher)*

REQUIRED: The difference between BEPS and DEPS for the extraordinary item.

DISCUSSION: BEPS for the extraordinary loss is $(3.49) [$(1,200,000) ÷ 344,000], whereas DEPS is $(2.70) [$(1,200,000) ÷ 444,000 shares].

Answer (A) is incorrect because $2.89 is the difference between DEPS and BEPS for the extraordinary loss. Answer (B) is incorrect because $2.10 is the difference between DEPS for the extraordinary loss and the BEPS for the net loss available to common shareholders after the extraordinary loss. Answer (D) is incorrect because $.60 is the BEPS for the net loss available to common shareholders after the extraordinary loss.

47. Refer to the information on page 396. DEPS for net income or loss is

A. $2.29

B. $(0.41)

C. $(0.53)

D. $(2.70)

Answer (B) is correct. *(Publisher)*

REQUIRED: The DEPS for net income or loss.

DISCUSSION: The numerator equals the income available to common shareholders, plus the effect of the assumed conversions, minus the extraordinary loss. The denominator equals the weighted-average of shares outstanding plus the dilutive potential common shares. Hence, DEPS for net loss is $(.41) [($994,000 + $23,500 – $1,200,000) ÷ 444,000].

Answer (A) is incorrect because $2.29 is DEPS for income before the extraordinary item. Answer (C) is incorrect because $(0.53) is based on the BEPS denominator. Answer (D) is incorrect because $(2.70) is DEPS for the extraordinary item.

16.3 Share-Based Payment

48. SFAS 123 (revised 2004), *Share-Based Payment*, normally requires entities to account for share-based employee compensation awards classified as equity in accordance with which of the following methods?

	Fair-Value Method	Intrinsic-Value Method
A.	Yes	Yes
B.	Yes	No
C.	No	Yes
D.	No	No

Answer (B) is correct. *(Publisher)*

REQUIRED: The method(s) prescribed for accounting for share-based employee compensations awards.

DISCUSSION: Entities must account for share-based payments classified as equity in accordance with the fair-value method except in the rare cases in which a nonpublic entity cannot reasonably estimate the fair value of the equity instruments at the grant date. In these cases, entities must account for such payments in accordance with the intrinsic-value method.

Answer (A) is incorrect because the pronouncement superseded by SFAS 123R permitted either method. However, an award classified as equity now must be measured at fair value except in rare cases. Answer (C) is incorrect because the pronouncement superseded by SFAS 123R permitted either method. However, an award classified as equity now must be measured at fair value except in rare cases. Answer (D) is incorrect because SFAS 123R prescribes the fair-value method except in rare cases.

49. The date on which an employer becomes contingently obligated to make share-based payments compensation to an employee who renders the requisite service is the

A. Grant date

B. Service inception date

C. Vesting date

D. Date of completion of the requisite service period

Answer (A) is correct. *(Publisher)*

REQUIRED: The date on which an employer becomes contingently obligated to issue share-based payments to an employee who renders the requisite service.

DISCUSSION: SFAS 123R generally requires a public entity to measure the cost of employee services received in exchange for equity instruments at the fair value of the instruments on the grant date and to allocate that cost to the requisite service period. The grant date is the date at which (1) a mutual understanding of the key terms and conditions of a share-based payment award is reached by an employer and an employee, (2) the employer becomes contingently obligated to issue share-based payments to an employee who renders the requisite service, (3) any necessary approvals are obtained, and (4) the subsequent changes in the market price of the underlying stock begin to benefit or adversely affect the employee.

Answer (B) is incorrect because the service inception date is the date on which the requisite service period begins. The service inception date usually is the same as, but under certain conditions may precede, the grant date. Answer (C) is incorrect because the vesting date is the date on which an employee has earned the right to receive the share-based payments. Answer (D) is incorrect because the requisite service period is the period during which an employee is required to provide services in exchange for an award.

50. SFAS 123R defines the service inception date as the date at which the requisite service period begins. The service inception date generally

A. Precedes the grant date.

B. Is the same as the grant date.

C. Follows the grant date.

D. Differs from the grant date.

Answer (B) is correct. *(Publisher)*

REQUIRED: The relationship between the grant date and the service inception date.

DISCUSSION: For more share-based payments, the service inception date is the same as the grant date. However, the service inception date precedes the grant date if (1) an award is authorized, (2) service begins before the employer and employee reach a mutual understanding of the key terms and conditions of the award, and (3) either (a) the terms of the award do not include a substantive future requisite service condition that exists at the grant date, or (b) the award includes a market or performance condition that will result in forfeiture of the award if not satisfied during the service period preceding the grant date and following the inception of the arrangement.

Answer (A) is incorrect because the service inception date usually is the grant date, but it will precede the grant date under certain conditions. Answer (C) is incorrect because the service inception date usually is the grant date, but it will precede the grant date under certain conditions. Answer (D) is incorrect because the service inception date usually is the grant date, but it will precede the grant date under certain conditions.

Questions 51 through 55 are based on the following information. On December 21, 2005, the board of directors of Oak Corporation approved a plan to award 600,000 share options to 20 key employees as additional compensation. Effective January 1, 2006, each employee was granted the option to purchase 30,000 shares of the company's $2 par value stock at an at-the-money exercise price equal to the January 1, 2006 market price of $36 per share. All share options cliff vest at December 31, 2008, the end of the 3-year requisite service period. They expire on December 31, 2015. None of the cost associated with this share-based compensation plan will be capitalized as an asset, and tax effects should be ignored in the calculations. Based on an appropriate option-pricing formula, the fair value of the options was estimated at $12 per option. During the most recent years, Oak Corporation has experienced a turnover rate of approximately 5% per year of employees eligible for the plan. Oak expected this turnover rate to continue during the 3-year requisite service period.

51. What amount of compensation expense should Oak Corporation recognize in accordance with the provisions of SFAS 123R in its annual income statement for the year ended December 31, 2006 based on an assumed 5% per year forfeiture rate?

A. $6,173,100

B. $2,400,000

C. $2,280,000

D. $2,057,700

Answer (D) is correct. *(Publisher)*

REQUIRED: The compensation expense recognized in 2006.

DISCUSSION: Total compensation cost recognized during the requisite service period should equal the grant-date fair value of all share options for which the requisite service is rendered. SFAS 123R requires an entity to (1) estimate the number of share options for which the requisite service is expected to be rendered, (2) measure the cost of employee services received in exchange for those options at their fair value on the grant date, and (3) allocate that cost to the requisite service period. Because both Oak Corporation and its employees were aware of the key terms and conditions of the share option plan at the date the options were awarded, the grant date is January 1, 2006. At January 1, 2006, based on an expected forfeiture rate of 5% per year, 514,425 [600,000 × $(1 - .05)^3$] options are expected to vest. Given that all options vest at the same time (cliff vesting), the $6,173,100 (514,425 shares × $12 estimated fair value) total compensation cost should be allocated proportionately to the 3-year requisite service period. Thus, $2,057,700 ($6,173,700 ÷ 3) should be expensed in the annual income statement for the year ended December 31, 2006.

Answer (A) is incorrect because $6,173,100 is the total estimated compensation cost. Answer (B) is incorrect because $2,400,000 is not adjusted for the expected forfeiture rate. Answer (C) is incorrect because $2,280,000 is adjusted for a 5% forfeiture rate for the 3-year period, not a 5% rate per year.

52. In 2006, Oak Corporation experienced a higher turnover of its employees eligible for the share option plan granted on January 1, 2006. Because Oak expected a return to the historical rate, it made no adjustment to the cumulative compensation cost at year-end 2006. However, when Oak again experienced a higher employee turnover rate in 2007, it decided to adjust the cumulative compensation cost. Accordingly, Oak changed its estimate of the estimated forfeiture rate from 5% to 10% per year for the entire award. If this change in estimate occurred prior to the release of the 2007 financial statements, what amount of compensation expense should Oak Corporation recognize in accordance with the provisions of SFAS 123R in its income statement for the year ended December 31, 2007?

A. $3,499,200

B. $2,057,700

C. $1,749,600

D. $1,441,500

Answer (D) is correct. *(Publisher)*

REQUIRED: The compensation expense recognized in 2007.

DISCUSSION: Total compensation cost recognized during the requisite service period should equal the grant-date fair value of all share options for which the requisite service is rendered. SFAS 123R requires an entity to estimate the number of share options for which the requisite service is expected to be rendered. If that estimate changes, it should be accounted for as a change in estimate, and its cumulative effect should be recognized in the period of change. At January 1, 2006, based on an expected forfeiture rate of 5% per year, 514,425 [600,000 × $(1 - .05)^3$] of the options were expected to vest. Thus, total estimated cost was $6,173,100 (514,425 shares × $12 estimated fair value), of which $2,057,700 ($6,173,700 ÷ 3) was allocated as compensation cost to 2006. Based on a revised forfeiture rate of 10% per year, the 437,400 [600,000 × $(1 - .10)^3$] options expected to vest result in total compensation cost of $5,248,800 (437,400 × $12), of which $3,499,200 [($5,248,800 ÷ 3) × 2 years] should be the cumulative compensation cost recognized at year-end 2007. Oak therefore should recognize 2007 compensation expense of $1,441,500, the difference between the $3,499,200 cumulative compensation cost that should be recognized at year-end 2007 and the $2,057,700 amount previously recognized in 2006.

Answer (A) is incorrect because $3,499,200 is the cumulative compensation cost that should be recognized at year-end 2007. Answer (B) is incorrect because $2,057,700 is the annual compensation cost based on a 5% forfeiture rate. Answer (C) is incorrect because $1,749,600 is the annual compensation cost based on a 10% forfeiture rate.

53. What amount of compensation expense should Oak report in the income statement for the year ended December 31, 2008 if Oak expected the forfeiture rate for the share options issued on January 1, 2006 to remain at 10% per year?

A. $5,248,800

B. $2,057,700

C. $1,749,600

D. $1,441,500

Answer (C) is correct. *(Publisher)*

REQUIRED: The compensation expense to be recognized in 2008.

DISCUSSION: Based on an expected forfeiture rate of 10% per year, the 437,400 [600,000 × $(1 - .10)^3$] options expected to vest result in total compensation cost of $5,248,800 (437,400 × $12), which should be recognized as cumulative compensation expense recognized at year-end 2008. The amount that Oak should recognize as compensation expense in 2008 is $1,749,600, the difference between $5,248,800 and $3,499,200, the cumulative compensation costs recognized at year-end 2008 and year-end 2007, respectively. Furthermore, $1,749,600 ($5,248,800 ÷ 3 years) is the amount that would have been allocated to each year had a 10% forfeiture rate been effective from the service inception date.

Answer (A) is incorrect because $5,248,800 is the cumulative compensation cost that should be recognized at year-end 2008. Answer (B) is incorrect because $2,057,700 is the annual compensation cost based on a 5% forfeiture rate. Answer (D) is incorrect because $1,441,500 is the compensation cost recognized in 2007 as a result of the change in accounting estimate.

54. Oak Corporation recognized total cumulative compensation cost of $5,248,800 during the 3-year requisite service period ending December 31, 2008. During the period from January 1, 2009 through December 31, 2015, 400,000 of the 437,400 share options that vested were exercised. Upon exercise, the amount that should be credited to additional paid-in capital in excess of par is

A. $19,200,000

B. $18,400,000

C. $13,600,000

D. $4,000,000

Answer (B) is correct. *(Publisher)*

REQUIRED: The credit to additional paid-in capital in excess of par when options are exercised.

DISCUSSION: Additional paid-in capital—share options should have been credited for $5,248,800 (437,400 × $12) when compensation expense was recognized during the requisite service period. During the period from January 1, 2009 through December 31, 2015, 400,000 options were exercised. Hence, additional paid-in capital in excess of par should be credited for $18,400,000 [400,000 shares × ($36 exercise price + $12 previously credited to additional paid-in capital—share options – $2 par value allocated to common stock)].

Answer (A) is incorrect because $19,200,000 includes the $2 par value allocated to the common stock account. Answer (C) is incorrect because $13,600,000 does not include the $12 fair value of the options determined at the grant date. Answer (D) is incorrect because $4,000,000 does not include the $36 exercise price.

55. During the period from January 1, 2009 though December 31, 2015, 400,000 of the 437,400 share options that vested were exercised. The remaining 37,400 were not exercised. What amount of the $5,248,800 previously recognized compensation expense should be adjusted upon expiration of the stock options.

A. $0

B. $74,800

C. $448,800

D. $1,720,000

Answer (A) is correct. *(Publisher)*

REQUIRED: The adjustment to previously recognized compensation expense when share options are not exercised.

DISCUSSION: Total compensation cost recognized during the requisite service period should equal the grant-date fair value of all share options for which the requisite service is rendered.

If the requisite service is provided, no adjustment to previously recognized compensation expense is permitted for options that expire.

Answer (B) is incorrect because $74,800 is the amount that would have been credited to the common stock account if the 37,400 options had been exercised. Answer (C) is incorrect because $448,800 is the compensation expense recognized for the 37,400 shares. Answer (D) is incorrect because $1,720,000 is the amount that would have been credited to additional paid-in capital in excess of par if the 37,400 options had been exercised.

56. On January 1, 2006, Yoshida Akinori entered into a three-year employment contract to serve as CEO of Wildpine Corporation. Terms of the contract stipulate that Akinori will be awarded 150,000 fully vested stock options at the end of each year for which he has provided service as CEO in accordance with the contract. If the exercise price of each 150,000-share award (three groups or tranches) will be set to equal to the market price at December 31 of each year in the three-year contract term, the grant date will be

A. January 1, 2006 for each of the three 150,000-share awards (tranches).

B. December 31, 2006 for each of the three 150,000-share awards (tranches).

C. January 1 of each year in the three-year contract.

D. December 31 of each year in the three-year contract.

Answer (D) is correct. *(Publisher)*

REQUIRED: The grant date included in a three-year share-based payment plan with a graded vesting schedule.

DISCUSSION: Because the exercise price for each tranche will not be known until the 150,000 share options for that year are awarded, the contract has three grant dates. December 31 of each year is the first date on which (1) the employer and employee will understand the key terms and conditions of the share-based payment award, (2) the employer will become contingently obligated to make share-based payments to the employee who renders the requisite service, (3) necessary approvals will have been obtained, and (4) subsequent changes in the market price of the underlying stock will begin to benefit or adversely affect the employee.

Answer (A) is incorrect because January 1, 2006 would be the grant date if the exercise price were set equal to the market price on January 1, 2006 for each tranche. Answer (B) is incorrect because December 31, 2006 would be the grant date if the exercise price were set equal to the market price on December 31, 2006 for each tranche. Answer (C) is incorrect because January 1 of each year would be the grant date if the exercise price were set equal to the market price on January 1 of each year.

57. On February 1, 2006, Atkins Corporation received final approval to offer the position of chief financial officer (CFO) to Carol Kirkland. The offer included an equity award of 50,000 share options in addition to salary and other benefits. Terms of the award require a 3-year vesting period scheduled to begin on the date the offer is accepted. On February 5, 2006, the offer was extended to Ms. Kirkland. On February 12, 2006, Ms. Kirkland accepted the offer subject to the provisions that she would neither provide any services as CFO nor receive any salary or benefits until March 1, 2006. These circumstances indicate that the service inception date and the grant date occur on

	Service Inception Date	Grant Date
A.	February 5	February 5
B.	February 12	February 12
C.	March 1	March 1
D.	February 12	March 1

Answer (C) is correct. *(Publisher)*

REQUIRED: The service inception date and the grant date.

DISCUSSION: On the grant date, a mutual understanding of the key terms and conditions of a share-based payment award is reached by an employer and an employee. Because March 1 is the first date the new CFO will function as an employee, March 1 is the earliest date that the mutual understanding between employer and employee can be reached. Moreover, on this date the employer is contingently obligated, and needed approvals have been received. Also, for this equity award, March 1 is when the employee begins to be affected by changes in the price of the employer's equity shares. Given that all four conditions are not met until March 1, that date is the grant date. For most share-based payments, the service inception date is the same as the grant date. However, the service inception date may differ from the grant date. It precedes the grant date when (1) the award is authorized; (2) the mutual understanding has not been reached; and (3) either (a) no substantive future requisite service period exists at the grant date, or (b) nonsatisfaction of a performance or market condition during the service period prior to the grant date will cause forfeiture of the award. Accordingly, the service inception date cannot precede the grant date (March 1) because (1) a substantive requisite service period of 3 years exists at the grant date, and (2) no service period or performance or market condition exists prior to the grant date.

Answer (A) is incorrect because the grant date cannot precede the date when the new CFO becomes an employee. In addition, the service inception date will only precede the grant date under conditions that are not met in the circumstances described. Answer (B) is incorrect because the grant date cannot precede the date when the new CFO becomes an employee. In addition, the service inception date will only precede the grant date under conditions that are not met in the circumstances described. Answer (D) is incorrect because the grant date cannot precede the date when the new CFO becomes an employee. In addition, the service inception date will only precede the grant date under conditions that are not met in the circumstances described.

58. On January 2, year 1, Kine Co. granted Morgan, its president, fully vested share options to buy 1,000 shares of Kine's $10 par common stock. The options have an exercise price of $20 per share and are exercisable for 3 years following the grant date. Morgan exercised the options on December 31, year 1. The market price of the shares was $50 on January 2, year 1 and $70 on the following December 31. If the fair value of the options is not reasonably estimable at the grant date, by what net amount should equity increase as a result of the grant and exercise of the options?

A. $20,000

B. $30,000

C. $50,000

D. $70,000

Answer (A) is correct. *(CIA, adapted)*

REQUIRED: The amount equity increases as a result of the grant and exercise of share options.

DISCUSSION: In the rare case in which an entity cannot reasonably estimate the fair value of equity instruments at the grant date, the accounting is based on intrinsic value (fair value of the underlying shares – exercise price of an option). Remeasurement is required at each reporting date and on final settlement. The measurement date is January 2, year 1. At that date, the intrinsic value of the options is $30,000 [1,000 shares × ($50 market price – $20 option price)]. This $30,000 will be recorded as both compensation expense and options outstanding. The net effect on equity is $0. When the options are exercised, the $20,000 (1,000 shares × $20 exercise price) cash received and the $30,000 of options outstanding will be allocated to share capital as $10,000 common stock and $40,000 additional paid-in capital. Moreover, compensation expense will be debited and additional paid-in capital will be credited for $20,000 to reflect the final measure of intrinsic value. The net effect on equity will be a $20,000 increase.

Answer (B) is incorrect because $30,000 is the amount of the initial debit to compensation expense and credit to options outstanding. Answer (C) is incorrect because $50,000 is the final measure of intrinsic value. Answer (D) is incorrect because $70,000 is the market price of the shares issued on the settlement date.

59. On January 1, year 1, the grant date, Public Entity entered into an equity-settled share-based payment transaction with its senior executives. This award of 1,000 share options has a four-year vesting period. The market prices of the options and the related shares on the grant date are $20 and $80, respectively. The exercise price is $85. Assuming that the requisite service was not completed for 100 of the options because of unexpected events in year 4, the entry to debit option expense at

A. December 31, year 4 is for $5,000.

B. December 31, year 3 is for $4,500.

C. December 31, year 2 is for $5,000.

D. January 1, year 1 is for $20,000.

Answer (C) is correct. *(Publisher)*

REQUIRED: The entry to debit option expense given that requisite service was not completed for some options.

DISCUSSION: The fair value of each share option is determined at the measurement date, which is usually the grant date for transactions with employees. Thus, the fair value of each share option was set at its market price of $20 on January 1, year 1. The periodic expense varies only with the expected number of equity instruments for which the requisite service is expected to be completed. Because the events causing the requisite service not to be completed for 100 options occurred unexpectedly in year 4, the entity presumably expected at each balance sheet date for the first three years of the requisite service period that all options would be expensed. Total expected expense was therefore $20,000, and the proportional expense recognized in each of the first three years was $5,000 [(1,000 options × $20) ÷ 4 years].

Answer (A) is incorrect because the year 4 expense is $3,000 [$20,000 total expected – $15,000 recognized in the first three years – (100 × $20) not vested]. Answer (B) is incorrect because no retrospective adjustment is made. The year 3 entry would have been $5,000 based on a then-expected total expense of $20,000. Answer (D) is incorrect because $20,000 would have been recognized at January 1, year 1 if the options had vested immediately.

60. SBP Co. is a public entity that granted share options for the purchase of 200,000 common shares on January 1, 20X3, the first day of its fiscal year. Under U.S. tax law, the options are not deemed to be incentive stock options. The option price and the quoted market price on that date were $20 per share, and the fair value of an option was $8 per share. Tax deductions are calculated based on the intrinsic-value method. Moreover, the vesting period is 4 years, and SBP presents basic statements only for the current year and the immediately preceding year. In accordance with SFAS 123(R), *Share-Based Payments*, SBP adopted the fair-value method of accounting for the options on January 1, 20X6. It chose modified retrospective application to all prior years for which fair value disclosures were required. Assuming all options were expected to vest, a 40% tax rate, and that the tax benefits of any deferred tax asset will be realized, SBP should recognize

A. In income a cumulative-effect adjustment of $960,000 for 20X6.

B. A debit of $320,000 to a deferred tax asset and a credit of $800,000 to additional paid-in capital for 20X5.

C. Share-based employee compensation cost of $1,200,000 in 20X5.

D. The change in accounting principle only prospectively.

Answer (B) is correct. *(Publisher)*

REQUIRED: The reporting of the transition to fair-value accounting for share options.

DISCUSSION: An entity may choose the modified retrospective application method of reporting the transition. Thus, SBP needs to adjust paid-in capital, retained earnings, and deferred taxes at the beginning of the first period presented. Under the MRA method, an entity may elect to apply it to all prior years for which SFAS 123 was effective. For all such years, presumably including 20X3 and 20X4, a public entity was required to make fair value disclosures related to its share-based payment arrangements. The date of the adjustments for SBP is January 1, 20X5. For 20X3 and 20X4, the cumulative compensation cost at fair value (given that all options were expected to vest) was $800,000 [$8 per share × 200,000 shares × (2 years ÷ 4-year vesting period)]. A deferred tax benefit arises because tax law applies the intrinsic-value method. Thus, a deferred tax asset for a deductible temporary difference is recorded equal to $320,000 ($800,000 compensation cost for 20X3 and 20X4 × 40%). Because the option price and the market price were the same at the grant (and measurement) date, the options had no intrinsic value recognizable under prior GAAP. Hence, no such amounts need to be reversed. SBP must therefore record a transition adjustment at January 1, 20X5 by debiting a deferred tax asset for $320,000. Furthermore, the beginning balance of retained earnings also must be adjusted. The after-tax cumulative effect on beginning retained earnings for 2005 is a debit of $480,000 [$800,000 compensation cost not previously recognized × (1.0 – .40 tax rate)]. Finally, SBP must increase paid-in capital by a credit of $800,000. If the fair-value method had been in effect in 20X3 and 20X4, the entry each year would have been a debit to compensation cost (an expense) and a credit to paid-in capital for $400,000.

Answer (A) is incorrect because SFAS 123(R) does not permit recognition of the cumulative effect of the change in income in the year of the change. Answer (C) is incorrect because the cost is $400,000 for 20X5 [$8 × 200,000 options × (1 year ÷ 4 years)]. Answer (D) is incorrect because the MRA method is permissible.

Questions 61 through 63 are based on the following information. Elfheim Co. is a public entity that granted share appreciation rights (SARs) to its employees on January 1, 20X1. Under U.S. tax law, the options are not deemed to be incentive stock options. Each right entitles the employee-holder to receive cash equal to the excess value of an Elfheim share over its $40 grant-date price. The SARs become fully vested on December 31, 20X3. Thus, the requisite service period is three years.

The number of SARs granted was 240,000, of which 98% were expected to vest and did vest. All vested SARs were exercised on the same date; the fair value of the SARs was the same on the exercise date as at December 31, 20X3; and current tax amounts were recognized before considering deductions for the exercise of the SARs.

The assumed fair values of the SARs at the end of 20X1, 20X2, and 20X3 were $14, $35, and $27, respectively. Elfheim's enacted tax rate is 30%, and no valuation allowance will be required for a deferred tax asset related to the SARs. Moreover, Elfheim at all times has sufficient taxable income to realize the full tax benefit of any recognized deferred tax asset.

61. Which entry should be made for 20X1?

A. Debit deferred tax asset for $329,280.

B. Debit compensation cost for $1,120,000.

C. Credit share-based compensation liability for $1,120,000.

D. Credit share-based compensation liability for $3,292,800.

Answer (A) is correct. *(Publisher)*

REQUIRED: The entry for 20X1.

DISCUSSION: A share-based compensation liability is recognized by a public entity based on fair value. Periodic compensation cost depends on the change (or part of the change depending on the requisite service performed to date) in fair value for the period. Remeasurement is required at each reporting date until settlement. The fair value of the SARs at December 31, 20X1 is $3,292,800 (240,000 SARs × 98% expected to vest × $14 assumed fair value per SAR). The debit to compensations cost and the credit to the liability for 20X1 equal $1,097,600 ($3,292,800 ÷ 3 years). The debit to deferred tax asset and the credit to deferred tax benefit equal $329,280 (30% × $1,097,600). A deferred tax asset is recognized because compensation cost is not deductible until the year the SARs are exercised.

Answer (B) is incorrect because $1,120,000 ignores the effect of expected forfeitures. Answer (C) is incorrect because $1,120,000 ignores the effect of expected forfeitures. Answer (D) is incorrect because $3,292,800 is the total fair value of the SARs at December 31, 20X1.

62. Which entry should be made for 20X2?

A. Credit deferred tax benefit for $1,646,000.

B. Debit compensation cost for $4,480,000.

C. Credit share-based compensation liability for $4,390,400.

D. Credit share-based compensation liability for $5,488,000.

Answer (C) is correct. *(Publisher)*

REQUIRED: The entry for 20X2.

DISCUSSION: The fair value of the SARs at December 31, 20X2 is $8,232,000 (240,000 SARs × 98% expected to vest × $35 assumed fair value per SAR). The share-based compensation liability after two years of requisite service have been provided is $5,488,000 [$8,232,000 × (2 ÷ 3)]. The debit to compensation cost and the credit to the liability equal $4,390,400 ($5,488,000 – $1,097,600 recognized for 20X1). The debit to deferred tax asset and credit to deferred tax benefit equal $1,317,120 (30% × $4,390,400).

Answer (A) is incorrect because $1,646,000 is 30% of the total liability at December 31, 20X2. Answer (B) is incorrect because $4,480,000 ignores the effect of expected forfeitures. Answer (D) is incorrect because $5,488,000 is the total expected liability for the SARs at December 31, 20X2.

63. Which entry should be made for 20X3 or at the exercise date?

A. Debit current tax expense at the exercise date for $1,905,120.

B. Debit share-based compensation liability at the exercise date for $862,400.

C. Credit $1,905,120 of deferred tax benefit for 20X3.

D. Credit $862,400 of share-based compensation cost for 20X3.

Answer (D) is correct. *(Publisher)*

REQUIRED: The entry for 20X3 or at the exercise date.

DISCUSSION: The fair value of the SARs and the share-based compensation liability on December 31, 20X3 is $6,350,000 (240,000 SARs × 98% fully vested × $27 assumed fair value per SAR). The debit to compensation cost and the credit to the liability equal $862,400 ($6,350,400 – $1,097,600 recognized cost for 20X1 – $4,390,400 recognized for 20X2). The debit to deferred tax asset and credit to deferred tax benefit equal $258,720 (30% × $862,400). At the exercise date, it is given that (1) the fair value of an SAR is $27 (Elfheim's share price is $67), (2) 98% of the SARs are exercised (actual forfeitures = estimated forfeitures), (3) current tax expense and taxes payable were calculated without regard to the exercise of the SARs, and (4) Elfheim has sufficient taxable income to realize the full tax benefit of any recognized deferred tax asset. Accordingly, Elfheim will debit the liability and credit cash for $6,350,400 on the exercise date. It also will debit deferred tax expense and credit deferred tax asset for $1,905,120 (30% × $6,350,400 liability at 12/31/X3) to reflect the realization (and reduction to $0) of the deferred tax asset. Furthermore, Elfheim will debit current taxes payable and credit current tax expense for $1,905,120 to recognize the current tax benefit.

Answer (A) is incorrect because, to recognize the current tax benefit of deductible compensation cost from exercise of the SARs, the entry is to debit current taxes payable and credit current tax expense. Answer (B) is incorrect because $862,400 is the amount of the credit to the liability for 20X3. Answer (C) is incorrect because the deferred tax benefit for 20X3 is $258,720.

64. On January 1, 20X1, an employer tells an executive whose substantive employment began on August 1, 20X0 that she will receive 500 fully vested share options on January 1, 20X2. The exercise price is the share price on the latter date. Required approvals, which were not mere formalities, were received on December 10, 20X0. If the executive is still an employee on January 1, 20X2 and receives the options, the grant date for the award is

A. August 1, 20X0.

B. December 10, 20X0.

C. January 1, 20X1.

D. January 1, 20X2.

Answer (D) is correct. *(Publisher)*

REQUIRED: The grant date for an award of fully vested share options.

DISCUSSION: On the grant date, the employer and employee have a mutual understanding of the key terms and conditions of the share-based payment arrangement, necessary approvals have been received, and (in the case of equity instruments) the employee has begun to benefit from (or be adversely affected by) changes in the share price. Accordingly, the grant date is January 1, 20X2, the post-approval date when (1) the employee will potentially benefit or not benefit from changes in the share price, and (2) a sufficient basis exists to understand the equity and compensatory relationship created by the award.

Answer (A) is incorrect because August 1, 20X0 precedes the service inception date and the grant date. Answer (B) is incorrect because December 10, 20X0 precedes the service inception date and the grant date. Answer (C) is incorrect because January 1, 20X1 is the service inception date. The requisite service period is from January 1, 20X1 to January 1, 20X2, the period during which the employee must perform service to receive the awards.

65. On January 1, year 1, Catt Corp. established an employee stock ownership plan (ESOP). Transactions relating to the ESOP during year 1 were as follows:

- On April 1, year 1, Catt lent $60,000 in cash to the ESOP, which used this amount to purchase 3,000 shares of no par common stock from Catt. All of these shares were allocated to employees.
- On July 1, year 1, the ESOP borrowed $100,000 from Union National Bank and acquired 5,000 shares of Catt's no par common stock from Catt. These shares were not allocated to employees. The note is for 1 year, bears interest at 10%, and is guaranteed by Catt.
- On October 1, year 1, Catt made a cash contribution of $62,500 to the ESOP. The plan used these funds to pay $2,500 of interest and to repay $60,000 of principal. As a result, 3,000 shares were released to employees. The market price on October 1, year 1, was $25 per share.
- On December 31, year 1, Catt declared a $.20 per common share cash dividend. The dividend does not reduce a liability.

In its year 1 income statement, what amount should Catt report as compensation expense relating to the ESOP (ignoring income taxes)?

A. $135,400

B. $77,400

C. $75,000

D. $62,400

Answer (A) is correct. *(Publisher)*

REQUIRED: The amount to be reported as compensation expense related to an ESOP.

DISCUSSION: According to SOP 93-6, *Accounting Practices for Employee Stock Ownership Plans*, the loan to the ESOP used to purchase shares from Catt that are allocated to employees is recognized by a debit to compensation expense and a credit to common stock (no par) for $60,000. The direct outside loan used to purchase shares from Catt is recognized by Catt (debit cash and credit loan payable for $100,000). However, the shares serve as collateral and may not be released to employees until the debit is paid. Accordingly, Catt offsets the $100,000 credit to common stock (no par) reflecting the issuance of shares with a $100,000 debit to the contra equity account "unearned ESOP shares." The debt service transactions are recognized by a debit to interest expense for $2,500, a debit to loan payable for $60,000, and a credit to cash for $62,500. Interest expense is recorded separately from compensation expense. The entry to recognize compensation expense related to the release of shares consists of a debit to compensation expense for their fair value on the release date of $75,000 (3,000 × $25), a credit to unearned ESOP shares at their cost of $60,000 (3,000 × $20), and a credit to additional paid-in capital of $15,000. The entry to record the dividend declaration pertaining to the ESOP shares is to debit retained earnings for $1,200 (6,000 allocated shares × $.20), debit compensation expense for $400 (2,000 unallocated shares × $0.20), and credit dividends payable for $2,400. The dividends on unallocated shares, that is, the shares not yet released and still serving as collateral, are not treated as dividends but as compensation expense. Accordingly, total compensation expense relating to the ESOP (ignoring income taxes) is $135,400 ($60,000 + $75,000 + $400).

Answer (B) is incorrect because $77,400 omits compensation for shares purchased from Catt with funds lent by Catt. It also includes dividends on the allocated shares. Answer (C) is incorrect because $75,000 omits compensation for shares purchased from Catt with funds lent by Catt. It also omits dividends. Answer (D) is incorrect because $62,400 omits compensation in the form of shares released after reduction of the debt. It also includes dividends on the allocated shares.

STUDY UNIT SEVENTEEN
ACCOUNTING FOR INCOME TAXES

The objectives of accounting for income taxes are to recognize (1) the amount of taxes payable or refundable for the current year and (2) deferred tax liabilities and assets for the future tax consequences of events recognized in financial statements or tax returns during current and preceding years. **SFAS 109**, *Accounting for Income Taxes*, prescribes a comprehensive recognition, asset, and liability approach to financial accounting and reporting for income taxes. In accordance with this approach, (1) a **current tax liability or asset** is recognized for the estimated taxes payable or refundable on tax returns for the current year; (2) a **deferred tax liability or asset** is recognized for the estimated future tax effects attributable to temporary differences and carryforwards; (3) a **deferred tax expense or benefit** is determined as the net change during a year in the enterprise's deferred tax liabilities and assets; and (4) total **income tax expense or benefit** for a year is recognized as the sum of the income taxes currently payable or refundable and the deferred tax expense or benefit. In addition, the tax benefit of an operating loss carryforward or carryback is reported in the same manner as the source of income or loss in the current year.

SFAS 109 requires the recognition of deferred tax liabilities and assets for temporary differences, operating loss carryforwards, and tax credit carryforwards existing at a balance sheet date. A **temporary difference (TD)** is a difference between the tax basis of an asset or liability and its reported amount in the financial statements that will result in taxable or deductible amounts in future years when the asset is recovered or the liability is settled at its reported amount (when the TD reverses). TDs arise from different transactions and events. Included among these transactions and events are timing differences which occur when revenues, expenses, gains, and losses are recognized in pretax financial income in earlier or later years than they are included in taxable income.

A TD is classified as taxable or deductible depending on whether it results in taxable or deductible amounts when it reverses. Pretax financial income will be higher (lower) than taxable income in the future because of deductible (taxable) amounts in the tax returns. **Taxable amounts** result when the effect of the reversal will be either (1) higher amounts of taxable items on the future tax return(s) than revenues and gains on the future income statement(s), or (2) lower deductions on the future tax return(s) than expenses and losses on the future income statement(s). In contrast, **deductible amounts** result when the effect of the reversal will be either (1) lower amounts of taxable items on the future tax return(s) than revenues and gains on the future income statement(s), or (2) higher deductions on the future tax return(s) than expenses and losses on the income statement(s).

A **permanent difference** is an event that is recognized either in pretax financial income or in taxable income but never in both. It does not result in a deferred tax asset or liability. **Examples** of items recognized in pretax financial income but not in taxable income are municipal bond interest, premiums on insurance policies for key executives, and the proceeds from such policies. **Examples** of items recognized in taxable income but not in financial income are the dividends received deduction and percentage depletion of natural resources. **Goodwill** acquired after August 10, 1993 is tax deductible. Deductibility is on a pro rata basis over a 15-year period. However, amortization of goodwill on the financial statements is not permitted under SFAS 142. Nevertheless, a **deferred tax liability** must be recognized for the taxable TD arising from tax deductions for goodwill. This treatment is required even though the deferred tax liability will not be settled until some indefinite future time when goodwill is impaired, sold, or otherwise disposed of. The same treatment applies to **other intangible assets** that are not amortized because their useful lives are indefinite.

The **computation of deferred tax amounts** is based on the following procedures: (1) Identify types and amounts of existing TDs, and the nature, amount, and remaining carryforward period of each type of operating loss and tax credit carryforward; (2) measure the total deferred tax liability for taxable TDs using the applicable tax rate; (3) measure the total deferred tax asset for deductible TDs and operating loss carryforwards using the applicable tax rate; (4) measure deferred tax assets for each type of tax credit carryforward; and (5) recognize a valuation allowance to reduce deferred tax assets to the amount that is more likely than not to be realized.

APB 4, *Accounting for the Investment Credit*, states that the deferral and flow-through methods of accounting for the credit are generally acceptable. The **deferral method** spreads the benefit of the credit over the depreciable life of the asset either by reducing its cost or by recording deferred income to be amortized over the life of the asset. The **flow-through method** accounts for the full credit as a decrease in federal income tax expense of the year of initial recognition.

The **applicable tax rate** is the **enacted tax rate** expected to apply to taxable income in the periods in which deferred tax liabilities or assets are estimated to be settled or realized. In the U.S. federal tax jurisdiction, the applicable tax rate is the regular tax rate. Provisions in the tax law that provide for different tax rates to be applicable to different categories of income are considered.

In determining whether a **valuation allowance** should be recognized, all available evidence should be carefully considered. Judgment must be used in evaluating the relative effects of positive and negative evidence. The weight given to those effects varies with the extent they can be objectively verified. The more negative evidence exists, the more positive evidence is needed and the more difficult it is to support a decision that no valuation allowance is necessary.

In a classified balance sheet, deferred tax liabilities and assets are classified as current or noncurrent. The **classification of deferred tax liabilities and assets** is based on the classification of the related asset or liability for financial reporting. Deferred tax liabilities and assets not related to an asset or liability for financial reporting, including deferred tax assets related to carryforwards, are classified based on the expected reversal date. A valuation allowance for a particular tax jurisdiction is allocated between current and noncurrent deferred tax assets on a pro rata basis.

Deferred tax liabilities and assets are **offset** and classified as net current and net noncurrent amounts for a particular tax-paying component of an enterprise and within a particular tax jurisdiction. Deferred tax liabilities and assets attributable to different tax-paying components of an enterprise or to different tax jurisdictions are not offset.

A deferred tax liability or asset is adjusted for the effect of a **change in tax law or rates**. The effect is included in income from continuing operations for the period that includes the date of enactment. The amount of the adjustment is disclosed as a component of income tax expense attributable to continuing operations.

A **change in tax status** requires an adjustment of deferred tax amounts. Thus, a deferred tax liability or asset is recognized for temporary differences at the date a nontaxable enterprise becomes a taxable enterprise. A deferred tax liability or asset generally is eliminated at the date an enterprise ceases to be a taxable enterprise. The effect of recognizing or eliminating a deferred tax liability or asset is included in income from continuing operations. The amount of the adjustment is disclosed as a component of income tax expense attributable to continuing operations.

Intraperiod tax allocation requires total income tax expense or benefit to be allocated among (1) continuing operations, (2) discontinued operations, (3) extraordinary items, (4) other comprehensive income, and (5) items charged or credited directly to equity. The amount of income tax expense or benefit allocated to items other than continuing operations is the portion of income tax expense or benefit incremental to the amount allocated to continuing operations.

QUESTIONS

17.1 Interperiod Tax Allocation

1. The provisions of SFAS 109, *Accounting for Income Taxes*, are applicable to

A. All foreign, state, and local taxes.

B. Domestic federal income taxes.

C. An enterprise's foreign operations accounted for by the cost method.

D. Financial statements of foreign enterprises required to pay U.S. federal income taxes.

Answer (B) is correct. *(Publisher)*

REQUIRED: The applicability of SFAS 109.

DISCUSSION: The principles and requirements of SFAS 109 are applicable to domestic federal income taxes (U.S. federal income taxes for U.S. enterprises) and to foreign, state, and local (including franchise) taxes based on income.

Answer (A) is incorrect because SFAS 109 is applicable only to foreign, state, and local taxes that are based on income. Answer (C) is incorrect because SFAS 109 applies to an enterprise's domestic and foreign operations that are consolidated, combined, or accounted for by the equity method. Answer (D) is incorrect because SFAS 109 applies to foreign enterprises for purposes of preparing financial statements in accordance with U.S. GAAP only.

2. Under current generally accepted accounting principles, which approach is used to determine income tax expense?

A. Asset and liability approach.

B. "With and without" approach.

C. Net-of-tax approach.

D. Deferred approach.

Answer (A) is correct. *(CPA, adapted)*

REQUIRED: The current approach used to determine income tax expense.

DISCUSSION: The asset and liability approach accrues liabilities or assets (taxes payable or refundable) for the current year. It also recognizes deferred tax liabilities and assets for the future tax consequences of events that have been previously recognized in the financial statements or tax returns. These liabilities and assets recognize the effects of temporary differences measured using the tax rate(s) expected to apply when the liabilities and assets are expected to be settled or realized.

Answer (B) is incorrect because APB 11 (superseded by SFAS 109) stated that the tax effect of a timing difference should "be measured by the differential between income taxes computed with and without inclusion of the transaction creating the difference between taxable income and pretax accounting income." Answer (C) is incorrect because the net-of-tax approach accounts for the effects of taxability or deductibility on assets and liabilities as reductions in their reported amounts. Answer (D) is incorrect because the deferred method used in APB 11 recognized deferred tax credits and charges. It attempted to match income tax expense with related revenues and expenses for the year when they were recognized in pretax financial income. Thus, APB 11 did not measure the cumulative taxes payable or refundable when temporary differences reverse in the future. APB 11 determined income tax expense by multiplying pretax financial income by the current tax rate, with the difference between taxes payable (refundable) and income tax expense (benefit) being recorded as a deferred credit or charge.

3. In its 2003 income statement, Small Co. reported income before income taxes of $600,000. Small estimated that, because of permanent differences, taxable income for 2003 would be $560,000. During 2003, Small made estimated tax payments of $100,000, which were debited to income tax expense. Small is subject to a 30% tax rate. What amount should Small report as income tax expense?

A. $68,000

B. $100,000

C. $168,000

D. $180,000

Answer (C) is correct. *(CPA, adapted)*

REQUIRED: The amount to be reported for income tax expense.

DISCUSSION: Income tax expense or benefit is the sum of current tax expense or benefit and deferred tax expense or benefit. A deferred tax expense or benefit is the change in an entity's deferred tax assets and liabilities. However, a permanent difference does not result in a change in a deferred tax asset or liability. Thus, income tax expense equals current income tax expense, which is the amount of taxes paid or payable for the year. Income taxes payable for 2003 equal $168,000 ($560,000 taxable income × 30%).

Answer (A) is incorrect because $68,000 equals the $168,000 of income taxes payable minus the $100,000 of income taxes paid. Answer (B) is incorrect because $100,000 equals income taxes paid, not the total current income tax expense. Answer (D) is incorrect because $180,000 is equal to the reported income of $600,000 times the tax rate.

4. SFAS 109, *Accounting for Income Taxes*, establishes standards of financial accounting and reporting for income taxes that are currently payable and for

A. The tax consequences of revenues and expenses included in taxable income in a different year from the year in which they are recognized for financial reporting purposes.

B. The method of accounting for the U.S. federal investment tax credit.

C. The discounting of income taxes.

D. The accounting for income taxes in general in interim periods.

Answer (A) is correct. *(Publisher)*

REQUIRED: The applicability of SFAS 109.

DISCUSSION: SFAS 109 establishes standards of financial accounting and reporting for (1) income taxes currently payable; (2) the tax consequences of revenues, expenses, gains, and losses included in taxable income of an earlier or later year than the year in which they are recognized in income for financial reporting purposes; (3) other events that create differences between the tax bases of assets and liabilities and their amounts for financial reporting purposes; and (4) operating loss or tax credit carrybacks for refunds of taxes paid in prior years and carryforwards to reduce taxes payable in future years.

Answer (B) is incorrect because this issue is excluded from the scope of SFAS 109. Answer (C) is incorrect because this issue is excluded from the scope of SFAS 109. Answer (D) is incorrect because, with certain exceptions, SFAS 109 does not address accounting for income taxes in interim periods. The exceptions relate to the recognition of tax benefits, the effects of enacted changes in tax law or rates, and changes in valuation allowance in interim periods.

5. For which of the following temporary differences is the recognition of a deferred tax liability or asset most likely not required by SFAS 109?

A. A warranty liability covering 10 future years.

B. Equipment whose depreciable life is twice its tax recovery life.

C. The excess of the reported investment in a foreign subsidiary over the tax basis.

D. A gain arising from an involuntary condemnation of a building.

Answer (C) is correct. *(Publisher)*

REQUIRED: The temporary difference for which recognition of deferred taxes is usually not required.

DISCUSSION: In general, SFAS 109 requires that a deferred tax be recognized for all temporary differences. Certain of the areas addressed by APB 23, *Accounting for Income Taxes - Special Areas*, are exceptions. As amended by SFAS 109, APB 23 states that a deferred tax liability is not recognized for the excess of the reported amount of an investment in a foreign subsidiary over its tax basis that meets the indefinite reversal criteria stated in APB 23. Deferred tax liabilities or assets also are not recognized for leveraged leases, goodwill for which amortization is not permitted for tax purposes, and unallocated excess over cost (also known as negative goodwill).

Answer (A) is incorrect because a deferred tax asset is recognized for a warranty liability covering 10 future years. Answer (B) is incorrect because a deferred tax asset is recognized for equipment whose depreciable life is twice its tax recovery life. Answer (D) is incorrect because a deferred tax asset is recognized for a gain arising from an involuntary condemnation of a building (a nonmonetary asset).

6. Temporary differences arise when expenses are deductible for tax purposes

	After They Are Recognized in Financial Income	Before They Are Recognized in Financial Income
A.	No	No
B.	No	Yes
C.	Yes	Yes
D.	Yes	No

Answer (C) is correct. *(CPA, adapted)*

REQUIRED: The situations in which temporary differences arise.

DISCUSSION: A temporary difference exists when (1) the reported amount of an asset or liability in the financial statements differs from the tax basis of that asset or liability, and (2) the difference will result in taxable or deductible amounts in future years when the asset is recovered or the liability is settled at its reported amount. A temporary difference may also exist although it cannot be identified with a particular asset or liability recognized for financial reporting purposes. A temporary difference relates to an asset or liability if reduction of the asset or liability causes the temporary difference to reverse. An example of a temporary difference not related to an asset or liability because it is not reduced when the asset or liability is reduced is a long-term contract accounted for by the percentage-of-completion method for financial reporting and the completed-contract method for tax purposes. In this case, the temporary difference reverses only when the contract is completed, not from collection of receivables resulting from progress billings (SFAS 37). Such a temporary difference must result from an event recognized in the financial statements and must also result in taxable or deductible amounts in future years based on the provisions of the tax laws. Temporary differences commonly arise when either expenses or revenues are recognized for tax purposes either earlier or later than in the determination of financial income.

7. Jackson Corp. leased a building and received the $36,000 annual rental payment on June 15, 2003. The beginning of the lease was July 1, 2003. Rental income is taxable when received. Jackson's tax rates are 30% for 2003 and 40% thereafter. Jackson had no other permanent or temporary differences. Jackson determined that no valuation allowance was needed. What amount of deferred tax asset should Jackson report in its December 31, 2003 balance sheet?

A. $5,400

B. $7,200

C. $10,800

D. $14,400

Answer (B) is correct. *(CPA, adapted)*

REQUIRED: The amount of deferred tax asset reported at year-end.

DISCUSSION: The $36,000 rental payment is taxable in full when received in 2003, but only $18,000 [$36,000 × (6 ÷ 12)] should be recognized in financial accounting income for the year. The result is a deductible temporary difference arising from the difference between the tax basis ($0) of the liability for unearned rent and its reported amount in the year-end balance sheet ($36,000 – $18,000 = $18,000). A deductible temporary difference results in a deferred tax asset. The income tax payable for 2003 based on the rental payment is $10,800 (30% tax rate for 2003 × $36,000), the deferred tax asset is $7,200 (40% enacted tax rate applicable after 2003 when the asset will be realized × $18,000 future deductible amount), and the income tax expense is $3,600 ($10,800 current tax expense – $7,200 deferred tax benefit). The deferred tax benefit equals the net change during the year in the enterprise's deferred tax liabilities and assets ($7,200 deferred tax asset recognized in 2003 – $0).

Answer (A) is incorrect because $5,400 is based on a 30% tax rate. Answer (C) is incorrect because $10,800 is income tax payable. Answer (D) is incorrect because $14,400 would be the income tax payable if the 40% tax rate applied in 2003.

8. Among the items reported on Perez Company's income statement for the year ended December 31 were the following:

Compensation expense for a stock option plan	$50,000
Insurance premium on life of an officer (Perez is the owner and beneficiary.)	25,000

Neither is deductible for tax purposes. Temporary differences amount to

A. $0

B. $25,000

C. $50,000

D. $75,000

Answer (A) is correct. *(CPA, adapted)*

REQUIRED: The amount of temporary differences.

DISCUSSION: Temporary differences arise when (1) the reported amount of an asset or a liability in the financial statements differs from the tax basis of that asset or liability, and (2) the difference will result in taxable or deductible amounts in future years when the asset is recovered or the liability is settled at its reported amount. It is given that expenses for compensation expense for a stock option plan and payment of the premium for life insurance covering a key executive are recognized in the financial statements but are not deductible for tax purposes. Because neither will result in taxable or deductible amounts in future years, neither meets the definition of a temporary difference.

9. Which one of the following temporary differences will result in a deferred tax asset?

A. Use of the straight-line depreciation method for financial statement purposes and the Modified Accelerated Cost Recovery System (MACRS) for income tax purposes.

B. Installment sale profits accounted for on the accrual basis for financial statement purposes and on a cash basis for income tax purposes.

C. Advance rental receipts accounted for on the accrual basis for financial statement purposes and on a cash basis for tax purposes.

D. Prepaid expenses accounted for on the accrual basis for financial statement purposes and on a cash basis for income tax purposes.

Answer (C) is correct. *(CMA, adapted)*

REQUIRED: The temporary difference that will result in a deferred tax asset.

DISCUSSION: A deferred tax asset records the deferred tax consequences attributable to deductible temporary differences and carryforwards. Advance rental receipts accounted for on the accrual basis for financial statement purposes and on a cash basis for tax purposes result in a deferred tax asset. The financial statements report no income and no related tax expense because the rental payments apply to future periods. The tax return, however, reports the rent as income when the cash is received, and a tax is due in the year of receipt. Because the tax is paid prior to recording the income for financial statement purposes, it represents an asset that will be recognized as an expense when income is finally recorded.

Answer (A) is incorrect because using accelerated depreciation on the tax return results in a deferred tax liability. Answer (B) is incorrect because recognizing installment income on the financial statements but not the tax return results in a taxable temporary difference. Answer (D) is incorrect because recognizing prepaid expenses earlier on the tax return than on the financial statements (a situation akin to the accelerated depreciation of fixed assets) gives rise to a deferred tax liability.

10. Vickers, Inc. reported deferred tax assets and deferred tax liabilities at the end of both 2002 and 2003. According to SFAS 109, for the year ended in 2003, Vickers should report deferred income tax expense or benefit equal to the

A. Sum of the net changes in deferred tax assets and deferred tax liabilities.

B. Decrease in the deferred tax assets.

C. Increase in the deferred tax liabilities.

D. Amount of the income tax liability plus the sum of the net changes in deferred tax assets and deferred tax liabilities.

Answer (A) is correct. *(CPA, adapted)*

REQUIRED: The method of determining deferred income tax expense or benefit.

DISCUSSION: The deferred tax expense or benefit recognized is the sum of the net changes in the deferred tax assets and deferred tax liabilities. The deferred income tax expense or benefit is aggregated with the income taxes currently payable or refundable to determine the amount of income tax expense or benefit for the year to be recorded in the income statement.

Answer (B) is incorrect because the deferred income tax expense or benefit is equal to the sum of the net changes in the deferred tax assets and deferred tax liabilities. Answer (C) is incorrect because the deferred income tax expense or benefit is equal to the sum of the net changes in the deferred tax assets and deferred tax liabilities. Answer (D) is incorrect because this calculation determines the income tax expense or benefit for the year.

11. Because Pittman Co. uses different methods to depreciate equipment for financial statement and income tax purposes, Pittman has temporary differences that will reverse during the next year and add to taxable income. Deferred income taxes that are based on these temporary differences should be classified in Pittman's balance sheet as a

A. Contra account to current assets.

B. Contra account to noncurrent assets.

C. Current liability.

D. Noncurrent liability.

Answer (D) is correct. *(CPA, adapted)*

REQUIRED: The classification of deferred income taxes based on temporary differences.

DISCUSSION: These temporary differences arise from use of an accelerated depreciation method for tax purposes. Future taxable amounts reflecting the difference between the tax basis and the reported amount of the asset will result when the reported amount is recovered. Accordingly, Pittman must recognize a deferred tax liability to record the tax consequences of these temporary differences. This liability is noncurrent because the related asset (equipment) is noncurrent.

Answer (A) is incorrect because a liability is not shown as an offset to assets. Answer (B) is incorrect because a liability is not shown as an offset to assets. Answer (C) is incorrect because the classification of the deferred tax liability is determined by the classification of the asset to which it relates.

12. Scottco Co. applies SFAS 109, *Accounting for Income Taxes*. At the end of the current year, the tax effects of temporary differences were as follows:

	Deferred Tax Assets (Liabilities)	Related Asset Classification
Accelerated tax depreciation	($150,000)	Noncurrent asset
Additional costs in inventory for tax purposes	50,000	Current asset
	($100,000)	

A valuation allowance was not considered necessary. Scottco anticipates that $20,000 of the deferred tax liability will reverse next year. In Scottco's current-year balance sheet, what amount should Scottco report as noncurrent deferred tax liability?

A. $80,000

B. $100,000

C. $130,000

D. $150,000

Answer (D) is correct. *(CPA, adapted)*

REQUIRED: The amount of noncurrent deferred tax liability.

DISCUSSION: In a classified balance sheet, deferred tax assets and liabilities are separated into current and noncurrent amounts (SFAS 37, *Balance Sheet Classification of Deferred Income Taxes*). Classification as current or noncurrent is based on the classification of the related asset or liability. Because the $150,000 deferred tax liability is related to a noncurrent asset, it should be classified as noncurrent.

Answer (A) is incorrect because $80,000 equals the $100,000 net deferred tax liability minus the $20,000 expected to reverse next year. Answer (B) is incorrect because $100,000 equals the net deferred tax liability. Answer (C) is incorrect because $130,000 equals the $150,000 noncurrent deferred tax liability minus the $20,000 expected to reverse next year.

13. SFAS 109, *Accounting for Income Taxes*, states that a deferred tax asset shall be reduced by a valuation allowance if it is

A. Probable that some portion will not be realized.

B. Reasonably possible that some portion will not be realized.

C. More likely than not that some portion will not be realized.

D. Likely that some portion will not be realized.

Answer (C) is correct. *(Publisher)*

REQUIRED: The standard established by SFAS 109 for recognizing a valuation allowance for a deferred tax asset.

DISCUSSION: A deferred tax asset shall be reduced by a valuation allowance if the weight of the available evidence, both positive and negative, indicates that it is more likely than not (that is, the probability is greater than 50%) that some portion will not be realized. The allowance should suffice to reduce the deferred tax asset to the amount that is more likely than not to be realized.

Answer (A) is incorrect because the FASB specifically rejected the term probable (likely) as used in SFAS 5, *Accounting for Contingencies*. Answer (B) is incorrect because the FASB believes that the appropriate criterion is the one that produces results that are closest to the expected outcome. A reasonable possibility does not meet that standard. Answer (D) is incorrect because the FASB specifically rejected the term probable (likely) as used in SFAS 5, *Accounting for Contingencies*.

14. The only temporary differences for a calendar-year firm arise from a major lease, which is capitalized for financial reporting purposes and treated as an operating lease for tax purposes. At December 31, the temporary difference amounts to $600,000, and the related deferred income tax asset account has a $240,000 debit balance. What portion of this deferred tax asset should be classified as noncurrent if the firm, in its next year, expects to deduct $480,000 for rental expense in its tax return and to expense a total of $420,000 as amortization and interest related to the lease in the income statement?

A. $0

B. $180,000

C. $216,000

D. $240,000

Answer (C) is correct. *(Publisher)*

REQUIRED: The balance of the December 31 noncurrent deferred income tax account.

DISCUSSION: When a temporary difference is not related to a specific asset or liability, the related deferred tax account should be classified based on the expected reversal date of the temporary difference (SFAS 109).

The temporary difference arising from the lease is not related to a specific asset or liability because it is related to both the capitalized fixed asset and the lease obligation. The temporary difference is being reversed because the expected tax deduction for the next year is greater by $60,000 than the expected financial reporting expenses. Given that the $60,000 reversing difference expected in the next year is 10% ($60,000 ÷ $600,000) of the temporary difference at December 31, $24,000 (10% × $240,000) of the deferred tax balance at December 31 should be classified as current, and $216,000 (90% × $240,000) should be classified as noncurrent.

Answer (A) is incorrect because $216,000 should be classified as noncurrent deferred tax asset. Answer (B) is incorrect because $180,000 results from the difference between the temporary difference and the amount of expense for depreciation and interest for next year. Answer (D) is incorrect because $240,000 is the total deferred tax asset.

15. SFAS 109 requires that deferred tax assets be reduced by a valuation allowance if, based on the weight of the evidence, it is more likely than not that some portion or all of the deferred tax assets will not be realized. Which of the following kinds of evidence is considered in making this determination?

	Positive Evidence	Negative Evidence
A.	Yes	No
B.	Yes	Yes
C.	No	Yes
D.	No	No

Answer (B) is correct. *(Publisher)*

REQUIRED: The evidence to be considered in determining whether a valuation allowance should be recognized.

DISCUSSION: In determining whether a valuation allowance is required to reduce deferred tax assets to the amount that is more likely than not to be realized, all available evidence should be considered. Available evidence includes both positive and negative evidence. In considering the relative impact of positive and negative evidence, the weight given to the potential effect of the evidence should be commensurate with the extent to which the evidence can be objectively verified. However, the more negative evidence in existence, the more positive evidence is necessary and the more difficult it is to support a conclusion that a valuation allowance is not necessary.

16. When a change in the tax law or rates occurs, the effect of the change on a deferred tax liability or asset is

A. Not recognized.

B. Recognized as an adjustment as of the effective date of the change.

C. Recognized as an adjustment as of the enactment date of the change.

D. Recognized as a prior-period adjustment.

Answer (C) is correct. *(Publisher)*

REQUIRED: The effect on a deferred tax liability or asset of a change in the tax law or rates.

DISCUSSION: When a change in the tax law or rates occurs, the effect of the change on a deferred tax liability or asset is recognized as an adjustment in the period that includes the enactment date of the change. The adjustment is allocated to income from continuing operations. It is not treated as an extraordinary item.

17. On June 15, 2003, the county in which Mills Company operates enacted changes in the county's tax law. These changes are to become effective on January 1, 2004. They will have a material effect on the deferred tax accounts that Mills reported in accordance with SFAS 109. In which of the following interim and annual financial statements issued by Mills should the effect of the changes in tax law initially be reported?

A. The interim financial statements for the 3-month period ending June 30, 2003.

B. The annual financial statements for the year ending December 31, 2003.

C. The interim financial statements for the 3-month period ending September 30, 2003.

D. The annual financial statements for the year ending December 31, 2004.

Answer (A) is correct. *(Publisher)*

REQUIRED: The financial statements in which the effects of a change in tax law should initially be reported.

DISCUSSION: The effects of a change in tax law or rates initially should be included in income from continuing operations in the first financial statements issued for the period that includes the enactment date.

Answer (B) is incorrect because the effect should initially be reported in the first statements issued for the period that includes the enactment date. Answer (C) is incorrect because the period covered includes the effective date, not the enactment date. Answer (D) is incorrect because the period covered includes the effective date, not the enactment date.

18. In late summer, the Parker-Williams Partnership incorporated as a taxable entity. On September 7, the Dowdy Corporation, a taxable entity, changed its status to a partnership. In accordance with the provisions of SFAS 109, a deferred tax liability, based on temporary differences existing at the time of the change in the tax status of these enterprises, should

	Parker-Williams	Dowdy
A.	Not be recognized	Not be eliminated
B.	Be recognized	Not be eliminated
C.	Be recognized	Be eliminated
D.	Not be recognized	Be eliminated

Answer (C) is correct. *(Publisher)*

REQUIRED: The effect on two enterprises of changes in tax status.

DISCUSSION: When an enterprise such as Parker-Williams changes its status from a nontaxable partnership to a taxable corporation, a deferred tax liability or asset should be recognized for taxable or deductible temporary differences or carryforwards existing at the date of the tax status change. When a company such as Dowdy changes its status from a taxable to a nontaxable enterprise, any existing deferred tax liability or asset should usually be eliminated at the date of the tax status change. The effect of either recognizing or eliminating a deferred tax liability or asset should be allocated to continuing operations. It should not be treated as an extraordinary item.

19. When an enterprise is acquired in a business combination, a deferred tax liability or asset is recognized for the difference between the assigned amount and the tax basis of

A. Goodwill for which amortization is not tax deductible.

B. A leveraged lease.

C. Inventory.

D. Unallocated excess of fair value of acquired net assets over cost.

Answer (C) is correct. *(Publisher)*

REQUIRED: The effect on a deferred tax liability or asset of a business combination.

DISCUSSION: SFAS 109 requires that a deferred tax liability or asset be recognized for differences between the assigned amounts and the tax bases of assets and liabilities recorded when an enterprise is acquired in a business combination. The exceptions are for goodwill for which no tax deduction is allowed, unallocated excess over cost, leveraged leases, and certain APB 23 differences. Accordingly, a difference between the assigned amount and the tax basis of inventory results in recognition of a deferred tax liability or asset in these circumstances. A deferred tax liability or asset is recognized if goodwill is tax deductible even though it is not amortizable on the financial statements. The reason is that tax deductible goodwill does not result in a permanent difference because it will eventually affect pretax financial income by being impaired, sold, or disposed of.

20. Which one of the following is true regarding disclosure of income taxes, including deferred taxes?

A. The manner of reporting the tax benefit of an operating loss carryforward or carryback is determined by the source of the income or loss in the current year.

B. The manner of reporting the tax benefit of an operating loss carryforward or carryback is determined by the source of expected future income that will result in realization of a deferred tax asset for an operating loss carryforward from the current year.

C. The tax benefit of an operating loss carryforward or carryback is disclosed only in a note to the financial statements.

D. The tax benefit of an operating loss carryforward or carryback is a component of net tax expense and is not separately disclosed.

Answer (A) is correct. *(CMA, adapted)*

REQUIRED: The true statement about disclosures relating to income taxes.

DISCUSSION: Under SFAS 109, with certain exceptions, the tax benefit of an operating loss carryforward is reported in the same manner as the source of the income offset by the carryforward in the current year. Similarly, the tax benefit of an operating loss carryback is reported in the same manner as the source of the current-year loss.

Answer (B) is incorrect because the manner of reporting is controlled by the source of the income or loss in the current year. Answer (C) is incorrect because the tax benefit is recorded. Answer (D) is incorrect because operating loss carryforwards and carrybacks should be separately disclosed.

21. SFAS 109 prescribes which of the following disclosures?

A. The reconciliation of the reported amount of income tax expense attributable to continuing operations to income taxes currently payable.

B. The amounts and expiration dates of operating loss carryforwards for both financial reporting and tax purposes.

C. The amounts and expiration dates of tax credit carryforwards for financial reporting purposes only.

D. The reconciliation of the reported amount of income tax expense attributable to continuing operations to the amount of income tax expense that would result from applying domestic federal statutory tax rates to pretax income from continuing operations.

Answer (D) is correct. *(Publisher)*

REQUIRED: The disclosure prescribed by SFAS 109.

DISCUSSION: SFAS 109 requires that the reported amount of income tax expense attributable to continuing operations for the year be reconciled to the amount of income tax expense that would result from applying domestic federal statutory tax rates to pretax income from continuing operations. Public enterprises must disclose the estimated amount and the nature of each significant reconciling item. Nonpublic enterprises must disclose the nature of significant reconciling items but may omit a numerical reconciliation.

Answer (A) is incorrect because the reconciliation is to the amount of income tax expense that would result from applying domestic federal statutory tax rates to pretax income from continuing operations. Answer (B) is incorrect because only the amounts and expiration dates of operating loss and tax credit carryforwards for tax purposes must be disclosed. Answer (C) is incorrect because only the amounts and expiration dates of operating loss and tax credit carryforwards for tax purposes must be disclosed.

22. On December 31, 2003, Thomas Company reported a $150,000 warranty expense in its income statement. The expense was based on actual warranty costs of $30,000 in 2003 and expected warranty costs of $35,000 in 2004, $40,000 in 2005, and $45,000 in 2006. At December 31, 2003, deferred taxes should be based on a

A. $120,000 deductible temporary difference.

B. $150,000 deductible temporary difference.

C. $120,000 taxable temporary difference.

D. $150,000 taxable temporary difference.

Answer (A) is correct. *(Publisher)*

REQUIRED: The taxable (deductible) temporary difference resulting from a warranty expense.

DISCUSSION: At year-end 2003, Thomas Company should report a $120,000 warranty liability in its balance sheet. The warranty liability is equal to the $150,000 warranty expense minus the $30,000 warranty cost actually incurred in 2003. Because warranty costs are not deductible until actually incurred, the tax basis of the warranty liability is $0. The result is a $120,000 temporary difference ($120,000 book basis – $0 tax basis). When the liability is settled through the actual incurrence of warranty costs, the amounts will be deductible. Thus, the temporary difference should be classified as a deductible temporary difference.

Answer (B) is incorrect because $150,000 equals the warranty expense, not the payable. Answer (C) is incorrect because warranty costs will result in a deductible amount. Answer (D) is incorrect because the warranty costs will result in a deductible amount, and the $30,000 actual warranty costs are currently deductible.

23. Ray Co. began operations in the current year and reported $225,000 in income before income taxes for the year. Ray's current-year tax depreciation exceeded its book depreciation by $25,000. Ray also had nondeductible book expenses of $10,000 related to permanent differences. Ray's tax rate for the current year was 40%, and 35% for the following years. In its current-year balance sheet, what amount of deferred income tax liability should Ray report?

A. $8,750

B. $10,000

C. $12,250

D. $14,000

Answer (A) is correct. *(CPA, adapted)*

REQUIRED: The deferred income tax liability reported on the balance sheet.

DISCUSSION: In measuring a deferred tax liability or asset, the objective is to use the enacted tax rate(s) expected to apply to taxable income in the periods in which the deferred tax liability or asset is expected to be settled or realized. At the end of the current year, the only temporary difference is the $25,000 excess of tax depreciation over the book depreciation. This temporary difference will give rise to a $25,000 taxable amount in the years following the current year. Given the enacted tax rate of 35% applicable after the current year, the total tax consequence attributable to the taxable temporary difference (the deferred tax liability) is $8,750 ($25,000 × 35%).

Answer (B) is incorrect because the 35% tax rate applicable when the deferred tax liability is expected to be settled should be used. Answer (C) is incorrect because permanent differences do not create deferred tax liabilities. Answer (D) is incorrect because permanent differences do not create deferred tax liabilities, and the 35% tax rate applicable when the deferred tax liability is expected to be settled should be used.

24. Based on its current operating levels, Ellis Corporation estimates that its annual level of taxable income in the foreseeable future will be $200,000 annually. Enacted tax rates for the tax jurisdiction in which Ellis operates are 15% for the first $50,000 of taxable income, 25% for the next $50,000 of taxable income, and 35% for taxable income in excess of $100,000. Which tax rate should Ellis use to measure a deferred tax liability or asset in accordance with SFAS 109, *Accounting for Income Taxes*?

A. 15%

B. 25%

C. 27.5%

D. 35%

Answer (C) is correct. *(Publisher)*

REQUIRED: The tax rate applicable to the measurement of a deferred tax liability or asset.

DISCUSSION: In measuring a deferred tax liability or asset, the objective is to use the enacted tax rate(s) expected to apply to taxable income in the periods in which the deferred tax liability or asset is expected to be settled or realized. If graduated tax rates are a significant factor for an enterprise, the applicable tax rate is the average graduated tax rate applicable to the amount of estimated future annual taxable income. As indicated, the applicable tax rate is 27.5%.

Taxable Income		Tax Rate		
$ 50,000	×	15%	=	$ 7,500
50,000	×	25%	=	12,500
100,000	×	35%	=	35,000
$200,000				$55,000

$55,000 ÷ $200,000 = 27.5%

Answer (A) is incorrect because 15% is the tax rate for the first $50,000 of income. Answer (B) is incorrect because 25% is the tax rate for income over $50,000 but less than $100,000. Answer (D) is incorrect because 35% is the tax rate for income over $100,000.

25. In its 2003 income statement, Orr Corp. reported depreciation of $400,000. Orr reported depreciation of $550,000 on its 2003 income tax return. The difference in depreciation is the only temporary difference, and it will reverse equally over the next 3 years. Assume that the enacted income tax rates are 35% for 2003, 30% for 2004, and 25% for 2005 and 2006. What amount should be included in the deferred income tax liability in Orr's December 31, 2003 balance sheet?

A. $37,500

B. $40,000

C. $45,000

D. $52,500

Answer (B) is correct. *(CPA, adapted)*

REQUIRED: The amount to be included in the deferred income tax liability at year-end.

DISCUSSION: At 12/31/03, the only temporary difference is the $150,000 ($550,000 – $400,000) excess of the tax depreciation over the book depreciation. This temporary difference will give rise to a $50,000 taxable amount in each of the years 2004 through 2006. Given the enacted tax rates of 30% in 2004 and 25% in 2005 and 2006, the total tax consequences are $40,000, which is the balance that should be reported in the deferred income tax liability at year-end.

Year	Taxable Amount	Enacted Tax Rates	Tax Consequences
2004	$50,000	30%	$15,000
2005	50,000	25%	12,500
2006	50,000	25%	12,500
			$40,000

Answer (A) is incorrect because $37,500 is based on a 25% tax rate. Answer (C) is incorrect because $45,000 is based on a 30% tax rate. Answer (D) is incorrect because $52,500 is based on a 35% tax rate.

26. Tharris Corp. uses the equity method to account for its 25% investment in Bailey, Inc. During the current year, Tharris received dividends of $30,000 from Bailey and recorded $180,000 as its equity in the earnings of Bailey. Additional information follows:

- All the undistributed earnings of Bailey will be distributed as dividends in future periods.
- The dividends received from Bailey are eligible for the 80% dividends received deduction.
- There are no other temporary differences.
- Enacted income tax rates are 30% for the current year and thereafter.

In its current-year balance sheet, what amount should Tharris report for deferred income tax liability?

A. $9,000

B. $10,800

C. $45,000

D. $54,000

Answer (A) is correct. *(CPA, adapted)*

REQUIRED: The deferred income tax liability reported on the balance sheet.

DISCUSSION: According to SFAS 109, the deferred tax liability constitutes the "deferred tax consequences attributable to taxable temporary differences. A deferred tax liability is measured using the applicable enacted tax rate and provisions of the enacted tax law." The recognition of $180,000 of equity-based earnings creates a temporary difference that will result in taxable amounts in future periods when dividends are distributed. The deferred tax liability arising from this temporary difference is measured using the 30% enacted tax rate and the dividends received deduction. Accordingly, given that all the undistributed earnings will be distributed, a deferred tax liability of $9,000 [($180,000 equity – $30,000 dividends received) × 20% not deductible × 30% tax rate applicable after the current year] should be reported.

Answer (B) is incorrect because $10,800 equals 30% of 20% of the equity in the earnings of Bailey. Answer (C) is incorrect because $45,000 is the net increase in the investment in Bailey account under the equity method multiplied by the 30% tax rate. Answer (D) is incorrect because $54,000 equals 30% of $180,000.

27. Ratliff Co., organized on January 2, 2003, had pretax accounting income of $500,000 and taxable income of $800,000 for the year ended December 31, 2003. Ratliff expected to maintain this level of taxable income in future years. The only temporary difference is for accrued product warranty costs expected to be paid as follows:

2004	$100,000
2005	50,000
2006	50,000
2007	100,000

The applicable enacted income tax rate is 30%. In Ratliff's December 31, 2003 balance sheet, the deferred income tax asset and related valuation allowance should be

	Deferred Tax Asset	Valuation Allowance
A.	$0	$0
B.	$90,000	$90,000
C.	$90,000	$0
D.	$0	$90,000

Answer (C) is correct. *(CPA, adapted)*

REQUIRED: The deferred tax asset and valuation allowance to be recognized at 12/31/03.

DISCUSSION: At 12/31/03, Ratliff should report an accrued product warranty liability of $300,000. The result is a deductible temporary difference of $300,000 because the liability will be settled and related amounts will be tax deductible when the warranty costs are incurred. A deferred tax asset should be measured for deductible temporary differences using the applicable tax rate. Hence, Ratliff should record a $90,000 ($300,000 × 30%) deferred tax asset. A valuation allowance should be used to reduce a deferred tax asset if, based on the weight of the available evidence, it is more likely than not that some portion will not be realized. In this case, however, Ratliff had taxable income of $800,000 for 2003 and expects to maintain that level of taxable income in future years. The positive evidence therefore indicates that sufficient taxable income will be available for the future realization of the tax benefit of the existing deductible temporary differences. Given no negative evidence, a valuation allowance is not necessary.

Answer (A) is incorrect because a deferred tax asset should be recognized. Answer (B) is incorrect because a valuation allowance should not be recognized. Answer (D) is incorrect because a deferred tax asset but not a valuation allowance should be recognized.

28. In preparing its current year-end financial statements, Guss Corp. must determine the proper accounting treatment of a $180,000 loss carryforward available to offset future taxable income. There are no temporary differences. The applicable current and future income tax rate is 30%. Available evidence is not conclusive as to the future existence of sufficient taxable income to provide for the future realization of the tax benefit of the $180,000 loss carryforward. However, based on the available evidence, Guss believes that it is more likely than not that future taxable income will be available to provide for the future realization of $100,000 of this loss carryforward. In its current-year statement of financial condition, Guss should recognize what amounts?

	Deferred Tax Asset	Valuation Allowance
A.	$0	$0
B.	$30,000	$0
C.	$54,000	$24,000
D.	$54,000	$30,000

Answer (C) is correct. *(Publisher)*

REQUIRED: The amounts to be recognized as a deferred tax asset and related valuation allowance.

DISCUSSION: The applicable tax rate should be used to measure a deferred tax asset for an operating loss carryforward that is available to offset future taxable income. Guss should therefore recognize a $54,000 ($180,000 × 30%) deferred tax asset. A valuation allowance should be recognized to reduce the deferred tax asset if, based on the weight of the available evidence, it is more likely than not (the likelihood is more than 50%) that some portion or all of a deferred tax asset will not be realized. The valuation allowance should be equal to an amount necessary to reduce the deferred tax asset to the amount that is more likely than not to be realized. Based on the available evidence, Guss believes that it is more likely than not that the tax benefit of $100,000 of the operating loss will be realized. Thus, the company should recognize a $24,000 valuation allowance to reduce the $54,000 deferred tax asset to $30,000 ($100,000 × 30%), the amount of the deferred tax asset that is more likely than not to be realized.

Answer (A) is incorrect because a deferred tax asset equal to $54,000 should be recognized, and a valuation allowance should be recognized equal to $24,000 to reduce the deferred tax asset to $30,000. Answer (B) is incorrect because a deferred tax asset of $30,000 results from netting the valuation allowance against the deferred tax asset. Answer (D) is incorrect because $30,000 is the deferred tax asset, not the valuation allowance, after the two are netted.

Questions 29 and 30 are based on the following information.

Zeff Co. prepared the following reconciliation of its pretax financial statement income to taxable income for the current year, its first year of operations:

Pretax financial income	$160,000
Nontaxable interest received on municipal securities	(5,000)
Long-term loss accrual in excess of deductible amount	10,000
Depreciation in excess of financial statement amount	(25,000)
Taxable income	$140,000

Zeff's tax rate is 40%.

29. In its current-year income statement, what amount should Zeff report as income tax expense – current portion?

A. $52,000

B. $56,000

C. $62,000

D. $64,000

Answer (B) is correct. *(CPA, adapted)*

REQUIRED: The current portion of income tax expense.

DISCUSSION: Pretax financial income is adjusted for permanent and temporary differences to arrive at the current taxable income. The current portion of income tax expense equals income taxes paid or payable as determined by applying enacted tax law. Thus, the current portion of income tax expense equals $56,000 ($140,000 × 40% tax rate).

Answer (A) is incorrect because $52,000 results from using taxable income of $130,000. Answer (C) is incorrect because $62,000 excludes the temporary differences from consideration. Answer (D) is incorrect because $64,000 is based on pretax financial income.

30. In its current-year balance sheet, what should Zeff report as deferred income tax liability?

A. $2,000

B. $4,000

C. $6,000

D. $8,000

Answer (C) is correct. *(CPA, adapted)*

REQUIRED: The amount of deferred income tax liability.

DISCUSSION: A deferred income tax liability arises from a taxable temporary difference. The $10,000 long-term loss accrual (a deductible temporary difference) results in a deferred tax asset. The $25,000 excess depreciation (a taxable temporary difference) is also a noncurrent item. It results in a deferred tax liability. These items should be netted because all noncurrent deferred tax assets and liabilities should be offset and presented as a single amount. Accordingly, the net deferred tax liability is $6,000 [($25,000 – $10,000) × .40].

Answer (A) is incorrect because $2,000 is 40% times the $5,000 permanent difference. Answer (B) is incorrect because $4,000 equals 40% of the deductible temporary difference. Answer (D) is incorrect because $8,000 results from combining the temporary differences and the permanent difference (municipal bond interest).

31. According to SFAS 109, *Accounting for Income Taxes*, which of the following items should affect current income tax expense for 2003?

A. Interest on a 2001 tax deficiency paid in 2003.

B. Penalty on a 2001 tax deficiency paid in 2003.

C. Change in income tax rate for 2003.

D. Change in income tax rate for 2004.

Answer (C) is correct. *(CPA, adapted)*

REQUIRED: The item that affects current income tax expense for 2002.

DISCUSSION: Current tax expense is the amount of income taxes paid or payable for a year as determined by applying the provisions of the enacted tax law to the taxable income for that year.

Answer (A) is incorrect because interest on a prior-year tax deficiency does not affect current income tax expense. Answer (B) is incorrect because penalties on a prior-year tax deficiency do not affect current income tax expense. Answer (D) is incorrect because a change in income tax rate for 2004 would affect the deferred tax expense or benefit for 2003, assuming scheduled effects of a temporary difference will occur in 2004.

32. Carter Corp.'s pretax income in the current year was $100,000. The temporary differences between amounts reported in the financial statements and the tax return are as follows:

Depreciation in the financial statements was $8,000 more than tax depreciation.

The equity method of accounting resulted in financial statement income of $35,000. A $25,000 dividend was received during the year, which is eligible for the 80% dividends-received deduction (DRD).

Carter's effective income tax rate was 30% in the current year. In its current-year income statement, Carter should report a current provision for income taxes of

A. $26,400

B. $23,400

C. $21,900

D. $18,600

Answer (B) is correct. *(CPA, adapted)*

REQUIRED: The current provision for income taxes.

DISCUSSION: Current tax expense is the amount of income taxes paid or payable for a year as determined by applying the provisions of the enacted tax law to the taxable income for that year. Pretax accounting income is given as $100,000. Financial statement depreciation exceeds tax depreciation by $8,000. Accounting income includes $35,000 of income determined in accordance with the equity method, but taxable income includes only $5,000 of this amount [$25,000 dividend received – (80% × $25,000) dividends-received deduction]. The reconciliation of pretax accounting income to taxable income is as follows:

Pretax accounting income	$100,000
Financial statement – tax depreciation	8,000
Equity-based income – taxable dividends	(30,000)
Taxable income	$ 78,000

Accordingly, the current provision for income taxes is $23,400 (30% applicable tax rate × $78,000).

Answer (A) is incorrect because $26,400 is based on the assumption that taxable income includes equity-based income minus the 80% DRD. Answer (C) is incorrect because $21,900 assumes a 100% DRD. Answer (D) is incorrect because $18,600 results from subtracting, not adding, the excess financial statement depreciation.

17.2 Intraperiod Tax Allocation

33. Intraperiod income tax allocation arises because

A. Items included in the determination of taxable income may be presented in different sections of the financial statements.

B. Income taxes must be allocated between current and future periods.

C. Certain revenues and expenses appear in the financial statements either before or after they are included in taxable income.

D. Certain revenues and expenses appear in the financial statements but are excluded from taxable income.

Answer (A) is correct. *(CPA, adapted)*

REQUIRED: The accounting reason for intraperiod allocation of income taxes.

DISCUSSION: To provide a fair presentation of the various components of the results of operations, SFAS 109 requires that income tax expense for the period be allocated among income from continuing operations, discontinued operations, extraordinary items, other comprehensive income, and items charged or credited directly to equity.

Answer (B) is incorrect because it describes interperiod tax allocation. Answer (C) is incorrect because differences in the timing of revenues and expenses for financial statement and tax return purposes create the need for interperiod income tax allocation. Answer (D) is incorrect because revenues and expenses included in the financial statements but not in taxable income cause permanent differences between the financial statements and tax returns, but do not create a need for tax allocation.

34. Last year, before providing for taxes, Dixon Company had income from continuing operations of $930,000 and an extraordinary gain of $104,000. The current effective tax rate on continuing operations income was 40% and the total tax liability was $398,000 ignoring any temporary differences. The amount of the extraordinary gain net of tax effect was

A. $41,600

B. $62,400

C. $78,000

D. $104,000

Answer (C) is correct. *(Publisher)*

REQUIRED: The amount of extraordinary gain net of the tax effect.

DISCUSSION: Given that the effective tax rate for continuing operations was 40%, the related tax expense was $372,000 ($930,000 × 40%). Because the total tax liability was $398,000, $26,000 ($398,000 – $372,000) was applicable to the extraordinary item. Accordingly, the extraordinary gain net of tax effect was $78,000 ($104,000 – $26,000).

Answer (A) is incorrect because $41,600 results from multiplying the extraordinary gain times the effective tax rate. Answer (B) is incorrect because $62,400 results from subtracting the extraordinary gain times the effective tax rate from the extraordinary gain. Answer (D) is incorrect because $104,000 results from not accounting for the tax effect.

STUDY UNIT EIGHTEEN
ACCOUNTING CHANGES AND ERROR CORRECTIONS

SFAS 154, *Accounting Changes and Error Corrections*, applies to business enterprises and not-for-profit organizations. It defines an **accounting change** as a change in an accounting principle, an accounting estimate, or the reporting entity. An accounting change does not include a correction of an accounting error in previously issued financial statements.

A **change in accounting principle** occurs when an entity (1) adopts a generally accepted accounting principle different from the one previously used, (2) changes the method of applying a generally accepted principle, or (3) changes to a generally accepted principle when the principle previously used is no longer generally accepted. A change in principle does not include the initial adoption of a principle because of an event or transaction occurring for the first time or that previously had an immaterial effect. It also does not include adoption or modification of a principle to account for an event or transaction that clearly differs in substance from the one previously occurring.

The **general presumption** in preparing financial statements is that a principle once adopted should be applied consistently. However, a change in principle is appropriate if the change is mandated by a newly issued official pronouncement, or the entity is able to justify it as preferable.

Retrospective application is required for all **direct effects** and the related income tax effects of a change in principle unless it is impracticable to determine the cumulative effect or the period-specific effects of the change. Furthermore, a new official pronouncement may prescribe a different transition method. Retrospective application, however, should not include **indirect effects**. These effects are changes in current or future cash flows resulting from retrospective application. An example is a required profit-sharing payment based on a reported amount (e.g., revenue). Indirect effects actually incurred are recognized when the change in principle is made.

Retrospective application requires that the carrying amounts of assets, liabilities, and retained earnings (or other appropriate components of equity or net assets) at the beginning of the first period reported be adjusted for the **cumulative effect** of the new principle on periods prior to the first period reported. Moreover, all periods reported must be individually adjusted for the **period-specific effects** of applying the new principle.

When it is **impracticable** to determine the **cumulative effect** of applying a new principle to any prior period (for example, when the change is from FIFO to LIFO), the new principle is applied prospectively at the earliest date practicable. When it is practicable to determine the cumulative effect of applying the new principle to all prior periods, but determining the period-specific effects on all prior periods is impracticable, cumulative-effect adjustments should be made to the beginning balances for the first period to which the new principle can be applied. Retrospective application is impracticable when (1) the entity cannot apply the new principle after making every reasonable effort; (2) assumptions about management's intent in a prior period are required that cannot be independently substantiated; or (3) significant estimates are required, and it is not possible to obtain objective evidence (a) about circumstances existing when amounts would have been recognized, measured, or disclosed, and (b) that would have been available when the prior statements were issued.

A **change in accounting estimate** results from new information and a reassessment of the current status and future benefits and obligations represented by assets and liabilities. The effects of a change in estimate should be accounted for **prospectively**. Thus, the effects should be recognized only in the period of change and any future periods affected. A **change in estimate inseparable from (effected by) a change in principle** is accounted for as a change in estimate. An example is a change in a method of depreciation, amortization, or depletion of long-lived, nonfinancial assets. When a change in estimate affects several future periods, **disclosures** include the effect on (1) income from continuing operations, (2) net income (or other appropriate captions), and (3) related per-share amounts of the current period.

A **change in reporting entity** results when (1) consolidated or combined financial statements are presented in place of financial statements of individual entities; (2) consolidated financial statements include subsidiaries different from those previously included; or (3) combined financial statements include entities different from those previously included. A change in reporting entity does not result from a business combination or consolidation of a variable interest entity. This change is retrospectively applied to interim and annual statements. (However, **interest cost** previously capitalized under **SFAS 58**, *Capitalization of Interest Cost in Financial Statements That Include Investments Accounted for by the Equity Method*, is not changed. According to SFAS 58, assets qualifying for interest capitalization may include an equity-method investment if the investee meets certain criteria.) In the period of change, **disclosures** must include (1) the nature of the change; (2) the reasons for it; and (3) the effect on income before extraordinary items, net income (or other appropriate captions), comprehensive income, and related per-share amounts for all periods presented.

For **all changes in principle**, the nature of and reason for the change should be disclosed when the change is made. **Additional disclosures** include (1) the method of applying the change; (2) the information adjusted; (3) the effects on income from continuing operations, any other affected line items, and any affected per-share amounts; (4) the cumulative-effect adjustment; and (5) a description of indirect effects (including amounts currently reported) and any related per-share amounts. If retrospective application is impracticable, disclosures of the reasons and the method used to report the change are required.

An **accounting error** results from (1) a mathematical mistake, (2) a mistake in the application of GAAP, or (3) an oversight or misuse of facts existing when the statements were prepared. An accounting error related to a prior period is accounted for as a **prior period adjustment**. When the statements are **restated**, the entity must disclose the restatement and the nature of the error. **Other required disclosures** include (1) the effect of the correction on each line item and per-share amount affected for all prior statements presented, (2) the cumulative effect on retained earnings, and (3) the disclosures required by **APB 9**, *Reporting the Results of Operations.*

QUESTIONS

18.1 General

1. Which of the following transactions should be classified as an accounting change?

I. Transition from a previously generally accepted accounting principle to a new accounting principle prescribed by a recently issued Statement of Financial Accounting Standards.

II. Transition from an accounting principle not generally accepted to a generally accepted accounting principle.

III. Change in the percentage used to determine an allowance for uncollectible accounts.

A. I, II, and III.

B. I and II only.

C. I and III only.

D. II and III only.

Answer (C) is correct. *(Publisher)*

REQUIRED: The transactions properly classified as accounting changes.

DISCUSSION: An accounting change is a change in an accounting principle, an accounting estimate, or the reporting entity. A correction of an accounting error in previously issued financial statements is not an accounting change. A transition to a newly prescribed SFAS is a change in accounting principle. A change from an accounting principle not generally accepted to one that is generally accepted is a correction of an accounting error. A change in the percentage used to determine an allowance for uncollectible accounts is a change in estimate.

Answer (A) is incorrect because a correction of an accounting error is not an accounting change. Answer (B) is incorrect because a change in the percentage used to determine an allowance for uncollectible accounts is a change in accounting estimate. Furthermore, the transition from an accounting principle not generally accepted to a generally accepted accounting principle is a correction of an accounting error. Answer (D) is incorrect because a transition from a previously generally accepted accounting principle to a new accounting principle prescribed by a recently issued Statement of Financial Accounting Standards is a change in accounting principle. Furthermore, the transition from an accounting principle not generally accepted to a generally accepted accounting principle is a correction of an accounting error.

2. For which of the following justified changes should previously issued financial statements be adjusted to report the effects of a newly adopted accounting principle as if the new principle had always been used?

A. A change from an accelerated method of depreciation of productive assets to the straight-line method.

B. A change from the weighted-average method of inventory valuation to the FIFO method.

C. A change in the percentages used to determine warranty expense.

D. Adoption of an accounting principle to account for a transaction clearly different in substance from previously occurring transactions.

Answer (B) is correct. *(Publisher)*

REQUIRED: The change that results in a retrospective adjustment.

DISCUSSION: Retrospective application changes previously issued financial statements to report the effects of a newly adopted accounting principle as if the new principle had always been used. It is required for all direct effects and the related income tax effects of a change in accounting principle, such as a change in inventory valuation methods, unless it is impracticable to determine either the cumulative effect or the period-specific effects of the change. An accounting principle is changed (1) to account for transition to a newly issued official pronouncement (unless the pronouncement prescribes a different method) or (2) when the entity justifies the change on the basis that it is preferable.

Answer (A) is incorrect because a change from an accelerated method of depreciation of productive assets to the straight-line method is a change in accounting estimate effected by a change in accounting principle. Answer (C) is incorrect because a change in the percentages used to determine warranty expense is a change in accounting estimate. Answer (D) is incorrect because the adoption of an accounting principle to account for a transaction clearly different in substance from previously occurring transactions is not considered a change in accounting principle.

3. The general presumption in preparing financial statements in accordance with generally accepted accounting principles is that

A. A change in accounting principle is permissible if the enterprise is able to justify the new principle as preferable to the existing principle.

B. A change is permissible only to correct the effect of an accounting error in previously issued financial statements.

C. A change to previously issued financial statements is never permissible.

D. A change is permissible only when a newly issued official pronouncement mandates a change in accounting principle.

Answer (A) is correct. *(Publisher)*

REQUIRED: The general presumption regarding when changes to previously issued financial statements are permitted.

DISCUSSION: The general presumption in preparing financial statements in accordance with GAAP is that an accounting principle once adopted should be applied on a consistent basis. However, a change in principle is appropriate if the change is mandated by a newly issued official pronouncement, or the entity is able to justify the new principle as preferable to the existing principle. In addition, when an accounting error is discovered, the error should be corrected as a retroactive restatement (prior period adjustment) of all periods presented.

Answer (B) is incorrect because an accounting principle also may be changed if it can be justified as preferable. Answer (C) is incorrect because a change in accounting principle may be justified, and a correction of an accounting error is required. Answer (D) is incorrect because an accounting principle also may be changed if it can be justified as preferable.

4. In January 2006, based on evidence that justified the change, Urban Corporation changed its method of depreciation of its productive assets from an accelerated method to the straight-line method. Urban should account for this change as a

A. Change in accounting estimate.

B. Correction of an error.

C. Change in accounting principle.

D. Change in the reporting entity.

Answer (A) is correct. *(Publisher)*

REQUIRED: The proper accounting for a change in depreciation method.

DISCUSSION: A change in a depreciation, amortization, or depletion method "is adopted in partial or complete recognition of a change in the estimated future benefits inherent in the asset, the pattern of consumption of those benefits, or the information available to the entity about those benefits" (SFAS 154). Thus, the effect of the change in accounting principle is considered to be inseparable from the effect of the change in accounting estimate. When a change in estimate is inseparable from (effected by) a change in principle, the change is accounted for as a change in estimate. The effects of a change in estimate should be accounted for prospectively, that is, by recognition in the period of change and any future periods affected by the change. The effects should not be recognized in prior periods.

Answer (B) is incorrect because a change in a depreciation, amortization, or depletion method is accounted for as a change in accounting estimate. Answer (C) is incorrect because a change in a depreciation, amortization, or depletion method is accounted for as a change in accounting estimate. Answer (D) is incorrect because a change in a depreciation, amortization, or depletion method is accounted for as a change in accounting estimate.

5. H. Will Company has justifiably changed its method of accounting for inventory. Retrospective application of the change is practicable. The cumulative effect on all prior periods of changing to the new accounting principle is included in the first period reported as an adjustment of

A. Retained earnings at the end of the year.

B. Retained earnings at the beginning of the year.

C. Net income.

D. Comprehensive income.

Answer (B) is correct. *(Publisher)*

REQUIRED: The proper accounting for the cumulative effect of a change in accounting principle.

DISCUSSION: A change in accounting principle is accounted for by retrospective application unless it is impracticable to determine either the cumulative effect or the period-specific effects of the change. Furthermore, a newly issued official pronouncement may prescribe a different transition method. Retrospective application changes previously issued financial statements to report the effects of the newly adopted principle as if it had always been used. Retrospective application requires that the carrying amounts of assets, liabilities, and retained earnings at the beginning of the first period reported be adjusted for the cumulative effect of the new principle on periods prior to the first period reported. Moreover, all periods reported must be individually adjusted for the period-specific effects of applying the new principle.

Answer (A) is incorrect because retained earnings at the beginning of the first period reported are adjusted. Answer (C) is incorrect because net income is adjusted for the period-specific effects. Answer (D) is incorrect because comprehensive income is adjusted for the period-specific effects.

18.2 Changes in Accounting Principle

6. When reporting a change in accounting principle, the general approach is to report the change

A. Prospectively, in the period of change and future periods affected by the change.

B. As a cumulative effect included in net income of the period of change.

C. By retrospective application to previously issued financial statements to report the effects of the new principle.

D. As a cumulative effect included in net income of the period of change and prospective application in future periods.

Answer (C) is correct. *(CMA, adapted)*

REQUIRED: The proper accounting for a change in accounting principle.

DISCUSSION: A change in accounting principle is recorded by retrospective application to previously issued financial statements unless it is impracticable to determine either the cumulative effect or the period-specific effects of the change. However, a newly issued official pronouncement may prescribe a different transition method.

Answer (A) is incorrect because retroactive application is required. Answer (B) is incorrect because retroactive application is required. Answer (D) is incorrect because retroactive application is required.

7. Retrospective application of a change in accounting principles is impracticable when

I. The costs of applying the new accounting principle to prior period financial statements are material.

II. Retrospective application requires that management's intent in a prior period be assumed without independent substantiation.

A. I only.

B. II only.

C. Both I and II.

D. Neither I nor II.

Answer (B) is correct. *(Publisher)*

REQUIRED: The condition(s) indicating that retroactive application is impracticable.

DISCUSSION: Retrospective application of a change in an accounting principle is deemed to be impracticable when (1) the entity cannot apply the new principle after making every reasonable effort; (2) assumptions about management's intent in a prior period are required that cannot be independently substantiated; or (3) significant estimates are required, and it is not possible to obtain objective evidence (a) about circumstances existing when amounts would have been recognized, measured, or disclosed, and (b) that would have been available when the prior statements were issued.

Answer (A) is incorrect because cost is not a condition of impracticability. Answer (C) is incorrect because cost is not a condition of impracticability. Answer (D) is incorrect because retrospective application is deemed to be impracticable when management's intent in a prior period must be assumed without independent substantiation.

8. P. Werner and Co. has made a justifiable change in an accounting principle. The cumulative effect of applying the change to all prior periods is determinable. However, it is not practicable to determine the period-specific effects on all prior periods presented. Consequently, the reported carrying amounts of the assets and liabilities should be adjusted for the effects of the new principle at the

A. Beginning of the earliest accounting period presented to which the new principle can be applied.

B. End of the latest accounting period presented for which retrospective application is impracticable.

C. Beginning of the current accounting period.

D. Beginning of the earliest accounting period presented.

Answer (A) is correct. *(Publisher)*

REQUIRED: The proper accounting when period-specific effects are not determinable.

DISCUSSION: When it is impracticable to determine the cumulative effect of applying a change in principle to any prior period, it is applied prospectively at the earliest date practicable. When the entity can determine the cumulative effect of applying the principle to all prior periods, but it is impracticable to determine the period-specific effects on all prior periods presented, the new principle should be applied to the reported carrying amounts of assets and liabilities at the beginning of the earliest period to which the new principle can be applied. An offsetting adjustment also may need to be made to beginning retained earnings.

Answer (B) is incorrect because, when period-specific effects are impracticable to determine, the accounting change should be recorded at the beginning of the earliest period to which the new principle can be applied. Answer (C) is incorrect because, when period-specific effects are impracticable to determine, the accounting change should be recorded at the beginning of the earliest period to which the new principle can be applied. Answer (D) is incorrect because, when period-specific effects are impracticable to determine, the accounting change should be recorded at the beginning of the earliest period to which the new principle can be applied.

9. JKC Corporation, a calendar year-end firm, changed its method for measuring inventory from FIFO to LIFO effective January 1, 2006. Records of inventory purchases and sales were not available for certain earlier years of its existence. Accordingly, it was impracticable for JKC to determine the cumulative effect of applying the change in accounting principle retrospectively. If records of inventory purchases and sales are available for recent years, JKC should retrospectively apply LIFO at the

A. End of the latest accounting period presented for which retrospective application is impracticable.

B. Beginning of the earliest accounting period presented for which retrospective application is practicable.

C. Beginning of the current accounting period.

D. Earliest date practicable.

Answer (D) is correct. *(CPA, adapted)*

REQUIRED: The proper accounting for a change in accounting principle.

DISCUSSION: When it is impracticable to determine the cumulative effect of applying a new accounting principle to any prior period, it should be applied prospectively at the earliest date practicable (SFAS 154). For example, if JKC has all the required information for applying LIFO beginning with January 1, 2004, it will carry forward the 2003 FIFO ending inventory balance. It will then begin using LIFO on January 1, 2004.

Answer (A) is incorrect because, when it is impracticable to determine the cumulative effect of a change in accounting principle on any prior period, the change should be applied prospectively at the earliest date practicable. Answer (B) is incorrect because, when it is impracticable to determine the cumulative effect of a change in accounting principle on any prior period, the change should be applied prospectively at the earliest date practicable. Answer (C) is incorrect because, when it is impracticable to determine the cumulative effect of a change in accounting principle on any prior period, the change should be applied prospectively at the earliest date practicable.

10. When the Sonia Corporation began business in 1994, its accountants decided to include such indirect costs of manufacturing as factory janitorial expenses, depreciation of machinery, and insurance on the factory as elements of inventory costs. At the beginning of 2006, the company began expensing all insurance costs in the period in which they are incurred. To comply with current standards, the company must justify and disclose the reason for the change. The reason that is most appropriate is that the new principle

A. Constitutes an improvement in financial reporting.

B. Has been and continues to be the treatment used for tax purposes.

C. Is easier to apply because no assumptions about allocation must be made.

D. Is one used by the company for insurance costs other than those on factory-related activities.

Answer (A) is correct. *(Publisher)*

REQUIRED: The most appropriate reason for making a change in accounting principle.

DISCUSSION: The presumption is that, once adopted, an accounting principle should not be changed in accounting for events and transactions of a similar type. This presumption in favor of continuity may be overcome if the enterprise justifies the use of an alternative acceptable principle. The new principle should be preferable because it constitutes an improvement in financial reporting. If the GAAP hierarchy is followed, preferability automatically is established if a pronouncement of the FASB (or other designated standard setter) (1) requires use of a new principle, (2) expresses a preference for a principle not being used, (3) interprets an existing principle, or (4) rejects a specific principle. FASB Interpretation No. 1, *Accounting Changes Related to the Cost of Inventory*, states that preferability should be determined on the basis of whether the new principle constitutes an improvement in financial reporting. Other bases are not sufficient justification.

Answer (B) is incorrect because it does not constitute sufficient justification. Answer (C) is incorrect because it does not constitute sufficient justification. Answer (D) is incorrect because it does not constitute sufficient justification.

Questions 11 through 13 are based on the following information. Loire Co., a calendar year-end firm, has used the FIFO method of inventory measurement since it began operations in 2003. Loire changed to the weighted-average method for determining inventory costs at the beginning of 2006. Justification for this change was that it better reflected inventory flow. The following schedule shows year-end inventory balances under FIFO and weighted-average methods:

Year	FIFO	Weighted-Average
2003	$90,000	$108,000
2004	156,000	142,000
2005	166,000	150,000

In its 2006 financial statements, Loire included comparative statements for both 2005 and 2004.

11. What adjustment, before taxes, should Loire make retrospectively to the balance reported for retained earnings at the beginning of 2004?

A. $18,000 increase.
B. $18,000 decrease.
C. $4,000 increase.
D. $0.

Answer (A) is correct. *(CPA, adapted)*

REQUIRED: The pretax retrospective adjustment to retained earnings as of the beginning of the first period reported.

DISCUSSION: Retrospective application requires that the carrying amounts of assets, liabilities, and retained earnings as of the beginning of the first period reported be adjusted for the cumulative effect of the new accounting principle on periods prior to the first period reported. Moreover, all periods reported must be individually adjusted for the period-specific effects of applying the new principle. The pretax cumulative-effect adjustment to retained earnings reported at the beginning of 2004 is equal to the $18,000 increase ($108,000 – $90,000) in inventory. If the weighted-average method had been applied in the first year of operations (2003), cost of goods sold would have been $18,000 lower. Pretax net income and ending retained earnings for 2003 and beginning retained earnings for 2004 would have been $18,000 greater.

Answer (B) is incorrect because beginning retained earnings as of the beginning of the first period reported (2004) is increased. Ending inventory would have been higher and cost of goods sold lower for 2003. Answer (C) is incorrect because $4,000 is equal to the difference at December 31, 2003 minus the difference at December 31, 2004. Answer (D) is incorrect because a cumulative-effect adjustment should be recorded.

12. What amount should Loire report as inventory in its financial statements for the year ended December 31, 2004 presented for comparative purposes?

A. $90,000
B. $108,000
C. $142,000
D. $156,000

Answer (C) is correct. *(Publisher)*

REQUIRED: The amount to be reported as inventory at December 31, 2004.

DISCUSSION: Retrospective application results in changing previously issued financial statements to reflect the direct effects of the newly adopted accounting principle as if it had always been used. Retrospective application requires that the carrying amounts of assets, liabilities, and retained earnings as of the beginning of the first period reported be adjusted for the cumulative effect of the new principle on periods prior to the first period reported. Moreover, all periods reported must be individually adjusted for the period-specific effects of applying the new principle. Thus, the December 31, 2004 inventory following the retrospective adjustment should be reported as the weighted-average amount of $142,000.

Answer (A) is incorrect because $90,000 is the FIFO amount at December 31, 2003. Answer (B) is incorrect because $108,000 is the weighted-average amount at December 31, 2003. Answer (D) is incorrect because $156,000 is the FIFO amount at December 31, 2004.

13. By what amount should cost of sales be retrospectively adjusted for the year ended December 31, 2005?

A. $0
B. $2,000 increase.
C. $14,000 increase.
D. $16,000 increase.

Answer (B) is correct. *(Publisher)*

REQUIRED: The retrospective adjustment to cost of sales for the year ended December 31, 2005.

DISCUSSION: Retrospective application changes previously issued financial statements to reflect the direct effects of the newly adopted principle as if it had always been used. Retrospective application requires that all periods reported be individually adjusted for the period-specific effects of applying the new principle. Cost of sales equals beginning inventory, plus purchases, minus ending inventory. Purchases are the same under FIFO and weighted average. Thus, the retrospective adjustment to cost of sales is equal to the change in beginning inventory resulting from the change from FIFO to weighted average minus the change in ending inventory. This adjustment equals an increase in cost of sales of $2,000 [($156,000 – $142,000) – ($166,000 – $150,000)].

Answer (A) is incorrect because period-specific adjustments are required. Answer (C) is incorrect because $14,000 is the difference between FIFO and weighted-average inventory amounts at December 31, 2004. Answer (D) is incorrect because $16,000 is the difference between FIFO and weighted-average inventory amounts at December 31, 2005.

14. On January 1, 2004, Colorado Corp. purchased a machine having an estimated useful life of 8 years and no salvage value. The machine was depreciated by the double-declining-balance (DDB) method for both financial statement and income tax reporting. On January 1, 2006, Colorado changed with justification to the straight-line method for both financial statement and income tax reporting. Accumulated depreciation at December 31, 2005 was $525,000. If the straight-line method had been used, the accumulated depreciation at December 31, 2005 would have been $300,000. The amount to be reported as a retroactive adjustment to the accumulated depreciation account as of January 1, 2006 as a result of the change in depreciation method is

A. $0

B. $225,000

C. $300,000

D. $525,000

Answer (A) is correct. *(CPA, adapted)*

REQUIRED: The retroactive adjustment to accumulated depreciation at the beginning of the year in which a change in depreciation method was made.

DISCUSSION: A change in accounting estimate inseparable from (effected by) a change in accounting principle includes a change in depreciation, amortization, or depletion method. When a change in accounting estimate and a change in accounting principle are inseparable, the transaction should be accounted for as a change in accounting estimate. The effects of a change in accounting estimate should be accounted for prospectively. Thus, the effects should be recognized in the period of change and any future periods affected by the change. The effects should not be recognized in prior periods. Consequently, the accumulated depreciation at January 1, 2006 should carry forth the $525,000 balance determined in accordance with the DDB method as of December 31, 2005.

Answer (B) is incorrect because $225,000 is equal to the difference between the DDB and straight-line methods. Answer (C) is incorrect because $300,000 is the balance determined under the straight-line method. Answer (D) is incorrect because $525,000 is the balance under the DDB method.

15. Volga Co. included a foreign subsidiary in its 2006 consolidated financial statements. The subsidiary was acquired in 2004 and was excluded from previous consolidations. The change was caused by the elimination of foreign currency controls. Including the subsidiary in the 2006 consolidated financial statements results in an accounting change that should be reported

A. By note disclosure only.

B. Currently and prospectively.

C. Currently with note disclosure of pro forma effects of retroactive application.

D. By restating the financial statements of all prior periods presented.

Answer (D) is correct. *(CPA, adapted)*

REQUIRED: The reporting of the change in the subsidiaries included in consolidated financial statements.

DISCUSSION: A change in the reporting entity requires retrospective application to all prior periods presented to report information for the new entity. The following are changes in the reporting entity: (1) presenting consolidated or combined statements in place of statements of individual entities, (2) changing the specific subsidiaries included in the group for which consolidated statements are presented, and (3) changing the entities included in combined statements.

18.3 Changes in Accounting Estimates

16. How should the effect of a change in accounting estimate be accounted for?

A. By retrospectively applying the change to amounts reported in financial statements of prior periods.

B. By reporting pro forma amounts for prior periods.

C. As a prior-period adjustment to beginning retained earnings.

D. By retroactively applying the change to all prior periods presented.

Answer (D) is correct. *(CPA, adapted)*

REQUIRED: The accounting for the effect of a change in accounting estimate.

DISCUSSION: The effect of a change in accounting estimate is accounted for in the period of change, if the change affects that period only, or in the period of change and future periods, if the change affects both. For a change in accounting estimate, the entity may not (1) restate or retrospectively adjust prior-period statements or (2) report pro forma amounts for prior periods.

Answer (A) is incorrect because retroactive application is required for a change in reporting entity. Answer (B) is incorrect because retroactive application is required for a change in reporting entity. Answer (C) is incorrect because retroactive application is required for a change in reporting entity. Disclosure of pro forma amounts is also not permitted.

17. For 2002, Suwanee Co. estimated its 2-year equipment warranty costs based on $100 per unit sold in 2002. Experience during 2003 indicated that the estimate should have been based on $110 per unit. The effect of this $10 difference from the estimate is reported

A. In 2003 income from continuing operations.

B. As an accounting change, net of tax, below 2003 income from continuing operations.

C. As an accounting change requiring 2002 financial statements to be retrospectively adjusted.

D. As a correction of an error requiring 2002 financial statements to be restated.

Answer (A) is correct. *(CPA, adapted)*

REQUIRED: The proper accounting for a change in estimate.

DISCUSSION: The effect of a change in accounting estimate is accounted for in the period of change, if the change affects that period only, or in the period of change and future periods, if the change affects both. For a change in accounting estimate, the entity may not (1) restate or retrospectively adjust prior-period statements or (2) report pro forma amounts for prior periods. A change in warranty costs is a change in estimate because it "is a consequence of the assessment, in conjunction with the periodic presentation of financial statements, of the present status and expected future benefits and obligations associated with assets and liabilities" (SFAS 154). Thus, it affects income from continuing operations.

Answer (B) is incorrect because a change in accounting estimate is included in the determination of income from continuing operations. Answer (C) is incorrect because a change in estimate is not reported retrospectively. Answer (D) is incorrect because a change in estimate is not a correction of an error.

18. On July 1, 2000, Allegheny Corp. purchased computer equipment at a cost of $360,000. This equipment was estimated to have a 6-year life with no residual value and was depreciated by the straight-line method. On January 3, 2003, Allegheny determined that this equipment could no longer process data efficiently, its value had been permanently impaired, and $70,000 could be recovered over the remaining useful life of the equipment. What carrying amount should Allegheny report on its December 31, 2003 balance sheet for this equipment?

A. $0

B. $50,000

C. $70,000

D. $150,000

Answer (B) is correct. *(CPA, adapted)*

REQUIRED: The carrying amount following a change in estimate.

DISCUSSION: At 1/3/03, the carrying amount of the computer equipment should be written down to $70,000. This $70,000 is expected to be recovered over the 3.5-year remaining useful life of the equipment. Under the straight-line method, the depreciation expense for the year ending 12/31/03 is $20,000 [($70,000 ÷ 42 months) × 12 months]. Thus, the carrying amount in the year-end balance sheet should be $50,000 ($70,000 – $20,000).

Answer (A) is incorrect because the computer should have a carrying amount of $50,000. Answer (C) is incorrect because $20,000 of depreciation must be taken on the asset for 2003. Answer (D) is incorrect because $150,000 reflects continued depreciation based on the original assumptions.

19. Missouri Company bought a machine on January 1, 2001 for $24,000, at which time it had an estimated useful life of 8 years, with no residual value. Straight-line depreciation is used for all of Missouri's depreciable assets. On January 1, 2003, the machine's estimated useful life was determined to be only 6 years from the acquisition date. Accordingly, the appropriate accounting change was made in 2003. The direct effects of this change were limited to the effect on depreciation and the related provision for income tax. Missouri's income tax rate was 40% in all the affected years. In Missouri's 2003 financial statements, how much should be reported as the cumulative effect on prior years because of the change in the estimated useful life of the machine?

A. $0

B. $1,200

C. $2,000

D. $2,800

Answer (A) is correct. *(CPA, adapted)*

REQUIRED: The proper accounting for a change in estimate.

DISCUSSION: An adjustment arising from a revision in an asset's estimated useful life is a change in accounting estimate that should be accounted for on a prospective basis. The remaining depreciable base should be allocated over the revised remaining life with no adjustment to the depreciation accumulated at the time of the change. Because no retrospective adjustment is made, the cumulative effect on prior years is $0. The remaining depreciable base of $18,000 ($24,000 cost – $6,000 accumulated depreciation based on a 6-year life) is allocated over the remaining expected life at $4,500 per year ($18,000 ÷ 4). A prior year's adjustment should not be made for a change in accounting estimate of the useful life of an asset.

Answer (B) is incorrect because a prior year's adjustment should not be made. Answer (C) is incorrect because a prior year's adjustment should not be made. Answer (D) is incorrect because a prior year's adjustment should not be made.

20. Tone Company is the defendant in a lawsuit filed by Witt in 2002 disputing the validity of a copyright held by Tone. At December 31, 2002, Tone determined that Witt would probably be successful against Tone for an estimated amount of $400,000. Appropriately, a $400,000 loss was accrued by a charge to income for the year ended December 31, 2002. On December 15, 2003, Tone and Witt agreed to a settlement providing for a cash payment of $250,000 by Tone to Witt and the transfer of Tone's copyright to Witt. The carrying amount of the copyright on Tone's accounting records was $60,000 at December 15, 2003. The settlement's effect on Tone's income before income tax in 2003 is

A. No effect.

B. $60,000 decrease.

C. $90,000 increase.

D. $150,000 increase.

Answer (C) is correct. *(CPA, adapted)*

REQUIRED: The accounting for the effect of a settlement at an amount different from that previously accrued.

DISCUSSION: In 2002, a $400,000 contingent loss and an accrued liability in the amount of $400,000 were properly recognized in accordance with SFAS 5. In 2003, the actual loss of $310,000 ($250,000 cash + $60,000 carrying amount of the copyright) was $90,000 less than the previously estimated amount. This new information should be treated as a change in estimate and accounted for in the period of change. Consequently, the $90,000 difference will be credited to 2003 income as a recovery of a previously recognized loss.

Answer (A) is incorrect because Tone's income before income tax will increase by $90,000. Answer (B) is incorrect because $60,000 is the carrying amount of the copyright. Answer (D) is incorrect because a $150,000 increase does not include the carrying amount of the copyright.

21. The effect of a change in accounting principle that is inseparable from the effect of a change in accounting estimate should be reported

A. By restating the financial statements of all prior periods presented.

B. As a correction of an error.

C. In the period of change and future periods if the change affects both.

D. As a separate disclosure after income from continuing operations, in the period of change and future periods if the change affects both.

Answer (C) is correct. *(CPA, adapted)*

REQUIRED: The reporting of the effect of a change in accounting principle.

DISCUSSION: When the effect of a change in principle is inseparable from the effect of a change in estimate, it should be accounted for in the same manner as a change in estimate only. An example of such a change is a change in the method of depreciation. Because the new method is adopted to recognize (1) a change in estimated future benefits, (2) their pattern of consumption, or (3) the information available to the entity about them, the effect of the change in principle is inseparable from the change in estimate. The effect of a change in estimate is accounted for in the period of change if the change affects that period only, or in the period of change and in future periods, if the change affects both.

Answer (A) is incorrect because prospective treatment is accorded to a change in principle inseparable from a change in estimate. Answer (B) is incorrect because a correction of an error is accounted for as a prior-period adjustment. Answer (D) is incorrect because the effect of the change in estimate is included in the determination of income from continuing operations. Moreover, disclosures about a change in estimate are made in the notes.

22. On January 1, 2004, Vicar Company purchased a machine for $240,000 with a useful life of 10 years and no salvage value. The machine was depreciated using the double-declining-balance (DDB) method, and the carrying amount of the machine was $153,600 on December 31, 2005. Vicar changed to the straight-line method on January 1, 2006. Vicar can justify the change. What should be the depreciation expense on this machine for the year ended December 31, 2006?

A. $15,360

B. $19,200

C. $24,000

D. $30,720

Answer (B) is correct. *(CPA, adapted)*

REQUIRED: The depreciation expense in the year in which a change in depreciation method is made.

DISCUSSION: A change in accounting estimate inseparable from (effected by) a change in accounting principle includes a change in depreciation, amortization, or depletion method. When a change in estimate and a change in principle are inseparable, the change should be accounted for as a change in estimate. The effects of a change in estimate should be accounted for prospectively. Thus, the effects should be recognized in the period of change and any future periods affected by the change. The effects should not be recognized in prior periods. Consequently, depreciation expense for the year ended December 31, 2006 should be $19,200 ($153,600 carrying amount at December 31, 2005 ÷ 8-year remaining useful life).

Answer (A) is incorrect because $15,360 is equal to the carrying amount at December 31, 2005 allocated using the straight-line method and assuming a 10-year remaining useful life. Answer (C) is incorrect because $24,000 is equal to the cost of the machine allocated using the straight-line method and assuming a 10-year remaining useful life. Answer (D) is incorrect because $30,720 is the result of continuing to depreciate the machine under the DDB method.

23. On January 2, 2000, Monongahela Co. purchased a machine for $264,000 and depreciated it by the straight-line method using an estimated useful life of 8 years with no salvage value. On January 2, 2003, the company determined that the machine had a useful life of 6 years from the date of acquisition and will have a salvage value of $24,000. An accounting change was made in 2003 to reflect the additional data. The accumulated depreciation for this machine should have a balance at December 31, 2003 of

A. $179,000

B. $160,000

C. $154,000

D. $146,000

Answer (D) is correct. *(CPA, adapted)*

REQUIRED: The accumulated depreciation for a machine given changes in estimates.

DISCUSSION: A change in estimated life is accounted for on a prospective basis. The new estimate affects the year of the change and subsequent years. For 2000 through 2002, the amount of depreciation was $33,000 per year ($264,000 ÷ 8). In 2003, the new estimates change annual depreciation to $47,000 [($264,000 – $99,000 accumulated depreciation – $24,000 expected salvage) ÷ 3 years remaining]. Thus, accumulated depreciation for 2003 is $146,000 ($99,000 + $47,000).

Answer (A) is incorrect because $179,000 does not include accumulated depreciation in calculating depreciation for 2003. Answer (B) is incorrect because $160,000 would be the accumulated depreciation if the revised estimates had been used from the date of acquisition. Answer (C) is incorrect because $154,000 does not include salvage value in calculating depreciation for 2003.

24. On January 1, 2004, Dickey Co. purchased a machine for $450,000 with an estimated life of 5 years with no salvage value. Dickey depreciated this machine under the sum-of-the-years-digits method (SYD) for 2 years. At January 1, 2006, when the carrying amount of the machine was $180,000 ($450,000 – $150,000 depreciation for 2004 – $120,000 depreciation for 2005), Dickey changed to the straight-line method. Dickey can justify the change. Dickey also determined that the remaining useful life of the machine had increased from 3 to 4 years. What is the amount of depreciation that Dickey should record in its income statement for the year ending December 31, 2006?

A. $90,000

B. $75,000

C. $60,000

D. $45,000

Answer (D) is correct. *(CPA, adapted)*

REQUIRED: The depreciation expense in the year in which a change in depreciation method is made.

DISCUSSION: A change in accounting estimate inseparable from (effected by) a change in accounting principle includes a change in depreciation, amortization, or depletion method. When a change in estimate and a change in principle are inseparable, the change should be accounted for as a change in estimate. The effects of a change in estimate should be accounted for prospectively. Thus, the effects should be recognized in the period of change and any future periods affected by the change. The effects should not be recognized in prior periods. Consequently, depreciation expense for the year ended December 31, 2006 should be $45,000 ($180,000 carrying amount at December 31, 2005 ÷ 4-year remaining useful life).

Answer (A) is incorrect because $90,000 is based on the $450,000 original cost allocated to the 5-year useful life under the straight-line method. Answer (B) is incorrect because $75,000 is equal to the original cost of the machine allocated under the straight-line method over its revised 6-year useful life. Answer (C) is incorrect because $60,000 is equal to the December 31, 2005 carrying amount allocated under the straight-line method over 3 years.

25. In early January 2006, Off-Line Co. changed its method of accounting for demo costs from writing off the costs over 2 years to expensing the costs immediately. Off-Line made the change in recognition that an increasing number of demos placed with potential customers did not result in sales. Off-Line had deferred demo costs of $500,000 at December 31, 2005, of which $300,000 were to be written off in 2006 and the remainder in 2007. Off-Line's income tax rate is 30%. In its 2006 statement of retained earnings, what amount should Off-Line report as a retrospective adjustment of its January 1, 2006 retained earnings?

A. $0

B. $210,000

C. $300,000

D. $500,000

Answer (A) is correct. *(CPA, adapted)*

REQUIRED: The retrospective adjustment of retained earnings at the beginning of the year in which an entity changed from capitalizing a cost to expensing it as incurred.

DISCUSSION: In general, the retrospective application method is used to account for a change in accounting principle. However, a change in accounting estimate inseparable from (effected by) a change in accounting principle should be accounted for as a change in accounting estimate. A change in estimate results from new information, such as the decreasing sales resulting from the demo placements. The effects of a change in estimate should be accounted for prospectively. Thus, the effects should be recognized in the period of change and any future periods affected by the change. Accordingly, the write-off of the $500,000 in deferred demo costs should be reported in the 2006 income statement. Retained earnings at the beginning of the year should not be retrospectively adjusted.

Answer (B) is incorrect because $210,000 is the after-tax effect of expensing $300,000 of the deferred costs in 2006. Answer (C) is incorrect because $300,000 is the amount that had been scheduled to be expensed in 2006. Answer (D) is incorrect because $500,000 is the pretax write-off to be recorded in the 2006 income statement.

18.4 Corrections of Accounting Errors

26. The correction of an error in the financial statements of a prior period should be reported, net of applicable income taxes, in the current

A. Retained earnings statement after net income but before dividends.

B. Retained earnings statement as an adjustment of the opening balance.

C. Income statement after income from continuing operations and before extraordinary items.

D. Income statement after income from continuing operations and after extraordinary items.

Answer (B) is correct. *(CPA, adapted)*

REQUIRED: The proper recording of a prior-period adjustment (correction of an error).

DISCUSSION: APB 9, *Reporting the Results of Operations*, as amended by SFAS 16, *Prior Period Adjustments*, requires that prior-period adjustments of single period statements be reported net of applicable income taxes as changes in the opening balance in the statement of retained earnings of the current period. In comparative financial statements, all prior periods affected by the prior-period adjustment should be restated to reflect the adjustment.

Answer (A) is incorrect because the correction of the error should be reported as an adjustment to beginning retained earnings. Answer (C) is incorrect because a prior-period adjustment is reported in the current retained earnings statement. Answer (D) is incorrect because a prior-period adjustment is reported in the current retained earnings statement.

27. Which of the following errors results in an overstatement of both current assets and equity?

A. Accrued sales expenses are understated.

B. Noncurrent note receivable principal is misclassified as a current asset.

C. Annual depreciation on manufacturing machinery is understated.

D. Holiday pay expense for administrative employees is misclassified as manufacturing overhead.

Answer (D) is correct. *(CIA, adapted)*

REQUIRED: The error that results in an overstatement of both current assets and equity.

DISCUSSION: The classification of holiday pay expense as manufacturing overhead overstates both current assets and equity. Holiday pay expense for administrative employees should be expensed as incurred. By classifying the expense as manufacturing overhead, inventory (a current asset) is overstated. If this inventory is not sold in the period, ending inventory will be overstated and expenses for the period will be understated. The effect is to overstate current assets, net income, retained earnings, and equity.

Answer (A) is incorrect because an understatement of accrued sales understates equity but affects current liabilities, not current assets. Answer (B) is incorrect because a misclassification of a noncurrent note receivable as a current asset does not affect equity. Answer (C) is incorrect because an understatement of depreciation on equipment does not affect current assets.

28. At the end of 2002, Dnieper Co. failed to accrue sales commissions earned during 2002 but paid in 2003. The error was not repeated in 2003. What was the effect of this error on 2002 ending working capital and on the 2003 ending retained earnings balance?

	2002 Ending Working Capital	2003 Ending Retained Earnings
A.	Overstated	Overstated
B.	No effect	Overstated
C.	No effect	No effect
D.	Overstated	No effect

Answer (D) is correct. *(CPA, adapted)*

REQUIRED: The effect of failure to accrue sales commissions.

DISCUSSION: The 2002 ending working capital (current assets – current liabilities) is overstated because the error understates current liabilities. The 2003 ending retained earnings balance is unaffected because it is a cumulative amount. Whether the sales commission expense is recognized in 2002 when it should have been accrued or in 2003 when it was paid affects the net income amounts for 2002 and 2003 but not 2003 ending retained earnings.

Answer (A) is incorrect because 2003 ending retained earnings is unaffected. Answer (B) is incorrect because 2002 ending working capital is overstated, and 2003 ending retained earnings is unaffected. Answer (C) is incorrect because 2002 ending working capital is overstated.

29. The 2002 financial statements of Essen Company reported net income for the year ended December 31, 2002 of $2 million. On July 1, 2003, subsequent to the issuance of the 2002 financial statements, Essen changed from an accounting principle that is not generally accepted to one that is generally accepted. If the generally accepted accounting principle had been used in 2002, net income for the year ended December 31, 2002 would have been decreased by $1 million. On August 1, 2003, Essen discovered a mathematical error relating to its 2002 financial statements. If this error had been discovered in 2002, net income for the year ended December 31, 2002 would have been increased by $500,000. What amount, if any, should be included in net income for the year ended December 31, 2003 because of the items noted above?

A. $0

B. $500,000 decrease.

C. $500,000 increase.

D. $1,000,000 decrease.

Answer (A) is correct. *(CPA, adapted)*

REQUIRED: The amount that should be included in net income because of an accounting change and an accounting error.

DISCUSSION: A change from an accounting principle that is not generally accepted to one that is generally accepted should be accounted for as the correction of an error. SFAS 16 requires that corrections of errors in financial statements of prior periods be accounted for as prior-period adjustments and thus excluded from the determination of net income for the current period. Accordingly, the mathematical error and the change in accounting method have no effect on 2003 net income.

Answer (B) is incorrect because the $500,000 decrease is the net amount by which 2002 income should be restated. Answer (C) is incorrect because it is part of the net amount by which 2002 income should be restated. Answer (D) is incorrect because it is part of the net amount by which 2002 income should be restated.

30. Eiger Co. reported a retained earnings balance of $400,000 at December 31, 2002. In August 2003, Eiger determined that insurance premiums of $60,000 for the 3-year period beginning January 1, 2002 had been paid and fully expensed in 2002. Eiger has a 30% income tax rate. What amount should Eiger report as adjusted beginning retained earnings in its 2003 statement of retained earnings?

A. $420,000

B. $428,000

C. $440,000

D. $442,000

Answer (B) is correct. *(CPA, adapted)*

REQUIRED: The adjusted beginning retained earnings after correction of an error.

DISCUSSION: APB 9, as amended by SFAS 16, requires that prior-period adjustments be reflected net of applicable income taxes as changes in the opening balance in the statement of retained earnings. The $60,000 insurance prepayment in 2002 should have been expensed ratably over the 3-year period. Consequently, 2002 net income was understated by $40,000, net of tax effect, and $40,000 [$60,000 – ($60,000 ÷ 3)] should have been reported as a prepaid expense (an asset) at the beginning of 2003. The prior-period adjustment to the beginning balance of retained earnings is therefore a credit of $28,000 [$40,000 × (1.0 – .3 tax rate)]. The adjusted balance is $428,000 ($400,000 + $28,000).

Answer (A) is incorrect because $420,000 is the sum of the beginning balance of retained earnings and the expense that should have been recognized in 2002. Answer (C) is incorrect because $440,000 does not consider the tax effect. Answer (D) is incorrect because $442,000 assumes that no insurance expense should have been recognized in 2002.

Questions 31 and 32 are based on the following information. On October 1, 2003, Eure Retailers signed a 4-month, 16% note payable to finance the purchase of holiday merchandise. At that date, there was no direct method of pricing the merchandise, and the note's market rate of interest was 11%. Eure recorded the purchase at the note's face amount. All of the merchandise was sold by December 1, 2003. Eure's 2003 financial statements reported interest payable and interest expense on the note for 3 months at 16%. All amounts due on the note were paid February 1, 2004.

31. Eure's 2003 cost of goods sold for the holiday merchandise was

A. Overstated by the difference between the note's face amount and the note's October 1, 2003 present value.

B. Overstated by the difference between the note's face amount and the note's October 1, 2003 present value plus 11% interest for 2 months.

C. Understated by the difference between the note's face amount and the note's October 1, 2003 present value.

D. Understated by the difference between the note's face amount and the note's October 1, 2003 present value plus 16% interest for 2 months.

Answer (C) is correct. *(CPA, adapted)*

REQUIRED: The cost of goods sold.

DISCUSSION: The general presumption when a note is exchanged for property, goods, or services in an arm's-length transaction is that the rate of interest is fair and adequate. If the rate is not stated or the stated rate is unreasonable, the note and the property, goods, or services should be recorded at the fair value of the property, goods, or services or the market value of the note, whichever is more clearly determinable. In the absence of these values, the present value of the note should be used as the basis for recording both the note and the property, goods, or services. This present value is obtained by discounting all future payments on the note using the market rate of interest, in accordance with APB 21, *Interest on Receivables and Payables.* Because the imputed rate (11%) is less than the nominal rate (16%), the note (and the purchase) should be recorded at a premium. The face amount is the present value at the nominal rate. The face amount plus a premium is the present value at the (lower) market rate. Thus, recording the note and purchase at the face amount of the note understates the cost of the inventory sold.

Answer (A) is incorrect because the cost of goods sold was understated. Answer (B) is incorrect because the cost of goods sold was understated. Answer (D) is incorrect because the understatement was equal to the note's present value at 11% on the date of purchase minus the face amount (present value at the 16% nominal rate).

32. As a result of Eure's accounting treatment of the note, interest, and merchandise, which of the following item(s) was (were) reported correctly?

	12/31/03 Retained Earnings	12/31/03 Interest Payable
A.	Yes	Yes
B.	No	No
C.	Yes	No
D.	No	Yes

Answer (D) is correct. *(CPA, adapted)*

REQUIRED: The item correctly reported as a result of incorrectly recording a note payable.

DISCUSSION: If the note's rate is not stated, or the stated rate is unreasonable, the note and any related property, goods, or services should be recorded at the fair value of the property, goods, services, or the market value of the note, whichever is more clearly determinable. Because the note was recorded at its face amount, cost of goods sold was understated by the difference between the note's face amount and its present value. Interest expense should be calculated based on the present value of the note at the market rate of interest. Interest payable is the stated rate times the face amount, and amortization of premium or discount is the difference between the payable and interest expense. In this situation, interest expense and interest payable are both recorded at the stated rate multiplied by the face amount. Thus, retained earnings is misstated as a result of the error in calculating cost of goods sold and interest expense. Interest payable is correctly reported.

Answer (A) is incorrect because retained earnings is misstated. Answer (B) is incorrect because interest payable is correctly stated. Answer (C) is incorrect because retained earnings is misstated and interest payable is correctly stated.

33. On December 30, 2003, Exmoor Corp. sold merchandise for $75,000 to Frinia Co. The terms of the sale were net 30, FOB shipping point. The merchandise was shipped on December 31, 2003 and arrived at Frinia on January 5, 2004. Because of a clerical error, the sale was not recorded until January 2004, and the merchandise, sold at a 25% markup, was included in Exmoor's inventory at December 31, 2003. As a result, Exmoor's cost of goods sold for the year ended December 31, 2003 was

A. Understated by $75,000.

B. Understated by $60,000.

C. Understated by $15,000.

D. Correctly stated.

Answer (B) is correct. *(CPA, adapted)*

REQUIRED: The cost of goods sold given delayed recording of a sale.

DISCUSSION: Under the shipping terms, the sale should have been recognized on December 31, 2003 because title and risk of loss passed to the buyer on that date; that is, an earning process was complete. Exmoor should have debited a receivable and credited sales for $75,000, the net amount, on the date of shipment. Exmoor should also have debited cost of sales and credited inventory at cost on the same date. The error therefore understated cost of goods sold by $60,000 ($75,000 sales price ÷ 125% of cost).

Answer (A) is incorrect because $75,000 is the selling price. Answer (C) is incorrect because $15,000 is the amount of the markup. Answer (D) is incorrect because cost of goods was understated by $60,000.

34. For the past 3 years, Gainesville Co. has failed to accrue unpaid wages earned by workers during the last week of the year. The amounts omitted, which are considered material, were as follows:

December 31, 2001	$56,000
December 31, 2002	51,000
December 31, 2003	64,000

The entry on December 31, 2003 to correct for these omissions would include a

A. Credit to wage expense for $64,000.

B. Debit to wage expense for $51,000.

C. Debit to wage expense for $13,000.

D. Credit to retained earnings for $64,000.

Answer (C) is correct. *(CMA, adapted)*

REQUIRED: The entry to correct for failure to accrue wages.

DISCUSSION: Failing to record accrued wages is a self-correcting error. Expenses are understated in one year and overstated in the next, resulting in the correction of the error over the 2-year period. The 2001 error overstated 2001 earnings and understated 2002 earnings by $56,000. Consequently, no correction is necessary for the 2001 error. The 2002 error overstated 2002 earnings and understated 2003 earnings by $51,000. The 2003 error overstated 2003 earnings by $64,000. Thus, the net effect in 2003 of the 2002 and 2003 errors is a $13,000 ($64,000 – $51,000) overstatement. The correcting entry is to debit expense for $13,000, debit retained earnings for $51,000, and credit wages payable for $64,000.

Answer (A) is incorrect because $64,000 is the accrued wages payable, not the amount of the adjustment. Answer (B) is incorrect because $51,000 is the correct wage accrual for 2002. Answer (D) is incorrect because retained earnings should be debited for $51,000.

35. An audit of Fundy Co. for 2003, its first year of operations, detected the following errors made at December 31, 2003:

- Failed to accrue $50,000 interest expense
- Failed to record depreciation expense on office equipment of $80,000
- Failed to amortize prepaid rent expense of $100,000
- Failed to delay recognition of prepaid advertising expense of $60,000

The net effect of these errors was to overstate net income for 2003 by

A. $130,000

B. $170,000

C. $230,000

D. $290,000

Answer (B) is correct. *(CIA, adapted)*

REQUIRED: The effect of certain errors on net income.

DISCUSSION: The failure to accrue interest expense, record depreciation expense on office equipment, and amortize prepaid rent expense overstates net income. Expensing the full amount of prepaid advertising instead of deferring recognition understates net income. Thus, net income would be overstated by $170,000 ($50,000 + $80,000 + $100,000 – $60,000).

Answer (A) is incorrect because $130,000 includes only the interest expense and depreciation expense. Answer (C) is incorrect because $230,000 results from not subtracting the prepaid advertising expense. Answer (D) is incorrect because $290,000 results from adding prepaid advertising expense.

36. While preparing its 2003 financial statements, Fulda Corp. discovered computational errors in its 2002 and 2001 depreciation expense. These errors resulted in overstatement of each year's income by $25,000, net of income taxes. The following amounts were reported in the previously issued financial statements:

	2002	2001
Retained earnings, 1/1	$700,000	$500,000
Net income	150,000	200,000
Retained earnings, 12/31	$850,000	$700,000

Fulda's 2003 net income is correctly reported at $180,000. Which of the following amounts should be reported as prior-period adjustments and net income in Fulda's 2003 and 2002 comparative financial statements?

	Year	Prior-Period Adjustment	Net Income
A.	2002	--	$150,000
	2003	$(50,000)	180,000
B.	2002	$(50,000)	$150,000
	2003	--	180,000
C.	2002	$(25,000)	$125,000
	2003	--	180,000
D.	2002	--	$125,000
	2003	--	180,000

Answer (C) is correct. *(CPA, adapted)*

REQUIRED: The amounts that should be reported as prior-period adjustments and net income in comparative financial statements.

DISCUSSION: In the comparative financial statements presented for 2002 and 2003, the 2002 statements should be restated to reflect the adjustment. The beginning balance of retained earnings for 2002 should be adjusted to correct the $25,000 overstatement of after-tax income for 2001, a year for which financial statements are not presented. The statements for 2002 should be restated to reflect the correction of the error in 2002 net income. This amount will be correctly reported in the 2003 and 2002 financial statements as $125,000 ($150,000 in the previously issued 2002 statements – $25,000 overstatement). No adjustments to the 2003 financial statements are necessary.

Answer (A) is incorrect because restated 2002 net income is $125,000, and the prior-period adjustment is made to the beginning balance of retained earnings for 2002. Answer (B) is incorrect because restated 2002 net income is $125,000, and the adjustment to 2002 retained earnings is for $25,000 (the overstatement of 2001 net income). Answer (D) is incorrect because a $25,000 prior-period adjustment must be made in the 2002 statements.

37. The following information appeared on Wight, Inc.'s December 31 financial statements:

	2002	2003
Assets	$1,000,000	$1,200,000
Liabilities	750,000	800,000
Contributed capital	120,000	120,000
Dividends paid	100,000	60,000

In preparing its 2003 financial statements, Wight discovered that it had misplaced a decimal in calculating depreciation for 2002. This error overstated 2002 depreciation by $10,000. In addition, changing technology had significantly shortened the useful life of Wight's computers. Based on this information, Wight determined that depreciation should be $30,000 higher in 2003 than was currently reflected in the 2003 financial statements. Assuming that no correcting or adjusting entries have been made and ignoring income taxes, how much should Wight report as 2003 net income?

A. $140,000

B. $170,000

C. $210,000

D. $230,000

Answer (B) is correct. *(C. Hall)*

REQUIRED: The net income following a correction of an error and a change in estimate.

DISCUSSION: Retained earnings are equal to assets minus liabilities minus contributed capital. Thus, 2002 retained earnings equal $130,000 ($1,000,000 – $750,000 – $120,000). Retained earnings for 2003 equal $280,000 ($1,200,000 – $800,000 – $120,000). The error in 2002 depreciation overstated expense and therefore understated 2002 net income and 2002 retained earnings. To correct for this error, a prior-period adjustment to 2002 ending retained earnings (2003 beginning retained earnings) should be made. Corrected 2002 ending retained earnings equal $140,000 ($130,000 previously reported + $10,000 adjustment). Unadjusted 2003 net income is equal to the $140,000 increase in retained earnings ($280,000 – $140,000) plus the $60,000 dividends paid. Hence, unadjusted 2003 net income equals $200,000. The $30,000 increase in depreciation attributable to the change in the asset life is a change in estimate that should be reflected in 2003 net income. Consequently, the adjusted 2003 net income is $170,000 ($200,000 – $30,000).

Answer (A) is incorrect because the increase in retained earnings must be adjusted for dividends paid and the additional depreciation to arrive at net income. Answer (C) is incorrect because the prior-period error in calculating depreciation does not affect current-period net income, and the current-period additional depreciation must be subtracted to arrive at net income. Answer (D) is incorrect because the additional depreciation for the current period must be subtracted from, not added to, retained earnings.

Questions 38 and 39 are based on the following information.
An audit of Brasilia Company has revealed the following four errors that have occurred but have not been corrected:

1. Inventory at December 31, 2002 - $40,000, Understated
2. Inventory at December 31, 2003 - $15,000, Overstated
3. Depreciation for 2002 - $7,000, Understated
4. Accrued expenses at December 31, 2003 - $10,000, Understated

38. The errors cause the reported net income for the year ending December 31, 2003 to be

A. Overstated by $72,000.

B. Overstated by $65,000.

C. Understated by $28,000.

D. Understated by $45,000.

Answer (B) is correct. *(CIA, adapted)*

REQUIRED: The effect of certain errors on net income.

DISCUSSION: Both the understatement of beginning inventory and the overstatement of ending inventory will understate cost of goods sold. The result understates cost of goods sold and overstates net income by $55,000 ($40,000 + $15,000). The understatement of 2002's depreciation has no effect on 2003's net income but results in an overstatement of 2002 and 2003 retained earnings of $7,000. The understatement of accrued expenses overstates net income by $10,000. Thus, net income is overstated by $65,000 ($40,000 + $15,000 + $10,000).

Answer (A) is incorrect because $72,000 results from including the $7,000 depreciation. Answer (C) is incorrect because a $28,000 understatement results from taking the difference between inventory errors ($40,000 – $15,000) and adding accrued expenses and subtracting depreciation expense. Answer (D) is incorrect because a $45,000 understatement results from adding beginning inventory and ending inventory and subtracting accrued expenses.

39. The errors cause the reported retained earnings at December 31, 2003 to be

A. Overstated by $65,000.

B. Overstated by $32,000.

C. Overstated by $25,000.

D. Understated by $18,000.

Answer (B) is correct. *(CIA, adapted)*

REQUIRED: The effect of errors on retained earnings.

DISCUSSION: The error in 12/31/02 inventory understates income in 2002 (cost of goods sold is overstated by $40,000) and overstates income in 2003 (cost of goods sold is understated by $40,000). The error in 12/31/03 inventory understates cost of goods sold, which overstates net income in 2003 by $15,000. The understatement of depreciation of $7,000 overstates 2002 net income. The understatement of accrued expenses overstates income in 2003 by $10,000. The effect of these errors on net income is reflected in retained earnings at 12/31/03. The result is an overstatement of retained earnings by $32,000 ($40,000 + $15,000 + $7,000 + $10,000 – $40,000).

Answer (A) is incorrect because an overstatement of $65,000 is the effect of the errors on 2003 net income. Answer (C) is incorrect because an overstatement of $25,000 results from taking into account only the ending inventory in 2003 and the accrued expenses. Answer (D) is incorrect because $18,000 results from subtracting, not adding, the effect of depreciation expense.

STUDY UNIT NINETEEN
STATEMENT OF CASH FLOWS

SFAS 95, *Statement of Cash Flows*, as amended by **SFAS 117**, *Financial Statements of Not-for-Profit Organizations*, establishes the reporting standards for the statement of cash flows for business and not-for-profit entities. Not-for-profit entities are covered in Study Unit 29.

The **primary purpose** of the statement of cash flows is to provide relevant information about the cash receipts and cash payments of an entity during an accounting period. A business enterprise (publicly or privately held) or not-for-profit organization that issues financial statements that report both financial position and results of operations is required to present a statement of cash flows for each accounting period for which results of operations are presented.

A statement of cash flows explains the changes in **cash and cash equivalents** during the period. Cash equivalents are short-term, highly liquid investments. Purchases and sales of these investments are cash management activities. Cash equivalents must be both readily convertible to known amounts of cash and so near their maturity that they present insignificant risk of changes in value because of changes in interest rates. Generally, cash equivalents include only investments with original maturities of 3 months or less. Examples of cash equivalents are Treasury bills, commercial paper, money market funds, and, for an enterprise engaged in banking operations, federal funds sold. However, not all short-term, highly liquid investments that qualify must be classified as cash equivalents. An entity should establish and consistently apply a **policy** that specifies which qualifying investments are to be treated as cash equivalents.

The net effect of the total cash flows is presented in a manner that **reconciles** beginning and ending cash and cash equivalents. The total amounts of cash and cash equivalents at the beginning and end of an accounting period presented in the statement of cash flows are the same amounts as similarly titled line items or subtotals presented in the statements of financial position as of those dates.

The statement discloses the cash effects of an entity's operating, financing, and investing activities. These cash inflows and outflows are usually reported at gross amounts rather than by netting related receipts and payments. **Operating activities** are all transactions and other events that are not classified as either financing or investing activities. In general, operating activities involve the production and delivery of goods and the provision of services, that is, transactions and other events the effects of which are included in the determination of net income or the change in net assets. In addition to this general guidance, certain cash receipts and disbursements are prescribed as operating cash flows. These include interest received, interest paid, and dividends received (**SFAS 95**); cash flows from purchases, sales, and maturities of trading securities (**SFAS 115**, *Accounting for Certain Investments in Debt and Equity Securities*); and cash that would have been paid for income taxes had increases in the value of equity instruments issued under share-based payment arrangements not included in either cost of goods or cost of services for financial reporting purposes also had not been deductible for tax purposes [**SFAS 123(R)**, *Share-Based Payment*].

Financing activities include (1) obtaining resources from owners; (2) paying dividends or making other distributions to owners; (3) returning investment principal to owners; (4) borrowing money; (5) repaying or otherwise settling the amounts borrowed; (6) obtaining and paying for other resources received from creditors on long-term credit; (7) receiving restricted resources that must be used for long-term purposes per donor stipulation; and (8) cash retained as excess tax benefits because of the deductibility of increases in the value of equity instruments issued under share-based payment arrangements that are not included in either cost of goods or cost of services for financial reporting purposes [**SFAS 123(R)**, *Share-Based Payment*].

Investing activities include (1) making and collecting loans; (2) acquiring and disposing of debt and equity instruments; and (3) acquiring and disposing of property, plant, equipment, and other productive assets held for or used in the production of goods or services (excluding inventory). However, transactions in cash equivalents, certain loans or other instruments acquired specifically for resale, and trading securities are operating activities, not investing activities (**SFAS 102** and **SFAS 145**). Cash flows from purchases, sales, and maturities of available-for-sale and held-to-maturity securities are cash flows from investing activities and are reported gross for each classification of security in the cash flows statement (SFAS 115).

Cash flows from derivative instruments accounted for as fair value hedges or cash flow hedges under **SFAS 133** may be classified in the same category as the flows from the hedged item, given disclosure of this policy (**SFAS 104**, as amended by SFAS 133).

Net cash flow from operating activities may be presented using the direct method or the indirect method. The **direct method** reports major classes of gross cash receipts and gross cash disbursements and their arithmetic sum (net operating cash flow). The **indirect method** adjusts net income of a business enterprise or the change in net assets of a not-for-profit organization to derive net operating cash flow. This reconciliation removes the effects of (1) all non-cash items, such as depreciation, (2) all deferrals of past operating cash flows, (3) all accruals of future cash flows, and (4) all investing and financing cash flows.

The statement of cash flows includes a **reconciliation of net income (change in net assets) and net cash flow from operating activities**. This reconciliation reports all major classes of reconciling items. At a minimum, changes in receivables related to operating activities, changes in inventory, and changes in payables related to operating activities are separately reported. If the direct method of reporting net cash flow from operating activities is used, the reconciliation of net income to net cash flow from operating activities is provided as a separate schedule. If the indirect method is used, the reconciliation may be reported within the statement of cash flows or in a separate schedule, with only the net cash flow from operating activities presented in the statement of cash flows. Furthermore, disclosures required when the indirect method is used include the amounts of interest paid (net of amounts capitalized) and income taxes paid.

Significant **noncash financing and investing activities** that affect recognized assets or liabilities are reported in related disclosures. These disclosures may be narrative in form, or they may be summarized in a schedule. The presentation must clearly distinguish between the cash and noncash aspects of the transaction. Examples of noncash financing and investing activities include (1) the conversion of debt to equity; (2) the acquisition of assets through the assumption of related liabilities, such as the purchase of a building by incurring a mortgage to the seller; (3) the exchange of noncash assets or liabilities for other noncash assets or liabilities; (4) the capital lease of an asset; and (5) obtaining a building or investment asset by receipt of a gift.

QUESTIONS

19.1 Statement of Cash Flows -- General

1. A statement of cash flows is to be presented in general-purpose external financial statements by which of the following?

A. Publicly held business enterprises only.

B. Privately held business enterprises only.

C. All business enterprises.

D. All business enterprises and not-for-profit organizations.

Answer (D) is correct. *(Publisher)*
REQUIRED: The entities required to present a statement of cash flows.
DISCUSSION: SFAS 95 as amended by SFAS 117 requires a statement of cash flows as part of a full set of financial statements of all business entities (both publicly held and privately held) and not-for-profit organizations. Defined benefit pension plans, certain other employee benefit plans, and certain highly liquid investment companies are exempted from this requirement by SFAS 102.

2. The primary purpose of a statement of cash flows of a business enterprise is to provide relevant information about

A. Differences between net income and associated cash receipts and disbursements.

B. An enterprise's ability to generate future positive net cash flows.

C. The cash receipts and cash disbursements of an enterprise during a period.

D. An enterprise's ability to meet cash operating needs.

Answer (C) is correct. *(CPA, adapted)*
REQUIRED: The purpose of a statement of cash flows.
DISCUSSION: The primary purpose is to provide information about the cash receipts and cash payments during a period. This information helps investors, creditors, and other users to assess the enterprise's ability to generate net cash inflows, meet its obligations, pay dividends, and secure external financing. It also helps assess reasons for the differences between net income and net cash flow and the effects of cash and noncash financing and investing activities.
Answer (A) is incorrect because reconciling net income with cash flows is a secondary purpose. Answer (B) is incorrect because assessing the ability to generate cash flows is a secondary purpose. Answer (D) is incorrect because assessing the ability to meet cash needs is a secondary purpose.

3. A corporation issues a balance sheet and income statement for the current year and comparative income statements for each of the 2 previous years. Under SFAS 95, a statement of cash flows

A. Should be issued for the current year only.

B. Should be issued for the current and the previous year only.

C. Should be issued for all 3 years.

D. May be issued at the company's option for any or all of the 3 years.

Answer (C) is correct. *(Publisher)*
REQUIRED: The circumstances in which a statement of cash flows should be issued.
DISCUSSION: When a business enterprise provides a set of financial statements that reports both financial position and results of operations, it must also present a statement of cash flows for each period for which the results of operations are provided.
Answer (A) is incorrect because a statement of cash flows must be provided for all 3 years. Answer (B) is incorrect because a statement of cash flows must be provided for all 3 years. Answer (D) is incorrect because the statement of cash flows is not optional in these circumstances.

4. Trans Co. had the following balances at December 31, year 1:

Cash in checking account	$ 35,000
Cash in money market account	75,000
U.S. Treasury bill, purchased 11/1/year 1, maturing 1/31/year 2	350,000
U.S. Treasury bill, purchased 12/1/year 1, maturing 3/31/year 2	400,000

Trans's policy is to treat as cash equivalents all highly liquid investments with a maturity of three months or less when purchased. What amount should Trans report as cash and cash equivalents in its December 31, year 1, balance sheet?

A. $110,000

B. $385,000

C. $460,000

D. $860,000

Answer (C) is correct. *(CPA, adapted)*
REQUIRED: The balance of cash and cash equivalents.
DISCUSSION: Cash is an asset that must be readily available for use by the business. It normally consists of (1) coin and currency on hand, (2) demand deposits (checking accounts), (3) time deposits (savings accounts), and (4) near-cash assets (e.g., money market accounts). In this case, cash equivalents include investments with original maturities of 3 months or less. The original maturity is the date on which the obligation becomes due. Accordingly, the amount to be reported as cash and cash equivalents is $460,000 ($35,000 + $75,000 + $350,000).
Answer (A) is incorrect because $110,000 excludes the T-bill maturing on 1/31/year 2. Answer (B) is incorrect because $385,000 excludes the cash in the money market account. Answer (D) is incorrect because $860,000 includes the T-bill maturing on 3/31/year 2.

5. Which of the following should be reported in a statement of cash flows issued by Grady Company?

A. Basic cash flows per share only.

B. Diluted cash flows per share only.

C. Both basic diluted cash flows per share.

D. Cash flows per share should not be reported.

Answer (D) is correct. *(CPA, adapted)*

REQUIRED: The cash flows per share reported in a statement of cash flows.

DISCUSSION: SFAS 95 prohibits reporting of a cash flow-per-share amount. Reporting a per-share amount might improperly imply that cash flow is an alternative to net income as a performance measure.

6. Ghent Co. purchased a 3-month U.S. Treasury bill. In preparing Ghent's statement of cash flows, this purchase would

A. Have no effect.

B. Be treated as an outflow from financing activities.

C. Be treated as an outflow from investing activities.

D. Be treated as an outflow from lending activities.

Answer (A) is correct. *(CPA, adapted)*

REQUIRED: The effect of purchasing a 3-month T-bill.

DISCUSSION: SFAS 95 defines cash equivalents as short-term, highly liquid investments that are both readily convertible to known amounts of cash and so near their maturity that they present insignificant risk of changes in value because of changes in interest rates. Moreover, cash equivalents ordinarily include only investments with original maturities to the holder of 3 months or less. The T-bill is therefore a cash equivalent and has no effect on the statement of cash flows.

7. The statement of cash flows may be presented in either a direct or an indirect (reconciliation) format. In which of these formats is cash collected from customers presented as a gross amount?

	Direct	Indirect
A.	No	No
B.	No	Yes
C.	Yes	Yes
D.	Yes	No

Answer (D) is correct. *(R. O'Keefe)*

REQUIRED: The format in which cash collected from customers is presented as a gross amount.

DISCUSSION: The statement of cash flows may report cash flows from operating activities in either an indirect (reconciliation) or a direct format. The direct format reports the major classes of operating cash receipts and cash payments as gross amounts. The indirect presentation reconciles net income (or the change in net assets of a not-for-profit organization) to the same amount of net cash flow from operations that would be determined in accordance with the direct method. To arrive at net operating cash flow, the indirect method adjusts net income by removing the effects of (1) all deferrals of past operating cash receipts and payments, (2) all accruals of expected future operating cash receipts and payments, and (3) all items whose cash effects are financing and investing cash flows.

8. Gascony Co. had the following activities during the current year:

- Acquired 2,000 shares of the common stock of Garmisch, Inc. (classified as available-for-sale) for $26,000.
- Sold common stock of Gastineau Motors (classified as available-for-sale) for $35,000 when the carrying amount was $33,000.
- Acquired a $50,000, 4-year certificate of deposit from a bank. (During the year, interest of $3,750 was paid to Gascony.)
- Collected dividends of $1,200 on stock investments.

In Gascony's current-year statement of cash flows, net cash outflow for investing activities should be

A. $37,250

B. $38,050

C. $39,800

D. $41,000

Answer (D) is correct. *(CPA, adapted)*

REQUIRED: The net cash outflow for investing activities.

DISCUSSION: Investing activities include (1) making and collecting loans; (2) acquiring and disposing of debt and equity instruments; and (3) acquiring and disposing of property, plant, equipment, and other productive assets held for, or used in, the production of goods or services (excluding inventory). However, transactions in cash equivalents, certain loans or other instruments acquired specifically for resale, and trading securities are operating, not investing, activities (SFAS 102 and SFAS 145). Cash flows from purchases, sales, and maturities of available-for-sale and held-to-maturity securities are cash flows from investing activities and are reported gross for each classification of security in the cash flows statement (SFAS 115). Thus, the purchase of available-for-sale securities, the sale of available-for-sale securities, and the acquisition of a long-term certificate of deposit (not a cash equivalent) are investing activities. The receipts of interest and dividends are cash flows from operating activities. The net cash used in investing activities therefore equals $41,000 ($26,000 – $35,000 + $50,000).

Answer (A) is incorrect because $37,250 treats interest received as an investing cash inflow. Answer (B) is incorrect because $38,050 treats interest and dividends received as investing cash inflows and uses the carrying amount of the investment sold. Answer (C) is incorrect because $39,800 treats dividends received as an investing cash inflow.

9. In a statement of cash flows, which of the following items is reported as a cash outflow from financing activities?

I. Payments to retire mortgage notes
II. Interest payments on mortgage notes
III. Dividend payments

A. I, II, and III.
B. II and III only.
C. I only.
D. I and III only.

Answer (D) is correct. *(CPA, adapted)*
REQUIRED: The cash outflows from financing activities.
DISCUSSION: Financing activities include issuance of stock, payment of dividends and other distributions to owners, treasury stock transactions, issuance of debt, receipt of donor-restricted resources to be used for long-term purposes, and repayment or other settlement of debt obligations. Thus, payment of the principal of a note and payment of dividends are outflows from financing activities.

Answer (A) is incorrect because interest payments are outflows from operating activities. Answer (B) is incorrect because interest payments are outflows from operating activities. Answer (C) is incorrect because dividend payments are outflows from financing activities.

10. The following information was taken from the accounting records of Gorky Corporation for the year ended December 31, year 1:

Proceeds from issuance of preferred stock	$8,000,000
Dividends paid on preferred stock	800,000
Bonds payable converted to common stock	4,000,000
Payment for purchase of machinery	1,000,000
Proceeds from sale of plant building	2,400,000
2% stock dividend on common stock	600,000
Gain on sale of plant building	400,000

The net cash flows from investing and financing activities that should be presented on Gorky's statement of cash flows for the year ended December 31, year 1 are, respectively

A. $1,400,000 and $7,200,000.
B. $1,400,000 and $7,800,000.
C. $1,800,000 and $7,800,000.
D. $1,800,000 and $7,200,000.

Answer (A) is correct. *(CMA, adapted)*
REQUIRED: The respective net cash flows from investing and financing activities.
DISCUSSION: Investing activities include (1) making and collecting loans; (2) acquiring and disposing of debt and equity instruments; and (3) acquiring and disposing of property, plant, equipment, and other productive assets held for, or used in, the production of goods or services (excluding inventory). However, transactions in cash equivalents, certain loans or other instruments acquired specifically for resale, and trading securities are operating, not investing, activities (SFAS 102 and SFAS 145). Financing activities include the issuance of stock, the payment of dividends, treasury stock transactions, the issuance of debt, the receipt of donor-restricted resources to be used for long-term purposes, and the repayment or other settlement of debt obligations. Investing activities include the purchase of machinery and the sale of a building. The net inflow from these activities is $1,400,000 ($2,400,000 – $1,000,000). Financing activities include the issuance of preferred stock and the payment of dividends. The net inflow is $7,200,000 ($8,000,000 – $800,000). The conversion of bonds into common stock and the stock dividend do not affect cash.

Answer (B) is incorrect because the stock dividend has no effect on cash flows from financing activities. Answer (C) is incorrect because the gain on the sale of the building is double counted in determining the net cash flow from investing activities. Answer (D) is incorrect because the gain on the sale of the building is double counted in determining the net cash flow from investing activities.

11. On September 1, year 1, Gardd Co. signed a 20-year building lease that it reported as a capital lease. Gardd paid the monthly lease payments when due. How should Gardd report the effect of the lease payments in the financing activities section of its year 1 statement of cash flows?

A. An inflow equal to the present value of future lease payments at September 1, year 1, minus year 1 principal and interest payments.
B. An outflow equal to the year 1 principal and interest payments on the lease.
C. An outflow equal to the year 1 principal payments only.
D. The lease payments should not be reported in the financing activities section.

Answer (C) is correct. *(CPA, adapted)*
REQUIRED: The effect of lease payments on the financing activities section in the statement of cash flows.
DISCUSSION: Financing activities include the repayment or settlement of debt obligations. Financing activities do not include the payment of interest. Thus, the payment of principal is an outflow from financing activities. The payments for interest are operating cash flows.

Answer (A) is incorrect because the payments made in year 1 are cash outflows, but the present value of future payments is not a cash item. Answer (B) is incorrect because the interest payments should not be included as cash flows from a financing activity. Answer (D) is incorrect because lease payments are considered cash outflows from financing activities.

12. In preparing its statement of cash flows, if Harlingen Co. omits the payment of cash dividends, the net cash provided by <List A> activities will be <List B>.

	List A	List B
A.	Operating	Understated
B.	Investing	Understated
C.	Investing	Overstated
D.	Financing	Overstated

Answer (D) is correct. *(CIA, adapted)*

REQUIRED: The effect of omitting payment of cash dividends.

DISCUSSION: Cash flows from financing activities include (1) obtaining resources from owners and providing them with a return on their investment, (2) borrowing from and repaying creditors, and (3) receiving restricted resources that by donor stipulation must be used for long-term purposes. This category of cash flows will be overstated if the use of cash to pay dividends to equity holders is omitted from the statement of cash flows.

Answer (A) is incorrect because cash flows from operating activities ordinarily arise from transactions that enter into the determination of net income. Cash dividends do not affect the cash flows from operating activities. Answer (B) is incorrect because cash flows from investing activities arise from making and collecting loans and acquiring and disposing of investments (both debt and equity) and property, plant, and equipment. Cash dividends do not affect the cash flows from investing activities. Answer (C) is incorrect because cash flows from investing activities arise from making and collecting loans and acquiring and disposing of investments (both debt and equity) and property, plant, and equipment. Cash dividends do not affect the cash flows from investing activities.

13. Which of the following related cash transactions should be disclosed by a bank in its statement of cash flows as gross amounts of cash receipts and cash payments rather than as net amounts?

A. The purchase and sale of fixed assets.

B. Changes in cash and cash equivalents.

C. The purchase and sale of federal funds.

D. The receipts and payments from demand deposits held for customers.

Answer (A) is correct. *(Publisher)*

REQUIRED: The related receipts and payments that should be classified as gross amounts.

DISCUSSION: In general, cash flows from operating, investing, and financing activities should be reported separately at gross amounts. Thus, cash flows related to investing activities, such as the purchase and sale of fixed assets, should be reported at gross amounts. In certain instances, however, the net amount of related cash receipts and cash payments may provide sufficient information about particular classes of cash flows. For example, SFAS 104 permits banks, saving institutions, and credit unions to report net amounts for (1) the placement and withdrawal of deposits with other financial institutions, (2) the acceptance and repayment of time deposits, and (3) the making of loans to customers and the collection of principal.

Answer (B) is incorrect because purchases and sales of cash equivalents, such as federal funds sold, may be presented as net amounts. These purchases and sales are usually part of the entity's cash management activities rather than its operating, investing, and financing activities. Hence, reporting of gross amounts is not required by SFAS 95. Answer (C) is incorrect because purchases and sales of cash equivalents, such as federal funds sold, may be presented as net amounts. These purchases and sales are usually part of the entity's cash management activities rather than its operating, investing, and financing activities. Hence, reporting of gross amounts is not required by SFAS 95. Answer (D) is incorrect because SFAS 95 states that net reporting is appropriate when turnover is quick, amounts are large, and maturities are short, for example, for the demand deposits of a bank.

14. Hanford Co. reported bonds payable of $47,000 on December 31, year 1, and $50,000 on December 31, year 2. During year 2, Hanford issued $20,000 of bonds payable in exchange for equipment. There was no amortization of bond premium or discount during the year. What amount should Hanford report in its year 2 statement of cash flows for redemption of bonds payable?

A. $3,000

B. $17,000

C. $20,000

D. $23,000

Answer (B) is correct. *(CPA, adapted)*

REQUIRED: The amount reported in the statement of cash flows for redemption of bonds payable.

DISCUSSION: Assuming no amortization of premium or discount, the net amount of bonds payable reported was affected solely by the issuance of bonds for equipment and the redemption of bonds. Given that $20,000 of bonds were issued and that the amount reported increased by only $3,000, $17,000 of bonds must have been redeemed. This amount should be reported in the statement of cash flows as a cash outflow from a financing activity.

Answer (A) is incorrect because $3,000 equals the increase in bonds payable. Answer (C) is incorrect because $20,000 is the amount of bonds issued. Answer (D) is incorrect because $23,000 is the sum of the bonds issued and the increase in bonds payable.

19.2 Operating Activities -- Indirect Presentation

15. Helicon Co. accrued a gain from the sale of used equipment for cash. The gain should be reported in a statement of cash flows using the indirect method in

A. Investment activities as a reduction of the cash inflow from the sale.

B. Investment activities as a cash outflow.

C. Operating activities as a deduction from income.

D. Operating activities as an addition to income.

Answer (C) is correct. *(CPA, adapted)*

REQUIRED: The presentation of a gain on the sale of used equipment in a statement of cash flows (indirect method).

DISCUSSION: Cash received from the sale of equipment is ordinarily classified in a statement of cash flows as a cash inflow from an investing activity. The cash inflow is equal to the carrying amount of the equipment plus any gain or minus any loss realized. Because the gain will be included in the determination of net income, it must be subtracted from the net income amount presented in the statement of cash flows (indirect method) in the reconciliation of net income to net cash flow from operating activities. The purpose of the adjustment is to remove the effect of the gain from both net income and the cash inflows from operating activities. In the cash flows from investing activities section, the amount reported is the sum of the gain and the carrying amount of the equipment.

16. In the indirect presentation of cash flows from operating activities, net income of a business enterprise is adjusted for noncash revenues, gains, expenses, and losses to determine the cash flows from operating activities. A reconciliation of net cash flows from operating activities to net income

A. Must be reported in the statement of cash flows.

B. Must be presented separately in a related disclosure.

C. May be either reported in the statement of cash flows or presented separately in a related disclosure.

D. Need not be presented.

Answer (C) is correct. *(Publisher)*

REQUIRED: The proper reporting of a reconciliation of net cash flows from operating activities to net income.

DISCUSSION: When an indirect presentation of net cash flows from operating activities is made by a business enterprise, a reconciliation with net income must be provided for all noncash revenues, gains, expenses, and losses. This reconciliation may be either reported in the statement of cash flows or provided separately in related disclosures, with the statement of cash flows presenting only the net cash flows from operating activities.

Answer (A) is incorrect because the reconciliation may be presented in a related disclosure. Answer (B) is incorrect because the reconciliation may be reported in the statement of cash flows. Answer (D) is incorrect because a reconciliation must be reported in an indirect presentation of the statement of cash flows.

17. If the indirect method is used to present the statement of cash flows of a business enterprise, depreciation expense is

A. Presented as an addition to net income in the operating section of the statement.

B. Presented as a deduction from net income in the operating section of the statement.

C. Reported as a cash outflow in the investing section of the statement.

D. Not disclosed on the statement.

Answer (A) is correct. *(R. Derstine)*

REQUIRED: The correct presentation of depreciation when the indirect method is used.

DISCUSSION: In an indirect presentation of net cash flows from operating activities by a business enterprise, the statement of cash flows should begin with net income adjusted for certain items, including those recognized in the determination of net income that did not affect cash during the period. The recognition of depreciation expense reduces net income without directly affecting cash. Thus, depreciation must be added back to net income in the determination of cash flows from operating activities.

Answer (B) is incorrect because depreciation is an addition to net income. Answer (C) is incorrect because depreciation is not a cash flow. Answer (D) is incorrect because depreciation is disclosed as an adjustment to net income.

18. Hellespont Company uses the indirect method to prepare its statement of cash flows. It should present the recognition of a loss from the impairment of goodwill as a(n)

A. Cash flow from investing activities.

B. Cash flow from financing activities.

C. Deduction from net income.

D. Addition to net income.

Answer (D) is correct. *(CMA, adapted)*

REQUIRED: The treatment of goodwill impairment in a statement of cash flows based on the indirect method.

DISCUSSION: The statement of cash flows may report operating activities in the form of either an indirect or a direct presentation. An indirect presentation by a business enterprise removes from net income the effects of all non-cash items, all deferrals of past operating cash flows, all accruals of expected future operating cash flows, and all items whose cash effects are financing or investing cash flows. The result is net operating cash flow. Goodwill impairment is a noncash loss and should be added to net income.

Answer (A) is incorrect because goodwill impairment is not a cash flow. Answer (B) is incorrect because goodwill impairment is not a cash flow. Answer (C) is incorrect because goodwill impairment is added to net income.

19. The net income for Hudson Co. was $3 million for the year ended December 31, year 1. Additional information is as follows:

Depreciation on fixed assets	$1,500,000
Gain from cash sale of land	200,000
Increase in accounts payable	300,000
Dividends paid on preferred stock	400,000

The net cash provided by operating activities in the statement of cash flows for the year ended December 31, year 1 should be

A. $4,200,000

B. $4,500,000

C. $4,600,000

D. $4,800,000

Answer (C) is correct. *(CMA, adapted)*

REQUIRED: The net cash provided by operations.

DISCUSSION: The statement of cash flows may be in the form of an indirect or a direct presentation. The indirect presentation by a business enterprise removes from net income the effects of all non-cash items, all deferrals of past operating cash flows, all accruals of expected future operating cash flows, and all items whose cash effects are financing or investing cash flows. The result is net operating cash flow. Depreciation is an expense not directly affecting cash flows that should be added back to net income. The increase in accounts payable is added to net income because it indicates that an expense has been recorded but not paid. The gain on the sale of land is an inflow from an investing, not an operating, activity and should be subtracted from net income. The dividends paid on preferred stock do not affect net income or net cash flow from operating activities and do not require an adjustment. Thus, net cash flow from operations is $4,600,000 ($3,000,000 + $1,500,000 – $200,000 + $300,000).

Answer (A) is incorrect because $4,200,000 equals net income, plus depreciation, minus the increase in accounts payable. Answer (B) is incorrect because $4,500,000 equals net income, plus depreciation. Answer (D) is incorrect because $4,800,000 equals net income, plus depreciation, plus the increase in accounts payable.

20. In a statement of cash flows (indirect method) of a business enterprise, an increase in inventories should be presented as

A. An outflow of cash.

B. An inflow and outflow of cash.

C. An addition to income from continuing operations.

D. A deduction from income from continuing operations.

Answer (D) is correct. *(CPA, adapted)*

REQUIRED: The presentation of an increase in inventories in a statement of cash flows (indirect method).

DISCUSSION: The objective of a statement of cash flows is to explain the cash receipts and cash disbursements of an entity during an accounting period. In a statement of cash flows of a business enterprise in which operating activities are presented on an indirect or reconciliation basis, cash flows from operating activities are determined by adjusting net income (which includes income from continuing operations) to remove the effects of all (1) non-cash items, (2) deferrals of past operating cash receipts and payments, (3) accruals of expected future operating cash receipts and payments, and (4) items whose cash effects are investing or financing activities. Cost of goods sold is included in the determination of net income. Cash paid to suppliers, however, should be the amount included in determining net cash flows from operating activities. To adjust net income to cash flow from operating activities for the difference between cost of goods sold and cash paid to suppliers, a two-step adjustment is necessary. The first step is to adjust net income for the change in the inventory account. This step adjusts for the difference between cost of goods sold and purchases. The second step is to adjust for the changes in the accounts payable account. This step adjusts for the difference between purchases and the amounts disbursed to suppliers. An increase in inventories indicates that purchases were greater than cost of goods sold. Thus, as part of the first step, an increase in inventories should be presented in a statement of cash flows (indirect method) as a deduction from net income.

21. Ionia Company reports operating activities in its statement of cash flows using the indirect method. Which of the following items, if any, should Ionia add back to net income to arrive at net operating cash flow?

	Excess of Treasury Stock Acquisition Cost over Sales Proceeds (Cost Method)	Bond Discount Amortization
A.	Yes	Yes
B.	No	No
C.	No	Yes
D.	Yes	No

Answer (C) is correct. *(CPA, adapted)*

REQUIRED: The item(s), if any, added back to net income when a business reports net operating cash flow by the indirect method.

DISCUSSION: Bond discount amortization is a noncash component of interest expense. Because the amortization decreases net income, it is added back in the reconciliation of net income to net operating cash flow. Treasury stock transactions involve cash flows that do not affect net income. They are also classified as financing activities, not operating activities.

Answer (A) is incorrect because cash flows from treasury stock transactions do not affect net income. Answer (B) is incorrect because the bond discount amortization should be added to net income. Answer (D) is incorrect because the bond discount amortization should be added to net income, and cash flows from treasury stock transactions do not affect net income.

22. Honshu Co. has provided the following current account balances for the preparation of the annual statement of cash flows:

	January 1	December 1
Accounts receivable	$11,500	$14,500
Allowance for uncollectible accounts	400	500
Prepaid rent expense	6,200	4,100
Accounts payable	9,700	11,200

Honshu's current-year net income is $75,000. Net cash provided by operating activities in the statement of cash flows should be

A. $72,700

B. $74,300

C. $75,500

D. $75,700

Answer (D) is correct. *(CPA, adapted)*

REQUIRED: The net cash provided by operating activities.

DISCUSSION: The net income of a business enterprise should be adjusted for the effects of items properly included in the determination of net income but having either a different effect or no effect on net operating cash flow. The increase in gross accounts receivable should be subtracted from net income. The increase indicates that sales exceeded cash received. The increase in the allowance for uncollectible accounts should be added to net income. This amount reflects a noncash expense. The decrease in prepaid rent expense should be added to net income. The cash was disbursed in a prior period, but the expense was recognized currently as a noncash item. The increase in accounts payable indicates that liabilities and related expenses were recognized without cash outlays. Thus, the change in this account should be added to net income. The net cash provided by operating activities is $75,700 ($75,000 NI – $3,000 change in A/R + $100 change in allowance + $2,100 decrease in prepaid rent + $1,500 increase in A/P).

Answer (A) is incorrect because $72,700 results from subtracting the increase in accounts payable. Answer (B) is incorrect because $74,300 results from adding the change in accounts receivable and subtracting the changes in the other balances. Answer (C) is incorrect because $75,500 results from subtracting the change in the allowance.

23. Jungfrau Company had net income of $150,000 for the year ended December 31, year 2 and paid $125,000 of dividends during year 2. The following is its comparative balance sheet:

	12/31/year 2	12/31/year 1
Cash	$150,000	$180,000
Accounts receivable	200,000	220,000
Total assets	$350,000	$400,000
Payables	$ 80,000	$160,000
Capital stock	130,000	125,000
Retained earnings	140,000	115,000
Total	$350,000	$400,000

The amount of net cash provided by operating activities during year 2 was

A. $70,000

B. $90,000

C. $150,000

D. $210,000

Answer (B) is correct. *(CIA, adapted)*

REQUIRED: The amount of net cash provided by operating activities during year 2.

DISCUSSION: A business enterprise adjusts net income to determine the net cash provided by operations. The payment of cash dividends is a cash flow from a financing activity. Hence, it is not a reconciling item. However, the decrease in accounts receivable ($220,000 – $200,000 = $20,000) during the period represents a cash inflow (collections of pre-year 1 receivables) not reflected in year 1 net income. Moreover, the decrease in payables ($160,000 – $80,000 = $80,000) indicates a cash outflow (payment of pre-year 1 liabilities) that also is not reflected in year 1 net income. Accordingly, net cash provided by operations was $90,000 ($150,000 + $20,000 – $80,000).

Answer (A) is incorrect because $70,000 fails to add to net income the reduction in accounts receivable. Answer (C) is incorrect because $150,000 is net income. Answer (D) is incorrect because $210,000 subtracts the reduction in receivables and adds the reduction in payables.

Questions 24 and 25 are based on the following information. Ithaca Co. reported net income of $300,000 for the current year. Changes occurred in several balance sheet accounts as follows:

Equipment	$25,000 increase
Accumulated depreciation	40,000 increase
Note payable	30,000 increase

Additional Information:

- During the current year, Ithaca sold equipment costing $25,000, with accumulated depreciation of $12,000, for a gain of $5,000.
- In December of the current year, Ithaca purchased equipment costing $50,000 with $20,000 cash and a 12% note payable of $30,000.
- Depreciation expense for the year was $52,000.

24. In Ithaca's current-year statement of cash flows, net cash provided by operating activities should be

A. $340,000

B. $347,000

C. $352,000

D. $357,000

Answer (B) is correct. *(CPA, adapted)*

REQUIRED: The net cash provided by operating activities in the statement of cash flows.

DISCUSSION: A business enterprise should adjust net income for the effects of items included in the determination of net income that have no effect on net cash provided by operating activities. Depreciation is included in the determination of net income but has no cash effect. Thus, depreciation should be added to net income. The sale of equipment resulted in a gain included in the determination of net income, but the cash effect is classified as an inflow from an investing activity. Thus, the gain should be subtracted from net income. The cash outflow for the purchase of equipment is from an investing activity and has no effect on net income. Hence, it requires no adjustment. Thus, the net cash provided by operating activities is $347,000 ($300,000 NI + $52,000 depreciation – $5,000 gain).

Answer (A) is incorrect because $340,000 reflects addition of the accumulated depreciation. Answer (C) is incorrect because $352,000 results from not deducting the gain. Answer (D) is incorrect because $357,000 results from adding the gain.

25. In Ithaca's current-year statement of cash flows, net cash used in investing activities should be

A. $2,000

B. $12,000

C. $18,000

D. $20,000

Answer (A) is correct. *(CPA, adapted)*

REQUIRED: The net cash used in investing activities.

DISCUSSION: Cash flows from investing activities include the cash inflow from the sale of equipment and the cash outflow from the purchase of equipment. The issuance of a note payable as part of the acquisition price of equipment is classified as a noncash financing and investing activity. The cash inflow from the sale of equipment (carrying amount + gain) is $18,000 [($25,000 – $12,000) + $5,000]. The cash outflow from the purchase of equipment is $20,000. Thus, net cash used is $2,000 ($20,000 – $18,000).

Answer (B) is incorrect because $12,000 assumes a $30,000 cash payment for the equipment. Answer (C) is incorrect because $18,000 is the cash inflow from the sale of equipment. Answer (D) is incorrect because $20,000 is the cash outflow from the purchase of equipment.

26. In its statement of cash flows issued for the year ending September 30, Berne Company reported a net cash inflow from operating activities of $123,000. The following adjustments were included in the supplementary schedule reconciling cash flow from operating activities with net income:

Depreciation	$38,000
Increase in net accounts receivable	31,000
Decrease in inventory	27,000
Increase in accounts payable	48,000
Increase in interest payable	12,000

Net income is

A. $29,000

B. $41,000

C. $79,000

D. $217,000

Answer (A) is correct. *(Publisher)*

REQUIRED: The net income given cash flow from operating activities and reconciling adjustments.

DISCUSSION: For a business enterprise to derive net income from net cash inflow from operating activities, various adjustments are necessary. The depreciation of $38,000 should be subtracted because it is a noncash item included in the determination of net income. The increase in net accounts receivable of $31,000 should be added because it signifies that sales revenue was greater than the cash collections from customers. The increase in accounts payable should be subtracted because it indicates that purchases were $48,000 greater than cash disbursements to suppliers. The second step of the transformation from cash paid to suppliers to cost of goods sold is to subtract the decrease in inventory. This change means that cost of goods sold was $27,000 greater than purchases. The $12,000 increase in interest payable should also be subtracted because it indicates that interest expense was greater than the cash paid to the lenders. Thus, the net adjustment to net cash inflow from operating activities is –$94,000 (–$38,000 + $31,000 – $27,000 – $48,000 – $12,000). Net income is $29,000 ($123,000 net cash inflow – $94,000 net adjustment).

Answer (B) is incorrect because the increase in interest payable is not subtracted. Answer (C) is incorrect because depreciation and the increase in interest payable are not subtracted. Answer (D) is incorrect because depreciation, the increase in accounts payable, the decrease in inventory, and the increase in interest payable should be subtracted. The increase in net accounts receivable should be added.

27. Jaffa Corp.'s statement of cash flows for the year ended October 31, year 1 was prepared using the indirect method and included the following:

Net income	$60,000
Noncash adjustments:	
Depreciation expense	9,000
Increase in accounts receivable	(5,000)
Decrease in inventory	40,000
Decrease in accounts payable	(12,000)
Net cash flows from operating activities	$92,000

Jaffa reported revenues from customers of $75,000 in its year 1 income statement. What amount of cash did Jaffa receive from its customers during the year ended October 31, year 1?

A. $80,000

B. $70,000

C. $65,000

D. $55,000

Answer (B) is correct. *(CPA, adapted)*

REQUIRED: The cash collected from customers.

DISCUSSION: Collections from customers equal sales revenue minus the increase in accounts receivable, or $70,000 ($75,000 – $5,000).

Answer (A) is incorrect because $80,000 adds the increase in accounts receivable. Answer (C) is incorrect because the only adjustment to the $75,000 of revenue from customers is for the $5,000 increase in accounts receivable. Answer (D) is incorrect because the only adjustment to the $75,000 of revenue from customers is for the $5,000 increase in accounts receivable.

19.3 Operating Activities -- Direct Presentation

28. In a statement of cash flows of a business enterprise, which of the following will increase reported cash flows from operating activities using the direct method? (Ignore income tax considerations.)

A. Dividends received from investments.

B. Gain on sale of equipment.

C. Gain on early retirement of bonds.

D. Change from straight-line to accelerated depreciation.

Answer (A) is correct. *(CPA, adapted)*

REQUIRED: The item that will increase reported cash flows from operating activities using the direct method.

DISCUSSION: Operating activities are transactions and other events not classified as investing and financing activities. In general, the cash effects of operating activities (other than gains and losses) enter into the determination of the net income of a business enterprise or the change in net assets of a not-for-profit organization. Thus, cash receipts from dividends is an operating activity.

Answer (B) is incorrect because the sale of equipment is an investing activity. Answer (C) is incorrect because an early retirement of bonds is a financing activity. Answer (D) is incorrect because a change in accounting principle is a noncash event.

29. Manitoba Company acquired copyrights from authors, in some cases paying advance royalties and in others paying royalties within 30 days of year-end. Manitoba reported royalty expense of $375,000 for the year ended December 31, year 2. The following data are included in Manitoba's balance sheet:

	Year 1	Year 2
Prepaid royalties	$60,000	$50,000
Royalties payable	75,000	90,000

In its year 2 statement of cash flows, Manitoba should report cash disbursements for royalty payments of

A. $350,000

B. $370,000

C. $380,000

D. $400,000

Answer (A) is correct. *(CPA, adapted)*

REQUIRED: The cash disbursements for royalty payments.

DISCUSSION: A decrease in a prepaid royalties asset account implies that royalty expense was greater than the related cash disbursements. Similarly, an increase in a royalties payable liability account indicates that royalties expense exceeded cash disbursements. Royalty expense therefore exceeds the amount of cash disbursements for royalty payments by the amount of the decrease in the prepaid royalties account plus the increase in the royalties payable account. Thus, Manitoba's year 2 cash disbursements for royalty payments total $350,000 ($375,000 royalty expense – $10,000 decrease in prepaid royalties – $15,000 increase in royalties payable).

Answer (B) is incorrect because the $10,000 decrease in prepaid royalties should be subtracted, not added. Answer (C) is incorrect because the $15,000 increase in royalties payable should be subtracted from royalty expense, not added. Answer (D) is incorrect because the decrease in prepaid royalties and the increase in royalties payable should be subtracted, not added.

30. Mukden Co. reported cost of goods sold of $270,000 for year 1. Additional information is as follows:

	December 31	January 1
Inventory	$60,000	$45,000
Accounts payable	26,000	39,000

If Mukden uses the direct method, what amount should Mukden report as cash paid to suppliers in its year 1 statement of cash flows?

A. $242,000

B. $268,000

C. $272,000

D. $298,000

Answer (D) is correct. *(CPA, adapted)*

REQUIRED: The amount reported as cash paid to suppliers in the statement of cash flows.

DISCUSSION: To reconcile cost of goods sold to cash paid to suppliers, a two-step adjustment is needed. First, determine purchases by adding the increase in inventory to cost of goods. Second, determine cash paid for goods sold by adding the decrease in accounts payable to purchases. Thus, cash paid for goods sold equals $298,000 [$270,000 + ($60,000 – $45,000) + ($39,000 – $26,000)].

Answer (A) is incorrect because $242,000 results from subtracting the changes in inventory and accounts payable. Answer (B) is incorrect because $268,000 results from subtracting the change in inventory. Answer (C) is incorrect because $272,000 results from subtracting the change in accounts payable.

31. The following balances were reported by Oland Co. at December 31, year 2 and year 1:

	12/31/year 2	12/31/year 1
Inventory	$260,000	$290,000
Accounts payable	75,000	50,000

Oland paid suppliers $490,000 during the year ended December 31, year 2. What amount should Oland report for cost of goods sold in year 2?

A. $545,000

B. $495,000

C. $485,000

D. $435,000

Answer (A) is correct. *(CPA, adapted)*

REQUIRED: The cost of goods sold.

DISCUSSION: If trade accounts increased by $25,000, purchases must have been $25,000 higher than the disbursements for purchases. Purchases thus are $515,000 ($490,000 + $25,000). The decrease in merchandise inventory indicates that cost of goods sold must have been $30,000 higher than purchases. Hence, CGS equals $545,000 ($515,000 + $30,000).

Answer (B) is incorrect because $495,000 results from subtracting the increase in accounts payable. Answer (C) is incorrect because $485,000 results from subtracting the decrease in inventory. Answer (D) is incorrect because $435,000 results from subtracting the decrease in inventory and the increase in accounts payable.

Questions 32 through 35 are based on the following information.

Pimlico Corp. uses the direct method to prepare its statement of cash flows. Pimlico's trial balances at December 31, year 2 and year 1 are as follows:

	December 31 Year 2	December 31 Year 1
Debits		
Cash	$ 35,000	$ 32,000
Accounts receivable	33,000	30,000
Inventory	31,000	47,000
Property, plant, & equipment	100,000	95,000
Unamortized bond discount	4,500	5,000
Cost of goods sold	250,000	380,000
Selling expenses	141,500	172,000
General and administrative expenses	137,000	151,300
Interest expense	4,300	2,600
Income tax expense	20,400	61,200
	$756,700	$976,100
Credits		
Allowance for uncollectible accounts	$ 1,300	$ 1,100
Accumulated depreciation	16,500	15,000
Trade accounts payable	25,000	17,500
Income taxes payable	21,000	27,100
Deferred income taxes	5,300	4,600
8% callable bonds payable	45,000	20,000
Common stock	50,000	40,000
Additional paid-in capital	9,100	7,500
Retained earnings	44,700	64,600
Sales	538,800	778,700
	$756,700	$976,100

- Pimlico purchased $5,000 in equipment during year 2.
- Pimlico allocated one-third of its depreciation expense to selling expenses and the remainder to general and administrative expenses.

32. What amounts should Pimlico report in its statement of cash flows for the year ended December 31, year 2 for cash collected from customers?

A. $541,800

B. $541,600

C. $536,000

D. $535,800

Answer (D) is correct. *(CPA, adapted)*

REQUIRED: The cash collected from customers.

DISCUSSION: Collections from customers equal sales minus the increase in gross accounts receivable, or $535,800 ($538,800 – $33,000 + $30,000).

Answer (A) is incorrect because $541,800 results from adding the increase in receivables. Answer (B) is incorrect because $541,600 results from adding the increase in receivables and subtracting the increase in the allowance for uncollectible accounts, that is, from adding net accounts receivable. Answer (C) is incorrect because $536,000 results from subtracting net accounts receivable.

33. What amounts should Pimlico report in its statement of cash flows for the year ended December 31, year 2 for cash paid for interest?

A. $4,800

B. $4,300

C. $3,800

D. $1,700

Answer (C) is correct. *(CPA, adapted)*

REQUIRED: The cash paid for interest.

DISCUSSION: Interest expense is $4,300. This amount includes $500 of discount amortization, a noncash item. Hence, the cash paid for interest was $3,800 ($4,300 – $500).

Answer (A) is incorrect because $4,800 results from adding the amortized discount. Answer (B) is incorrect because $4,300 is the total interest expense. Answer (D) is incorrect because $1,700 is the increase in interest expense.

34. What amounts should Pimlico report in its statement of cash flows for the year ended December 31, year 2 for cash paid for income taxes?

A. $25,800

B. $20,400

C. $19,700

D. $15,000

Answer (A) is correct. *(CPA, adapted)*

REQUIRED: The cash paid for income taxes.

DISCUSSION: To reconcile income tax expense to cash paid for income taxes, a two-step adjustment is needed. The first step is to add the decrease in income taxes payable. The second step is to subtract the increase in deferred income taxes. Hence, cash paid for income taxes equals $25,800 [$20,400 + ($27,100 – $21,000) – ($5,300 – $4,600)].

Answer (B) is incorrect because $20,400 is income tax expense. Answer (C) is incorrect because $19,700 equals income tax expense minus the increase in deferred income taxes. Answer (D) is incorrect because $15,000 results from subtracting the decrease in income taxes payable and adding the increase in deferred taxes payable.

35. Refer to the information preceding question 32. What amounts should Pimlico report in its statement of cash flows for the year ended December 31, year 1 for cash paid for selling expenses?

A. $142,000

B. $141,500

C. $141,000

D. $140,000

Answer (C) is correct. *(CPA, adapted)*

REQUIRED: The cash paid for selling expenses.

DISCUSSION: Cash paid for selling expenses equals selling expenses minus the depreciation allocated to selling expenses. Total depreciation expense equals the $1,500 ($16,500 – $15,000) change in accumulated depreciation. Thus, cash paid for selling expenses equals $141,000 ($141,500 expense for year 1 – $1,500 depreciation for year 1 × 33 1/3% allocated to selling).

Answer (A) is incorrect because $142,000 results from adding the depreciation allocated to selling expenses. Answer (B) is incorrect because $141,500 equals the selling expenses for year 1. Answer (D) is incorrect because $140,000 results from subtracting 100% of depreciation expense from selling expenses.

36. The Marburg Corporation owns extensive rental property. For some of this property, rent is paid in advance. For other property, rent is paid following the end of the year. In the income statement for the year ended December 31, year 2, Marburg reported $140,000 in rental income. The following data are included in Marburg's December 31 balance sheet:

	Year 2	Year 1
Rent receivable	$95,000	$120,000
Deferred rent income	40,000	50,000

In its statement of cash flows for the year ended December 31, year 2, Marburg should report cash receipts from rental properties totaling

A. $105,000

B. $125,000

C. $155,000

D. $175,000

Answer (C) is correct. *(K.M. Boze)*

REQUIRED: The amount of total rental cash receipts.

DISCUSSION: No write-offs of rent receivables are mentioned. Consequently, a decrease in the rent receivable asset account implies that Marburg collected more in cash receipts from rental customers than it recognized as rental income in year 2. In contrast, a decrease in the deferred rent income liability account signifies that Marburg recognized more rental income than it received in cash payments. To determine cash receipts from rental properties, the rental income of $140,000 should be increased by the $25,000 change in the rent receivable account and decreased by the $10,000 reduction in the deferred rent income account. Cash receipts from rental properties were therefore $155,000.

Answer (A) is incorrect because the $25,000 decrease in rent receivable should be added to rental income, not subtracted. Answer (B) is incorrect because the $25,000 decrease in rent receivable should be added to rental income, not subtracted, and the $10,000 decrease in deferred rental income should be subtracted, not added. Answer (D) is incorrect because the $10,000 decrease in deferred rental income should be subtracted from rental income, not added.

37. The following information was taken from the year 1 financial statements of Hofburg Corp.:

Accounts receivable, January 1, year 1	$ 21,600
Accounts receivable, December 31, year 1	30,400
Sales on account and cash sales	438,000
Uncollectible accounts	1,000

No accounts receivable were written off or recovered during the year. If the direct method is used in the year 1 statement of cash flows, Hofburg should report cash collected from customers as

A. $447,800

B. $446,800

C. $429,200

D. $428,200

Answer (C) is correct. *(CPA, adapted)*

REQUIRED: The cash collected from customers.

DISCUSSION: Collections from customers equal sales revenue adjusted for the change in gross accounts receivable and write-offs and recoveries. Because no accounts receivable were written off or recovered during the year, no adjustment for these transactions is needed. Accounts receivable increased by $8,800 ($30,400 – $21,600), which represents an excess of revenue recognized over cash received. Hofburg thus should report cash collected from customers of $429,200 ($438,000 – $8,800).

Answer (A) is incorrect because $447,800 results from adding the increase in accounts receivable and the uncollectible accounts balance. Answer (B) is incorrect because $446,800 results from adding the increase in accounts receivable. Answer (D) is incorrect because $428,200 results from subtracting the uncollectible accounts balance.

STUDY UNIT TWENTY
ACCOUNTING FOR CHANGING PRICES

The accounting method primarily (but not exclusively) used in general-purpose financial statements presented by U.S. entities in accordance with generally accepted accounting principles is based on historical transactions measured in terms of dollars unadjusted for changes in purchasing power (**historical cost-nominal purchasing power**). However, this position is being modified as the Financial Accounting Standards Board moves to change the recording of assets and liabilities classified as financial instruments to fair value. For example, **SFAS 133**, *Accounting for Derivatives and Hedging Activities*, requires all derivative instruments to be measured at fair value (Study Unit 10).

In **SFAS 89**, *Financial Reporting and Changing Prices*, the FASB encourages (but does not require) business enterprises to provide supplemental information on the effects of changing prices, for example, with regard to purchasing power gains and losses on net monetary items and changes in the current cost or lower recoverable amount of inventory and property, plant, and equipment. Currently, most business enterprises do not provide this information. The suggested disclosures are based on measures of **current cost or lower recoverable amounts** in units of dollars, each of which has the same general purchasing power (**current cost-constant purchasing power**). However, SFAS 89 does not discourage disclosure of other forms of information on the effects of changing prices, such as information based on current market value or information based on historical transactions measured in terms of dollars adjusted for changes in purchasing power (historical cost-constant purchasing power).

QUESTIONS

20.1 General

1. Which of the following items is included in the 5-year summary of selected financial data recommended by SFAS 89, *Financial Reporting and Changing Prices*?

A. Net income.

B. Income from continuing operations on a current cost basis.

C. Purchasing power gain or loss on net nonmonetary items.

D. Cash dividends paid per common share.

Answer (B) is correct. *(Publisher)*

REQUIRED: The item included in the 5-year summary of selected financial data.

DISCUSSION: SFAS 89 recommends that an enterprise disclose the following information for each of the 5 most recent years:

a) Net sales and other operating revenues.
b) Income from continuing operations on a current cost basis.
c) Purchasing power gain or loss on net monetary items.
d) Increase or decrease in the current cost or lower recoverable amount of inventory and property, plant, and equipment, net of inflation.
e) The aggregate foreign currency translation adjustment on a current cost basis (if applicable).
f) Net assets at year-end on a current cost basis.
g) Income per common share from continuing operations on a current cost basis.
h) Cash dividends declared per common share.
i) Market price per common share at year-end.

2. Which of the following is a method of accounting based on measures of current cost or lower recoverable amount in units of currency having the same general purchasing power?

A. Historical cost-constant purchasing power accounting.

B. Historical cost-nominal dollar accounting.

C. Current cost-constant purchasing power accounting.

D. Current cost-nominal dollar accounting.

Answer (C) is correct. *(CPA, adapted)*

REQUIRED: The method of accounting based on measures of current cost or lower recoverable amount in units of the same general purchasing power.

DISCUSSION: Current cost accounting attempts to present an enterprise's assets and liabilities on the basis of current worth (current cost or lower recoverable amount). Constant purchasing power accounting reports financial statement elements in units of currency with the same general purchasing power.

Answer (A) is incorrect because, in historical cost accounting, items are measured and reported at their historical prices. Answer (B) is incorrect because, in historical cost accounting, items are measured and reported at their historical prices. Also, under nominal dollar accounting, dollars are not restated into units with the same general purchasing power. Answer (D) is incorrect because, under nominal dollar accounting, dollars are not restated into units with the same general purchasing power.

3. Financial statements that are presented assuming a stable monetary unit are

A. General price-level financial statements.

B. Nominal dollar financial statements.

C. Current value financial statements.

D. Fair value financial statements.

Answer (B) is correct. *(CPA, adapted)*

REQUIRED: The financial statements that assume a stable monetary unit.

DISCUSSION: Nominal dollar financial statements assume that the unit of measure does not fluctuate in value significantly. Although this assumption has the virtues of simplicity and objectivity, it results in financial statement amounts that do not reflect general price-level changes.

Answer (A) is incorrect because general price-level statements recognize that monetary units change in value and require price-level adjustments. Answer (C) is incorrect because current fair value takes into account the effect of specific price-level indexes. Answer (D) is incorrect because current fair value takes into account the effect of specific price-level indexes.

4. SFAS 89, *Financial Reporting and Changing Prices*, recommends that the information presented in the 5-year summary of selected financial data be stated in terms of

A. Beginning-of-the-year units of constant purchasing power.

B. Average-for-the-year units of constant purchasing power.

C. Nominal units of money.

D. Dollars equivalent in purchasing power to dollars used in calculating the current period Consumer Price Index for All Urban Consumers.

Answer (B) is correct. *(Publisher)*

REQUIRED: The unit of measure used to state the selected financial data included in the 5-year summary.

DISCUSSION: SFAS 89 recommends that the information presented in the 5-year summary be stated in average-for-the-year units of constant purchasing power, in end-of-year units of constant purchasing power, or in dollars having a purchasing power equal to that of the dollars of the base period used by the Bureau of Labor Statistics in calculating the Consumer Price Index for All Urban Consumers.

Answer (A) is incorrect because SFAS 89 does not recommend that information presented in the 5-year summary be stated in beginning-of-the-year units of constant purchasing power. Answer (C) is incorrect because SFAS 89 does not recommend that information presented in the 5-year summary be stated in nominal units of money. Answer (D) is incorrect because SFAS 89 does not recommend that information presented in the 5-year summary be stated in dollars equivalent in purchasing power to dollars used in calculating the current period Consumer Price Index for All Urban Consumers.

5. SFAS 89 recommends that a 5-year summary of certain selected financial data be presented. If the current year income from continuing operations on a current cost-constant purchasing power basis differs significantly from income from continuing operations in the primary financial statements, an enterprise should also disclose

A. All components of income from continuing operations for the current year on a current cost basis.

B. All components of net income for the current year on a current cost basis.

C. Certain components of income from continuing operations for the current year on a current cost basis.

D. All operating expenses for the current year on a current cost basis.

Answer (C) is correct. *(Publisher)*

REQUIRED: The information for the current year that should be disclosed.

DISCUSSION: When income from continuing operations on a current cost-constant purchasing power basis differs significantly from income from continuing operations reported in the primary financial statements, SFAS 89 recommends that certain components of income from continuing operations for the current year be disclosed on a current cost basis. The information may be presented in a statement format, in a reconciliation format, or in notes to the 5-year summary. Whichever format is used, the presentation should disclose or allow the reader to determine the difference between the amount in the primary statements and the current cost amount of the following: cost of goods sold, depreciation, depletion, and amortization expense.

6. A company that wishes to disclose information about the effect of changing prices in accordance with SFAS 89, *Financial Reporting and Changing Prices*, should report this information in

A. The body of the financial statements.

B. The notes to the financial statements.

C. Supplementary information to the financial statements.

D. Management's report to shareholders.

Answer (C) is correct. *(CPA, adapted)*

REQUIRED: The reporting of the effect of changing prices.

DISCUSSION: SFAS 89 encourages, but does not require, disclosure of supplementary current cost-constant purchasing power information.

Answer (A) is incorrect because voluntary disclosures about the effects of changing prices should not be reported in the body of the financial statements or the notes. Answer (B) is incorrect because voluntary disclosures about the effects of changing prices should not be reported in the body of the financial statements or the notes. Answer (D) is incorrect because information about the effect of changing prices is meaningful to users of financial statements other than shareholders.

20.2 Current Cost

7. Griffin Co. adjusted its historical cost income statement by applying specific price indexes to its depreciation expense and cost of goods sold. Griffin's adjusted income statement is prepared according to

A. Fair value accounting.

B. General purchasing power accounting.

C. Current cost accounting.

D. Current cost-general purchasing power accounting.

Answer (C) is correct. *(CPA, adapted)*

REQUIRED: The basis of accounting that applies specific price indexes to historical cost items.

DISCUSSION: According to SFAS 89, current cost is the estimated cost of acquiring the service potential provided by an asset, adjusted for depreciation, etc. An enterprise that chooses to report supplementary information on the effects of changing prices should disclose income from continuing operations on a current cost basis. This basis measures cost of goods sold at current cost or lower recoverable amount at the date of sale or at the date resources are used on, or committed to, a specific contract. Depreciation is measured on the basis of the average current cost of the assets' service potential or lower recoverable amount during the period of use.

Answer (A) is incorrect because fair value accounting presents the current fair values of assets and the changes in those values with or without separate identification of the effects of general price-level changes. Current cost is one possible estimate of current fair value. Exit value and capitalization of net cash inflows are other possible estimates. Answer (B) is incorrect because general (constant) purchasing power accounting reports financial statement elements in units of currency with the same general purchasing power. Thus, it applies a general price index. Answer (D) is incorrect because the term "current cost-general purchasing power accounting" is internally contradictory. General (constant) purchasing power accounting reports financial statement elements in units of currency with the same general purchasing power. Thus, it applies a general price index, not a price index specific to the item measured.

8. At December 31, Poplin Corp. owned two assets as follows:

	Equipment	Inventory
Current cost	$200,000	$160,000
Recoverable amount	190,000	180,000

Poplin voluntarily disclosed supplementary information about current cost at December 31. In such a disclosure, at what amount would Poplin report total assets?

A. $350,000

B. $360,000

C. $370,000

D. $380,000

Answer (A) is correct. *(CPA, adapted)*

REQUIRED: The amount at which supplementary information about the current cost of equipment and inventory should be reported.

DISCUSSION: According to SFAS 89, inventory is measured at current cost or lower recoverable amount at the measurement date. Property, plant, and equipment are measured at the current cost or lower recoverable amount of the remaining service potential at the measurement date. Thus, the equipment should be reported at $190,000 and the inventory at $160,000, a total of $350,000.

Answer (B) is incorrect because $360,000 results from using the current cost for equipment instead of the recoverable amount. Answer (C) is incorrect because $370,000 results from using the recoverable amount for inventory instead of current cost. Answer (D) is incorrect because $380,000 results from using the current cost for equipment and recoverable amount for inventory.

9. Dinah Co. prepares supplementary reports on income from continuing operations on a current cost basis in accordance with SFAS 89, *Financial Reporting and Changing Prices*. How should Dinah compute cost of goods sold on a current cost basis?

A. Number of units sold times average current cost of units during the year.

B. Number of units sold times current cost of units at year-end.

C. Number of units sold times current cost of units at the beginning of the year.

D. Beginning inventory at current cost, plus cost of goods purchased, minus ending inventory at current cost.

Answer (A) is correct. *(CPA, adapted)*

REQUIRED: The method of computing cost of goods sold on a current cost basis.

DISCUSSION: If an enterprise provides supplementary information about the effects of changing prices in accordance with SFAS 89 and operating income on a current cost-constant purchasing power basis differs significantly from that reported in the primary statements, it should, among other items, disclose the difference between the cost of goods sold in the primary financial statements and the current cost amount. SFAS 89 calculates the latter by multiplying the units sold during the period by the average of the unit current cost or lower recoverable amounts at the beginning and end of the period.

10. The following information pertains to each unit of merchandise purchased for resale by Denton Co.:

March 1, year 1	
Purchase price	$ 16
Selling price	$ 24
Price level index	110
December 31, year 1	
Replacement cost	$ 20
Selling price	$ 30
Price level index	121

Under current cost accounting, what is the amount of Denton's holding gain on each unit of this merchandise?

A. $0

B. $1.60

C. $2.40

D. $4.00

Answer (D) is correct. *(CPA, adapted)*

REQUIRED: The holding gain on each unit under current cost accounting.

DISCUSSION: SFAS 89, *Financial Reporting and Changing Prices*, defines the current cost of inventory as the current cost of purchasing the goods or the current cost of the resources needed to produce the goods (including an allowance for the current overhead costs according to the allocation bases used under GAAP), whichever is applicable in the circumstances. Thus, the current cost at 12/31/year 1 was the $20 replacement cost, and the holding gain, calculated without restatement into units of constant purchasing power, is $4.00 ($20 – $16 historical cost).

Answer (A) is incorrect because a holding gain occurred. Replacement cost exceeds historical cost. Answer (B) is incorrect because $1.60 is the adjustment necessary to inflate the 3/1/year 1 unit purchase price to the 12/31/year 1 price level. Answer (C) is incorrect because $2.40 equals the difference between replacement cost and the historical cost if the latter is restated into units of constant purchasing power to reflect the 12/31/year 1 price level.

Questions 11 and 12 are based on the following information.

In a period of rising general price levels, Jayhawk Corp. discloses income on a current cost basis in accordance with SFAS 89, *Financial Reporting and Changing Prices.*

11. Compared with historical cost income from continuing operations, which of the following conditions increases Jayhawk's current cost income from continuing operations?

A. Current cost of equipment is greater than historical cost.

B. Current cost of land is greater than historical cost.

C. Current cost of cost of goods sold is less than historical cost.

D. Ending net monetary assets are less than beginning net monetary assets.

Answer (C) is correct. *(CPA, adapted)*

REQUIRED: The condition that increases current cost income from continuing operations compared with historical cost income.

DISCUSSION: Revenues generally reflect current cost when they are earned. Thus, they are stated at current cost in the historical cost income statement. Expenses, such as cost of goods sold, however, will vary because the current cost and historical cost of nonmonetary items, such as inventory, differ over time. If the current cost or lower recoverable amount is less than the historical cost, the effect is that current cost of goods sold is lower than historical cost of goods sold. Hence, current cost operating income (sales – CGS – operating expenses) will be greater than historical cost operating income.

Answer (A) is incorrect because holding gains (excess of current cost over the historical cost) are not included in current cost operating income. They are added to that amount in the determination of current cost net income. Answer (B) is incorrect because holding gains (excess of current cost over the historical cost) are not included in current cost operating income. They are added to that amount in the determination of current cost net income. Answer (D) is incorrect because the income statement effects of a change during the period in the amount of net monetary assets are the same under the historical cost and current cost bases. The reason is that monetary items are already stated at current cost in the historical cost financial statements.

12. Could Jayhawk Corp.'s current cost financial statements report holding gains for goods sold during the period and holding gains on inventory at the end of the period?

	Goods Sold	Inventory
A.	Yes	Yes
B.	Yes	No
C.	No	Yes
D.	No	No

Answer (A) is correct. *(CPA, adapted)*

REQUIRED: The true statement as to whether current cost financial statements may report holding gains for goods sold during the period and holding gains on inventory at the end of the period.

DISCUSSION: According to SFAS 89, the change in the current cost amounts of inventory and property, plant, and equipment is the difference between the measures of the assets at their entry dates for the year (beginning of the year or dates of acquisition) and their exit dates (end of the year or dates of use, sale, or commitment to a specific contract). A change in the current cost of inventory is reflected in the current cost income statement. A holding gain for inventory is the excess of the current cost at the exit date over the current cost at the entry date. Consequently, a realized holding gain is recognized when inventory is sold, and an unrealized holding gain is recognized on inventory held at the end of the period.

13. Syracuse Company purchased a machine for $230,000 on January 1, the company's first day of operations. At the end of the year, the current cost of the machine was $250,000. The machine has no salvage value, has a 5-year life, and is depreciated by the straight-line method. For the first year of operations, the amount of the current cost depreciation expense that would appear in supplementary current cost financial statements is

A. $28,000

B. $46,000

C. $48,000

D. $50,000

Answer (C) is correct. *(CPA, adapted)*

REQUIRED: The depreciation expense for the year on the current cost basis using the straight-line method.

DISCUSSION: Depreciation, depletion, and amortization expense of property, plant, and equipment should be measured on the basis of the average current cost or lower recoverable amount during the period of use. The average current cost for Syracuse Company's machine is $240,000 [($230,000 + $250,000) ÷ 2]. Based on the straight-line depreciation method over a 5-year expected useful life with no salvage value, the depreciation expense determined on a current cost basis is $48,000 ($240,000 ÷ 5).

Answer (A) is incorrect because $28,000 results when the difference between the end of the year current cost and the purchase price is subtracted from the current cost depreciation expense. Answer (B) is incorrect because the historical cost of the machine is used ($230,000 ÷ 5). Answer (D) is incorrect because the current cost of the machine is used ($250,000 ÷ 5).

Questions 14 and 15 are based on the following information.

Niner Company accounts for inventory on a FIFO basis. There were 8,000 units in inventory on January 1. Costs were incurred and goods purchased during the year as presented in the next column. Niner estimates that the current cost per unit of inventory was $57 at January 1 and $71 at December 31.

	Historical Costs	Units Purchased	Units Sold
1st quarter	$ 410,000	7,000	7,500
2nd quarter	550,000	8,500	7,300
3rd quarter	425,000	6,500	8,200
4th quarter	630,000	9,000	7,000
	$2,015,000	31,000	30,000

14. In Niner's voluntary supplementary information restated into current cost, the December 31 inventory should be reported at

A. $576,000
B. $585,000
C. $630,000
D. $639,000

Answer (D) is correct. *(CPA, adapted)*
REQUIRED: The current cost of the year-end inventory.
DISCUSSION: SFAS 89 states that the current cost amounts of inventory should be measured at current cost or lower recoverable amount at the measurement date. At December 31, the current cost per unit is $71. Because 9,000 units are in the ending inventory (8,000 BI + 31,000 units purchased – 30,000 units sold), the current cost of the ending inventory is $639,000 (9,000 units × $71).
Answer (A) is incorrect because $576,000 results from applying the average of current cost from the beginning- and end-of-year costs. Answer (B) is incorrect because $585,000 results from multiplying ending inventory times $65 (the average purchase price for the year). Answer (C) is incorrect because $630,000 is the cost of purchases during the fourth quarter.

15. In Niner's voluntary supplementary information restated into current cost, the cost of goods sold for the year is

A. $1,920,000
B. $1,944,000
C. $2,100,000
D. $2,130,000

Answer (A) is correct. *(CPA, adapted)*
REQUIRED: The cost of goods sold restated into current cost.
DISCUSSION: To restate cost of goods sold into current cost, the number of units sold (30,000) is multiplied by the average current cost per unit. The average current cost per unit is $64 [($57 + $71) ÷ 2]. The current cost of goods sold is therefore $1,920,000 (30,000 units × $64).
Answer (B) is incorrect because $1,944,000 results from calculating cost of goods sold using an average cost of $64.80. Answer (C) is incorrect because $2,100,000 results from calculating cost of goods sold using an average cost of $70 (the cost per unit during the fourth quarter). Answer (D) is incorrect because $2,130,000 results from using an average current cost of $71 (the current cost at December 31).

16. Details of Edgar Corp.'s plant assets at December 31, year 3 are as follows:

Year Acquired	Percentage Depreciated	Historical Cost	Estimated Current Cost
1	30	$200,000	$280,000
2	20	60,000	76,000
3	10	80,000	88,000

Edgar uses straight-line depreciation at 10% per annum. A full year's depreciation is charged in the year of acquisition. There were no disposals of plant assets. In Edgar's voluntary supplementary information restated into current cost, the net current cost (after accumulated depreciation) of the plant assets at December 31, year 3 should be

A. $364,000
B. $336,000
C. $260,000
D. $232,000

Answer (B) is correct. *(CPA, adapted)*
REQUIRED: The net current cost of the plant assets after accumulated depreciation.
DISCUSSION: The net current cost of plant assets is equal to the estimated current cost of the assets minus the depreciation to date. Depreciation is based on the average current cost of an asset's service potential or lower recoverable amount during the period of use. The net current cost calculated below is thus equal to $336,000.

Year Acquired	Current Cost	Depreciation	Current Cost Depreciation
1	$280,000	30%	$ 84,000
2	76,000	20%	15,200
3	88,000	10%	8,800
	$444,000		$108,000

$444,000 – $108,000 = $336,000

Answer (A) is incorrect because depreciation incorrectly calculated using historical cost for depreciation [($200,000 × 30%) + ($60,000 × 20%) + ($80,000 × 10%)] is deducted from current cost ($444,000 – $80,000). Answer (C) is incorrect because depreciation incorrectly calculated using historical cost for depreciation is deducted from the historical cost ($340,000 – $80,000). Answer (D) is incorrect because depreciation correctly calculated using current cost ($108,000) is incorrectly deducted from the historical cost ($340,000 – $108,000).

20.3 Constant Purchasing Power

17. In its financial statements, Monster Co. discloses supplemental information on the effects of changing prices in accordance with SFAS 89, *Financial Reporting and Changing Prices.* Monster computed the increase in current cost of inventory as follows:

Increase in current cost (nominal dollars)	$30,000
Increase in current cost (constant dollars)	$24,000

What amount should Monster disclose as the inflation component of the increase in current cost of inventories?

A. $6,000

B. $24,000

C. $30,000

D. $54,000

Answer (A) is correct. *(CPA, adapted)*

REQUIRED: The inflation component of the increase in current cost of inventories.

DISCUSSION: If supplemental information on the effects of changing prices is presented in accordance with SFAS 89, the change in current cost amounts of inventory and property, plant, and equipment is reported both before and after eliminating the effects of general inflation. The inflation component of the increase in current cost (the change attributable to general price-level changes) is the difference between the nominal dollar and constant dollar measures, or $6,000 ($30,000 – $24,000).

Answer (B) is incorrect because $24,000 is the increase in current cost stated in constant dollars. Answer (C) is incorrect because $30,000 is the increase in current cost stated in nominal dollars. Answer (D) is incorrect because $54,000 is the sum of the increase in current cost stated in constant dollars plus the increase in current cost stated in nominal dollars.

18. A method of accounting based on measures of historical prices in dollars, each of which has the same general purchasing power, is

A. Current cost-constant purchasing power accounting.

B. Current cost-nominal dollar accounting.

C. Historical cost-constant purchasing power accounting.

D. Historical cost-nominal dollar accounting.

Answer (C) is correct. *(CPA, adapted)*

REQUIRED: The method of accounting based on measures of historical prices in dollars, each of which has the same general purchasing power.

DISCUSSION: In historical cost-constant purchasing power accounting, the historical cost principle is retained, but the unit of measure is restated to reflect changes in the general purchasing power of the dollar.

Answer (A) is incorrect because current cost accounting is based on measures of current cost or lower recoverable amount. Answer (B) is incorrect because current cost accounting is based on measures of current cost or lower recoverable amount and nominal dollar accounting is based on measures of dollars unadjusted for in general purchasing power. Answer (D) is incorrect because nominal dollar accounting is based on measures of dollars unadjusted for changes in general purchasing power.

19. During a period of inflation in which an asset account remains constant, which of the following occurs?

A. A purchasing power gain, if the item is a monetary asset.

B. A purchasing power gain, if the item is a nonmonetary asset.

C. A purchasing power loss, if the item is a monetary asset.

D. A purchasing power loss, if the item is a nonmonetary asset.

Answer (C) is correct. *(CPA, adapted)*

REQUIRED: The effect of an asset account's remaining constant during a period of inflation.

DISCUSSION: A monetary asset is "money or a claim to receive a sum of money the amount of which is fixed or determinable without reference to future prices of specific goods or services" (SFAS 89). A purchasing power gain or loss is determined by restating in units of constant purchasing power the opening and closing balances of, and transactions in, a monetary item. If the balance of a monetary asset has remained constant in nominal dollars despite a decline in the general purchasing power of money, the ending balance will reflect less purchasing power than the beginning balance, that is, a purchasing power loss.

20. When computing purchasing power gain or loss on net monetary items, which of the following accounts is classified as nonmonetary?

A. Accumulated depreciation of equipment.

B. Advances to unconsolidated subsidiaries.

C. Allowance for doubtful accounts.

D. Unamortized premium on bonds payable.

Answer (A) is correct. *(CPA, adapted)*

REQUIRED: The item classified as nonmonetary in historical cost-constant purchasing power accounting.

DISCUSSION: A monetary asset is either money or a claim to receive a sum of money the amount of which is fixed or determinable without reference to future prices of specific goods or services. A monetary liability is an obligation to pay a sum of money the amount of which is fixed or determinable without reference to future prices of specific goods and services. Equipment and the related accumulated depreciation account are an asset and a contra asset, respectively, the value of which will change in relationship to future prices of specific goods and services. Hence, accumulated depreciation is a nonmonetary item.

21. When computing information on a historical cost-constant purchasing power basis, which of the following is classified as nonmonetary?

A. Cash surrender value of life insurance.

B. Long-term receivables.

C. Allowance for doubtful accounts.

D. Inventories, other than inventories used on contracts.

Answer (D) is correct. *(CPA, adapted)*

REQUIRED: The item classified as nonmonetary on a historical cost-constant purchasing power basis.

DISCUSSION: Nonmonetary assets include goods held primarily for resale or assets held primarily for direct use in providing services to the enterprise. SFAS 89 classifies inventories as nonmonetary, with the exception of inventories used on contracts. They are effectively rights to receive fixed sums of money if the future cash receipts on the contracts will not vary with future changes in specific prices.

Answer (A) is incorrect because SFAS 89 specifically classifies this as a monetary item. Answer (B) is incorrect because SFAS 89 specifically classifies this as a monetary item. Answer (C) is incorrect because SFAS 89 specifically classifies this as a monetary item.

22. In the context of general price-level adjustments, which of the following is a nonmonetary item?

A. Receivables under capitalized leases.

B. Obligations under capitalized leases.

C. Goodwill.

D. Unamortized discount on bonds payable.

Answer (C) is correct. *(CPA, adapted)*

REQUIRED: The nonmonetary item in the context of general price-level adjustments.

DISCUSSION: SFAS 89 specifically states that nonmonetary items include residual rights such as goodwill and equity interests.

Answer (A) is incorrect because it involves a fixed dollar amount that will not vary with fluctuations in the future prices of specific goods or services. Answer (B) is incorrect because it involves a fixed dollar amount that will not vary with fluctuations in the future prices of specific goods or services. Answer (D) is incorrect because it involves a fixed dollar amount that will not vary with fluctuations in the future prices of specific goods or services.

23. When computing information on the historical cost-constant purchasing power basis, which of the following is classified as monetary?

A. Equity investment in unconsolidated subsidiaries.

B. Obligations under warranties.

C. Unamortized discount on bonds payable.

D. Deferred investment tax credits.

Answer (C) is correct. *(CPA, adapted)*

REQUIRED: The item treated as monetary in historical cost-constant purchasing power accounting.

DISCUSSION: SFAS 89 defines a monetary item as one that is fixed in amount by contract or otherwise. Because an unamortized discount on bonds payable is inseparable from the debt (a monetary item) to which it relates, the discount is a monetary item.

24. All of the following are monetary liabilities except

A. Bonds payable that are due in 2002.

B. Accounts payable.

C. Unearned subscription revenue.

D. A note payable due in 6 months.

Answer (C) is correct. *(CMA, adapted)*

REQUIRED: The item that is not a monetary liability.

DISCUSSION: Monetary liabilities are obligations to pay sums of money that are fixed or determinable without reference to future prices of specific goods or services. Unearned subscription revenue is not a monetary liability because it is deferred revenue, which involves an obligation to furnish goods or services in the future that may vary in cost (price).

Answer (A) is incorrect because bonds payable that are due in 2002 are payable in a fixed amount. Answer (B) is incorrect because accounts payable are payable in a fixed amount. Answer (D) is incorrect because a note payable due in 6 months is payable in a fixed amount.

25. The following assets were among those that appeared on Astarte Co.'s books at the end of the year:

Demand bank deposits	$1,300,000
Net long-term receivables	800,000
Patents and trademarks	300,000

In preparing constant dollar financial statements, how much should Astarte classify as monetary assets?

A. $2,400,000

B. $2,100,000

C. $1,600,000

D. $1,300,000

Answer (B) is correct. *(CPA, adapted)*

REQUIRED: The amount that should be classified as monetary assets.

DISCUSSION: Monetary assets are either cash or a claim to receive a sum of cash the amount of which is fixed or determinable without reference to future prices of specific goods or services. The value of nonmonetary assets will change in relationship to future prices of specific goods and services. The demand bank deposits of $1,300,000 and the long-term receivables of $800,000 meet the criteria for monetary assets. The patents and trademarks satisfy the definition of nonmonetary assets. Thus, Astarte should classify $2,100,000 ($1,300,000 + $800,000) as monetary assets.

Answer (A) is incorrect because $2,400,000 results from including the patents and trademarks as monetary assets. Answer (C) is incorrect because $1,600,000 results from not including the net long-term receivables and including the patents and trademarks as monetary assets. Answer (D) is incorrect because $1,300,000 results from not including the net long-term receivables as a monetary asset.

26. The following schedule lists the average Consumer Price Index for All Urban Consumers of the indicated year:

Year 1	100
Year 2	125
Year 3	150

Carl Corporation's plant and equipment data at December 31, year 3 follow:

Year Acquired	Percentage Depreciated	Historical Cost
1	30	$30,000
2	20	20,000
3	10	10,000
		$60,000

Depreciation is calculated at 10% per annum, straight-line. A full year's depreciation is charged in the year of acquisition. No disposals occurred in year 3. What amount of depreciation expense should be included in the income statement adjusted for general inflation (historical cost-constant purchasing power accounting)?

A. $6,000

B. $7,200

C. $7,900

D. $9,000

Answer (C) is correct. *(CPA, adapted)*

REQUIRED: The amount of depreciation expense after adjustment for general inflation on the historical cost-constant purchasing power basis.

DISCUSSION: The historical cost of each asset must be restated in terms of constant purchasing power. This adjustment is achieved by multiplying each asset's historical cost by a fraction with a numerator equal to the current consumer price index and a denominator equal to the price index for the year of acquisition. As shown below, the total constant purchasing power cost of the plant and equipment is $79,000. Given straight-line depreciation at 10% per year, the historical cost-constant purchasing power depreciation expense is $7,900.

Year 1 (150 ÷ 100) × $30,000 =	$45,000
Year 2 (150 ÷ 125) × $20,000 =	24,000
Year 3 (150 ÷ 150) × $10,000 =	10,000
Constant purchasing power cost	$79,000
	× 10%
Constant purchasing power depreciation	$ 7,900

Answer (A) is incorrect because the historical cost without any adjustments for general inflation is used to calculate depreciation expense ($60,000 × 10%). Answer (B) is incorrect because the plant and equipment accounts are adjusted using the year 2 average CPI [$60,000 × (150 ÷ 125) × 10%]. Answer (D) is incorrect because the plant and equipment accounts are adjusted using the year 3 average CPI [$60,000 × (150 ÷ 100) × 10%].

27. Rigel Corp. purchased a machine in year 1 when the average Consumer Price Index (CPI) was 180. The average CPI was 190 for year 2 and 200 for year 3. Rigel prepares supplementary constant dollar statements (adjusted for changing prices). Depreciation on this machine is $200,000 a year. In Rigel's supplementary constant purchasing power statements for year 3, the amount of depreciation expense should be stated as

A. $180,000

B. $190,000

C. $210,526

D. $222,222

Answer (D) is correct. *(CPA, adapted)*

REQUIRED: The amount of depreciation expense in the supplementary constant purchasing power statement.

DISCUSSION: Given that the machine was purchased when the CPI was 180 and the CPI for year 3 is 200, the adjustment to depreciation for the change in the general price level involves multiplying the historical cost depreciation of $200,000 by a fraction with a numerator equal to the year 3 CPI and a denominator equal to the year 1 CPI (200 ÷ 180). Rigel's price-level-adjusted depreciation expense is therefore $222,222.

Answer (A) is incorrect because the year 1 index is incorrectly used in the numerator, and the year 3 index is incorrectly used in the denominator [(180 ÷ 200) × $200,000]. Answer (B) is incorrect because the year 2 CPI is incorrectly used in the numerator, and the year 3 CPI is incorrectly used in the denominator [(190 ÷ 200) × $200,000]. Answer (C) is incorrect because the year 2 CPI is incorrectly used in the denominator [(200 ÷ 190) × $200,000].

28. The following data summarize a company's fixed asset acquisitions:

Year	Cost of Acquisitions	Price Index
1	$5,000	80
11	5,000	150
16	5,000	200

The total of these assets in constant purchasing power at the end of year 16 is

A. $24,167

B. $17,500

C. $10,750

D. $10,000

Answer (A) is correct. *(CIA, adapted)*

REQUIRED: The total fixed assets in constant purchasing power at the end of the current period.

DISCUSSION: The historical cost of each asset must be restated in terms of constant purchasing power. This adjustment is achieved by multiplying each asset's historical cost by a fraction with a numerator equal to the current consumer price index and a denominator equal to the price index for the year of acquisition. The year 1 acquisition should be valued at $12,500 [(200 ÷ 80) × $5,000], the year 11 acquisition at $6,667 [(200 ÷ 150) × $5,000], and the year 16 acquisition at $5,000 [(200 ÷ 200) × $5,000]. The total in constant purchasing power is $24,167 ($12,500 + $6,667 + $5,000).

Answer (B) is incorrect because it omits the purchasing power for the assets purchased in year 11. Answer (C) is incorrect because it reverses the fraction by which the assets' historical costs must be multiplied. Answer (D) is incorrect because it is the sum of the historical cost of two of the acquisition years' purchases.

29. Clark Company was formed on January 1, year 1. Selected balances from the historical cost balance sheet at December 31, year 2 follow:

Land (purchased in year 1)	$120,000
Investment in nonconvertible bonds (purchased in year 1, and expected to be held to maturity)	60,000
Long-term debt	80,000

The average Consumer Price Index was 100 for year 1 and 110 for year 2. In a supplementary constant purchasing power balance sheet (adjusted for changing prices) at December 31, year 2, these selected account balances should be shown at

	Land	Investment	Long-term Debt
A.	$120,000	$60,000	$88,000
B.	$120,000	$66,000	$88,000
C.	$132,000	$60,000	$80,000
D.	$132,000	$66,000	$80,000

Answer (C) is correct. *(CPA, adapted)*

REQUIRED: The amounts at which selected account balances should be shown in a supplementary constant purchasing power balance sheet.

DISCUSSION: Monetary items by their nature are already stated in terms of constant purchasing power. Nonmonetary items, on the other hand, require restatement. Monetary items are those that involve claims or obligations that are fixed in monetary terms. Nonmonetary items are those the valuations of which will change as the general price level fluctuates. The investment in nonconvertible bonds and the long-term debt are fixed claims and obligations. Accordingly, only the land should be restated in terms of constant purchasing power. The $120,000 historical cost is multiplied by a fraction with a numerator equal to the year 2 CPI of 110 and a denominator equal to the year 1 CPI of 100. Land should therefore appear in the supplementary constant purchasing power balance sheet at $132,000 ($120,000 × 110 ÷ 100), whereas the investment in nonconvertible bonds and the long-term debt should be recorded at their face values of $60,000 and $80,000, respectively.

Answer (A) is incorrect because long-term debt is a monetary item and should not be adjusted. Also, land is a nonmonetary account that should be adjusted. Answer (B) is incorrect because long-term debt is a monetary item and should not be adjusted. Land is a nonmonetary account that should be adjusted, and the investment in nonconvertible bonds is a monetary account and should not be adjusted. Answer (D) is incorrect because the investment in nonconvertible bonds is a monetary account and should not be adjusted.

30. A corporation has gathered the following data in order to compute the purchasing power gain or loss to be included in its supplementary information for the year ended December 31, year 2:

	Amount in Nominal Dollars	
	December 31, year 1	December 31, year 2
Net monetary assets	$800,000	$943,000

	Index Number
Consumer Price Index at December 31, yr 1	200
Consumer Price Index at December 31, yr 2	230
Average Consumer Price Index for year 2	220

The purchasing power gain or loss on net monetary items (expressed in average-for-the-year dollars for year 2) should be reported at what amount for the year ended December 31, year 2?

A. $121,000 purchasing power loss.

B. $121,000 purchasing power gain.

C. $126,500 purchasing power loss.

D. $126,500 purchasing power gain.

Answer (A) is correct. *(CIA, adapted)*

REQUIRED: The amount to be reported as purchasing power gain or loss on net monetary items.

DISCUSSION: Purchasing power gain or loss expressed in average constant monetary units equals the beginning net monetary position restated to average constant monetary units, plus the actual change in the net monetary position during the year expressed in average constant monetary units, minus the ending net monetary position restated to average constant monetary units. The restatement to average constant monetary units requires multiplying the nominal dollar amount by a fraction with a numerator equal to the average CPI (220) and the denominator equal to the CPI at the date of the recording of the net monetary assets. For December 31, year 1, the denominator is 200. For the $943,000 December 31, year 2 balance, the denominator is 230. For the $143,000 difference between the beginning and ending balances, the denominator is 220, based on the assumption this change occurred evenly throughout the year. As indicated below, a purchasing power loss (inflation is unfavorable to holders of monetary assets) of $121,000 results.

Nominal Dollars	Adjustment Fraction	Constant Dollars
$800,000	220 ÷ 200	$ 880,000
+143,000	220 ÷ 220	+143,000
−943,000	220 ÷ 230	−902,000
Purchasing power loss		$ 121,000

31. Shipp Corporation prepared the following data needed to compute the purchasing power gain or loss on net monetary items for inclusion in its supplementary information for the year ended December 31, year 2:

	Amount in Nominal Dollars	
	December 31, year 1	December 31, year 2
Monetary assets	$ 600,000	$1,000,000
Monetary liabilities	1,566,000	2,449,000
Net monetary liabilities	966,000	1,449,000
Assumed Consumer Price Index numbers:		
At December 31, yr 1	210	
At December 31, yr 2	230	
Average for year 2	220	

Shipp's purchasing power gain or loss (expressed in average year 2 constant purchasing power) on net monetary items for the year ended December 31, year 2 should be

A. $109,000 gain.

B. $109,000 loss.

C. $111,000 gain.

D. $111,000 loss.

Answer (A) is correct. *(CPA, adapted)*

REQUIRED: The purchasing power gain or loss on net monetary items expressed in average constant purchasing power.

DISCUSSION: Purchasing power gain or loss expressed in average constant monetary units equals the beginning net monetary position restated to average constant monetary units, plus the actual change in the net monetary position during the year, minus the ending net monetary position restated to average constant monetary units. The actual changes are assumed to be in average dollars for the year. The beginning balance is the year 1 net liability of $966,000. The ending balance is the year 2 net liability of $1,449,000. The change is $483,000 ($1,449,000 – $966,000). Restatement requires multiplying by a fraction with a numerator equal to the average CPI (220). The denominator is either the CPI at the beginning of the year (210) or the end of the year (230), as appropriate. Shipp's purchasing power gain (inflation favors debtors) is therefore $109,000.

	Nominal $$	Index		Avg. Year 2 Constant $$
12/31/year 1	$ 966,000	× (220 ÷ 210)	=	$1,012,000
Year 2 actual increase	483,000			483,000
				$1,495,000
12/31/year 2	1,449,000	× (220 ÷ 230)	=	(1,386,000)
Purchasing power gain				$ 109,000

Answer (B) is incorrect because Shipp has a purchasing power gain. Answer (C) is incorrect because $111,000 is the loss that results from switching the denominators of the fractions used to adjust the beginning and ending balances. Answer (D) is incorrect because $111,000 is the loss that results from switching the denominators of the fractions used to adjust the beginning and ending balances.

Questions 32 and 33 are based on the following information. Corporate records disclose the information below.

	Historical Cost	Current Replacement Cost
Inventory (as of 1/1)	$100,000	$120,000
Inventory (as of 12/31)	120,000	180,000
Cost of sales (as of date of sale)	200,000	220,000
Purchases (as of date of purchase)	220,000	220,000

The corporation follows the LIFO method of inventory. The beginning inventory was all acquired when the general price-level index was 100 (1/1 of last year). The general price-level index at various dates was as follows:

1/1:	120
12/31:	150
This year's average:	125

Assume that sales and purchases were made evenly throughout the year (that is, use this year's average index if any adjustments of those items are necessary).

32. What is the difference between ending inventory at historical cost adjusted for inflation and at replacement cost?

A. $0

B. $30,000

C. $60,000

D. $6,000

Answer (D) is correct. *(CIA, adapted)*

REQUIRED: The difference between ending inventory at historical cost adjusted for inflation and at replacement cost.

DISCUSSION: The ending inventory at replacement cost is given as $180,000. The ending LIFO inventory at historical cost is given as $120,000, including a $100,000 component acquired when the price-level index was 100 and a $20,000 component acquired when the average index was 125. To adjust for inflation, the $100,000 component should be multiplied by the ratio of the 12/31 index (150) divided by last year's 1/1 index (100). The product is $150,000. The $20,000 component was acquired evenly throughout this year and should be multiplied by the ratio of the 12/31 index (150) divided by the average index for this year (125), giving a product of $24,000. The price-level-adjusted ending inventory value is thus $174,000 ($150,000 + $24,000), which is $6,000 less than replacement cost.

Answer (A) is incorrect because the ending inventory adjusted for inflation {[$100,000 × (150 ÷ 100)] + [$20,000 × (150 ÷ 125)]} is less than the current replacement cost ($180,000). Answer (B) is incorrect because the ending inventory balance is used and is incorrectly adjusted with the ending index (150) divided by the beginning index (120) [$120,000 × (150 ÷ 120)]. Answer (C) is incorrect because historical cost of inventory is not adjusted for inflation.

33. The cost of sales at historical cost adjusted for inflation is

A. $200,000

B. $220,000

C. $240,000

D. $264,000

Answer (C) is correct. *(CIA, adapted)*

REQUIRED: The cost of sales at historical cost adjusted for inflation.

DISCUSSION: Purchases for this year exceeded sales. Given a LIFO flow assumption, sales are deemed to have come entirely from purchases. Accordingly, the adjustment for inflation should use the average index for this year. The $200,000 historical cost of sales should be multiplied by the ratio of the 12/31 price-level index (150) divided by the average index for this year (125), giving an adjusted cost of sales of $240,000.

Answer (A) is incorrect because $200,000 is not adjusted for inflation. Answer (B) is incorrect because $220,000 is the cost of sales at current replacement cost. Answer (D) is incorrect because $264,000 is equal to the purchases adjusted by the beginning index (120) divided by last year's beginning index (100).

STUDY UNIT TWENTY-ONE
FINANCIAL STATEMENT DISCLOSURES

Entities are required to disclose their **significant accounting policies**. The disclosure includes those principles and methods that involve a selection from existing acceptable methods, those methods peculiar to the industry in which the entity operates, and any unusual or innovative applications. The summary of accounting policies preferably is included as a separate section immediately preceding the notes or as the initial note.

Entities are required to disclose if they are in the **development stage**. An enterprise is considered to be in the development stage if planned principal operations have not commenced or if these operations have not yet begun to generate significant revenue. Development stage enterprise financial statements ordinarily are presented in conformity with GAAP similar to those presented by more mature enterprises. However, while in the development stage, an entity is also required to disclose (1) the nature of its development stage activities and (2) certain additional information accumulated since inception (cumulative net losses, cumulative revenue and expense, cumulative cash flows, and information about stock issuances).

Entities are required to disclose material **related party transactions** other than compensation arrangements, expense allowances, and other similar items occurring in the ordinary course of business. Related party disclosures include (1) the nature of the relationship involved, (2) a description of each transaction for each period for which an income statement is presented, (3) the dollar amount of each transaction for each period for which an income statement is presented, (4) related party receivables and payables for each balance sheet, and (5) certain tax information.

Under **SFAS 131**, *Disclosures about Segments of an Enterprise and Related Information*, public business entities are required to disclose information about the different types of business activities in which they engage and the different economic environments in which they operate. The disclosures should be made in annual financial statements and in interim financial reports issued to shareholders. These disclosures include certain information about operating segments and related information about products and services, countries in which the enterprise earns revenues and holds assets, and major customers. This information should reflect management's approach to organizing segments within the enterprise for the purposes of making operating decisions and assessing performance. Consistent with what the FASB calls the management approach, the segment information disclosed ordinarily shall be on the same basis as that used internally by the chief operating decision maker.

Operating segments are components of a business enterprise (1) that engage in business activities (including intersegment activities) from which they may earn revenues and incur expenses, and (2) for which discrete financial information is available that is evaluated regularly by the chief operating decision maker in deciding how to allocate resources and in assessing performance. An enterprise shall report information separately for each operating segment for which a **materiality threshold** is reached: (1) The reported revenue, including both sales to external customers and intersegment sales or transfers, is at least 10% of the combined revenue, external and internal, of all operating segments; (2) the absolute amount of the reported profit or loss is at least 10% of the greater, in absolute terms, of (a) the combined reported profit of all operating segments that did not report a loss or (b) the combined reported loss of all operating segments that reported a loss; or (3) the assets are at least 10% of the combined assets of all operating segments. However, an operating segment not meeting one of these criteria may be treated as reportable, and may be separately disclosed, if management believes that information about that segment would be useful. If the **total external revenue** of the enterprise's operating segments is **less than 75%** of total consolidated revenue, additional operating segments must be treated as reportable even if they do not meet the specified criteria. The enterprise must report combined information for nonreportable operating segments and other business activities.

An enterprise is required to disclose for **each period for which an income statement is presented** (1) the factors it used to identify its reportable segments; (2) the types of products and services from which each reportable segment derives its revenues; (3) information about each segment's operating profit or loss and total assets, and the basis of measurement of these amounts; and (4) reconciliations of the totals of segment revenues, reported profit or loss, assets, and other significant items to corresponding amounts in the entity's general-purpose financial statements. However, **reconciliations** of balance sheet items are required only for years in which a balance sheet is presented. Moreover, an enterprise is not required to disclose information that is not prepared for internal use if reporting it would be impracticable.

SOP 94-6, *Disclosure of Certain Significant Risks and Uncertainties*, requires disclosure of risks and uncertainties that could significantly affect reported amounts in the near term. One set of nonquantified disclosures relates to the **nature of operations**: major products or services, principal markets, industries in which the entity operates and the relative importance of each, and the basis for determining the relative importance. A second type of disclosure concerns the **use of estimates** in the preparation of financial statements. Conformity with GAAP requires management to use numerous estimates. A third category concerns certain **significant estimates.** Disclosure of an estimate used to value assets, liabilities, or contingencies is required when the estimate is subject to a **reasonable possibility** of change in the near term and the effect of the change will be material. If an estimate is of a **loss contingency**, the disclosure should include the estimated range of loss or a statement that an estimate cannot be made. A fourth set of disclosures concerns **current vulnerability due to concentrations**, for example, when entities fail to diversify. Disclosure is necessary if management knows prior to issuance of the statements that the concentration exists at the balance sheet date, it makes the entity vulnerable to a near-term **severe impact**, and such impact is at least **reasonably possible** in the near term. Disclosable concentrations include the following: volume of business with a given customer, supplier, lender, grantor, or contributor; revenue from given products, services, or fund-raising events; the available suppliers of materials, labor, services, or rights (e.g., licenses) used in operations; and the market or geographic area where the entity operates.

SFAS 47, *Disclosure of Long-Term Obligations*, requires disclosure of commitments under **unconditional purchase obligations** associated with suppliers. Such obligations are commitments to transfer funds in the future for fixed or minimum amounts of goods or services at fixed or minimum prices. SFAS 47 applies to an unconditional purchase obligation that (1) was negotiated as part of the financing arrangement for facilities that will provide contracted goods or services, (2) has a remaining term of more than 1 year, and (3) is either noncancelable or cancelable only under terms that make continuation or replacement (but not cancelation) of the agreement reasonably assured. A purchase obligation cancelable upon the payment of a nominal penalty is not unconditional. **Disclosure** of the following is required for **recorded obligations** for each of the 5 years following the date of the latest balance sheet: (1) the aggregate payments for unconditional purchase obligations, and (2) the aggregate amount of maturities and sinking-fund requirements for all long-term borrowings. If an unconditional purchase obligation is **not recorded**, the **disclosures** required are: (1) the nature and term of the obligation; (2) its variable components; (3) the amounts purchased under the obligation for each period; and (4) the amount of the fixed and determinable portion of the obligation at the latest balance sheet date and, if determinable, for each of the 5 succeeding fiscal years.

AU 560, *Subsequent Events*, concerns certain material events or transactions that occur after the balance sheet date and prior to the issuance of the financial statements. These events and transactions require adjustment of, or disclosure in, the statements. One type of subsequent event provides additional evidence about **conditions at the date of the balance sheet**. It affects the estimates inherent in statement preparation. An example is a loss on an uncollectible receivable as a result of a customer's bankruptcy. The financial statements should be **adjusted** for any resulting changes in estimates. Subsequent events affecting the realization of assets (such as receivables and inventories) or the settlement of estimated liabilities ordinarily require **adjustment**. They usually reflect the resolution of conditions that existed over a relatively long period. A second type of subsequent event provides evidence about **conditions that did not exist at the date of the balance sheet**. Some of these events require disclosure but not adjustment. Examples of subsequent events requiring disclosure only are (1) sale of a bond or capital stock issue, (2) purchase of a business, (3) settlement of litigation when the precipitating event occurred after the balance sheet date, (4) loss of plant or inventories as a result of fire or flood, and (5) losses on receivables resulting from conditions (e.g., a customer's major casualty) arising after the balance sheet date. Some events of the second type may be so significant that the most appropriate disclosure is to supplement the historical statements with **pro forma financial data**.

QUESTIONS

21.1 Disclosure of Accounting Policies

1. The specific accounting policies and methods considered to be appropriate by management and used for reporting purposes

A. Should be disclosed parenthetically in the tabular portion of the financial statements.

B. Should be disclosed in a separate summary of significant accounting policies preceding the notes to the financial statements or in the initial note to the financial statements.

C. Should be disclosed in management's discussion of operations.

D. Need not be disclosed unless they are at variance with generally accepted accounting principles.

Answer (B) is correct. *(CMA, adapted)*

REQUIRED: The most appropriate statement concerning disclosure of accounting policies.

DISCUSSION: APB 22 requires that all significant accounting policies of a reporting entity be disclosed as an integral part of its financial statements. APB 22 expresses a preference for including a summary of accounting policies in a separate section preceding the notes or in the initial note. Disclosure should encompass those principles and methods that involve a selection from existing acceptable alternatives, those methods peculiar to the industry in which the entity operates, and any unusual or innovative applications of GAAP.

Answer (A) is incorrect because necessary disclosures should precede the notes to the financial statements or appear in the initial note. Answer (C) is incorrect because necessary disclosures should precede the notes to the financial statements or appear in the initial note. Answer (D) is incorrect because accounting policies and methods must be disclosed.

2. When it is appropriate to issue one of the basic financial statements without the others, disclosure of the pertinent accounting policies is

A. Not required.

B. Not required if a complete set of financial statements has not or will not be issued separately.

C. Required only for an annual financial statement.

D. Usually required.

Answer (D) is correct. *(Publisher)*

REQUIRED: The most appropriate statement about disclosure of accounting policies when only one financial statement is issued.

DISCUSSION: When it is appropriate to issue one or more of the basic financial statements without the others, purporting to present fairly the information given in accordance with GAAP, the statements should also include disclosure of the pertinent accounting policies.

Answer (A) is incorrect because pertinent accounting policies must be disclosed regardless of whether a complete set of statements is issued separately or whether the statement is for an annual or interim period. Answer (B) is incorrect because pertinent accounting policies must be disclosed regardless of whether a complete set of statements is issued separately or whether the statement is for an annual or interim period. Answer (C) is incorrect because pertinent accounting policies must be disclosed regardless of whether a complete set of statements is issued separately or whether the statement is for an annual or interim period.

3. Disclosure of accounting policies is not necessary when

A. Selection of an accounting principle or method has been made from existing acceptable alternatives.

B. The accounting principles and methods used by an entity are peculiar to the entity's industry, provided that such principles and methods are predominantly followed in that industry.

C. Unaudited financial statements are issued as of a date between annual reporting dates and the reporting entity has not changed its accounting policies since the end of its preceding fiscal year.

D. An entity makes unusual or innovative applications of GAAP.

Answer (C) is correct. *(Publisher)*

REQUIRED: The situation in which disclosure of accounting policies is not necessary.

DISCUSSION: APB 22 does not require disclosure of accounting policies in unaudited interim financial statements when the reporting entity has not changed its policies since the end of the preceding fiscal year. Users of such interim statements will presumably consult the disclosure concerning significant accounting policies in the statements issued at the close of the preceding fiscal year.

4. Which of the following information should be disclosed in the summary of significant accounting policies?

A. Refinancing of debt subsequent to the balance sheet date.

B. Guarantees of indebtedness of others.

C. Criteria for determining which investments are treated as cash equivalents.

D. Adequacy of pension plan assets relative to vested benefits.

Answer (C) is correct. *(CPA, adapted)*

REQUIRED: The disclosure of the summary of significant accounting policies.

DISCUSSION: APB 22 requires that all significant accounting policies be disclosed as an integral part of the financial statements. SFAS 95 amended APB 22 to require disclosure of the policy for determining which investments are treated as cash equivalents.

Answer (A) is incorrect because the refinancing of debt subsequent to the balance sheet date is not an accounting policy but is an item disclosed in the notes. Answer (B) is incorrect because guarantees of the indebtedness of others is not an accounting policy but is an item disclosed in the notes. Answer (D) is incorrect because the adequacy of pension plan benefits is not an accounting policy but is an item disclosed in the notes.

5. The accounting profession has adopted various standards to be followed when reporting inventory in the financial statements. All of the following are required to be reported in the financial statements or disclosed in notes to the financial statements except for

A. Inventory detail, such as raw materials, work-in-process, and finished goods.

B. Significant financing agreements, such as product financing arrangements and pledging of inventories.

C. The method used in determining cost.

D. Unrealized profit on inventories.

Answer (D) is correct. *(CMA, adapted)*

REQUIRED: The item not a required disclosure about inventory.

DISCUSSION: APB 22 requires disclosure of accounting policies in a separate summary of significant policies or as the first note to the financial statements. The disclosure should specify accounting principles adopted and the method of applying those principles. Examples include inventory valuation methods; inventory details, such as the mix of finished goods, work-in-progress, and raw materials; methods used in determining costs; and any significant financing agreements, such as leases, related party transactions, product financing arrangements, firm purchase commitments, pledging of inventories, and involuntary liquidation of LIFO layers. Unrealized profit on inventories is not reported because the company usually has no assurance that the inventories will be sold.

Answer (A) is incorrect because inventory details should be disclosed in the notes. Answer (B) is incorrect because financing agreements should be disclosed in the notes. Answer (C) is incorrect because cost determinants should be disclosed in the notes.

6. Which of the following information should be included in Mariah Company's current-year summary of significant accounting policies?

A. Property, plant, and equipment is recorded at cost with depreciation computed principally by the straight-line method.

B. During the current year, the consulting services operating segment was sold.

C. Operating segment current-year sales are $2 million for the software segment, $4 million for the book production segment, and $6 million for the technical services segment.

D. Future common share dividends are expected to approximate 60% of earnings.

Answer (A) is correct. *(CPA, adapted)*

REQUIRED: The item properly disclosed in the summary of significant accounting policies.

DISCUSSION: APB 22 explicitly lists certain items as commonly required disclosures in a summary of significant accounting policies. These items include the basis of consolidation, depreciation methods, amortization of intangible assets, inventory pricing, recognition of profit on long-term construction-type contracts, and recognition of revenue from franchising and leasing operations. Hence, the summary of significant accounting policies should include information about property, plant, and equipment depreciated by the straight-line method.

Answer (B) is incorrect because the sale of an operating segment is a transaction, not an accounting principle. It is reflected in the discontinued operations section of the income statement. Answer (C) is incorrect because specific operating segment information does not constitute an accounting policy. An accounting policy is a specific principle or a method of applying it. Answer (D) is incorrect because future dividend policy is not an accounting policy.

7. Which of the following should be disclosed in the summary of significant accounting policies?

	Composition of Inventories	Maturity Dates of Long-Term Debt
A.	Yes	Yes
B.	Yes	No
C.	No	No
D.	No	Yes

Answer (C) is correct. *(CPA, adapted)*

REQUIRED: The item(s) properly disclosed in the summary of significant accounting policies.

DISCUSSION: APB 22 explicitly lists certain items as commonly required disclosures in a summary of significant accounting policies. These items include the basis of consolidation, depreciation methods, amortization of intangible assets, inventory pricing, recognition of profit on long-term construction-type contracts, and recognition of revenue from franchising and leasing operations. APB 22 also recognizes that financial statement disclosure of accounting policies should not duplicate details presented elsewhere in the financial statements. Details about the composition of inventories and the maturity dates of long-term debts are disclosed elsewhere in the financial statements. Hence, the summary of significant accounting policies should refer to these details but need not duplicate them.

8. APB 22, *Disclosure of Accounting Policies*, recommends that, when financial statements are issued, a statement identifying the accounting policies adopted by the reporting entity be presented as part of the financial statements. All of the following are required to be disclosed with respect to accounting policies except the

A. Depreciation methods used for plant assets.

B. Accounting for long-term construction contracts.

C. Estimated lives of depreciable assets.

D. Principles of consolidation.

Answer (C) is correct. *(CMA, adapted)*

REQUIRED: The item not a required disclosure by APB 22.

DISCUSSION: APB 22 requires disclosure of accounting policies in a separate summary of significant accounting policies or in the initial footnote to the financial statements. The disclosures should identify the principles followed and the methods of applying them that materially affect the statements. Moreover, the disclosures should encompass principles and methods involving a selection from acceptable alternatives, accounting principles peculiar to a particular industry, and innovative or unusual applications of GAAP. However, the disclosures should not repeat details presented elsewhere, e.g., the estimated lives of depreciable assets.

Answer (A) is incorrect because examples of required disclosures include depreciation and amortization methods. Answer (B) is incorrect because examples of required disclosures include means of accounting for long-term construction contracts. Answer (D) is incorrect because examples of required disclosures include basis of consolidation.

9. The summary of significant accounting policies should disclose the

A. Pro forma effect of retroactive application of an accounting change.

B. Basis of profit recognition on long-term construction contracts.

C. Adequacy of pension plan assets in relation to vested benefits.

D. Future minimum lease payments in the aggregate and for each of the 5 succeeding fiscal years.

Answer (B) is correct. *(CPA, adapted)*

REQUIRED: The item disclosed in the summary of significant accounting policies.

DISCUSSION: APB 22 explicitly lists certain items as commonly required disclosures in a summary of significant accounting policies. These items include the basis of consolidation, depreciation methods, amortization of intangible assets, inventory pricing, recognition of profit on long-term construction-type contracts, and recognition of revenue from franchising and leasing operations.

Answer (A) is incorrect because APB 20, *Accounting Changes*, states that the pro forma effect of retroactive application of an accounting change should be shown on the face of the income statement. Answer (C) is incorrect because the adequacy of pension plan assets in relation to vested benefits is not a disclosure required by SFAS 132, *Employers' Accounting for Pensions*. Answer (D) is incorrect because the future minimum lease payments in the aggregate and for each of the 5 succeeding fiscal years should be disclosed in the notes, but not in the summary of significant accounting policies.

10. A note must be included in the financial statements commenting on normal transactions concerning each of the following except

A. Assets acquired by lease.

B. Trade accounts receivable.

C. Pension plans.

D. Employee stock options.

Answer (B) is correct. *(CPA, adapted)*

REQUIRED: The subject not requiring a note commenting on normal transactions.

DISCUSSION: Trade accounts receivable that arise in the ordinary course of business are not specialized or unusual and accordingly do not require disclosure. In addition, no official pronouncement requires a note commenting on normal transactions in trade accounts receivable.

Answer (A) is incorrect because SFAS 13, *Accounting for Leases*, requires note disclosure of certain transactions involving assets acquired by lease. Answer (C) is incorrect because SFAS 132 requires note disclosure regarding certain transactions relating to pension plans. Answer (D) is incorrect because SFAS 123 requires note disclosure of data related to employee stock options.

21.2 Development Stage Enterprises

11. A statement of cash flows for a development stage enterprise

A. Is the same as that of an established operating enterprise and, in addition, shows cumulative amounts from the enterprise's inception.

B. Shows only cumulative amounts from the enterprise's inception.

C. Is the same as that of an established operating enterprise, but does not show cumulative amounts from the enterprise's inception.

D. Is not presented.

Answer (A) is correct. *(CPA, adapted)*

REQUIRED: The true statement about a statement of cash flows for a development stage enterprise.

DISCUSSION: Development stage enterprises must present financial statements in conformity with GAAP together with certain additional information accumulated since the enterprise's inception. Cumulative net losses must be disclosed in the equity section of the balance sheet, cumulative amounts of revenue and expense in the income statement, cumulative amounts of cash inflows and outflows in the statement of cash flows, and information about each issuance of stock in the statement of equity.

Answer (B) is incorrect because the statement of cash flows must also conform with GAAP applicable to established enterprises. Answer (C) is incorrect because the statement of cash flows must also show cumulative amounts from the enterprise's inception. Answer (D) is incorrect because a statement of cash flows is required as part of a full set of financial statements.

12. Current authoritative literature requires an enterprise to disclose that it had been in the development stage until the

A. Planned principal operations have commenced.

B. Planned principal operations have commenced to generate revenue.

C. Planned principal operations have commenced to generate significant revenue.

D. Second fiscal year in which an enterprise is no longer considered to be in the development stage.

Answer (D) is correct. *(Publisher)*

REQUIRED: The time when an enterprise no longer must disclose that it had been in a development stage.

DISCUSSION: During the development stage, an enterprise's financial statements should be identified as those of a development stage enterprise, the nature of the development stage activities should be disclosed, and certain additional information should be included in the financial statements. When the development stage has been completed, the financial statements for the first fiscal year thereafter must disclose that, in prior years, the enterprise had been in the development stage. No further disclosure is required. The development stage is considered to be complete when significant revenue is generated from the planned principal operations.

13. According to SFAS 7, *Accounting and Reporting by Development Stage Enterprises*, an enterprise is considered to be in the development stage if

A. 12 months of operations have not been completed.

B. Planned principal operations have commenced but have not yet begun to produce significant revenue.

C. The enterprise has not previously shown a profit from operations.

D. The enterprise has not obtained 50% of the initial planned activity level.

Answer (B) is correct. *(Publisher)*

REQUIRED: The statement that describes the development stage of an enterprise.

DISCUSSION: An enterprise is considered to be in the development stage if planned principal operations have not yet commenced or if they have not yet begun to generate significant revenue.

Answer (A) is incorrect because the development stage has no time limit. Answer (C) is incorrect because amounts of profit or loss do not define the development stage. Answer (D) is incorrect because the development stage is not defined by a level of planned activity.

14. Financial reporting by a development stage enterprise differs from financial reporting for an established operating enterprise in regard to note disclosures

A. Only.

B. And expense recognition principles only.

C. And revenue recognition principles only.

D. And revenue and expense recognition principles.

Answer (A) is correct. *(CPA, adapted)*

REQUIRED: The way in which financial reporting by a development stage enterprise differs from financial reporting for an established operating enterprise.

DISCUSSION: Development stage enterprises must present financial statements in conformity with GAAP together with certain additional information accumulated since the firm's inception. Cumulative net losses must be disclosed in the equity section of the balance sheet, cumulative amounts of revenue and expense in the income statement, cumulative amounts of cash inflows and outflows in the statement of cash flows, and information about each issuance of stock in the statement of equity.

15. Juris Corp. was a development stage enterprise from October 10, 2001 (inception) through December 31, 2002. The year ended December 31, 2003 was the first year in which Juris qualified as an established operating enterprise. The following are among the costs incurred by Juris:

	For the Period 10/10/01 – 12/31/02	For the Year Ended 12/31/03
Leasehold improvements, equipment, and furniture	$1,000,000	$ 300,000
Security deposits	60,000	30,000
Research and development	750,000	900,000
Laboratory operations	175,000	550,000
General and administrative	225,000	685,000
Depreciation	25,000	115,000
	$2,235,000	$2,580,000

From its inception through the period ended December 31, 2003, what is the total amount of costs incurred by Juris that should be charged to operations?

A. $3,425,000

B. $2,250,000

C. $1,775,000

D. $1,350,000

Answer (A) is correct. *(CPA, adapted)*

REQUIRED: The total amount of costs that a development stage enterprise should charge to operations.

DISCUSSION: Development stage enterprises must use the same GAAP as established operating enterprises. An established operating enterprise would have capitalized the entire $1,300,000 of leasehold improvements, equipment, and furniture, as well as the $90,000 of security deposits. Consequently, Juris Corp., a development stage enterprise, should also capitalize these costs. An established operating enterprise would have expensed the $1,650,000 of research and development costs, the $725,000 of laboratory operations costs, the $910,000 of general and administrative costs, and the $140,000 of depreciation. Juris Corp. should also expense these costs. The total to be expensed by Juris therefore equals $3,425,000 ($1,650,000 + $725,000 + $910,000 + $140,000).

Answer (B) is incorrect because $2,250,000 equals costs incurred in 2003 minus security deposits and leasehold improvements, equipment, and furniture. Answer (C) is incorrect because $1,775,000 excludes R&D costs. Answer (D) is incorrect because $1,350,000 equals costs incurred during the development stage, minus leasehold improvements, equipment, and furniture, plus 2003 depreciation.

21.3 Related Party Disclosures

16. SFAS 57 requires the disclosure of certain related party transactions. Which of the following is not a related party transaction?

A. The Eli Company borrowed money from the Peyton Company at the prevailing market rate of interest. Both companies are subsidiaries of the Arch Corporation.

B. The Kerwin Corporation established a profit-sharing trust fund administered by an independently owned bank located in the same community. The trustees invested part of the trust fund in Kerwin Corporation's outstanding bonds.

C. The Perry Company provided management services to its subsidiary without charge.

D. The Peace Company lent $25,000 to the son of the company's president at the prevailing market rate of interest.

Answer (B) is correct. *(Publisher)*

REQUIRED: The transaction that is not between related parties.

DISCUSSION: Related parties include

1. A parent and its subsidiaries.
2. Subsidiaries of a common parent.
3. An enterprise and employee trusts managed by or under the trusteeship of the enterprise's management.
4. An enterprise and its principal owners, management, or members of their immediate families.
5. Affiliates.
6. An enterprise and its equity-based investees.
7. An enterprise and any other entity if one party can significantly influence the other to the extent that one party may be prevented from fully pursuing its own interests.
8. Parties all of which can be significantly influenced by another party.

If a trust fund established to benefit employees is administered by an independent party (the bank), the investment of trust assets in the bonds of the reporting enterprise is not a transaction between related parties.

Answer (A) is incorrect because transactions between subsidiaries of a common parent are considered related party transactions even if they were consummated at arm's length and at prevailing market interest rates. Answer (C) is incorrect because transactions between a parent and subsidiary are considered related party transactions even if they are not recorded when they occur. Answer (D) is incorrect because a transaction between a reporting enterprise and a member of the immediate family of one of its policy makers is a related party transaction.

17. Related party transactions include transactions between the enterprise and

A. The principal owners, management, and any of their relatives.

B. Affiliates.

C. Trusts for the benefit of employees whether or not the trustee is independent of management.

D. Beneficial owners of at least 5% of the voting interests of the entity.

Answer (B) is correct. *(Publisher)*

REQUIRED: The parties to related party transactions.

DISCUSSION: According to SFAS 57, *Related Party Disclosures*, related party transactions include transactions between

1. A parent and its subsidiaries.
2. Subsidiaries of a common parent.
3. An enterprise and employee trusts managed by or under the trusteeship of the enterprise's management.
4. An enterprise and its principal owners, management, or members of their immediate families.
5. Affiliates.
6. An enterprise and its equity-based investees.
7. An enterprise and any other entity if one party can significantly influence the other to the extent that one party may be prevented from fully pursuing its own interests.
8. Parties all of which can be significantly influenced by another party.

Answer (A) is incorrect because only immediate family members of the principal owners and management are considered related parties. Answer (C) is incorrect because employee benefit trusts that are not managed by the entity are not related parties. Answer (D) is incorrect because only those owners of record or known beneficial owners of more than 10% of the voting interests of the entity are related parties.

18. Dex Co. has entered into a joint venture with an affiliate to secure access to additional inventory. Under the joint venture agreement, Dex will purchase the output of the venture at prices negotiated on an arm's-length basis. Which of the following is(are) required to be disclosed about the related party transaction?

I. The amount due to the affiliate at the balance sheet date.

II. The dollar amount of the purchases during the year.

A. I only.

B. II only.

C. Both I and II.

D. Neither I nor II.

Answer (C) is correct. *(CPA, adapted)*

REQUIRED: The disclosures for a related party transaction.

DISCUSSION: SFAS 57 requires disclosure of (1) the nature of the relationship involved; (2) a description of the transactions for each period an income statement is presented and such other information as is deemed necessary to an understanding of the effects of the transactions; (3) the dollar amounts of transactions for each period an income statement is presented and the effects of any change in the method of establishing their terms; (4) amounts due from or to related parties as of the date of each balance sheet, including the terms of settlement; and (5) certain tax information required by SFAS 109 if the enterprise is part of a group that files a consolidated tax return.

19. For purposes of SFAS 57, *Related Party Disclosures*, principal owners are

A. Parties that, directly or indirectly, through one or more intermediaries, control, are controlled by, or are under common control with an enterprise.

B. Owners of record or known beneficial owners of more than 10% of the voting interests of that enterprise.

C. Owners of record or known beneficial owners of more than 30% of the voting interests of that enterprise.

D. Persons who are responsible for achieving the objectives of the enterprise and who have the authority to establish policies and make decisions by which those objectives are pursued.

Answer (B) is correct. *(Publisher)*

REQUIRED: The definition of a principal owner for the purpose of disclosing related party transactions.

DISCUSSION: SFAS 57 defines principal owners as owners of record or known beneficial owners of more than 10% of the voting interests of the enterprise.

Answer (A) is incorrect because it states the definition of an affiliate. Answer (C) is incorrect because the threshold percentage of ownership is 10%, not 30%. Answer (D) is incorrect because it defines management.

20. The material transaction between related parties that must be disclosed in financial statements is the

A. Compensation arrangement between a company and its president.

B. Loan made by a parent to its consolidated subsidiary.

C. Intercompany loan between a parent entity and its unconsolidated equity-based investee.

D. Expense allowance provided by a company to its chief executive officer.

Answer (C) is correct. *(Publisher)*

REQUIRED: The transaction between related parties that must be disclosed.

DISCUSSION: SFAS 57 requires the disclosure of material related party transactions other than compensation arrangements, expense allowances, and other similar items in the ordinary course of business. Related party transactions that are eliminated in the preparation of consolidated or combined financial statements are also not required to be disclosed in those financial statements. A loan made by a parent to an unconsolidated equity-based investee (or vice versa) is not eliminated, so the transaction must be disclosed.

Answer (A) is incorrect because a compensation agreement in the ordinary course of business need not be disclosed. Answer (B) is incorrect because transactions that will be eliminated in the preparation of consolidated statements need not be disclosed. Answer (D) is incorrect because expense allowances in the ordinary course of business need not be disclosed.

21. The disclosure of certain related party transactions is considered useful to financial statement users in formulating their investment and credit decisions. Which of the following statements about related party transactions is true?

A. A reporting company need only disclose that it is the subsidiary of another company when transactions have taken place between it and its parent.

B. Representations about transactions between related parties may not indicate that they were equivalent to arm's-length transactions.

C. Transactions between related parties are not considered to be related party transactions unless they are given accounting recognition.

D. Transactions between related parties cannot ordinarily be presumed to be carried out on an arm's-length basis.

Answer (D) is correct. *(Publisher)*

REQUIRED: The true statement about related party transactions.

DISCUSSION: Transactions reflected in financial statements are usually presumed to have been consummated between independent parties on an arm's-length basis. When transactions occur between related parties, the required conditions of competitive, free-market dealings may not be present, and this general presumption is not applicable.

Answer (A) is incorrect because, even if there were no transactions between the enterprises, disclosure of the control relationship is required when common ownership or management control could result in financial position or operating results of a reporting enterprise materially different from those obtainable if the enterprises were independent. Answer (B) is incorrect because such representations may be made if they can be substantiated. Answer (C) is incorrect because accounting recognition is not a requirement of a related party transaction.

22. Julia Co. acquired 100% of Amsterdam Corp. prior to 2003. During 2003, the individual companies included in their financial statements the following:

	Julia	Amsterdam
Officers' salaries	$150,000	$100,000
Officers' expenses	40,000	20,000
Loans to officers	250,000	100,000
Intercompany sales	300,000	--

What amount should be reported as related party disclosures in the notes to Julia's 2003 consolidated financial statements?

A. $300,000

B. $310,000

C. $350,000

D. $660,000

Answer (C) is correct. *(CPA, adapted)*

REQUIRED: The amount to be reported as related party disclosures.

DISCUSSION: SFAS 57 requires the disclosure of material related party transactions other than compensation arrangements, expense allowances, and other similar items in the ordinary course of business. Related party transactions that are eliminated in the preparation of consolidated or combined financial statements also are not required to be disclosed in those financial statements. Accordingly, the compensation arrangements (officers' salaries and expenses) and the intercompany sales, which will be eliminated in the consolidated financial statements, need not be disclosed. However, other transactions between an enterprise and its management, such as borrowings and lendings, must be disclosed. Julia should therefore report as related party disclosures the $350,000 ($250,000 + $100,000) of loans to officers.

Answer (A) is incorrect because $300,000 equals the intercompany sales. Answer (B) is incorrect because $310,000 equals the officers' salaries and officers' expenses. Answer (D) is incorrect because $660,000 equals the officers' salaries and officers' expenses plus the loans to officers.

23. If the reporting enterprise and another enterprise are under common ownership or management control, what is the criterion for disclosure of the control relationship?

A. The existence of that control could result in financial position or operating results of the reporting enterprise significantly different from those that would have been obtained if the enterprises were autonomous.

B. Related party transactions have taken place.

C. Related party transactions have taken place that might not have been the same if they had occurred at arm's length.

D. One or more of the enterprises involved is publicly held.

Answer (A) is correct. *(Publisher)*

REQUIRED: The basis for disclosing the relationship between commonly owned or controlled entities.

DISCUSSION: When common ownership or management control could result in financial position or operating results of the reporting enterprise significantly different from those that would have been obtained if common control did not exist, that control relationship should be disclosed even if there were no transactions between the commonly controlled enterprises.

Answer (B) is incorrect because the control relationship must be disclosed regardless of whether related party transactions occurred or were at arm's length. Answer (C) is incorrect because the control relationship must be disclosed regardless of whether related party transactions occurred or were at arm's length. Answer (D) is incorrect because no distinction is made between public and nonpublic companies with respect to related party disclosures.

21.4 Segment Information

24. SFAS 131, *Disclosures about Segments of an Enterprise and Related Information*, requires the disclosure of information about operating segments in annual financial statements of

A. Public business enterprises.

B. Public and nonpublic business enterprises.

C. Public business enterprises, nonpublic business enterprises, and not-for-profit organizations.

D. Public business enterprises and not-for-profit organizations.

Answer (A) is correct. *(Publisher)*

REQUIRED: The entities for which operating segment disclosures are required in annual financial statements.

DISCUSSION: SFAS 131 requires public business enterprises to disclose information about operating segments in their annual financial statements. SFAS 131 further requires these enterprises to disclose selected information about operating segments in interim financial reports issued to shareholders.

Answer (B) is incorrect because SFAS 131 is applicable only to public business enterprises. Answer (C) is incorrect because SFAS 131 is applicable only to public business enterprises. Answer (D) is incorrect because SFAS 131 is applicable only to public business enterprises.

25. Which of the following is not one of the three criteria used by SFAS 131 to define an operating segment?

A. Discrete financial information about the segment is available.

B. The segment's operating results are regularly reviewed by the chief operating decision maker.

C. The segment is involved with business activities from which it may earn revenues and incur expenses.

D. The segment is primarily involved in business activities with unaffiliated enterprises.

Answer (D) is correct. *(Publisher)*

REQUIRED: The criterion not included in the definition of an operating segment.

DISCUSSION: An operating segment is a component of an enterprise (1) engaged in business activities from which it may earn revenues and incur expenses, (2) whose operating results regularly are reviewed by the chief operating officer as a basis for allocating resources and assessing performance, and (3) for which discrete information is available. The segment's business activities may involve affiliated components as well as unaffiliated enterprises.

Answer (A) is incorrect because it is included in the definition of an operating segment. Answer (B) is incorrect because it is included in the definition of an operating segment. Answer (C) is incorrect because it is included in the definition of an operating segment.

26. In determining the segment profit or loss to be included in the annual performance review of reportable operating segments, a public company's chief operating decision maker receives information about both unusual items and extraordinary items. Which of these items, if any, must be disclosed?

	Unusual Items	Extraordinary Items
A.	Yes	No
B.	No	Yes
C.	Yes	Yes
D.	No	No

Answer (C) is correct. *(Publisher)*

REQUIRED: The item(s), if any, required to be disclosed about reportable segments.

DISCUSSION: SFAS 131 requires disclosure of the measure of operating profit or loss and of total assets evaluated by the chief operating decision maker in deciding resource allocations and performance evaluations. SFAS 131 further requires the disclosure of certain items if they are included in the measure of operating segment profit or loss. These items include (1) revenues from unaffiliated customers; (2) revenues from affiliated customers; (3) interest revenue; (4) interest expense; (5) depreciation, depletion, amortization, and other significant noncash items; (6) unusual items as defined by APB 30; (7) income from equity-basis investees; (8) income tax provisions; and (9) extraordinary items.

27. Arktos Co. is a multidivisional corporation that makes both intersegment sales and sales to unaffiliated customers. Arktos should report operating segment financial information for each segment meeting which one of the following criteria?

A. Segment operating profit or loss is 10% or more of consolidated profit or loss.

B. Segment operating profit or loss is 10% or more of combined operating profit or loss of all company segments.

C. Segment revenue is 10% or more of combined revenue of all the company segments.

D. Segment revenue is 10% or more of consolidated revenue.

Answer (C) is correct. *(CPA, adapted)*

REQUIRED: The criterion used to identify operating segments as reportable segments.

DISCUSSION: An operating segment is classified as a reportable segment when it is significant to the enterprise. An operating segment is considered significant if it satisfies one or more of three tests: its revenue (including sales to both affiliated and unaffiliated customers) is at least 10% of the combined revenue (including sales to both affiliated and unaffiliated customers) of all the enterprise's operating segments; its identifiable assets are at least 10% of the combined identifiable assets of all its operating segments; and the absolute amount of its operating profit or operating loss is at least 10% of the greater, in absolute amount, of the combined operating profit of all operating segments that did not incur an operating loss or the combined loss of all operating segments that did incur an operating loss.

Answer (A) is incorrect because it is not specified as a test by SFAS 131. Answer (B) is incorrect because it is not specified as a test by SFAS 131. Answer (D) is incorrect because it is not specified as a test by SFAS 131.

28. The following information pertains to revenue earned by Meadows Co.'s operating segments for the year ended December 31:

Segment	Sales to Unaffiliated Customers	Intersegment Sales	Total Revenue
Alpha	$ 5,000	$ 3,000	$ 8,000
Beta	8,000	4,000	12,000
Delta	4,000	--	4,000
Gamma	43,000	16,000	59,000
Combined	60,000	$23,000	83,000
Elimination	--	(23,000)	(23,000)
Consolidated	$60,000	--	$60,000

In conformity with the revenue test, the company's reportable segments were

A. Only Gamma.

B. Only Beta and Gamma.

C. Only Alpha, Beta, and Gamma.

D. Alpha, Beta, Delta, and Gamma.

Answer (B) is correct. *(CPA, adapted)*

REQUIRED: The reportable segments in conformity with the revenue test.

DISCUSSION: For the purpose of identifying reportable segments, SFAS 131 defines revenue to include sales to unaffiliated customers and intersegment sales. In accordance with the revenue test, a reportable operating segment has revenue equal to 10% or more of the total combined revenue of all of the enterprise's operating segments. Given combined revenue of $83,000, only Beta ($12,000) and Gamma ($59,000) qualify because their revenues are at least $8,300 (10% × $83,000).

29. Greque Co. operates in four industries. Which of the following operating segments should be identified as a reportable segment under the operating profit or loss test?

Segment	Operating Profit (Loss)
Rho	$ 90,000
Sigma	(100,000)
Tau	910,000
Upsilon	(420,000)

A. Segment Tau only.

B. Segments Tau and Upsilon.

C. Segments Sigma, Tau, and Upsilon.

D. Segments Rho, Sigma, Tau, and Upsilon.

Answer (C) is correct. *(Publisher)*

REQUIRED: The reportable segments under the operating profit or loss test.

DISCUSSION: Under SFAS 131, an operating segment is identified as a reportable segment if it meets the profit or loss test (among others). The segment is reportable if the absolute amount of the operating profit or loss equals at least 10% of the greater, in absolute amount, of (1) the combined operating profit of all segments not reporting an operating loss or (2) the combined operating loss of all segments reporting an operating loss.

Segments Sigma, Tau, and Upsilon are reportable segments. As shown below, the sum of the operating profits of Rho and Tau ($1,000,000) is greater than the sum of the operating losses of Sigma and Upsilon ($520,000). Consequently, the test criterion is $100,000 (10% × $1,000,000).

Segment	Operating Profit	Operating Loss
Rho	$ 90,000	$ 0
Sigma	0	100,000
Tau	910,000	0
Upsilon	0	420,000
	$1,000,000	$520,000

30. Selected data for an operating segment of a business enterprise are to be separately reported in accordance with SFAS 131 when the revenue of the segment exceeds 10% of the

A. Combined net income of all segments reporting profits.

B. Total revenue obtained in transactions with outsiders.

C. Total revenue of all the enterprise's operating segments.

D. Total combined revenue of all segments reporting profits.

Answer (C) is correct. *(CPA, adapted)*

REQUIRED: The revenue test for selecting reportable segments.

DISCUSSION: An operating segment is a reportable segment if it satisfies one or more of three tests. One test is whether its revenue is 10% or more of the combined revenue of all the enterprise's operating segments.

Answer (A) is incorrect because whether an operating segment reported a profit is not a factor in the revenue test. Answer (B) is incorrect because the test for revenue applies both to sales to unaffiliated customers and to intersegment sales or transfers. Answer (D) is incorrect because whether an operating segment reported a profit is not a factor in the revenue test.

31. Salaam Co.'s four operating segments have revenues and identifiable assets expressed as percentages of Salaam's total revenues and total assets as follows:

	Revenues	Assets
Un	64%	66%
Deux	14%	18%
Trois	14%	4%
Quatre	8%	12%
	100%	100%

Which of these operating segments are deemed to be reportable segments?

A. Un only.

B. Un and Deux only.

C. Un, Deux, and Trois only.

D. Un, Deux, Trois, and Quatre.

Answer (D) is correct. *(CPA, adapted)*

REQUIRED: The operating segment(s) deemed to be reportable.

DISCUSSION: An operating segment is a reportable segment if it satisfies one or more of three tests. One test is whether its revenue is 10% or more of the combined revenue of all the enterprise's operating segments. According to the identifiable assets test, an operating segment with identifiable assets equal to 10% or more of the combined identifiable assets of all operating segments is a reportable segment. Un, Deux, and Trois meet the revenue test, and Un, Deux, and Quatre meet the identifiable assets test.

32. Dillon Corp. and its divisions are engaged solely in manufacturing operations. The following data (consistent with prior years' data) pertain to the industries in which operations were conducted for the year ended December 31, 2003:

Industry	Total Revenue	Operating Profit	Identifiable Assets at 12/31/03
A	$10,000,000	$1,750,000	$20,000,000
B	8,000,000	1,400,000	17,500,000
C	6,000,000	1,200,000	12,500,000
D	3,000,000	550,000	7,500,000
E	4,250,000	675,000	7,000,000
F	1,500,000	225,000	3,000,000
	$32,750,000	$5,800,000	$67,500,000

In its operating segment information for 2003, how many reportable operating segments does Dillon have?

A. Three.

B. Four.

C. Five.

D. Six.

Answer (C) is correct. *(CPA, adapted)*

REQUIRED: The number of reportable segments.

DISCUSSION: Four operating segments (A, B, C, and E) have segment revenue equal to or greater than 10% of the $32,750,000 total revenue. These four operating segments also have segment operating profit equal to or greater than 10% of the $5,800,000 total operating profit. Five operating segments (A, B, C, D, and E) have identifiable assets greater than 10% of the $67,500,000 total identifiable assets. Because an operating segment is reportable if it meets one or more of the three tests established by SFAS 131, Dillon Corp. has five reportable segments for 2003.

33. The disclosure of information about major customers is required when the amount of sales to a single customer is 10% or more of the revenue of an enterprise. Which of the following must be disclosed?

A. The identity of the major customer.

B. The percentage of total revenue derived from the major customer.

C. The operating segment or segments making the sale.

D. The geographic area or areas from which the sales were made.

Answer (C) is correct. *(Publisher)*

REQUIRED: The required disclosure for sales to major customers.

DISCUSSION: If 10% or more of the revenue of an enterprise is derived from sales to any single customer, that fact and the amount of revenue from each such customer (without disclosing the identity of the customer) must be disclosed according to SFAS 131. The identity of the operating segment or segments making the sales must also be disclosed.

34. Which of the following materiality tests is required to determine whether the operating segments of an enterprise that have been identified as reportable operating segments represent a substantial portion of the total operations of the enterprise?

A. The combined revenue of all reportable segments equals or exceeds 75% of the combined revenue of all operating segments.

B. The combined revenue from sales to unaffiliated customers by all reportable segments equals or exceeds 75% of the combined revenue of all operating segments.

C. The combined revenue from sales to unaffiliated customers by all reportable segments equals or exceeds 75% of total consolidated revenue.

D. The combined revenue of all reportable segments equals or exceeds 75% of the combined revenue from sales to unaffiliated customers by all operating segments.

Answer (C) is correct. *(Publisher)*

REQUIRED: The test for determining whether the reportable segments represent a substantial portion of the enterprise's total operations.

DISCUSSION: SFAS 131 requires that the reportable segments represent a substantial portion of the enterprise's total operations. To determine materiality, the combined revenue from sales to unaffiliated customers by all reportable segments must equal or exceed 75% of total consolidated revenue. The test should be applied separately for each fiscal year for which financial statements are presented. When the test criterion is not met, additional segments must be identified as reportable until the criterion is met. Segments may have to be combined to meet one of the 10% tests.

35. Zan Corp., a publicly owned corporation, is subject to the requirements for segment reporting. In its income statement for the current-year end, Zan reported revenues of $100,000,000, operating expenses of $94,000,000, and net income of $6,000,000. Operating expenses include payroll costs of $30,000,000. Zan's combined identifiable assets of all operating segments in the current year were $80,000,000. In its current-year financial statements, Zan should disclose major customer data if sales to any single customer amount to at least

A. $600,000

B. $3,000,000

C. $8,000,000

D. $10,000,000

Answer (D) is correct. *(CPA, adapted)*

REQUIRED: The sales level requiring disclosure of major customer data.

DISCUSSION: If 10% or more of the revenue of an enterprise is derived from sales to any single customer, that fact and the amount of revenue from each such customer (without disclosing the identity of the customer) must be disclosed according to SFAS 131. The identity of the operating segment or segments making the sales must also be disclosed. Hence, Zan's sales to a single customer of $10,000,000 (10% × $100,000,000 total revenue) will necessitate disclosure of major customer data.

Answer (A) is incorrect because $600,000 is 10% of net income. Answer (B) is incorrect because $3,000,000 is 10% of payroll costs. Answer (C) is incorrect because $8,000,000 is 10% of combined identifiable assets of all industry segments.

36. For each of the following groups of customers, purchases amounted to 10% or more of the revenue of a publicly held company. For which of these groups must the company disclose information about major customers?

A. Federal governmental agencies, 6%; state governmental agencies, 4%.

B. French governmental agencies, 6%; Italian governmental agencies, 4%.

C. Parent company, 6%; subsidiary of parent company, 4%.

D. Federal governmental agencies, 6%; foreign governmental agencies, 4%.

Answer (C) is correct. *(Publisher)*

REQUIRED: The set of circumstances requiring disclosure about major customers.

DISCUSSION: For purposes of SFAS 131, a group of customers under common control must be regarded as a single customer in determining whether 10% or more of the revenue of an enterprise is derived from sales to any single customer. A parent and a subsidiary are under common control, and they should be regarded as a single customer. Major customer disclosure is required in situation (C) because total combined revenue is 10% (6% + 4%).

37. Listed below are the most recent year's sales to the three largest customers of the Oxford Company, a publicly held firm.

Federal government	$5,000,000
State of Florina	4,000,000
State of Carolida	3,000,000

If Oxford's total revenue amounts to $44,000,000, Oxford should disclose the total amount of sales to major customers as which of the following amounts?

A. $0

B. $5,000,000

C. $9,000,000

D. $12,000,000

Answer (B) is correct. *(Publisher)*

REQUIRED: The total amount of sales to major customers required to be separately reported.

DISCUSSION: An enterprise should disclose information about the extent of the enterprise's reliance on its major customers. If 10% or more of the revenue of an enterprise is derived from sales to any single customer, that fact, the identity of the operating segment or segments making the sale, and the amount of revenue from such customer must be disclosed. A single customer includes a group of entities under common control, the federal government, a state government, a local government, or a foreign government. Total revenue for Oxford is $44,000,000. Thus, Oxford should disclose the amount of sales to any major customer from whom sales revenue totals $4,400,000 (10% × $44,000,000). Because the year's sales to the federal government totaled $5,000,000, such disclosure must be made (but not necessarily identifying the customer).

21.5 Risks and Uncertainties

38. According to SOP 94-6, *Disclosure of Certain Significant Risks and Uncertainties*, financial statements must disclose significant risks and uncertainties. The required disclosures include

A. Quantified comparisons of the relative importance of the different businesses in which the entity operates.

B. Factors making a significant estimate sensitive to change.

C. Risk-reduction techniques that have successfully mitigated losses.

D. Vulnerability due to a concentration if a near-term severe impact is at least reasonably possible.

Answer (D) is correct. *(Publisher)*

REQUIRED: The required disclosure.

DISCUSSION: The current vulnerability due to concentrations must be disclosed if certain conditions are met. Disclosure is necessary if management knows prior to issuance of the statements that the concentration exists at the balance sheet date, it makes the entity vulnerable to a near-term severe impact, and such impact is at least reasonably possible in the near term. A severe impact may result from loss of all or a part of a business relationship, price or demand changes, loss of a patent, changes in the availability of a resource or right, or the disruption of operations in a market or geographic area.

Answer (A) is incorrect because disclosures about the nature of operations need not be quantified. Answer (B) is incorrect because disclosure is encouraged, but not required, for factors making a significant estimate sensitive to change. Answer (C) is incorrect because the criteria for required disclosures about significant estimates may not be met if the entity has successfully employed risk-reduction techniques. In these circumstances, disclosure of those techniques is encouraged but not required.

39. Certain significant risks and uncertainties must be disclosed. Disclosures about a significant estimate are required when

I. The estimate is subject to at least a reasonable possibility of change.
II. The estimate is subject to change that is at least remotely possible.
III. The change will be material.
IV. The change will be material or immaterial.

A. I and III.

B. I and IV.

C. II and III.

D. II and IV.

Answer (A) is correct. *(Publisher)*

REQUIRED: The circumstances in which disclosures about a significant estimate are required.

DISCUSSION: Disclosures about an estimate used to value assets, liabilities, or contingencies are required when the estimated financial statement effect of a condition, situation, or set of circumstances at the balance sheet date is subject to a reasonable possibility of change in the near term, and the effect of the change will be material. The effect of using a different estimate determines materiality. The disclosure must include the nature of the uncertainty, that it is reasonably possible, and that the estimate may change in the near term.

21.6 Unconditional Purchase Obligations

40. SFAS 47 specifies disclosure requirements for long-term obligations as a group. The FASB believed that a particular group of long-term obligations frequently was not disclosed adequately. Thus, this statement was specifically addressed to the group of items referred to as

A. Loss contingencies.

B. Unconditional purchase obligations.

C. Long-term borrowings.

D. Pension plans.

Answer (B) is correct. *(CMA, adapted)*

REQUIRED: The long-term obligations covered by SFAS 47.

DISCUSSION: SFAS 47, *Disclosure of Long-Term Obligations*, requires that a company disclose commitments under unconditional purchase obligations that are associated with suppliers. Unconditional purchase obligations are commitments to transfer funds in the future for fixed or minimum amounts of goods or services at fixed or minimum prices.

Answer (A) is incorrect because loss contingencies are covered by SFAS 5, *Accounting for Contingencies*. Answer (C) is incorrect because long-term borrowings is a broad financial accounting topic for which there is no single authoritative pronouncement. Answer (D) is incorrect because pension plans are covered by SFAS 35, *Accounting and Reporting by Defined Benefit Pension Plans*; SFAS 87, *Employers' Accounting for Pensions*; SFAS 88, *Employers' Accounting for Settlements and Curtailments of Defined Benefit Pension Plans and for Termination Benefits*; and SFAS 132 (revised 2003), *Employers' Disclosures about Pensions and Other Postretirement Benefits*.

41. SFAS 47, *Disclosure of Long-Term Obligations*, does not apply to an unconditional purchase obligation that is cancelable under which of the following conditions?

A. Upon the occurrence of a remote contingency.

B. With the permission of the other party.

C. If a replacement agreement is signed between the same parties.

D. Upon payment of a nominal penalty.

Answer (D) is correct. *(Publisher)*

REQUIRED: The condition excluding unconditional purchase obligation coverage by SFAS 47.

DISCUSSION: SFAS 47 provides the standards of accounting for an unconditional purchase obligation that

1. Was negotiated as part of the financing arrangement for facilities that will provide contracted goods or services
2. Has a remaining term of more than 1 year
3. Is either noncancelable or cancelable only under specific terms that make continuation or replacement of the agreement reasonably assured

Excluded from these terms and from the provisions of SFAS 47 is a purchase obligation cancelable upon the payment of a nominal penalty.

Answer (A) is incorrect because cancelability only upon the occurrence of a remote contingency is a condition indicating that the obligation is noncancelable in substance. Answer (B) is incorrect because cancelability only with the permission of the other party is a condition indicating that the obligation is noncancelable in substance. Answer (C) is incorrect because cancelability only if a replacement agreement is signed between the same parties is a condition indicating that the obligation is noncancelable in substance.

42. Denmark Corp. has unconditional purchase obligations associated with product financing arrangements. These obligations are reported as liabilities on Denmark's balance sheet, with the related assets also recognized. In the notes to Denmark's financial statements, the aggregate amount of payments for these obligations should be disclosed for each of how many years following the date of the balance sheet?

A. 0

B. 1

C. 5

D. 10

Answer (C) is correct. *(CPA, adapted)*

REQUIRED: The disclosure about reported unconditional purchase obligations.

DISCUSSION: SFAS 47, *Disclosure of Long-Term Obligations*, states that the following disclosures must be made for recorded unconditional purchase obligations for each of the 5 years after the date of the latest balance sheet: (1) the aggregate amount of the payments for the recognized obligations, and (2) the combined amount of maturities and sinking fund requirements for all long-term borrowing.

Answer (A) is incorrect because SFAS 47 requires disclosures for 5 years. Answer (B) is incorrect because SFAS 47 requires disclosures for 5 years. Answer (D) is incorrect because SFAS 47 requires disclosures for 5 years.

43. If an unconditional purchase obligation is not presented in the balance sheet, certain disclosures are required. A disclosure that is not required is

A. The nature and term of the obligation.

B. The variable components of the obligation.

C. The imputed interest necessary to reduce the unconditional purchase obligation to its present value.

D. The amounts purchased under the obligation for each period an income statement is presented.

Answer (C) is correct. *(Publisher)*

REQUIRED: The item not required to be disclosed if an unconditional purchase obligation is not recognized in the balance sheet.

DISCUSSION: When an unconditional purchase obligation is not recorded in the balance sheet, SFAS 47 encourages but does not require the disclosure of the amount of imputed interest necessary to reduce the unconditional purchase obligation to its present value. This disclosure is explicitly required by SFAS 47 when an unconditional purchase obligation is not recorded in the balance sheet. SFAS 47 also requires disclosure of the amount of the fixed and determinable portion of the obligation in the aggregate as of the latest balance sheet date and the amounts due in each of the next 5 years.

44. Witt Corp. has outstanding at December 31, 2003 two long-term borrowings with annual sinking-fund requirements and maturities as follows:

	Sinking-Fund Requirements	Maturities
2004	$1,000,000	$ --
2005	1,500,000	2,000,000
2006	1,500,000	2,000,000
2007	2,000,000	2,500,000
2008	2,000,000	3,000,000
	$8,000,000	$9,500,000

In the notes to its December 31, 2002 balance sheet, how should Witt report the above data?

A. No disclosure is required.

B. Only sinking-fund payments totaling $8,000,000 for the next 5 years detailed by year need be disclosed.

C. Only maturities totaling $9,500,000 for the next 5 years detailed by year need be disclosed.

D. The combined aggregate of $17,500,000 of maturities and sinking-fund requirements detailed by year should be disclosed.

Answer (D) is correct. *(CPA, adapted)*

REQUIRED: The required note disclosure of sinking fund payments and maturities for long-term borrowings.

DISCUSSION: In addition to the disclosures required by other official pronouncements, SFAS 47 requires the disclosure of the following information for recorded obligations for each of the 5 years following the date of the latest balance sheet presented: (1) the aggregate amount of payments for unconditional purchase obligations and (2) the aggregate amount of maturities and sinking-fund requirements for all long-term borrowings. Thus, Witt Corp. should disclose in the notes to the December 31, 2003 balance sheet the combined aggregate of $17,500,000 ($8,000,000 + $9,500,000) of maturities and sinking-fund requirements detailed by year.

45. When an entity discloses the imputed interest rate necessary to reduce an unconditional purchase obligation, not recorded in the balance sheet, to its present value, the interest rate disclosed should be which of the following?

A. If known by the purchaser, the effective initial interest rate of the debt that financed the facilities providing the contracted goods or services.

B. The purchaser's incremental borrowing rate.

C. The prime rate.

D. The current Aa bond interest rate.

Answer (A) is correct. *(Publisher)*

REQUIRED: The interest rate to be used in determining the present value of an unconditional purchase obligation.

DISCUSSION: SFAS 47 encourages, but does not require, disclosure of the imputed interest rate. If known by the purchaser, the rate disclosed should be the initial effective interest rate of the debt that financed the facilities providing the contracted goods or services. If that rate cannot be determined by the purchaser, the purchaser's incremental borrowing rate should be used.

Answer (B) is incorrect because the purchaser's incremental borrowing rate is used only if the purchaser does not know the initial interest rate on the debt that financed the facilities providing the contracted goods or services. Answer (C) is incorrect because the prime rate is not discussed in SFAS 47. Answer (D) is incorrect because the current Aa bond interest rate is not discussed in SFAS 47.

21.7 Subsequent Events

46. On January 15, 20X1, before the Mapleview Co. released its financial statements for the year ended December 31, 20X0, it settled a long-standing lawsuit. A material loss resulted, and no prior liability had been recorded. How should this loss be disclosed or recognized?

A. The loss should be disclosed in notes to the financial statements, but the financial statements themselves need not be adjusted.

B. The loss should be disclosed in an explanatory paragraph in the auditor's report.

C. No disclosure or recognition is required.

D. The financial statements should be adjusted to recognize the loss.

Answer (D) is correct. *(Publisher)*

REQUIRED: The proper disclosure of a material loss on an existing lawsuit after year-end.

DISCUSSION: Subsequent events that provide additional evidence with the respect to conditions that existed at the balance sheet date and that affect the estimates inherent in the process of preparing the financial statements should be reflected in the current financial statements. Settlement of a lawsuit is indicative of conditions existing at year-end and calls for adjustment of the statements (AU 560, *Subsequent Events*).

Answer (A) is incorrect because the financial statements should be adjusted to reflect the loss. Answer (B) is incorrect because the audit report need not be modified. Answer (C) is incorrect because failure to adjust the statements for a material loss on an asset that existed at year-end would be misleading.

47. Zero Corp. suffered a loss that would have a material effect on its financial statements on an uncollectible trade account receivable due to a customer's bankruptcy. This occurred suddenly due to a natural disaster ten days after Zero's balance sheet date but one month before the issuance of the financial statements. Under these circumstances,

	The Financial Statements Should Be Adjusted	The Event Requires Financial Statement Disclosure, but No Adjustment	The Auditor's Report Should Be Modified for a Lack of Consistency
A.	Yes	No	No
B.	Yes	No	Yes
C.	No	Yes	Yes
D.	No	Yes	No

Answer (D) is correct. *(CPA, adapted)*

REQUIRED: The effect on the financial statements and the auditor's report.

DISCUSSION: Certain subsequent events may provide additional evidence about conditions at the date of the balance sheet and affect estimates inherent in the preparation of statements. These events require adjustment by the client in the financial statements at year-end. Other subsequent events provide evidence about conditions not existing at the date of the balance sheet but arising subsequent to that date and affecting the interpretation of the year-end financial statements. An example is the inability to collect a material receivable caused solely by a post-balance-sheet-date event, such as a natural disaster. These events may require disclosure in notes to the financial statements but do not require adjustment of the financial statement balances. Thus, Zero's financial statements should not be adjusted, but disclosure should be made in the notes. The auditor's report is unaffected.

STUDY UNIT TWENTY-TWO
LONG-TERM CONSTRUCTION-TYPE CONTRACTS, INSTALLMENT SALES, AND CONSIGNMENTS

The **percentage-of-completion method** is used to recognize revenue and gross profit (total revenue – total costs) on long-term construction-type contracts when (1) the extent of progress toward completion, contract revenue, and contract costs are reasonably estimable; (2) the enforceable rights regarding goods or services to be provided, the consideration to be exchanged, and the manner and terms of settlement are clearly specified; and (3) the contractual obligations of both the buyer and the contractor are expected to be fulfilled. The **completed-contract method** is used when the percentage-of-completion method is inappropriate. (**SOP 81-1**, *Accounting for Performance of Construction-Type and Certain Production-Type Contracts.*)

The percentage-of-completion method recognizes revenue and gross profit based on the progress of the construction contract. The completed-contract method recognizes revenue and gross profit when the contract is complete or substantially complete. However, under either method, losses are recognized immediately.

An **installment sale** occurs when the receivable associated with the sale will be collected over an extended period of time. Revenue from an installment sale is recognized when realized and earned, which usually is at the point of sale. Under unusual circumstances, when there is no reasonable basis for estimating the degree of collectibility of the receivable, recognition of the gross profit may be deferred until cash is collected. Either the installment method or the cost-recovery method may be appropriate in these circumstances.

Under the **installment method**, a proportional amount of installment gross profit is realized as the installment receivable is collected. This amount is equal to the gross profit margin associated with the receivable multiplied by the amount of the receivable collected. Under the **cost-recovery method**, gross profit during the term of an installment receivable is not realized until the full cost of the item sold is recovered. Subsequent amounts collected are recognized as realized gross profit.

Under a **consignment** sales arrangement, the consignor ships inventory items to the consignee who acts as a sales agent of the consignor. The items are in the physical possession of the consignee, but they remain in the inventory of the consignor.

QUESTIONS

22.1 Long-Term Construction-Type Contracts

1. A building contractor has a contract to construct a large building. It is estimated that the building will take 2 years to complete. Progress billings will be sent to the customer at quarterly intervals. Which of the following describes the preferable point for revenue and gross profit recognition for this contract?

A. After the contract is signed.

B. As progress is made toward completion of the contract.

C. As cash is received.

D. When the contract is completed.

Answer (B) is correct. *(CIA, adapted)*

REQUIRED: The moment when revenue and gross profit should be recognized.

DISCUSSION: There are two methods used for revenue and gross profit recognition for long-term construction-type contracts: the percentage-of-completion method and the completed-contract method. Under the percentage-of-completion method, revenue and gross profit are recognized each period based upon the progress of the construction. The presumption is that the percentage-of-completion approach is the better method and that the completed-contract method should be used only when the percentage-of-completion method is inappropriate.

Answer (A) is incorrect because revenue and gross profit are not earned until progress has been made toward completion. Answer (C) is incorrect because an accrual method, such as the percentage-of-completion method, should be used. Answer (D) is incorrect because the completed-contract method should be used only if conditions for using the percentage-of-completion method cannot be met.

2. Saskia Company's construction projects extend over several years, and collection of receivables is reasonably certain. Each project has a firm contract price, reliable estimates of the extent of progress and cost to finish, and a contract that is specific as to the rights and obligations of all parties. The contractor and the buyer are expected to fulfill their contractual obligations on each project. The method that the company should use to account for construction revenue and gross profit is

A. Installment sales.

B. Percentage-of-completion.

C. Completed-contract.

D. Point-of-sale.

Answer (B) is correct. *(CIA, adapted)*

REQUIRED: The method appropriate to account for construction revenue.

DISCUSSION: SFAC 5 states that revenue should be recognized when it is both realized or realizable and earned. If a project is contracted for before production and is long in relation to reporting periods, revenue and gross profit may be recognized by a percentage-of-completion method as they are earned (as production occurs), provided reasonable estimates of results at completion and reliable measures of progress are available. This information is more relevant and representationally faithful than information based on waiting for delivery, completion of the project, or payment.

Answer (A) is incorrect because the installment method is appropriate if collectibility is doubtful. Answer (C) is incorrect because the completed-contract method is appropriate if reasonable estimates of results at completion and reliable measures of progress are not available. Answer (D) is incorrect because the point-of-sale method is appropriate when the product or merchandise is delivered or services are rendered directly to customers.

3. The calculation of the gross profit recognized in the third year of a 5-year construction contract accounted for using the percentage-of-completion method includes the ratio of

A. Total costs incurred to date to total estimated costs.

B. Total costs incurred to date to total billings to date.

C. Costs incurred in year 3 to total estimated costs.

D. Costs incurred in year 3 to total billings to date.

Answer (A) is correct. *(CPA, adapted)*

REQUIRED: The ratio used in the calculation of gross profit recognized for a construction contract using the percentage-of-completion method.

DISCUSSION: The percentage-of-completion method provides for the recognition of gross profit based on the relationship between costs incurred to date and estimated total costs for completion of the contract. (But ARB 45 permits any other measure of progress "as may be appropriate having due regard to work performed.") The amount recognized in the third year of a 5-year contract is calculated as follows: The total anticipated gross profit (based on the latest available estimated costs) is multiplied by the ratio of costs incurred to date to the latest available total estimated costs, and the product is reduced by previously recognized income.

Answer (B) is incorrect because the ratio of total costs incurred to date to total billings to date is not relevant. Answer (C) is incorrect because total costs incurred must be used. Answer (D) is incorrect because neither the issuance nor the collection of billings results in income recognition.

4. How should the balances of progress billings and construction in progress be shown at reporting dates prior to the completion of a long-term contract?

A. Progress billings as deferred income, construction in progress as a deferred expense.

B. Progress billings as income, construction in progress as inventory.

C. Net, as a current asset if debit balance and current liability if credit balance.

D. Net, as gross profit from construction if credit balance, and loss from construction if debit balance.

Answer (C) is correct. *(CPA, adapted)*
REQUIRED: The proper balance sheet presentation of progress billings and construction in progress.
DISCUSSION: ARB 45, *Long-Term Construction-Type Contracts*, requires that the difference between construction in progress (costs and recognized gross profit) and progress billings to date be shown as a current asset if construction in progress exceeds total billings, and as a current liability if billings exceed construction in progress. Separate recognition is required for each project.
Answer (A) is incorrect because progress billings and construction in progress should be netted for balance sheet presentation as a current asset or liability. Answer (B) is incorrect because progress billings and construction in progress should be netted for balance sheet presentation as a current asset or liability. Answer (D) is incorrect because neither gross profit nor loss results from progress billings.

5. A company used the percentage-of-completion method of accounting for a 4-year construction contract. Which of the following items should be used to calculate the gross profit recognized in the second year?

	Gross Profit Previously Recognized	Progress Billings to Date
A.	Yes	Yes
B.	No	Yes
C.	Yes	No
D.	No	No

Answer (C) is correct. *(CPA, adapted)*
REQUIRED: The item(s) used in computing gross profit in the second year.
DISCUSSION: The percentage-of-completion method provides for the recognition of gross profit based on the relationship between the costs incurred to date and estimated total costs for the completion of the contract. The amount of gross profit (based on the latest available estimated costs) recognized in the second year of a 4-year contract is calculated as follows: The total anticipated gross profit is multiplied by the ratio of the costs incurred to date to the total estimated costs, and the product is reduced by previously recognized gross profit. Gross profit previously recognized is therefore used to calculate gross profit to be recognized in the second year. However, progress billings to date have no effect on the amount of gross profit to be recognized in the second year.

6. A company uses the percentage-of-completion method to account for a 4-year construction contract. Which of the following should be used in the calculation of the gross profit recognized in the first year?

	Progress Billings	Collections on Progress Billings
A.	Yes	Yes
B.	Yes	No
C.	No	No
D.	No	Yes

Answer (C) is correct. *(CPA, adapted)*
REQUIRED: The effect that progress billings and collections have on the determination of gross profit.
DISCUSSION: Under GAAP, revenue should be recognized when it is realized or realizable and earned. For long-term construction contracts, these criteria are met in accordance with either the percentage-of-completion or the completed-contract method. Neither the issuance of a progress billing (debit accounts receivable, credit progress billings) nor the collection of cash (debit cash, credit accounts receivable) results in recognition of gross profit.

7. During year 1, Lynx Co. began construction on a project scheduled for completion in year 3. At December 31, year 1, an overall loss was anticipated at contract completion. What would be the effect of the project on year 1 operating income under the percentage-of-completion method and the completed-contract method?

	Percentage-of-Completion	Completed-Contract
A.	No effect	No effect
B.	No effect	Decrease
C.	Decrease	No effect
D.	Decrease	Decrease

Answer (D) is correct. *(CPA, adapted)*
REQUIRED: The effect of the project on year 1 operating income under the percentage-of-completion method and the completed-contract method.
DISCUSSION: When the current estimate of total contract costs indicates a loss, an immediate provision for the entire loss should be made regardless of method. Thus, under either method, year 1 operating income is decreased by the projected loss.

8. Cinnabar Construction Company has consistently used the percentage-of-completion method of recognizing gross profit. During year 1, Cinnabar entered into a fixed-price contract to construct an office building for $10 million. Information relating to the contract is as follows:

	December 31	
	Year 1	Year 2
Percentage of completion	20%	60%
Estimated total costs at completion	$7,500,000	$8,000,000
Gross profit recognized (cumulative)	500,000	1,200,000

Contract costs incurred during year 2 were

A. $3,200,000

B. $3,300,000

C. $3,500,000

D. $4,800,000

Answer (B) is correct. *(CPA, adapted)*

REQUIRED: The contract cost incurred during the second year of a long-term contract.

DISCUSSION: If the percentage of completion is based on the relationship of the cumulative costs incurred to date to estimated total costs at completion, the cumulative amount incurred at 12/31/year 1 was $1,500,000 (20% × $7,500,000). At 12/31/year 2, the cumulative amount incurred was $4,800,000 (60% × $8,000,000). The difference of $3,300,000 ($4,800,000 – $1,500,000) equals contract costs incurred during year 2.

Answer (A) is incorrect because $3,200,000 equals the $8,000,000 estimated total costs multiplied by the 40% (60% – 20%) change in the percentages of completion. Answer (C) is incorrect because $3,500,000 equals the $10,000,000 contract price multiplied by the 40% change in the percentage of completion minus the $500,000 gross profit recognized in year 1. Answer (D) is incorrect because $4,800,000 equals the $8,000,000 estimated total costs multiplied by the 60% percentage of completion.

9. Kechara Corp. started a long-term construction project in year 1. The following data relate to this project:

Contract price	$4,200,000
Costs incurred in year 1	1,750,000
Estimated costs to complete	1,750,000
Progress billings	900,000
Collections on progress billings	800,000

The project is accounted for by the percentage-of-completion method of accounting. In Kechara's year 1 income statement, what amount of gross profit should be reported for this project?

A. $350,000

B. $150,000

C. $133,333

D. $100,000

Answer (A) is correct. *(CPA, adapted)*

REQUIRED: The gross profit for the first year of a long-term construction contract.

DISCUSSION: In year 1, one-half of the estimated costs of this construction project were incurred [$1,750,000 ÷ ($1,750,000 + $1,750,000)]. The company should therefore recognize one-half of the estimated gross profit in year 1. At year-end, the estimated gross profit is $700,000, equal to the contract price minus total estimated costs [$4,200,000 – ($1,750,000 + $1,750,000)]. In year 1, $350,000 should be recognized as gross profit ($700,000 × 50%).

10. Ashke Co. recognizes construction revenue and gross profit using the percentage-of-completion method. During year 1, a single long-term project was begun, which continued through year 2. Information on the project follows:

	Year 1	Year 2
Accounts receivable from construction contract	$100,000	$300,000
Construction expenses	105,000	192,000
Construction in progress	122,000	364,000
Partial billings on contract	100,000	420,000

Gross profit recognized on the long-term construction contract in year 2 should be

A. $50,000

B. $108,000

C. $120,000

D. $228,000

Answer (A) is correct. *(CPA, adapted)*

REQUIRED: The gross profit recognized on the long-term construction contract.

DISCUSSION: Construction in progress includes gross profit recognized and costs incurred. Costs incurred through year 2 equal $297,000 ($105,000 + $192,000). Hence, gross profit recognized in year 1 and year 2 is $67,000 ($364,000 construction in progress – $297,000 cumulative costs). Because gross profit was recognized in year 1 ($122,000 construction in progress – $105,000 of costs), $50,000 ($67,000 – $17,000) should be recognized in year 2.

Answer (B) is incorrect because $108,000 equals the year 2 accounts receivable minus year 2 costs. Answer (C) is incorrect because $120,000 equals year 2 billings minus year 2 accounts receivable. Answer (D) is incorrect because $228,000 equals year 2 billings minus year 2 costs.

11. Ailouros Construction, Inc. has consistently used the percentage-of-completion method of recognizing gross profit. During year 1, Ailouros started work on a $6 million fixed-price construction contract. The accounting records disclosed the following data for the year ended December 31, year 1:

Costs incurred	$1,860,000
Estimated costs to complete	4,340,000
Progress billings	2,200,000
Collections	1,400,000

How much loss should Ailouros have recognized in year 1?

A. $460,000

B. $200,000

C. $60,000

D. $0

Answer (B) is correct. *(CPA, adapted)*

REQUIRED: The loss to be recorded in the first year of a long-term construction contract.

DISCUSSION: The total of the costs incurred in year 1 plus estimated costs to complete is $6,200,000 ($1,860,000 + $4,340,000). Because this sum exceeds the $6 million fixed-price construction contract amount, a $200,000 loss should be recognized.

Answer (A) is incorrect because $460,000 is the difference between the costs incurred and the collections ($1,860,000 – $1,400,000). Answer (C) is incorrect because $60,000 results from multiplying the loss that should be recognized by the ratio of estimated costs incurred to total costs [$1,860,000 ÷ ($1,860,000 + $4,340,000) × $200,000 = $60,000]. Answer (D) is incorrect because a loss is recognized in the period in which it occurs.

12. Felis Corp. began construction work under a 3-year contract this year. The contract price is $800,000. Felis uses the percentage-of-completion method for financial accounting purposes. The gross profit to be recognized each year is based on the proportion of costs incurred to total estimated costs for completing the contract. The following financial statement presentations relate to this contract at December 31 of the first year:

Accounts receivable-construction contract billings		$30,000
Construction in progress	$100,000	
Minus contract billings	(94,000)	
Costs of uncompleted contract in excess of billings		6,000
Gross profit (before tax) on the contract recognized in year 1		$20,000

How much cash was collected in the first year on this contract?

A. $30,000

B. $64,000

C. $70,000

D. $94,000

Answer (B) is correct. *(CPA, adapted)*

REQUIRED: The cash collections in the first year on a contract accounted for under the percentage-of-completion method.

DISCUSSION: Billings on a construction contract are debited to a receivable and credited to a cumulative contract billings account (progress billings). Collections are debited to cash and credited to the receivable. The billings account, however, will not be reduced until it is closed at the end of the contract. Consequently, the difference between the billings and receivable accounts is the amount collected. For Felis Corp., collections equal $64,000 ($94,000 contract billings – $30,000 accounts receivable).

Answer (A) is incorrect because $30,000 is the accounts receivable balance for the contract billings. Answer (C) is incorrect because $70,000 is the difference between construction in progress and the accounts receivable balance. Answer (D) is incorrect because $94,000 is the amount of contract billings.

13. A company uses the completed-contract method to account for a long-term construction contract. Revenue and gross profit are recognized when recorded progress billings

	Are Collected	Exceed Recorded Costs
A.	Yes	Yes
B.	No	No
C.	Yes	No
D.	No	Yes

Answer (B) is correct. *(CPA, adapted)*

REQUIRED: The effect of the completed-contract method on revenue recognition.

DISCUSSION: Under the completed-contract method of accounting for long-term construction contracts, recorded progress billings have no effect on the recognition of revenue and gross profit.

Questions 14 and 15 are based on the following information. Data pertaining to Catus Co.'s construction jobs, which commenced during year 1 are as follows:

	Project 1	Project 2
Contract price	$420,000	$300,000
Costs incurred during year 1	240,000	280,000
Estimated costs to complete	120,000	40,000
Billed to customers during year 1	150,000	270,000
Received from customers during year 1	90,000	250,000

14. If Catus uses the completed-contract method, what amount of gross profit (loss) should Catus report in its year 1 income statement?

A. $(20,000)

B. $0

C. $340,000

D. $420,000

Answer (A) is correct. *(CPA, adapted)*

REQUIRED: The amount of gross profit (loss) reported in the income statement under the completed-contract method.

DISCUSSION: Under the completed-contract method, gross profit is recognized when the contract is completed. Neither project will be completed by the end of year 1. Hence, no gross profit is recognized for Project 1 even though estimated data predict a gross profit of $60,000 ($420,000 contract price – $240,000 costs incurred – $120,000 additional estimated costs). However, when the current estimate of total contract costs indicates a loss, an immediate provision for the entire loss should be made regardless of the method of accounting used. Thus, a $20,000 loss ($300,000 contract price – $280,000 costs incurred – $40,000 additional estimated costs) will be reported for Project 2.

Answer (B) is incorrect because estimated losses must be recognized. Answer (C) is incorrect because gross profit is not recognized until the contract is completed. Answer (D) is incorrect because gross profit is not recognized until the contract is completed.

15. If Catus uses the percentage-of-completion method, what amount of gross profit (loss) should Catus report in its year 1 income statement?

A. $(20,000)

B. $20,000

C. $22,500

D. $40,000

Answer (B) is correct. *(CPA, adapted)*

REQUIRED: The amount of gross profit (loss) reported in the income statement using the percentage-of-completion method.

DISCUSSION: Percentages of completion are normally based on the ratio of cumulative costs incurred to date to the total estimated costs. At the end of year 1, Project 1 is 66 2/3% complete [$240,000 ÷ ($240,000 + $120,000)] and Project 2 is 87 1/2% complete [$280,000 ÷ ($280,000 + $40,000)]. Each project's percentage of completion is multiplied by its expected total gross profit. Accordingly, Catus recognizes $40,000 [66 2/3% × ($420,000 contract price – $240,000 costs incurred – $120,000 additional estimated costs)] of gross profit for Project 1. However, Project 2 estimates indicate a loss of $20,000 ($300,000 – $280,000 – $40,000). Because the full amount of a loss is reported immediately irrespective of the accounting method used, a gross profit of $20,000 [$40,000 Project 1 + $(20,000) Project 2] is recognized.

Answer (A) is incorrect because $(20,000) does not include the gross profit from Project 1. Answer (C) is incorrect because the entire loss projected for Project 2 is reported. Answer (D) is incorrect because $40,000 excludes the loss on Project 2.

16. Haft Construction Co. has consistently used the percentage-of-completion method. On January 10, year 1, Haft began work on a $3 million construction contract. At the inception date, the estimated cost of construction was $2,250,000. The following data relate to the progress of the contract:

Gross profit recognized at 12/31/year 1	$ 300,000
Costs incurred 1/10/X1 through 12/31/year 2	1,800,000
Estimated cost to complete at 12/31/year 2	600,000

In its income statement for the year ended December 31, year 2, what amount of gross profit should Haft report?

A. $450,000

B. $300,000

C. $262,500

D. $150,000

Answer (D) is correct. *(CPA, adapted)*

REQUIRED: The amount of gross profit reported using the percentage-of-completion method.

DISCUSSION: The percentage-of-completion method normally provides for the recognition of gross profit based on the relationship between the costs incurred to date and estimated total costs for the completion of the contract. The total anticipated gross profit is multiplied by the ratio of the costs incurred to date to the total estimated costs, and the product is reduced by previously recognized gross profit. The percentage-of-completion at 12/31/year 2 is 75% [$1,800,000 ÷ ($1,800,000 + $600,000)]. The total anticipated gross profit is $600,000 ($3,000,000 contract price – $2,400,000 expected total costs). Consequently, a gross profit of $150,000 [(75% × $600,000 total gross profit) – $300,000 previously recognized gross profit] is recognized for year 2.

Answer (A) is incorrect because the year 2 gross profit equals the cumulative gross profit minus the previously recognized gross profit. Answer (B) is incorrect because $300,000 is the previously recognized gross profit. Answer (C) is incorrect because $262,500 assumes the total estimated gross profit is $750,000 ($3,000,000 price – $2,250,000 originally estimated total cost).

17. Felidae Company uses the completed-contract method to account for a 4-year construction contract that is currently in its third year. Progress billings were recorded and collected in the third year. Based on events occurring in the third year, a loss is now anticipated on the contract. When will the effect of each of the following be reported in the company's income statement?

	Third-Year Progress Billings	Anticipated Loss
A.	Not third year	Third year
B.	Not third year	Fourth year
C.	Third year	Third year
D.	Third year	Fourth year

Answer (A) is correct. *(CPA, adapted)*

REQUIRED: The effect of progress billings and an anticipated loss on the company's income statement.

DISCUSSION: Under the completed-contract method, the gross profit on the contract should be recognized upon the completion of the contract. If a loss is anticipated, however, the loss should be recognized immediately. Under GAAP, the entries to record progress billings and their collection do not affect the recognition of gross profit or loss. Thus, the third-year progress billings have no effect on the income statement, but the loss anticipated in the third year should be recognized in full in that year.

22.2 Installment Sales

18. Cash collection is a critical event for income recognition in the

	Cost-Recovery Method	Installment Method
A.	No	No
B.	Yes	Yes
C.	No	Yes
D.	Yes	No

Answer (B) is correct. *(CPA, adapted)*

REQUIRED: The method(s), if any, under which cash collection is important for recognizing income.

DISCUSSION: When receivables are collected over an extended period and no reasonable basis exists for estimating the degree of collectibility, the installment method or the cost-recovery method of accounting may be used. Under the installment method, gross profit recognized during each period of the term of an installment receivable is equal to the gross profit ratio on the installment sales for the period in which the receivable is recognized multiplied by the amount of cash collected on that receivable during the period. The cost-recovery method recognizes gross profit only after collections exceed the cost of the item sold, that is, when the full cost has been recovered. Subsequent amounts collected are treated entirely as realized gross profit.

19. Leopard Co. uses the installment sales method to recognize revenue. Customers pay the installment notes in 24 equal monthly amounts, which include 12% interest. What is the balance of an installment note receivable 6 months after the sale?

A. 75% of the original sales price.

B. Less than 75% of the original sales price.

C. The present value of the remaining monthly payments discounted at 12%.

D. Less than the present value of the remaining monthly payments discounted at 12%.

Answer (C) is correct. *(CPA, adapted)*

REQUIRED: The balance of an installment note 6 months after sale.

DISCUSSION: The balance of an installment note receivable equals the unpaid principal. The difference between the gross receivable and the unpaid principal equals interest. Thus, the balance of the note is equal to the present value of the remaining payments discounted at the contract interest rate.

Answer (A) is incorrect because the balance will be greater than 75% of the price. Because early payments contain a greater interest component than later payments, the sum of the principal components of the first six payments will be less than 25% of the price. Answer (B) is incorrect because the balance will be greater than 75% of the price. Because early payments contain a greater interest component than later payments, the sum of the principal components of the first six payments will be less than 25% of the price. Answer (D) is incorrect because the principal balance equals the present value of the remaining payments.

20. On January 2, year 1, Ishmael Co. sold a plant to Merchant Co. for $1.5 million. On that date, the plant's carrying cost was $1 million. Merchant gave Ishmael $300,000 cash and a $1.2 million note, payable in four annual installments of $300,000 plus 12% interest. Merchant made the first principal and interest payment of $444,000 on December 31, year 1. Ishmael uses the installment method of revenue recognition. In its year 1 income statement, what amount of realized gross profit should Ishmael report?

A. $344,000

B. $200,000

C. $148,000

D. $100,000

Answer (B) is correct. *(CPA, adapted)*

REQUIRED: The amount of realized gross profit under the installment method of revenue recognition.

DISCUSSION: The installment method recognizes gross profit on a sale as the related receivable is collected. The amount recognized each period is the gross profit ratio (gross profit ÷ selling price) multiplied by the cash collected. In addition, interest income must be accounted for separately from the gross profit on the sale. The cash collected is the $300,000 paid to Ishmael on 1/2/year 1, plus the $300,000 principal paid on 12/31/year 1. The gross profit is $500,000 ($1,500,000 – $1,000,000), and the gross profit ratio is 33 1/3% ($500,000 ÷ $1,500,000). Thus, the amount of realized profit is $200,000 ($600,000 × 33 1/3%).

Answer (A) is incorrect because $344,000 includes the interest income of $144,000 ($1,200,000 × 12%). Answer (C) is incorrect because $148,000 equals the gross profit ratio applied to the total payment of interest and principal (33 1/3% × $444,000). Answer (D) is incorrect because $100,000 is equal to the gross profit ratio applied to $300,000.

21. Decorum Co., which began operations on January 1, year 1, appropriately uses the installment method of accounting to record revenues. The following information is available for the years ended December 31, year 1 and year 2:

	Year 1	Year 2
Sales	$1,000,000	$2,000,000
Gross profit realized on sales made in:		
Year 1	150,000	90,000
Year 2	--	200,000
Gross profit percentages	30%	40%

What amount of installment accounts receivable should Decorum report in its December 31, year 2, balance sheet?

A. $1,100,000

B. $1,300,000

C. $1,700,000

D. $1,900,000

Answer (C) is correct. *(CPA, adapted)*

REQUIRED: The amount of installment accounts receivable.

DISCUSSION: Gross profit realized equals the gross profit percentage times cash collected. Cash collected may be calculated by dividing gross profit realized by the gross profit percentage. Hence, cash collected on year 1 sales was $800,000 [($150,000 + $90,000) ÷ 30%], and cash collected on year 2 sales was $500,000 ($200,000 ÷ 40%). Because installment accounts receivable equals sales minus collections, the remaining balance of installment receivables is $1,700,000 ($1,000,000 + $2,000,000 – $800,000 – $500,000).

Answer (A) is incorrect because $1,100,000 equals total gross profit (both realized and unrealized) for year 1 and year 2. Answer (B) is incorrect because $1,300,000 is total cash collected. Answer (D) is incorrect because $1,900,000 equals total sales minus total gross profit for year 1 and year 2.

22. Curling Co., which began operations on January 2, year 1, appropriately uses the installment sales method of accounting. The following information is available for year 1:

Installment accounts receivable, December 31, year 1	$800,000
Deferred gross profit, December 31, year 1 (before recognition of realized gross profit for year 1)	560,000
Gross profit on sales	40%

For the year ended December 31, year 1, cash collections and realized gross profit on sales should be

	Cash Collections	Realized Gross Profit
A.	$480,000	$320,000
B.	$480,000	$240,000
C.	$600,000	$320,000
D.	$600,000	$240,000

Answer (D) is correct. *(CPA, adapted)*

REQUIRED: The amount of cash collections and realized gross profit under the installment sales method.

DISCUSSION: Under the installment method, the periodic recognition of gross profit over the term of the installment receivable is equal to the gross profit margin on the sale multiplied by the amount of cash collected. Given that year 1 was the first year of operations for Curling, the $560,000 of total deferred gross profit before recognition of realized gross profit represents 40% of all sales. Hence, sales during year 1 were $1,400,000 ($560,000 ÷ 40%). The $800,000 in accounts receivable at year-end is the difference between total sales and cash collections; therefore, cash collections must have been $600,000 ($1,400,000 – $800,000). Because gross profit is recognized in proportion to cash collections, the realized gross profit for year 1 is equal to $240,000 ($600,000 cash collections × 40% gross margin).

Answer (A) is incorrect because $320,000 is the deferred gross profit after recognition of the realized gross profit, and $480,000 equals year-end installment receivables minus the deferred gross profit. Answer (B) is incorrect because $480,000 equals year-end installment receivables minus the deferred gross profit. Answer (C) is incorrect because $320,000 is the deferred gross profit after recognition of the realized gross profit.

23. On January 1, year 1, Seven Co. sold a used machine to Union, Inc. for $525,000. On this date, the machine had a depreciated cost of $367,500. Union paid $75,000 cash on January 1, year 1 and signed a $450,000 note bearing interest at 10%. The note was payable in three annual installments of $150,000 beginning January 1, year 2. Seven appropriately accounted for the sale under the installment method. Union made a timely payment of the first installment on January 1, year 2 of $195,000, which included interest of $45,000 to date of payment. At December 31, year 2, Seven has deferred gross profit of

A. $105,000

B. $99,000

C. $90,000

D. $76,500

Answer (C) is correct. *(CPA, adapted)*

REQUIRED: The deferred gross profit.

DISCUSSION: The deferred gross profit balance at the end of year 2 is equal to the amount of installment sales for which cash has not been collected times the gross profit margin. The uncollected amount of installment sales is $300,000 ($525,000 price – $75,000 down payment – $150,000 installment payment). The gross profit margin is 30% [($525,000 price – $367,500 carrying amount) ÷ $525,000]. Hence, the deferred gross profit is $90,000 (30% × $300,000).

Answer (A) is incorrect because $105,000 is equal to the $150,000 first installment payment minus the $45,000 interest. Answer (B) is incorrect because $99,000 includes 30% of the interest that will be due on January 1, year 3. Answer (D) is incorrect because $76,500 results from deducting the interest paid as part of the first installment from the balance of the installment receivable.

24. Feld Co., which began operations on January 1, year 1, appropriately uses the installment method of accounting. The following information pertains to its operations for the year 1:

Installment sales	$1,000,000
Regular sales	600,000
Cost of installment sales	500,000
Cost of regular sales	300,000
General and administrative expenses	100,000
Collections on installment sales	200,000

The balance in the deferred gross profit account in Feld's December 31, year 1 balance sheet should be

A. $200,000

B. $320,000

C. $400,000

D. $500,000

Answer (C) is correct. *(CPA, adapted)*

REQUIRED: The deferred gross profit at the end of the first year of operations.

DISCUSSION: The installment method recognizes gross profit as collections on installment sales are made. Gross profit recognized equals the cash collected multiplied by the gross profit margin on the installment sale that gave rise to the receivable. The ending balance in the deferred gross profit account equals the year-end balance of installment accounts receivable times the gross profit margin on the installment sales. The installment accounts receivable have a year-end balance of $800,000 ($1,000,000 installment sales – $200,000 collections on installment sales). The gross profit margin is equal to the installment sales minus their cost, divided by the installment sales. As indicated below, the gross profit margin on year 1 installment sales is 50%. At 12/31/year 1, Feld should record a deferred gross profit of $400,000 ($800,000 × 50%).

$$\frac{\$1,000,000 - \$500,000}{\$1,000,000} = 50\% \text{ gross profit margin}$$

Answer (A) is incorrect because $200,000 equals collections on installment sales. Answer (B) is incorrect because $320,000 results from including the general and administrative expenses in the cost of installment sales. Answer (D) is incorrect because $500,000 is the total of deferred and recognized gross profit.

25. When assets that have been sold and accounted for by the installment method are subsequently repossessed and returned to inventory, they should be recorded on the books at

A. Selling price.

B. The amount of the installment receivable less associated deferred gross profit.

C. Net realizable value.

D. Net realizable value minus normal profit.

Answer (D) is correct. *(Publisher)*

REQUIRED: The recorded amount of repossessed assets accounted for by the installment method.

DISCUSSION: Repossessed assets returned to inventory should usually be recorded at their net realizable value minus normal profit. Net realizable value is the selling price minus costs of completion, reconditioning, and reselling. Normal profit should be recognized upon resale.

Answer (A) is incorrect because, if repossessed goods are recorded at selling price, a loss would occur upon resale if reconditioning or selling costs were incurred. Answer (B) is incorrect because the installment receivable minus the associated deferred gross profit is usually not equal to the net realizable value of the asset. Answer (C) is incorrect because recording at net realizable value precludes recognition of normal profit upon resale.

26. Christopher Co. sells equipment on installment contracts. Which of the following statements best justifies Christopher's use of the cost-recovery method of revenue recognition to account for these installment sales?

A. The sales contract provides that title to the equipment passes to the purchaser only when all payments have been made.

B. No cash payments are due until one year from the date of sale.

C. Sales are subject to a high rate of return.

D. There is no reasonable basis for estimating collectibility.

Answer (D) is correct. *(CPA, adapted)*

REQUIRED: The best justification for the cost-recovery method.

DISCUSSION: APB 10 states that revenues ordinarily should be accounted for when a transaction is completed, with appropriate provision for uncollectible accounts. However, when there is no reasonable basis for estimating the degree of collectibility, either the installment method or the cost-recovery method may be used. The cost-recovery method recognizes gross profit only after collections exceed the cost of the item sold.

Answer (A) is incorrect because passage of title is not a recognition criterion. Answer (B) is incorrect because a delayed due date does not necessarily indicate that collectibility cannot be reasonably estimated. Answer (C) is incorrect because a high rate of return does not necessarily indicate that collectibility cannot be reasonably estimated.

27. Several of Pitt, Inc.'s customers are having cash flow problems. Information pertaining to these customers for the years ended March 31, year 1 and year 2 follows:

	3/31/year 1	3/31/year 2
Sales	$10,000	$15,000
Cost of sales	8,000	9,000
Cash collections		
on year 1 sales	7,000	3,000
on year 2 sales	--	12,000

If the cost-recovery method is used, what amount should Pitt report as gross profit from sales to these customers for the year ended March 31, year 2?

A. $2,000

B. $3,000

C. $5,000

D. $15,000

Answer (C) is correct. *(CPA, adapted)*

REQUIRED: The gross profit from sales if the cost-recovery method is used.

DISCUSSION: The cost-recovery method recognizes profit only after collections exceed the cost of the item sold, that is, when the full cost has been recovered. Subsequent amounts collected are treated entirely as realized gross profit. The sum of collections in excess of costs to be recognized as gross profit is $5,000 [($3,000 of year 2 collections on year 1 sales + $7,000 of year 1 collections on year 1 sales – $8,000 cost) + ($12,000 of collections on year 2 sales – $9,000 cost)].

Answer (A) is incorrect because $2,000 excludes the profit on year 2 sales. Answer (B) is incorrect because $3,000 excludes the gross profit on year 1 sales. Answer (D) is incorrect because $15,000 equals year 2 sales.

28. The following information pertains to a sale of real estate by South Co. to Nord Co. on December 31, year 1:

Carrying amount		$4,000,000
Sales price:		
Cash	$ 600,000	
Purchase money mortgage	5,400,000	6,000,000

The mortgage is payable in nine annual installments of $600,000 beginning December 31, year 2, plus interest of 10%. The December 31, year 2 installment was paid as scheduled, together with interest of $540,000. South uses the cost-recovery method to account for the sale. What amount of gross profit should South recognize in year 2 from the real estate sale and its financing?

A. $1,140,000

B. $740,000

C. $540,000

D. $0

Answer (D) is correct. *(CPA, adapted)*

REQUIRED: The gross profit recognized under the cost-recovery method.

DISCUSSION: The cost-recovery method recognizes gross profit only after collections exceed the cost of the item sold, that is, when the full cost has been recovered. As of 12/31/year 2, only $1,200,000 of the $4,000,000 cost has been recovered. Consequently, no gross profit should be recognized.

22.3 Consignments

29. In accounting for sales on consignment, sales revenue and the related cost of goods sold should be recognized by the

A. Consignor when the goods are shipped to the consignee.

B. Consignee when the goods are shipped to the third party.

C. Consignor when notification is received that the consignee has sold the goods.

D. Consignee when cash is received from the customer.

Answer (C) is correct. *(CIA, adapted)*

REQUIRED: The basis for recognition of sales revenue and related cost of goods sold for goods on consignment.

DISCUSSION: Under a consignment sales arrangement, the consignor ships merchandise to the consignee, who acts as agent for the consignor in selling the goods. The goods are in the physical possession of the consignee but remain the property of the consignor and are included in the consignor's inventory count. Sales revenue and the related cost of goods sold from these consigned goods should be recognized by the consignor only when the merchandise is sold and delivered to the ultimate customer. Accordingly, recognition occurs when notification is received that the consignee has sold the goods.

Answer (A) is incorrect because, at the date of shipment to the consignee, the goods are still the property of the consignor. Answer (B) is incorrect because the consignee does not recognize sales revenue or cost of goods sold for these goods. The consignee recognizes commission revenue only when the goods are sold and delivered to the third party. Answer (D) is incorrect because the consignee does not recognize sales revenue or cost of goods sold for these goods. The consignee recognizes commission revenue only when the goods are sold and delivered to the third party.

30. Consignor Co. paid the in-transit insurance premium for consignment goods shipped to Consignee Co. In addition, Consignor advanced part of the commissions that will be due when Consignee sells the goods. Should Consignor include the in-transit insurance premium and the advanced commissions in inventory costs?

	Insurance Premiums	Advanced Commissions
A.	Yes	Yes
B.	No	No
C.	Yes	No
D.	No	Yes

Answer (C) is correct. *(CPA, adapted)*

REQUIRED: The item(s) included in a consignor's inventory costs.

DISCUSSION: Inventoriable costs include all costs of making the inventory ready for sale. Costs incurred by a consignor on the transfer of goods to a consignee are costs necessary to prepare the inventory for sale. Consequently, these costs are inventoriable, and therefore the in-transit insurance premium is inventoried. The advanced commissions constitute a receivable or prepaid expense, not an element of inventory cost.

Answer (A) is incorrect because the advanced commissions are not an element of inventory cost. Answer (B) is incorrect because the in-transit insurance premium is inventoried. Answer (D) is incorrect because the in-transit insurance premium is inventoried, but the advanced commissions are not an element of inventory cost.

Questions 31 and 32 are based on the following information. Glazier Co. sells all of its glassware on a consignment basis. The consignees receive reimbursement of expenses plus a sales commission of 10% of retail value. During the current year, Glazier shipped 11,800 units with a cost of $24 per unit and a retail value of $44 per unit to the Glass Retailers. Freight paid by Glazier on these shipments totaled $26,600. Glass reported that it sold 9,500 units and incurred expenses relating to the sold units, exclusive of commissions, in the amount of $19,200. Glass remitted cash for the units sold minus commissions and expenses.

31. The cash collected during the year by Glazier from Glass is

A. $208,800

B. $357,000

C. $186,000

D. $398,800

Answer (B) is correct. *(CMA, adapted)*

REQUIRED: The cash collected by the consignor.

DISCUSSION: The consignor will receive cash equal to the sales price of the units sold, minus expenses of $19,200, minus a 10% sales commission. The units sold for $418,000 ($44 × 9,500). Cash collected equaled $357,000 [$418,000 – (10% × $418,000) – $19,200].

Answer (A) is incorrect because $208,800 is based on the cost of $24 per unit, not the retail selling price, and ignores the sales commissions. Answer (C) is incorrect because $186,000 is based on the cost of $24 per unit, not the retail selling price of $44. Answer (D) is incorrect because $398,800 omits the 10% sales commission.

32. Glazier's profit before taxes from consignment sales made by Glass for the current year is

A. $129,000

B. $138,280

C. $102,400

D. $107,585

Answer (D) is correct. *(CMA, adapted)*

REQUIRED: The consignor's profit before taxes.

DISCUSSION: The consignor will receive cash equal to the sales price of the units sold, minus expenses of $19,200, minus a 10% sales commission. The units sold for $418,000 ($44 × 9,500). Cash collected equaled $357,000 [$418,000 – (10% × $418,000) – $19,200]. Freight costs attributable to the units sold were $21,415 [(9,500 units sold ÷ 11,800 units consigned) × $26,600]. Thus, pretax profit is $107,585 [$357,000 – $21,415 freight costs – ($24 unit cost × 9,500)].

Answer (A) is incorrect because $129,000 ignores the freight costs of $26,600. Answer (B) is incorrect because $138,280 assumes 11,800 units were sold. Answer (C) is incorrect because $102,400 expenses all of the freight costs (inventoriable costs).

33. Jel Co., a consignee, paid the freight costs for goods shipped from Dale Co., a consignor. These freight costs are to be deducted from Jel's payment to Dale when the consignment goods are sold. Until Jel sells the goods, the freight costs should be included in Jel's

A. Cost of goods sold.

B. Freight-out costs.

C. Selling expenses.

D. Accounts receivable.

Answer (D) is correct. *(CPA, adapted)*

REQUIRED: The consignee's classification of freight costs paid by the consignee on behalf of the consignor.

DISCUSSION: The consignee should debit consignment-in for the freight costs. Consignment-in is a receivable/payable account used by consignees. It represents the amount payable to the consignor if it has a credit balance. If it has a debit balance, it reflects the amount receivable from the consignor. Before consigned goods are sold, expenditures chargeable to the consignor are recorded in the consignment-in account as a receivable. After the consigned goods are sold, the consignee's net liability to the consignor is reflected in the account.

34. The following information was derived from the current-year accounting records of Niche Co.:

	Niche's Central Warehouse	Niche's Goods Held by Consignees
Beginning inventory	$110,000	$12,000
Purchases	480,000	60,000
Freight-in	10,000	
Transportation to consignees		5,000
Freight-out	30,000	8,000
Ending inventory	145,000	20,000

Niche's cost of sales for the current year is

A. $455,000

B. $485,000

C. $507,000

D. $512,000

Answer (D) is correct. *(CPA, adapted)*
REQUIRED: The total cost of sales for goods sold from a central warehouse and by consignees.
DISCUSSION: Cost of sales is equal to the cost of goods available for sale minus the ending inventory. Cost of goods available for sale is equal to beginning inventory, plus purchases, plus additional costs (such as freight-in and transportation to consignees) that are necessary to prepare the inventory for sale. As indicated below, the cost of sales for the inventory items held in the central warehouse is $455,000. The cost of sales for the inventory held by consignees is $57,000. Hence, total cost of sales equals $512,000 ($455,000 + $57,000). Freight-out is a selling cost and therefore not included in the determination of cost of sales.

Central Warehouse Inventory

1/1	$110,000	$455,000	Cost of sales
Purchases	480,000		
Freight-in	10,000		
12/31	$145,000		

Consigned Inventory

1/1	$12,000	$57,000	Cost of sales
Purchases	60,000		
Transportation	5,000		
12/31	$20,000		

Answer (A) is incorrect because $455,000 is the cost of sales for the central warehouse inventory. Answer (B) is incorrect because $485,000 is the cost of sales for the central warehouse inventory assuming freight-out is included as a cost of sales. Answer (C) is incorrect because $507,000 is the cost of sales minus the cost of transportation to consignees ($512,000 – $5,000).

35. On October 1, the Ajax Company consigned 100 television sets to M & R Retailers, Inc. Each television set had a cost of $150. Freight on the shipment was paid by Ajax in the amount of $200. On December 1, M & R submitted an "account sales" stating that it had sold 60 sets, and it remitted the $12,840 balance due. The remittance was net of the following deductions from the sales price of the televisions sold:

Commission	20% of sales price
Advertising	$500
Delivery and installation charges	100

What was the total sales price of the television sets sold by M & R?

A. $13,440

B. $15,000

C. $16,800

D. $17,000

Answer (C) is correct. *(CPA, adapted)*
REQUIRED: The total sales price of the consigned goods sold during the period.
DISCUSSION: Because the television sets are on consignment from Ajax, M & R should make no accounting entry to record the receipt of the sets. The inventory should remain on the books of Ajax. A consignment-in account is used by M & R to record reimbursable expenses in connection with the consignment and sales of the consigned goods. Assuming the advertising and delivery and installation charges are expenses of Ajax, they are debits to consignment-in (reimbursable cash outlays). Moreover, the commission of 20% of the sales price due M & R should be debited to the account. The calculation of sales price is given below:

Consignment-In

Adv.	$ 500	X	Sales
Del. & inst.	100		
Commission	.2 X		
Remit to Ajax	$12,840		

$$
\begin{aligned}
\$500 + \$100 + .2X + \$12{,}840 &= X \\
\$13{,}440 &= X - .2X \\
\$13{,}440 &= .8X \\
\$16{,}800 &= X
\end{aligned}
$$

Answer (A) is incorrect because $13,440 is the total sales price if the amount of commission is excluded. Answer (B) is incorrect because $15,000 is the amount of consigned television sets multiplied by the cost per set (100 × $150). Answer (D) is incorrect because $17,000 is the total sales price plus the freight costs paid by Ajax ($16,800 + $200).

36. Mora Co.'s December 31 balance sheet reported the following current assets:

Cash	$ 70,000
Accounts receivable	120,000
Inventories	60,000
Total	$250,000

An analysis of the accounts disclosed that accounts receivable consisted of the following:

Trade accounts	$ 96,000
Allowance for uncollectible accounts	(2,000)
Selling price of Mora's unsold goods out on consignment, at 130% of cost, not included in Mora's ending inventory	26,000
Total	$120,000

At December 31, the total of Mora's current assets is

A. $224,000

B. $230,000

C. $244,000

D. $270,000

Answer (C) is correct. *(CPA, adapted)*

REQUIRED: The amount of total current assets to be reported at year-end.

DISCUSSION: Under a consignment sales agreement, the goods are in the physical possession of the consignee but remain the property of the consignor and are included in the consignor's inventory. Thus, unsold consigned goods should be included in inventory at cost ($26,000 ÷ 130% = $20,000), not in receivables at their sale price. Current assets should therefore be $244,000 ($70,000 cash + $94,000 net receivables + $80,000 inventory).

Answer (A) is incorrect because $224,000 does not include the cost of the consigned goods in inventory. Answer (B) is incorrect because $230,000 results from subtracting the cost of the consigned goods from the total reported current assets. Answer (D) is incorrect because $270,000 results from adding the cost of the consigned goods to the total reported current assets.

37. Petra Co. had the following consignment transactions during December:

Inventory shipped on consignment to Rock Co.	$18,000
Freight paid by Petra	900
Inventory received on consignment from Jeter Co.	12,000
Freight paid by Jeter	500

No sales of consigned goods were made through December 31. Petra's December 31 balance sheet should include consigned inventory at

A. $12,000

B. $12,500

C. $18,000

D. $18,900

Answer (D) is correct. *(CPA, adapted)*

REQUIRED: The recognition of inventory for consignment sales.

DISCUSSION: In a consignment, the consignor ships merchandise to the consignee, who acts as agent for the consignor in selling the goods. The goods are in the physical possession of the consignee but remain the physical property of the consignor and are included in the consignor's inventory. Costs incurred by a consignor on the transfer of goods to a consignee are inventoriable. Thus, Petra's inventory account should include $18,900 equal to the $18,000 inventory shipped to Rock on consignment and the $900 associated freight charges.

Answer (A) is incorrect because $12,000 is the inventory received from Jeter, which is not the property of Petra. Answer (B) is incorrect because $12,500 is the inventory received from Jeter and the associated freight charges. Answer (C) is incorrect because $18,000 does not include the $900 freight cost.

38. On December 1, New Co. received 505 sweaters on consignment from Olden. Olden's cost for the sweaters was $80 each, and they were priced to sell at $100. New's commission on consigned goods is 10%. At December 31, five sweaters remained. In its December 31 balance sheet, what amount should New report as payable for consigned goods?

A. $49,000

B. $45,400

C. $45,000

D. $40,400

Answer (C) is correct. *(CPA, adapted)*

REQUIRED: The payable reported by the consignee for consigned goods.

DISCUSSION: Consignment-in is a receivable/payable account used by consignees. It is the amount payable to the consignor if it has a credit balance. The amount of the payable equals total sales minus 10% commission on the goods sold, or $45,000 [($100 × 500) sales – 10% × ($100 × 500)].

Answer (A) is incorrect because $49,000 equals sales minus 10% of the gross margin on sales. Answer (B) is incorrect because $45,400 equals the cost of 505 sweaters, plus the commissions on the 500 sweaters sold. Answer (D) is incorrect because $40,400 is the cost of 505 sweaters.

STUDY UNIT TWENTY-THREE
FINANCIAL STATEMENT ANALYSIS BASED ON PERCENTAGE RELATIONSHIPS

Converting the information contained in financial statements to percentage relationships often enhances financial statement analysis. Common-size analysis and ratio analysis are the primary methods based on percentage relationships.

Common-size financial statements are expressed in percentages. **Horizontal common-size analysis** focuses on changes in operating results and financial position during two or more accounting periods. The changes are expressed in terms of percentages of corresponding amounts in a base period.

Vertical common-size analysis concerns the relationships among financial statement items of a single accounting period expressed in terms of a percentage relationship to a base item. For example, income statement items may be expressed as percentages of sales or cost of goods sold, and balance sheet items may be expressed as a percentage of total assets.

Ratio analysis focuses on the relationship of two or more related financial statement items. Ratios commonly measure financial attributes such as liquidity, activity, profitability, and stability. They are used for internal comparisons of an enterprise's operations over a number of accounting periods; they also are used for external comparisons of an enterprise's performance with that of other enterprises.

Liquidity or solvency ratios, e.g., current ratio and quick (acid-test) ratio, analyze short-term viability, that is, the ability of the enterprise to satisfy its short-term obligations. Activity ratios, e.g., receivables turnover ratio and inventory turnover ratio, analyze the enterprise's ability to generate revenue and operating income. Profitability ratios, e.g., earnings per share, rate of return, and price-earnings ratio, analyze the firm's effectiveness in meeting its return objectives. Stability ratios, e.g., debt ratio and times-interest-earned ratio, analyze the enterprise's long-term solvency.

QUESTIONS

23.1 General

1. Of the several methods of financial analysis, the most basic and widely used is fundamental analysis, which values common stock based upon

A. All available information concerning the company in relation to similar companies.

B. Daily volume of trading and price changes.

C. The stock's risk relative to its rate of return.

D. The relationship of past stock prices and earnings.

Answer (A) is correct. *(Publisher)*

REQUIRED: The description of fundamental analysis.

DISCUSSION: Fundamental analysis is based on the assumption that the inherent worth of a security can be determined by consideration of the facts. An investor will then make buy and sell decisions based on the relation of the inherent worth to the market price of the security. Ratio analysis is a form of fundamental analysis.

Answer (B) is incorrect because technical analysis concerns daily volume of trading and price changes. Answer (C) is incorrect because capital market analysis (based on the efficient market hypothesis) values stock based on its risk and return. Answer (D) is incorrect because linear regression analysis considers the relationship of past stock prices and earnings.

2. A useful tool in financial statement analysis is the common-size financial statement. What does this tool enable the financial analyst to do?

A. Evaluate financial statements of companies within a given industry of approximately the same value.

B. Determine which companies in the same industry are at approximately the same stage of development.

C. Compare the mix of assets, liabilities, capital, revenue, and expenses within a company over time or between companies within a given industry without respect to relative size.

D. Ascertain the relative potential of companies of similar size in different industries.

Answer (C) is correct. *(CPA, adapted)*

REQUIRED: The purposes of a common-size financial statement.

DISCUSSION: A common-size financial statement presents the items in a financial statement as percentages of a common base amount. In vertical common-size analysis, the items in a balance sheet are usually stated in percentages of total assets, and the items in the income statement are usually expressed as a percentage of sales. Thus, comparisons among firms in the same industry are made possible despite differences in size. Comparison of firms in different industries has drawbacks because the optimum mix of assets, liabilities, etc., will vary from industry to industry. Horizontal common-size analysis focuses on changes in operating results and financial position during two or more accounting periods. The changes are expressed in terms of percentages of corresponding amounts in a base period.

Answer (A) is incorrect because common-size statements are designed to permit comparison of different-sized companies. Answer (B) is incorrect because common-size statements do not reveal the stage of development of a company and are more useful for comparing companies in the same industries than in different ones. Answer (D) is incorrect because common-size statements do not reveal the stage of development of a company and are more useful for comparing companies in the same industries than in different ones.

3. In financial statement analysis, the expression of all financial statement figures as a percentage of base-year figures is

A. Horizontal common-size analysis.

B. Vertical common-size analysis.

C. Cross-sectional analysis.

D. Ratio analysis.

Answer (A) is correct. *(CMA, adapted)*

REQUIRED: The financial statement analysis based on the expression of financial statement figures as a percentage of base-year figures.

DISCUSSION: Horizontal common-size analysis is a percentage analysis technique in which financial data from two or more accounting periods are expressed in terms of a single designated base. Percentage analysis is a technique used to highlight trends in individual line items or accounts of financial statements.

Answer (B) is incorrect because, in vertical analysis, all of the line items or accounts in a particular financial statement are presented as a percentage of a single designated line item or account in that financial statement. Answer (C) is incorrect because cross-sectional analysis is a technique that is not time related. Answer (D) is incorrect because ratio analysis is an analysis technique that concerns the relationship between two or more line items or accounts in the financial statements.

4. In capital market analysis, the nonsystematic risk

A. Is correlated with qualitative aspects of the underlying entity.

B. Is correlated with quantitative aspects of the underlying entity.

C. Cannot easily be overcome by individual investors.

D. Is considered random.

Answer (D) is correct. *(Publisher)*

REQUIRED: The true statement about nonsystematic risk in capital market analysis.

DISCUSSION: Nonsystematic risk is considered to be unique to a firm and therefore random. In capital market theory, nonsystematic risk can largely be avoided through diversified investments.

Answer (A) is incorrect because nonsystematic risk cannot be correlated with any variable, whether qualitative or quantitative. Answer (B) is incorrect because nonsystematic risk cannot be correlated with any variable, whether qualitative or quantitative. Answer (C) is incorrect because nonsystematic risk may be reduced through diversification.

5. The relationship of the total debt to the total equity of a corporation is a measure of

A. Liquidity.

B. Profitability.

C. Creditor risk.

D. Solvency.

Answer (C) is correct. *(CMA, adapted)*

REQUIRED: The information provided by the debt-to-equity ratio.

DISCUSSION: The ratio of total debt to total equity is a measure of risk to creditors. It helps in the evaluation of a company's relative reliance on debt and equity financing (leverage).

Answer (A) is incorrect because liquidity measures describe the ability of a company to meet its short-term obligations. Answer (B) is incorrect because profitability ratios measure the relative success of a firm in earning a return on its assets, sales, equity, etc. Answer (D) is incorrect because solvency measures describe the ability of a company to meet its short-term obligations.

6. What type of ratio is earnings per share?

A. Profitability ratio.

B. Activity ratio.

C. Liquidity ratio.

D. Leverage ratio.

Answer (A) is correct. *(Publisher)*

REQUIRED: The proper classification of the earnings-per-share ratio.

DISCUSSION: Earnings per share is a profitability ratio. It measures the level of profitability of the entity on a per-share basis.

Answer (B) is incorrect because activity ratios measure management's efficiency in using specific resources. Answer (C) is incorrect because liquidity ratios indicate the ability of an entity to meet short-term obligations. Answer (D) is incorrect because leverage ratios concern the relationship of debt to equity and measure the impact of the debt on profitability and risk.

7. Are the following ratios useful in assessing the liquidity position of a company?

	Defensive-Interval Ratio	Return on Equity
A.	Yes	Yes
B.	Yes	No
C.	No	Yes
D.	No	No

Answer (B) is correct. *(CPA, adapted)*

REQUIRED: The ratio(s) useful in assessing the liquidity position of a company.

DISCUSSION: The defensive-interval ratio is equal to defensive assets divided by average daily expenditures for operations. Defensive assets include cash, short-term marketable securities, and net short-term receivables. This ratio provides information about a company's ability to survive in the absence of external cash flows. It is therefore useful in assessing liquidity (the ability to meet obligations as they mature). In contrast, return on equity is equal to net income minus preferred dividends, divided by average common equity. Return on equity provides information about the profitability of the firm. It does not provide information that is useful in assessing liquidity.

23.2 Quick (Acid-Test) Ratio

8. Which of the following ratios is(are) useful in assessing a company's ability to meet currently maturing or short-term obligations?

	Acid-Test Ratio	Debt-to-Equity Ratio
A.	No	No
B.	No	Yes
C.	Yes	Yes
D.	Yes	No

Answer (D) is correct. *(CPA, adapted)*

REQUIRED: The ratio(s) useful in assessing a company's ability to meet currently maturing obligations.

DISCUSSION: Liquidity ratios measure the ability of a company to meet its short-term obligations. A commonly used liquidity ratio is the acid-test or quick ratio, which equals quick assets (net accounts receivable, current marketable securities, and cash) divided by current liabilities. The debt-to-equity ratio is a leverage ratio. Leverage ratios measure the impact of debt on profitability and risk.

9. How is the average inventory used in the calculation of each of the following?

	Acid-Test (Quick) Ratio	Inventory Turnover Ratio
A.	Numerator	Numerator
B.	Numerator	Denominator
C.	Not used	Denominator
D.	Not used	Numerator

Answer (C) is correct. *(CPA, adapted)*
REQUIRED: The use of average inventories in the acid-test (quick) ratio and the inventory turnover ratio.
DISCUSSION: Assets included in the numerator of the acid-test (quick) ratio include cash, current marketable securities, and net accounts receivable. The inventory turnover ratio is equal to cost of goods sold divided by average inventory. Thus, average inventory is included in the denominator of the inventory turnover ratio but is not used in the acid-test ratio.

10. Selected financial data from Barrymore Co. are

	As of December 31
Cash	$ 75,000
Accounts receivable (net)	225,000
Merchandise inventory	270,000
Trading securities (current)	40,000
Land and building (net)	500,000
Mortgage payable-current portion	30,000
Accounts payable and accrued liabilities	120,000
Short-term notes payable	50,000
	Year Ended December 31
Sales	$1,500,000
Cost of goods sold	900,000

Barrymore's quick (acid-test) ratio as of December 31 is

A. 3.6 to 1.
B. 3.1 to 1.
C. 2.0 to 1.
D. 1.7 to 1.

Answer (D) is correct. *(CPA, adapted)*
REQUIRED: The company's quick (acid-test) ratio.
DISCUSSION: The quick or acid-test ratio is a measure of the firm's ability to pay its maturing liabilities in the short run. It is defined as quick assets divided by current liabilities. Quick assets are current monetary assets, such as cash, current marketable securities, and net accounts receivable. The company's quick assets equal $340,000 ($75,000 + $225,000 + $40,000). The current liabilities equal $200,000 ($30,000 + $120,000 + $50,000). Dividing the $340,000 of quick assets by the $200,000 of current liabilities results in a quick (acid-test) ratio of 1.7 to 1.
Answer (A) is incorrect because 3.6 to 1 includes inventory in the quick assets and does not include the current portion of the mortgage payable in the current liabilities. Answer (B) is incorrect because 3.1 to 1 includes inventory in the current monetary assets. Answer (C) is incorrect because 2.0 to 1 does not include the current portion of the mortgage payable in the current liabilities.

11. North Bank is analyzing Belle Corp.'s financial statements for a possible extension of credit. Belle's quick ratio is significantly better than the industry average. Which of the following factors should North consider as a possible limitation of using this ratio when evaluating Belle's creditworthiness?

A. Fluctuating market prices of short-term investments may adversely affect the ratio.
B. Increasing market prices for Belle's inventory may adversely affect the ratio.
C. Belle may need to sell its available-for-sale investments to meet its current obligations.
D. Belle may need to liquidate its inventory to meet its long-term obligations.

Answer (A) is correct. *(CPA, adapted)*
REQUIRED: The possible limitation of using the quick ratio to evaluate creditworthiness.
DISCUSSION: The quick ratio equals current assets minus inventory, divided by current liabilities. Because short-term marketable securities are included in the numerator, fluctuating market prices of short-term investments may adversely affect the ratio if Belle holds a substantial amount of such current assets.
Answer (B) is incorrect because inventory is excluded from the calculation of the quick ratio. Answer (C) is incorrect because, if the available-for-sale securities are not current, they are not included in the calculation of the ratio. If they are classified as current, their sale to meet current obligations is consistent with normal current assets management practices. Answer (D) is incorrect because inventory is excluded from the calculation of the quick ratio.

12. Given an acid-test ratio of 2.0, current assets of $5,000, and inventory of $2,000, and assuming no prepaid expenses, the value of current liabilities is

A. $1,500

B. $2,500

C. $3,500

D. $6,000

Answer (A) is correct. *(CIA, adapted)*

REQUIRED: The value of current liabilities given the acid-test ratio, current assets, and inventory.

DISCUSSION: The acid-test or quick ratio equals the ratio of the quick assets divided by current liabilities. Current assets equal the quick assets plus inventory and prepaid expenses. This question assumes that the entity has no prepaid expenses. Given current assets of $5,000, inventory of $2,000, and no prepaid expenses, the quick assets must be $3,000. Because the acid test ratio is 2.0, the quick assets are double the current liabilities. Current liabilities therefore are equal to $1,500 ($3,000 quick assets ÷ 2.0).

Answer (B) is incorrect because $2,500 results from dividing the current assets by 2.0. Current assets include inventory, which should not be included in the calculation of the acid-test ratio. Answer (C) is incorrect because $3,500 results from adding inventory to current assets rather than subtracting it. Answer (D) is incorrect because $6,000 results from multiplying the quick assets by 2 instead of dividing by 2.

23.3 Current Ratio and Net Working Capital

13. At December 30, Agnon Co. had cash of $200,000, a current ratio of 1.5:1, and a quick ratio of .5:1. On December 31, all cash was used to reduce accounts payable. How did these cash payments affect the ratios?

	Current Ratio	Quick Ratio
A.	Increased	Decreased
B.	Increased	No effect
C.	Decreased	Increased
D.	Decreased	No effect

Answer (A) is correct. *(CPA, adapted)*

REQUIRED: The effect of the cash payments on the current and quick ratios.

DISCUSSION: The current ratio (1.5) equals current assets (cash, net accounts receivable, current marketable securities, certain available-for-sale and held-to-maturity securities, inventory, prepaid expenses) divided by current liabilities (accounts payable, etc.). If a ratio is greater than 1.0, equal decreases in the numerator and denominator (debit accounts payable and credit cash for $200,000) increase the ratio. The quick ratio (.5) equals quick assets divided by current liabilities. If a ratio is less than 1.0, equal decreases in the numerator and denominator (debit accounts payable and credit cash for $200,000) decrease the ratio.

14. Information from Dominic Company's year-end financial statements is as follows:

	Year 1	Year 2
Current assets	$ 4,000,000	$ 4,200,000
Current liabilities	2,000,000	1,800,000
Equity	5,000,000	5,400,000
Net sales	16,600,000	17,600,000
Cost of goods sold	12,400,000	12,800,000
Operating income	1,000,000	1,100,000

What is the current ratio at December 31, year 2?

A. 1.20 to 1.

B. 2.25 to 1.

C. 2.33 to 1.

D. 7.33 to 1.

Answer (C) is correct. *(CPA, adapted)*

REQUIRED: The current ratio at the end of the second year.

DISCUSSION: The current ratio equals current assets divided by current liabilities. For year 2, the current ratio equals $4,200,000 divided by $1,800,000, or 2.33. The other information is irrelevant.

15. In comparing the current ratios of two companies, why is it invalid to assume that the company with the higher current ratio is the better company?

A. The current ratio includes assets other than cash.

B. A high current ratio may indicate inadequate inventory on hand.

C. A high current ratio may indicate inefficient use of various assets and liabilities.

D. The two companies may define working capital in different terms.

Answer (C) is correct. *(CPA, adapted)*

REQUIRED: The reason comparison of firms' current ratios does not indicate the better company.

DISCUSSION: The current ratio measures only the ratio of current assets to current liabilities. It does not measure the efficiency of handling the individual current asset accounts. A high ratio may indicate, for example, slow collection of accounts receivable, holding of excess inventory, or retention of more cash than needed for the cash flow requirements of the firm. The weaker and less efficient company may have the higher current ratio.

Answer (A) is incorrect because the composition of the assets in the current ratio does not, by itself, indicate whether a higher or lower ratio is preferable. Answer (B) is incorrect because a high ratio more likely indicates excess inventory on hand. Answer (D) is incorrect because working capital is always defined as the excess of current assets over current liabilities.

16. Badoglio Co.'s current ratio is 3:1. Which of the following transactions would normally increase its current ratio?

A. Purchasing inventory on account.

B. Selling inventory on account.

C. Collecting an account receivable.

D. Purchasing machinery for cash.

Answer (B) is correct. *(CPA, adapted)*

REQUIRED: The transaction that would increase a current ratio.

DISCUSSION: The current ratio is equal to current assets divided by current liabilities. Given that the company has a current ratio of 3:1, an increase in current assets or decrease in current liabilities would cause this ratio to increase. If the company sold merchandise on open account that earned a normal gross margin, receivables would be increased at the time of recording the sales revenue in an amount greater than the decrease in inventory from recording the cost of goods sold. The effect would be an increase in the current assets and no change in the current liabilities. Thus, the current ratio would be increased.

Answer (A) is incorrect because the purchase of inventory on open account increases current assets and current liabilities by the same amount. Equal increases in the numerator and denominator of a fraction that exceeds one decrease the fraction. Answer (C) is incorrect because collecting an account receivable decreases one current asset and increases another by the same amount. Answer (D) is incorrect because purchasing machinery for cash decreases a current asset and increases a noncurrent asset, thereby decreasing the ratio.

17. Mogul Co. wrote off obsolete inventory during the current year. What was the effect of this write-off on Mogul's ratio analysis?

A. Decrease in current ratio but not in quick ratio.

B. Decrease in quick ratio but not in current ratio.

C. Increase in current ratio but not in quick ratio.

D. Increase in quick ratio but not in current ratio.

Answer (A) is correct. *(CPA, adapted)*

REQUIRED: The effect of writing off obsolete inventory.

DISCUSSION: The entry is to debit a loss and credit inventory, an asset that is included in the numerator of the current ratio, but not the quick ratio. Hence the write-off decreases the current ratio, but not the quick ratio.

18. Galad Corp. has current assets of $180,000 and current liabilities of $360,000. Which of the following transactions would improve Galad's current ratio?

A. Refinancing a $60,000 long-term mortgage with a short-term note.

B. Purchasing $100,000 of merchandise inventory with a short-term account payable.

C. Paying $40,000 of short-term accounts payable.

D. Collecting $20,000 of short-term accounts receivable.

Answer (B) is correct. *(CPA, adapted)*

REQUIRED: The transaction that improves the current ratio.

DISCUSSION: If a current ratio is less than 1.0, a transaction that results in equal increases in the numerator and denominator will improve the ratio. The current ratio is .5 ($180,000 ÷ $360,000). Debiting inventory and crediting accounts payable increases the ratio to .61 ($280,000 ÷ $460,000).

Answer (A) is incorrect because refinancing a $60,000 long-term mortgage with a short-term note results in an increase in the denominator and no change in the numerator. Answer (C) is incorrect because decreasing the denominator and the numerator by the same amount decreases a current ratio that is lower than 1.0. Answer (D) is incorrect because collecting $20,000 of short-term accounts receivable has no effect on the amount of the numerator or denominator.

19. Austen, Inc. uses the allowance method to account for uncollectible accounts. An account receivable that was previously determined to be uncollectible and written off was collected during September. The effect of the collection on Austen's current ratio and total working capital is

	Current Ratio	Working Capital
A.	None	None
B.	Increase	Increase
C.	Decrease	Decrease
D.	None	Increase

Answer (A) is correct. *(CMA, adapted)*

REQUIRED: The effect of the collection of a previously written off account receivable on the current ratio and total working capital.

DISCUSSION: The current ratio is the ratio of current assets to current liabilities. Working capital is equal to the difference between current assets and current liabilities. When an account receivable is written off, the allowance for uncollectible accounts and the gross receivables are decreased by the same amount. Thus, there is no effect on net accounts receivable. When an account receivable that was previously determined to be uncollectible and written off is collected, the amounts previously written off must be reestablished (debit accounts receivable, credit the allowance). This entry also has no net effect on net accounts receivable. The collection is then recorded as an equal increase in cash and a decrease in accounts receivable. The changes in these accounts are equal, so net current assets is unchanged. Because the net amount of current assets remains the same, neither the current ratio nor working capital is affected.

20. A company has a current ratio of 1.5. This ratio will decrease if the company

A. Receives a 10% stock dividend on one of its marketable securities.

B. Pays a large account payable that had been a current liability.

C. Borrows cash on a 9-month note.

D. Sells merchandise for more than cost and records the sale using the perpetual inventory method.

Answer (C) is correct. *(CPA, adapted)*

REQUIRED: The transaction reducing a positive current ratio.

DISCUSSION: If a current ratio is greater than 1.0, an equal increase in current assets and current liabilities, like borrowing cash on a short-term basis, decreases the ratio.

Answer (A) is incorrect because stock dividends do not affect the carrying value of the securities. Answer (B) is incorrect because paying a current liability decreases current assets and liabilities equally, thereby increasing the ratio. Answer (D) is incorrect because it increases the numerator with no effect on the denominator, which causes the ratio to increase.

21. If a company converts a short-term note payable into a long-term note payable, this transaction will

A. Decrease working capital only.

B. Decrease both working capital and the current ratio.

C. Increase working capital only.

D. Increase both working capital and the current ratio.

Answer (D) is correct. *(CPA, adapted)*

REQUIRED: The effect of converting a short-term note to a long-term note.

DISCUSSION: Converting a short-term note to a long-term note reduces current liabilities but not current assets. Thus, the transaction increases both working capital and the current ratio.

Answer (A) is incorrect because a reduction in current liabilities increases working capital. Answer (B) is incorrect because a reduction in current liabilities with no change in current assets increases both working capital and the current ratio. Answer (C) is incorrect because a decrease in current liabilities increases the current ratio as well as working capital.

Questions 22 and 23 are based on the following information. Calculation of ratios and the determination of other factors are considered important in analysis of financial statements. Prior to the independent events described below, the corporation concerned had current and quick ratios in excess of one to one and reported a net income (as opposed to a loss) for the period just ended. Income tax effects are to be ignored. The corporation had only one class of shares outstanding.

22. The effect of recording a 2-for-1 stock split is to

A. Decrease the current ratio, decrease working capital, and decrease book value per share.

B. Leave inventory turnover unaffected, decrease working capital, and decrease book value per share.

C. Leave working capital unaffected, decrease earnings per share, and decrease book value per share.

D. Leave working capital unaffected, decrease earnings per share, and decrease the debt-to-equity ratio.

Answer (C) is correct. *(CPA, adapted)*
REQUIRED: The effect of recording a 2-for-1 stock split.
DISCUSSION: A 2-for-1 stock split involves an increase in shares outstanding with no increase in the capital stock account. Thus, the par or stated value of the shares is adjusted so that the total is unchanged. It has no effect on assets, liabilities, working capital, or total equity. Thus, the current ratio, the working capital, and the debt-to-equity ratio are unaffected. EPS and book value per share decline because more shares are outstanding.

23. Recording the payment (as distinguished from the declaration) of a cash dividend, the declaration of which was already recorded, will

A. Increase the current ratio but have no effect on working capital.

B. Decrease both the current ratio and working capital.

C. Increase both the current ratio and working capital.

D. Have no effect on the current ratio or earnings per share.

Answer (A) is correct. *(CPA, adapted)*
REQUIRED: The effect of the payment of a cash dividend.
DISCUSSION: The payment of a previously declared cash dividend reduces current assets and current liabilities equally. An equal reduction in current assets and current liabilities causes an increase in a positive (greater than 1.0) current ratio.

23.4 Receivable and Inventory Ratios

24. The following information is available from Alden Corp.'s financial records for the current year:

Sales:	
Net credit sales	$500,000
Net cash sales	250,000
	$750,000

Accounts Receivable:	
Balance, January 1	$ 75,000
Balance, December 31	50,000

How many times did Alden's accounts receivable turn over in the current year?

A. 15

B. 12

C. 10

D. 8

Answer (D) is correct. *(CPA, adapted)*
REQUIRED: The accounts receivable turnover.
DISCUSSION: The accounts receivable turnover is equal to net credit sales divided by the average accounts receivable. Net credit sales is $500,000. The average accounts receivable is $62,500 [($75,000 + $50,000) ÷ 2]. Accounts receivable turnover is 8 ($500,000 ÷ $62,500).

Answer (A) is incorrect because 15 results from dividing total sales by ending accounts receivable. Answer (B) is incorrect because 12 results from dividing total sales by average accounts receivable. Answer (C) is incorrect because 10 results from dividing net credit sales by ending accounts receivable.

25. Kline Co. had the following sales and accounts receivable balances at the end of the current year:

Cash sales	$1,000,000
Net credit sales	3,000,000
Net accounts receivable, 1/1	100,000
Net accounts receivable, 12/31	400,000

Assuming a 360-day year, what is Kline's average collection period for its accounts receivable?

A. 48.0 days.

B. 30.0 days.

C. 22.5 days.

D. 12.0 days.

Answer (B) is correct. *(CPA, adapted)*

REQUIRED: The average collection period for accounts receivable.

DISCUSSION: The average collection period for accounts receivable is calculated by dividing 360 days by the accounts receivable turnover. Accounts receivable turnover is equal to net credit sales divided by average accounts receivable. Average accounts receivable equals $250,000 [($100,000 beginning balance + $400,000 ending balance) ÷ 2]. Accounts receivable turnover is 12 times ($3,000,000 ÷ $250,000). Thus, the average collection period for accounts receivable is 30 days (360 days ÷ 12).

Answer (A) is incorrect because 48 days is based on a turnover rate calculated using ending accounts receivable instead of average accounts receivable. Answer (C) is incorrect because cash sales should not be included when calculating the turnover ratio. Answer (D) is incorrect because 12 is the receivables turnover ratio.

26. During the current year, Rand Co. purchased $960,000 of inventory. The cost of goods sold for the year was $900,000, and the ending inventory at December 31 was $180,000. What was the inventory turnover for the year?

A. 6.4

B. 6.0

C. 7.2

D. 5.0

Answer (B) is correct. *(CPA, adapted)*

REQUIRED: The inventory turnover.

DISCUSSION: Inventory turnover is equal to cost of goods sold divided by the average inventory. Average inventory is equal to the average of beginning inventory and ending inventory [(BI+EI) ÷ 2]. As calculated below, beginning inventory is equal to $120,000. Average inventory is therefore equal to $150,000 [($120,000 + $180,000) ÷ 2]. Inventory turnover is 6.0 ($900,000 cost of goods sold ÷ $150,000 average inventory).

Cost of goods sold	$ 900,000
Ending inventory	180,000
Goods available	$1,080,000
Purchases	(960,000)
Beginning inventory	$ 120,000

Answer (A) is incorrect because 6.4 equals purchases divided by average inventory. Answer (C) is incorrect because 7.2 results from dividing goods available for sale by average inventory. Answer (D) is incorrect because 5.0 results from dividing cost of goods sold by ending inventory.

27. On July 14, Avila Co. collected a receivable due from a major customer. Which of the following ratios is increased by this transaction?

A. Inventory turnover ratio.

B. Receivable turnover ratio.

C. Current ratio.

D. Quick ratio.

Answer (B) is correct. *(CPA, adapted)*

REQUIRED: The ratio increased by collection of a receivable.

DISCUSSION: The accounts receivable turnover is equal to net credit sales divided by the average accounts receivable. Collection of a receivable decreases the denominator and increases the ratio.

Answer (A) is incorrect because the inventory turnover ratio equals the cost of goods sold divided by the average inventory. Collection of a receivable does not affect it. Answer (C) is incorrect because a decrease in a receivable and an equal increase in cash have no effect on the current ratio or the quick ratio. Answer (D) is incorrect because a decrease in a receivable and an equal increase in cash have no effect on the current ratio or the quick ratio.

28. Selected data from Baez Corporation's year-end financial statements are presented below. The difference between average and ending inventory is immaterial.

Current ratio	3.0
Quick ratio	2.0
Current liabilities	$120,000
Inventory turnover (based on cost of goods sold)	6 times
Gross profit margin	50%

Net sales for the year were

A. $1,440,000

B. $720,000

C. $1,800,000

D. $360,000

Answer (A) is correct. *(CMA, adapted)*

REQUIRED: The net sales for the year.

DISCUSSION: Net sales may be calculated indirectly from the inventory turnover ratio and the other ratios given. If the current ratio is 3.0 and current liabilities are $120,000, current assets must be $360,000 (3.0 × $120,000). Similarly, if the quick ratio is 2.0, the total quick assets must be $240,000 (2.0 × $120,000). The major difference between quick assets and current assets is that inventory is not included in the definition of quick assets. Consequently, ending inventory must be $120,000 ($360,000 – $240,000). The inventory turnover ratio (CGS ÷ average inventory) is 6. Thus, cost of goods sold must be 6 times average inventory, or $720,000, given no material difference between average and ending inventory. If the gross profit margin is 50%, the cost of goods sold percentage is 50%, cost of goods sold equals 50% of sales, and sales must be $1,440,000 ($720,000 ÷ 50%).

Answer (B) is incorrect because $1,440,000 is cost of goods sold. Answer (C) is incorrect because $1,800,000 is based on a 60% gross profit margin. Answer (D) is incorrect because $360,000 equals current assets.

29. Which one of the following inventory cost flow assumptions will result in a higher inventory turnover ratio in an inflationary economy?

A. FIFO.

B. LIFO.

C. Weighted average.

D. Specific identification.

Answer (B) is correct. *(CMA, adapted)*

REQUIRED: The cost flow assumption that will result in a higher inventory turnover ratio in an inflationary economy.

DISCUSSION: The inventory turnover ratio equals the cost of goods sold divided by the average inventory. LIFO assumes that the last goods purchased are the first goods sold and that the oldest goods purchased remain in inventory. The result is a higher cost of goods sold and a lower average inventory than under other inventory cost flow assumptions if prices are rising. Because cost of goods sold (the numerator) will be higher and average inventory (the denominator) will be lower than under other inventory cost flow assumptions, LIFO produces the highest inventory turnover ratio.

30. If a company changes from the first-in, first-out (FIFO) inventory method to the last-in, first-out (LIFO) method during a period of rising prices, its

A. Current ratio will be reduced.

B. Inventory turnover ratio will be reduced.

C. Cash flow will be decreased.

D. Debt-to-equity ratio will be decreased.

Answer (A) is correct. *(CMA, adapted)*

REQUIRED: The effect of changing from FIFO to LIFO during a period of rising prices.

DISCUSSION: Changing from FIFO to LIFO during a period of rising prices will result in a lower inventory valuation and a higher cost of goods sold. Thus, the current ratio will be reduced because current assets are lower under LIFO.

Answer (B) is incorrect because inventory turnover will increase. Cost of goods sold (the numerator) will increase, and the average inventory (the denominator) will decline. Answer (C) is incorrect because cash flow will be unchanged except for the tax savings from switching to LIFO. The tax savings will result in increased cash flow. Answer (D) is incorrect because the debt-to-equity ratio will increase. Assets and equity will be lower, but debt will be unchanged.

31. Which of the following ratios should be used in evaluating the effectiveness with which the company uses its assets?

	Receivables Turnover	Dividend Payout Ratio
A.	Yes	Yes
B.	No	No
C.	Yes	No
D.	No	Yes

Answer (C) is correct. *(CPA, adapted)*

REQUIRED: The ratios that should be used in evaluating the effectiveness with which assets are used by a company.

DISCUSSION: The receivables turnover is equal to net credit sales divided by average accounts receivable, which is an estimate of the number of times a year that receivables are collected. It may indicate the quality of receivables and the success of collection efforts. Accordingly, this ratio is a measure of the effectiveness with which a company uses its assets. In contrast, the dividend payout ratio is equal to the declared cash dividends divided by income available to common shareholders (net income – preferred dividends). It measures the extent to which a company distributes its assets and may be useful to investors desiring regular income from equity securities. However, the payout ratio does not reflect the efficiency and effectiveness of management.

32. Blasso Company's net accounts receivable were $500,000 at December 31, year 1 and $600,000 at December 31, year 2. Net cash sales for year 2 were $200,000. The accounts receivable turnover for year 2 was 5.0. What were Blasso's total net sales for year 2?

A. $2,950,000

B. $3,000,000

C. $3,200,000

D. $5,500,000

Answer (A) is correct. *(CPA, adapted)*

REQUIRED: The net sales given accounts receivable, net cash sales, and the accounts receivable turnover.

DISCUSSION: Total sales equal cash sales plus credit sales. Blasso's cash sales were $200,000. Credit sales may be determined from the accounts receivable turnover formula, which equals net credit sales divided by average accounts receivable. Net credit sales are equal to 5.0 times average receivables [($500,000 + $600,000) ÷ 2], or $2,750,000. Total sales were equal to $2,950,000 ($2,750,000 + $200,000).

Answer (B) is incorrect because $3,000,000 equals ending accounts receivable multiplied by the accounts receivable turnover ratio. Answer (C) is incorrect because $3,200,000 equals cash sales plus the product of ending accounts receivable and the accounts receivable turnover ratio. Answer (D) is incorrect because $5,500,000 equals beginning accounts receivable plus ending accounts receivable multiplied by the accounts receivable turnover ratio.

33. Selected information from the accounting records of Bolingbroke Company follows:

Net sales	$1,800,000
Cost of goods sold	1,200,000
Inventories at January 1	336,000
Inventories at December 31	288,000

Assuming there are 300 working days per year, what is the number of days' sales in average inventories for the year?

A. 78

B. 72

C. 52

D. 48

Answer (A) is correct. *(CPA, adapted)*

REQUIRED: The number of days' sales in average inventories.

DISCUSSION: The number of days' sales in average inventories (average number of days to sell inventories) equals the number of working days in the year (300) divided by the inventory turnover ratio (CGS ÷ average inventory). CGS is given as $1,200,000, and average inventory is $312,000 [($336,000 + $288,000) ÷ 2]. The number of days' sales in average inventories is therefore 78 [300 ÷ ($1,200,000 ÷ $312,000)].

Answer (B) is incorrect because 72 results from using ending inventory rather than average inventory in the inventory turnover ratio. Answer (C) is incorrect because 52 results from using net sales rather than cost of goods sold in the inventory turnover ratio. Answer (D) is incorrect because 48 results from using net sales and ending inventory rather than cost of goods sold and average inventory in the inventory turnover ratio.

34. Selected information from the accounting records of the Blackwood Company is as follows:

Net A/R at December 31, year 1	$ 900,000
Net A/R at December 31, year 2	$1,000,000
Accounts receivable turnover	5 to 1
Inventories at December 31, year 1	$1,100,000
Inventories at December 31, year 2	$1,200,000
Inventory turnover	4 to 1

What was the gross margin for year 2?

A. $150,000

B. $200,000

C. $300,000

D. $400,000

Answer (A) is correct. *(CPA, adapted)*

REQUIRED: The gross margin given inventory, receivables, and the related turnover ratios.

DISCUSSION: Gross margin is net sales minus cost of goods sold. Net sales may be calculated from the accounts receivable turnover ratio, which is net sales divided by average receivables. The average accounts receivable is $950,000 [($900,000 + $1,000,000) ÷ 2]. Sales equal average receivables multiplied by the related turnover ratio, or $4,750,000 (5 × $950,000).

Cost of goods sold may be calculated from the inventory turnover ratio, which is cost of goods sold divided by average inventory. Average inventory is $1,150,000 [($1,100,000 + $1,200,000) ÷ 2]. Cost of goods sold equals average inventory multiplied by the inventory turnover ratio, or $4,600,000 (4 × $1,150,000). Thus, the gross margin is $150,000 ($4,750,000 net sales – $4,600,000 cost of goods sold).

Answer (B) is incorrect because $200,000 results from subtracting the ending inventory times the inventory turnover from the ending accounts receivable times the accounts receivable turnover. Answer (C) is incorrect because $300,000 results from subtracting the sum of the beginning and ending inventories times the inventory turnover from the sum of the beginning and ending accounts receivable times the accounts receivable turnover. Answer (D) is incorrect because $400,000 results from subtracting the sum of the beginning and ending accounts receivable from the sum of the beginning and ending inventories.

35. In a comparison of year 2 with year 1, Baliol Co.'s inventory turnover ratio increased substantially although sales and inventory amounts were essentially unchanged. Which of the following statements explains the increased inventory turnover ratio?

A. Cost of goods sold decreased.

B. Accounts receivable turnover increased.

C. Total asset turnover increased.

D. Gross profit percentage decreased.

Answer (D) is correct. *(CPA, adapted)*

REQUIRED: The statement that explains the increased inventory turnover ratio.

DISCUSSION: The inventory turnover ratio is equal to cost of goods sold divided by average inventory. If inventory is unchanged, an increase in cost of goods sold increases the inventory turnover ratio. A decrease in the gross profit percentage [(sales – cost of goods sold) ÷ sales] signifies an increase in cost of goods sold given that the amount of sales is constant.

Answer (A) is incorrect because a decrease in cost of goods sold results in a decrease in the inventory turnover ratio. Answer (B) is incorrect because the accounts receivable turnover does not affect the inventory turnover ratio. Answer (C) is incorrect because total asset turnover does not affect the inventory turnover ratio.

36. The following computations were made from Bruckner Co.'s current-year books:

Number of days' sales in inventory	55
Number of days' sales in trade accounts receivable	26

What was the number of days in Bruckner's current-year operating cycle?

A. 26

B. 40.5

C. 55

D. 81

Answer (D) is correct. *(CPA, adapted)*

REQUIRED: The number of days in the operating cycle.

DISCUSSION: The operating cycle is the time needed to turn cash into inventory, inventory into receivables, and receivables back into cash. It is equal to the sum of the number of days' sales in inventory (average number of days to sell inventory) and the number of days' sales in receivables (the average collection period). The number of days' sales in inventory is given as 55 days. The number of days' sales in receivables is given as 26 days. Hence, the number of days in the operating cycle is 81 (55 + 26).

Answer (A) is incorrect because 26 is the number of days' sales in receivables. Answer (B) is incorrect because 40.5 equals the sum of the number of days' sales in inventory and the number of days' sales in receivables, divided by 2. Answer (C) is incorrect because 55 is the number of days' sales in inventory.

37. Based on the data presented below, what is the cost of sales for the Canfield Corporation for year 2?

Current ratio	3.5
Acid test ratio	3.0
Current liabilities 12/31/year 2	$600,000
Inventory 12/31/year 1	$500,000
Inventory turnover	8.0

A. $1,600,000

B. $2,400,000

C. $3,200,000

D. $6,400,000

Answer (C) is correct. *(CMA, adapted)*

REQUIRED: The cost of sales given various ratios, ending liabilities, and beginning inventory.

DISCUSSION: Inventory turnover equals cost of sales divided by average inventory. The turnover ratio and the beginning inventory are known. If ending inventory can be determined, average inventory and cost of sales can also be calculated. The relationship among the current ratio, acid test ratio, and current liabilities facilitates this calculation. The current ratio is the ratio of current assets to current liabilities. Thus, current assets are 3.5 times current liabilities. Given that current liabilities at year-end are $600,000, current assets at year-end must be $2,100,000 (3.5 × $600,000). The acid test ratio is equal to the ratio of the sum of cash, net accounts receivable, and short-term marketable securities to current liabilities. Accordingly, quick assets are 3.0 times current liabilities. If current liabilities at year-end are $600,000, the quick assets are $1,800,000 (3.0 × $600,000). The difference between current assets and quick assets is equal to inventory (assuming no prepaid expenses are included in current assets). Because current assets at year-end are $2,100,000 and quick assets are $1,800,000, ending inventory must be $300,000. Average inventory is equal to $400,000 [($500,000 beginning inventory + $300,000 ending inventory) ÷ 2]. An inventory turnover (cost of sales ÷ average inventory) of 8.0 indicates that cost of sales is 8.0 times average inventory. Cost of sales is therefore equal to $3,200,000 (8.0 × $400,000).

23.5 Equity Ratios

38. Calderone Corp.'s equity balances, which include no accumulated other comprehensive income, were as follows at December 31:

6% noncumulative preferred stock, $100 par (liquidation value $105 per share)	$100,000
Common stock, $10 par	300,000
Retained earnings	95,000

At December 31, book value per common share was

A. $13.17

B. $13.00

C. $12.97

D. $12.80

Answer (B) is correct. *(CPA, adapted)*

REQUIRED: The book value per share of common stock at year-end.

DISCUSSION: The preferred stock is noncumulative, so the equity of the preferred shareholders equals the liquidation value. The liquidation value is $105,000 ($105 per share × 1,000 shares). Given total equity of $495,000 ($100,000 + $300,000 + $95,000), common equity is $390,000 ($495,000 – $105,000). Therefore, book value per share of common stock equals $13.00 ($390,000 ÷ 30,000 shares).

Answer (A) is incorrect because $13.17 equals the sum of common stock and retained earnings divided by the shares outstanding of common stock. Answer (C) is incorrect because $12.97 equals the sum of common stock and retained earnings, minus the preferred stock dividend, divided by the number of common stock shares outstanding. Answer (D) is incorrect because $12.80 results from deducting the preferred stock dividend from common equity and dividing by the number of common shares outstanding.

39. The following data pertain to Canova, Inc., for the year ended December 31:

Net sales	$ 600,000
Net income	150,000
Total assets, January 1	2,000,000
Total assets, December 31	3,000,000

What was Canova's rate of return on assets for the year?

A. 5%

B. 6%

C. 20%

D. 24%

Answer (B) is correct. *(CPA, adapted)*

REQUIRED: The rate of return on assets.

DISCUSSION: Return on assets equals net income divided by average total assets, or 6% ($150,000 ÷ $2,500,000).

Answer (A) is incorrect because 5% results from using ending total assets instead of the average total assets. Answer (C) is incorrect because 20% results from dividing net sales by ending total assets. Answer (D) is incorrect because 24% results from dividing net sales by average total assets.

40. Cloisters Corp.'s current balance sheet reports the following equity:

5% cumulative preferred stock, par value $100 per share; 2,500 shares issued and outstanding	$250,000
Common stock, par value $3.50 per share; 100,000 shares issued and outstanding	350,000
Additional paid-in capital in excess of par value of common stock	125,000
Retained earnings	300,000
Accumulated other comprehensive income	100,000

Dividends in arrears on the preferred stock amount to $25,000. If Cloisters were to be liquidated, the preferred shareholders would receive par value plus a premium of $50,000. The book value per share of common stock is

A. $8.75

B. $8.50

C. $8.25

D. $8.00

Answer (D) is correct. *(CPA, adapted)*

REQUIRED: The book value per share of common stock upon liquidation.

DISCUSSION: Given that the preferred stock is cumulative, the liquidation value of the preferred stock equals the par value, plus the premium, plus the dividends in arrears. Liquidation value equals $325,000 ($250,000 + $50,000 + $25,000). Given total equity of $1,125,000 ($250,000 + $350,000 + $125,000 + $300,000 + $100,000), common equity is $800,000 ($1,125,000 – $325,000). Thus, book value per share of common stock equals $8.00 ($800,000 ÷ 100,000 shares outstanding).

Answer (A) is incorrect because $8.75 does not include the dividends in arrears or the premium. Answer (B) is incorrect because $8.50 does not include the premium. Answer (C) is incorrect because $8.25 does not include the dividends in arrears.

41. Return on investment may be calculated by multiplying total asset turnover by

A. Average collection period.

B. Profit margin.

C. Debt ratio.

D. Fixed-charge coverage.

Answer (B) is correct. *(CIA, adapted)*

REQUIRED: The method of calculating return on investment.

DISCUSSION: Return on investment is equal to profit divided by the average total assets. Asset turnover is equal to net sales divided by average total assets. Profit margin is equal to the profit divided by net sales. Thus, multiplying the asset turnover by the profit margin results in the cancelation of net sales from both ratios, leaving a ratio composed of profit in the numerator and average total assets in the denominator, which equals return on investment.

42. What would be the effect on book value per share and earnings per share if the corporation purchased its own shares in the open market at a price greater than the carrying amount?

A. No effect on book value per share but increase earnings per share.

B. Increase both book value per share and earnings per share.

C. Decrease both book value per share and earnings per share.

D. Decrease book value per share and increase earnings per share.

Answer (D) is correct. *(CPA, adapted)*

REQUIRED: The effect of a treasury stock purchase for more than the carrying amount on book value per share and EPS.

DISCUSSION: When treasury stock is purchased, the number of shares of stock outstanding is decreased, causing an increase in EPS. When the price paid is greater than the existing carrying amount, the book value per share of the remaining stock outstanding is decreased.

43. If Day Company has a higher rate of return on assets than Night Company, the reason may be that Day has a <List A> profit margin on sales, or a <List B> asset turnover ratio, or both.

	List A	List B
A.	Higher	Higher
B.	Higher	Lower
C.	Lower	Higher
D.	Lower	Lower

Answer (A) is correct. *(CIA, adapted)*

REQUIRED: The reason for a higher rate of return on assets.

DISCUSSION: The return on assets equals the product of the profit margin and the asset turnover.

Return on assets = Profit margin × Asset turnover

$$\frac{\textit{Net income}}{\textit{Assets}} = \frac{\textit{Net income}}{\textit{Sales}} \times \frac{\textit{Sales}}{\textit{Assets}}$$

If one company has a higher return on assets than another, it may have a higher profit margin, a higher asset turnover, or both.

44. Selected information for Dayan Company is as follows:

	December 31, Year 1	Year 2
Preferred stock, 8%, par $100, nonconvertible, noncumulative	$125,000	$125,000
Common stock	300,000	400,000
Retained earnings	75,000	185,000
Accumulated other comprehensive income	0	40,000
Dividends paid on preferred stock for year ended	10,000	10,000
Net income for year ended	60,000	120,000

Dayan's return on common equity, rounded to the nearest percentage point, for year 2 is

A. 16%

B. 17.6%

C. 22%

D. 24%

Answer (C) is correct. *(CPA, adapted)*

REQUIRED: The return on common equity for the year.

DISCUSSION: Return on common equity is equal to the earnings available to common shareholders divided by the average common equity. The numerator is therefore net income ($120,000) minus preferred dividends (8% × $125,000 = $10,000), that is, $110,000. Average common equity is equal to the average of beginning and ending common equity, or $500,000 [($375,000 + $625,000) ÷ 2]. Thus, return on common equity equals 22% ($110,000 ÷ $500,000).

Answer (A) is incorrect because 16% results from dividing net income for year 2 by total equity. Answer (B) is incorrect because 17.6% results from dividing earnings available to common shareholders by ending common equity. Answer (D) is incorrect because 24% results from dividing net income for year 2 by average common equity without subtracting the preferred dividends from net income.

45. Share options are frequently provided to officers of companies. Share options that are exercised improve

A. The debt-to-equity ratio.

B. Earnings per share.

C. The ownership interest of existing shareholders.

D. The total asset turnover.

Answer (A) is correct. *(CMA, adapted)*
REQUIRED: The effect of exercising share options.
DISCUSSION: Exercising share options improves (decreases) the debt-to-equity ratio because equity is increased with no effect on debt. When stock is issued, common stock and paid-in capital are credited and cash is debited.
Answer (B) is incorrect because EPS decreases when the number of shares outstanding increases. Answer (C) is incorrect because share options exercised increase the number of shares outstanding, thereby diluting the existing ownership interest. Answer (D) is incorrect because asset turnover equals net sales divided by average assets. The exercise of share options increases assets, thereby decreasing the ratio.

46. Sharif Co. has total debt of $420,000 and equity of $700,000. Sharif is seeking capital to fund an expansion. Sharif is planning to issue an additional $300,000 in common stock and is negotiating with a bank to borrow additional funds. The bank requires a debt-to-equity ratio of .75. What is the maximum additional amount Sharif will be able to borrow?

A. $225,000

B. $330,000

C. $525,000

D. $750,000

Answer (B) is correct. *(CPA, adapted)*
REQUIRED: The maximum additional borrowing allowed to satisfy a specific debt-to-equity ratio.
DISCUSSION: Sharif will have $1 million ($700,000 + $300,000) in total equity. The debt-to-equity restriction allows up to $750,000 ($1,000,000 × .75) in debt. Sharif already has $420,000 in debt, so the additional borrowing cannot exceed $330,000 ($750,000 – $420,000).
Answer (A) is incorrect because $225,000 results from multiplying the $300,000 of additional common stock by the debt-to-equity ratio. Answer (C) is incorrect because $525,000 equals the $700,000 of equity times the debt-to-equity ratio. Answer (D) is incorrect because $750,000 is the total debt allowed.

47. A company has 100,000 outstanding common shares with a market value of $20 per share. Dividends of $2 per share were paid in the current year, and the company has a dividend-payout ratio of 40%. The price-earnings (P-E) ratio of the company is

A. 2.5

B. 4

C. 10

D. 50

Answer (B) is correct. *(CIA, adapted)*
REQUIRED: The P-E ratio.
DISCUSSION: The P-E ratio equals the share price divided by EPS. If the dividends per share equaled $2 and the dividend-payout ratio was 40%, EPS must have been $5 ($2 ÷ .4). Accordingly, the P-E ratio is 4 ($20 share price ÷ $5 EPS).
Answer (A) is incorrect because 2.5 equals EPS divided by dividends per share. Answer (C) is incorrect because 10 equals share price divided by dividends per share. Answer (D) is incorrect because 50 equals price per share divided by the dividend-payout percentage.

48. Information concerning Rashad Company's common stock is presented below for the fiscal year ended May 31, year 2.

Common shares outstanding	750,000
Stated value per share	$15.00
Market price per share	45.00
Year 1 dividends paid per share	4.50
Year 2 dividends paid per share	7.50
Basic earnings per share	11.25
Diluted earnings per share	9.00

The price-earnings ratio for Rashad's common stock is

A. 3.0 times.

B. 4.0 times.

C. 5.0 times.

D. 6.0 times.

Answer (C) is correct. *(CMA, adapted)*
REQUIRED: The price-earnings ratio for the common stock.
DISCUSSION: The price-earnings ratio is calculated by dividing the current market price of the stock by the earnings per share. Diluted earnings per share is used if disclosed. Thus, Rashad's price-earnings ratio is 5.0 ($45 market price ÷ $9 DEPS).
Answer (A) is incorrect because the 3.0 figure is based on the stated value per share in the denominator. Answer (B) is incorrect because 4.0 is based on the basic earnings per share in the denominator. Answer (D) is incorrect because 6.0 is derived by using year 2 dividends per share in the denominator.

49. Ehrenburg Company had net income of $5.3 million and earnings per share on common stock of $2.50. Included in the net income was $500,000 of bond interest expense related to its long-term debt. The income tax rate was 50%. Dividends on preferred stock were $300,000. The dividend-payout ratio on common stock was 40%. What were the dividends on common stock?

A. $1,800,000

B. $1,900,000

C. $2,000,000

D. $2,120,000

Answer (C) is correct. *(CPA, adapted)*
REQUIRED: The dividends on common stock given the dividend-payout ratio.
DISCUSSION: The dividend-payout ratio is equal to the dividends on common stock divided by the earnings available to common. If earnings available to common were $5,000,000 ($5,300,000 net income – $300,000 preferred dividends) and the payout ratio was 40%, the dividends on common stock were $2,000,000.

50. How are the following used in the calculation of the dividend-payout ratio for a company with only common stock outstanding?

	Dividends Per Share	Earnings Per Share	Book Value Per Share
A.	Denominator	Numerator	Not used
B.	Denominator	Not used	Numerator
C.	Numerator	Denominator	Not used
D.	Numerator	Not used	Denominator

Answer (C) is correct. *(CPA, adapted)*
REQUIRED: The components of the dividend-payout ratio.
DISCUSSION: In the absence of preferred stock, the dividend-payout ratio may be stated as the dividends per share (numerator) divided by the earnings per share (denominator).
Answer (A) is incorrect because dividends per share is the numerator and earnings per share is the denominator in the dividend-payout ratio. Answer (B) is incorrect because dividends per share is the numerator, earnings per share is the denominator, and book value per share is not used in the dividend-payout ratio. Answer (D) is incorrect because earnings per share is the denominator and book value per share is not used in the dividend-payout ratio.

51. A drop in the market price of a firm's common stock will immediately affect its

A. Return on equity.

B. Dividend-payout ratio.

C. Debt-to-net-worth ratio.

D. Dividend yield.

Answer (D) is correct. *(CMA, adapted)*
REQUIRED: The effect of a drop in the market price of a firm's common stock.
DISCUSSION: Dividend yield equals dividends per common share divided by the market price per common share. Hence, a drop in the market price of the stock will affect this ratio.
Answer (A) is incorrect because this ratio is based on book values in their calculation rather than the market price of the common stock. Answer (B) is incorrect because this ratio is based on book values in their calculation rather than the market price of the common stock. Answer (C) is incorrect because this ratio is based on book values in their calculation rather than the market price of the common stock.

52. The ratio of earnings before interest and taxes to total interest expense is a measure of

A. Liquidity.

B. Risk.

C. Activity.

D. Profitability.

Answer (B) is correct. *(CPA, adapted)*
REQUIRED: The function of the times-interest-earned ratio.
DISCUSSION: The ratio of earnings before interest and taxes to total interest expense is the times-interest-earned ratio. This ratio assists a creditor in estimating risk by measuring a firm's ability to pay interest expense.
Answer (A) is incorrect because the current (liquidity) ratio measures the ability to pay short-term liabilities out of current assets. Answer (C) is incorrect because turnover ratios measure a firm's activity. Answer (D) is incorrect because EPS measures return to owners.

Questions 53 and 54 are based on the following information. Selected financial data of Draco Corporation for the year ended December 31 are as follows. Common stock dividends were $120,000.

Operating income	$900,000
Interest expense	(100,000)
Income before income tax	$800,000
Income tax expense	(320,000)
Net income	$480,000
Preferred stock dividends	(200,000)
Net income available to common shareholders	$280,000

53. The times-interest-earned ratio is

A. 2.8 to 1.

B. 4.8 to 1.

C. 8.0 to 1.

D. 9.0 to 1.

Answer (D) is correct. *(CPA, adapted)*

REQUIRED: The times-interest-earned ratio.

DISCUSSION: The times-interest-earned ratio is a measure of the firm's ability to pay interest on debt. It equals the sum of net income, interest expense, and taxes divided by the amount of interest. Taxes are added back to the numerator because the ability to pay interest is not affected by the taxes to be paid in the future. That is, if all available income were used to pay interest, the entity would have no tax liability. Thus, times-interest-earned ratio is 9.0 to 1.

$$\frac{\$480{,}000 + \$100{,}000 + \$320{,}000}{\$100{,}000} = 9.0$$

Answer (A) is incorrect because 2.8 to 1 results from dividing net income available to common shareholders by interest expense. Answer (B) is incorrect because 4.8 to 1 results from dividing net income by interest expense. Answer (C) is incorrect because 8.0 to 1 results from dividing income before income tax by interest expense.

54. The times-preferred-dividend-earned ratio is

A. 1.4 to 1.

B. 1.7 to 1.

C. 2.4 to 1.

D. 4.0 to 1.

Answer (C) is correct. *(CPA, adapted)*

REQUIRED: The times-preferred-dividend-earned ratio.

DISCUSSION: The times-preferred-dividend-earned ratio is a measure of the company's ability to pay preferred dividends. It equals net income divided by preferred dividends. Preferred dividends are not added back to net income in the numerator because they are not deducted in arriving at net income. Income taxes are also not added back to net income in the numerator because preferred dividends are not tax deductible and are paid only after senior claims to income, such as interest and taxes, have been satisfied. The times-preferred-dividend-earned ratio is 2.4 to 1 ($480,000 net income ÷ $200,000 preferred dividends).

23.6 Questions on More Than One Ratio

Questions 55 and 56 are based on the following information. Selected data pertaining to Castile Co. for the current calendar year is as follows:

Net cash sales	$ 3,000
Cost of goods sold	18,000
Inventory at beginning of year	6,000
Purchases	24,000
Accounts receivable at beginning of year	20,000
Accounts receivable at end of year	22,000

55. The accounts receivable turnover for the current year was 5.0 times. What were Castile's current-year net credit sales?

A. $105,000

B. $107,000

C. $110,000

D. $210,000

Answer (A) is correct. *(CPA, adapted)*
REQUIRED: The net credit sales.
DISCUSSION: Credit sales may be determined from the accounts receivable turnover formula (credit sales ÷ average accounts receivable). Credit sales are equal to 5.0 times average receivables [($20,000 + $22,000) ÷ 2], or $105,000.
Answer (B) is incorrect because $107,000 equals ending accounts receivable multiplied by the accounts receivable turnover ratio, minus cash sales. Answer (C) is incorrect because $110,000 equals ending accounts receivable multiplied by the accounts receivable turnover ratio. Answer (D) is incorrect because $210,000 equals beginning accounts receivable plus ending accounts receivable, multiplied by the accounts receivable turnover ratio.

56. What was the inventory turnover for the current year?

A. 1.2 times.

B. 1.5 times.

C. 2.0 times.

D. 3.0 times.

Answer (C) is correct. *(CPA, adapted)*
REQUIRED: The inventory turnover ratio.
DISCUSSION: Inventory turnover is equal to cost of goods sold divided by average inventory. Ending inventory equals beginning inventory, plus purchases, minus cost of goods sold, or $12,000 ($6,000 + $24,000 – $18,000). Average inventory is $9,000 [($6,000 + $12,000) ÷ 2]. Inventory turnover is 2.0 times ($18,000 cost of goods sold ÷ $9,000 average inventory).
Answer (A) is incorrect because 1.2 times uses the average of beginning inventory and purchases. Answer (B) is incorrect because 1.5 times uses ending inventory instead of average inventory. Answer (D) is incorrect because 3.0 times uses beginning inventory instead of average inventory.

Questions 57 through 59 are based on the following information. The following inventory and sales data are available for the current year for Dylan Company, which uses a 365-day year when computing ratios.

	November 30, Year 2	November 30, Year 1
Net credit sales	$6,205,000	
Gross receivables	350,000	320,000
Inventory	960,000	780,000
Cost of goods sold	4,380,000	

57. Dylan Company's average number of days to collect accounts receivable for the current year is

A. 18.82 days.

B. 19.43 days.

C. 19.71 days.

D. 20.59 days.

Answer (C) is correct. *(CMA, adapted)*

REQUIRED: The average collection period.

DISCUSSION: The average collection period (the number of days' sales in receivables) equals 365 days divided by the receivables turnover (net credit sales ÷ average accounts receivable). Turnover is 18.52 times {$6,205,000 sales ÷ [($350,000 + $320,000) ÷ 2]}. Hence, the average collection period is 19.71 days (365 ÷ 18.52).

Answer (A) is incorrect because 18.82 days is based on receivables of $320,000. Answer (B) is incorrect because 19.43 days is based on a 360-day year. Answer (D) is incorrect because 20.59 days is based on receivables of $350,000.

58. Dylan Company's average number of days to sell inventory for the current year is

A. 51.18 days.

B. 65.00 days.

C. 71.51 days.

D. 72.50 days.

Answer (D) is correct. *(CMA, adapted)*

REQUIRED: The average days to sell inventory.

DISCUSSION: The average number of days to sell inventory (the number of days' sales in inventory) equals 365 days divided by the inventory turnover (cost of goods sold ÷ average inventory). Thus, turnover is 5.0345 times {$4,380,000 CGS ÷ [($960,000 + $780,000) ÷ 2]}. The average number of days to sell inventory is 72.5 days (365 ÷ 5.0345).

Answer (A) is incorrect because 51.18 days is based on sales, not cost of sales. Sales are recorded at retail prices. Answer (B) is incorrect because 65.00 days is based on the beginning inventory. Answer (C) is incorrect because 71.51 days is based on a 360-day year, not a 365-day year.

59. Dylan Company's operating cycle for the current year is

A. 70.61 days.

B. 93.09 days.

C. 92.21 days.

D. 99.71 days.

Answer (C) is correct. *(CMA, adapted)*

REQUIRED: The length of the firm's operating cycle.

DISCUSSION: The operating cycle is the length of time required to complete normal operating activities. Thus, the operating cycle is a cash-to-cash cycle equivalent to the average time that inventory is held plus the average time that receivables are held. Dylan holds its inventory 72.50 days [365 days ÷ ($4,380,000 CGS ÷ $870,000 average inventory)] and its receivables 19.71 days [365 days ÷ ($6,205,000 sales ÷ $335,000 average receivables)]. Its operating cycle is 92.21 days (72.50 + 19.71).

Answer (A) is incorrect because the inventory alone is held for 72.50 days. Answer (B) is incorrect because 93.09 days is based on the ending receivables balance. Answer (D) is incorrect because 99.71 days is based on the ending inventory.

Questions 60 through 62 are based on the following information. The selected data below pertain to Patel Company at December 31, year 1:

Quick assets	$208,000
Acid test ratio	2.6 to 1
Current ratio	3.5 to 1
Net sales for year 1	$1,800,000
Cost of sales for year 1	$990,000
Average total assets for year 1	$1,200,000

60. Patel's current liabilities at December 31, year 1 amount to

A. $59,429

B. $80,000

C. $134,857

D. $187,200

Answer (B) is correct. *(CIA, adapted)*

REQUIRED: Current liabilities at year-end.

DISCUSSION: The acid-test ratio is equal to quick assets divided by current liabilities. Thus, current liabilities equal the $208,000 of quick assets divided by the 2.6 acid-test ratio. Hence, current liabilities equal $80,000.

61. Patel's inventory balance at December 31, year 1, is

A. $72,000

B. $187,200

C. $231,111

D. $282,857

Answer (A) is correct. *(CIA, adapted)*

REQUIRED: The inventory balance at year-end.

DISCUSSION: Inventory is equal to the difference between current assets and quick assets (assuming no prepaid expenses are included in current assets). The current ratio is equal to current assets divided by current liabilities. Accordingly, multiplying the current liabilities of $80,000 (determined by dividing the quick assets by the acid test ratio) by the current ratio of 3.5 gives current assets of $280,000. Subtracting the $208,000 of quick assets from the $280,000 of current assets results in an inventory balance of $72,000.

62. Patel's asset turnover for year 1 is

A. .675

B. .825

C. 1.21

D. 1.50

Answer (D) is correct. *(CIA, adapted)*

REQUIRED: The asset turnover for the year.

DISCUSSION: Asset turnover equals $1,800,000 of net sales divided by $1,200,000 of average total assets. The asset turnover for year 1 is therefore equal to 1.5.

Questions 63 and 64 are based on the following information. Eisenstein Co. had the following account information:

Accounts receivable	$200,000
Accounts payable	80,000
Bonds payable, due in 10 years	300,000
Cash	100,000
Interest payable, due in 3 months	10,000
Inventory	400,000
Land	250,000
Notes payable, due in 6 months	50,000
Prepaid expenses	40,000

The company has an operating cycle of 5 months.

63. The current ratio for Eisenstein is

A. 1.68

B. 2.14

C. 5.00

D. 5.29

Answer (D) is correct. *(CMA, adapted)*

REQUIRED: The current ratio.

DISCUSSION: The current ratio equals current assets divided by current liabilities. This company's current assets consist of accounts receivable, cash, inventory, and prepaid expenses, which total $740,000 ($200,000 + $100,000 + $400,000 + $40,000). The current liabilities consist of accounts payable, interest payable, and notes payable, which total $140,000 ($80,000 + $10,000 + $50,000). Thus, the current ratio is 5.29 ($740,000 ÷ $140,000).

Answer (A) is incorrect because 1.68 treats bonds payable as a current liability. Answer (B) is incorrect because 2.14 is the quick ratio. Answer (C) is incorrect because 5.00 excludes prepaid expenses from current assets.

64. What is the company's acid-test (quick) ratio?

A. 0.68

B. 1.68

C. 2.14

D. 2.31

Answer (C) is correct. *(CMA, adapted)*

REQUIRED: The acid-test (quick) ratio.

DISCUSSION: The acid-test, or quick, ratio equals quick assets divided by current liabilities. Quick assets consist of cash ($100,000) and accounts receivable ($200,000), for a total of $300,000. The current liabilities consist of accounts payable, interest payable, and notes payable, for a total of $140,000 ($80,000 + $10,000 + $50,000). Hence, the quick ratio is 2.14 ($300,000 ÷ $140,000).

Answer (A) is incorrect because 0.68 equals the quick assets divided by the sum of the current liabilities and the bonds payable. Answer (B) is incorrect because 1.68 equals current assets divided by the sum of current liabilities and the bonds payable. Answer (D) is incorrect because 2.31 omits interest payable from the current liabilities.

Questions 65 through 67 are based on the following information. Ellington Company reports the following account balances at year-end:

Account	Balance
Long-term debt	$200,000
Cash	50,000
Net sales	600,000
Fixed assets (net)	370,000
Tax expense	67,500
Inventory	25,000
Common stock	100,000
Interest expense	20,000
Administrative expense	35,000
Retained earnings	150,000
Accumulated other comprehensive income	50,000
Accounts payable	65,000
Accounts receivable	120,000
Cost of goods sold	400,000
Depreciation expense	10,000

Additional Information:

The opening balance of common stock was $100,000.

The opening balance of retained earnings was $82,500.

The opening balance of accumulated other comprehensive income was $17,500.

The company had 10,000 common shares outstanding all year.

No dividends were paid during the year.

65. For the year just ended, Ellington has times-interest-earned of

A. 3.375 times.

B. 6.75 times.

C. 7.75 times.

D. 9.5 times.

Answer (C) is correct. *(CIA, adapted)*

REQUIRED: The times-interest-earned ratio (TIE).

DISCUSSION: The TIE ratio is a leverage ratio. It indicates the company's ability to pay interest expense. The ratio equals income before interest and taxes divided by interest.

$$= \frac{(\textit{Sales} - \textit{CGS} - \textit{Administrative expense} - \textit{Depreciation})}{(\textit{Interest expense})}$$

$$= \frac{\$600{,}000 - \$400{,}000 - \$35{,}000 - \$10{,}000}{\$20{,}000} = 7.75 \text{ times}$$

Answer (A) is incorrect because 3.375 times results from including in the numerator deductions for taxes and interest. Answer (B) is incorrect because 6.75 times results from including in the numerator a deduction for interest. Answer (D) is incorrect because 9.5 times results from failing to deduct the administrative expenses from the numerator.

66. At year-end, Ellington has a book value per share of

A. $15

B. $20

C. $25

D. $30

Answer (D) is correct. *(CIA, adapted)*

REQUIRED: The book value per share at year-end.

DISCUSSION: Book value per share, based on balance sheet amounts, measures the per-share amount that would be received if the company were liquidated. The ratio is calculated as common equity divided by the number of outstanding shares.

$$= \frac{\textit{Common stock} + \textit{Retained earnings} + \textit{AOCI}}{\textit{Outstanding shares}}$$

$$= \frac{\$100{,}000 + \$150{,}000 + \$50{,}000}{10{,}000 \text{ shares}} = \underline{\underline{\$30}}$$

Answer (A) is incorrect because $15 excludes retained earnings from the numerator. Answer (B) is incorrect because $20 excludes common stock from the numerator. Answer (C) is incorrect because $25 is based on average equity.

67. For the year just ended, Ellington had a rate of return on common equity, rounded to two decimals, of

A. 27.00%

B. 45.00%

C. 50.47%

D. 62.00%

Answer (A) is correct. *(CIA, adapted)*

REQUIRED: The rate of return on common equity for the year just ended.

DISCUSSION: Rate of return on common equity, a profitability ratio, measures the rate of return on investment. The ratio equals net income divided by average equity.

$$= \frac{\textit{Sales} - \textit{CGS} - \textit{Adm. exp.} - \textit{Deprec.} - \textit{Interest} - \textit{Tax}}{(\textit{Beginning equity} + \textit{Ending equity}) \div 2}$$

$$= \frac{\$600{,}000 - \$400{,}000 - \$35{,}000 - \$10{,}000 - \$20{,}000 - \$67{,}500}{(\$200{,}000 + 300{,}000) \div 2} = \frac{\$67{,}500}{250{,}000} = 27.00\%$$

Answer (B) is incorrect because 45.00% excludes common stock from the denominator. Answer (C) is incorrect because 50.47% excludes retained earnings from the denominator. Answer (D) is incorrect because 62.00% excludes interest expense and tax expense from the numerator.

Questions 68 through 70 are based on the following information. Hopper Company is a manufacturer of industrial products and employs a calendar year for financial reporting purposes. These questions present several of Hopper's transactions during the year. Assume that total quick assets exceeded total current liabilities both before and after each transaction described. Further assume that Hopper has positive profits during the year and a credit balance throughout the year in its retained earnings account.

---

68. Payment of a trade account payable of $64,500 will

A. Increase the current ratio, but the quick ratio would not be affected.

B. Increase the quick ratio, but the current ratio would not be affected.

C. Increase both the current and quick ratios.

D. Decrease both the current and quick ratios.

Answer (C) is correct. *(CMA, adapted)*

REQUIRED: The effect of paying a trade account payable on the current and quick ratios.

DISCUSSION: Given that the quick assets exceed current liabilities, both the current and quick ratios exceed one because the numerator of the current ratio includes other current assets in addition to the quick assets of cash, net accounts receivable, and short-term marketable securities. An equal reduction in the numerator and the denominator, such as a payment of a trade payable, will cause each ratio to increase.

69. The purchase of raw materials for $85,000 on open account will

A. Increase the current ratio.

B. Decrease the current ratio.

C. Increase net working capital.

D. Decrease net working capital.

Answer (B) is correct. *(CMA, adapted)*

REQUIRED: The effect of a credit purchase of raw materials on the current ratio and working capital.

DISCUSSION: The purchase increases both the numerator and denominator of the current ratio by adding inventory to the numerator and payables to the denominator. Because the ratio before the purchase was greater than one, the ratio is decreased.

Answer (A) is incorrect because the current ratio is decreased. Answer (C) is incorrect because the purchase of raw materials on account has no effect on working capital (current assets and current liabilities change by the same amount). Answer (D) is incorrect because the purchase of raw materials on account has no effect on working capital (current assets and current liabilities change by the same amount).

70. The collection of a current accounts receivable of $29,000 will

A. Increase the current ratio.

B. Decrease the current ratio and the quick ratio.

C. Increase the quick ratio.

D. Not affect the current or quick ratios.

Answer (D) is correct. *(CMA, adapted)*

REQUIRED: The effect of collection of a current account receivable on the current and quick ratios.

DISCUSSION: Collecting current accounts receivable has no effect on either the current ratio or the quick ratio because current assets, quick assets, and current liabilities are unchanged by the collection.

71. Obsolete inventory of $125,000 was written off during the year. This transaction

A. Decreased the quick ratio.

B. Increased the quick ratio.

C. Increased net working capital.

D. Decreased the current ratio.

Answer (D) is correct. *(CMA, adapted)*

REQUIRED: The effect of writing off obsolete inventory.

DISCUSSION: Writing off obsolete inventory reduced current assets but not quick assets (cash, receivables, and marketable securities). Thus, the current ratio was reduced, and the quick ratio was unaffected.

Answer (A) is incorrect because the quick ratio was not affected. Answer (B) is incorrect because the quick ratio was not affected. Answer (C) is incorrect because working capital was decreased.

72. The issuance of new shares in a five-for-one split of common stock

A. Decreases the book value per share of common stock.

B. Increases the book value per share of common stock.

C. Increases total equity.

D. Decreases total equity.

Answer (A) is correct. *(CMA, adapted)*

REQUIRED: The effect of a five-for-one split of common stock.

DISCUSSION: Given that five times as many shares of stock are outstanding after the split, the book value per share of common stock is one-fifth of the former value.

Answer (B) is incorrect because the book value per share is decreased. Answer (C) is incorrect because the stock split does not change the amount of equity. Answer (D) is incorrect because the stock split does not change the amount of equity.

73. The issuance of serial bonds in exchange for an office building, with the first installment of the bonds due late this year,

A. Decreases net working capital.

B. Decreases the current ratio.

C. Decreases the quick ratio.

D. Affects all of the above as indicated.

Answer (D) is correct. *(CMA, adapted)*

REQUIRED: The effect of issuing serial bonds with the first installment due late this year.

DISCUSSION: The first installment is a current liability; thus the amount of current liabilities increases with no corresponding increase in current assets. The effect is to decrease working capital, the current ratio, and the quick ratio.

74. The early liquidation of a long-term note with cash affects the

A. Current ratio to a greater degree than the quick ratio.

B. Quick ratio to a greater degree than the current ratio.

C. Current and quick ratio to the same degree.

D. Current ratio but not the quick ratio.

Answer (B) is correct. *(CMA, adapted)*

REQUIRED: The effect of an early liquidation of a long-term note with cash.

DISCUSSION: The numerators of the quick and current ratios are decreased when cash is expended. Early payment of a long-term liability has no effect on the denominator (current liabilities). Because the numerator of the quick ratio, which includes cash, net receivables, and marketable securities, is less than the numerator of the current ratio, which includes all current assets, the quick ratio is affected to a greater degree.

STUDY UNIT TWENTY-FOUR
GAAP ACCOUNTING FOR PARTNERSHIPS

Partnership law in the U.S. is based on the Uniform Partnership Act (UPA). However, a later version of this act, the **Revised Uniform Partnership Act (RUPA)** has been widely adopted. Accordingly, the following summary is based on the RUPA, to the extent it is relevant.

A **partnership**, as defined by the RUPA, is "the association of two or more persons to carry on as co-owners a business for profit." The recognition of assets, liabilities, revenues, expenses, gains, and losses in accordance with GAAP ordinarily is the same for partnerships as for corporations and proprietorships. GAAP accounting for ownership interests, however, is different.

These differences may involve the use of individual capital and drawing accounts for each partner. Individual **capital accounts** reflect the partners' initial contributions, additional investments, shares of profits and losses, withdrawals, and adjustments for ownership changes. They facilitate the accounting for partnership interests when partners elect to share differently in the profits or losses generated by the partnership. Different shares may be determined in accordance with a **profit-and-loss ratio**. Different shares also may include adjustments for salaries, bonuses, and returns on capital balances in addition to a residual profit-and-loss ratio. Provisions for salaries and bonuses usually are included to reward partners for their involvement in partnership activities. Returns on capital are provided to reward levels of capital investment. Still another possibility employed by many international accounting firms is to apportion profits and losses exclusively on the basis of capital balances, with partners required to maintain minimum balances related to levels of responsibility. However, unless the partnership agreement states otherwise, the RUPA specifies that partners will share profits equally and that they will share losses in proportion to their shares of the profits.

Drawing accounts are nominal accounts used to record periodic removals of money in anticipation of the distribution of partnership income. Drawings differ from withdrawals in that drawings do not affect partners' capital balances until the drawings are closed at year-end. Withdrawals are removals of cash that reduce partners' capital balances as the withdrawals occur.

The differences in accounting for ownership interests also may be reflected in partnership formation, dissociation of a partner with or without dissolution, and winding up. In contrast with a corporation, a partnership usually is easier to form, dissolve, liquidate, and terminate. It may be formed by a simple oral agreement. Tangible net assets contributed to the initial formation of a partnership should be recorded at fair value.

Under the RUPA, the process of ending the partnership begins with dissociation of partner(s). Dissolution, winding up, and termination may or may not follow. **Dissociation** is the legal effect of a partner's ceasing to be associated in carrying on the business of the partnership. After dissociation, the business either continues after purchase of the dissociated partner's interest or the process of dissolution begins. Dissociation may result from circumstances such as a partner's express will to withdraw, expulsion, bankruptcy, death, or determination of incapacity. Dissociation causes dissolution only if it is by express will. If dissociation does not cause dissolution, the partnership must purchase the **partner's interest**. The price is the amount distributable in a winding up if, at the time of dissociation, the assets had been sold at the greater of liquidation value or going-concern value. Dissociation by express will is the only one of the listed circumstances that results in dissolution. **Dissolution** may also result from an event specified in the partnership agreement, the illegality of the partnership business, the expiration of its stated term, and certain judicial determinations. However, dissolution will not proceed in these situations if all partners waive the right of winding up and termination.

When a new partner is admitted (an event requiring unanimous consent of the partners, unless the partnership agreement specifies otherwise), GAAP permits the recognition of partners' capital accounts at fair value as if a new partnership had been formed. This recognition will result in the revaluation of existing net assets or the recognition of goodwill (**goodwill method**). If the partners elect to focus on the continuation of the business activities and also agree that their capital balances should reflect their proportionate ownership, only the capital balances will be adjusted (**bonus method**), and no revaluation of net assets or recognition of goodwill will occur.

When a partner's dissociation results in **winding up** the partnership business, the RUPA specifies that the partnership's assets, including any required partner contributions, must be used first to pay its creditors, including creditors that are partners (to the extent permitted by law). Gains and losses from liquidation are credited or debited to the partners' accounts, with each partner entitled to a distribution if credits exceed debits, or liable to make a contribution if debits exceed credits. If a partner fails to contribute, the others must contribute the amount needed. Each such partner then has a right to recover his/her excess contributions from the other partners. A trustee in bankruptcy of a partner or partnership, or an assignee for the benefit of creditors of a partner or partnership, may enforce the obligation of a partner to contribute. Thus, for example, a trustee in bankruptcy of a partnership will have the status of a general unsecured creditor of a bankrupt partner. This rule is consistent with federal bankruptcy law.

In general, a liquidation involves converting noncash assets into cash, recognizing the related gains and losses, determining profit or loss during the liquidation phase, allocating profit or loss to the partners' capital accounts, settling liabilities, and distributing remaining cash to partners based on their capital balances. The distribution to partners can be made as a single payment or in installments as safe cash becomes available. **Safe cash** is cash that can be distributed to partners with reasonable assurance that it will not have to be returned to the partnership. Safe cash can be estimated by preparing a safe payments schedule or a cash distribution plan.

QUESTIONS

24.1 Formation

1. The Revised Uniform Partnership Act defines a partnership as

A. Any association of two or more persons or entities.

B. An association of two or more persons to carry on as co-owners a business for profit.

C. A separate legal entity for most legal purposes.

D. An entity created by following statutory requirements.

Answer (B) is correct. *(Publisher)*
REQUIRED: The definition of a partnership.
DISCUSSION: A partnership, as defined by the Revised Uniform Partnership Act, is "the association of two or more persons to carry on as co-owners a business for profit."
Answer (A) is incorrect because a partnership must be a profit-oriented business arrangement among co-owners. Answer (C) is incorrect because a partnership is viewed for most legal purposes as a group of individuals rather than a separate entity. Answer (D) is incorrect because no statutory requirements need be met to create a general partnership. A partnership may arise regardless of the intent of the parties when an arrangement satisfies the definition. However, specific statutory requirements must be followed to create a limited partnership.

2. The partnership agreement is an express contract among the partners (the owners of the business). Such an agreement generally does not include

A. A limitation on a partner's liability to creditors.

B. The rights and duties of the partners.

C. The allocation of income between the partners.

D. The rights and duties of the partners in the event of partnership dissolution.

Answer (A) is correct. *(Publisher)*
REQUIRED: The item not usually included in the partnership agreement.
DISCUSSION: Unlike corporations, general partnerships do not insulate a partner from liability to creditors. Each general partner has unlimited liability for partnership debts. The partners may agree among themselves to limit a partner's liability, but such a provision cannot limit direct liability to creditors.
Answer (B) is incorrect because this is typically found in the agreement among partners that establishes the partnership. A written agreement is not necessary for the creation of a partnership, but such an agreement is commonly used to define the rights and duties among the partners. Answer (C) is incorrect because this is typically found in the agreement among partners that establishes the partnership. A written agreement is not necessary for the creation of a partnership, but such an agreement is commonly used to define the rights and duties among the partners. Answer (D) is incorrect because this is typically found in the agreement among partners that establishes the partnership. A written agreement is not necessary for the creation of a partnership, but such an agreement is commonly used to define the rights and duties among the partners.

3. Pilates and Wesson drafted a partnership agreement that lists the following assets contributed at the partnership's formation:

	Contributed by	
	Pilates	Wesson
Cash	$40,000	$60,000
Inventory	--	30,000
Building	--	80,000
Furniture and equipment	30,000	--

The building is subject to a mortgage of $20,000, which the partnership has assumed. The partnership agreement also specifies that profits and losses are to be distributed evenly. What amounts should be recorded as capital for Pilates and Wesson at the formation of the partnership?

	Pilates	Wesson
A.	$70,000	$170,000
B.	$70,000	$150,000
C.	$110,000	$110,000
D.	$120,000	$120,000

Answer (B) is correct. *(CPA, adapted)*
REQUIRED: The capital balances of partners at the formation of the partnership.
DISCUSSION: The balances should reflect the fair values of the assets contributed. The building should be valued net of the mortgage. Hence, the capital balances for Pilates and Wesson are $70,000 ($40,000 + $30,000) and $150,000 ($60,000 + $30,000 + $80,000 – $20,000), respectively.
Answer (A) is incorrect because the building should be included net of the mortgage. Answer (C) is incorrect because the partners did not agree to divide capital equally. Answer (D) is incorrect because the partners did not agree to divide capital equally, and the building should be included net of the mortgage.

4. When property other than cash is invested in a partnership, at what amount should the noncash property be credited to the contributing partner's capital account?

A. Fair value at the date of contribution.

B. Contributing partner's original cost.

C. Assessed valuation for property tax purposes.

D. Contributing partner's tax basis.

Answer (A) is correct. *(CPA, adapted)*

REQUIRED: The credit to the contributing partner's capital account when noncash assets are invested.

DISCUSSION: The capital account should be credited for the current fair value of the assets at the date of the contribution.

5. Byrd and Katt formed a partnership and agreed to divide initial capital equally, even though Byrd contributed $200,000 and Katt contributed $168,000 in identifiable assets. Under the bonus approach to adjust the capital accounts, Katt's unidentifiable asset should be debited for

A. $92,000

B. $32,000

C. $16,000

D. $0

Answer (D) is correct. *(CPA, adapted)*

REQUIRED: The unidentifiable asset debited under the bonus approach.

DISCUSSION: The goodwill and the bonus methods are two means of adjusting for differences between the carrying amount and the fair value of partnership net assets. Under the goodwill method, assets are revalued. Under the bonus method, assets are not revalued. Instead, adjustments are made to partnership capital accounts. Consequently, total partnership capital differs between the two methods, and an unidentifiable asset may be debited under the goodwill but not the bonus method.

Answer (A) is incorrect because $92,000 is 50% of the balance in each partner's capital account under the bonus method. Answer (B) is incorrect because $32,000 is the unidentifiable asset recognized under the goodwill method. Answer (C) is incorrect because $16,000 is the amount transferred from Byrd's capital account to Katt's capital account under the bonus method.

6. The Gray-Redd Partnership was formed on January 2 of the current year. Under the partnership agreement, each partner has an equal initial capital balance accounted for under the goodwill method. Partnership net income or loss is allocated 60% to Gray and 40% to Redd. To form the partnership, Gray originally contributed assets costing $30,000 with a fair value of $60,000 on January 2 of the current year, and Redd contributed $20,000 in cash. Drawings by the partners during the current year totaled $3,000 by Gray and $9,000 by Redd. The partnership's current-year net income was $25,000. Redd's initial capital balance in the partnership is

A. $20,000

B. $25,000

C. $40,000

D. $60,000

Answer (D) is correct. *(CPA, adapted)*

REQUIRED: The initial capital balance credited to Redd based on the goodwill method.

DISCUSSION: If $60,000 (the fair value of Gray's original contribution) is 50% of the partnership capital, the total initial capital is $120,000, and goodwill of $40,000 should be recognized ($120,000 – $60,000 – $20,000 cash contributed by Redd). Thus, Redd's initial capital is $60,000.

Answer (A) is incorrect because $20,000 is Redd's initial cash contribution. Answer (B) is incorrect because $25,000 equals 50% of the cost of assets contributed by Gray plus the cash contributed by Redd. Answer (C) is incorrect because $40,000 is the goodwill recorded.

7. Partnership capital and drawing accounts are similar to the corporate

A. Paid-in capital, retained earnings, and dividends accounts.

B. Retained earnings account.

C. Paid-in capital and retained earnings accounts.

D. Preferred and common stock accounts.

Answer (A) is correct. *(Publisher)*

REQUIRED: The corporate accounts similar to partnership capital and drawing accounts.

DISCUSSION: Partnership capital accounts are similar to corporate paid-in capital and retained earnings accounts. Partnership drawing accounts are similar to corporate dividends accounts. They are nominal accounts that are closed to partnership capital and corporate retained earnings, respectively, at the end of each period.

Answer (B) is incorrect because drawing accounts are comparable to dividends accounts. Answer (C) is incorrect because drawing accounts are comparable to dividends accounts. Answer (D) is incorrect because drawing accounts are not like preferred and common stock accounts.

24.2 Distribution of Income

8. If the partnership agreement does not specify how income is to be allocated, profits should be allocated

A. Equally.

B. In proportion to the weighted average of capital invested during the period.

C. Equitably so that partners are compensated for the time and effort expended on behalf of the partnership.

D. In accordance with an established ratio.

Answer (A) is correct. *(Publisher)*

REQUIRED: The profit and loss allocation among partners absent a provision in the partnership agreement.

DISCUSSION: Under the RUPA, profits are to be distributed equally among partners and losses are to be distributed in the same manner as profits unless the partnership agreement provides otherwise. This equal distribution should be based on the number of partners rather than in proportion to the partners' capital balances.

9. The partnership agreement of Moe, Berg & Tyrus provides for the year-end allocation of net income in the following order:

- First, Moe is to receive 10% of net income up to $100,000 and 20% over $100,000.
- Second, Berg and Tyrus are each to receive 5% of the remaining income over $150,000.
- The balance of income is to be allocated equally among the three partners.

The partnership's net income was $250,000 before any allocations to partners. What amount should be allocated to Moe?

A. $101,000

B. $106,667

C. $108,000

D. $110,000

Answer (C) is correct. *(CPA, adapted)*

REQUIRED: The amount of partnership net income allocated to Moe.

DISCUSSION: Partners may elect to allocate income on any basis that is legal. Common elements of an income distribution are salary, bonus, return on capital, and a residual ratio. This agreement includes bonus and residual ratio provisions. Moe initially receives $40,000 {(10% × $100,000) + [20% × ($250,000 – $100,000)]}. The remaining income is $210,000 ($250,000 – $40,000). Of this amount, Berg and Tyrus each receive $3,000 [5% × ($210,000 – $150,000)], a total of $6,000. The balance is allocated equally [($250,000 – $40,000 – $6,000) ÷ 3 = $68,000]. Thus, Moe receives a total of $108,000 ($40,000 + $68,000).

Answer (A) is incorrect because $101,000 omits the 10% of net income up to $100,000 paid to Moe. Answer (B) is incorrect because $106,667 assumes, in the calculation of amounts paid to Berg and Tyrus, that the remaining income over $150,000 is $100,000. Answer (D) is incorrect because $110,000 omits the 5% of remaining income over $150,000 paid to both Berg and Tyrus.

10. Moore, the active partner in Moore & Besser, receives an annual bonus of 25% of partnership net income after deducting the bonus. For the current year ended December 31, partnership net income before the bonus amounted to $300,000. Moore's current-year bonus should be

A. $56,250

B. $60,000

C. $75,000

D. $100,000

Answer (B) is correct. *(CPA, adapted)*

REQUIRED: The amount of a bonus defined as a percentage of income after deduction of the bonus.

DISCUSSION: Calculating the bonus requires formulating an equation with one unknown. The bonus is formulated by subtracting the bonus variable B from net income and multiplying the result by 25%.

$$\begin{aligned} B &= .25(NI - B) \\ B &= .25(\$300{,}000 - B) \\ B &= \$75{,}000 - .25B \\ 1.25B &= \$75{,}000 \\ B &= \$60{,}000 \end{aligned}$$

Answer (A) is incorrect because $56,250 is the result of taking 25% of $300,000, subtracting that amount from $300,000, and then multiplying the remainder by 25%. Answer (C) is incorrect because $75,000 is 25% of the net income before the bonus. Answer (D) is incorrect because $100,000 is 25% of the sum of net income plus the bonus.

11. Kaspar and Karp formed a partnership on January 2 and agreed to share profits 90% and 10%, respectively. Kaspar contributed capital of $25,000. Karp contributed no capital but has a specialized expertise and manages the firm full-time. There were no withdrawals during the year. The partnership agreement provides that capital accounts are to be credited annually with interest at 5% of beginning capital; Karp is to be paid a salary of $1,000 a month; Karp is to receive a bonus of 20% of income calculated before deducting her salary, the bonus, and interest on both capital accounts; and bonus, interest, and Karp's salary are to be considered partnership expenses. The partnership annual income statement follows:

Revenues	$96,450
Expenses (including salary, interest, and bonus)	(49,700)
Net income	$46,750

What is Karp's bonus?

A. $11,688
B. $12,000
C. $14,687
D. $15,000

Answer (D) is correct. *(CPA, adapted)*
REQUIRED: The amount of a bonus calculated as a percentage of income before salary and interest.
DISCUSSION: The bonus payable to Karp is equal to 20% of the income before deduction of her salary and interest on both capital accounts. Net income after deduction of salary, interest, and the bonus is $46,750. The solution requires adding back salary ($1,000 × 12 months), interest (.05 × $25,000), and the bonus (B) to the net income. The bonus (B) equals 20% of the sum of these items.

$$\begin{aligned} B &= .2(\$46{,}750 + \$12{,}000 + \$1{,}250 + B) \\ B &= .2(\$60{,}000 + B) \\ B &= \$12{,}000 + .2B \\ .8B &= \$12{,}000 \\ B &= \$15{,}000 \end{aligned}$$

Answer (A) is incorrect because $11,688 results from omitting salary and interest from the bonus computation. Answer (B) is incorrect because $12,000 is the amount of the salary. Answer (C) is incorrect because $14,687 results from omitting interest from the bonus computation.

12. The Oxide and Ferris partnership agreement provides for Oxide to receive a 20% bonus on profits before the bonus. Remaining profits and losses are divided between Oxide and Ferris in the ratio of 2 to 3, respectively. Which partner has a greater advantage when the partnership has a profit and when it has a loss?

	Profit	Loss
A.	Oxide	Ferris
B.	Oxide	Oxide
C.	Ferris	Oxide
D.	Ferris	Ferris

Answer (B) is correct. *(CPA, adapted)*
REQUIRED: The partner with a greater advantage when the partnership has a profit and when it has a loss.
DISCUSSION: When the partnership has a loss, Ferris is allocated 60% and Oxide 40%. Hence, Oxide has the advantage when the partnership has a loss. When the partnership has a profit, Oxide receives 20% plus 40% of the remaining 80%, a total of 52% [20% + (40% × 80%)]. Thus, Oxide also has the advantage in this situation.

13. The partnership agreement of Orion and Hunt provides that interest at 10% per year is to be credited to each partner on the basis of weighted-average capital balances. A summary of Hunt's capital account for the current year ended December 31 is as follows:

Balance, January 1	$280,000
Additional investment, July 1	80,000
Withdrawal, August 1	(30,000)
Balance, December 31	330,000

What amount of interest should be credited to Hunt's capital account for the current year?

A. $28,000
B. $30,750
C. $33,000
D. $36,000

Answer (B) is correct. *(CPA, adapted)*
REQUIRED: The amount of interest credited to Hunt's capital account.
DISCUSSION: Hunt's balance was $280,000 for 6 months, $360,000 for 1 month, and $330,000 for 5 months. Consequently, the weighted-average balance was $307,500, as shown below, and interest was $30,750 (10% × $307,500).

(6 ÷ 12) × $280,000	=	$140,000
(1 ÷ 12) × $360,000	=	30,000
(5 ÷ 12) × $330,000	=	137,500
		$307,500

Answer (A) is incorrect because $28,000 is based on the beginning balance. Answer (C) is incorrect because $33,000 is based on the year-end balance. Answer (D) is incorrect because $36,000 is based on the July 1 balance.

14. During the current year, Jung and Freud maintained average capital balances in their partnership of $160,000 and $100,000, respectively. The partners receive 10% interest on average capital balances, and residual profit or loss is divided equally. Partnership profit before interest was $4,000. By what amount should Freud's capital account change for the year?

A. $1,000 decrease.

B. $2,000 increase.

C. $11,000 decrease.

D. $12,000 increase.

Answer (A) is correct. *(CPA, adapted)*

REQUIRED: The change in a partner's capital account.

DISCUSSION: The partners are to receive 10% interest and then split the residual profit or loss. Because interest exceeds partnership profit before interest, the residual loss is $22,000 {[10% × ($160,000 + $100,000)] – $4,000}. Freud's account is increased by $10,000 (10% × $100,000) and decreased by $11,000 (50% × $22,000 loss), a net decrease of $1,000.

Answer (B) is incorrect because $2,000 is 50% of the partnership profit before interest. Answer (C) is incorrect because an $11,000 decrease does not include the $10,000 of interest owed to Freud. Answer (D) is incorrect because a $12,000 increase equals 10% of capital plus 50% of the partnership profit before interest.

15. Porter and Saint-Lucie are partners who share profits and losses in the ratio of 6:4, respectively. Porter's salary is $20,000 and Saint-Lucie's is $10,000. The partners also are paid interest on their average capital balances. In 2003, Porter received $10,000 of interest and Saint-Lucie $4,000. The profit and loss allocation is determined after deductions for the salary and interest payments. If Saint-Lucie's share of partnership income was $40,000 in 2003, what was the total partnership income?

A. $65,000

B. $95,000

C. $100,000

D. $109,000

Answer (D) is correct. *(P. Lockett)*

REQUIRED: The partnership income given the distribution of income to one partner.

DISCUSSION: Given that Saint-Lucie's share of partnership income was $40,000, her share of residual income must have been $26,000 ($40,000 – $10,000 salary – $4,000 interest on his average capital balance). This amount represents 40% of the residual income, so total residual income was $65,000 ($26,000 ÷ 40%). Consequently, Porter's share of residual income was $39,000 (60% × $65,000). Moreover, Porter's share of partnership income was equal to $69,000 ($10,000 interest + $20,000 salary + $39,000 residual income). Total partnership income was therefore $109,000 ($69,000 + $40,000).

Answer (A) is incorrect because $65,000 was the residual income. Answer (B) is incorrect because $95,000 was the sum of residual income and salaries. Answer (C) is incorrect because $100,000 was the residual income assuming Saint-Lucie's share of residual income was $40,000.

24.3 Admission of New Partners

16. The goodwill and bonus methods are two means of adjusting for differences between the net book value and the fair value of partnerships when new partners are admitted. Which of the following statements about these methods is true?

A. The bonus method does not revalue assets to market values.

B. The bonus method revalues assets to market values.

C. Both methods result in the same balances in partner capital accounts.

D. Both methods result in the same total value of partner capital accounts, but the individual capital accounts vary.

Answer (A) is correct. *(Publisher)*

REQUIRED: The true statement about the bonus and goodwill methods.

DISCUSSION: The goodwill method revalues assets to adjust the total value of partnership capital. The bonus method simply readjusts capital accounts and makes no changes in existing asset accounts.

Answer (B) is incorrect because the bonus method does not revalue assets. Answer (C) is incorrect because the goodwill method revalues assets and the bonus method adjusts capital accounts. Consequently, total partnership capital differs between the two methods. Answer (D) is incorrect because the goodwill method revalues assets and the bonus method adjusts capital accounts. Consequently, total partnership capital differs between the two methods.

17. Tinker and Evers are partners with capital balances of $60,000 and $20,000, respectively. Profits and losses are divided in the ratio of 60:40. Tinker and Evers decided to admit Chance as a new partner. Chance invested land valued at $15,000 for a 20% capital interest in the new partnership. The cost of the land was $12,000. The partnership elected to use the bonus method to record the admission of Chance into the partnership. Chance's capital account should be credited for

A. $12,000

B. $15,000

C. $16,000

D. $19,000

Answer (D) is correct. *(CPA, adapted)*

REQUIRED: The amount to be credited to a new partner's capital account.

DISCUSSION: This transaction is to be accounted for under the bonus method. The incoming partner invests $15,000 fair value of land for a 20% interest in the capital of the new partnership. Hence, the incoming partner's capital account should be credited for 20% of the total capital following the investment. The total capital following the investment by the new partner equals $95,000 ($60,000 + $20,000 + $15,000). Because 20% of this amount is $19,000, Chance's capital account should be credited for $19,000.

Answer (A) is incorrect because $12,000 is the cost of the land. Answer (B) is incorrect because $15,000 is the fair value of the land. Answer (C) is incorrect because $16,000 equals 20% of the capital of the original partners.

18. Presented below is the condensed balance sheet of the partnership of Charles, Foster, and Welles, who share profits and losses in the ratio of 6:3:1, respectively:

Cash	$ 85,000
Other assets	415,000
	$500,000
Liabilities	$ 80,000
Charles, capital	252,000
Foster, capital	126,000
Welles, capital	42,000
	$500,000

Assume that the partners agree to sell to Orson 20% of their respective capital and profit and loss interests for a total payment of $90,000. The payment by Orson is to be made directly to the individual partners. The partners agree that implied goodwill is to be recorded prior to the acquisition by Orson. What are the capital balances of Charles, Foster, and Welles, respectively, after the acquisition by Orson?

A. $198,000; $99,000; $33,000

B. $201,600; $100,800; $33,600

C. $216,000; $108,000; $36,000

D. $270,000; $135,000; $45,000

Answer (C) is correct. *(CPA, adapted)*

REQUIRED: The capital balances of the original partners after recording goodwill and selling an interest to a new partner.

DISCUSSION: If Orson is to purchase a 20% interest in the partnership for $90,000, the partnership is estimated to be worth $450,000 ($90,000 ÷ 20%). But the sum of the original capital balances is only $420,000. Because goodwill is to be recognized prior to the purchase, $30,000 must be allocated to the capital accounts of the original partners. This amount will be shared in the profit and loss ratio of 6:3:1. The final step is to debit the capital accounts of the original partners for 20% of their respective interests and to credit the new partner's account for $90,000.

	Charles	Foster	Welles	Orson
Beginning capital	$252	$126	$42	
Goodwill	18	9	3	
	$270	$135	$45	
Minus 20% sold	(54)	(27)	(9)	$90
Ending capital	$216	$108	$36	$90

Answer (A) is incorrect because $198,000, $99,000, and $33,000 equal the balances of Charles, Foster, and Welles, respectively, if $90,000 is allocated according to the profit-and-loss ratio from the partners' original balances to Orson's account. Answer (B) is incorrect because $201,600, $100,800, and $33,600 are the original partners' balances if no goodwill is recognized and 20% of the original balances (20% × $420,000 = $84,000) is deemed to have been sold. Answer (D) is incorrect because $270,000, $135,000, and $45,000 are the original partners' balances after allocation of goodwill but before deduction of the interest sold.

19. Redd and White are partners with capital account balances of $60,000 and $90,000, respectively. They agree to admit Blue as a partner with a one-third interest in capital and profits, for an investment of $100,000, after revaluing the assets of Redd and White. Goodwill to the original partners should be

A. $0

B. $33,333

C. $50,000

D. $66,667

Answer (C) is correct. *(CPA, adapted)*

REQUIRED: The goodwill to the original partners.

DISCUSSION: If a one-third interest is worth an investment of $100,000, the value of the partnership must be $300,000 ($100,000 ÷ 331/3%). The total of the existing capital balances and Blue's investment is $250,000 ($60,000 + $90,000 + $100,000). Thus, goodwill is $50,000 ($300,000 – $250,000). The entry will be to debit cash (or property at fair value) for $100,000 and goodwill for $50,000, and to credit Blue's capital balance for $100,000 and the capital balances of Redd and White for a total of $50,000.

Answer (A) is incorrect because goodwill should be recognized and credited to the capital balances of Redd and White. Answer (B) is incorrect because $33,333 is one-third of the new partner's investment. Answer (D) is incorrect because $66,667 is two-thirds of the new partner's investment.

20. Orange and Blue have a partnership with capital balances of $50,000 and $70,000, respectively. They wish to admit Jeri White into the partnership partly because of the prestige that she will bring to the partnership. If White purchases a one-fourth interest in capital and future profit and loss for $25,000, her capital account should reflect assigned goodwill in what amount?

A. $10,000

B. $11,250

C. $15,000

D. $25,000

Answer (C) is correct. *(Publisher)*

REQUIRED: The goodwill assigned to a new partner.

DISCUSSION: The partnership capital is $120,000 prior to the admission of White, and she is to receive 25% of the capital for her contribution of cash and goodwill. Thus, $120,000 equals 75% of the new capital after her admission. The total capital will therefore be $160,000 ($120,000 ÷ .75), and White's capital account will be credited for $40,000. Because she contributed only $25,000 in cash, a debit to goodwill of $15,000 also is required.

Answer (A) is incorrect because $10,000 is the difference between the cash contribution and the goodwill assigned. Answer (B) is incorrect because $11,250 equals 25% of the capital excluding goodwill, minus the cash contribution. Answer (D) is incorrect because $25,000 equals the cash contribution.

21. Gordon and Rogers are partners who share profits and losses in the ratio of 6:4, respectively. On May 1 of the current year, their respective capital accounts were as follows:

Gordon	$60,000
Rogers	50,000

On that date, Corbett was admitted as a partner with a one-third interest in capital and profits for an investment of $40,000. The new partnership began with total capital of $150,000. Immediately after Corbett's admission, Gordon's capital should be

A. $50,000

B. $54,000

C. $56,667

D. $60,000

Answer (B) is correct. *(CPA, adapted)*

REQUIRED: The capital balance of an existing partner following the admission of a new partner.

DISCUSSION: Following the entrance of Corbett, the partnership began with total capital of $150,000. Corbett received a one-third interest; therefore, the new partner's capital balance must be credited for $50,000 ($150,000 ÷ 3). But Corbett contributed only $40,000, so the $10,000 difference ($50,000 – $40,000) must be allocated to the existing partners in the ratio of 6:4. The result will be debits to the capital accounts of Gordon and Rogers of $6,000 ($10,000 × 60%) and $4,000 ($10,000 × 40%), respectively. Consequently, immediately after Corbett's admission, Gordon's capital is $54,000 ($60,000 – $6,000).

Answer (A) is incorrect because $50,000 is Corbett's capital balance. Answer (C) is incorrect because $56,667 assumes Gordon's balance was reduced by one-third of the difference between Corbett's balance and his contribution. Answer (D) is incorrect because $60,000 was Gordon's original capital balance.

22. Presented below is the condensed balance sheet for the partnership of Lever, Polen, and Quint, who share profits and losses in the ratio of 4:3:3, respectively.

Cash	$ 90,000
Other assets	830,000
Lever, loan	20,000
	$940,000
Accounts payable	$210,000
Quint, loan	30,000
Lever, capital	310,000
Polen, capital	200,000
Quint, capital	190,000
	$940,000

Assume that the assets and liabilities are fairly valued on the balance sheet and that the partnership decides to admit Fahn as a new partner with a 20% interest. No goodwill or bonus is to be recorded. How much should Fahn contribute in cash or other assets?

A. $140,000

B. $142,000

C. $175,000

D. $177,500

Answer (C) is correct. *(CPA, adapted)*

REQUIRED: The amount to be contributed by a new partner when neither goodwill nor bonus is to be recorded.

DISCUSSION: The carrying amount of the partnership is the sum of the capital accounts of Lever, Polen, and Quint, i.e., $700,000. If Fahn is to have a 20% interest without recording goodwill or bonus, the current sum of the capital accounts will be equal to 80% of the carrying amount after the admission of Fahn. Dividing the original carrying amount of $700,000 by 80% yields the new carrying amount after Fahn's admission ($875,000). The difference between the respective carrying amounts is the amount the new partner must contribute.

New partnership ($700,000 ÷ 80%)	$875,000
Old partnership	(700,000)
Fahn's contribution	$175,000

Answer (A) is incorrect because $140,000 equals 20% of the $700,000 carrying amount. Answer (B) is incorrect because $142,000 equals 20% of the $700,000 carrying amount plus the $10,000 excess of the Quint payable over the Lever receivable. Answer (D) is incorrect because $177,500 assumes that the $10,000 excess of the Quint payable over the Lever receivable is added to the sum of the existing capital accounts before being divided by 80%.

23. In the Alex and Amy partnership, Alex and Amy had a capital ratio of 3:1 and a profit and loss ratio of 2:1, respectively. The bonus method was used to record Mark's admittance as a new partner. What ratio would be used to allocate to Alex and Amy the excess of Mark's contribution over the amount credited to Mark's capital account?

A. Alex and Amy's new relative capital ratio.

B. Alex and Amy's new relative profit and loss ratio.

C. Alex and Amy's old capital ratio.

D. Alex and Amy's old profit and loss ratio.

Answer (D) is correct. *(CPA, adapted)*

REQUIRED: The ratio used to allocate to the original partners the excess of the new partner's contribution over the amount credited to his/her capital account.

DISCUSSION: The bonus method makes no changes in existing asset accounts. Capital accounts of existing partners are adjusted in accordance with the old profit and loss ratio to reflect the bonus. The entry will be to debit cash (or the fair value of the property) contributed and to credit Mark's capital account for a lesser amount. The excess will be credited in the ratio of 2:1 to the original partners' capital balances.

24.4 Retirement of Partners

24. Hi Shade, a partner in an accounting firm, decided to withdraw from the partnership. Shade's share of the partnership profits and losses was 20%. Upon withdrawing from the partnership, he was paid $74,000 in final settlement of his interest. The total of the partners' capital accounts before recognition of partnership goodwill prior to Shade's withdrawal was $210,000. After his withdrawal, the remaining partners' capital accounts, excluding their share of goodwill, totaled $160,000. The total agreed upon goodwill of the firm was

A. $120,000

B. $160,000

C. $210,000

D. $250,000

Answer (A) is correct. *(CPA, adapted)*

REQUIRED: The amount of goodwill agreed upon prior to Shade's withdrawal.

DISCUSSION: The balance in Shade's account prior to recognition of goodwill was $50,000 ($210,000 – $160,000). Given that he was paid $74,000 upon withdrawing, Shade's account must have been credited with $24,000 in goodwill. If his share of partnership profits and losses was 20%, the total agreed upon goodwill equals $120,000 ($24,000 ÷ 20%).

Answer (B) is incorrect because $160,000 was the sum of the remaining partners' capital balances exclusive of goodwill. Answer (C) is incorrect because $210,000 was the sum of the partners' capital balances prior to Shade's withdrawal. Answer (D) is incorrect because $250,000 assumes that Shade was assigned $50,000 of goodwill.

25. On June 30, the condensed balance sheet for the partnership of Anna Lowe, Ben High, and Cam Meany, together with their respective profit and loss sharing percentages, was as follows:

Assets, net of liabilities	$320,000
Lowe, capital (50%)	$160,000
High, capital (30%)	96,000
Meany, capital (20%)	64,000
	$320,000

Lowe decided to retire from the partnership and by mutual agreement is to be paid $180,000 out of partnership funds for her interest. Total goodwill implicit in the agreement is to be recorded. After Lowe's retirement, what are the capital balances of the other partners?

	High	Meany
A.	$84,000	$56,000
B.	$102,000	$68,000
C.	$108,000	$72,000
D.	$120,000	$80,000

Answer (C) is correct. *(CPA, adapted)*

REQUIRED: The capital balances of the remaining partners following the retirement of a partner.

DISCUSSION: The $180,000 paid to Lowe represents Lowe's 50% interest in the partnership. The total value of the partnership is therefore $360,000 ($180,000 ÷ 50%), and the goodwill implicit in the retirement agreement is $40,000 ($360,000 total value – $320,000 net assets prior to the recording of goodwill). This $40,000 should be allocated 50% ($20,000) to Lowe, 30% ($12,000) to High, and 20% ($8,000) to Meany. High's capital balance following the recording of goodwill is $108,000 ($96,000 + $12,000), and Meany's is $72,000 ($64,000 + $8,000).

Answer (A) is incorrect because it assumes no goodwill is recognized, and the additional $20,000 paid to Lowe is deducted from the balances of High and Meany in the ratio of 3:2. Answer (B) is incorrect because $20,000, not $10,000, of goodwill should be allocated to High and Meany. Answer (D) is incorrect because the entire amount of goodwill should not be allocated to High and Meany.

26. On June 30, the balance sheet for the partnership of Ace, Deuce, and Trey, including their respective profit and loss ratios, was as follows:

Assets, at cost	$300,000
Ace, loan	$ 15,000
Ace, capital (20%)	70,000
Deuce, capital (20%)	65,000
Trey, capital (60%)	150,000
Total	$300,000

Ace has decided to retire from the partnership and by mutual agreement the assets are to be adjusted to their fair value of $360,000 at June 30. It was agreed that the partnership would pay Ace $102,000 cash for Ace's partnership interest exclusive of the amount due on the loan, which is to be repaid in full. No goodwill is to be recorded in this transaction. After Ace's retirement, what are the capital account balances of Deuce and Trey, respectively?

A. $65,000 and $150,000.

B. $72,000 and $171,000.

C. $73,000 and $174,000.

D. $77,000 and $186,000.

Answer (B) is correct. *(CPA, adapted)*

REQUIRED: The capital account balances of the remaining partners after a partner's retirement.

DISCUSSION: The first step is to record $60,000 to reflect the appreciation of the assets. This amount should be allocated according to the profit-and-loss ratio of 2:2:6. Writeup of specific assets has nothing to do with the recording of goodwill.

After the distribution, Ace has an account balance of $82,000. If Ace is to be paid $102,000, exclusive of the repayment of the loan and without recording goodwill, a $20,000 bonus must be deducted from the capital accounts of Deuce and Trey. Because they share profits and losses in the ratio of 2:6, their accounts will be reduced by $5,000 and $15,000, respectively.

	Ace	Deuce	Trey
Beginning capital	$ 70	$65	$150
Appreciation	12	12	36
	$ 82	$77	$186
Bonus	20	(5)	(15)
Ending capital	$102	$72	$171

Answer (A) is incorrect because the accounts must be adjusted for appreciation and bonus. Answer (C) is incorrect because the accounts must be increased for appreciation in the ratio of 2:2:6 and decreased in Deuce's and Trey's accounts for the bonus in the ratio of 2:6. Answer (D) is incorrect because the accounts must be reduced by the amount of the bonus.

27. When Brown retired from the partnership of Brown, Dart, and Prince, the final settlement of Brown's interest exceeded Brown's capital balance. Under the bonus method, the excess

A. Was recorded as goodwill.

B. Was recorded as an expense.

C. Reduced the capital balances of Dart and Prince.

D. Had no effect on the capital balances of Dart and Prince.

Answer (C) is correct. *(CPA, adapted)*

REQUIRED: The treatment of the excess of the settlement of a partner's interest over the capital balance.

DISCUSSION: The bonus method reduces the capital accounts of the other partners because the bonus, that is, the excess of settlement value over the retiring partner's capital balance, is deemed to be paid to the withdrawing partner by the remaining partners.

Answer (A) is incorrect because goodwill is not recorded under the bonus method. Answer (B) is incorrect because the excess is not an expense. Answer (D) is incorrect because the excess reduces the capital accounts.

24.5 Liquidation of Partnerships

28. The following condensed balance sheet is presented for the Iota and Theta partnership, who share profits and losses in the ratio of 60:40, respectively:

Other assets	$450,000
Iota, loan	20,000
	$470,000
Accounts payable	$120,000
Iota, capital	195,000
Theta, capital	155,000
	$470,000

The partners have decided to liquidate. If the other assets are sold for $385,000, what amount of the available cash should be distributed to Iota?

A. $136,000

B. $156,000

C. $159,000

D. $195,000

Answer (A) is correct. *(CPA, adapted)*

REQUIRED: The amount of cash to be distributed to a partner.

DISCUSSION: When the partnership sells the other assets, it must recognize a loss of $65,000 ($450,000 – $385,000). This loss must be allocated to the partners based on their loss ratio of 60:40. Thus, Iota's capital account is reduced to $156,000 [$195,000 – (60% × $65,000)] and Theta's to $129,000 [$155,000 – (40% × $65,000)]. The accounts payable are then paid, leaving assets of $265,000. Finally, the balance of the loan is subtracted from Iota's capital account balance, and each partner receives the balance in his/her capital account. Thus, Iota should receive $136,000 in cash ($156,000 – $20,000).

Answer (B) is incorrect because $156,000 results from not subtracting the loan from Iota's capital account. Answer (C) is incorrect because $159,000 equals 60% of the assets remaining after the liabilities have been settled. Answer (D) is incorrect because $195,000 equals Iota's unadjusted capital balance.

29. The following condensed balance sheet is presented for the partnership of Axel, Barr, and Cain, who share profits and losses in the ratio of 4:3:3, respectively:

Cash	$100,000
Other assets	300,000
Total	$400,000
Liabilities	$150,000
Axel, capital	40,000
Barr, capital	180,000
Cain, capital	30,000
Total	$400,000

The partners agreed to wind up the partnership after selling the other assets for $200,000. Upon winding up, Axel should have received

A. $0

B. $40,000

C. $60,000

D. $70,000

Answer (A) is correct. *(CPA, adapted)*

REQUIRED: The amount Axel should receive upon liquidation.

DISCUSSION: When the other assets with a carrying value of $300,000 were sold for $200,000, a loss of $100,000 resulted. When this loss is distributed in the ratio of 4:3:3 to the capital balances, Axel's and Cain's capital balances are eliminated. Thus, upon winding up of the partnership, neither Axel nor Cain will receive any cash. Of the $300,000 available ($100,000 cash on hand + $200,000 proceeds from the sale of other assets), $150,000 will be distributed to creditors (liabilities) and $150,000 to Barr.

	Axel	Barr	Cain
Beginning capital	$40,000	$180,000	$30,000
Loss on sale	(40,000)	(30,000)	(30,000)
Distribution of cash	$ 0	$150,000	$ 0

Answer (B) is incorrect because $40,000 is the beginning balance in Axel's capital account. Answer (C) is incorrect because $60,000 assumes that Axel is due 40% of the $150,000 available to distribute to partners. Answer (D) is incorrect because $70,000 is the sum of the capital balances of Axel and Cain.

30. Quinn, Rob, Sam, and Tod are partners sharing profits and losses equally. The partnership is insolvent and is to be liquidated. The status of the partnership and each partner is as follows:

	Partnership Capital Balance	Personal Assets (Exclusive of Partnership Interest)	Personal Liabilities (Exclusive of Partnership Interest)
Quinn	$ 15,000	$100,000	$40,000
Rob	10,000	30,000	60,000
Sam	(20,000)	80,000	5,000
Tod	(30,000)	1,000	28,000
	$(25,000)		

Assuming the partnership operates in a state where the Uniform Partnership Act applies, the partnership creditors

A. Must first seek recovery against Sam because he is solvent personally and has a negative capital balance.

B. Will not be paid in full regardless of how they proceed legally because the partnership assets are less than the partnership liabilities.

C. Will have to share Rob's interest in the partnership on a pro rata basis with his personal creditors.

D. Have first claim to the partnership assets before any partner's personal creditors have rights to the partnership assets.

Answer (D) is correct. *(CPA, adapted)*

REQUIRED: The rights of partnership creditors under the Uniform Partnership Act.

DISCUSSION: The Uniform Partnership Act follows the legal concept of marshaling of assets. Accordingly, the assets of the partnership are made available first to the partnership creditors. Only after their claims are fully satisfied will the personal creditors of the partners be able to proceed against partnership assets. Similarly, the personal creditors of each general partner have first claim to the personal assets of that general partner. The federal Bankruptcy Reform Act of 1978, however, altered the marshaling of assets concept with regard to the personal assets of a bankrupt partner when the partnership is also bankrupt. The trustee of a bankrupt partnership shares pro rata with the other general unsecured creditors of a bankrupt general partner. However, partnership creditors retain their priority in partnership assets under bankruptcy law. The Revised Uniform Partnership Act follows the federal law.

Answer (A) is incorrect because, after exhausting the partnership assets, the creditors must seek recovery against all partners in one legal proceeding; i.e., the partners are jointly liable. Answer (B) is incorrect because the partnership creditors ultimately have recourse to the personal assets of all the general partners. Answer (C) is incorrect because, under the UPA, the partnership creditors have first claim to the partnership assets.

Questions 31 and 32 are based on the following information.

December 31 balance sheet accounts of the Dan, Jim, and Mary Partnership follow:

Cash	$ 20,000
Inventory	120,000
Plant assets – net	300,000
Accounts payable	170,000
Dan, capital	100,000
Jim, capital	90,000
Mary, capital	80,000

The partners' profit and loss percentages are Dan, 50%; Jim, 30%; and Mary, 20%.

On January 1 of the next year, the partners decide to liquidate the partnership. They agree that all cash should be distributed as soon as it becomes available during the liquidation process. They also agree that a cash predistribution plan is necessary to facilitate the distribution of cash.

31. The predistribution plan should be based on relative vulnerability to losses. For the Dan, Jim, and Mary Partnership, the relative vulnerability should show that

A. Dan is the most vulnerable.

B. Dan is the least vulnerable.

C. Jim is the most vulnerable.

D. Jim is the least vulnerable.

Answer (A) is correct. *(Publisher)*

REQUIRED: The true statement about relative vulnerability.

DISCUSSION: A cash predistribution plan is based on the partners' relative vulnerability to losses under the assumption that a partner would not repay a deficit capital balance. This vulnerability is determined by projecting the loss that, in accordance with the profit-and-loss ratio, would eliminate each partner's account. Because Dan would be allocated 50% of each loss, a projected loss of $200,000 ($100,000 capital balance ÷ 50%) would eliminate his account. Projected losses of $300,000 ($90,000 ÷ 30%) and $400,000 ($80,000 ÷ 20%) would eliminate Jim's and Mary's balances, respectively. Accordingly, Dan is the most vulnerable because his capital balance would be eliminated by the smallest projected loss.

32. If cash of $220,000, including the $20,000 cash on hand, becomes available, it should be distributed in accordance with the cash predistribution plan. How much should be distributed to the creditors and partners respectively?

	Creditors	Dan	Jim	Mary
A.	$170,000	$25,000	$15,000	$10,000
B.	$170,000	$0	$26,000	$24,000
C.	$170,000	$10,000	$32,000	$8,000
D.	$170,000	$0	$18,000	$32,000

Answer (D) is correct. *(Publisher)*

REQUIRED: The distribution of cash to partners and creditors using a cash predistribution plan.

DISCUSSION: To prepare a cash predistribution plan, the smallest projected loss that will eliminate the partner most vulnerable to losses is allocated in the profit-loss ratio. Then, based on the newly calculated capital balances, the projected loss that will eliminate the next most vulnerable partner is allocated. The projected loss and its allocation are based on a profit-and-loss ratio adjusted for the previous elimination of more vulnerable partners. Once projected losses to eliminate all partners are calculated, the plan sets forth a distribution of cash that prevents an overpayment to an insolvent partner. Liabilities to outside creditors must be satisfied before cash is distributed to the partners. After satisfying the accounts payable of $170,000, $50,000 remains to be distributed to partners. The first $20,000 is to be distributed to Mary. Of the remaining $30,000, 60% ($18,000) will be distributed to Jim and 40% ($12,000) to Mary. The $50,000 should therefore be distributed $0 to Dan, $18,000 to Jim, and $32,000 to Mary.

Cash Distribution Plan

Projected Loss	Dan-50%	Jim-30%	Mary-20%
	$100,000	$90,000	$80,000
$200,000	(100,000)	(60,000)	(40,000)
	$ -0-	$30,000	$40,000
$ 50,000		(30,000)	(20,000)
		$ -0-	$20,000
$ 20,000			(20,000)
			$ -0-

Cash Distribution		Creditors	Dan	Jim	Mary
First	$170,000	100%			
Next	20,000				100%
Next	50,000			60%	40%
Then			50%	30%	20%

33. On January 1, the partners of Hornsby, Wagner, and Waner, who share profits and losses in the ratio of 5:3:2, respectively, decided to liquidate their partnership. On this date, the partnership condensed balance sheet was as follows:

Assets	
Cash	$ 50,000
Other assets	250,000
	$300,000

Liabilities and Capital	
Liabilities	$ 60,000
Hornsby, capital	80,000
Wagner, capital	90,000
Waner, capital	70,000
	$300,000

On January 15, the first cash sale of other assets with a carrying amount of $150,000 realized $120,000. Safe installment payments to the partners were made the same date. How much cash should be distributed to each partner?

	Hornsby	Wagner	Waner
A.	$15,000	$51,000	$44,000
B.	$40,000	$45,000	$35,000
C.	$55,000	$33,000	$22,000
D.	$60,000	$36,000	$24,000

Answer (A) is correct. *(CPA, adapted)*

REQUIRED: The safe installment payments to partners after the initial sale of assets.

DISCUSSION: When the liquidation of a partnership proceeds over time, a conservative approach must be taken to the distribution of assets (cash) to partners. This conservative approach incorporates three steps. In the first step, a gain or loss realized from the actual sale of assets ($120,000 – $150,000 = $30,000 loss) is allocated to the partners' capital accounts in accordance with the profit-and-loss ratio. In the second step, remaining assets are assumed to have a fair value of $0, which results in an assumed loss equal to their carrying amount. For this partnership, an assumed loss of $100,000 ($250,000 of other assets – $150,000 of other assets sold) results. This assumed loss is also allocated to the partners' accounts in accordance with the profit-and-loss ratio. The third step is taken only if at least one of the partners' capital accounts has a deficit balance. If a deficit results, the conservative approach requires allocation of the deficit to the remaining partners' accounts. This step is not necessary in this example. The final balances in the partnership accounts equal the amounts of cash that may be distributed in a safe installment payment schedule.

	Hornsby	Wagner	Waner
Beginning capital	$80,000	$90,000	$70,000
Realized loss ($30,000)	(15,000)	(9,000)	(6,000)
Assumed loss ($100,000)	(50,000)	(30,000)	(20,000)
Resulting capital	$15,000	$51,000	$44,000

Answer (B) is incorrect because a maximum of $110,000 in cash can be distributed given available cash of $170,000 and liabilities of $60,000. Answer (C) is incorrect because $55,000, $33,000, and $22,000 are equal to 50%, 30%, and 20%, respectively, of the excess of the total cash available over the liabilities. Answer (D) is incorrect because $60,000, $36,000, and $24,000 are equal to 50%, 30%, and 20%, respectively, of the $120,000 of cash realized from the sale of other assets.

34. Prior to partnership liquidation, a schedule of possible losses is frequently prepared to determine the amount of cash that may be safely distributed to the partners. The schedule of possible losses

A. Consists of each partner's capital account plus loan balance, divided by that partner's profit-and-loss sharing ratio.

B. Shows the successive losses necessary to eliminate the capital accounts of partners (assuming no contribution of personal assets by the partners).

C. Indicates the distribution of successive amounts of available cash to each partner.

D. Assumes contribution of personal assets by partners unless there is a substantial presumption of personal insolvency by the partners.

Answer (B) is correct. *(Publisher)*

REQUIRED: The true statement about a schedule of possible losses.

DISCUSSION: A schedule of possible losses presents a series of incremental losses to indicate the amount of loss in a liquidation that will eliminate each partner's capital account. The presumption is that losses or partners' capital deficits will not be repaid by individual partners. The schedule is used to determine the amount of cash that may be safely distributed to the individual partners without potential impairment of the rights of any party.

Answer (A) is incorrect because it describes the computation that determines the order in which partners' capital accounts will be eliminated by losses, not the amounts thereof. Answer (C) is incorrect because it describes a cash distribution schedule. Answer (D) is incorrect because the presumption (for the schedule) is that losses or deficits will not be repaid by individual partners.

STUDY UNIT TWENTY-FIVE
BUSINESS COMBINATIONS, CONSOLIDATIONS, AND BRANCH ACCOUNTING

A **business combination** is an entity's acquisition of net assets constituting a business or of controlling equity interests of one or more other entities. **SFAS 141**, *Business Combinations*, applies when (1) entities are merged or become subsidiaries, (2) one entity's net assets or equity interests are transferred to another entity, or (3) net assets or equity interests of the existing entities are transferred to a newly formed entity. The customary **historical-cost accounting** principles relevant to initial recognition and measurement of assets, liabilities, and equity interests issued; cost allocation; and subsequent accounting also apply to business combinations. **Cost allocation** to the elements of an asset (net asset) group is based on the elements' fair values. If the cost of the group acquired in a business combination is greater than the sum of the fair values assigned to the acquired assets (tangible assets, financial assets, and separately recognized intangible assets) minus the liabilities assumed, the difference is recognized as **goodwill**. Goodwill is tested for impairment but not amortized. A business combination subject to SFAS 141 is accounted for using the **purchase method**. An acquisition of a **minority interest** is also accounted for in this way. The **acquiring entity** must be identified. Thus, when no equity interests are exchanged, the entity that distributes cash or other assets or incurs liabilities is the acquiring entity. However, if a business combination is consummated through an exchange of equity interests, the determination is often more difficult because neither the issuer of equity interests nor the larger entity is necessarily the acquirer. Thus, all facts and circumstances should be considered. **Direct costs of the business combination** are accounted for as costs of the acquired entity, the fair value of securities issued is reduced by their **registration and issuance costs**, and **indirect and general expenses** are expensed as incurred. **Contingent consideration** results when an issuance of securities or the payment of other consideration may be contingent upon specified future events or transactions. The **cost of the acquired entity** includes the determinable amount of contingent consideration at the acquisition date. When resolution of a contingency based on **future earnings** levels results in the issuance or issuability of additional consideration, its fair value should be treated as an additional cost of the acquired entity. Resolution of a contingency based on **security prices** does not result in an adjustment of the cost of the acquired entity. The additional consideration currently distributable because of failure to achieve or maintain a security price is recorded at current fair value, but securities previously issued at the acquisition date are reduced to the lower current fair value.

The **cost of the acquired entity** is determined at the acquisition date. It is **allocated** to the assets acquired and liabilities assumed in accordance with their fair values at the acquisition date. **Preacquisition goodwill and deferred tax amounts** on the acquired entity's balance sheet are not recognized by the acquiring entity. However, it should recognize deferred tax amounts for differences between assigned values and tax bases of assets acquired and liabilities assumed. An **intangible asset distinct from goodwill** is recognized if it arises from **contractual or other legal rights** even if it is not transferable or separable. If this criterion is not met, an intangible asset distinct from goodwill may still be recognized if it is **separable**. If an intangible asset acquired in a business combination does not meet these recognition criteria, it is included in goodwill. A **preacquisition contingency** is a contingent asset, liability, or impairment of an asset of the acquired entity that existed prior to the business combination. It is normally included in the allocation of the purchase price at fair value unless the fair value is not determinable during the **allocation period**. This period ends when the acquiring entity no longer is waiting for information it has arranged to obtain and that is available or obtainable. The allocation period ordinarily is not more than 1 year after the combination is completed. If a preacquisition contingency's fair value is not determinable during the allocation period, it is included in the allocation based on principles applying to contingencies.

The total amount assigned to assets acquired and liabilities assumed may exceed the cost of the acquired entity. This **excess over cost** is allocated proportionately to reduce the amounts assignable to certain acquired assets. The acquired assets to which the excess over cost is **not** allocated are (1) financial assets (excluding equity-method investments); (2) assets to be disposed of by sale; (3) deferred tax assets; (4) prepaid assets of postretirement benefit plans, including pension plans; and (5) other current assets. The excess over cost may not be fully allocated because a partial allocation has reduced to zero the amounts assignable to acquired assets other than those assets just mentioned. The **remaining excess over cost** is treated as an **extraordinary gain** in accordance with APB 30 when the combination is completed.

Subsequent accounting for goodwill and other intangible assets acquired in a business combination is prescribed by **SFAS 142**, *Goodwill and Other Intangible Assets* (Study Unit 9).

Under SFAS 142, assets and liabilities must be assigned to **reporting units**. Hence, the determination of the purchase price of the acquired entity and related factors (e.g., reasons for the acquisition) should be **documented** at the acquisition date.

SFAS 94, *Consolidation of All Majority-Owned Subsidiaries*, amended **ARB 51**, *Consolidated Financial Statements*, to require that all entities in which a parent has a controlling financial interest through direct or indirect ownership of a majority voting interest be consolidated. However, a subsidiary is not consolidated when control does not rest with the majority owner. In **consolidated financial statements**, the results of operations, financial position, and cash flows of the parent and its subsidiaries are presented as those of a single accounting entity. Thus, interentity balances and transactions are eliminated. Consolidated statements should be prepared only when the controlling financial interest is held by one of the consolidated entities. When consolidated statements are not prepared, **combined statements** may be more meaningful than the separate statements of commonly controlled entities. For example, they are useful when one individual owns a controlling interest in several entities with related operations, entities are under common management, or the financial position and results of a group of unconsolidated subsidiaries are to be presented. Combined statements are prepared in much the same way as consolidated statements. Interentity transactions, profits, and losses must be eliminated. Moreover, such matters as minority interests, foreign operations, different fiscal periods, and income taxes are treated in the same way as in consolidated statements.

FASB Interpretation No. 46 (revised 2003), *Consolidation of Variable Interest Entities*, is a response to accounting scandals. A **variable interest entity (VIE)** is an off-balance-sheet arrangement that may take any legal form. The **primary beneficiary (PB)** consolidates a VIE. The PB is an enterprise with a variable interest(s) that will absorb a majority of the VIE's expected losses if losses occur or receive a majority of expected residual returns if returns occur. **Variable interests** are ownership, contractual, or monetary interests that vary with the fair value of the VIE's **net assets**.

Examples of variable interests are equity at risk, subordinated debt, subordinated beneficial interests (e.g., in a trust), and guarantees. The determination of the PB is made when the enterprise **becomes involved** with the VIE. If one enterprise meets the loss criterion and a second enterprise meets the return criterion, the former consolidates the VIE. A VIE exists and must be consolidated if, **by design**, either of two conditions exists: (1) Its **equity at risk** is insufficient to finance its operations without subordinated financial support from other entities, or (2) the equity investors lack one of the essential characteristics of a **controlling financial interest**. These characteristics are (a) decision-making ability based on voting or similar rights, (b) an obligation to absorb expected losses if they occur, or (c) the right to receive expected residual returns if they occur. The PB consolidates the VIE at **fair value**. A loss from this initial measurement is **goodwill** if the the VIE is a business and an **extraordinary item** if it is not. A gain is allocated to reduce assets as described in **SFAS 141**. A gain or loss is the excess of (1) the sum of the fair value of the consolidated VIE's assets and the reported amounts of assets transferred by the PB to the VIE over (2) the sum of the fair value of the consideration paid, the reported amount of previously held interests in the VIE, and the fair value of the consolidated VIE's liabilities and noncontrolling interests. The PB recognizes **no gain or loss on transfers** of assets or liabilities to a VIE made shortly before, at, or any time after the date it became the PB. Thus, the PB continues to measure them as if they had not been transferred.

In **branch accounting**, the term **branch** is used to describe a business subunit at a location different from the **home office**. A branch is not a separate legal entity. It is merely the extension of the existing legal entity and therefore need not maintain its own accounting records. Home offices may choose between a centralized or decentralized accounting system. In a **centralized system**, the branch does not maintain a separate general ledger. This system is most feasible when the operations of the branch do not involve complex transactions. In a **decentralized system**, the branch maintains a complete set of accounting records similar to those of an independent business. A branch with complex or extensive operations uses this system. When a branch uses a decentralized system, it records transactions with **external parties** in the normal way. Transactions between the home office and the branch also are recorded in the normal way, except that intraentity accounts are needed. **Intraentity accounts** are **reciprocal accounts** between the home office and the branch. They have equal and offsetting balances on the home office and branch books if both are up to date. They are used by both business units to record transactions between the units or made on behalf of one unit by the other. Thus, if the home office has a debit balance, the branch will have a credit balance for the same amount. The home office uses an **investment in branch** account to record its claim on branch assets. The balance reflects the home office's transfers of assets to the branch and the periodic results of branch operations (change in net assets from operations). Hence, it is the equity of the home office in the branch. The investment in branch account records **debits** for asset transfers and branch net income and **credits** for assets received from the branch and branch net losses. The **home office account** is used by the branch to record transactions with the home office. The branch's obligations to the home office are reflected in the account. The home office account records **debits** for assets transferred to the home office and branch net losses and **credits** for assets received and branch net income. Under normal business conditions, the investment in branch has a debit balance, and the home office account has a credit balance. The decentralized system is used solely for **internal reporting**. Because the home office and its branches are a single legal entity, the firm will prepare **combined statements** for external purposes. The firm must **eliminate reciprocal balances** when combining the balances of the home office and the branch. They represent transactions within the legal entity rather than with external parties.

QUESTIONS

25.1 General Concepts

1. A business combination may be structured as a merger, a transfer of equity interests, a direct acquisition of net assets, or a transfer of equity interests or net assets to a newly formed entity. Which of the following describes a business combination that is structured as a merger?

A. The surviving entity is one of the two combining entities.

B. The surviving entity is neither of the two combining entities.

C. An investor-investee relationship is established.

D. A parent-subsidiary relationship is established.

Answer (A) is correct. *(Publisher)*

REQUIRED: The characteristic of a business combination structured as a merger.

DISCUSSION: In a business combination structured as a merger, the assets and liabilities of one of the combining entities are transferred to the books of the other combining entity (the surviving entity). The surviving entity continues to exist as a separate legal entity. The nonsurviving entity generally ceases to exist as a separate entity, and its books are closed.

Answer (B) is incorrect because, in a consolidation, a new entity is formed to account for the assets and liabilities of the combining entities. This term should not be confused with the consolidation of the financial statements of legally separate entities. Answer (C) is incorrect because it describes an investment. A parent-subsidiary relationship exists when the investor holds more than 50% of the outstanding voting interests of the investee. Answer (D) is incorrect because it describes an investment. A parent-subsidiary relationship exists when the investor holds more than 50% of the outstanding voting interests of the investee.

2. Business combinations are accomplished either through acquisition of net assets constituting a business, or acquisition of controlling equity interests of one or more other entities. A parent-subsidiary relationship always arises from a

A. Tax-free reorganization.

B. Vertical combination.

C. Horizontal combination.

D. Greater than 50% investment in the voting interests of another entity.

Answer (D) is correct. *(Publisher)*

REQUIRED: The situation creating a parent-subsidiary relationship.

DISCUSSION: A parent-subsidiary relationship arises from an effective ownership of the voting interests of another entity in excess of 50%. The financial statements for the two entities ordinarily should be presented on a consolidated basis. To the extent the acquired entity is not wholly owned, a minority interest is presented.

Answer (A) is incorrect because a tax-free reorganization may or may not be a combination, and it may or may not result in a parent-subsidiary relationship. Answer (B) is incorrect because vertical combinations may also be accomplished by a merger or a consolidation, in which case the combining entities become one. A vertical combination combines a supplier and customer. Answer (C) is incorrect because horizontal combinations may also be accomplished by a merger or a consolidation, in which case the combining entities become one. A horizontal combination combines competitors.

3. A business combination structured as a merger has one set of books and accounting records (the surviving entity's) to account for the consolidated operations. On the other hand, if the combination is accomplished by a transfer of equity interests, each of the combining entities continues to maintain its own individual books and accounting records. For a transfer of equity interests, the books and accounting records of the consolidated entity are usually

A. Maintained by the parent separately from the surviving entity's books.

B. Prepared in worksheet form each time consolidated statements are prepared.

C. Maintained by each entity in the same manner that branch-home office accounting is accomplished.

D. Maintained by the subsidiary.

Answer (B) is correct. *(Publisher)*

REQUIRED: The true statement about the books and accounting records of a consolidated entity created by a transfer of equity interests.

DISCUSSION: No formal books are kept and no formal journal entries are prepared for a consolidated entity created by a transfer of equity interests. When consolidated financial statements are prepared, the normal procedure is to start with the output of the formal accounting systems of the parent and the subsidiary and, on a worksheet only, prepare the informal (worksheet) adjusting and elimination entries necessary to prepare the consolidated financial statements. These consolidating adjusting entries must be cumulative because previous worksheet entries were not recorded in the accounts of either the parent or the subsidiary.

4. When a parent-subsidiary relationship exists, consolidated financial statements are prepared in recognition of the accounting concept of

A. Reliability.

B. Materiality.

C. Legal entity.

D. Economic entity.

Answer (D) is correct. *(CPA, adapted)*

REQUIRED: The accounting concept recognized in consolidated financial statements.

DISCUSSION: Consolidated financial statements should reflect the economic activities of a business enterprise measured without regard to the boundaries of the legal entity. Accounting information pertains to a business enterprise, the boundaries of which are not necessarily those of the legal entity. For instance, a parent and subsidiary are legally separate but are treated as a single business enterprise in consolidated statements.

Answer (A) is incorrect because reliability reflects the quality of information assuring that it is reasonably free from error and bias and faithfully represents what it purports to represent. Answer (B) is incorrect because materiality requires reporting of information that has a value significant enough to affect decisions of those using the financial statements. Answer (C) is incorrect because the boundaries of the legal entity are disregarded in the preparation of consolidated financial statements.

5. In the period when a material business combination occurs, what supplemental information should be disclosed on a pro forma basis in the notes to the financial statements of a combined entity that is a public business enterprise?

A. Contingent payments, options, or commitments specified in the acquisition agreement.

B. If comparative statements are presented, the results of operations for all periods reported as though the combination had been completed at the beginning of the earliest period.

C. If comparative financial statements are presented, the results of operations for the comparable prior period as though the combination had been completed at the beginning of that period.

D. The period for which the results of operations of the acquired entity are included in the income statement of the combined entity.

Answer (C) is correct. *(Publisher)*

REQUIRED: The pro forma disclosure required.

DISCUSSION: SFAS 141, *Business Combinations*, requires pro forma disclosure of the results of operations (1) for the current period, as though the combination had been completed at the beginning of the period, unless the acquisition was at or near the beginning of the period, and (2) for the comparable prior period, as though the combination had been completed at the beginning of that period, if comparative financial statements are presented. However, pro forma disclosures for nonpublic entities are not required.

Answer (A) is incorrect because it is a required disclosure of actual data. Answer (B) is incorrect because disclosure is required only for the comparable prior period. Answer (D) is incorrect because it is a required disclosure of actual data.

6. Primor, a manufacturer, owns 75% of the voting interests of Sublette, an investment entity. Sublette owns 60% of the voting interests of Minos, an insurer. In Primor's consolidated financial statements, should consolidation accounting or equity method accounting be used for Sublette and Minos?

A. Consolidation used for Sublette and equity method used for Minos.

B. Consolidation used for both Sublette and Minos.

C. Equity method used for Sublette and consolidation used for Minos.

D. Equity method used for both Sublette and Minos.

Answer (B) is correct. *(CPA, adapted)*

REQUIRED: The method of accounting used by an entity that has a direct controlling interest in one entity and an indirect interest in another.

DISCUSSION: SFAS 94, *Consolidation of All Majority-Owned Subsidiaries*, amended ARB 51, *Consolidated Financial Statements*, to require that all entities in which a parent has a controlling financial interest through direct or indirect ownership of a majority voting interest be consolidated. However, a subsidiary is not consolidated when control does not rest with the majority owner. Primor has direct control of Sublette and indirect control of Minos and should consolidate both.

7. A 70%-owned subsidiary declares and pays a cash dividend. What effect does the dividend have on the retained earnings and minority interest balances in the parent's consolidated balance sheet?

A. No effect on either retained earnings or minority interest.

B. No effect on retained earnings and a decrease in minority interest.

C. Decreases in both retained earnings and minority interest.

D. A decrease in retained earnings and no effect on minority interest.

Answer (B) is correct. *(CPA, adapted)*

REQUIRED: The effect on retained earnings and minority interest balances in the parent's consolidated balance sheet after a subsidiary's payment of a cash dividend.

DISCUSSION: The parent's investment in subsidiary accounts and its proportionate share of the subsidiary's equity accounts, which include retained earnings, are eliminated in a consolidation. The remainder of the subsidiary's equity is reported separately as the minority interest. Thus, consolidated retained earnings is essentially the parent's retained earnings at year-end. The subsidiary's cash dividend reduces its retained earnings balance and therefore the minority interest but not the parent's.

8. Consolidated financial statements are typically prepared when one entity has a controlling financial interest in another unless

A. The subsidiary is a finance entity.

B. The fiscal year-ends of the two entities are more than 3 months apart.

C. Control does not rest with the majority owner(s).

D. The two entities are in unrelated industries, such as manufacturing and real estate.

Answer (C) is correct. *(CPA, adapted)*

REQUIRED: The exception to consolidation.

DISCUSSION: SFAS 94 usually requires consolidation when one entity owns, directly or indirectly, more than 50% of the outstanding voting interests of another entity. However, a majority-owned subsidiary is not consolidated if control does not rest with the majority owner.

Answer (A) is incorrect because the nature of the subsidiary's business is irrelevant under SFAS 94. Answer (B) is incorrect because a difference in fiscal periods is irrelevant under SFAS 94. Answer (D) is incorrect because whether the parent and subsidiary are in related industries is irrelevant under SFAS 94.

9. When a parent sells part of its interest in a subsidiary, it should account for the difference at the time of sale between the selling price and the carrying amount of the interest sold as which of the following?

A. A gain or loss.

B. A direct adjustment to paid-in capital.

C. A direct adjustment to retained earnings.

D. Either a gain or loss or a direct adjustment to paid-in capital.

Answer (A) is correct. *(Publisher)*

REQUIRED: The proper treatment of the difference between the selling price and the carrying amount in a sale of a parent's interest in a subsidiary.

DISCUSSION: When an investor sells part of its interest in an investee, APB 18, *Equity Method for Investments in Common Stock*, requires that the difference at the time of the sale between the selling price and the carrying amount be accounted for as a gain or loss. This principle also applies to the sale of an interest in a subsidiary by a parent.

10. For the past several years, Mozza Company has invested in the common stock of Chedd Company. As of July 1, 2003, Mozza owned approximately 13% of the total of Chedd's outstanding voting common stock. Recently, managements of the two companies have discussed a possible combination of the two entities. However, no public announcement has been made, and no notice to owners has been given. The resulting business combination should be accounted for as a

A. Pooling of interests.

B. Purchase.

C. Part purchase, part pooling.

D. Joint venture.

Answer (B) is correct. *(Publisher)*

REQUIRED: The accounting for a business combination, given 13% ownership of one combining entity by the other.

DISCUSSION: A business combination is an entity's acquisition of (1) net assets constituting a business or (2) controlling equity interests of one or more other entities. A business combination initiated after June 30, 2001 must be accounted for using the purchase method. A business combination is initiated at the earlier of the date the major terms (including the ratio of exchange) are announced publicly or formally made known to owners of any combining entity or the date owners of a combining entity are notified in writing of an exchange offer. Thus, no combination was initiated before July 1, 2001, and any subsequent combination of these entities must be accounted for using the purchase method.

Answer (A) is incorrect because the pooling-of-interests method may not be used to account for a business combination initiated after June 30, 2001. Answer (C) is incorrect because accounting for a business combination as part purchase and part pooling is not allowed. Answer (D) is incorrect because a joint venture does not meet the definition of a business combination.

25.2 Purchase Accounting--Valuation

11. To effect a business combination initiated on July 1, 2003, Proper Co. acquired all the outstanding common shares of Scapula Co. for cash equal to the carrying amount of Scapula's net assets. The carrying amounts of Scapula's assets and liabilities approximated their fair values, except that the carrying amount of its building was more than fair value. In preparing Proper's December 31, 2003 consolidated income statement, what is the effect of recording the assets acquired and liabilities assumed at fair value, and should goodwill amortization be recognized?

	Depreciation Expense	Goodwill Amortization
A.	Lower	Yes
B.	Higher	Yes
C.	Lower	No
D.	Higher	No

Answer (C) is correct. *(CPA, adapted)*

REQUIRED: The adjustments made in preparing the consolidated income statement.

DISCUSSION: A business combination initiated after June 30, 2001 is accounted for as a purchase regardless of the form of consideration given. Under purchase accounting, assets acquired and liabilities assumed should be recorded at their fair values. The differences between fair values and carrying amounts will affect net income when related expenses are incurred. The effect of recording the building at fair value in the consolidated balance sheet instead of its higher carrying amount on Scapula's books will be to decrease future depreciation. If the building is to be used, fair value is its current replacement cost for similar capacity unless expected use indicates a lower value to the acquirer. If the building is to be sold, it should be reported at fair value minus cost to sell. The excess of the cost over fair value of the net assets acquired will be recognized as goodwill, but, under SFAS 142, this amount will be tested for impairment but not amortized.

12. Zuider Corp. acquired 100% of the outstanding common stock of Zee Corp. in a business combination. The cost of the acquisition exceeded the fair value of the acquired net assets. The general guidelines for assigning amounts to the inventories acquired provide for

A. Raw materials to be valued at original cost.

B. Work-in-process to be valued at the estimated selling prices of finished goods, minus both costs to complete and costs of disposal.

C. Finished goods to be valued at replacement cost.

D. Finished goods to be valued at estimated selling prices, minus both costs of disposal and a reasonable profit allowance.

Answer (D) is correct. *(CPA, adapted)*

REQUIRED: The proper accounting for inventories when the cost of the acquisition exceeds the fair value of the net assets acquired.

DISCUSSION: According to SFAS 141, a business combination is accounted for as a purchase, and its cost should be assigned based on fair values at the acquisition date to the assets acquired and liabilities assumed. Finished goods and merchandise should be assigned amounts equal to estimated selling prices minus the sum of (1) costs of disposal and (2) a reasonable profit allowance for the selling effort of the acquiring entity.

Answer (A) is incorrect because raw materials should be valued at current replacement cost. Answer (B) is incorrect because work-in-process should be valued at estimated selling prices of finished goods minus the sum of (1) costs to complete, (2) costs of disposal, and (3) a reasonable profit allowance for the completing and selling effort of the acquiring entity based on profit for similar finished goods. Answer (C) is incorrect because finished goods are valued at estimated selling prices minus the sum of (1) costs of disposal and (2) a reasonable profit allowance.

13. Dire Co. purchased Wall Co. at a cost that resulted in recognition of goodwill having an expected 10-year benefit period. However, Dire plans to make additional expenditures to maintain goodwill for a total of 40 years. What costs should be capitalized and over how many years should they be amortized?

	Costs Capitalized	Amortization Period
A.	Acquisition costs only	0 years
B.	Acquisition costs only	40 years
C.	Acquisition and maintenance costs	10 years
D.	Acquisition and maintenance costs	40 years

Answer (A) is correct. *(CPA, adapted)*

REQUIRED: The costs to be capitalized and the amortization period.

DISCUSSION: SFAS 141 requires that goodwill (the excess of the cost of the acquired entity over the fair value of the acquired net assets) from a business combination be capitalized. Subsequent accounting for goodwill is governed by SFAS 142, which provides that goodwill is tested for impairment but not amortized. In contrast, the cost of developing, maintaining, or restoring intangible assets that (1) are not specifically identifiable, (2) have indeterminate lives, or (3) are inherent in a continuing business and related to an enterprise as a whole should be expensed as incurred.

Answer (B) is incorrect because the goodwill acquired externally is not amortized. Answer (C) is incorrect because the goodwill acquired externally is not amortized, and the costs of maintaining goodwill should be expensed as incurred. Answer (D) is incorrect because the goodwill acquired externally is not amortized, and the costs of maintaining goodwill should be expensed as incurred.

Questions 14 and 15 are based on the following information. On January 1, year 1, Pathan Corp. purchased 80% of Samoa Corp.'s $10 par common stock for $975,000. On the purchase date, the carrying amount of Samoa's net assets was $1 million. The fair values of the assets acquired and liabilities assumed were the same as their carrying amounts on Samoa's balance sheet except for plant assets (net), the fair value of which was $100,000 in excess of the carrying amount. For the year ended December 31, year 1, Samoa had net income of $190,000 and paid cash dividends totaling $125,000.

14. The goodwill recognized at the date of the business combination is

A. $0

B. $75,000

C. $95,000

D. $175,000

Answer (C) is correct. *(CPA, adapted)*

REQUIRED: The goodwill to be recorded at the date of the business combination.

DISCUSSION: A business combination is accounted for as a purchase. The excess of the cost of the acquired entity over the fair value of the acquired net assets is goodwill. As indicated below, the fair value of 80% of the acquired net assets is $880,000. Goodwill is therefore $95,000.

Cost	$975,000
Fair value of acquired net assets:	
Carrying amount: $1,000,000 × 80%	(800,000)
Undervalued plant: $100,000 × 80%	(80,000)
Goodwill	$ 95,000

Answer (A) is incorrect because the cost exceeds the fair value of the net assets acquired. Hence, goodwill should be recognized. Answer (B) is incorrect because $75,000 assumes that 100% of the undervaluation is included in Pathan's 80% interest. Answer (D) is incorrect because $175,000 assumes that carrying amount equals fair value.

15. In the December 31, year 1 consolidated balance sheet, the minority interest should be reported at

A. $200,000

B. $213,000

C. $220,000

D. $233,000

Answer (B) is correct. *(CPA, adapted)*

REQUIRED: The minority interest to be reported in the consolidated balance sheet at year-end.

DISCUSSION: The minority interest is equal to the 20% (100% – 80%) interest in Samoa not held by Pathan (the parent). Although the parent's interest equals the fair value of the net assets acquired at the date of purchase, the minority interest is recorded at the carrying amount recorded on the subsidiary's books. As indicated below, the minority interest to be reported in the year-end balance sheet equals 20% of the equity (net assets) at the beginning of the year, plus 20% of the net income, minus 20% of the dividends. Thus, the minority interest is reported at $213,000.

	20% Minority Interest
Equity at 1/1	$200,000
Net income (20% × $190,000)	38,000
Dividends (20% × $125,000)	(25,000)
Minority interest at 12/31	$213,000

Answer (A) is incorrect because $200,000 was the minority interest at 1/1. Answer (C) is incorrect because $220,000 is the minority interest measured at fair value at 1/1. Answer (D) is incorrect because $233,000 is the minority interest measured at fair value at 1/1, plus its share of net income, minus its share of dividends.

16. Pindar Co. purchased for cash at $30 per share all 250,000 shares of the outstanding common stock of Shimoda Co. At November 30, year 1, Shimoda's balance sheet showed a carrying amount of net assets of $6 million. At that date, the fair value of Shimoda's property, plant, and equipment exceeded its carrying amount by $800,000. In its November 30, year 1 consolidated balance sheet, what amount should Pindar report as goodwill?

A. $1,500,000

B. $800,000

C. $700,000

D. $0

Answer (C) is correct. *(CPA, adapted)*

REQUIRED: The goodwill to be recorded at the date of the business combination.

DISCUSSION: A business combination is accounted for as a purchase. The excess of the cost of the acquired entity over the fair value of the net assets acquired equals goodwill. Thus, goodwill is $700,000 [($30 × 250,000 shares) – $6,000,000 carrying amount – $800,000 additional fair value of PPE].

Answer (A) is incorrect because $1,500,000 equals the excess of the cost over the carrying amount. Answer (B) is incorrect because $800,000 is the fair value in excess of the carrying amount of the acquired net assets. Answer (D) is incorrect because goodwill should be recognized. The price exceeds the fair value of the net assets acquired.

17. Pellew Corp. paid $600,000 for the outstanding common stock of Samos Co. in a business combination initiated and completed in December, year 1. At that time, Samos had the following condensed balance sheet:

	Carrying Amounts
Current assets	$ 80,000
Plant and equipment, net	760,000
Liabilities	400,000
Equity	440,000

The fair value of the plant and equipment was $120,000 more than its carrying amount. The fair values and carrying amounts were equal for all other assets and liabilities. What amount of goodwill, related to Samos's acquisition, should Pellew report in its consolidated balance sheet?

A. $40,000

B. $80,000

C. $120,000

D. $160,000

Answer (A) is correct. *(CPA, adapted)*

REQUIRED: The amount of goodwill reported in the consolidated balance sheet.

DISCUSSION: A business combination is accounted for as a purchase regardless of the form of the consideration given. Under purchase accounting, assets acquired and liabilities assumed should be recorded at their fair values. Any excess of cost over the fair value of the net assets acquired is recorded as goodwill. After adjusting the net plant and equipment, and assuming other items are stated at fair value, the fair value of the net assets acquired is $560,000 [$80,000 current assets + ($760,000 + $120,000) plant and equipment – $400,000 liabilities]. Hence, goodwill is $40,000 ($600,000 cost – $560,000).

Answer (B) is incorrect because $80,000 is the amount of current assets. Answer (C) is incorrect because $120,000 is the amount plant and equipment is undervalued. Answer (D) is incorrect because $160,000 is the difference between the $600,000 cost and the $440,000 carrying amount of the net assets.

18. Costs incurred in completing a business combination are listed below.

Direct acquisition costs	$240,000
Indirect acquisition expenses	120,000
Cost to register and issue equity securities	80,000

The amount charged to the expenses of business combination account should be

A. $80,000

B. $120,000

C. $200,000

D. $240,000

Answer (B) is correct. *(CMA, adapted)*

REQUIRED: The treatment of the costs of a business combination.

DISCUSSION: Three types of costs may be incurred in effecting a business combination: direct costs of acquisition, costs of registering and issuing equity securities, and indirect and general expenses. Direct costs, such as finders' and consultants' fees, should be included in the determination of the cost of the acquired entity. Costs of registering and issuing equity securities should be treated as a reduction of their otherwise determinable fair value. Indirect and general expenses related to a combination should be expensed as incurred. Thus, only the $120,000 in indirect acquisition expenses should be charged to the expenses of the business combination.

Answer (A) is incorrect because $80,000 equals the cost to register and issue equity securities, which reduces their otherwise determinable fair value. Answer (C) is incorrect because $200,000 includes the cost to register and issue equity securities. Answer (D) is incorrect because $240,000 equals direct acquisition costs, which are included in the cost of the acquired entity.

19. On August 31, year 1, Parr Corp. issued 100,000 shares of its $40 par value common stock for the net assets of Vestee Co. in a business combination initiated after July 15, year 1. The market value of Parr's common stock on August 31 was $72 per share. Parr paid a fee of $320,000 to the consultant who arranged this acquisition. Costs of registering and issuing the equity securities amounted to $160,000. No goodwill was involved in the purchase. What amount should Parr capitalize as the cost of acquiring Vestee's net assets?

A. $7,200,000

B. $7,360,000

C. $7,520,000

D. $7,680,000

Answer (C) is correct. *(CPA, adapted)*

REQUIRED: The amount capitalized as the cost of acquiring the net assets.

DISCUSSION: Three types of costs may be incurred in effecting a business combination: direct costs of acquisition, costs of registering and issuing equity securities, and indirect and general expenses. Direct costs, such as finders' and consultants' fees, should be included in the determination of the cost of the company acquired. Costs of registering and issuing equity securities should be treated as a reduction in the otherwise determinable fair value of the securities. Indirect and general expenses should be included in the determination of net income when incurred.

An asset acquired by issuing stock is usually recorded at the fair value of the asset. However, the fair value of securities is normally more clearly evident than the fair value of an acquired company. Hence, the quoted price at the acquisition date (August 31) of the equity securities issued to effect the combination may be used to approximate the fair value of the acquired company. The investment should be debited for $7,520,000 [(100,000 shares × $72) + $320,000 consultant's fee], and additional paid-in capital should be debited for $160,000 (the registration and issuance costs). The credits are to common stock for $4,000,000 ($40 × 100,000 shares), additional paid-in capital for $3,200,000 [($72 – $40 par) × 100,000 shares], and cash for $480,000 ($320,000 + $160,000).

Answer (A) is incorrect because $7,200,000 ignores the other costs of the combination. Answer (B) is incorrect because $7,360,000 treats the registration and issuance costs as a reduction of the investment instead of paid-in capital. Answer (D) is incorrect because $7,680,000 treats the registration and issuance costs as an addition to the investment instead of as a reduction of paid-in capital.

20. In a business combination, Major Corporation issued nonvoting, nonconvertible preferred stock with a fair value of $8 million in exchange for all of the outstanding common stock of Minor Corporation. On the acquisition date, Minor had tangible net assets with a carrying amount of $4 million and a fair value of $5 million. In addition, Major issued preferred stock valued at $800,000 to an individual as a finder's fee in arranging the transaction. As a result of this transaction, Major should record an increase in net assets of

A. $4,000,000

B. $5,000,000

C. $5,800,000

D. $8,800,000

Answer (D) is correct. *(CPA, adapted)*

REQUIRED: The initial amount recorded for net assets acquired in a business combination.

DISCUSSION: In applying the purchase method, the cost to the purchasing entity of acquiring another entity is the amount of cash paid or the fair value of other assets given up, liabilities assumed, or equity interests issued in the transaction. This fair value is the more clearly evident and therefore the more reliably measurable of (1) the fair value of the consideration given or (2) the asset (net assets) acquired. In addition, any direct fees paid related to the combination are added to the consideration given.

Although the principle of recording the fair value of consideration received for issued shares applies to senior securities (e.g., preferred stock), the cost of an entity acquired for preferred stock with characteristics similar to debt securities (e.g., nonvoting and nonconvertible) may be determined on the same basis as debt securities. Thus, the fair value of the preferred stock given up is used to measure this transaction. It equals $8 million, and the fair value of the finder's fee paid is $800,000. Accordingly, Major should recognize an increase in net assets at the acquisition date of $8,800,000 ($8,000,000 + $800,000).

Answer (A) is incorrect because $4,000,000 is the carrying amount of Minor's tangible net assets. Answer (B) is incorrect because $5,000,000 is the fair value of Minor's tangible net assets. Answer (C) is incorrect because $5,800,000 equals the fair value of Minor's tangible net assets plus the finder's fee.

21. In a business combination, the sum of the amounts assigned by the acquiring entity to assets acquired and liabilities assumed exceeds the cost of the acquired entity. The excess should be reported as a

A. Deferred credit.

B. Reduction of the amounts assigned to current assets and a deferred credit for any unallocated portion.

C. Reduction of the amounts assigned to certain acquired assets and an extraordinary gain for any unallocated portion.

D. Pro rata reduction of the amounts assigned to all acquired assets and an extraordinary gain for any unallocated portion.

Answer (C) is correct. *(CPA, adapted)*

REQUIRED: The accounting for the excess of the fair value of acquired net assets over cost.

DISCUSSION: In a business combination, any excess of the fair value assigned to the net assets acquired over the cost of the purchase must be allocated proportionately to reduce the amounts otherwise assignable to all of the acquired assets except (a) financial assets (excluding equity-method investments), (b) assets to be disposed of by sale, (c) deferred tax assets, (d) prepaid assets relating to post-retirement benefit plans, and (e) other current assets. Any remainder after the amounts otherwise assignable to those assets have been reduced to zero is reported as an extraordinary gain (SFAS 141).

Answer (A) is incorrect because a deferred credit is never recognized for the excess of the fair value of acquired net assets over cost. Answer (B) is incorrect because a deferred credit is never recognized for the excess of the fair value of acquired net assets over cost. Answer (D) is incorrect because the amounts assigned to certain acquired assets (most financial assets, assets to be disposed of by sale, etc.) are not reduced.

22. Purchase Corporation purchased for cash at $10 per share all 100,000 shares of the outstanding common stock of Seller Company. The total fair value of the assets acquired minus liabilities assumed of Seller was $1.4 million on the acquisition date, including the fair value of Seller's property, plant, and equipment (its only noncurrent asset) of $250,000. The consolidated financial statements of Purchase Corporation and its wholly owned subsidiary should reflect

A. A deferred credit of $150,000.

B. Goodwill of $150,000.

C. An extraordinary gain of $150,000.

D. Goodwill of $400,000.

Answer (C) is correct. *(CPA, adapted)*

REQUIRED: The accounting treatment of the excess of the fair value of net assets acquired over cost.

DISCUSSION: In a business combination, any excess of the fair value assigned to the net assets acquired over the cost of the purchase must be allocated proportionately to reduce the amounts otherwise assignable to all of the acquired assets except (a) financial assets (excluding equity-method investments), (b) assets to be disposed of by sale, (c) deferred tax assets, (d) prepaid assets relating to post-retirement benefit plans, and (e) other current assets. Any remainder after the amounts otherwise assignable to those assets have been reduced to zero is reported as an extraordinary gain (SFAS 141).

The excess over cost in this transaction is $400,000 ($1,400,000 fair value – $1,000,000 cash paid). Given that the only assets to which the excess over cost may be allocated are those classified as property, plant, and equipment (all other acquired assets are current), only $250,000 of the excess is allocable. Hence, the excess of $150,000 ($400,000 – $250,000) remaining after allocation is recognized as an extraordinary gain.

Answer (A) is incorrect because a deferred credit is never recognized for the excess of the fair value of acquired net assets over cost. Answer (B) is incorrect because goodwill is recognized when cost exceeds the fair value of acquired net assets. Answer (D) is incorrect because goodwill is recognized when cost exceeds the fair value of acquired net assets.

23. Startup Company has properly treated as expense $200,000 of research and development costs that resulted in a patent. When Venture Company acquired Startup Company, it was determined that the patent had a fair value of $500,000. Which of the following statements is true?

A. On the books of Venture Company, the patent should be recorded at $200,000 because that was the cost to produce it.

B. The cost of the patent on the books of Venture Company should be $500,000.

C. The cost of the patent on the books of Venture Company should be the same as on the books of Startup Company.

D. The cost of the patent on the books of Venture Company should be represented by the legal costs involved in the patent process.

Answer (B) is correct. *(Publisher)*

REQUIRED: The accounting for the fair value of an asset not recorded in the books of the acquired entity at the acquisition date.

DISCUSSION: In applying the purchase method, the acquiring entity allocates the cost of the acquired entity to the assets acquired and liabilities assumed based on their estimated fair values at the acquisition date. This principle applies to intangible assets, even if they are not recorded on the books of the acquired entity. Thus, an acquired intangible asset is recognized separately from goodwill if it arises from contractual or other legal rights. If this criterion is not met, an acquired intangible asset may still be recognized if it is separable from the acquired entity. Thus, the patent, which arises from legal rights, should be recognized at its estimated fair value at the acquisition date.

Answer (A) is incorrect because purchase accounting requires use of fair values in recording the acquired net assets. Answer (C) is incorrect because purchase accounting requires use of fair values in recording the acquired net assets. Answer (D) is incorrect because purchase accounting requires use of fair values in recording the acquired net assets.

24. An entire acquired entity is sold. The goodwill remaining from the acquisition should be

A. Included in the carrying amount of the net assets sold.

B. Charged to retained earnings of the current period.

C. Expensed in the period sold.

D. Charged to retained earnings of prior periods.

Answer (A) is correct. *(Publisher)*
REQUIRED: The accounting for goodwill when an acquired entity is sold.
DISCUSSION: When a reporting unit is disposed of in its entirety, goodwill of that reporting unit (to the extent an impairment loss has not been recognized) is included in the carrying amount of the reporting unit to determine the gain or loss on disposal (SFAS 142). Consequently, the unimpaired goodwill of each reporting unit of the acquired entity is included in the total carrying amount of that entity.

25. Included in the assets of an acquired subsidiary are a patent that was internally developed, equipment used in research and development (R&D) with an alternative use, and equipment used in R&D with no alternative use. FASB Interpretation No. 4, *Applicability of SFAS 2 to Business Combinations Accounted for by the Purchase Method*, requires that the purchase price be allocated to these three asset categories based on their fair values at the date of the business combination. Which of these asset types is (are) subsequently accounted for by immediately expensing the fair value assigned?

A. All three asset types.

B. The two types of equipment to be used in R&D.

C. The equipment to be used in R&D with no alternative use.

D. The equipment to be used in R&D with an alternative use.

Answer (C) is correct. *(Publisher)*
REQUIRED: The accounting for R&D costs arising from a business combination.
DISCUSSION: FASB Interpretation No. 4 requires the allocation of the purchase price to all identifiable assets, whether tangible or intangible. FASB Interpretation No. 4 further requires that the cost assigned to assets that are to be used in a particular R&D project and that have no alternative future use be charged to R&D expense at the date of the consummation of the combination.

Answer (A) is incorrect because only the R&D equipment with no alternative future use is charged to R&D expense. The patent and the R&D equipment with alternative uses are capitalized. Answer (B) is incorrect because only the R&D equipment with no alternative future use is charged to R&D expense. The patent and the R&D equipment with alternative uses are capitalized. Answer (D) is incorrect because only the R&D equipment with no alternative future use is charged to R&D expense. The patent and the R&D equipment with alternative uses are capitalized.

26. Which of the following statements is true about a lease held by an entity acquired in a business combination?

A. The classification of a lease in accordance with the criteria of SFAS 13 is based on the amounts assigned to the lease at the date of the business combination.

B. The provisions of a lease that are modified in connection with the business combination are disregarded in the classification of the lease.

C. The lease is accounted for by the acquiring entity in the same manner that it was accounted for (both classification and measurement) by the acquired entity.

D. The amounts assigned to the lease asset and obligation are based on their fair values as of the date of the business combination.

Answer (D) is correct. *(Publisher)*
REQUIRED: The true statement about the accounting for a lease of a subsidiary acquired in a business combination.
DISCUSSION: FASB Interpretation No. 21, *Accounting for Leases in a Business Combination*, requires that the amounts assigned to lease assets acquired and lease liabilities assumed at the date of the business combination be determined in accordance with SFAS 141, *Business Combinations*. Thus, the cost of the acquired entity is allocated based on the estimated fair values of assets acquired and liabilities assumed at the acquisition date.

Answer (A) is incorrect because the classification of a lease is changed only if the provisions of the lease are modified in the business combination. The modified lease is then classified by the acquiring entity in accordance with the criteria in SFAS 13, *Accounting for Leases*. Answer (B) is incorrect because the classification of a lease is changed only if the provisions of the lease are modified in the business combination. The modified lease is then classified by the acquiring entity in accordance with the criteria in SFAS 13, *Accounting for Leases*. Answer (C) is incorrect because the measurement of the lease asset acquired and the lease liability assumed depends on the allocation of the cost of the acquired entity, which is based on estimated fair values. The classification does not change unless the lease is modified in the business combination.

25.3 Purchase Accounting--Implementation

27. On January 1, 2003, Pane Corp. exchanged 150,000 shares of its $20 par value common stock for all of Sky Corp.'s common stock. At that date, the fair value of Pane's common stock issued was equal to the carrying amount of Sky's net assets. Both corporations continued to operate as separate businesses, maintaining accounting records with years ending December 31. Information from separate company operations follows:

	Pane	Sky
Retained earnings – 12/31/02	$3,200,000	$925,000
Net income – 6 months ended 6/30/03	800,000	275,000
Dividends paid – 3/25/03	750,000	--

What amount of retained earnings should Pane report in its June 30, 2003 consolidated balance sheet?

A. $5,200,000

B. $4,450,000

C. $3,525,000

D. $3,250,000

Answer (D) is correct. *(CPA, adapted)*

REQUIRED: The retained earnings at the date of a business combination.

DISCUSSION: The purchase method must be used to account for a business combination. It accounts for a business combination on the basis of the values exchanged. Hence, the cost of the acquired entity is allocated to the assets acquired and liabilities assumed based on their fair values, with possible adjustments for goodwill or the excess of fair value over cost. Moreover, no minority interest is recorded in this combination. Accordingly, only the cost of the acquired entity is included in a consolidated balance sheet prepared using the purchase method. The equity, including retained earnings of the acquired entity, is excluded. Pane's separate retained earnings is therefore equal to the amount in the consolidated balance sheet, i.e., $3,250,000 ($3,200,000 beginning RE + $800,000 NI – $750,000 dividends).

Answer (A) is incorrect because $5,200,000 includes Sky's retained earnings at 6/30/03 and does not deduct the dividends paid. Answer (B) is incorrect because $4,450,000 equals the consolidated retained earnings if the combination had been accounted for as a pooling, a method not applicable to a combination initiated after June 30, 2001. Answer (C) is incorrect because $3,525,000 double counts Sky's net income through 6/30/03. The income statement of the acquiring entity for the period in which a business combination occurs includes the income of the acquired entity after the acquisition date, with revenues and expenses based on the cost to the acquiring entity.

28. Rolan Corporation issued 10,000 shares of common stock in exchange for all of Sandin Corporation's outstanding stock on September 1, 2003. Rolan's common stock had a market price of $60 per share on September 1. The market price of Sandin's stock was not readily ascertainable. Condensed balance sheets of Rolan and Sandin immediately prior to the combination are indicated below.

	Rolan	Sandin
Total assets	$1,000,000	$500,000
Liabilities	$ 300,000	$150,000
Common stock ($10 par)	200,000	100,000
Retained earnings	500,000	250,000
Total equities	$1,000,000	$500,000

Rolan's investment in Sandin's stock will be stated in Rolan's balance sheet immediately after the combination in the amount of

A. $100,000

B. $350,000

C. $500,000

D. $600,000

Answer (D) is correct. *(CPA, adapted)*

REQUIRED: The recorded amount of the acquired entity.

DISCUSSION: A business combination is accounted for using the purchase method. Hence, the cost to the acquiring entity is measured by the amount of cash disbursed. If the consideration given is not cash, measurement is based on the more clearly evident of the fair value of the consideration given or the fair value of the asset (net assets) acquired. Given that Rolan issued 10,000 shares of common stock with a fair value of $60 per share to effect the purchase, the total cost is $600,000, the amount to be recorded as Rolan's investment in Sandin.

Answer (A) is incorrect because $100,000 equals the par value of the stock issued. Answer (B) is incorrect because $350,000 equals the carrying amount of Sandin's net assets. Answer (C) is incorrect because $500,000 equals the fair value of the stock issued minus its par value.

29. On December 31, 2003, Saxe Corporation was merged into Poe Corporation in a business combination. On December 31, Poe issued 200,000 shares of its $10 par common stock, with a market price of $18 a share, for all of Saxe's common stock. The equity section of each entity's balance sheet immediately before the combination are presented below:

	Poe	Saxe
Common stock	$3,000,000	$1,500,000
Additional paid-in capital	1,300,000	150,000
Retained earnings	2,500,000	850,000
	$6,800,000	$2,500,000

In the December 31, 2003 consolidated balance sheet, additional paid-in capital should be reported at

A. $950,000

B. $1,300,000

C. $1,450,000

D. $2,900,000

Answer (D) is correct. *(CPA, adapted)*

REQUIRED: The additional paid-in capital to be reported in the consolidated balance sheet.

DISCUSSION: A business combination is accounted for using the purchase method. To effect the acquisition, the 200,000 shares were issued for $3,600,000 (200,000 shares × $18 market price per share). Of this amount, $2,000,000 (200,000 shares × $10 par) should be allocated to the common stock of Poe, with the remaining $1,600,000 ($3,600,000 – $2,000,000) allocated to additional paid-in capital. The additional paid-in capital recorded on Poe's (the parent's) books is $2,900,000 ($1,300,000 + $1,600,000). This balance is also reported on the 2003 consolidated balance sheet.

Answer (A) is incorrect because $950,000 is the additional paid-in capital reported under the pooling-of-interests method, which may not be applied to combinations initiated after June 30, 2001. Answer (B) is incorrect because $1,300,000 is the amount reported by Poe immediately before the combination. Answer (C) is incorrect because $1,450,000 is the sum of the amounts reported by Poe and Saxe immediately before the combination.

Questions 30 through 34 are based on the following information.

Parma Corp. and Seville Corp. condensed balance sheets on January 1, year 1 are presented in the opposite column.

On January 2, year 1, Parma borrowed $60,000 and used the proceeds to purchase 90% of the outstanding common shares of Seville. Ten equal principal and interest payments begin December 30, year 1. The excess cost of the investment over Seville's carrying amount of acquired net assets should be allocated 60% to inventory and 40% to goodwill.

	Parma	Seville
Current assets	$70,000	$20,000
Noncurrent assets	90,000	40,000
Total assets	$160,000	$60,000
Current liabilities	$30,000	$10,000
Long-term debt	50,000	--
Equity	80,000	50,000
Total liabilities and equity	$160,000	$60,000

30. On Parma's January 2, year 1 consolidated balance sheet, current assets should be

A. $99,000

B. $96,000

C. $90,000

D. $79,000

Answer (A) is correct. *(CPA, adapted)*

REQUIRED: The current assets to be reported in a consolidated balance sheet at the date of the combination.

DISCUSSION: Parma's 90% interest in the carrying amount of the net assets of Seville equals $45,000 [($60,000 assets – $10,000 liabilities) × 90%]. The excess cost of the investment over the carrying amount of the acquired net assets is $15,000 ($60,000 price – $45,000). Of this amount, $9,000 ($15,000 × 60%) should be allocated to inventory, presumably because it is the only asset whose fair value differs from its carrying amount. The remaining $6,000 ($15,000 × 40%) is goodwill (excess of acquisition cost over the fair value of the acquired net assets). ARB 51 requires that 100% of the net assets of a subsidiary be included in the consolidated financial statements. Thus, the amount of current assets to be reported in the consolidated balance sheet should be $99,000 ($70,000 current assets of Parma + $20,000 current assets of Seville + $9,000 allocation to inventory).

Answer (B) is incorrect because $96,000 assumes an allocation of $6,000 to inventory. Answer (C) is incorrect because $90,000 ignores the excess cost of the investment. Answer (D) is incorrect because $79,000 excludes Seville's current assets.

31. On Parma's January 2, year 1 consolidated balance sheet, noncurrent assets should be

A. $130,000

B. $134,000

C. $136,000

D. $140,000

Answer (C) is correct. *(CPA, adapted)*

REQUIRED: The noncurrent assets reported in the consolidated balance sheet at the date of the combination.

DISCUSSION: The noncurrent assets should be recorded at $136,000 ($90,000 noncurrent assets of Parma + $40,000 noncurrent assets of Seville + $6,000 allocation to goodwill).

Answer (A) is incorrect because $130,000 ignores goodwill. Answer (B) is incorrect because $134,000 assumes that a 100% interest was acquired and that goodwill was therefore $4,000 [($60,000 – $50,000) × 40%]. Answer (D) is incorrect because $140,000 assumes that a 100% interest was acquired and that goodwill was $10,000.

32. On Parma's January 2, year 1 consolidated balance sheet, current liabilities should be

A. $50,000

B. $46,000

C. $40,000

D. $30,000

Answer (B) is correct. *(CPA, adapted)*

REQUIRED: The current liabilities to be reported in the consolidated balance sheet at the date of the combination.

DISCUSSION: The total current liabilities include the $30,000 of current liabilities on Parma's books, the $10,000 on Seville's books, and the $6,000 ($60,000 debt ÷ 10 equal annual principal payments) that will be due and payable on December 30, year 1. Thus, current liabilities should be recorded at $46,000.

Answer (A) is incorrect because $50,000 is the preexisting long-term debt. Answer (C) is incorrect because $40,000 ignores the new borrowing. Answer (D) is incorrect because $30,000 is the amount of Parma's preexisting current liabilities.

33. On Parma's January 2, year 1 consolidated balance sheet, noncurrent liabilities, including the minority interest, should be

A. $115,000

B. $109,000

C. $104,000

D. $55,000

Answer (B) is correct. *(CPA, adapted)*

REQUIRED: The noncurrent liabilities, including the minority interest, that should be recorded in a consolidated balance sheet at the date of the business combination.

DISCUSSION: The noncurrent liabilities include the $50,000 in long-term debt on Parma's books on January 1, year 1, the $54,000 ($60,000 total debt – $6,000 current portion) noncurrent portion of the debt used to effect the business combination, and the minority interest. The minority interest is equal to $5,000 ($50,000 equity of the acquired entity × 10% minority interest). Accordingly, the noncurrent liabilities, including the minority interest, total $109,000.

Answer (A) is incorrect because $115,000 assumes the entire new borrowing is a noncurrent liability. Answer (C) is incorrect because $104,000 omits the minority interest. Answer (D) is incorrect because $55,000 ignores the new borrowing.

34. On Parma's January 2, year 1 consolidated balance sheet, equity should be

A. $80,000

B. $85,000

C. $90,000

D. $130,000

Answer (A) is correct. *(CPA, adapted)*

REQUIRED: The equity that should be reported in the consolidated balance sheet at the date of a business combination.

DISCUSSION: The minority interest was treated as part of noncurrent liabilities. Thus, the equity section of the current parent company balance sheet is the same as the equity section of the consolidated balance sheet. Consequently, equity is $80,000.

Answer (B) is incorrect because $85,000 equals Parma's equity plus the minority interest. Answer (C) is incorrect because $90,000 equals the total liabilities of the two companies at 1/1/X1. Answer (D) is incorrect because $130,000 is the sum of the equity amounts for Parma and Seville at 1/1/X1.

Questions 35 through 38 are based on the following information. The separate condensed balance sheets and income statements of Pater Corp. and its wholly owned subsidiary, Subito Corp., are as follows:

BALANCE SHEETS
December 31, year 1

	Pater	Subito
Assets		
Current assets		
Cash	$ 80,000	$ 60,000
Accounts receivable (net)	140,000	25,000
Inventories	90,000	50,000
Total current assets	$ 310,000	$135,000
Property, plant, and equipment (net)	515,000	280,000
Intangible assets	100,000	--
Investment in Subito (equity method)	400,000	--
Total assets	$1,325,000	$415,000
Liabilities and Equity		
Current liabilities		
Accounts payable	$ 160,000	$ 95,000
Accrued liabilities	110,000	30,000
Total current liabilities	$ 270,000	$125,000
Equity		
Common stock ($10 par)	$ 300,000	$ 50,000
Additional paid-in capital		10,000
Retained earnings	755,000	230,000
Total equity	$1,055,000	$290,000
Total liabilities and equity	$1,325,000	$415,000

INCOME STATEMENTS
For the year Ended December 31, 2002

	Pater	Subito
Sales	$2,000,000	$750,000
Cost of goods sold	1,540,000	500,000
Gross margin	$ 460,000	$250,000
Operating expenses	260,000	150,000
Operating income	$ 200,000	$100,000
Equity in earnings of Subito	70,000	--
Income before income taxes	$ 270,000	$100,000
Provision for income taxes	70,000	30,000
Net income	$ 200,000	$ 70,000

Additional Information:

- On January 1, year 1, Pater purchased for $360,000 all of Subito's $10 par, voting common stock. On January 1, year 1, the fair value of Subito's assets and liabilities equaled their carrying amounts of $410,000 and $160,000, respectively, except that the fair values of certain items identifiable in Subito's inventory were $10,000 more than their carrying amounts. These items were still on hand on December 31, year 1. Pater amortizes intangible assets over a 10-year period.
- During year 1, Pater and Subito paid cash dividends of $100,000 and $30,000, respectively. For tax purposes, Pater receives the 100% exclusion for dividends received from Subito.
- There were no interentity transactions, except for Pater's receipt of dividends from Subito and Pater's recording of its share of Subito's earnings.
- No transactions affected other comprehensive income.
- Both Pater and Subito paid income taxes at the rate of 30%.
- Pater treats Subito as a reporting unit, and all goodwill acquired in the business combination is assigned to Subito for the purpose of testing impairment. However, goodwill was not impaired on December 31, year 1.

35. In the December 31, year 1 consolidated financial statements of Pater and its subsidiary, total current assets should be

A. $455,000

B. $445,000

C. $310,000

D. $135,000

Answer (A) is correct. *(CPA, adapted)*

REQUIRED: The consolidated total current assets.

DISCUSSION: In a business combination, the excess of the acquisition cost over the subsidiary's equity is allocated to assets acquired and liabilities assumed based on their estimated fair values. Any remaining excess is treated as goodwill. As stated, $10,000 was allocated to inventory items that were still on hand at year-end. Hence, total current assets at year-end equals $455,000 ($310,000 Pater current assets + $135,000 Subito current assets + $10,000 excess fair value attributable to inventory).

Answer (B) is incorrect because $445,000 does not reflect the fair value of the inventory. Answer (C) is incorrect because $310,000 equals the parent's current assets. Answer (D) is incorrect because $135,000 equals the unadjusted current assets of the subsidiary.

36. In the December 31, year 1 consolidated financial statements of Pater and its subsidiary, total assets should be

A. $1,740,000

B. $1,450,000

C. $1,350,000

D. $1,325,000

Answer (B) is correct. *(CPA, adapted)*

REQUIRED: The consolidated total assets.

DISCUSSION: All of a subsidiary's assets should be included in a consolidated balance sheet after elimination of interentity transactions. Given that the only interentity transaction in year 1 was the dividend payment, no adjustment for interentity transactions is needed. The amount of total assets is determined as follows:

Total assets (12/31/X1) ($1,325,000 + $415,000)		$1,740,000
Minus: Investment in Subito		(400,000)
Add: Increase in inventory and unimpaired goodwill:		
Cost of investment	$360,000	
Equity acquired ($410,000 – $160,000)	(250,000)	
Excess	$110,000	
Applied to inventory	(10,000)	10,000
Goodwill	$100,000	
Goodwill impairment	0	100,000
		$1,450,000

Answer (A) is incorrect because $1,740,000 is the unadjusted sum of the assets of Pater and Subito. Answer (C) is incorrect because $1,350,000 is not adjusted for goodwill. Answer (D) is incorrect because $1,325,000 equals the parent's total assets.

37. In the December 31, year 1 consolidated financial statements of Pater and its subsidiary, total retained earnings should be?

A. $985,000

B. $825,000

C. $795,000

D. $755,000

Answer (D) is correct. *(CPA, adapted)*

REQUIRED: The consolidated total retained earnings.

DISCUSSION: Pater acquired Subito in a purchase transaction and properly accounts for the investment using the equity method. Thus, Pater's $755,000 of retained earnings equals consolidated retained earnings.

Answer (A) is incorrect because $985,000 includes the subsidiary's retained earnings. Answer (B) is incorrect because $825,000 includes the subsidiary's net income, an amount already reflected in the parent's retained earnings under the equity method. Answer (C) is incorrect because $795,000 includes the subsidiary's net income minus the dividends paid, an amount already accounted for using the equity method.

38. In the December 31, year 1 consolidated financial statements of Pater and its subsidiary, net income should be

A. $270,000

B. $200,000

C. $190,000

D. $170,000

Answer (B) is correct. *(CPA, adapted)*

REQUIRED: The consolidated net income.

DISCUSSION: The equity in the earnings of the subsidiary recorded on the parent's income statement is recorded in accordance with the equity method. Thus, the parent's $200,000 of net income equals consolidated net income.

Answer (A) is incorrect because $270,000 equals the sum of the net incomes of Pater and Subito. Answer (C) is incorrect because $190,000 equals Pater's net income minus goodwill amortization ($100,000 ÷ 10 years). However, goodwill is tested for impairment but not amortized. Goodwill was not impaired at December 31, year 1. Answer (D) is incorrect because $170,000 equals Pater's net income minus the dividend payment, which does not affect equity-based net income.

Questions 39 through 42 are based on the following information.

December 31, year 1 balance sheet items of the Subic Company are presented in the opposite column on both a historical cost and a fair value basis.

	Historical Cost	Fair Value
Current assets	$250,000	$300,000
Fixed assets	350,000	500,000
Liabilities	100,000	100,000
Common stock, $5 par	150,000	
Additional paid-in capital	150,000	
Retained earnings	200,000	

39. On January 2, year 2, Rent Company issued 25,000 shares of its $10 par value stock in exchange for all of the outstanding shares of Subic Company. If the market price of Rent's stock was $40 at the date of acquisition, which entry records Rent's investment in its new subsidiary?

A. Investment in subsidiary	$500,000	
Common stock		$250,000
Additional paid-in capital		250,000
B. Investment in subsidiary	$1,000,000	
Common stock		$250,000
Additional paid-in capital		750,000
C. Investment in subsidiary	$500,000	
Common stock		$250,000
Additional paid-in capital		50,000
Retained earnings		200,000
D. Current assets	$300,000	
Fixed assets	500,000	
Goodwill	300,000	
Liabilities		$100,000
Common stock		250,000
Additional paid-in capital		750,000

Answer (B) is correct. *(Publisher)*

REQUIRED: The journal entry to record a business combination effected by issuance of equity securities.

DISCUSSION: The investment in subsidiary account should be debited for the $1,000,000 fair value of the shares issued (25,000 shares x $40). The common stock account should be credited for $250,000 (25,000 shares x $10 par), and the remaining $750,000 should be credited to additional paid-in capital.

Answer (A) is incorrect because fair value, not carrying amount, is the appropriate measurement of a purchase. Answer (C) is incorrect because it reflects a pooling of interests, a method no longer permitted under GAAP. Answer (D) is incorrect because it reflects a merger rather than a stock investment.

40. Assume that Rent Company issues 25,000 shares of stock with a market price of $40 per share on January 2, year 2, for all Subic's outstanding shares, and also that the purchase agreement provides for the contingent issuance of 5,000 shares of Rent's stock to the previous shareholders of Subic in year 1 if a certain level of earnings is attained. If the required level of earnings is attained and the 5,000 additional shares are issued when the market price of Rent's shares is $45, the journal entry to reflect this transaction is which of the following?

A. No entry is necessary.

B. Investment in subsidiary	$225,000	
Common stock		$225,000
C. Investment in subsidiary	$225,000	
Common stock		$ 50,000
Additional paid-in capital		175,000
D. Investment in subsidiary	$200,000	
Common stock		$ 50,000
Additional paid-in capital		150,000

Answer (C) is correct. *(Publisher)*

REQUIRED: The journal entry to reflect a contingent issuance of shares based on earnings.

DISCUSSION: SFAS 141 states that, when a contingency based on earnings is resolved and additional consideration is distributable, the acquiring entity should record the current fair value of the consideration issued or issuable as an additional cost of the acquired entity. Thus, Rent should debit investment in subsidiary for an additional $225,000 (5,000 shares x $45). The common stock account should be credited for $50,000 (5,000 shares x $10), and additional paid-in capital should be credited for the $175,000 remainder ($225,000 – $50,000).

Answer (A) is incorrect because an entry is necessary. Answer (B) is incorrect because the $225,000 must be allocated between common stock and additional paid-in capital. Answer (D) is incorrect because the fair value of the shares issued should be used, rather than the $40 fair value at the date of the original acquisition.

41. Assume that Rent Company issues 25,000 shares of stock with a market price of $40 on January 2, year 2, for all Subic's outstanding shares, and also that the purchase agreement provides for the contingent issuance of additional shares necessary to pay a $1 million purchase price if the market price of Rent's stock is not equal to $40 on December 31, year 2. If the market price of Rent's shares is $25 on December 31, year 2, which of the following entries is necessary to reflect the issuance of the contingent shares?

A. No entry is necessary.

B.	Additional paid-in capital	$150,000	
	Common stock		$150,000

C.	Investment in subsidiary	$375,000	
	Common stock		$150,000
	Additional paid-in capital		225,000

D.	Investment in subsidiary	$150,000	
	Common stock		$150,000

Answer (B) is correct. *(Publisher)*

REQUIRED: The journal entry to reflect the issuance of shares to resolve a contingency based on valuation of the acquiring entity's stock.

DISCUSSION: SFAS 141 states that the cost of an acquired entity recorded at the date of acquisition represents the entire payment when an issuance of additional securities or distribution of other consideration depends on resolution of a contingency based on security prices. Given a contingency based on share prices, for any additional shares distributed at a later date, the acquiring entity (Rent) should reduce the fair value previously allocated to the shares issued. In this situation, Rent must issue an additional 15,000 shares of $10 par stock at a market price of $25 so that the total shares issued ($1,000,000 ÷ $25 current share price = 40,000 shares) will have a fair value equal to the purchase price. Thus, $400,000 (40,000 shares × $10 par) must be allocated to the common stock account and $600,000 to additional paid-in capital. To adjust the existing common stock balance of $250,000 and the additional paid-in capital balance of $750,000, the additional paid-in capital account must be debited and common stock credited for $150,000.

Answer (A) is incorrect because an entry is necessary. Answer (C) is incorrect because the cost of the acquired entity is not changed, so an adjustment to the investment account is unnecessary. Answer (D) is incorrect because the cost of the acquired entity is not changed, so an adjustment to the investment account is unnecessary.

42. Assume that, in addition to the assets and liabilities among Subic Company's December 31, year 1 balance sheet items, Subic has brought suit against a competitor for an infringement of a patent. If sufficient evidence exists to indicate that settlement of the lawsuit in the amount of $75,000 is probable, the allocation of the $1 million purchase price (25,000 shares × $40) should include goodwill of

A. $0

B. $225,000

C. $375,000

D. $425,000

Answer (B) is correct. *(Publisher)*

REQUIRED: The determination of goodwill when a preacquisition contingency exists.

DISCUSSION: According to SFAS 141, if the fair value of a preacquisition contingency is determinable during the allocation period, it is included in the allocation of the purchase price based on that fair value. However, the fair value may not be determinable during the allocation period. In that case, the preacquisition contingency is included in the purchase price allocation based on the amount determined according to the following criteria: information available before the end of the allocation period indicates that it is probable an asset existed, a liability had been incurred, or an asset had been impaired at the date of the combination; and the amount of the asset or liability can be reasonably estimated. The fair value of the net assets acquired is $775,000 ($300,000 current assets + $500,000 noncurrent assets – $100,000 liabilities + $75,000 contingent settlement). The excess of the $1,000,000 cost over the $775,000 fair value of the net assets acquired is $225,000 of goodwill.

Answer (A) is incorrect because goodwill must be recognized when cost exceeds fair value of the net assets acquired. Answer (C) is incorrect because $375,000 assumes that a contingent liability has been incurred by Subic. Answer (D) is incorrect because $425,000 is based on historical costs, not fair values.

43. Pent Corp. purchased 100% of Subtle Corp.'s outstanding capital stock for $860,000 cash. Immediately before the purchase, the balance sheets of both corporations reported the following:

	Pent	Subtle
Assets	$4,000,000	$1,500,000
Liabilities	$1,400,000	$ 720,000
Common stock	2,000,000	620,000
Retained earnings	500,000	80,000
Accumulated other comprehensive income	100,000	80,000
Liabilities and equity	$4,000,000	$1,500,000

At the date of purchase, the fair value of Subtle's assets was $100,000 more than the aggregate carrying amounts. In the consolidated balance sheet prepared immediately after the purchase, the consolidated equity should equal

A. $3,460,000

B. $3,480,000

C. $3,380,000

D. $2,600,000

Answer (D) is correct. *(CPA, adapted)*

REQUIRED: The consolidated equity after the purchase.

DISCUSSION: A purchase is viewed as an acquisition of net assets. Thus, only the fair value of the net assets of a subsidiary is included in a consolidated balance sheet prepared using the purchase method. The equity, including retained earnings, is excluded. Thus, the equity section of the current balance sheet of the acquiring entity is the same as the equity section of the consolidated balance sheet. Consequently, equity is $2,600,000 ($2,000,000 common stock + $500,000 retained earnings + $100,000 accumulated OCI).

Answer (A) is incorrect because $3,460,000 is the sum of the equity of Pent plus the cash price. Answer (B) is incorrect because $3,480,000 is the sum of the equity of Pent and Subtle plus the excess fair value of Subtle's assets. Answer (C) is incorrect because $3,380,000 is the sum of the equity of Pent and Subtle.

44. On July 1, the Par Company acquired 90% of the Subside Company for cash in an amount equal to the carrying amount of the net assets on Subside Company's books. During the year, Subside Company, a nonseasonal company, declared net income of $800,000, and it paid dividends of $100,000 on June 30 and December 31. The preferred presentation of the year-end consolidated income statement should contain which of the following amounts?

A. Minority income of $20,000.

B. Minority income of $40,000.

C. Preacquisition earnings of $360,000.

D. Preacquisition earnings of $400,000.

Answer (C) is correct. *(Publisher)*

REQUIRED: The amount arising from a midyear purchase contained in a consolidated income statement.

DISCUSSION: ARB 51, *Consolidated Financial Statements*, states that, when a subsidiary is purchased during the year, the preferred method of presenting the results of operations is to include the subsidiary's operations in the consolidated income statement as though it had been acquired at the beginning of the year and to deduct from the total earnings the preacquisition earnings. The minority interest income for the entire year is also deducted. Preacquisition or purchased earnings are earnings of a subsidiary earned prior to the date of the acquisition of the subsidiary by the parent. These earnings are included in determining the purchase price. The minority income equals the subsidiary's income for the annual period multiplied by the year-end minority interest. Because the purchase of Subside Company occurred at midyear, the minority interest was 10% at year-end, and the subsidiary is nonseasonal, the preacquisition earnings are $360,000 [50% × ($800,000 total income – $80,000 minority interest income)].

Answer (A) is incorrect because minority income subtracted is $80,000 (10% year-end minority interest × $800,000 annual net income). Answer (B) is incorrect because minority income subtracted is $80,000 (10% year-end minority interest × $800,000 annual net income). Answer (D) is incorrect because the preacquisition earnings do not include the minority income earned prior to the date of the acquisition.

45. A preacquisition contingency is a contingency of an entity acquired in a business combination that was in existence before the consummation of the combination. A preacquisition contingency will be excluded from the allocation of the purchase price if it involves an infringement of patent lawsuit brought

A. Against the acquired entity that was settled before the consummation of the business combination.

B. By the acquired entity against a competitor that was settled before the consummation of the business combination.

C. By the acquired entity against a competitor for which information available prior to the end of the allocation period indicates that it is probable that the lawsuit will be favorably settled for an amount that is reasonably estimable.

D. By the acquired entity against a competitor for which information available prior to the end of the allocation period indicates that it is reasonably possible that the lawsuit will be favorably settled for an amount that is reasonably estimable.

Answer (D) is correct. *(Publisher)*

REQUIRED: The preacquisition contingency to which part of the purchase price will not be allocated.

DISCUSSION: A preacquisition contingency may be a contingent asset, a contingent liability, or a contingent impairment of an asset. A preacquisition contingency, other than the potential tax effects of (1) temporary differences and carryforwards of an acquired entity at the acquisition date and (2) income tax uncertainties relating to the acquisition, must be included in the allocation of the purchase price at fair value if that fair value is determinable during the allocation period. However, the fair value may not be determinable during the allocation period. In that case, the preacquisition contingency is included in the purchase price allocation based on the amount determined according to the following criteria: Information available before the end of the allocation period indicates that it is probable an asset existed, a liability had been incurred, or an asset had been impaired at the date of the combination; and the amount of the asset or liability can be reasonably estimated. If these conditions are not met, the preacquisition contingency is not included in the allocation of the purchase price. Accordingly, a reasonably possible preacquisition contingency concerning the patent infringement lawsuit is included in the determination of net income in the period in which settlement is reached.

46. Submit Company repurchased 10,000 shares of its outstanding stock for $600,000 on December 31. Submit's equity sections immediately before and immediately after this treasury stock transaction are presented below.

	Before	After
Common stock, $10 par	$1,000,000	$1,000,000
Additional paid-in capital	1,500,000	1,500,000
Retained earnings	2,500,000	2,500,000
Treasury stock	-0-	(600,000)
Total equity	$5,000,000	$4,400,000

Assume that Submit repurchased this stock from the general public. By what amount should Paren Company, which holds 75,000 shares of the outstanding stock of Submit, adjust its investment in subsidiary account because of Submit's treasury stock transaction?

A. $0

B. $83,333 debit.

C. $83,333 credit.

D. $3,666,667 debit.

Answer (C) is correct. *(Publisher)*

REQUIRED: The investment in subsidiary account adjustment to reflect the repurchase of shares by the subsidiary from the minority interest.

DISCUSSION: Immediately before this treasury stock transaction, the parent's interest in the subsidiary was 75% (75,000 shares held ÷ 100,000 shares outstanding). Immediately after the transaction, it was 83 1/3% (75,000 shares held ÷ 90,000 shares outstanding). The parent's proportionate interest in the total recorded equity of the subsidiary decreased from $3,750,000 (75% × $5,000,000) to $3,666,667 (83 1/3% × $4,400,000). Thus, the investment account should be credited (decreased) by $83,333 ($3,750,000 – $3,666,667). The carrying amount of the investment account is not needed to calculate the adjustment because the adjustment relates only to the parent's proportionate interest in the subsidiary's equity.

Answer (A) is incorrect because the investment account should be adjusted for the change in the parent's proportionate interest. Answer (B) is incorrect because the $83,333 decrease should be credited, not debited. Answer (D) is incorrect because $3,666,667 is the parent's proportionate interest in the subsidiary.

47. SFAS 72, *Accounting for Certain Acquisitions of Banking or Thrift Institutions*, as amended by SFAS 147, *Acquisitions of Certain Financial Institutions*, is applicable to a business combination involving mutual enterprises that are banking or thrift institutions. If the fair value of liabilities assumed exceeds the fair value of the tangible and identifiable intangible assets acquired in such an acquisition, the unidentifiable intangible asset that is recognized for that excess should be amortized over

A. Its expected useful life using the straight-line method.

B. Its expected useful life, not to exceed 40 years, using the straight-line method.

C. Its expected useful life, not to exceed 40 years, using the interest method.

D. A period no longer than that over which the discount on the long-term interest-bearing assets acquired is to be recognized as interest income, not to exceed 40 years, using the interest method.

Answer (D) is correct. *(Publisher)*

REQUIRED: The proper method of accounting for an unidentifiable intangible asset recognized in a business combination involving mutual enterprises that are financial institutions.

DISCUSSION: When the fair value of liabilities assumed exceeds the fair value of tangible and identifiable intangible assets acquired, the unidentifiable intangible asset recognized for that excess should usually be amortized over a period no greater than the estimated remaining life of the long-term interest-bearing assets acquired. Amortization is applied at a constant rate to the carrying amount of the interest-bearing assets expected to be outstanding at the beginning of each subsequent period. Thus, the amortization period is no longer than the period over which the discount on the long-term interest-bearing assets acquired is to be recognized as interest income using the interest method. According to SFAS 142, an entity should evaluate the remaining useful life of an amortizable intangible asset each reporting period. However, SFAS 72 states that the period of amortization of the unidentifiable intangible asset should not exceed 40 years or be revised upward. In other words, low-rate interest-bearing assets may have been discounted to fair value by applying current (higher) interest rates, and the fair value of the liabilities assumed may then exceed the fair value of the assets acquired. In that case, the unidentifiable intangible asset and the discount on the long-term interest-bearing assets acquired will be amortized to income using the interest method over the same period.

SFAS 147 narrowed the scope of SFAS 72. A business combination that is not between two or more mutual enterprises that are financial institutions is accounted for under SFAS 141, *Business Combinations*, which provides for reviewing goodwill for impairment but prohibits amortization of goodwill.

Answer (A) is incorrect because the amortization period of the unidentifiable intangible asset is measured by the estimated remaining useful life of the long-term interest-bearing assets acquired, and the method of amortization is based on application of a constant rate, not recognition of a constant periodic amount (the straight-line method). Answer (B) is incorrect because the amortization period of the unidentifiable intangible asset is measured by the estimated remaining useful life of the long-term interest-bearing assets acquired, and the method of amortization is based on application of a constant rate, not recognition of a constant periodic amount (the straight-line method). Answer (C) is incorrect because the amortization period of the unidentifiable intangible asset is measured by the estimated remaining useful life of the long-term interest-bearing assets acquired, and the method of amortization is based on application of a constant rate, not recognition of a constant periodic amount (the straight-line method).

Questions 48 and 49 are based on the following information.

Suwannee Company issued 20,000 additional shares of its common stock for $1.6 million. Suwannee Company's equity sections immediately before and immediately after this issuance of stock transaction are presented below.

	Before	After
Common stock, $10 par	$1,000,000	$1,200,000
Additional paid-in capital	2,500,000	3,900,000
Retained earnings	3,900,000	3,900,000
Total equity	$7,400,000	$9,000,000

48. Assume that Suwannee Company issued this stock to the general public. By what amount should Palatka Corporation, the owner of 80,000 of the outstanding shares of Suwannee Company, adjust its investment in subsidiary account because of the issuance of stock by Suwannee Company?

A. $0

B. $80,000 debit.

C. $80,000 credit.

D. $1,280,000 debit.

Answer (B) is correct. *(Publisher)*

REQUIRED: The investment in subsidiary account adjustment to reflect the issuance of stock by a subsidiary to the general public.

DISCUSSION: Immediately prior to the issuance of the additional shares of stock by Suwannee Company, Palatka's ownership interest was 80% (80,000 shares held ÷ 100,000 shares outstanding). Its proportionate interest in the subsidiary's recorded equity was $5,920,000 (80% × $7,400,000). Immediately after the issuance of the shares, Palatka's ownership interest was 66 2/3% (80,000 shares held ÷ 120,000 shares outstanding), and its proportionate ownership interest was $6,000,000 (66 2/3% × $9,000,000). Thus, its investment in subsidiary account should be debited (increased) for the $80,000 difference ($6,000,000 after – $5,920,000 before). The corresponding credit is to paid-in capital.

Answer (A) is incorrect because the investment in subsidiary account should be adjusted for the change in the parent's proportionate interest. Answer (C) is incorrect because the increase should be debited. Answer (D) is incorrect because $1,280,000 assumes that the ownership percentage remained at 80%.

49. Assume that Suwannee Company issued the stock to Palatka Corporation, whose ownership interest in Suwannee increased from 80,000 shares to 100,000 shares. If the carrying amount of the acquired net assets of Suwannee is equal to their fair value at the time the additional shares are issued, the goodwill indicated in the purchase of the additional shares equals

A. $0

B. $20,000

C. $320,000

D. $1,580,000

Answer (B) is correct. *(Publisher)*

REQUIRED: The determination of goodwill when the parent purchases additional stock issued by the subsidiary.

DISCUSSION: Prior to the issuance of the new securities, the parent owned 80% of the outstanding stock of the subsidiary, resulting in a proportionate ownership in the subsidiary's recorded equity of $5,920,000. Following the issuance of the 20,000 shares, the parent holds an 83 1/3% interest (100,000 shares held ÷ 120,000 shares outstanding), resulting in a proportionate ownership interest in the subsidiary's equity of $7,500,000 (83 1/3% × $9,000,000). The difference is $1,580,000 ($7,500,000 – $5,920,000). Hence, goodwill of $20,000 results ($1,600,000 price paid – $1,580,000).

Answer (A) is incorrect because goodwill must be recognized. The purchase price exceeded the fair value of the net assets acquired. Answer (C) is incorrect because $320,000 assumes the ownership percentage did not change. Answer (D) is incorrect because $1,580,000 is the increase in the proportionate interest.

Questions 50 through 53 are based on the following information.

ADA, Inc. owns 80% of the capital stock of BLT Co. and 70% of the capital stock of CDC, Inc. BLT Co. owns 15% of the capital stock of CDC, Inc. CDC, Inc., in turn, owns 25% of the capital stock of ADA, Inc. These ownership interrelationships are illustrated in the following diagram:

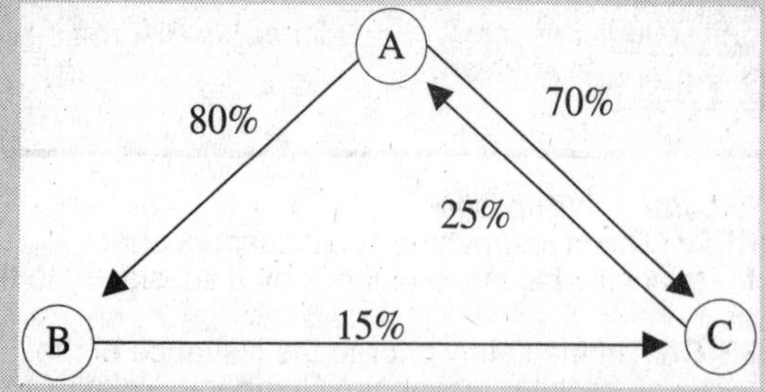

Net income before adjusting for interests in interentity net income for each corporation follows:

ADA, Inc.	$190,000
BLT Co.	170,000
CDC, Inc.	230,000

Ignore all income tax considerations.

A = ADA's consolidated net income, i.e., its net income plus its share of BLT and CDC.

B = BLT's consolidated net income, i.e., its net income plus its share of the consolidated net income of CDC.

C = CDC's consolidated net income, i.e., its net income plus its share of the consolidated net income of ADA.

50. The equation, in a set of simultaneous equations, that computes A is

A. A = .75($190,000 + .8B + .7C)

B. A = $190,000 + .8B + .7C

C. A = .75($190,000) + .8($170,000) + .7($230,000)

D. A = .75($190,000) + .8B + .7C

Answer (B) is correct. *(CPA, adapted)*

REQUIRED: The equation that computes ADA's consolidated net income.

DISCUSSION: ADA's consolidated net income is its net income of $190,000, plus 80% of BLT's consolidated net income, plus 70% of CDC's consolidated net income.

Answer (A) is incorrect because there is no reduction in ADA's consolidated net income for the ownership by CDC from a consolidated point of view. Answer (C) is incorrect because there is no reduction in ADA's consolidated net income for the ownership by CDC from a consolidated point of view. Answer (D) is incorrect because there is no reduction in ADA's consolidated net income for the ownership by CDC from a consolidated point of view.

51. The equation, in a set of simultaneous equations, that computes B is

A. B = $170,000 + .15C – .75A

B. B = $170,000 + .15C

C. B = .2($170,000) + .15($230,000)

D. B = .2($170,000) + .15C

Answer (B) is correct. *(CPA, adapted)*

REQUIRED: The equation that computes BLT's consolidated net income.

DISCUSSION: BLT's consolidated net income is its net income plus 15% of CDC's consolidated net income.

Answer (A) is incorrect because being ADA's subsidiary does not affect BLT's consolidated net income. Answer (C) is incorrect because BLT's consolidated income includes its entire net income, not only its minority shareholders' share, and because BLT includes its share of CDC's consolidated net income, not only its share of CDC's net income. Answer (D) is incorrect because BLT's consolidated income includes its entire net income, not only its minority shareholders' share.

52. CDC's minority interest in consolidated net income is

A. 15($130,000)

B. $230,000 + .25A

C. 15($230,000) + .25A

D. 15C

Answer (D) is correct. *(CPA, adapted)*

REQUIRED: The share of consolidated net income attributable to CDC's minority interest.

DISCUSSION: From a consolidated point of view, 15% of CDC is held outside the consolidated entity because 70% of CDC is owned by ADA and 15% by BLT.

Answer (A) is incorrect because CDC's consolidated net income is $230,000 plus 25% of ADA's consolidated net income. Answer (B) is incorrect because CDC's minority interest is only 15% (not 100%) of CDC's consolidated net income. Answer (C) is incorrect because the second term (.25A) of the expression should also be multiplied by 15%.

53. BLT's minority interest in consolidated net income is

A. $34,000

B. $45,755

C. $58,774

D. $161,824

Answer (B) is correct. *(CPA, adapted)*

REQUIRED: The share of consolidated net income attributable to BLT's minority interest.

DISCUSSION: The minority interest in BLT's income is 20% (100% – 80% owned by ADA), which may be computed by solving a set of simultaneous equations. Each of the first three equations below represents the consolidated net income of one of the three companies. Equations (4), (5), and (6) provide the algebraic solution for CDC's consolidated net income. Equation (7) is BLT's consolidated income. Equation (8) is BLT's minority interest in consolidated net income.

(1) A = $190,000 + .8B + .7C
(2) B = $170,000 + .15C
(3) C = $230,000 + .25A
(4) –A = $920,000 – 4C
(5) 0 = $1,110,000 + .8B – 3.3C
(6) 0 = $1,110,000 + $136,000 + .12C – 3.3C
3.18C = $1,246,000
C = $391,824
(7) B = $170,000 + .15($391,824) = $228,774
(8) .20B = $45,755

Answer (A) is incorrect because $34,000 is 20% of BLT's unadjusted net income. Answer (C) is incorrect because $58,774 equals the minority interest in CDC's net income. Answer (D) is incorrect because $161,824 equals CDC's share of ADA's consolidated net income.

54. Subpar Company had net assets according to its books of $1 million on January 1, year 1. On the same date, Pariah Company owned 9,000 of the 12,000 outstanding shares of Subpar's only class of stock, and its investment in Subpar Company account had a balance of $795,000. If, on January 1, year 1, Subpar repurchased 2,000 shares from Pariah for $200,000, the gain on the sale of the stock recognized by Pariah was

A. $3,000

B. $7,000

C. $10,000

D. $23,333

Answer (B) is correct. *(Publisher)*

REQUIRED: The gain on a purchase of treasury stock by a subsidiary from its parent.

DISCUSSION: The gain recognized by the parent equals the difference between the amount received and the credit to the investment account. The latter has two components: (1) the decrease in the parent's equity in the net assets of the subsidiary and (2) the reduction in the differential (investment balance – equity in the subsidiary's net assets) attributable to the decrease in the percentage of ownership. Prior to the treasury stock transaction, the parent's equity in the subsidiary's net assets was $750,000 [$1,000,000 × (9,000 shares ÷ 12,000 total shares)]. Hence, the differential was $45,000 ($795,000 investment balance – $750,000 interest in net assets). The equity in the subsidiary after the treasury stock transaction was $560,000 [(7,000 shares ÷ 10,000 total shares) × $800,000], and the decrease in the equity was therefore $190,000 ($750,000 – $560,000). Given a reduction in percentage stock ownership from 75% (9,000 ÷ 12,000) to 70% (7,000 ÷ 10,000), the reduction in the differential was $3,000 {[(75% – 70%) ÷ 75%] × $45,000}. Accordingly, the total decrease in the investment account was $193,000 ($190,000 + $3,000), and the parent realized a gain of $7,000 ($200,000 proceeds – $193,000 credit to the investment account). The journal entry in the parent's books was

Cash	$200,000	
Investment in Subpar Company		$193,000
Gain on sale		7,000

Answer (A) is incorrect because $3,000 is the reduction in the differential. Answer (C) is incorrect because $10,000 ignores the reduction in the differential. Answer (D) is incorrect because $23,333 assumes that the investment balance is reduced by approximately 22.22% (2,000 shares ÷ 9,000 shares).

25.4 Interentity Transactions

55. Wright Corp. has several subsidiaries that are included in its consolidated financial statements. In its December 31, year 1 trial balance, Wright had the following interentity balances before eliminations:

	Debit	Credit
Current receivable due from Main Co.	$ 32,000	
Noncurrent receivable from Main	114,000	
Cash advance to Corn Corp.	6,000	
Cash advance from King Co.		$ 15,000
Intercompany payable to King		101,000

In its December 31, year 1 consolidated balance sheet, what amount should Wright report as interentity receivables?

A. $152,000

B. $146,000

C. $36,000

D. $0

Answer (D) is correct. *(CPA, adapted)*

REQUIRED: The interentity receivables reported in a consolidated balance sheet.

DISCUSSION: In a consolidated balance sheet, reciprocal balances, such as receivables and payables, between a parent and a consolidated subsidiary should be eliminated in their entirety regardless of the portion of the subsidiary's stock held by the parent. Thus, Wright should report $0 as interentity receivables.

56. Pelota Co. owns 80% of Saginaw Co.'s outstanding common stock. Saginaw, in turn, owns 10% of Pelota's outstanding common stock. What percentage of the common stock cash dividends declared by the individual companies should be reported as dividends declared in the consolidated financial statements?

	Dividends Declared by Pelota	Dividends Declared by Saginaw
A.	90%	0%
B.	90%	20%
C.	100%	0%
D.	100%	20%

Answer (A) is correct. *(CPA, adapted)*

REQUIRED: The percentage of common stock cash dividends declared by the individual companies that should be reported as dividends declared in the consolidated financial statements.

DISCUSSION: Because the parent owns 80% of the subsidiary and the subsidiary owns 10% of the parent, 80% of the dividends declared by the subsidiary and 10% of the dividends declared by the parent are not transferred outside of the consolidated entity. These amounts are eliminated as interentity transactions. Consequently, 90% of the parent's and 20% of the subsidiary's dividend payments are to third parties. The 90% declared by the parent will be reported as dividends declared under the parent company theory of consolidation. The 20% declared by the subsidiary is treated as a reduction of the minority interest in the consolidated financial statements, not as consolidated dividends declared.

Answer (B) is incorrect because 90% of the parent's dividends and 0% of the subsidiary's are treated as consolidated dividends declared. Answer (C) is incorrect because 90% of the parent's dividends and 0% of the subsidiary's are treated as consolidated dividends declared. Answer (D) is incorrect because 90% of the parent's dividends and 0% of the subsidiary's are treated as consolidated dividends declared.

57. Shep Co. has a receivable from its parent, Pep Co. Should this receivable be separately reported in Shep's balance sheet and in Pep's consolidated balance sheet?

	Shep's Balance Sheet	Pep's Consolidated Balance Sheet
A.	Yes	No
B.	Yes	Yes
C.	No	No
D.	No	Yes

Answer (A) is correct. *(CPA, adapted)*

REQUIRED: The treatment of an interentity receivable in the balance sheet of a subsidiary and in the consolidated balance sheet.

DISCUSSION: In a consolidated balance sheet, reciprocal balances, such as receivables and payables, between a parent and a consolidated subsidiary should be eliminated in their entirety regardless of the portion of the subsidiary's stock held by the parent. However, interentity transactions should not be eliminated from the separate financial statements of the entities.

58. At December 31, year 1, Grey, Inc. owned 90% of Winn Corp., a consolidated subsidiary, and 20% of Carr Corp., an investee over which Grey cannot exercise significant influence. On the same date, Grey had receivables of $300,000 from Winn and $200,000 from Carr. In its December 31, year 1 consolidated balance sheet, Grey should report accounts receivable from affiliates of

A. $500,000

B. $340,000

C. $230,000

D. $200,000

Answer (D) is correct. *(CPA, adapted)*
REQUIRED: The accounts receivable from a consolidated subsidiary and an investee over which significant influence cannot be exercised.
DISCUSSION: In a consolidated balance sheet, reciprocal balances, such as receivables and payables, between a parent and a consolidated subsidiary should be eliminated completely, regardless of the portion of the subsidiary's stock held by the parent. Hence, the $300,000 receivable from Winn should be eliminated in its entirety. Because Grey cannot exercise significant influence over Carr, even though it holds 20% of the outstanding shares, this investment should be accounted for on the fair-value basis if the fair value of the equity securities is readily determinable. If it is not, it should be accounted for on the cost basis. Receivables owed by an investee over which significant influence cannot be exercised should be reported on the consolidated balance sheet. Grey should therefore report $200,000 in accounts receivable from affiliates.
Answer (A) is incorrect because the $300,000 receivable from Winn should be eliminated. Answer (B) is incorrect because $340,000 includes the receivable from Winn and 20% of the receivable from Carr. Answer (C) is incorrect because $230,000 includes 10% of the receivable from the consolidated subsidiary.

59. Perez, Inc. owns 80% of Senior, Inc. During year 1, Perez sold goods with a 40% gross profit to Senior. Senior sold all of these goods in year 1. In its year 1 consolidated financial statements, how should the summation of Perez and Senior income statement items be adjusted?

A. Sales and cost of goods sold should be reduced by the interentity sales.

B. Sales and cost of goods sold should be reduced by 80% of the interentity sales.

C. Net income should be reduced by 80% of the gross profit on interentity sales.

D. No adjustment is necessary.

Answer (A) is correct. *(CPA, adapted)*
REQUIRED: The adjustment, if any, to prepare consolidated financial statements given a sale by the parent to the subsidiary.
DISCUSSION: Given that all of the goods were sold, no adjustment is necessary for interentity profit in ending inventory. Accordingly, the parent's cost should be included in consolidated cost of goods sold, and the price received by the subsidiary should be included in consolidated sales. The required adjustment is to eliminate the sale recorded by the parent and the cost of goods sold recorded by the subsidiary.
Answer (B) is incorrect because the elimination is made without regard to the minority interest. Answer (C) is incorrect because no profit should be eliminated. All of the goods sold to Senior have been resold. Answer (D) is incorrect because sales and cost of sales should be reduced.

60. Parker Corp. owns 80% of Smith, Inc.'s common stock. During year 1, Parker sold Smith $250,000 of inventory on the same terms as sales made to third parties. Smith sold all of the inventory purchased from Parker in year 1. The following information pertains to Smith and Parker's sales for year 1:

	Parker	Smith
Sales	$1,000,000	$700,000
Cost of sales	400,000	350,000
	$ 600,000	$350,000

What amount should Parker report as cost of sales in its year 1 consolidated income statement?

A. $750,000

B. $680,000

C. $500,000

D. $430,000

Answer (C) is correct. *(CPA, adapted)*
REQUIRED: The cost of sales in the consolidated income statement.
DISCUSSION: Given that Smith purchased inventory from Parker for $250,000 and sold all of it during the year, $250,000 must be eliminated from consolidated cost of goods sold. Hence, the cost of sales in the consolidated income statement is $500,000 [($400,000 + $350,000) – $250,000].
Answer (A) is incorrect because $750,000 is the total of the amounts reported separately by Parker and Smith. Answer (B) is incorrect because $680,000 equals Parker's CGS plus 80% of Smith's. Answer (D) is incorrect because $430,000 equals Parker's CGS plus 80% of Smith's, minus $250,000.

Questions 61 and 62 are based on the following information.

Scroll, Inc., a wholly owned subsidiary of Pirn, Inc., began operations on January 1, year 1. The following information is from the condensed year 1 income statements of Pirn and Scroll:

	Pirn	Scroll
Sales to Scroll	$100,000	$ --
Sales to others	400,000	300,000
	$500,000	$300,000
Cost of goods sold:		
Acquired from Pirn	--	80,000
Acquired from others	350,000	190,000
Gross profit	$150,000	30,000
Depreciation	40,000	10,000
Other expenses	60,000	15,000
Income from operations	$ 50,000	$ 5,000
Gain on sale of equipment to Scroll	12,000	--
Income before income taxes	$ 38,000	$ 5,000

Additional Information

- Sales by Pirn to Scroll are made on the same terms as those made to third parties.
- Equipment purchased by Scroll from Pirn for $36,000 on January 1, year 1 is depreciated using the straight-line method over 4 years.

61. In Pirn's December 31, year 1 consolidating worksheet, how much interentity profit should be eliminated from Scroll's inventory?

A. $30,000
B. $20,000
C. $10,000
D. $6,000

Answer (D) is correct. *(CPA, adapted)*

REQUIRED: The interentity profit eliminated from Scroll's inventory.

DISCUSSION: Sales by Pirn to Scroll totaled $100,000, and Scroll reported related CGS of $80,000. Thus, the remaining inventory of these items must have been $20,000. Because Pirn's gross profit rate was 30% ($150,000 gross profit ÷ $500,000 sales), the interentity profit eliminated from Scroll's inventory should be $6,000 (30% × $20,000).

Answer (A) is incorrect because $30,000 is Scroll's total gross profit. Answer (B) is incorrect because $20,000 is the interentity inventory. Answer (C) is incorrect because $10,000 equals the total gross profit minus the interentity obtained from Pirn.

62. What amount should be reported as depreciation expense in Pirn's year 1 consolidated income statement?

A. $50,000
B. $47,000
C. $44,000
D. $41,000

Answer (B) is correct. *(CPA, adapted)*

REQUIRED: The depreciation expense in the consolidated income statement.

DISCUSSION: The depreciation attributable to the gain on sale of equipment to Scroll should be eliminated. Thus, the depreciation expense in the consolidated income statement should be $47,000 [($40,000 Pirn depreciation + $10,000 Scroll depreciation) – ($12,000 ÷ 4 years)].

Answer (A) is incorrect because $50,000 does not eliminate the effect of the gain. Answer (C) is incorrect because $44,000 equals total depreciation minus the inventory profit. Answer (D) is incorrect because $41,000 equals total depreciation minus the inventory profit and the effect of the gain.

63. Clark Co. had the following transactions with affiliated parties during year 1:

- Sales of $50,000 to Dean, Inc., with $20,000 gross profit. Dean had $15,000 of this inventory on hand at year-end. Clark owns a 15% interest in Dean and does not exert significant influence.
- Purchases of raw materials totaling $240,000 from Kent Corp., a wholly owned subsidiary. Kent's gross profit on the sale was $48,000. Clark had $60,000 of this inventory remaining on December 31, year 1.

Before eliminating entries, Clark had consolidated current assets of $320,000. What amount should Clark report in its December 31, year 1 consolidated balance sheet for current assets?

A. $320,000

B. $314,000

C. $308,000

D. $302,000

Answer (C) is correct. *(CPA, adapted)*

REQUIRED: The amount reported on the consolidated balance sheet for current assets.

DISCUSSION: When an investor buys inventory from an investee that is neither a consolidated subsidiary nor an equity-method investee, no adjustment for interentity profit is made. Thus, no adjustment is made to the inventory purchased from Dean. When a parent buys inventory from a subsidiary, the inventory on the consolidated balance sheet must be adjusted to remove any interentity profit. Hence, the inventory must be reduced by the pro rata share of interentity profit made on the sale by Kent. The reduction is $12,000 [($60,000 EI ÷ $240,000 purchases) × $48,000 gross profit]. Thus, current assets equal $308,000 ($320,000 – $12,000).

Answer (A) is incorrect because $320,000 does not eliminate interentity transactions. Answer (B) is incorrect because $314,000 does not eliminate the effect of the transactions with Kent but deducts the gross profit included in the inventory held by Dean. Answer (D) is incorrect because $302,000 treats the sales between Clark and Dean as an interentity transaction.

64. Port Inc. owns 100% of Salem, Inc. On January 1, year 1, Port sold Salem delivery equipment at a gain. Port had owned the equipment for 2 years and used a 5-year straight-line depreciation rate with no residual value. Salem is using a 3-year straight-line depreciation rate with no residual value for the equipment. In the consolidated income statement, Salem's recorded depreciation expense on the equipment for year 1 will be decreased by

A. 20% of the gain on sale.

B. 33 1/3% of the gain on sale.

C. 50% of the gain on sale.

D. 100% of the gain on sale.

Answer (B) is correct. *(CPA, adapted)*

REQUIRED: The consolidated depreciation expense on equipment sold by a parent to a subsidiary.

DISCUSSION: The effects of interentity transactions should be eliminated. Consequently, the equipment and the related depreciation expense should be reported at amounts that exclude the gain on the sale to Salem. Given that the equipment was held by Port for 2 of its 5 years of estimated useful life, that it has no salvage value, and that Salem is depreciating it over 3 years, Salem recognizes as depreciation expense in its separate year 1 statements 33 1/3% of the acquisition cost, which equals the gain recognized by Port plus Port's carrying amount. Thus, 33 1/3% of the gain is included in the year 1 depreciation expense recorded on the equipment and should be eliminated.

Answer (A) is incorrect because 20% assumes a 5-year life. Answer (C) is incorrect because 50% assumes a 2-year life. Answer (D) is incorrect because 100% assumes a 1-year life.

65. On January 1, year 1, Poe Corp. sold a machine for $900,000 to Saxe Corp., its wholly owned subsidiary. Poe paid $1.1 million for this machine, which had accumulated depreciation of $250,000. Poe estimated a $100,000 salvage value and depreciated the machine on the straight-line method over 20 years, a policy that Saxe continued. In Poe's December 31, year 1 consolidated balance sheet, this machine should be included in cost and accumulated depreciation as

	Cost	Accumulated Depreciation
A.	$1,100,000	$300,000
B.	$1,100,000	$290,000
C.	$900,000	$40,000
D.	$850,000	$42,500

Answer (A) is correct. *(CPA, adapted)*

REQUIRED: The cost and accumulated depreciation in the consolidated balance sheet.

DISCUSSION: The effect of the interentity transaction should be eliminated. Thus, the machine should be carried at cost ($1,100,000) minus accumulated depreciation of $300,000 {$250,000 + [($1,100,0000 – $100,000) ÷ 20]}.

Answer (B) is incorrect because $290,000 assumes that year 1 depreciation is based on a $900,000 cost, $100,000 salvage value, and a remaining 20-year life. Answer (C) is incorrect because $900,000 is the sales price, and $40,000 is the depreciation based on a $900,000 cost, $100,000 salvage value, and a remaining 20-year life. Answer (D) is incorrect because $850,000 was the carrying amount at the time of sale, and $42,500 would be the depreciation in Saxe's separate financial statements assuming the $850,000 cost, a 20-year life, and no salvage value.

66. At January 1, Seacoast Company, an 80%-owned subsidiary of Plantation Corporation, had $1 million face amount of 14% bonds outstanding. They had been issued at face amount. Market conditions at January 1 provided a 10% yield rate when Plantation purchased these bonds in the open market for $1.1 million. Which of the following amounts should be included in a consolidated income statement for the year?

A. Bond interest expense of $140,000.

B. Bond interest revenue of $110,000.

C. Constructive loss of $100,000.

D. Constructive loss of $80,000.

Answer (C) is correct. *(Publisher)*

REQUIRED: The amount of an interentity bond transaction in consolidated net income.

DISCUSSION: Because a consolidated financial statement should include both Plantation and Seacoast as a single (consolidated) reporting entity, the purchase of the $1 million outstanding bonds of Seacoast by Plantation for $1.1 million was in substance a retirement of debt for $100,000 more than the debt's carrying amount. This transaction should be reflected in the consolidated income statement as a constructive loss from the retirement of debt in the amount of $100,000.

Answer (A) is incorrect because it represents the interentity interest reflected on the subsidiary's and parent's books that must be eliminated in the consolidated financial statements. Answer (B) is incorrect because it represents the interentity interest reflected on the subsidiary's and parent's books that must be eliminated in the consolidated financial statements. Answer (D) is incorrect because ARB 51 requires an adjustment for the total loss, not just the parent's share.

67. Wagner, a holder of a $1 million Palmer, Inc. bond, collected the interest due on March 31, year 1, and then sold the bond to Seal, Inc. for $975,000. On that date, Palmer, a 75% owner of Seal, had a $1,075,000 carrying amount for this bond. What was the effect of Seal's purchase of Palmer's bond on the retained earnings and minority interest amounts reported in Palmer's March 31, year 1 consolidated balance sheet?

	Retained Earnings	Minority Interest
A.	$100,000 increase	$0
B.	$75,000 increase	$25,000 increase
C.	$0	$25,000 increase
D.	$0	$100,000 increase

Answer (A) is correct. *(CPA, adapted)*

REQUIRED: The effect of the purchase by the subsidiary of the parent's debt.

DISCUSSION: The purchase was in substance a retirement of debt by the consolidated entity for less than its carrying amount. The transaction resulted in a constructive gain of $100,000 ($1,075,000 carrying amount – $975,000 price) and therefore a $100,000 increase in consolidated retained earnings. The minority interest was unaffected. The minority interest is based on the subsidiary's carrying amounts adjusted for subsidiary income and dividends. This transaction did not result in gain or loss for Seal.

Answer (B) is incorrect because the gain is not allocated. Answer (C) is incorrect because retained earnings is increased by $100,000, but the minority interest is not affected. Answer (D) is incorrect because retained earnings is increased by $100,000, but the minority interest is not affected.

68. During year 1, Pard Corp. sold goods to its 80%-owned subsidiary, Seed Corp. At December 31, year 1, one-half of these goods were included in Seed's ending inventory. Reported year 1 selling expenses were $1.1 million and $400,000 for Pard and Seed, respectively. Pard's selling expenses included $50,000 in freight-out costs for goods sold to Seed. What amount of selling expenses should be reported in Pard's year 1 consolidated income statement?

A. $1,500,000

B. $1,480,000

C. $1,475,000

D. $1,450,000

Answer (D) is correct. *(CPA, adapted)*

REQUIRED: The selling expenses reported in the consolidated income statement.

DISCUSSION: The effects of interentity transactions should be eliminated from consolidated financial statements in their entirety regardless of the parent's percentage of ownership. Consequently, consolidated selling expense is $1,450,000 ($1,100,000 + $400,000 – $50,000 of freight-out incurred on a sale by Pard to Seed). Seed's inventory balance is not relevant to this calculation because selling expenses, including freight-out, are not inventoried.

Answer (A) is incorrect because $1,500,000 assumes no elimination of the effects of the intercompany transaction. Answer (B) is incorrect because $1,480,000 assumes that the selling expense eliminated is related to the inventory held by Seed and that a minority interest in the remainder (20% × $25,000) is also not eliminated. Answer (C) is incorrect because $1,475,000 assumes that the selling expense eliminated is related to the inventory held by Seed.

25.5 Combined Financial Statements

69. Combined statements may be used to present the results of operations of

	Entities under Common Management	Commonly Controlled Entities
A.	No	Yes
B.	Yes	No
C.	No	No
D.	Yes	Yes

Answer (D) is correct. *(CPA, adapted)*

REQUIRED: The condition(s) in which combined financial statements are appropriate.

DISCUSSION: ARB 51 states that combined (as distinguished from consolidated) statements of commonly controlled entities may be more meaningful than separate statements. For example, combined statements may be used (1) to combine the statements of several entities with related operations when one individual owns a controlling interest in them, (2) to present financial position and results of operations of a group of unconsolidated subsidiaries, or (3) to combine the statements of entities under common management.

70. At December 31, year 1, S Corp. owned 80% of J Corp.'s common stock and 90% of C Corp.'s common stock. J's year 1 net income was $200,000 and C's year 1 net income was $400,000. C and J had no interentity ownership or transactions during year 1. Combined year 1 financial statements are being prepared for C and J in contemplation of their sale to an outside party. In the combined income statement, combined net income should be reported at

A. $420,000

B. $520,000

C. $560,000

D. $600,000

Answer (D) is correct. *(CPA, adapted)*

REQUIRED: The combined net income.

DISCUSSION: Combined financial statements are appropriate when a relationship such as common management or common ownership exists for two or more entities not subject to consolidation. The calculation of combined net income is similar to the calculation for consolidated net income. Thus, combined net income should be recorded at the total of the net income reported by the combined entities, adjusted for any profits or losses from transactions between the combined entities. In the combined income statement issued for J Corp. and C Corp., net income should be reported at $600,000 ($200,000 + $400,000).

Answer (A) is incorrect because $420,000 is 70% of the combined net income. Answer (B) is incorrect because $520,000 equals 80% of the net income of J and 90% of the net income of C. Answer (C) is incorrect because $560,000 equals 80% of J's net income and 100% of C's net income.

71. Selected data for two subsidiaries of Dunn Corp. taken from December 31, year 1 preclosing trial balances are as follows:

	Banks Co. Debit	Lamm Co. Credit
Shipments to Banks	--	$150,000
Shipments from Lamm	$200,000	--
Interentity inventory profit on total shipments	--	50,000

Additional data relating to the December 31, year 1 inventory are as follows:

Inventory acquired from outside parties	$175,000	$250,000
Inventory acquired from Lamm	60,000	--

At December 31, year 1, the inventory reported on the combined balance sheet of the two subsidiaries should be

A. $425,000

B. $435,000

C. $470,000

D. $485,000

Answer (C) is correct. *(CPA, adapted)*

REQUIRED: The inventory to be reported on the combined balance sheet of two subsidiaries.

DISCUSSION: When combined financial statements are prepared for unconsolidated subsidiaries, interentity profits should be eliminated. The $60,000 of ending inventory acquired by Banks from Lamm is equal to 30% ($60,000 inventory remaining ÷ $200,000 shipments) of the total received from Lamm. Accordingly, $15,000 (30% × $50,000 inventory profit on total shipments) should be eliminated. Given that $425,000 ($175,000 + $250,000) of the ending inventory held by Banks and Lamm was obtained from outside parties, the combined balance sheet of the two subsidiaries should report inventory of $470,000 ($425,000 + $60,000 – $15,000).

Answer (A) is incorrect because $425,000 is the total inventory acquired from outside parties. Answer (B) is incorrect because $435,000 excludes the profit on inventory acquired from Lamm and subsequently sold. Answer (D) is incorrect because $485,000 does not exclude the interentity inventory profit.

72. Mr. Cord owns four corporations. Combined financial statements are being prepared for these corporations, which have interentity loans of $200,000 and interentity profits of $500,000. What amount of these loans and profits should be included in the combined financial statements?

	Interentity	
	Loans	Profits
A.	$200,000	$0
B.	$200,000	$500,000
C.	$0	$0
D.	$0	$500,000

Answer (C) is correct. *(CPA, adapted)*

REQUIRED: The amount of interentity loans and profits that should be included in combined financial statements.

DISCUSSION: According to ARB 51, combined financial statements are appropriately issued when two or more entities have a common relationship, such as a common ownership interest or common management. When combined financial statements are issued, interentity loans and profits should be eliminated in their entirety. Consequently, $200,000 in loans and $500,000 in profits should not be included in the combined financial statements.

73. Ahm Corp. owns 90% of Bee Corp.'s common stock and 80% of Cee Corp.'s common stock. The remaining common shares of Bee and Cee are owned by their respective employees. Bee sells exclusively to Cee, Cee buys exclusively from Bee, and Cee sells exclusively to unrelated entities. Selected year 1 information for Bee and Cee follows:

	Bee Corp.	Cee Corp.
Sales	$130,000	$91,000
Cost of sales	100,000	65,000
Beginning inventory	None	None
Ending inventory	None	65,000

What amount should be reported as gross profit in Bee and Cee's combined income statement for the year ended December 31, year 1?

A. $26,000

B. $41,000

C. $47,800

D. $56,000

Answer (B) is correct. *(CPA, adapted)*

REQUIRED: The gross profit in the combined income statement.

DISCUSSION: Cee buys exclusively from Bee. Thus, Cee's cost of sales equals the sales price charged by Bee, which represented a 30% [($130,000 – $100,000) ÷ $100,000] markup on the cost to the combined entity. Consequently, the gross profit of the combined entity on sales to unrelated entities should include Bee's markup as well as Cee's gross profit. Because Bee's sales were 130% of its cost, the cost to the entity of Cee's sales was $50,000 ($65,000 cost of sales ÷ 130%). The gross profit in the combined income statement was therefore $41,000 ($91,000 – $50,000).

Answer (A) is incorrect because $26,000 was Cee's gross profit. Answer (C) is incorrect because $47,800 is the sum of 90% of Bee's and 80% of Cee's gross profits. Answer (D) is incorrect because $56,000 is the sum of Bee's and Cee's gross profits.

25.6 Variable Interest Entities

74. According to FASB Interpretation No. 46 (revised December 2003), *Consolidation of Variable Interest Entities*, which of the following most likely should be treated as VIEs?

I. An enterprise is controlled by its equity investors but has sustained large operating losses.

II. A development stage enterprise has minority owners with veto rights.

III. An entity's investors have voting rights that are not proportional to their obligations to absorb expected losses, and substantially all of its activities involve an investor with disproportionately fewer voting rights.

IV. The right of an entity's investors to receive expected residual returns is capped.

A. I and II only.

B. II and III only.

C. III and IV only.

D. I, II, III, and IV.

Answer (C) is correct. *(Publisher)*

REQUIRED: The variable interest entities.

DISCUSSION: An entity is a VIE if, by design, the equity at risk does not suffice to finance entity activities without additional subordinated financial support. An entity is also a VIE if at least one of the essential characteristics of a controlling financial interest is not present; that is, the holders of equity at risk do not have (1) decision-making ability based on voting or similar rights, (2) an obligation to absorb the VIE's expected losses, or (3) the right to receive the expected residual returns. Item (1) is satisfied if (a) some investors' votes are disproportionate to their obligations to absorb expected losses or to receive expected residual returns and (b) substantially all of the VIE's activities involve or are performed for an investor with disproportionately few voting rights. Item (3) is satisfied if the investors' return is capped by the entity's governing documents or by arrangements with the entity or other holders of variable interests. However, an enterprise controlled by its equity investors that was not initially a VIE does not change its status by reason of operating losses, regardless of the amount. Moreover, veto rights of minority shareholders are not a basis for classification of the entity as a VIE if the shareholders as a whole control the enterprise, and the equity at risk is sufficient to finance the entity's activities.

75. According to FASB Interpretation No. 46 (revised December 2003), *Consolidation of Variable Interest Entities,*

A. A not-for-profit organization may not be treated as a variable interest entity.

B. A variable interest entity has an equity investment of more than 10% of its total assets.

C. A variable interest entity is consolidated by its primary beneficiary when it becomes involved with the entity.

D. Corporations may not be organized as variable interest entities.

Answer (C) is correct. *(Publisher)*

REQUIRED: The true statement about VIEs.

DISCUSSION: In essence, a variable interest entity (VIE) is any legal structure with insufficient equity investment or whose equity investors lack one of the essential characteristics of financial control. When an enterprise becomes involved with a VIE, it must determine whether it is the primary beneficiary (PB) and therefore must consolidate the VIE. A PB holds a variable interest(s) that will absorb a majority of the VIE's expected losses or receive a majority of its expected residual returns (or both).

Answer (A) is incorrect because this Interpretation applies to NPOs if they are used to avoid the requirements of the pronouncement. Answer (B) is incorrect because an entity qualifies as a VIE if the equity at risk does not suffice to finance entity activities without additional subordinated financial support (other variable interests that will absorb expected losses). An equity investment of less than 10% of total assets is usually considered to be insufficient. But a greater investment also may not suffice if, for example, assets or entity activities are high risk. Answer (D) is incorrect because a VIE may take any form.

25.7 Branch Accounting

76. An enterprise uses a branch accounting system in which it establishes separate formal accounting systems for its home office operations and its branch office operations. Which of the following statements about this arrangement is false?

A. The home office account on the books of a branch office represents the equity interest of the home office in the net assets of the branch.

B. The branch office account on the books of the home office represents the equity interest of the branch office in the net assets of the home office.

C. The home office and branch office accounts are reciprocal accounts that must be eliminated in the preparation of the enterprise's financial statements that are presented in accordance with GAAP.

D. Unrealized profit from internal transfers between the home office and a branch must be eliminated in the preparation of the enterprise's financial statements that are presented in accordance with GAAP.

Answer (B) is correct. *(Publisher)*

REQUIRED: The false statement about branch accounting.

DISCUSSION: In branch accounting, the branch office account on the books of the home office represents the investment by the home office in the net assets of the branch, not the branch's equity in the home office.

77. Allen Corporation bills its branch office for shipments of goods at a 20% markup on cost and records the billed prices in its shipments to branch account. During the first year of operation of the branch, Allen sent merchandise to the branch at a billed price of $24,000 (cost $20,000). Some of the goods were returned as spoiled (billed price $600). Branch cost of goods sold for the period totaled $13,800. Assuming no losses of inventory items, by how much should Allen adjust the reported income of the branch?

A. $1,800

B. $2,300

C. $2,760

D. $4,000

Answer (B) is correct. *(J.R. Barnhart)*

REQUIRED: The year-end adjustment to branch income.

DISCUSSION: Cost of goods sold as reported by the branch includes the 20% markup of $2,300 [$13,800 – ($13,800 ÷ 120%)]. Allen should adjust the reported branch income and the balance in shipments to its branch account for the amount of the billed markup realized during the year. The home office entry at year-end when the shipments to branch account has been credited at billed cost is first to debit the shipments to branch account (reducing it to cost) and to credit an unrealized profit in branch inventories account for the markup on the shipments. The second part of the entry is to debit the unrealized profit account and credit branch income for the amount of the markup realized on branch sales to outside entities ($2,300, as calculated above).

Answer (A) is incorrect because $1,800 equals the markup included in branch cost of goods sold minus the cost to the company of the goods returned. Answer (C) is incorrect because $2,760 equals 20% of branch cost of goods sold. Answer (D) is incorrect because $4,000 equals the total markup on goods sent to the branch.

78. The following information pertains to shipments of merchandise from Home Office to Branch during year 1:

Home Office's cost of merchandise	$160,000
Intraentity billing	200,000
Sales by Branch	250,000
Unsold merchandise at Branch on December 31, year 1	20,000

In the combined income statement of Home Office and Branch for the year ended December 31, year 1, what amount should be included in sales?

A. $250,000

B. $230,000

C. $200,000

D. $180,000

Answer (A) is correct. *(CPA, adapted)*

REQUIRED: The sales reported on the combined income statement.

DISCUSSION: Reciprocal balances and transactions should be eliminated. The only sales to be recognized in the income statement are Branch's sales to outside parties.

Answer (B) is incorrect because $230,000 equals sales minus year-end inventory. Answer (C) is incorrect because $200,000 equals intraoffice billing. Answer (D) is incorrect because $180,000 equals intraoffice billing minus year-end inventory.

79. Which represents the proper journal entry for a periodic inventory system that should be made on the books of the home office when goods that cost the home office $100,000 to manufacture are shipped to a branch at a transfer price of $125,000 and the billed price is not recorded in the branch account?

A. Branch office	$100,000	
Shipments to branch		$100,000
B. Branch office	$125,000	
Shipments to branch		$125,000
C. Branch office	$125,000	
Shipments to branch		$100,000
Unrealized profit		25,000
D. Shipments to branch	$100,000	
Unrealized profit	25,000	
Shipments from home office		$125,000

Answer (C) is correct. *(Publisher)*

REQUIRED: The home office journal entry to reflect merchandise shipments at cost plus a markup.

DISCUSSION: When goods are shipped from a home office to a branch at a transfer price that reflects original cost plus a markup, the branch must record the shipment at the transfer price. The home office most often reflects the shipments to branch at original cost. To maintain a reciprocal relationship between the home office and the branch office accounts, an unrealized profit in branch inventories account reflects the markup.

Answer (A) is incorrect because this does not reflect the unrealized profit and the branch office should be recorded at $125,000. Answer (B) is incorrect because this does not reflect the unrealized profit and the shipments to the branch should be recorded at the original cost of $100,000. Answer (D) is incorrect because it is the worksheet entry necessary to eliminate this intercompany transaction in the preparation of the financial statements.

80. Which represents the proper journal entry for a periodic inventory system that should be made on the books of the branch when goods that cost the home office $100,000 to manufacture are shipped to the branch at a price of $125,000?

A. Shipments from home office	$100,000	
Home office		$100,000
B. Shipments from home office	$125,000	
Home office		$125,000
C. Shipments from home office	$125,000	
Unrealized profit		$ 25,000
Home office		100,000
D. Shipments to branch	$100,000	
Unrealized profit	25,000	
Shipments from home office		$125,000

Answer (B) is correct. *(Publisher)*

REQUIRED: The journal entry on the branch books to reflect the receipt of merchandise shipments at a transfer price that reflects cost plus a markup.

DISCUSSION: In a periodic system, when merchandise is received by a branch from the home office, the merchandise should be reflected as a shipment from the home office in the amount of the transfer price, with a corresponding entry to the home office account to indicate the equity of the home office in the net assets of the branch.

Answer (A) is incorrect because the shipments should be reflected at the transfer price. Answer (C) is incorrect because the home office equity should be reflected at the transfer price. Answer (D) is incorrect because it is the worksheet entry used to eliminate this intercompany transaction in the preparation of the enterprise's financial statements.

STUDY UNIT TWENTY-SIX
INTERIM FINANCIAL REPORTING

An interim accounting period is a period less than an annual accounting period. **APB 28**, *Interim Financial Reporting*, applies whenever entities issue interim financial information. It characterizes interim periods as **integral parts of an annual period** rather than as discrete periods. Hence, the results for an interim period ordinarily are based on the same accounting principles and practices used in the preparation of the most recent annual financial statements. In addition, certain principles and practices used for annual reporting may require modification in interim periods so that the interim report may relate more closely to the results of operations for the annual period.

Revenues and costs associated directly with revenues (product costs) are usually recognized on the same basis in interim and annual accounting periods, but certain modifications are made in accounting for **inventory**. These modifications are that (1) an **estimated gross profit rate** may be used to determine cost of sales during an interim period; (2) a **LIFO liquidation** at an interim period is not recognized if the inventory is expected to be replaced by year-end, and interim cost of sales should reflect the expected replacement cost; (3) the **LCM** rule is not applicable if the market decline is temporary, i.e., if it is expected to reverse by year-end; and (4), in a standard cost accounting system, purchase price variances or volume or capacity cost variances that are planned or expected to be absorbed by year-end are not recognized in interim periods.

Costs and expenses other than product costs are recognized in interim periods as incurred, or they are allocated among interim periods based on an estimate of time expired, benefits received, or activity associated with the periods. Arbitrary allocations, however, are not permitted. In addition, (1) costs and expenses that cannot be readily identified with the activities or benefits of another interim period are recognized as incurred, and (2) gains and losses similar to those that would not be deferred at year-end are recognized immediately.

An enterprise subject to seasonal fluctuations must disclose the nature of the seasonality.

According to **SFAS 154**, *Accounting Changes and Error Corrections*, a **change in an accounting principle** made in an interim period is reported by **retrospective application** unless it is **impracticable** to measure the **cumulative or period-specific effects** of the change. However, the impracticability exception is not applicable to prior interim periods of the year of change. When application to prechange interim periods is impracticable, the change is made at the beginning of the next annual period. Information reported for each post-change interim period must **disclose** the effect of the change on (1) income from continuing operations, (2) net income (or other appropriate captions), and (3) related per-share amounts. The disclosures required for all changes in principle are described in Study Unit 18.

A **change in an accounting estimate** is accounted for on a prospective basis. The effect of the change is therefore recognized in the interim period in which the change in estimate is made and in future periods. Prior-period financial information is not restated.

Corrections of accounting errors in interim financial information are treated as prior-period adjustments. Moreover, according to **SFAS 16**, *Prior Period Adjustments*, restatement of prior interim period financial information of the current year also may be required for adjustment or settlement of litigation, income taxes (except for the effects of retroactive tax legislation), renegotiation proceedings, or utility revenue under rate-making processes. If all or part of the adjustment or settlement relates specifically to a prior interim period of the current year, if the effect is material, and if the amount became reasonably estimable in the current interim period, the financial information for prior interim periods affected is restated for the applicable amounts. In addition, any portion of the adjustment or settlement that is directly related to prior fiscal years is included in the determination of income of the first interim period of the current year. However, these adjustments affect only interim reporting. In annual statements, these items are reported in current income.

Income taxes related to income (loss) from continuing operations recognized in an interim period are based on the tax rate expected to be applicable for the annual period. In determining the provision for the current interim period, an enterprise estimates its **expected annual effective rate** and multiplies the year-to-date "ordinary" income (loss) by this estimated rate to determine the year-to-date tax provision. **"Ordinary"** in this context means excluding unusual or infrequent items, extraordinary items, and discontinued operations. The provision for the current interim period then is determined by subtracting the tax provision previously recognized in prior interim periods from the year-to-date provision. Tax provisions for discontinued operations and extraordinary items are determined on an incremental basis. "Ordinary" income (loss) in this context means excluding unusual or infrequent items, extraordinary items, and discontinued operations.

APB 28 addresses the proper accounting for interim periods when financial information is presented. APB 28 also requires publicly traded companies to disclose certain minimum information when they present **summarized financial information** at interim dates.

QUESTIONS

26.1 Basic Concepts

1. In considering interim financial reporting, how did the Accounting Principles Board conclude that such reporting should be viewed?

A. As a "special" type of reporting that need not follow generally accepted accounting principles.

B. As useful only if activity is evenly spread throughout the year so that estimates are unnecessary.

C. As reporting for a basic accounting period.

D. As reporting for an integral part of an annual period.

Answer (D) is correct. *(CPA, adapted)*

REQUIRED: The APB's view of interim financial reporting.

DISCUSSION: APB 28, *Interim Financial Reporting*, characterizes each interim period primarily as an integral part of an annual period. Ordinarily, the results for an interim period should be based on the same accounting principles the enterprise uses in preparing annual statements. Certain principles and practices used for annual reporting, however, may require modification at interim dates so that interim reports may relate more closely to the results of operations for the annual period.

Answer (A) is incorrect because interim reporting is not a "special" type of reporting, and GAAP should be followed. Answer (B) is incorrect because interim reports may be useful for seasonal and unevenly spread activities. Answer (C) is incorrect because the APB rejected the view that the interim period is a discrete accounting period.

2. The Hoity-Toity Country Club offers membership privileges for a 3-year period under the following arrangements:

1) The applicant pays the entire $200,000 membership fee in eight quarterly installments during the first 2 years of the contract period.
2) The applicant is entitled to unlimited use of the facilities during the 3-year contract period.

Based on experience, Hoity-Toity is able to reasonably estimate uncollectible receivables. It prepares quarterly financial statements. In which accounting period(s) should Hoity-Toity recognize the membership fee as revenue for financial statement reporting?

A. In the quarter that the membership contract is signed.

B. Evenly over the eight quarters in which the installment payments are to be received.

C. In the quarter that the membership period terminates.

D. Evenly over the 12-quarter membership period.

Answer (D) is correct. *(CIA, adapted)*

REQUIRED: The accounting period in which revenue should be recognized.

DISCUSSION: In general, APB 28 states that the results for an interim period should be based on the same accounting principles that the enterprise uses in preparing annual statements. SFAC 5 states that revenue should be recognized when it is realized or realizable and earned. For revenue associated with membership privileges, the earning process is completed in proportion to the amount of the membership period elapsed. This principle is applicable in both annual and interim periods. Thus, the membership fee should be allocated evenly over the 12-quarter membership period.

3. Which of the following statements is a true description of the disclosure requirements when a publicly traded company that regularly reports interim information does not issue a separate fourth quarter interim report?

A. Such omission is not permitted if the company is publicly traded.

B. A note to the annual financial statements must include certain disclosures concerning the fourth interim period that are more limited than those required in a separate fourth quarter report.

C. All three prior interim reports must be revised and reissued if the aggregate effect of year-end adjustments is material to the results of the fourth quarter.

D. Current year-to-date interim data must be disclosed.

Answer (B) is correct. *(Publisher)*

REQUIRED: The true statement about disclosures for a company that does not issue a separate fourth quarter interim report.

DISCUSSION: When interim financial information is not reported separately for the fourth quarter, certain disclosures required by APB 28 must be made in a note to the annual financial statements. These disclosures are less extensive than the minimum information required when a publicly traded company chooses to report at interim dates. The disclosures must include disposals of components of an entity; extraordinary, unusual, or infrequent items; and the aggregate effect of material year-end adjustments. Moreover, if an accounting change is made in the fourth quarter, the appropriate disclosures about accounting changes required by GAAP also should be included in the note.

Answer (A) is incorrect because APB 28 specifically permits disclosure of fourth quarter data in a note to the annual statements. Answer (C) is incorrect because APB 28 does not require restatement or revision of prior interim reports, even if year-end adjustments are necessary. Answer (D) is incorrect because the current year-to-date interim data are the annual statements themselves.

4. How should material seasonal variations in revenue be reflected in interim financial statements?

A. The seasonal variation should be disclosed by showing pro forma financial statements for subsequent interim periods within the fiscal year.

B. Because the total revenue pattern of the current annual period is not known with certainty, any statements about seasonal patterns may be misleading and must be omitted from interim statements.

C. Disclosures should warn the statement reader that revenues are subject to seasonal variation, but no supplemental schedules of past seasonality should be shown.

D. The seasonal nature should be disclosed. Revenue information for 12-month periods ended at the interim date may be disclosed.

Answer (D) is correct. *(Publisher)*

REQUIRED: The proper method of reflecting material seasonal variations in revenue in interim financial statements.

DISCUSSION: If they issue interim information, APB 28 makes certain disclosures mandatory for businesses that have material seasonal fluctuations. Such disclosures safeguard the user of the statements from being misled into believing that interim results from such businesses are fairly representative of annual results. Businesses must disclose the seasonal nature of their activities and should consider supplementing interim reports with information for the 12-month period that ended at the interim date for the current and preceding years.

Answer (A) is incorrect because the disclosure requirement may be met by providing financial data for prior, not subsequent, interim periods within the fiscal year. Answer (B) is incorrect because businesses must disclose the seasonal nature of their activities. Answer (C) is incorrect because supplemental schedules with information for the 12-month period ending at the interim date for the current and preceding years are proper disclosures.

5. Interim reporting disclosures should include all of the following except

A. Basic and diluted earnings per share.

B. Significant changes in estimates or provisions for income tax.

C. Changes in accounting principles or estimates.

D. Changes in investment policy.

Answer (D) is correct. *(CMA, adapted)*

REQUIRED: The interim financial reporting disclosures not required.

DISCUSSION: APB 28 does not require presentation of interim income statements, statements of financial position, or statements of cash flows. Nor does it require disclosure of changes in investment policy. Although interim financial statements may be presented, minimum disclosures required when a publicly held company does issue a financial summary of interim operations include

1) Sales or gross revenues, provision for income taxes, extraordinary items, net income, and comprehensive income.
2) Basic and diluted EPS.
3) Seasonal revenues, costs, or expenses.
4) Significant changes in estimates or provisions for income taxes.
5) Disposal of a component of an entity and unusual or infrequent items.
6) Contingent items.
7) Changes in accounting principles or estimates.
8) Significant changes in financial position (disclosure of balance sheet and cash flow data is encouraged).
9) Certain information about reportable operating segments determined in accordance with SFAS 131.
10) Certain information about defined benefit pension plans and other defined benefit postretirement benefit plans required by SFAS 132(R).

Answer (A) is incorrect because disclosures required by APB 28 include BEPS and DEPS. Answer (B) is incorrect because disclosures required by APB 28 include estimates or provisions for income tax. Answer (C) is incorrect because disclosures required by APB 28 include changes in estimates and principles.

6. For interim financial reporting, an extraordinary gain occurring in the second quarter should be

A. Recognized ratably over the last three quarters.

B. Recognized ratably over all four quarters, with the first quarter being restated.

C. Recognized in the second quarter.

D. Disclosed by note only in the second quarter.

Answer (C) is correct. *(CPA, adapted)*

REQUIRED: The appropriate recognition of an extraordinary gain in an interim report.

DISCUSSION: Extraordinary items are material gains or losses that are unusual in nature and infrequent in occurrence within the environment in which the business operates. APB 28 requires that extraordinary items be disclosed separately and included in the determination of net income for the interim period in which they occur. Gains and losses similar to those that would not be deferred at year-end should not be deferred to later interim periods of the same year. Hence, the extraordinary gain should not be prorated.

Answer (A) is incorrect because the gain should be recognized in the quarter in which it occurs. Answer (B) is incorrect because the gain should be recognized in the quarter in which it occurs. Answer (D) is incorrect because the gain should be recognized in income. Disclosure in notes is not sufficient.

7. Direct response advertising costs are capitalized (deferred) to provide an appropriate expense in each period for

	Interim Financial Reporting	Year-end Financial Reporting
A.	Yes	No
B.	Yes	Yes
C.	No	No
D.	No	Yes

Answer (B) is correct. *(CPA, adapted)*

REQUIRED: The type(s) of reporting in which direct response advertising costs may be deferred.

DISCUSSION: Direct response advertising costs are capitalized (deferred) for annual reporting purposes if (1) the primary objective is to make sales to customers who respond specifically to the advertising, and (2) probable future economic benefits result. An entity that capitalizes these costs must document that customers have specifically responded to the advertising. It also must document the benefits from prior direct response advertising (SOP 93-7, *Reporting on Advertising Costs*). Moreover, the deferral of advertising costs is appropriate for interim financial reporting if their benefits clearly apply to more than one interim period. Thus, if a cost that would be fully expensed in an annual report benefits more than one interim period, it may be allocated to those interim periods (APB 28).

8. On March 15 of the current year, Chen Company paid property taxes of $120,000 on its factory building for the current calendar year. On April 1, Chen made $240,000 in unanticipated repairs to its plant equipment. The repairs will benefit operations for the remainder of the calendar year. What total amount of these expenses should be included in Chen's quarterly income statement for the 3 months ended June 30?

A. $60,000

B. $110,000

C. $150,000

D. $270,000

Answer (B) is correct. *(CPA, adapted)*

REQUIRED: The proper accounting for payments of property taxes and major repair costs in a quarterly income statement.

DISCUSSION: The benefit from the payment of the property taxes relates to all four quarters of the current year and should be prorated at $30,000 ($120,000 ÷ 4) per quarter. The benefit from the unanticipated repairs to plant equipment relates to the second, third, and fourth quarters. It should be spread evenly over these quarters at $80,000 ($240,000 ÷ 3) per quarter. The total amount of expenses that should be included in the quarterly income statement for the 3 months ended June 30 is therefore $110,000.

Answer (A) is incorrect because $60,000 results from not prorating the property taxes and from prorating the repair cost over all four quarters. Answer (C) is incorrect because $150,000 assumes that the entire repair cost is allocated to the first two quarters. Answer (D) is incorrect because $270,000 results from not allocating the repair expense.

9. Napier Corp. has estimated that total depreciation expense for the year ending December 31 will amount to $120,000 and that year-end bonuses to employees will total $240,000. In Napier's interim income statement for the 6 months ended June 30, what is the total amount of expense relating to these two items that should be reported?

A. $0

B. $60,000

C. $180,000

D. $360,000

Answer (C) is correct. *(CPA, adapted)*

REQUIRED: The amount of expenses related to depreciation and year-end bonuses that should be reported in the 6-month income statement.

DISCUSSION: APB 28 states that costs and expenses other than product costs should be either charged to income in interim periods as incurred or allocated among interim periods based on the benefits received. The depreciation and the bonuses to employees clearly provide benefits throughout the year, and they should be allocated ratably to all interim periods. In the interim income statement for the 6 months ended June 30, the total amount of expense that should be recorded is $180,000 [($360,000 ÷ 12 months) × 6 months].

Answer (A) is incorrect because depreciation and bonus expenses should be allocated ratably. Answer (B) is incorrect because $60,000 excludes the allocation of bonuses. Answer (D) is incorrect because $360,000 allocates the expenses entirely to the 6-month interim period ending June 30.

10. In August 2003, Snow Company spent $300,000 on an advertising campaign for subscriptions to the magazine it publishes concerning preparing for the winter sports season. The only two issues appear in October and in November. The magazine is sold only on a subscription basis, and the subscriptions started in October 2003. Assuming Snow's fiscal year ends on March 31, 2004, what amount of expense should be included in Snow's quarterly income statement for the 3 months ended December 31, 2003 as a result of this expenditure?

A. $75,000

B. $100,000

C. $150,000

D. $300,000

Answer (D) is correct. *(CPA, adapted)*

REQUIRED: The amount of advertising expense included in the third quarter's income statement.

DISCUSSION: Even if payments are received in advance, subscription revenue may be recognized only when it has been realized and earned. Because the magazine is published only during October and November, recognition of subscription revenue and related expenses is appropriate only during that quarter. Accordingly, the entire advertising expense of $300,000 should be recognized in that period.

Answer (A) is incorrect because $75,000 results from allocating the $300,000 expense ratably to four quarters. Answer (B) is incorrect because $100,000 results from allocating 33 1/3% of the $300,000 expense. Answer (C) is incorrect because $150,000 results from allocating 50% of the $300,000 expense.

11. On June 30, Tun Corp. incurred a $200,000 net loss from disposal of a component. Also, on June 30, Tun paid $80,000 for property taxes assessed for the calendar year. What amount of the foregoing items should be included in the determination of Tun's net income or loss for the 6-month interim period ended June 30?

A. $280,000

B. $240,000

C. $180,000

D. $140,000

Answer (B) is correct. *(CPA, adapted)*

REQUIRED: The amount of property taxes and loss from disposal of a component that should be included in the determination of net income or loss for the interim period.

DISCUSSION: Costs other than product costs, such as rent, interest, or property taxes, that will clearly benefit two or more interim periods should be allocated among those periods based on estimates of time expired, the benefit received, or the activity associated with each period. Thus, Tun should allocate $40,000 [(6 ÷ 12) × $80,000] of the property taxes to the 6-month interim period ended June 30. Gains and losses that arise in an interim period that are similar to gains and losses that would not be deferred at year-end should not be deferred to later interim periods within the same fiscal year. Consequently, gains or losses from disposal of a component should not be prorated over the balance of the fiscal year, so the loss on disposal ($200,000) should be recognized in full for the interim period ended June 30. The total included in the interim income statement for the two items is therefore $240,000 ($40,000 + $200,000).

Answer (A) is incorrect because $280,000 reflects a failure to prorate the property taxes. Answer (C) is incorrect because $180,000 reflects proration of the loss on disposal of a segment and the full amount of the property taxes. Answer (D) is incorrect because $140,000 reflects proration of the loss on disposal of a component.

26.2 Inventory

12. Which of the following reporting practices is permissible for interim financial reporting?

A. Use of the gross profit method for interim inventory pricing.

B. Use of the direct costing method for determining manufacturing inventories.

C. Deferral of unplanned variances under a standard cost system until year-end.

D. Deferral of inventory market declines until year-end.

Answer (A) is correct. *(CPA, adapted)*
REQUIRED: The inventory reporting practice permissible in interim financial reporting.
DISCUSSION: Certain accounting principles and practices followed for annual reporting purposes may be modified for interim reporting. For example, the gross profit method may be used for estimating cost of goods sold and inventory because a physical inventory count at the interim date may not be feasible.
Answer (B) is incorrect because the direct costing method is never permissible for external financial reporting. Answer (C) is incorrect because only variances that are planned and expected to be absorbed by the end of the annual period may be deferred. Answer (D) is incorrect because only market declines that can reasonably be expected to be restored within the fiscal year may be deferred.

13. Wilson Corp. experienced a $50,000 decline in the market value of its inventory in the first quarter of its fiscal year. Wilson had expected this decline to reverse in the third quarter, and in fact, the third quarter recovery exceeded the previous decline by $10,000. Wilson's inventory did not experience any other declines in market value during the fiscal year. What amounts of loss or gain should Wilson report in its interim financial statements for the first and third quarters?

	First Quarter	Third Quarter
A.	$0	$0
B.	$0	$10,000 gain
C.	$50,000 loss	$50,000 gain
D.	$50,000 loss	$60,000 gain

Answer (A) is correct. *(CPA, adapted)*
REQUIRED: The loss or gain reported for changes in market value of inventory in interim statements.
DISCUSSION: A market decline reasonably expected to be restored within the fiscal year may be deferred at an interim reporting date because no loss is anticipated for the year. Inventory losses from nontemporary market declines, however, must be recognized at the interim reporting date. If the loss is recovered later during the fiscal year (in another quarter), it should be treated as a change in estimate. The price recovery recognized is limited to the extent of the losses previously recognized.
Answer (B) is incorrect because gains in the market value of inventory that are not recoveries of nontemporary declines are not recognized. Answer (C) is incorrect because a loss reasonably expected to be restored in a later interim period is deferred, and gains in the market value of inventory that are not recoveries of nontemporary declines are not recognized. Answer (D) is incorrect because a loss reasonably expected to be restored in a later interim period is deferred, and gains in the market value of inventory that are not recoveries of nontemporary declines are not recognized.

14. A store uses the gross profit method to estimate inventory and cost of goods sold for interim reporting purposes. Past experience indicates that the average gross profit rate is 25% of sales. The following data relate to the month of June:

Inventory cost, June 1	$25,000
Purchases during the month at cost	67,000
Sales	84,000
Sales returns	3,000

Based on the data above, what is the estimated ending inventory at June 30?

A. $20,250

B. $21,000

C. $29,000

D. $31,250

Answer (D) is correct. *(CIA, adapted)*
REQUIRED: The estimated ending inventory under the gross profit method.
DISCUSSION: In accordance with the gross profit method, cost of goods sold is estimated by multiplying the net sales figure by one minus the gross profit rate. In this example, the estimate of cost of goods sold is $60,750 [($84,000 sales – $3,000 sales returns) × (1 – .25)]. As indicated below, subtracting the estimated cost of goods sold from the goods available for sale results in an estimated ending inventory at June 30 of $31,250.

Beginning inventory	$25,000
June purchases	67,000
Goods available for sale	$92,000
Estimated CGS	(60,750)
Estimated ending inventory	$31,250

Answer (A) is incorrect because $20,250 is the gross profit. Answer (B) is incorrect because purchases are subtracted from beginning inventory, and cost of goods sold ($84,000 × 75% = 63,000) is not adjusted for sales returns and is added to beginning inventory (25,000 – 67,000 + 63,000 = 21,000). Answer (C) is incorrect because cost of goods sold is not adjusted for sales returns.

15. An inventory loss from a market price decline occurred in the first quarter. The loss was not expected to be restored in the fiscal year. However, in the third quarter the inventory had a market price recovery that exceeded the market decline that occurred in the first quarter. For interim financial reporting, the dollar amount of net inventory should

A. Decrease in the first quarter by the amount of the market price decline and increase in the third quarter by the amount of the market price recovery.

B. Decrease in the first quarter by the amount of the market price decline and increase in the third quarter by the amount of decrease in the first quarter.

C. Decrease in the first quarter by the amount of the market price decline and not be affected in the third quarter.

D. Not be affected in either the first quarter or the third quarter.

Answer (B) is correct. *(CPA, adapted)*

REQUIRED: The proper interim financial reporting of a market decline and subsequent recovery.

DISCUSSION: APB 28 requires that a market price decline in inventory be recognized in the interim period in which it occurs unless it is expected to be temporary, i.e., unless the decline is expected to be restored by the end of the fiscal year. Because this loss was not expected to be restored in the fiscal year, the company should report the dollar amount of the market price decline as a loss in the first quarter. When a market price recovery occurs in an interim period, it should be treated as a change in estimate. The market price recovery recognized in the third quarter is limited, however, to the extent of losses previously recognized. Accordingly, the inventory should be written up to its original cost.

Answer (A) is incorrect because the recovery recognized in the third quarter is limited to the amount of the losses previously recognized. Answer (C) is incorrect because the first quarter loss and the third quarter recovery are offsetting. Answer (D) is incorrect because the first quarter loss and the third quarter recovery are offsetting.

16. An inventory loss from a permanent market decline of $360,000 occurred in May. Richter Co. appropriately recorded this loss in May after its March 31 quarterly report was issued. What amount of inventory loss should be reported in Richter's quarterly income statement for the 3 months ended June 30?

A. $0

B. $90,000

C. $180,000

D. $360,000

Answer (D) is correct. *(CPA, adapted)*

REQUIRED: The permanent inventory loss from a market decline reported in a quarterly income statement.

DISCUSSION: APB 28 requires that an inventory loss from market decline not be deferred beyond the interim period in which it occurs, unless it is expected to be recovered within the fiscal year. The $360,000 market decline occurring in the quarter ended June 30 is not considered temporary. Hence, it should be recognized in full in that quarter.

Answer (A) is incorrect because the decline should be recognized in full in the quarter ended June 30. Answer (B) is incorrect because $90,000 assumes proration over four quarters. Answer (C) is incorrect because $180,000 assumes proration over two quarters.

17. When a standard cost system of accounting is used to determine costs for valuation of inventory in interim financial statements,

A. Unanticipated variances should be spread prospectively to the remaining interim periods in the current annual reporting period.

B. Unplanned variances should be recognized in the interim period in which they are incurred.

C. Unplanned volume variances should be retroactively allocated to prior interim periods in the current annual reporting period if they occur after the first quarter.

D. Unplanned variances should be deferred to the fourth quarter and recognized as a component of year-end adjustments.

Answer (B) is correct. *(Publisher)*

REQUIRED: The true statement about interim reporting of unplanned variances when using standard costs.

DISCUSSION: APB 28 allows planned standard cost variances to be deferred if they are expected to be absorbed in subsequent interim periods of a year. Unplanned or unanticipated variances, however, should be recognized in the interim period in which they are incurred.

Answer (A) is incorrect because unanticipated variances should be expensed in the interim period in which they are incurred. Answer (C) is incorrect because an unplanned volume variance is not a basis for a retroactive restatement. Answer (D) is incorrect because unplanned variances should be expensed in the interim period in which they are incurred.

18. A company that uses the last-in, first-out (LIFO) method of inventory pricing at an interim reporting date has encountered a partial liquidation of the base-period inventory level. The decline is considered temporary, and the partial liquidation will be replaced prior to year-end. The amount shown as inventory at the interim reporting date should

A. Not give effect to the LIFO liquidation, and cost of sales for the interim reporting period should include the expected cost of replacement of the liquidated LIFO base.

B. Be shown at the actual level, and cost of sales for the interim reporting period should reflect the decrease in LIFO base-period inventory level.

C. Not give effect to the LIFO liquidation, and cost of sales for the interim reporting period should reflect the decrease in the LIFO base-period inventory level.

D. Be shown at the actual level, and the decrease in inventory level should not be reflected in the cost of sales for the interim reporting period.

Answer (A) is correct. *(CPA, adapted)*

REQUIRED: The true statement about inventory valuation at an interim reporting date when a temporary LIFO liquidation has occurred.

DISCUSSION: Interim financial reporting may depart in certain respects from GAAP applied in annual financial statements. Thus, given that the partial liquidation of the base-period inventory is only temporary and will be replaced within the fiscal year, APB 28 states that the partial liquidation need not be given effect in the interim financial statements, and the cost of sales for the interim period should include the expected cost of replacement of the liquidated base.

Answer (B) is incorrect because no effect should be given to the LIFO liquidation. The cost of sales should reflect the expected cost of replacement, not the decrease in the base-period inventory level. Answer (C) is incorrect because no effect should be given to the LIFO liquidation. The cost of sales should reflect the expected cost of replacement, not the decrease in the base-period inventory level. Answer (D) is incorrect because no effect should be given to the LIFO liquidation. The cost of sales should reflect the expected cost of replacement, not the decrease in the base-period inventory level.

26.3 Accounting Changes

19. A change in accounting principle is permitted in an interim period subsequent to the first interim period of an entity's fiscal year

A. Under no circumstances.

B. If the change can be justified.

C. If the change can be justified and it is practicable to determine the cumulative effect of applying the change at the beginning of the year of the change.

D. If the change can be justified and it is practicable to determine period-specific effects of applying the change to prechange interim periods of the year of the change.

Answer (D) is correct. *(Publisher)*

REQUIRED: When a change in accounting principle is permitted in an interim period other than the first interim period.

DISCUSSION: A change in accounting principle introduced in an interim period is reported by retrospective application similar to a change made in an annual financial statement, provided that it is practicable to determine period-specific effects of the change on prechange interim periods of the year in which the change is made. If it is impracticable to determine period-specific effects of retrospective application to prior interim periods of the year of the change, the change may not be made until the beginning of a subsequent annual period.

20. In the third quarter of calendar year 2006, Preboske Corp. documented justification for a change in accounting principle. Preboske also determined the cumulative effects of applying the new principle at January 1, 2003 and the period-specific effects of applying it to the current quarter and the previously reported quarterly interim periods of the current and previous three fiscal years. If Preboske makes this change in the third quarter, the cumulative effect of applying the change to periods prior to the periods presented should be

A. Included in net income in the first quarter of calendar year 2006.

B. Included in net income in the third quarter of calendar year 2006.

C. Included in net income in the first period presented.

D. Reflected in the carrying amounts of assets and liabilities as of the beginning of the first period presented.

Answer (D) is correct. *(Publisher)*

REQUIRED: The proper treatment of the cumulative effect of applying the change to periods prior to the periods presented.

DISCUSSION: Retroactive application is generally required when it is practicable to determine the cumulative effect and the period-specific effects of a change in accounting principle in an interim period. Retroactive application results in changing previously issued financial statements to reflect the effects of the newly adopted accounting principle as if the new principle had always been used. Retroactive application requires that the carrying value of assets, liabilities, and retained earnings as of the beginning of the first period reported be adjusted for the cumulative effect of the new accounting principle on periods prior to the first period reported, and that all periods reported be individually adjusted for the period-specific effects of applying the new accounting principle.

21. Andrews Corp.'s $190,000 net income for the quarter ended September 30, 2006 included the following after-tax items:

- A $120,000 extraordinary gain, realized on April 30, 2006, was allocated equally to the second, third, and fourth quarters of 2006.
- A $32,000 loss (a period-specific effect of a change in accounting principle during the quarter) was recognized on September 30, 2006. While the cumulative effect of the change at July 1, 2006 could be determined, it was not practicable to determine the period-specific effects of the change on first and second net income of 2006.

In addition, Andrews paid $96,000 on February 1, 2006 for 2006 calendar-year property taxes. Of this amount, $24,000 was allocated to the third quarter of 2006. For the quarter ended September 30, 2006, Andrews should report net income of

A. $222,000

B. $206,000

C. $182,000

D. $150,000

Answer (C) is correct. *(CPA, adapted)*

REQUIRED: The net income reported for the quarter.

DISCUSSION: APB 28 requires that extraordinary items be disclosed separately and included in the determination of net income for the interim period in which they occur. Gains and losses similar to those that would not be deferred at year-end should not be deferred to later interim periods of the same year. Hence, the $120,000 extraordinary gain should be recognized in net income for the second quarter. No effect is permitted in third quarter income. A voluntary change in accounting principle is not permitted to take effect in an interim period if it is impracticable to differentiate between the cumulative effect of the change on prior years and the period-specific effects on prior interim period of the year of the change. Thus, Andrews is not permitted to change this accounting principle until January 1, 2007. Accordingly, the $32,000 loss should not be included in third quarter income. Since property taxes were proportionally allocated among the four quarters, the $24,000 is properly included in third quarter income. As a result, Andrews should report third quarter net income of $182,000 [$190,000 – ($120,000 ÷ 3) + $32,000].

Answer (A) is incorrect because $222,000 does not include the adjustment for the proportionate extraordinary gain. Answer (B) is incorrect because $206,000 includes an adjustment for the $24,000 allocation of property taxes. Answer (D) is incorrect because $150,000 does not include an adjustment for the $32,000 period-specific effects of the accounting change.

22. The following information is applicable to a change in accounting principle made in the second quarter of the year from FIFO to LIFO. The firm is able to apply the new principle retrospectively. For all relevant periods, prices have risen. The effect of the change is limited to the effects on the inventory balance and income tax provisions (a 40% tax rate).

Period	Net Income on the Basis of FIFO	Gross Effect of Change	Gross Effect Minus Income Taxes
Prior to 1st Qtr	$6,262,000	$300,000	$180,000
1st Qtr	1,032,400	60,000	36,000
2nd Qtr	1,282,400	60,000	36,000
3rd Qtr	1,298,600	90,000	54,000
4th Qtr	1,164,800	120,000	72,000

Net income for the first quarter should be restated as

A. $1,068,400

B. $1,032,400

C. $816,400

D. $996,400

Answer (D) is correct. *(Publisher)*

REQUIRED: The restated net income for the first quarter resulting from a change in principle in the second quarter.

DISCUSSION: The change in accounting principle should be effected by retrospective application unless determination of the cumulative effect or the period-specific effects is impracticable. (However, the impracticability exception is not applicable to prior interim periods of the year of change.) The period-specific effects are adjustments made to the individual periods reported. Beginning balances of the first period reported are adjusted to reflect the cumulative effects of the change on all prior periods. Accordingly, given the period-specific effects for the first quarter, restated net income based on retrospective application is $996,400 ($1,032,400 – $36,000 gross after-tax effect of applying the new principle). Changing to LIFO when prices are rising decreases net income.

Answer (A) is incorrect because $1,068,400 results from adding, not subtracting, the gross effect minus income taxes. Given rising prices, the change to LIFO lowers after-tax income. Answer (B) is incorrect because first quarter net income must be adjusted. Answer (C) is incorrect because $816,400 results from subtracting the cumulative after-tax effect on prior periods as well as the adjustment for the first quarter.

23. When an entity makes a change in accounting principle during an interim period, which disclosure need not be made in the financial reports of a postchange interim period in the same fiscal year?

A. The effect of the change on interim net income.

B. The nature of and reason for the change to the newly adopted accounting principle.

C. The effect of the change on per-share amounts.

D. The effect of the change on interim income from continuing operations.

Answer (B) is correct. *(Publisher)*

REQUIRED: The item that need not be disclosed in subsequent interim reports when an entity changes an accounting principle.

DISCUSSION: In a postchange interim period of the fiscal year of the change, the effect on income from continuing operations, net income (or other appropriate captions), and related per-share amounts must be disclosed for that interim period. However, the nature of and reason for the change in principle should be disclosed in the period of change.

24. When a public company that regularly reports interim information makes an accounting change in the fourth quarter, it must

A. Issue a separate fourth quarter financial statement explaining the change and make the other disclosures required by GAAP.

B. Make the required interim-period disclosures in a note to the annual financial statements if fourth quarter summarized interim data are not reported.

C. Either issue a separate interim statement or, in the annual financial statements, label a separate note Accounting Change in the Fourth Quarter.

D. Not make a special disclosure because GAAP require the disclosure to be made annually.

Answer (B) is correct. *(Publisher)*

REQUIRED: The requirement for disclosing an accounting change in the fourth quarter.

DISCUSSION: When a public company makes an accounting change in the last quarter, full interim-period disclosures must be made in a note to the annual financial statements of the year of change in the absence of disclosure in a separate fourth quarter report or the annual report.

Answer (A) is incorrect because fourth quarter statements are not required if disclosures are made in the annual report or a note to the annual financial statements. Answer (C) is incorrect because the note need not be labeled Accounting Change in the Fourth Quarter. Answer (D) is incorrect because separate disclosure with respect to the effect on interim statements must be made in (1) an interim report, (2) the annual report, or (3) a note to the annual statements.

26.4 Prior Interim Period Adjustments

25. During the third quarter of 2003, the accountant at the Laurie Company discovered that a machine purchased January 2, 2001 for $120,000 had been erroneously charged against first quarter net income in 2001. The machine should have been depreciated at a rate of $2,000 per month. The correction of this error should include

A. A charge of $66,000 to income before taxes of the third quarter of 2003.

B. An adjustment of $48,000 to the previously declared income before taxes of the first quarter of 2003.

C. An adjustment of $54,000 to the previously declared income before taxes of the first quarter of 2003.

D. An adjustment of $6,000 to the previously declared income before taxes of the first quarter of 2003.

Answer (D) is correct. *(Publisher)*

REQUIRED: The proper treatment of an accounting error.

DISCUSSION: An error was committed when the full cost of the asset was expensed in the period of acquisition. Instead, the cost should have been capitalized and the asset depreciated over its useful life. The correction of this error should be accounted for as a prior-period adjustment. Ignoring tax effects, this requires an entry to beginning retained earnings for the year to correct the understatement of income (and of retained earnings) that resulted from the error. If comparative statements are issued, a restatement of prior-period financial statements is also necessary. The previously reported income of the first quarter of 2003 (as well as that for the second quarter) should be restated to reflect the $6,000 ($2,000 × 3 months) depreciation that should have been taken on the asset during that period.

26. On June 15, 2003, a court of law found the Panther Corporation, a calendar-year company, guilty of patent infringement and awarded damages of $5,000,000 to the plaintiff. Of this amount, $2,000,000 related to each of the years 2001 and 2002; $500,000 related to each of the two quarters of 2003. No provision for loss had been recorded previously. If the applicable tax rate is 40%, this event should result in a

A. Charge of $3,000,000 to income reported for the second quarter of 2003.

B. Restatement of the previously reported net income for the first quarter of 2003 to include a charge of $300,000.

C. Restatement of the previously reported net income for the first quarter of 2003 to include a charge of $2,700,000.

D. Restatement of the previously reported net income for the first quarter of 2003 to include a charge of $3,000,000.

Answer (C) is correct. *(Publisher)*

REQUIRED: The proper treatment of the settlement of litigation related to a prior interim period and prior fiscal years.

DISCUSSION: According to SFAS 16, *Prior Period Adjustments*, if an item of profit or loss that relates to settlement of litigation occurs in other than the first interim period of the fiscal year and all or a part of the item meets the criteria for an adjustment related to prior interim periods of that fiscal year, the financial statements for the prior interim periods should be restated to include their allocable portions of the adjustment. The portion of the adjustment directly related to prior fiscal years should also be included in the determination of net income of the first interim period of the current fiscal year. The settlement in this case occurred in the second quarter; thus the first quarter should be restated for the $500,000 directly related to first-quarter operations and the $4,000,000 directly related to prior years' operations. The restated net income for the first quarter of 2003 should therefore include a $2,700,000 adjustment ($4,500,000 – the tax savings of $1,800,000).

27. On September 30, 2003, the Cantata Corporation, a calendar-year company, reached an agreement with the Internal Revenue Service. The company agreed to pay additional income taxes of $2,000,000 that directly related to a loss claimed in the third quarter of 2001. In accordance with current authoritative literature, this transaction should be recorded as a

A. Component of the net income reported for the third quarter of 2003.

B. Restatement of the net income previously reported for the first quarter of 2003.

C. Restatement of the beginning retained earnings previously reported for the third quarter of 2003.

D. Restatement of the beginning retained earnings previously reported for the first quarter of 2003.

Answer (A) is correct. *(Publisher)*

REQUIRED: The proper recording of an income tax settlement reached in the third quarter of the current year relating to the third quarter of a prior year.

DISCUSSION: SFAS 16 may require a prior interim period adjustment for an adjustment or settlement of litigation, income taxes (except for the effects of retroactive tax legislation), renegotiation proceedings, and utility revenue under rate-making processes. All or part of the adjustment or settlement must relate specifically to a prior interim period of the current year, its effect must be material, and the amount must have become reasonably estimable only in the current interim period. XYZ's transaction does not qualify as a prior interim period adjustment because no portion of the item is related to prior interim periods of the current fiscal year. Thus, the tax settlement liability should be included in net income in the third quarter of 2003.

Answer (B) is incorrect because the item does not qualify for treatment as a prior interim period adjustment in the current fiscal year. Answer (C) is incorrect because the item does not qualify for treatment as a prior interim period adjustment in the current fiscal year. Answer (D) is incorrect because a tax settlement related to a prior fiscal year is not treated as a prior-period adjustment.

28. On June 1, 2003, the Adipose Corporation, a calendar-year company, settled a patent infringement lawsuit. The court awarded Adipose $3,000,000 in damages. Of this amount, $1,000,000 related to each of the years 2001 and 2002, and $500,000 related to each of the first two quarters in 2003. The applicable tax rate is 40%. What effect does the settlement have on the net income of the second quarter of 2003?

A. $200,000

B. $300,000

C. $600,000

D. $1,800,000

Answer (B) is correct. *(Publisher)*

REQUIRED: The effect of a patent lawsuit settlement on second quarter net income.

DISCUSSION: Under SFAS 16, if an item of profit related to settlement of litigation occurs in other than the first interim period of the fiscal year (here, the second quarter of a calendar-year company), and all or part of the item of profit meets the criteria for an adjustment related to a prior interim period of the current fiscal year, the portion of the item allocable to the current interim period should be included in the determination of net income for that period. Prior interim periods should be restated to include their allocable portions of the adjustment. Accordingly, $500,000 of the settlement should be included in the determination of net income for the second quarter. Given a tax rate of 40%, the settlement increases net income of the second quarter by $300,000.

Answer (A) is incorrect because $200,000 is the amount of the income tax. Answer (C) is incorrect because $600,000 is the adjustment to be made to each year (2002 and 2001). Answer (D) is incorrect because the income should not be recognized entirely in 2003.

26.5 Annual Effective Tax Rate

29. For interim financial reporting, a company's income tax provision for the second quarter should be determined using the

A. Statutory tax rate for the year.

B. Effective tax rate expected to be applicable for the full year as estimated at the end of the first quarter.

C. Effective tax rate expected to be applicable for the full year as estimated at the end of the second quarter.

D. Effective tax rate expected to be applicable for the second quarter.

Answer (C) is correct. *(CPA, adapted)*

REQUIRED: The tax rate used to determine the interim income tax provision.

DISCUSSION: APB 28 requires that, at the end of each interim period, an enterprise make its best estimate of the effective tax rate expected to be applicable for the full fiscal year. That rate should be used in providing for income taxes on a current year-to-date basis.

30. For interim financial reporting, the computation of a company's second quarter provision for income taxes uses an effective tax rate expected to be applicable for the full fiscal year. The effective tax rate should reflect anticipated

	Foreign Tax Rates	Available Tax Planning Alternatives
A.	No	Yes
B.	No	No
C.	Yes	No
D.	Yes	Yes

Answer (D) is correct. *(CPA, adapted)*

REQUIRED: The factors used to estimate the annual effective tax rate for interim statements.

DISCUSSION: The estimated effective annual tax rate should be based upon the statutory rate adjusted for the current year's expected conditions. These conditions include anticipated investment tax credits, foreign tax rates, percentage depletion, capital gain rates, and other tax planning alternatives.

31. The computation of a company's third quarter provision for income taxes should be based upon "ordinary" income (loss)

A. For the quarter at an expected annual effective income tax rate.

B. For the quarter at the statutory rate.

C. To date at an expected annual effective income tax rate, minus prior quarters' provisions.

D. To date at the statutory rate, minus prior quarters' provisions.

Answer (C) is correct. *(CPA, adapted)*

REQUIRED: The correct computation of a third quarter provision for income taxes.

DISCUSSION: According to FASB Interpretation No. 18, the income tax provision for an interim period should be calculated by applying the estimated annual effective tax rate to the "ordinary" income (loss) for the year to date and then deducting the prior interim periods' income tax provisions. "Ordinary" in this context means excluding unusual or infrequent items, extraordinary items, discontinued operations, and cumulative effects of changes in accounting principles.

Answer (A) is incorrect because the calculation must apply the expected annual effective income tax rate to the cumulative "ordinary" income (loss) for the year to date, and then subtract prior quarters' tax provisions. Answer (B) is incorrect because the company must use an estimated annual effective income tax rate. Answer (D) is incorrect because the company must use an estimated annual effective income tax rate.

32. In interim financial statements, income tax (benefit) for extraordinary items and discontinued operations is shown net of tax just as in annual statements. The tax (benefit) is computed

A. By applying the estimated annual tax rate of the company to the particular item.

B. As the difference between the tax (benefit) on income including the other items and the tax (benefit) on income excluding the other items.

C. At the statutory rate on both extraordinary items and discontinued operations.

D. At the estimated tax rate for the particular interim period in which the extraordinary item or discontinued item occurred.

Answer (B) is correct. *(Publisher)*

REQUIRED: The method of computing the income tax (benefit) for extraordinary items and discontinued operations in interim financial statements.

DISCUSSION: Under FASB Interpretation No. 18, the income tax (benefit) for extraordinary items and discontinued operations is determined based on an incremental calculation. It is the difference between the tax (benefit) on the interim period "ordinary" income (loss) and the total tax (benefit) on the sum of "ordinary" income (loss) and the other items.

Answer (A) is incorrect because the tax effect for extraordinary items and discontinued operations is based on an incremental calculation. Answer (C) is incorrect because the tax effect for extraordinary items and discontinued operations is based on an incremental calculation. Answer (D) is incorrect because the tax effect for extraordinary items and discontinued operations is based on an incremental calculation.

33. During the first quarter of 2003, Lipid Co. had income before taxes of $200,000, and its effective income tax rate was 15%. Lipid's 2002 effective annual income tax rate was 30%, but Lipid expects its 2003 effective annual income tax rate to be 25%. In its first quarter interim income statement, what amount of income tax expense should Lipid report?

A. $0

B. $30,000

C. $50,000

D. $60,000

Answer (C) is correct. *(CPA, adapted)*

REQUIRED: The provision for income taxes for the first interim period.

DISCUSSION: According to APB 28, "At the end of each interim period the company should make its best estimate of the effective tax rate expected to be applicable for the full fiscal year. The rate so determined should be used in providing for income taxes on a current year-to-date basis." The "ordinary" income before taxes for the first quarter is $200,000, and the estimated annual effective tax rate for 2003 is 25%. The income tax expense for the first interim period is therefore $50,000 (25% × $200,000).

Answer (A) is incorrect because $0 excludes any income tax expense. Answer (B) is incorrect because $30,000 is based on the quarterly effective income tax rate. Answer (D) is incorrect because $60,000 is based on the 2002 effective annual income tax rate.

34. The following information was used in preparing Nocturne Company's quarterly income statements during the first half of 2003:

Quarter	Income Before Income Taxes	Estimated Effective Annual Income Tax Rate
1	$80,000	45%
2	70,000	45%

For the third quarter of 2003, income before income taxes was $50,000, and the estimated effective annual income tax rate was 40%. The income statement for the third quarter of 2003 should include a provision for income taxes of

A. $12,500

B. $17,500

C. $20,000

D. $22,500

Answer (A) is correct. *(CIA, adapted)*

REQUIRED: The provision for income taxes in the interim income statement for the third quarter.

DISCUSSION: According to FASB Interpretation No. 18, the tax provision for the third quarter is calculated by multiplying the estimated annual effective tax rate determined at the end of the third quarter times the cumulative year-to-date "ordinary" income (loss) and then subtracting the cumulative tax provision for the first two quarters. At the end of the third quarter, the year-to-date "ordinary" income is $200,000 ($80,000 + $70,000 + $50,000), and the cumulative tax provision is $80,000 ($200,000 × 40%). Because the cumulative tax provision at the end of the second quarter was $67,500 [($80,000 + $70,000) × 45%], $12,500 ($80,000 – $67,500) should be reported as a provision for income taxes in the income statement for the third quarter.

Answer (B) is incorrect because $17,500 adds the estimated income tax of $50,000 at 40% to the cumulative tax provision and then subtracts $150,000 (80,000 + 70,000) × 40%. Answer (C) is incorrect because $20,000 is the third-quarter effective annual income tax rate multiplied by income before taxes (40% × $50,000). Answer (D) is incorrect because $22,500 is the second-quarter effective annual income tax rate multiplied by income before taxes (45% × $50,000).

35. Prelude Corporation expects to sustain an operating loss of $100,000 for the full year ending December 31, its first year of operations. It operates entirely in one jurisdiction where the tax rate is 40%. Tax credits for the year total $10,000. No permanent differences are expected. Realization of the full tax benefit of the expected operating loss and of the anticipated tax credits is more likely than not. Thus, Prelude expects to recognize the full tax benefit at year-end as a deferred tax asset with a valuation allowance of $0. For the quarter ended March 31, Prelude reports an operating loss of $20,000. How much of a tax benefit should Prelude report for the interim period ended March 31?

A. $0

B. $8,000

C. $10,000

D. $12,500

Answer (C) is correct. *(CPA, adapted)*

REQUIRED: The tax benefit to be reported for an interim period.

DISCUSSION: The current effective tax rate is based on the statutory rate adjusted for the current year's expected conditions, e.g., tax credits. The interim period tax benefit for the first quarter is the estimated annual effective tax rate applied to the loss for the quarter (because the full benefit of the operating loss and tax credits is more likely than not to be realized). The tax benefit of the annual operating loss is $40,000 (40% tax rate × $100,000). The total tax benefit is therefore $50,000 ($40,000 + $10,000 tax credit), and the annual effective tax rate is 50% ($50,000 benefit ÷ $100,000 loss). The quarterly loss was $20,000; thus, the quarterly tax benefit is $10,000 (50% × $20,000).

Answer (A) is incorrect because a tax benefit should be realized. Answer (B) is incorrect because $8,000 is the operating loss multiplied by the statutory tax rate. Answer (D) is incorrect because $12,500 is the operating loss multiplied by the tax rate ($20,000 × 40%) plus the tax credits multiplied by the average of the annual effective tax rate and the regular tax rate.

STUDY UNIT TWENTY-SEVEN
FOREIGN CURRENCY TRANSLATION AND TRANSACTIONS

Foreign currency translation involves changing amounts denominated or measured in a different currency into the currency in which consolidated financial statements are reported. For example, the financial statements of a Japanese subsidiary are changed from yen to dollar amounts to be included in the consolidated financial statements issued by a U.S. parent. One purpose of translation is to include in consolidated financial statements the financial results and relationships of each entity as measured in that entity's functional currency. The **functional currency** is the currency of the primary economic environment in which an entity generates and expends cash. For a foreign entity that is a direct and integral component or extension of a U.S. parent, the functional currency ordinarily is the U.S. dollar. For a foreign entity whose operations are relatively self-contained and integrated within a foreign country, the functional currency is most often the currency of that country. However, for a foreign entity whose operations are conducted in a **highly inflationary economy**, the functional currency is the currency in which the consolidated financial statements are reported.

The **functional currency translation approach** requires (1) identifying a foreign entity's functional currency; (2) if the foreign entity's functional currency is different from the currency in which the foreign entity's financial statements are measured, remeasuring those statements into the functional currency; and (3) if the foreign entity's functional currency is different from the currency in which the consolidated financial statements are reported, translating the foreign entity's financial statements into the reporting currency. Current exchange rates are used to remeasure monetary accounts; historical exchange rates are used to remeasure nonmonetary accounts. A current exchange rate is used to translate all accounts.

Another purpose of translation is to reflect the expected economic effect of an exchange rate change on consolidated cash flows and equity. Exchange rate changes involving foreign operations that are a direct extension of the U.S. parent are considered to affect parent cash flows directly. Thus, exchange rate gains and losses arising from **remeasurement of monetary assets and liabilities** are included in **current income**. Exchange rate changes involving foreign operations that are self-contained in a foreign country are considered to relate to the net investment in that operation and not to affect parent cash flows directly. Thus, exchange rate gains and losses arising from **translation** are not included in the determination of net income. Instead, they are included in **other comprehensive income (OCI)**.

Foreign currency transactions are transactions whose terms are denominated in a currency different from the entity's functional currency. For example, a company whose functional currency is the U.S. dollar purchases inventory on credit from a German company, and terms of the purchase require payment in euros. Foreign currency **transaction gains and losses** arise as a result of changes in the exchange rate between the functional currency and the currency in which a foreign currency transaction is denominated. These gains and losses are included in the determination of net income in the period the exchange rate changes. However, if the transaction is effective as a hedge of a **net investment in a foreign entity** or is an **intercompany transaction of a long-term investment nature**, the gains and losses are accounted for in the same manner as translation adjustments.

This study unit addresses the accounting for **hedges** of foreign currency exposures. Hedging the foreign currency exposures of a net investment in a foreign operation, an unrecognized firm commitment, a recognized asset or liability (including an available-for-sale security), and a forecasted transaction (including a forecasted intercompany transaction) is discussed in the summary of Study Unit 10. The general provisions of SFAS 133, *Accounting for Derivative Instruments and Hedging Activities*, as amended, also are covered in Study Unit 10.

A foreign currency exposure exists when an entity is subject to the risks resulting from changes in foreign currency exchange rates. This risk is present when a transaction, asset, liability, or net investment is denominated in a currency different from the entity's functional currency. Thus, for example, a U.S. entity is subject to a foreign currency exposure when it is involved in a purchase transaction that is payable in Japanese yen, when it holds a receivable to be satisfied in Mexican pesos, or when it is the parent company of a German subsidiary whose functional currency is the euro. Companies commonly hedge their exposure to changes in foreign currency exchange rates.

SFAS 133 permits a **fair value hedge** of a foreign-currency denominated unrecognized firm commitment or a recognized asset or liability (including an available-for-sale security). A derivative or nonderivative that may result in a **foreign currency transaction gain or loss** may be designated as a hedge of the changes in fair value of all (or part) of an **unrecognized firm commitment** that are attributable to exchange rates. If the fair value hedge criteria are met (they are too complex to be described here), the gain or loss on the hedging instrument and the offsetting loss or gain on the hedged item is recognized in current **earnings**. A derivative (but **NOT** a nonderivative) may be designated as a hedge of all (or part) of a **recognized asset or liability** for which a **foreign currency transaction gain or loss** is recognized. If the fair value hedge criteria and certain other conditions are met, the gain or loss on the hedging derivative and the offsetting loss or gain on the hedged item is recognized in current **earnings**.

SFAS 133 states that a nonderivative instrument may not be the hedging instrument in a **foreign currency cash flow hedge**. However, a derivative instrument may be designated as a hedge of "the foreign currency exposure to variability in the functional-currency-equivalent cash flows associated with a forecasted transaction, a recognized asset or liability, an unrecognized firm commitment, or a forecasted intercompany transaction" (e.g., a forecasted sale to a foreign subsidiary). Accordingly, if the cash flow hedge criteria are met (also too complex to be described here), the effective portion of the gain or loss on the hedging derivative instrument in a foreign currency cash flow hedge is recognized as a component of **OCI**, and the ineffective portion is recognized in earnings in the period in which the gain or loss is recognized. The gain or loss recognized in OCI is reclassified into earnings in the same period(s) during which the hedged item affects earnings.

SFAS 133 requires the effective portion of the gain or loss on the hedging derivative or hedging nonderivative instrument in a hedge of a **net investment in a foreign operation** to be recognized in OCI as part of the cumulative translation adjustment. The ineffective portion is recognized in earnings in the period in which the gain or loss is recognized.

QUESTIONS

27.1 Foreign Currency Translation

1. The economic effects of a change in foreign exchange rates on a relatively self-contained and integrated operation within a foreign country relate to the net investment by the reporting enterprise in that operation. Consequently, translation adjustments that arise from the consolidation of that operation

A. Directly affect cash flows but should not be reflected in income.

B. Directly affect cash flows and should be reflected in income.

C. Do not directly affect cash flows and should not be reflected in income.

D. Do not directly affect cash flows but should be reflected in income.

Answer (C) is correct. *(Publisher)*

REQUIRED: The true statement about translation adjustments arising from consolidation of a self-contained foreign operation with its U.S. parent/investor.

DISCUSSION: SFAS 52, *Foreign Currency Translation*, concludes that foreign currency translation adjustments for a foreign operation that is relatively self-contained and integrated within its environment do not affect cash flows of the reporting enterprise and should be excluded from net income. When an operation is relatively self-contained, the cash generated and expended by the entity is normally in the currency of the foreign country, and that currency is deemed to be the operation's functional currency.

Answer (A) is incorrect because, when an operation is relatively self-contained, the assumption is that translation adjustments do not affect cash flows. Answer (B) is incorrect because, when an operation is relatively self-contained, the assumption is that translation adjustments do not affect cash flows, and translation adjustments should be included in other comprehensive income, not recognized in income. Answer (D) is incorrect because translation adjustments should be included in OCI, not recognized in income.

2. The financial results and relationships of foreign subsidiaries that are presented in the consolidated financial statements of a U.S.-based parent company should be measured in accordance with the

A. Functional currency translation method.

B. Current/noncurrent translation method.

C. Monetary/nonmonetary translation method.

D. Temporal translation method.

Answer (A) is correct. *(Publisher)*

REQUIRED: The method used to convert foreign subsidiary financial statements for consolidation purposes.

DISCUSSION: According to SFAS 52, the functional currency translation approach is appropriate for use in accounting for and reporting the financial results and relationships of foreign subsidiaries in consolidated statements. It involves identifying the functional currency of the entity (the currency of the primary economic environment in which the entity operates), measuring all elements of the financial statements in the functional currency, and using a current exchange rate for translation from the functional currency to the reporting currency.

3. In preparing consolidated financial statements of a U.S. parent company with a foreign subsidiary, the foreign subsidiary's functional currency is the currency

A. In which the subsidiary maintains its accounting records.

B. Of the country in which the subsidiary is located.

C. Of the country in which the parent is located.

D. Of the environment in which the subsidiary primarily generates and expends cash.

Answer (D) is correct. *(CPA, adapted)*

REQUIRED: The foreign subsidiary's functional currency.

DISCUSSION: The method used to convert foreign currency amounts into units of the reporting currency is the functional currency translation approach. It is appropriate for use in accounting for and reporting the financial results and relationships of foreign subsidiaries in consolidated statements. This method identifies the functional currency of the entity (the currency of the primary economic environment in which the foreign entity operates), measures all elements of the financial statements in the functional currency, and uses a current exchange rate for translation from the functional currency to the reporting currency.

Answer (A) is incorrect because the currency in which the subsidiary maintains its accounting records may not be the currency indicated by the salient economic indicators, such as cash flows, sales prices, sales markets, expenses, financing, and intercompany transactions. Answer (B) is incorrect because the currency of the country in which the subsidiary is located may not be the currency indicated by the salient economic indicators, such as cash flows, sales prices, sales markets, expenses, financing, and intercompany transactions. Answer (C) is incorrect because the currency of the country in which the parent is located may not be the currency indicated by the salient economic indicators, such as cash flows, sales prices, sales markets, expenses, financing, and intercompany transactions.

4. SFAS 52, *Foreign Currency Translation*, provides specific guidelines for translating foreign currency financial statements. The translation process begins with a determination of whether a foreign affiliate's functional currency is also its local reporting currency. Which one of the following factors indicates that a foreign affiliate's functional currency is the U.S. dollar?

A. Cash flows are primarily in foreign currency and do not affect parent's cash flows.

B. Financing is primarily obtained from local foreign sources and from the affiliate's operations.

C. Sales prices are responsive to short-term changes in exchange rates and worldwide competition.

D. Labor, materials, and other costs consist primarily of local costs to the foreign affiliate.

Answer (C) is correct. *(CMA, adapted)*

REQUIRED: The factor indicating that a foreign affiliate's functional currency is the U.S. dollar.

DISCUSSION: The functional currency is the currency of the primary economic environment in which an entity operates. It is normally the currency of the environment in which an entity primarily generates and expends cash. If a U.S. company's foreign affiliate's sales prices are responsive to short-term changes in exchange rates and worldwide competition, its functional currency is likely to be the U.S. dollar.

Answer (A) is incorrect because cash flows that are primarily in a foreign currency indicate that the foreign currency is the functional currency. Answer (B) is incorrect because, when financing is obtained primarily from foreign sources and operations, the foreign currency is likely to be the functional currency. Answer (D) is incorrect because, when costs are primarily paid in the foreign country, the foreign currency is likely to be the functional currency.

5. The financial results of three foreign subsidiaries are included along with those of a U.S. parent company in consolidated financial statements. The subsidiaries are distinct and separable from the parent and from each other. If the four operations are conducted in four different economic environments, how many different functional currencies are necessary to measure these operations?

A. One.

B. Two.

C. Three.

D. Four.

Answer (D) is correct. *(Publisher)*

REQUIRED: The number of functional currencies involved in measuring the financial activities of a parent and three distinct subsidiaries operating in different environments.

DISCUSSION: The activities of an entity must be measured in terms of the currency of the primary economic environment in which the entity operates, that is, the functional currency. Because the four operations (parent and three subsidiaries) are distinct and separable from each other and are conducted in four different economic environments, each entity will use a different functional currency to measure its operations.

6. Which of the following is not an integral part of the functional currency translation approach?

A. The functional currency of each foreign operation must be identified.

B. All elements of the financial statements of a foreign operation must be measured in the functional currency.

C. If the functional currency of a foreign operation differs from the reporting currency, translation using the current exchange rate method is required.

D. The gain or loss arising from translation must be included in the determination of the current period's income.

Answer (D) is correct. *(Publisher)*

REQUIRED: The item that is not an element of the functional currency translation approach.

DISCUSSION: According to SFAS 52, a gain or loss arising from translation from the functional currency into the reporting currency is not reflected in the current period's net income. Translation adjustments are reported in OCI.

Answer (A) is incorrect because it is an integral part of the functional currency translation approach. Answer (B) is incorrect because it is an integral part of the functional currency translation approach. Answer (C) is incorrect because it is an integral part of the functional currency translation approach.

7. Certain balance sheet accounts of a foreign subsidiary of Rowan, Inc., have been translated into U.S. dollars on December 31 as follows:

	Translated at	
	Current Rates	Historical Rates
Note receivable, long-term	$240,000	$200,000
Prepaid rent	85,000	80,000
Patent	150,000	170,000
	$475,000	$450,000

The subsidiary's functional currency is the currency of the country in which it is located. What total amount should be included in Rowan's December 31 consolidated balance sheet for the above accounts?

A. $450,000

B. $455,000

C. $475,000

D. $495,000

Answer (C) is correct. *(CPA, adapted)*

REQUIRED: The total translated amount to be included in the consolidated balance sheet.

DISCUSSION: When the currency used to prepare a foreign entity's financial statements is its functional currency, SFAS 52 specifies that the current rate method be used to translate the foreign entity's financial statements into the reporting currency. The translation gains and losses arising from applying this method are included in OCI in the equity section of the consolidated balance sheet. Thus, the listed assets translated at current rates should be included in the consolidated balance sheet at $475,000.

Answer (A) is incorrect because $450,000 reflects translation at historical rates. Answer (B) is incorrect because the note and patent are translated at historical rates. Answer (D) is incorrect because the patent is translated at historical rates.

8. If an entity's books of accounts are not maintained in its functional currency, SFAS 52, *Foreign Currency Translation*, requires remeasurement into the functional currency prior to the translation process. An item that should be remeasured by use of the current exchange rate is

A. An investment in bonds to be held until maturity.

B. A plant asset and the associated accumulated depreciation.

C. A patent and the associated accumulated amortization.

D. The revenue from a long-term construction contract.

Answer (A) is correct. *(CMA, adapted)*

REQUIRED: The item that should be remeasured into the functional currency using the current exchange rate.

DISCUSSION: The current rate should be used for all items except common nonmonetary balance sheet accounts and their related revenues, expenses, gains, and losses, which are remeasured at historical rates. Thus, most monetary items, such as an investment in bonds, are remeasured at the current exchange rate.

Answer (B) is incorrect because plant assets are remeasured at historical rates. Answer (C) is incorrect because a patent is remeasured at historical rates. Answer (D) is incorrect because the revenue from a long-term construction contract is one of the exceptions for which the current rate is not to be used.

9. If all assets and liabilities of a firm's foreign subsidiary are translated into the parent's currency at the current exchange rate (the rate in effect at the date of the balance sheet), the extent of the parent firm's translation gain or loss is based on the subsidiary's

A. Current assets minus current liabilities.

B. Total assets minus total liabilities.

C. Monetary assets minus monetary liabilities.

D. Operating cash flows.

Answer (B) is correct. *(CIA, adapted)*

REQUIRED: The basis for the parent's translation gain or loss if all assets and liabilities of the foreign subsidiary are translated at the current exchange rate.

DISCUSSION: When the functional currency of a foreign subsidiary is the local (foreign) currency, translation of all assets and liabilities is required at the current rate as of the balance sheet date.

10. A wholly owned subsidiary of Ward, Inc. has certain expense accounts for the year ended December 31, 2003 stated in local currency units (LCUs) as follows:

	LCU
Depreciation of equipment (related assets purchased Jan. 1, 2001)	120,000
Provision for doubtful accounts	80,000
Rent	200,000

The exchange rates at various dates are as follows:

	Dollar Equivalent of 1 LCU
December 31, 2003	$.40
Average for year ended 12/31/03	.44
January 1, 2001	.50

Assume that the LCU is the subsidiary's functional currency and that the charges to the expense accounts occurred approximately evenly during the year. What total dollar amount should be included in Ward's 2003 consolidated income statement to reflect these expenses?

A. $160,000

B. $168,000

C. $176,000

D. $183,200

Answer (C) is correct. *(CPA, adapted)*

REQUIRED: The amount of expenses in the consolidated income statement.

DISCUSSION: When the local currency of the subsidiary is the functional currency, translation into the reporting currency is necessary. Assets and liabilities are translated at the exchange rate at the balance sheet date, and revenues, expenses, gains, and losses are usually translated at average rates for the period. Thus, the $400,000 in total expenses should be translated at the average exchange rate of $.44, resulting in expenses reflected in the consolidated income statement of $176,000 ($400,000 × $.44).

Answer (A) is incorrect because the average exchange rate, not the current year-end rate, should be used. Answer (B) is incorrect because the average exchange rate, not a combination of rates, should be used. Answer (D) is incorrect because the average exchange rate, not a combination of rates, should be used.

11. A foreign subsidiary's functional currency is its local currency, which has not experienced significant inflation. The weighted-average exchange rate for the current year is the appropriate exchange rate for translating

	Wages Expense	Sales to Customers
A.	Yes	No
B.	Yes	Yes
C.	No	Yes
D.	No	No

Answer (B) is correct. *(CPA, adapted)*

REQUIRED: The item(s) translated at the weighted-average exchange rate for the current year.

DISCUSSION: When an entity's local currency is the functional currency and this currency has not experienced significant inflation, translation into the reporting currency of all elements of the financial statements must be at a current exchange rate. Assets and liabilities are translated at the exchange rate at the balance sheet date. Revenues (e.g., sales), expenses (e.g., wages), gains, and losses should be translated at the rates in effect when they were recognized. However, translation of income statement items at a weighted-average rate for the period is permitted.

12. Park Co.'s wholly owned subsidiary, Schnell Corp., maintains its accounting records in euros. Because all of Schnell's branch offices are in Switzerland, its functional currency is the Swiss franc. Remeasurement of Schnell's current-year financial statements resulted in a $7,600 gain, and translation of its financial statements resulted in an $8,100 gain. What amount should Park report as a gain in its income statement for the current year ended December 31?

A. $0

B. $7,600

C. $8,100

D. $15,700

Answer (B) is correct. *(CPA, adapted)*

REQUIRED: The gain reported as a result of translation and remeasurement.

DISCUSSION: The financial statements must be remeasured into the functional currency (Swiss francs) and then translated into the reporting currency (U.S. dollar). The $7,600 gain arising from remeasurement should be reported in current income. The $8,100 translation gain should be reported in OCI. Translation gains are not reflected in net income.

Answer (A) is incorrect because the gain on remeasurement should be reported in the income statement. Answer (C) is incorrect because the $8,100 translation gain is not reported in the income statement. Answer (D) is incorrect because the $8,100 translation gain is not reported in the income statement.

13. SFAS 52, *Foreign Currency Translation*, requires the current rate of exchange to be used for remeasuring certain balance sheet items and the historical rate of exchange for other balance sheet items. An item that should be remeasured using the historical exchange rate is

A. Accounts and notes receivable.

B. Accounts and notes payable.

C. Taxes payable.

D. Prepaid expenses.

Answer (D) is correct. *(CMA, adapted)*

REQUIRED: The item that should be remeasured using the historical exchange rate.

DISCUSSION: Financial statements are remeasured using the temporal rate method. In general, this method adjusts monetary items at the current rate and nonmonetary items at the historical rate. Prepaid expenses, a nonmonetary item, should be remeasured using the historical rate.

Answer (A) is incorrect because accounts and notes receivable are monetary items. Thus, they should be remeasured using the current rate of exchange. Answer (B) is incorrect because accounts and notes payable are monetary items. Thus, they should be remeasured using the current rate of exchange. Answer (C) is incorrect because taxes payable is a monetary item. Thus, it should be remeasured using the current rate of exchange.

14. A wholly owned foreign subsidiary of Union Corporation has certain expense accounts for the year ended December 31, 2003 stated in local currency units (LCUs) as follows:

	LCU
Amortization of patent (related patent acquired Jan. 1, 2001)	40,000
Provision for doubtful accounts	100,000
Rent	200,000

The exchange rates at various dates are as follows:

	Dollar Equivalent of 1 LCU
December 31, 2003	$.20
Average for year ended 12/31/03	.22
January 1, 2001	.25

The subsidiary's operations were an extension of the parent company's operations. What total dollar amount should be included in Union's income statement to reflect the above expenses for the year ended December 31, 2003?

A. $40,000

B. $42,000

C. $44,000

D. $45,200

Answer (D) is correct. *(CPA, adapted)*

REQUIRED: The dollar amount of remeasured expenses of a foreign subsidiary whose operations are an extension of the parent's.

DISCUSSION: Given that the foreign subsidiary's operations are an extension of the parent company's, the functional currency of the subsidiary is considered to be the U.S. dollar. Thus, remeasurement from the local currency to the U.S. dollar is required for financial statement purposes.

Nonmonetary balance sheet items and related revenues and expenses (e.g., cost of sales, depreciation, and amortization) should be remeasured using historical rates to produce the same results as if those items had been initially recorded in the functional currency (U.S. dollar). Accordingly, the amortization of patent expense (LCUs = 40,000) should be remeasured at the rate of exchange in effect at the date the patent was acquired, $.25. Monetary and current value items should be remeasured at a current rate. Hence, provision for doubtful accounts and rent should be remeasured at the average 2003 exchange rate of $.22, which is the customary approximation of the current rate used to remeasure expenses not related to nonmonetary items.

Patent amortization	40,000 × $.25	=	$10,000
Provision for doubtful accounts	60,000 × $.22	=	13,200
Rent	100,000 × $.22	=	22,000
Total remeasured expenses			$45,200

Answer (A) is incorrect because $40,000 results from applying the year-end exchange rate to the total expenses. Answer (B) is incorrect because $42,000 results from applying the average rate to the patent and the year-end rate to the rent. Answer (C) is incorrect because $44,000 results from applying the average rate to the total expenses.

15. A foreign subsidiary of a U.S. parent reports its financial statements in its local currency although its functional currency is the U.S. dollar. In the consolidated financial statements, all of the following accounts of the subsidiary are remeasured into the functional currency at the historical rate except

A. Marketable securities carried at cost.

B. Inventories carried at market.

C. Property, plant, and equipment.

D. Goodwill.

Answer (B) is correct. *(J.W. Mantooth)*

REQUIRED: The account that is not remeasured at the historical rate.

DISCUSSION: When a foreign subsidiary's functional currency is the U.S. dollar, all accounts of that subsidiary reported in a foreign currency must be remeasured as if they had been recorded in the U.S. dollar. Nonmonetary balance sheet items and related revenue, expense, gain, and loss accounts are remeasured at the historical rate. Monetary accounts are remeasured at the current rate. Inventories carried at market value are classified as monetary assets and should therefore be remeasured at the current rate.

16. When remeasuring foreign currency financial statements into the functional currency, which of the following items is remeasured using historical exchange rates?

A. Inventories carried at cost.

B. Equity securities reported at fair values.

C. Bonds payable.

D. Accrued liabilities.

Answer (A) is correct. *(CPA, adapted)*

REQUIRED: The item that is remeasured using historical exchange rates.

DISCUSSION: SFAS 52 requires the current rate of exchange to be used for remeasuring certain balance sheet items and the historical rate of exchange for other balance sheet items. Nonmonetary balance sheet items and related revenue, expense, gain, and loss accounts are remeasured at the historical rate. Monetary accounts are remeasured at the current rate. Inventories valued at cost are nonmonetary items and are measured at historical rates.

Answer (B) is incorrect because equity securities reported at fair values is a monetary item valued at the current rate. Answer (C) is incorrect because bonds payable is a monetary item valued at the current rate. Answer (D) is incorrect because accrued liabilities is a monetary item valued at the current rate.

17. The Brinjac Company owns a foreign subsidiary. Included among the subsidiary's liabilities for the year just ended are 400,000 LCUs of revenue received in advance, recorded when $.50 was the dollar equivalent per LCU, and a deferred tax liability for 187,500 LCU, recognized when $.40 was the dollar equivalent per LCUs. The rate of exchange in effect at year-end was $.35 per LCU. If the accounting is in accordance with SFAS 52 and SFAS 109 and the dollar is the functional currency, what total should be included for these two liabilities on Brinjac's consolidated balance sheet at year-end?

A. $205,625

B. $215,000

C. $265,625

D. $275,000

Answer (D) is correct. *(C.J. Skender)*

REQUIRED: The total of two liability accounts of a foreign subsidiary in the consolidated statements if the functional currency is the U.S. dollar.

DISCUSSION: When a foreign entity's functional currency is the U.S. dollar, the financial statements of the entity recorded in a foreign currency must be remeasured in terms of the U.S. dollar. In accordance with SFAS 52, revenue received in advance (deferred income) is considered a nonmonetary balance sheet item and is remeasured at the applicable historical rate (400,000 LCUs × $.50 per LCU = $200,000). Deferred charges and credits (except policy acquisition costs for life insurance companies) are also remeasured at historical exchange rates. Deferred taxes were formerly not subject to this rule, but SFAS 109 amended SFAS 52 to eliminate the exception. Consequently, the deferred tax liability (a deferred credit) should be remeasured at the historical rate (187,500 LCUs × $.40 per LCU) = $75,000). The total for these liabilities is therefore $275,000 ($200,000 + $75,000).

Answer (A) is incorrect because $205,625 results from applying the year-end rate to the total liabilities. Answer (B) is incorrect because the historical, not current, rate should be used to remeasure the deferred income. Answer (C) is incorrect because the historical rate is used to remeasure nonmonetary balance sheet items, including deferred tax assets and liabilities.

18. For the purpose of remeasuring financial statements of a foreign entity into the functional currency, a highly inflationary economy is considered to be one that has a(n)

A. Inflation rate of 100% or more per year for a 3-year period.

B. Inflation rate 100% greater than that of the reporting currency for a 3-year period.

C. Inflation rate of 100% per year for 3 out of 5 years.

D. Cumulative inflation rate of 100% or more over a 3-year period.

Answer (D) is correct. *(J. Bruno)*

REQUIRED: The test for a highly inflationary economy applied to a foreign economic environment.

DISCUSSION: The financial statements of a foreign entity in a highly inflationary economy should be remeasured into the reporting currency; that is, the reporting currency should be treated as if it were the functional currency. SFAS 52 defines a highly inflationary economy as one that has cumulative inflation of approximately 100% or more over a 3-year period.

19. The Dease Company owns a foreign subsidiary with 3,600,000 local currency units (LCUs) of property, plant, and equipment before accumulated depreciation on December 31, 2003. The subsidiary's functional currency is the U.S. dollar. Of this amount, 2,400,000 LCUs were acquired in 1996 when the rate of exchange was 1.6 LCUs to $1, and 1,200,000 LCUs were acquired in 1999 when the rate of exchange was 1.8 LCUs to $1. The rate of exchange in effect at December 31, 2003 was 2 LCUs to $1. The weighted average of exchange rates in effect during 2003 was 1.92 LCUs to $1. Assuming that the property, plant, and equipment are depreciated using the straight-line method over a 10-year period with no salvage value, how much depreciation expense relating to the foreign subsidiary's property, plant, and equipment should be charged in Dease's income statement for 2003 if SFAS 52 is followed?

A. $180,000

B. $187,500

C. $200,000

D. $216,667

Answer (D) is correct. *(CPA, adapted)*

REQUIRED: The amount of remeasured depreciation expense recognized in consolidating a foreign subsidiary whose functional currency is the U.S. dollar.

DISCUSSION: Given that the subsidiary's functional currency is the U.S. dollar, the financial statements of the subsidiary must be remeasured in terms of the dollar. Nonmonetary assets and the related revenues and expenses should be remeasured based on the historical rates in effect at the dates of the transactions. Depreciation expense relates to the property, plant, and equipment (nonmonetary assets), so the rate of exchange in effect when these fixed assets were acquired should be used in remeasuring depreciation expense for the period.

Because 2,400,000 LCUs of fixed assets were acquired when the rate of exchange was 1.6, depreciation expense can be remeasured by multiplying the LCU depreciation by $1 ÷ 1.6, resulting in $150,000 of remeasured depreciation expense [(2,400,000 ÷ 10) × ($1 ÷ 1.6)]. Depreciation related to the asset that cost 1,200,000 LCUs is $66,667 in remeasured terms [(1,200,000 ÷ 10) × ($1 ÷ 1.8)]. Total depreciation expense equals $216,667 ($150,000 + $66,667).

Answer (A) is incorrect because $180,000 results from applying the current (year-end) rate to the total depreciation expense. Answer (B) is incorrect because $187,500 results from applying the average rate to the total depreciation expense. Answer (C) is incorrect because the rate prevailing at the time the assets were acquired should be used for each group of assets.

20. When the foreign operations are conducted in a highly inflationary economy, at what exchange rates should the following balance sheet accounts in foreign statements be remeasured into U.S. dollars?

	Equipment	Accumulated Depreciation of Equipment
A.	Current	Current
B.	Current	Average for year
C.	Historical	Current
D.	Historical	Historical

Answer (D) is correct. *(CPA, adapted)*

REQUIRED: The proper exchange rates used for balance sheet items of a foreign operation in a highly inflationary economy.

DISCUSSION: When a foreign entity operates in an environment that is highly inflationary (approximately 100% or more inflation over a 3-year period), SFAS 52 requires that financial statements be remeasured into the reporting currency; that is, the reporting currency is treated as if it were the functional currency. A nonmonetary asset, such as equipment, and its related expense or revenue items are remeasured at applicable historical rates. The results should be the same as if those items had initially been recorded in the currency (the U.S. dollar) into which they are being remeasured.

21. A widely diversified U.S. corporation sold portions of three wholly owned foreign subsidiaries in the same year. The functional currency of each subsidiary was the currency of the country in which it was located. The percentage sold and the amount of the translation adjustment attributable to each subsidiary at the time of sale follow:

	% Sold	Translation Adjustment
Sub A	100%	$90,000 credit
Sub B	50%	40,000 debit
Sub C	10%	25,000 debit

What total amount of the translation adjustment should be reported as part of the gain on sale of the three subsidiaries?

A. $90,000 credit.

B. $70,000 net credit.

C. $67,500 net credit.

D. $0

Answer (C) is correct. *(Publisher)*

REQUIRED: The total translation adjustment included in the gain on the sale of subsidiaries.

DISCUSSION: FASB Interpretation No. 37, *Accounting for Translation Adjustments upon Sale of Part of an Investment in a Foreign Entity*, clarifies SFAS 52. A pro rata portion of the accumulated translation adjustment attributable to an investment shall be recognized in measuring the gain or loss on the sale of all or part of a company's interest in a foreign entity. Here, the total amount to be reported is a $67,500 net credit [(100% × $90,000) – (50% × $40,000) – (10% × $25,000)].

Answer (A) is incorrect because a $90,000 credit fails to consider Subs B and C. Answer (B) is incorrect because a $70,000 net credit fails to consider Sub C. Answer (D) is incorrect because a translation adjustment is recognized as part of the gain on the sale of the subsidiaries.

27.2 Foreign Currency Transactions

22. On October 1, 2003, Velec Co., a U.S. company, contracted to purchase foreign goods requiring payment in local currency units (LCUs) 1 month after the receipt of the goods at Velec's factory. Title to the goods passed on December 15, 2003. The goods were still in transit on December 31, 2003. Exchange rates were one dollar to 22 LCUs, 20 LCUs, and 21 LCUs on October 1, December 15, and December 31, 2003, respectively. Velec should account for the exchange rate fluctuation in 2003 as

A. A loss included in net income before extraordinary items.

B. A gain included in net income before extraordinary items.

C. An extraordinary gain.

D. An extraordinary loss.

Answer (B) is correct. *(CPA, adapted)*

REQUIRED: The classification of a gain or loss due to exchange rate fluctuations.

DISCUSSION: SFAS 52 requires that a receivable or payable denominated in a foreign currency be adjusted to its current exchange rate at each balance sheet date. "Denominated in a foreign currency" means that the contract is settled in that currency. The transaction gain or loss arising from this adjustment should ordinarily be reflected in current income. Because title passed on December 15, the liability fixed in LCUs should have been recorded on that date at the 20-LCU exchange rate. The increase to 21 LCUs per dollar at year-end decreases the dollar value of the liability and results in a foreign currency transaction gain. Such a gain is ordinarily treated as a component of income from continuing operations.

Answer (A) is incorrect because the strengthening of the dollar resulted in a gain. Answer (C) is incorrect because an extraordinary item is infrequent and unusual in nature. Exchange rates change frequently. Answer (D) is incorrect because an extraordinary item is infrequent and unusual in nature. Exchange rates change frequently.

23. On October 1, 2003, Mild Co., a U.S. company, purchased machinery from Grund, a German company, with payment due on April 1, 2004. If Mild's 2003 operating income included no foreign currency transaction gain or loss, the transaction could have

A. Resulted in an extraordinary gain.

B. Been denominated in U.S. dollars.

C. Caused a foreign currency transaction gain to be reported as a contra account against machinery.

D. Caused a foreign currency translation gain to be reported in OCI.

Answer (B) is correct. *(CPA, adapted)*

REQUIRED: The reason no foreign currency transaction gain or loss occurred when a U.S. company purchased machinery from a German company.

DISCUSSION: A foreign currency transaction gives rise to a receivable or a payable, fixed in terms of the amount of foreign currency. A change in the exchange rate between the functional currency and the currency in which the transaction is denominated is a gain or loss that ordinarily should be included as a component of income from continuing operations in the period in which the exchange rate changes. If Mild Co.'s functional currency is the U.S. dollar and the transaction was denominated in U.S. dollars, the transaction is a foreign transaction, not a foreign currency transaction. Thus, no foreign currency transaction gain or loss occurred.

Answer (A) is incorrect because foreign currency transaction gains and losses are ordinarily treated as operating items. Answer (C) is incorrect because foreign currency transaction gains and losses are included in the determination of net income. Answer (D) is incorrect because foreign currency translation gains and losses result from translating functional currency amounts into the reporting currency. If the transaction was denominated in U.S. dollars, no translation was needed.

24. SFAS 52 states that transaction gains and losses have direct cash flow effects when foreign-denominated monetary assets are settled in amounts greater or less than the functional currency equivalent of the original transactions. These transaction gains and losses should be reflected in income

A. At the date the transaction originated.

B. On a retroactive basis.

C. In the period the exchange rate changes.

D. Only at the year-end balance sheet date.

Answer (C) is correct. *(CMA, adapted)*

REQUIRED: The time when foreign currency transaction gains and losses should be reflected in income.

DISCUSSION: When a foreign currency transaction gives rise to a receivable or a payable that is fixed in terms of the amount of foreign currency to be received or paid, a change in the exchange rate between the functional currency and the currency in which the transaction is denominated results in a gain or loss that ordinarily should be included as a component of income from continuing operations in the period in which the exchange rate changes.

Answer (A) is incorrect because the extent of any gain or loss cannot be known at the date of the original transaction. Answer (B) is incorrect because retroactive recognition is not permitted. Answer (D) is incorrect because gains and losses are to be recognized in the period of the rate change.

25. Shore Co. records its transactions in U.S. dollars. A sale of goods resulted in a receivable denominated in Japanese yen, and a purchase of goods resulted in a payable denominated in euros. Shore recorded a foreign currency transaction gain on collection of the receivable and a transaction loss on settlement of the payable. The exchange rates are expressed as so many units of foreign currency to one dollar. Did the number of foreign currency units exchangeable for a dollar increase or decrease between the contract and settlement dates?

	Yen Exchangeable for $1	Euros Exchangeable for $1
A.	Increase	Increase
B.	Decrease	Decrease
C.	Decrease	Increase
D.	Increase	Decrease

Answer (B) is correct. *(CPA, adapted)*

REQUIRED: The movements in exchange rates.

DISCUSSION: A gain on a receivable denominated in a foreign currency results when the fixed amount of the foreign currency can be exchanged for a greater number of dollars at the date of collection, that is, when the number of foreign currency units exchangeable for a dollar decreases. A loss on a payable denominated in a foreign currency results when the number of dollars needed to purchase the fixed amount of the foreign currency increases, that is, when the number of foreign currency units exchangeable for a dollar decreases.

26. Ball Corp. had the following foreign currency transactions during 2003:

- Merchandise was purchased from a foreign supplier on January 20, 2003 for the U.S. dollar equivalent of $90,000. The invoice was paid on March 20, 2003 at the U.S. dollar equivalent of $96,000.
- On July 1, 2003, Ball borrowed the U.S. dollar equivalent of $500,000 evidenced by a note that was payable in the lender's local currency on July 1, 2005. On December 31, 2003, the U.S. dollar equivalents of the principal amount and accrued interest were $520,000 and $26,000, respectively. Interest on the note is 10% per annum.

In Ball's 2003 income statement, what amount should be included as foreign currency transaction loss?

A. $0

B. $6,000

C. $21,000

D. $27,000

Answer (D) is correct. *(CPA, adapted)*

REQUIRED: The amount to be included as foreign currency transaction loss.

DISCUSSION: When a foreign currency transaction gives rise to a receivable or a payable that is fixed in terms of the foreign currency, a change in the exchange rate between the functional currency and the currency in which the transaction is denominated is a gain or loss that ordinarily should be included as a component of income from continuing operations in the period in which the exchange rate changes. In the 2003 income statement, the foreign currency transaction loss should include the $6,000 difference between the $90,000 initially recorded as a payable and the $96,000 payment amount, the $20,000 difference between the $500,000 equivalent amount of the principal of the note on December 31 and its $520,000 equivalent on July 1, and the $1,000 difference between the $26,000 equivalent of the interest accrued and the $25,000 ($500,000 × 10% × 6 ÷ 12) interest on the initially recorded amount of the loan. The foreign currency transaction loss therefore equals $27,000 ($6,000 + $20,000 + $1,000).

Answer (A) is incorrect because the loss must be recognized. Answer (B) is incorrect because the differences in principal and interest on the $500,000 note are excluded. Answer (C) is incorrect because $21,000 excludes the $6,000 difference in the recording and payment for the foreign purchase.

27. On September 1, 2002, Cano & Co., a U.S. corporation, sold merchandise to a foreign firm for 250,000 local currency units (LCUs). Terms of the sale require payment in LCUs on February 1, 2003. On September 1, 2002, the spot exchange rate was $0.20 per LCU. On December 31, 2002, Cano's year-end, the spot rate was $0.19, but the rate increased to $0.22 by February 1, 2003, when payment was received. How much should Cano report as foreign currency transaction gain or loss in its 2003 income statement?

A. $0

B. $2,500 loss.

C. $5,000 gain.

D. $7,500 gain.

Answer (D) is correct. *(CPA, adapted)*

REQUIRED: The foreign currency transaction gain or loss in the 2003 income statement.

DISCUSSION: A receivable or payable denominated in a foreign currency should be recorded at the current exchange rate and then adjusted to the current exchange rate at each balance sheet date. That adjustment is a foreign currency transaction gain or loss that is ordinarily included in the determination of net income for the period of change. Furthermore, a gain or loss measured from the transaction date or the most recent intervening balance sheet date is recognized when the transaction is settled. Accordingly, Cano should recognize a foreign currency transaction gain of $7,500 [($0.22 – $0.19) × 250,000 LCUs receivable] in 2003.

Answer (A) is incorrect because the exchange rate changed between the balance sheet date and the settlement date. Answer (B) is incorrect because a $2,500 loss was incurred in 2002. Answer (C) is incorrect because $5,000 is the net transaction gain.

28. On November 2, 2002, Platt Co. entered into a 90-day futures contract to purchase 50,000 Swiss francs when the contract quote was $.70. The purchase was for speculation in price movement. The following exchange rates existed during the contract period:

	30-day Futures	Spot Rate
November 2, 2002	$.62	$.63
December 31, 2002	.65	.64
January 30, 2003	.65	.68

What amount should Platt report as foreign currency transaction loss in its income statement for the year ended December 31, 2002?

A. $2,500

B. $3,000

C. $3,500

D. $4,000

Answer (A) is correct. *(CPA, adapted)*

REQUIRED: The foreign currency transaction loss that should be reported on the income statement.

DISCUSSION: Under SFAS 52, foreign currency transaction gains and losses from fluctuations in the exchange rate are ordinarily reflected in income when the rates change. The foreign currency transaction loss is the difference between the contract price on the date the transaction originates and the futures rate at the balance sheet date. Hence, the foreign currency transaction loss for Platt Co. is $2,500 [($.70 – $.65) × 50,000 Swiss francs].

Answer (B) is incorrect because $3,000 is the result of using the spot rate on 12/31/02. Answer (C) is incorrect because $3,500 results from using the spot rate on 11/02/02. Answer (D) is incorrect because $4,000 is the result of using the 30-day rate on 11/02/02.

29. Fay Corp. had a realized foreign currency transaction loss of $15,000 for the year ended December 31, 2003 and must also determine whether the following items will require year-end adjustment:

- Fay had an $8,000 loss resulting from the translation of the accounts of its wholly owned foreign subsidiary for the year ended December 31, 2003.
- Fay had an account payable to an unrelated foreign supplier payable in the supplier's local currency. The U.S. dollar equivalent of the payable was $64,000 on the October 31, 2003 invoice date and $60,000 on December 31, 2003. The invoice is payable on January 30, 2004.

In Fay's 2003 consolidated income statement, what amount should be included as foreign currency transaction loss?

A. $11,000

B. $15,000

C. $19,000

D. $23,000

Answer (A) is correct. *(CPA, adapted)*

REQUIRED: The amount to be included as foreign currency transaction loss.

DISCUSSION: SFAS 52 requires that translation adjustments (gains and losses) be reported in OCI. Translation adjustments are therefore not included in the determination of income. SFAS 52 further requires that a receivable or payable denominated in a foreign currency be recorded at the date of the transaction at the current rate of exchange. This receivable or payable must then be adjusted to its current value at each balance sheet date. The gain or loss from this adjustment is included in the determination of net income. Accordingly, the $4,000 ($64,000 – $60,000) gain adjustment arising from the foreign currency transaction should be included along with the realized foreign currency transaction loss of $15,000 in the 2003 consolidated income statement. The amount to be reported is an $11,000 ($15,000 loss – $4,000 gain) foreign currency transaction loss.

Answer (B) is incorrect because $15,000 excludes the $4,000 gain. Answer (C) is incorrect because the gain was added to, rather than subtracted from, the loss. Answer (D) is incorrect because the translation loss is added to the loss, and the transaction gain is not included.

27.3 Foreign Currency Hedges

30. According to SFAS 133, *Accounting for Derivative Instruments and Hedging Activities*, as amended by SFAS 138, *Accounting for Certain Derivative Instruments and Certain Hedging Activities*, the effective portion of a loss associated with a change in fair value of a derivative instrument must be reported as a component of other comprehensive income (OCI) only if the derivative is appropriately designated as a

A. Cash flow hedge of the foreign currency exposure of a forecasted transaction.

B. Fair value hedge of the foreign currency exposure of an unrecognized firm commitment.

C. Fair value hedge of the foreign currency exposure of a recognized asset or liability for which a foreign currency transaction gain or loss is recognized in earnings.

D. Speculation in a foreign currency.

Answer (A) is correct. *(Publisher)*

REQUIRED: The designation of a derivative when the effective portion of a loss from its change in fair value is reported in OCI.

DISCUSSION: The hedge of the foreign currency exposure of a forecasted transaction is designated as a cash flow hedge. The effective portion of gains and losses associated with changes in fair value of a derivative instrument designated and qualifying as a cash flow hedge is reported in OCI.

Answer (B) is incorrect because a hedge of the foreign currency exposure of either an unrecognized firm commitment or a recognized asset or liability for which a foreign currency transaction gain or loss is recognized in earnings may be a fair value hedge or a cash flow hedge. The effective portion of gains and losses arising from changes in fair value of a derivative classified as a fair value hedge is included in earnings of the period of change. It is offset by losses and gains on the hedged item that are attributable to the risk being hedged. Answer (C) is incorrect because a hedge of the foreign currency exposure of either an unrecognized firm commitment or a recognized asset or liability for which a foreign currency transaction gain or loss is recognized in earnings may be a fair value hedge or a cash flow hedge. The effective portion of gains and losses arising from changes in fair value of a derivative classified as a fair value hedge is included in earnings of the period of change. It is offset by losses and gains on the hedged item that are attributable to the risk being hedged. Answer (D) is incorrect because gains and losses associated with changes in fair value of a derivative used as a speculation in a foreign currency are included in earnings of the period of change.

31. The effective portion of a gain arising from an increase in the fair value of a derivative is included in earnings in the period of change if the derivative is appropriately designated and qualifies as a hedge of

A. A foreign currency exposure of a net investment in a foreign operation.

B. A foreign currency exposure of a forecasted transaction.

C. A foreign currency exposure of an available-for-sale security.

D. The variable cash flows of a forecasted transaction.

Answer (C) is correct. *(Publisher)*

REQUIRED: The item hedged if the effective portion of a gain from a change in the hedging derivative's fair value is included in earnings when the change in fair value occurs.

DISCUSSION: A fair value hedge includes a hedge of an exposure to changes in the fair value of a recognized asset or liability or an unrecognized firm commitment. Such a hedge minimizes the risk associated with fixed cash flows. A foreign currency fair value hedge includes a hedge of a foreign currency exposure of an unrecognized firm commitment. It also includes a hedge of a foreign currency exposure of a recognized asset or liability (including an available-for-sale security) for which a foreign currency transaction gain or loss is recognized in earnings under SFAS 52. Gains and losses arising from changes in fair value of a derivative classified as either a fair value or a foreign fair value hedge are included in earnings in the period of change. They are offset by losses or gains on the hedged item attributable to the risk being hedged. Thus, earnings of the period of change are affected only by the net gain or loss attributable to the ineffective aspect of the hedge.

Answer (A) is incorrect because the effective portion of gains and losses on this hedge is reported in the same manner as translation adjustments, that is, in OCI. Answer (B) is incorrect because the effective portion of gains and losses on this hedge is included in OCI until periods in which the forecasted transaction affects earnings. Answer (D) is incorrect because the effective portion of gains and losses on this hedge is included in OCI until periods in which the forecasted transaction affects earnings.

Questions 32 through 34 are based on the following information.

On November 15, 2002, Hector Corp., a calendar-year-end U.S. company, signed a legally binding contract to purchase equipment from Diego Corp., a foreign company. The negotiated price is FC1,000,000. The scheduled delivery date is February 15, 2003. Terms require payment by Hector Corp. upon delivery. The terms also impose a 10% penalty on Diego Corp. if the equipment is not delivered by February 15, 2003.

To hedge its agreement to pay FC1,000,000, Hector entered into a foreign currency forward contract on November 15, 2002 to receive FC1,000,000 on February 15, 2003 at an exchange rate of FC1.00 = U.S.$0.36. Additional exchange rate information:

Date	Spot Rates	Forward Rates for February 15, 2003
11/15/02	1 FC = $0.35 U.S.	1 FC = $0.36 U.S.
12/31/02	1 FC = $0.36 U.S.	1 FC = $0.38 U.S.
02/15/03	1 FC = $0.39 U.S.	1 FC = $0.39 U.S.

Quotes obtained from dealers indicate the following incremental changes in the fair values of the forward contract based on the changes in forward rates discounted on a net-present-value basis:

Date	Gain/(Loss)
11/15/02	$0
12/31/02	$19,600
02/15/03	$10,400

Hector formally documented its objective and strategy for entering into this hedge. Hector also decided to assess hedge effectiveness based on an assessment of the difference between changes in value of the forward contract and the U.S.-dollar equivalent of the purchase agreement with Diego. Because both changes are based on changes in forward rates, Hector further determined that the hedge is 100% effective.

32. The contract signed by Hector Corp. to purchase the equipment from Diego Corp. meets the definition of a

	Firm Commitment	Forecasted Transaction
A.	Yes	Yes
B.	No	No
C.	Yes	No
D.	No	Yes

Answer (C) is correct. *(Publisher)*

REQUIRED: The type of contract described.

DISCUSSION: SFAS 133 defines a firm commitment as an agreement between unrelated parties, binding on both and usually legally enforceable, that specifies all significant terms and includes a disincentive for nonperformance. SFAS 133 defines a forecasted transaction as a transaction that is expected to occur for which there is no firm commitment.

33. What are the amounts reported for the forward contract receivable and the liability for the purchase from Diego at December 31, 2002 and February 15, 2003 (prior to the settlement of the contract)?

	12/31/02	02/15/03
A.	$10,000	$40,000
B.	$19,600	$30,000
C.	$19,600	$10,400
D.	$20,000	$30,000

Answer (B) is correct. *(Publisher)*

REQUIRED: The amounts to be recorded for a forward contract receivable and the hedged item at 12/31/02 and 02/15/03 (prior to the settlement of the contract).

DISCUSSION: This hedge is a foreign currency fair value hedge because it hedges a foreign currency exposure of an unrecognized firm commitment whose cash flows are fixed. Thus, unlike a foreign currency cash flow hedge, it does not hedge the foreign currency exposure to variability in the functional-currency-equivalent cash flows associated with an unrecognized firm commitment. SFAS 133 requires recognition of the forward contract receivable as an asset at fair value, with the changes in fair value recognized in earnings. SFAS 133 further requires recognition of the changes in the fair value of the firm commitment that are attributable to the changes in exchange rates. These changes in fair value are recognized in earnings and as entries to a liability. Fair values should reflect changes in the forward exchange rates on a net-present-value basis. Thus, the forward contract receivable should be debited and a gain credited for $19,600 at 12/31/02. A loss should be debited and a firm commitment liability should be credited in the same amount at the same date. Under current GAAP, no asset or liability is recognized for a firm commitment when the contract is signed. At 2/15/03, a further $10,400 forward contract gain and firm commitment loss should be recorded. Because the changes in value of both the forward contract and the U.S. dollar equivalent of the firm commitment are based on changes in forward rates, the hedge is completely effective; the changes in fair values ($19,600 and $10,400) of the forward contract receivable (gains) and the firm commitment (losses) offset each other in the income statement.

Answer (A) is incorrect because the balance sheet amounts should be based on the discounted changes in forward rates, not the undiscounted changes in spot rates. Answer (C) is incorrect because $19,600 and $10,400 are the respective income statement effects. Answer (D) is incorrect because $20,000 is the undiscounted change in the forward rates at 12/31/02.

34. As a result of this hedging transaction, at what amount should Hector recognize the equipment on February 15, 2003?

A. $350,000

B. $360,000

C. $390,000

D. $420,000

Answer (B) is correct. *(Publisher)*

REQUIRED: The amount at which the equipment should be recognized as a result of the hedging transaction.

DISCUSSION: The equipment should be recorded at $360,000. This amount equals $390,000 (FC1,000,000 × $0.39 spot rate at 2/15/03) minus the $30,000 balance in the firm commitment liability account. The entry is to debit equipment for $360,000, debit the firm commitment liability for $30,000, and credit a payable for $390,000. On the same date, Hector will debit the payable for $390,000, credit the forward contract receivable for $30,000, and credit cash for $360,000. The latter entry reflects settlement of the payable and of the forward contract.

Answer (A) is incorrect because $350,000 is the amount that would have been recognized if the equipment had been delivered on 11/15/02. Answer (C) is incorrect because $390,000 is the amount that would have been recognized if the firm commitment had not been hedged. Answer (D) is incorrect because $420,000 equals $390,000 plus the $30,000 balance in the firm commitment liability account.

35. On October 1, 2003, Weeks Co., a calendar-year-end U.S. company, forecasts that, near the end of March 2004, Sullivan Corp., a foreign entity, will purchase 50,000 gallons of Weeks's primary product for FC500,000. Sullivan has not firmly committed to the purchase. However, based on Sullivan's purchasing pattern, Weeks believes that the sale is probable. Weeks's risk-management policy includes avoiding foreign currency exposure through the use of foreign currency forward contracts. Thus, on October 1, 2003, Weeks enters into a 6-month foreign currency forward contract to sell FC500,000 to a dealer on March 31, 2004. Weeks designates the contract as a hedge and determines that hedge effectiveness will be based on changes in forward rates. The following information is available:

	Value of FC500,000 Based on Spot Rates	Value of FC500,000 Based on Forward Rates for 03/31/04	Incremental Discounted Changes in Value of Forward Contract Based on Changes in Forward Rates
10/02/03	$570,000	$500,000	$ 0
12/31/03	$540,000	$490,000	$ 9,800
03/31/04	$475,000	$475,000	$15,200

At what amounts should Weeks record the forward contract on December 31, 2003 and March 31, 2004?

	12/31/03	03/31/04
A.	$9,800	$25,000
B.	$10,000	$25,000
C.	$540,000	$475,000
D.	$490,000	$475,000

Answer (A) is correct. *(Publisher)*

REQUIRED: The amounts at which the forward contract should be recognized.

DISCUSSION: Weeks should record the forward contract as a receivable at fair value. Fair value is based on changes in forward rates discounted on a net present value basis. Thus, the receivable should be recorded at $9,800 on December 31, 2003 and $25,000 ($9,800 + $15,200) on March 31, 2004. Because a hedge of the foreign currency exposure of a forecasted transaction is a cash flow hedge, Weeks should also credit these amounts to OCI. On March 31, the sale should be recorded at $500,000 ($475,000 value based on the spot rate at March 31 + $25,000 balance in OCI). The amount of cash received also is equal to $500,000 ($475,000 + $25,000 balance in the forward contract receivable).

Answer (B) is incorrect because the change in forward rates should be adjusted for the time value of money. Answer (C) is incorrect because $540,000 and $475,000 reflect the value of FC500,000 at spot rates. Answer (D) is incorrect because $490,000 and $475,000 reflect the value of FC500,000 at forward rates.

STUDY UNIT TWENTY-EIGHT
ACCOUNTING FOR STATE AND LOCAL GOVERNMENT ENTITIES

The **Governmental Accounting Standards Board (GASB)** is the authoritative body for determining the accounting and reporting requirements for state and local governments (SLGs). **SGAS 34**, *Basic Financial Statements - and Management's Discussion and Analysis - for State and Local Governments*, is the primary GASB pronouncement concerning financial reporting requirements. **SGAS 35**, *Basic Financial Statements - and Management's Discussion and Analysis - for Public Colleges and Universities*, applies SGAS 34 to governmental institutions of higher learning. SGAS 35 allows such institutions to follow the guidance of SGAS 34 with respect to **special-purpose governments**.

The accounting and reporting requirements of an SLG require an accounting system that makes it possible to (1) present fairly and with full disclosure the funds and activities of the SLG in conformity with GAAP and (2) determine and demonstrate compliance with finance-related legal and contractual provisions. To satisfy these objectives, SLG accounting systems should be organized on a fund basis. A **fund** is "a fiscal and accounting entity with a self-balancing set of accounts recording cash and other financial resources, together with all related liabilities and residual equities or balances, and changes therein, which are segregated for the purpose of carrying on specific activities or attaining certain objectives in accordance with special regulations, restrictions, or limitations" (SGAS 1). SLGs should prepare an annual (or, in some states, biennial) comprehensive budget covering all fund categories. SLG accounting uses three categories of funds: governmental, proprietary, and fiduciary.

SLGs use **governmental funds** to account for most functions that are uniquely governmental. Governmental funds always include one general fund. They also may include special revenue, capital projects, debt service, and permanent funds. The **general fund** is used to account for all financial resources except those accounted for in other funds. **Special revenue funds** are used to account for the proceeds of special revenue sources (other than those accounted for in certain trust funds or in capital projects funds) that are legally restricted to expenditure for specified purposes. **Capital projects funds** are used to account for financial resources to be used for the acquisition or construction of major capital projects (other than those financed by proprietary and certain trust funds). **Debt service funds** are used to account for the accumulation of resources for, and the payment of, general long-term debt principal and interest. **Permanent funds** account for resources legally restricted so that earnings only, not principal, maybe expended for the benefit of the government or its citizens. SLGs should establish and maintain the minimum number of funds consistent with their legal and operating requirements.

Governmental funds are accounting segregations of financial resources. Each fund consists of expendable assets assigned based on the fund's purpose, current liabilities to be paid from these assets, and a fund balance. Governmental funds often integrate **budgetary accounts** (e.g., estimated revenue, appropriation, and encumbrance accounts) into the formal accounting systems of general funds, special revenue funds, and other annually budgeted governmental funds that have numerous types of revenues, expenditures, and transfers. Governmental funds have a **current financial**

resources measurement focus and are accounted for in accordance with the **modified accrual basis**. This basis requires **revenues** (inflows of resources other than by transfer) to be recognized when they become available and measurable and **expenditures** (uses of financial resources other than by transfer) to be recognized when related liabilities are incurred. The exception is unmatured interest on long-term debt, which is recognized when due.

SLGs use **proprietary funds** to account for governmental activities similar to those of business entities. Proprietary funds focus on operating income, net assets (or cost recovery), financial position, and cash flows. Proprietary funds include enterprise and internal service funds. **Enterprise funds** may be used to account for any activity for which external users are charged a fee for goods and services. **Internal service funds** are used to account for goods and services provided to the reporting government's funds, departments, or agencies; to component units of the reporting government; or to other governments. Activities of proprietary funds are reported using an **economic resources measurement focus** and the **accrual basis** of accounting.

SLGs use **fiduciary funds** to account for assets held in a trustee or agency relationship for individuals, private organizations, or other governments. Fiduciary funds include **pension (and other employee benefit) trust funds, investment trust funds, private-purpose trust funds, and agency funds**. The focus of fiduciary funds is on net assets and changes in net assets. Activities of fiduciary funds generally are reported using an **economic resources measurement focus** and the **accrual basis** of accounting.

SLGs are required to prepare and publish a **comprehensive annual financial report (CAFR)**. The CAFR should cover all activities of (1) the primary government, (2) organizations for which the primary government is financially accountable, and (3) other organizations, the exclusion of which would cause the financial statements to be misleading or incomplete. As a minimum, the CAFR should include (1) an introductory section, (2) management's discussion and analysis (MD&A), (3) the basic financial statements, (4) required supplementary information in addition to the MD&A, (5) combining and individual fund statements, (6) schedules, (7) narrative explanations, and (8) a statistical section.

MD&A should precede the basic financial statements. It should contain an objective and easily readable analysis of the government's financial activities based on currently known facts, decisions, and conditions. It should focus on the current year while providing comparisons of the current year with prior years.

The **basic financial statements** include (1) government-wide financial statements, (2) fund financial statements, and (3) notes to the financial statements. **Government-wide financial statements** report information about the overall government other than fiduciary activities. They should include a **statement of net assets** and a **statement of activities**. Net assets are displayed in three components: invested in capital assets, net of related debt; restricted net assets; and unrestricted net assets. Capital assets to be reported include **infrastructure assets**. These statements should display information about the reporting government as a whole. Separate rows and columns should be used to distinguish between **governmental and business-type activities** of the primary government and between the primary government and its discretely presented component units. Government-wide financial statements should reflect the **economic resources measurement focus** and the **accrual basis of accounting**.

Fund financial statements should be used to report additional and detailed information about the primary government. They must be reconciled to the government-wide statements. The focus of governmental and enterprise fund financial statements is on **major funds**. Major funds always include the general fund. They also include any governmental or enterprise fund with total assets, liabilities, revenues, or expenditures/expenses that are (1) at least 10% of the corresponding element total for all funds of that category or type (i.e., total governmental or total enterprise funds) and (2) at least 5% of the corresponding element total for all governmental and enterprise funds combined. Separate columns should be used to present financial information for each major fund and for nonmajor funds in the aggregate. SLGs should present a **summary reconciliation** to the government-wide financial statements at either the bottom of the fund financial statements or in an accompanying schedule. **Required financial statements** for **governmental funds** are (1) a balance sheet and (2) a statement of revenues, expenditures, and changes in fund balances. Required financial statements for **proprietary funds** are (1) a balance sheet or statement of net assets; (2) a statement of revenues, expenses, and changes in fund equity or net assets; and (3) a statement of cash flows. Required financial statements for **fiduciary fund**s are (1) a statement of fiduciary net assets and (2) a statement of changes in fiduciary net assets. Fiduciary fund financial statements should provide a separate column for each fund type.

Notes communicate information not displayed on the face of the financial statements that is essential to fair presentation. **Required supplementary information** in addition to MD&A should include a budgetary comparison schedule for the general fund and for each special revenue fund that has a legally adopted annual budget. This comparison should include the original budget; the final appropriated budget; and the actual inflows, outflows, and balances stated on the SLG's budgetary basis.

Under **SGAS 33**, *Accounting and Financial Reporting for Nonexchange Transactions*, **derived tax revenues** are assessments on exchange transactions (e.g., income taxes or sales taxes). **Imposed nonexchange revenues** are assessments on nongovernmental entities other than assessments on exchange transactions (e.g., property taxes and fines). **Government-mandated nonexchange transactions** occur when one government provides resources to a government at another level and requires that they be used for a specific purpose (e.g., federal programs that state or local governments must implement). **Voluntary nonexchange transactions** arise from legislative or contractual agreements, other than exchanges, entered into willingly by the parties (e.g., certain grants and private donations). The timing of recognition of **assets**, **liabilities**, and **expenses or expenditures** arising from nonexchange transactions is not affected by the basis of accounting. **Revenue recognition** on the modified accrual basis, however, requires that the accrual-basis criteria be met and that the revenues be **available**. For **derived tax revenues**, assets are recognized when the underlying exchange transaction occurs or resources are received, whichever is earlier. Revenues are recognized when the underlying exchange transaction occurs. For **imposed nonexchange revenues**, assets are recognized when an enforceable legal claim to the resources has arisen or resources are received, whichever is earlier. Revenues are recognized when the resources are required to be used or when their use is first allowed by the time requirements. For property taxes, revenue recognition is in the period for which they are levied, regardless of when the due date occurs or the enforceable legal claim arises. For **government-mandated and voluntary nonexchange transactions**, assets are recognized by recipients and liabilities by providers when all eligibility requirements are met or resources are received, whichever is earlier. Revenues are recognized by recipients and expenses or expenditures by providers when all eligibility requirements are met. **SGAS 33** requires a provider of shared nonexchange revenues (originally derived tax revenues or imposed nonexchange revenues) to account for the sharing as a government-mandated or voluntary nonexchange transaction. **SGAS 36**, *Recipient Reporting for Certain Shared Nonexchange Revenues*, amends SGAS 33 to require the recipient to account for the sharing in the same way. The recipient may use any reasonable estimate of the amount to be accrued if provider notice is not timely.

QUESTIONS

28.1 General

1. What body primarily determines the measurement focus and basis of accounting standards for governmental financial statements?

A. Governmental Accounting Standards Board.

B. National Council on Governmental Accounting.

C. Governmental Accounting and Auditing Committee of the AICPA.

D. Financial Accounting Standards Board.

Answer (A) is correct. *(CPA, adapted)*

REQUIRED: The authoritative body that issues pronouncements on GAAP for state and local governments.

DISCUSSION: The GASB is currently the primary standard-setting body for state and local governments.

Answer (B) is incorrect because the NCGA was a predecessor of the GASB. Answer (C) is incorrect because the GAAC is not currently an active and functioning committee of the AICPA. Answer (D) is incorrect because the FASB is the primary authoritative standard-setting board for private sector accounting.

2. Governmental financial reporting should provide information to assist users in which situation(s)?

I. Making social and political decisions

II. Assessing whether current-year citizens received services but shifted part of the payment burden to future-year citizens

A. I only.

B. II only.

C. Both I and II.

D. Neither I nor II.

Answer (C) is correct. *(CPA, adapted)*

REQUIRED: The use(s) of governmental reporting.

DISCUSSION: GASB Concepts Statement 1 states, "Financial reporting by state and local governments is used in making economic, social, and political decisions and in assessing accountability." It also states that "interperiod equity is a significant part of accountability and is fundamental to public administration." Thus, "financial reporting should help users assess whether current-year revenues are sufficient to pay for the services provided that year and whether future taxpayers will be required to assume burdens for services previously provided."

3. Thornton County is required under state law to report its financial statements on a basis that conflicts with generally accepted governmental accounting principles. On which basis of accounting should Thornton County's financial statements be prepared?

A. Generally accepted governmental accounting basis only.

B. State law basis only.

C. State law basis with supplemental disclosure of generally accepted governmental accounting reconciliation schedules.

D. Generally accepted governmental accounting basis with supplemental supporting schedules as necessary to comply with state law.

Answer (D) is correct. *(J.P. Trebby)*

REQUIRED: The proper presentation of county financial statements when state law conflicts with GAAP.

DISCUSSION: Certain state laws and regulatory requirements conflict with generally accepted accounting and financial reporting practices. When such a conflict exists, the governmental entity should prepare basic financial statements conforming with GAAP and also present supporting schedules and narrative explanations in the CAFR as necessary to clearly report upon compliance with legal responsibilities.

Answer (A) is incorrect because the financial statements should include supplemental supporting schedules to comply with state law. Answer (B) is incorrect because the financial statements should be prepared in accordance with GAAP. Answer (C) is incorrect because the financial statements should be prepared in accordance with GAAP.

4. The accounting systems of state and local governmental entities (SLGs) should be organized and operated on which of the following bases?

A. Proprietary fund.

B. Fiduciary fund.

C. Governmental fund.

D. Fund.

Answer (D) is correct. *(Publisher)*

REQUIRED: The basis on which governmental accounting systems of SLGs should be organized and operated.

DISCUSSION: The accounting and reporting requirements of SLGs require an accounting system that makes it possible to (1) present fairly and with full disclosure the funds and activities of SLGs in conformity with GAAP and (2) determine and demonstrate compliance with finance-related legal and contractual provisions. To satisfy these objectives, SLG accounting systems should be organized on a fund basis. A fund is defined as "a fiscal and accounting entity with a self-balancing set of accounts recording cash and other financial resources, together with all related liabilities and residual equities or balances, and changes therein, which are segregated for the purpose of carrying on specific activities or attaining certain objectives in accordance with special regulations, restrictions, or limitations" (SGAS 1). The three categories of funds used by SLGs are governmental, proprietary, and fiduciary.

28.2 Funds

5. A local governmental unit may use which of the following types of funds?

	Fiduciary	Proprietary
A.	Yes	No
B.	Yes	Yes
C.	No	Yes
D.	No	No

Answer (B) is correct. *(CPA, adapted)*

REQUIRED: The types of funds that may be used by a local governmental unit.

DISCUSSION: Three broad categories of funds may be used by a state or local governmental unit for general purpose financial statements.

1) Governmental - general, special revenue, debt service, capital projects, and permanent funds
2) Proprietary - internal service and enterprise funds
3) Fiduciary - trust and agency funds

6. Park City uses encumbrance accounting and formally integrates its budget into the general fund's accounting records.

For the year ending July 31, the following budget was adopted:

Estimated revenues	$30,000,000
Appropriations	27,000,000
Estimated transfer to debt service fund	900,000

When Park's budget is adopted and recorded, Park's budgetary fund balance should have a

A. $3,000,000 credit balance.

B. $3,000,000 debit balance.

C. $2,100,000 credit balance.

D. $2,100,000 debit balance.

Answer (C) is correct. *(CPA, adapted)*

REQUIRED: The budgetary fund balance when a budget is adopted and recorded.

DISCUSSION: The initial entry to record the budget consists of a $30,000,000 debit to estimated revenues, a $27,000,000 credit to appropriations, and a $900,000 credit to estimated transfer to debt service fund; the $2,100,000 residual is credited to budgetary fund balance. Some accountants prefer to use budgetary fund balance in the budgetary entry rather than unreserved fund balances. The former is a budgetary account that is eliminated at the end of the period, and the latter is a balance sheet account.

Answer (A) is incorrect because the $900,000 estimated transfer to debt service fund must be credited. Answer (B) is incorrect because the estimated revenues should be debited. Answer (D) is incorrect because the estimated revenues should be debited.

7. For the budgetary year ending December 31, Maple City's general fund expects the following inflows of resources:

Property taxes, licenses, and fines	$9,000,000
Proceeds of debt issue	5,000,000
Interfund transfers for debt service	1,000,000

In the budgetary entry, what amount should Maple record for estimated revenues?

A. $9,000,000

B. $10,000,000

C. $14,000,000

D. $15,000,000

Answer (A) is correct. *(CPA, adapted)*

REQUIRED: The amount to be recorded as estimated revenues.

DISCUSSION: Revenues are recognized in governmental funds when they are measurable and available. They are increases in (sources of) fund financial resources other than from interfund transfers, debt issue proceeds, and redemptions of demand bonds. The major source classifications are taxes, licenses and permits, intergovernmental revenues, charges for services, fines and forfeits, and miscellaneous revenues. Hence, Maple's revenues include taxes, licenses, and fines equal to $9 million.

Answer (B) is incorrect because $10,000,000 incorrectly includes the interfund transfers. Answer (C) is incorrect because $14,000,000 incorrectly includes the debt issue proceeds. Answer (D) is incorrect because $15,000,000 incorrectly includes the debt issue proceeds and interfund transfers.

8. In the current year, New City issued purchase orders and contracts of $850,000 that were chargeable against the current year's budgeted appropriations of $1,000,000. The journal entry to record the issuance of the purchase orders and contracts should include a

A. Credit to vouchers payable of $1,000,000.

B. Credit to reserve for encumbrances of $850,000.

C. Debit to expenditures of $1,000,000.

D. Debit to appropriations of $850,000.

Answer (B) is correct. *(CPA, adapted)*

REQUIRED: The entry for issuance of purchase orders and contracts.

DISCUSSION: When a purchase order is approved or a contract is signed, an estimated liability is recorded in the encumbrances account for the amount of the purchase order. The entry is a debit to encumbrances and a credit to reserve for encumbrances.

Answer (A) is incorrect because expenditures will be debited and vouchers payable credited for $850,000 when the liability has been incurred. Answer (C) is incorrect because expenditures will be debited and vouchers payable credited for $850,000 when the liability has been incurred. Answer (D) is incorrect because appropriations is debited when the budgetary accounts are closed.

9. When a snowplow purchased by a governmental unit is received, it should be recorded in the general fund as a(n)

A. Encumbrance.

B. Expenditure.

C. General capital asset.

D. Appropriation.

Answer (B) is correct. *(CPA, adapted)*

REQUIRED: The effect of receipt of equipment.

DISCUSSION: When previously ordered goods are received, the entry includes a debit to expenditures for the actual amount to be paid. An expenditure is recognized when a liability is incurred, that is, when an executory contract is complete or virtually complete.

Answer (A) is incorrect because an encumbrance is recorded for the purchase commitment. Answer (C) is incorrect because general capital assets are reported only in the government-wide statement of net assets. Answer (D) is incorrect because appropriations are accounted for when recording the budget.

10. Which of the following amounts are included in a general fund's encumbrances account?

I. Outstanding vouchers payable amounts
II. Outstanding purchase order amounts
III. Excess of the amount of a purchase order over the actual expenditure for that order

A. I only.

B. Both I and III.

C. II only.

D. Both II and III.

Answer (C) is correct. *(CPA, adapted)*

REQUIRED: The amounts included in a general fund's encumbrances account.

DISCUSSION: The encumbrances account is debited when goods are approved to be purchased, and a purchase order is prepared. When the goods are actually received, it is credited. Thus, the encumbrances account includes only those amounts that represent outstanding purchase orders.

Answer (A) is incorrect because the encumbrances account does not include vouchers payable amounts, only outstanding purchase order amounts. Answer (B) is incorrect because the encumbrances account does not include vouchers payable amounts, only outstanding purchase order amounts. Answer (D) is incorrect because excesses of the actual expenditure over the purchase order are recorded in the expenditures control account.

11. Gold County received goods that had been approved for purchase but for which payment had not yet been made. Should the accounts listed below be increased?

	Encumbrances	Expenditures
A.	No	No
B.	No	Yes
C.	Yes	No
D.	Yes	Yes

Answer (B) is correct. *(CPA, adapted)*

REQUIRED: The effect of receipt of previously ordered goods on the encumbrances and expenditures accounts.

DISCUSSION: The encumbrances account will be decreased when previously ordered goods have been received. Expenditures and vouchers payable will be increased for the actual amount to be paid for the goods.

Answer (A) is incorrect because the expenditures control account is increased upon receipt of goods previously ordered. Answer (C) is incorrect because the encumbrances account is decreased and the expenditures account is increased at the time goods are received. Answer (D) is incorrect because the encumbrances account is decreased when the goods are received.

12. Which of the following fund types used by a government most likely would have a fund balance reserved for inventory of supplies?

A. General.

B. Internal service.

C. Private-purpose trust.

D. Capital projects.

Answer (A) is correct. *(CPA, adapted)*

REQUIRED: The fund type most likely to have a fund balance reserved for inventory of supplies.

DISCUSSION: Governmental units normally record the purchases of supplies inventory in an internal service fund or in the general fund. However, an internal service fund is a proprietary fund for which an amount for net assets, not fund balance, is reported. A fund balance is reported for the general fund. In accounting for supplies, the expenditure account may be charged (debited) when the materials and supplies are purchased or when they are consumed. Under either method, the inventory of supplies remaining at year-end must be recorded on the balance sheet as an asset. Under the purchases method, resources have already been deemed to be expended to acquire these supplies. Thus, a fund balance reserved for inventory of supplies must be established (credited) to indicate the unavailability of resources in this amount for other expenditures.

Answer (B) is incorrect because an internal service fund is a proprietary fund. Thus, net assets, not fund balance, are reported for an internal service fund. Answer (C) is incorrect because a private-purpose trust is a fiduciary fund. Thus, net assets, not fund balance, are reported for a private-purpose trust fund. Answer (D) is incorrect because supplies are not generally recognized as an asset of a capital projects fund.

13. During its fiscal year ended June 30, year 1, Cliff City issued purchase orders totaling $5,000,000, which were properly charged to encumbrances at that time. Cliff received goods and related invoices at the encumbered amounts totaling $4,500,000 before year-end. The remaining goods of $500,000 were not received until after year-end. Cliff paid $4,200,000 of the invoices received during the year. What amount of Cliff's encumbrances were outstanding at June 30, year 1?

A. $0

B. $300,000

C. $500,000

D. $800,000

Answer (C) is correct. *(CPA, adapted)*

REQUIRED: The amount of encumbrances outstanding.

DISCUSSION: In fund accounting, when a commitment is made to expend monies, the encumbrances account is debited and reserve for encumbrances is credited. When the goods are received, this entry is reversed. Because goods totaling $500,000 were not received at year-end, encumbrances outstanding total $500,000 ($5,000,000 – $4,500,000).

Answer (A) is incorrect because not all of the goods related to the encumbrance amounts were received during the year. Answer (B) is incorrect because $300,000 is the excess of goods received over amount actually paid on the invoices during the year. Answer (D) is incorrect because $800,000 is the excess of total encumbrances over the amount paid on the invoices.

14. Elm City issued a purchase order for supplies with an estimated cost of $5,000. When the supplies were received, the accompanying invoice indicated an actual price of $4,950. What amount should Elm have debited (credited) to the reserve for encumbrances after the supplies and invoice were received?

A. $(50)

B. $50

C. $4,950

D. $5,000

Answer (D) is correct. *(CPA, adapted)*

REQUIRED: The debit (credit) to the reserve for encumbrances after the supplies and invoice were received.

DISCUSSION: Expenditures are actual decreases in net financial resources. They are recognized in the governmental funds when fund liabilities are incurred, if measurable. When goods are received by, or services are rendered to, a governmental unit, a journal entry is made to debit expenditures control and to credit vouchers payable. In addition, a previously recorded encumbrance must be reversed by debiting the fund balance reserved for encumbrances and crediting encumbrances control. Because the original budgetary entry is reversed, reserve for encumbrances must be debited for the previously recognized estimated cost of $5,000.

Answer (A) is incorrect because reserve for encumbrances is debited, not credited, for the original estimated cost. Answer (B) is incorrect because $50 is the difference between the estimated and actual price. Answer (C) is incorrect because $4,950 is the actual, not the estimated price.

15. When Rolan County adopted its budget for the year ending June 30, $20,000,000 was recorded for estimated revenues control. Actual revenues for the year ended June 30, amounted to $17,000,000. In closing the budgetary accounts at June 30,

A. Revenues control should be debited for $3,000,000.

B. Estimated revenues control should be debited for $3,000,000.

C. Revenues control should be credited for $20,000,000.

D. Estimated revenues control should be credited for $20,000,000.

Answer (D) is correct. *(CPA, adapted)*

REQUIRED: The journal entry to close estimated revenues control and revenues control.

DISCUSSION: Estimated revenues control is a budgetary account recognized upon the adoption of the budget. Revenues control is a nominal account in which revenues are recorded when they meet the criteria of being available and measurable. At year-end, both accounts are closed to fund balance. The journal entry to close estimated revenues control and actual revenues to fund balance is

Revenues control	$17,000,000	
Fund balance	3,000,000	
Estimated revenues control		$20,000,000

16. A budgetary fund balance reserved for encumbrances in excess of a balance of encumbrances indicates

A. An excess of vouchers payable over encumbrances.

B. An excess of purchase orders over invoices received.

C. An excess of appropriations over encumbrances.

D. A recording error.

Answer (D) is correct. *(CPA, adapted)*

REQUIRED: The reason the reserve for encumbrances balance would exceed the encumbrance balance.

DISCUSSION: The entry to record an encumbrance is a debit to encumbrances and a credit to reserve for encumbrances. Thus, reserve for encumbrances should never exceed encumbrances. If it does, a recording error must exist.

17. Governmental expenditures for insurance extending over more than one accounting period

A. Must be accounted for as expenditures of the period of acquisition.

B. Must be accounted for as expenditures of the periods subsequent to acquisition.

C. Must be allocated between or among accounting periods.

D. May be allocated between or among accounting periods or may be accounted for as expenditures of the period of acquisition.

Answer (D) is correct. *(CPA, adapted)*

REQUIRED: The proper treatment of expenditures extending over more than one period.

DISCUSSION: Prepaid insurance may be reported by either the purchase method or the consumption method. Under the purchase method, an expenditure is reported when the policy is purchased. Under the consumption method, an expenditure is reported when the asset is consumed.

18. The following information pertains to Park Township's general fund at December 31, year 1:

Total assets, including $200,000 of cash	$1,000,000
Total liabilities	600,000
Reserved for encumbrances	100,000

Appropriations do not lapse at year-end. At December 31, year 1, what amount should Park report as unreserved fund balance for the general fund in its governmental funds balance sheet?

A. $200,000

B. $300,000

C. $400,000

D. $500,000

Answer (B) is correct. *(CPA, adapted)*

REQUIRED: The amount to be reported as unreserved fund balance.

DISCUSSION: The amount in the unreserved fund balance is equal to the amount of assets available to finance expenditures of the current and succeeding years. The fund balance is $400,000 ($1,000,000 assets – $600,000 liabilities). Given that $100,000 is reserved for encumbrances, the unreserved fund balance is $300,000 ($400,000 – $100,000).

Answer (A) is incorrect because $200,000 is the amount of cash available. Answer (C) is incorrect because $400,000 incorrectly includes the reserve for encumbrances. Answer (D) is incorrect because $500,000 is net assets (assets minus liabilities) plus the reserve for encumbrances.

19. During the current year, a city's electric utility, which is operated as an enterprise fund, rendered billings for electricity supplied to the general fund. Which of the following accounts should be debited by the general fund?

A. Appropriations.

B. Expenditures.

C. Due to electric utility enterprise fund.

D. Other financing uses – interfund transfer-out.

Answer (B) is correct. *(CPA, adapted)*

REQUIRED: The account debited by the general fund for receipt of services supplied by an enterprise fund.

DISCUSSION: Enterprise funds are used to account for operations similar to those of private businesses. This rendition of services by the enterprise fund to the general fund is presumably at prices equivalent to external exchange values. Thus, it is classified as an interfund service provided and used. The result is revenue to the seller (the enterprise fund) and an expenditure to the buyer (the general fund). Unpaid amounts are interfund receivables or payables. The entry is to debit expenditures control and credit due to enterprise fund.

Answer (A) is incorrect because appropriations is debited when the budgetary accounts are closed. Answer (C) is incorrect because due to enterprise fund should be credited. Answer (D) is incorrect because this transaction is an interfund service provided and used, not an interfund transfer.

20. Which of the following funds of a governmental unit recognizes revenues in the accounting period in which they become available and measurable?

	General Fund	Enterprise Fund
A.	Yes	No
B.	No	Yes
C.	Yes	Yes
D.	No	No

Answer (A) is correct. *(CPA, adapted)*

REQUIRED: The criteria for revenue recognition for general and enterprise funds.

DISCUSSION: The general fund is accounted for on the modified accrual basis. This basis of accounting recognizes revenues in the period in which they are measurable and available. The enterprise fund is a proprietary fund that is accounted for on the accrual basis. This basis of accounting recognizes revenues in the accounting period in which the exchange occurs. Revenues from nonexchange transactions are recognized in accordance with SGAS 33.

Answer (B) is incorrect because the opposite situation is true. Answer (C) is incorrect because the enterprise fund recognizes revenues when the exchange occurs. Revenues from nonexchange transactions are recognized in accordance with SGAS 33. Answer (D) is incorrect because the general fund recognizes revenues when they are available and measurable.

21. On December 31 of the current year, Elm Village paid a contractor $4,500,000 for the total cost of a new Village Hall built during the current year on Village-owned land. Financing for the capital project was provided by a $3,000,000 general obligation bond issue sold at face amount on December 31 of the current year, with the remaining $1,500,000 transferred from the general fund. What account and amount should be reported in Elm's current-year financial statements for the general fund?

A. Other financing sources control $4,500,000

B. Expenditures control $4,500,000

C. Other financing sources control $3,000,000

D. Other financing uses control $1,500,000

Answer (D) is correct. *(CPA, adapted)*

REQUIRED: The account and amount to be reported in the financial statements for the general fund.

DISCUSSION: Accounting for state and local governments requires that transfers be reported as other financing sources by the governmental fund receiving the transfer and other financing uses by the governmental fund making the transfer. However, the bond issue proceeds and the cost of construction will be accounted for in the capital projects fund. Accordingly, the general fund should record only the interfund transfer out. The appropriate entry is to debit other financing uses control -- interfund transfer for $1,500,000 and to credit a liability. The capital projects fund should credit other financing sources -- interfund transfer for $1,500,000 and debit a receivable.

Answer (A) is incorrect because other financing uses control is debited to record transfers out of a fund. Furthermore, the $3,000,000 from the bond issue was not transferred in or out of the general fund. Answer (B) is incorrect because the sum paid to the contractor is reflected in the capital projects fund. Answer (C) is incorrect because the capital projects fund credits other financing sources control-bond issue proceeds for $3,000,000.

22. Cal City maintains several major fund types. The following were among Cal's cash receipts during the current year:

Unrestricted state grant	$1,000,000
Interest on bank accounts held for employees' pension plan	200,000

What amount of these cash receipts should be accounted for in Cal's general fund?

A. $1,200,000

B. $1,000,000

C. $200,000

D. $0

Answer (B) is correct. *(CPA, adapted)*

REQUIRED: The amount of cash receipts to be accounted for in the general fund.

DISCUSSION: The general fund is used to account for all transactions of a governmental unit that are not accounted for in another fund. The interest is accounted for in a pension trust fund. Thus, the general fund accounts for only the $1,000,000 grant.

Answer (A) is incorrect because $1,200,000 incorrectly includes the interest. Answer (C) is incorrect because $200,000 incorrectly includes the interest and excludes the unrestricted state grant. Answer (D) is incorrect because $0 excludes the unrestricted state grant.

23. In which situation(s) are property taxes due to a governmental unit recorded as deferred revenue?

I. Property taxes receivable are recognized in advance of the year for which they are levied.

II. Property taxes receivable are collected in advance of the year in which they are levied.

A. I only.

B. Both I and II.

C. II only.

D. Neither I nor II.

Answer (B) is correct. *(CPA, adapted)*

REQUIRED: The situation(s) when taxes due are recorded as deferred revenue.

DISCUSSION: A property tax assessment is made to finance the budget of a specific period. Hence, the revenue produced should be recognized in the period for which the assessment was levied, provided it meets the criteria of being available and measurable. When property taxes are recognized or collected in advance, they should be recorded as deferred revenue in a governmental fund. They are not recognized as revenue until the year for which they are levied. Under SGAS 33, a property tax assessment is classified as an imposed nonexchange revenue transaction. In such a transaction, assets (not revenues) should be recognized when an enforceable legal claim arises or when resources are received, whichever is earlier. Thus, under SGAS 33, recognition of a receivable in a year prior to that for which the property taxes were levied implies that, under the enabling statute, the enforceable legal claim arose in that prior year.

Answer (A) is incorrect because property taxes collected in advance should be initially recorded as deferred revenue. Answer (C) is incorrect because property taxes recognized in advance should be initially recorded as deferred revenue. Answer (D) is incorrect because property taxes recognized or collected in advance should be initially recorded as deferred revenue.

24. When a capital lease of a governmental unit represents the acquisition of a general capital asset, the acquisition should be reflected in the governmental fund financial statements as

A. An expenditure but not as an other financing source.

B. An other financing source but not as an expenditure.

C. An expenditure and an other financing source.

D. Neither an expenditure nor an other financing source.

Answer (C) is correct. *(CPA, adapted)*

REQUIRED: The accounting treatment of general capital assets acquired by capital lease.

DISCUSSION: General capital assets that are acquired by capital lease are recorded in the same manner as capital assets acquired by outright purchase. The principal amount of the lease is initially debited as an expenditure, and "other financing sources – capital lease" is credited.

25. Revenues that are legally restricted to expenditures for specified purposes should be accounted for in special revenue funds, including

A. Accumulation of resources for payment of general long-term debt principal and interest.

B. Pension trust fund revenues.

C. Gasoline taxes to finance road repairs.

D. Proprietary fund revenues.

Answer (C) is correct. *(CPA, adapted)*

REQUIRED: The revenues legally restricted to expenditures for specified purposes that should be accounted for in special revenue funds.

DISCUSSION: A special revenue fund is used to account for the proceeds of specific revenue sources (other than those accounted for in certain trust funds or in capital projects funds) that are legally restricted to expenditure for certain specified purposes. Gasoline taxes levied to finance road repair are revenues legally restricted to expenditures for specified purposes that should be accounted for in special revenue funds.

Answer (A) is incorrect because these resources are accounted for in the debt service fund. Answer (B) is incorrect because pension trust fund revenues are accounted for in the pension trust fund. Answer (D) is incorrect because proprietary fund revenues are accounted for in either enterprise or internal service funds.

26. The following pertains to Grove City's interfund receivables and payables at December 31:

Due to special revenue fund from general fund	$10,000
Due to agency fund from special revenue fund	4,000

How should Grove report these interfund amounts for the special revenue fund in its governmental fund balance sheet at December 31?

A. As an asset of $6,000.

B. As a liability of $6,000.

C. As an asset of $4,000 and liability of $10,000.

D. As an asset of $10,000 and liability of $4,000.

Answer (D) is correct. *(CPA, adapted)*

REQUIRED: The reporting of interfund amounts in the special revenue fund.

DISCUSSION: In a special revenue fund, funds due "to" the special revenue fund are receivables (assets), and funds due to another fund "from" the special revenue fund are payables (liabilities). Thus, Grove should report a $10,000 asset and a $4,000 liability in the special revenue fund.

Answer (A) is incorrect because, in a special revenue fund, assets are not reported net of liabilities. Answer (B) is incorrect because $6,000 is the amount of net assets. Answer (C) is incorrect because "due to special revenue fund" is a receivable (asset) and "due from special revenue fund" is a payable (liability).

27. Kew City received a $15,000,000 federal grant to finance the construction of a center for rehabilitation of drug addicts. The proceeds of this grant should be accounted for in the

A. Special revenue funds.

B. General fund.

C. Capital projects funds.

D. Trust funds.

Answer (C) is correct. *(CPA, adapted)*

REQUIRED: The fund used to account for a federal grant earmarked to finance the construction of a center for rehabilitation of drug addicts.

DISCUSSION: The capital projects fund is used to account for the receipt and disbursement of resources restricted to acquisition of major capital facilities (other than those financed by proprietary and trust funds) through purchase or construction.

Answer (A) is incorrect because this fund does not record resources to be used for major capital facilities. Answer (B) is incorrect because this fund does not record resources to be used for major capital facilities. Answer (D) is incorrect because a grant for a drug rehabilitation center is not accounted for in a trust fund. A trust fund accounts for assets held by a governmental entity in the capacity of a trustee for individuals, private organizations, or other governments.

28. Should a special revenue fund with a legally adopted budget maintain its accounts on an accrual basis and integrate budgetary accounts into its accounting system?

	Maintain on Accrual Basis	Integrate Budgetary Accounts
A.	Yes	Yes
B.	Yes	No
C.	No	Yes
D.	No	No

Answer (C) is correct. *(CPA, adapted)*

REQUIRED: The accounting by a special revenue fund with a legally adopted budget.

DISCUSSION: The current financial resources measurement focus and the modified accrual basis of accounting are required in the financial statements of governmental funds. Because a special revenue fund is a governmental fund, it should maintain its accounts on the modified accrual basis.

The integration of budgetary accounts into the formal accounting system is a management control technique used to assist in controlling expenditures and enforcing revenue provisions. The extent to which the budgetary accounts should be integrated varies among governmental fund types and according to the nature of fund transactions. However, integration is considered essential in the general fund, special revenue funds, and other annually budgeted governmental funds with numerous types of revenues, expenditures, and transfers. Thus, a special revenue fund with a legally adopted budget should integrate its budgetary accounts into its accounting system.

Answer (A) is incorrect because special revenue funds are maintained on the modified accrual basis. Answer (B) is incorrect because special revenue funds are maintained on the modified accrual basis. Answer (D) is incorrect because the special revenue fund with a legally adopted budget should integrate its budgetary accounts into its accounting system.

29. The renovation of Fir City's municipal park was accounted for in a capital projects fund. Financing for the renovation which was begun and completed in year 1, came from the following sources:

Grant from state government	$400,000
Proceeds from general obligation bond issue	500,000
Transfer from Fir's general fund	100,000

In its year 1 governmental funds statement of revenues, expenditures, and changes in fund balances, Fir should report these amounts as

	Revenues	Other Financing Sources
A.	$1,000,000	$0
B.	$900,000	$100,000
C.	$400,000	$600,000
D.	$0	$1,000,000

Answer (C) is correct. *(CPA, adapted)*

REQUIRED: The amounts to be reported in the governmental funds statement of revenues, expenditures, and changes in fund balances.

DISCUSSION: Governmental fund revenues are increases in fund financial resources other than from interfund transfers, debt issue proceeds, and redemptions of demand bonds. Thus, revenues of a capital projects fund include grants. Under SGAS 33, the grant (a voluntary nonexchange transaction) is recognized when all eligibility requirements, including time requirements, have been met. When modified accrual accounting is used, as in a capital projects fund, the grant must also be "available." Other financing sources include proceeds from bonds and interfund transfers. Thus, Fir reports revenues of $400,000 and other financing sources of $600,000 ($500,000 + $100,000) in its governmental fund statement of revenues, expenditures, and changes in fund balances.

Answer (A) is incorrect because the proceeds from the bond issue and the transfer from the general fund should be reported under other financing sources. Answer (B) is incorrect because the proceeds from bond issue should be reported under other financing sources. Answer (D) is incorrect because the grant should be reported under revenues.

30. In year 1, Menton City received $5,000,000 of bond proceeds to be used for capital projects. Of this amount, $1,000,000 was expended in year 1 with the balance expected to be incurred in year 2. When should the bond proceeds be recorded in a capital projects fund?

A. $5,000,000 in year 1.

B. $5,000,000 in year 2.

C. $1,000,000 in 2002 and $4,000,000 in year 2.

D. $1,000,000 in year 1 and in the general fund for $4,000,000 in year 1.

Answer (A) is correct. *(CPA, adapted)*

REQUIRED: The date(s) bond proceeds should be recorded in a capital projects fund.

DISCUSSION: The general obligation debt will be reported as a general long-term liability in the governmental activities column of the government-wide statements of net assets, and expenditures will be recorded in year 1 and year 2. The face amount of long-term debt, issuance premium or discount, certain payments to escrow agents for bond refundings, transfers, and sales of capital assets not qualifying as special items are reported as other financing sources and uses in the governmental funds statement of revenues, expenditures, and changes in fund balances. Thus, the entry in the capital projects fund in year 1, the year of receipt, to record the bond proceeds is a debit to cash and a credit to other financing sources -- bond issue proceeds for $5,000,000.

31. Grove Township issued $50,000 of bond anticipation notes at face amount and placed the proceeds in its capital projects fund. All legal steps were taken to refinance the notes, but Grove was unable to consummate refinancing. In the capital projects fund, which account should be credited to record the $50,000 proceeds?

A. Other financing sources control.

B. Revenues control.

C. Deferred revenues.

D. Bond anticipation notes payable.

Answer (D) is correct. *(CPA, adapted)*

REQUIRED: The account to be credited to record the proceeds from bond anticipation notes.

DISCUSSION: Bond anticipation notes of governmental funds should be reported as general long-term liabilities in the governmental activities column of the government-wide statement of net assets if (1) all legal steps have been taken to refinance them and (2) the intent is supported by an ability to consummate the refinancing on a long-term basis. If both criteria are not met, the bond anticipation notes should be reported as a liability in the governmental fund in which the proceeds are recorded and in the government-wide statement of net assets. Thus, because Grove was unable to consummate the refinancing, the proceeds should be recorded as a bond anticipation note payable in the capital projects fund.

Answer (A) is incorrect because the notes should be recorded in the capital projects fund by a debit to cash and a credit to bond anticipation notes payable. Answer (B) is incorrect because the notes should be recorded in the capital projects fund by a debit to cash and a credit to bond anticipation notes payable. Answer (C) is incorrect because the notes should be recorded in the capital projects fund by a debit to cash and a credit to bond anticipation notes payable.

32. A public school district should recognize revenue from property taxes levied for its debt service fund when

A. Bonds to be retired by the levy are due and payable.

B. Assessed valuations of property subject to the levy are known.

C. Funds from the levy are measurable and available to the district.

D. Proceeds from collection of the levy are deposited in the district's bank account.

Answer (C) is correct. *(CPA, adapted)*

REQUIRED: The timing of property tax recognition.

DISCUSSION: Debt service funds apply the modified accrual basis of accounting. Thus, revenues are recognized when they are measurable and available. Moreover, under SGAS 33, assets from imposed nonexchange revenue transactions, such as property tax levies, should be recognized when an enforceable legal claim arises or the resources are received, whichever is earlier. If the legal claim arises in the period after that for which the property taxes are levied, a receivable is recognized when revenues are recognized. Revenues are recognized in the period for which the taxes are levied if the availability criterion is met. For property taxes, this criterion is met if the taxes are collected within the current period or soon enough afterward (not exceeding 60 days) to pay current liabilities.

Answer (A) is incorrect because revenues are recognized when property taxes are levied. Answer (B) is incorrect because the assessed valuations are necessary for calculating the amount of tax but do not make the tax revenue available. Answer (D) is incorrect because revenue recognition is not on the cash basis.

33. Tott City's serial bonds are serviced through a debt service fund with cash provided by the general fund. In the financial statements of the governmental funds, how are cash receipts and cash payments reported?

	Cash Receipts	Cash Payments
A.	Revenues	Expenditures
B.	Revenues	Interfund transfers
C.	Interfund transfers	Expenditures
D.	Interfund transfers	Interfund transfers

Answer (C) is correct. *(CPA, adapted)*

REQUIRED: The reporting of cash receipts and payments in the governmental-fund financial statements.

DISCUSSION: Cash receipts of a debt service fund provided by the general fund are interfund transfers (other financing sources), not revenues. The cash receipts are interfund transfers because they are nonreciprocal activities with no repayment required. Cash payments made to retire principal and interest payments of serial bonds are recorded as expenditures of the governmental unit's resources. An expenditure is recognized in a governmental fund when the liability is incurred, if measurable, except for the unmatured principal and interest on general long-term debt (e.g., the serial bonds), which are recognized when due.

34. In which of the following fund types of a city government are revenues and expenditures recognized on the same basis of accounting as the general fund?

A. Private-purpose trust.

B. Internal service.

C. Enterprise.

D. Debt service.

Answer (D) is correct. *(CPA, adapted)*

REQUIRED: The fund that recognizes revenues and expenditures in the same manner as the general fund.

DISCUSSION: The debt service fund is the only fund listed that is classified as a governmental fund. The other funds are proprietary or fiduciary. Governmental funds use the modified accrual basis, and proprietary and fiduciary funds use the accrual basis.

Answer (A) is incorrect because a private-purpose trust fund is a fiduciary fund. It is accounted for in a manner similar to that of proprietary funds. Answer (B) is incorrect because the internal service fund is a proprietary fund. It uses the accrual basis of accounting. Answer (C) is incorrect because the enterprise fund is a proprietary fund. It uses the accrual basis of accounting.

35. Wood City, which is legally obligated to maintain a debt service fund, issued the following general obligation bonds on July 1, year 1:

Term of bonds	10 years
Face amount	$1,000,000
Issue price	101
Stated interest rate	6%

Interest is payable January 1 and July 1. What amount of bond issuance premium should be amortized in Wood's debt service fund for the year ended December 31, year 1?

A. $1,000

B. $500

C. $250

D. $0

Answer (D) is correct. *(CPA, adapted)*

REQUIRED: The amount of bond premium amortized in the debt service fund.

DISCUSSION: The debt service fund of a governmental unit is a governmental fund used to account for the accumulation of resources for, and the payment of, general long-term debt principal and interest. Bond issuance premium may be recorded as an other financing source in the debt service fund. However, because this fund has a current financial resources measurement focus, that is, a focus on fiscal accountability for current spendable resources, premium is not amortized in the debt service fund.

36. In connection with Albury Township's long-term debt, the following cash accumulations are available to cover payment of principal and interest on

Bonds for financing of water treatment plant construction	$1,000,000
General long-term obligations	400,000

The amount of these cash accumulations that should be accounted for in Albury's debt service funds is

A. $0

B. $400,000

C. $1,000,000

D. $1,400,000

Answer (B) is correct. *(CPA, adapted)*

REQUIRED: The amount of cash accumulations to be accounted for in debt service funds.

DISCUSSION: A debt service fund is used to account for resources raised to pay the principal and interest of general obligation long-term debt issued by a governmental unit. Water treatment plants and other utilities are customarily accounted for in enterprise funds because they tend to be financed and operated in the same manner as private businesses. Cash accumulations to cover payment of principal and interest on enterprise fund obligations are accounted for in the enterprise fund itself. Hence, only the $400,000 of proceeds from general long-term obligations should be accounted for in the debt service funds.

Answer (A) is incorrect because the amount accumulated for payment of the general long-term obligations is properly accounted for in the debt service fund. Answer (C) is incorrect because the amount accumulated for the bonds should be accounted for in the water-utility enterprise fund. Answer (D) is incorrect because $1,400,000 includes the bonds for the water-utility fund project.

37. Dale City is accumulating financial resources that are legally restricted to payments of general long-term debt principal and interest maturing in future years. At December 31 of the current year, $5,000,000 has been accumulated for principal payments, and $300,000 has been accumulated for interest payments. These restricted funds should be accounted for in the

	Debt Service Fund	General Fund
A.	$0	$5,300,000
B.	$300,000	$5,000,000
C.	$5,000,000	$300,000
D.	$5,300,000	$0

Answer (D) is correct. *(CPA, adapted)*

REQUIRED: The funds in which to account for financial resources reserved for principal and interest.

DISCUSSION: Debt service funds are created to accumulate financial resources for repayment of principal and interest of long-term general obligation debt. The general fund does not account for these transactions, except to record transfers to the debt service fund.

38. A major exception to the general rule of expenditure accrual for governmental funds of a state or local government relates to unmatured

	Principal of General Long-Term Debt	Interest on General Long-Term Debt
A.	Yes	Yes
B.	Yes	No
C.	No	Yes
D.	No	No

Answer (A) is correct. *(CPA, adapted)*

REQUIRED: The major exception to the general rule of expenditure accrual for governmental units.

DISCUSSION: According to the modified accrual basis of accounting, expenditures are recognized when liabilities are incurred. For general long-term debt, however, principal and interest expenditures ordinarily are recognized when payments on the debt are due.

39. If a capital asset is donated to a governmental unit, the asset is accounted for in an enterprise fund, and eligibility requirements are met, it should be recorded

A. At the donor's carrying amount as revenue.

B. At estimated fair value as revenue.

C. At the lower of the donor's carrying amount or estimated fair value as deferred revenues.

D. As a memorandum entry only.

Answer (B) is correct. *(CPA, adapted)*

REQUIRED: The method of recording capital assets donated to a governmental unit.

DISCUSSION: The amount to be reported for a capital asset ordinarily is its cost. However, if a capital asset is donated to a governmental unit, it should be recorded at its estimated fair value at the time of acquisition plus any ancillary charges. If the capital asset is accounted for in a proprietary fund, it should be reported in the government-wide statement of net assets and in the proprietary funds statement of net assets. For a voluntary nonexchange transaction, such as a contribution, assets are recognized when all eligibility requirements are met or the resources are provided, whichever is earlier. Revenue is recognized in the government-wide statement of activities and the proprietary funds statement of revenues, expenses, and changes in fund net assets (or fund equity) when eligibility requirements are met. Because an enterprise fund uses the accrual basis of accounting, the resources need not be "available."

Answer (A) is incorrect because the donor's carrying amount may not reflect the asset's fair value at the time of the governmental unit's receipt of the asset. Moreover, the enterprise fund should recognize revenue. Answer (C) is incorrect because the donor's carrying amount may not reflect the asset's fair value at the time of the governmental unit's receipt of the asset. Moreover, the enterprise fund should recognize revenue. Answer (D) is incorrect because the value of the donated asset should be recognized.

40. The debt service transactions of a special assessment bond issue for which the government is not obligated in any manner should be reported in a(n)

A. Agency fund.

B. Enterprise fund.

C. Special revenue fund.

D. Debt service fund.

Answer (A) is correct. *(CPA, adapted)*

REQUIRED: The reporting of debt service transactions of a special assessment bond issue for which the government is not obligated.

DISCUSSION: The debt service transactions of a special assessment issue for which the government is not obligated in any manner should be reported in an agency fund rather than a debt service fund. This treatment reflects the limitation of the government's duty to act as an agent for the assessed property owners and the bondholders.

Answer (B) is incorrect because an enterprise fund is a proprietary fund used to account for activities for which fees are charged to external users. Answer (C) is incorrect because a special revenue fund is a governmental fund used to account for the proceeds of specific revenue sources that are legally restricted and expended for a specific purpose. Answer (D) is incorrect because the government is not obligated for this special assessment bond issue.

41. The following equity balances are among those maintained by Cole City:

Enterprise funds	$1,000,000
Internal service funds	400,000

Cole's proprietary equity balances amount to

A. $1,400,000

B. $1,000,000

C. $400,000

D. $0

Answer (A) is correct. *(CPA, adapted)*

REQUIRED: The amount of proprietary equity balances.

DISCUSSION: Proprietary funds include enterprise funds and internal service funds. Thus, the proprietary equity balances equal $1,400,000 ($1,000,000 + $400,000).

Answer (B) is incorrect because $1,000,000 excludes the equity balance of the internal service funds. Answer (C) is incorrect because $400,000 excludes the equity balance of the enterprise funds. Answer (D) is incorrect because $0 excludes the equity balances of the enterprise funds and the internal service funds.

42. Bay Creek's municipal motor pool maintains all city-owned vehicles and charges the various departments for the cost of rendering the maintenance services. In which of the following funds should Bay account for the cost of such maintenance?

A. General fund.

B. Internal service fund.

C. Special revenue fund.

D. Special assessment fund.

Answer (B) is correct. *(CPA, adapted)*

REQUIRED: The fund in which to account for the cost of vehicle maintenance provided by the motor pool to other departments.

DISCUSSION: An internal service fund is used when one governmental entity provides goods or services to other subunits of the primary government and its component units or to other governments on a cost-reimbursement basis. However, if the reporting government is not the predominant participant, the activity should be reported as an enterprise fund.

Answer (A) is incorrect because the general fund is used to account for transactions not accounted for in other governmental funds. Answer (C) is incorrect because the special revenue fund is used to account for certain restricted categories of revenue. Answer (D) is incorrect because the special assessment fund type is not used in general-purpose financial statements.

43. Nox City reported a $25,000 net increase in the fund balances for total governmental funds. Nox also reported an increase in net assets for the following funds:

Motor pool internal service fund	$ 9,000
Water enterprise fund	12,000
Employee pension fund	7,000

The motor pool internal service fund provides service to the general fund departments. What amount should Nox report as the change in net assets for governmental activities?

A. $25,000

B. $34,000

C. $41,000

D. $46,000

Answer (B) is correct. *(CPA, adapted)*

REQUIRED: The change in net assets for governmental activities.

DISCUSSION: Separate rows and columns are used in the government-wide financial statements to distinguish between governmental and business-type activities of the primary government. Governmental activities are normally reported in governmental funds and internal service funds. The latter are proprietary funds. Business-type activities are reported in enterprise funds, which are proprietary funds (SGAS 34). Thus, the change in net assets for governmental activities is $34,000 ($25,000 net increase for all governmental funds + $9,000 net increase for the internal service funds). Fiduciary activities, such as those of an employee pension fund, are reported only in the fiduciary fund financial statements because their resources are not available for the government's programs.

Answer (A) is incorrect because $25,000 omits the internal service fund's increase in net assets. Answer (C) is incorrect because $41,000 includes the pension fund's increase in net assets. Answer (D) is incorrect because $46,000 includes the enterprise fund's increase in net assets.

44. Through an internal service fund, New County operates a centralized data processing center to provide services to New's other governmental units. This internal service fund billed New's parks and recreation fund $150,000 for data processing services. What account should New's internal service fund credit to record this $150,000 billing to the parks and recreation fund?

A. Data processing department expenses.

B. Interfund transfers.

C. Interfund reimbursements.

D. Operating revenues control.

Answer (D) is correct. *(CPA, adapted)*

REQUIRED: The account to be credited by an internal service fund to record a billing to other governmental units.

DISCUSSION: Interfund services provided and used are sales and purchases of goods and services at prices equivalent to external exchange values. They result in revenues to seller funds and expenditures or expenses to buyer funds. Unpaid amounts are interfund receivables or payables. Thus, billings issued for services rendered by an internal service data processing center to other governmental units should be recorded as a debit to a receivable and a credit to operating revenues control.

Answer (A) is incorrect because the services provided should be recorded as a revenue, not a decrease in an expense. Answer (B) is incorrect because interfund services provided and used are reciprocal interfund activities. Interfund transfers are nonreciprocal interfund activities. Answer (C) is incorrect because interfund services provided and used are reciprocal interfund activities. Interfund reimbursements are nonreciprocal interfund activities.

45. The following transactions were among those reported by Corfe City's electric utility enterprise fund for year 1:

Capital contributed by subdividers	$ 900,000
Cash received from customer households	2,700,000
Proceeds from sale of revenue bonds	4,500,000

In the electric utility enterprise fund's statement of cash flows for the year ended December 31, year 1, what amount should be reported as cash flows from capital and related financing activities?

A. $4,500,000

B. $5,400,000

C. $7,200,000

D. $8,100,000

Answer (B) is correct. *(CPA, adapted)*

REQUIRED: The amount reported as cash flows from capital and related financing activities.

DISCUSSION: Cash flows should be classified as operating, noncapital financing, capital and related financing, or investing. Operating activities include producing and delivering goods and providing services. Thus, cash from customer households is a revenue item reported under cash flows from operating activities. Capital and related financing activities include (1) acquiring and disposing of capital assets used to provide goods or services; (2) borrowings and repayments of debt related to acquiring, constructing, or improving capital assets; and (3) paying for capital assets obtained on credit. Assuming the sale of revenue bonds and the capital contributions by subdividers are for the acquisition or improvement of capital assets, the amount to report under capital and related financing activities is $5,400,000 ($900,000 + $4,500,000).

Answer (A) is incorrect because $4,500,000 omits the capital contributed by subdividers. Answer (C) is incorrect because $7,200,000 includes customer fees revenue and omits capital contributed by subdividers. Answer (D) is incorrect because $8,100,000 includes customer fees.

46. Cy City's Municipal Solid Waste Landfill Enterprise Fund was established when a new landfill was opened January 3, year 1. The landfill is expected to close December 31, year 20. Cy's year 1 expenses include a portion of which of the year 21's expected disbursements?

I. Cost of a final cover to be applied to the landfill
II. Cost of equipment to be installed to monitor methane gas buildup

A. I only.

B. II only.

C. Both I and II.

D. Neither I nor II.

Answer (C) is correct. *(CPA, adapted)*
REQUIRED: The accounting for municipal solid waste landfill (MSWLF) closure and postclosure care costs.
DISCUSSION: Owners and operators of MSWLF sites must incur a variety of costs to protect the environment during the period of operation and during the postclosure period. Certain costs result in disbursements near or after the date that the MSWLF stops accepting solid waste and during the postclosure period. The costs of final cover and of gas monitoring systems are included in the estimated total current closure and postclosure care costs. A proprietary fund (e.g., an enterprise fund) should recognize a portion of the estimated total current cost as an expense and a liability in each period that the MSWLF accepts solid waste.
Answer (A) is incorrect because portions of the cost of gas monitoring systems are included in year 1 expenses. Answer (B) is incorrect because portions of the cost of a final cover are included in year 1 expenses. Answer (D) is incorrect because portions of the costs of a final cover and of gas monitoring systems are included in year 1 expenses.

47. Dogwood City's water enterprise fund received interest of $10,000 on long-term investments. How should this amount be reported on the Statement of Cash Flows?

A. Operating activities.

B. Noncapital financing activities.

C. Capital and related financing activities.

D. Investing activities.

Answer (D) is correct. *(CPA, adapted)*
REQUIRED: The classification of interest received on long term investments in the statement of cash flows of a governmental utility.
DISCUSSION: SGAS 9 requires reporting of cash flows of proprietary funds and entities engaged in business-type activities, e.g., public benefit corporations and authorities, governmental utilities, governmental healthcare providers, and public colleges and universities. Cash flows should be classified as operating, financing, and investing. Investing activities include making and collecting loans (other than program loans) and acquiring and disposing of debt and equity instruments. Cash inflows from investing include interest and dividends received as returns on loans (not program loans), debt of other entities, equity securities, and each management or investment pools. Thus, interest on investments is a cash inflow from an investing activity.
Answer (A) is incorrect because operating activities are all transactions and other events that are not classified as either financing or investing activities. In general, operating activities involve transactions and other events, the effects of which are included in the determination of operating income. Answer (B) is incorrect because noncapital financing activities include borrowings for purposes other than acquiring, constructing, or improving capital assets and debt. Cash flows may include grants and subsidies received or paid, tax receipts, debt proceeds, and cash received from or paid to other funds (excluding flows from interfund services provided or used). Answer (C) is incorrect because capital and related financing activities include borrowings and repayments of debt related to acquiring, constructing, or improving capital assets; acquiring and disposing of capital assets used to provide goods or services; and paying for capital assets obtained on credit.

48. A state government had the following activities:

I. State-operated lottery $10,000,000
II. State-operated hospital $3,000,000

Which of the above activities may be accounted for in an enterprise fund?

A. Neither I nor II.

B. I only.

C. II only.

D. Both I and II.

Answer (D) is correct. *(CPA, adapted)*
REQUIRED: The activities to be accounted for in the enterprise fund.
DISCUSSION: Enterprise funds may be used to account for any activity of a state or local government that provides goods or services to external users for a fee. Both a state-operated hospital and a state-operated lottery are typical enterprise fund activities.
Answer (A) is incorrect because a state-run hospital and a state-run lottery provide services to external users for a fee. Answer (B) is incorrect because a state-run hospital provides services to external users for a fee. Answer (C) is incorrect because a state-run lottery provides services to external users for a fee.

49. According to SGAS 31, *Accounting and Financial Reporting for Certain Investments and for External Investment Pools*, how should a state or local governmental unit that sponsors an external investment pool report the external portion of the pool?

	Fund	Measurement Focus	Basis of Accounting
A.	Enterprise fund	Income determination	Accrual
B.	Special revenue	Current financial resources	Modified accrual
C.	Investment trust fund	Economic resources	Accrual
D.	General fund	Current financial resources	Modified accrual

Answer (C) is correct. *(Publisher)*

REQUIRED: The reporting of the external portion of an external investment pool.

DISCUSSION: According to SGAS 31, an investment trust fund (a fiduciary fund) is used by a sponsoring government to report the external portion of an external investment pool (the portion belonging to legally separate entities not part of the sponsor's reporting entity). Moreover, the sponsor should report each external pool as a separate fund. Transactions and balances are reported on the accrual basis with an economic resources measurement focus. This measurement focus differs from the shorter-term current-financial-resources approach used in governmental funds. It measures revenues and expenses in the same way as in proprietary funds or commercial accounting but does not necessarily emphasize net income. Instead, the emphasis is on a longer-range measure of revenues earned or levied (and accrued immediately if measurable). Moreover, the economic resources model focuses on cost of services.

50. River City has a defined contribution pension plan. How should River report the pension plan in its financial statements?

A. Amortize any transition asset over the estimated number of years of current employees' service.

B. Disclose in the notes to the financial statements the amount of the pension benefit obligation and the net assets available for benefits.

C. Disclose in the notes to the financial statements the classes of employees covered and the employer's and employees' obligations to contribute to the fund.

D. Accrue a liability for benefits earned but not paid to fund participants.

Answer (C) is correct. *(CPA, adapted)*

REQUIRED: The method for reporting a defined contribution pension plan.

DISCUSSION: GASB 25, *Financial Reporting for Defined Benefit Pension Plans and Note Disclosures for Defined Contribution Plans*, requires that a defined contribution pension plan report a plan description, a summary of significant accounting policies, and information about investment concentrations. The plan description should identify the plan as a defined contribution plan and disclose the number of participating employers and other contributing entities. The description should also include the classes of employees covered and the total current membership, a brief description of plan provisions and the authority under which they are established (or may be amended), and contribution requirements.

Answer (A) is incorrect because no transition asset arises under a defined contribution plan. Answer (B) is incorrect because a pension benefit obligation arises under a defined benefit pension plan. Answer (D) is incorrect because, under a defined contribution plan, the governmental employer's obligation is for contributions, not benefits.

51. Glen County uses governmental fund accounting and is the administrator of a multiple-jurisdiction deferred compensation plan covering both its own employees and those of other governments participating in the plan. This plan is an eligible deferred compensation plan under the U.S. Internal Revenue Code and Income Tax Regulations, and it meets the criteria for a pension (and other employee benefit) trust fund. Glen has legal access to the plan's $40 million in assets, of which $2 million pertain to Glen and $38 million to the other participating governments. In Glen's balance sheet, what amount should be reported in an agency fund for plan assets and as a corresponding liability?

A. $0

B. $2,000,000

C. $38,000,000

D. $40,000,000

Answer (A) is correct. *(CPA, adapted)*

REQUIRED: The deferred compensation plan assets and liability to record in an agency fund.

DISCUSSION: Under SGAS 32, *Accounting and Financial Reporting for Internal Revenue Code Section 457 Deferred Compensation Plans*, the plan should be reported in a pension (and other employee benefit) trust fund in the statements of fiduciary net assets and changes in fiduciary net assets if it meets the criteria for that fund type. This treatment is in accordance with a 1996 amendment to IRC Sec. 457 that required all assets and income of the plan to be held in trust for the exclusive benefit of participants and their beneficiaries. Consequently, no amounts should be reported in an agency fund.

Questions 52 and 53 are based on the following information. During year 1, Todd City received two state grants, one to buy a bus and one for bus operation. In year 1, 90% of the capital grant was used for the bus purchase, but 100% of the operating grant was disbursed. Todd accounts for its bus operations in an enterprise fund. Todd is liable for general obligation bonds issued for the water and sewer fund, which will service the debt, and for revenue bonds to be repaid from admission fees collected from users of the municipal recreation center. Both issues are expected to be paid from enterprise funds and to be secured by Todd's full faith and credit, as well as its taxing power.

52. In reporting the state grants for the bus purchase and operation, what should Todd include as grant revenues for the year ended December 31, year 1?

	90% of the Capital Grant	100% of the Capital Grant	Operating Grant
A.	Yes	No	No
B.	No	Yes	No
C.	No	Yes	Yes
D.	Yes	No	Yes

Answer (C) is correct. *(CPA, adapted)*

REQUIRED: The grant revenues for the year.

DISCUSSION: The grants for bus purchase and operation are voluntary nonexchange transactions. Revenues are recognized in such transactions when all eligibility requirements, including time requirements, are met. If the modified accrual method is used to account for the transaction, resources also should be "available" (SGAS 33), Todd has apparently met the eligibility requirements because it has what are presumably the characteristics of a recipient (it is a local government with a bus operation), and the period when the resources are required to be used or when use is first permitted has begun. Other eligibility requirements are not relevant based on the stated facts. The availability criterion has been met but is not relevant because the bus operation is accounted for in an enterprise fund, which uses the accrual method. The requirement to use the grants for bus purchase and operation is a purpose restriction and has no bearing on revenue recognition. Its effect is to cause the recipient to classify the unused resources as restricted. Thus, 100% of both grants should be recognized as revenues.

53. Which of Todd's long-term obligations should be accounted for only in the government-wide financial statements?

	General Obligation Bonds	Revenue Bonds
A.	Yes	Yes
B.	Yes	No
C.	No	Yes
D.	No	No

Answer (D) is correct. *(CPA, adapted)*

REQUIRED: The bonds reported in the government-wide financial statements.

DISCUSSION: When long-term liabilities are directly related to and expected to be paid from a proprietary fund, such as an enterprise fund, they are not general long-term liabilities and should be reported in the proprietary fund statement of net assets as well as the government-wide statement of net assets. They are specific fund liabilities even though they are backed by the full faith and credit of the governmental unit. The water and sewer fund and the municipal recreation center fund are both enterprise funds.

54. State University received two contributions during the current year that must be used to provide scholarships. Contribution A for $10,000 was collected during the year, and $8,000 was spent on scholarships. Contribution B is a pledge for $30,000 to be received next fiscal year. What amount of contribution revenue should the university report in its statement of activities?

A. $8,000

B. $10,000

C. $38,000

D. $40,000

Answer (D) is correct. *(CPA, adapted)*

REQUIRED: The contribution revenue reported in the statement of activities of a public university.

DISCUSSION: The contributions are voluntary nonexchange transactions (legislative or contractual agreements, other than exchanges, entered into willingly by the parties). No eligibility requirements (such as types of recipients) must be met, so the donee recognizes cash and revenue in the amount of $10,000 when Contribution A is received. However, Contribution B was announced one fiscal year in advance. Nevertheless, if the promise is verifiable, the resources are measurable, and collection is deemed to be probable. State University should debit a receivable and credit contribution revenue in the amount of $30,000 at the time of the announcement. Total contribution revenue is therefore $40,000 ($10,000 + $30,000).

As a result of the issuance of SGAS 35, the GASB reporting model, not the AICPA College Guide model, must be applied by public colleges and universities. Thus, SGAS 33, *Accounting and Financial Reporting for Nonexchange Transactions*, governs the reporting of Contributions A and B.

Answer (A) is incorrect because $8,000 is the amount that may be reclassified as unrestricted net assets (or fund balance) as a result of its use for the purpose to which it was restricted. Answer (B) is incorrect because the pledge may be recognized as revenue if its collection is probable. Answer (C) is incorrect because the full amount of Contribution A may be reported although part was not spent.

55. Grants that are to be transferred to secondary recipients by a local government should be accounted for in which funds if the government has no administrative or direct involvement in the program?

A. Cash and investment agency funds.

B. Tax agency funds.

C. Agency funds.

D. Special assessment funds.

Answer (C) is correct. *(Publisher)*

REQUIRED: The funds that account for grants to be transferred to secondary recipients.

DISCUSSION: Agency funds may account for certain grants and other financial assistance to be transferred to, or spent on behalf of, secondary recipients (individuals, private organizations, or other governments). The agency fund acts purely as a conduit. It receives the monies and passes them through to the ultimate recipients. However, if the recipient government has administrative or direct financial involvement in the program, the pass-through grant is accounted for in an appropriate governmental, proprietary, or trust fund (SGAS 24).

56. Chase City imposes a 2% tax on hotel charges. Revenues from this tax will be used to promote tourism in the city. Chase should record this tax as what type of nonexchange transaction?

A. Derived tax revenue.

B. Imposed nonexchange revenue.

C. Government-mandated transaction.

D. Voluntary nonexchange transaction.

Answer (A) is correct. *(CPA, adapted)*

REQUIRED: The type of nonexchange transaction.

DISCUSSION: Derived tax revenues are assessments on exchange transactions, for example, income, sales, and, in this case, hotel room rentals. The government recognizes assets when the underlying exchange occurs (or when resources are received, if earlier). Revenues (net of estimated refunds) are recognized when the underlying exchange occurs. The requirements to use the proceeds for promotion of tourism is a purpose restriction, and the resulting net assets, equity, or fund balance is restricted until used (SGAS 33).

Answer (B) is incorrect because imposed nonexchange revenues (e.g., property taxes and fines) are assessments on nongovernmental entities, including individuals, other than assessments on exchange transactions. Answer (C) is incorrect because government-mandated nonexchange transactions occur when one government provides resources to a government at another level and requires that they be used for a specific purpose (e.g., federal programs that state or local governments are required to implement). Answer (D) is incorrect because voluntary nonexchange transactions arise from legislative or contractual agreements, other than exchanges, entered into willingly by the parties (e.g., certain grants and private donations).

28.3 Comprehensive Annual Financial Report

57. Government-wide financial statements

A. Display individual funds.

B. Display aggregated information about fund types.

C. Exclude information about discretely presented component units.

D. Use separate columns to distinguish between governmental and business-type activities.

Answer (D) is correct. *(Publisher)*

REQUIRED: The information reported in government-wide financial statements.

DISCUSSION: The basic financial statements include government-wide financial statements, fund financial statements, and the notes to the financial statements. Government-wide financial statements do not display funds or fund types but instead report information about the overall government. They distinguish between the primary government and its discretely presented component units and between the governmental activities and business-type activities of the primary government by reporting such information in separate rows and columns.

Answer (A) is incorrect because fund information is reported in the fund financial statements. Answer (B) is incorrect because fund information is reported in the fund financial statements. Answer (C) is incorrect because separate rows and columns report information about discretely presented component units.

58. According to SGAS 34, *Basic Financial Statements--and Management's Discussion and Analysis--for State and Local Governments*, financial reporting by general-purpose governments includes presentation of MD&A as

A. Required supplementary information after the notes to the financial statements.

B. Part of the basic financial statements.

C. A description of currently known facts, decisions, or conditions expected to have significant effects on financial activities.

D. Information that may be limited to highlighting the amounts and percentages of change from the prior to the current year.

Answer (C) is correct. *(Publisher)*

REQUIRED: The nature of MD&A.

DISCUSSION: Management's discussion and analysis (MD&A) is required supplementary information (RSI) that precedes the basic financial statements and provides an analytical overview of financial activities. It is based on currently known facts, decisions, or conditions and includes comparisons of the current and prior years, with an emphasis on the current year, based on government-wide information. Currently known facts are those of which management is aware at the audit report date (SGAS 34). However, the information presented should be confined to the topics discussed in SGAS 34 (SGAS 37, *Basic Financial Statements--and Management's Discussion and Analysis--for State and Local Governments: Omnibus*).

Answer (A) is incorrect because MD&A precedes the basic financial statements. Answer (B) is incorrect because MD&A precedes the basic financial statements. Answer (D) is incorrect because MD&A should state the reasons for change from the prior year, not merely the amounts or percentages of change.

59. Government-wide financial statements are prepared using the

	Economic Resources Measurement Focus	Current Financial Resources Measurement Focus	Accrual Basis	Modified Accrual Basis
A.	Yes	No	Yes	No
B.	No	Yes	No	Yes
C.	Yes	No	No	Yes
D.	No	Yes	Yes	No

Answer (A) is correct. *(Publisher)*

REQUIRED: The measurement focus and basis of accounting used in government-wide financial statements.

DISCUSSION: Government-wide financial statements are prepared using the economic resources measurement focus and the accrual basis of accounting and should report all of the government's assets, liabilities, revenues, expenses, gains, and losses. The economic resources measurement focus differs from the shorter-term flow-of-current-financial-resources approach used in governmental funds. It measures revenues and expenses in the same way as in proprietary funds or commercial accounting but does not necessarily emphasize net income. Instead, the emphasis is on a longer-range measure of revenues earned or levied (and accrued immediately if measurable). Moreover, the economic resources model focuses on cost of services. The accrual basis of accounting recognizes most transactions when they occur, regardless of when cash is received or paid.

60. The government-wide financial statements report capital assets

A. In the general fixed assets account group.

B. At historical cost, including ancillary charges.

C. Only in the notes if they are donated.

D. At estimated fair value.

Answer (B) is correct. *(Publisher)*

REQUIRED: The reporting of capital assets in the government-wide financial statements.

DISCUSSION: Capital assets include land, land improvements, easements, buildings, vehicles, machinery, equipment, works of art, historical treasures, infrastructure, and other tangible and intangible operating assets with useful lives greater than one reporting period. They are reported at historical cost, including ancillary charges necessary to put them in their intended location and condition for use. Ancillary charges, e.g., freight, site preparation, and professional fees, are directly attributable to acquisition of the assets.

Answer (A) is incorrect because presentation of government-wide financial statements eliminates the need for the general fixed assets account group and the general long-term debt account group. Answer (C) is incorrect because capital assets are reported at historical cost, including ancillary charges, in the statements. Answer (D) is incorrect because only donated capital assets are reported at estimated fair value at the time of acquisition plus ancillary charges.

61. Items reported only in the fund financial statements of a general-purpose government are those arising from

A. Proprietary activities.

B. Fiduciary activities.

C. Exchange-like transactions.

D. Nonexchange-like transactions.

Answer (B) is correct. *(Publisher)*

REQUIRED: The items reported only in the fund financial statements.

DISCUSSION: The resources of fiduciary activities are not available to finance the government's programs. Thus, they are reported only in the fund financial statements. Fiduciary activities are reported in or with the fiduciary funds of the primary government. Fiduciary component units are reported with the primary government's fiduciary funds only in the fund financial statements.

Answer (A) is incorrect because government-wide statements report governmental and business-type (proprietary) activities. Answer (C) is incorrect because government-wide statements recognize exchange or exchange-like transactions when the exchange occurs. Answer (D) is incorrect because government-wide statements recognize nonexchange-like transactions in accordance with SGAS 33.

62. Which capital assets must be depreciated in the government-wide financial statements?

A. All capitalized collections of works of art.

B. All infrastructure assets.

C. All noncapitalized collections of historical treasures.

D. All capitalized collections that are exhaustible.

Answer (D) is correct. *(Publisher)*

REQUIRED: The capital assets that must be depreciated.

DISCUSSION: Individual items or collections of works of art, historical treasures, and similar assets ordinarily must be capitalized. However, if a collection is held in furtherance of public service and not for gain; protected, preserved, cared for, and kept unencumbered; and subject to a policy that sale proceeds are to be used to obtain other collection items, capitalization is not required. If capitalized collections or individual items are exhaustible, for example, because their useful lives are reduced by display, educational, or research uses, they must be depreciated.

Answer (A) is incorrect because capitalized collections or individual items that are inexhaustible need not be depreciated. Answer (B) is incorrect because infrastructure assets that are part of a network or a subsystem of a network need not be depreciated if the assets are managed using a system with certain characteristics and if the government documents preservation of the assets at an established and disclosed condition. Answer (C) is incorrect because capitalization is needed for depreciation.

63. If a state or local government reports eligible infrastructure assets using the modified approach,

A. Complete condition assessments must be performed annually.

B. Expenditures for the assets are capitalized.

C. No depreciation expense is required to be recognized.

D. The assets are not being preserved at or above the established and disclosed condition level.

Answer (C) is correct. *(Publisher)*

REQUIRED: The implication of reporting eligible infrastructure assets using the modified approach.

DISCUSSION: Under the modified approach permitted by SGAS 34, infrastructure assets that are part of a network or subsystem of a network (eligible infrastructure assets) need not be depreciated if the government uses an asset management system with certain characteristics and documents that the assets are being preserved approximately at (or above) a condition level established and disclosed by the government. An asset management system should include an updated inventory of eligible infrastructure assets, perform condition assessments and summarize results using a measurement scale, and make annual estimates of the annual amounts needed to maintain the assets at the established condition level.

Answer (A) is incorrect because a government using the modified approach must document that complete condition assessments are performed in a consistent manner every 3 years and that the three most recent assessments provide reasonable assurance that the assets are being preserved at or above the established and disclosed condition level. Answer (B) is incorrect because, under the modified approach, expenditures (except those for additions and improvements) are expensed when incurred. Answer (D) is incorrect because, if the assets are not being preserved at or above the established and disclosed condition level, the modified approach must be abandoned, and depreciation must be recognized.

64. Which of the following capital assets are least likely to be considered infrastructure assets of a state or local government?

A. Buildings.

B. Sewer systems.

C. Roads.

D. Lighting systems.

Answer (A) is correct. *(Publisher)*

REQUIRED: The capital assets least likely to be considered infrastructure assets.

DISCUSSION: Infrastructure assets are capital assets that normally are stationary and can be preserved for a longer time than most capital assets, e.g., roads, bridges, water and sewer systems, drainage systems, and lighting systems. However, buildings, other than those that are ancillary parts of a network of infrastructure assets, are not deemed to be infrastructure assets.

Answer (B) is incorrect because sewer systems are considered infrastructure assets. Answer (C) is incorrect because roads are considered infrastructure assets. Answer (D) is incorrect because lighting systems are considered infrastructure assets.

65. The government-wide statement of net assets must

A. Be presented in a classified format.

B. Present assets and liabilities in order of liquidity.

C. Use the balance sheet format.

D. Display net assets in three components.

Answer (D) is correct. *(Publisher)*

REQUIRED: The required presentation of the government-wide statement of net assets.

DISCUSSION: The GASB requires that the government-wide statement of net assets display net assets in three components: invested in capital assets, net of related debt; restricted net assets; and unrestricted net assets.

Answer (A) is incorrect because a classified format is acceptable but not required. Answer (B) is incorrect because the GASB encourages but does not require governments to present assets and liabilities in order of liquidity. Answer (C) is incorrect because the GASB permits governments to use the balance sheet format, although it prefers the net asset format.

66. In the government-wide statement of net assets, restricted capital assets should be included in the

A. Expendable component of restricted net assets.

B. Nonexpendable component of restricted net assets.

C. Invested in capital assets, net of related debt, component of net assets.

D. Designated component of net assets.

Answer (C) is correct. *(Publisher)*

REQUIRED: The classification of restricted capital assets in the statement of net assets.

DISCUSSION: Invested in capital assets, net of related debt, includes unrestricted and restricted capital assets, net of accumulated depreciation and related liabilities for borrowings. However, debt related to significant unspent proceeds is classified in the same net assets component as those proceeds.

Answer (A) is incorrect because restricted net assets are subject to constraints imposed by external entities (creditors, grantors, or other governments) or by law (constitutional provisions or enabling legislation). If permanent endowments or permanent fund principal amounts are included, restricted net assets should be displayed as expendable and nonexpendable. Nonexpendable means that the net assets are retained in perpetuity. However, capital assets must be included in the invested in capital assets, net of related debt, component of net assets, even if they are restricted. Answer (B) is incorrect because restricted net assets are subject to constraints imposed by external entities (creditors, grantors, or other governments) or by law (constitutional provisions or enabling legislation). If permanent endowments or permanent fund principal amounts are included, restricted net assets should be displayed as expendable and nonexpendable. Nonexpendable means that the net assets are retained in perpetuity. However, capital assets must be included in the invested in capital assets, net of related debt, component of net assets, even if they are restricted. Answer (D) is incorrect because designations of net assets are not reported on the face of the statement.

67. The statement of activities of the government-wide financial statements is designed primarily to provide information to assess which of the following?

A. Operational accountability.

B. Financial accountability.

C. Fiscal accountability.

D. Functional accountability.

Answer (A) is correct. *(CPA, adapted)*

REQUIRED: The primary form of accountability provided by government-wide financial statements.

DISCUSSION: SGAS 34 defines fiscal accountability to be the responsibility of governments to justify that their actions currently comply with public decisions concerning the raising and spending of public monies in the short term. Operational accountability is the governments' responsibility to report the extent to which they have met their accounting objectives efficiently and effectively, using all resources available, and whether they can continue to do so in the near future. The governmental funds financial statements continue to focus on the fiscal accountability of governmental activities. However, government-wide financial statements focus on the operational accountability of the governmental and business-type activities of the government as a whole. The fiduciary funds financial statements and the proprietary funds financial statements provide information about the operational accountability of each fund, respectively.

Answer (B) is incorrect because the government-wide statements focus on operational accountability. Moreover, financial accountability is not as accurate a phase as fiscal accountability. The term "fiscal" is preferable because it means having to do with the public treasury or revenues. Answer (C) is incorrect because fiscal accountability remains the main focus of governmental funds financial statements under SGAS 34. Answer (D) is incorrect because operational accountability includes but is not limited to functional accountability.

68. The government-wide statement of activities reports

A. Activities accounted for in governmental funds by segment.

B. Activities accounted for in enterprise funds at the fund level of detail.

C. Net (expense) revenue for each function equal to expenses minus program revenues.

D. Net (expense) revenue for each function equal to expenses minus general revenues.

Answer (C) is correct. *(Publisher)*

REQUIRED: The reporting in the government-wide statement of activities.

DISCUSSION: The statement of activities presents operations in a format that displays net (expense) revenue for each function, thereby reporting the relative financial burden to the taxpayers for that function. The net (expense) revenue for each governmental or business-type function equals expenses (at a minimum, the direct expenses of the function) minus program revenues, i.e., charges or fees and fines deriving directly from the function or program, and contributions that are restricted to the function or program (SGAS 34 and SGAS 37).

Answer (A) is incorrect because the minimum levels of detail for activities accounted for in governmental funds and activities accounted for in enterprise funds are by function and by different identifiable activities, respectively. However, the word "function" is also used in SGAS 34 to include the minimum levels of detail for both types of activities. Answer (B) is incorrect because the minimum levels of detail for activities accounted for in governmental funds and activities accounted for in enterprise funds are by function and by different identifiable activities, respectively. However, the word "function" is also used in SGAS 34 to include the minimum levels of detail for both types of activities. Answer (D) is incorrect because general revenues are reported separately after total net (expense) revenue for all functions.

69. How are expenses reported in the government-wide statement of activities?

A. Interest on general long-term liabilities is ordinarily treated as a direct expense.

B. At a minimum, direct expenses should be reported for each function.

C. If indirect expenses are allocated, a full-cost approach must be used.

D. Direct and allocated indirect expenses are aggregated in a single column.

Answer (B) is correct. *(Publisher)*

REQUIRED: The reporting of expenses in the statement of activities.

DISCUSSION: Direct expenses are specifically associated with a service, program, or department. Hence, they are clearly identifiable with a given function. The net (expense) revenue for each function equals expenses (at a minimum, the direct expenses of the function) minus program revenues. However, indirect expenses need not be allocated and included in the determination of net (expense) revenue for each function.

Answer (A) is incorrect because interest on general long-term liabilities is a direct expense only in unusual circumstances, that is, when the borrowing is essential to establishing or maintaining a program and omitting the interest from the program's direct expenses would be misleading. Answer (C) is incorrect because direct expenses must be reported by function, whereas indirect expenses may or may not be allocated. A government may choose to allocate some indirect expenses, to adopt a full-cost allocation approach, or not to allocate. Answer (D) is incorrect because, if indirect expenses are allocated, direct and indirect expenses should be displayed in separate columns.

70. In the government-wide statement of activities, depreciation of

A. Capital assets shared by some of the government's functions is an indirect expense.

B. Capital assets shared by all of the government's functions is not required to be included in the direct expenses of those functions.

C. General infrastructure assets should be allocated to the various functions.

D. General infrastructure assets must be presented as a separate line item.

Answer (B) is correct. *(Publisher)*

REQUIRED: The treatment of depreciation in the statement of activities.

DISCUSSION: Depreciation of shared capital assets, such as a structure that houses the offices of the tax assessor, election supervisor, and building inspector, should be apportioned to, and included in the direct expenses of, the sharing functions. However, if a capital asset, such as a city hall, serves all of the government's functions, depreciation of that asset need not be reported as a direct expense of the various functions. It may be displayed as a separate line item or as part of the general government function and, in either case, may or may not be allocated.

Answer (A) is incorrect because depreciation of shared capital assets should be apportioned to, and included in the direct expenses of, the sharing functions. Answer (C) is incorrect because depreciation of infrastructure assets is not allocated to other functions. It is reported either as a separate line item or as a direct expense of the function associated with capital outlays for, and maintenance of, the infrastructure assets. Answer (D) is incorrect because depreciation of infrastructure assets is not allocated to other functions. It is reported either as a separate line item or as a direct expense of the function associated with capital outlays for, and maintenance of, the infrastructure assets.

71. In accordance with SGAS 34, *Basic Financial Statements – and Management's Discussion and Analysis – for State and Local Governments*, general revenues reported in the government-wide statement of activities

A. Include all taxes.

B. Exclude taxes levied for a specific purpose.

C. Are aggregated with contributions, special and extraordinary items, and transfers in a line item.

D. Exclude interest and grants.

Answer (A) is correct. *(Publisher)*

REQUIRED: The true statement about general revenues.

DISCUSSION: General revenues are revenues not required to be reported as program revenues. They are reported separately after total net (expense) revenue for all functions in the government-wide statement of activities. All taxes, including those levied for a special purpose, are general revenues.

Answer (B) is incorrect because all taxes are general revenues but should be reported by type of tax, e.g., income, sales, and property. Answer (C) is incorrect because contributions to endowments, contributions to permanent fund principal, transfers between governmental and business-type activities, and special and extraordinary items are reported separately in the same manner as general revenues (at the bottom of the statement of activities to determine the change in net assets for the period). Answer (D) is incorrect because general revenues are all revenues not required to be reported as program revenues.

72. The government-wide statement of activities should report which of the following categories of program revenues?

I. Charges for services
II. Earnings of permanent funds that finance general fund programs
III. Program-specific capital grants and contributions.

A. I only.
B. I and III only.
C. II and III only.
D. I, II, and III.

Answer (B) is correct. *(Publisher)*
REQUIRED: The categories of program revenues.
DISCUSSION: Program revenues include (a) charges for services (fees for specific services, licenses and permits; operating special assessments; other amounts charged to service recipients; and fines and forfeitures) and (b) program-specific grants and contributions, both operating and capital. They may also include earnings on endowments, permanent fund investments, or other investments restricted to a given program. Earnings of endowments or permanent funds that finance general fund programs or general operating expenses are not program revenues. However, when earnings on a program's invested accumulated resources are legally restricted for use by the program, those earnings are program revenues.
Answer (A) is incorrect because program revenues also include program-specific grants and contributions, both operating and capital. Answer (C) is incorrect because earnings of endowments or permanent funds that finance general fund programs or general operating expenses are not program revenues. Answer (D) is incorrect because earnings of endowments or permanent funds that finance general fund programs or general operating expenses are not program revenues.

73. Preparation of government-wide financial statements requires elimination of

A. Receivables from fiduciary funds from the statement of net assets.
B. The effects on the statement of activities of interfund services provided and used between functions.
C. Internal balances from the total primary government column in the statement of net assets.
D. Net residual amounts due between governmental and business-type activities from those columns in the statement of net assets.

Answer (C) is correct. *(Publisher)*
REQUIRED: The elimination necessary in the preparation of government-wide financial statements.
DISCUSSION: Numerous eliminations and reclassifications are necessary in preparing the government-wide statements. Thus, interfund receivables and payables are eliminated in the governmental and business-type activities columns of the statement of net assets, except for net residual amounts due (presented as internal balances). However, the total primary government column excludes internal balances.
Answer (A) is incorrect because fund receivables from, or payables to, fiduciary funds are treated in the statement of net assets as arising from transactions with external parties, not as internal balances. Answer (B) is incorrect because eliminations are not made in the statement of activities for the effects of interfund services provided and used between functions (e.g., the sale of power by a utility to the general government). Answer (D) is incorrect because net residual amounts due between governmental and business-type activities are presented as interfund balances in the appropriate columns but are eliminated in the total primary government column.

74. State and local governments report various funds to the extent their activities meet the fund criteria. Governmental funds include

A. Internal service funds.
B. Nonexpendable trust funds.
C. Enterprise funds.
D. Permanent funds.

Answer (D) is correct. *(Publisher)*
REQUIRED: The governmental funds.
DISCUSSION: Governmental funds (the general fund, special revenue funds, capital projects funds, debt service funds, and permanent funds) emphasize sources, uses, and balances of current financial resources, often with use of budgetary accounts. Expendable assets are assigned to funds based on their intended use, liabilities are assigned to the funds from which they will be paid, and the difference (fund equity) is the fund balance. Permanent funds report resources legally restricted so that earnings only, not principal, may be expended for the benefit of the government or its citizenry, that is, to support the government's programs. An example is a perpetual-care fund for a public cemetery. Permanent funds should be distinguished from private-purpose trust funds.
Answer (A) is incorrect because internal service funds are proprietary funds. Answer (B) is incorrect because SGAS 34 eliminated the expendable and nonexpendable trust fund types. Answer (C) is incorrect because enterprise funds are proprietary funds.

75. In the government-wide statement of activities, special items are transactions or other events that are

A. Unusual in nature and infrequent in occurrence.

B. Unusual in nature or infrequent in occurrence but not within management's control.

C. Unusual in nature and infrequent in occurrence and within management's control.

D. Unusual in nature or infrequent in occurrence and within management's control.

Answer (D) is correct. *(Publisher)*

REQUIRED: The characteristics of special items.

DISCUSSION: Extraordinary items are unusual in nature and infrequent in occurrence. Special items are significant transactions or other events within the control of management that are either unusual or infrequent. They are reported separately after extraordinary items. The terms "unusual" and "infrequent" are defined in the same way as in APB 30.

Answer (A) is incorrect because extraordinary items are unusual in nature and infrequent in occurrence. Answer (B) is incorrect because special items are within management's control. Answer (C) is incorrect because extraordinary items are unusual in nature and infrequent in occurrence.

76. The focus of certain fund financial statements is on major funds. Accordingly,

A. Major internal service funds must be presented separately in the statement of net assets for proprietary funds.

B. The main operating fund is always reported as a major fund.

C. Combining statements for nonmajor funds are required.

D. Enterprise funds not meeting the quantitative criteria are not eligible for presentation as major funds.

Answer (B) is correct. *(Publisher)*

REQUIRED: The true statement about major fund reporting.

DISCUSSION: The focus of governmental and proprietary fund financial statements is on major funds (but major fund reporting is not required for internal service funds). Each major fund is presented in a separate column, and nonmajor funds are aggregated in one column. Combining statements are not required for nonmajor funds. The main operating fund (e.g., the general fund) is always reported as a major fund, and any governmental or enterprise fund believed to be particularly important to users may also be reported in this way. Other individual governmental or enterprise funds must be reported as major if they meet the quantitative thresholds.

Answer (A) is incorrect because major fund reporting requirements apply to governmental and enterprise funds but not to internal service funds. Answer (C) is incorrect because combining statements for nonmajor funds are not required but may be reported as supplementary information. Answer (D) is incorrect because a government may report any governmental or enterprise individual fund as major if it is believed to be particularly important to users.

77. A capital projects fund must be reported as major if

A. Total assets of that fund are 5% of the total assets of all governmental funds and 2% of the total assets of all governmental and enterprise funds combined.

B. Total expenditures of that fund are 10% of the total expenditures of all governmental funds and 2% of the total expenditures of all governmental and enterprise funds combined.

C. Total liabilities of that fund are 10% of the total liabilities of all governmental funds and 5% of the total liabilities of all governmental and enterprise funds combined.

D. Total revenues of that fund are 6% of the total revenues of all governmental funds and 3% of the total revenues of all governmental and enterprise funds combined.

Answer (C) is correct. *(Publisher)*

REQUIRED: The criteria for requiring major fund reporting.

DISCUSSION: The main operating fund (e.g., the general fund) is always reported as a major fund, and any governmental or enterprise fund believed to be particularly important to users may also be reported as a major fund. Moreover, any fund must be reported as major if revenues, expenditures/expenses, assets, or liabilities (excluding revenues and expenditures/expenses reported as extraordinary items) of the fund are (1) at least 10% of the corresponding element total for all funds of the same category or type, that is, for all governmental or all enterprise funds, and (2) the same element that met the 10% criterion is at least 5% of the corresponding element total for all governmental and enterprise funds combined (SGAS 34 and SGAS 37).

78. A summary reconciliation of the government-wide and fund financial statements

A. Must be presented at the bottom of the fund statements or in an accompanying schedule.

B. Must be presented as required supplementary information.

C. Must be presented in the notes.

D. Is recommended but not required.

Answer (A) is correct. *(Publisher)*

REQUIRED: The presentation of a summary reconciliation of the government-wide and fund financial statements.

DISCUSSION: A government must provide a summary reconciliation to the government-wide statements at the bottom of the fund statements or in a schedule. Brief explanations on the face of the statements may suffice, but a more detailed explanation in the notes may be necessary.

Answer (B) is incorrect because RSI consists of MD&A, budgetary comparison schedules, and information about infrastructure assets reported using the modified approach. Answer (C) is incorrect because the summary reconciliation must be presented at the bottom of the fund statements or in an accompanying schedule. Additional detail may need to be given in the notes. Answer (D) is incorrect because the summary reconciliation is required.

79. Tree City reported a $1,500 net increase in fund balance for governmental funds for the current year. During the year, Tree purchased general capital assets of $9,000 and recorded depreciation expense of $3,000. What amount should Tree report as the change in net assets for governmental activities?

A. ($4,500)

B. $1,500

C. $7,500

D. $10,500

Answer (C) is correct. *(CPA, adapted)*

REQUIRED: The change in net assets for governmental activities.

DISCUSSION: General capital assets are not specifically related to activities reported in nongovernmental funds, usually result from expenditure of governmental fund financial resources, and should be reported at historical cost in the governmental activities column of the government-wide statement of net assets. They are not reported as assets in the fund financial statements. Moreover, capital assets must be depreciated unless they are infrastructure assets that meet certain requirements. The modified accrual basis of accounting is required in the financial statements of governmental funds, and the accrual basis of accounting is required in the government-wide statements (SGAS 34). Thus, the calculation of the $1,500 net increase in the fund balance for governmental funds most likely reflects a $9,000 expenditure (modified accrual basis) to acquire the general capital assets. The effect of the expenditure is a decrease in current financial resources of $9,000. However the government-wide statements report an expense of $3,000 (accrual basis) for depreciation and a depreciated asset with a carrying amount of $6,000 ($9,000 cost – $3,000 depreciation). The effect of recognizing depreciation expense is a decrease in economic resources of $3,000. Reconciling the net increase in fund balance for governmental funds to the change in net assets for governmental activities therefore requires adding $6,000 ($9,000 modified accrual basis expenditure – $3,000 accrual basis expense). The change in net assets for governmental activities is $7,500 ($1,500 + $6,000 reconciling item).

Answer (A) is incorrect because ($4,500) is the excess of the expenditure over the sum of the expense and the increase in fund balance. Answer (B) is incorrect because $1,500 is the increase in fund balance. Answer (D) is incorrect because $10,500 assumes depreciation is not recognized.

80. Governmental fund financial statements are prepared using the

	Economic Resources Measurement Focus	Current Financial Resources Measurement Focus	Accrual Basis	Modified Accrual Basis
A.	Yes	No	Yes	No
B.	No	Yes	No	Yes
C.	Yes	No	No	Yes
D.	No	Yes	Yes	No

Answer (B) is correct. *(Publisher)*

REQUIRED: The measurement focus and basis of accounting used in governmental fund financial statements.

DISCUSSION: The current financial resources measurement focus and the modified accrual basis of accounting are required in the financial statements of governmental funds. The emphasis is on determination of financial position and changes therein (sources, uses, and balances of financial resources). Revenues should be recognized when they become available and measurable; expenditures should be recognized when the fund liability is incurred, if measurable. However, unmatured interest on general long-term liabilities is recognized when due.

81. General capital assets and general long-term liabilities must be reported in the

A. Governmental funds financial statements.

B. General account groups.

C. General fund's balance sheet.

D. Governmental activities column of the government-wide statement of net assets.

Answer (D) is correct. *(Publisher)*

REQUIRED: The reporting of general capital assets and general long-term liabilities.

DISCUSSION: General capital assets are not specifically related to activities reported in nongovernmental funds, usually result from expenditure of governmental fund financial resources, and should be reported in the governmental activities column of the government-wide statement of net assets. They are not reported as assets in governmental funds or in a general fixed assets account group. General long-term liabilities are not reported as liabilities in governmental funds or in a general long-term debt account group. They should be reported in the governmental activities column of the government-wide statement of net assets. General long-term liabilities include the unmatured principal amounts of general obligation indebtedness (such as bonds, warrants, and notes); lease-purchase agreements and other commitments not recorded as current liabilities in governmental funds; and the noncurrent portions of liabilities for capital leases, operating leases with scheduled rent increases, compensated absences, claims and judgments, pensions, special termination benefits, and landfill closure and postclosure care.

Answer (A) is incorrect because general capital assets and general long-term liabilities traditionally have not been reported in any given fund or funds. The reason is that they apply to all governmental activities. Moreover, general capital assets are not financial, and general long-term liabilities are not current; thus, they do not meet the criteria for recognition in governmental funds, which have a current financial resources measurement focus. Answer (B) is incorrect because SGAS 34 has eliminated the general fixed assets and general long-term debt account groups. Answer (C) is incorrect because general capital assets and general long-term liabilities traditionally have not been reported in any given fund or funds. The reason is that they apply to all governmental activities. Moreover, general capital assets are not financial, and general long-term liabilities are not current; thus, they do not meet the criteria for recognition in governmental funds, which have a current financial resources measurement focus.

82. A state or local government must present which financial statements for proprietary funds?

I. A statement of activities
II. A statement in net assets or balance sheet format
III. A statement of cash flows

A. I only.

B. I and III only.

C. II and III only.

D. I, II, and III.

Answer (C) is correct. *(Publisher)*

REQUIRED: The statement(s) required for proprietary funds.

DISCUSSION: Proprietary funds emphasize determination of operating income, changes in net assets (or cost recovery), financial position, and cash flows. A statement of net assets or balance sheet is required for proprietary funds, with assets and liabilities classified as current or noncurrent. Either a net assets format (assets – liabilities = net assets) or a balance sheet format (assets = liabilities + net assets) may be used. A statement of revenues, expenses, and changes in fund net assets or fund equity (either label may be used) is the required operating statement for proprietary funds. A statement of cash flows prepared in accordance with SGAS 9 is also required for proprietary funds. However, SGAS 34 requires that the direct method (including a reconciliation of operating cash flows to operating income) be used. The direct method reports major classes of gross operating cash receipts and payments and their sum (net cash flow from operating activities). The minimum classes to be reported are cash receipts from customers, cash receipts from interfund services provided, other operating cash receipts, cash payments to employees for services, cash payments to other suppliers, cash payments for interfund services used, and other operating cash payments.

83. Which financial statement must be presented for governmental funds?

A. A statement of activities.

B. A statement of cash flows.

C. A statement of revenues, expenses, and changes in fund net assets.

D. A financial statement in balance sheet format.

Answer (D) is correct. *(Publisher)*

REQUIRED: The governmental fund financial statement.

DISCUSSION: A balance sheet is required for governmental funds. It should be in balance sheet format (assets = liabilities + fund balances) with a total column and segregation of fund balances into reserved and unreserved amounts.

Answer (A) is incorrect because a statement of activities is a required government-wide statement. Answer (B) is incorrect because a statement of net assets or balance sheet; a statement of revenues, expenses, and changes in fund net assets; and a statement of cash flows are required for proprietary funds. Answer (C) is incorrect because a statement of net assets or balance sheet; a statement of revenues, expenses, and changes in fund net assets; and a statement of cash flows are required for proprietary funds.

84. A statement of revenues, expenditures, and changes in fund balances must be reported for governmental funds. In that statement,

A. Debt refundings are treated as extraordinary items.

B. Revenues are classified, at a minimum, by function.

C. Proceeds of long-term debt should be reported in the other financing sources and uses classification.

D. Expenditures are classified by major expenditure source.

Answer (C) is correct. *(Publisher)*

REQUIRED: The appropriate reporting in the statement of revenues, expenditures, and changes in fund balances.

DISCUSSION: A statement of revenues, expenditures, and changes in fund balances is required for governmental funds. It reports inflows, outflows, and balances of current financial resources for each major fund, for nonmajor funds in the aggregate, and in a total column. In this statement, the other financing sources and uses classification appears after excess (deficiency) of revenues over expenditures. Other financing sources and uses include the face amount of long-term debt, issuance premium or discount, some payments to escrow agents for bond refundings, transfers, and sales of most capital assets (SGAS 34 and SGAS 37).

Answer (A) is incorrect because debt refundings in governmental funds are not extraordinary items. They result in other financing sources or uses, not gains or losses. Answer (B) is incorrect because revenues are classified in this statement by major source. Answer (D) is incorrect because expenditures are classified in this statement by, at a minimum, function.

85. SGAS 34 establishes criteria for the required reporting of activities as enterprise funds. Based on these criteria, and assuming the amounts involved are derived from principal revenue sources, enterprise fund reporting is most likely to be optional if

A. Fees are charged to external users for goods or services.

B. The activity is financed with debt, and the only security is a pledge of the activity's net revenues from fees and charges.

C. The activity's costs are legally required to be recovered from fees and charges.

D. The activity's pricing policies set fees and charges to recover costs.

Answer (A) is correct. *(Publisher)*

REQUIRED: The circumstances in which enterprise fund reporting may be optional.

DISCUSSION: Enterprise funds need not be used to report insignificant activities. They may be used for activities for which fees are charged to external users, but they must be used if one of three criteria (applied in the context of the activity's principal revenue sources) is satisfied. The activity should be reported as an enterprise fund if it is financed with debt, and the only security is a pledge of the activity's net revenues from fees and charges. If the debt is also secured by the full faith and credit of a related governmental entity, the debt is not payable solely from the activity's net revenues. The activity also should be reported as an enterprise fund if its costs (including capital costs) of providing services are legally required to be recovered from fees and charges, not taxes or similar revenues. Furthermore, the activity should be reported as an enterprise fund if its pricing policies set fees and charges to recover its costs (including capital costs). The focus of these criteria is primarily on fees charged to external users (SGAS 34 and SGAS 37).

Answer (B) is incorrect because, in the context of an activity's principal revenue sources, enterprise fund reporting is required if the financing of an activity is secured by fees and charges. Answer (C) is incorrect because, in the context of an activity's principal revenue sources, enterprise fund reporting is required if there is a legal requirement to recover costs from fees and charges. Answer (D) is incorrect because, in the context of an activity's principal revenue sources, enterprise fund reporting is required if there is a policy that sets fees and charges to recover costs.

86. An activity that provides goods to other subunits of the primary government on a cost reimbursement basis should be reported as a(n)

A. Fiduciary fund.

B. Agency fund.

C. Enterprise fund in some cases.

D. Internal service fund in all cases.

Answer (C) is correct. *(Publisher)*

REQUIRED: The fund used to report an activity providing goods to other subunits of the primary government on a cost reimbursement basis.

DISCUSSION: Internal service funds may be used for activities that provide goods and services to other subunits of the primary government and its component units or to other governments on a cost-reimbursement basis. However, if the reporting government is not the predominant participant, the activity should be reported as an enterprise fund.

Answer (A) is incorrect because fiduciary funds emphasize net assets and changes in net assets. They report assets that cannot be used to support the government's own programs because they are held in trust or in an agency capacity. Answer (B) is incorrect because fiduciary funds emphasize net assets and changes in net assets. They report assets that cannot be used to support the government's own programs because they are held in trust or in an agency capacity. Answer (D) is incorrect because use of an internal service fund is inappropriate if the reporting government is not the predominant participant.

87. Under SGAS 34, proprietary fund financial statements are prepared using the

	Economic Resources Measure-ment Focus	Current Financial Resources Measure-ment Focus	Accrual Basis	Modified Accrual Basis
A.	Yes	No	Yes	No
B.	No	Yes	No	Yes
C.	Yes	No	No	Yes
D.	No	Yes	Yes	No

Answer (A) is correct. *(Publisher)*

REQUIRED: The measurement focus and basis of accounting used in proprietary fund financial statements.

DISCUSSION: The economic resources measurement focus and the accrual basis of accounting are required in the proprietary fund financial statements. The economic resources measurement focus differs from the shorter-term flow-of-current-financial-resources approach used in governmental funds. It measures revenues and expenses in the same way as in commercial accounting but does not necessarily emphasize net income. Instead, the emphasis is on a longer-range measure of revenues earned or levied (and accrued immediately if measurable). Moreover, the economic resources model focuses on cost of services. The accrual basis of accounting recognizes most transactions when they occur, regardless of when cash is received or paid.

88. In a statement of net assets or balance sheet for proprietary funds,

A. Net assets must be reported in two components: restricted or unrestricted.

B. Capital contributions must be reported in a separate component of net assets.

C. Designations must be shown on the face of the statement.

D. Assets and liabilities must be classified.

Answer (D) is correct. *(Publisher)*

REQUIRED: The appropriate display in the statement of net assets or balance sheet for proprietary funds.

DISCUSSION: A statement of net assets or balance sheet is required for proprietary funds, and assets and liabilities must be classified as current or noncurrent. Either a net assets format (assets – liabilities = net assets) or a balance sheet format (assets = liabilities + net assets) may be used. Furthermore, net assets should be reported in three components (invested in capital assets, net of related debt; restricted; and unrestricted), capital contributions should not be displayed as a separate component, and designations should not be shown on the face of the statements.

Answer (A) is incorrect because net assets should be reported in three components, including invested in capital assets, net of related debt. Answer (B) is incorrect because one of the three components of net assets is not capital contributions. Answer (C) is incorrect because designations are removable at the discretion of the reporting government and should not be reported in the statement.

89. Enterprise funds may be reported using GASB pronouncements and

A. Any nonconflicting, relevant FASB Statements and Interpretations elected by the reporting government.

B. Relevant FASB Statements and Interpretations issued after November 30, 1989 that were developed for businesses and that do not conflict with or contradict GASB pronouncements.

C. All relevant FASB Statements and Interpretations, APB Opinions, and ARBs whether or not developed for businesses.

D. No pronouncements of the FASB and its predecessors.

Answer (B) is correct. *(Publisher)*

REQUIRED: The pronouncements used to report enterprise funds.

DISCUSSION: Proprietary funds apply not only GASB pronouncements but also FASB Statements and Interpretations, APB Opinions, and ARBs issued on or before November 30, 1989 that do not conflict with or contradict GASB pronouncements. Enterprise funds (but not internal service funds) may elect to apply either all or none of the FASB Statements and Interpretations issued after that date that were developed for business enterprises and that do not conflict with or contradict GASB pronouncements.

Answer (A) is incorrect because an enterprise fund must be reported based on relevant FASB Statements and Interpretations that were issued on or before November 30, 1989 and that do not conflict with or contradict GASB pronouncements. Answer (C) is incorrect because enterprise funds should not apply FASB Statements and Interpretations that were issued after November 30, 1989 that were not developed for businesses, that is, those limited to or addressing matters that primarily concern not-for-profit organizations. Answer (D) is incorrect because enterprise funds must be reported based on FASB Statements and Interpretations, APB Opinions, and ARBs issued on or before November 30, 1989 that do not conflict with or contradict GASB pronouncements.

90. The statement of revenues, expenses, and changes in fund net assets for proprietary funds

A. Combines special and extraordinary items in a subtotal presented before nonoperating revenues and expenses.

B. Must report revenues at gross amounts, with discounts and allowances disclosed parenthetically.

C. Distinguishes between operating and nonoperating revenues and expenses.

D. Must define operating items in the same way as in the statement of cash flows.

Answer (C) is correct. *(Publisher)*

REQUIRED: The true statement about the statement of revenues, expenses, and changes in fund net assets.

DISCUSSION: A statement of revenues, expenses, and changes in fund net assets or fund equity (either label may be used) is the required operating statement for proprietary funds. Operating and nonoperating revenues and expenses should be distinguished, with separate subtotals for operating revenues, operating expenses, and operating income.

Answer (A) is incorrect because nonoperating revenues and expenses are presented immediately after operating income (loss). Moreover, special and extraordinary items are reported separately. Answer (B) is incorrect because revenues are reported by major source either net with disclosure of discounts and allowances or gross with discounts and allowances reported beneath the revenue amounts. Answer (D) is incorrect because a government should consistently follow appropriate definitions of operating items. SGAS 34 provides general guidelines and mandates consistent use of definitions, but it does not require that the categorization of items in the statement of cash flows control the definitions of operating items in the statement of revenues, expenses, and changes in fund net assets.

91. A statement of cash flows for proprietary funds

A. Is optional.

B. Must be prepared using either the direct method or the indirect method.

C. Must be prepared using the direct method.

D. Need not reconcile operating cash flows to operating income if the direct method is used.

Answer (C) is correct. *(Publisher)*

REQUIRED: The true statement about the statement of cash flows for proprietary funds.

DISCUSSION: A statement of cash flows prepared in accordance with SGAS 9 is required for proprietary funds. However, SGAS 34 requires that the direct method (including a reconciliation of operating cash flows to operating income) be used. The direct method reports major classes of gross operating cash receipts and payments and their sum (net cash flow from operating activities). The minimum classes to be reported are cash receipts from customers, cash receipts from interfund services provided, other operating cash receipts, cash payments to employees for services, cash payments to other suppliers, cash payments for interfund services used, and other operating cash payments.

Answer (A) is incorrect because a statement of cash flows for proprietary funds is required. Answer (B) is incorrect because the direct method is required. Answer (D) is incorrect because the reconciliation is required.

92. A state or local government may report which fiduciary funds?

A. Private-purpose trust funds.

B. Expendable trust funds.

C. Nonexpendable trust funds.

D. Permanent funds.

Answer (A) is correct. *(Publisher)*

REQUIRED: The fiduciary funds.

DISCUSSION: Under SGAS 34, fiduciary funds include pension (and other employee benefit) trust funds, investment trust funds, private-purpose trust funds, and agency funds. Pension (and other employee benefit) trust funds report resources held for members and beneficiaries of pension plans (defined benefit or contribution), other postemployment benefit plans, or other employee benefit plans. Investment trust funds are used by a sponsoring government to report the external portions of external investment pools (SGAS 31). Private-purpose trust funds are used for all other trust arrangements, whether the beneficiaries are individuals, private organizations, or other governments.

Answer (B) is incorrect because expendable trust funds were eliminated by SGAS 34. Answer (C) is incorrect because nonexpendable trust funds were eliminated by SGAS 34. Answer (D) is incorrect because permanent funds are governmental funds.

93. Which financial statements must be reported for fiduciary funds?

I. Statement of fiduciary net assets

II. Statement of changes in fiduciary net assets

III. Statement of revenues, expenditures, and changes in fund balances

IV. Statement of cash flows

A. I and II only.

B. I, II, and III only.

C. II, III, and IV only.

D. I, II, III, and IV.

Answer (A) is correct. *(Publisher)*

REQUIRED: The financial statements reported by fiduciary funds.

DISCUSSION: Fiduciary fund financial statements include information about all fiduciary funds and similar component units. The statements report information in a separate column for each fund type but not by major fund. The notes present financial statements for individual pension plans and postemployment health-care plans unless separate GAAP reports have been issued. A statement of fiduciary net assets (equivalent to the statement of plan net assets required by SGAS 25 for defined benefit pension plans) is required for fiduciary funds. It reports assets, liabilities, and net assets for each fiduciary fund type but does not present the three components of net assets reported in the government-wide statement of net assets or in the proprietary fund statement of net assets. A statement of changes in fiduciary net assets (equivalent to the statement of changes in plan net assets required by SGAS 25 for defined benefit pension plans) is required for fiduciary funds. It reports additions to, subtractions from, and the annual net change in net assets for each fiduciary fund type.

94. Liabilities of a defined benefit pension plan for benefits and refunds are reported in a state or local government's fiduciary fund financial statements using the

	Economic Resources Measurement Focus	Current Financial Resources Measurement Focus	Accrual Basis	Modified Accrual Basis
A.	Yes	No	Yes	No
B.	No	Yes	No	Yes
C.	Yes	No	No	Yes
D.	No	Yes	Yes	No

Answer (A) is correct. *(Publisher)*

REQUIRED: The measurement focus and basis of accounting used in fiduciary fund financial statements.

DISCUSSION: The economic resources measurement focus and the accrual basis of accounting are required in the fiduciary fund financial statements. Liabilities of defined benefit pension plans and of postemployment benefit plans other than pensions are recognized on the accrual basis, that is, when the transaction or event occurs. For plan liabilities for benefits and refunds, the transaction occurs when the benefits and refunds become due and payable under the plan's terms (SGAS 25 and SGAS 43).

95. Fiduciary fund financial statements report

A. Information by major fund.

B. Three components of net assets.

C. A separate column for each fund type.

D. No separate statements for individual pension plans.

Answer (C) is correct. *(Publisher)*

REQUIRED: The reporting in fiduciary fund financial statements.

DISCUSSION: Fiduciary fund financial statements include information about all fiduciary funds and similar component units. The statements report information in a separate column for each fund type but not by major fund. The notes present financial statements for individual pension plans and postemployment health-care plans unless separate GAAP reports have been issued. A statement of fiduciary net assets is required for fiduciary funds. It reports assets, liabilities, and net assets for each fiduciary fund type but does not present the three components of net assets reported in the government-wide statement of net assets or in the proprietary fund statement of net assets.

Answer (A) is incorrect because major funds are reported only in governmental and enterprise fund statements. Answer (B) is incorrect because three components of net assets are reported only in the government-wide statement of net assets and in the proprietary fund statement of net assets. Answer (D) is incorrect because separate financial statements for individual pension plans and postemployment health-care plans are reported in the notes. However, if separate GAAP financial statements have been issued for such plans, information is given in the notes about how those statements may be obtained.

96. Which of the following is a reporting requirement for agency funds?

A. They should be reported in a statement of fiduciary net assets and a statement of changes in fiduciary net assets.

B. Agency fund assets should equal liabilities in the statement of fiduciary net assets.

C. An agency fund used as a clearing account should report as assets the amounts pertaining to the other funds.

D. An agency fund should not be used as a clearing account.

Answer (B) is correct. *(Publisher)*

REQUIRED: The reporting requirement for agency funds.

DISCUSSION: Agency fund assets should equal liabilities in the statement of fiduciary net assets, but agency funds are not reported in the statement of changes in fiduciary net assets.

Answer (A) is incorrect because agency funds are not reported in the statement of changes in fiduciary net assets. Answer (C) is incorrect because an agency fund may be used as a clearing account to distribute resources to other funds as well as to other entities, for example, by a county tax collector to distribute taxes to other funds and other governments. Assets pertaining to other funds are reported in those funds, not in the agency fund. Answer (D) is incorrect because an agency fund may be used as a clearing account to distribute resources to other funds as well as to other entities, for example, by a county tax collector to distribute taxes to other funds and other governments. Assets pertaining to other funds are reported in those funds, not in the agency fund.

97. Interfund activity is classified as

A. Operating transfers and residual equity transfers.

B. Operating transfers, residual equity transfers, and reimbursements.

C. Quasi-external transfers and residual equity transfers.

D. Reciprocal and nonreciprocal.

Answer (D) is correct. *(Publisher)*

REQUIRED: The classification of interfund activity.

DISCUSSION: Interfund activity may be reciprocal or nonreciprocal. Reciprocal interfund activity is analogous to exchange and exchange-like transactions, for example, interfund loans and services provided and used. Nonreciprocal interfund activity is analogous to nonexchange transactions, for example, interfund transfers and reimbursements.

98. An internal service provided and used

A. Is the internal counterpart to a nonexchange transaction.

B. Results in expenditures or expenses to buyer funds and revenues to seller funds.

C. Normally is accounted for as a reimbursement.

D. Requires recognition of an other financing source by the transferee fund and an other financing use by the transferor fund.

Answer (B) is correct. *(Publisher)*

REQUIRED: The treatment of an internal service provided and used.

DISCUSSION: Interfund services provided and used are transactions at prices equivalent to external exchange values. They result in revenues to seller funds and expenditures or expenses to buyer funds. Unpaid amounts are interfund receivables or payables.

Answer (A) is incorrect because an internal service provided and used is a reciprocal interfund activity, which is analogous to an exchange or an exchange-like transaction. Answer (C) is incorrect because interfund services provided and used normally result in revenues to sellers and expenditures or expenses to buyers. Reimbursements are not displayed in the statements. Answer (D) is incorrect because a transfer (nonreciprocal interfund activity) is an other financing source (use) in a transferee (transferor) governmental fund. An internal service provided and used is reciprocal interfund activity.

99. An interfund transfer

A. Is the internal counterpart to an exchange or an exchange-like transaction.

B. Results in a receivable and a payable.

C. Is reported in a proprietary fund's statements after nonoperating revenues and expenses.

D. Is reported in a proprietary fund as an other financing source or use.

Answer (C) is correct. *(Publisher)*

REQUIRED: The treatment of an interfund transfer.

DISCUSSION: Interfund transfers are one-way asset flows with no repayment required. In a governmental fund, a transfer is an other financing use (source) in the transferor (transferee) fund. In a proprietary fund's statement of revenues, expenses, and changes in fund net assets, transfers should be reported separately after nonoperating revenues and expenses in the same component as capital contributions, additions to endowments, and special and extraordinary items.

Answer (A) is incorrect because nonreciprocal interfund activity is analogous to nonexchange transactions. Answer (B) is incorrect because reciprocal interfund activity results in a receivable and a payable. Answer (D) is incorrect because, in a governmental fund, a transfer is an other financing use (source) in the transferor (transferee) fund.

100. The summary of significant accounting policies must make which of the following general disclosures?

A. The policy for applying FASB pronouncements issued before November 30, 1989 to business-type activities.

B. The policy for defining operating and nonoperating revenues of proprietary funds.

C. The measurement focus and basis of accounting of the fund financial statements.

D. The capital acquisitions for the period presented by major classes.

Answer (B) is correct. *(Publisher)*

REQUIRED: The general disclosure required to be made in the summary of significant accounting policies.

DISCUSSION: A government should have a policy that defines operating items in a way that is consistent with the nature of the activity, disclose that policy in the summary of significant accounting policies, and apply it consistently. How transactions would be categorized in a statement of cash flows is a consideration in defining operating items for proprietary funds. For example, cash flows classified as from capital and related financing activities, noncapital financing activities, and investing activities ordinarily are not included in operating income.

Answer (A) is incorrect because a government must apply all nonconflicting FASB Statements and Interpretations, APB Opinions, and ARBs issued on or before November 30, 1989. It must disclose its election regarding whether to apply nonconflicting FASB Statements and Interpretations issued after November 30, 1989 that were developed for business enterprises. Answer (C) is incorrect because a government must disclose in the summary of significant accounting policies the measurement focus and basis of accounting used in the government-wide financial statements. Answer (D) is incorrect because the capital acquisitions for the period presented by major classes are details required to be disclosed in a note but not in the summary of significant accounting policies.

101. State and local governments must disclose segment information for activities reported using enterprise fund accounting and reporting standards. For this purpose, a segment is

A. An individual enterprise fund of a state or local government.

B. A separate major line of business or class of customer.

C. A component of an enterprise that engages in business activities from which it may earn revenues and incur expenses.

D. An identifiable activity that has debt outstanding, with a revenue stream pledged in support of that debt.

Answer (D) is correct. *(Publisher)*

REQUIRED: The definition of a segment.

DISCUSSION: A segment is an identifiable activity (or grouping of activities) reported as or within an enterprise fund or another stand-alone entity that has revenue-backed debt (for example, certificates of participation) outstanding. Thus, a segment has a revenue stream pledged in support of that debt. Moreover, a segment's revenues, expenses, gains, losses, assets, and liabilities must be accounted for separately. Segment disclosures should identify the types of goods or services provided and present condensed financial information: statements of net assets; revenues, expenses, and changes in net assets; and cash flows (SGAS 34 and SGAS 37).

Answer (A) is incorrect because NCGA Interpretation 2 (superseded by SGAS 34) defines a segment as an individual enterprise fund of a state or local government. Answer (B) is incorrect because APB 30 defines a segment of a business as a separate major line of business or class of customer. Answer (C) is incorrect because SFAS 131 defines an operating segment as a component of an enterprise that engages in business activities from which it may earn revenues and incur expenses, whose operating results are regularly reviewed by the enterprise's chief operating decision maker to make resource allocation decisions and assess performance, and for which discrete financial information is available.

102. What approach to presentation of the notes to the financial statements has been adopted for financial reporting by state and local governments?

A. The notes are essential for fair presentation of the statements.

B. The notes are required supplementary information.

C. The notes have the same status as MD&A.

D. The notes give equal focus to the primary government and its discretely presented component units.

Answer (A) is correct. *(Publisher)*

REQUIRED: The approach to presentation of the notes to the financial statements.

DISCUSSION: Notes to the financial statements are an integral part of the basic financial statements because they disclose information essential to fair presentation that is not reported on the face of the statements. The focus is on the primary government's governmental activities, business-type activities, major funds, and nonmajor funds in the aggregate.

Answer (B) is incorrect because RSI mandated by SGAS 34 includes MD&A, budgetary comparison schedules for governmental funds, and information about infrastructure assets reported using the modified approach. Answer (C) is incorrect because RSI mandated by SGAS 34 includes MD&A, budgetary comparison schedules for governmental funds, and information about infrastructure assets reported using the modified approach. Answer (D) is incorrect because the notes focus on the primary government.

103. Budgetary comparison schedules presented by a state or local government must

A. Be reported for the general fund and each major special revenue fund with a legally adopted budget.

B. Be presented instead of budgetary comparison statements included in the basic statements.

C. Convert the appropriated budget information to the GAAP basis for comparison with actual amounts reported on that basis.

D. Compare only the final appropriated budget with actual amounts.

Answer (A) is correct. *(Publisher)*

REQUIRED: The true statement about budgetary comparison schedules.

DISCUSSION: Under SGAS 34, certain information must be presented as RSI in addition to MD&A. Budgetary comparison schedules must be reported for the general fund and each major special revenue fund with a legally adopted annual budget. A schedule includes the original budgets, that is, the first complete appropriated budgets; the final appropriated budgets; and the actual inflows, outflows, and balances stated on the budgetary basis of accounting. Thus, budgetary comparison schedules are not required for proprietary funds, fiduciary funds, and governmental funds other than the general fund and major special revenue funds.

Answer (B) is incorrect because a government may elect to report budgetary comparison information in a statement as part of the basic statements. Answer (C) is incorrect because the budgetary comparison schedules compare the budgets with actual inflows, outflows, and balances stated on the government's budgetary basis. However, a reconciliation to GAAP is required. Answer (D) is incorrect because the original and final appropriated budgets are compared with the actual inflows, outflows, and balances.

104. Users of a government's financial statements should be able to distinguish between the primary government and its component units. Furthermore, an overview of the discretely presented component units should be provided. Accordingly,

A. The government-wide statements provide discrete presentation of component unit data, including data for fiduciary component units.

B. Condensed financial statements for major component units must be presented in the notes to the basic statements.

C. Information about each major component unit must be provided in the reporting entity's basic statements.

D. Major component unit information must be provided in the form of combining statements.

Answer (C) is correct. *(Publisher)*

REQUIRED: The appropriate presentation of component unit data.

DISCUSSION: To provide an overview of component units, discrete presentation of component unit data is required in the government-wide statements, but fiduciary component units are included only in the fund statements. Blended component units are reported in accordance with SGAS 14. Each major component unit should be reported in the basic statements by presentation (1) in a separate column in the government-wide statements, (2) in combining statements of major component units after the fund statements, or (3) of condensed statements (a statement of net assets and a statement of activities) in the notes. The aggregated total component unit information should be the entity totals derived from the component units' statements of net assets and activities. However, major component unit information is not required for fiduciary component units (SGAS 34 and SGAS 37).

Answer (A) is incorrect because information for fiduciary component units is presented only in the fund financial statements with information for the primary government's fiduciary funds. Answer (B) is incorrect because major component units may be presented in combining statements after the fund statements, in separate columns in the government-wide statements, or in condensed statements in the notes. Answer (D) is incorrect because major component units may be presented in combining statements after the fund statements, in separate columns in the government-wide statements, or in condensed statements in the notes.

105. According to GASB 34, *Basic Financial Statements -- and Management's Discussion and Analysis -- for State and Local Governments*, certain budgetary schedules are required supplementary information (RSI). What is the minimum budgetary information required to be reported in those schedules?

A. A schedule for unfavorable variances at the functional level.

B. A schedule showing the final appropriations budget and actual expenditures on a budgetary basis.

C. A schedule showing the original budget, the final appropriations budget, and actual inflows, outflows, and balances on a budgetary basis.

D. A schedule showing the proposed budget, the approved budget, the final amended budget, actual inflows and outflows on a budgetary basis, and variances between budget and actual.

Answer (C) is correct. *(CPA, adapted)*

REQUIRED: The minimum information in required budgetary schedules.

DISCUSSION: Under SGAS 34, certain information must be presented as RSI in addition to MD&A. Budgetary comparison schedules must be reported for the general fund and each major special revenue fund with a legally adopted annual budget. A schedule includes the original budgets (the first complete appropriated budgets); the final appropriate budgets; and the actual inflows, outflows, and balances stated on the budgetary basis of accounting. Furthermore, a reconciliation of budgetary and GAAP information must be provided.

Answer (A) is incorrect because a budgetary comparison schedule may include a separate column to report the variance between the final budget and actual amounts. This treatment is encouraged but not required. Answer (B) is incorrect because the original budget and actual inflows, outflows, and balances on the budgetary basis are also required. Answer (D) is incorrect because SGAS 34 states that a schedule showing the original budget, the final appropriations budget, and actual inflows, outflows, and balances on a budgetary basis is required.

106. If infrastructure assets are reported using the modified approach, SGAS 34 requires which of the following to be presented as required supplementary information?

A. The assessment of condition, done at least every 3 years, for the last three complete assessments.

B. The amounts needed to maintain the current condition level.

C. The amounts actually expensed for maintenance of the condition level for each period of the infrastructure assets' service life.

D. The original condition level of the eligible infrastructure assets.

Answer (A) is correct. *(Publisher)*

REQUIRED: The information about infrastructure assets reported as RSI.

DISCUSSION: Information about infrastructure assets reported using the modified approach is also RSI. It includes schedules presenting the assessed condition of all eligible infrastructure assets for at least the last three complete assessments (done at least every 3 years), the amounts needed to maintain the assets at or above the condition level established and disclosed, and the amounts actually expensed for each of the last five periods. Disclosures in addition to the schedules include the basis for the condition measurement, the measurement scale used, and the condition level at which the government intends to preserve the assets.

Answer (B) is incorrect because the amounts needed to maintain and preserve the assets at or above the established and disclosed condition level should be compared with the amounts actually expensed for each of the last five reporting periods. Answer (C) is incorrect because the amounts needed to maintain and preserve the assets at or above the established and disclosed condition level should be compared with the amounts actually expensed for each of the last five reporting periods. Answer (D) is incorrect because the government must disclose the condition level at which it intends to preserve the eligible infrastructure assets reported using the modified approach.

107. A state or local government is reported as a special-purpose government if it

A. Has governmental and business-type activities.

B. Is engaged in two or more governmental programs.

C. Is not a legally separate entity.

D. Is engaged in one governmental program.

Answer (D) is correct. *(Publisher)*

REQUIRED: The entity that may be reported as a special-purpose government.

DISCUSSION: Special-purpose governments are legally separate entities that are component units or other stand-alone governments. If they have governmental and business-type activities or are engaged in two or more governmental programs, they should be reported as general-purpose governments. If a special-purpose government is engaged in one governmental program (e.g., an assessment or drainage district), it may combine the government-wide and fund statements in a format that reconciles individual items of fund data to government-wide data in a separate column. It may also report separate government-wide and fund statements, with the government-wide statement of activities presented in a different format.

Answer (A) is incorrect because a government that has governmental and business-type activities should be reported in the same manner as a general-purpose government. Answer (B) is incorrect because a government that is engaged in two or more governmental programs should be reported in the same manner as a general-purpose government. Answer (C) is incorrect because a special-purpose government is a legally separate entity.

STUDY UNIT TWENTY-NINE
NOT-FOR-PROFIT ORGANIZATIONS

According to **SFAS 117**, *Financial Statements of Not-for-Profit Organizations*, a complete set of financial statements for a not-for-profit organization includes a statement of financial position as of the end of the reporting period, a statement of activities and a statement of cash flows for the reporting period, and accompanying notes. The focus of financial statements is the organization as a whole. The degree of aggregation and order of presentation of accounts is similar to those required or permitted for business enterprises.

A **statement of financial position** reports total amounts of assets, liabilities, and net assets. Assets and liabilities are aggregated into reasonably homogeneous groups. Information about liquidity is provided by (1) sequencing assets according to their nearness of conversion to cash and liabilities according to their nearness to their maturity and resulting use of cash, (2) classifying assets and liabilities as current and noncurrent, or (3) disclosing relevant information in notes to the financial statements. Amounts of **net assets** are classified and reported as (1) **unrestricted**, (2) **temporarily restricted**, and (3) **permanently restricted**. These classifications are based on the existence or absence of donor-imposed restrictions.

A **statement of activities** reports the amount of changes in net assets for the period. It reports the changes in unrestricted, temporarily restricted, and permanently restricted net assets. The statement of activities uses descriptive terminology such as "change in net assets" or "change in equity." The change in net assets articulates with the net assets or equity in the statement of financial position. Events that simultaneously increase one class of net assets and decrease another (reclassifications) are reported separately. **Revenues** are reported as increases in unrestricted net assets unless the use of the assets received is subject to a donor-imposed restriction. **Expenses** are reported as decreases in unrestricted net assets. Information about expenses is reported by their functional classification in the statement of activities or in notes to the financial statements. Primary functional classifications are program services and supporting activities. Supporting activities include management and general, fund-raising, and membership-development activities. Voluntary health and welfare organizations are also required to report expenses by their natural classification.

According to **SFAS 116**, *Accounting for Contributions Received and Contributions Made*, a pronouncement applicable to business enterprises and not-for-profit organizations, a **contribution** is an unconditional transfer of cash or other assets to an entity or a settlement or cancelation of its liabilities in a voluntary nonreciprocal transfer by another entity acting other than as an owner. Contributions received ordinarily are measured at their fair values and recognized as revenues or gains in the period received.

However, SFAS 116 does not apply to tax exemptions, abatements, or incentives, or to transfers of assets from a government to a business enterprise. Nevertheless, SFAS 116 does not preclude accounting for this contribution as a revenue or gain. Indeed, such treatment would be consistent with the accounting for most contributions.

Contributions **without donor-imposed restrictions** are reported as unrestricted revenues and increases in unrestricted net assets. Contributions subject to **permanent donor-imposed restrictions** are reported as restricted support and as increases in permanently restricted net assets. Contributions subject to **temporary donor-imposed restrictions** are reported as restricted support and as increases in temporarily restricted net assets. However, donor-restricted contributions may be recognized as unrestricted support when the restrictions are met in the period the contribution is received, and the entity consistently applies and discloses this policy. **Expiration of a donor-imposed restriction** on a contribution is recognized in the period in which the restriction expires. Restrictions expire when the stipulated purpose for which the resource was restricted has been fulfilled or the stipulated time has elapsed. Expirations are reported simultaneously as increases in one class of net assets and decreases in another. These expirations are reclassifications that are reported as separate items.

Receipts of **unconditional promises to give** with payments due in future periods usually are reported as restricted support and increases in temporarily restricted net assets. However, if the donor clearly intended that current-period activities be supported, the promise is reported as unrestricted revenue and an increase in unrestricted net assets. **Contributions of long-lived assets** received without donor restrictions may be reported as restricted support if implying a time restriction on their use is an established accounting policy of the recipient organization. **Contributions of services** are recognized only if they either (1) create or enhance nonfinancial assets, or (2) require specialized skills, are provided by individuals possessing those skills, and would typically need to be purchased if not provided by donation. **Contributions of works of art, historical treasures, and similar assets** need not be recognized if the assets are to be added to collections that (1) are held for public exhibition, education, or research in furtherance of public service rather than financial gain; (2) are protected, kept unencumbered, cared for, and preserved; and (3) are subject to an organizational policy that requires the proceeds from the sales of collection items to be used to acquire other items for collections. **Conditional promises to give** are recognized when the conditions on which they depend are substantially met.

Contributions made by a not-for-profit entity are measured at their fair values. The donor entity recognizes them as expenses in the period made.

Under **SOP 94-3**, *Reporting of Related Entities by Not-for-Profit Organizations*, an NPO **consolidates** a **for-profit entity** if it has a direct or indirect majority voting interest unless control does not rest with the majority owner. If an NPO exercises **significant influence** as defined in APB 18 over the for-profit entity, it accounts for its ownership interest using the **equity method**. However, certain NPOs may report certain investments at market value in lieu of applying the equity method. An NPO may have a **controlling financial interest** in another NPO through direct or indirect ownership of a **majority voting interest in the other NPO**. An NPO **consolidates another NPO** in these circumstances unless control does not rest with the majority owner. **Consolidation** is also necessary if the NPO controls another NPO by exercising a majority voting interest in the board or a **majority ownership interest** that is not a majority voting interest. This distinction arises because NPOs have differing legal forms, such as joint ventures, partnerships, or corporations that issue membership certificates. **Control** other than by ownership of a majority voting interest in the other NPO is deemed to exist only if the NPO also has an **economic interest** in the other NPO. Control is the "direct or indirect ability to determine the direction of management and policies through ownership, contract, or otherwise." An economic interest arises when "(a) the other entity holds or uses significant resources that must be used for the unrestricted or restricted purposes of the NPO, either directly or indirectly by producing income or providing services, or (b) the reporting organization is responsible for the liabilities of the other entity." If an NPO has an economic interest and control through other than majority ownership or a majority voting interest (in the other NPO or in its board), consolidation is optional. For example, such control may be conferred by a contract. If consolidation is not chosen, various **disclosures** are required.

QUESTIONS

29.1 Objectives of Nonbusiness Organizations

1. Which of the following is ordinarily not considered one of the major distinguishing characteristics of nonbusiness organizations?

A. Significant amounts of resources are provided by donors in nonreciprocal transactions.

B. There is an absence of defined, transferable ownership interests.

C. Performance indicators similar to a business enterprise's profit are readily available.

D. The primary operating purpose is not to provide goods or services at a profit.

Answer (C) is correct. *(Publisher)*

REQUIRED: The statement not ordinarily considered a major characteristic of nonbusiness organizations.

DISCUSSION: SFAC 4, *Objectives of Financial Reporting by Nonbusiness Organizations*, states that the objectives of financial reporting are derived from the common interests of those who provide the resources to nonbusiness organizations. Such organizations ordinarily have no single indicator of performance comparable to a business enterprise's profit. Thus, nonbusiness organization performance is usually evaluated in terms of management stewardship.

Answer (A) is incorrect because SFAC 4 specifically gives significant amounts of resources provided by donors in nonreciprocal transactions as a distinguishing characteristic of nonbusiness organizations. Answer (B) is incorrect because SFAC 4 specifically gives an absence of defined, transferable ownership interests as a distinguishing characteristic of nonbusiness organizations. Answer (D) is incorrect because SFAC 4 specifically gives the primary operating purpose is not to provide goods or services at a profit as a distinguishing characteristic of nonbusiness organizations.

2. Which of the following is a characteristic of nonbusiness organizations?

A. Noneconomic reasons seldom underlie the decision to provide resources to nonbusiness enterprises.

B. Business and nonbusiness organizations usually obtain resources in the same way.

C. Both nonbusiness and business organizations use scarce resources in the production and distribution of goods and services.

D. The operating environment of nonbusiness organizations ordinarily differs from that of business organizations.

Answer (C) is correct. *(Publisher)*

REQUIRED: The characteristic of nonbusiness organizations.

DISCUSSION: The operating environments of nonbusiness and business organizations are similar in many ways. Both produce and distribute goods and services using scarce resources.

Answer (A) is incorrect because many noneconomic factors affect decisions to provide resources to nonbusiness enterprises. Answer (B) is incorrect because business organizations obtain resources by providing goods and services. Many nonbusiness organizations obtain resources from contributors and are accountable to the providers of those resources or to their representatives. Answer (D) is incorrect because the operating environments of nonbusiness and business organizations are similar.

3. Financial reporting by nonbusiness organizations should provide information useful in

A. Making resource allocation decisions.

B. Assessing services and the ability to continue to provide services.

C. Assessing management stewardship and performance.

D. All of the answers are correct.

Answer (D) is correct. *(Publisher)*

REQUIRED: The objective(s) of financial reporting by nonbusiness organizations.

DISCUSSION: Making resource allocation decisions, assessing services and the ability to continue to provide services, and assessing management stewardship and performance are included among the basic objectives of financial reporting for nonbusiness organizations stated in SFAC 4. Additional objectives are to provide information about the liquidity of the organization, economic resources, obligations, net resources, and changes in them, including managers' explanations and interpretations.

Answer (A) is incorrect because financial reporting by nonbusiness organizations should provide information useful in making resource allocation decisions. Answer (B) is incorrect because financial reporting by nonbusiness organizations should provide information useful in assessing services and the ability to continue to provide services. Answer (C) is incorrect because financial reporting by nonbusiness organizations should provide information useful in assessing management stewardship and performance.

4. Typical users of financial reports of nonbusiness organizations include which of the following?

A. Resource providers.

B. Constituents.

C. Governing and oversight bodies.

D. All of the answers are correct.

Answer (D) is correct. *(Publisher)*

REQUIRED: The typical users of financial reports prepared by nonbusiness organizations.

DISCUSSION: In addition to resource providers, constituents, and governing and oversight bodies, others potentially interested in the financial information provided by nonbusiness organizations include managers, organization members, taxpayers, contributors, grantors, lenders, suppliers, creditors, employees, directors and trustees, service beneficiaries, financial analysts and advisers, brokers, underwriters, lawyers, economists, taxing authorities, regulatory authorities, legislators, the financial press, labor unions, trade associations, researchers, teachers, and students.

Answer (A) is incorrect because resource providers are typical users. Answer (B) is incorrect because constituents are typical users. Answer (C) is incorrect because governing and oversight bodies are typical users.

29.2 Not-for-Profit Organizations

5. SFAS 117, *Financial Statements of Not-for-Profit Organizations*, establishes standards for general-purpose external financial statements issued by not-for-profit organizations. A complete set of financial statements should include

A. Statements of financial position as of the beginning and end of the reporting period, a statement of cash flows, and a statement of activities.

B. A statement of financial position as of the end of the reporting period, a statement of cash flows prepared on the direct basis, and a statement of activities.

C. A statement of financial position as of the end of the reporting period, a statement of cash flows, and a statement of activities.

D. Statements of financial position as of the beginning and end of the reporting period, comparative statements of cash flows, and comparative statements of activities.

Answer (C) is correct. *(Publisher)*

REQUIRED: The statements included in a complete set of financial statements of not-for-profit organizations.

DISCUSSION: SFAS 117 states that "a complete set of financial statements of a not-for-profit organization shall include a statement of financial position as of the end of the reporting period, a statement of activities and a statement of cash flows for the reporting period, and accompanying notes to financial statements."

Answer (A) is incorrect because the statement of financial position should be as of the end of the reporting period. Answer (B) is incorrect because SFAS 117 does not specify how the statement of cash flows is to be prepared. Answer (D) is incorrect because the statement of financial position should be as of the end of the reporting period, and comparative statements are not required.

6. SFAS 117, *Financial Statements of Not-for-Profit Organizations*, focuses on

A. Basic information for the organization as a whole.

B. Standardization of funds nomenclature.

C. Inherent differences of not-for-profit organizations that affect reporting presentations.

D. Distinctions between current fund and noncurrent fund presentations.

Answer (A) is correct. *(CPA, adapted)*

REQUIRED: The focus of SFAS 117.

DISCUSSION: SFAS 117 is intended to promote the relevance, understandability, and comparability of financial statements issued by not-for-profit organizations by requiring that certain basic information be reported. The focus of the financial statements required by SFAS 117 is on the not-for-profit organization as a whole and on reporting assets, liabilities, and net assets; changes in net assets; flows of economic resources; cashflows, borrowing and repayment of borrowing, and other factors affecting liquidity; and service efforts.

7. In a statement of financial position, a not-for-profit organization should report amounts for which of the following classes of net assets?

I. Unrestricted
II. Temporarily restricted
III. Permanently restricted

A. I, II, and III.

B. I and II only.

C. I and III only.

D. II and III only.

Answer (A) is correct. *(Publisher)*
REQUIRED: The classes of net assets reported in a statement of financial position of a not-for-profit organization.
DISCUSSION: SFAS 117, *Financial Statements of Not-for-Profit Organizations*, requires a not-for-profit organization to report amounts for all three classes: permanently restricted net assets, temporarily restricted net assets, and unrestricted net assets. Information regarding the nature and amounts of permanently or temporarily restricted net assets should be provided by reporting amounts on the face of the statement or by including details in the notes to financial statements.

8. In 2003, Gamma, a not-for-profit organization, deposited at a bank $1 million given to it by a donor to purchase endowment securities. The securities were purchased January 2, 2004. At December 31, 2003, the bank recorded $2,000 interest on the deposit. In accordance with the bequest, this $2,000 was used to finance ongoing program expenses in March 2004. At December 31, 2003, what amount of the bank balance should be included as current assets in Gamma's classified balance sheet?

A. $0

B. $2,000

C. $1,000,000

D. $1,002,000

Answer (B) is correct. *(CPA, adapted)*
REQUIRED: The amount of the bank balance classified as current assets.
DISCUSSION: In accordance with SFAS 117, a not-for-profit organization may classify its assets and liabilities as current or noncurrent as defined in ARB 43, Chapter 3A. That pronouncement defines current assets as those reasonably expected to be realized in cash, sold, or consumed during the operating cycle or within 1 year, whichever is longer. Accordingly, the $2,000 of interest recorded at December 31, 2003 should be classified as current because the bequest stipulated that it be used for ongoing program expenses. However, the $1 million restricted to the purchase of endowment securities is not classified as current. SFAS 117 states that assets received with a donor-imposed restriction limiting their use to long-term purposes should not be classified with assets available for current use.

9. In its statement of activities, a not-for-profit organization may report expenses as decreases in which of the following classes of net assets?

	Unrestricted	Permanently Restricted	Temporarily Restricted
A.	Yes	Yes	No
B.	Yes	No	Yes
C.	Yes	No	No
D.	Yes	Yes	Yes

Answer (C) is correct. *(Publisher)*
REQUIRED: The reporting of expenses in a not-for-profit organization's statement of activities.
DISCUSSION: In a statement of activities, revenues and expenses ordinarily should be reported as gross amounts. Revenues may be reported as increases in either unrestricted or restricted (temporarily or permanently) net assets. Expenses ordinarily should be reported as decreases in unrestricted net assets. However, investment revenues, reported as increases in unrestricted or restricted net assets, may be reported net of related fees such as custodial fees and investment advisory fees provided that these fees are disclosed either on the face of the statement or in the related notes.

10. Pharm, a nongovernmental not-for-profit organization, is preparing its year-end financial statements. Which of the following statements is required?

A. Statement of changes in financial position.

B. Statement of cash flows.

C. Statement of changes in fund balance.

D. Statement of revenue, expenses, and changes in fund balance.

Answer (B) is correct. *(CPA, adapted)*
REQUIRED: The statements required in a complete set of financial statements of not-for-profit organizations.
DISCUSSION: SFAS 117 states that "a complete set of financial statements of a not-for-profit organization shall include a statement of financial position as of the end of the reporting period, a statement of activities and a statement of cash flows for the reporting period, and accompanying notes to financial statements."
Answer (A) is incorrect because a statement of changes in financial position is not required for nongovernmental not-for-profit organizations by SFAS 117. Answer (C) is incorrect because a statement of changes in fund balance is not required for nongovernmental not-for-profit organizations by SFAS 117. Answer (D) is incorrect because a statement of revenue, expenses, and changes in fund balance is not required for nongovernmental not-for-profit organizations by SFAS 117.

11. Forkin Manor, a nongovernmental not-for-profit organization, is interested in having its financial statements reformatted using terminology that is more readily associated with for-profit entities. The director believes that the term "operating profit" and the practice of segregating recurring and nonrecurring items more accurately depict the organization's activities. Under what condition will Forkin be allowed to use "operating profit" and to segregate its recurring items from its nonrecurring items in its statement of activities?

A. The organization reports the change in unrestricted net assets for the period.

B. A parenthetical disclosure in the notes implies that the not-for-profit organization is seeking for-profit entity status.

C. Forkin receives special authorization from the Internal Revenue Service that this wording is appropriate.

D. At a minimum, the organization reports the change in permanently restricted net assets for the period.

Answer (A) is correct. *(CPA, adapted)*

REQUIRED: The condition allowing an NPO to use the term operating profit and to segregate recurring and nonrecurring items in its statement of activities.

DISCUSSION: In its statement of activities, an NPO classifies revenues, expenses, gains, and losses within the three classes of changes in net assets (permanently restricted, temporarily restricted, and unrestricted). Within a class or classes, other classifications are permitted, for example, operating and nonoperating, expendable and nonexpendable, earned and unearned, and recurring and nonrecurring. Furthermore, a term such as operating income or operating profit is permitted when an intermediate measure of operations is reported. However, this measure must be in a financial statement that reports the change in unrestricted net assets for the period (SFAS 117).

Answer (B) is incorrect because the NPO need not seek for-profit status or obtain IRS authorization to report in the described manner. Answer (C) is incorrect because the NPO need not seek for-profit status or obtain IRS authorization to report in the described manner. Answer (D) is incorrect because the NPO should report the changes in all three classes of net assets regardless of whether additional classifications are included in the statement of activities.

12. For which of the following assets held by a religious organization should depreciation be recognized in the organization's general purpose external financial statements?

A. The house of worship.

B. A priceless painting.

C. A nationally recognized historical treasure.

D. Land used for a building site.

Answer (A) is correct. *(Publisher)*

REQUIRED: The asset held by a nonprofit organization for which depreciation should be recognized.

DISCUSSION: SFAS 93, *Recognition of Depreciation by Not-for-Profit Organizations*, requires all nonprofit organizations to recognize the cost of using up long-lived tangible assets (depreciation) in their general purpose external financial statements. Hence, a building used for religious activity is ordinarily depreciable.

Answer (B) is incorrect because depreciation does not have to be recognized for certain works of art whose economic benefit or service potential is used up so slowly that their estimated useful lives are extraordinarily long. Answer (C) is incorrect because depreciation does not have to be recognized for historical treasures whose economic benefit or service potential is used up so slowly that their estimated useful lives are extraordinarily long. Answer (D) is incorrect because land is normally not depreciated by any organization.

13. On December 31, 2003, Dahlia, a nongovernmental not-for-profit organization, purchased a vehicle with $15,000 unrestricted cash and received a donated second vehicle having a fair value of $12,000. Dahlia expects each vehicle to provide it with equal service value over each of the next five years and then to have no residual value. Dahlia has an accounting policy implying a time restriction on gifts of long-lived assets. In Dahlia's 2004 statement of activities, what depreciation expense should be included under changes in unrestricted net assets?

A. $0

B. $2,400

C. $3,000

D. $5,400

Answer (D) is correct. *(CPA, adapted)*

REQUIRED: The depreciation expense included under changes in unrestricted net assets.

DISCUSSION: The expiration of a restriction is recognized when it expires. Expiration occurs when the stipulated time has elapsed, the purpose of the restriction has been fulfilled, or both. It is reported separately as a reclassification in the statement of activities as net assets released from restrictions. The effect is to increase one class of net assets and decrease another. For example, an implied time restriction on a long-lived depreciable asset expires as the economic benefits are used. Depreciation expense is reported as a decrease in unrestricted net assets (SFAS 116). Consequently, Dahlia should record a decrease in unrestricted net assets related to depreciation of $5,400 [($15,000 + $12,000) ÷ 5-year useful life], assuming no residual value.

14. United Donees, a not-for-profit organization, received the following pledges:

Unrestricted	$400,000
Restricted for capital additions	300,000

All pledges are legally enforceable and are expected to be received in the upcoming year. The experience of United Donees indicates that 10% of all pledges prove to be uncollectible. What amount may United Donees report as a reasonable estimate of the fair value of pledges receivable?

A. $270,000

B. $360,000

C. $630,000

D. $700,000

Answer (C) is correct. *(CPA, adapted)*

REQUIRED: The amount to report as a reasonable estimate of the fair value of pledges receivable.

DISCUSSION: SFAS 116, *Accounting for Contributions Received and Contributions Made*, requires not-for-profit organizations to recognize unconditional promises to give at fair value. The present value of estimated future cash flows is an appropriate measure of fair value. However, unconditional promises to give expected to be collected in less than one year may be recognized at net realizable value. United Donees may therefore report net pledges receivable of $630,000 [($400,000 + $300,000) × (1.0 – 10%)].

Answer (A) is incorrect because $270,000 is based on the assumption that only the pledges "restricted for capital additions" are reported as receivables, net of 10% of the amount. Answer (B) is incorrect because $360,000 is based on the assumption that only the unrestricted pledges are reported, net of 10% of that amount. Answer (D) is incorrect because pledges receivable expected to be collected in less than one year may be reported at net realizable value.

15. During 2004, Jones Foundation received the following support:

- A cash contribution of $875,000 to be used at the board of directors' discretion
- A promise to contribute $500,000 in 2005 from a supporter who has made similar contributions in prior periods
- Contributed legal services with a value of $100,000, which Jones would have otherwise purchased

At what amounts should Jones classify and record these transactions?

	Unrestricted Revenue	Temporarily Restricted Revenue
A.	$1,375,000	$0
B.	$875,000	$500,000
C.	$975,000	$0
D.	$975,000	$500,000

Answer (D) is correct. *(CPA, adapted)*

REQUIRED: The amounts recorded for unrestricted and temporarily restricted revenues from contributions.

DISCUSSION: The cash contribution ($875,000) was a revenue received in 2004 that was without restrictions. Thus, it is classified as unrestricted support and increases unrestricted net assets. The unconditional promise to give ($500,000) with the amount due in 2005 meets the definition of a contribution, assuming sufficient evidence in the form of verifiable documentation exists to recognize a promise to give. The promisee should recognize an asset and contribution revenue. However, the unconditional promise to give is reported ordinarily as restricted support unless the circumstances clearly indicate that the donor intended support for current activities. Thus, unconditional promises of future cash amounts usually increase temporarily restricted net assets. Contributions of services are recognized as revenues at fair value ($100,000) if they require special skills (e.g., legal training), are provided by those having such special skills, and would usually be purchased if not obtained by donations. They are classified as unrestricted support because the services presumably have been rendered and any purpose for which the resource was restricted has been fulfilled. Consequently, Jones should recognize unrestricted revenue of $975,000 ($875,000 + $100,000) and restricted revenue of $500,000.

Answer (A) is incorrect because the promise to contribute is temporarily restricted until actually received, and the contribution of legal services should be reported as an unrestricted contribution. Answer (B) is incorrect because contributions of services are recognized as revenues at fair value if they require special skills, are provided by those having such special skills, and would usually be purchased if not obtained by donations. Answer (C) is incorrect because the promise to contribute is temporarily restricted revenue.

16. A family lost its home in a fire. On December 25, 2003, a philanthropist sent money to the Benevolent Society to purchase furniture for the family. The resource provider did not explicitly grant the Society the unilateral power to redirect the use of the assets. During January 2004, the Society purchased this furniture for the Addams family. The Society, a not-for-profit organization, should report the receipt of the money in its 2003 financial statements as a(n)

A. Unrestricted contribution.

B. Temporarily restricted contribution.

C. Permanently restricted contribution.

D. Liability.

Answer (D) is correct. *(CPA, adapted)*

REQUIRED: The reporting of a transfer to an NPO with a direction that the assets be used to aid a specific beneficiary.

DISCUSSION: SFAS 136, *Transfer of Assets to a Not-for-Profit Organization or Charitable Trust That Raises or Holds Contributions for Others*, applies when a donor makes a contribution to a recipient entity that agrees either to use the assets for the benefit of another entity designated by the donor or to transfer the assets to the beneficiary. The recipient entity should recognize the receipt of the assets as a contribution if the donor explicitly grants the entity variance power to redirect the use of the assets or if the recipient and the beneficiary are financially interrelated. However, if neither of these conditions applies, the recipient entity should recognize the fair value of the assets as a liability.

17. Pica, a nongovernmental not-for-profit organization, received unconditional promises of $100,000 expected to be collected within one year. Pica received $10,000 prior to year end. Pica anticipates collecting 90% of the contributions and has a June 30 fiscal year end. What amount should Pica record as contribution revenue as of June 30?

A. $10,000

B. $80,000

C. $90,000

D. $100,000

Answer (C) is correct. *(CPA, adapted)*

REQUIRED: The contribution revenue recorded at fiscal year-end.

DISCUSSION: An unconditional promise to give may be recognized as a contribution given sufficient verifiable documentation. Contributions received ordinarily are accounted for at fair value as credits to revenues or gains and as debits to assets, liabilities, or expenses (SFAS 116). For an unconditional promise to give, the present value of estimated future cash flows is an appropriate measure of fair value. However, unconditional promises to give expected to be collected in less than 1 year may be recognized at net realizable value. The latter amount equals $90,000 (90% collection percentage × $100,000 unconditionally promised).

Answer (A) is incorrect because $10,000 is the amount collected. Answer (B) is incorrect because the amount collected also should be recognized as revenue. Answer (D) is incorrect because revenue equals the net realizable value, not the gross amount promised.

18. In Bow Co.'s current year annual report, Bow described its social awareness expenditures during the year as follows:

The Company contributed $250,000 in cash to youth and educational programs. The Company also gave $140,000 to health and human-service organizations, of which $80,000 was contributed by employees through payroll deductions. In addition, consistent with the Company's commitment to the environment, the Company spent $100,000 to redesign product packaging.

What amount of the above should be included in Bow's income statement as charitable contributions expense?

A. $310,000

B. $390,000

C. $410,000

D. $490,000

Answer (A) is correct. *(CPA, adapted)*

REQUIRED: The amount of charitable contribution expense included in the income statement.

DISCUSSION: The company cannot deduct a charitable expense for money donated by employees. In addition, the redesign of a product's package cannot be considered a charitable expense. Accordingly, the charitable contribution expense is $310,000 ($250,000 + $140,000 – $80,000).

Answer (B) is incorrect because $390,000 includes the employees' charitable contribution. Answer (C) is incorrect because $410,000 includes the redesign costs. Answer (D) is incorrect because $490,000 includes the employees' charitable contribution and the redesign costs.

19. On December 30 of the current year, the Geology Museum, a not-for-profit organization, received a $14,000,000 donation of Knight Co. shares with donor-stipulated requirements as follows:

- Shares valued at $10,000,000 are to be sold with the proceeds used to erect a public viewing building.
- Shares valued at $4,000,000 are to be retained, with the dividends used to support current operations

As a consequence of the receipt of the Knight shares, how much should the Museum report as temporarily restricted net assets on its current year statement of financial position?

A. $0

B. $4,000,000

C. $10,000,000

D. $14,000,000

Answer (C) is correct. *(CPA, adapted)*

REQUIRED: The amount to report as temporarily restricted net assets.

DISCUSSION: A temporary restriction permits the donee organization to "expend the donated assets as specified and is satisfied either by the passage of time or by actions of the organization" (SFAS 116). The shares valued at $10,000,000 meet this definition because they are to be sold and used for a specified project. A permanent restriction requires that the "resources be maintained permanently but permits the organization to use up or expend part or all of the income derived" (SFAS 116). The $4,000,000 stock donation meets this definition and should be reported as permanently restricted net assets. The Museum should report $10,000,000 as temporarily restricted net assets.

Answer (A) is incorrect because the shares valued at $10,000,000 are temporarily restricted. Answer (B) is incorrect because the shares valued at $4,000,000 are permanently restricted, and the shares valued at $10,000,000 have temporary restrictions. Answer (D) is incorrect because only the shares valued at $10,000,000 have temporary restrictions.

20. Resource Provider transferred assets to Recipient Organization and specified itself as the beneficiary. The transfer meets the criteria for an equity transaction. In accordance with SFAS 136, *Transfers of Assets to a Not-for-Profit Organization or Charitable Trust That Raises or Holds Contributions for Others*, Resource Provider should

A. Debit an asset and credit equity.

B. Debit equity.

C. Debit an interest in net assets of Recipient.

D. Make no entry.

Answer (C) is correct. *(Publisher)*

REQUIRED: The accounting for a resource provider's transfer of assets in an equity transaction in which it specified itself as the beneficiary.

DISCUSSION: No contribution is involved when the resource provider or its affiliate is the specified beneficiary. If the transfer also involves a recipient that is financially interrelated with the resource provider and if neither party expects payment of the transferred assets, an equity transaction must be accounted for. If the resource provider itself is the specified beneficiary, its entry is to debit an interest in net assets of the recipient (similar to the investment account when the equity method is used) and to credit an asset or payable.

Answer (A) is incorrect because the recipient debits an asset and credits equity (reported as a separate line in the statement of activities). Answer (B) is incorrect because a debit to equity (reported as a separate line in the statement of activities) is appropriate if the resource provider's affiliate is its specified beneficiary. Answer (D) is incorrect because the resource provider should record an interest in the recipient's net assets.

21. Donor Organization transfers an asset to Recipient Organization, a not-for-profit entity that does not serve as a trustee. Recipient accepts the asset and agrees to use it on behalf of Beneficiary, an entity specified by Donor but not financially related or affiliated with Donor. In accordance with SFAS 136, *Transfers of Assets to a Not-for-Profit Organization or Charitable Trust That Raises or Holds Contributions for Others*, if

A. Donor does not grant Recipient variance power, and if Recipient and Beneficiary are not financially interrelated, Recipient must record an asset and a liability to Beneficiary if the asset transferred is a nonfinancial asset.

B. Donor does not grant Recipient variance power, and if Recipient and Beneficiary are not financially interrelated, Recipient records an asset and contribution revenue.

C. Donor explicitly grants Recipient variance power, Recipient must record an asset and contribution revenue only if the asset transferred is a financial asset.

D. Beneficiary recognizes a right to the asset.

Answer (B) is correct. *(Publisher)*

REQUIRED: The accounting for a donor's transfer of an asset to a recipient NPO that agrees to use it on behalf of an unaffiliated beneficiary.

DISCUSSION: Given that Recipient and Beneficiary are financially interrelated and that Recipient is not a trustee (SFAS 136 does not apply to a trustee's reporting), Recipient is treated as a donee. It should therefore recognize a contribution by debiting an asset and crediting contribution revenue, regardless of the nature of the asset transferred.

Answer (A) is incorrect because, if the asset transferred is a nonfinancial asset, Recipient does not have explicit variance power, and Recipient and Beneficiary are not financially interrelated, the transfer is not a contribution. Recipient is permitted but not required to recognize the asset and the liability, provided the accounting policy chosen is disclosed and consistently applied. Answer (C) is incorrect because, if Donor has explicitly granted Recipient variance power and Beneficiary is not affiliated with Donor, Recipient is a donee and must debit an asset and credit contribution revenue regardless of the nature of the asset transferred. Variance power is the unilateral power to redirect the use of the transferred asset to another beneficiary. Answer (D) is incorrect because Beneficiary recognizes its right to financial or nonfinancial assets held by Recipient unless Recipient has explicit variance power.

22. The Art Museum, a not-for-profit organization, received a contribution of historical artifacts. It need not recognize the contribution if the artifacts are to be sold and the proceeds used to

A. Support general museum activities.

B. Acquire other items for collections.

C. Repair existing collections.

D. Purchase buildings to house collections.

Answer (B) is correct. *(CPA, adapted)*

REQUIRED: The circumstance under which a contribution of artifacts to be sold need not be recognized.

DISCUSSION: Contributions of such items as art works and historical treasures need not be capitalized and recognized as revenues if they are added to collections that are (1) subject to a policy that requires the proceeds of sale of collection items to be used to acquire other collection items; (2) protected, kept unencumbered, cared for, and preserved; and (3) held for public exhibition, education, or research for public service purposes rather than financial gain (SFAS 116).

Answer (A) is incorrect because, if the proceeds are used to support general museum activities, the contribution must be recognized. Answer (C) is incorrect because, if the proceeds are used to repair existing collections, the contribution must be recognized. Answer (D) is incorrect because, if the proceeds are used to purchase buildings to house collections, the contribution must be recognized.

23. According to SFAS 116, *Accounting for Contributions Received and Contributions Made*, what classification(s), if any, should be used by not-for-profit organizations to report receipts of contributions?

	Unrestricted Support	Restricted Support
A.	No	No
B.	No	Yes
C.	Yes	No
D.	Yes	Yes

Answer (D) is correct. *(Publisher)*

REQUIRED: The classification(s), if any, of contributions received by not-for-profit organizations.

DISCUSSION: SFAS 116 requires that contributions received by not-for-profit organizations be reported as restricted support or unrestricted support. Contributions with donor-imposed restrictions are reported as restricted support. Restricted support increases permanently restricted net assets or temporarily restricted net assets. Contributions without donor-imposed restrictions are reported as unrestricted support.

24. SFAS 116 requires not-for-profit organizations to recognize a conditional promise to give when

A. The promise is received.

B. The promise is received in writing.

C. The conditions are met.

D. It is reasonably possible that the conditions will be met.

Answer (C) is correct. *(Publisher)*

REQUIRED: The timing of recognition of a conditional promise to give.

DISCUSSION: A conditional promise to give is one that depends on the occurrence of a specified future, uncertain event to establish the promisor's obligation. It is recognized when the conditions are substantially met, i.e., when the conditional promise becomes unconditional. If the possibility is remote that the condition will not be met, the recognition criterion is satisfied.

Answer (A) is incorrect because receipt of the promise is not sufficient for recognition of a contribution. Answer (B) is incorrect because receipt of the promise is not sufficient for recognition of a contribution. Answer (D) is incorrect because the possibility that the condition will not be met must be remote before a contribution is recognized.

Questions 25 through 27 are based on the following information. On June 30 of the current year, Older Relatives Community Assistance (ORCA), a not-for-profit organization, received a building and the land on which it was constructed as a gift from Sapient Corporation. The building is intended to support the organization's education and training mission or any other purpose consistent with the organization's mission. Immediately prior to the contribution, the fair values of the building and land had been appraised as $700,000 and $300,000, respectively. Carrying amounts on Sapient's books at June 30 of the current year were $580,000 and $150,000, respectively.

25. If ORCA does not have a policy of implying time restrictions on gifts of long-lived assets, the gift should be recorded by the organization as

	Unrestricted Support	Restricted Support
A.	$300,000	$700,000
B.	$1,000,000	$0
C.	$0	$1,000,000
D.	$150,000	$580,000

Answer (B) is correct. *(Publisher)*

REQUIRED: The amount at which a contribution of long-lived assets should be recorded by the donee.

DISCUSSION: The terms of this contribution allow the long-lived assets to be used for any purpose consistent with the NPO's mission. It does not have a policy of implying time restrictions on gifts of long-lived assets. Thus, the building and land on which it was constructed should be recorded at fair value as assets and unrestricted support.

26. If ORCA has a policy of implying time restrictions on gifts of long-lived assets, the gift should be recorded by the organization as

	Unrestricted Support	Restricted Support
A.	$300,000	$700,000
B.	$1,000,000	$0
C.	$0	$1,000,000
D.	$150,000	$580,000

Answer (C) is correct. *(Publisher)*

REQUIRED: The amount at which a contribution of long-lived assets should be recorded by the donee.

DISCUSSION: The terms of this gift allow the long-lived assets to be used for any purpose consistent with the NPO's mission. In the absence of a policy implying time restrictions on gifts of long-lived assets, the contribution should be recorded as unrestricted support. However, given that ORCA has a policy of implying a time restriction, the building and land on which it was constructed should be recorded at fair value as assets and restricted support. The restriction will expire over the expected useful life of the building.

27. Sapient Corporation should record its contribution of the building and land as a

A. $730,000 reduction in contributed capital.

B. $1,000,000 reduction in contributed capital.

C. $730,000 expense.

D. $1,000,000 expense.

Answer (D) is correct. *(Publisher)*
REQUIRED: The amount at which a contribution of long-lived assets should be recorded by the donor.
DISCUSSION: Contributions made should be recognized as expenses in the period made. They should be measured at the fair value of the assets contributed.

28. Napro Charities, a not-for-profit agency, receives free electricity on a continuous basis from a local utility company. The utility company's contribution is made subject to cancelation by the donor. Napro should account for this contribution as a(n)

A. Unrestricted revenue only.

B. Restricted revenue only.

C. Unrestricted revenue and an expense.

D. Restricted revenue and an expense.

Answer (C) is correct. *(Publisher)*
REQUIRED: The amount at which a contribution of electricity should be recorded by the donee.
DISCUSSION: SFAS 116 defines a contribution of utilities, such as electricity, as a contribution of other assets, not a contribution of services. A simultaneous receipt and use of utilities should be recognized as both an unrestricted revenue and an expense in the period of receipt and use. The revenue and expense should be measured at estimated fair value. This estimate can be obtained from the rate schedule used by the utility company to determine rates charged to a similar customer.

29. Oz, a nongovernmental not-for-profit organization, received $50,000 from Ame Company to sponsor a play given by Oz at the local theater. Oz gave Ame 25 tickets, which generally cost $100 each. Ame received no other benefits. What amount of ticket sales revenue should Oz record?

A. $0

B. $2,500

C. $47,500

D. $50,000

Answer (B) is correct. *(CPA, adapted)*
REQUIRED: The amount of ticket sales revenue.
DISCUSSION: This transaction involves both a contribution and an exchange. In an exchange, the parties receive and sacrifice something of approximately equal value. Hence, Oz should recognize $2,500 of ticket revenue (25 tickets × $100), the fair value of the exchange element of the transaction. The fair value of the contribution element ($50,000 – $2,500) is recorded as contribution revenue in the period received. It is classified as temporarily restricted support until it is expended in fulfillment of the donor restriction.
Answer (A) is incorrect because ticket sales revenue is recorded to account for the exchange element of the transaction. Answer (C) is incorrect because $47,500 is the contribution revenue. Answer (D) is incorrect because $50,000 is the ticket sales revenue plus the contribution revenue.

30. On December 31 of the current year, Communities Organized for Social Improvement (COSI), a not-for-profit organization, holds an investment in common stock of one publicly traded entity and an investment in debt securities of another. The not-for-profit organization holds the common stock as a long-term investment, and has the intent and the ability to hold the debt securities until maturity.

	Investment in Common Stock	Investment in Debt Securities
Original cost	$50,000	$35,000
Amortized cost		$28,000
Fair value	$63,000	$40,000

In the December 31 statement of financial position for the current year, COSI should value these investments as

	Investment in Common Stock	Investment in Debt Securities
A.	$50,000	$28,000
B.	$50,000	$40,000
C.	$63,000	$28,000
D.	$63,000	$40,000

Answer (D) is correct. *(Publisher)*
REQUIRED: The amount to be recorded by a not-for-profit organization for investments in equity and debt securities.
DISCUSSION: SFAS 124, *Accounting for Certain Investments Held by Not-for-Profit Organizations*, requires not-for-profit entities to measure investments in equity securities with readily determinable fair values and all investments in debt securities at fair value in the statement of financial position.

Questions 31 through 35 are based on the following information. Early in 2003, a not-for-profit organization (NPO) received a $2,000,000 gift from a wealthy benefactor. This benefactor specified that the gift be invested in perpetuity with income restricted to provide speaker fees for a lecture series named for the benefactor. The NPO is permitted to choose suitable investments and is responsible for all other costs associated with initiating and administering this series. Neither the donor's stipulation nor the law addresses gains and losses on this permanent endowment. In 2003, the investments purchased with the gift earned $50,000 in dividend income. The fair value of the investments increased by $120,000.

31. The $2,000,000 gift should be recorded in the 2003 statement of activity as an increase in

A. Unrestricted net assets.

B. Temporarily restricted net assets.

C. Permanently restricted net assets.

D. Either unrestricted or temporarily restricted net assets.

Answer (C) is correct. *(Publisher)*

REQUIRED: The classification of a gift to be invested in perpetuity.

DISCUSSION: A donor-imposed restriction limits the use of contributed assets. This gift is unconditional in the sense that no condition is imposed on the transfer, but it includes a permanent restriction on the use of the assets. Under SFAS 117, the gift should therefore be classified as an increase in permanently restricted net assets.

32. Three presentations in the lecture series were held in 2003. The speaker fees for the 3 presentations amounted to $90,000. The not-for-profit organization used the $50,000 dividend income to cover part of the total fees. Because the board of directors did not wish to sell part of the investments, the organization used $40,000 in unrestricted resources to pay the remainder of the speaker fees. In the 2003 statement of activity, the $50,000 of dividend income should be recorded as an increase in

A. Unrestricted net assets.

B. Temporarily restricted net assets.

C. Permanently restricted net assets.

D. Either unrestricted or temporarily restricted net assets.

Answer (D) is correct. *(Publisher)*

REQUIRED: The classification of expended dividend income generated from investments held in perpetuity.

DISCUSSION: SFASs 117 and 124 require that income from donor-restricted permanent endowments be classified as an increase in temporarily restricted or permanently restricted net assets if the donor restricts its use. However, if the donor-imposed restrictions are met in the same reporting period as the gains and investment income are recognized, the gains and income may be reported as increases in unrestricted net assets, provided that the organization has a similar policy for reporting contributions received, reports on a consistent basis from period to period, and adequately discloses its accounting policy. The temporary restriction on the $50,000 of investment income was met by expenditure in 2003, the year the gain and income were recognized. Thus, the dividend revenue may be classified as an increase in either unrestricted or temporarily restricted net assets, depending on the NPO's accounting policy.

33. The NPO's accounting policy is to record gains and investment income, for which a donor-imposed restriction is met in the same accounting period as the gains and investment income are recognized, as increases in unrestricted net assets. In the 2003 statement of activity, the $120,000 unrealized gain should be recorded as

A. A $40,000 increase in unrestricted net assets and an $80,000 increase in temporarily restricted net assets.

B. A $120,000 increase in unrestricted net assets.

C. A $120,000 increase in temporarily restricted net assets.

D. A $120,000 increase in permanently restricted net assets.

Answer (B) is correct. *(Publisher)*

REQUIRED: The classification of unrealized gain from investments held in perpetuity.

DISCUSSION: SFASs 117 and 124 permit the recognition of gains and investment income as increases in unrestricted net assets if the donor-imposed restrictions are met in the same reporting period as the gains and investment income are recognized, provided that the organization has a similar policy for reporting contributions received, reports on a consistent basis from period to period, and adequately discloses its accounting policy. The temporary restriction on the income was met by expenditure in 2002, the year the income and the gain were recognized. Thus, consistent with its policy, the NPO should treat the gain as an increase in unrestricted net assets. Given that the donor of the endowment allows the NPO to choose suitable investments and that no permanent restriction is imposed on the gain by the donor or by the law, the classification of the gain is the same as that of the income.

34. If the lecture series were not scheduled to begin until 2004, the $50,000 dividend income would be recorded in the 2003 statement of activity as an increase in

A. Unrestricted net assets.

B. Temporarily restricted net assets.

C. Permanently restricted net assets.

D. Either unrestricted or temporarily restricted net assets.

Answer (B) is correct. *(Publisher)*

REQUIRED: The classification of unexpended dividend income generated from investments held in perpetuity.

DISCUSSION: SFAS 117 requires that gains and investment income from donor-restricted permanent endowments be classified as increases in temporarily restricted net assets if the donor restricts the use of these resources to a specific purpose that either expires with the passage of time or can be met by actions of the organization. The restriction is temporary because it will expire when the income is expended in a future period. Moreover, the income cannot be classified as unrestricted because recognition and the expiration of the restriction do not occur in the same period.

35. If the lecture series were not scheduled to begin until 2004, the $120,000 unrealized gain should be recorded in the 2004 statement of activity as an increase in

A. Unrestricted net assets.

B. Temporarily restricted net assets.

C. Permanently restricted net assets.

D. Either unrestricted or temporarily restricted net assets.

Answer (B) is correct. *(Publisher)*

REQUIRED: The classification of an unrealized gain on investments held in perpetuity.

DISCUSSION: Given that the NPO has the discretion to choose suitable investments (as opposed to holding specific securities in perpetuity), the gain is not permanently restricted absent a donor stipulation or a legal requirement. Rather, the gain has the same classification as the income. The latter is temporarily restricted because it is to be expended in a future period. Hence, the gain is also temporarily restricted.

36. A not-for-profit voluntary health and welfare organization received a $500,000 permanent endowment. The donor stipulated that the income be used for a mental health program. The endowment fund reported $60,000 net decrease in fair value and $30,000 investment income. The organization spent $45,000 on the mental health program during the year. What amount of change in temporarily restricted net assets should the organization report?

A. $75,000 decrease.

B. $15,000 decrease.

C. $0

D. $425,000 increase.

Answer (C) is correct. *(CPA, adapted)*

REQUIRED: The change in temporarily restricted net assets.

DISCUSSION: The contribution of $500,000 to be maintained in an endowment as a permanent source of income is classified as an increase in permanently restricted net assets. The income is restricted to use for a mental health program. SFASs 117 and 124 require that income from donor-restricted permanent endowments be classified as an increase in temporarily restricted or permanently restricted net assets if the donor restricts its use. However, if the donor-imposed restrictions are met in the same reporting period as the investment income is recognized, it may be reported as an increase in unrestricted net assets, provided that the organization has a similar policy for reporting contributions received, reports on a consistent basis from period to period, and adequately discloses its accounting policy. The restriction on the use of the $30,000 of income expired when it was spent (along with the additional $15,000, presumably from other sources). Absent donor stipulations or contrary legal requirements, losses on investments of a permanent endowment reduce temporarily restricted net assets to the extent that a donor's temporary restriction on net appreciation of the fund has not expired prior to the losses. Any remaining losses are reductions of unrestricted net assets. Accordingly, in the absence of any such donor restriction, the $60,000 decrease in the fair value of the endowment's investments reduced unrestricted net assets. The effect on temporarily restricted net assets of (1) creation of the endowment, (2) the receipt and expenditure in the same period of investment income, and (3) the decline in the fair value of the principal of the endowment (absent a donor restriction) is therefore $0.

Answer (A) is incorrect because $75,000 is the sum of the fair value decrease and the excess of expenditures over income. Answer (B) is incorrect because $15,000 is the excess of the amount spent over the income. Answer (D) is incorrect because $425,000 equals the contribution minus the sum of the fair value decrease and the excess of expenditures over income.

37. Following the destruction of its house of worship by fire, a religious organization held a rebuilding party. Part of the labor was donated by professional carpenters. The remainder was donated by members of the organization. Capitalization is required for the value of the services provided by

A. The professional carpenters only.

B. The members only.

C. The professional carpenters and the members.

D. Neither the professional carpenters nor the members.

Answer (C) is correct. *(Publisher)*

REQUIRED: The contributed services to be capitalized.

DISCUSSION: Contributions of services by the professional carpenters should be capitalized. Under SFAS 116, the contributions of services requiring specialized skills, such as those of carpenters and electricians, should be recognized if they are provided by individuals possessing those skills and would typically need to be purchased if not provided by donation. SFAS 116 also requires that donated services creating or enhancing nonfinancial assets be recognized even though specialized skills are not involved. Because the members' labor helped rebuild the church, their contributions of services also should be capitalized.

38. Health Policy Foundation (HPF), a voluntary health and welfare organization supported by contributions from the general public, included the following costs in its statement of functional expenses for the year:

Fund-raising	$1,000,000
Administrative (including data processing)	600,000
Research	200,000

HPF's functional expenses for program services included

A. $1,800,000

B. $1,000,000

C. $600,000

D. $200,000

Answer (D) is correct. *(CPA, adapted)*

REQUIRED: The amount of functional expenses for program services incurred by a VHWO.

DISCUSSION: An NPO's statement of activities or notes thereto should classify expenses by function. The major functional classes include program services and supporting services. Management and general expenses, along with fund-raising expenses, are classified in the supporting services category. Program services expenses are those directly related to the administration of programs. Of the costs given, only the research costs ($200,000) are program services expenses.

Answer (A) is incorrect because $1,800,000 includes $1,000,000 of fund-raising expenses and $600,000 of administrative expenses, which should be included in supporting services expenses. Answer (B) is incorrect because $1,000,000 of fund-raising expenses should be classified as supporting services expenses. Answer (C) is incorrect because $600,000 of administrative expenses should be classified as supporting services expenses.

39. For the fall semester of the current year, Micanopy University, a private not-for-profit institution, assessed its students $3,000,000 for tuition and fees. The net amount realized was only $2,500,000 because scholarships of $400,000 were granted to students and tuition remissions of $100,000 were allowed to faculty members' children attending Micanopy. What amount should Micanopy report for the period as revenues for tuition and fees?

A. $2,500,000

B. $2,600,000

C. $2,900,000

D. $3,000,000

Answer (D) is correct. *(CPA, adapted)*

REQUIRED: The amount reported as revenues for tuition and fees.

DISCUSSION: In accounting for tuition and fees for private, not-for-profit colleges and universities, the full amount of the tuition assessed is reported as revenue. Tuition waivers, scholarships, and like items are recorded as expenses if given in exchange transactions. Refunds are handled by merely debiting revenues and crediting cash, so tuition is automatically reported net of refunds.

Answer (A) is incorrect because $2,500,000 assumes that only net tuition is recorded. Answer (B) is incorrect because $2,600,000 assumes that scholarships are deducted before recording tuition revenues. Answer (C) is incorrect because $2,900,000 assumes that tuition remissions are deducted before recording tuition revenues.

40. Eleemosynary Institution (EI) received a donation of equity securities with readily determinable fair values. The securities had appreciated in value after they were purchased by the donor, and they continued to appreciate through the end of EI's fiscal year. At what amount should EI report its investment in donated securities in its year-end balance sheet?

A. Donor's cost.

B. Fair value at the date of receipt.

C. Fair value at the balance sheet date.

D. Fair value at either the date of receipt or the balance sheet date.

Answer (C) is correct. *(CPA, adapted)*

REQUIRED: The valuation of donated equity securities.

DISCUSSION: In its statement of financial position, a not-for-profit organization should measure the following investments at fair value: (1) equity securities with readily determinable fair values and (2) debt securities. Thus, the total change in the fair value of the donated securities from the date of receipt to the balance sheet date must be reported in the statement of activities (SFAS 124).

41. VHWO is a voluntary welfare organization funded by contributions from the general public. During 2003, unrestricted pledges of $600,000 were received, of which it was estimated that $72,000 would be uncollectible. By the end of 2003, $480,000 of the pledges had been collected, and it was expected that an additional $48,000 of these pledges would be collected in 2004, with the balance to be written off as uncollectible. Donors did not specify any periods during which the donations were to be used. Also during 2003, VHWO sold a computer for $18,000. Its cost was $21,000, and its book value was $15,000. VHWO made the correct entry to record the gain on the sale. What amount should VHWO include as unrestricted support in 2003 for contributions?

A. $480,000

B. $528,000

C. $531,000

D. $600,000

Answer (B) is correct. *(CPA, adapted)*

REQUIRED: The net contributions.

DISCUSSION: Because donors placed no restrictions on the pledges, none of them will be considered restricted support. Moreover, the pledge receivables are expected to be collected within 1 year and should be reported at their net realizable value. Amounts estimated as uncollectible should be deducted from pledges received, and an allowance for uncollectible pledges account should be established. Accordingly, unrestricted support from contributions equaled the net realizable value of $528,000 ($480,000 + $48,000).

Answer (A) is incorrect because $480,000 assumes that unrestricted support is recorded on a cash basis. Answer (C) is incorrect because $531,000 assumes that the gain from the sale of the computer is added to unrestricted support. The gain is considered separately under the revenue category in the statement of activities. Answer (D) is incorrect because $600,000 assumes that pledge receivables are reported on a gross basis.

42. Cancer Educators, a not-for-profit organization, incurred costs of $10,000 in its combined program services and fund-raising activities. Which of the following cost allocations might Cancer report in its statement of activities?

	Program Services	Fund-Raising	General Services
A.	$0	$0	$10,000
B.	$0	$6,000	$4,000
C.	$6,000	$4,000	$0
D.	$10,000	$0	$0

Answer (C) is correct. *(CPA, adapted)*

REQUIRED: The allocation of costs for combined functions.

DISCUSSION: NPOs must provide information about expenses reported by functional classification. The $10,000 of costs should therefore be divided between program services and fund-raising.

43. Environs, a community foundation, incurred $10,000 in management and general expenses during the current year. In Environs' statement of activities for the current year ended December 31, the $10,000 should be reported as

A. A direct reduction of fund balance.

B. Part of supporting services.

C. Part of program services.

D. A contra account to offset revenue.

Answer (B) is correct. *(CPA, adapted)*

REQUIRED: The expense classification for management and general expenses in the statement of activities.

DISCUSSION: Two functional categories of expenses for an NPO are program services expenses and supporting services expenses. Supporting services expenses, which do not relate to the primary mission of the organization, may be further subdivided into (1) management and general expenses, (2) fund-raising expenses, and (3) membership development costs.

Answer (A) is incorrect because a direct reduction of fund balance would be the result of a transfer or a refund to a donor. Moreover, fund accounting information is not required to be externally reported. Answer (C) is incorrect because program services expenses relate directly to the primary mission of the NPO. Answer (D) is incorrect because only costs directly related to a certain source of support, such as a special event or estimated uncollectible pledges, may be offset against revenue.

44. The following expenditures were made by Green Services, a society for the protection of the environment:

Printing of the annual report	$12,000
Unsolicited merchandise sent to encourage contributions	25,000
Cost of an audit performed by a CPA firm	3,000

What amount should be classified as fund-raising costs in the society's statement of activities?

A. $37,000

B. $28,000

C. $25,000

D. $0

Answer (C) is correct. *(CPA, adapted)*

REQUIRED: The amount to be reported as fund-raising costs in the activity statement.

DISCUSSION: There are two major classifications of expenses for an NPO: program service expenses and supporting services expenses. Program service expenses relate directly to the primary purpose or mission of the organization. Supporting services expenses are further classified as management and general expenses, fund-raising expenses, and membership development costs. The only cost here that is related to fund-raising is the unsolicited merchandise sent to encourage contributions.

Answer (A) is incorrect because $37,000 classifies all of the expenses as fund-raising expenses when only the unsolicited merchandise is related to fund-raising. Answer (B) is incorrect because the cost of an audit is a management-related expense. Answer (D) is incorrect because this answer assumes that none of the expenses listed are related to fund-raising when the unsolicited merchandise is a fund-raising expense.

45. A not-for-profit organization combines fund-raising efforts with its program services directed toward prevention of drug use. The joint activity involves sending educational materials to parents of senior and junior high school students. These materials (1) inform parents about the dangers and warning signs of drug use, (2) provide advice about counseling children regarding these matters, (3) urge such counseling, and (4) seek contributions. Moreover, the compensation of the executive director of the organization, who is involved in the distribution of the materials, is unaffected by the amount of contributions received. Similar activities using the same media are conducted on a larger scale without the fund-raising appeal. Given that no combined costs are identifiable with a specific function, the total combined costs incurred are

A. Reported as program services expenses.

B. Allocated between fund-raising and program services expenses on a rational and systematic basis.

C. Reported as fund-raising costs.

D. Reported as management and general expenses.

Answer (B) is correct. *(Publisher)*

REQUIRED: The accounting for combined fundraising and program services costs.

DISCUSSION: SOP 98-2, *Accounting for Costs of Activities of Not-For-Profit Organizations and State and Local Governmental Entities that Include Fund Raising*, applies to allocation of costs of joint activities. These activities include not only fund raising but also program or management and general functions. If the criteria of purpose, audience, and content are met, any costs of a joint activity that are identifiable with a given function are assigned to that function. The remaining costs of the joint activity (joint costs) are allocated on a rational and systematic basis between fund raising and the given program or management and general function. The purpose criterion is met because the joint activity accomplishes a program function. The program component calls for specific purpose-related action, and a similar component is conducted (1) without the fund-raising appeal, (2) using the same media, and (3) on the same or a larger scale. Furthermore, the audience criterion is met because the parents have a reasonable potential for use of the program component of the activity. Finally, the content criterion is met because the joint activity supports the program function. The specific called-for action by recipients will help accomplish the mission of the organization.

Answer (A) is incorrect because the costs should be allocated. Answer (C) is incorrect because the costs should be allocated. Answer (D) is incorrect because only program services and fund-raising are involved.

46. On January 2 of the current year, a nonprofit botanical society received a gift of an exhaustible fixed asset with an estimated useful life of 10 years and no salvage value. The donor's cost of this asset was $20,000, and its fair value at the date of the gift was $30,000. What amount of depreciation of this asset should the society recognize in its current year financial statements?

A. $3,000

B. $2,500

C. $2,000

D. $0

Answer (A) is correct. *(CPA, adapted)*

REQUIRED: The amount of depreciation to be recognized in the financial statements.

DISCUSSION: SFAS 93 requires not-for-profit organizations to recognize depreciation in the statement of activities. Moreover, contributions are recorded at their fair value when received. Assuming the straight-line method is used, the amount of depreciation that the nonprofit botanical society should recognize is $3,000 [($30,000 fair value – $0 salvage value) ÷ 10 years].

47. Lane Foundation received a permanent endowment of $500,000 in 2002 from Gant Enterprises. The endowment assets were invested in publicly traded securities, and Lane is permitted to choose suitable investments. Gant did not specify how gains and losses from dispositions of endowment assets were to be treated. No restrictions were placed on the use of dividends received and interest earned on fund resources. In 2003, Lane realized gains of $50,000 on sales of fund investments and received total interest and dividends of $40,000 on fund securities. What amount of these capital gains, interest, and dividends increases unrestricted net assets?

A. $0

B. $40,000

C. $50,000

D. $90,000

Answer (D) is correct. *(CPA, adapted)*

REQUIRED: The amount of capital gains, interest, and dividends that increases unrestricted net assets.

DISCUSSION: Absent an explicit donor stipulation or law to the contrary, assuming the donee is allowed to choose suitable investments, income and gains or losses on a donor-restricted endowment fund's assets are changes in unrestricted net assets. Thus, the increase in unrestricted net assets is $90,000 ($50,000 gains + $40,000 interest and dividends).

Answer (A) is incorrect because $0 assumes the income and gains are restricted. Answer (B) is incorrect because $40,000 assumes the gains are restricted. Answer (C) is incorrect because $50,000 assumes the income is restricted.

48. In year 1, a nonprofit trade association enrolled five new member companies, each of which was obligated to pay nonrefundable initiation fees of $1,000. These fees were receivable by the association in year 2. Three of the new members paid the initiation fees in year 2, and the other two new members paid their initiation fees in year 3. Annual dues (excluding initiation fees) received by the association from all of its members have always covered the organization's costs of services provided to its members. It can be reasonably expected that future dues will cover all costs of the organization's future services to members. Average membership duration is 10 years because of mergers, attrition, and economic factors. What amount of initiation fees from these five new members should the association recognize as revenue in year 2?

A. $5,000

B. $3,000

C. $500

D. $0

Answer (A) is correct. *(CPA, adapted)*

REQUIRED: The amount of initiation fees to be reported as revenue.

DISCUSSION: Membership dues received or receivable in exchange transactions that relate to several accounting periods should be allocated and recognized as revenue in those periods. Nonrefundable initiation and life membership fees are recognized as revenue when they are receivable if future dues and fees can be reasonably expected to cover the costs of the organization's services. Otherwise, they are amortized to future periods. Hence, given that future dues are expected to cover the organization's costs, the $5,000 in nonrefundable initiation fees should be recognized as revenue when assessed and reported as such in the year 2 statement of activities.

49. In July year 1, Ross irrevocably donated $200,000 cash to be invested and held in trust by a church. Ross stipulated that the revenue generated from this gift be paid to Ross during Ross's lifetime. After Ross dies, the principal is to be used by the church for any purpose chosen by its governing body. The church received interest of $16,000 on the $200,000 for the year ended June 30, year 2, and the interest was remitted to Ross. In the church's June 30, year 2, annual financial statements

A. $200,000 should be reported as revenue.

B. $184,000 should be reported as revenue.

C. $16,000 should be reported as revenue.

D. The gift and its terms should be disclosed only in notes to the financial statements.

Answer (A) is correct. *(CPA, adapted)*

REQUIRED: The proper accounting for a split-interest agreement.

DISCUSSION: An NPO should report an irrevocable split-interest agreement. Assets under the control of the NPO are recorded at fair value at the time of initial recognition, and the contribution is recognized as revenue. Because the NPO has a remainder interest, it should not recognize revenue from receipt of the income of the trust. Thus, the NPO should recognize revenue of $200,000 (the presumed fair value of the contributed cash).

Answer (B) is incorrect because the contribution is not reduced by the income paid to the donor. Answer (C) is incorrect because the income paid to the donor is not revenue of the NPO. Answer (D) is incorrect because the contribution should be recognized at fair value.

50. Maple Church has cash available for investments from contributions with different restrictions. Maple's policy is to maximize its financial resources. How may Maple pool its investments?

A. Maple may not pool its investments.

B. Maple may pool all investments but must equitably allocate realized and unrealized gains and losses among participants.

C. Maple may pool only unrestricted investments but must equitably allocate realized and unrealized gains and losses among participating funds.

D. Maple may pool only restricted investments but must equitably allocate realized and unrealized gains and losses among participating funds.

Answer (B) is correct. *(CPA, adapted)*

REQUIRED: The true statement about pooling of investments by an NPO.

DISCUSSION: Investment pools, including investments from contributions with different restrictions, are created for portfolio management. Ownership interests are assigned (ordinarily in terms of units) to the pool categories (participants) based on the market value of the cash and securities obtained from each participant. Current market value also determines the units allocated to additional assets placed in the pool and to value withdrawals. Investment income, realized gains and losses, and recognized unrealized gains and losses are allocated based on the units assigned.

Answer (A) is incorrect because pooling of investments is allowed to obtain investment flexibility and reduce risk. Answer (C) is incorrect because no prohibition exists as to the types of investments that may be pooled. Answer (D) is incorrect because no prohibition exists as to the types of investments that may be pooled.

Questions 51 through 53 are based on the following information. United Together, a labor union, had the following receipts and expenses for the current year ended December 31:

Receipts:	
Per capita dues	$680,000
Initiation fees	90,000
Sales of organizational supplies	60,000
Gift restricted by donor for loan purposes for 10 years	30,000
Gift restricted by donor for loan purposes in perpetuity	25,000

Expenses:	
Labor negotiations	$500,000
Fund-raising	100,000
Membership development	50,000
Administrative and general	200,000

Additional information: The union's constitution provides that 10% of the per capita dues are designated for the Strike Insurance Fund to be distributed for strike relief at the discretion of the union's executive board.

51. In United Together's statement of activities for the current year ended December 31, what amount should be reported as revenue?

A. $795,000

B. $830,000

C. $825,000

D. $885,000

Answer (D) is correct. *(CPA, adapted)*

REQUIRED: The amount classified as revenue.

DISCUSSION: NPOs generate resources through contributions, exchange transactions, and agency transactions. Revenues are recognized on contributions and exchange transactions. Contributions of resources by donors result from nonreciprocal transactions. Thus, revenue includes not only the resources provided as membership dues, initiation fees, sales revenue, investment income, gains and losses on the disposal of fixed assets and investments, and fees for services rendered but also the contributions received as restricted support. United Together should recognize $885,000 ($680,000 dues + $90,000 initiation fees + $60,000 sales + $30,000 gift + $25,000 gift) of revenue in the current year.

Answer (A) is incorrect because the initiation fees of $90,000 should be included as revenue. Answer (B) is incorrect because the revenue should include the amounts for gifts. Answer (C) is incorrect because the amount for sales of organizational supplies should be included as revenue.

52. In United Together's statement of activities for the current year ended December 31, what amount should be reported under the classification of program services expenses?

A. $850,000

B. $600,000

C. $550,000

D. $500,000

Answer (D) is correct. *(CPA, adapted)*

REQUIRED: The amount to be reported.

DISCUSSION: Program services include the expenses that relate directly to the primary missions of the NPO. These expenses include both the direct expenses clearly identified with the program and a systematic and rational allocation of indirect costs. Because the $500,000 labor negotiation expenses are the only expenses that relate directly to the primary mission of the labor union, $500,000 should be reported in the statement of activities.

Answer (A) is incorrect because fund-raising, membership development, and administrative costs relate to supporting services. Answer (B) is incorrect because the fund-raising amount should be supporting services expenses. Answer (C) is incorrect because the expenses for membership development are supporting services expenses.

53. In United Together's statement of activities for the current year ended December 31, what amount should be reported under the classification of restricted support?

A. $55,000

B. $30,000

C. $25,000

D. $0

Answer (A) is correct. *(CPA, adapted)*

REQUIRED: The amount of restricted support.

DISCUSSION: Contributions with donor-imposed restrictions, whether temporary or permanent, are reported as restricted support. Restricted support increases temporarily or permanently restricted net assets. Thus, $55,000 ($30,000 temporarily restricted gift + $25,000 permanently restricted gift) should be reported.

Answer (B) is incorrect because $30,000 omits the nonexpendable gift in perpetuity. Answer (C) is incorrect because $25,000 omits the nonexpendable gift for loan purposes that is donor-restricted for 10 years. Answer (D) is incorrect because both donor-restricted gifts are capital additions.

54. One not-for-profit organization (NPO) has control of another NPO (NPO-1) through a majority ownership interest in its board. Must NPO consolidate NPO-1?

A. No. Consolidation is required only if NPO has a controlling financial interest through ownership of a majority voting interest.

B. Yes, provided that NPO has an economic interest in NPO-1 and control rests with the majority owner.

C. No. Consolidation is required only if NPO has control through a majority ownership interest or a financial interest.

D. Yes, without any majority ownership or voting interest, if NPO has an economic interest in NPO-1 and exercises control conferred by a contract.

Answer (B) is correct. *(Publisher)*

REQUIRED: The circumstances in which an NPO must consolidate another NPO.

DISCUSSION: An NPO may have a controlling financial interest in another NPO through direct or indirect ownership of a majority voting interest in the other NPO. An NPO consolidates another NPO in these circumstances unless control does not rest with the majority owner. Consolidation is also necessary if the NPO controls another NPO by exercising a majority voting interest in the board or a majority ownership interest that is not a majority voting interest. This distinction arises because NPOs have differing legal forms, such as joint ventures, partnerships, or corporations that issue membership certificates. Control other than by ownership of a majority voting interest in the other NPO is deemed to exist only if the NPO also has an economic interest in the other NPO. Control is the ability to determine the direction of management and policies through ownership, contract, or otherwise. An economic interest exists when the other entity has significant resources that must be used for the purposes of the NPO, or the NPO is responsible for the other entity's liabilities.

Answer (A) is incorrect because, if NPO has an economic interest in NPO-1, its exercise of control through a majority voting interest in the board or a majority ownership interest that is not a majority voting interest requires consolidation. Answer (C) is incorrect because consolidation is required if an NPO (1) has an economic interest in the other entity and (2) exercises control through a majority interest in the board or a majority ownership interest that is not a majority voting interest. Answer (D) is incorrect because consolidation in these circumstances is optional.

29.3 Health Care Organizations

55. Monies from educational programs of a hospital normally are included in

A. Premium revenue.

B. Patient service revenue.

C. Nonoperating gains.

D. Other revenue.

Answer (D) is correct. *(CPA, adapted)*

REQUIRED: The classification of monies derived from educational programs of a hospital.

DISCUSSION: Revenues of an HCO include patient service revenue, premium revenue, resident service revenue, and other revenue. Other revenue, gains, or losses derive from services other than providing health care services or coverage to patients, enrollees, or residents. One source of other revenue is student tuition and fees. Thus, the monies received from an educational program conducted by a hospital should be classified as other revenue.

Answer (A) is incorrect because premium revenue is derived from a capitation arrangement, that is, from a contract under which a prepaid health care plan pays a per-individual fee to a provider. Answer (B) is incorrect because educational program revenue is not directly related to patient care and is therefore not includible in patient service revenues. Answer (C) is incorrect because nonoperating gains typically arise from activities such as sales of investments or fixed assets.

56. Which of the following should normally be considered ongoing or central transactions for a not-for-profit hospital?

I. Room and board fees from patients
II. Recovery room fees

A. Neither I nor II.

B. Both I and II.

C. II only.

D. I only.

Answer (B) is correct. *(CPA, adapted)*

REQUIRED: The item(s), if any, that are ongoing or central transactions for a not-for-profit hospital.

DISCUSSION: Revenues arise from an entity's ongoing major or central operations. Revenue from health care services includes inpatient and outpatient services provided directly to patients for their medical care. The resulting revenues derive from furnishing room and board and nursing services. Health care service revenues are also earned by the operating room, recovery room, labor and delivery room, and other ancillary departments that provide patient care.

57. Valley's community hospital normally includes proceeds from the sale of cafeteria meals in

A. Deductions from dietary service expenses.

B. Ancillary service revenues.

C. Patient service revenues.

D. Other revenues.

Answer (D) is correct. *(CPA, adapted)*

REQUIRED: The classification of revenue from cafeteria meals.

DISCUSSION: Other revenues are derived from services other than providing health care services or coverage to patients, residents, or enrollees. This category includes proceeds from sale of cafeteria meals and guest trays to employees, medical staff, and visitors.

Answer (A) is incorrect because revenues from cafeteria sales are accounted for separately and not as a component of any related expenses. Answer (B) is incorrect because "ancillary service revenues" is not a proper classification for hospital revenues. Answer (C) is incorrect because patient service revenues are health care services revenues.

58. Under Cura Hospital's established rate structure, health care services revenues of $9,000,000 would have been earned for the current year ended December 31. However, only $6,750,000 was collected because of charity allowances of $1,500,000 and discounts of $750,000 to third-party payors. For the current year ended December 31, what amount should Cura report as net health care services revenues in the statement of operations?

A. $6,750,000

B. $7,500,000

C. $8,250,000

D. $9,000,000

Answer (A) is correct. *(CPA, adapted)*

REQUIRED: The health care services revenues reported in the statement of operations.

DISCUSSION: Gross health care services revenues do not include charity care, which is disclosed separately in the notes to the financial statements. Moreover, such revenues are reported in the financial statements net of contractual and other adjustments. Thus, health care services revenues are recorded in the accounting records at the gross amount (excluding charity care) of $7,500,000 but reported in the financial statements at the net realizable value of $6,750,000.

Answer (B) is incorrect because $7,500,000 equals gross revenues. Answer (C) is incorrect because $8,250,000 assumes that charity allowances are included in gross and net revenues. Answer (D) is incorrect because charity care is excluded from gross revenue, and contractual adjustments are subtracted to arrive at net revenue.

59. Palma Hospital's patient service revenue for services provided in the current year at established rates amounted to $8,000,000 on the accrual basis. For internal reporting, Palma uses the discharge method. Under this method, patient service revenue is recognized only when patients are discharged, with no recognition given to revenue accruing for services to patients not yet discharged. Patient service revenue at established rates using the discharge method amounted to $7,000,000 for the current year. According to generally accepted accounting principles, Palma should report patient service revenue for the current year of

A. Either $8,000,000 or $7,000,000, at the option of the hospital.

B. $8,000,000

C. $7,500,000

D. $7,000,000

Answer (B) is correct. *(CPA, adapted)*

REQUIRED: The amount of patient service revenue to be reported.

DISCUSSION: The general principle is that gross service revenue is recorded on the accrual basis at the health care organization's established rates, regardless of whether it expects to collect the full amount. Contractual and other adjustments are also recorded on the accrual basis and subtracted from gross service revenue to arrive at net service revenue. Charity care is excluded from service revenue for financial reporting purposes. Thus, the discharge method currently used by Palma Hospital for internal reporting is not acceptable under GAAP. In its general purpose external financial statements, Palma should report $8,000,000 of patient service revenue based on established rates.

Answer (A) is incorrect because the $7,000,000 resulting from the discharge method is not acceptable under GAAP. Answer (C) is incorrect because $7,500,000 is the average of the $8,000,000 accrual basis amount and the $7,000,000 discharge method amount. Answer (D) is incorrect because the $7,000,000 resulting from the discharge method is not acceptable under GAAP.

60. In health care accounting, restricted net assets are

A. Not available unless the directors remove the restrictions.

B. Restricted as to use only for board-designated purposes.

C. Not available for current operating use; however, the income generated is available for current operating use.

D. Restricted as to use by the donor, grantor, or other source of the resources.

Answer (D) is correct. *(CPA, adapted)*

REQUIRED: The definition of restricted net assets.

DISCUSSION: In health care organization accounting, the term "restricted" is used to describe resources that have been restricted as to their use by the donors or grantors of those resources. Temporarily restricted net assets are those donor-restricted net assets that can be used by the not-for-profit organization for their specified purpose once the donor's restriction is met. Permanently restricted net assets are those with donor restrictions that do not expire with the passage of time and cannot be removed by any actions taken by the entity.

Answer (A) is incorrect because donor restrictions are not removable by the board. Temporary restrictions expire by passage of time or by actions by the entity consistent with the donor's restrictions. Answer (B) is incorrect because board-designated restrictions are board-removable. Answer (C) is incorrect because income generated by restricted net assets can be restricted for specific purposes.

61. In April of the current year, Delta Hospital purchased medicines from Field Pharmaceutical Co. at a cost of $5,000. However, Field notified Delta that the invoice was being canceled and that the medicines were being donated to Delta. Delta should record this donation of medicines as

A. A memorandum entry only.

B. A $5,000 credit to nonoperating expenses.

C. A $5,000 credit to operating expenses.

D. Other operating revenue of $5,000.

Answer (D) is correct. *(CPA, adapted)*

REQUIRED: The accounting for a donation of medicine.

DISCUSSION: Contributions of noncash assets that are not long-lived are reported at fair value in the statement of operations. Donated medicines, office supplies, and other materials that normally would be purchased by a hospital should be credited at fair value as other revenue because they directly relate to ongoing major operations but are not derived from services directly provided to patients, residents, or enrollees.

Answer (A) is incorrect because donated assets should be recorded at their fair value when received. Answer (B) is incorrect because this donation should be credited to another revenue account or a gain account. Answer (C) is incorrect because this donation should be credited to another revenue account or a gain account.

62. Which of the following normally is included in the revenue of a hospital?

	Revenue from Educational Programs	Unrestricted Gifts
A.	No	No
B.	No	Yes
C.	Yes	No
D.	Yes	Yes

Answer (C) is correct. *(CPA, adapted)*

REQUIRED: The items(s), if any, of revenue of a hospital.

DISCUSSION: Other revenue, gains, or losses may appropriately be recognized by a hospital for services other than health care or coverage provided to patients, residents, or enrollees. Other revenue may include cafeteria sales, tuition from educational programs, sales of medical supplies, and office space rentals. Revenue or expense results from an entity's ongoing major or central operations. Gains or losses result from peripheral or incidental transactions and from all transactions and other events and circumstances that do not generate revenue or expense (SFAC 6). Thus, contributions, either unrestricted or for a specific purpose, should be treated as gains unless fund-raising is an ongoing major activity of the hospital. They are recognized at fair value.

63. An organization of high school seniors performs services for patients at Leer Hospital. These students are volunteers and perform services that the hospital would not otherwise provide, such as wheeling patients in the park and reading to patients. They donated 5,000 hours of service to Leer in the current year. At a minimum wage rate, these services would amount to $18,750, while it is estimated that the fair value of these services was $25,000. In Leer's current year statement of activities, what amount should be reported as nonoperating revenue?

A. $25,000

B. $18,750

C. $6,250

D. $0

Answer (D) is correct. *(CPA, adapted)*

REQUIRED: The nonoperating revenue to record for services by volunteers.

DISCUSSION: Contributed services are recognized if they (1) create or enhance nonfinancial assets or (2) require special skills, are provided by persons possessing those skills, and would ordinarily be purchased if not provided by donation. Hence, the hospital should report no revenue. Nonfinancial assets are not involved, and no special skills, such as those of professionals or craftsmen, are required.

64. General purpose external financial reporting by a health care organization requires presentation of

A. Fund group information by a not-for-profit organization.

B. A statement of operations.

C. A separate statement of changes in equity, net assets, or fund balance.

D. A performance indicator only by for-profit entities.

Answer (B) is correct. *(Publisher)*

REQUIRED: The true statement about external reporting by a health care organization.

DISCUSSION: The basic financial statements of a health care organization include a balance sheet; a statement of operations; a statement of changes in equity, net assets, or fund balance; and a statement of cash flows.

Answer (A) is incorrect because fund accounting may be used for internal purposes but is not required or encouraged for external reporting. Answer (C) is incorrect because the statement of changes in equity, net assets, or fund balance may be combined with the statement of operations. Answer (D) is incorrect because the statement of operations of all HCOs, including NPOs, should report a performance indicator and other changes in net assets.

STUDY UNIT THIRTY
SPECIALIZED ACCOUNTING ISSUES

In **personal financial statements** prepared in accordance with GAAP, assets are presented at their estimated current values and liabilities at their estimated current amounts at the date of the financial statements. The estimated current value is the amount at which the asset could be exchanged between a buyer and a seller, both of whom are informed and willing and neither of whom is compelled to buy or sell. The estimated current amount is the lower of the estimated future cash to be paid, discounted at the interest rate implicit in the transaction in which the debt was incurred, or the amount at which the liability currently could be settled.

Prospective financial statements are either financial forecasts or financial projections. Financial forecasts present an entity's expected financial position, results of operations, and changes in cash flows. Financial projections present an entity's expected financial position, results of operations, and changes in cash flows based on one or more hypothetical assumptions.

Regulated industries may have rates set at levels intended to recover the estimated costs of providing regulated services or products. They should account for certain costs differently from nonregulated industries. For example, if regulation provides assurance that incurred costs will be recoverable in the future, those costs should be capitalized. If current recovery is provided for costs that are expected to be incurred in the future, those current receipts should be recognized as liabilities.

Oil and gas producing activities involve exploration, development, production, and the acquisition of mineral interests in properties. These activities may be accounted for in accordance with either the successful-efforts method or the full-cost method. Under the **successful-efforts method**, the producing activity costs that are associated with recoverable oil and gas should be capitalized and subsequently amortized. Producing activity costs associated with unsuccessful efforts are expensed. Under the **full-cost method**, the producing activity costs that are associated with oil and gas properties in large geographical areas should be capitalized and subsequently amortized, regardless of whether the costs are associated with successful or unsuccessful projects. A comprehensive set of disclosures is required for oil and gas producing activities regardless of the accounting method used.

Specialized accounting principles and practices for the **record and music industry** require a licensing fee to be recognized as revenue if the license agreement is an outright sale in substance and collectibility of the fee is reasonably assured. In addition, minimum guarantees paid in advance by a licensee to a licensor should be capitalized and expensed in accordance with the terms of the licensing agreement unless all or a portion of the guarantee appears nonrecoverable.

A **cable television company** must partially capitalize and partially expense costs related to both current and future operations that are incurred during a prematurity period. A **prematurity period** is the period in which a cable television system is partially under construction and partially in service.

A **broadcaster** must recognize the rights acquired and obligations incurred under a **license agreement** for program material as assets and liabilities when the license period begins and (1) the cost of each program is known or determinable, (2) the program material has been accepted, and (3) the program material is available for viewing or telecast. In addition, when a broadcaster barters unsold advertising time for goods and services, barter revenue should be recognized when the commercials are broadcast.

Insurance enterprises must classify insurance contracts as short-duration or long-duration contracts. Premiums from **short-duration contracts** ordinarily are recognized as revenue over the period of the contract in proportion to the amount of insurance protection provided. Premiums from **long-duration contracts** are recognized as revenue when due from policyholders.

Enterprises that use a **title plant** in their operations must capitalize costs directly incurred to construct a title plant until the enterprise can use the title plant to do title searches. A title plant should not be depreciated. Costs of maintaining a title plant and of conducting searches should be expensed as incurred.

Mortgage loans held for sale must be reported at the lower of cost or market value. Loan origination fees and direct loan origination costs related to loans held for investment are deferred and recognized as an adjustment of yield in accordance with the interest method. Loan origination fees and direct loan origination costs related to loans held for resale are deferred until the related loan is sold.

According to **SFAS 66**, *Accounting for Sales of Real Estate*, recognition of profit or loss on **retail land sales** should be recognized in accordance with the full accrual basis if the seller's receivables from the land sales are collectible and the seller has no significant remaining obligations for construction or development. If these criteria are not met, retail land sales should be recognized in accordance with either the percentage-of-completion method or the installment method. For **other real estate sales**, specific criteria determine whether profit or loss should be recognized in accordance with the full accrual method or other methods. These criteria relate to whether the sale has been consummated, the extent of the buyer's investment in the property, whether the seller's receivable is subject to further subordination, and the degree of the seller's continuing involvement with the property after the sale. Under **SFAS 152**, *Accounting for Real Estate Time-Sharing Transactions*, such transactions are accounted for as nonretail land sales.

Certain costs associated with **real estate projects** should be capitalized. These costs include preacquisition costs, taxes and insurance, acquisition, development and construction costs (project costs), costs of amenities, incidental operation costs, and selling and rental costs. Costs generally should no longer be capitalized when a rental project is substantially completed and held available for occupancy (**SFAS 67**, *Accounting for Costs and Initial Rental Operations of Real Estate Projects*). However, SFAS 67 does not apply to (1) costs of selling real estate projects or (2) incidental operations if such costs or operations are related to time-sharing transactions (SFAS 152).

QUESTIONS

30.1 Personal Financial Statements

1. Personal financial statements should report assets and liabilities at

A. Estimated current values and amounts at the date of the financial statements and, as additional information, at historical cost and historical proceeds.

B. Estimated current values and amounts at the date of the financial statements.

C. Historical cost and historical proceeds and, as additional information, at estimated current values and amounts at the date of the financial statements.

D. Historical cost and historical proceeds.

Answer (B) is correct. *(CPA, adapted)*

REQUIRED: The measurement attributes of assets and liabilities in personal financial statements.

DISCUSSION: SOP 82-1, *Accounting and Financial Reporting for Personal Financial Statements*, requires personal financial statements to present assets at their estimated current values and liabilities at their estimated current amounts at the date of the statement. The estimated current value of an asset is defined as the amount at which the asset could be exchanged between informed and willing sellers and buyers, neither of whom is compelled to buy or sell. Estimated current amounts of liabilities are defined as the lower of either the amount of future cash to be paid discounted at the interest rate implicit in the transaction in which the debt was incurred or the amount at which the debt could currently be settled.

Answer (A) is incorrect because the historical cost and historical proceeds of assets and liabilities do not have to be reported. Answer (C) is incorrect because the historical cost and historical proceeds of assets and liabilities do not have to be reported. Answer (D) is incorrect because estimated current values and current amounts should be used.

2. Personal financial statements require which of the following statements?

	Financial Condition	Changes in Net Worth	Cash Flows
A.	No	Yes	Yes
B.	Yes	No	No
C.	Yes	Yes	No
D.	Yes	Yes	Yes

Answer (B) is correct. *(CPA, adapted)*

REQUIRED: The basic financial statements that should be included in personal financial statements.

DISCUSSION: SOP 82-1 requires that personal financial statements include at least a statement of financial condition. SOP 82-1 further recommends, but does not require, a statement of changes in net worth and comparative financial statements. A personal statement of cash flows, however, is neither required nor recommended.

3. Mayerling owns several works of art. At what amount should these artworks be reported in Mayerling's personal financial statements?

A. Original cost.

B. Insured amount.

C. Smith's estimate.

D. Appraised value.

Answer (D) is correct. *(CPA, adapted)*

REQUIRED: The amount at which works of art should be reported in personal financial statements.

DISCUSSION: SOP 82-1 requires that assets be presented at their estimated current values in a personal statement of financial condition. Current value may be based on discounted cash flow, market price, appraisal value, or other basis, depending on the asset. Appraisal value is appropriate for works of art.

4. The following information pertains to an insurance policy that Oshima owns on his life:

Face amount	$200,000
Accumulated premiums paid up to December 31, 2003	16,000
Cash value at December 31, 2003	24,000
Policy loan	6,000

In Oshima's personal statement of financial condition at December 31, 2003, what amount should be reported for the investment in life insurance?

A. $194,000

B. $24,000

C. $18,000

D. $16,000

Answer (C) is correct. *(CPA, adapted)*

REQUIRED: The amount reported for the investment in life insurance.

DISCUSSION: SOP 82-1 requires that a life insurance policy be reported at its cash value minus any loans against it. Accordingly, the amount reported should be $18,000 ($24,000 – $6,000).

Answer (A) is incorrect because $194,000 equals the face amount of the policy minus the loan. Answer (B) is incorrect because $24,000 equals the cash value. Answer (D) is incorrect because $16,000 equals the premiums paid.

5. Doyle is preparing a personal statement of financial condition as of April 30. Included in Doyle's assets are the following:

- 50% of the voting stock of Conan Corp. A shareholders' agreement restricts the sale of the stock and, under certain circumstances, requires Conan to repurchase the stock based on carrying amounts of net assets plus an agreed amount for goodwill. At April 30, the buyout value of this stock is $675,000. Doyle's tax basis for the stock is $430,000.
- Jewelry with a fair value aggregating $70,000 based on an independent appraisal on April 30 for insurance purposes. This jewelry was acquired by purchase and gift over a 10-year period and has a total tax basis of $40,000.

At what total amount should the Conan stock and jewelry be reported in Doyle's April 30 personal statement of financial condition?

A. $745,000

B. $715,000

C. $500,000

D. $470,000

Answer (A) is correct. *(CPA, adapted)*

REQUIRED: The amount at which stock and jewelry should be reported in a personal statement of financial condition.

DISCUSSION: SOP 82-1 requires that all assets be reported at estimated current value. An interest in a closely held business is an asset and should be shown at its estimated current value. The buyout value is a better representation of the current value of the Conan stock than the tax basis. The appraisal value is the appropriate basis for reporting the jewelry. Thus, the stock and jewelry should be reported at $745,000 ($675,000 + $70,000).

Answer (B) is incorrect because $715,000 includes the jewelry's tax basis rather than fair value. The tax basis is used only when the jewelry is sold to determine taxable profit. Answer (C) is incorrect because $500,000 includes the stock at its tax basis. Answer (D) is incorrect because $470,000 reports both assets at their tax bases.

6. Hudson has been employed by Moriarty Co. since February 1, 2001 and is covered by a Section 401(k) deferred compensation plan. Hudson's contributions have been 10% of salaries. Moriarty has made matching contributions of 5%. Hudson's salaries were $21,000 in 2001, $23,000 in 2002, and $26,000 in 2003. Employer contributions vest after an employee completes 3 years of continuous employment. The balance in Hudson's 401(k) account was $11,900 at December 31, 2003, which included earnings of $1,200 on Hudson's contributions. What amount should be reported for the vested interest in the 401(k) plan in Hudson's December 31, 2003 personal statement of financial condition?

A. $11,900

B. $8,200

C. $7,000

D. $1,200

Answer (B) is correct. *(CPA, adapted)*

REQUIRED: The amount reported for the vested interest in the 401(k) plan in the personal statement of financial condition.

DISCUSSION: The employee's contributions equaled $7,000 [10% x ($21,000 + $23,000 + $26,000)], and earnings on those contributions were $1,200, for a total of $8,200. The remainder of the balance in the 401(k) account consists of employer contributions that have not yet vested. The employee should report the employee contributions and earnings on these contributions, but not the nonvested employer contributions. The latter do not constitute nonforfeitable rights to receive future sums.

Answer (A) is incorrect because $11,900 includes the nonvested employer contributions. Answer (C) is incorrect because $7,000 excludes earnings on the employee contributions. Answer (D) is incorrect because $1,200 excludes the employee contributions.

7. On December 31 of the current year, Watson had the following noncancelable personal commitments:

- $10,000 pledge to be paid to Gator State University 30 days after volunteers refurbish the campus meditation center
- $50,000 pledge to be paid to Gator State University when Watson's youngest son attains the age of 40

What amount should be included in liabilities in Watson's current year personal statement of financial condition at December 31?

A. $0

B. $10,000

C. $50,000

D. $60,000

Answer (A) is correct. *(CPA, adapted)*

REQUIRED: The amount included in liabilities for noncancelable personal commitments.

DISCUSSION: SOP 82-1 requires that noncancelable commitments to pay future sums be presented at their estimated current amounts as liabilities in personal financial statements if they (1) are for fixed or determinable amounts, (2) are not contingent on another's life expectancy or the occurrence of a particular event such as disability or death, and (3) do not require the future performance of service by another. Consequently, neither of Watson's commitments qualifies for inclusion.

Answer (B) is incorrect because the pledge to the Gator State University requires the future performance of service by another. Answer (C) is incorrect because the pledge to Gator State University is contingent on another's life expectancy. Answer (D) is incorrect because neither pledge qualifies for inclusion.

8. John, a calendar-year taxpayer, is preparing a personal statement of financial condition as of April 30, 2003. John's 2002 income tax liability was paid in full on April 15, 2003. John's tax on income earned from January through April 2003 is estimated at $60,000. In addition, $50,000 is estimated for income tax on the differences between the estimated current values of John's assets and the current amounts of liabilities and their tax bases at April 30, 2003. No withholdings or payments have been made toward the 2003 income tax liability. In John's statement of financial condition at April 30, 2003, what is the total of the amount or amounts that should be reported for income taxes?

A. $0

B. $50,000

C. $60,000

D. $110,000

Answer (D) is correct. *(CPA, adapted)*

REQUIRED: The total of the amount(s) that should be reported for income taxes.

DISCUSSION: No amount should be reported for 2002 taxes because the 2002 liability was paid in full. John should report estimated income taxes for amounts earned through April 2003 and for the differences between the estimated current values of assets and the estimated current amounts of liabilities and their tax bases, a sum of $110,000.

Answer (A) is incorrect because John must report estimated income taxes. Answer (B) is incorrect because $50,000 excludes the estimated income taxes on 2003 income earned to date. Answer (C) is incorrect because $60,000 excludes estimated income taxes for the differences between the estimated current values of assets and the estimated current amounts of liabilities and their tax bases.

9. Stone had the following personal investments at December 31, 2003:

- Realty held as a limited business activity not conducted in a separate business entity. Mortgage payments were made with funds from sources unrelated to the realty. The cost of this realty was $1,000,000, and the related mortgage payable was $200,000 at December 31, 2003.
- Sole proprietorship marketable as a going concern. Its cost was $1,800,000, and it had related accounts payable of $160,000 at December 31, 2003.

The costs of both investments equal estimated current values. The balances of liabilities equal their estimated current amounts. How should the foregoing information be reported in Stone's statement of financial condition at December 31, 2003?

		Assets	Liabilities
A.	Investment in real estate	$ 800,000	
	Investment in sole proprietorship	1,640,000	
B.	Investment in real estate	$1,000,000	
	Investment in sole proprietorship	1,640,000	
	Mortgage payable		$200,000
C.	Investment in real estate	$1,000,000	
	Investment in sole proprietorship	1,800,000	
	Mortgage payable		$200,000
	Accounts payable		160,000
D.	Investments	$2,800,000	
	Accounts and mortgage payable		$360,000

Answer (B) is correct. *(CPA, adapted)*

REQUIRED: The reporting of personal investments.

DISCUSSION: For an investment in a limited business activity not conducted in a separate business entity (such as an investment in real estate and a related mortgage), SOP 82-1 requires that the assets and liabilities should be presented as separate assets at their estimated current values and separate liabilities at their estimated current amount rather than as a net amount. This presentation is particularly important if a large portion of the liabilities may be satisfied with funds from sources unrelated to the investments. SOP 82-1 requires that a business interest constituting a large part of an individual's total assets be presented in a personal statement of financial condition as a single amount equal to the estimated current value of the business interest. This investment should be disclosed separately from other investments if the entity is marketable as a going concern. Thus, the realty and the related mortgage should be presented as separate amounts at $1,000,000 and $200,000, respectively, and the sole proprietorship should be disclosed separately as a single amount equal to $1,640,000 ($1,800,000 – $160,000).

Answer (A) is incorrect because the realty and the related mortgage should be presented as separate amounts. Answer (C) is incorrect because the sole proprietorship should be disclosed separately as a single amount. Answer (D) is incorrect because the realty and the related mortgage should be presented as separate amounts, and the sole proprietorship should be disclosed separately as a single amount.

10. On December 31, 2003, Jean is a fully vested participant in a company-sponsored pension plan. According to the plan's administrator, Jean has at that date the nonforfeitable right to receive a lump sum of $200,000 on December 28, 2004. The discounted amount of $200,000 is $180,000 at December 31, 2003. The right is not contingent on Jean's life expectancy and requires no future performance on Jean's part. In Jean's December 31, 2003 personal statement of financial condition, the vested interest in the pension plan should be reported at

A. $0

B. $180,000

C. $190,000

D. $200,000

Answer (B) is correct. *(CPA, adapted)*

REQUIRED: The amount at which the vested interest in a pension plan should be reported in a personal statement of financial condition.

DISCUSSION: SOP 82-1 requires that noncancelable rights to receive future sums be presented at their estimated current value as assets in personal financial statements if they (1) are for fixed or determinable amounts; (2) are not contingent on the holder's life expectancy or the occurrence of a particular event, such as disability or death; and (3) do not require the future performance of service by the holder. The fully vested rights in the company-sponsored pension plan therefore should be reported at their current value, which is equal to the $180,000 discounted amount.

Answer (A) is incorrect because the current value of the right should be reported. Answer (C) is incorrect because $190,000 is the average of the discounted and nondiscounted amounts. Answer (D) is incorrect because $200,000 is the undiscounted amount.

30.2 Prospective Financial Statements

The questions in this subheading are based on the AICPA's Statements on Standards for Attestation Engagements (SSAEs). References to a statement of changes in financial position or to changes in financial position should be read in the light of the requirement of SFAS 95 that the basic financial statements include a statement of cash flows.

11. Financial forecasts and financial projections should preferably be in the format of the historical financial statements that would be issued for the future period(s) covered if the responsible party and potential users do not have an agreement specifying another format. Financial forecasts and financial projections may take the form of complete basic financial statements or may be limited to a presentation of certain minimum items. Which of the following is not one of the minimum items?

A. Net income.

B. Discontinued operations or extraordinary items, if any.

C. Significant changes in financial position.

D. Statement of financial position.

Answer (D) is correct. *(Publisher)*

REQUIRED: The item not required in prospective financial statements.

DISCUSSION: Prospective financial statements may be limited to certain minimum items of financial data (when such items would be presented for historical financial statements for the period). These items are (1) sales or gross revenue, (2) gross profit or cost of sales, (3) unusual or infrequently occurring items, (4) provision for income taxes, (5) discontinued operations or extraordinary items, (6) income from continuing operations, (7) net income, (8) basic and diluted earnings per share, and (9) significant changes in financial position. Omission of any of items (1) through (9) results in a partial presentation. Such a presentation ordinarily is not appropriate for general use. Moreover, with respect to item (9), the responsible party should disclose cash flows and other significant changes in balance sheet accounts, but no balance sheet or cash flow statement is required to be disclosed.

The following disclosures should also accompany prospective financial statements, whatever their form: (1) a description of what the responsible party intends the prospective financial statements to present, a statement that the assumptions are based on the responsible party's judgment at the time the prospective information was prepared, and a caveat that the prospective results may not be achieved; (2) a summary of significant assumptions; and (3) a summary of significant accounting policies.

Answer (A) is incorrect because net income is a required item when prospective financial statements are presented in a limited form. Answer (B) is incorrect because discontinued operations or extraordinary items, if any, are required items when prospective financial statements are presented in a limited form. Answer (C) is incorrect because significant changes in cash flows are required items when prospective financial statements are presented in a limited form.

12. Prospective financial information is any financial information about the future. Prospective financial information represents financial position, results of operations, and cash flows. Prospective financial statements include which of the following?

A. Financial forecasts and pro forma financial statements.

B. Financial forecasts and financial projections.

C. Financial projections and pro forma financial statements.

D. Financial forecasts and partial presentations.

Answer (B) is correct. *(Publisher)*

REQUIRED: The types of information defined as prospective financial statements.

DISCUSSION: Prospective financial statements consist of either financial forecasts or financial projections, including the summaries of significant assumptions and accounting policies. Financial forecasts are prospective financial statements that present, to the best of the responsible party's knowledge and belief, an entity's expected financial position, results of operations, and cash flows. Financial projections are prospective financial statements that present, to the best of the responsible party's knowledge and belief given one or more hypothetical assumptions, an entity's expected financial position, results of operations, and cash flows.

Answer (A) is incorrect because pro forma financial statements demonstrate the effect of a future or hypothetical transaction on financial statements of a past period as if the transaction had been consummated during the period covered by those statements. Thus, pro forma financial statements are not prospective. Answer (C) is incorrect because pro forma financial statements demonstrate the effect of a future or hypothetical transaction on financial statements of a past period as if the transaction had been consummated during the period covered by those statements. Thus, pro forma financial statements are not prospective. Answer (D) is incorrect because a partial presentation omits one or more items of financial data required of prospective financial statements.

13. Prospective financial statements may be used in certain instances. Which of the following best describes an authorized use?

A. Financial forecasts expressed as a single point estimate are appropriate for general use; financial forecasts expressed as a range are appropriate only for limited use.

B. Financial projections expressed as a single point estimate are appropriate for general use; financial projections expressed as a range are appropriate only for limited use.

C. Financial forecasts expressed as either a single point estimate or a range are appropriate only for limited use.

D. Financial forecasts expressed as either a single point estimate or a range are appropriate for general use.

Answer (D) is correct. *(Publisher)*

REQUIRED: The use(s) appropriate for financial forecasts or financial projections.

DISCUSSION: Prospective financial statements are designated as for general use or limited use. General use refers to use by persons with whom the responsible party is not negotiating directly. Limited use refers to use by the responsible party alone or by the responsible party and third parties with whom the responsible party is negotiating directly. Financial forecasts expressed as either a single point estimate or a range are appropriate for either of these uses. However, a financial projection expressed as either a single point estimate or a range is appropriate only for limited use, unless the projection is used to supplement a financial forecast.

14. Certain items are basic to an entity's operations and serve as a foundation for prospective financial statements. Which is the best term for these significant matters?

A. Key factors.

B. Assumptions.

C. Hypothetical assumptions.

D. Responsible parties.

Answer (A) is correct. *(Publisher)*

REQUIRED: The term for the items basic to an entity's operations.

DISCUSSION: Key factors are the significant matters on which an entity's future results are expected to depend, i.e., the basis for the assumptions underlying the prospective financial statements. They encompass matters affecting the entity's sales, service, production, and financing activities.

Answer (B) is incorrect because an assumption reflects conditions the responsible party expects to exist in the future. Answer (C) is incorrect because a hypothetical assumption represents a condition or course of action that is not necessarily expected to occur but is consistent with the purpose of a projection. Answer (D) is incorrect because responsible parties (usually management) are the persons responsible for establishing the assumptions underlying the prospective financial statements.

15. Which of the following statements best describes the use of appropriate accounting principles in the preparation of prospective financial statements?

A. The accounting principles used in prospective financial statements should always be the same as those used in the historical financial statements.

B. Accounting changes should be reflected in financial projections only if the responsible party expects to make the change in the historical statements for that period.

C. A basis of accounting used in prospective financial statements may differ from that used in the historical financial statements.

D. Accounting changes reflected in prospective financial statements should be recorded as a cumulative-effect type of change.

Answer (C) is correct. *(Publisher)*

REQUIRED: The statement that best describes the appropriate use of accounting principles in prospective financial statements.

DISCUSSION: Occasionally, a basis of accounting used in a financial forecast or financial projection may differ from that used in the historical financial statements for that period; e.g., a cash-basis statement may be prepared rather than an accrual-basis statement. When a different basis of accounting is used, it should be reconciled to results that would be obtained using the basis of accounting found in the historical financial statements.

Answer (A) is incorrect because a different basis of accounting may occasionally be used. Answer (B) is incorrect because an accounting change may be reflected in a financial projection for analytical purposes, even if there is no intention of actually changing the method of accounting. Answer (D) is incorrect because accounting changes reflected in prospective financial statements should be reflected on the same basis as in historical financial statements, which may or may not be cumulative.

16. Which of the following disclosures should prospective financial statements include?

	Summary of Significant Accounting Policies	Summary of Significant Assumptions
A.	Yes	Yes
B.	Yes	No
C.	No	Yes
D.	No	No

Answer (A) is correct. *(CPA, adapted)*

REQUIRED: The disclosures in prospective financial statements.

DISCUSSION: Under the minimum presentation guidelines for prospective financial statements (PFSs), PFSs may take the form of complete basic statements or be limited to certain minimum items (when the items would be presented for the period's historical statements). Among these items are the summary of significant accounting policies and the summary of significant assumptions.

17. In a financial forecast, the disclosures concerning the assumptions underlying the forecast ordinarily should include all except

A. Assumptions for which there is a reasonable possibility of the occurrence of a variation that may significantly affect the forecasted results.

B. Assumptions about anticipated conditions that are expected to be significantly different from current conditions that are not otherwise reasonably apparent.

C. Assumptions implicit in the forecast that have enormous potential impact on the forecast, such as conditions of peace, absence of natural disasters, etc.

D. Other matters deemed important to the forecast or to its interpretation.

Answer (C) is correct. *(Publisher)*

REQUIRED: The assumptions not requiring disclosure in a financial forecast.

DISCUSSION: Assumptions are the single most important ingredient of a financial forecast. At a minimum, they should include the assumptions described in answers (A), (B), and (D). Basic assumptions that are implicit in a forecast and have enormous potential impact, such as conditions of peace and absence of natural disasters, need be disclosed only when there is a reasonable probability that the current conditions will not prevail.

30.3 Regulated Industries

18. Which of the following is a true statement about enterprises with regulated operations to which SFAS 71, *Accounting for the Effects of Certain Types of Regulation*, applies?

A. Profit on sales to regulated affiliates normally should be eliminated in general purpose financial statements.

B. In all circumstances, the amount of interest that should be capitalized on a construction project should be calculated in accordance with SFAS 34, *Capitalization of Interest Cost.*

C. Refunds to customers required by a regulator should be recorded as liabilities only in the period in which they must be refunded.

D. Rate actions of a regulator may result in the required capitalization of an incurred cost that would be charged to expense by a nonregulated enterprise.

Answer (D) is correct. *(Publisher)*

REQUIRED: The true statement about the required accounting for an enterprise with regulated operations to which SFAS 71 applies.

DISCUSSION: If rate actions of a regulator are such that reasonable assurance is provided of the existence of an asset, an enterprise subject to the provisions of SFAS 71 should capitalize the cost incurred even though a nonregulated enterprise normally would charge it to expense.

Answer (A) is incorrect because profit on sales to regulated affiliates should not be eliminated if the sales price is reasonable and if it is probable that, through the rate-making process, future revenues approximately equal to the sales price will result from the use of the products by the regulated affiliates. Answer (B) is incorrect because SFAS 34 does not apply when a regulator requires the capitalization of financing costs on a construction project that is financed partially by borrowings and partially by equity. Answer (C) is incorrect because, if a regulator requires refunds to customers, a liability should be recorded when it is both probable and reasonably estimable.

19. The basic question addressed by SFAS 71 is whether accounting prescribed by regulatory authorities should be considered in and of itself generally accepted for purposes of financial reporting by rate-regulated enterprises. Which of the following statements best describes the authoritative position taken relative to this basic issue?

A. Accounting prescribed by regulatory authorities in and of itself is considered generally accepted for purposes of financial reporting by rate-regulated enterprises.

B. GAAP as currently prescribed for nonrate-regulated enterprises are equally appropriate for rate-regulated enterprises.

C. Certain differences should exist between the application of GAAP as currently prescribed for nonrate-regulated enterprises and rate-regulated enterprises.

D. GAAP as currently prescribed for nonrate-regulated enterprises are not applicable to rate-regulated enterprises.

Answer (C) is correct. *(Publisher)*

REQUIRED: The authoritative position on the application of GAAP to rate-regulated enterprises.

DISCUSSION: SFAS 71 states that accounting prescribed by regulatory agencies should not be considered generally accepted in and of itself. The board concluded that differences should exist between the application of generally accepted accounting principles as currently prescribed for nonrate-regulated enterprises and rate-regulated enterprises. Thus, SFAS 71 applies GAAP in the regulatory environment.

Answer (A) is incorrect because SFAS 71 states that accounting prescribed by regulatory agencies should not be considered GAAP in and of itself. Answer (B) is incorrect because GAAP for nonrate-regulated enterprises are not always appropriate for rate-regulated enterprises. Answer (D) is incorrect because GAAP, as currently presented for nonrate-regulated enterprises, are appropriate for rate-regulated enterprises under many circumstances.

20. SFAS 71 is applicable to the general-purpose external financial statements of an enterprise with regulated operations that meet certain specified criteria. Which of the following is not one of the criteria that must be met?

A. The enterprise's rates for regulated services or products are established by, or are subject to, approval by an independent third-party regulator.

B. The enterprise's rates for regulated services or products are established by, or are subject to, a contractual arrangement with a governmental agency.

C. The regulated rates are designed to recover the specific enterprise's costs of providing the regulated services or products.

D. Reasonable assurance must exist that the regulated environment and its economic effect will continue to exist.

Answer (B) is correct. *(Publisher)*

REQUIRED: The criterion not required to be met for SFAS 71 to be applicable.

DISCUSSION: SFAS 71 requires the existence of an independent third-party regulator. This criterion is intended to exclude contractual arrangements in which the government or another party that could be viewed as the regulator is a party to a contract and is the principal customer of the enterprise. If an enterprise's regulated operations cease meeting these criteria for any reason, SFAS 101, *Regulated Enterprises – Accounting for the Discontinuation of Application of FASB Statement No. 71*, requires that the enterprise discontinue the application of SFAS 71.

Answer (A) is incorrect because it is one of the three criteria that must be met for SFAS 71 to be applicable to the operations of the enterprise. Answer (C) is incorrect because it is one of the three criteria that must be met for SFAS 71 to be applicable to the operations of the enterprise. Answer (D) is incorrect because it is one of the three criteria that must be met for SFAS 71 to be applicable to the operations of the enterprise.

21. A major difference between nonregulated and regulated enterprises is the ability of a regulatory action to create a future economic benefit that in substance is an asset. Which of the following actions relative to the rate-making process results in the creation of a future economic benefit that should be recognized as an asset by a regulated entity?

A. A regulator provides current rates intended to recover costs expected to be incurred in the future with the understanding that, if the costs are not incurred, future rates will be reduced.

B. A regulator requires that a gain or other reduction of net allowable costs be passed on to customers over future periods.

C. A regulator allows future rates to be increased by the amount of the excess cost of reacquired debt over the debt's net carrying amount.

D. A regulator allows a regulated enterprise to bill for requested rate increases before the regulator has ruled on the request.

Answer (C) is correct. *(Publisher)*

REQUIRED: The action by a regulator that results in the recognition of an asset through the creation of a future economic benefit.

DISCUSSION: If debt is reacquired for an amount in excess of its net carrying amount and the regulator allows an increase in future rates to provide for this difference, reasonable assurance is considered to have been given of the existence of a future economic benefit that should be recognized as an asset.

Answer (A) is incorrect because the regulator's action in this instance would give rise to the creation and recognition of a liability under SFAS 71, not a benefit. Answer (B) is incorrect because the regulator's action in this instance would give rise to the creation and recognition of a liability under SFAS 71, not a benefit. Answer (D) is incorrect because the regulator's action in this instance would give rise to the creation and recognition of a liability under SFAS 71, not a benefit.

22. Power Company has reached a decision to discontinue construction on a partially completed generating plant. Based on previous action by the rate-making board, Power believes that recovery of certain of the construction costs incurred plus a full return on investment for these costs will be allowed. Based on this information, it should

A. Write off the construction costs incurred immediately.

B. Amortize the construction costs incurred over the normal recovery period.

C. Write down the construction costs incurred to an amount equal to the allowable costs.

D. Write down the construction costs incurred to the present value of the future revenues expected to be provided.

Answer (C) is correct. *(Publisher)*

REQUIRED: The accounting for a plant abandonment by a regulated enterprise.

DISCUSSION: SFAS 90, *Regulated Enterprises – Accounting for Abandonments and Disallowances of Plant Costs*, states that, when it becomes probable that an operating asset or an asset under construction will be abandoned, its cost should be removed from construction work-in-process or plant-in-service. Any disallowance of all or part of the cost of the abandoned plant that is probable and reasonably estimable should be recognized as a loss. If a full return on investment is likely to be provided by the regulator, the carrying amount of the recorded asset should be similarly reduced, and the remainder of the cost should be reported as a separate new asset. The amount of the allowable cost should then be amortized in the same manner as that used for rate-making purposes.

Answer (A) is incorrect because an immediate write-off is not appropriate. Answer (B) is incorrect because only the allowable construction costs should be amortized over the normal recovery period. Answer (D) is incorrect because a write-down of the construction costs incurred to the present value of the future revenues expected to be provided is appropriate when a partial return or no return on investment is likely to be provided.

23. When a utility completes a new plant, conventional rate-making procedures usually establish rates to provide recovery of the current operating costs of the plant, depreciation, interest, and shareholder earnings on the investment. However, if regulatory agencies defer recovery of part of these costs because of the significantly increased cost of the new plant, the deferred cost to be recovered under a phase-in plan can be capitalized if certain specified criteria are met. For plants that were completed or on which substantial physical construction was performed before January 1, 1988, which of the following criteria must be met before all allowable costs deferred for future recovery may be capitalized for financial reporting?

A. It is probable that the regulator will agree to the plan.

B. The plan specifies the timing of recovery of all deferred allowable costs.

C. All allowable costs deferred under the plan are scheduled for recovery within 40 years.

D. The percentage increase in rates under the plan is the same for each future year.

Answer (B) is correct. *(Publisher)*

REQUIRED: The criterion used to determine whether capitalization is appropriate.

DISCUSSION: According to SFAS 92, *Regulated Enterprises - Accounting for Phase-in Plans*, if a phase-in plan is ordered by a regulatory body in connection with a plant that either was completed before January 1, 1988 or on which substantial physical construction was performed before that date, certain criteria must be met before all allowable costs deferred by the regulator under the phase-in plan may be capitalized for financial reporting as a separate asset. One of the criteria is that the plan must specify the timing of recovery of all allowable costs that will be deferred.

Answer (A) is incorrect because the regulator must have agreed to the plan. Answer (C) is incorrect because the recovery period must be within 10 years of the date when deferrals begin. Answer (D) is incorrect because the percentage increase in rates scheduled under the plan for each future year may not be greater than the percentage increase scheduled for each immediately preceding year.

30.4 Oil and Gas

24. Exploil Company drilled two wells in a remote area. The first, a dry hole, cost $50,000. The second cost $100,000 and had estimated recoverable reserves of 25,000 barrels, of which 10,000 were sold this year. If Exploil uses the successful-efforts method of accounting, what will be its total expense for the year related to oil exploration and production in the remote area?

A. $40,000

B. $60,000

C. $90,000

D. $150,000

Answer (C) is correct. *(CIA, adapted)*

REQUIRED: The total expense for the year related to oil exploration and production using the successful-efforts method of accounting.

DISCUSSION: Under the successful-efforts method, exploration costs are capitalized and subsequently amortized for the cost of finding recoverable oil and gas. This method expenses costs of unsuccessful efforts in the year incurred. The alternative is the full-cost method, under which all of the costs of acquiring, exploring, and developing oil and gas properties in very large geographical areas are capitalized and subsequently amortized, whether the costs are related to successful or unsuccessful projects. The successful-efforts method capitalizes the $100,000 cost of the second well, expenses the $50,000 cost of the first well, and amortizes an amount of the capitalized cost of the second well that is proportionate to the oil produced. Amortization for the year equals $40,000 [$100,000 capitalized cost × (10,000 barrels sold ÷ 25,000 barrels of resources)]. Consequently, the total expense is $90,000 ($50,000 + $40,000).

Answer (A) is incorrect because $40,000 is amortization for the year. Answer (B) is incorrect because $60,000 is based on the full-cost method [(10,000 ÷ 25,000) × ($100,000 + $50,000)]. Answer (D) is incorrect because $150,000 equals the cost of both wells.

25. An oil company has acquired the right to use 2,000 acres of land to explore for oil. The lease cost is $100,000; the related exploration costs for a discovered oil deposit on the property are $400,000; and intangible development costs in erecting and drilling the well are $1,500,000. It is estimated that the well will provide approximately 1,000,000 barrels of oil. If 200,000 barrels are withdrawn and sold in the first year, and the successful-efforts approach is used, the amount to be reported for depletion for the first year is

A. $100,000

B. $300,000

C. $400,000

D. $2,000,000

Answer (C) is correct. *(CPA, adapted)*

REQUIRED: The amount to be reported for depletion for the first year under the successful-efforts method.

DISCUSSION: Under the successful-efforts method, the costs of finding recoverable oil and gas are capitalized and subsequently amortized. This method expenses costs of unsuccessful efforts in the year incurred. The alternative is the full-cost method, under which all of the costs of acquiring, exploring, and developing oil and gas properties in very large geographical areas are capitalized and subsequently amortized, whether the costs are related to successful or unsuccessful projects. The costs of natural resources include (1) acquisition cost of the deposit, (2) exploration costs, and (3) development costs. These costs are spread evenly over the estimated recoverable units in the deposit to calculate the estimated cost of the units removed from the well during the period. The capitalizable depletion cost is $2,000,000 ($100,000 + $400,000 + $1,500,000). Thus, unit depletion cost is $2 ($2,000,000 ÷ 1,000,000 barrels), and total depletion for the first year is $400,000 ($2 × 200,000 barrels).

Answer (A) is incorrect because $100,000 omits the $1,500,000 intangible development costs from the depletion base. Answer (B) is incorrect because $300,000 omits the $100,000 cost of the lease and the $400,000 related exploration costs from the depletion base. Answer (D) is incorrect because $2,000,000 is based on the assumption that all costs are expensed immediately.

26. SFAS 19, *Financial Accounting and Reporting by Oil and Gas Producing Companies*, required the successful-efforts method of accounting. SFAS 25, *Suspension of Certain Accounting Requirements for Oil and Gas Producing Companies*, amended SFAS 19 to permit the full-cost accounting method as well as the successful-efforts method. Why was SFAS 25 issued?

A. The oil and gas industry refused to abide by SFAS 19.

B. The SEC indicated its continued acceptance of the full-cost method.

C. Political pressures from the oil and gas industry forced the FASB to reverse its position.

D. Congress threatened legislation to permit continued use of full costing.

Answer (B) is correct. *(Publisher)*

REQUIRED: The reason SFAS 25 was issued to amend SFAS 19.

DISCUSSION: Prior to SFAS 19, both the full-cost and successful-efforts methods were acceptable ways to account for the exploration and development activities of oil- and gas-producing companies. SFAS 19 indicated that only the successful-efforts method was acceptable. SFAS 25 reinstated full cost because the SEC manifested its continued acceptance of this method through Accounting Series Release 253.

Answer (A) is incorrect because the SEC's action forced the FASB to issue SFAS 25, although the oil and gas industry's refusal to abide by SFAS 19 contributed to the SEC's decision. Answer (C) is incorrect because the SEC's action forced the FASB to issue SFAS 25, although political pressures from the oil and gas industry contributed to the SEC's decision. Answer (D) is incorrect because the SEC's action forced the FASB to issue SFAS 25, although Congress' threatened legislation to permit continued use of full costing contributed to the SEC's decision.

27. Gigaoil Ltd. transferred assets used in oil and gas producing activities to Teraoil in exchange for other assets also used in oil and gas producing activities. Gigaoil may recognize a loss on the transfer in accordance with SFAS 144, *Accounting for the Impairment or Disposal of Long-Lived Assets*, if the transferred assets related to

	Proved Properties	Unproved Properties
A.	Yes	Yes
B.	Yes	No
C.	No	Yes
D.	No	No

Answer (B) is correct. *(Publisher)*

REQUIRED: The circumstances, if any, in which an impairment loss may be recognized.

DISCUSSION: According to SFAS 19, as amended by SFAS 144, if assets used in oil and gas producing activities related to proved properties are exchanged for other assets used in oil and gas producing activities, an impairment loss, if any, is recognized at the time of the disposal if the carrying amount of the transferred assets exceeds their fair value.

28. SFAS 69, *Disclosures about Oil and Gas Producing Activities*, requires publicly traded enterprises with significant oil and gas activities to disclose certain supplemental information in complete sets of annual financial statements. The disclosures include

A. Proved oil and gas reserve quantities and standardized measure of discounted future net cash flows relating to them.

B. Capitalized costs relating to oil- and gas-producing activities and costs incurred in oil and gas property acquisition, exploration, and development activities.

C. Results of operations for oil- and gas-producing activities.

D. All of the answers are correct.

Answer (D) is correct. *(Publisher)*
REQUIRED: The disclosure(s) required by SFAS 69 regarding oil and gas activities.
DISCUSSION: Each of the listed disclosures is required by SFAS 69. Most important to SFAS 69 is the requirement of disclosure of a standardized measure of discounted future net cash flows relating to proved oil and gas quantities. This disclosure reflects some, but not all, characteristics of a fair-value measurement in accordance with the SEC's requirements.

29. According to SFAS 69, the standard measure of discounted future net cash flows relating to proved oil and gas reserve quantities should include consideration of which of the following?

A. Future cash inflows based on year-end prices applied to the proved year-end reserves.

B. Future development and production costs based on year-end costs.

C. Future income tax expenses based on applying year-end statutory tax rates.

D. All of the answers are correct.

Answer (D) is correct. *(Publisher)*
REQUIRED: The factor(s) included in the determination of discounted future net cash flows of oil and gas reserves.
DISCUSSION: SFAS 69 requires disclosure of a standardized measure of discounted future net cash flows relating to an enterprise's interests in both proved oil and gas reserves and oil and gas subject to purchase under long-term supply agreements and contracts for oil- and gas-producing properties. Future cash inflows based on year-end prices applied to the proved year-end reserves, development and production costs based on year-end costs, and future income tax based on applying year-end statutory tax rates should be considered. Additionally, the future cash flows should be discounted at 10% per year. The standardized measure equals the future net cash flows (A-B-C) minus the calculated discount.

30. SFAS 69 requires that publicly traded enterprises with significant oil- and gas-producing activities make certain disclosures. Activity is significant if

A. Revenue from oil- and gas-producing activities related to unaffiliated customers and internal operations is 25% of total sales to unaffiliated customers and internal operations.

B. Revenue from oil- and gas-producing activities related to unaffiliated customers and internal operations is 20% of total sales to unaffiliated customers and internal operations.

C. The amount of reported revenue, profit or loss, or assets of the activity meets the criteria for an operating segment established in SFAS 131, *Disclosures about Segments of an Enterprise and Related Information.*

D. Revenue, current or prospective, is of probable interest to financial statement users as defined by management.

Answer (C) is correct. *(Publisher)*
REQUIRED: The definition of significant oil- and gas-producing activities.
DISCUSSION: Under SFAS 69, oil- and gas-producing activities are considered significant if, in general, the activities satisfy the criteria in SFAS 131 that define an operating segment. Under SFAS 131, an operating segment is "a component of an enterprise that engages in business activities from which it may earn revenues and incur expenses (including revenues and expenses relating to transactions with other components of the same enterprise), whose operating results are regularly reviewed by the enterprise's chief operating decision maker to make decisions about resources to be allocated to the segment and assess its performance, and for which discrete financial information is available." Moreover, an enterprise separately reports information about an operating segment if it satisfies one of three tests: its revenue (including sales to external customers and intersegment sales or transfers) is equal to at least 10% of the combined revenue, internal and external, of all the enterprise's operating segments; its assets are equal to at least 10% of the combined assets of all operating segments; and the absolute amount of its reported profit or loss is equal to at least 10% of the greater, in absolute amount, of the combined reported profit of all operating segments that did not report a loss or the combined reported loss of all operating segments that did report a loss.
Answer (A) is incorrect because the quantitative criteria include profit or loss and assets as well as revenue. Also, the amounts must be at or above the 10% level. Answer (B) is incorrect because the quantitative criteria include profit or loss and assets as well as revenue. Also, the amounts must be at or above the 10% level. Answer (D) is incorrect because the decision is not left to management but is based on the relative level of oil- and gas-producing revenue, profit or loss, or assets.

31. FASB Interpretation No. 36, *Accounting for Exploratory Wells in Progress at the End of a Period*, provides a clarification of SFAS 19's requirement that the costs of exploratory wells that do not locate proved oil and gas reserves be charged to expense. Which of the following statements reflects the proper accounting treatment?

A. The costs incurred for exploratory wells in progress at the end of the reporting period should be expensed unless it is probable at the end of the reporting period that proved reserves will be discovered.

B. The cost of all exploratory wells in progress at the end of the period should be expensed.

C. The costs of all exploratory wells in progress at the end of the year should be deferred.

D. The costs of exploratory wells in progress at the end of the period that are completed without finding proved reserves before the financial statements are issued should be expensed in the period for which the statements are issued.

Answer (D) is correct. *(Publisher)*

REQUIRED: The proper accounting for exploratory wells in progress at year-end.

DISCUSSION: FASB Interpretation No. 36 states that the costs of exploratory wells in progress at year-end should be expensed if the wells are determined to be unsuccessful (i.e., determined not to have proved reserves) before the financial statements for that period are issued.

Answer (A) is incorrect because it cannot be deemed probable that proved reserves exist until they are located. Answer (B) is incorrect because the cost of exploratory wells may be deferred under the full-cost approach if they are successful, i.e., when proved reserves have been found. Answer (C) is incorrect because the costs of exploratory wells should be expensed in the period for which the statements are issued if the wells have been completed without locating proved reserves prior to the issuance of the statements.

32. SFAS 19 and SFAS 25 define proved, proved developed, and proved undeveloped oil and gas reserves. Proved oil and gas reserves are defined as quantities of oil and gas

A. Expected to be recovered from new wells on undrilled acreage or from existing wells when a relatively major expenditure is required for completion.

B. Expected to be recoverable in future years from known reservoirs under existing economic and operating conditions.

C. In a single reservoir or multiple reservoirs grouped or related to the same geological condition.

D. Expected to be recovered through existing wells developed with existing equipment and operating methods, including those available under improved recovery techniques.

Answer (B) is correct. *(Publisher)*

REQUIRED: The definition of proved oil and gas reserves.

DISCUSSION: Proved reserves are those expected to be recoverable in future years from known reservoirs under existing economic and operating conditions.

Answer (A) is incorrect because it defines proved undeveloped reserves. Answer (C) is incorrect because it defines a field. Answer (D) is incorrect because it defines proved developed reserves.

30.5 Record and Music Industry, Cable TV, and Broadcasters

33. SFAS 50, *Financial Reporting in the Record and Music Industry*, establishes standards of financial reporting for licensors and licensees. A licensor may recognize income when

A. The licensor has delivered the usable rights to the licensee and collectibility of the license fee is reasonably assured.

B. Payment of the licensing fee by the licensee is guaranteed by a third party.

C. The licensor has delivered the usable rights to the licensee and has no remaining significant obligations pursuant to a noncancelable contract, and collection is reasonably assured.

D. A minimum guarantee is paid in advance.

Answer (C) is correct. *(Publisher)*

REQUIRED: The requirement(s) for recognition of income by the licensor of record and music masters and copyrights.

DISCUSSION: A licensing agreement may, in substance, be an outright sale. A licensor may recognize income if the licensor has signed a noncancelable contract, has agreed to a fixed fee, and has delivered the rights to the licensee with the right to use them; if no significant obligations remain; and if collection is reasonably assured. The earning process is then complete.

Answer (A) is incorrect because, in addition, the licensor must have signed a noncancelable contract and have no remaining significant obligations. Answer (B) is incorrect because there is no third-party guarantee requirement, and assurance of collection does not mean the earning process is complete. Answer (D) is incorrect because minimum guarantees that are received in advance should be recorded initially as a liability and recognized as revenue when the license fee is earned under the agreement.

34. According to SFAS 50, *Financial Reporting in the Record and Music Industry*, a licensee of music copyrights accounts for minimum guarantees paid in advance as

A. Expense in the year paid.

B. An asset and charged to expense in accord with the license agreement.

C. An asset if the record master is estimated to be profitable in the future based upon the performer's past performance and current popularity.

D. An advance royalty to the artist if it is probable that the advance will be recoverable from future royalties earned by the artist.

Answer (B) is correct. *(Publisher)*

REQUIRED: The accounting by licensees of record and music copyrights for advance payments to licensors.

DISCUSSION: Advance payments by a licensee to a licensor should be capitalized as an asset and charged to expense according to the terms of the license agreement, unless all or a portion of the guarantee appears nonrecoverable. In that event, the amount should be expensed.

Answer (A) is incorrect because the advance payment is usually deferred as an asset and amortized. Answer (C) is incorrect because it describes the accounting for record masters by the licensor, not minimum guarantees by the licensee. Answer (D) is incorrect because it states the proper accounting by licensors for advance royalties paid to artists.

35. SFAS 51, *Financial Reporting by Cable Television Companies*, prescribes accounting by cable TV companies during the prematurity period. This period begins with the first subscriber revenue and ends when a predetermined subscriber level is reached, when no additional investment for the cable TV plant is required, or when the first major construction period is completed. During the prematurity period,

A. Costs of cable television plant are capitalized.

B. Subscriber-related costs and general administrative expenses should be capitalized.

C. Programming costs and other system costs should be capitalized in full.

D. Depreciation should not be recognized.

Answer (A) is correct. *(Publisher)*

REQUIRED: The accounting procedure applicable to the prematurity period of a cable TV company.

DISCUSSION: During the prematurity period, SFAS 51 requires that the cost of the cable television plant, including materials, direct labor, and overhead, be capitalized in full.

Answer (B) is incorrect because subscriber-related costs and general administrative expenses should be expensed during, as well as after, the prematurity period. Answer (C) is incorrect because programming and other system costs and depreciation are expensed according to the relationship of the current level of subscription revenue to the amount expected at the end of the prematurity stage. Answer (D) is incorrect because programming and other system costs and depreciation are expensed according to the relationship of the current level of subscription revenue to the amount expected at the end of the prematurity stage.

36. According to SFAS 51, the initial hookup revenue of cable television companies should be

A. Deferred and amortized to income over the estimated average period that subscribers are expected to remain connected to the system.

B. Recognized as revenue immediately to the extent direct selling costs are incurred, with the remainder deferred and amortized.

C. Recognized as revenue upon receipt.

D. Recognized as revenue systematically and rationally over a period of not less than 5 and not more than 10 years.

Answer (B) is correct. *(Publisher)*

REQUIRED: The proper accounting for cable television company initial hookup revenue.

DISCUSSION: Initial hookup revenue is recognized as revenue to the extent that direct selling costs are incurred. Direct selling costs include commissions, salespersons' compensation, local advertising, document processing, etc. Any remaining initial hookup revenue should be deferred and amortized over the estimated average period that subscribers are expected to remain connected to the system.

Answer (A) is incorrect because all or part of hookup revenue is used to offset direct selling costs. Answer (C) is incorrect because hookup revenue is deferred and amortized to the extent it exceeds direct selling costs. Answer (D) is incorrect because hookup revenue is deferred and amortized to the extent it exceeds direct selling costs.

37. Initial subscriber installation costs for cable television service, including materials, labor, and overhead, should be

A. Expensed as incurred.

B. Expensed in the periods that initial hookup revenue is recognized.

C. Capitalized and depreciated.

D. Capitalized and expensed at the point that reconnection fees are earned.

Answer (C) is correct. *(Publisher)*

REQUIRED: The accounting for initial subscriber installation costs.

DISCUSSION: Initial subscriber installation costs should be capitalized and depreciated over a period not to exceed the expected useful life of the cable TV plant. The costs of subsequent disconnecting and reconnecting are expensed as incurred.

Answer (A) is incorrect because initial installation costs are capitalized. Answer (B) is incorrect because capitalization and depreciation are required. Answer (D) is incorrect because capitalization and depreciation are required.

38. Broadcasters frequently barter unsold advertising time for products or services. According to SFAS 63, *Financial Reporting by Broadcasters*, barter revenue should be recognized when

A. The barter agreement is signed.

B. The commercials are broadcast.

C. The merchandise or services are received or used.

D. An enforceable contract is entered into to sell the products or services.

Answer (B) is correct. *(Publisher)*

REQUIRED: The timing of recognition by broadcasters of barter revenue.

DISCUSSION: Barter revenue should be recognized in appropriate amounts when the commercials are broadcast. The amounts should be reported at the estimated fair value of the product or service received in accordance with APB 29, *Accounting for Nonmonetary Transactions.*

Answer (A) is incorrect because the revenue has not been earned until the commercials are broadcast. Answer (C) is incorrect because an asset should be recognized if the commercials are broadcast before the merchandise or services are received. A liability should be recognized if the merchandise or services are received before the commercials are broadcast. Answer (D) is incorrect because the merchandise or services need not be resold for revenue to be recognized.

39. When a broadcaster enters into a license agreement for program material, the broadcaster should report

A. An asset and a liability for the rights acquired and obligations incurred when the agreement is reached.

B. An asset and a liability when the cost of each program is known or determinable, the program material has been accepted, and the program is available for viewing or telecast.

C. The related assets and liability as current if the license period expires within 1 year and as noncurrent if the license period expires in more than 1 year.

D. An asset and a liability but only for the present value of future payments in accordance with the procedures set forth in APB 21.

Answer (B) is correct. *(Publisher)*

REQUIRED: The proper accounting by the broadcaster for a license agreement for program material.

DISCUSSION: Broadcasters (licensees) should report the rights acquired and obligations incurred under a license agreement when the license period begins and when

1. The cost of each program is known or determinable.
2. The program material has been accepted by the licensee.
3. The program is available for viewing or telecast.

Answer (A) is incorrect because the license period must have begun and the three criteria specified in SFAS 63 must be met. Answer (C) is incorrect because the asset should be allocated in the balance sheet between current and noncurrent based on the time of usage, and the liability should be allocated between current and noncurrent based on payment terms. Answer (D) is incorrect because SFAS 63 permits the asset and liability to be valued at either the present value or the gross amount of the liability.

40. Network affiliation agreements of a broadcaster should be reported as

A. Intangible assets.

B. Expenses when incurred.

C. Deferred charges in equity.

D. Deferred network program advertising.

Answer (A) is correct. *(Publisher)*

REQUIRED: The reporting of network affiliation agreements in the financial statements of a broadcaster.

DISCUSSION: Network affiliation agreements are intangible assets that should be accounted for in accordance with SFAS 142, *Goodwill and Other Intangible Assets.*

Answer (B) is incorrect because intangible assets must be capitalized if they meet the criteria in SFAS 141 or SFAS 142. Answer (C) is incorrect because intangible assets are an asset rather than a contra equity item. Answer (D) is incorrect because it is a nonsense term.

30.6 Investment Companies, Insurance Enterprises, Title Plants, and Mortgage Banking

41. Investment companies should report their securities portfolios at fair value. In the case of short-term investment (money market) instruments, fair value may be approximated by valuing the short-term instruments at

A. Amortized cost.

B. Quoted sales prices.

C. Bid and asked prices.

D. Quotations by established market makers.

Answer (A) is correct. *(Publisher)*

REQUIRED: The method used to approximate the fair value of money market instruments that mature within a short time.

DISCUSSION: Short-term investments (e.g., commercial paper, short-term governmental obligations, or CDs) may be bought at face amount or at a discount from the face amount. According to *AICPA Audit and Accounting Guide, Audits of Investment Companies*, the SEC does not object if an investment company determines in good faith that amortized cost approximates the fair value of debt securities with remaining maturities of 60 days or less, unless particular circumstances require securities to be valued at marked or fair value. In the case of events such as the impairment of the credit standing of the issuer or unusual changes in interest rates, amortized cost may not approximate the value of short-term money market instruments.

Answer (B) is incorrect because quoted sales prices are measures of fair value. Answer (C) is incorrect because quoted bid and asked prices are measures of fair value. Answer (D) is incorrect because quotations by established market makers are measures of fair value.

42. SFAS 60, *Accounting and Reporting by Insurance Enterprises*, sets forth specialized accounting principles and practices for insurance enterprises. With respect to short-term insurance contracts (primarily property and liability contracts),

A. Claim costs are expensed when paid.

B. Premiums are recognized as revenue over the contract period in proportion to the amount of insurance protection provided.

C. Claim costs relating to insured events that have occurred but have not yet been reported are not expensed until reported.

D. If premiums are subject to adjustment as in retroactively rated policies, the premium should ordinarily be accounted for by the cost-recovery or the deposit method.

Answer (B) is correct. *(Publisher)*

REQUIRED: The correct statement about accounting for short-term insurance contracts.

DISCUSSION: Premiums for short-term contracts are recognized as revenue over the period of the contract in proportion to the amount of insurance protection provided.

Answer (A) is incorrect because claim costs are expensed when the insured events occur, not when the claims are settled. Answer (C) is incorrect because claim costs expense should include estimates of insured events that have occurred but have not yet been reported. Answer (D) is incorrect because, only if the ultimate premium cannot be easily estimated, which is unusual, should the cost-recovery or deposit method be used. Normally, the ultimate premium is reasonably estimable and is recognized as revenue over the contract period.

43. Which of the following is true concerning accounting for investments by insurance enterprises?

A. All investments in debt securities are measured at amortized cost.

B. Mortgage loans are reported at outstanding principal or amortized cost.

C. Real estate to be held and used is reported at depreciated cost minus an allowance for any impairment in value.

D. Equity securities that do not have readily determinable fair values are reported at cost.

Answer (B) is correct. *(Publisher)*

REQUIRED: The true statement concerning investments by insurance enterprises.

DISCUSSION: Insurance enterprises covered by SFAS 60 value mortgage loans at outstanding principal balances, if acquired at par value, or at amortized cost, if purchased at a premium or discount, with an allowance for estimated uncollectible accounts, if any.

Answer (A) is incorrect because, if debt securities are not classifiable as held to maturity, a business enterprise accounts for them at fair value. Answer (C) is incorrect because real estate is recorded at cost minus accumulated depreciation, but no impairment allowance is recorded. An impairment of an asset to be held and used is recognized as a realized loss, and the reduced carrying amount is the new cost basis. Restoration of an impairment loss is prohibited. Answer (D) is incorrect because equity securities that do not have "readily determinable fair values" are not addressed by SFASs 115 or 124. Nevertheless, they are accounted for by insurers at fair value, with changes in fair value reported in other comprehensive income by a business enterprise and in the statement of activities by a not-for-profit organization.

44. SFAS 97, *Accounting and Reporting by Insurance Enterprises for Certain Long-Duration Contracts and for Realized Gains and Losses from the Sale of Investments*, establishes standards of financial accounting and reporting for investment contracts, limited-payment contracts, and universal life-type contracts. Under SFAS 97,

A. Investment contracts issued by an insurance enterprise are accounted for as insurance contracts.

B. The collection of premiums on a limited-payment contract represents the completion of an earning process.

C. Premiums collected on universal life-type contracts are reported as revenue in the statement of earnings.

D. Premiums from long-duration contracts, such as whole-life contracts, are recognized as revenue when due from policyholders.

Answer (D) is correct. *(Publisher)*

REQUIRED: The accounting provision established by SFAS 97.

DISCUSSION: SFAS 60, *Accounting and Reporting by Insurance Enterprises*, was amended by SFAS 97 to require that premiums from long-duration contracts, such as whole-life contracts, guaranteed renewable term life contracts, and title insurance contracts, be recognized as revenue when due from policyholders.

Answer (A) is incorrect because investment contracts, as defined by SFAS 97, do not incorporate significant insurance risk and shall not be accounted for as insurance contracts. Answer (B) is incorrect because the collection of premiums does not represent the completion of an earning process. Any gross premium (the premium charged for an insurance contract) exceeding the net premium (the part of the gross premium required to provide for benefits and expenses) is deferred and recognized in income in a constant relationship with insurance in force (life insurance) or with expected future payments (annuity contracts). Answer (C) is incorrect because the collection of premiums on universal life-type contracts shall not be recorded as revenue. Revenue is based on amounts assessed against policyholders and is ordinarily reported in the period of assessment.

45. SFAS 61, *Accounting for Title Plant*, applies to title insurance enterprises. It defines title plant as including

A. Indexed and cataloged information concerning ownership and encumbrances on parcels of the land in a geographic area.

B. Information relating to persons having an interest in real estate.

C. Maps and plots, copies of prior title insurance contracts, and other documents and records.

D. All of the answers are correct.

Answer (D) is correct. *(Publisher)*

REQUIRED: The components of a title plant as defined in SFAS 61.

DISCUSSION: A title plant constitutes a historical record of all matters affecting title to parcels of land in a particular geographic area. It includes all of the items in (A) through (C). Updated on a daily or other frequent basis, title plants are maintained for the number of years required by regulation and for the minimum information period considered necessary to issue title insurance policies efficiently. Title plant does not include the building, furniture, or fixtures of the title insurance firm.

Answer (A) is incorrect because title plant includes information about ownership and encumbrances. Answer (B) is incorrect because title plant includes information about persons having an interest in real estate. Answer (C) is incorrect because title plant includes information about various documents and records.

46. SFAS 65, *Accounting for Certain Mortgage Banking Activities*, as amended by SFAS 91, *Accounting for Nonrefundable Fees and Costs Associated with Originating or Acquiring Loans and Initial Direct Costs of Leases*, establishes accounting and reporting standards for the mortgage banking industry. Which of the following is an appropriate method of accounting for this industry?

A. Loan origination fees related to loans held for investment are recognized as revenue when the loans are consummated.

B. Direct loan origination costs related to loans held for investment are recognized as revenue when the loans are consummated.

C. Fees for services performed by third parties and loan placement fees are recognized as revenue over the life of the loan.

D. Loan origination fees related to loans held for resale are deferred until the related loan is sold.

Answer (D) is correct. *(Publisher)*

REQUIRED: The accounting prescribed for the mortgage banking industry.

DISCUSSION: SFAS 65 as amended by SFAS 91 states that if a loan is held for resale, loan origination fees and the direct loan origination costs specified in SFAS 91 are deferred until the related loan is sold.

Answer (A) is incorrect because, if the loan is held for investment, loan origination fees and the direct loan origination costs specified in SFAS 91 are deferred and recognized as an adjustment of yield by the interest method. Answer (B) is incorrect because, if the loan is held for investment, loan origination fees and the direct loan origination costs specified in SFAS 91 are deferred and recognized as an adjustment of yield by the interest method. Answer (C) is incorrect because fees for services performed by third parties and loan placement fees are recognized as revenue when all significant services have been performed.

47. SFAS 61 applies to title insurance enterprises, title abstract enterprises, and title agents that use a title plant in their operations. Which is the false statement about accounting for title plants?

A. The costs of a title plant should not be depreciated.

B. The costs of maintaining a title plant and doing title searches should be expensed as incurred.

C. The cost incurred to construct a title plant should be capitalized.

D. Costs subsequent to initial operations to convert to another information retrieval system should be capitalized but not depreciated.

Answer (D) is correct. *(Publisher)*

REQUIRED: The false statement about accounting for title plants.

DISCUSSION: The costs of title plants should be capitalized as they are developed. After completion, they should not be depreciated. All the costs of updating (maintaining) the title plant and doing title searches should be expensed as incurred. Costs of subsequent modernization of the information retrieval system or conversion to another retrieval system should be capitalized and expensed systematically and rationally (i.e., depreciated).

48. SFAS 91 is an attempt to standardize the accounting by financial institutions for nonrefundable loan origination fees and direct loan origination costs. The adjustment for these items is recognized in accordance with which of the following methods?

A. Straight-line method.

B. Sum-of-the-years'-digits method.

C. Interest method.

D. Double-declining-balance method.

Answer (C) is correct. *(P.E. Bayes)*

REQUIRED: The method used to amortize loan origination fees and direct loan origination costs.

DISCUSSION: Loan origination fees and direct loan origination costs are deferred and recognized over the life of the related loan as an adjustment of yield. Such fees and costs for a given loan are offset, and only the net amount is deferred and amortized. The net amount of fees or costs that is required to be recognized as an adjustment of yield over the life of the related loan is normally recognized by the interest method.

Answer (A) is incorrect because it should ordinarily be accounted for either on the equity basis or as a subsidiary. Answer (B) is incorrect because it should ordinarily be accounted for either on the equity basis or as a subsidiary. Answer (D) is incorrect because it should ordinarily be accounted for either on the equity basis or as a subsidiary.

30.7 Real Estate

49. For which of the following forms of investment in real estate or real estate development projects by two or more entities may the cost basis of accounting be more appropriate for the investor than the equity basis?

A. An undivided interest that is subject to joint control by the owners.

B. A corporate joint venture.

C. A noncontrolling interest in a general partnership.

D. A controlling interest in a limited partnership.

Answer (A) is correct. *(Publisher)*

REQUIRED: The form of investment in real estate or real estate development projects that ordinarily may be accounted for by an investor on the cost basis.

DISCUSSION: SOP 78-9, *Accounting for Investments in Real Estate Ventures*, states that an undivided interest that is subject to joint control by both the owners and a noncontrolling interest in a limited partnership may, if the investment is minor, be more appropriately accounted for on the cost basis than the equity basis.

Answer (B) is incorrect because it should ordinarily be accounted for either on the equity basis or as a subsidiary. Answer (C) is incorrect because it should ordinarily be accounted for either on the equity basis or as a subsidiary. Answer (D) is incorrect because it should ordinarily be accounted for either on the equity basis or as a subsidiary.

50. A commitment fee is defined, in general, as any fee paid by a potential borrower to a potential lender for a promise to lend money in the future. For a REIT, the recognition of income from commitment fees should be in accordance with which of the following?

A. Immediate recognition.

B. Deferral and amortization over the commitment period.

C. Deferral and amortization over the loan period.

D. Deferral and amortization over the combined commitment and loan periods.

Answer (D) is correct. *(Publisher)*

REQUIRED: The basis for the recognition by a REIT of income from commitment fees.

DISCUSSION: SOP 75-2 requires that income from commitment fees be recognized by a REIT by deferral and amortization over the combined commitment and loan periods.

Answer (A) is incorrect because this alternative is not permitted by SOP 75-2. Answer (B) is incorrect because this alternative is not permitted by SOP 75-2. Answer (C) is incorrect because this alternative is not permitted by SOP 75-2.

51. For a real estate investment trust, the method for determining a provision for loan losses should be based on which of the following?

A. An evaluation of the individual loans and foreclosed properties.

B. The percentages of loan balances outstanding.

C. A percentage of income.

D. Actual loan defaults.

Answer (A) is correct. *(Publisher)*
REQUIRED: The basis for determining a provision for loan losses of REITs.
DISCUSSION: The allowance for losses of REITs should be based on an evaluation of the recoverability of individual loans and properties. Consideration should be given to the circumstances at the time of the evaluation and to reasonable probabilistic estimates of future economic conditions and other relevant information (SOP 75-2). Methods other than evaluation of the individual laws and foreclosed properties are not permitted.

52. SOP 75-2 states that the recognition of interest revenue by a REIT should be discontinued when it is no longer reasonable to expect that the revenue will be received. Which of the following conditions establishes a presumption that interest revenue will not be received?

A. The borrower is in default.

B. The payments of principal or interest are past due.

C. The creditworthiness of the borrower is in doubt because of pending or actual bankruptcy.

D. All of the answers are correct.

Answer (D) is correct. *(Publisher)*
REQUIRED: The condition(s) establishing a presumption that interest revenue will not be received.
DISCUSSION: The borrower's default or bankruptcy or overdue payments should each be regarded as a condition that establishes a presumption that revenue will not be received and that recognition of interest revenue should be discontinued. Other considerations that establish this presumption are that the loan has been renegotiated, foreclosure procedures have been or are expected to be initiated, and cost overruns and/or delays in construction cast doubt on the economic viability of the project.
Answer (A) is incorrect because the presumption is established when the borrower is in default. Answer (B) is incorrect because the presumption is established when payments are overdue. Answer (C) is incorrect because the presumption is established when the borrower is bankrupt.

53. SFAS 67, *Accounting for Costs and Initial Rental Operations of Real Estate Projects*, requires that certain costs be capitalized as part of the cost of a real estate project. Which of the following costs is not capitalized?

A. Payment to obtain an option to acquire real property.

B. Property taxes and insurance during the construction period.

C. Indirect project costs that relate to several real estate projects.

D. Incremental costs from incidental operations in excess of incremental revenues.

Answer (D) is correct. *(Publisher)*
REQUIRED: The cost that should not be capitalized as part of the cost of a real estate project.
DISCUSSION: SFAS 67 states that incremental revenue from incidental operations in excess of incremental costs (e.g., profits from an adjacent golf course) should be accounted for as a reduction of the capitalized project costs. However, incremental costs in excess of incremental revenues should not be capitalized. They should be expensed because the incidental operations did not reduce the cost of developing the property for its intended use.

54. According to SFAS 67, preacquisition costs such as payments to obtain an option to acquire real property should be capitalized. Other costs related to real property that are incurred before the enterprise acquires the property should be capitalized if certain conditions are met. Which of the following is not one of the conditions required to be met before other preacquisition costs are capitalized?

A. The costs are directly identifiable with a specific property.

B. The costs would be capitalized if the property had already been acquired.

C. Acquisition of an option to acquire the property is probable.

D. Acquisition of the property is reasonably possible.

Answer (D) is correct. *(Publisher)*
REQUIRED: The condition that is not required to be met before preacquisition costs are capitalized as part of the cost of a real estate project.
DISCUSSION: The reasonable possibility that a real estate property may be acquired is not sufficient. One of the conditions required by SFAS 67 is that acquisition of the property or of an option to acquire the property be probable.

55. Which of the following statements about accounting for costs of real estate projects is true?

A. All costs incurred to sell real estate projects should be expensed as incurred.

B. All costs incurred to rent real estate projects should be expensed as incurred.

C. A real estate project is considered substantially completed and held available for occupancy no later than 1 year from the cessation of major construction activities.

D. If portions of a project are under construction and other portions are substantially completed and held available for occupancy, they should be accounted for as a single project.

Answer (C) is correct. *(Publisher)*

REQUIRED: The correct statement about costs incurred to sell and rent real estate projects.

DISCUSSION: SFAS 67 states that a real estate project should be considered substantially completed and held available for occupancy upon completion of tenant improvements by the developer, but no later than 1 year from the cessation of major construction activity. When the project is substantially complete, costs are expensed as they accrue and previously capitalized costs should be amortized.

Answer (A) is incorrect because costs incurred to sell real estate projects should be capitalized if they are incurred for tangible assets used directly throughout the selling period to aid in the sale of the project. Answer (B) is incorrect because costs incurred to rent a real estate project should be capitalized if they directly relate to the rental of the real estate project and their recovery is reasonably expected. Answer (D) is incorrect because costs related to a rental project for which some portions are substantially completed and others are still under construction should be allocated to each portion, which then should be treated as separate projects.

56. According to SFAS 67, *Accounting for Costs and Initial Rental Operations of Real Estate Projects*, allocation of capitalized costs to the components of a real estate project may not be done on the basis of

A. Relative fair value before construction.

B. Relative sales value.

C. Land area.

D. An equal amount to each component.

Answer (D) is correct. *(CMA, adapted)*

REQUIRED: The inappropriate basis for allocation of the capitalized cost to the components of a real estate project.

DISCUSSION: SFAS 67 states that the preferable method of allocating capitalized costs of a real estate project to its individual components is specific identification. If specific identification is not practicable, however, land costs should be allocated based on the relative fair values of the individual land parcels before construction, and construction costs should be allocated to the individual units on the basis of the relative sales value of each unit. Furthermore, if allocation based on relative value is also not practicable, the capitalized cost should be allocated based on an area method such as square footage or other value method appropriate under the circumstances.

57. On July 1, Berlin Company purchased a tract of land for $900,000. Additional costs of $150,000 were incurred in subdividing the land during July through December. Of the tract acreage, 70% was subdivided into residential lots, as shown below, and 30% was conveyed to the city for roads and a park.

Lot Class	Number of Lots	Sales Price per Lot
A	100	$12,000
B	100	8,000
C	200	5,000

Under the relative sales value method, the cost allocated to each Class A lot should be

A. $2,625

B. $2,940

C. $3,600

D. $4,200

Answer (D) is correct. *(CPA, adapted)*

REQUIRED: The cost to be allocated to each Class A lot under the relative sales value method.

DISCUSSION: SFAS 67, *Accounting for Costs and Initial Rental Operations of Real Estate Projects*, states that real estate donated to municipalities or other governmental agencies for uses that will benefit the project shall be allocated as a common cost of the project. Thus, none of the costs of the project should be allocated to the land donated to the city. The total cost of acquiring the land ($900,000 + $150,000 = $1,050,000) should be allocated to the lots that will generate revenue. Using the relative sales value method as indicated below, 40% of the total cost, or $420,000 (40% × $1,050,000), should be allocated to the Class A lots. The amount per lot will be $4,200 ($420,000 ÷ 100).

Lot Class	Number of Lots	Sales Price	Sales Value	Relative Value
A	100	$12,000	$1,200,000	40 %
B	100	8,000	800,000	26 2/3%
C	200	5,000	1,000,000	33 1/3%
			$3,000,000	100 %

Answer (A) is incorrect because $2,625 results from the relative value based on the number of lots per lot class. Answer (B) is incorrect because $2,940 incorrectly allocates only 70% of the total costs to the residential lots. Answer (C) is incorrect because $3,600 excludes the cost of subdividing the land.

58. Under SFAS 66, *Accounting for Sales of Real Estate*, which of the following statements is true about the recognition of profit for sales transactions within a retail land sales project?

A. A single method of recognizing profit will be determined and used without change for all sales transactions within a project.

B. A single method of recognizing profit that will be changed when certain conditions are met for the entire project should be applied to all sales transactions within a project.

C. The full accrual method of recognizing profit should be applied to all sales transactions within a project.

D. The installment method of recognizing profit should be applied to all sales transactions within a project.

Answer (B) is correct. *(Publisher)*

REQUIRED: The correct statement about the recognition of profit on sales transactions.

DISCUSSION: SFAS 66 requires that a single method be used to recognize profit from all sales transactions within a retail land sales project. However, when certain conditions change for the entire project, the method of recognizing profit should be changed to reflect the new conditions.

Answer (A) is incorrect because the single method should be changed to reflect changed conditions. Answer (C) is incorrect because certain criteria specified in SFAS 66 must be met before the installment method can be used, and still more criteria must be met before the full accrual method can be used in a retail land sales project. Answer (D) is incorrect because certain criteria specified in SFAS 66 must be met before the installment method can be used, and still more criteria must be met before the full accrual method can be used in a retail land sales project.

59. For a particular retail land development project, the Developer Company requires at least a 25% down payment. Moreover, (1) the period of cancelation with refund for this project has expired on the lots sold, and (2) the receivables from the sale are not subject to subordination to new loans. Under what additional condition should the full accrual basis of accounting for the profit be used to account for the sales transactions?

A. The seller is financially capable.

B. The development is practical.

C. Progress has been made on improvements.

D. The development has been completed.

Answer (D) is correct. *(Publisher)*

REQUIRED: The additional condition that must be met before the full accrual method may be used.

DISCUSSION: SFAS 66 requires that the full accrual method of accounting be applied to a retail land sale if all of the following conditions are met:

1. The period of cancelation with refund has expired.
2. Cumulative payments equal or exceed 10% of the contract sales price.
3. The receivables are collectible.
4. The receivables are not subject to subordination.
5. The development is complete.

A down payment of at least 20% is considered an acceptable indication of the collectibility of receivables. Furthermore, it satisfies the cumulative payment condition. Because all other conditions are met, the full accrual method should be used if the development has been completed.

Answer (A) is incorrect because the installment method is used when the seller is financially capable, the period of cancelation with refund has expired, and cumulative payments equal or exceed 10% of the contract sales price. Answer (B) is incorrect because this condition, together with the first four of the five conditions listed above, indicate that the percentage-of-completion method should be used. Answer (C) is incorrect because this condition, together with the first four of the five conditions listed above, indicate that the percentage-of-completion method should be used.

60. Which method of recognizing profit should be applied to all sales transactions within a retail land sales project if (1) the period of cancelation with refund has expired for the project, (2) the cumulative payments are at least equal to 10% of the sales price, (3) the receivables are collectible and are not subject to subordination, (4) there has been progress on improvements, and (5) the development is practical?

A. The full accrual method.

B. The percentage-of-completion method.

C. The installment method.

D. The deposit method.

Answer (B) is correct. *(Publisher)*
REQUIRED: The accounting method that should be applied given the conditions listed.
DISCUSSION: SFAS 66 requires that the percentage-of-completion method of accounting be applied to sales transactions within a retail land sales project if all of the following criteria are met:

1. The period of cancelation with refund has expired.
2. Cumulative payments equal or exceed 10% of the contract sales price.
3. The receivables are collectible.
4. The receivables are not subject to subordination.
5. There has been progress on improvements.
6. The development is practical.

Answer (A) is incorrect because the full accrual method should be used if, in addition to the first four criteria, the development has been completed. Answer (C) is incorrect because the installment method should be used if, in addition to the first two criteria, the seller is financially capable. Answer (D) is incorrect because the deposit method should be used when the necessary criteria for the other three methods are not met.

61. Which of the following methods should be used to account for retail land sales when (1) the period of cancelation with refund has expired, (2) the cumulative payments of principal and interest equal at least 10% of the contract sales price, (3) the seller is financially capable, and (4) the receivables are not subject to subordination?

A. Full accrual.

B. Percentage-of-completion.

C. Installment.

D. Deposit.

Answer (C) is correct. *(Publisher)*
REQUIRED: The accounting method for the described retail land sales.
DISCUSSION: SFAS 66 requires that the installment method of accounting be applied to a retail land sales transaction for which the period of cancelation with refund has expired, the cumulative payments equal or exceed 10% of the contract sales price, and the seller is financially capable.
Answer (A) is incorrect because this method is appropriate only when conditions have been met in addition to those required for the installment method. Answer (B) is incorrect because this method is appropriate only when conditions have been met in addition to those required for the installment method. Answer (D) is incorrect because the deposit method should be used only when the criteria for all the other methods have not been met.

62. According to SFAS 66, which of the following conditions does not indicate that a sale has been consummated in a real estate sales transaction other than a retail land sale?

A. The parties are bound by the terms of a contract.

B. All consideration has been exchanged.

C. Any permanent financing for which the seller is responsible has been arranged.

D. An agreement to sell is signed.

Answer (D) is correct. *(Publisher)*
REQUIRED: The condition that is not indicative of the consummation of a real estate sale.
DISCUSSION: In addition to the conditions listed in (A) through (C), SFAS 66 requires that all conditions precedent to closing must have been performed. The four conditions required are usually met at the time of closing or after closing, not when an agreement to sell is signed or at a preclosing.

63. Profit is recognized in full on real estate sales transactions other than retail land sales, provided that the profit is determinable and the earning process is virtually complete. Which of the following criteria must be met before the full accrual method may be used to recognize profit on real estate sales transactions other than retail land sales?

A. The sale is consummated.

B. The buyer demonstrates a commitment to pay for the property.

C. The seller's receivable is not subject to future subordination.

D. All of the answers are correct.

Answer (D) is correct. *(Publisher)*

REQUIRED: The condition(s) that must be met before the full accrual method of accounting for profit may be used for a nonretail land sale.

DISCUSSION: SFAS 66 requires that the sale be consummated, the buyer demonstrate a commitment to pay, and the seller's receivable not be subordinated. In addition, the seller must not have a substantial continuing involvement with the property.

Answer (A) is incorrect because consummation of the sale is a condition for use of the full accrual method. Answer (B) is incorrect because demonstration of the buyer's commitment to pay is a condition for use of the full accrual method. Answer (C) is incorrect because the priority of the seller's receivable is a condition for use of the full accrual method.

64. One of the conditions required by SFAS 66 before the full accrual method of accounting for nonretail real estate sales may be used is that the buyer's initial and continuing investments are adequate to demonstrate a commitment to pay for the property. In measuring the adequacy of a buyer's initial investment, which of the following payments should be included in the determination of the initial investment?

A. Payments by the buyer to third parties to reduce existing indebtedness on the property.

B. A permanent loan commitment by an independent third party to replace a loan made by the seller.

C. Payments by the buyer to third parties for improvements to the property.

D. Funds that have been or will be lent, refunded, or directly or indirectly provided to the buyer by the seller.

Answer (A) is correct. *(Publisher)*

REQUIRED: The consideration that should be included in the determination of the buyer's initial investment.

DISCUSSION: SFAS 66 states that the buyer's initial investment should include only the following:

1. Cash paid as a down payment.
2. The buyer's notes supported by irrevocable letters of credit from an independent, established lending institution.
3. Amounts paid by the buyer that are part of the sales value.
4. Payments by the buyer to third parties to reduce existing indebtedness on the property.

Answer (B) is incorrect because it is explicitly excluded by SFAS 66 from the determination of the buyer's initial investment. Answer (C) is incorrect because it is explicitly excluded by SFAS 66 from the determination of the buyer's initial investment. Answer (D) is incorrect because it is explicitly excluded by SFAS 66 from the determination of the buyer's initial investment.

65. If a real estate sale is not a retail land sale, the seller has transferred substantially all of the risks and rewards of ownership, and the buyer's initial or continuing investment does not qualify for the full accrual method, but the recovery of the cost of the property is reasonably assured if the buyer defaults, which method of accounting should be used?

A. Deposit method or cost-recovery method.

B. Installment method or cost-recovery method.

C. Deposit method or installment method.

D. Installment method only.

Answer (B) is correct. *(Publisher)*

REQUIRED: The appropriate accounting method(s) for real estate sales when recovery of the cost of the property is reasonably assured.

DISCUSSION: For real estate sales other than retail land sales, SFAS 66 states that if the buyer's initial investment does not meet the criteria for the accrual method, but recovery of the cost of the property is reasonably assured if the buyer defaults, the installment method should be used. The cost-recovery method may also be used to account for nonretail sales of real estate for which the installment method would be appropriate.

Answer (A) is incorrect because the deposit method is appropriate only when recovery of the cost of the property is not reasonably assured if the buyer defaults. Answer (C) is incorrect because the deposit and installment methods are never appropriate for the same transaction. Answer (D) is incorrect because the cost-recovery method may also be used when the installment method is appropriate.

APPENDIX A
SUBUNIT CROSS-REFERENCES TO INTERMEDIATE AND ADVANCED FINANCIAL ACCOUNTING TEXTBOOKS

The following ten pages contain the tables of contents of current intermediate and advanced financial accounting textbooks with cross-references to the related subunits or study units in this study manual. The books are listed in alphabetical order by the first author. As you study a particular chapter in your intermediate or advanced textbook, you can easily determine which subunit(s) to study in this manual. You should review all questions in the subunit.

INTERMEDIATE ACCOUNTING TEXTBOOKS

Chasteen, Flaherty, and O'Connor, *Intermediate Accounting*, Sixth Edition, McGraw-Hill, Inc., 1998.

Dyckman, Davis, and Dukes, *Intermediate Accounting*, Fifth Edition, McGraw-Hill, Inc., 2001.

Kieso, Warfield, and Weygandt, *Intermediate Accounting*, Eleventh Edition, John Wiley & Sons, Inc., 2004.

Needles and Powers, *Financial Accounting*, Eighth Edition, Houghton Mifflin Co., 2004.

Nikolai and Bazley, *Intermediate Accounting*, Ninth Edition, South-Western College Publishing Co., 2004.

Skousen, Stice, and Stice, *Intermediate Accounting with Thompson Analytics*, Fifteenth Edition, South-Western College Publishing Co., 2004.

Stice and Stice, *Financial Accounting: Reporting and Analysis*, Seventh Edition, South-Western College Publishing Co., 2006.

Warren, Reeve, and Fess, *Corporate Financial Accounting*, Eighth Edition, South-Western College Publishing Co., 2005.

Williams, Stanga, and Holder, *Intermediate Accounting*, Fifth Edition, Harcourt Brace College Publishers, 1997.

ADVANCED ACCOUNTING TEXTBOOKS

Anthony, Beams, Clement, and Lowensohn, *Advanced Accounting*, Eighth Edition, Prentice-Hall, Inc., 2003.

Baker, Lembke, and King, *Advanced Financial Accounting*, Sixth Edition, McGraw-Hill, Inc., 2005.

Fischer, Taylor, and Cheng, *Advanced Accounting*, Ninth Edition, South-Western College Publishing Co., 2006.

Hoyle, Schaefer, and Doupnik, *Advanced Accounting*, Seventh Edition, McGraw-Hill, Inc., 2004.

Huefner, Largay, and Hamlen, *Advanced Financial Accounting*, Eighth Edition, Thomson Custom Publishing, 2002.

Jeter and Chaney, *Advanced Accounting*, Second Edition, John Wiley & Sons, Inc., 2003.

Larsen, *Modern Advanced Accounting*, Tenth Edition, McGraw-Hill, Inc., 2006.

Pahler, *Advanced Accounting: Concepts and Practice*, Ninth Edition, South-Western College Publishing Co., 2006.

INTERMEDIATE ACCOUNTING TEXTBOOKS

Chasteen, Flaherty, and O'Connor, *Intermediate Accounting*, Sixth Edition, McGraw-Hill, Inc., 1998.

Chapter 1 - Financial Accounting and Reporting: An Introduction - 1.1
Chapter 2 - Financial Accounting and Reporting: A Theoretical Structure - 1.2
Chapter 3 - The Accounting Process: An Overview - 2.1-2.3
Chapter 4 - The Income Statement - SU 3
Chapter 5 - The Balance Sheet (Statement of Financial Position) - 5.1-5.2
Chapter 6 - The Statement of Cash Flows - SU 19
Chapter 7 - Revenue Recognition and Income Determination - 1.3-1.4
Chapter 8 - A. Cash and Current Receivables - 5.3-5.6
B. Current Payables and Contingencies - SU 11
Chapter 9 - Inventory Valuation: Determining Cost and Using Cost Flow Assumptions - 6.1-6.2
Chapter 10 - Inventory Valuation: Departures from Historical Cost and Methods of Estimating Inventory Cost - 6.1-6.6
Chapter 11 - Plant Assets and Intangibles: Acquisition and Subsequent Expenditures - SU 7
Chapter 12 - Plant Assets and Intangibles: Depreciation, Depletion, Amortization, and Disposition - SU 8
Chapter 13 - Financial Instruments: Equity Securities - 10.1-10.5
Chapter 14 - Financial Instruments: Debt Securities - 10.1-12.5
Chapter 15 - Leases - SU 14
Chapter 16 - Pensions and Other Post-Retirement Benefits - SU 13
Chapter 17 - Accounting for Income Taxes - SU 17
Chapter 18 - Stockholders' Equity - SU 15
Chapter 19 - Accounting Changes and Error Analysis - SU 18
Chapter 20 - Earnings Per Share - SU 16
Chapter 21 - A. Revisiting the Statement of Cash Flows - SU 19
B. Additional Disclosure Topics - SU 21

Dyckman, Davis, and Dukes, *Intermediate Accounting*, Fifth Edition, McGraw-Hill, Inc., 2001.

Part I - Foundation and Review
Chapter 1 - The Environment of Accounting - 1.1
Chapter 2 - The FASB's Conceptual Framework of Accounting - 1.2
Chapter 3 - Review: The Accounting Information Processing System - SU 2
Chapter 4 - Review: The Income Statement and the Retained Earnings Statement - 3.1-3.5
Chapter 5 - Review: The Balance Sheet and the Statement of Cash Flows - 5.1-5.2, SU 19
Chapter 6 - Interest: Concepts of Future and Present Value - SU 4
Part II - Asset Recognition and Measurement
Chapter 7 - Revenue and Expense Recognition - 1.3-1.4
Chapter 8 - Cash and Receivables - 5.3-5.6
Chapter 9 - Inventory: Basic Valuation Methods - SU 6
Chapter 10 - Inventory: Alternative Valuation Methods - SU 6
Chapter 11 - Operational Assets: Acquisition, Disposal, and Exchange - SU 7
Chapter 12 - Operational Assets: Depreciation and Impairment - SU 8
Chapter 13 - Intangible Assets and Natural Resources - SU 9
Chapter 14 - Investments in Debt and Equity Securities - SU 10
Part III - Liabilities
Chapter 15 - Short-Term Liabilities - SU 11
Chapter 16 - Long-Term Liabilities - SU 12
Chapter 17 - Accounting for Leases - SU 14
Chapter 18 - Accounting for Pensions and Other Postemployment Benefits - SU 13
Chapter 19 - Accounting for Income Taxes - SU 17
Part IV - Owners' Equity
Chapter 20 - Corporations: Contributed Capital - SU 15
Chapter 21 - Corporations: Retained Earnings and Stock Options - SU 15
Chapter 22 - Earnings per Share - SU 16
Part V - Special Topics
Chapter 23 - Statement of Cash Flows - SU 19
Chapter 24 - Accounting Changes and Error Corrections - SU 18
Chapter 25 - Special Topics: Disclosures, Segment Reporting, and Interim Reporting - SU 26, 27

Kieso, Warfield, and Weygandt, *Intermediate Accounting*, Eleventh Edition, John Wiley & Sons, Inc., 2004.

Chapter 1 - Financial Accounting and Accounting Standards - 1.1
Chapter 2 - Conceptual Framework Underlying Financial Accounting - 1.1-1.3
Chapter 3 - The Accounting Information System - 2.1-2.3
Chapter 4 - Income Statement and Related Information - 3.1-3.5
Chapter 5 - Balance Sheet and Statement of Cash Flows - 5.1, 5.2, SU 19
Chapter 6 - Accounting and the Time Value of Money - SU 4
Chapter 7 - Cash and Receivables - 5.3, 5.4, 5.5, 5.6
Chapter 8 - Valuation of Inventories: A Cost Basis Approach - 6.1-6.3, 6.7, 6.8
Chapter 9 - Inventories: Additional Valuation Issues - 6.4-6.6, 26.2
Chapter 10 - Acquisition and Disposition of Property, Plant, and Equipment - 7.1-7.5
Chapter 11 - Depreciation, Impairments, and Depletion - SU 8
Chapter 12 - Intangible Assets - SU 9
Chapter 13 - Current Liabilities and Contingencies - SU 11
Chapter 14 - Long-Term Liabilities - SU 12
Chapter 15 - Stockholders' Equity - 15.1, 15.4
Chapter 16 - Dilutive Securities and Earnings Per Share - 15.6-15.7, SU 16
Chapter 17 - Investments - 10.1-10.5, 15.6
Chapter 18 - Revenue Recognition - 1.4, 22.1-22.3
Chapter 19 - Accounting for Income Taxes - SU 17
Chapter 20 - Accounting for Pensions and Postretirement Benefits - SU 13
Chapter 21 - Accounting for Leases - SU 14
Chapter 22 - Accounting Changes and Error Analysis - SU 18
Chapter 23 - Statement of Cash Flows - SU 19
Chapter 24 - Full Disclosure in Financial Reporting - SU 21, 26, 30.2

Needles and Powers, *Financial Accounting*, Eighth Edition, Houghton Mifflin Co., 2004.

Part I - Accounting as an Information System
  Chapter 1 - Uses of Accounting Information and the Financial Statements - SU 1, 2.1
  Chapter 2 - Measuring Business Transactions - 2.1, 2.3
  Chapter 3 - Measuring Business Income - 2.2
  Chapter 4 - Accounting Systems - N/A
Part II - Measuring and Reporting the Operating Cycle
  Chapter 5 - Financial Reporting and Analysis - 1.2, 3.2
  Chapter 6 - Merchandising Operations and Internal Control - 6.1, 22.2, 22.3
  Chapter 7 - Short-Term Liquid Assets - SU 5, 10.1
  Chapter 8 - Inventories - SU 6, 20
  Chapter 9 - Current Liabilities and the Time Value of Money - SU 4, 11
Part III - Measuring and Reporting Long-Term Assets and Long-Term Financing
  Chapter 10 - Long-Term Assets - SU 7, 8, 9
  Chapter 11 - Long-Term Liabilities - SU 12, 13, 14.1, 14.2, 14.4, 14.5
  Chapter 12 - Contributed Capital - SU 15
Part IV - Expanded Presentation and Analysis of Accounting Information
  Chapter 13 - The Corporate Income Statement and the Statement of Stockholders' Equity - SU 3, 15, 16, 17, 18
  Chapter 14 - The Statement of Cash Flows - SU 19
  Chapter 15 - Financial Statement Analysis - SU 23
  Chapter 16 - International Accounting and Long-Term Investments - SU 25, 27

Nikolai and Bazley, *Intermediate Accounting,* Ninth Edition, South-Western College Publishing Co., 2004.

Part I - Financial Reporting: Concepts, Financial Statements, and Related Disclosures
Chapter 1 - The Environment of Financial Reporting - 1.1-1.4
Chapter 2 - Financial Reporting: Its Conceptual Framework - 1.1-1.4
Chapter 3 - The Balance Sheet and Statement of Changes in Stockholders' Equity - 5.1-5.2, SU 15
Chapter 4 - The Income Statement and Statement of Cash Flows - SU 3, 15, 19
Chapter 5 - Additional Aspects of Financial Reporting and Financial Analysis - SU 23
Part II - Financial Reporting: Asset Measurement and Income Determination
Chapter 6 - Cash and Receivables - 5.3-5.6
Chapter 7 - Inventories: Cost Measurement and Flow Assumptions - 6.1-6.3, 6.7, 6.8
Chapter 8 - Inventories: Special Valuation Issues - 6.4-6.6, 6.9
Chapter 9 - Property, Plant, and Equipment: Acquisition and Disposal - 7.1-7.5
Chapter 10 - Depreciation and Depletion - SU 8
Chapter 11 - Intangibles - SU 9
Part III - Financial Reporting: Valuation of Liabilities and Investments
Chapter 12 - Current Liabilities and Contingencies - SU 11
Chapter 13 - Long-Term Liabilities and Receivables - SU 12
Chapter 14 - Investments - 10.1-10.5
Part IV - Financial Reporting: Stockholders' Equity
Chapter 15 - Contributed Capital - 15.1-15.3, 15.6
Chapter 16 - Earnings Per Share and Retained Earnings - SU 16
Part V - Financial Reporting: Special Topics
Chapter 17 - Income Recognition and Measurement of Net Assets - 1.4, 22.1-22.3
Chapter 18 - Accounting for Income Taxes - SU 17
Chapter 19 - Accounting for Postemployment Benefits - SU 13
Chapter 20 - Accounting for Leases - SU 14
Chapter 21 - The Statement of Cash Flows - SU 19
Chapter 22 - Accounting Changes and Errors - SU 18

Skousen, Stice, and Stice, *Intermediate Accounting with Thompson Analytics,* Fifteenth Edition, South-Western College Publishing Co., 2004.

Part 1 - Foundations of Financial Accounting
Chapter 1 - Financial Reporting - 1.1-1.4
Chapter 2 - A Review of the Accounting Cycle - 2.1-2.3
Chapter 3 - The Balance Sheet and Notes to the Financial Statements - 5.1-5.2, SU 21
Chapter 4 - The Income Statement - 3.1-3.5
Chapter 5 - The Statement of Cash Flows - SU 19
Part 2 - Primary Activities of a Business
Section 1 - Operating Activities
Chapter 6 - Earnings Management - SU 1
Chapter 7 - The Revenue/Receivables/Cash Cycle - 1.3, 22.1-22.3
Chapter 8 - Revenue Recognition -- Identification and Valuation - SU 6
Chapter 9 - Cost of Goods Sold and Inventory - SU 6
Section 2 - Financing Activities
Chapter 10 - Debt Financing - 12.1-12.4, 12.6
Chapter 11 - Equity Financing - 15.1-15.4, 15.6
Section 3 - Investing Activities
Chapter 12 - Investments in Noncurrent Operating Assets -- Acquisition - SU 7, 9
Chapter 13 - Investments in Noncurrent Operating Assets -- Utilization and Retirement - SU 8
Chapter 14 - Investments in Debt and Equity Securities - SU 10
Part 3 - Additional Activities and Common Disclosures of a Business
Chapter 15 - Leases - SU 14
Chapter 16 - Income Taxes - SU 17
Chapter 17 - Employee Compensation -- Payroll, Pensions, and Other Compensation Issues - SU 13, 18
Chapter 18 - Derivatives, Contingencies, Business Segments, and Interim Reports - 10.5, 11.8, 21.4, SU 26
Part 4 - Other Dimensions of Financial Reporting
Chapter 19 - Earnings Per Share - SU 18
Chapter 20 - Accounting Changes for Error Corrections - SU 16
Chapter 21 - Analysis of Financial Statements - SU 23

Stice and Stice, *Financial Accounting: Reporting and Analysis*, Seventh Edition, South-Western College Publishing Co., 2006.

Part 1 - Introduction to Financial Statements
Chapter 1 - The Nature and Purpose of Financial Accounting - 1.1
Chapter 2 - Overview of the Financial Statements - 1.3
Chapter 3 - Introduction to Financial Statement Analysis - SU 23
Chapter 4 - The Balance Sheet - 5.1-5.2
Chapter 5 - The Income Statement - SU 3
Chapter 6 - The Statement of Cash Flows - SU 19
Part 2 - The Accounting Information System
Chapter 7 - The Accounting Information System - 2.1-2.3
Part 3 - Operating Decisions
Chapter 8 - Revenue Cycle: Sales, Receivables, and Cash - 1.3-1.4
Chapter 9 - Cost of Goods Sold and Inventory - SU 6
Chapter 10 - Expenditure Cycle: Other Operating Items - SU 10, 12, 15
Part 4 - Investing Decisions
Chapter 11 - Investments in Operating Assets - SU 7
Chapter 12 - Investments in Securities - SU 10
Part 5 - Financial Decisions
Chapter 13 - Financing with Debt - 12.1-12.4, 12.6
Chapter 14 - Financing with Equity - 15.1-15.4, 15.6
Part 6 - Additional Reporting and Analysis
Chapter 15 - Accounting in a Global Market - N/A

Warren, Reeve, and Fess, *Corporate Financial Accounting*, Eighth Edition, South-Western College Publishing Co., 2005.

Chapter 1 - Introduction to Accounting and Business - SU 1
Chapter 2 - Analyzing Transactions - SU 1
Chapter 3 - The Matching Concept and the Adjusting Process - 1.4, SU 2
Chapter 4 - Completing the Accounting Cycle - SU 2
Chapter 5 - Accounting for Merchandising Businesses - SU 6
Chapter 6 - Accounting Systems, Internal Controls, and Cash - SU 2, 5.3
Chapter 7 - Receivables - SU 5
Chapter 8 - Inventories - SU 6
Chapter 9 - Fixed Assets and Intangible Assets - SU 7, 8, 9
Chapter 10 - Current Liabilities - SU 11
Chapter 11 - Corporations: Organization, Capital Stock Transactions, and Dividends - SU 15
Chapter 12 - Income Taxes, Unusual Income Items, Stockholders' Equity, and Investments in Stocks - 10.1, 10.3, SU 15, 17
Chapter 13 - Bonds Payable and Investments in Bonds - 10.1, 10.2, 10.6, SU 12, 19, 23
Chapter 14 - Statement of Cash Flows
Chapter 15 - Financial Statement Analysis

Williams, Stanga, and Holder, *Intermediate Accounting*, Fifth Edition, Harcourt Brace College Publishers, 1997.

Part I - Theoretical Foundation for Financial Reporting
Chapter 1 - The Financial Accounting Environment - 1.1
Chapter 2 - Financial Accounting Theory -- A Model - 1.2
Chapter 3 - Nature and Measurement of the Elements of Financial Statements - 1.2-1.4
Chapter 4 - Basic Financial Statements - 3.1, 3.6, 5.1-5.2
Part II - Tools of Accounting
Chapter 5 - The Accounting Cycle - 2.1-2.3
Chapter 6 - Compound Interest Concepts - 4.1-4.3
Part III - Asset Accounting
Chapter 7 - Cash and Receivables - 5.3, 5.4-5.6
Chapter 8 - Inventories: Basic Valuation Methods - SU 6
Chapter 9 - Inventories: Additional Valuation Methods - SU 6
Chapter 10 - Investments and Funds - 10.1-10.5
Chapter 11 - Property, Plant, and Equipment: Acquisition and Disposal - SU 7
Chapter 12 - Property, Plant, and Equipment: Depreciation, Depletion, and Special Problems - SU 8
Chapter 13 - Intangible Assets - SU 9
Part IV - Liability and Stockholders' Equity Accounting
Chapter 14 - Current and Contingent Liabilities -- Characteristics of Liabilities - SU 11
Chapter 15 - Long-Term Debt - SU 12
Chapter 16 - Stockholders' Equity: Corporate Formation and Contributed Capital - SU 15
Chapter 17 - Stockholders' Equity: Operations, Earnings, Dividends, and Other Issues - SU 15
Chapter 18 - Earnings Per Share - SU 16
Part V - Additional Financial Reporting Issues
Chapter 19 - Financial Reporting of Income Taxes - SU 17
Chapter 20 - Accounting Changes and Corrections of Errors - SU 18
Chapter 21 - Revenue Measurement and Income Presentation - 1.3, 3.1-3.5
Chapter 22 - Reporting Cash Flow Information - SU 19
Chapter 23 - Leases - SU 14
Chapter 24 - Accounting for Retirement Benefits - SU 13
Chapter 25 - Additional Disclosure Issues and Financial Analysis - SU 21, 23
Chapter 26 - Financial Reporting and Changing Prices - SU 20

ADVANCED ACCOUNTING TEXTBOOKS

Anthony, Beams, Clement, and Lowensohn, *Advanced Accounting*, Eighth Edition, Prentice-Hall, Inc., 2003.

Chapter 1 - Business Combinations - 25.1
Chapter 2 - Stock Investments and Investor Accounting and Reporting - 10.4-10.5
Chapter 3 - An Introduction to Consolidated Financial Statements - 25.1
Chapter 4 - Consolidation Techniques and Procedures - SU 25
Chapter 5 - Intercompany Profit Transactions and Inventories - 25.6
Chapter 6 - Intercompany Profit Transactions and Plant Assets - 25.6
Chapter 7 - Intercompany Profit Transactions and Bonds - 25.6
Chapter 8 - Consolidations and Changes in Ownership Interests - 25.5
Chapter 9 - Indirect and Mutual Holdings - 25.5
Chapter 10 - Subsidiary Preferred Stock, Consolidated Earnings Per Share, and Consolidated Income Taxation - N/A
Chapter 11 - Consolidation Theories, Push-Down Accounting, and Corporate Joint Ventures - 25.1, 25.7
Chapter 12 - Foreign Currency Concepts and Transactions - 27.2
Chapter 13 - Foreign Currency Financial Statements - 27.1
Chapter 14 - Segment and Interim Financial Reporting - 21.4, SU 26
Chapter 15 - Partnerships -- Formation, Operations, and Changes in Ownership Interests - 24.1-24.4
Chapter 16 - Dissolution and Liquidation of a Partnership - 24.4-24.5
Chapter 17 - Corporate Liquidations and Reorganizations - 12.6, 15.5
Chapter 18 - An Introduction to Accounting for State and Local Governmental Units - Governmental Funds - SU 28
Chapter 19 - An Introduction to Accounting for State and Local Governmental Units - Proprietary and Fiduciary Funds - SU 28
Chapter 20 - Accounting for Not-For-Profit Organizations - SU 29

Baker, Lembke, and King, *Advanced Financial Accounting*, Sixth Edition, McGraw-Hill, Inc., 2005.

Chapter 1 - Intercorporate Acquisitions & Instruments in Other Entities - 25.1
Chapter 2 - Reporting Intercorporate Interests - 25.3
Chapter 3 - The Reporting Entity and Consolidated Financial Statements - 21.4, 25.1
Chapter 4 - Consolidation as of the Date of Acquisition - 25.2
Chapter 5 - Consolidation Following Acquisition - 25.3
Chapter 6 - Intercorporate Transfers: Noncurrent Assets - 25.4
Chapter 7 - Intercompany Inventory Transactions - 25.4
Chapter 8 - Intercompany Indebtedness - 25.4
Chapter 9 - Consolidation Ownership Issues - 25.1-25.4
Chapter 10 - Additional Consolidation Reporting Issues - 25.1-25.4
Chapter 11 - Multinational Accounting: Foreign Currency Transactions and Financial Instruments - 27.2-27.3
Chapter 12 - Multinational Accounting: Translation of Foreign Entity Statements - 27.1
Chapter 13 - Segment and Interim Reporting - 21.4, 26.1-26.5
Chapter 14 - SEC Reporting - N/A
Chapter 15 - Partnerships: Formation, Operation, and Changes of Membership - 24.1-24.4
Chapter 16 - Partnerships: Liquidations - 24.5
Chapter 17 - Governmental Entities: Introduction and General Fund Accounting - 28.1-28.2
Chapter 18 - Governmental Entities: Special Funds and Government-Wide Financial Statements - 28.2-28.3
Chapter 19 - Not-For-Profit Entities - SU 29
Chapter 20 - Corporations in Financial Difficulty - 15.5

Fischer, Taylor, and Cheng, *Advanced Accounting*, Ninth Edition, South-Western College Publishing Co., 2006.

Part 1 - Combined Corporate Entities and Consolidations
Chapter 1 - Business Combinations: America's Most Popular Business Activity, Bringing an End to the Controversy - 25.1
Chapter 2 - Consolidated Statements: Date of Acquisition - 25.3-25.5
Chapter 3 - Consolidated Statements: Subsequent to Acquisition - 25.3-25.5
Special Appendix 1. Possible New Consolidation Procedure - Goodwill
Chapter 4 - Intercompany Sales - 25.6
Chapter 5 - Intercompany Debt - 25.6
Chapter 6 - Cash Flow, EPS, Taxation, and Unconsolidated Investments - N/A
Chapter 7 - Special Issues in Accounting for an Investment in a Subsidiary - 25.7
Chapter 8 - Subsidiary Equity Transactions, Indirect and Mutual Holdings - 25.5
Special Appendix 2. Leveraged Buyouts.
Part 2 - Multinational Accounting and Other Reporting Concerns
Chapter 9 - The International Accounting Environment Module - 27.3
Chapter 10 - Foreign Currency Transactions - 27.2
Chapter 11 - Translation of Foreign Financial Statements - 27.1
Chapter 12 - Interim Reporting and Disclosures About Segments of an Enterprise - 21.4, 26
Part 3 - Partnerships
Chapter 13 - Partnerships: Characteristics, Formation, and Accounting for Activities - 24.1, 24.2
Chapter 14 - Partnerships: Ownership Changes and Liquidations - 24.3, 24.5
Part 4 - Governmental and Not-For-Profit Accounting
Chapter 15 - Governmental Accounting: General Fund and the Account Groups - 28.1, 28.2
Chapter 16 - Governmental Accounting: Other Governmental Funds, Proprietary and Fiduciary Funds - 28.2
Chapter 17 - Financial Reporting Issues - 28.3
Chapter 18 - Accounting for Private Not-For-Profit Organizations Including Voluntary Health and Welfare Organizations - 29.1, 29.2
Chapter 19 - Public and Private College and University and Health Care Accounting - 29.2, 29.3
Part 5 - Fiduciary Accounting
Chapter 20 - Estates and Trusts: Their Nature and the Accountant's Role - N/A
Chapter 21 - Debt Restructuring, Corporate Reorganizations, and Liquidations - 12.6, 15.5

Hoyle, Schaefer, and Doupnik, *Advanced Accounting*, Seventh Edition, McGraw-Hill, Inc., 2004.

Chapter 1 - The Equity Method of Accounting for Investments - 10.3
Chapter 2 - Consolidation of Financial Information - SU 25
Chapter 3 - Consolidations -- Subsequent to the Date of Acquisition - SU 25
Chapter 4 - Consolidated Financial Statements and Outside Ownership - SU 25
Chapter 5 - Consolidated Financial Statements -- Intercompany Asset Transactions - 25.6
Chapter 6 - Variable Interest Entities, Intercompany Debt, Consolidated Statement of Cash Flows, and Other Issues - 25.6
Chapter 7 - Consolidated Financial Statements -- Ownership Patterns and Income Taxes - SU 25
Chapter 8 - Segment and Interim Reporting - 25.8
Chapter 9 - Foreign Currency Transactions and Hedging Foreign Exchange Risk - 27.2-27.3
Chapter 10 - Translation of Foreign Currency Financial Statements - 27.1
Chapter 11 - Worldwide Accounting Diversity and International Accounting Standards - N/A
Chapter 12 - Financial Reporting and the Securities and Exchange Commission - 21.4
Chapter 13 - Accounting for Legal Reorganizations and Liquidations - 15.5
Chapter 14 - Partnerships: Formation and Operation - 24.1-24.3
Chapter 15 - Partnerships: Termination and Liquidation - 24.4-24.5
Chapter 16 - Accounting for State and Local Governments, Part I - SU 28
Chapter 17 - Accounting for State and Local Governments, Part II - SU 28
Chapter 18 - Accounting and Reporting for Not-For-Profit Organizations - SU 29
Chapter 19 - Accounting for Estates and Trusts - N/A

Huefner, Largay, and Hamlen, *Advanced Financial Accounting*, Eighth Edition, Thomson Custom Publishing, 2002.

Volume I

Chapter 1 - Accounting for Mergers and Acquisitions - SU 25
Chapter 2 - Special Topics in Mergers and Acquisitions - SU 25
Chapter 3 - Introduction to Consolidation: The Balance Sheet - 25.3-25.5
Chapter 4 - Consolidation After Date of Acquisition - 25.3-25.5
Chapter 5 - Consolidated Financial Statements: Intercompany Transactions I - 25.6
Chapter 6 - Consolidated Financial Statements: Intercompany Transactions II - 25.6
Chapter 7 - Consolidated Financial Statements: Special Topics - 25.7
Chapter 8 - Bankruptcy and Reorganization - 15.5
Chapter 9 - Translating Foreign Currency Financial Statements - 27.1
Chapter 10 - Accounting for Foreign Currency Transactions - 27.2
Chapter 11 - Derivative Financial Instruments: Futures, Options, and Interest Rate Swaps - 10.6
Chapter 12 - Accounting and Reporting for Routine Activities of State and Local Government - 28.1-28.2
Chapter 13 - Accounting for Nonroutine Activities and External Reporting for State and Local Government - 28.2-28.3
Chapter 14 - Accounting and Reporting by Not-For-Profit Organizations - SU 29
Chapter 15 - Partnerships: Formation, Operation, and Expansion - 24.1-24.2
Chapter 16 - Partnerships: Contraction, Termination, and Liquidation - 24.3-24.5
Module A Conceptual Issues and Consolidated Financial Reporting - SU 25
Module B Tax Accounting in Mergers and Consolidated Statements - N/A
Module C Consolidating Internal Operation; Branch Accounting - 25.8
Module D Segment Reporting - 21.4
Module E The SEC and Its Role in Financial Reporting - N/A
Module F Environmental Liabilities - N/A
Module G Personal Financial Statements - 30.1
Module H Accounting and Reporting for Estates and Trusts - N/A

Jeter and Chaney, *Advanced Accounting,* Second Edition, John Wiley & Sons, Inc., 2003.

Part I - Accounting for Mergers and Acquisitions
- Chapter 1 - Introduction to Business Combinations - 25.1
- Chapter 2 - Accounting for Business Combinations - 25.1
- Chapter 3 - Consolidated Financial Statements - Date of Acquisition - 25.3-25.5
- Chapter 4 - Consolidated Financial Statements After Acquisition - 25.3-25.5
- Chapter 5 - Allocation and Depreciation of Differences Between Cost and Book Values - 25.4
- Chapter 6 - Elimination of Unrealized Profit on Intercompany Sales of Inventory - 25.6
- Chapter 7 - Elimination of Unrealized Gains and Losses on Intercompany Sales of Property and Equipment - 25.6
- Chapter 8 - Changes in Ownership Interest - SU 25
- Chapter 9 - Intercompany Bond Holding and Miscellaneous Topics - Consolidated Financial Statements - SU 25
- Chapter 10 - Insolvency - Liquidation and Reorganization - N/A

Part II - Accounting in the International Marketplace
- Chapter 11 - International Accounting and the Global Economy - SU 27
- Chapter 12 - Accounting for Foreign Currency Transactions and Hedging Foreign Exchange Risk - 27.2
- Chapter 13 - Translations of Financial Statements of Foreign Affiliates - 27.1
- Chapter 14 - Reporting for Segments and for Interim Financial Periods - 21.4, SU 26

Part III - Partnership Accounting
- Chapter 15 - Partnerships: Formation, Operation, and Ownership Changes - 24.1-24.4
- Chapter 16 - Partnership Liquidation - 24.5

Part IV - Fund and Nonprofit Accounting
- Chapter 17 - Introduction to Fund Accounting - SU 28
- Chapter 18 - Introduction to Accounting for State and Local Governmental Units - SU 28
- Chapter 19 - Accounting for Nongovernment Nonbusiness Organizations: Colleges and Universities, Hospitals, and Other Health Care Organizations - SU 29

Larsen, *Modern Advanced Accounting,* Tenth Edition, McGraw-Hill, Inc., 2006.

- Chapter 1 - Ethical Issues in Advanced Accounting - N/A

Part One: Accounting for Partnerships and Branches
- Chapter 2 - Partnerships: Organization and Operation - 24.1-24.4
- Chapter 3 - Partnership Liquidation and Incorporation; Joint Ventures - 24.5
- Chapter 4 - Accounting for Branches; Combined Financial Statements - 25.8

Part Two: Business Combinations and Consolidated Financial Statements
- Chapter 5 - Business Combinations - 25.1
- Chapter 6 - Consolidated Financial Statements: On Date of Business Combination - 25.5
- Chapter 7 - Consolidated Financial Statements: Subsequent to Date Business - 25.5
- Chapter 8 - Consolidated Financial Statements: Intercompany Transactions - 25.6
- Chapter 9 - Consolidated Financial Statements: Income Taxes, Cash Flows, and Installment Acquisitions - 25.5
- Chapter 10 - Consolidated Financial Statements: Special Programs - 25.7

Part Three: International Accounting; Reporting of Segments for Interim Periods, and to the SEC
- Chapter 11 - International Accounting Standards; Accounting for Foreign Currency Transactions - 27.2
- Chapter 12 - Translation of Foreign Currency Financial Statements - 27.1
- Chapter 13 - Reporting for Components; Interim Reports; Reporting for the SEC - 21.4, SU 26

Part Four: Accounting for Fiduciaries
- Chapter 14 - Bankruptcy: Liquidation and Reorganization - 15.5
- Chapter 15 - Estates and Trusts - N/A

Part Five: Accounting for Nonbusiness Organizations
- Chapter 16 - Nonprofit Organizations - SU 29
- Chapter 17 - Governmental Entities: General Fund - 28.1-28.2
- Chapter 18 - Governmental Entities: Other Governmental Funds and Account Groups - 28.2
- Chapter 19 - Governmental Entities: Proprietary Funds, Fiduciary Funds, and Comprehensive Annual Financial Reports - 28.2-28.3

Pahler, *Advanced Accounting: Concepts and Practice*, Ninth Edition, South-Western College Publishing Co., 2006.

Part I - Consolidated Financial Statements: Internal Expansion Issues
- Chapter 1 - Wholly Owned Subsidiaries: At Date of Creation - SU 25
- Chapter 2 - Wholly Owned Subsidiaries: Postcreation Periods - SU 25
- Chapter 3 - Partially Owned Created Subsidiaries - SU 25

Part II - Consolidated Financial Statements: External Expansion Issues
- Chapter 4 - Introduction to Business Combinations - 25.1
- Chapter 5 - The Purchase Method: At Date of Acquisition -- 100% Ownership - SU 25
- Chapter 6 - The Purchase Method: Postacquisition Periods and Partial Ownerships - 25.5
- Chapter 7 - New Basis of Accounting - N/A

Part III - Consolidated Financial Statements: Intercompany Transactions
- Chapter 8 - Introduction to Intercompany Transactions - 25.6
- Chapter 9 - Intercompany Inventory Transfers - 25.6
- Chapter 10 - Intercompany Fixed Asset Transfers and Bond Holdings - 25.6

Part IV - Consolidated Financial Statements: Other Topics
- Chapter 11 - Changes in a Parent's Ownership Interest - SU 25
- Chapter 12 - Reporting Segment and Related Information - SU 21

Part V - Foreign Transactions and Foreign Operations
- Chapter 13 - International Accounting and Translating Foreign Currency Transactions - 27.1
- Chapter 14 - Using Derivatives to Manage Foreign Currency Exposures - 27.3
- Chapter 15 - Translating Foreign Statements: The Current Rate Method - 27.1-27.2
- Chapter 16 - Translating Foreign Statements: The Temporal Method and the Functional Currency Concept - 27.1-27.2

Part VI - Miscellaneous Corporate Reporting Topics
- Chapter 17 - Interim Period Reporting - SU 26
- Chapter 18 - Securities and Exchange Commission Reporting
- Chapter 19 - Bankruptcy Reorganizations and Liquidations - 15.5

Part VII - Partnerships and Estates and Trusts
- Chapter 20 - Partnerships: Formation and Operation - 24.1-24.2
- Chapter 21 - Partnerships: Changes in Ownership - 24.3-24.4
- Chapter 22 - Partnerships: Liquidations - 24.5
- Chapter 23 - Estates and Trusts - N/A

Part VIII - Government and Nonprofit Organizations
- Chapter 24 - Governmental Accounting: Basic Principles and the General Fund - 28.1-28.2
- Chapter 25 - Governmental Accounting: The Special Purpose Funds and Special General Ledger - 28.2
- Chapter 26 - Not-For-Profit Organizations: Introduction and Private NPOs - SU 29

INDEX

CPA CMA/CFM CIA EA EQE CPE

COMPLETE GLEIM CPA SYSTEM with REVIEW ONLINE

All 4 parts, including books*, software, audio cds, Review Online, plus bonus book bag. ☐ $924.95
Also available by exam part @ $256.95 (does not include book bag).

*Fifth book: *CPA Review: A System for Success*

$________

COMPLETE GLEIM CMA/CFM SYSTEM with ONLINE COURSE for the UNCHANGED EXAM

Includes: books, software, audio cds, and Online Course, plus bonus book bag.

☐ CMA $681.95 ☐ CFM $681.95 ☐ CMA/CFM $855.95

Also available by exam part @ $198.95 (does not include book bag).

COMPLETE GLEIM CMA SYSTEM with ONLINE COURSE for the "REORGANIZED" EXAM

Includes: books, software, audio cds, and Online Course, plus bonus book bag.

☐ CMA $739.95 ☐ CMA/CFM $913.95

Also available by exam part @ $213.95 (does not include book bag).

$________

COMPLETE GLEIM CIA SYSTEM with ONLINE COURSE

Includes: books, software, audio cds, and Online Course, plus bonus book bag. ☐ $824.95
Also available by exam part @ $224.95 (does not include book bag).

GLEIM CIA SET

All 4 parts, including books, software, audio cds, plus bonus book bag. ☐ $483.80
Also available by exam part @ $120.95 (does not include book bag).

$________

GLEIM EA REVIEW SYSTEM

Includes: books and software. ☐ $279.80
Also available by exam part @ $69.95 (does not include book bag).

$________

"THE GLEIM SERIES" EXAM QUESTIONS AND EXPLANATIONS

Includes: 5 books and EQE Test Prep software. ☐ $112.25
Also available by part @ $29.95.

GLEIM CPE

Includes book and service. ☐ Financial Acctg ☐ Auditing ☐ Federal Tax ☐ $200 each

For our Online CPE courses and course catalogue, please visit www.gleim.com/CPE

$________

Contact **GLEIM PUBLICATIONS** for further assistance:

www.gleim.com
(800) 874-5346
sales@gleim.com

SUBTOTAL $________

Complete your order on the next page

GLEIM PUBLICATIONS, INC.

P. O. Box 12848 Gainesville, FL 32604

TOLL FREE: (800) 874-5346
LOCAL: (352) 375-0772
FAX: (888) 375-6940 (toll free)
INTERNET: www.gleim.com
E-MAIL: sales@gleim.com

Customer service is available (Eastern Time):
8:00 a.m. - 7:00 p.m., Mon. - Fri.
9:00 a.m. - 2:00 p.m., Saturday
Please have your credit card ready,
or save time by ordering online!

SUBTOTAL (from previous page) $______
Add applicable sales tax for shipments within Florida. ______
Shipping (nonrefundable) 15.00

TOTAL $______

Fax or write for prices/instructions on shipments outside the 48 contiguous states, or simply order online.

NAME (please print) ______________________________

ADDRESS ______________________________ Apt. ______
(street address required for UPS)

CITY ______________________ STATE ______ ZIP ______

____ MC/VISA/DISC ____ Check/M.O. Daytime Telephone ( ) ______________

Credit Card No. ________ - ________ - ________ - ________

Exp. ____/____ Signature ______________________________
Month / Year

E-mail address ______________________________

1. We process and ship orders daily, within one business day over 98.8% of the time. Call by 3:00 pm for same-day service.
2. Please PHOTOCOPY this order form for others.
3. No CODs. Orders from individuals must be prepaid.
4. Gleim Publications, Inc. guarantees the immediate refund of all resalable texts and unopened software and audios if returned within 30 days. Applies only to items purchased direct from Gleim Publications, Inc. Our shipping charge is nonrefundable.
5. Components of specially priced package deals are nonrefundable.

Prices subject to change without notice.

For updates and other important information, visit our website.

GLEIM KNOWLEDGE TRANSFER SYSTEMS®

www.gleim.com

GLEIM CPE

Continuing Professional Education
Self-Study Course Catalog

© Stockbyte/Picture Quest; Reprinted w/ permission.

GLEIM

provides a wide variety of CPE courses in a user-friendly learning format to maintain your interest and to enhance your expertise.

Increase your competitive advantage with GLEIM.

- Dr. Gleim has decades of experience developing effective Knowledge Transfer Systems that provide you with sophisticated, yet versatile, CPE courses to help increase your competitive edge.
- Earn CPE credits while enhancing your employment opportunities by studying for the CMA/CFM and CIA exams!

GLEIM provides CPE in 2 formats:

- ***ONLINE***
  - ✓ Convenient
  - ✓ Flexible
- ***PAPER AND PENCIL***
  - ✓ Mobile
  - ✓ Economical

All GLEIM CPE courses are NASBA Registry and QAS approved.

Gleim Publications, Inc. is registered with the National Association of State Boards of Accountancy (NASBA), as a Quality Service Assurance sponsor of continuing professional education. State boards of accountancy have final authority of the acceptance of individual courses for CPE credit. Complaints regarding QAS program sponsors may be addressed to NASBA,150 Fourth Avenue North, Suite 700, Nashville, TN, 37219-2417. NASBA phone number: 615.880.4200 Web site: www.nasba.org

Gleim Publications, Inc. is registered with the National Association of State Boards of Accountancy (NASBA), as a Quality Service Assurance sponsor of continuing professional education. State boards of accountancy have final authority of the acceptance of individual courses for CPE credit. Complaints regarding QAS program sponsors may be addressed to NASBA,150 Fourth Avenue North, Suite 700, Nashville, TN, 37219-2417. NASBA phone number: 615.880.4200 Web site: www.nasba.org

Please forward your suggestions, corrections, and comments concerning typographical errors, etc., to **Irvin N. Gleim • c/o Gleim Publications, Inc. • P.O. Box 12848 • University Station • Gainesville, Florida • 32604.** Please include your name and address so we can properly thank you for your interest.

1. ____________________

2. ____________________

3. ____________________

4. ____________________

5. ____________________

6. ____________________

7. ____________________

8. ____________________

9. ____________________

10. ____________________

11. ____________________

12. ____________________

13. ____________________

14. ____________________

15. ____________________

16. ____________________

17. ____________________

18. ____________________

Remember, for superior service: Mail, e-mail, or fax questions about our books or software.
Telephone questions about orders, prices, shipments, or payments.

Name: ____________________

Address: ____________________

City/State/Zip: ____________________

Telephone: Home: __________ Work: __________ Fax: __________

E-mail: ____________________